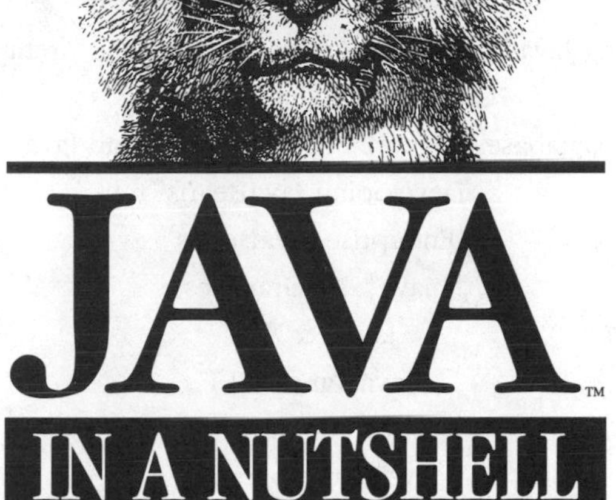

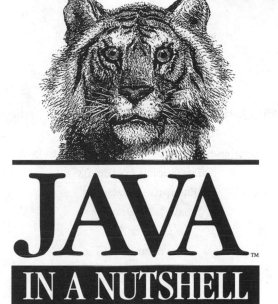

JAVA™ IN A NUTSHELL

A Desktop Quick Reference

Related Titles from O'Reilly

J2ME™ in a Nutshell
Java™ Enterprise in a Nutshell
Java™ Examples in a Nutshell
Java™ Foundation Classes in a Nutshell

Building Java™ Enterprise Applications Vol. 1: Architecture
Creating Effective JavaHelp™
Database Programming with JDBC and Java™
Developing JavaBeans™
Enterprise JavaBeans™
Java™ 2D Graphics
Java™ & XML
Java™ and XSLT
Java™ Cookbook
Java™ Cryptography
Java™ Distributed Computing
Java™ I/O
Java™ Internationalization
Java™ Message Service
Java™ Network Programming
Java™ Performance Tuning
Java™ Programming with Oracle SQLJ
Java™ RMI
Java™ Security
JavaServer™ Pages
JavaServer™ Pages Pocket Reference
Java™ Servlet Programming
Java™ Swing
Java™ Threads
Java™ Web Services
Jini™ in a Nutshell
Learning Java™
Learning Wireless Java™

JAVA™ IN A NUTSHELL

A Desktop Quick Reference

Fourth Edition

David Flanagan

O'REILLY®

Beijing • Cambridge • Farnham • Köln • Paris • Sebastopol • Taipei • Tokyo

Java™ in a Nutshell, Fourth Edition

by David Flanagan

Published by O'Reilly & Associates, Inc., 1005 Gravenstein Highway North, Sebastopol, CA 95472.

O'Reilly & Associates books may be purchased for educational, business, or sales promotional use. Online editions are also available for most titles (*safari.oreilly.com*). For more information contact our corporate/institutional sales department: (800) 998-9938 or *corporate@oreilly.com*.

Editors: Paula Ferguson and Robert Eckstein

Production Editor: Matt Hutchinson

Cover Designer: Edie Freedman

Printing History:

February 1996:	First Edition.
May 1997:	Second Edition.
November 1999:	Third Edition.
March 2002:	Fourth Edition.

ISBN: 0-596-00283-1
[M] [12/02]

This book is dedicated to all

who teach peace and resist violence.

Table of Contents

Chapter 3—Object-Oriented Programming in Java *88*

Chapter 4—The Java Platform *142*

Part II: API Quick Reference

Preface

This book is a desktop quick reference for Java™ programmers, designed to sit faithfully by your keyboard while you program. Part I of the book is a fast-paced, "no-fluff" introduction to the Java programming language and the core APIs of the Java platform. Part II is a quick-reference section that succinctly details most classes and interfaces of those core APIs. The book covers Java 1.0, 1.1, 1.2, 1.3, and 1.4.

Changes in the Fourth Edition

Once again, the Java platform has grown dramatically larger with the release of Java 1.4, and this book has grown in response. Some of the important new features of Java 1.4 (and of this book) are:

Assert statement
: The Java language has been extended to support assertions with the `assert` statement. This new statement is documented in Chapter 2.

JavaBeans persistence
: JavaBeans and related objects can now be serialized to XML documents. See `java.beans.XMLEncoder` in Chapter 9 for more information.

New I/O API
: Java 1.4 includes a new API for high-performance, nonblocking file and network input and output. See the `java.nio` package and its subpackages in Chapter 14. Chapter 4 contains a number of examples of this important new API.

Certification path API
: The `java.security.cert` package has been extended with new classes and interfaces for creating certificate chains, or "certification paths," which are commonly used in network authentication.

Logging API
: The new `java.util.logging` package defines a powerful and flexible logging framework for Java applications.

Preferences API
: `java.util.prefs` defines an API that allows applications to persistently store and query user preference values and systemwide configuration options.

Pattern matching with regular expressions
: One more new utility package, `java.util.regex`, provides support for textual pattern matching with Perl-style regular expressions.

Secure network sockets
: The Java Secure Sockets Extension (JSSE) API defined by the new `javax.net` and `javax.net.ssl` packages provides support for secure networking with the SSL and TLS protocols.

Network authentication and authorization
: The Java Authentication and Authorization Service (JAAS) is defined by the `javax.security.auth` package and its subpackages. JAAS enables a Java application to securely establish the identity of a user and run code under a security policy based on the set of permissions granted to that user.

XML parsing and transformations
: The Java API for XML Processing (JAXP) is defined by the `javax.xml.parsers` package and the `javax.xml.transform` package and subpackages. JAXP provides facilities for parsing XML documents using the SAX and DOM APIs and for transforming the content of those documents using XSLT. Along with JAXP, the DOM and SAX APIs have also been made part of the Java 1.4 platform. You'll find them in the `org.w3c.dom` package in Chapter 23 and in the `org.xml.sax` package and subpackages in Chapter 24.

You'll find examples illustrating how to use most of these new APIs in Chapter 4.

In addition to all the new content, there have been a few organizational changes to the book. In previous editions, the quick reference was organized with one package to a chapter. This edition documents 46 distinct packages, which would make for an excessive number of chapters. In this edition, therefore, related packages (those with a common prefix) are grouped into a single chapter, shortening the quick reference to a more manageable 15 chapters. Because the quick reference has a purely alphabetical organization, however, the chapter boundaries are largely irrelevant, and you can find what you need simply by flipping through the quick reference as you would flip through a dictionary or phone book.

Another change caused by the dramatically increased number of packages is that I was forced to cut the package hierarchy figures that appeared at the start of each chapter in previous editions. These figures were all carefully hand-drawn and have become an increasingly large burden on the technical illustration staff at O'Reilly & Associates, Inc. Furthermore, the figures simply haven't proven to be as useful as they once seemed. In this edition, I decided that the figures' benefit simply didn't justify their cost. If you are one of the minority of readers who was fond of those diagrams, I apologize for their removal.

There are two new features of the quick reference that should compensate for the loss of the package hierarchy diagrams. First, the reference entry for each package now includes a listing of all interfaces and classes in the package. The entries in this list are grouped by category (interfaces, classes, and exceptions, for example) and by hierarchy. This listing, while not graphical, provides exactly the same information as the old hierarchy diagrams. Second, the class hierarchy subsection of each class and interface quick reference has been converted from an awkward textual format to an improved graphical format.

Contents of This Book

The first eight chapters of this book document the Java language, the Java platform, and the Java development tools that are supplied with Sun's Java SDK (software development kit). The first four chapters are essential; the next four cover topics of interest to some, but not all Java programmers.

Chapter 1: Introduction
: This chapter is an overview of the Java language and the Java platform that explains the important features and benefits of Java. It concludes with an example Java program and walks the new Java programmer through it line by line.

Chapter 2: Java Syntax From the Ground Up
: This chapter explains the details of the Java programming language. It is a long and detailed chapter. Experienced Java programmers can use it as a language reference. Programmers with substantial experience with languages such as C and C++ should be able to pick up Java syntax by reading this chapter. The chapter does not assume years of programming experience, however, and does not even require familiarity with C or C++. Even beginning programmers, with only a modest amount of experience should be able to learn Java programming by studying this chapter carefully.

Chapter 3: Object-Oriented Programming in Java
: This chapter describes how the basic Java syntax documented in Chapter 2 is used to write object-oriented programs in Java. The chapter assumes no prior experience with OO programming. It can be used as a tutorial by new programmers or as a reference by experienced Java programmers.

Chapter 4: The Java Platform
: This chapter is an overview of the essential Java APIs covered in this book. It contains numerous short examples that demonstrate how to perform common tasks with the classes and interfaces that comprise the Java platform. Programmers who are new to Java, and especially those who learn best by example, should find this a valuable chapter.

Chapter 5: Java Security
: This chapter explains the Java security architecture that allows untrusted code to run in a secure environment from which it cannot do any malicious damage to the host system. It is important for all Java programmers to have at least a passing familiarity with Java security mechanisms.

Chapter 6: JavaBeans

This chapter documents the JavaBeans™ component framework and explains what programmers need to know to create and use the reusable, embeddable Java classes known as beans.

Chapter 7: Java Programming and Documentation Conventions

This chapter documents important and widely adopted Java programming conventions and also explains how you can make your Java code self-documenting by including specially formatted documentation comments.

Chapter 8: Java Development Tools

The Java SDK shipped by Sun includes a number of useful Java development tools, most notably the Java interpreter and the Java compiler. This chapter documents those tools.

These first eight chapters teach you the Java language and get you up and running with the Java APIs. The bulk of the book, however, is the API quick reference, Chapters 9 through 24, which is a succinct but detailed API reference formatted for optimum ease of use. Please be sure to read Chapter 1, which appears at the beginning of the reference section; it explains how to get the most out of this section. Also, please note that the quick-reference chapters are followed by one final chapter entitled "Class, Method, and Field Index". This special index allows you to look up the name of a class and find the package it is defined in or look up the name of a method or field and find the class it is defined in.

Related Books

O'Reilly publishes an entire series of books on Java programming, including several companion books to this one. The companion books are:

Java Enterprise in a Nutshell

This book is a succinct tutorial and quick reference for the Java "Enterprise" APIs such as JDBC, RMI, JNDI, and CORBA.

Java Foundation Classes in a Nutshell

This book is a tutorial and quick reference for the graphics, graphical user interface, and related APIs of the Java platform. It includes coverage of Applets, AWT, Java2D, and Swing.

Java Examples in a Nutshell

This book contains hundreds of complete, working examples illustrating many common Java programming tasks using the core, enterprise, and foundation classes APIs. *Java Examples in a Nutshell* is like Chapter 4 of this book, greatly expanded in breadth and depth, and with all the code snippets fully fleshed out into working examples. This is a particularly valuable book for readers who learn well by experimenting with existing code.

J2ME in a Nutshell

This book is a tutorial and quick reference for the graphics, networking, and database APIs of the Java 2 Micro Edition (J2ME) platform.

You can find a complete list of Java books from O'Reilly at *http://java.oreilly.com/*. Books that focus on the core Java APIs, as this one does, include:

Learning Java, by Pat Niemeyer and Jonathan Knudsen
: A comprehensive tutorial introduction to Java, with an emphasis on client-side Java programming.

Java Threads, by Scott Oaks and Henry Wong
: Java makes multithreaded programming easy, but doing it right can still be tricky. This book explains everything you need to know.

Java I/O, by Elliotte Rusty Harold
: Java's stream-based input/output architecture is a thing of beauty. This book covers it in the detail it deserves.

Java Network Programming, by Elliotte Rusty Harold
: This book documents the Java networking APIs in detail.

Java Security, by Scott Oaks
: This book explains the Java access-control mechanisms in detail and also documents the authentication mechanisms of digital signatures and message digests.

Java Cryptography, by Jonathan Knudsen
: Thorough coverage of the Java Cryptography Extension, the `javax.crypto.*` packages, and everything you need to know about cryptography in Java.

Developing Java Beans, by Robert Englander
: A complete guide to writing components that work with the JavaBeans API.

Java Programming Resources Online

This book is a quick reference designed for speedy access to frequently needed information. It does not, and cannot, tell you everything you need to know about Java. In addition to the books listed earlier, there are several valuable (and free) electronic sources of information about Java programming.

Sun's main web site for all things related to Java is *http://java.sun.com/*. The web site specifically for Java developers is *http://developer.java.sun.com/*. Much of the content on this developer site is password-protected, and access to it requires (free) registration.

Sun distributes electronic documentation for all Java classes and methods in its *javadoc* HTML format. Although this documentation is somewhat difficult to navigate and is rough or outdated in places, it is still an excellent starting point when you need to know more about a particular Java package, class, method, or field. If you do not already have the *javadoc* files with your Java distribution, see *http://java.sun.com/docs/* for a link to the latest available version. Sun also distributes its excellent *Java Tutorial* online. You can browse and download it from *http://java.sun.com/docs/books/tutorial/*.

For Usenet discussion (in English) about Java, try the *comp.lang.java.programmer* and related *comp.lang.java.** newsgroups. You can find the very comprehensive *comp.lang.java.programmer* FAQ by Peter van der Linden at *http://www.afu.com/javafaq.htm*.

Finally, don't forget O'Reilly's Java web site. *http://java.oreilly.com/* contains Java news and commentary. The O'Reilly Network (*www.oreillynet.com*) includes the *onjava.com* site which has a focus on Enterprise Java.

Examples Online

The examples in this book are available online and can be downloaded from the home page for the book at *http://www.oreilly.com/catalog/javanut4*. You also may want to visit this site to see if any important notes or errata about the book have been published there.

Conventions Used in This Book

We use the following formatting conventions in this book:

Italic
: Used for emphasis and to signify the first use of a term. Italic is also used for commands, email addresses, web sites, FTP sites, file and directory names, and newsgroups.

Bold
: Occasionally used to refer to particular keys on a computer keyboard or to portions of a user interface, such as the **Back** button or the **Options** menu.

`Constant Width`
: Used in all Java code and generally for anything that you would type literally when programming, including keywords, data types, constants, method names, variables, class names, and interface names.

`Constant Width Italic`
: Used for the names of function arguments and generally as a placeholder to indicate an item that should be replaced with an actual value in your program.

Franklin Gothic Book Condensed
: Used for the Java class synopses in the quick-reference section. This very narrow font allows us to fit a lot of information on the page without a lot of distracting line breaks. This font is also used for code entities in the descriptions in the quick-reference section.

Franklin Gothic Demi Condensed
: Used for highlighting class, method, field, property, and constructor names in the quick-reference section, which makes it easier to scan the class synopses.

Franklin Gothic Book Condensed Italic
: Used for method parameter names and comments in the quick-reference section.

Request for Comments

Please address comments and questions concerning this book to the publisher:

O'Reilly & Associates, Inc.
1005 Gravenstein Highway North
Sebastopol, CA 95472
(800) 998-9938 (in the United States or Canada)
(707) 829-0515 (international or local)
(707) 829-1014 (fax)

There is a web page for this book, which lists errata, examples, and any additional information. You can access this page at:

http://www.oreilly.com/catalog/javanut4/

To ask technical questions or comment on this book, send email to:

bookquestions@oreilly.com

For more information about books, conferences, Resource Centers, and the O'Reilly Network, see the O'Reilly web site at:

http://www.oreilly.com/

How the Quick Reference Is Generated

For the curious reader, this section explains a bit about how the quick-reference material in *Java in a Nutshell* and related books is created.

As Java has evolved, so has my system for generating Java quick-reference material. The current system is part of a larger commercial documentation browser system I'm developing (visit *http://www.davidflanagan.com/Jude/* for more information about it). The program works in two passes: the first pass collects and organizes the API information, and the second pass outputs that information in the form of quick-reference chapters.

The first pass begins by reading the class files for all of the classes and interfaces to be documented. Almost all of the API information in the quick reference is available in these class files. The notable exception is the names of method arguments, which are not stored in class files. These argument names are obtained by parsing the Java source file for each class and interface. Where source files are not available, I obtain method argument names by parsing the API documentation generated by *javadoc*. The parsers I use to extract API information from the source files and *javadoc* files are created using the Antlr parser generator developed by Terrence Parr of the Magelang Institute. (See *http://www.antlr.org/* for details on this very powerful programming tool.)

Once the API information has been obtained by reading class files, source files, and *javadoc* files, the program spends some time sorting and cross-referencing everything. Then it stores all the API information into a single large data file.

The second pass reads API information from that data file and outputs quick-reference chapters using a custom XML doctype. Once I've generated the XML output, I hand it off to the production team at O'Reilly. They process it and convert it to troff source code. The troff source is processed with the GNU *groff* program (*ftp://ftp.gnu.org/gnu/groff/*) and a custom set of troff macros to produce PostScript output that is shipped directly to the printer.

Acknowledgments

Many people helped in the creation of this book, and I am grateful to them all. I am indebted to the many, many readers of the first three editions who wrote in with comments, suggestions, bug reports, and praise. Their many small contributions are scattered throughout the book. Also, my apologies to those who made the many good suggestions that could not be incorporated into this edition.

Paula Ferguson, a friend and colleague, was the editor of the first three editions of this book. Her careful reading and always-practical suggestions have made the book stronger, clearer, and more useful. Paula's editorial duties have moved her away from Java books and into Web programming books, and this fourth edition was edited by Bob Eckstein, a careful editor with a great sense of humor.

The new material I wrote for this edition has been reviewed by a number of engineers at Sun, and often these engineers were the very ones who created or worked on the APIs for which they were reviewers. I am fortunate to have been able to go "straight to the source" for these reviews, and am very grateful to these engineers, who made time in their very busy schedules to read and comment on my drafts. In alphabetical order, the reviewers were:

- Josh Bloch, author of the excellent book *Effective Java Programming Language Guide*, reviewed the new material on assertions and the Preferences API.
- Graham Hamilton reviewed the Logging API material.
- Jonathan Knudsen (who is also an O'Reilly author) reviewed the JSSE and Certification Path material.
- Charlie Lai reviewed the JAAS material.
- Ram Marti reviewed the JGSS material.
- Philip Milne, a former Sun employee, now at Dresdner Kleinwort Wasserstein, reviewed the material on the Java Beans persistence mechanism.
- Mark Reinhold reviewed the `java.nio` material. Mark deserves special thanks for having been a reviewer for the second, third, and fourth editions of this book.
- Andreas Sterbenz and Brad Wetmore reviewed the JSSE material.

In addition to these reviewers from Sun, Ron Hitchens reviewed my New I/O material, and my editor, Bob Eckstein, did double duty as the technical reviewer for the XML material. My sincere thanks to each of these gentlemen for their careful work. Any mistakes that remain in this book are, of course, my own.

The third edition also benefited greatly from the contributions of reviewers who are intimately familiar with the Java platform. Joshua Bloch, one of the primary authors of the Java collections framework, reviewed my descriptions of the collections classes and interfaces. Joshua was also helpful in discussing the `Timer` and `TimerTask` classes of Java 1.3 with me. Mark Reinhold, creator of the `java.lang.ref` package, explained the package to me and reviewed my documentation of it. Scott Oaks reviewed my descriptions of the Java security and cryptography classes and interfaces. Joshua, Mark, and Scott are all engineers with Sun Microsystems, and I'm very grateful for their time. The documentation of the `javax.crypto` package and its subpackages was also reviewed by Jon Eaves. Jon worked on a clean-room implementation of the Java Cryptography Extension (which is available from *http://www.aba.net.au/*), and his comments were quite helpful. Jon now works for Fluent Technologies (*http://www.fluent.com.au/*) consulting in Java and electronic commerce. Finally, Chapter 1 was improved by the comments of reviewers who were *not* already familiar with the Java platform: Christina Byrne reviewed it from the standpoint of a novice programmer, and Judita Byrne of Virginia Power offered her comments as a professional COBOL programmer.

For the second edition, John Zukowski reviewed my Java 1.1 AWT quick-reference material, and George Reese reviewed most of the remaining new material. The second edition was also blessed with a "dream team" of technical reviewers from Sun. John Rose, the author of the Java inner class specification, reviewed the chapter on inner classes. Mark Reinhold, author of the new character stream classes in `java.io`, reviewed my documentation of these classes. Nakul Saraiya, the designer of the new Java Reflection API, reviewed my documentation of the `java.lang.reflect` package. I am very grateful to these engineers and architects; their efforts made this a stronger, more accurate book.

Mike Loukides provided high-level direction and guidance for the first edition of the book. Eric Raymond and Troy Downing reviewed that first edition—they helped spot my errors and omissions and offered good advice on making the book more useful to Java programmers.

The O'Reilly production team has done its usual fine work of creating a book out of the electronic files I submit. My thanks to them all.

As always, my thanks and love to Christie.

David Flanagan
http://www.davidflanagan.com/
January 2002

PART I

Introducing Java

Part I is an introduction to the Java language and the Java platform. These chapters provide enough information for you to get started using Java right away.

CHAPTER 1

Introduction

Welcome to Java. This chapter begins by explaining what Java is and describing some of the features that distinguish it from other programming languages. Then, as a tutorial introduction to the language, it walks you through a simple Java program you can type in, compile, and run.

What Is Java?

In discussing Java, it is important to distinguish between the Java programming language, the Java Virtual Machine, and the Java platform. The Java programming language is the language in which Java applications (including applets, servlets, and JavaBeans components) are written. When a Java program is compiled, it is converted to byte codes that are the portable machine language of a CPU architecture known as the Java Virtual Machine (also called the Java VM or JVM). The JVM can be implemented directly in hardware, but it is usually implemented in the form of a software program that interprets and executes byte codes.

The Java platform is distinct from both the Java language and Java VM. The Java platform is the predefined set of Java classes that exist on every Java installation; these classes are available for use by all Java programs. The Java platform is also sometimes referred to as the Java runtime environment or the core Java APIs (application programming interfaces). The Java platform can be extended with optional standard extensions. These extension APIs exist in some Java installations, but are not guaranteed to exist in all installations.

The Java Programming Language

The Java programming language is a state-of-the-art, object-oriented language that has a syntax similar to that of C. The language designers strove to make the Java language powerful, but, at the same time, they tried to avoid the overly complex features that have bogged down other object-oriented languages, such as C++. By keeping the language simple, the designers also made it easier for programmers to write robust, bug-free code. As a result of its elegant design and next-generation features, the Java language has proved popular with programmers, who typically find it a pleasure to work with Java after struggling with more difficult, less powerful languages.

The Java Virtual Machine

The Java Virtual Machine, or Java interpreter, is the crucial piece of every Java installation. By design, Java programs are portable, but they are only portable to platforms to which a Java interpreter has been ported. Sun ships VM implementations for its own Solaris operating system and for Microsoft Windows and Linux platforms. Many other vendors, including Apple and various commercial Unix vendors, provide Java interpreters for their platforms. The Java VM is not only for desktop systems, however. It has been ported to set-top boxes, and scaled-down versions are even available for hand-held devices that run Windows CE and PalmOS.

Although interpreters are not typically considered high-performance systems, Java VM performance is remarkably good and has been improving steadily. Of particular note is a VM technology called just-in-time (JIT) compilation, whereby Java byte codes are converted on-the-fly into native-platform machine language, boosting execution speed for code that is run repeatedly. Sun's new Hotspot technology is a particularly good implementation of JIT compilation.

The Java Platform

The Java platform is just as important as the Java programming language and the Java Virtual Machine. All programs written in the Java language rely on the set of predefined classes* that comprise the Java platform. Java classes are organized into related groups known as *packages*. The Java platform defines packages for functionality such as input/output, networking, graphics, user-interface creation, security, and much more.

The Java 1.2 release was a major milestone for the Java platform. This release almost tripled the number of classes in the platform and introduced significant new functionality. In recognition of this, Sun named the new version the Java 2 Platform. This is a trademarked name created for marketing purposes; it serves to emphasize how much Java has grown since its first release. However, most programmers refer to the Java platform by its official version number, which, at the time of this writing, is 1.4.

It is important to understand what is meant by the term platform. To a computer programmer, a platform is defined by the APIs he or she can rely on when writing programs. These APIs are usually defined by the operating system of the target computer. Thus, a programmer writing a program to run under Microsoft Windows must use a different set of APIs than a programmer writing the same program for the Macintosh or for a Unix-based system. In this respect, Windows, Macintosh, and Unix are three distinct platforms.

---

* A *class* is a module of Java code that defines a data structure and a set of methods (also called procedures, functions, or subroutines) that operate on that data.

Java is not an operating system. Nevertheless, the Java platform provides APIs with a comparable breadth and depth to those defined by an operating system. With the Java platform, you can write applications in Java without sacrificing the advanced features available to programmers writing native applications targeted at a particular underlying operating system. An application written on the Java platform runs on any operating system that supports the Java platform. This means you do not have to create distinct Windows, Macintosh, and Unix versions of your programs, for example. A single Java program runs on all these operating systems, which explains why "Write once, run anywhere" is Sun's motto for Java.

It also explains why companies like Microsoft might feel threatened by Java. The Java platform is not an operating system, but for programmers, it is an alternative development target and a very popular one at that. The Java platform reduces programmers' reliance on the underlying operating system, and, by allowing programs to run on top of any operating system, it increases end users' freedom to choose an operating system.

Versions of Java

As of this writing, there have been five major versions of Java. They are:

Java 1.0
: This was the first public version of Java. It contained 212 classes organized in 8 packages. It was simple and elegant but is now completely outdated.

Java 1.1
: This release of Java doubled the size of the Java platform to 504 classes in 23 packages. It introduced inner classes, an important change to the Java language itself, and included significant performance improvements in the Java VM. There is a large installed base of web browsers that run Java 1.1, so although this version is outdated, it is still used for writing simple applets—Java programs that are included in web pages. See *Java Foundation Classes in a Nutshell* (O'Reilly) for a discussion of applets.

Java 1.2
: This was a very significant release of Java; it tripled the size of the Java platform to 1,520 classes in 59 packages. Important additions included the new Swing GUI API and a powerful and flexible Collections API for working with sets, lists, and maps of objects. Because of the many new features included in the 1.2 release, the platform was rebranded as "the Java 2 Platform."

Java 1.3
: This was primarily a maintenance release, focused on bug fixes, stability, and performance improvements (including the high-performance "HotSpot" virtual machine). New additions to the platform included the JNDI and Java Sound APIs, which were previously available as extensions to the platform. The most interesting new classes are probably `java.util.Timer` and `java.lang.reflect.Proxy`. In total, Version 1.3 of the Java platform contains 1,842 classes in 76 packages.

Java 1.4

This is another big release, adding important new functionality and increasing the size of the platform by 62% to 2,991 classes and interfaces in 135 packages. New features include a high-performance, low-level I/O API; support for pattern matching with regular expressions; a logging API; a user preferences API; new Collections classes; an XML-based persistence mechanism for JavaBeans; support for XML parsing using both the DOM and SAX APIs; user authentication with the JAAS API; support for secure network connections using the SSL protocol; support for cryptography; a new API for reading and writing image files; an API for network printing; a handful of new GUI components in the Swing API; and a simplified drag-and-drop architecture for Swing. In addition to these platform changes, the Java 1.4 release introduces an `assert` statement to the Java language.

To work with Java 1.0 or Java 1.1, you must obtain the Java Development Kit (JDK) for that release. As of Java 1.2, the JDK has been renamed and is now called a Software Development Kit (SDK), so we have the Java 2 SDK or, more precisely, the Java 2 SDK, Standard Edition, Version 1.4. Despite the new name, many programmers still refer to the development kit as the JDK.

Don't confuse the JDK (or SDK) with the Java Runtime Environment (JRE). The JRE contains everything you need to run Java programs, but it does not contain the tools you need to develop Java programs (primarily the compiler). You should also be aware of the Java Plug-in, a version of the JRE that is designed to be integrated into the Netscape Navigator and Microsoft Internet Explorer web browsers.

In addition to the Standard Edition of Java used by most Java developers and documented in this book, Sun has also released the Java 2 Platform, Enterprise Edition (or J2EE) for enterprise developers and the Java 2 Platform, Micro Edition (J2ME) for consumer electronic systems, such as handheld PDAs and cellular telephones. See *Java Enterprise in a Nutshell* and *Java Micro Edition in a Nutshell* (both by O'Reilly) for more information on these other editions.

Key Benefits of Java

Why use Java at all? Is it worth learning a new language and a new platform? This section explores some of the key benefits of Java.

Write Once, Run Anywhere

Sun identifies "Write once, run anywhere" as the core value proposition of the Java platform. Translated from business jargon, this means that the most important promise of Java technology is that you only have to write your application once—for the Java platform—and then you'll be able to run it *anywhere.*

Anywhere, that is, that supports the Java platform. Fortunately, Java support is becoming ubiquitous. It is integrated, or being integrated, into practically all major operating systems. It is built into the popular web browsers, which places it on virtually every Internet-connected PC in the world. It is even being built into consumer electronic devices, such as television set-top boxes, PDAs, and cell phones.

Security

Another key benefit of Java is its security features. Both the language and the platform were designed from the ground up with security in mind. The Java platform allows users to download untrusted code over a network and run it in a secure environment in which it cannot do any harm: untrusted code cannot infect the host system with a virus, cannot read or write files from the hard drive, and so forth. This capability alone makes the Java platform unique.

Java 1.2 took the security model a step further. It made security levels and restrictions highly configurable and extended them beyond applets. As of Java 1.2, any Java code, whether it is an applet, a servlet, a JavaBeans component, or a complete Java application, can be run with restricted permissions that prevent it from doing harm to the host system.

The security features of the Java language and platform have been subjected to intense scrutiny by security experts around the world. In the earlier days of Java, security-related bugs, some of them potentially serious, were found and promptly fixed. Because of the strong security promises Java makes, it is big news when a new security bug is found. No other mainstream platform can make security guarantees nearly as strong as those Java makes. No one can say that Java security holes will not be found in the future, but if Java's security is not yet perfect, it has been proven strong enough for practical day-to-day use and is certainly better than any of the alternatives.

Network-Centric Programming

Sun's corporate motto has always been "The network is the computer." The designers of the Java platform believed in the importance of networking and designed the Java platform to be network-centric. From a programmer's point of view, Java makes it easy to work with resources across a network and to create network-based applications using client/server or multitier architectures.

Dynamic, Extensible Programs

Java is both dynamic and extensible. Java code is organized in modular object-oriented units called *classes*. Classes are stored in separate files and are loaded into the Java interpreter only when needed. This means that an application can decide as it is running what classes it needs and can load them when it needs them. It also means that a program can dynamically extend itself by loading the classes it needs to expand its functionality.

The network-centric design of the Java platform means that a Java application can dynamically extend itself by loading new classes over a network. An application that takes advantage of these features ceases to be a monolithic block of code. Instead, it becomes an interacting collection of independent software components. Thus, Java enables a powerful new metaphor of application design and development.

Internationalization

The Java language and the Java platform were designed from the start with the rest of the world in mind. When it was created, Java was the only commonly used programming language that had internationalization features at its core, rather than tacked on as an afterthought. While most programming languages use 8-bit characters that represent only the alphabets of English and Western European languages, Java uses 16-bit Unicode characters that represent the phonetic alphabets and ideographic character sets of the entire world. Java's internationalization features are not restricted to just low-level character representation, however. The features permeate the Java platform, making it easier to write internationalized programs with Java than it is with any other environment.

Performance

As described earlier, Java programs are compiled to a portable intermediate form known as byte codes, rather than to native machine-language instructions. The Java Virtual Machine runs a Java program by interpreting these portable byte-code instructions. This architecture means that Java programs are faster than programs or scripts written in purely interpreted languages, but they are typically slower than C and C++ programs compiled to native machine language. Keep in mind, however, that although Java programs are compiled to byte code, not all of the Java platform is implemented with interpreted byte codes. For efficiency, computationally intensive portions of the Java platform—such as the string-manipulation methods—are implemented using native machine code.

Although early releases of Java suffered from performance problems, the speed of the Java VM has improved dramatically with each new release. The VM has been highly tuned and optimized in many significant ways. Furthermore, most current implementations include a just-in-time (JIT) compiler, which converts Java byte codes to native machine instructions on the fly. Using sophisticated JIT compilers, Java programs can execute at speeds comparable to the speeds of native C and C++ applications.

Java is a portable, interpreted language; Java programs run almost as fast as native, non-portable C and C++ programs. Performance used to be an issue that made some programmers avoid using Java. Now, with the improvements made in Java 1.2, 1.3 and 1.4, performance issues should no longer keep anyone away.

Programmer Efficiency and Time-to-Market

The final, and perhaps most important, reason to use Java is that programmers like it. Java is an elegant language combined with a powerful and (usually) well-designed set of APIs. Programmers enjoy programming in Java and are often amazed at how quickly they can get results with it. Because Java is a simple and elegant language with a well-designed, intuitive set of APIs, programmers write better code with fewer bugs than for other platforms, again reducing development time.

An Example Program

Example 1-1 shows a Java program to compute factorials.* The numbers at the beginning of each line are not part of the program; they are there for ease of reference when we dissect the program line-by-line.

Example 1-1. Factorial.java: a program to compute factorials

```
 1 /**
 2  * This program computes the factorial of a number
 3  */
 4 public class Factorial {                           // Define a class
 5   public static void main(String[] args) { // The program starts here
 6     int input = Integer.parseInt(args[0]); // Get the user's input
 7     double result = factorial(input);      // Compute the factorial
 8     System.out.println(result);            // Print out the result
 9   }                                        // The main() method ends here
10
11   public static double factorial(int x) { // This method computes x!
12     if (x < 0)                             // Check for bad input
13       return 0.0;                          // If bad, return 0
14     double fact = 1.0;                     // Begin with an initial value
15     while(x > 1) {                         // Loop until x equals 1
16       fact = fact * x;                     // Multiply by x each time
17       x = x - 1;                           // And then decrement x
18     }                                      // Jump back to start of loop
19     return fact;                           // Return the result
20   }                                        // factorial() ends here
21 }                                          // The class ends here
```

Compiling and Running the Program

Before we look at how the program works, we must first discuss how to run it. In order to compile and run the program, you need a Java software development kit (SDK) of some sort. Sun Microsystems created the Java language and ships a free Java SDK for its Solaris operating system and also for Linux and Microsoft Windows platforms. At the time of this writing, the current version of Sun's SDK is entitled Java 2 SDK, Standard Edition, Version 1.4 and is available for download from *http://java.sun.com/*. Be sure to get the SDK and not the Java Runtime Environment. The JRE enables you to run existing Java programs, but not to write and compile your own.

Sun supports its SDK only on Solaris, Linux, and Windows platforms. Many other companies have licensed and ported the SDK to their platforms, however. Contact your operating-system vendor to find if a version of the Java SDK is available for your system.

The Sun SDK is not the only Java programming environment you can use. Companies such as Borland, Inprise, Metrowerks, Oracle, Sybase, and Symantec offer commercial products that enable you to write Java programs. This book assumes

* The factorial of an integer is the product of the number and all positive integers less than the number. So, for example, the factorial of 4, which is also written 4!, is 4 times 3 times 2 times 1, or 24. By definition, 0! is 1.

that you are using Sun's SDK. If you are using a product from some other vendor, be sure to read that vendor's documentation to learn how to compile and run a simple program, like that shown in Example 1-1.

Once you have a Java programming environment installed, the first step towards running our program is to type it in. Using your favorite text editor, enter the program as it is shown in Example 1-1. Omit the line numbers, as they are just there for reference. Note that Java is a case-sensitive language, so you must type lowercase letters in lowercase and uppercase letters in uppercase. You'll notice that many of the lines of this program end with semicolons. It is a common mistake to forget these characters, but the program won't work without them, so be careful! If you are not a fast typist, you can omit everything from // to the end of a line. Those are *comments*; they are there for your benefit and are ignored by Java.*

When writing Java programs, you should use a text editor that saves files in plain-text format, not a word processor that supports fonts and formatting and saves files in a proprietary format. My favorite text editor on Unix systems is *emacs*. If you use a Windows system, you might use *Notepad* or *WordPad*, if you don't have a more specialized programmer's editor. If you are using a commercial Java programming environment, it probably includes an appropriate text editor; read the documentation that came with the product. When you are done entering the program, save it in a file named *Factorial.java*. This is important; the program will not work if you save it by any other name.

After writing a program like this one, the next step is to compile it. With Sun's SDK, the Java compiler is known as *javac*. *javac* is a command-line tool, so you can only use it from a terminal window, such as an MS-DOS window on a Windows system or an *xterm* window on a Unix system. Compile the program by typing the following command line:†

```
C:\> javac Factorial.java
```

If this command prints any error messages, you probably got something wrong when you typed in the program. If it does not print any error messages, however, the compilation has succeeded, and *javac* creates a file called *Factorial.class*. This is the compiled version of the program.

Once you have compiled a Java program, you must still run it. Unlike some other languages, Java programs are not compiled into native machine language, so they cannot be executed directly by the system. Instead, they are run by another program known as the Java interpreter. In Sun's SDK, the interpreter is a command-line program named, appropriately enough, *java*. To run the factorial program, type:

```
C:\> java Factorial 4
```

---

* I recommend that you type this example in by hand, to get a feel for the language. If you *really* don't want to, however, you can download this, and all examples in the book, from *http://www.oreilly.com/catalog/javanut4/*.

† The "C:\>" characters represent the command-line prompt; *don't* type these characters yourself.

java is the command to run the Java interpreter, *Factorial* is the name of the Java program we want the interpreter to run, and *4* is the input data—the number we want the interpreter to compute the factorial of. The program prints a single line of output, telling us that the factorial of 4 is 24:

```
C:\> java Factorial 4
24.0
```

Congratulations! You've just written, compiled, and run your first Java program. Try running it again to compute the factorials of some other numbers.

Analyzing the Program

Now that you have run the factorial program, let's analyze it line by line, to see what makes a Java program tick.

Comments

The first three lines of the program are a comment. Java ignores them, but they tell a human programmer what the program does. A comment begins with the characters /* and ends with the characters */. Any amount of text, including multiple lines of text, may appear between these characters. Java also supports another type of comment, which you can see in lines 4 through 21. If the characters // appear in a Java program, Java ignores those characters and any other text that appears between those characters and the end of the line.

Defining a class

Line 4 is the beginning of the program. It says that we are defining a class named `Factorial`. This explains why the program had to be stored in a file named *Factorial.java*. That filename indicates that the file contains Java source code for a class named `Factorial`. The word `public` is a *modifier*; it says that the class is publicly available and that anyone may use it. The open curly-brace character ({) marks the beginning of the body of the class, which extends all the way to line 21, where we find the matching close curly-brace character (}). The program contains a number of pairs of curly braces; the lines are indented to show the nesting within these braces.

A class is the fundamental unit of program structure in Java, so it is not surprising that the first line of our program declares a class. All Java programs are classes, although some programs use many classes instead of just one. Java is an object-oriented programming language, and classes are a fundamental part of the object-oriented paradigm. Each class defines a unique kind of object. Example 1-1 is not really an object-oriented program, however, so I'm not going to go into detail about classes and objects here. That is the topic of Chapter 3. For now, all you need to understand is that a class defines a set of interacting *members*. Those members may be fields, methods, or other classes. The `Factorial` class contains two members, both of which are methods. They are described in upcoming sections.

Defining a method

Line 5 begins the definition of a *method* of our `Factorial` class. A method is a named chunk of Java code. A Java program can call, or *invoke*, a method to execute the code in it. If you have programmed in other languages, you have probably seen methods before, but they may have been called functions, procedures, or subroutines. The interesting thing about methods is that they have *parameters* and *return values*. When you call a method, you pass it some data you want it to operate on, and it returns a result to you. A method is like an algebraic function:

```
y = f(x)
```

Here, the mathematical function `f` performs some computation on the value represented by `x` and returns a value, which we represent by `y`.

To return to line 5, the `public` and `static` keywords are modifiers. `public` means the method is publicly accessible; anyone can use it. The meaning of the `static` modifier is not important here; it is explained in Chapter 3. The `void` keyword specifies the return value of the method. In this case, it specifies that this method does not have a return value.

The word `main` is the name of the method. `main` is a special name. When you run the Java interpreter, it reads in the class you specify, then looks for a method named `main()`.* When the interpreter finds this method, it starts running the program at that method. When the `main()` method finishes, the program is done, and the Java interpreter exits. In other words, the `main()` method is the main entry point into a Java program. It is not actually sufficient for a method to be named `main()`, however. The method must be declared `public static void` exactly as shown in line 5. In fact, the only part of line 5 you can change is the word `args`, which you can replace with any word you want. You'll be using this line in all of your Java programs, so go ahead and commit it to memory now!†

Following the name of the `main()` method is a list of method parameters, contained in parentheses. This `main()` method has only a single parameter. `String[]` specifies the type of the parameter, which is an array of strings (i.e., a numbered list of strings of text). `args` specifies the name of the parameter. In the algebraic equation `f(x)`, `x` is simply a way of referring to an unknown value. `args` serves the same purpose for the `main()` method. As we'll see, the name `args` is used in the body of the method to refer to the unknown value that is passed to the method.

---

* By convention, when this book refers to a method, it follows the name of the method by a pair of parentheses. As you'll see, parentheses are an important part of method syntax, and they serve here to keep method names distinct from the names of classes, fields, variables, and so on.

† All Java programs that are run directly by the Java interpreter must have a `main()` method. Programs of this sort are often called *applications*. It is possible to write programs that are not run directly by the interpreter, but are dynamically loaded into some other already running Java program. Examples are *applets*, which are programs run by a web browser, and *servlets*, which are programs run by a web server. Applets are discussed in *Java Foundation Classes in a Nutshell* (O'Reilly), while servlets are discussed in *Java Enterprise in a Nutshell* (O'Reilly). In this book, we consider only applications.

As I've just explained, the `main()` method is a special one that is called by the Java interpreter when it starts running a Java class (program). When you invoke the Java interpreter like this:

```
C:\> java Factorial 4
```

the string "4" is passed to the `main()` method as the value of the parameter named `args`. More precisely, an array of strings containing only one entry, "4", is passed to `main()`. If we invoke the program like this:

```
C:\> java Factorial 4 3 2 1
```

then an array of four strings, "4", "3", "2", and "1", are passed to the `main()` method as the value of the parameter named `args`. Our program looks only at the first string in the array, so the other strings are ignored.

Finally, the last thing on line 5 is an open curly brace. This marks the beginning of the body of the `main()` method, which continues until the matching close curly brace on line 9. Methods are composed of *statements*, which the Java interpreter executes in sequential order. In this case, lines 6, 7, and 8 are three statements that compose the body of the `main()` method. Each statement ends with a semicolon to separate it from the next. This is an important part of Java syntax; beginning programmers often forget the semicolons.

Declaring a variable and parsing input

The first statement of the `main()` method, line 6, declares a variable and assigns a value to it. In any programming language, a *variable* is simply a symbolic name for a value. We've already seen that in this program the name `args` refers to the parameter value passed to the `main()` method. Method parameters are one type of variable. It is also possible for methods to declare additional "local" variables. Methods can use local variables to store and reference the intermediate values they use while performing their computations.

This is exactly what we are doing on line 6. That line begins with the words `int input`, which declare a variable named `input` and specify that the variable has the type `int`; that is, it is an integer. Java can work with several different types of values, including integers, real or floating-point numbers, characters (e.g., letters and digits), and strings of text. Java is a *strongly typed* language, which means that all variables must have a type specified and can refer only to values of that type. Our `input` variable always refers to an integer; it cannot refer to a floating-point number or a string. Method parameters are also typed. Recall that the `args` parameter had a type of `String[]`.

Continuing with line 6, the variable declaration `int input` is followed by the = character. This is the assignment operator in Java; it sets the value of a variable. When reading Java code, don't read = as "equals," but instead read it as "is assigned the value." As we'll see in Chapter 2, there is a different operator for "equals."

The value being assigned to our `input` variable is `Integer.parseInt(args[0])`. This is a method invocation. This first statement of the `main()` method invokes another method whose name is `Integer.parseInt()`. As you might guess, this method "parses" an integer; that is, it converts a string representation of an integer, such as "4", to the integer itself. The `Integer.parseInt()` method is not part of the Java language, but it is a core part of the Java API or Application Programming Interface. Every Java program can use the powerful set of classes and methods defined by this core API. The second half of this book is a quick reference that documents that core API.

When you call a method, you pass values (called *arguments*) that are assigned to the corresponding parameters defined by the method, and the method returns a value. The argument passed to `Integer.parseInt()` is `args[0]`. Recall that `args` is the name of the parameter for `main()`; it specifies an array (or list) of strings. The elements of an array are numbered sequentially, and the first one is always numbered 0. We only care about the first string in the `args` array, so we use the expression `args[0]` to refer to that string. Thus, when we invoke the program as shown earlier, line 6 takes the first string specified after the name of the class, "4", and passes it to the method named `Integer.parseInt()`. This method converts the string to the corresponding integer and returns the integer as its return value. Finally, this returned integer is assigned to the variable named `input`.

Computing the result

The statement on line 7 is a lot like the statement on line 6. It declares a variable and assigns a value to it. The value assigned to the variable is computed by invoking a method. The variable is named `result`, and it has a type of `double`. `double` means a double-precision floating-point number. The variable is assigned a value that is computed by the `factorial()` method. The `factorial()` method, however, is not part of the standard Java API. Instead, it is defined as part of our program, by lines 11 through 19. The argument passed to `factorial()` is the value referred to by the `input` variable, which was computed on line 6. We'll consider the body of the `factorial()` method shortly, but you can surmise from its name that this method takes an input value, computes the factorial of that value, and returns the result.

Displaying output

Line 8 simply calls a method named `System.out.println()`. This commonly used method is part of the core Java API; it causes the Java interpreter to print out a value. In this case, the value that it prints is the value referred to by the variable named `result`. This is the result of our factorial computation. If the `input` variable holds the value `4`, the `result` variable holds the value `24`, and this line prints out that value.

The `System.out.println()` method does not have a return value, so there is no variable declaration or `=` assignment operator in this statement, since there is no value to assign to anything. Another way to say this is that, like the `main()` method of line 5, `System.out.println()` is declared `void`.

The end of a method

Line 9 contains only a single character, `}`. This marks the end of the method. When the Java interpreter gets here, it is done executing the `main()` method, so it stops running. The end of the `main()` method is also the end of the *variable scope* for the `input` and `result` variables declared within `main()` and for the `args` parameter of `main()`. These variable and parameter names have meaning only within the `main()` method and cannot be used elsewhere in the program, unless other parts of the program declare different variables or parameters that happen to have the same name.

Blank lines

Line 10 is a blank line. You can insert blank lines, spaces, and tabs anywhere in a program, and you should use them liberally to make the program readable. A blank line appears here to separate the `main()` method from the `factorial()` method that begins on line 11. You'll notice that the program also uses spaces and tabs to indent the various lines of code. This kind of indentation is optional; it emphasizes the structure of the program and greatly enhances the readability of the code.

Another method

Line 11 begins the definition of the `factorial()` method that was used by the `main()` method. Compare this line to line 5 to note its similarities and differences. The `factorial()` method has the same `public` and `static` modifiers. It takes a single integer parameter, which we call `x`. Unlike the `main()` method, which had no return value (`void`), `factorial()` returns a value of type `double`. The open curly brace marks the beginning of the method body, which continues past the nested braces on lines 15 and 18 to line 20, where the matching close curly brace is found. The body of the `factorial()` method, like the body of the `main()` method, is composed of statements, which are found on lines 12 through 19.

Checking for valid input

In the `main()` method, we saw variable declarations, assignments, and method invocations. The statement on line 12 is different. It is an `if` statement, which executes another statement conditionally. We saw earlier that the Java interpreter executes the three statements of the `main()` method one after another. It always executes them in exactly that way, in exactly that order. An `if` statement is a flow-control statement; it can affect the way the interpreter runs a program.

The `if` keyword is followed by a parenthesized expression and a statement. The Java interpreter first evaluates the expression. If it is `true`, the interpreter executes the statement. If the expression is `false`, however, the interpreter skips the statement and goes to the next one. The condition for the `if` statement on line 12 is `x < 0`. It checks whether the value passed to the `factorial()` method is less than zero. If it is, this expression is `true`, and the statement on line 13 is executed. Line 12 does not end with a semicolon because the statement on line 13 is part of the `if` statement. Semicolons are required only at the end of a statement.

Line 13 is a `return` statement. It says that the return value of the `factorial()` method is 0.0. `return` is also a flow-control statement. When the Java interpreter sees a `return`, it stops executing the current method and returns the specified value immediately. A `return` statement can stand alone, but in this case, the `return` statement is part of the `if` statement on line 12. The indentation of line 13 helps emphasize this fact. (Java ignores this indentation, but it is very helpful for humans who read Java code!) Line 13 is executed only if the expression on line 12 is `true`.

Before we move on, we should pull back a bit and talk about why lines 12 and 13 are necessary in the first place. It is an error to try to compute a factorial for a negative number, so these lines make sure that the input value `x` is valid. If it is not valid, they cause `factorial()` to return a consistent invalid result, 0.0.

An important variable

Line 14 is another variable declaration; it declares a variable named `fact` of type `double` and assigns it an initial value of 1.0. This variable holds the value of the factorial as we compute it in the statements that follow. In Java, variables can be declared anywhere; they are not restricted to the beginning of a method or block of code.

Looping and computing the factorial

Line 15 introduces another type of statement: the `while` loop. Like an `if` statement, a `while` statement consists of a parenthesized expression and a statement. When the Java interpreter sees a `while` statement, it evaluates the associated expression. If that expression is `true`, the interpreter executes the statement. The interpreter repeats this process, evaluating the expression and executing the statement if the expression is `true`, until the expression evaluates to `false`. The expression on line 15 is `x > 1`, so the `while` statement loops *while* the parameter `x` holds a value that is greater than 1. Another way to say this is that the loop continues *until* `x` holds a value less than or equal to 1. We can assume from this expression that if the loop is ever going to terminate, the value of `x` must somehow be modified by the statement that the loop executes.

The major difference between the `if` statement on lines 12–13 and the `while` loop on lines 15–18 is that the statement associated with the `while` loop is a *compound statement*. A compound statement is zero or more statements grouped between curly braces. The `while` keyword on line 15 is followed by an expression in parentheses and then by an open curly brace. This means that the body of the loop consists of all statements between that opening brace and the closing brace on line 18. Earlier in the chapter, I said that all Java statements end with semicolons. This rule does not apply to compound statements, however, as you can see by the lack of a semicolon at the end of line 18. The statements inside the compound statement (lines 16 and 17) do end with semicolons, of course.

The body of the `while` loop consists of the statements on line 16 and 17. Line 16 multiplies the value of `fact` by the value of `x` and stores the result back into `fact`. Line 17 is similar. It subtracts 1 from the value of `x` and stores the result back into `x`. The `*` character on line 16 is important: it is the multiplication *operator*. And, as you can probably guess, the `-` on line 17 is the subtraction operator. An operator is a key part of Java syntax: it performs a computation on one or two *operands* to produce a new value. Operands and operators combine to form *expressions*, such as `fact * x` or `x - 1`. We've seen other operators in the program. Line 15, for example, uses the greater-than operator (>) in the expression `x > 1`, which compares the value of the variable `x` to 1. The value of this expression is a boolean truth value—either `true` or `false`, depending on the result of the comparison.

To understand this `while` loop, it is helpful to think like the Java interpreter. Suppose we are trying to compute the factorial of 4. Before the loop starts, `fact` is 1.0, and `x` is 4. After the body of the loop has been executed once—after the first *iteration*—`fact` is 4.0, and `x` is 3. After the second iteration, `fact` is 12.0, and `x` is 2. After the third iteration, `fact` is 24.0, and `x` is 1. When the interpreter tests the loop condition after the third iteration, it finds that `x > 1` is no longer true, so it stops running the loop, and the program resumes at line 19.

Returning the result

Line 19 is another `return` statement, like the one we saw on line 13. This one does not return a constant value like 0.0, but instead returns the value of the `fact` variable. If the value of `x` passed into the `factorial()` function is 4, then, as we saw earlier, the value of `fact` is 24.0, so this is the value returned. Recall that the `factorial()` method was invoked on line 7 of the program. When this `return` statement is executed, control returns to line 7, where the return value is assigned to the variable named `result`.

Exceptions

If you've made it all the way through the line-by-line analysis of Example 1-1, you are well on your way to understanding the basics of the Java language.* It is a simple but nontrivial program that illustrates many of the features of Java. There is one more important feature of Java programming I want to introduce, but it is one that does not appear in the program listing itself. Recall that the program computes the factorial of the number you specify on the command line. What happens if you run the program without specifying a number?

```
C:\> java Factorial
java.lang.ArrayIndexOutOfBoundsException: 0
        at Factorial.main(Factorial.java:6)
C:\>
```

And what happens if you specify a value that is not a number?

```
C:\> java Factorial ten
java.lang.NumberFormatException: ten
        at java.lang.Integer.parseInt(Integer.java)
        at java.lang.Integer.parseInt(Integer.java)
        at Factorial.main(Factorial.java:6)
C:\>
```

* If you didn't understand all the details of this factorial program, don't worry. We'll cover the details of the Java language a lot more thoroughly in Chapter 2 and Chapter 3. However, if you feel like you didn't understand any of the line-by-line analysis, you may also find that the upcoming chapters are over your head. In that case, you should probably go elsewhere to learn the basics of the Java language and return to this book to solidify your understanding, and, of course, to use as a reference. One resource you may find useful in learning the language is Sun's online Java tutorial, available at *http://java.sun.com/docs/books/tutorial/*.

In both cases, an error occurs or, in Java terminology, an *exception* is thrown. When an exception is thrown, the Java interpreter prints out a message that explains what type of exception it was and where it occurred (both exceptions above occurred on line 6). In the first case, the exception is thrown because there are no strings in the `args` list, meaning we asked for a nonexistent string with `args[0]`. In the second case, the exception is thrown because `Integer.parseInt()` cannot convert the string "ten" to a number. We'll see more about exceptions in Chapter 2 and learn how to handle them gracefully as they occur.

CHAPTER 2

Java Syntax

Java Syntax from the Ground Up

This chapter is a terse but comprehensive introduction to Java syntax. It is written primarily for readers who are new to the language, but have at least some previous programming experience. Determined novices with no prior programming experience may also find it useful. If you already know Java, you should find it a useful language reference. In previous editions of this book, this chapter was written explicitly for C and C++ programmers making the transition to Java. It has been rewritten for this edition to make it more generally useful, but it still contains comparisons to C and C++ for the benefit of programmers coming from those languages.*

This chapter documents the syntax of Java programs by starting at the very lowest level of Java syntax and building from there, covering increasingly higher orders of structure. It covers:

- The characters used to write Java programs and the encoding of those characters.
- Data types, literal values, identifiers, and other tokens that comprise a Java program.
- The operators used in Java to group individual tokens into larger expressions.
- Statements, which group expressions and other statements to form logical chunks of Java code.
- Methods (also called functions, procedures, or subroutines), which are named collections of Java statements that can be invoked by other Java code.

---

* Readers who want even more thorough coverage of the Java language should consider *The Java Programming Language, Second Edition*, by Ken Arnold and James Gosling (the creator of Java) (Addison Wesley Longman). And hardcore readers may want to go straight to the primary source: *The Java Language Specification*, by James Gosling, Bill Joy, and Guy Steele (Addison Wesley Longman). This specification is available in printed book form, but is also freely available for download from Sun's web site at *http://java.sun.com/docs/books/jls/*. I found both documents quite helpful while writing this chapter.

- Classes, which are collections of methods and fields. Classes are the central program element in Java and form the basis for object-oriented programming. Chapter 3 is devoted entirely to a discussion of classes and objects.
- Packages, which are collections of related classes.
- Java programs, which consist of one or more interacting classes that may be drawn from one or more packages.

The syntax of most programming languages is complex, and Java is no exception. In general, it is not possible to document all elements of a language without referring to other elements that have not yet been discussed. For example, it is not really possible to explain in a meaningful way the operators and statements supported by Java without referring to objects. But it is also not possible to document objects thoroughly without referring to the operators and statements of the language. The process of learning Java, or any language, is therefore an iterative one. If you are new to Java (or a Java-style programming language), you may find that you benefit greatly from working through this chapter and the next *twice*, so that you can grasp the interrelated concepts.

The Unicode Character Set

Java programs are written using the Unicode character set. Unlike the 7-bit ASCII encoding, which is useful only for English, and the 8-bit ISO Latin-1 encoding, which is useful only for major Western European languages, the 16-bit Unicode encoding can represent virtually every written language in common use on the planet. Very few text editors support Unicode, however, and in practice, most Java programs are written in plain ASCII. 16-bit Unicode characters are typically written to files using an encoding known as UTF-8, which converts the 16-bit characters into a stream of bytes. The format is designed so that plain ASCII and Latin-1 text are valid UTF-8 byte streams. Thus, you can simply write plain ASCII programs, and they will work as valid Unicode.

If you want to embed a Unicode character within a Java program that is written in plain ASCII, use the special Unicode escape sequence `\u`*`xxxx`*. That is, a backslash and a lowercase u, followed by four hexadecimal characters. For example, `\u0020` is the space character, and `\u03c0` is the character π. You can use Unicode characters anywhere in a Java program, including comments and variable names.

Comments

Java supports three types of comments. The first type is a single-line comment, which begins with the characters // and continues until the end of the current line. For example:

```
int i = 0;   // Initialize the loop variable
```

The second kind of comment is a multiline comment. It begins with the characters /* and continues, over any number of lines, until the characters */. Any text between the /* and the */ is ignored by the Java compiler. Although this style of comment is typically used for multiline comments, it can also be used for single-line comments. This type of comment cannot be nested (i.e., one /* */ comment cannot appear within another one). When writing multiline comments, programmers often use extra * characters to make the comments stand out. Here is a typical multiline comment:

```
/*
 * Step 4: Print static methods, both public and protected,
 *         but don't list deprecated ones.
 */
```


The third type of comment is a special case of the second. If a comment begins with /**, it is regarded as a special *doc comment*. Like regular multiline comments, doc comments end with */ and cannot be nested. When you write a Java class you expect other programmers to use, use doc comments to embed documentation about the class and each of its methods directly into the source code. A program named *javadoc* extracts these comments and processes them to create online documentation for your class. A doc comment can contain HTML tags and can use additional syntax understood by *javadoc*. For example:

```
/**
 * Display a list of classes, many to a line.
 *
 * @param classes The classes to display
 * @return <tt>true</tt> on success,
 * <tt>false</tt> on failure.
 * @author David Flanagan
 */
```

See Chapter 7 for more information on the doc-comment syntax and Chapter 8 for more information on the *javadoc* program.

Identifiers and Reserved Words

An *identifier* is any symbolic name that refers to something in a Java program. Class, method, parameter, and variable names are all identifiers. An identifier must begin with a letter, an underscore (_), or a Unicode currency symbol (e.g., $, £, ¥). This initial letter can be followed by any number of letters, digits, underscores, or currency symbols. Remember that Java uses the Unicode character set, which contains quite a few letters and digits other than those in the ASCII character set. The following are legal identifiers:

```
i
engine3
theCurrentTime
the_current_time
θ
```

Identifiers can include numbers, but cannot begin with a number. In addition, they cannot contain any punctuation characters other than underscores and currency characters. By convention, dollar signs and other currency characters are reserved for identifiers automatically generated by a compiler or some kind of code preprocessor. It is best to avoid these characters in your own identifiers.

Another important restriction on identifiers is that you cannot use any of the keywords and literals that are part of the Java language itself. These reserved words are listed in Table 2-1.

Table 2-1. Java reserved words

`abstract`	`default`	`if`	`package`	`synchronized`
`assert`	`do`	`implements`	`private`	`this`
`boolean`	`double`	`import`	`protected`	`throw`
`break`	`else`	`instanceof`	`public`	`throws`
`byte`	`extends`	`int`	`return`	`transient`
`case`	`false`	`interface`	`short`	`true`
`catch`	`final`	`long`	`static`	`try`
`char`	`finally`	`native`	`strictfp`	`void`
`class`	`float`	`new`	`super`	`volatile`
`const`	`for`	`null`	`switch`	`while`
`continue`	`goto`			

Note that `const` and `goto` are reserved words but aren't part of the Java language. `assert` is a reserved word as of Java 1.4

Primitive Data Types

Java supports eight basic data types known as *primitive types*. In addition, it supports classes and arrays as composite data types, or reference types. Classes and arrays are documented later in this chapter. The primitive types are: a boolean type, a character type, four integer types, and two floating-point types. The four integer types and the two floating-point types differ in the number of bits that represent them, and therefore in the range of numbers they can represent. Table 2-2 summarizes these primitive data types.

Table 2-2. Java primitive data types

Type	*Contains*	*Default*	*Size*	*Range*
`boolean`	`true` or `false`	`false`	1 bit	NA
`char`	Unicode character	`\u0000`	16 bits	`\u0000` to `\uFFFF`
`byte`	Signed integer	0	8 bits	–128 to 127
`short`	Signed integer	0	16 bits	–32768 to 32767
`int`	Signed integer	0	32 bits	–2147483648 to 2147483647
`long`	Signed integer	0	64 bits	–9223372036854775808 to 9223372036854775807
`float`	IEEE 754 floating point	0.0	32 bits	±1.4E–45 to ±3.4028235E+38

Table 2-2. Java primitive data types (continued)

Type	*Contains*	*Default*	*Size*	*Range*
`double`	IEEE 754 floating point	0.0	64 bits	±4.9E–324 to ±1.7976931348623157E+308

Java Syntax

The boolean Type

The `boolean` type represents truth values. There are only two possible values of this type, representing the two boolean states: on or off, yes or no, true or false. Java reserves the words `true` and `false` to represent these two boolean values.

C and C++ programmers should note that Java is quite strict about its `boolean` type: `boolean` values can never be converted to or from other data types. In particular, a `boolean` is not an integral type, and integer values cannot be used in place of a `boolean`. In other words, you cannot take shortcuts such as the following in Java:

```
if (o) {
  while(i) {
  }
}
```

Instead, Java forces you to write cleaner code by explicitly stating the comparisons you want:

```
if (o != null) {
  while(i != 0) {
  }
}
```

The char Type

The `char` type represents Unicode characters. It surprises many experienced programmers to learn that Java `char` values are 16 bits long, but in practice this fact is totally transparent. To include a character literal in a Java program, simply place it between single quotes (apostrophes):

```
char c = 'A';
```

You can, of course, use any Unicode character as a character literal, and you can use the `\u` Unicode escape sequence. In addition, Java supports a number of other escape sequences that make it easy both to represent commonly used nonprinting ASCII characters such as newline and to escape certain punctuation characters that have special meaning in Java. For example:

```
char tab = '\t', apostrophe = '\'', nul = '', aleph='\u05D0';
```

Table 2-3 lists the escape characters that can be used in `char` literals. These characters can also be used in string literals, which are covered later in this chapter.

Table 2-3. Java escape characters

Escape sequence	*Character value*
`\b`	Backspace
`\t`	Horizontal tab
`\n`	Newline
`\f`	Form feed
`\r`	Carriage return
`\"`	Double quote
`\'`	Single quote
`\\`	Backslash
`\`*xxx*	The Latin-1 character with the encoding *xxx*, where *xxx* is an octal (base 8) number between 000 and 377. The forms `\`*x* and `\`*xx* are also legal, as in `'\0'`, but are not recommended because they can cause difficulties in string constants where the escape sequence is followed by a regular digit.
`\u`*xxxx*	The Unicode character with encoding *xxxx*, where *xxxx* is four hexadecimal digits. Unicode escapes can appear anywhere in a Java program, not only in character and string literals.

`char` values can be converted to and from the various integral types. Unlike `byte`, `short`, `int`, and `long`, however, `char` is an unsigned type. The `Character` class defines a number of useful `static` methods for working with characters, including `isDigit()`, `isJavaLetter()`, `isLowerCase()`, and `toUpperCase()`.

Integer Types

The integer types in Java are `byte`, `short`, `int`, and `long`. As shown in Table 2-2, these four types differ only in the number of bits and, therefore, in the range of numbers each type can represent. All integral types represent signed numbers; there is no `unsigned` keyword as there is in C and C++.

Literals for each of these types are written exactly as you would expect: as a string of decimal digits, optionally preceded by a minus sign.* Here are some legal integer literals:

```
0
1
123
-42000
```

* Technically, the minus sign is an operator that operates on the literal, not part of the literal itself. Also, all integer literals are 32-bit `int` values unless followed by the letter L, in which case they are 64-bit `long` values. There is no special syntax for `byte` and `short` literals, but `int` literals are usually converted to these shorter types as needed. For example, in the code:

```
byte b = 123;
```

123 is a 32-bit `int` literal that is automatically converted (without requiring a cast) to a byte in the assignment statement.

Integer literals can also be expressed in hexadecimal or octal notation. A literal that begins with 0x or 0X is taken as a hexadecimal number, using the letters A to F (or a to f) as the additional digits required for base-16 numbers. Integer literals beginning with a leading 0 are taken to be octal (base-8) numbers and cannot include the digits 8 or 9. Java does not allow integer literals to be expressed in binary (base-2) notation. Legal hexadecimal and octal literals include:

```
0xff              // Decimal 255, expressed in hexadecimal
0377              // The same number, expressed in octal (base 8)
0xCAFEBABE        // A magic number used to identify Java class files
```

Integer literals are 32-bit int values unless they end with the character L or l, in which case they are 64-bit long values:

```
1234        // An int value
1234L       // A long value
0xffL       // Another long value
```

Integer arithmetic in Java is modular, which means that it never produces an overflow or an underflow when you exceed the range of a given integer type. Instead, numbers just wrap around. For example:

```
byte b1 = 127, b2 = 1;          // Largest byte is 127
byte sum = (byte)(b1 + b2);     // Sum wraps to -128, which is the smallest byte
```

Neither the Java compiler nor the Java interpreter warns you in any way when this occurs. When doing integer arithmetic, you simply must ensure that the type you are using has a sufficient range for the purposes you intend. Integer division by zero and modulo by zero are illegal and cause an ArithmeticException to be thrown.

Each integer type has a corresponding wrapper class: Byte, Short, Integer, and Long. Each of these classes defines MIN_VALUE and MAX_VALUE constants that describe the range of the type. The classes also define useful static methods, such as Byte.parseByte() and Integer.parseInt(), for converting strings to integer values.

Floating-Point Types

Real numbers in Java are represented with the float and double data types. As shown in Table 2-2, float is a 32-bit, single-precision floating-point value, and double is a 64-bit, double-precision floating-point value. Both types adhere to the IEEE 754-1985 standard, which specifies both the format of the numbers and the behavior of arithmetic for the numbers.

Floating-point values can be included literally in a Java program as an optional string of digits, followed by a decimal point and another string of digits. Here are some examples:

```
123.45
0.0
.01
```

Floating-point literals can also use exponential, or scientific, notation, in which a number is followed by the letter e or E (for exponent) and another number. This second number represents the power of ten by which the first number is multiplied. For example:

```
1.2345E02       // 1.2345 × 10², or 123.45
1e-6            // 1 × 10⁻⁶, or 0.000001
6.02e23         // Avogadro's Number: 6.02 × 10²³
```

Floating-point literals are `double` values by default. To include a `float` value literally in a program, follow the number by the character `f` or `F`:

```
double d = 6.02E23;
float f = 6.02e23f;
```

Floating-point literals cannot be expressed in hexadecimal or octal notation.

Most real numbers, by their very nature, cannot be represented exactly in any finite number of bits. Thus, it is important to remember that `float` and `double` values are only approximations of the numbers they are meant to represent. A `float` is a 32-bit approximation, which results in at least 6 significant decimal digits, and a `double` is a 64-bit approximation, which results in at least 15 significant digits. In practice, these data types are suitable for most real-number computations.

In addition to representing ordinary numbers, the `float` and `double` types can also represent four special values: positive and negative infinity, zero, and NaN. The infinity values result when a floating-point computation produces a value that overflows the representable range of a `float` or `double`. When a floating-point computation underflows the representable range of a `float` or a `double`, a zero value results. The Java floating-point types make a distinction between positive zero and negative zero, depending on the direction from which the underflow occurred. In practice, positive and negative zero behave pretty much the same. Finally, the last special floating-point value is NaN, which stands for not-a-number. The NaN value results when an illegal floating-point operation, such as 0.0/0.0, is performed. Here are examples of statements that result in these special values:

```
double inf = 1.0/0.0;               // Infinity
double neginf = -1.0/0.0;           // -Infinity
double negzero = -1.0/inf;          // Negative zero
double NaN = 0.0/0.0;               // Not-a-Number
```

Because the Java floating-point types can handle overflow to infinity and underflow to zero and have a special NaN value, floating-point arithmetic never throws exceptions, even when performing illegal operations, like dividing zero by zero or taking the square root of a negative number.

The `float` and `double` primitive types have corresponding classes, named `Float` and `Double`. Each of these classes defines the following useful constants: `MIN_VALUE`, `MAX_VALUE`, `NEGATIVE_INFINITY`, `POSITIVE_INFINITY`, and `NaN`.

The infinite floating-point values behave as you would expect. Adding or subtracting any finite value to or from infinity, for example, yields infinity. Negative zero behaves almost identically to positive zero, and, in fact, the == equality operator reports that negative zero is equal to positive zero. One way to distinguish negative zero from positive, or regular, zero is to divide by it. 1.0/0.0 yields positive infinity, but 1.0 divided by negative zero yields negative infinity. Finally, since NaN is not-a-number, the == operator says that it is not equal to any other number, including itself! To check whether a `float` or `double` value is NaN, you must use the `Float.isNaN()` and `Double.isNaN()` methods.

Strings

In addition to the boolean, character, integer, and floating-point data types, Java also has a data type for working with strings of text (usually simply called *strings*). The `String` type is a class, however, and is not one of the primitive types of the language. Because strings are so commonly used, though, Java does have a syntax for including string values literally in a program. A `String` literal consists of arbitrary text within double quotes. For example:

```
"Hello, world"
"'This' is a string!"
```

String literals can contain any of the escape sequences that can appear as `char` literals (see Table 2-3). Use the \" sequence to include a double-quote within a `String` literal. Strings and string literals are discussed in more detail later in this chapter. Chapter 4 demonstrates some of the ways you can work with `String` objects in Java.

Type Conversions

Java allows conversions between integer values and floating-point values. In addition, because every character corresponds to a number in the Unicode encoding, `char` values can be converted to and from the integer and floating-point types. In fact, `boolean` is the only primitive type that cannot be converted to or from another primitive type in Java.

There are two basic types of conversions. A *widening conversion* occurs when a value of one type is converted to a wider type—one that has a larger range of legal values. Java performs widening conversions automatically when, for example, you assign an `int` literal to a `double` variable or a `char` literal to an `int` variable.

Narrowing conversions are another matter, however. A *narrowing conversion* occurs when a value is converted to a type that is not wider than it. Narrowing conversions are not always safe: it is reasonable to convert the integer value 13 to a `byte`, for example, but it is not reasonable to convert 13000 to a `byte`, since `byte` can only hold numbers between –128 and 127. Because you can lose data in a narrowing conversion, the Java compiler complains when you attempt any narrowing conversion, even if the value being converted would in fact fit in the narrower range of the specified type:

```
int i = 13;
byte b = i;    // The compiler does not allow this
```

The one exception to this rule is that you can assign an integer literal (an `int` value) to a `byte` or `short` variable, if the literal falls within the range of the variable.

If you need to perform a narrowing conversion and are confident you can do so without losing data or precision, you can force Java to perform the conversion using a language construct known as a *cast*. Perform a cast by placing the name of the desired type in parentheses before the value to be converted. For example:

```
int i = 13;
byte b = (byte) i;      // Force the int to be converted to a byte
i = (int) 13.456;       // Force this double literal to the int 13
```

Casts of primitive types are most often used to convert floating-point values to integers. When you do this, the fractional part of the floating-point value is simply truncated (i.e., the floating-point value is rounded towards zero, not towards the nearest integer). The methods `Math.round()`, `Math.floor()`, and `Math.ceil()` perform other types of rounding.

The `char` type acts like an integer type in most ways, so a `char` value can be used anywhere an `int` or `long` value is required. Recall, however, that the `char` type is *unsigned*, so it behaves differently than the `short` type, even though both of them are 16 bits wide:

```
short s = (short) 0xffff; // These bits represent the number -1
char c = '\uffff';        // The same bits, representing a Unicode character
int i1 = s;               // Converting the short to an int yields -1
int i2 = c;               // Converting the char to an int yields 65535
```

Table 2-4 is a grid that shows which primitive types can be converted to which other types and how the conversion is performed. The letter N in the table means that the conversion cannot be performed. The letter Y means that the conversion is a widening conversion and is therefore performed automatically and implicitly by Java. The letter C means that the conversion is a narrowing conversion and requires an explicit cast. Finally, the notation Y* means that the conversion is an automatic widening conversion, but that some of the least significant digits of the value may be lost by the conversion. This can happen when converting an `int` or `long` to a `float` or `double`. The floating-point types have a larger range than the integer types, so any `int` or `long` can be represented by a `float` or `double`. However, the floating-point types are approximations of numbers and cannot always hold as many significant digits as the integer types.

Table 2–4. Java primitive type conversions

Convert	*Convert to:*							
from:	`boolean`	`byte`	`short`	`char`	`int`	`long`	`float`	`double`
`boolean`	–	N	N	N	N	N	N	N
`byte`	N	–	Y	C	Y	Y	Y	Y
`short`	N	C	–	C	Y	Y	Y	Y
`char`	N	C	C	–	Y	Y	Y	Y
`int`	N	C	C	C	–	Y	Y*	Y
`long`	N	C	C	C	C	–	Y*	Y*
`float`	N	C	C	C	C	C	–	Y
`double`	N	C	C	C	C	C	C	–

Reference Types

In addition to its eight primitive types, Java defines two additional categories of data types: classes and arrays. Java programs consist of class definitions; each class defines a new data type that can be manipulated by Java programs. For example, a program might define a class named `Point` and use it to store and manipulate X,Y points in a Cartesian coordinate system. This makes `Point` a new data type in that program. An array type represents a list of values of some other type. `char` is a data type, and an array of `char` values is another data type, written `char[]`. An array of `Point` objects is a data type, written `Point[]`. And an array of `Point` arrays is yet another type, written `Point[][]`.

As you can see, there are an infinite number of possible class and array data types. Collectively, these data types are known as *reference types*. The reason for this name will become clear later in this chapter. For now, however, what is important to understand is that class and array types differ significantly from primitive types, in that they are compound, or composite, types. A primitive data type holds exactly one value. Classes and arrays are aggregate types that contain multiple values. The `Point` type, for example, holds two `double` values representing the X and Y coordinates of the point. And `char[]` is obviously a compound type because it represents a list of characters. By their very nature, class and array types are more complicated than the primitive data types. We'll discuss classes and arrays in detail later in this chapter and examine classes in even more detail in Chapter 3.

Expressions and Operators

So far in this chapter, we've learned about the primitive types that Java programs can manipulate and seen how to include primitive values as *literals* in a Java program. We've also used *variables* as symbolic names that represent, or hold, values. These literals and variables are the tokens out of which Java programs are built.

An *expression* is the next higher level of structure in a Java program. The Java interpreter *evaluates* an expression to compute its value. The very simplest expressions are called *primary expressions* and consist of literals and variables. So, for example, the following are all expressions:

```
1.7          // A floating-point literal
true         // A boolean literal
sum          // A variable
```

When the Java interpreter evaluates a literal expression, the resulting value is the literal itself. When the interpreter evaluates a variable expression, the resulting value is the value stored in the variable.

Primary expressions are not very interesting. More complex expressions are made by using *operators* to combine primary expressions. For example, the following expression uses the assignment operator to combine two primary expressions—a variable and a floating-point literal—into an assignment expression:

```
sum = 1.7
```

But operators are used not only with primary expressions; they can also be used with expressions at any level of complexity. Thus, the following are all legal expressions:

```
sum = 1 + 2 + 3*1.2 + (4 + 8)/3.0
sum/Math.sqrt(3.0 * 1.234)
(int)(sum + 33)
```

Operator Summary

The kinds of expressions you can write in a programming language depend entirely on the set of operators available to you. Table 2-5 summarizes the operators available in Java. The P and A columns of the table specify the precedence and associativity of each group of related operators, respectively.

Table 2-5. Java operators

P	*A*	*Operator*	*Operand type(s)*	*Operation performed*
15	L	.	object, member	object member access
		[]	array, int	array element access
		(*args*)	method, arglist	method invocation
		++, --	variable	post-increment, decrement
14	R	++, --	variable	pre-increment, decrement
		+, -	number	unary plus, unary minus
		~	integer	bitwise complement
		!	boolean	boolean NOT
13	R	new	class, arglist	object creation
		(*type*)	type, any	cast (type conversion)
12	L	*, /, %	number, number	multiplication, division, remainder
11	L	+, -	number, number	addition, subtraction
		+	string, any	string concatenation
10	L	<<	integer, integer	left shift
		>>	integer, integer	right shift with sign extension
		>>>	integer, integer	right shift with zero extension
9	L	<, <=	number, number	less than, less than or equal
		>, >=	number, number	greater than, greater than or equal
		instanceof	reference, type	type comparison
8	L	==	primitive, primitive	equal (have identical values)
		!=	primitive, primitive	not equal (have different values)
		==	reference, reference	equal (refer to same object)

Table 2-5. Java operators (continued)

<table>
<tr><th>P</th><th>A</th><th>Operator</th><th>Operand type(s)</th><th>Operation performed</th></tr>
<tr><td></td><td></td><td>!=</td><td>reference, reference</td><td>not equal (refer to different objects)</td></tr>
<tr><td>7</td><td>L</td><td>&</td><td>integer, integer</td><td>bitwise AND</td></tr>
<tr><td></td><td></td><td>&</td><td>boolean, boolean</td><td>boolean AND</td></tr>
<tr><td>6</td><td>L</td><td>^</td><td>integer, integer</td><td>bitwise XOR</td></tr>
<tr><td></td><td></td><td>^</td><td>boolean, boolean</td><td>boolean XOR</td></tr>
<tr><td>5</td><td>L</td><td>|</td><td>integer, integer</td><td>bitwise OR</td></tr>
<tr><td></td><td></td><td>|</td><td>boolean, boolean</td><td>boolean OR</td></tr>
<tr><td>4</td><td>L</td><td>&&</td><td>boolean, boolean</td><td>conditional AND</td></tr>
<tr><td>3</td><td>L</td><td>||</td><td>boolean, boolean</td><td>conditional OR</td></tr>
<tr><td>2</td><td>R</td><td>?:</td><td>boolean, any, any</td><td>conditional (ternary) operator</td></tr>
<tr><td>1</td><td>R</td><td>=</td><td>variable, any</td><td>assignment</td></tr>
<tr><td></td><td></td><td>*=, /=, %=,
|=, =, <<=,
>>=, >>>=,
&=, ^=, |=</td><td>variable, any</td><td>assignment with operation</td></tr>
</table>

Precedence

The P column of Table 2-5 specifies the *precedence* of each operator. Precedence specifies the order in which operations are performed. Consider this expression:

```
a + b * c
```

The multiplication operator has higher precedence than the addition operator, so a is added to the product of b and c. Operator precedence can be thought of as a measure of how tightly operators bind to their operands. The higher the number, the more tightly they bind.

Default operator precedence can be overridden through the use of parentheses, to explicitly specify the order of operations. The previous expression can be rewritten as follows to specify that the addition should be performed before the multiplication:

```
(a + b) * c
```

The default operator precedence in Java was chosen for compatibility with C; the designers of C chose this precedence so that most expressions can be written naturally without parentheses. There are only a few common Java idioms for which parentheses are required. Examples include:

```
// Class cast combined with member access
((Integer) o).intValue();

// Assignment combined with comparison
```

```
while((line = in.readLine()) != null) { ... }

// Bitwise operators combined with comparison
if ((flags & (PUBLIC | PROTECTED)) != 0) { ... }
```

Associativity

When an expression involves several operators that have the same precedence, the operator associativity governs the order in which the operations are performed. Most operators are left-to-right associative, which means that the operations are performed from left to right. The assignment and unary operators, however, have right-to-left associativity. The A column of Table 2-5 specifies the associativity of each operator or group of operators. The value L means left to right, and R means right to left.

The additive operators are all left-to-right associative, so the expression `a+b-c` is evaluated from left to right: `(a+b)-c`. Unary operators and assignment operators are evaluated from right to left. Consider this complex expression:

```
a = b += c = -~d
```

This is evaluated as follows:

```
a = (b += (c = -(~d)))
```

As with operator precedence, operator associativity establishes a default order of evaluation for an expression. This default order can be overridden through the use of parentheses. However, the default operator associativity in Java has been chosen to yield a natural expression syntax, and you rarely need to alter it.

Operand number and type

The fourth column of Table 2-5 specifies the number and type of the operands expected by each operator. Some operators operate on only one operand; these are called unary operators. For example, the unary minus operator changes the sign of a single number:

```
-n              // The unary minus operator
```

Most operators, however, are binary operators that operate on two operand values. The – operator actually comes in both forms:

```
a - b           // The subtraction operator is a binary operator
```

Java also defines one ternary operator, often called the conditional operator. It is like an `if` statement inside an expression. Its three operands are separated by a question mark and a colon; the second and third operands must be convertible to the same type:

```
x > y ? x : y  // Ternary expression; evaluates to the larger of x and y
```

In addition to expecting a certain number of operands, each operator also expects particular types of operands. Column four of the table lists the operand types. Some of the codes used in that column require further explanation:

number
: An integer, floating-point value, or character (i.e., any primitive type except `boolean`)

integer
: A `byte`, `short`, `int`, `long`, or `char` value (`long` values are not allowed for the array access operator `[]`)

reference
: An object or array

variable
: A variable or anything else, such as an array element, to which a value can be assigned

Return type

Just as every operator expects its operands to be of specific types, each operator produces a value of a specific type. The arithmetic, increment and decrement, bitwise, and shift operators return a `double` if at least one of the operands is a `double`. Otherwise, they return a `float` if at least one of the operands is a `float`. Otherwise, they return a `long` if at least one of the operands is a `long`. Otherwise, they return an `int`, even if both operands are `byte`, `short`, or `char` types that are narrower than `int`.

The comparison, equality, and boolean operators always return `boolean` values. Each assignment operator returns whatever value it assigned, which is of a type compatible with the variable on the left side of the expression. The conditional operator returns the value of its second or third argument (which must both be of the same type).

Side effects

Every operator computes a value based on one or more operand values. Some operators, however, have *side effects* in addition to their basic evaluation. If an expression contains side effects, evaluating it changes the state of a Java program in such a way that evaluating the expression again may yield a different result. For example, the ++ increment operator has the side effect of incrementing a variable. The expression `++a` increments the variable `a` and returns the newly incremented value. If this expression is evaluated again, the value will be different. The various assignment operators also have side effects. For example, the expression `a*=2` can also be written as `a=a*2`. The value of the expression is the value of `a` multiplied by 2, but the expression also has the side effect of storing that value back into `a`. The method invocation operator `()` has side effects if the invoked method has side effects. Some methods, such as `Math.sqrt()`, simply compute and return a value without side effects of any kind. Typically, however, methods do have side effects. Finally, the `new` operator has the profound side effect of creating a new object.

Order of evaluation

When the Java interpreter evaluates an expression, it performs the various operations in an order specified by the parentheses in the expression, the precedence of the operators, and the associativity of the operators. Before any operation is performed, however, the interpreter first evaluates the operands of the operator. (The exceptions are the `&&`, `||`, and `?:` operators, which do not always evaluate all their operands.) The interpreter always evaluates operands in order from left to right. This matters if any of the operands are expressions that contain side effects. Consider this code, for example:

```
int a = 2;
int v = ++a + ++a * ++a;
```

Although the multiplication is performed before the addition, the operands of the + operator are evaluated first. Thus, the expression evaluates to 3+4*5, or 23.

Arithmetic Operators

Since most programs operate primarily on numbers, the most commonly used operators are often those that perform arithmetic operations. The arithmetic operators can be used with integers, floating-point numbers, and even characters (i.e., they can be used with any primitive type other than `boolean`). If either of the operands is a floating-point number, floating-point arithmetic is used; otherwise, integer arithmetic is used. This matters because integer arithmetic and floating-point arithmetic differ in the way division is performed and in the way underflows and overflows are handled, for example. The arithmetic operators are:

Addition (+)
: The + operator adds two numbers. As we'll see shortly, the + operator can also be used to concatenate strings. If either operand of + is a string, the other one is converted to a string as well. Be sure to use parentheses when you want to combine addition with concatenation. For example:

```
System.out.println("Total: " + 3 + 4);    // Prints "Total: 34", not 7!
```

Subtraction (–)
: When – is used as a binary operator, it subtracts its second operand from its first. For example, 7–3 evaluates to 4. The – operator can perform unary negation.

Multiplication (*)
: The * operator multiplies its two operands. For example, 7*3 evaluates to 21.

Division (/)
: The / operator divides its first operand by its second. If both operands are integers, the result is an integer, and any remainder is lost. If either operand is a floating-point value, however, the result is a floating-point value. When dividing two integers, division by zero throws an `ArithmeticException`. For floating-point calculations, however, division by zero simply yields an infinite result or NaN:

```
7/3         // Evaluates to 2
7/3.0f      // Evaluates to 2.333333f
7/0         // Throws an ArithmeticException
7/0.0       // Evaluates to positive infinity
0.0/0.0     // Evaluates to NaN
```

Modulo (%)
: The % operator computes the first operand modulo the second operand (i.e., it returns the remainder when the first operand is divided by the second operand an integral number of times). For example, 7%3 is 1. The sign of the result is the same as the sign of the first operand. While the modulo operator is typically used with integer operands, it also works for floating-point values. For example, 4.3%2.1 evaluates to 0.1. When operating with integers, trying to compute a value modulo zero causes an `ArithmeticException`. When working with floating-point values, anything modulo 0.0 evaluates to `NaN`, as does infinity modulo anything.

Unary minus (–)
: When - is used as a unary operator, before a single operand, it performs unary negation. In other words, it converts a positive value to an equivalently negative value, and vice versa.

Java Syntax

String Concatenation Operator

In addition to adding numbers, the + operator (and the related += operator) also concatenates, or joins, strings. If either of the operands to + is a string, the operator converts the other operand to a string. For example:

```
System.out.println("Quotient: " + 7/3.0f);  // Prints "Quotient: 2.3333333"
```

As a result, you must be careful to put any addition expressions in parentheses when combining them with string concatenation. If you do not, the addition operator is interpreted as a concatenation operator.

The Java interpreter has built-in string conversions for all primitive types. An object is converted to a string by invoking its `toString()` method. Some classes define custom `toString()` methods, so that objects of that class can easily be converted to strings in this way. An array is converted to a string by invoking the built-in `toString()` method, which, unfortunately, does not return a useful string representation of the array contents.

Increment and Decrement Operators

The ++ operator increments its single operand, which must be a variable, an element of an array, or a field of an object, by one. The behavior of this operator depends on its position relative to the operand. When used before the operand, where it is known as the *pre-increment* operator, it increments the operand and evaluates to the incremented value of that operand. When used after the operand, where it is known as the *post-increment* operator, it increments its operand, but evaluates to the value of that operand before it was incremented.

For example, the following code sets both i and j to 2:

```
i = 1;
j = ++i;
```

But these lines set i to 2 and j to 1:

```
i = 1;
j = i++;
```

Similarly, the -- operator decrements its single numeric operand, which must be a variable, an element of an array, or a field of an object, by one. Like the ++ operator, the behavior of -- depends on its position relative to the operand. When used before the operand, it decrements the operand and returns the decremented value. When used after the operand, it decrements the operand, but returns the *undecremented* value.

The expressions x++ and x-- are equivalent to x=x+1 and x=x-1, respectively, except that when using the increment and decrement operators, x is only evaluated once. If x is itself an expression with side effects, this makes a big difference. For example, these two expressions are not equivalent:

```
a[i++]++;              // Increments an element of an array
a[i++] = a[i++] + 1;   // Adds one to an array element and stores it in another
```

These operators, in both prefix and postfix forms, are most commonly used to increment or decrement the counter that controls a loop.

Comparison Operators

The comparison operators consist of the equality operators that test values for equality or inequality and the relational operators used with ordered types (numbers and characters) to test for greater than and less than relationships. Both types of operators yield a boolean result, so they are typically used with if statements and while and for loops to make branching and looping decisions. For example:

```
if (o != null) ...;          // The not equals operator
while(i < a.length) ...;     // The less than operator
```

Java provides the following equality operators:

Equals (==)

The == operator evaluates to true if its two operands are equal and false otherwise. With primitive operands, it tests whether the operand values themselves are identical. For operands of reference types, however, it tests whether the operands refer to the same object or array. In other words, it does not test the equality of two distinct objects or arrays. In particular, note that you cannot test two distinct strings for equality with this operator.

If == is used to compare two numeric or character operands that are not of the same type, the narrower operand is converted to the type of the wider operand before the comparison is done. For example, when comparing a short to a float, the short is first converted to a float before the comparison is performed. For floating-point numbers, the special negative zero value tests equal to the regular, positive zero value. Also, the special NaN (not-a-number) value is not equal to any other number, including itself. To test whether a floating-point value is NaN, use the `Float.isNan()` or `Double.isNan()` method.

Not equals (!=)
: The != operator is exactly the opposite of the == operator. It evaluates to `true` if its two primitive operands have different values or if its two reference operands refer to different objects or arrays. Otherwise, it evaluates to `false`.

The relational operators can be used with numbers and characters, but not with `boolean` values, objects, or arrays because those types are not ordered. Java provides the following relational operators:

Less than (<)
: Evaluates to `true` if the first operand is less than the second.

Less than or equal (<=)
: Evaluates to `true` if the first operand is less than or equal to the second.

Greater than (>)
: Evaluates to `true` if the first operand is greater than the second.

Greater than or equal (>=)
: Evaluates to `true` if the first operand is greater than or equal to the second.

Boolean Operators

As we've just seen, the comparison operators compare their operands and yield a `boolean` result, which is often used in branching and looping statements. In order to make branching and looping decisions based on conditions more interesting than a single comparison, you can use the boolean (or logical) operators to combine multiple comparison expressions into a single, more complex, expression. The boolean operators require their operands to be `boolean` values and they evaluate to `boolean` values. The operators are:

Conditional AND (&&)
: This operator performs a boolean AND operation on its operands. It evaluates to `true` if and only if both its operands are `true`. If either or both operands are `false`, it evaluates to `false`. For example:

```
if (x < 10 && y > 3) ... // If both comparisons are true
```

This operator (and all the boolean operators except the unary `!` operator) have a lower precedence than the comparison operators. Thus, it is perfectly legal to write a line of code like the one above. However, some programmers prefer to use parentheses to make the order of evaluation explicit:

```
if ((x < 10) && (y > 3)) ...
```

You should use whichever style you find easier to read.

This operator is called a conditional AND because it conditionally evaluates its second operand. If the first operand evaluates to `false`, the value of the expression is `false`, regardless of the value of the second operand. Therefore, to increase efficiency, the Java interpreter takes a shortcut and skips the second operand. Since the second operand is not guaranteed to be evaluated, you must use caution when using this operator with expressions that have side effects. On the other hand, the conditional nature of this operator allows us to write Java expressions such as the following:

```
if (data != null && i < data.length && data[i] != -1) ...
```

The second and third comparisons in this expression would cause errors if the first or second comparisons evaluated to `false`. Fortunately, we don't have to worry about this because of the conditional behavior of the `&&` operator.

Conditional OR (`||`)
This operator performs a boolean OR operation on its two `boolean` operands. It evaluates to `true` if either or both of its operands are `true`. If both operands are `false`, it evaluates to `false`. Like the `&&` operator, `||` does not always evaluate its second operand. If the first operand evaluates to `true`, the value of the expression is `true`, regardless of the value of the second operand. Thus, the operator simply skips that second operand in that case.

Boolean NOT (`!`)
This unary operator changes the `boolean` value of its operand. If applied to a `true` value, it evaluates to `false`, and if applied to a `false` value, it evaluates to `true`. It is useful in expressions like these:

```
if (!found) ...          // found is a boolean variable declared somewhere
while (!c.isEmpty()) ... // The isEmpty() method returns a boolean value
```

Because `!` is a unary operator, it has a high precedence and often must be used with parentheses:

```
if (!(x > y && y > z))
```

Boolean AND (`&`)
When used with `boolean` operands, the `&` operator behaves like the `&&` operator, except that it always evaluates both operands, regardless of the value of the first operand. This operator is almost always used as a bitwise operator with integer operands, however, and many Java programmers would not even recognize its use with `boolean` operands as legal Java code.

Boolean OR (`|`)
This operator performs a boolean OR operation on its two `boolean` operands. It is like the `||` operator, except that it always evaluates both operands, even if the first one is `true`. The `|` operator is almost always used as a bitwise operator on integer operands; its use with `boolean` operands is very rare.

Boolean XOR (`^`)
When used with `boolean` operands, this operator computes the Exclusive OR (XOR) of its operands. It evaluates to `true` if exactly one of the two operands is `true`. In other words, it evaluates to `false` if both operands are `false` or if both operands are `true`. Unlike the `&&` and `||` operators, this one must always evaluate both operands. The `^` operator is much more commonly used as a bitwise operator on integer operands. With `boolean` operands, this operator is equivalent to the `!=` operator.

Bitwise and Shift Operators

The bitwise and shift operators are low-level operators that manipulate the individual bits that make up an integer value. The bitwise operators are most commonly used for testing and setting individual flag bits in a value. In order to understand their behavior, you must understand binary (base-2) numbers and the twos-complement format used to represent negative integers. You cannot use these operators with floating-point, `boolean`, array, or object operands. When used with `boolean` operands, the `&`, `|`, and `^` operators perform a different operation, as described in the previous section.

If either of the arguments to a bitwise operator is a `long`, the result is a `long`. Otherwise, the result is an `int`. If the left operand of a shift operator is a `long`, the result is a `long`; otherwise, the result is an `int`. The operators are:

Bitwise complement (`~`)
: The unary `~` operator is known as the bitwise complement, or bitwise NOT, operator. It inverts each bit of its single operand, converting ones to zeros and zeros to ones. For example:

```
byte b = ~12;           // ~00001100 ==> 11110011 or -13 decimal
flags = flags & ~f;     // Clear flag f in a set of flags
```

Bitwise AND (`&`)
: This operator combines its two integer operands by performing a boolean AND operation on their individual bits. The result has a bit set only if the corresponding bit is set in both operands. For example:

```
10 & 7                  // 00001010 & 00000111 ==> 00000010 or 2
if ((flags & f) != 0)   // Test whether flag f is set
```

When used with `boolean` operands, `&` is the infrequently used boolean AND operator described earlier.

Bitwise OR (`|`)
: This operator combines its two integer operands by performing a boolean OR operation on their individual bits. The result has a bit set if the corresponding bit is set in either or both of the operands. It has a zero bit only where both corresponding operand bits are zero. For example:

```
10 | 7                  // 00001010 | 00000111 ==> 00001111 or 15
flags = flags | f;      // Set flag f
```

When used with `boolean` operands, `|` is the infrequently used boolean OR operator described earlier.

Bitwise XOR (`^`)
: This operator combines its two integer operands by performing a boolean XOR (Exclusive OR) operation on their individual bits. The result has a bit set if the corresponding bits in the two operands are different. If the corresponding operand bits are both ones or both zeros, the result bit is a zero. For example:

```
10 ^ 7                // 00001010 ^ 00000111 ==> 00001101 or 13
```

When used with `boolean` operands, ^ is the infrequently used boolean XOR operator.

Left shift (<<)

The << operator shifts the bits of the left operand left by the number of places specified by the right operand. High-order bits of the left operand are lost, and zero bits are shifted in from the right. Shifting an integer left by *n* places is equivalent to multiplying that number by 2^n. For example:

```
10 << 1     // 00001010 << 1 = 00010100 = 20 = 10*2
7 << 3      // 00000111 << 3 = 00111000 = 56 = 7*8
-1 << 2     // 0xFFFFFFFF << 2 = 0xFFFFFFFC = -4 = -1*4
```

If the left operand is a `long`, the right operand should be between 0 and 63. Otherwise, the left operand is taken to be an `int`, and the right operand should be between 0 and 31.

Signed right shift (>>)

The >> operator shifts the bits of the left operand to the right by the number of places specified by the right operand. The low-order bits of the left operand are shifted away and are lost. The high-order bits shifted in are the same as the original high-order bit of the left operand. In other words, if the left operand is positive, zeros are shifted into the high-order bits. If the left operand is negative, ones are shifted in instead. This technique is known as *sign extension*; it is used to preserve the sign of the left operand. For example:

```
10 >> 1       // 00001010 >> 1 = 00000101 = 5 = 10/2
27 >> 3       // 00011011 >> 3 = 00000011 = 3 = 27/8
-50 >> 2      // 11001110 >> 2 = 11110011 = -13 != -50/4
```

If the left operand is positive and the right operand is *n*, the >> operator is the same as integer division by 2^n.

Unsigned right shift (>>>)

This operator is like the >> operator, except that it always shifts zeros into the high-order bits of the result, regardless of the sign of the left-hand operand. This technique is called *zero extension*; it is appropriate when the left operand is being treated as an unsigned value (despite the fact that Java integer types are all signed). Examples:

```
0xff >>> 4     // 11111111 >>> 4 = 00001111 = 15  = 255/16
-50 >>> 2      // 0xFFFFFFCE >>> 2 = 0x3FFFFF33 = 107371811
```

Assignment Operators

The assignment operators store, or assign, a value into some kind of variable. The left operand must evaluate to an appropriate local variable, array element, or object field. The right side can be any value of a type compatible with the variable. An assignment expression evaluates to the value that is assigned to the variable. More importantly, however, the expression has the side effect of actually performing the assignment. Unlike all other binary operators, the assignment operators are right-associative, which means that the assignments in `a=b=c` are performed right-to-left, as follows: `a=(b=c)`.

The basic assignment operator is =. Do not confuse it with the equality operator, ==. In order to keep these two operators distinct, I recommend that you read = as "is assigned the value."

In addition to this simple assignment operator, Java also defines 11 other operators that combine assignment with the 5 arithmetic operators and the 6 bitwise and shift operators. For example, the += operator reads the value of the left variable, adds the value of the right operand to it, stores the sum back into the left variable as a side effect, and returns the sum as the value of the expression. Thus, the expression x+=2 is almost the same as x=x+2. The difference between these two expressions is that when you use the += operator, the left operand is evaluated only once. This makes a difference when that operand has a side effect. Consider the following two expressions, which are not equivalent:

Java Syntax

```
a[i++] += 2;
a[i++] = a[i++] + 2;
```

The general form of these combination assignment operators is:

```
var op= value
```

This is equivalent (unless there are side effects in var) to:

```
var = var op value
```

The available operators are:

```
+=    -=    *=    /=    %=      // Arithmetic operators plus assignment
&=    |=    ^=                  // Bitwise operators plus assignment
<<=   >>=   >>>=                // Shift operators plus assignment
```

The most commonly used operators are += and -=, although &= and |= can also be useful when working with boolean flags. For example:

```
i += 2;           // Increment a loop counter by 2
c -= 5;           // Decrement a counter by 5
flags |= f;       // Set a flag f in an integer set of flags
flags &= ~f;      // Clear a flag f in an integer set of flags
```

The Conditional Operator

The conditional operator ?: is a somewhat obscure ternary (three-operand) operator inherited from C. It allows you to embed a conditional within an expression. You can think of it as the operator version of the if/else statement. The first and second operands of the conditional operator are separated by a question mark (?), while the second and third operands are separated by a colon (:). The first operand must evaluate to a boolean value. The second and third operands can be of any type, but they must be convertible to the same type.

The conditional operator starts by evaluating its first operand. If it is true, the operator evaluates its second operand and uses that as the value of the expression. On the other hand, if the first operand is false, the conditional operator evaluates and returns its third operand. The conditional operator never evaluates both its second and third operand, so be careful when using expressions with side effects with this operator. Examples of this operator are:

```
int max = (x > y) ? x : y;
String name = (name != null) ? name : "unknown";
```

Note that the `?:` operator has lower precedence than all other operators except the assignment operators, so parentheses are not usually necessary around the operands of this operator. Many programmers find conditional expressions easier to read if the first operand is placed within parentheses, however. This is especially true because the conditional `if` statement always has its conditional expression written within parentheses.

The instanceof Operator

The `instanceof` operator requires an object or array value as its left operand and the name of a reference type as its right operand. It evaluates to `true` if the object or array is an *instance* of the specified type; it returns `false` otherwise. If the left operand is `null`, `instanceof` always evaluates to `false`. If an `instanceof` expression evaluates to `true`, it means that you can safely cast and assign the left operand to a variable of the type of the right operand.

The `instanceof` operator can be used only with array and object types and values, not primitive types and values. Object and array types are discussed in detail later in this chapter. Examples of `instanceof` are:

```
"string" instanceof String      // True: all strings are instances of String
"" instanceof Object            // True: strings are also instances of Object
null instanceof String          // False: null is never instanceof anything

Object o = new int[] {1,2,3};
o instanceof int[]   // True: the array value is an int array
o instanceof byte[]  // False: the array value is not a byte array
o instanceof Object  // True: all arrays are instances of Object

// Use instanceof to make sure that it is safe to cast an object
if (object instanceof Point) {
  Point p = (Point) object;
}
```

Special Operators

There are five language constructs in Java that are sometimes considered operators and sometimes considered simply part of the basic language syntax. These "operators" are listed in Table 2-5 in order to show their precedence relative to the other true operators. The use of these language constructs is detailed elsewhere in this chapter, but is described briefly here, so that you can recognize these constructs when you encounter them in code examples:

Object member access (`.`)
: An *object* is a collection of data and methods that operate on that data; the data fields and methods of an object are called its members. The dot (`.`) operator accesses these members. If `o` is an expression that evaluates to an

object reference, and f is the name of a field of the object, o.f evaluates to the value contained in that field. If m is the name of a method, o.m refers to that method and allows it to be invoked using the () operator shown later.

Array element access ([])
An *array* is a numbered list of values. Each element of an array can be referred to by its number, or *index*. The [] operator allows you to refer to the individual elements of an array. If a is an array, and i is an expression that evaluates to an int, a[i] refers to one of the elements of a. Unlike other operators that work with integer values, this operator restricts array index values to be of type int or narrower.

Method invocation (())
A *method* is a named collection of Java code that can be run, or *invoked*, by following the name of the method with zero or more comma-separated expressions contained within parentheses. The values of these expressions are the *arguments* to the method. The method processes the arguments and optionally returns a value that becomes the value of the method invocation expression. If o.m is a method that expects no arguments, the method can be invoked with o.m(). If the method expects three arguments, for example, it can be invoked with an expression such as o.m(x,y,z). Before the Java interpreter invokes a method, it evaluates each of the arguments to be passed to the method. These expressions are guaranteed to be evaluated in order from left to right (which matters if any of the arguments have side effects).

Object creation (new)
In Java, objects (and arrays) are created with the new operator, which is followed by the type of the object to be created and a parenthesized list of arguments to be passed to the object *constructor*. A constructor is a special method that initializes a newly created object, so the object creation syntax is similar to the Java method invocation syntax. For example:

```
new ArrayList();
new Point(1,2)
```

Type conversion or casting (())
As we've already seen, parentheses can also be used as an operator to perform narrowing type conversions, or casts. The first operand of this operator is the type to be converted to; it is placed between the parentheses. The second operand is the value to be converted; it follows the parentheses. For example:

```
(byte) 28           // An integer literal cast to a byte type
(int) (x + 3.14f)   // A floating-point sum value cast to an integer value
(String)h.get(k)    // A generic object cast to a more specific string type
```

Statements

A *statement* is a single command executed b the Java interpreter. By default, the Java interpreter runs one statement after another, in the order they are written. Many of the statements defined by Java, however, are flow-control statements, such as conditionals and loops, that alter this default order of execution in well-defined ways. Table 2-6 summarizes the statements defined by Java.

Table 2-6. Java statements

Statement	*Purpose*	*Syntax*

expression	side effects	`var = expr;`
		`expr++;`
		`method();`
		`new Type();`

compound	group statements	`{ statements }`
empty	do nothing	`;`
labeled	name a statement	`label : statement`
variable	declare a variable	`[final] type name [= value] [, name [= value]] ... ;`
`if`	conditional	`if ( expr ) statement [ else statement]`

`switch`	conditional	`switch ( expr ) {`
		`[ case expr : statements ] ...`
		`[ default: statements ]`
		`}`

`while`	loop	`while ( expr ) statement`
`do`	loop	`do statement while ( expr );`
`for`	simplified loop	`for ( init ; test ; increment ) statement`
`break`	exit block	`break [ label ] ;`
`continue`	restart loop	`continue [ label ] ;`
`return`	end method	`return [ expr ] ;`
`synchronized`	critical section	`synchronized ( expr ) { statements }`
`throw`	throw exception	`throw expr ;`

`try`	handle exception	`try { statements }`
		`[ catch ( type name ) { statements } ]`
		`...`
		`[ finally { statements } ]`

`assert`	verify invariant	`assert invariant [ : error] ;` (Java 1.4 and later)

Expression Statements

As we saw earlier in the chapter, certain types of Java expressions have side effects. In other words, they do not simply evaluate to some value, but also change the program state in some way. Any expression with side effects can be used as a statement simply by following it with a semicolon. The legal types of expression statements are assignments, increments and decrements, method calls, and object creation. For example:

```
a = 1;                          // Assignment
x *= 2;                         // Assignment with operation
i++;                            // Post-increment
--c;                            // Pre-decrement
System.out.println("statement"); // Method invocation
```

Compound Statements

A *compound statement* is any number and kind of statements grouped together within curly braces. You can use a compound statement anywhere a *statement* is required by Java syntax:


```
for(int i = 0; i < 10; i++) {
  a[i]++;                    // Body of this loop is a compound statement.
  b[i]--;                    // It consists of two expression statements
}                            // within curly braces.
```

The Empty Statement

An *empty statement* in Java is written as a single semicolon. The empty statement doesn't do anything, but the syntax is occasionally useful. For example, you can use it to indicate an empty loop body of a for loop:

```
for(int i = 0; i < 10; a[i++]++)  // Increment array elements
    /* empty */;                  // Loop body is empty statement
```

Labeled Statements

A *labeled statement* is simply a statement that has been given a name by prepending an identifier and a colon to it. Labels are used by the break and continue statements. For example:

```
rowLoop: for(int r = 0; r < rows.length; r++) {        // A labeled loop
  colLoop: for(int c = 0; c < columns.length; c++) {   // Another one
    break rowLoop;                                     // Use a label
  }
}
```

Local Variable Declaration Statements

A *local variable*, often simply called a variable, is a symbolic name for a location where a value can be stored that is defined within a method or compound statement. All variables must be declared before they can be used; this is done with a variable declaration statement. Because Java is a strongly typed language, a variable declaration specifies the type of the variable, and only values of that type can be stored in the variable.

In its simplest form, a variable declaration specifies a variable's type and name:

```
int counter;
String s;
```

A variable declaration can also include an *initializer*: an expression that specifies an initial value for the variable. For example:

```
int i = 0;
String s = readLine();
int[] data = {x+1, x+2, x+3};  // Array initializers are documented later
```

The Java compiler does not allow you to use a local variable that has not been initialized, so it is usually convenient to combine variable declaration and initialization into a single statement. The initializer expression need not be a literal value or a constant expression that can be evaluated by the compiler; it can be an arbitrarily complex expression whose value is computed when the program is run.

A single variable declaration statement can declare and initialize more than one variable, but all variables must be of the same type. Variable names and optional initializers are separated from each other with commas:

```
int i, j, k;
float x = 1.0, y = 1.0;
String question = "Really Quit?", response;
```

In Java 1.1 and later, variable declaration statements can begin with the `final` keyword. This modifier specifies that once an initial value is specified for the variable, that value is never allowed to change:

```
final String greeting = getLocalLanguageGreeting();
```

C programmers should note that Java variable declaration statements can appear anywhere in Java code; they are not restricted to the beginning of a method or block of code. Local variable declarations can also be integrated with the *`initialize`* portion of a `for` loop, as we'll discuss shortly.

Local variables can be used only within the method or block of code in which they are defined. This is called their *scope* or *lexical scope*:

```
void method() {            // A generic method
  int i = 0;               // Declare variable i
  while (i < 10) {         // i is in scope here
    int j = 0;             // Declare j; the scope of j begins here
    i++;                   // i is in scope here; increment it
  }                        // j is no longer in scope; can't use it anymore
  System.out.println(i);   // i is still in scope here
}                          // The scope of i ends here
```

The if/else Statement

The `if` statement is the fundamental control statement that allows Java to make decisions or, more precisely, to execute statements conditionally. The `if` statement has an associated expression and statement. If the expression evaluates to `true`, the interpreter executes the statement. If the expression evaluates to `false`, however, the interpreter skips the statement. For example:

```
if (username == null)         // If username is null,
  username = "John Doe";      // define it
```

Although they look extraneous, the parentheses around the expression are a required part of the syntax for the `if` statement.

As I already mentioned, a block of statements enclosed in curly braces is itself a statement, so we can also write `if` statements that look as follows:

```
if ((address == null) || (address.equals(""))) {
  address = "[undefined]";
  System.out.println("WARNING: no address specified.");
}
```

An `if` statement can include an optional `else` keyword that is followed by a second statement. In this form of the statement, the expression is evaluated, and, if it is `true`, the first statement is executed. Otherwise, the second statement is executed. For example:

```
if (username != null)
  System.out.println("Hello " + username);
else {
  username = askQuestion("What is your name?");
  System.out.println("Hello " + username + ". Welcome!");
}
```

When you use nested `if/else` statements, some caution is required to ensure that the `else` clause goes with the appropriate `if` statement. Consider the following lines:

```
if (i == j)
  if (j == k)
    System.out.println("i equals k");
else
  System.out.println("i doesn't equal j");    // WRONG!!
```

In this example, the inner `if` statement forms the single statement allowed by the syntax of the outer `if` statement. Unfortunately, it is not clear (except from the hint given by the indentation) which `if` the `else` goes with. And in this example, the indentation hint is wrong. The rule is that an `else` clause like this is associated with the nearest `if` statement. Properly indented, this code looks like this:

```
if (i == j)
  if (j == k)
    System.out.println("i equals k");
  else
    System.out.println("i doesn't equal j");    // WRONG!!
```

This is legal code, but it is clearly not what the programmer had in mind. When working with nested `if` statements, you should use curly braces to make your code easier to read. Here is a better way to write the code:

```
if (i == j) {
  if (j == k)
    System.out.println("i equals k");
}
else {
  System.out.println("i doesn't equal j");
}
```

The else if clause

The `if/else` statement is useful for testing a condition and choosing between two statements or blocks of code to execute. But what about when you need to choose between several blocks of code? This is typically done with an `else if` clause, which is not really new syntax, but a common idiomatic usage of the standard `if/else` statement. It looks like this:

```
if (n == 1) {
   // Execute code block #1
}
else if (n == 2) {
   // Execute code block #2
}
else if (n == 3) {
   // Execute code block #3
}
else {
   // If all else fails, execute block #4
}
```

There is nothing special about this code. It is just a series of `if` statements, where each `if` is part of the `else` clause of the previous statement. Using the `else if` idiom is preferable to, and more legible than, writing these statements out in their fully nested form:

```
if (n == 1) {
  // Execute code block #1
}
else {
  if (n == 2) {
    // Execute code block #2
  }
  else {
    if (n == 3) {
      // Execute code block #3
    }
    else {
      // If all else fails, execute block #4
    }
  }
}
```

The switch Statement

An `if` statement causes a branch in the flow of a program's execution. You can use multiple `if` statements, as shown in the previous section, to perform a multiway branch. This is not always the best solution, however, especially when all of the branches depend on the value of a single variable. In this case, it is inefficient to repeatedly check the value of the same variable in multiple `if` statements.

A better solution is to use a `switch` statement, which is inherited from the C programming language. Although the syntax of this statement is not nearly as elegant as other parts of Java, the brute practicality of the construct makes it worthwhile. If you are not familiar with the `switch` statement itself, you may at least be familiar with the basic concept, under the name computed goto or jump table. A `switch` statement has an integer expression and a body that contains various numbered entry points. The expression is evaluated, and control jumps to the entry point specified by that value. For example, the following `switch` statement is equivalent to the repeated `if` and `else/if` statements shown in the previous section:

```
switch(n) {
  case 1:                      // Start here if n == 1
    // Execute code block #1
    break;                     // Stop here
  case 2:                      // Start here if n == 2
    // Execute code block #2
    break;                     // Stop here
  case 3:                      // Start here if n == 3
    // Execute code block #3
    break;                     // Stop here
  default:                     // If all else fails...
                               // Execute code block #4
    break;                     // Stop here
}
```

As you can see from the example, the various entry points into a `switch` statement are labeled either with the keyword `case`, followed by an integer value and a colon, or with the special `default` keyword, followed by a colon. When a `switch` statement executes, the interpreter computes the value of the expression in parentheses and then looks for a `case` label that matches that value. If it finds one, the interpreter starts executing the block of code at the first statement following the `case` label. If it does not find a `case` label with a matching value, the interpreter starts execution at the first statement following a special-case `default:` label. Or, if there is no `default:` label, the interpreter skips the body of the `switch` statement altogether.

Note the use of the `break` keyword at the end of each `case` in the previous code. The `break` statement is described later in this chapter, but, in this case, it causes the interpreter to exit the body of the `switch` statement. The `case` clauses in a `switch` statement specify only the *starting point* of the desired code. The individual cases are not independent blocks of code, and they do not have any implicit ending point. Therefore, you must explicitly specify the end of each case with a `break` or related statement. In the absence of `break` statements, a `switch` statement begins executing code at the first statement after the matching `case` label and continues executing statements until it reaches the end of the block. On rare occasions, it is useful to write code like this that falls through from one `case` label to the next, but 99% of the time you should be careful to end every `case` and `default` section with a statement that causes the `switch` statement to stop executing. Normally you use a `break` statement, but `return` and `throw` also work.

A `switch` statement can have more than one `case` clause labeling the same statement. Consider the `switch` statement in the following method:

```
boolean parseYesOrNoResponse(char response) {
  switch(response) {
    case 'y':
    case 'Y': return true;
    case 'n':
    case 'N': return false;
    default: throw new IllegalArgumentException("Response must be Y or N");
```

```
    }
  }
```

There are some important restrictions on the `switch` statement and its `case` labels. First, the expression associated with a `switch` statement must have a `byte`, `char`, `short`, or `int` value. The floating-point and `boolean` types are not supported, and neither is `long`, even though `long` is an integer type. Second, the value associated with each `case` label must be a constant value or a constant expression the compiler can evaluate. A `case` label cannot contain a runtime expression involving variables or method calls, for example. Third, the `case` label values must be within the range of the data type used for the `switch` expression. And finally, it is obviously not legal to have two or more `case` labels with the same value or more than one `default` label.

The while Statement

Just as the `if` statement is the basic control statement that allows Java to make decisions, the `while` statement is the basic statement that allows Java to perform repetitive actions. It has the following syntax:

```
while (expression)
  statement
```

The `while` statement works by first evaluating the *`expression`*. If it is `false`, the interpreter skips the *`statement`* associated with the loop and moves to the next statement in the program. If it is `true`, however, the *`statement`* that forms the body of the loop is executed, and the *`expression`* is reevaluated. Again, if the value of *`expression`* is `false`, the interpreter moves on to the next statement in the program; otherwise it executes the *`statement`* again. This cycle continues while the *`expression`* remains `true` (i.e., until it evaluates to `false`), at which point the `while` statement ends, and the interpreter moves on to the next statement. You can create an infinite loop with the syntax `while(true)`.

Here is an example `while` loop that prints the numbers 0 to 9:

```
int count = 0;
while (count < 10) {
  System.out.println(count);
  count++;
}
```

As you can see, the variable `count` starts off at 0 in this example and is incremented each time the body of the loop runs. Once the loop has executed 10 times, the expression becomes `false` (i.e., `count` is no longer less than 10), the `while` statement finishes, and the Java interpreter can move to the next statement in the program. Most loops have a counter variable like `count`. The variable names `i`, `j`, and `k` are commonly used as a loop counters, although you should use more descriptive names if it makes your code easier to understand.

The do Statement

A `do` loop is much like a `while` loop, except that the loop expression is tested at the bottom of the loop, rather than at the top. This means that the body of the loop is always executed at least once. The syntax is:

```
do
  statement
while ( expression ) ;
```


There are a couple of differences to notice between the `do` loop and the more ordinary `while` loop. First, the `do` loop requires both the `do` keyword to mark the beginning of the loop and the `while` keyword to mark the end and introduce the loop condition. Also, unlike the `while` loop, the `do` loop is terminated with a semicolon. This is because the `do` loop ends with the loop condition, rather than simply ending with a curly brace that marks the end of the loop body. The following `do` loop prints the same output as the `while` loop shown above:

```
int count = 0;
do {
  System.out.println(count);
  count++;
} while(count < 10);
```

Note that the `do` loop is much less commonly used than its `while` cousin. This is because, in practice, it is unusual to encounter a situation where you are sure you always want a loop to execute at least once.

The for Statement

The `for` statement provides a looping construct that is often more convenient than the `while` and `do` loops. The `for` statement takes advantage of a common looping pattern. Most loops have a counter, or state variable of some kind, that is initialized before the loop starts, tested to determine whether to execute the loop body, and then incremented, or updated somehow, at the end of the loop body before the test expression is evaluated again. The initialization, test, and update steps are the three crucial manipulations of a loop variable, and the `for` statement makes these three steps an explicit part of the loop syntax:

```
for(initialize ; test ; update)
    statement
```

This `for` loop is basically equivalent to the following `while` loop:*

```
initialize;
while(test) {
  statement;
  update;
}
```

Placing the *`initialize`*, *`test`*, and *`update`* expressions at the top of a `for` loop makes it especially easy to understand what the loop is doing, and it prevents

* As you'll see when we consider the `continue` statement, this `while` loop is not exactly equivalent to the `for` loop.

mistakes such as forgetting to initialize or update the loop variable. The interpreter discards the values of the *initialize* and *update* expressions, so in order to be useful, these expressions must have side effects. *initialize* is typically an assignment expression, while *update* is usually an increment, decrement, or some other assignment.

The following `for` loop prints the numbers 0 to 9, just as the previous `while` and `do` loops have done:

```
int count;
for(count = 0 ; count < 10 ; count++)
  System.out.println(count);
```

Notice how this syntax places all the important information about the loop variable on a single line, making it very clear how the loop executes. Placing the update expression in the `for` statement itself also simplifies the body of the loop to a single statement; we don't even need to use curly braces to produce a statement block.

The `for` loop supports some additional syntax that makes it even more convenient to use. Because many loops use their loop variables only within the loop, the `for` loop allows the *initialize* expression to be a full variable declaration, so that the variable is scoped to the body of the loop and is not visible outside of it. For example:

```
for(int count = 0 ; count < 10 ; count++)
  System.out.println(count);
```

Furthermore, the `for` loop syntax does not restrict you to writing loops that use only a single variable. Both the *initialize* and *update* expressions of a `for` loop can use a comma to separate multiple initializations and update expressions. For example:

```
for(int i = 0, j = 10 ; i < 10 ; i++, j--)
    sum += i * j;
```

Even though all the examples so far have counted numbers, `for` loops are not restricted to loops that count numbers. For example, you might use a `for` loop to iterate through the elements of a linked list:

```
for(Node n = listHead; n != null; n = n.nextNode())
  process(n);
```

The *initialize*, *test*, and *update* expressions of a `for` loop are all optional; only the semicolons that separate the expressions are required. If the *test* expression is omitted, it is assumed to be `true`. Thus, you can write an infinite loop as `for(;;)`.

The break Statement

A `break` statement causes the Java interpreter to skip immediately to the end of a containing statement. We have already seen the `break` statement used with the switch statement. The break statement is most often written as simply the keyword break followed by a semicolon:

```
break;
```

When used in this form, it causes the Java interpreter to immediately exit the innermost containing while, do, for, or switch statement. For example:

```
for(int i = 0; i < data.length; i++) {  // Loop through the data array.
  if (data[i] == target) {              // When we find what we're looking for,
    index = i;                          // remember where we found it
    break;                              // and stop looking!
  }
}   // The Java interpreter goes here after executing break
```


The break statement can also be followed by the name of a containing labeled statement. When used in this form, break causes the Java interpreter to immediately exit from the named block, which can be any kind of statement, not just a loop or switch. For example:

```
testfornull: if (data != null) {             // If the array is defined,
  for(int row = 0; row < numrows; row++) {   // loop through one dimension,
    for(int col = 0; col < numcols; col++) { // then loop through the other.
      if (data[row][col] == null)            // If the array is missing data,
        break testfornull;                   // treat the array as undefined.
    }
  }
}  // Java interpreter goes here after executing break testfornull
```

The continue Statement

While a break statement exits a loop, a continue statement quits the current iteration of a loop and starts the next one. continue, in both its unlabeled and labeled forms, can be used only within a while, do, or for loop. When used without a label, continue causes the innermost loop to start a new iteration. When used with a label that is the name of a containing loop, it causes the named loop to start a new iteration. For example:

```
for(int i = 0; i < data.length; i++) {  // Loop through data.
  if (data[i] == -1)                    // If a data value is missing,
    continue;                           // skip to the next iteration.
  process(data[i]);                     // Process the data value.
}
```

while, do, and for loops differ slightly in the way that continue starts a new iteration:

- With a while loop, the Java interpreter simply returns to the top of the loop, tests the loop condition again, and, if it evaluates to true, executes the body of the loop again.
- With a do loop, the interpreter jumps to the bottom of the loop, where it tests the loop condition to decide whether to perform another iteration of the loop.

- With a `for` loop, the interpreter jumps to the top of the loop, where it first evaluates the *update* expression and then evaluates the *test* expression to decide whether to loop again. As you can see, the behavior of a `for` loop with a `continue` statement is different from the behavior of the "basically equivalent" `while` loop I presented earlier; *update* gets evaluated in the `for` loop, but not in the equivalent `while` loop.

The return Statement

A `return` statement tells the Java interpreter to stop executing the current method. If the method is declared to return a value, the `return` statement is followed by an expression. The value of the expression becomes the return value of the method. For example, the following method computes and returns the square of a number:

```
double square(double x) {       // A method to compute x squared
  return x * x;                 // Compute and return a value
}
```

Some methods are declared `void` to indicate they do not return any value. The Java interpreter runs methods like this by executing its statements one by one until it reaches the end of the method. After executing the last statement, the interpreter returns implicitly. Sometimes, however, a `void` method has to return explicitly before reaching the last statement. In this case, it can use the `return` statement by itself, without any expression. For example, the following method prints, but does not return, the square root of its argument. If the argument is a negative number, it returns without printing anything:

```
void printSquareRoot(double x) {     // A method to print square root of x
  if (x < 0) return;                 // If x is negative, return explicitly
  System.out.println(Math.sqrt(x));  // Print the square root of x
}                                    // End of method: return implicitly
```

The synchronized Statement

Since Java is a multithreaded system, you must often take care to prevent multiple threads from modifying an object simultaneously in a way that might corrupt the object's state. Sections of code that must not be executed simultaneously are known as *critical sections*. Java provides the `synchronized` statement to protect these critical sections. The syntax is:

```
synchronized ( expression ) {
  statements
}
```

expression is an expression that must evaluate to an object or an array. The *statements* constitute the code of the critical section and must be enclosed in curly braces. Before executing the critical section, the Java interpreter first obtains an exclusive lock on the object or array specified by *expression*. It holds the lock until it is finished running the critical section, then releases it. While a thread holds the lock on an object, no other thread can obtain that lock. Therefore, no other thread can execute this or any other critical sections that require a lock on the same object. If a thread cannot immediately obtain the lock required to execute a critical section, it simply waits until the lock becomes available.

Note that you do not have to use the synchronized statement unless your program creates multiple threads that share data. If only one thread ever accesses a data structure, there is no need to protect it with synchronized. When you do have to use synchronized, it might be in code like the following:

```
public static void SortIntArray(int[] a) {
  // Sort the array a. This is synchronized so that some other thread
  // cannot change elements of the array while we're sorting it (at
  // least not other threads that protect their changes to the array
  // with synchronized).
  synchronized (a) {
  // Do the array sort here
  }
}
```


The synchronized keyword is also available as a modifier in Java and is more commonly used in this form than as a statement. When applied to a method, the synchronized keyword indicates that the entire method is a critical section. For a synchronized class method (a static method), Java obtains an exclusive lock on the class before executing the method. For a synchronized instance method, Java obtains an exclusive lock on the class instance. (Class and instance methods are discussed in Chapter 3.)

The throw Statement

An *exception* is a signal that indicates some sort of exceptional condition or error has occurred. To *throw* an exception is to signal an exceptional condition. To *catch* an exception is to handle it—to take whatever actions are necessary to recover from it.

In Java, the throw statement is used to throw an exception:

```
throw expression ;
```

The *expression* must evaluate to an exception object that describes the exception or error that has occurred. We'll talk more about types of exceptions shortly; for now, all you need to know is that an exception is represented by an object. Here is some example code that throws an exception:

```
public static double factorial(int x) {
  if (x < 0)
    throw new IllegalArgumentException("x must be >= 0");
  double fact;
  for(fact=1.0; x > 1; fact *= x, x--)
    /* empty */ ;          // Note use of the empty statement
  return fact;
}
```

When the Java interpreter executes a throw statement, it immediately stops normal program execution and starts looking for an exception handler that can catch, or handle, the exception. Exception handlers are written with the try/catch/finally statement, which is described in the next section. The Java interpreter first looks at the enclosing block of code to see if it has an associated exception handler. If so, it exits that block of code and starts running the exception-handling code associated with the block. After running the exception handler, the interpreter continues execution at the statement immediately following the handler code.

If the enclosing block of code does not have an appropriate exception handler, the interpreter checks the next higher enclosing block of code in the method. This continues until a handler is found. If the method does not contain an exception handler that can handle the exception thrown by the `throw` statement, the interpreter stops running the current method and returns to the caller. Now the interpreter starts looking for an exception handler in the blocks of code of the calling method. In this way, exceptions propagate up through the lexical structure of Java methods, up the call stack of the Java interpreter. If the exception is never caught, it propagates all the way up to the `main()` method of the program. If it is not handled in that method, the Java interpreter prints an error message, prints a stack trace to indicate where the exception occurred, and then exits.

Exception types

An exception in Java is an object. The type of this object is `java.lang.Throwable`, or more commonly, some subclass of `Throwable` that more specifically describes the type of exception that occurred.* `Throwable` has two standard subclasses: `java.lang.Error` and `java.lang.Exception`. Exceptions that are subclasses of `Error` generally indicate unrecoverable problems: the virtual machine has run out of memory, or a class file is corrupted and cannot be read, for example. Exceptions of this sort can be caught and handled, but it is rare to do so. Exceptions that are subclasses of `Exception`, on the other hand, indicate less severe conditions. These are exceptions that can be reasonably caught and handled. They include such exceptions as `java.io.EOFException`, which signals the end of a file, and `java.lang.ArrayIndexOutOfBoundsException`, which indicates that a program has tried to read past the end of an array. In this book, I use the term "exception" to refer to any exception object, regardless of whether the type of that exception is `Exception` or `Error`.

Since an exception is an object, it can contain data, and its class can define methods that operate on that data. The `Throwable` class and all its subclasses include a `String` field that stores a human-readable error message that describes the exceptional condition. It's set when the exception object is created and can be read from the exception with the `getMessage()` method. Most exceptions contain only this single message, but a few add other data. The `java.io.InterruptedIOException`, for example, adds a field named `bytesTransferred` that specifies how much input or output was completed before the exceptional condition interrupted it.

Declaring exceptions

In addition to making a distinction between `Error` and `Exception` classes, the Java exception-handling scheme also makes a distinction between checked and unchecked exceptions. Any exception object that is an `Error` is unchecked. Any exception object that is an `Exception` is checked, unless it is a subclass of `java.lang.RuntimeException`, in which case it is unchecked. (`RuntimeException`

* We haven't talked about subclasses yet; they are covered in detail in Chapter 3.

is a subclass of Exception.) The reason for this distinction is that virtually any method can throw an unchecked exception, at essentially any time. There is no way to predict an OutOfMemoryError, for example, and any method that uses objects or arrays can throw a NullPointerException if it is passed an invalid null argument. Checked exceptions, on the other hand, arise only in specific, well-defined circumstances. If you try to read data from a file, for example, you must at least consider the possibility that a FileNotFoundException will be thrown if the specified file cannot be found.

Java has different rules for working with checked and unchecked exceptions. If you write a method that throws a checked exception, you must use a throws clause to declare the exception in the method signature. The reason these types of exceptions are called checked exceptions is that the Java compiler checks to make sure you have declared them in method signatures and produces a compilation error if you have not. The factorial() method shown earlier throws an exception of type java.lang.IllegalArgumentException. This is a subclass of RuntimeException, so it is an unchecked exception, and we do not have to declare it with a throws clause (although we can if we want to be explicit).

Even if you never throw an exception yourself, there are times when you must use a throws clause to declare an exception. If your method calls a method that can throw a checked exception, you must either include exception-handling code to handle that exception or use throws to declare that your method can also throw that exception.

How do you know if the method you are calling can throw a checked exception? You can look at its method signature to find out. Or, failing that, the Java compiler will tell you (by reporting a compilation error) if you've called a method whose exceptions you must handle or declare. The following method reads the first line of text from a named file. It uses methods that can throw various types of java.io.IOException objects, so it declares this fact with a throws clause:

```
public static String readFirstLine(String filename) throws IOException {
  BufferedReader in = new BufferedReader(new FileReader(filename));
  return in.readLine();
}
```

We'll talk more about method declarations and method signatures later in this chapter.

The try/catch/finally Statement

The try/catch/finally statement is Java's exception-handling mechanism. The try clause of this statement establishes a block of code for exception handling. This try block is followed by zero or more catch clauses, each of which is a block of statements designed to handle a specific type of exception. The catch clauses are followed by an optional finally block that contains cleanup code guaranteed to be executed regardless of what happens in the try block. Both the catch and finally clauses are optional, but every try block must be accompanied by at least one or the other. The try, catch, and finally blocks all begin and end with curly braces. These are a required part of the syntax and cannot be omitted, even if the clause contains only a single statement.

The following code illustrates the syntax and purpose of the try/catch/finally statement:

```
try {
  // Normally this code runs from the top of the block to the bottom
  // without problems. But it can sometimes throw an exception,
  // either directly with a throw statement or indirectly by calling
  // a method that throws an exception.
}
catch (SomeException e1) {
  // This block contains statements that handle an exception object
  // of type SomeException or a subclass of that type. Statements in
  // this block can refer to that exception object by the name e1.
}
catch (AnotherException e2) {
  // This block contains statements that handle an exception object
  // of type AnotherException or a subclass of that type. Statements
  // in this block can refer to that exception object by the name e2.
}
finally {
  // This block contains statements that are always executed
  // after we leave the try clause, regardless of whether we leave it:
  //   1) normally, after reaching the bottom of the block;
  //   2) because of a break, continue, or return statement;
  //   3) with an exception that is handled by a catch clause above; or
  //   4) with an uncaught exception that has not been handled.
  // If the try clause calls System.exit(), however, the interpreter
  // exits before the finally clause can be run.
}
```

try

The try clause simply establishes a block of code that either has its exceptions handled or needs special cleanup code to be run when it terminates for any reason. The try clause by itself doesn't do anything interesting; it is the catch and finally clauses that do the exception-handling and cleanup operations.

catch

A try block can be followed by zero or more catch clauses that specify code to handle various types of exceptions. Each catch clause is declared with a single argument that specifies the type of exceptions the clause can handle and also provides a name the clause can use to refer to the exception object it is currently handling. The type and name of an exception handled by a catch clause are exactly like the type and name of an argument passed to a method, except that for a catch clause, the argument type must be Throwable or one of its subclasses.

When an exception is thrown, the Java interpreter looks for a catch clause with an argument of the same type as the exception object or a superclass of that type. The interpreter invokes the first such catch clause it finds. The code within a catch block should take whatever action is necessary to cope with the exceptional condition. If the exception is a java.io.FileNotFoundException exception, for example, you might handle it by asking the user to check his spelling and try again. It is not required to have a catch clause for every possible exception; in some cases the correct response is to allow the exception to propagate up and be caught by the invoking method. In other cases, such as a programming error signaled by NullPointerException, the correct response is probably not to catch the exception at all, but allow it to propagate and have the Java interpreter exit with a stack trace and an error message.

finally

The finally clause is generally used to clean up after the code in the try clause (e.g., close files, shut down network connections). What is useful about the finally clause is that it is guaranteed to be executed if any portion of the try block is executed, regardless of how the code in the try block completes. In fact, the only way a try clause can exit without allowing the finally clause to be executed is by invoking the System.exit() method, which causes the Java interpreter to stop running.

In the normal case, control reaches the end of the try block and then proceeds to the finally block, which performs any necessary cleanup. If control leaves the try block because of a return, continue, or break statement, the finally block is executed before control transfers to its new destination.

If an exception occurs in the try block, and there is an associated catch block to handle the exception, control transfers first to the catch block and then to the finally block. If there is no local catch block to handle the exception, control transfers first to the finally block, and then propagates up to the nearest containing catch clause that can handle the exception.

If a finally block itself transfers control with a return, continue, break, or throw statement or by calling a method that throws an exception, the pending control transfer is abandoned, and this new transfer is processed. For example, if a finally clause throws an exception, that exception replaces any exception that was in the process of being thrown. If a finally clause issues a return statement, the method returns normally, even if an exception has been thrown and has not been handled yet.

try and finally can be used together without exceptions or any catch clauses. In this case, the finally block is simply cleanup code that is guaranteed to be executed, regardless of any break, continue, or return statements within the try clause.

In previous discussions of the for and continue statements, we've seen that a for loop cannot be naively translated into a while loop because the continue statement behaves slightly differently when used in a for loop than it does when used in a while loop. The finally clause gives us a way to write a while loop that handles the continue statement in the same way that a for loop does. Consider the following generalized for loop:

```
for( initialize ; test ; update )
    statement
```

The following while loop behaves the same, even if the statement block contains a continue statement:

```
initialize ;
while ( test ) {
```

```
    try { statement }
    finally { update ; }
}
```

Note, however, that placing the update statement within a `finally` block causes this `while` loop to respond to `break` statements differently than the `for` loop does.

The assert Statement

An `assert` statement is used to document and verify design assumptions in Java code. This statement was added in Java 1.4 and cannot be used with previous versions of the language. An *assertion* consists of the `assert` keyword followed by a boolean expression that the programmer believes should always evaluate to `true`. By default, assertions are not enabled, and the `assert` statement does not actually do anything. It is possible to enable assertions as a debugging and testing tool, however; when this is done, the `assert` statement evaluates the expression. If it is indeed `true`, `assert` does nothing. On the other hand, if the expression evaluates to `false`, the assertion fails, and the `assert` statement throws a `java.lang.AssertionError`.

The `assert` statement may include an optional second expression, separated from the first by a colon. When assertions are enabled, and the first expression evaluates to `false`, the value of the second expression is taken as an error code or error message and is passed to the `AssertionError()` constructor. The full syntax of the statement is:

```
assert assertion ;
```

or:

```
assert assertion : errorcode ;
```

It is important to remember that the `assertion` *must* be a boolean expression, which typically means that it contains a comparison operator or invokes a boolean-valued method.

Compiling assertions

Because the `assert` statement was added in Java 1.4, and because `assert` was not a reserved word prior to Java 1.4, the introduction of this new statement can cause code that uses "assert" as an identifier to break. For this reason, the *javac* compiler does not recognize the `assert` statement by default. To compile Java code that uses the `assert` statement, you must use the command-line argument `-source 1.4`. For example:

```
javac -source 1.4 ClassWithAssertions.java
```

The *javac* compiler allows "assert" to be used as an identifier unless `-source 1.4` is specified. If it finds `assert` used as an identifier, it issues an incompatibility warning. In future releases, the command-line option may no longer be required, and the `assert` statement may be recognized by default, so code that uses `assert` as an identifier should be phased out or fixed.

Enabling assertions

assert statements encode assumptions that should always be true. For efficiency, it does not make sense to test assertions each time code is executed. Thus, by default, assertions are disabled, and assert statements have no effect. The assertion code remains compiled in the class files, however, so it can always be enabled for testing, diagnostic, and debugging purposes. You can enable assertions, either across the board or selectively, with command-line arguments to the Java interpreter. To enable assertions in all classes except for system classes, use the -ea argument. To enable assertions in system classes, use -esa. To enable assertions within a specific class, use -ea followed by a colon and the classname:

```
java -ea:com.example.sorters.MergeSort com.example.sorters.Test
```

To enable assertions for all classes in a package and in all of its subpackages, follow the -ea argument with a colon, the package name, and three dots:

```
java -ea:com.example.sorters... com.example.sorters.Test
```

You can disable assertions in the same way, using the -da argument. For example, to enable assertions throughout a package and then disable them in a specific class or subpackage, use:

```
java -ea:com.example.sorters... -da:com.example.sorters.QuickSort
java -ea:com.example.sorters... -da:com.example.sorters.plugins...
```

If you prefer verbose command-line arguments, you can use -enableassertions and -disableassertions instead of -ea and -da and -enablesystemassertions instead of -esa.

Java 1.4 adds to java.lang.ClassLoader methods for enabling and disabling the assertions for classes loaded through that ClassLoader. If you use a custom class loader in your program and want to turn on assertions, you may be interested in these methods. See ClassLoader in Chapter 11.

Using assertions

Because assertions are disabled by default and impose no performance penalty on your code, you can use them liberally to document any assumptions you make while programming. It may take some time to get used to this, but as you do, you'll find more and more uses for the assert statement. Suppose, for example, that you're writing a method in such a way that you know that the variable x is either 0 or 1. Without assertions, you might code an if statement that looks like this:

```
if (x == 0) {
  ...
}
else {  // x is 1
  ...
}
```

The comment in this code is an informal assertion indicating that you believe that within the body of the else clause, x will always equal 1.

Now suppose that your code is later modified in such a way that x can take on a value other than 0 and 1. The comment and the assumption that go along with it are no longer valid, and this may cause a bug that is not immediately apparent or is difficult to localize. The solution in this situation is to convert your comment into an assert statement. The code becomes:

```
if (x == 0) {
  ...
}
else {
  assert x == 1 : x  // x must be 0 or 1
  ...
}
```

Now, if x somehow ends up holding an unexpected value, an AssertionError is thrown, which makes the bug immediately apparent and easy to pinpoint. Furthermore, the second expression (following the colon) in the assert statement includes the unexpected value of x as the "error message" of the AssertionError. This message is not intended to mean anything to an end user, but to provide enough information so that you know not just that an assertion failed but also what caused it to fail.

A similar technique is useful with switch statements. If you write a switch statement without a default clause, you make an assumption about the set of possible values for the switch expression. If you believe that no other value is possible, you can add an assert statement to document and validate that fact. For example:

```
switch(x) {
  case -1: return LESS;
  case 0: return EQUALS;
  case 1: return GREATER;
  default: assert false:x; // Throw AssertionError if x is not -1, 0, or 1.
}
```

Note that assert false; always fails. This form of the statement is a useful "dead-end" statement when you believe that the statement can never be reached.

Another common use of the assert statement is to test whether the arguments passed to a method all have values that are legal for that method; this is also known as enforcing method preconditions. For example:

```
private static Object[] subArray(Object[] a, int x, int y) {
  assert x <= y : "subArray: x > y";   // Precondition: x must be <= y
  // Now go on to create and return a subarray of a...
}
```

Note that this is a private method. The programmer has used an assert statement to document a precondition of the subArray() method and state that she believes that all methods that invoke this private method do in fact honor that precondition. She can state this because she has control over all the methods that invoke subArray(). She can verify her belief by enabling assertions while testing the code. But once the code is tested, if assertions are left disabled, the method does not suffer the overhead of testing its arguments each time it is called. Note that the programmer did not use an assert statement to test that argument *a* is non-null and that the *x* and *y* arguments were legal indexes into that array. These implicit preconditions are always tested by Java at runtime, and a failure results in an unchecked NullPointerException or an ArrayIndexOutOfBoundsException, so an assertion is not required for them.

It is important to understand that the assert statement is not suitable for enforcing preconditions on public methods. A public method can be called from anywhere, and the programmer cannot assert in advance that it will be invoked correctly. To be robust, a public API must explicitly test its arguments and enforce its preconditions each time it is called, whether or not assertions are enabled.

A related use of the assert statement is to verify a class invariant. Suppose you are creating a class that represents a list of objects and allows objects to be inserted and deleted, but always maintains the list in sorted order. You can assert this invariant by writing a method that tests whether the list is actually sorted, then using an assert statement to invoke the method at the end of each method that modifies the list. For example:

```
public void insert(Object o) {
  ...                  // Do the insertion here
  assert isSorted();  // Assert the class invariant here
}
```

When writing code that must be thread-safe, you must obtain locks (using a synchronized method or statement) when required. One common use of the assert statement in this situation is to verify that the current thread holds the lock it requires:

```
assert Thread.holdsLock(data);
```

The Thread.holdsLock() method was added in Java 1.4 primarily for use with the assert statement.

To use assertions effectively, there are a couple of things that you should avoid doing. First, remember that your programs will sometimes run with assertions enabled and sometimes with assertions disabled. This means that you should be careful not to write assertion expressions that contain side effects. If you do, your code will run differently when assertions are enabled than it will when they are disabled. There are a few exceptions to this rule, of course. For example, if a method contains two assert statements, the first can include a side effect that affects only the second assertion. Another use of side effects in assertions is the following idiom that determines whether assertions are enabled (which is not something that your code should ever really need to do):

```
boolean assertions = false;  // Whether assertions are enabled
assert assertions = true;    // This assert never fails but has a side effect
```

Note that the expression in the assert statement is an assignment, not a comparison. The value of an assignment expression is always the value assigned, so this expression always evaluates to true, and the assertion never fails. Because this assignment expression is part of an assert statement, the assertions variable is set to true only if assertions are enabled.

In addition to avoiding side effects in your assertions, another rule for working with the assert statement is that you should never try to catch an AssertionError (unless you catch it at the top level simply so that you can display the error in a more user-friendly fashion). If an AssertionError is thrown, it indicates that one of the programmer's assumptions has not held up. This means that the code is being used outside of the parameters for which it was designed, and it cannot be expected to work correctly. In short, there is no plausible way to recover from an `AssertionError`, and you should not attempt to catch it.

Methods

A *method* is a named sequence of Java statements that can be invoked by other Java code. When a method is invoked, it is passed zero or more values known as arguments. The method performs some computations and, optionally, returns a value. A method invocation is an expression that is evaluated by the Java interpreter. Because method invocations can have side effects, however, they can also be used as expression statements.

You already know how to define the body of a method; it is simply an arbitrary sequence of statements enclosed within curly braces. What is more interesting about a method is its *signature*. The signature specifies:*

- The name of the method
- The number, order, type and name of the parameters used by the method
- The type of the value returned by the method
- The checked exceptions that the method can throw (the signature may also list unchecked exceptions, but these are not required)
- Various method modifiers that provide additional information about the method

A method signature defines everything you need to know about a method before calling it. It is the method *specification* and defines the API for the method. The reference section of this book is essentially a list of method signatures for all publicly accessible methods of all publicly accessible classes of the Java platform. In order to use the reference section of this book, you need to know how to read a method signature. And, in order to write Java programs, you need to know how to define your own methods, each of which begins with a method signature.

A method signature looks like this:

```
modifiers type name ( paramlist ) [ throws exceptions ]
```

The signature (the method specification) is followed by the method body (the method implementation), which is simply a sequence of Java statements enclosed in curly braces. In certain cases (described in Chapter 3), the implementation is omitted, and the method body is replaced with a single semicolon.

Here are some example method definitions. The method bodies have been omitted, so we can focus on the signatures:

```
public static void main(String[] args) { ... }
public final synchronized int indexOf(Object element, int startIndex) { ... }
```

---

* In the Java Language Specification, the term "signature" has a technical meaning that is slightly different than that used here. This book uses a less formal definition of method signature.

```
double distanceFromOrigin() { ... }
static double squareRoot(double x) throws IllegalArgumentException { ... }
protected abstract String readText(File f, String encoding)
          throws FileNotFoundException, UnsupportedEncodingException;
```

modifiers is zero or more special modifier keywords, separated from each other by spaces. A method might be declared with the `public` and `static` modifiers, for example. Other valid method modifiers are `abstract`, `final`, `native`, `private`, `protected`, and `synchronized`. The meanings of these modifiers are not important here; they are discussed in Chapter 3.

The *type* in a method signature specifies the return type of the method. If the method returns a value, this is the name of a primitive type, an array type, or a class. If the method does not return a value, *type* must be `void`. A *constructor* is a special kind of method used to initialize newly created objects. As we'll see in Chapter 3, constructors are defined just like methods, except that their signatures do not include this *type* specification.

The *name* of a method follows the specification of its modifiers and type. Method names, like variable names, are Java identifiers and, like all Java identifiers, may contain letters in any language represented by the Unicode character set. It is legal (and sometimes useful) to define more than one method with the same name, as long as each version of the method has a different parameter list. Defining multiple methods with the same name is called *method overloading*. The `System.out.println()` method we've seen so much of is an overloaded method. There is one method by this name that prints a string and other methods by the same name that print the values of the various primitive types. The Java compiler decides which method to call based on the type of the argument passed to the method.

When you are defining a method, the name of the method is always followed by the method's parameter list, which must be enclosed in parentheses. The parameter list defines zero or more arguments that are passed to the method. The parameter specifications, if there are any, each consist of a type and a name and are separated from each other by commas (if there are multiple parameters). When a method is invoked, the argument values it is passed must match the number, type, and order of the parameters specified in this method signature line. The values passed need not have exactly the same type as specified in the signature, but they must be convertible to those types without casting. C and C++ programmers should note that when a Java method expects no arguments, its parameter list is simply `()`, not `(void)`.

The final part of a method signature is the `throws` clause, which I first described when we discussed the `throw` statement. If a method uses the `throw` statement to throw a checked exception, or if it calls some other method that throws a checked exception and does not catch or handle that exception, the method must declare that it can throw that exception. If a method can throw one or more checked exceptions, it specifies this by placing the `throws` keyword after the argument list and following it by the name of the exception class or classes it can throw. If a method does not throw any exceptions, it does not use the `throws` keyword. If a method throws more than one type of exception, separate the names of the exception classes from each other with commas.

Classes and Objects

Now that we have introduced operators, expressions, statements, and methods, we can finally talk about classes. A *class* is a named collection of fields that hold data values and methods that operate on those values. Some classes also contain nested inner classes. Classes are the most fundamental structural element of all Java programs. You cannot write Java code without defining a class. All Java statements appear within methods, and all methods are defined within classes.

Classes are more than just another structural level of Java syntax. Just as a cell is the smallest unit of life that can survive and reproduce on its own, a class is the smallest unit of Java code that can stand alone. The Java compiler and interpreter do not recognize fragments of Java code that are smaller than a class. A class is the basic unit of execution for Java, which makes classes very important. Java actually defines another construct, called an *interface*, that is quite similar to a class. The distinction between classes and interfaces will become clear in Chapter 3, but for now I'll use the term "class" to mean either a class or an interface.

Classes are important for another reason: every class defines a new data type. For example, you can define a class named `Point` to represent a data point in the two-dimensional Cartesian coordinate system. This class can define fields (each of type `double`) to hold the X and Y coordinates of a point and methods to manipulate and operate on the point. The `Point` class is a new data type.

When discussing data types, it is important to distinguish between the data type itself and the values the data type represents. `char` is a data type: it represents Unicode characters. But a `char` value represents a single specific character. A class is a data type; a class value is called an *object*. We use the name class because each class defines a type (or kind, or species, or class) of objects. The `Point` class is a data type that represents X,Y points, while a `Point` object represents a single specific X,Y point. As you might imagine, classes and their objects are closely linked. In the sections that follow, we will discuss both.

Defining a Class

Here is a possible definition of the `Point` class we have been discussing:

```
/** Represents a Cartesian (x,y) point */
public class Point {
  public double x, y;                    // The coordinates of the point
  public Point(double x, double y) {     // A constructor that
    this.x = x; this.y = y;              // initializes the fields
  }

  public double distanceFromOrigin() {   // A method that operates on
    return Math.sqrt(x*x + y*y);         // the x and y fields
  }
}
```

This class definition is stored in a file named *Point.java* and compiled to a file named *Point.class*, at which point it is available for use by Java programs and other classes. This class definition is provided here for completeness and to provide context, but don't expect to understand all the details just yet; most of

Chapter 3 is devoted to the topic of defining classes. Do pay extra attention to the first (non-comment) line of the class definition, however. Just as the first line of a method definition—the method signature—defines the API for the method, this line defines the basic API for a class (as described in the next chapter).

Keep in mind that you don't have to define every class you want to use in a Java program. The Java platform consists of over 1,500 predefined classes that are guaranteed to be available on every computer that runs Java.

Creating an Object

Now that we have defined the `Point` class as a new data type, we can use the following line to declare a variable that holds a `Point` object:

```
Point p;
```

Declaring a variable to hold a `Point` object does not create the object itself, however. To actually create an object, you must use the `new` operator. This keyword is followed by the object's class (i.e., its type) and an optional argument list in parentheses. These arguments are passed to the constructor method for the class, which initializes internal fields in the new object:

```
// Create a Point object representing (2,-3.5) and store it in variable p
Point p = new Point(2.0, -3.5);

// Create some other objects as well
Date d = new Date();          // A Date object that represents the current time
Vector list = new Vector();   // A Vector object to hold a list of objects
```

The `new` keyword is by far the most common way to create objects in Java. There are a few other ways that are worth mentioning, however. First, there are a couple of classes so important that Java defines special literal syntax for creating objects of those types (as we'll discuss in the next section). Second, Java supports a dynamic loading mechanism that allows programs to load classes and create instances of those classes dynamically. This dynamic instantiation is done with the `newInstance()` methods of `java.lang.Class` and `java.lang.reflect.Constructor`. Finally, in Java 1.1 and later, objects can also be created by deserializing them. In other words, an object that has had its state saved, or serialized, usually to a file, can be recreated using the `java.io.ObjectInputStream` class.

Object Literals

As I just said, Java defines special syntax for creating instances of two very important classes. The first class is `String`, which represents text as a string of characters. Since programs usually communicate with their users through the written word, the ability to manipulate strings of text is quite important in any programming language. In some languages, strings are a primitive type, on a par with integers and characters. In Java, however, strings are objects; the data type used to represent text is the `String` class.

Because strings are such a fundamental data type, Java allows you to include text literally in programs by placing it between double-quote (") characters. For example:

```
String name = "David";
System.out.println("Hello, " + name);
```

Don't confuse the double-quote characters that surround string literals with the single-quote (or apostrophe) characters that surround `char` literals. String literals can contain any of the escape sequences `char` literals can (see Table 2-3). Escape sequences are particularly useful for embedding double-quote characters within double-quoted string literals. For example:

```
String story = "\t\"How can you stand it?\" he asked sarcastically.\n";
```

String literals cannot contain comments, and may consist of only a single line. Java does not support any kind of continuation-character syntax that allows two separate lines to be treated as a single line. If you need to represent a long string of text that does not fit on a single line, break it into independent string literals and use the + operator to concatenate the literals. For example:

```
String s = "This is a test of the        // This is illegal; string literals
            emergency broadcast system"; // cannot be broken across lines.

String s = "This is a test of the " +    // Do this instead
           "emergency broadcast system";
```

This concatenation of literals is done when your program is compiled, not when it is run, so you do not need to worry about any kind of performance penalty.

The second class that supports its own special object literal syntax is the class named `Class`. `Class` is a (self-referential) data type that represents all Java data types, including primitive types and array types, not just class types. To include a `Class` object literally in a Java program, follow the name of any data type with `.class`. For example:

```
Class typeInt = int.class;
Class typeIntArray = int[].class;
Class typePoint = Point.class;
```

This feature is supported by Java 1.1 and later.

The Java reserved word `null` is a special literal that can be used with any class. Instead of representing a literal object, it represents the absence of an object. For example:

```
String s = null;
Point p = null;
```

Finally, objects can also be included literally in a Java program through the use of a construct known as an anonymous inner class. Anonymous classes are discussed in Chapter 3.

Using an Object

Now that we've seen how to define classes and instantiate them by creating objects, we need to look at the Java syntax that allows us to use those objects. Recall that a class defines a collection of fields and methods. Each object has its own copies of those fields and has access to those methods. We use the dot character (.) to access the named fields and methods of an object. For example:

```
Point p = new Point(2, 3);          // Create an object
double x = p.x;                     // Read a field of the object
p.y = p.x * p.x;                    // Set the value of a field
double d = p.distanceFromOrigin(); // Access a method of the object
```

This syntax is central to object-oriented programming in Java, so you'll see it a lot. Note, in particular, the expression `p.distanceFromOrigin()`. This tells the Java compiler to look up a method named `distanceFromOrigin()` defined by the class `Point` and use that method to perform a computation on the fields of the object `p`. We'll cover the details of this operation in Chapter 3.

Array Types

Array types are the second kind of reference types in Java.* An array is an ordered collection, or numbered list, of values. The values can be primitive values, objects, or even other arrays, but all of the values in an array must be of the same type. The type of the array is the type of the values it holds, followed by the characters `[]`. For example:

```
byte b;                        // byte is a primitive type
byte[] arrayOfBytes;           // byte[] is an array type: array of byte
byte[][] arrayOfArrayOfBytes;  // byte[][] is another type: array of byte[]
Point[] points;                // Point[] is an array of Point objects
```

For compatibility with C and C++, Java also supports another syntax for declaring variables of array type. In this syntax, one or more pairs of square brackets follow the name of the variable, rather than the name of the type:

```
byte arrayOfBytes[];            // Same as byte[] arrayOfBytes
byte arrayOfArrayOfBytes[][];   // Same as byte[][] arrayOfArrayOfBytes
byte[] arrayOfArrayOfBytes[];   // Ugh! Same as byte[][] arrayOfArrayOfBytes
```

This is often a confusing syntax, however, and should be avoided.

With classes and objects, we have separate terms for the type and the values of that type. With arrays, the single word array does double duty as the name of both the type and the value. Thus, we can speak of the array type `int[]` (a type) and an array of `int` (a particular array value). In practice, it is usually clear from context whether a type or a value is being discussed.

* Arrays are actually Java objects, but they have specialized syntax and behavior, which makes it easy to consider them separately.

Creating Arrays

To create an array value in Java, you use the new keyword, just as you do to create an object. Arrays don't need to be initialized like objects do, however, so you don't pass a list of arguments between parentheses. What you must specify, though, is how big you want the array to be. If you are creating a byte[], for example, you must specify how many byte values you want it to hold. Array values have a fixed size in Java. Once an array is created, it can never grow or shrink. Specify the desired size of your array as a non-negative integer between square brackets:

```
byte[] buffer = new byte[1024];
String[] lines = new String[50];
```

When you create an array with this syntax, each of the values held in the array is automatically initialized to its default value. This is false for boolean values, '\u0000' for char values, 0 for integer values, 0.0 for floating-point values, and null for objects or array values.

Using Arrays

Once you've created an array with the new operator and the square-bracket syntax, you also use square brackets to access the individual values contained in the array. Remember that an array is an ordered collection of values. The elements of an array are numbered sequentially, starting with 0. The number of an array element refers to the element. This number is often called the *index*, and the process of looking up a numbered value in an array is sometimes called *indexing* the array.

To refer to a particular element of an array, simply place the index of the desired element in square brackets after the name of the array. For example:

```
String[] responses = new String[2];   // Create an array of two strings
responses[0] = "Yes";                 // Set the first element of the array
responses[1] = "No";                  // Set the second element of the array

// Now read these array elements
System.out.println(question + " (" + responses[0] + "/" +
                   responses[1] + " ): ");
```

In some programming languages, such as C and C++, it is a common bug to write code that tries to read or write array elements that are past the end of the array. Java does not allow this. Every time you access an array element, the Java interpreter automatically checks that the index you have specified is valid. If you specify a negative index or an index that is greater than the last index of the array, the interpreter throws an exception of type ArrayIndexOutOfBoundsException. This prevents you from reading or writing nonexistent array elements.

Array index values are integers; you cannot index an array with a floating-point value, a boolean, an object, or another array. char values can be converted to int values, so you *can* use characters as array indexes. Although long is an integer data type, long values cannot be used as array indexes. This may seem surprising at first, but consider that an int index supports arrays with over two billion elements. An int[] with this many elements would require eight gigabytes of memory. When you think of it this way, it is not surprising that long values are not allowed as array indexes.

Besides setting and reading the value of array elements, there is one other thing you can do with an array value. Recall that whenever we create an array, we must specify the number of elements the array holds. This value is referred to as the length of the array; it is an intrinsic property of the array. If you need to know the length of the array, append .length to the array name:

```
if (errorCode < errorMessages.length)
  System.out.println(errorMessages[errorCode]);
```


Every array has a length field that specifies the number of elements it contains. Note that this field is read-only: you can use it to read the length of the array, but you cannot assign any value to it or use it to set or change the length of an array.

In the previous example, the array index within square brackets is a variable, not an integer literal. In fact, arrays are most often used with loops, particularly for loops, where they are indexed using a variable that is incremented or decremented each time through the loop:

```
int[] values;            // Assume array is created and initialized elsewhere
int total = 0;                             // Store sum of elements here
for(int i = 0; i < values.length; i++) // Loop through array elements
  total += values[i];                      // Add them up
```

In Java, the first element of an array is always element number 0. If you are accustomed to a programming language that numbers array elements beginning with 1, this will take some getting used to. For an array a, the first element is a[0], the second element is a[1], and the last element is:

```
a[a.length - 1]         // The last element of any array named a
```

Array Literals

The null literal used to represent the absence of an object can also be used to represent the absence of an array. For example:

```
char[] password = null;
```

In addition to the null literal, Java also defines special syntax that allows you to specify array values literally in your programs. There are actually two different syntaxes for array literals. The first, and more commonly used, syntax can be used only when declaring a variable of array type. It combines the creation of the array object with the initialization of the array elements:

```
int[] powersOfTwo = {1, 2, 4, 8, 16, 32, 64, 128};
```

This creates an array that contains the eight int elements listed within the curly braces. Note that we don't use the new keyword or specify the type of the array in this array literal syntax. The type is implicit in the variable declaration of which the initializer is a part. Also, the array length is not specified explicitly with this syntax; it is determined implicitly by counting the number of elements listed between the curly braces. There is a semicolon following the close curly brace in this array literal. This is one of the fine points of Java syntax. When curly braces delimit classes, methods, and compound statements, they are not followed by semicolons. However, for this array literal syntax, the semicolon is required to terminate the variable declaration statement.

The problem with this array literal syntax is that it works only when you are declaring a variable of array type. Sometimes you need to do something with an array value (such as pass it to a method) but are going to use the array only once, so you don't want to bother assigning it to a variable. In Java 1.1 and later, there is an array literal syntax that supports this kind of anonymous arrays (so called because they are not assigned to variables, so they don't have names). This kind of array literal looks as follows:

```
// Call a method, passing an anonymous array literal that contains two strings
String response = askQuestion("Do you want to quit?",
                              new String[] {"Yes", "No"});

// Call another method with an anonymous array (of anonymous objects)
double d = computeAreaOfTriangle(new Point[] { new Point(1,2),
                                               new Point(3,4),
                                               new Point(3,2) });
```

With this syntax, you use the `new` keyword and specify the type of the array, but the length of the array is not explicitly specified.

It is important to understand that the Java Virtual Machine architecture does not support any kind of efficient array initialization. In other words, array literals are created and initialized when the program is run, not when the program is compiled. Consider the following array literal:

```
int[] perfectNumbers = {6, 28};
```

This is compiled into Java byte codes that are equivalent to:

```
int[] perfectNumbers = new int[2];
perfectNumbers[0] = 6;
perfectNumbers[1] = 28;
```

Thus, if you want to include a large amount of data in a Java program, it may not be a good idea to include that data literally in an array, since the Java compiler has to create lots of Java byte codes to initialize the array, and then the Java interpreter has to laboriously execute all that initialization code. In cases like this, it is better to store your data in an external file and read it into the program at runtime.

The fact that Java does all array initialization explicitly at runtime has an important corollary, however. It means that the elements of an array literal can be arbitrary expressions that are computed at runtime, rather than constant expressions that are resolved by the compiler. For example:

```
Point[] points = { circle1.getCenterPoint(), circle2.getCenterPoint() };
```

Multidimensional Arrays

As we've seen, an array type is simply the element type followed by a pair of square brackets. An array of char is char[], and an array of arrays of char is char[][]. When the elements of an array are themselves arrays, we say that the array is *multidimensional*. In order to work with multidimensional arrays, there are a few additional details you must understand.

Imagine that you want to use a multidimensional array to represent a multiplication table:

```
int[][] products;      // A multiplication table
```

Each of the pairs of square brackets represents one dimension, so this is a two-dimensional array. To access a single int element of this two-dimensional array, you must specify two index values, one for each dimension. Assuming that this array was actually initialized as a multiplication table, the int value stored at any given element would be the product of the two indexes. That is, products[2][4] would be 8, and products[3][7] would be 21.

To create a new multidimensional array, use the new keyword and specify the size of both dimensions of the array. For example:

```
int[][] products = new int[10][10];
```

In some languages, an array like this would be created as a single block of 100 int values. Java does not work this way. This line of code does three things:

- Declares a variable named products to hold an array of arrays of int.
- Creates a 10-element array to hold 10 arrays of int.
- Creates 10 more arrays, each of which is a 10-element array of int. It assigns each of these 10 new arrays to the elements of the initial array. The default value of every int element of each of these 10 new arrays is 0.

To put this another way, the previous single line of code is equivalent to the following code:

```
int[][] products = new int[10][];     // An array to hold 10 int[] values
for(int i = 0; i < 10; i++)          // Loop 10 times...
  products[i] = new int[10];          // ...and create 10 arrays
```

The new keyword performs this additional initialization automatically for you. It works with arrays with more than two dimensions as well:

```
float[][][] globalTemperatureData = new float[360][180][100];
```

When using new with multidimensional arrays, you do not have to specify a size for all dimensions of the array, only the leftmost dimension or dimensions. For example, the following two lines are legal:

```
float[][][] globalTemperatureData = new float[360][][];
float[][][] globalTemperatureData = new float[360][180][];
```

The first line creates a single-dimensional array, where each element of the array can hold a float[][]. The second line creates a two-dimensional array, where each element of the array is a float[]. If you specify a size for only some of the dimensions of an array, however, those dimensions must be the leftmost ones. The following lines are not legal:

```
float[][][] globalTemperatureData = new float[360][][100];  // Error!
float[][][] globalTemperatureData = new float[][180][100];  // Error!
```

Like a one-dimensional array, a multidimensional array can be initialized using an array literal. Simply use nested sets of curly braces to nest arrays within arrays. For example, we can declare, create, and initialize a 5×5 multiplication table like this:

```
int[][] products = { {0, 0, 0, 0, 0},
                     {0, 1, 2, 3, 4},
                     {0, 2, 4, 6, 8},
                     {0, 3, 6, 9, 12},
                     {0, 4, 8, 12, 16} };
```

Or, if you want to use a multidimensional array without declaring a variable, you can use the anonymous initializer syntax:

```
boolean response = bilingualQuestion(question, new String[][] {
                                                  { "Yes", "No" },
                                                  { "Oui", "Non" }});
```

When you create a multidimensional array using the new keyword, you always get a *rectangular* array: one in which all the array values for a given dimension have the same size. This is perfect for rectangular data structures, such as matrixes. However, because multidimensional arrays are implemented as arrays of arrays in Java, instead of as a single rectangular block of elements, you are in no way constrained to use rectangular arrays. For example, since our multiplication table is symmetrical about the diagonal from top left to bottom right, we can represent the same information in a nonrectangular array with fewer elements:

```
int[][] products = { {0},
                     {0, 1},
                     {0, 2, 4},
                     {0, 3, 6, 9},
                     {0, 4, 8, 12, 16} };
```

When working with multidimensional arrays, you'll often find yourself using nested loops to create or initialize them. For example, you can create and initialize a large triangular multiplication table as follows:

```
int[][] products = new int[12][];            // An array of 12 arrays of int.
for(int row = 0; row < 12; row++) {          // For each element of that array,
  products[row] = new int[row+1];            // allocate an array of int.
  for(int col = 0; col < row+1; col++)       // For each element of the int[],
    products[row][col] = row * col;          // initialize it to the product.
}
```

Reference Types

Now that we have discussed the syntax for working with objects and arrays, we can return to the issue of why classes and array types are known as reference types. As we saw in Table 2-2, all the Java primitive types have well-defined standard sizes, so all primitive values can be stored in a fixed amount of memory (between one and eight bytes, depending on the type). But classes and array types are composite types; objects and arrays contain other values, so they do not have a standard size, and they often require quite a bit more memory than eight bytes. For this reason, Java does not manipulate objects and arrays directly. Instead, it manipulates *references* to objects and arrays. Because Java handles objects and arrays by reference, classes and array types are known as reference types. In contrast, Java handles values of the primitive types directly, or by value.

A reference to an object or an array is simply some fixed-size value that refers to the object or array in some way.* When you assign an object or array to a variable, you are actually setting the variable to hold a reference to that object or array. Similarly, when you pass an object or array to a method, what really happens is that the method is given a reference to the object or array through which it can manipulate the object or array.

C and C++ programmers should note that Java does not support the & address-of operator or the * and -> dereference operators. In Java, primitive types are always handled exclusively by value, and objects and arrays are always handled exclusively by reference: the `.` operator in Java is more like the -> operator in C and C++ than like the `.` operator of those languages. It is very important to understand that, unlike pointers in C and C++, references in Java are entirely opaque: they cannot be converted to or from integers, and they cannot be incremented or decremented.

Although references are an important part of how Java works, Java programs cannot manipulate references in any way. Despite this, there are significant differences between the behavior of primitive types and reference types in two important areas: the way values are copied and the way they are compared for equality.

Copying Objects and Arrays

Consider the following code that manipulate a primitive `int` value:

```
int x = 42;
int y = x;
```

After these lines execute, the variable `y` contains a copy of the value held in the variable `x`. Inside the Java VM, there are two independent copies of the 32-bit integer 42.

Now think about what happens if we run the same basic code but use a reference type instead of a primitive type:

```
Point p = new Point(1.0, 2.0);
Point q = p;
```

After this code runs, the variable `q` holds a copy of the reference held in the variable `p`. There is still only one copy of the `Point` object in the VM, but there are

* Typically, a reference is the memory address at which the object or array is stored. However, since Java references are opaque and cannot be manipulated in any way, this is an implementation detail.

now two copies of the reference to that object. This has some important implications. Suppose the two previous lines of code are followed by this code:

```
System.out.println(p.x);  // Print out the X coordinate of p: 1.0
q.x = 13.0;               // Now change the X coordinate of q
System.out.println(p.x);  // Print out p.x again; this time it is 13.0
```

Since the variables p and q hold references to the same object, either variable can be used to make changes to the object, and those changes are visible through the other variable as well.

This behavior is not specific to objects; the same thing happens with arrays, as illustrated by the following code:

```
char[] greet = { 'h','e','l','l','o' };  // greet holds an array reference
char[] cuss = greet;                     // cuss holds the same reference
cuss[4] = '!';                           // Use reference to change an element
System.out.println(greet);               // Prints "hell!"
```

A similar difference in behavior between primitive types and reference types occurs when arguments are passed to methods. Consider the following method:

```
void changePrimitive(int x) {
  while(x > 0)
    System.out.println(x--);
}
```

When this method is invoked, the method is given a copy of the argument used to invoke the method in the parameter x. The code in the method uses x as a loop counter and decrements it to zero. Since x is a primitive type, the method has its own private copy of this value, so this is a perfectly reasonable thing to do.

On the other hand, consider what happens if we modify the method so that the parameter is a reference type:

```
void changeReference(Point p) {
  while(p.x > 0)
    System.out.println(p.x--);
}
```

When this method is invoked, it is passed a private copy of a reference to a Point object and can use this reference to change the Point object. Consider the following:

```
Point q = new Point(3.0, 4.5);  // A point with an X coordinate of 3
changeReference(q);             // Prints 3,2,1 and modifies the Point
System.out.println(q.x);        // The X coordinate of q is now 0!
```

When the changeReference() method is invoked, it is passed a copy of the reference held in variable q. Now both the variable q and the method parameter p hold references to the same object. The method can use its reference to change the contents of the object. Note, however, that it cannot change the contents of the variable q. In other words, the method can change the Point object beyond recognition, but it cannot change the fact that the variable q refers to that object.

The title of this section is "Copying Objects and Arrays," but, so far, we've only seen copies of references to objects and arrays, not copies of the objects and arrays themselves. To make an actual copy of an object or an array, you must use the special `clone()` method (inherited by all objects from `java.lang.Object`):

```
Point p = new Point(1,2);    // p refers to one object
Point q = (Point) p.clone(); // q refers to a copy of that object
q.y = 42;                    // Modify the copied object, but not the original

int[] data = {1,2,3,4,5};            // An array
int[] copy = (int[]) data.clone();   // A copy of the array
```

Note that a cast is necessary to coerce the return value of the `clone()` method to the correct type. The reason for this will become clear later in this chapter. There are a couple of points you should be aware of when using `clone()`. First, not all objects can be cloned. Java only allows an object to be cloned if the object's class has explicitly declared itself to be cloneable by implementing the `Cloneable` interface. (We haven't discussed interfaces or how they are implemented yet; that is covered in Chapter 3.) The definition of `Point` that we showed earlier does not actually implement this interface, so our `Point` type, as implemented, is not cloneable. Note, however, that arrays are always cloneable. If you call the `clone()` method for a non-cloneable object, it throws a `CloneNotSupportedException`, so when you use the `clone()` method, you may want to use it within a `try` block to catch this exception.

The second thing you need to understand about `clone()` is that, by default, it is implemented to create a shallow copy of an object or array. The copied object or array contains copies of all the primitive values and references in the original object or array. In other words, any references in the object or array are copied, not cloned; `clone()` does not recursively make copies of the objects or arrays referred to by those references. A class may need to override this shallow copy behavior by defining its own version of the `clone()` method that explicitly performs a deeper copy where needed. To understand the shallow copy behavior of `clone()`, consider cloning a two-dimensional array of arrays:

```
int[][] data = {{1,2,3}, {4,5}};         // An array of two references
int[][] copy = (int[][]) data.clone();   // Copy the two refs to a new array
copy[0][0] = 99;                         // This changes data[0][0] too!
copy[1] = new int[] {7,8,9};             // This does not change data[1]
```

If you want to make a deep copy of this multidimensional array, you have to copy each dimension explicitly:

```
int[][] data = {{1,2,3}, {4,5}};         // An array of two references
int[][] copy = new int[data.length][];   // A new array to hold copied arrays
for(int i = 0; i < data.length; i++)
  copy[i] = (int[]) data[i].clone();
```

Comparing Objects and Arrays

We've seen that primitive types and reference types differ significantly in the way they are assigned to variables, passed to methods, and copied. The types also differ in the way they are compared for equality. When used with primitive values, the equality operator (==) simply tests whether two values are identical (i.e., whether they have exactly the same bits). With reference types, however, == compares references, not actual objects or arrays. In other words, == tests whether two references refer to the same object or array; it does not test whether two objects or arrays have the same content. For example:

```
String letter = "o";
String s = "hello";                       // These two String objects
String t = "hell" + letter;               // contain exactly the same text.
if (s == t) System.out.println("equal"); // But they are not equal!

byte[] a = { 1, 2, 3 };                   // An array.
byte[] b = (byte[]) a.clone();            // A copy with identical content.
if (a == b) System.out.println("equal"); // But they are not equal!
```

When working with reference types, there are two kinds of equality: equality of reference and equality of object. It is important to distinguish between these two kinds of equality. One way to do this is to use the word "equals" when talking about equality of references and the word "equivalent" when talking about two distinct object or arrays that have the same contents. Unfortunately, the designers of Java didn't use this nomenclature, as the method for testing whether one object is equivalent to another is named `equals()`. To test two objects for equivalence, pass one of them to the `equals()` method of the other:

```
String letter = "o";
String s = "hello";                       // These two String objects
String t = "hell" + letter;               // contain exactly the same text.
if (s.equals(t))                          // And the equals() method
  System.out.println("equivalent");       // tells us so.
```

All objects inherit an `equals()` method (from `Object`), but the default implementation simply uses == to test for equality of references, not equivalence of content. A class that wants to allow objects to be compared for equivalence can define its own version of the `equals()` method. Our `Point` class does not do this, but the `String` class does, as indicated by the code above. You can call the `equals()` method on an array, but it is the same as using the == operator, because arrays always inherit the default `equals()` method that compares references rather than array content. Starting in Java 1.2, you can compare arrays for equivalence with the convenience method `java.util.Arrays.equals()`. Prior to Java 1.2, however, you must loop through the elements of the arrays and compare them yourself.

The null Reference

We've seen the `null` keyword in our discussions of objects and arrays. Now that we have described references, it is worth revisiting `null` to point out that it is a special value that is a reference to nothing, or an absence of a reference. The default value for all reference types is `null`. The `null` value is unique in that it can be assigned to a variable of any reference type whatsoever.

Terminology: Pass by Value

I've said that Java handles arrays and objects "by reference." Don't confuse this with the phrase "pass by reference."* "Pass by reference" is a term used to

* Unfortunately, previous editions of this book may have contributed to the confusion!

describe the method-calling conventions of some programming languages. In a pass-by-reference language, values—even primitive values—are not passed directly to methods. Instead, methods are always passed references to values. Thus, if the method modifies its parameters, those modifications are visible when the method returns, even for primitive types.

Java does *not* do this; it is a "pass by value" language. However, when a reference type is involved, the value that is passed is a reference. But this is not the same as pass-by-reference. If Java were a pass-by-reference language, when a reference type was passed to a method, it would be passed as a reference to the reference.

Memory Allocation and Garbage Collection

As we've already noted, objects and arrays are composite values that can contain a number of other values and may require a substantial amount of memory. When you use the new keyword to create a new object or array or use an object or array literal in your program, Java automatically creates the object for you, allocating whatever amount of memory is necessary. You don't need to do anything to make this happen.

In addition, Java also automatically reclaims that memory for reuse when it is no longer needed. It does this through a process called *garbage collection*. An object is considered garbage when there are no longer any references to it stored in any variables, the fields of any objects, or the elements of any arrays. For example:

```
Point p = new Point(1,2);             // Create an object
double d = p.distanceFromOrigin();    // Use it for something
p = new Point(2,3);                   // Create a new object
```

After the Java interpreter executes the third line, a reference to the new Point object has replaced the reference to the first one. There are now no remaining references to the first object, so it is garbage. At some point, the garbage collector will discover this and reclaim the memory used by the object.

C programmers, who are used to using malloc() and free() to manage memory, and C++ programmers, who are used to explicitly deleting their objects with delete, may find it a little hard to relinquish control and trust the garbage collector. Even though it seems like magic, it really works! There is a slight performance penalty due to the use of garbage collection, and Java programs may sometimes slow down noticeably while the garbage collector is actively reclaiming memory. However, having garbage collection built into the language dramatically reduces the occurrence of memory leaks and related bugs and almost always improves programmer productivity.

Reference Type Conversions

When we discussed primitive types earlier in this chapter, we saw that values of certain types can be converted to values of other types. Widening conversions are performed automatically by the Java interpreter, as necessary. Narrowing conversions, however, can result in lost data, so the interpreter does not perform them unless explicitly directed to do so with a cast.

Java does not allow any kind of conversion from primitive types to reference types or vice versa. Java does allow widening and narrowing conversions among certain reference types, however. As we've seen, there are an infinite number of potential reference types. In order to understand the conversions that can be performed among these types, you need to understand that the types form a hierarchy, usually called the *class hierarchy*.

Every Java class *extends* some other class, known as its *superclass*. A class inherits the fields and methods of its superclass and then defines its own additional fields and methods. There is a special class named `Object` that serves as the root of the class hierarchy in Java. It does not extend any class, but all other Java classes extend `Object` or some other class that has `Object` as one of its ancestors. The `Object` class defines a number of special methods that are inherited (or overridden) by all classes. These include the `toString()`, `clone()`, and `equals()` methods described earlier.

The predefined `String` class and the `Point` class we defined earlier in this chapter both extend `Object`. Thus, we can say that all `String` objects are also `Object` objects. We can also say that all `Point` objects are `Object` objects. The opposite is not true, however. We cannot say that every `Object` is a `String` because, as we've just seen, some `Object` objects are `Point` objects.

With this simple understanding of the class hierarchy, we can return to the rules of reference type conversion:

- An object cannot be converted to an unrelated type. The Java compiler does not allow you to convert a `String` to a `Point`, for example, even if you use a cast operator.
- An object can be converted to the type of its superclass or of any ancestor class. This is a widening conversion, so no cast is required. For example, a `String` value can be assigned to a variable of type `Object` or passed to a method where an `Object` parameter is expected. Note that no conversion is actually performed; the object is simply treated as if it were an instance of the superclass.
- An object can be converted to the type of a subclass, but this is a narrowing conversion and requires a cast. The Java compiler provisionally allows this kind of conversion, but the Java interpreter checks at runtime to make sure it is valid. Only cast an object to the type of a subclass if you are sure, based on the logic of your program, that the object is actually an instance of the subclass. If it is not, the interpreter throws a `ClassCastException`. For example, if we assign a `String` object to a variable of type `Object`, we can later cast the value of that variable back to type `String`:

  ```
  Object o = "string";    // Widening conversion from String to Object
  // Later in the program...
  String s = (String) o;  // Narrowing conversion from Object to String
  ```

Arrays are objects and follow some conversion rules of their own. First, any array can be converted to an `Object` value through a widening conversion. A narrowing conversion with a cast can convert such an object value back to an array. For example:

```
Object o = new int[] {1,2,3};  // Widening conversion from array to Object
// Later in the program...
int[] a = (int[]) o;           // Narrowing conversion back to array type
```

In addition to converting an array to an object, you can convert an array to another type of array if the "base types" of the two arrays are reference types that can themselves be converted. For example:

```
// Here is an array of strings
String[] strings = new String[] { "hi", "there" };
// A widening conversion to CharSequence[] is allowed because String
// can widened to CharSequence.
CharSequence[] sequences = strings;
// The narrowing conversion back to String[] requires a cast
strings = (String[]) sequences;
// This is an array of arrays of strings
String[][] s = new String[][] { strings };
// It cannot be converted to CharSequence[] because String[] cannot be
// converted to CharSequence; the number of dimensions don't match.
sequences = s;  // This line will not compile
// s can be converted to Object or Object[], however, because all array types
// (including String[] and String[][]) can be converted to Object.
Object[] objects = s;
```

Note that these array conversion rules apply only to arrays of objects and arrays of arrays. An array of a primitive type cannot be converted to any other array type, even if the primitive base types can be converted:

```
// Can't convert int[] to double[] even though int can be widened to double
double[] data = new int[] {1,2,3};  // This line causes a compilation error
// This line is legal, however, since int[] can be converted to Object
Object[] objects = new int[][] {{1,2},{3,4}};
```

Packages and the Java Namespace

A *package* is a named collection of classes (and possibly subpackages). Packages serve to group related classes and define a namespace for the classes they contain.

The Java platform includes packages with names that begin with `java`, `javax`, and `org.omg`. (Sun also defines standard extensions to the Java platform in packages whose names begin with `javax`.) The most fundamental classes of the language are in the package `java.lang`. Various utility classes are in `java.util`. Classes for input and output are in `java.io`, and classes for networking are in `java.net`. Some of these packages contain subpackages. For example, `java.lang` contains two more specialized packages, named `java.lang.reflect` and `java.lang.ref`, and `java.util` contains a subpackage, `java.util.zip`, that contains classes for working with compressed ZIP archives.

Every class has both a simple name, which is the name given to it in its definition, and a fully qualified name, which includes the name of the package of which it is a part. The `String` class, for example, is part of the `java.lang` package, so its fully qualified name is `java.lang.String`.

Defining a Package

To specify the package a class is to be part of, you use a `package` directive. The `package` keyword, if it appears, must be the first token of Java code (i.e., the first thing other than comments and space) in the Java file. The keyword should be followed by the name of the desired package and a semicolon. Consider a file of Java code that begins with this directive:

```
package com.davidflanagan.jude;
```

All classes defined by this file are part of the package named `com.davidflanagan.jude`.

If no `package` directive appears in a file of Java code, all classes defined in that file are part of a default unnamed package. As we'll see in Chapter 3, classes in the same package have special access to each other. Thus, except when you are writing simple example programs, you should always use the `package` directive to prevent access to your classes from totally unrelated classes that also just happen to be stored in the unnamed package.

Importing Classes and Packages

A class in a package `p` can refer to any other class in `p` by its simple name. And, since the classes in the `java.lang` package are so fundamental to the Java language, any Java code can refer to any class in this package by its simple name. Thus, you can always type `String`, instead of `java.lang.String`. By default, however, you must use the fully qualified name of all other classes. So, if you want to use the `File` class of the `java.io` package, you must type `java.io.File`.

Specifying package names explicitly all the time quickly gets tiring, so Java includes an `import` directive you can use to save some typing. `import` is used to specify classes and packages of classes that can be referred to by their simple names instead of by their fully qualified names. The `import` keyword can be used any number of times in a Java file, but all uses must be at the top of the file, immediately after the `package` directive, if there is one. There can be comments between the `package` directive and the `import` directives, of course, but there cannot be any other Java code.

The `import` directive is available in two forms. To specify a single class that can be referred to by its simple name, follow the `import` keyword with the name of the class and a semicolon:

```
import java.io.File;    // Now we can type File instead of java.io.File
```

To import an entire package of classes, follow `import` with the name of the package, the characters `.*`, and a semicolon. Thus, if you want to use several other classes from the `java.io` package in addition to the `File` class, you can simply import the entire package:

```
import java.io.*;   // Now we can use simple names for all classes in java.io
```

This package `import` syntax does not apply to subpackages. If I import the `java.util` package, I must still refer to the `java.util.zip.ZipInputStream` class by its fully qualified name. If two classes with the same name are both imported from different packages, neither one can be referred to by its simple name; to resolve this naming conflict unambiguously, you must use the fully qualified name of both classes.

Globally Unique Package Names

One of the important functions of packages is to partition the Java namespace and prevent name collisions between classes. It is only their package names that keep the `java.util.List` and `java.awt.List` classes distinct, for example. In order for this to work, however, package names must themselves be distinct. As the developer of Java, Sun controls all package names that begin with `java`, `javax`, and `sun`.

For the rest of us, Sun proposes a package-naming scheme, which, if followed correctly, guarantees globally unique package names. The scheme is to use your Internet domain name, with its elements reversed, as the prefix for all your package names. My web site is *davidflanagan.com*, so all my Java packages begin with `com.davidflanagan`. It is up to me to decide how to partition the namespace below `com.davidflanagan`, but since I own that domain name, no other person or organization who is playing by the rules can define a package with the same name as any of mine.

Java File Structure

This chapter has taken us from the smallest to the largest elements of Java syntax, from individual characters and tokens to operators, expressions, statements, and methods, and on up to classes and packages. From a practical standpoint, the unit of Java program structure you will be dealing with most often is the Java file. A Java file is the smallest unit of Java code that can be compiled by the Java compiler. A Java file consists of:

- An optional `package` directive
- Zero or more `import` directives
- One or more class definitions

These elements can be interspersed with comments, of course, but they must appear in this order. This is all there is to a Java file. All Java statements (except the `package` and `import` directives, which are not true statements) must appear within methods, and all methods must appear within a class definition.

There are a couple of other important restrictions on Java files. First, each file can contain at most one class that is declared `public`. A `public` class is one that is designed for use by other classes in other packages. We'll talk more about `public` and related modifiers in Chapter 3. This restriction on public classes only applies to top-level classes; a class can contain any number of nested or inner classes that are declared `public`, as we'll see in Chapter 3.

The second restriction concerns the filename of a Java file. If a Java file contains a `public` class, the name of the file must be the same as the name of the class, with the extension *.java* appended. Thus, if `Point` is defined as a `public` class, its source code must appear in a file named *Point.java*. Regardless of whether your classes are `public` or not, it is good programming practice to define only one per file and to give the file the same name as the class.

When a Java file is compiled, each of the classes it defines is compiled into a separate *class file* that contains Java byte codes to be interpreted by the Java Virtual Machine. A class file has the same name as the class it defines, with the extension *.class* appended. Thus, if the file *Point.java* defines a class named `Point`, a Java compiler compiles it to a file named *Point.class*. On most systems, class files are stored in directories that correspond to their package names. Thus, the class `com.davidflanagan.jude.DataFile` is defined by the class file *com/davidflanagan/jude/DataFile.class*.

The Java interpreter knows where the class files for the standard system classes are located and can load them as needed. When the interpreter runs a program that wants to use a class named `com.davidflanagan.jude.DataFile`, it knows that the code for that class is located in a directory named *com/davidflanagan/jude* and, by default, it "looks" in the current directory for a subdirectory of that name. In order to tell the interpreter to look in locations other than the current directory, you must use the `-classpath` option when invoking the interpreter or set the `CLASSPATH` environment variable. For details, see the documentation for the Java interpreter, *java*, in Chapter 8.

Defining and Running Java Programs

A Java program consists of a set of interacting class definitions. But not every Java class or Java file defines a program. To create a program, you must define a class that has a special method with the following signature:

```
public static void main(String[] args)
```

This `main()` method is the main entry point for your program. It is where the Java interpreter starts running. This method is passed an array of strings and returns no value. When `main()` returns, the Java interpreter exits (unless `main()` has created separate threads, in which case the interpreter waits for all those threads to exit).

To run a Java program, you run the Java interpreter, *java*, specifying the fully qualified name of the class that contains the `main()` method. Note that you specify the name of the class, *not* the name of the class file that contains the class. Any additional arguments you specify on the command line are passed to the `main()` method as its `String[]` parameter. You may also need to specify the `-classpath` option (or `-cp`) to tell the interpreter where to look for the classes needed by the program. Consider the following command:

```
% java -classpath /usr/local/Jude com.davidflanagan.jude.Jude datafile.jude
```

java is the command to run the Java interpreter. *-classpath /usr/local/Jude* tells the interpreter where to look for *.class* files. `com.davidflanagan.jude.Jude` is the name of the program to run (i.e., the name of the class that defines the `main()` method). Finally, *datafile.jude* is a string that is passed to that `main()` method as the single element of an array of `String` objects.

In Java 1.2, there is an easier way to run programs. If a program and all its auxiliary classes (except those that are part of the Java platform) have been properly bundled in a Java archive (JAR) file, you can run the program simply by specifying the name of the JAR file:

```
% java -jar /usr/local/Jude/jude.jar datafile.jude
```

Some operating systems make JAR files automatically executable. On those systems, you can simply say:

```
% /usr/local/Jude/jude.jar datafile.jude
```

See Chapter 8 for details.

Differences Between C and Java

If you are a C or C++ programmer, you should have found much of the syntax of Java—particularly at the level of operators and statements—to be familiar. Because Java and C are so similar in some ways, it is important for C and C++ programmers to understand where the similarities end. There are a number of important differences between C and Java, which are summarized in the following list:

No preprocessor
: Java does not include a preprocessor and does not define any analogs of the `#define`, `#include`, and `#ifdef` directives. Constant definitions are replaced with `static final` fields in Java. (See the `java.lang.Math.PI` field for an example.) Macro definitions are not available in Java, but advanced compiler technology and inlining has made them less useful. Java does not require an `#include` directive because Java has no header files. Java class files contain both the class API and the class implementation, and the compiler reads API information from class files as necessary. Java lacks any form of conditional compilation, but its cross-platform portability means that this feature is rarely needed.

No global variables
: Java defines a very clean namespace. Packages contain classes, classes contain fields and methods, and methods contain local variables. But there are no global variables in Java, and, thus, there is no possibility of namespace collisions among those variables.

Well-defined primitive type sizes
: All the primitive types in Java have well-defined sizes. In C, the size of `short`, `int`, and `long` types is platform-dependent, which hampers portability.

No pointers
: Java classes and arrays are reference types, and references to objects and arrays are akin to pointers in C. Unlike C pointers, however, references in Java are entirely opaque. There is no way to convert a reference to a primitive type, and a reference cannot be incremented or decremented. There is no address-of operator like &, dereference operator like * or −>, or `sizeof` operator. Pointers are a notorious source of bugs. Eliminating them simplifies the language and makes Java programs more robust and secure.

Garbage collection

The Java Virtual Machine performs garbage collection so that Java programmers do not have to explicitly manage the memory used by all objects and arrays. This feature eliminates another entire category of common bugs and all but eliminates memory leaks from Java programs.

No goto statement

Java doesn't support a `goto` statement. Use of `goto` except in certain well-defined circumstances is regarded as poor programming practice. Java adds exception handling and labeled `break` and `continue` statements to the flow-control statements offered by C. These are a good substitute for `goto`.

Variable declarations anywhere

C requires local variable declarations to be made at the beginning of a method or block, while Java allows them anywhere in a method or block. Many programmers prefer to keep all their variable declarations grouped together at the top of a method, however.

Forward references

The Java compiler is smarter than the C compiler, in that it allows methods to be invoked before they are defined. This eliminates the need to declare functions in a header file before defining them in a program file, as is done in C.

Method overloading

Java programs can define multiple methods with the same name, as long as the methods have different parameter lists.

No struct and union types

Java doesn't support C `struct` and `union` types. A Java `class` can be thought of as an enhanced `struct`, however.

No enumerated types

Java doesn't support the `enum` keyword used in C to define types that consist of fixed sets of named values. This is surprising for a strongly typed language like Java, but there are ways to simulate this feature with object constants.

No bitfields

Java doesn't support the (infrequently used) ability of C to specify the number of individual bits occupied by fields of a `struct`.

No typedef

Java doesn't support the `typedef` keyword used in C to define aliases for type names. Java's lack of pointers makes its type-naming scheme simpler and more consistent than C's, however, so many of the common uses of `typedef` are not really necessary in Java.

No method pointers

C allows you to store the address of a function in a variable and pass this function pointer to other functions. You cannot do this with Java methods, but you can often achieve similar results by passing an object that implements a particular interface. Also, a Java method can be represented and invoked through a `java.lang.reflect.Method` object.

No variable-length argument lists

Java doesn't allow you to define methods such as C's `printf()` that take a variable number of arguments. Method overloading allows you to simulate C varargs functions for simple cases, and arguments can also be passed as an `Object[]`, but there's no general replacement for this feature.

CHAPTER 3

Object-Oriented Programming in Java

Java is an object-oriented programming language. As we discussed in Chapter 2, all Java programs use objects, and every Java program is defined as a class. The previous chapter explained the basic syntax of the Java programming language, including data types, operators, and expressions, and even showed how to define simple classes and work with objects. This chapter continues where that one left off, explaining the details of object-oriented programming in Java.

If you do not have any object-oriented (OO) programming background, don't worry; this chapter does not assume any prior experience. If you do have experience with OO programming, however, be careful. The term "object-oriented" has different meanings in different languages. Don't assume that Java works the same way as your favorite OO language. This is particularly true for C++ programmers. We saw in the last chapter that close analogies can be drawn between Java and C. The same is not true for Java and C++, however. Java uses object-oriented programming concepts that are familiar to C++ programmers and even borrows C++ syntax in a number of places, but the similarities between Java and C++ are not nearly as strong as those between Java and C. Don't let your experience with C++ lull you into a false familiarity with Java.

The Members of a Class

As we discussed in Chapter 2, a class is a collection of data, stored in named fields, and code, organized into named methods, that operates on that data. The fields and methods are called *members* of a class. In Java 1.1 and later, classes can also contain other classes. These member classes, or inner classes, are an advanced feature that is discussed later in the chapter. For now, we are going to discuss only fields and methods. The members of a class come in two distinct types: class, or static, members are associated with the class itself, while instance members are associated with individual instances of the class (i.e., with objects). Ignoring member classes for now, this gives us four types of members:

- Class fields
- Class methods
- Instance fields
- Instance methods

The simple class definition for the class `Circle`, shown in Example 3-1, contains all four types of members.

Example 3-1. A simple class and its members

```
public class Circle {
  // A class field
  public static final double PI= 3.14159;     // A useful constant

  // A class method: just compute a value based on the arguments
  public static double radiansToDegrees(double rads) {
    return rads * 180 / PI;
  }

  // An instance field
  public double r;                  // The radius of the circle

  // Two instance methods: they operate on the instance fields of an object
  public double area() {            // Compute the area of the circle
    return PI * r * r;
  }
  public double circumference() {   // Compute the circumference of the circle
    return 2 * PI * r;
  }
}
```

Object-Oriented

Class Fields

A *class field* is associated with the class in which it is defined, rather than with an instance of the class. The following line declares a class field:

```
public static final double PI = 3.14159;
```

This line declares a field of type `double` named `PI` and assigns it a value of 3.14159. As you can see, a field declaration looks quite a bit like the local variable declarations we discussed in Chapter 2. The difference, of course, is that variables are defined within methods, while fields are members of classes.

The `static` modifier says that the field is a class field. Class fields are sometimes called static fields because of this `static` modifier. The `final` modifier says that the value of the field does not change. Since the field `PI` represents a constant, we declare it `final` so that it cannot be changed. It is a convention in Java (and many other languages) that constants are named with capital letters, which is why our field is named `PI`, not `pi`. Defining constants like this is a common use for class fields, meaning that the `static` and `final` modifiers are often used together. Not all class fields are constants, however. In other words, a field can be declared `static` without declaring it `final`. Finally, the `public` modifier says that anyone can use the field. This is a visibility modifier, and we'll discuss it and related modifiers in more detail later in this chapter.

The key point to understand about a static field is that there is only a single copy of it. This field is associated with the class itself, not with instances of the class. If you look at the various methods of the Circle class, you'll see that they use this field. From inside the Circle class, the field can be referred to simply as PI. Outside the class, however, both class and field names are required to uniquely specify the field. Methods that are not part of Circle access this field as Circle.PI.

A class field is essentially a global variable. The names of class fields are qualified by the unique names of the classes that contain them, however. Thus, Java does not suffer from the name collisions that can affect other languages when different modules of code define global variables with the same name.

Class Methods

As with class fields, *class methods* are declared with the static modifier:

```
public static double radiansToDegrees(double rads) { return rads * 180 / PI; }
```

This line declares a class method named radiansToDegrees(). It has a single parameter of type double and returns a double value. The body of the method is quite short; it performs a simple computation and returns the result.

Like class fields, class methods are associated with a class, rather than with an object. When invoking a class method from code that exists outside the class, you must specify both the name of the class and the method. For example:

```
// How many degrees is 2.0 radians?
double d = Circle.radiansToDegrees(2.0);
```

If you want to invoke a class method from inside the class in which it is defined, you don't have to specify the class name. However, it is often good style to specify the class name anyway, to make it clear that a class method is being invoked.

Note that the body of our Circle.radiansToDegrees() method uses the class field PI. A class method can use any class fields and class methods of its own class (or of any other class). But it cannot use any instance fields or instance methods because class methods are not associated with an instance of the class. In other words, although the radiansToDegrees() method is defined in the Circle class, it does not use any Circle objects. The instance fields and instance methods of the class are associated with Circle objects, not with the class itself. Since a class method is not associated with an instance of its class, it cannot use any instance methods or fields.

As we discussed earlier, a class field is essentially a global variable. In a similar way, a class method is a global method, or global function. Although radiansToDegrees() does not operate on Circle objects, it is defined within the Circle class because it is a utility method that is sometimes useful when working with circles. In many non-object-oriented programming languages, all methods, or functions, are global. You can write complex Java programs using only class methods. This is not object-oriented programming, however, and does not take advantage of the power of the Java language. To do true object-oriented programming, we need to add instance fields and instance methods to our repertoire.

Instance Fields

Any field declared without the `static` modifier is an *instance field*:

```
public double r;      // The radius of the circle
```

Instance fields are associated with instances of the class, rather than with the class itself. Thus, every `Circle` object we create has its own copy of the `double` field `r`. In our example, `r` represents the radius of a circle. Thus, each `Circle` object can have a radius independent of all other `Circle` objects.

Inside a class definition, instance fields are referred to by name alone. You can see an example of this if you look at the method body of the `circumference()` instance method. In code outside the class, the name of an instance method must be prepended by a reference to the object that contains it. For example, if we have a `Circle` object named `c`, we can refer to its instance field `r` as `c.r`:

```
Circle c = new Circle(); // Create a new Circle object; store it in variable c
c.r = 2.0;               // Assign a value to its instance field r
Circle d = new Circle(); // Create a different Circle object
d.r = c.r * 2;           // Make this one twice as big
```

Instance fields are key to object-oriented programming. Instance fields define an object; the values of those fields make one object distinct from another.

Instance Methods

Any method not declared with the `static` keyword is an instance method. An *instance method* operates on an instance of a class (an object) instead of operating on the class itself. It is with instance methods that object-oriented programming starts to get interesting. The `Circle` class defined in Example 3-1 contains two instance methods, `area()` and `circumference()`, that compute and return the area and circumference of the circle represented by a given `Circle` object.

To use an instance method from outside the class in which it is defined, we must prepend a reference to the instance that is to be operated on. For example:

```
Circle c = new Circle();    // Create a Circle object; store in variable c
c.r = 2.0;                  // Set an instance field of the object
double a = c.area();        // Invoke an instance method of the object
```

If you're new to object-oriented programming, that last line of code may look a little strange. I did not write:

```
a = area(c);
```

Instead, I wrote:

```
a = c.area();
```

This is why it is called object-oriented programming; the object is the focus here, not the function call. This small syntactic difference is perhaps the single most important feature of the object-oriented paradigm.

The point here is that we don't have to pass an argument to `c.area()`. The object we are operating on, `c`, is implicit in the syntax. Take a look at Example 3-1 again.

You'll notice the same thing in the signature of the `area()` method: it doesn't have a parameter. Now look at the body of the `area()` method: it uses the instance field `r`. Because the `area()` method is part of the same class that defines this instance field, the method can use the unqualified name `r`. It is understood that this refers to the radius of whatever `Circle` instance invokes the method.

Another important thing to notice about the bodies of the `area()` and `circumference()` methods is that they both use the class field `PI`. We saw earlier that class methods can use only class fields and class methods, not instance fields or methods. Instance methods are not restricted in this way: they can use any member of a class, whether it is declared `static` or not.

How instance methods work

Consider this line of code again:

```
a = c.area();
```

What's going on here? How can a method that has no parameters know what data to operate on? In fact, the `area()` method does have a parameter. All instance methods are implemented with an implicit parameter not shown in the method signature. The implicit argument is named `this`; it holds a reference to the object through which the method is invoked. In our example, that object is a `Circle`.

The implicit `this` parameter is not shown in method signatures because it is usually not needed; whenever a Java method accesses the fields in its class, it is implied that it is accessing fields in the object referred to by the `this` parameter. The same is true when an instance method invokes another instance method in the same class. I said earlier that to invoke an instance method you must prepend a reference to the object to be operated on. When an instance method is invoked within another instance method in the same class, however, you don't need to specify an object. In this case, it is implicit that the method is being invoked on the `this` object.

You can use the `this` keyword explicitly when you want to make it clear that a method is accessing its own fields and/or methods. For example, we can rewrite the `area()` method to use `this` explicitly to refer to instance fields:

```
public double area() {
  return Circle.PI * this.r * this.r;
}
```

This code also uses the class name explicitly to refer to class field `PI`. In a method this simple, it is not necessary to be explicit. In more complicated cases, however, you may find that it increases the clarity of your code to use an explicit `this` where it is not strictly required.

There are some cases in which the `this` keyword *is* required, however. For example, when a method parameter or local variable in a method has the same name as one of the fields of the class, you must use `this` to refer to the field, since the field name used alone refers to the method parameter or local variable. For example, we can add the following method to the `Circle` class:

```
public void setRadius(double r) {
  this.r = r;       // Assign the argument (r) to the field (this.r)
                    // Note that we cannot just say r = r
}
```

Finally, note that while instance methods can use the `this` keyword, class methods cannot. This is because class methods are not associated with objects.

Instance methods or class methods?

Instance methods are one of the key features of object-oriented programming. That doesn't mean, however, that you should shun class methods. There are many cases in which is is perfectly reasonable to define class methods. When working with the `Circle` class, for example, you might find there are many times you want to compute the area of a circle with a given radius, but don't want to bother creating a `Circle` object to represent that circle. In this case, a class method is more convenient:

```
public static double area(double r) { return PI * r * r; }
```

It is perfectly legal for a class to define more than one method with the same name, as long as the methods have different parameters. Since this version of the `area()` method is a class method, it does not have an implicit `this` parameter and must have a parameter that specifies the radius of the circle. This parameter keeps it distinct from the instance method of the same name.

As another example of the choice between instance methods and class methods, consider defining a method named `bigger()` that examines two `Circle` objects and returns whichever has the larger radius. We can write `bigger()` as an instance method as follows:

```
// Compare the implicit "this" circle to the "that" circle passed
// explicitly as an argument and return the bigger one.
public Circle bigger(Circle that) {
  if (this.r > that.r) return this;
  else return that;
}
```

We can also implement `bigger()` as a class method as follows:

```
// Compare circle a to circle b and return the one with the larger radius
public static Circle bigger(Circle a, Circle b) {
  if (a.r > b.r) return a;
  else return b;
}
```

Given two `Circle` objects, `x` and `y`, we can use either the instance method or the class method to determine which is bigger. The invocation syntax differs significantly for the two methods, however:

```
Circle biggest = x.bigger(y);           // Instance method: also y.bigger(x)
Circle biggest = Circle.bigger(x, y);   // Static method
```

Both methods work well, and from an object-oriented design standpoint, neither of these methods is "more correct" than the other. The instance method is more formally object-oriented, but its invocation syntax suffers from a kind of asymmetry. In a case like this, the choice between an instance method and a class method is simply a design decision. Depending on the circumstances, one or the other will likely be the more natural choice.

A Mystery Solved

As we saw in Chapters 1 and 2, the way to display textual output to the terminal in Java is with a method named `System.out.println()`. Those chapters never explained why this method has such an long, awkward name or what those two periods are doing in it. Now that you understand class and instance fields and class and instance methods, it is easier to understand what is going on. Here's the story: `System` is a class. It has a class field named `out`. The field `System.out` refers to an object. The object `System.out` has an instance method named `println()`. Mystery solved! If you want to explore this in more detail, you can look up the `java.lang.System` class in Chapter 12. The class synopsis there tells you that the field `out` is of type `java.io.PrintStream`, which you can look up in Chapter 11.

Creating and Initializing Objects

Take another look at how we've been creating `Circle` objects:

```
Circle c = new Circle();
```

What are those parentheses doing there? They make it look like we're calling a method. In fact, that is exactly what we're doing. Every class in Java has at least one *constructor*, which is a method that has the same name as the class and whose purpose is to perform any necessary initialization for a new object. Since we didn't explicitly define a constructor for our `Circle` class in Example 3-1, Java gave us a default constructor that takes no arguments and performs no special initialization.

Here's how a constructor works. The `new` operator creates a new, but uninitialized, instance of the class. The constructor method is then called, with the new object passed implicitly (a `this` reference, as we saw earlier), and whatever arguments that are specified between parentheses passed explicitly. The constructor can use these arguments to do whatever initialization is necessary.

Defining a Constructor

There is some obvious initialization we could do for our circle objects, so let's define a constructor. Example 3-2 shows a new definition for `Circle` that contains a constructor that lets us specify the radius of a new `Circle` object. The constructor also uses the `this` reference to distinguish between a method parameter and an instance field that have the same name.

Example 3-2. A constructor for the Circle class

```
public class Circle {
    public static final double PI = 3.14159;  // A constant
    public double r;   // An instance field that holds the radius of the circle

    // The constructor method: initialize the radius field
```

Example 3-2. A constructor for the Circle class (continued)

```
    public Circle(double r) { this.r = r; }

    // The instance methods: compute values based on the radius
    public double circumference() { return 2 * PI * r; }
    public double area() { return PI * r*r; }
}
```

When we relied on the default constructor supplied by the compiler, we had to write code like this to initialize the radius explicitly:

```
Circle c = new Circle();
c.r = 0.25;
```

With this new constructor, the initialization becomes part of the object creation step:

```
Circle c = new Circle(0.25);
```

Here are some important notes about naming, declaring, and writing constructors:

- The constructor name is always the same as the class name.
- Unlike all other methods, a constructor is declared without a return type, not even `void`.
- The body of a constructor should initialize the `this` object.
- A constructor should not return `this` or any other value.

Defining Multiple Constructors

Sometimes you want to initialize an object in a number of different ways, depending on what is most convenient in a particular circumstance. For example, we might want to initialize the radius of a circle to a specified value or a reasonable default value. Since our `Circle` class has only a single instance field, there aren't too many ways we can initialize it, of course. But in more complex classes, it is often convenient to define a variety of constructors. Here's how we can define two constructors for `Circle`:

```
public Circle() { r = 1.0; }
public Circle(double r) { this.r = r; }
```

It is perfectly legal to define multiple constructors for a class, as long as each constructor has a different parameter list. The compiler determines which constructor you wish to use based on the number and type of arguments you supply. This is simply an example of method overloading, which we discussed in Chapter 2.

Invoking One Constructor from Another

There is a specialized use of the `this` keyword that arises when a class has multiple constructors; it can be used from a constructor to invoke one of the other constructors of the same class. In other words, we can rewrite the two previous `Circle` constructors as follows:

```
// This is the basic constructor: initialize the radius
public Circle(double r) { this.r = r; }
// This constructor uses this() to invoke the constructor above
public Circle() { this(1.0); }
```

The `this()` syntax is a method invocation that calls one of the other constructors of the class. The particular constructor that is invoked is determined by the number and type of arguments, of course. This is a useful technique when a number of constructors share a significant amount of initialization code, as it avoids repetition of that code. This would be a more impressive example, of course, if the one-parameter version of the `Circle()` constructor did more initialization than it does.

There is an important restriction on using `this()`: it can appear only as the first statement in a constructor. It may, of course, be followed by any additional initialization a particular version of the constructor needs to do. The reason for this restriction involves the automatic invocation of superclass constructor methods, which we'll explore later in this chapter.

Field Defaults and Initializers

Not every field of a class requires initialization. Unlike local variables, which have no default value and cannot be used until explicitly initialized, the fields of a class are automatically initialized to the default values shown in Table 2-2. Essentially, every field of a primitive type is initialized to a default value of `false` or zero, as appropriate. All fields of reference type are, by default, initialized to `null`. These default values are guaranteed by Java. If the default value of a field is appropriate, you can simply rely on it without explicitly initializing the field. This default initialization applies to both instance fields and class fields.

As we've seen, the syntax for declaring a field of a class is a lot like the syntax for declaring a local variable. Both class and instance field declarations can be followed by an equals sign and an initial value, as in:

```
public static final double PI = 3.14159;
public double r = 1.0;
```

As we discussed in Chapter 2, a variable declaration is a statement that appears within a Java method; the variable initialization is performed when the statement is executed. Field declarations, however, are not part of any method, so they cannot be executed as statements are. Instead, the Java compiler generates instance-field initialization code automatically and puts it in the constructor or constructors for the class. The initialization code is inserted into a constructor in the order it appears in the source code, which means that a field initializer can use the initial values of fields declared before it. Consider the following code excerpt, which shows a constructor and two instance fields of a hypothetical class:

```
public class TestClass {
  ... public int len = 10;
  public int[] table = new int[len];

  public TestClass() {
```

```
    for(int i = 0; i < len; i++) table[i] = i;
  }

  // The rest of the class is omitted...
}
```

In this case, the code generated for the constructor is actually equivalent to the following:

```
public TestClass() {
  len = 10;
  table = new int[len];
  for(int i = 0; i < len; i++) table[i] = i;
}
```

If a constructor begins with a `this()` call to another constructor, the field initialization code does not appear in the first constructor. Instead, the initialization is handled in the constructor invoked by the `this()` call.

So, if instance fields are initialized in constructor methods, where are class fields initialized? These fields are associated with the class, even if no instances of the class are ever created, so they need to be initialized even before a constructor is called. To support this, the Java compiler generates a class initialization method automatically for every class. Class fields are initialized in the body of this method, which is is invoked exactly once before the class is first used (often when the class is first loaded).* As with instance field initialization, class field initialization expressions are inserted into the class initialization method in the order they appear in the source code. This means that the initialization expression for a class field can use the class fields declared before it. The class initialization method is an internal method that is hidden from Java programmers. If you disassemble the byte codes in a Java class file, however, you'll see the class initialization code in a method named `<clinit>`.

Initializer blocks

So far, we've seen that objects can be initialized through the initialization expressions for their fields and by arbitrary code in their constructor methods. A class has a class initialization method, which is like a constructor, but we cannot explicitly define the body of this method as we can for a constructor. Java does allow us to write arbitrary code for the initialization of class fields, however, with a construct known as a *static initializer*. A static initializer is simply the keyword `static` followed by a block of code in curly braces. A static initializer can appear in a class definition anywhere a field or method definition can appear. For example, consider the following code that performs some nontrivial initialization for two class fields:

```
// We can draw the outline of a circle using trigonometric functions
// Trigonometry is slow, though, so we precompute a bunch of values
public class TrigCircle {
  // Here are our static lookup tables and their own simple initializers
```

* It is actually possible to write a class initializer for a class C that calls a method of another class that creates an instance of C. In this contrived recursive case, an instance of C is created before the class C is fully initialized. This situation is not common in everyday practice, however.

```
    private static final int NUMPTS = 500;
    private static double sines[] = new double[NUMPTS];
    private static double cosines[] = new double[NUMPTS];

    // Here's a static initializer that fills in the arrays
    static {
      double x = 0.0;
      double delta_x = (Circle.PI/2)/(NUMPTS-1);
      for(int i = 0, x = 0.0; i < NUMPTS; i++, x += delta_x) {
        sines[i] = Math.sin(x);
        cosines[i] = Math.cos(x);
      }
    }
    // The rest of the class is omitted...
  }
```

A class can have any number of static initializers. The body of each initializer block is incorporated into the class initialization method, along with any static field initialization expressions. A static initializer is like a class method in that it cannot use the `this` keyword or any instance fields or instance methods of the class.

In Java 1.1 and later, classes are also allowed to have instance initializers. An instance initializer is like a static initializer, except that it initializes an object, not a class. A class can have any number of instance initializers, and they can appear anywhere a field or method definition can appear. The body of each instance initializer is inserted at the beginning of every constructor for the class, along with any field initialization expressions. An instance initializer looks just like a static initializer, except that it doesn't use the `static` keyword. In other words, an instance initializer is just a block of arbitrary Java code that appears within curly braces.

Instance initializers can initialize arrays or other fields that require complex initialization. They are sometimes useful because they locate the initialization code right next to the field, instead of separating it off in a constructor method. For example:

```
private static final int NUMPTS = 100;
private int[] data = new int[NUMPTS];
{ for(int i = 0; i < NUMPTS; i++) data[i] = i; }
```

In practice, however, this use of instance initializers is fairly rare. Instance initializers were introduced in Java to support anonymous inner classes, and that is their main utility (we'll discuss anonymous inner classes later in this chapter).

Destroying and Finalizing Objects

Now that we've seen how new objects are created and initialized in Java, we need to study the other end of the object life cycle and examine how objects are finalized and destroyed. *Finalization* is the opposite of initialization.

As I mentioned in Chapter 2, the memory occupied by an object is automatically reclaimed when the object is no longer needed. This is done through a process known as *garbage collection*. Garbage collection is not some newfangled technique; it has been around for years in languages such as Lisp. It just takes some getting used to for programmers accustomed to such languages as C and C++, in which you must call the `free()` function or the `delete` operator to reclaim memory. The fact that you don't need to remember to destroy every object you create is one of the features that makes Java a pleasant language to work with. It is also one of the features that makes programs written in Java less prone to bugs than those written in languages that don't support automatic garbage collection.

Garbage Collection

The Java interpreter knows exactly what objects and arrays it has allocated. It can also figure out which local variables refer to which objects and arrays, and which objects and arrays refer to which other objects and arrays. Thus, the interpreter is able to determine when an allocated object is no longer referred to by any other object or variable. When the interpreter finds such an object, it knows it can destroy the object safely and does so. The garbage collector can also detect and destroy cycles of objects that refer to each other, but are not referenced by any other active objects. Any such cycles are also reclaimed.

The Java garbage collector runs as a low-priority thread, so it does most of its work when nothing else is going on, such as during idle time while waiting for user input. The only time the garbage collector must run while something high-priority is going on (i.e., the only time it will actually slow down the system) is when available memory has become dangerously low. This doesn't happen very often because the low-priority thread cleans things up in the background.

This scheme may sound slow and wasteful of memory. Actually though, modern garbage collectors can be surprisingly efficient. Garbage collection will never be as efficient as well-written, explicit memory allocation and deallocation. But it does make programming a lot easier and less prone to bugs. And for most real-world programs, rapid development, lack of bugs, and easy maintenance are more important features than raw speed or memory efficiency.

Memory Leaks in Java

The fact that Java supports garbage collection dramatically reduces the incidence of a class of bugs known as *memory leaks*. A memory leak occurs when memory is allocated and never reclaimed. At first glance, it might seem that garbage collection prevents all memory leaks because it reclaims all unused objects. A memory leak can still occur in Java, however, if a valid (but unused) reference to an unused object is left hanging around. For example, when a method runs for a long time (or forever), the local variables in that method can retain object references much longer than they are actually required. The following code illustrates:

```
public static void main(String args[]) {
  int big_array[] = new int[100000];

  // Do some computations with big_array and get a result.
  int result = compute(big_array);

  // We no longer need big_array. It will get garbage collected when there
  // are no more references to it. Since big_array is a local variable,
  // it refers to the array until this method returns. But this method
  // doesn't return. So we've got to explicitly get rid of the reference
  // ourselves, so the garbage collector knows it can reclaim the array.
  big_array = null;
```


Object-Oriented

```
    // Loop forever, handling the user's input
    for(;;) handle_input(result);
  }
```

Memory leaks can also occur when you use a hashtable or similar data structure to associate one object with another. Even when neither object is required anymore, the association remains in the hashtable, preventing the objects from being reclaimed until the hashtable itself is reclaimed. If the hashtable has a substantially longer lifetime than the objects it holds, this can cause memory leaks.

Object Finalization

A *finalizer* in Java is the opposite of a constructor. While a constructor method performs initialization for an object, a finalizer method performs finalization for the object. Garbage collection automatically frees up the memory resources used by objects, but objects can hold other kinds of resources, such as open files and network connections. The garbage collector cannot free these resources for you, so you need to write a finalizer method for any object that needs to perform such tasks as closing files, terminating network connections, deleting temporary files, and so on.

A finalizer is an instance method that takes no arguments and returns no value. There can be only one finalizer per class, and it must be named `finalize()`.* A finalizer can throw any kind of exception or error, but when a finalizer is automatically invoked by the garbage collector, any exception or error it throws is ignored and serves only to cause the finalizer method to return. Finalizer methods are typically declared `protected` (which we have not discussed yet), but can also be declared `public`. An example finalizer looks like this:

```
protected void finalize() throws Throwable {
  // Invoke the finalizer of our superclass
  // We haven't discussed superclasses or this syntax yet
  super.finalize();

  // Delete a temporary file we were using
  // If the file doesn't exist or tempfile is null, this can throw
  // an exception, but that exception is ignored.
  tempfile.delete();
}
```

Here are some important points about finalizers:

- If an object has a finalizer, the finalizer method is invoked sometime after the object becomes unused (or unreachable), but before the garbage collector reclaims the object.
- Java makes no guarantees about when garbage collection will occur or in what order objects will be collected. Therefore, Java can make no guarantees about when (or even whether) a finalizer will be invoked, in what order finalizers will be invoked, or what thread will execute finalizers.

---

* C++ programmers should note that although Java constructor methods are named like C++ constructors, Java finalization methods are not named like C++ destructor methods. As we will see, they do not behave quite like C++ destructor methods, either.

- The Java interpreter can exit without garbage collecting all outstanding objects, so some finalizers may never be invoked. In this case, though, any outstanding resources are usually freed by the operating system. In Java 1.1, the `Runtime` method `runFinalizersOnExit()` can force the virtual machine to run finalizers before exiting. Unfortunately, however, this method can cause deadlock and is inherently unsafe; it has been deprecated as of Java 1.2. In Java 1.3, the `Runtime` method `addShutdownHook()` can safely execute arbitrary code before the Java interpreter exits.
- After a finalizer is invoked, objects are not freed right away. This is because a finalizer method can resurrect an object by storing the `this` pointer somewhere so that the object once again has references. Thus, after `finalize()` is called, the garbage collector must once again determine that the object is unreferenced before it can garbage-collect it. However, even if an object is resurrected, the finalizer method is never invoked more than once. Resurrecting an object is never a useful thing to do—just a strange quirk of object finalization. As of Java 1.2, the `java.lang.ref.PhantomReference` class can implement an alternative to finalization that does not allow resurrection.

In practice, it is relatively rare for an application-level class to require a `finalize()` method. Finalizer methods are more useful, however, when writing Java classes that interface to native platform code with `native` methods. In this case, the native implementation can allocate memory or other resources that are not under the control of the Java garbage collector and need to be reclaimed explicitly by a `native finalize()` method.

While Java supports both class and instance initialization through static initializers and constructors, it provides only a facility for instance finalization. The original Java specification called for a `classFinalize()` method that could finalize a class when the class itself became unused and was unloaded from the VM. This feature was never implemented, however, and because it has proved to be unnecessary, class finalization has been removed from the language specification.

Subclasses and Inheritance

The `Circle` defined earlier is a simple class that distinguishes circle objects only by their radii. Suppose, instead, that we want to represent circles that have both a size and a position. For example, a circle of radius 1.0 centered at point 0,0 in the Cartesian plane is different from the circle of radius 1.0 centered at point 1,2. To do this, we need a new class, which we'll call `PlaneCircle`. We'd like to add the ability to represent the position of a circle without losing any of the existing functionality of the `Circle` class. This is done by defining `PlaneCircle` as a subclass of `Circle`, so that `PlaneCircle` inherits the fields and methods of its superclass, `Circle`. The ability to add functionality to a class by subclassing, or extending, it is central to the object-oriented programming paradigm.

Extending a Class

Example 3-3 shows how we can implement PlaneCircle as a subclass of the Circle class.

Example 3-3. Extending the Circle class

```
public class PlaneCircle extends Circle {
  // We automatically inherit the fields and methods of Circle,
  // so we only have to put the new stuff here.
  // New instance fields that store the center point of the circle
  public double cx, cy;

  // A new constructor method to initialize the new fields
  // It uses a special syntax to invoke the Circle() constructor
  public PlaneCircle(double r, double x, double y) {
    super(r);       // Invoke the constructor of the superclass, Circle()
    this.cx = x;    // Initialize the instance field cx
    this.cy = y;    // Initialize the instance field cy
  }

  // The area() and circumference() methods are inherited from Circle
  // A new instance method that checks whether a point is inside the circle
  // Note that it uses the inherited instance field r
  public boolean isInside(double x, double y) {
    double dx = x - cx, dy = y - cy;             // Distance from center
    double distance = Math.sqrt(dx*dx + dy*dy);  // Pythagorean theorem
    return (distance < r);                       // Returns true or false
  }
}
```

Note the use of the keyword extends in the first line of Example 3-3. This keyword tells Java that PlaneCircle extends, or subclasses, Circle, meaning that it inherits the fields and methods of that class.* The definition of the isInside() method shows field inheritance; this method uses the field r (defined by the Circle class) as if it were defined right in PlaneCircle itself. PlaneCircle also inherits the methods of Circle. Thus, if we have a PlaneCircle object referenced by variable pc, we can say:

```
double ratio = pc.circumference() / pc.area();
```

This works just as if the area() and circumference() methods were defined in PlaneCircle itself.

Another feature of subclassing is that every PlaneCircle object is also a perfectly legal Circle object. Thus, if pc refers to a PlaneCircle object, we can assign it to a Circle variable and forget all about its extra positioning capabilities:

```
PlaneCircle pc = new PlaneCircle(1.0, 0.0, 0.0);  // Unit circle at the origin
Circle c = pc;     // Assigned to a Circle variable without casting
```

This assignment of a PlaneCircle object to a Circle variable can be done without a cast. As we discussed in Chapter 2, this is a widening conversion and is always legal. The value held in the Circle variable c is still a valid PlaneCircle object,

* C++ programmers should note that extends is the Java equivalent of : in C++; both are used to indicate the superclass of a class.

but the compiler cannot know this for sure, so it doesn't allow us to do the opposite (narrowing) conversion without a cast:

```
// Narrowing conversions require a cast (and a runtime check by the VM)
PlaneCircle pc2 = (PlaneCircle) c;
boolean origininside = ((PlaneCircle) c).isInside(0.0, 0.0);
```

Final classes

When a class is declared with the `final` modifier, it means that it cannot be extended or subclassed. `java.lang.System` is an example of a `final` class. Declaring a class `final` prevents unwanted extensions to the class, and it also allows the compiler to make some optimizations when invoking the methods of a class. We'll explore this in more detail later in this chapter, when we talk about method overriding.

Superclasses, Object, and the Class Hierarchy

In our example, `PlaneCircle` is a subclass of `Circle`. We can also say that `Circle` is the superclass of `PlaneCircle`. The superclass of a class is specified in its `extends` clause:

```
public class PlaneCircle extends Circle { ... }
```

Every class you define has a superclass. If you do not specify the superclass with an `extends` clause, the superclass is the class `java.lang.Object`. `Object` is a special class for a couple of reasons:

- It is the only class in Java that does not have a superclass.
- All Java classes inherit the methods of `Object`.

Because every class has a superclass, classes in Java form a class hierarchy, which can be represented as a tree with `Object` at its root. Figure 3-1 shows a class hierarchy diagram that includes our `Circle` and `PlaneCircle` classes, as well as some of the standard classes from the Java API.

Subclass Constructors

Look again at the `PlaneCircle()` constructor method of Example 3-3:

```
public PlaneCircle(double r, double x, double y) {
  super(r);        // Invoke the constructor of the superclass, Circle()
  this.cx = x;     // Initialize the instance field cx
  this.cy = y;     // Initialize the instance field cy
}
```

This constructor explicitly initializes the `cx` and `cy` fields newly defined by `PlaneCircle`, but it relies on the superclass `Circle()` constructor to initialize the inherited fields of the class. To invoke the superclass constructor, our constructor calls `super()`. `super` is a reserved word in Java. One of its uses is to invoke the constructor method of a superclass from within the constructor method of a subclass. This use is analogous to the use of `this()` to invoke one constructor method of a class from within another constructor method of the same class. Using

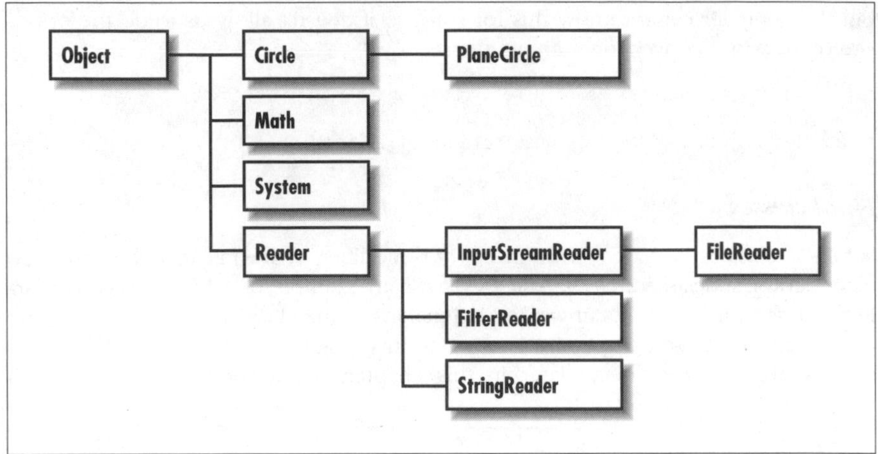

Figure 3-1. A class hierarchy diagram

`super()` to invoke a constructor is subject to the same restrictions as using `this()` to invoke a constructor:

- `super()` can be used in this way only within a constructor method.
- The call to the superclass constructor must appear as the first statement within the constructor method, even before local variable declarations.

The arguments passed to `super()` must match the parameters of the superclass constructor. If the superclass defines more than one constructor, `super()` can be used to invoke any one of them, depending on the arguments passed.

Constructor Chaining and the Default Constructor

Java guarantees that the constructor method of a class is called whenever an instance of that class is created. It also guarantees that the constructor is called whenever an instance of any subclass is created. In order to guarantee this second point, Java must ensure that every constructor method calls its superclass constructor method. Thus, if the first statement in a constructor does not explicitly invoke another constructor with `this()` or `super()`, Java implicitly inserts the call `super()`; that is, it calls the superclass constructor with no arguments. If the superclass does not have a constructor that takes no arguments, this implicit invocation causes a compilation error.

Consider what happens when we create a new instance of the `PlaneCircle` class. First, the `PlaneCircle` constructor is invoked. This constructor explicitly calls `super(r)` to invoke a `Circle` constructor, and that `Circle()` constructor implicitly calls `super()` to invoke the constructor of its superclass, `Object`. The body of the `Object` constructor runs first. When it returns, the body of the `Circle()` constructor runs. Finally, when the call to `super(r)` returns, the remaining statements of the `PlaneCircle()` constructor are executed.

What all this means is that constructor calls are chained; any time an object is created, a sequence of constructor methods is invoked, from subclass to superclass on up to Object at the root of the class hierarchy. Because a superclass constructor is always invoked as the first statement of its subclass constructor, the body of the Object constructor always runs first, followed by the constructor of its subclass and on down the class hierarchy to the class that is being instantiated. There is an important implication here; when a constructor is invoked, it can count on the fields of its superclass to be initialized.

The default constructor

There is one missing piece in the previous description of constructor chaining. If a constructor does not invoke a superclass constructor, Java does so implicitly. But what if a class is declared without a constructor? In this case, Java implicitly adds a constructor to the class. This default constructor does nothing but invoke the superclass constructor. For example, if we don't declare a constructor for the PlaneCircle class, Java implicitly inserts this constructor:

```
public PlaneCircle() { super(); }
```

If the superclass, Circle, doesn't declare a no-argument constructor, the super() call in this automatically inserted default constructor for PlaneCircle() causes a compilation error. In general, if a class does not define a no-argument constructor, all its subclasses must define constructors that explicitly invoke the superclass constructor with the necessary arguments.

If a class does not declare any constructors, it is given a no-argument constructor by default. Classes declared public are given public constructors. All other classes are given a default constructor that is declared without any visibility modifier: such a constructor has default visibility. (The notion of visibility is explained later in this chapter.) If you are creating a public class that should not be publicly instantiated, you should declare at least one non-public constructor to prevent the insertion of a default public constructor. Classes that should never be instantiated (such as java.lang.Math or java.lang.System) should define a private constructor. Such a constructor can never be invoked from outside of the class, but it prevents the automatic insertion of the default constructor.

Finalizer chaining?

You might assume that, since Java chains constructor methods, it also automatically chains the finalizer methods for an object. In other words, you might assume that the finalizer method of a class automatically invokes the finalizer of its superclass, and so on. In fact, Java does *not* do this. When you write a finalize() method, you must explicitly invoke the superclass finalizer. (You should do this even if you know that the superclass does not have a finalizer because a future implementation of the superclass might add a finalizer.)

As we saw in our example finalizer earlier in the chapter, you can invoke a superclass method with a special syntax that uses the super keyword:

```
// Invoke the finalizer of our superclass
super.finalize();
```

We'll discuss this syntax in more detail when we consider method overriding. In practice, the need for finalizer methods, and thus finalizer chaining, rarely arises.

Shadowing Superclass Fields

For the sake of example, imagine that our PlaneCircle class needs to know the distance between the center of the circle and the origin (0,0). We can add another instance field to hold this value:

```
public double r;
```

Adding the following line to the constructor computes the value of the field:

```
this.r = Math.sqrt(cx*cx + cy*cy);  // Pythagorean theorem
```

But wait, this new field r has the same name as the radius field r in the Circle superclass. When this happens, we say that the field r of PlaneCircle *shadows* the field r of Circle. (This is a contrived example, of course: the new field should really be called distanceFromOrigin. Although you should attempt to avoid it, subclass fields do sometimes shadow fields of their superclass.)

With this new definition of PlaneCircle, the expressions r and this.r both refer to the field of PlaneCircle. How, then, can we refer to the field r of Circle that holds the radius of the circle? There is a special syntax for this that uses the super keyword:

```
r        // Refers to the PlaneCircle field
this.r   // Refers to the PlaneCircle field
super.r  // Refers to the Circle field
```

Another way to refer to a shadowed field is to cast this (or any instance of the class) to the appropriate superclass and then access the field:

```
((Circle) this).r   // Refers to field r of the Circle class
```

This casting technique is particularly useful when you need to refer to a shadowed field defined in a class that is not the immediate superclass. Suppose, for example, that classes A, B, and C all define a field named x and that C is a subclass of B, which is a subclass of A. Then, in the methods of class C, you can refer to these different fields as follows:

```
x                // Field x in class C
this.x           // Field x in class C
super.x          // Field x in class B
((B)this).x      // Field x in class B
((A)this).x      // Field x in class A
super.super.x    // Illegal; does not refer to x in class A
```

You cannot refer to a shadowed field x in the superclass of a superclass with super.super.x. This is not legal syntax.

Similarly, if you have an instance c of class C, you can refer to the three fields named x like this:

```
c.x              // Field x of class C
((B)c).x         // Field x of class B
((A)c).x         // Field x of class A
```

So far, we've been discussing instance fields. Class fields can also be shadowed. You can use the same super syntax to refer to the shadowed value of the field, but this is never necessary since you can always refer to a class field by prepending the name of the desired class. Suppose that the implementer of PlaneCircle decides that the Circle.PI field does not express π to enough decimal places. She can define her own class field PI:

```
public static final double PI = 3.14159265358979323846;
```

Now, code in PlaneCircle can use this more accurate value with the expressions PI or PlaneCircle.PI. It can also refer to the old, less accurate value with the expressions super.PI and Circle.PI. Note, however, that the area() and circumference() methods inherited by PlaneCircle are defined in the Circle class, so they use the value Circle.PI, even though that value is shadowed now by PlaneCircle.PI.

Overriding Superclass Methods

When a class defines an instance method using the same name, return type, and parameters as a method in its superclass, that method *overrides* the method of the superclass. When the method is invoked for an object of the class, it is the new definition of the method that is called, not the superclass's old definition.

Method overriding is an important and useful technique in object-oriented programming. PlaneCircle does not override either of the methods defined by Circle, but suppose we define another subclass of Circle, named Ellipse.* In this case, it is important for Ellipse to override the area() and circumference() methods of Circle, since the formulas used to compute the area and circumference of a circle do not work for ellipses.

The upcoming discussion of method overriding considers only instance methods. Class methods behave quite differently, and there isn't much to say. Like fields, class methods can be shadowed by a subclass, but not overridden. As I noted earlier in this chapter, it is good programming style to always prefix a class method invocation with the name of the class in which it is defined. If you consider the class name part of the class method name, the two methods have different names, so nothing is actually shadowed at all. It is, however, illegal for a class method to shadow an instance method.

Before we go any further with the discussion of method overriding, you need to be sure you understand the difference between method overriding and method overloading. As we discussed in Chapter 2, method overloading refers to the practice of defining multiple methods (in the same class) that have the same name, but different parameter lists. This is very different from method overriding, so don't get them confused.

Overriding is not shadowing

Although Java treats the fields and methods of a class analogously in many ways, method overriding is not like field shadowing at all. You can refer to shadowed

* Mathematical purists may argue that since all circles are ellipses, Ellipse should be the superclass and Circle the subclass. A pragmatic engineer might counterargue that circles can be represented with fewer instance fields, so Circle objects should not be burdened by inheriting unnecessary fields from Ellipse. In any case, this is a useful example here.

fields simply by casting an object to an instance of the appropriate superclass, but you cannot invoke overridden instance methods with this technique. The following code illustrates this crucial difference:

```
class A {                          // Define a class named A
  int i = 1;                       // An instance field
  int f() { return i; }            // An instance method
  static char g() { return 'A'; }  // A class method
}

class B extends A {                // Define a subclass of A
  int i = 2;                       // Shadows field i in class A
  int f() { return -i; }           // Overrides instance method f in class A
  static char g() { return 'B'; }  // Shadows class method g() in class A
}

public class OverrideTest {
  public static void main(String args[]) {
    B b = new B();                 // Creates a new object of type B
    System.out.println(b.i);       // Refers to B.i; prints 2
    System.out.println(b.f());     // Refers to B.f(); prints -2
    System.out.println(b.g());     // Refers to B.g(); prints B
    System.out.println(B.g());     // This is a better way to invoke B.g()

    A a = (A) b;                   // Casts b to an instance of class A
    System.out.println(a.i);       // Now refers to A.i; prints 1
    System.out.println(a.f());     // Still refers to B.f(); prints -2
    System.out.println(a.g());     // Refers to A.g(); prints A
    System.out.println(A.g());     // This is a better way to invoke A.g()
  }
}
```

While this difference between method overriding and field shadowing may seem surprising at first, a little thought makes the purpose clear. Suppose we have a bunch of `Circle` and `Ellipse` objects we are manipulating. To keep track of the circles and ellipses, we store them in an array of type `Circle[]`. (We can do this because `Ellipse` is a subclass of `Circle`, so all `Ellipse` objects are legal `Circle` objects.) When we loop through the elements of this array, we don't have to know or care whether the element is actually a `Circle` or an `Ellipse`. What we do care about very much, however, is that the correct value is computed when we invoke the `area()` method of any element of the array. In other words, we don't want to use the formula for the area of a circle when the object is actually an ellipse! Seen in this context, it is not surprising at all that method overriding is handled differently by Java than field shadowing.

Dynamic method lookup

If we have a `Circle[]` array that holds `Circle` and `Ellipse` objects, how does the compiler know whether to call the `area()` method of the `Circle` class or the `Ellipse` class for any given item in the array? In fact, the compiler does not know this because it cannot know it. The compiler knows that it does not know, however, and produces code that uses dynamic method lookup at runtime. When the interpreter runs the code, it looks up the appropriate `area()` method to call for each of the objects in the array. That is, when the interpreter interprets the expression `o.area()`, it checks the actual type of the object referred to by the variable `o` and then finds the area() method that is appropriate for that type. It does not simply use the area() method that is statically associated with the type of the variable o. This process of dynamic method lookup is sometimes also called virtual method invocation.*

Final methods and static method lookup

Virtual method invocation is fast, but method invocation is faster when no dynamic lookup is necessary at runtime. Fortunately, there are a number of situations in which Java does not need to use dynamic method lookup. In particular, if a method is declared with the final modifier, it means that the method definition is the final one; it cannot be overridden by any subclasses. If a method cannot be overridden, the compiler knows that there is only one version of the method, and dynamic method lookup is not necessary.† In addition, all methods of a final class are themselves implicitly final and cannot be overridden. As we'll discuss later in this chapter, private methods are not inherited by subclasses and, therefore, cannot be overridden (i.e., all private methods are implicitly final). Finally, class methods behave like fields (i.e., they can be shadowed by subclasses but not overridden). Taken together, this means that all methods of a class that is declared final, as well as all methods that are final, private, or static, are invoked without dynamic method lookup. These methods are also candidates for inlining at runtime by a just-in-time compiler (JIT) or similar optimization tool.

Invoking an overridden method

We've seen the important differences between method overriding and field shadowing. Nevertheless, the Java syntax for invoking an overridden method is quite similar to the syntax for accessing a shadowed field: both use the super keyword. The following code illustrates:

```
class A {
  int i = 1;                  // An instance field shadowed by subclass B
  int f() { return i; }       // An instance method overridden by subclass B
}
class B extends A {
  int i;                      // This field shadows i in A
  int f() {                   // This method overrides f() in A
    i = super.i + 1;          // It can retrieve A.i like this
    return super.f() + i;     // It can invoke A.f() like this
  }
}
```

Recall that when you use super to refer to a shadowed field, it is the same as casting this to the superclass type and accessing the field through that. Using super to invoke an overridden method, however, is not the same as casting this. In

* C++ programmers should note that dynamic method lookup is what C++ does for virtual functions. An important difference between Java and C++ is that Java does not have a virtual keyword. In Java, methods are virtual by default.

† In this sense, the final modifier is the opposite of the virtual modifier in C++. All non-final methods in Java are virtual.

other words, in the previous code, the expression `super.f()` is not the same as `((A)this).f()`.

When the interpreter invokes an instance method with this `super` syntax, a modified form of dynamic method lookup is performed. The first step, as in regular dynamic method lookup, is to determine the actual class of the object through which the method is invoked. Normally, the dynamic search for an appropriate method definition would begin with this class. When a method is invoked with the `super` syntax, however, the search begins at the superclass of the class. If the superclass implements the method directly, that version of the method is invoked. If the superclass inherits the method, the inherited version of the method is invoked.

Note that the `super` keyword invokes the most immediately overridden version of a method. Suppose class `A` has a subclass `B` that has a subclass `C`, and all three classes define the same method `f()`. Then the method `C.f()` can invoke the method `B.f()`, which it overrides directly, with `super.f()`. But there is no way for `C.f()` to invoke `A.f()` directly: `super.super.f()` is not legal Java syntax. Of course, if `C.f()` invokes `B.f()`, it is reasonable to suppose that `B.f()` might also invoke `A.f()`. This kind of chaining is relatively common when working with overridden methods: it is a way of augmenting the behavior of a method without replacing the method entirely. We saw this technique in the the example `finalize()` method shown earlier in the chapter: that method invoked `super.finalize()` to run its superclass finalization method.

Don't confuse the use of `super` to invoke an overridden method with the `super()` method call used in constructor methods to invoke a superclass constructor. Although they both use the same keyword, these are two entirely different syntaxes. In particular, you can use `super` to invoke an overridden method anywhere in the overriding class, while you can use `super()` only to invoke a superclass constructor as the very first statement of a constructor.

It is also important to remember that `super` can be used only to invoke an overridden method from within the class that overrides it. Given an `Ellipse` object `e`, there is no way for a program that uses an object (with or without the `super` syntax) to invoke the `area()` method defined by the `Circle` class on this object.

I've already explained that class methods can shadow class methods in superclasses, but cannot override them. The preferred way to invoke class methods is to include the name of the class in the invocation. If you do not do this, however, you can use the `super` syntax to invoke a shadowed class method, just as you would invoke an instance method or refer to a shadowed field.

Data Hiding and Encapsulation

We started this chapter by describing a class as "a collection of data and methods." One of the important object-oriented techniques we haven't discussed so far is hiding the data within the class and making it available only through the methods. This technique is known as *encapsulation* because it seals the data (and internal methods) safely inside the "capsule" of the class, where it can be accessed only by trusted users (i.e., by the methods of the class).

Why would you want to do this? The most important reason is to hide the internal implementation details of your class. If you prevent programmers from relying on those details, you can safely modify the implementation without worrying that you will break existing code that uses the class.

Another reason for encapsulation is to protect your class against accidental or willful stupidity. A class often contains a number of interdependent fields that must be in a consistent state. If you allow a programmer (including yourself) to manipulate those fields directly, he may change one field without changing important related fields, thus leaving the class in an inconsistent state. If, instead, he has to call a method to change the field, that method can be sure to do everything necessary to keep the state consistent. Similarly, if a class defines certain methods for internal use only, hiding these methods prevents users of the class from calling them.

Here's another way to think about encapsulation: when all the data for a class is hidden, the methods define the only possible operations that can be performed on objects of that class. Once you have carefully tested and debugged your methods, you can be confident that the class will work as expected. On the other hand, if all the fields of the class can be directly manipulated, the number of possibilities you have to test becomes unmanageable.

There are other reasons to hide fields and methods of a class, as well:

- Internal fields and methods that are visible outside the class just clutter up the API. Keeping visible fields to a minimum keeps your class tidy and therefore easier to use and understand.
- If a field or method is visible to the users of your class, you have to document it. Save yourself time and effort by hiding it instead.

Access Control

All the fields and methods of a class can always be used within the body of the class itself. Java defines access control rules that restrict members of a class from being used outside the class. In an number of examples in this chapter, you've seen the `public` modifier used in field and method declarations. This `public` keyword, along with `protected` and `private`, are *access control modifiers*; they specify the access rules for the field or method.

Access to packages

A package is always accessible to code defined within the package. Whether it is accessible to code from other packages depends on the way the package is deployed on the host system. When the class files that comprise a package are stored in a directory, for example, a user must have read access to the directory and the files within it in order to have access to the package. Package access is not part of the Java language itself. Access control is usually done at the level of classes and members of classes instead.

Access to classes

By default, top-level classes are accessible within the package in which they are defined. However, if a top-level class is declared `public`, it is accessible everywhere (or everywhere that the package itself is accessible). The reason that we've restricted these statements to top-level classes is that, as we'll see later in this chapter, classes can also be defined as members of other classes. Because these inner classes are members of a class, they obey the member access-control rules.

Access to members

As I've already said, the members of a class are always accessible within the body of the class. By default, members are also accessible throughout the package in which the class is defined. This implies that classes placed in the same package should trust each other with their internal implementation details. This default level of access is often called *package access*. It is only one of four possible levels of access. The other three levels of access are defined by the `public`, `protected`, and `private` modifiers. Here is some example code that uses these modifiers:

```
public class Laundromat {       // People can use this class.
  private Laundry[] dirty;      // They cannot use this internal field,
  public void wash() { ... }    // but they can use these public methods
  public void dry() { ... }     // to manipulate the internal field.
}
```

Here are the access rules that apply to members of a class:

- If a member of a class is declared with the `public` modifier, it means that the member is accessible anywhere the containing class is accessible. This is the least restrictive type of access control.
- If a member of a class is declared `private`, the member is never accessible, except within the class itself. This is the most restrictive type of access control.
- If a member of a class is declared `protected`, it is accessible to all classes within the package (the same as the default package accessibility) and also accessible within the body of any subclass of the class, regardless of the package in which that subclass is defined. This is more restrictive than `public` access, but less restrictive than package access.
- If a member of a class is not declared with any of these modifiers, it has the default package access: it is accessible to code within all classes that are defined in the same package, but inaccessible outside of the package.

`protected` access requires a little more elaboration. Suppose class `A` declares a `protected` field `x` and is extended by a class `B`, which is defined in a different package (this last point is important). Class `B` inherits the `protected` field `x`, and its code can access that field in the current instance of `B` or in any other instances of `B` that the code can refer to. This does not mean, however, that the code of class `B` can start reading the protected fields of arbitrary instances of `A`! If an object is an instance of `A`, but is not an instance of `B`, then its fields are obviously not inherited by `B`, and the code of class `B` cannot read them.

Access control and inheritance

The Java specification states that a subclass inherits all the instance fields and instance methods of its superclass accessible to it. If the subclass is defined in the same package as the superclass, it inherits all non-`private` instance fields and methods. If the subclass is defined in a different package, however, it inherits all `protected` and `public` instance fields and methods. `private` fields and methods are never inherited; neither are class fields or class methods. Finally, constructors are not inherited; they are chained, as described earlier in this chapter.

The statement that a subclass does not inherit the inaccessible fields and methods of its superclass can be a confusing one. It would seem to imply that when you create an instance of a subclass, no memory is allocated for any `private` fields defined by the superclass. This is not the intent of the statement, however. Every instance of a subclass does, in fact, include a complete instance of the superclass within it, including all inaccessible fields and methods. It is simply a matter of terminology. Because the inaccessible fields cannot be used in the subclass, we say they are not inherited. I stated earlier in this section that the members of a class are always accessible within the body of the class. If this statement is to apply to all members of the class, including inherited members, then we have to define "inherited members" to include only those members that are accessible. If you don't care for this definition, you can think of it this way instead:

- A class inherits *all* instance fields and instance methods (but not constructors) of its superclass.
- The body of a class can always access all the fields and methods it declares itself. It can also access the *accessible* fields and members it inherits from its superclass.

Member access summary

Table 3-1 summarizes the member access rules.

Table 3-1. Class member accessibility

	Member visibility			
Accessible to	*public*	*protected*	*package*	*private*
Defining class	Yes	Yes	Yes	Yes
Class in same package	Yes	Yes	Yes	No
Subclass in different package	Yes	Yes	No	No
Non-subclass different package	Yes	No	No	No

Here are some simple rules of thumb for using visibility modifiers:

- Use `public` only for methods and constants that form part of the public API of the class. Certain important or frequently used fields can also be `public`, but it is common practice to make fields non-`public` and encapsulate them with `public` accessor methods.

- Use `protected` for fields and methods that aren't required by most programmers using the class, but that may be of interest to anyone creating a subclass as part of a different package. Note that `protected` members are technically part of the exported API of a class. They should be documented and cannot be changed without potentially breaking code that relies on them.
- Use the default package visibility for fields and methods that are internal implementation details, but are used by cooperating classes in the same package. You cannot take real advantage of package visibility unless you use the `package` directive to group your cooperating classes into a package.
- Use `private` for fields and methods that are used only inside the class and should be hidden everywhere else.

If you are not sure whether to use `protected`, package, or `private` accessibility, it is better to start with overly restrictive member access. You can always relax the access restrictions in future versions of your class, if necessary. Doing the reverse is not a good idea because increasing access restrictions is not a backwards-compatible change.

Data Accessor Methods

In the `Circle` example we've been using, we've declared the circle radius to be a `public` field. The `Circle` class is one in which it may well be reasonable to keep that field publicly accessible; it is a simple enough class, with no dependencies between its fields. On the other hand, our current implementation of the class allows a `Circle` object to have a negative radius, and circles with negative radii should simply not exist. As long as the radius is stored in a `public` field, however, any programmer can set the field to any value she wants, no matter how unreasonable. The only solution is to restrict the programmer's direct access to the field and define `public` methods that provide indirect access to the field. Providing `public` methods to read and write a field is not the same as making the field itself `public`. The crucial difference is that methods can perform error checking.

Example 3-4 shows how we might reimplement `Circle` to prevent circles with negative radii. This version of `Circle` declares the `r` field to be `protected` and defines accessor methods named `getRadius()` and `setRadius()` to read and write the field value while enforcing the restriction on negative radius values. Because the `r` field is `protected`, it is directly (and more efficiently) accessible to subclasses.

Example 3-4. The Circle class using data hiding and encapsulation

```
package shapes;           // Specify a package for the class

public class Circle {     // The class is still public
  // This is a generally useful constant, so we keep it public
  public static final double PI = 3.14159;

  protected double r;     // Radius is hidden, but visible to subclasses

  // A method to enforce the restriction on the radius
  // This is an implementation detail that may be of interest to subclasses
  protected void checkRadius(double radius) {
```

```
    if (radius < 0.0)
      throw new IllegalArgumentException("radius may not be negative.");
  }

  // The constructor method
  public Circle(double r) {
    checkRadius(r);
    this.r = r;
  }

  // Public data accessor methods
  public double getRadius() { return r; }
  public void setRadius(double r) {
    checkRadius(r);
    this.r = r;
  }

  // Methods to operate on the instance field
  public double area() { return PI * r * r; }
  public double circumference() { return 2 * PI * r; }
}
```


We have defined the `Circle` class within a package named `shapes`. Since `r` is `protected`, any other classes in the `shapes` package have direct access to that field and can set it however they like. The assumption here is that all classes within the `shapes` package were written by the same author or a closely cooperating group of authors, and that the classes all trust each other not to abuse their privileged level of access to each other's implementation details.

Finally, the code that enforces the restriction against negative radius values is itself placed within a `protected` method, `checkRadius()`. Although users of the `Circle` class cannot call this method, subclasses of the class can call it and even override it if they want to change the restrictions on the radius.

Note particularly the `getRadius()` and `setRadius()` methods of Example 3-4. It is almost universal in Java that data accessor methods begin with the prefixes "get" and "set." If the field being accessed is of type `boolean`, however, the `get()` method may be replaced with an equivalent method that begins with "is." For example, the accessor method for a `boolean` field named `readable` is typically called `isReadable()` instead of `getReadable()`. In the programming conventions of the JavaBeans component model (covered in Chapter 6), a hidden field with one or more data accessor methods whose names begin with "get," "is," or "set" is called a *property*. An interesting way to study a complex class is to look at the set of properties it defines. Properties are particularly common in the AWT and Swing APIs, which are covered in *Java Foundation Classes in a Nutshell* (O'Reilly).

Abstract Classes and Methods

In Example 3-4, we declared our `Circle` class to be part of a package named `shapes`. Suppose we plan to implement a number of shape classes: `Rectangle`, `Square`, `Ellipse`, `Triangle`, and so on. We can give these shape classes our two basic `area()` and `circumference()` methods. Now, to make it easy to work with an array of shapes, it would be helpful if all our shape classes had a common superclass, Shape. If we structure our class hierarchy this way, every shape object, regardless of the actual type of shape it represents, can be assigned to variables, fields, or array elements of type Shape. We want the Shape class to encapsulate whatever features all our shapes have in common (e.g., the area() and circumference() methods). But our generic Shape class doesn't represent any real kind of shape, so it cannot define useful implementations of the methods. Java handles this situation with *abstract methods*.

Java lets us define a method without implementing it by declaring the method with the abstract modifier. An abstract method has no body; it simply has a signature definition followed by a semicolon.* Here are the rules about abstract methods and the abstract classes that contain them:

- Any class with an abstract method is automatically abstract itself and must be declared as such.
- An abstract class cannot be instantiated.
- A subclass of an abstract class can be instantiated only if it overrides each of the abstract methods of its superclass and provides an implementation (i.e., a method body) for all of them. Such a class is often called a *concrete* subclass, to emphasize the fact that it is not abstract.
- If a subclass of an abstract class does not implement all the abstract methods it inherits, that subclass is itself abstract.
- static, private, and final methods cannot be abstract, since these types of methods cannot be overridden by a subclass. Similarly, a final class cannot contain any abstract methods.
- A class can be declared abstract even if it does not actually have any abstract methods. Declaring such a class abstract indicates that the implementation is somehow incomplete and is meant to serve as a superclass for one or more subclasses that will complete the implementation. Such a class cannot be instantiated.

There is an important feature of the rules of abstract methods. If we define the Shape class to have abstract area() and circumference() methods, any subclass of Shape is required to provide implementations of these methods so it can be instantiated. In other words, every Shape object is guaranteed to have implementations of these methods defined. Example 3-5 shows how this might work. It defines an abstract Shape class and two concrete subclasses of it.

Example 3-5. An abstract class and concrete subclasses

```
public abstract class Shape {
  public abstract double area();            // Abstract methods: note
  public abstract double circumference();   // semicolon instead of body.
}
```

* An abstract method in Java is something like a pure virtual function in C++ (i.e., a virtual function that is declared = 0). In C++, a class that contains a pure virtual function is called an abstract class and cannot be instantiated. The same is true of Java classes that contain abstract methods.

Example 3-5. An abstract class and concrete subclasses (continued)

```
class Circle extends Shape {
  public static final double PI = 3.14159265358979323846;
  protected double r;                              // Instance data
  public Circle(double r) { this.r = r; }          // Constructor
  public double getRadius() { return r; }          // Accessor
  public double area() { return PI*r*r; }          // Implementations of
  public double circumference() { return 2*PI*r; } // abstract methods.
}

class Rectangle extends Shape {
  protected double w, h;                               // Instance data
  public Rectangle(double w, double h) {               // Constructor
    this.w = w;  this.h = h;
  }
  public double getWidth() { return w; }               // Accessor method
  public double getHeight() { return h; }              // Another accessor
  public double area() { return w*h; }                 // Implementations of
  public double circumference() { return 2*(w + h); }  // abstract methods.
}
```

Each abstract method in Shape has a semicolon right after its parentheses. There are no curly braces, and no method body is defined. Using the classes defined in Example 3-5, we can now write code such as:

```
Shape[] shapes = new Shape[3];          // Create an array to hold shapes
shapes[0] = new Circle(2.0);            // Fill in the array
shapes[1] = new Rectangle(1.0, 3.0);
shapes[2] = new Rectangle(4.0, 2.0);

double total_area = 0;
for(int i = 0; i < shapes.length; i++)
    total_area += shapes[i].area();     // Compute the area of the shapes
```

There are two important points to notice here:

- Subclasses of Shape can be assigned to elements of an array of Shape. No cast is necessary. This is another example of a widening reference type conversion (discussed in Chapter 2).
- You can invoke the area() and circumference() methods for any Shape object, even though the Shape class does not define a body for these methods. When you do this, the method to be invoked is found using dynamic method lookup, so the area of a circle is computed using the method defined by Circle, and the area of a rectangle is computed using the method defined by Rectangle.

Interfaces

Let's extend our shapes package further. Suppose we now want to implement a number of shapes that not only know their sizes, but also know the position of their center point in the Cartesian coordinate plane. One way to do this is to define an abstract CenteredShape class and then implement various subclasses of it, such as CenteredCircle, CenteredRectangle, and so on.

But we also want these positionable shape classes to support the `area()` and `circumference()` methods we've already defined, without reimplementing these methods. So, for example, we'd like to define `CenteredCircle` as a subclass of `Circle`, so that it inherits `area()` and `circumference()`. But a class in Java can have only one immediate superclass. If `CenteredCircle` extends `Circle`, it cannot also extend the `abstract CenteredShape` class!*

Java's solution to this problem is called an interface. Although a Java class can extend only a single superclass, it can *implement* any number of interfaces.

Defining an Interface

An interface is a reference type that is closely related to a class. Almost everything you've read so far in this book about classes applies equally to interfaces. Defining an interface is a lot like defining an abstract class, except that the keywords `abstract` and `class` are replaced with the keyword `interface`. When you define an interface, you are creating a new reference type, just as you are when you define a class. As its name implies, an *interface* specifies an interface, or API, for certain functionality. It does not define any implementation of that API, however. There are a number of restrictions that apply to the members of an interface:

- An interface contains no implementation whatsoever. All methods of an interface are implicitly `abstract`, even if the `abstract` modifier is omitted. Interface methods have no implementation; a semicolon appears in place of the method body. Because interfaces can contain only `abstract` methods, and class methods cannot be abstract, the methods of an interface must all be instance methods.
- An interface defines a public API. All methods of an interface are implicitly `public`, even if the `public` modifier is omitted. It is an error to define a `protected` or `private` method in an interface.
- Although a class defines data and methods that operate on that data, an interface cannot define instance fields. Fields are an implementation detail, and an interface is a pure specification without any implementation. The only fields allowed in an interface definition are constants that are declared both `static` and `final`.
- An interface cannot be instantiated, so it does not define a constructor.

Example 3-6 shows the definition of an interface named `Centered`. This interface defines the methods a `Shape` subclass should implement if it knows the x,y coordinate of its center point.

Example 3-6. An interface definition

```
public interface Centered {
  public void setCenter(double x, double y);
  public double getCenterX();
```

* C++ allows classes to have more than one superclass, using a technique known as multiple inheritance. Multiple inheritance adds a lot of complexity to a language; Java supports what many believe is a more elegant solution.

Example 3-6. An interface definition (continued)

```
  public double getCenterY();
}
```

Implementing an Interface

Just as a class uses `extends` to specify its superclass, it can use `implements` to name one or more interfaces it supports. `implements` is a Java keyword that can appear in a class declaration following the `extends` clause. `implements` should be followed by the name or names of the interface(s) the class implements, with multiple names separated by commas.

When a class declares an interface in its `implements` clause, it is saying that it provides an implementation (i.e., a body) for each method of that interface. If a class implements an interface but does not provide an implementation for every interface method, it inherits those unimplemented `abstract` methods from the interface and must itself be declared `abstract`. If a class implements more than one interface, it must implement every method of each interface it implements (or be declared `abstract`).

Example 3-7 shows how we can define a `CenteredRectangle` class that extends our `Rectangle` class and implements the `Centered` interface we defined in Example 3-6.

Example 3-7. Implementing an interface

```
public class CenteredRectangle extends Rectangle implements Centered {
  // New instance fields
  private double cx, cy;

  // A constructor
  public CenteredRectangle(double cx, double cy, double w, double h) {
    super(w, h);
    this.cx = cx;
    this.cy = cy;
  }

  // We inherit all the methods of Rectangle, but must
  // provide implementations of all the Centered methods.
  public void setCenter(double x, double y) { cx = x; cy = y; }
  public double getCenterX() { return cx; }
  public double getCenterY() { return cy; }
}
```

As I noted earlier, constants can appear in an interface definition. Any class that implements the interface inherits the constants and can use them as if they were defined directly in the class. There is no need to prefix them with the name of the interface or provide any kind of implementation of the constants. When you have a set of constants used by more than one class (e.g., a port number and other protocol constants used by a client and server), it can be convenient to define the necessary constants in an interface that contains no methods. Then, any class that wants to use those constants needs only to declare that it implements the interface. `java.io.ObjectStreamConstants` is just such an interface.

Using Interfaces

Suppose we implement CenteredCircle and CenteredSquare just as we implemented CenteredRectangle in Example 3-7. Since each class extends Shape, instances of the classes can be treated as instances of the Shape class, as we saw earlier. Since each class implements Centered, instances can also be treated as instances of that type. The following code demonstrates both techniques:

```
Shape[] shapes = new Shape[3];          // Create an array to hold shapes

// Create some centered shapes, and store them in the Shape[]
// No cast necessary: these are all widening conversions
shapes[0] = new CenteredCircle(1.0, 1.0, 1.0);
shapes[1] = new CenteredSquare(2.5, 2, 3);
shapes[2] = new CenteredRectangle(2.3, 4.5, 3, 4);

// Compute average area of the shapes and average distance from the origin
double totalArea = 0;
double totalDistance = 0;
for(int i = 0; i < shapes.length; i++) {
  totalArea += shapes[i].area();        // Compute the area of the shapes
  if (shapes[i] instanceof Centered) { // The shape is a Centered shape
    // Note the required cast from Shape to Centered (no cast would
    // be required to go from CenteredSquare to Centered, however).
    Centered c = (Centered) shapes[i]; // Assign it to a Centered variable
    double cx = c.getCenterX();         // Get coordinates of the center
    double cy = c.getCenterY();         // Compute distance from origin
    totalDistance += Math.sqrt(cx*cx + cy*cy);
  }
}
System.out.println("Average area: " + totalArea/shapes.length);
System.out.println("Average distance: " + totalDistance/shapes.length);
```

This example demonstrates that interfaces are data types in Java, just like classes. When a class implements an interface, instances of that class can be assigned to variables of the interface type. Don't interpret this example, however, to imply that you must assign a CenteredRectangle object to a Centered variable before you can invoke the setCenter() method or to a Shape variable before you can invoke the area() method. CenteredRectangle defines setCenter() and inherits area() from its Rectangle superclass, so you can always invoke these methods.

When to Use Interfaces

When defining an abstract type (e.g., Shape) that you expect to have many subtypes (e.g., Circle, Rectangle, Square), you are often faced with a choice between interfaces and abstract classes. Since they have similar features, it is not always clear when to use one over the other.

An interface is useful because any class can implement it, even if that class extends some entirely unrelated superclass. But an interface is a pure API specification and contains no implementation. If an interface has numerous methods, it can become tedious to implement the methods over and over, especially when much of the implementation is duplicated by each implementing class.

On the other hand, a class that extends an abstract class cannot extend any other class, which can cause design difficulties in some situations. However, an abstract class does not need to be entirely abstract; it can contain a partial implementation that subclasses can take advantage of. In some cases, numerous subclasses can rely on default method implementations provided by an abstract class.

Another important difference between interfaces and abstract classes has to do with compatibility. If you define an interface as part of a public API and then later add a new method to the interface, you break any classes that implemented the previous version of the interface. If you use an abstract clas, however, you can safely add nonabstract methods to that class without requiring modifications to existing classes that extend the abstract class.

In some situations, it will be clear that an interface or an abstract class is the right design choice. In other cases, a common design pattern is to use both. First, define the type as a totally abstract interface. Then create an abstract class that implements the interface and provides useful default implementations subclasses can take advantage of. For example:

```
// Here is a basic interface. It represents a shape that fits inside
// of a rectangular bounding box. Any class that wants to serve as a
// RectangularShape can implement these methods from scratch.
public interface RectangularShape {
  public void setSize(double width, double height);
  public void setPosition(double x, double y);
  public void translate(double dx, double dy);
  public double area();
  public boolean isInside();
}

// Here is a partial implementation of that interface. Many
// implementations may find this a useful starting point.
public abstract class AbstractRectangularShape implements RectangularShape {
  // The position and size of the shape
  protected double x, y, w, h;

  // Default implementations of some of the interface methods
  public void setSize(double width, double height) { w = width; h = height; }
  public void setPosition(double x, double y) { this.x = x; this.y = y; }
  public void translate (double dx, double dy) { x += dx; y += dy; }
}
```

Implementing Multiple Interfaces

Suppose we want shape objects that can be positioned in terms of not only their center points, but also their upper-right corners. And suppose we also want shapes that can be scaled larger and smaller. Remember that although a class can extend only a single superclass, it can implement any number of interfaces. Assuming we have defined appropriate `UpperRightCornered` and `Scalable` interfaces, we can declare a class as follows:

```
public class SuperDuperSquare extends Shape
       implements Centered, UpperRightCornered, Scalable {
   // Class members omitted here
}
```

When a class implements more than one interface, it simply means that it must provide implementations for all abstract methods in all its interfaces.

Extending Interfaces

Interfaces can have subinterfaces, just as classes can have subclasses. A subinterface inherits all the abstract methods and constants of its superinterface and can define new abstract methods and constants. Interfaces are different from classes in one very important way, however: an interface can have an `extends` clause that lists more than one superinterface. For example, here are some interfaces that extend other interfaces:

```
public interface Positionable extends Centered {
  public void setUpperRightCorner(double x, double y);
  public double getUpperRightX();
  public double getUpperRightY();
}
public interface Transformable extends Scalable, Translatable, Rotatable {}
public interface SuperShape extends Positionable, Transformable {}
```

An interface that extends more than one interface inherits all the abstract methods and constants from each of those interfaces and can define its own additional abstract methods and constants. A class that implements such an interface must implement the abstract methods defined directly by the interface, as well as all the abstract methods inherited from all the superinterfaces.

Marker Interfaces

Sometimes it is useful to define an interface that is entirely empty. A class can implement this interface simply by naming it in its `implements` clause without having to implement any methods. In this case, any instances of the class become valid instances of the interface. Java code can check whether an object is an instance of the interface using the `instanceof` operator, so this technique is a useful way to provide additional information about an object. The `Cloneable` interface in `java.lang` is an example of this type of *marker interface*. It defines no methods, but identifies the class as one that allows its internal state to be cloned by the `clone()` method of the `Object` class. As of Java 1.1, `java.io.Serializable` is another such marker interface. Given an arbitrary object, you can determine whether it has a working `clone()` method with code such as:

```
Object o;      // Initialized elsewhere
Object copy;
if (o instanceof Cloneable) copy = o.clone();
else copy = null;
```

Inner Class Overview

The classes and interfaces we have seen so far in this chapter have all been top-level classes (i.e., they are direct members of packages, not nested within any other classes). Starting in Java 1.1, however, there are four other types of classes, loosely known as *inner classes*, that can be defined in a Java program. Used correctly, inner classes are an elegant and powerful feature of the Java language. These four types of classes are summarized here:

Static member classes
: A static member class is a class (or interface) defined as a `static` member of another class. A `static` method is called a class method, so, by analogy, we could call this type of inner class a "class class," but this terminology would obviously be confusing. A static member class behaves much like an ordinary top-level class, except that it can access the `static` members of the class that contains it. Interfaces can be defined as static members of classes.

Member classes
: A member class is also defined as a member of an enclosing class, but is not declared with the `static` modifier. This type of inner class is analogous to an instance method or field. An instance of a member class is always associated with an instance of the enclosing class, and the code of a member class has access to all the fields and methods (both `static` and non-`static`) of its enclosing class. There are several features of Java syntax that exist specifically to work with the enclosing instance of a member class. Interfaces can only be defined as static members of a class, not as non-`static` members.

Local classes
: A local class is a class defined within a block of Java code. Like a local variable, a local class is visible only within that block. Although local classes are not member classes, they are still defined within an enclosing class, so they share many of the features of member classes. Additionally, however, a local class can access any `final` local variables or parameters that are accessible in the scope of the block that defines the class. Interfaces cannot be defined locally.

Anonymous classes
: An anonymous class is a kind of local class that has no name; it combines the syntax for class definition with the syntax for object instantiation. While a local class definition is a Java statement, an anonymous class definition (and instantiation) is a Java expression, so it can appear as part of a larger expression, such as method invocation. Interfaces cannot be defined anonymously.

Java programmers have not reached a consensus on the appropriate names for the various kinds of inner classes. Thus, you may find them referred to by different names in different situations. In particular, static member classes are sometimes called "nested top-level" classes, and the term "nested classes" may refer to all types of inner classes. The term "inner classes" is itself overloaded and sometimes refers specifically to member classes. On other occasions, "inner classes" refers to member classes, local classes, and anonymous classes, but not static member classes. In this book, I use "inner class" to mean any class other than a standard top-level class and the names shown previously to refer to the individual types of inner classes.

Static Member Classes

A *static member class* (or interface) is much like a regular top-level class (or interface). For convenience, however, it is nested within another class or interface. Example 3-8 shows a helper interface defined as a static member of a containing class. The example also shows how this interface is used both within the class that contains it and by external classes. Note the use of its hierarchical name in the external class.

Example 3-8. Defining and using a static member interface

```
// A class that implements a stack as a linked list
public class LinkedStack {
  // This static member interface defines how objects are linked
  public static interface Linkable {
    public Linkable getNext();
    public void setNext(Linkable node);
  }

  // The head of the list is a Linkable object
  Linkable head;

  // Method bodies omitted
  public void push(Linkable node) { ... }
  public Object pop() { ... }
}

// This class implements the static member interface
class LinkableInteger implements LinkedStack.Linkable {
  // Here's the node's data and constructor
  int i;
  public LinkableInteger(int i) { this.i = i; }

  // Here are the data and methods required to implement the interface
  LinkedStack.Linkable next;
  public LinkedStack.Linkable getNext() { return next; }
  public void setNext(LinkedStack.Linkable node) { next = node; }
}
```

Features of Static Member Classes

A static member class or interface is defined as a `static` member of a containing class, making it analogous to the class fields and methods that are also declared `static`. Like a class method, a static member class is not associated with any instance of the containing class (i.e., there is no `this` object). A static member class does, however, have access to all the `static` members (including any other static member classes and interfaces) of its containing class. A static member class can use any other static member without qualifying its name with the name of the containing class.

A static member class has access to all static members of its containing class, including `private` members. The reverse is true as well: the methods of the containing class have access to all members of a static member class, including the `private` members. A static member class even has access to all the members of any other static member classes, including the `private` members of those classes.

Since static member classes are themselves class members, a static member class can be declared with its own access control modifiers. These modifiers have the same meanings for static member classes as they do for other members of a class. In Example 3-8, the `Linkable` interface is declared `public`, so it can be implemented by any class that is interested in being stored on a `LinkedStack`.

Restrictions on Static Member Classes

A static member class cannot have the same name as any of its enclosing classes. In addition, static member classes and interfaces can be defined only within top-level classes and other static member classes and interfaces. This is actually part of a larger prohibition against `static` members of any sort within member, local, and anonymous classes.

Object-Oriented

New Syntax for Static Member Classes

In code outside of the containing class, a static member class or interface is named by combining the name of the outer class with the name of the inner class (e.g., `LinkedStack.Linkable`). You can use the `import` directive to import a static member class:

```
import LinkedStack.Linkable;  // Import a specific inner class
import LinkedStack.*;         // Import all inner classes of LinkedStack
```

Importing inner classes is not recommended, however, because it obscures the fact that the inner class is tightly associated with its containing class.

Member Classes

A *member class* is a class that is declared as a non-`static` member of a containing class. If a static member class is analogous to a class field or class method, a member class is analogous to an instance field or instance method. Example 3-9 shows how a member class can be defined and used. This example extends the previous `LinkedStack` example to allow enumeration of the elements on the stack by defining an `enumerate()` method that returns an implementation of the `java.util.Enumeration` interface. The implementation of this interface is defined as a member class.

Example 3-9. An enumeration implemented as a member class

```
public class LinkedStack {
  // Our static member interface; body omitted here...
  public static interface Linkable { ... }

  // The head of the list
  private Linkable head;

  // Method bodies omitted here
  public void push(Linkable node) { ... }
  public Linkable pop() { ... }

  // This method returns an Enumeration object for this LinkedStack
```

Example 3-9. An enumeration implemented as a member class (continued)

```
  public java.util.Enumeration enumerate() { return new Enumerator(); }

  // Here is the implementation of the Enumeration interface,
  // defined as a member class.
  protected class Enumerator implements java.util.Enumeration {
    Linkable current;
    // The constructor uses the private head field of the containing class
    public Enumerator() { current = head; }
    public boolean hasMoreElements() {  return (current != null); }
    public Object nextElement() {
      if (current == null) throw new java.util.NoSuchElementException();
      Object value = current;
      current = current.getNext();
      return value;
    }
  }
}
```

Notice how the `Enumerator` class is nested within the `LinkedStack` class. Since `Enumerator` is a helper class used only within `LinkedStack`, there is a real elegance to having it defined so close to where it is used by the containing class.

Features of Member Classes

Like instance fields and instance methods, every member class is associated with an instance of the class within which it is defined (i.e., every instance of a member class is associated with an instance of the containing class). This means that the code of a member class has access to all the instance fields and instance methods (as well as the `static` members) of the containing class, including any that are declared `private`.

This crucial feature is illustrated in Example 3-9. Here is the body of the `LinkedStack.Enumerator()` constructor again:

```
current = head;
```

This single line of code sets the `current` field of the inner class to the value of the `head` field of the containing class. The code works as shown, even though `head` is declared as a `private` field in the containing class.

A member class, like any member of a class, can be assigned one of three visibility levels: `public`, `protected`, or `private`. If none of these visibility modifiers is specified, the default package visibility is used. In Example 3-9, the `Enumerator` class is declared `protected`, so it is inaccessible to code (in a different package) using the `LinkedStack` class, but accessible to any class that subclasses `LinkedStack`.

Restrictions on Member Classes

There are three important restrictions on member classes:

- A member class cannot have the same name as any containing class or package. This is an important rule, and one not shared by fields and methods.

- Member classes cannot contain any `static` fields, methods, or classes (with the exception of constant fields declared both `static` and `final`). `static` fields, methods, and classes are top-level constructs not associated with any particular object, while every member class is associated with an instance of its enclosing class. Defining a `static` top-level member within a non-top-level member class simply promotes confusion and bad programming style, so you are required to define all static members within a top-level or static member class or interface.
- Interfaces cannot be defined as member classes. An interface cannot be instantiated, so there is no object to associate with an instance of the enclosing class. If you declare an interface as a member of a class, the interface is implicitly `static`, making it a static member class.

Object-Oriented

New Syntax for Member Classes

The most important feature of a member class is that it can access the instance fields and methods in its containing object. We saw this in the `LinkedStack.Enumerator()` constructor of Example 3-9:

```
public Enumerator() { current = head; }
```

In this example, `head` is a field of the `LinkedStack` class, and we assign it to the `current` field of the `Enumerator` class. The current code works, but what if we want to make these references explicit? We could try code like this:

```
public Enumerator() { this.current = this.head; }
```

This code does not compile, however. `this.current` is fine; it is an explicit reference to the `current` field in the newly created `Enumerator` object. It is the `this.head` expression that causes the problem; it refers to a field named `head` in the `Enumerator` object. Since there is no such field, the compiler generates an error. To solve this problem, Java defines a special syntax for explicitly referring to the containing instance of the `this` object. Thus, if we want to be explicit in our constructor, we can use the following syntax:

```
public Enumerator() { this.current = LinkedStack.this.head; }
```

The general syntax is *`classname`*`.this`, where *`classname`* is the name of a containing class. Note that member classes can themselves contain member classes, nested to any depth. Since no member class can have the same name as any containing class, however, the use of the enclosing class name prepended to `this` is a perfectly general way to refer to any containing instance. This syntax is needed only when referring to a member of a containing class that is hidden by a member of the same name in the member class.

Accessing superclass members of the containing class

When a class shadows or overrides a member of its superclass, you can use the keyword `super` to refer to the hidden member. This `super` syntax can be extended to work with member classes as well. On the rare occasion when you need to refer to a shadowed field `f` or an overridden method `m` of a superclass of a containing class `C`, use the following expressions:

```
C.super.f
C.super.m()
```

This syntax was not implemented by Java 1.1 compilers, but it works correctly as of Java 1.2.

Specifying the containing instance

As we've seen, every instance of a member class is associated with an instance of its containing class. Look again at our definition of the `enumerate()` method in Example 3-9:

```
public Enumeration enumerate() { return new Enumerator(); }
```

When a member class constructor is invoked like this, the new instance of the member class is automatically associated with the `this` object. This is what you would expect to happen and exactly what you want to occur in most cases. Occasionally, however, you may want to specify the containing instance explicitly when instantiating a member class. You can do this by preceding the `new` operator with a reference to the containing instance. Thus, the `enumerate()` method shown above is shorthand for the following:

```
public Enumeration enumerate() { return this.new Enumerator(); }
```

Let's pretend we didn't define an `enumerate()` method for `LinkedStack`. In this case, the code to obtain an `Enumerator` object for a given `LinkedStack` object might look like this:

```
LinkedStack stack = new LinkedStack();     // Create an empty stack
Enumeration e = stack.new Enumerator();    // Create an Enumeration for it
```

The containing instance implicitly specifies the name of the containing class; it is a syntax error to explicitly specify that containing class:

```
Enumeration e = stack.new LinkedStack.Enumerator();  // Syntax error
```

There is one other special piece of Java syntax that specifies an enclosing instance for a member class explicitly. Before we consider it, however, let me point out that you should rarely, if ever, need to use this syntax. It is one of the pathological cases that snuck into the language along with all the elegant features of inner classes.

As strange as it may seem, it is possible for a top-level class to extend a member class. This means that the subclass does not have a containing instance, but its superclass does. When the subclass constructor invokes the superclass constructor, it must specify the containing instance. It does this by prepending the containing instance and a period to the `super` keyword. If we had not declared our `Enumerator` class to be a `protected` member of `LinkedStack`, we could subclass it. Although it is not clear why we would want to do so, we could write code like the following:

```
// A top-level class that extends a member class
class SpecialEnumerator extends LinkedStack.Enumerator {
  // The constructor must explicitly specify a containing instance
  // when invoking the superclass constructor.
  public SpecialEnumerator(LinkedStack s) { s.super(); }
```

```
    // Rest of class omitted...
}
```

Scope Versus Inheritance for Member Classes

We've just noted that a top-level class can extend a member class. With the introduction of member classes, there are two separate hierarchies that must be considered for any class. The first is the *class hierarchy*, from superclass to subclass, that defines the fields and methods a member class inherits. The second is the *containment hierarchy*, from containing class to contained class, that defines a set of fields and methods that are in the scope of (and are therefore accessible to) the member class.

The two hierarchies are entirely distinct from each other; it is important that you do not confuse them. This should not be a problem if you refrain from creating naming conflicts, where a field or method in a superclass has the same name as a field or method in a containing class. If such a naming conflict does arise, however, the inherited field or method takes precedence over the field or method of the same name in the containing class. This behavior is logical: when a class inherits a field or method, that field or method effectively becomes part of that class. Therefore, inherited fields and methods are in the scope of the class that inherits them and take precedence over fields and methods by the same name in enclosing scopes.

A good way to prevent confusion between the class hierarchy and the containment hierarchy is to avoid deep containment hierarchies. If a class is nested more than two levels deep, it is probably going to cause more confusion than it is worth. Furthermore, if a class has a deep class hierarchy (i.e., it has many superclass ancestors), consider defining it as a top-level class, rather than as a member class.

Local Classes

A *local class* is declared locally within a block of Java code, rather than as a member of a class. Typically, a local class is defined within a method, but it can also be defined within a static initializer or instance initializer of a class. Because all blocks of Java code appear within class definitions, all local classes are nested within containing classes. For this reason, local classes share many of the features of member classes. It is usually more appropriate, however, to think of them as an entirely separate kind of inner class. A local class has approximately the same relationship to a member class as a local variable has to an instance variable of a class.

The defining characteristic of a local class is that it is local to a block of code. Like a local variable, a local class is valid only within the scope defined by its enclosing block. If a member class is used only within a single method of its containing class, for example, there is usually no reason it cannot be coded as a local class, rather than a member class. Example 3-10 shows how we can modify the `enumerate()` method of the `LinkedStack` class so it defines `Enumerator` as a local class instead of a member class. By doing this, we move the definition of the class even closer to where it is used and hopefully improve the clarity of the code even further. For brevity, Example 3-10 shows only the enumerate() method, not the entire LinkedStack class that contains it.

Example 3-10. Defining and using a local class

```
// This method creates and returns an Enumeration object
public java.util.Enumeration enumerate() {

  // Here's the definition of Enumerator as a local class
  class Enumerator implements java.util.Enumeration {
    Linkable current;
    public Enumerator() { current = head; }
    public boolean hasMoreElements() {  return (current != null); }
    public Object nextElement() {
      if (current == null) throw new java.util.NoSuchElementException();
      Object value = current;
      current = current.getNext();
      return value;
    }
  }

  // Now return an instance of the Enumerator class we just defined
  return new Enumerator();
}
```

Features of Local Classes

Local classes have the following interesting features:

- Like member classes, local classes are associated with a containing instance, and can access any members, including private members, of the containing class.
- In addition to accessing fields defined by the containing class, local classes can access any local variables, method parameters, or exception parameters that are in the scope of the local method definition and declared final.

Restrictions on Local Classes

Local classes are subject to the following restrictions:

- A local class is visible only within the block that defines it; it can never be used outside that block.
- Local classes cannot be declared public, protected, private, or static. These modifiers are for members of classes; they are not allowed with local variable declarations or local class declarations.
- Like member classes, and for the same reasons, local classes cannot contain static fields, methods, or classes. The only exception is for constants that are declared both static and final.
- Interfaces cannot be defined locally.

- A local class, like a member class, cannot have the same name as any of its enclosing classes.
- As noted earlier, a local class can use the local variables, method parameters, and even exception parameters that are in its scope, but only if those variables or parameters are declared `final`. This is because the lifetime of an instance of a local class can be much longer than the execution of the method in which the class is defined. For this reason, a local class must have a private internal copy of all local variables it uses (these copies are automatically generated by the compiler). The only way to ensure that the local variable and the private copy are always the same is to insist that the local variable is `final`.

New Syntax for Local Classes

In Java 1.0, only fields, methods, and classes can be declared `final`. The addition of local classes in Java 1.1 has required a liberalization in the use of the `final` modifier. It can now be applied to local variables, method parameters, and even the exception parameter of a `catch` statement. The meaning of the `final` modifier remains the same in these new uses: once the local variable or parameter has been assigned a value, that value cannot be changed.

Instances of local classes, like instances of member classes, have an enclosing instance that is implicitly passed to all constructors of the local class. Local classes can use the same `this` syntax as member classes, to refer explicitly to members of enclosing classes. Because local classes are never visible outside the blocks that define them, however, there is never a need to use the `new` and `super` syntax used by member classes to specify the enclosing instance explicitly.

Scope of a Local Class

In discussing member classes, we saw that a member class can access any members inherited from superclasses and any members defined by its containing classes. The same is true for local classes, but local classes can also access `final` local variables and parameters. The following code illustrates the many fields and variables that may be accessible to a local class:

```
class A { protected char a = 'a'; }
class B { protected char b = 'b'; }

public class C extends A {
  private char c = 'c';          // Private fields visible to local class
  public static char d = 'd';
  public void createLocalObject(final char e)
  {
    final char f = 'f';
    int i = 0;                   // i not final; not usable by local class
    class Local extends B
    {
      char g = 'g';
      public void printVars()
      {
        // All of these fields and variables are accessible to this class
```

```
            System.out.println(g);  // (this.g) g is a field of this class
            System.out.println(f);  // f is a final local variable
            System.out.println(e);  // e is a final local parameter
            System.out.println(d);  // (C.this.d) d -- field of containing class
            System.out.println(c);  // (C.this.c) c -- field of containing class
            System.out.println(b);  // b is inherited by this class
            System.out.println(a);  // a is inherited by the containing class
        }
    }
    Local l = new Local();          // Create an instance of the local class
    l.printVars();                  // and call its printVars() method.
  }
}
```

Local Classes and Local Variable Scope

A local variable is defined within a block of code, which defines its scope. A local variable ceases to exist outside of its scope. Java is a *lexically scoped* language, which means that its concept of scope has to do with the way the source code is written. Any code within the curly braces that define the boundaries of a block can use local variables defined in that block.*

Lexical scoping simply defines a segment of source code within which a variable can be used. It is common, however, to think of a scope as a temporal scope—to think of a local variable as existing from the time the Java interpreter begins executing the block until the time the interpreter exits the block. This is usually a reasonable way to think about local variables and their scope.

The introduction of local classes confuses the picture, however, because local classes can use local variables, and instances of a local class can have a lifetime much longer than the time it takes the interpreter to execute the block of code. In other words, if you create an instance of a local class, the instance does not automatically go away when the interpreter finishes executing the block that defines the class, as shown in the following code:

```
public class Weird {
  // A static member interface used below
  public static interface IntHolder { public int getValue(); }

  public static void main(String[] args) {
    IntHolder[] holders = new IntHolder[10];    // An array to hold 10 objects
    for(int i = 0; i < 10; i++) {               // Loop to fill the array up
      final int fi = i;                         // A final local variable
      class MyIntHolder implements IntHolder {  // A local class
         public int getValue() { return fi; }   // It uses the final variable
      }
      holders[i] = new MyIntHolder();           // Instantiate the local class
    }

    // The local class is now out of scope, so we can't use it. But
    // we have 10 valid instances of that class in our array. The local
    // variable fi is not in our scope here, but it is still in scope for
    // the getValue() method of each of those 10 objects. So call getValue()
```

* This section covers advanced material; first-time readers may want to skip it for now and return to it later.

```
        // for each object and print it out. This prints the digits 0 to 9.
        for(int i = 0; i < 10; i++) System.out.println(holders[i].getValue());
    }
}
```

The behavior of the previous program is pretty surprising. To make sense of it, remember that the lexical scope of the methods of a local class has nothing to do with when the interpreter enters and exits the block of code that defines the local class. Here's another way to think about it: each instance of a local class has an automatically created private copy of each of the final local variables it uses, so, in effect, it has its own private copy of the scope that existed when it was created.

Anonymous Classes

An *anonymous class* is a local class without a name. An anonymous class is defined and instantiated in a single succinct expression using the `new` operator. While a local class definition is a statement in a block of Java code, an anonymous class definition is an expression, which means that it can be included as part of a larger expression, such as a method call. When a local class is used only once, consider using anonymous class syntax, which places the definition and use of the class in exactly the same place.

Consider Example 3-11, which shows the `Enumeration` class implemented as an anonymous class within the `enumerate()` method of the `LinkedStack` class. Compare it with Example 3-10, which shows the same class implemented as a local class.

Example 3-11. An enumeration implemented with an anonymous class

```
public java.util.Enumeration enumerate() {
  // The anonymous class is defined as part of the return statement
  return new java.util.Enumeration() {
    Linkable current;
    { current = head; }  // Replace constructor with an instance initializer
    public boolean hasMoreElements() {  return (current != null); }
    public Object nextElement() {
      if (current == null) throw new java.util.NoSuchElementException();
      Object value = current;
      current = current.getNext();
      return value;
    }
  };  // Note the required semicolon. It terminates the return statement
}
```

One common use for an anonymous class is to provide a simple implementation of an adapter class. An *adapter class* is one that defines code that is invoked by some other object. Take, for example, the `list()` method of the `java.io.File` class. This method lists the files in a directory. Before it returns the list, though, it passes the name of each file to a `FilenameFilter` object you must supply. This `FilenameFilter` object accepts or rejects each file. When you implement the `FilenameFilter` interface, you are defining an adapter class for use with the `File.list()` method. Since the body of such a class is typically quite short, it is easy to define an adapter class as an anonymous class. Here's how you can define a `FilenameFilter` class to list only those files whose names end with *.java*:

```
File f = new File("/src");      // The directory to list

// Now call the list() method with a single FilenameFilter argument
// Define and instantiate an anonymous implementation of FilenameFilter
// as part of the method invocation expression.
String[] filelist = f.list(new FilenameFilter() {
  public boolean accept(File f, String s) { return s.endsWith(".java"); }
}); // Don't forget the parenthesis and semicolon that end the method call!
```

As you can see, the syntax for defining an anonymous class and creating an instance of that class uses the `new` keyword, followed by the name of a class and a class body definition in curly braces. If the name following the `new` keyword is the name of a class, the anonymous class is a subclass of the named class. If the name following `new` specifies an interface, as in the two previous examples, the anonymous class implements that interface and extends `Object`. The syntax does not include any way to specify an `extends` clause, an `implements` clause, or a name for the class.

Because an anonymous class has no name, it is not possible to define a constructor for it within the class body. This is one of the basic restrictions on anonymous classes. Any arguments you specify between the parentheses following the superclass name in an anonymous class definition are implicitly passed to the superclass constructor. Anonymous classes are commonly used to subclass simple classes that do not take any constructor arguments, so the parentheses in the anonymous class definition syntax are often empty. In the previous examples, each anonymous class implemented an interface and extended `Object`. Since the `Object()` constructor takes no arguments, the parentheses were empty in those examples.

Features of Anonymous Classes

One of the most elegant things about anonymous classes is that they allow you to define a one-shot class exactly where it is needed. In addition, anonymous classes have a succinct syntax that reduces clutter in your code.

Restrictions on Anonymous Classes

Because an anonymous class is just a type of local class, anonymous classes and local classes share the same restrictions. An anonymous class cannot define any `static` fields, methods, or classes, except for `static final` constants. Interfaces cannot be defined anonymously, since there is no way to implement an interface without a name. Also, like local classes, anonymous classes cannot be `public`, `private`, `protected`, or `static`.

Since an anonymous class has no name, it is not possible to define a constructor for an anonymous class. If your class requires a constructor, you must use a local class instead. However, you can often use an instance initializer as a substitute for a constructor. In fact, instance initializers were introduced into the language for this very purpose.

The syntax for defining an anonymous class combines definition with instantiation. Thus, using an anonymous class instead of a local class is not appropriate if you need to create more than a single instance of the class each time the containing block is executed.

New Syntax for Anonymous Classes

We've already seen examples of the syntax for defining and instantiating an anonymous class. We can express that syntax more formally as:

```
new class-name ( [ argument-list ] ) { class-body }
```

or:

```
new interface-name () { class-body }
```


As I already mentioned, instance initializers are another specialized piece of Java syntax that was introduced to support anonymous classes. As we discussed earlier in the chapter, an instance initializer is a block of initialization code contained within curly braces inside a class definition. The contents of an instance initializer for a class are automatically inserted into all constructors for the class, including any automatically created default constructor. An anonymous class cannot define a constructor, so it gets a default constructor. By using an instance initializer, you can get around the fact that you cannot define a constructor for an anonymous class.

When to Use an Anonymous Class

As we've discussed, an anonymous class behaves just like a local class and is distinguished from a local class merely in the syntax used to define and instantiate it. In your own code, when you have to choose between using an anonymous class and a local class, the decision often comes down to a matter of style. You should use whichever syntax makes your code clearer. In general, you should consider using an anonymous class instead of a local class if:

- The class has a very short body.
- Only one instance of the class is needed.
- The class is used right after it is defined.
- The name of the class does not make your code any easier to understand.

Anonymous Class Indentation and Formatting

The common indentation and formatting conventions we are familiar with for block-structured languages like Java and C begin to break down somewhat once we start placing anonymous class definitions within arbitrary expressions. Based on their experience with inner classes, the engineers at Sun recommend the following formatting rules:

- The opening curly brace should not be on a line by itself; instead, it should follow the close parenthesis of the `new` operator. Similarly, the `new` operator should, when possible, appear on the same line as the assignment or other expression of which it is a part.
- The body of the anonymous class should be indented relative to the beginning of the line that contains the `new` keyword.
- The closing curly brace of an anonymous class should not be on a line by itself either; it should be followed by whatever tokens are required by the rest of the expression. Often this is a semicolon or a close parenthesis followed by a semicolon. This extra punctuation serves as a flag to the reader that this is not just an ordinary block of code and makes it easier to understand anonymous classes in a code listing.

How Inner Classes Work

The preceding sections have explained the features and behavior of the various types of inner classes. Strictly speaking, that should be all you need to know about inner classes. In practice, however, some programmers find it easier to understand the details of inner classes if they understand how they are implemented.

Inner classes were introduced in Java 1.1. Despite the dramatic changes to the Java language, the introduction of inner classes did not change the Java Virtual Machine or the Java class file format. As far as the Java interpreter is concerned, there is no such thing as an inner class: all classes are normal top-level classes. In order to make an inner class behave as if it is actually defined inside another class, the Java compiler ends up inserting hidden fields, methods, and constructor arguments into the classes it generates. You may want to use the *javap* disassembler to disassemble some of the class files for inner classes so you can see what tricks the compiler has used to make inner classes work. (See Chapter 8 for information on *javap*.)

Static Member Class Implementation

Recall our first `LinkedStack` example (Example 3-8), which defined a static member interface named `Linkable`. When you compile this `LinkedStack` class, the compiler actually generates two class files. The first one is *LinkedStack.class*, as expected. The second class file, however, is called *LinkedStack$Linkable.class*. The `$` in this name is automatically inserted by the Java compiler. This second class file contains the implementation of the static member interface.

As we discussed earlier, a static member class can access all the `static` members of its containing class. If a static member class does this, the compiler automatically qualifies the member access expression with the name of the containing class. A static member class is even allowed to access the `private static` fields of its containing class. Since the static member class is compiled into an ordinary top-level class, however, there is no way it can directly access the `private` members of its container. Therefore, if a static member class uses a `private` member of its containing class (or vice versa), the compiler automatically generates non-`private` access methods and converts the expressions that access the `private` members into expressions that access these specially generated methods. These methods are given the default package access, which is sufficient, as the member class and its containing class are guaranteed to be in the same package.

Member Class Implementation

A member class is implemented much like a static member class. It is compiled into a separate top-level class file, and the compiler performs various code manipulations to make interclass member access work correctly.

The most significant difference between a member class and a static member class is that each instance of a member class is associated with an instance of the enclosing class. The compiler enforces this association by defining a synthetic field named `this$0` in each member class. This field is used to hold a reference to the enclosing instance. Every member class constructor is given an extra parameter that initializes this field. Every time a member class constructor is invoked, the compiler automatically passes a reference to the enclosing class for this extra parameter.

As we've seen, a member class, like any member of a class, can be declared `public`, `protected`, or `private`, or given the default package visibility. However, as I mentioned earlier, there have been no changes to the Java Virtual Machine to support member classes. Member classes are compiled to class files just like top-level classes, but top-level classes can only have public or package access. Therefore, as far as the Java interpreter is concerned, member classes can only have public or package visibility. This means that a member class declared `protected` is actually treated as a public class, and a member class declared `private` actually has package visibility. This does not mean you should never declare a member class as `protected` or `private`. Although the interpreter cannot enforce these access control modifiers, the modifiers are noted in the class file. This allows any conforming Java compiler to enforce the access modifiers and prevent the member classes from being accessed in unintended ways.

Local and Anonymous Class Implementation

A local class is able to refer to fields and methods in its containing class for exactly the same reason that a member class can; it is passed a hidden reference to the containing class in its constructor and saves that reference away in a `private` field added by the compiler. Also, like member classes, local classes can use `private` fields and methods of their containing class because the compiler inserts any required accessor methods.

What makes local classes different from member classes is that they have the ability to refer to local variables in the scope that defines them. The crucial restriction on this ability, however, is that local classes can only reference local variables and parameters that are declared `final`. The reason for this restriction becomes apparent from the implementation. A local class can use local variables because the compiler automatically gives the class a `private` instance field to hold a copy of each local variable the class uses. The compiler also adds hidden parameters to each local class constructor to initialize these automatically created `private` fields. Thus, a local class does not actually access local variables, but merely its own private copies of them. The only way this can work correctly is if the local variables are declared `final`, so that they are guaranteed not to change. With this guarantee, the local class can be assured that its internal copies of the variables are always in sync with the real local variables.

Since anonymous classes have no names, you may wonder what the class files that represent them are named. This is an implementation detail, but the Java compiler from Sun uses numbers to provide anonymous class names. If you compile the example shown in Example 3-11, you'll find that it produces a file with a name like *LinkedStack$1.class*. This is the class file for the anonymous class.

Modifier Summary

As we've seen, classes, interfaces, and their members can be declared with one or more *modifiers*—keywords such as `public`, `static`, and `final`. This chapter has introduced the `public`, `protected`, and `private` access modifiers, as well as the `abstract`, `final`, and `static` modifiers. In addition to these six, Java defines five other less commonly used modifiers. Table 3-2 lists the Java modifiers, explains what types of Java constructs they can modify, and explains what they do.

Table 3-2. Java modifiers

Modifier	*Used on*	*Meaning*
`abstract`	Class	The class contains unimplemented methods and cannot be instantiated.
	Interface	All interfaces are `abstract`. The modifier is optional in interface declarations.
`abstract`	Method	No body is provided for the method; it is provided by a subclass. The signature is followed by a semicolon. The enclosing class must also be `abstract`.
`final`	Class	The class cannot be subclassed.
	Method	The method cannot be overridden (and is not subject to dynamic method lookup).
	Field	The field cannot have its value changed. `static final` fields are compile-time constants.
	Variable	A local variable, method parameter, or exception parameter cannot have its value changed (Java 1.1 and later). Useful with local classes.
`native`	Method	The method is implemented in some platform-dependent way (often in C). No body is provided; the signature is followed by a semicolon.

Table 3-2. Java modifiers (continued)

Modifier	*Used on*	*Meaning*
None (package)	Class	A non-`public` class is accessible only in its package.
	Interface	A non-`public` interface is accessible only in its package.
	Member	A member that is not `private`, `protected`, or `public` has package visibility and is accessible only within its package.
`private`	Member	The member is accessible only within the class that defines it.
`protected`	Member	The member is accessible only within the package in which it is defined and within subclasses.
`public`	Class	The class is accessible anywhere its package is.
	Interface	The interface is accessible anywhere its package is.
	Member	The member is accessible anywhere its class is.
`strictfp`	Class	All methods of the class are implicitly `strictfp` (Java 1.2 and later).
`strictfp`	Method	All floating-point computation done by the method must be performed in a way that strictly conforms to the IEEE 754 standard. In particular, all values, including intermediate results, must be expressed as IEEE `float` or `double` values and cannot take advantage of any extra precision or range offered by native platform floating-point formats or hardware (Java 1.2 and later). This modifier is rarely used.
`static`	Class	An inner class declared `static` is a top-level class, not associated with a member of the containing class (Java 1.1 and later).
	Method	A `static` method is a class method. It is not passed an implicit `this` object reference. It can be invoked through the class name.
	Field	A `static` field is a class field. There is only one instance of the field, regardless of the number of class instances created. It can be accessed through the class name.
	Initializer	The initializer is run when the class is loaded, rather than when an instance is created.

Table 3-2. Java modifiers (continued)

Modifier	*Used on*	*Meaning*
`synchronized`	Method	The method makes non-atomic modifications to the class or instance, so care must be taken to ensure that two threads cannot modify the class or instance at the same time. For a `static` method, a lock for the class is acquired before executing the method. For a non-`static` method, a lock for the specific object instance is acquired.
`transient`	Field	The field is not part of the persistent state of the object and should not be serialized with the object. Used with object serialization; see `java.io.ObjectOutputStream`.
`volatile`	Field	The field can be accessed by unsynchronized threads, so certain optimizations must not be performed on it. This modifier can sometimes be used as an alternative to `synchronized`. This modifier is very rarely used.

C++ Features Not Found in Java

Throughout this chapter, I've noted similarities and differences between Java and C++ in footnotes. Java shares enough concepts and features with C++ to make it an easy language for C++ programmers to pick up. There are several features of C++ that have no parallel in Java, however. In general, Java does not adopt those features of C++ that make the language significantly more complicated.

C++ supports multiple inheritance of method implementations from more than one superclass at a time. While this seems like a useful feature, it actually introduces many complexities to the language. The Java language designers chose to avoid the added complexity by using interfaces instead. Thus, a class in Java can inherit method implementations only from a single superclass, but it can inherit method declarations from any number of interfaces.

C++ supports templates that allow you, for example, to implement a `Stack` class and then instantiate it as `Stack<int>` or `Stack<double>` to produce two separate types: a stack of integers and a stack of floating-point values. Java does not allow this, but efforts are underway to add this feature to the language in a robust and standardized way. Furthermore, the fact that every class in Java is a subclass of `Object` means that every object can be cast to an instance of `Object`. Thus, in Java it is often sufficient to define a data structure (such as a `Stack` class) that operates on `Object` values; the objects can be cast back to their actual types whenever necessary.

C++ allows you to define operators that perform arbitrary operations on instances of your classes. In effect, it allows you to extend the syntax of the language. This is a nifty feature, called operator overloading, that makes for elegant examples. In practice, however, it tends to make code quite difficult to understand. After much debate, the Java language designers decided to omit such operator overloading from the language. Note, though, that the use of the + operator for string concatenation in Java is at least reminiscent of operator overloading.

C++ allows you to define conversion functions for a class that automatically invoke an appropriate constructor method when a value is assigned to a variable of that class. This is simply a syntactic shortcut (similar to overriding the assignment operator) and is not included in Java.

In C++, objects are manipulated by value by default; you must use `&` to specify a variable or function argument automatically manipulated by reference. In Java, all objects are manipulated by reference, so there is no need for this `&` syntax.

CHAPTER 4

The Java Platform

Chapters 2 and 3 documented the Java programming language. This chapter switches gears and covers the Java platform—a vast collection of predefined classes available to every Java program, regardless of the underlying host system on which it is running. The classes of the Java platform are collected into related groups, known as *packages*. This chapter begins with an overview of the packages of the Java platform that are documented in this book. It then moves on to demonstrate, in the form of short examples, the most useful classes in these packages. Most of the examples are code snippets only, not full programs you can compile and run. For fully fleshed-out, real-world examples, see *Java Examples in a Nutshell* (O'Reilly). That book expands greatly on this chapter and is intended as a companion to this one.

Java Platform Overview

Table 4-1 summarizes the key packages of the Java platform that are covered in this book.

Table 4-1. Key packages of the Java platform

Package	*Description*
`java.beans`	The JavaBeans component model for reusable, embeddable software components.
`java.beans.beancontext`	Additional classes that define bean context objects that hold and provide services to the JavaBeans objects they contain.
`java.io`	Classes and interfaces for input and output. Although some of the classes in this package are for working directly with files, most are for working with streams of bytes or characters.

Table 4-1. Key packages of the Java platform (continued)

Package	*Description*
`java.lang`	The core classes of the language, such as `String`, `Math`, `System`, `Thread`, and `Exception`.
`java.lang.ref`	Classes that define weak references to objects. A weak reference is one that does not prevent the referent object from being garbage-collected.
`java.lang.reflect`	Classes and interfaces that allow Java programs to reflect on themselves by examining the constructors, methods, and fields of classes.
`java.math`	A small package that contains classes for arbitrary-precision integer and floating-point arithmetic.
`java.net`	Classes and interfaces for networking with other systems.
`java.nio`	Buffer classes for the New I/O API.
`java.nio.channels`	Channel and selector interfaces and classes for high-performance, nonblocking I/O.
`java.nio.charset`	Character set encoders and decoders for converting Unicode strings to and from bytes.
`java.security`	Classes and interfaces for access control and authentication. Supports cryptographic message digests and digital signatures.
`java.security.acl`	A package that supports access control lists. Deprecated and unused as of Java 1.2.
`java.security.cert`	Classes and interfaces for working with public-key certificates.
`java.security.interfaces`	Interfaces used with DSA and RSA public-key encryption.
`java.security.spec`	Classes and interfaces for transparent representations of keys and parameters used in public-key cryptography.
`java.text`	Classes and interfaces for working with text in internationalized applications.
`java.util`	Various utility classes, including the powerful collections framework for working with collections of objects.
`java.util.jar`	Classes for reading and writing JAR files.
`java.util.logging`	A flexible logging facility.

Table 4-1. Key packages of the Java platform (continued)

Package	*Description*
`java.util.prefs`	An API to read and write user and system preferences.
`java.util.regex`	Text pattern matching using regular expressions.
`java.util.zip`	Classes for reading and writing ZIP files.
`javax.crypto`	Classes and interfaces for encryption and decryption of data.
`javax.crypto.interfaces`	Interfaces that represent the Diffie-Hellman public/private keys used in the Diffie-Hellman key agreement protocol.
`javax.crypto.spec`	Classes that define transparent representations of keys and parameters used in cryptography.
`javax.net`	Defines factory classes for creating sockets and server sockets. Enables the creation of socket types other than the default.
`javax.net.ssl`	Classes for encrypted network communication using the Secure Sockets Layer (SSL).
`javax.security.auth`	The top-level package for the JAAS API for authentication and authorization.
`javax.security.auth.callback`	Classes that facilitate communication between a low-level login module and a user through a user interface.
`javax.security.auth.kerberos`	Utility classes to support network authentication using the Kerberos protocol.
`javax.security.auth.login`	The `LoginContext` and related classes for user authentication.
`javax.security.auth.spi`	Defines the `LoginModule` interface that is implemented by plugable user-authentication modules.
`javax.security.auth.x500`	Utility classes that represent X.500 certificate information.
`javax.xml.parsers`	A high-level API for parsing XML documents using plugable DOM and SAX parsers.
`javax.xml.transform`	A high-level API for transforming XML documents using a plugable XSLT transformation engine and for converting XML documents between streams, DOM trees, and SAX events.

Table 4-1. Key packages of the Java platform (continued)

Package	*Description*
`javax.xml.transform.dom`	Concrete XML transformation classes for DOM.
`javax.xml.transform.sax`	Concrete XML transformation classes for SAX.
`javax.xml.transform.stream`	Concrete XML transformation classes for XML streams.
`org.ietf.jgss`	The Java binding of the Generic Security Services API, which defines a single API for underlying security mechanisms such as Kerberos.
`org.w3c.dom`	Interfaces defined by the World Wide Web Consortium to represent an XML document as a DOM tree.
`org.xml.sax`	Classes and interfaces for parsing XML documents using the event-based SAX (Simple API for XML) API.
`org.xml.sax.ext`	Extension classes for the SAX API.
`org.xml.sax.helpers`	Utility classes for the SAX API.

Table 4-1 does not list all the packages in the Java platform, only those documented in this book. (And it omits a few "spi" packages that are documented in this book but are of interest only to low-level "service providers.") Java also defines numerous packages for graphics and graphical user interface programming and for distributed, or enterprise, computing. The graphics and GUI packages are `java.awt` and `javax.swing` and their many subpackages. These packages, along with the `java.applet` package, are documented in *Java Foundation Classes in a Nutshell* (O'Reilly). The enterprise packages of Java include `java.rmi`, `java.sql`, `javax.jndi`, `org.omg.CORBA`, `org.omg.CosNaming`, and all of their subpackages. These packages, as well as several standard extensions to the Java platform, are documented in *Java Enterprise in a Nutshell* (O'Reilly).

Strings and Characters

Strings of text are a fundamental and commonly used data type. In Java, however, strings are not a primitive type, like `char`, `int`, and `float`. Instead, strings are represented by the `java.lang.String` class, which defines many useful methods for manipulating strings. `String` objects are *immutable*: once a `String` object has been created, there is no way to modify the string of text it represents. Thus, each method that operates on a string typically returns a new `String` object that holds the modified string.

This code shows some of the basic operations you can perform on strings:

```
// Creating strings
String s = "Now";                    // String objects have a special literal syntax
```

```
String t = s + " is the time."; // Concatenate strings with + operator
String t1 = s + " " + 23.4;     // + converts other values to strings
t1 = String.valueOf('c');       // Get string corresponding to char value
t1 = String.valueOf(42);        // Get string version of integer or any value
t1 = object.toString();         // Convert objects to strings with toString()

// String length
int len = t.length();           // Number of characters in the string: 16

// Substrings of a string
String sub = t.substring(4);    // Returns char 4 to end: "is the time."
sub = t.substring(4, 6);        // Returns chars 4 and 5: "is"
sub = t.substring(0, 3);        // Returns chars 0 through 2: "Now"
sub = t.substring(x, y);        // Returns chars between pos x and y-1
int numchars = sub.length();    // Length of substring is always (y-x)

// Extracting characters from a string
char c = t.charAt(2);           // Get the 3rd character of t: w
char[] ca = t.toCharArray();    // Convert string to an array of characters
t.getChars(0, 3, ca, 1);        // Put 1st 3 chars of t into ca[1]-ca[3]

// Case conversion
String caps = t.toUpperCase();  // Convert to uppercase
String lower = t.toLowerCase(); // Convert to lowercase

// Comparing strings
boolean b1 = t.equals("hello");         // Returns false: strings not equal
boolean b2 = t.equalsIgnoreCase(caps);  // Case-insensitive compare: true
boolean b3 = t.startsWith("Now");       // Returns true
boolean b4 = t.endsWith("time.");       // Returns true
int r1 = s.compareTo("Pow");            // Returns < 0: s comes before "Pow"
int r2 = s.compareTo("Now");            // Returns 0: strings are equal
int r3 = s.compareTo("Mow");            // Returns > 0: s comes after "Mow"
r1 = s.compareToIgnoreCase("pow");      // Returns < 0 (Java 1.2 and later)

// Searching for characters and substrings
int pos = t.indexOf('i');          // Position of first 'i': 4
pos = t.indexOf('i', pos+1);       // Position of the next 'i': 12
pos = t.indexOf('i', pos+1);       // No more 'i's in string, returns -1
pos = t.lastIndexOf('i');          // Position of last 'i' in string: 12
pos = t.lastIndexOf('i', pos-1);   // Search backwards for 'i' from char 11

pos = t.indexOf("is");             // Search for substring: returns 4
pos = t.indexOf("is", pos+1);      // Only appears once: returns -1
pos = t.lastIndexOf("the ");       // Search backwards for a string
String noun = t.substring(pos+4);  // Extract word following "the"

// Replace all instances of one character with another character
String exclaim = t.replace('.', '!');  // Works only with chars, not substrings

// Strip blank space off the beginning and end of a string
String noextraspaces = t.trim();

// Obtain unique instances of strings with intern()
String s1 = s.intern();         // Returns s1 equal to s
String s2 = "Now".intern();     // Returns s2 equal to "Now"
boolean equals = (s1 == s2);    // Now can test for equality with ==
```

The Character Class

As you know, individual characters are represented in Java by the primitive char type. The Java platform also defines a Character class, which contains useful class methods for checking the type of a character and for converting the case of a character. For example:

```
char[] text;  // An array of characters, initialized somewhere else
int p = 0;    // Our current position in the array of characters
// Skip leading whitespace
while((p < text.length) && Character.isWhitespace(text[p])) p++;
// Capitalize the first word of text
while((p < text.length) && Character.isLetter(text[p])) {
  text[p] = Character.toUpperCase(text[p]);
  p++;
}
```

The StringBuffer Class

Since String objects are immutable, you cannot manipulate the characters of an instantiated String. If you need to do this, use a java.lang.StringBuffer instead:

```
// Create a string buffer from a string
StringBuffer b = new StringBuffer("Mow");

// Get and set individual characters of the StringBuffer
char c = b.charAt(0);          // Returns 'M': just like String.charAt()
b.setCharAt(0, 'N');           // b holds "Now": can't do that with a String!

// Append to a StringBuffer
b.append(' ');                 // Append a character
b.append("is the time.");      // Append a string
b.append(23);                  // Append an integer or any other value

// Insert Strings or other values into a StringBuffer
b.insert(6, "n't");            // b now holds: "Now isn't the time.23"

// Replace a range of characters with a string (Java 1.2 and later)
b.replace(4, 9, "is");         // Back to "Now is the time.23"

// Delete characters
b.delete(16, 18);              // Delete a range: "Now is the time"
b.deleteCharAt(2);             // Delete 2nd character: "No is the time"
b.setLength(5);                // Truncate by setting the length: "No is"

// Other useful operations
b.reverse();                   // Reverse characters: "si oN"
String s = b.toString();       // Convert back to an immutable string
s = b.substring(1,2);          // Or take a substring: "i"
b.setLength(0);                // Erase buffer; now it is ready for reuse
```

The CharSequence Interface

In Java 1.4, both the String and the StringBuffer classes implement the new java.lang.CharSequence interface, which is a standard interface for querying the length of and extracting characters and subsequences from a readable sequence of characters. This interface is also implemented by the `java.nio.CharBuffer` interface, which is part of the New I/O API that was introduced in Java 1.4. `CharSequence` provides a way to perform simple operations on strings of characters regardless of the underlying implementation of those strings. For example:

```
/**
 * Return a prefix of the specified CharSequence that starts at the first
 * character of the sequence and extends up to (and includes) the first
 * occurrence of the character c in the sequence. Returns null if c is
 * not found. s may be a String, StringBuffer, or java.nio.CharBuffer.
 */
public static CharSequence prefix(CharSequence s, char c) {
  int numChars = s.length();             // How long is the sequence?
  for(int i = 0; i < numChars; i++) {    // Loop through characters in sequence
    if (s.charAt(i) == c)                // If we find c,
      return s.subSequence(0,i+1);       // then return the prefix subsequence
  }
  return null;                           // Otherwise, return null
}
```

Pattern Matching with Regular Expressions

In Java 1.4 and later, you can perform textual pattern matching with regular expressions. Regular expression support is provided by the `Pattern` and `Matcher` classes of the `java.util.regex` package, but the `String` class defines a number of convenient methods that allow you to use regular expressions even more simply. Regular expressions use a fairly complex grammar to describe patterns of characters. The Java implementation uses the same regex syntax as the Perl programming language. See the `java.util.regex.Pattern` class in Chapter 17 for a summary of this syntax or consult a good Perl programming book for further details. For a complete tutorial on Perl-style regular expressions, see *Mastering Regular Expressions* (O'Reilly).

The simplest `String` method that accepts a regular expression argument is `matches()`; it returns `true` if the string matches the pattern defined by the specified regular expression:

```
// This string is a regular expression that describes the pattern of a typical
// sentence. In Perl-style regular expression syntax, it specifies
// a string that begins with a capital letter and ends with a period,
// a question mark, or an exclamation point.
String pattern = "^[A-Z].*[\\.?!]$";
String s = "Java is fun!";
s.matches(pattern);    // The string matches the pattern, so this returns true.
```

The `matches()` method returns `true` only if the entire string is a match for the specified pattern. Perl programmers should note that this differs from Perl's behavior, in which a match means only that some portion of the string matches the pattern. To determine if a string or any substring matches a pattern, simply alter the regular expression to allow arbitrary characters before and after the desired pattern. In the following code, the regular expression characters `.*` match any number of arbitrary characters:

```
s.matches(".*\\bJava\\b.*"); // True if s contains the word "Java" anywhere
                             // The b specifies a word boundary
```

If you are already familiar with Perl's regular expression syntax, you know that it relies on the liberal use of backslashes to escape certain characters. In Perl, regular expressions are language primitives, and their syntax is part of the language itself. In Java, however, regular expressions are described using strings and are typically embedded in programs using string literals. The syntax for Java string literals also uses the backslash as an escape character, so to include a single backslash in the regular expression, you must use two backslashes. Thus, in Java programming, you will often see double backslashes in regular expressions.

In addition to matching, regular expressions can be used for search-and-replace operations. The `replaceFirst()` and `replaceAll()` methods search a string for the first substring or all substrings that match a given pattern and replace the string or strings with the specified replacement text, returning a new string that contains the replacements. For example, you could use this code to ensure that the word "Java" is correctly capitalized in a string `s`:

```
s.replaceAll("(?i)\\bjava\\b",// Pattern: the word "java", case-insensitive
             "Java");          // The replacement string, correctly capitalized
```

The replacement string passed to `replaceAll()` and `replaceFirst()` need not be a simple literal string; it may also include references to text that matched parenthesized subexpressions within the pattern. These references take the form of a dollar sign followed by the number of the subexpression. (If you are not familiar with parenthesized subexpressions within a regular expression, see `java.util.regex.Pattern` in Chapter 17.) For example, to search for words such as JavaBean, JavaScript, JavaOS, and JavaVM (but not Java or Javanese), and to replace the Java prefix with the letter J without altering the suffix, you could use code such as:

```
s.replaceAll("\\bJava([A-Z]\\w+)",  // The pattern
             "J$1");        // J followed by the suffix that matched the
                            // subexpression in parentheses: [A-Z]\\w+
```

The other new Java 1.4 `String` method that uses regular expressions is `split()`, which returns an array of the substrings of a string, separated by delimiters that match the specified pattern. To obtain an array of words in a string separated by any number of spaces, tabs, or newlines, do this:

```
String sentence = "This is a\n\ttwo-line sentence";
String[] words = sentence.split("[ \t\n\r]+");
```

An optional second argument specifies the maximum number of entries in the returned array.

The `matches()`, `replaceFirst()`, `replaceAll()`, and `split()` methods are suitable for when you use a regular expression only once. If you want to use a regular expression for multiple matches, you should explicitly use the `Pattern` and `Matcher` classes of the `java.util.regex` package. First, create a `Pattern` object to represent your regular expression with the static `Pattern.compile()` method. (Another reason to use the `Pattern` class explicitly instead of the `String` convenience methods is that `Pattern.compile()` allows you to specify flags such as `Pattern.CASE_INSENSITIVE` that globally alter the way the pattern matching is done.) Note that the `compile()` method can throw a `PatternSyntaxException` if you pass it an invalid regular expression string. (This exception is also thrown by the various String convenience methods.) The Pattern class defines split() methods that are similar to the String.split() methods. For all other matching, however, you must create a Matcher object with the matcher() method and specify the text to be matched against:

```
import java.util.regex.*;

Pattern javaword = Pattern.compile("\\bJava(\\w*)", Pattern.CASE_INSENSITIVE);
Matcher m = javaword.matcher(sentence);
boolean match = m.matches();  // True if text matches pattern exactly
```

Once you have a Matcher object, you can compare the string to the pattern in various ways. One of the more sophisticated ways is to find all substrings that match the pattern:

```
String text = "Java is fun; JavaScript is funny.";
m.reset(text);  // Start matching against a new string
// Loop to find all matches of the string and print details of each match
while(m.find()) {
  System.out.println("Found '" + m.group(0) + "' at position " + m.start(0));
  if (m.start(1) < m.end(1)) System.out.println("Suffix is " + m.group(1));
}
```

See the Matcher class in Chapter 17 for further details.

String Comparison

The compareTo() and equals() methods of the String class allow you to compare strings. compareTo() bases its comparison on the character order defined by the Unicode encoding, while equals() defines string equality as strict character-by-character equality. These are not always the right methods to use, however. In some languages, the character ordering imposed by the Unicode standard does not match the dictionary ordering used when alphabetizing strings. In Spanish, for example, the letters "ch" are considered a single letter that comes after "c" and before "d." When comparing human-readable strings in an internationalized application, you should use the java.text.Collator class instead:

```
import java.text.*;

// Compare two strings; results depend on where the program is run
// Return values of Collator.compare() have same meanings as String.compareTo()
Collator c = Collator.getInstance();        // Get Collator for current locale
int result = c.compare("chica", "coche");  // Use it to compare two strings
```

StringTokenizer

There are a number of other Java classes that operate on strings and characters. One notable class is java.util.StringTokenizer, which you can use to break a string of text into its component words:

```
String s = "Now is the time";
java.util.StringTokenizer st = new java.util.StringTokenizer(s);
while(st.hasMoreTokens()) {
  System.out.println(st.nextToken());
}
```

You can even use this class to tokenize words that are delimited by characters other than spaces:

```
String s = "a:b:c:d";
java.util.StringTokenizer st = new java.util.StringTokenizer(s, ":");
```

Numbers and Math

Java provides the byte, short, int, long, float, and double primitive types for representing numbers. The java.lang package includes the corresponding Byte, Short, Integer, Long, Float, and Double classes, each of which is a subclass of Number. These classes can be useful as object wrappers around their primitive types, and they also define some useful constants:

```
// Integral range constants: Integer, Long, and Character also define these
Byte.MIN_VALUE      // The smallest (most negative) byte value
Byte.MAX_VALUE      // The largest byte value
Short.MIN_VALUE     // The most negative short value
Short.MAX_VALUE     // The largest short value

// Floating-point range constants: Double also defines these
Float.MIN_VALUE     // Smallest (closest to zero) positive float value
Float.MAX_VALUE     // Largest positive float value

// Other useful constants
Math.PI             // 3.14159265358979323846
Math.E              // 2.7182818284590452354
```


Converting Numbers from and to Strings

A Java program that operates on numbers must get its input values from somewhere. Often, such a program reads a textual representation of a number and must convert it to a numeric representation. The various Number subclasses define useful conversion methods:

```
String s = "-42";
byte b = Byte.parseByte(s);                // s as a byte
short sh = Short.parseShort(s);            // s as a short
int i = Integer.parseInt(s);               // s as an int
long l = Long.parseLong(s);                // s as a long
float f = Float.parseFloat(s);             // s as a float (Java 1.2 and later)
f = Float.valueOf(s).floatValue();         // s as a float (prior to Java 1.2)
double d = Double.parseDouble(s);          // s as a double (Java 1.2 and later)
d = Double.valueOf(s).doubleValue();       // s as a double (prior to Java 1.2)

// The integer conversion routines handle numbers in other bases
byte b = Byte.parseByte("1011", 2);        // 1011 in binary is 11 in decimal
short sh = Short.parseShort("ff", 16);     // ff in base 16 is 255 in decimal

// The valueOf() method can handle arbitrary bases between 2 and 36
int i = Integer.valueOf("egg", 17).intValue();    // Base 17!

// The decode() method handles octal, decimal, or hexadecimal, depending
// on the numeric prefix of the string
short sh = Short.decode("0377").byteValue();    // Leading 0 means base 8
int i = Integer.decode("0xff").shortValue();    // Leading 0x means base 16
```

```
long l = Long.decode("255").intValue();          // Other numbers mean base 10

// Integer class can convert numbers to strings
String decimal = Integer.toString(42);
String binary = Integer.toBinaryString(42);
String octal = Integer.toOctalString(42);
String hex = Integer.toHexString(42);
String base36 = Integer.toString(42, 36);
```

Formatting Numbers

Numeric values are often printed differently in different countries. For example, many European languages use a comma to separate the integral part of a floating-point value from the fractional part (instead of a decimal point). Formatting differences can diverge even further when displaying numbers that represent monetary values. When converting numbers to strings for display, therefore, it is best to use the `java.text.NumberFormat` class to perform the conversion in a locale-specific way:

```
import java.text.*;

// Use NumberFormat to format and parse numbers for the current locale
NumberFormat nf = NumberFormat.getNumberInstance();  // Get a NumberFormat
System.out.println(nf.format(9876543.21)); // Format number for current locale
try {
  Number n = nf.parse("1.234.567,89");       // Parse strings according to locale
} catch (ParseException e) { /* Handle exception */ }

// Monetary values are sometimes formatted differently than other numbers
NumberFormat moneyFmt = NumberFormat.getCurrencyInstance();
System.out.println(moneyFmt.format(1234.56)); // Prints $1,234.56 in U.S.
```

Mathematical Functions

The `Math` class defines a number of methods that provide trigonometric, logarithmic, exponential, and rounding operations, among others. This class is primarily useful with floating-point values. For the trigonometric functions, angles are expressed in radians. The logarithm and exponentiation functions are base *e*, not base 10. Here are some examples:

```
double d = Math.toRadians(27);        // Convert 27 degrees to radians
d = Math.cos(d);                      // Take the cosine
d = Math.sqrt(d);                     // Take the square root
d = Math.log(d);                      // Take the natural logarithm
d = Math.exp(d);                      // Do the inverse: e to the power d
d = Math.pow(10, d);                  // Raise 10 to this power
d = Math.atan(d);                     // Compute the arc tangent
d = Math.toDegrees(d);                // Convert back to degrees
double up = Math.ceil(d);             // Round to ceiling
double down = Math.floor(d);          // Round to floor
long nearest = Math.round(d);         // Round to nearest
```

Random Numbers

The Math class also defines a rudimentary method for generating pseudo-random numbers, but the java.util.Random class is more flexible. If you need *very* random pseudo-random numbers, you can use the java.security.SecureRandom class:

```
// A simple random number
double r = Math.random();     // Returns d such that: 0.0 <= d < 1.0

// Create a new Random object, seeding with the current time
java.util.Random generator = new java.util.Random(System.currentTimeMillis());
double d = generator.nextDouble();   // 0.0 <= d < 1.0
float f = generator.nextFloat();     // 0.0 <= f < 1.0
long l = generator.nextLong();       // Chosen from the entire range of long
int i = generator.nextInt();         // Chosen from the entire range of int
i = generator.nextInt(limit);        // 0 <= i < limit (Java 1.2 and later)
boolean b = generator.nextBoolean(); // true or false (Java 1.2 and later)
d = generator.nextGaussian();        // Mean value: 0.0; std. deviation: 1.0
byte[] randomBytes = new byte[128];
generator.nextBytes(randomBytes);    // Fill in array with random bytes

// For cryptographic strength random numbers, use the SecureRandom subclass
java.security.SecureRandom generator2 = new java.security.SecureRandom();
// Have the generator generate its own 16-byte seed; takes a *long* time
generator2.setSeed(generator2.generateSeed(16));  // Extra random 16-byte seed
// Then use SecureRandom like any other Random object
generator2.nextBytes(randomBytes);   // Generate more random bytes
```

The Java Platform

Big Numbers

The java.math package contains the BigInteger and BigDecimal classes. These classes allow you to work with arbitrary-size and arbitrary-precision integers and floating-point values. For example:

```
import java.math.*;

// Compute the factorial of 1000
BigInteger total = BigInteger.valueOf(1);
for(int i = 2; i <= 1000; i++)
  total = total.multiply(BigInteger.valueOf(i));
System.out.println(total.toString());
```

In Java 1.4, BigInteger has a method to randomly generate large prime numbers, which is useful in many cryptographic applications:

```
BigInteger prime =
  BigInteger.probablePrime(1024,        // 1024 bits long
                           generator2); // Source of randomness; from
                                        // preceding example
```

Dates and Times

Java uses several different classes for working with dates and times. The `java.util.Date` class represents an instant in time (precise down to the millisecond). This class is nothing more than a wrapper around a `long` value that holds the number of milliseconds since midnight GMT, January 1, 1970. Here are two ways to determine the current time:

```
long t0 = System.currentTimeMillis();          // Current time in milliseconds
java.util.Date now = new java.util.Date(); // Basically the same thing
long t1 = now.getTime();                    // Convert a Date to a long value
```

The `Date` class has a number of interesting-sounding methods, but almost all of them have been deprecated in favor of methods of the `java.util.Calendar` and `java.text.DateFormat` classes.

Formatting Dates with DateFormat

To print a date or a time, use the `DateFormat` class, which automatically handles locale-specific conventions for date and time formatting. `DateFormat` even works correctly in locales that use a calendar other than the common era (Gregorian) calendar in use throughout much of the world:

```
import java.util.Date;
import java.text.*;

// Display today's date using a default format for the current locale
DateFormat defaultDate = DateFormat.getDateInstance();
System.out.println(defaultDate.format(new Date()));

// Display the current time using a short time format for the current locale
DateFormat shortTime = DateFormat.getTimeInstance(DateFormat.SHORT);
System.out.println(shortTime.format(new Date()));

// Display date and time using a long format for both
DateFormat longTimestamp =
  DateFormat.getDateTimeInstance(DateFormat.FULL, DateFormat.FULL);
System.out.println(longTimestamp.format(new Date()));

// Use SimpleDateFormat to define your own formatting template
// See java.text.SimpleDateFormat for the template syntax
DateFormat myformat = new SimpleDateFormat("yyyy.MM.dd");
System.out.println(myformat.format(new Date()));
try {   // DateFormat can parse dates too
  Date leapday = myformat.parse("2000.02.29");
}
catch (ParseException e) { /* Handle parsing exception */ }
```

Date Arithmetic with Calendar

The `Date` class and its millisecond representation allow only a very simple form of date arithmetic:

```
long now = System.currentTimeMillis();          // The current time
long anHourFromNow = now + (60 * 60 * 1000);    // Add 3,600,000 milliseconds
```

To perform more sophisticated date and time arithmetic and manipulate dates in ways humans (rather than computers) typically care about, use the `java.util.Calendar` class:

```
import java.util.*;

// Get a Calendar for current locale and time zone
Calendar cal = Calendar.getInstance();

// Figure out what day of the year today is
cal.setTime(new Date());                      // Set to the current time
int dayOfYear = cal.get(Calendar.DAY_OF_YEAR); // What day of the year is it?

// What day of the week does the leap day in the year 2000 occur on?
cal.set(2000, Calendar.FEBRUARY, 29);         // Set year, month, day fields
int dayOfWeek = cal.get(Calendar.DAY_OF_WEEK); // Query a different field

// What day of the month is the 3rd Thursday of May, 2001?
cal.set(Calendar.YEAR, 2001);                         // Set the year
cal.set(Calendar.MONTH, Calendar.MAY);                // Set the month
cal.set(Calendar.DAY_OF_WEEK, Calendar.THURSDAY);     // Set the day of week
cal.set(Calendar.DAY_OF_WEEK_IN_MONTH, 3);            // Set the week
int dayOfMonth = cal.get(Calendar.DAY_OF_MONTH);      // Query the day in month

// Get a Date object that represents 30 days from now
Date today = new Date();                   // Current date
cal.setTime(today);                        // Set it in the Calendar object
cal.add(Calendar.DATE, 30);                // Add 30 days
Date expiration = cal.getTime();           // Retrieve the resulting date
```

Arrays

The `java.lang.System` class defines an `arraycopy()` method that is useful for copying specified elements in one array to a specified position in a second array. The second array must be the same type as the first, and it can even be the same array:

```
char[] text = "Now is the time".toCharArray();
char[] copy = new char[100];
// Copy 10 characters from element 4 of text into copy, starting at copy[0]
System.arraycopy(text, 4, copy, 0, 10);

// Move some of the text to later elements, making room for insertions
System.arraycopy(copy, 3, copy, 6, 7);
```

In Java 1.2 and later, the `java.util.Arrays` class defines useful array-manipulation methods, including methods for sorting and searching arrays:

```
import java.util.Arrays;

int[] intarray = new int[] { 10, 5, 7, -3 }; // An array of integers
Arrays.sort(intarray);                       // Sort it in place
int pos = Arrays.binarySearch(intarray, 7);  // Value 7 is found at index 2
pos = Arrays.binarySearch(intarray, 12);     // Not found: negative return value

// Arrays of objects can be sorted and searched too
String[] strarray = new String[] { "now", "is", "the", "time" };
Arrays.sort(strarray);      // { "is", "now", "the", "time" }
```

```
// Arrays.equals() compares all elements of two arrays
String[] clone = (String[]) strarray.clone();
boolean b1 = Arrays.equals(strarray, clone);  // Yes, they're equal

// Arrays.fill() initializes array elements
byte[] data = new byte[100];           // An empty array; elements set to 0
Arrays.fill(data, (byte) -1);          // Set them all to -1
Arrays.fill(data, 5, 10, (byte) -2);  // Set elements 5, 6, 7, 8, 9 to -2
```

Arrays can be treated and manipulated as objects in Java. Given an arbitrary object o, you can use code such as the following to find out if the object is an array and, if so, what type of array it is:

```
Class type = o.getClass();
if (type.isArray()) {
  Class elementType = type.getComponentType();
}
```

Collections

The Java collection framework is a set of important utility classes and interfaces in the `java.util` package for working with collections of objects. The collection framework defines two fundamental types of collections. A `Collection` is a group of objects, while a `Map` is a set of mappings, or associations, between objects. A `Set` is a type of `Collection` in which there are no duplicates, and a `List` is a `Collection` in which the elements are ordered. `SortedSet` and `SortedMap` are specialized sets and maps that maintain their elements in a sorted order. `Collection`, `Set`, `List`, `Map`, `SortedSet`, and `SortedMap` are all interfaces, but the `java.util` package also defines various concrete implementations, such as lists based on arrays and linked lists, and maps and sets based on hashtables or binary trees. (See the `java.util` package in Chapter 17 for a complete list.) Other important interfaces are `Iterator` and `ListIterator`, which allow you to loop through the objects in a collection. The collection framework is new as of Java 1.2, but prior to that release you can use `Vector` and `Hashtable`, which are approximately the same as `ArrayList` and `HashMap`.

In Java 1.4, the Collections API has grown with the addition of the `RandomAccess` marker interface, which is implemented by `List` implementations that support efficient random access (i.e., it is implemented by `ArrayList` and `Vector` but not by `LinkedList`.) Java 1.4 also introduces `LinkedHashMap` and `LinkedHashSet`, which are hashtable-based maps and sets that preserve the insertion order of elements. Finally, `IdentityHashMap` is a hashtable-based `Map` implementation that uses the == operator to compare key objects rather than using the `equals()` method to compare them.

The following code demonstrates how you might create and perform basic manipulations on sets, lists, and maps:

```
import java.util.*;

Set s = new HashSet();              // Implementation based on a hashtable
s.add("test");                      // Add a String object to the set
```

```
boolean b = s.contains("test2"); // Check whether a set contains an object
s.remove("test");                // Remove a member from a set

Set ss = new TreeSet();          // TreeSet implements SortedSet
ss.add("b");                     // Add some elements
ss.add("a");
// Now iterate through the elements (in sorted order) and print them
for(Iterator i = ss.iterator(); i.hasNext();)
  System.out.println(i.next());

List l = new LinkedList();       // LinkedList implements a doubly linked list
l = new ArrayList();             // ArrayList is more efficient, usually
Vector v = new Vector();         // Vector is an alternative in Java 1.1/1.0
l.addAll(ss);                    // Append some elements to it
l.addAll(1, ss);                 // Insert the elements again at index 1
Object o = l.get(1);             // Get the second element
l.set(3, "new element");         // Set the fourth element
l.add("test");                   // Append a new element to the end
l.add(0, "test2");               // Insert a new element at the start
l.remove(1);                     // Remove the second element
l.remove("a");                   // Remove the element "a"
l.removeAll(ss);                 // Remove elements from this set
if (!l.isEmpty())                // If list is not empty,
  System.out.println(l.size());  // print out the number of elements in it
boolean b1 = l.contains("a");    // Does it contain this value?
boolean b2 = l.containsAll(ss);  // Does it contain all these values?
List sublist = l.subList(1,3);   // A sublist of the 2nd and 3rd elements
Object[] elements = l.toArray(); // Convert it to an array
l.clear();                       // Delete all elements

Map m = new HashMap();           // Hashtable an alternative in Java 1.1/1.0
m.put("key", new Integer(42));   // Associate a value object with a key object
Object value = m.get("key");     // Look up the value associated with a key
m.remove("key");                 // Remove the association from the Map
Set keys = m.keySet();           // Get the set of keys held by the Map
```

Converting to and from Arrays

Arrays of objects and collections serve similar purposes. It is possible to convert from one to the other:

```
Object[] members = set.toArray();         // Get set elements as an array
Object[] items = list.toArray();          // Get list elements as an array
Object[] keys = map.keySet().toArray();   // Get map key objects as an array
Object[] values = map.values().toArray(); // Get map value objects as an array

List l = Arrays.asList(a);                // View array as an ungrowable list
List l = new ArrayList(Arrays.asList(a)); // Make a growable copy of it
```

Collections Utility Methods

Just as the `java.util.Arrays` class defined methods to operate on arrays, the `java.util.Collections` class defines methods to operate on collections. Most notable are methods to sort and search the elements of collections:

```
Collections.sort(list);
int pos = Collections.binarySearch(list, "key"); // list must be sorted first
```

Here are some other interesting Collections methods:

```
Collections.copy(list1, list2); // Copy list2 into list1, overwriting list1
Collections.fill(list, o);      // Fill list with Object o
Collections.max(c);             // Find the largest element in Collection c
Collections.min(c);             // Find the smallest element in Collection c

Collections.reverse(list);      // Reverse list
Collections.shuffle(list);      // Mix up list

Set s = Collections.singleton(o); // Return an immutable set with one element o
List ul = Collections.unmodifiableList(list); // Immutable wrapper for list
Map sm = Collections.synchronizedMap(map);    // Synchronized wrapper for map
```

Types, Reflection, and Dynamic Loading

The java.lang.Class class represents data types in Java and, along with the classes in the java.lang.reflect package, gives Java programs the capability of introspection (or self-reflection); a Java class can look at itself, or any other class, and determine its superclass, what methods it defines, and so on.

Class Objects

There are several ways you can obtain a Class object in Java:

```
// Obtain the Class of an arbitrary object o
Class c = o.getClass();

// Obtain a Class object for primitive types with various predefined constants
c = Void.TYPE;          // The special "no-return-value" type
c = Byte.TYPE;          // Class object that represents a byte
c = Integer.TYPE;       // Class object that represents an int
c = Double.TYPE;        // etc; see also Short, Character, Long, Float

// Express a class literal as a type name followed by ".class"
c = int.class;          // Same as Integer.TYPE
c = String.class;       // Same as "dummystring".getClass()
c = byte[].class;       // Type of byte arrays
c = Class[][].class;    // Type of array of arrays of Class objects
```

Reflecting on a Class

Once you have a Class object, you can perform some interesting reflective operations with it:

```
import java.lang.reflect.*;

Object o;                    // Some unknown object to investigate
Class c = o.getClass();      // Get its type

// If it is an array, figure out its base type
while (c.isArray()) c = c.getComponentType();

// If c is not a primitive type, print its class hierarchy
if (!c.isPrimitive()) {
  for(Class s = c; s != null; s = s.getSuperclass())
```

```
        System.out.println(s.getName() + " extends");
    }

    // Try to create a new instance of c; this requires a no-arg constructor
    Object newobj = null;
    try { newobj = c.newInstance(); }
    catch (Exception e) {
      // Handle InstantiationException, IllegalAccessException
    }

    // See if the class has a method named setText that takes a single String
    // If so, call it with a string argument
    try {
      Method m = c.getMethod("setText", new Class[] { String.class });
      m.invoke(newobj, new Object[] { "My Label" });
    } catch(Exception e) { /* Handle exceptions here */ }
```

Dynamic Class Loading

`Class` also provides a simple mechanism for dynamic class loading in Java. For more complete control over dynamic class loading, however, you should use a `java.lang.ClassLoader` object, typically a `java.net.URLClassLoader`. This technique is useful, for example, when you want to load a class that is named in a configuration file instead of being hardcoded into your program:

```
// Dynamically load a class specified by name in a config file
String classname =                         // Look up the name of the class
    config.getProperty("filterclass",      // The property name
                       "com.davidflanagan.filters.Default"); // A default

try {
  Class c = Class.forName(classname);  // Dynamically load the class
  Object o = c.newInstance();          // Dynamically instantiate it
} catch (Exception e) { /* Handle exceptions */ }
```

The preceding code works only if the class to be loaded is in the class path. If this is not the case, you can create a custom `ClassLoader` object to load a class from a path (or URL) you specify yourself:

```
import java.net.*;
String classdir = config.getProperty("filterDirectory"); // Look up class path
trying {
  ClassLoader loader = new URLClassLoader(new URL[] { new URL(classdir) });
  Class c = loader.loadClass(classname);
}
catch (Exception e) { /* Handle exceptions */ }
```

Dynamic Proxies

Java 1.3 added the `Proxy` class and `InvocationHandler` interface to the `java.lang.reflect` package. `Proxy` is a powerful but infrequently used class that allows you to dynamically create a new class or instance that implements a specified interface or set of interfaces. It also dispatches invocations of the interface methods to an `InvocationHandler` object.

Threads

Java makes it easy to define and work with multiple threads of execution within a program. `java.lang.Thread` is the fundamental thread class in the Java API. There are two ways to define a thread. One is to subclass `Thread`, override the `run()` method, and then instantiate your `Thread` subclass. The other is to define a class that implements the `Runnable` method (i.e., define a `run()` method) and then pass an instance of this `Runnable` object to the `Thread()` constructor. In either case, the result is a `Thread` object, where the `run()` method is the body of the thread. When you call the `start()` method of the `Thread` object, the interpreter creates a new thread to execute the `run()` method. This new thread continues to run until the `run()` method exits, at which point it ceases to exist. Meanwhile, the original thread continues running itself, starting with the statement following the `start()` method. The following code demonstrates:

```
final List list;  // Some long unsorted list of objects; initialized elsewhere

/** A Thread class for sorting a List in the background */
class BackgroundSorter extends Thread {
  List l;
  public BackgroundSorter(List l) { this.l = l; }    // Constructor
  public void run() { Collections.sort(l); }         // Thread body
}

// Create a BackgroundSorter thread
Thread sorter = new BackgroundSorter(list);
// Start it running; the new thread runs the run() method above, while
// the original thread continues with whatever statement comes next.
sorter.start();

// Here's another way to define a similar thread
Thread t = new Thread(new Runnable() {          // Create a new thread
  public void run() { Collections.sort(list); } // to sort the list of objects.
});
t.start();                                      // Start it running
```

Thread Priorities

Threads can run at different priority levels. A thread at a given priority level does not typically run unless there are no higher-priority threads waiting to run. Here is some code you can use when working with thread priorities:

```
// Set a thread t to lower-than-normal priority
t.setPriority(Thread.NORM_PRIORITY-1);

// Set a thread to lower priority than the current thread
t.setPriority(Thread.currentThread().getPriority() - 1);

// Threads that don't pause for I/O should explicitly yield the CPU
// to give other threads with the same priority a chance to run.
Thread t = new Thread(new Runnable() {
  public void run() {
    for(int i = 0; i < data.length; i++) {  // Loop through a bunch of data
      process(data[i]);                     // Process it
      if ((i % 10) == 0)                    // But after every 10 iterations,
        Thread.yield();                     // pause to let other threads run.
```

```
    }
  }
});
```

Making a Thread Sleep

Often, threads are used to perform some kind of repetitive task at a fixed interval. This is particularly true when doing graphical programming that involves animation or similar effects. The key to doing this is making a thread *sleep*, or stop running for a specified amount of time. This is done with the static `Thread.sleep()` method:

```
public class Clock extends Thread {
  java.text.DateFormat f =      // How to format the time for this locale
    java.text.DateFormat.getTimeInstance(java.text.DateFormat.MEDIUM);
  volatile boolean keepRunning = true;

  public Clock() {              // The constructor
    setDaemon(true);            // Daemon thread: interpreter can exit while it runs
    start();                    // This thread starts itself
  }

  public void run() {           // The body of the thread
    while(keepRunning) {        // This thread runs until asked to stop
      String time = f.format(new java.util.Date()); // Current time
      System.out.println(time);                     // Print the time
      try { Thread.sleep(1000); }                   // Wait 1,000 milliseconds
      catch (InterruptedException e) {}             // Ignore this exception
    }
  }

  // Ask the thread to stop running
  public void pleaseStop() { keepRunning = false; }
}
```

Notice the `pleaseStop()` method in this example. You can forcefully terminate a thread by calling its `stop()` method, but this method has been deprecated because a thread that is forcefully stopped can leave objects it is manipulating in an inconsistent state. If you need a thread that can be stopped, you should define a method such as `pleaseStop()` that stops the thread in a controlled way.

Timers

In Java 1.3, the `java.util.Timer` and `java.util.TimerTask` classes make it even easier to run repetitive tasks. Here is some code that behaves much like the previous `Clock` class:

```
import java.util.*;

// How to format the time for this locale
final java.text.DateFormat timeFmt =
  java.text.DateFormat.getTimeInstance(java.text.DateFormat.MEDIUM);
// Define the time-display task
TimerTask displayTime = new TimerTask() {
  public void run() { System.out.println(timeFmt.format(new Date())); }
};
```

```
// Create a timer object to run the task (and possibly others)
Timer timer = new Timer();
// Now schedule that task to be run every 1,000 milliseconds, starting now
Timer.schedule(displayTime, 0, 1000);

// To stop the time-display task
displayTime.cancel();
```

Waiting for a Thread to Finish

Sometimes one thread needs to stop and wait for another thread to complete. You can accomplish this with the `join()` method:

```
List list;  // A long list of objects to be sorted; initialized elsewhere

// Define a thread to sort the list: lower its priority, so it runs only
// when the current thread is waiting for I/O, and then start it running.
Thread sorter = new BackgroundSorter(list);                // Defined earlier
sorter.setPriority(Thread.currentThread.getPriority()-1); // Lower priority
sorter.start();                                            // Start sorting

// Meanwhile, in this original thread, read data from a file
byte[] data = readData();  // Method defined elsewhere

// Before we can proceed, we need the list to be fully sorted, so
// we must wait for the sorter thread to exit, if it hasn't already.
try { sorter.join(); } catch(InterruptedException e) {}
```

Thread Synchronization

When using multiple threads, you must be very careful if you allow more than one thread to access the same data structure. Consider what would happen if one thread was trying to loop through the elements of a `List` while another thread was sorting those elements. Preventing this problem is called *thread synchronization* and is one of the central problems of multithreaded computing. The basic technique for preventing two threads from accessing the same object at the same time is to require a thread to obtain a lock on the object before the thread can modify it. While any one thread holds the lock, another thread that requests the lock has to wait until the first thread is done and releases the lock. Every Java object has the fundamental ability to provide such a locking capability.

The easiest way to keep objects thread-safe is to declare all sensitive methods `synchronized`. A thread must obtain a lock on an object before it can execute any of its `synchronized` methods, which means that no other thread can execute any other `synchronized` method at the same time. (If a `static` method is declared `synchronized`, the thread must obtain a lock on the class, and this works in the same manner.) To do finer-grained locking, you can specify `synchronized` blocks of code that hold a lock on a specified object for a short time:

```
// This method swaps two array elements in a synchronized block
public static void swap(Object[] array, int index1, int index2) {
  synchronized(array) {
    Object tmp = array[index1];
    array[index1] = array[index2];
    array[index2] = tmp;
```

```
    }
}

// The Collection, Set, List, and Map implementations in java.util do
// not have synchronized methods (except for the legacy implementations
// Vector and Hashtable). When working with multiple threads, you can
// obtain synchronized wrapper objects.
List synclist = Collections.synchronizedList(list);
Map syncmap = Collections.synchronizedMap(map);
```

Deadlock

When you are synchronizing threads, you must be careful to avoid *deadlock*, which occurs when two threads end up waiting for each other to release a lock they need. Since neither can proceed, neither one can release the lock it holds, and they both stop running:

```
// When two threads try to lock two objects, deadlock can occur unless
// they always request the locks in the same order.
final Object resource1 = new Object();   // Here are two objects to lock
final Object resource2 = new Object();
Thread t1 = new Thread(new Runnable() {  // Locks resource1 then resource2
  public void run() {
    synchronized(resource1) {
      synchronized(resource2) { compute(); }
    }
  }
});

Thread t2 = new Thread(new Runnable() {  // Locks resource2 then resource1
  public void run() {
    synchronized(resource2) {
      synchronized(resource1) { compute(); }
    }
  }
});

t1.start();  // Locks resource1
t2.start();  // Locks resource2 and now neither thread can progress!
```

Coordinating Threads with wait() and notify()

Sometimes a thread needs to stop running and wait until some kind of event occurs, at which point it is told to continue running. This is done with the `wait()` and `notify()` methods. These aren't methods of the `Thread` class, however; they are methods of `Object`. Just as every Java object has a lock associated with it, every object can maintain a list of waiting threads. When a thread calls the `wait()` method of an object, any locks the thread holds are temporarily released, and the thread is added to the list of waiting threads for that object and stops running. When another thread calls the `notify()` method of the same object, the object wakes up one of the waiting threads and allows it to continue running:

```
/**
 * A queue. One thread calls push() to put an object on the queue.
 * Another calls pop() to get an object off the queue. If there is no
 * data, pop() waits until there is some, using wait()/notify().
```

```
 * wait() and notify() must be used within a synchronized method or
 * block.
 */
import java.util.*;

public class Queue {
  LinkedList q = new LinkedList();  // Where objects are stored
  public synchronized void push(Object o) {
    q.add(o);       // Append the object to the end of the list
    this.notify(); // Tell waiting threads that data is ready
  }
  public synchronized Object pop() {
    while(q.size() == 0) {
      try { this.wait(); }
      catch (InterruptedException e) { /* Ignore this exception */ }
    }
    return q.remove(0);
  }
}
```

Thread Interruption

In the examples illustrating the `sleep()`, `join()`, and `wait()` methods, you may have noticed that calls to each of these methods are wrapped in a `try` statement that catches an `InterruptedException`. This is necessary because the `interrupt()` method allows one thread to interrupt the execution of another. Interrupting a thread is not intended to stop it from executing, but to wake it up from a blocking state.

If the `interrupt()` method is called on a thread that is not blocked, the thread continues running, but its "interrupt status" is set to indicate that an interrupt has been requested. A thread can test its own interrupt status by calling the static `Thread.interrupted()` method, which returns `true` if the thread has been interrupted and, as a side effect, clears the interrupt status. One thread can test the interrupt status of another thread with the instance method `isInterrupted()`, which queries the status but does not clear it.

If a thread calls `sleep()`, `join()`, or `wait()` while its interrupt status is set, it does not block but immediately throws an `InterruptedException` (the interrupt status is cleared as a side effect of throwing the exception). Similarly, if the `interrupt()` method is called on a thread that is already blocked in a call to `sleep()`, `join()`, or `wait()`, that thread stops blocking by throwing an `InterruptedException`.

One of the most common times that threads block is while doing input/output; a thread often has to pause and wait for data to become available from the filesystem or from the network. (The `java.io`, `java.net`, and `java.nio` APIs for performing I/O operations are discussed later in this chapter.) Unfortunately, the `interrupt()` method does not wake up a thread blocked in an I/O method of the `java.io` package. This is one of the shortcomings of `java.io` that is cured by the New I/O API in `java.nio`. If a thread is interrupted while blocked in an I/O operation on any channel that implements `java.nio.channels.InterruptibleChannel`, the channel is closed, the thread's interrupt status is set, and the thread wakes up by throwing a `java.nio.channels.ClosedByInterruptException`. The same thing happens if a thread tries to call a blocking I/O method while its interrupt status is set. Similarly, if a thread is interrupted while it is blocked in the `select()` method of a `java.nio.channels.Selector` (or if it calls `select()` while its interrupt status is set), `select()` will stop blocking (or will never start) and will return immediately. No exception is thrown in this case; the interrupted thread simply wakes up, and the `select()` call returns.

Files and Directories

The `java.io.File` class represents a file or a directory and defines a number of important methods for manipulating files and directories. Note, however, that none of these methods allow you to read the contents of a file; that is the job of `java.io.FileInputStream`, which is just one of the many types of I/O streams used in Java and discussed in the next section. Here are some things you can do with `File`:

```
import java.io.*;
import java.util.*;

// Get the name of the user's home directory and represent it with a File
File homedir = new File(System.getProperty("user.home"));
// Create a File object to represent a file in that directory
File f = new File(homedir, ".configfile");

// Find out how big a file is and when it was last modified
long filelength = f.length();
Date lastModified = new java.util.Date(f.lastModified());

// If the file exists, is not a directory, and is readable,
// move it into a newly created directory.
if (f.exists() && f.isFile() && f.canRead()) {        // Check config file
  File configdir = new File(homedir, ".configdir"); // A new config directory
  configdir.mkdir();                                  // Create that directory
  f.renameTo(new File(configdir, ".config"));         // Move the file into it
}

// List all files in the home directory
String[] allfiles = homedir.list();

// List all files that have a ".java" suffix
String[] sourcecode = homedir.list(new FilenameFilter() {
  public boolean accept(File d, String name) { return name.endsWith(".java"); }
});
```

The `File` class provides some important additional functionality as of Java 1.2:

```
// List all filesystem root directories; on Windows, this gives us
// File objects for all drive letters (Java 1.2 and later).
File[] rootdirs = File.listRoots();

// Atomically, create a lock file, then delete it (Java 1.2 and later)
File lock = new File(configdir, ".lock");
if (lock.createNewFile()) {
  // We successfully created the file, so do something
  ...
  // Then delete the lock file
  lock.delete();
}
```

```
else {
  // We didn't create the file; someone else has a lock
  System.err.println("Can't create lock file; exiting.");
  System.exit(1);
}

// Create a temporary file to use during processing (Java 1.2 and later)
File temp = File.createTempFile("app", ".tmp");  // Filename prefix and suffix

// Make sure file gets deleted when we're done with it (Java 1.2 and later)
temp.deleteOnExit();
```

RandomAccessFile

The `java.io` package also defines a `RandomAccessFile` class that allows you to read binary data from arbitrary locations in a file. This can be a useful thing to do in certain situations, but most applications read files sequentially, using the stream classes described in the next section. Here is a short example of using `RandomAccessFile`:

```
// Open a file for read/write ("rw") access
File datafile = new File(configdir, "datafile");
RandomAccessFile f = new RandomAccessFile(datafile, "rw");
f.seek(100);                     // Move to byte 100 of the file
byte[] data = new byte[100];     // Create a buffer to hold data
f.read(data);                    // Read 100 bytes from the file
int i = f.readInt();             // Read a 4-byte integer from the file
f.seek(100);                     // Move back to byte 100
f.writeInt(i);                   // Write the integer first
f.write(data);                   // Then write the 100 bytes
f.close();                       // Close file when done with it
```

Input and Output Streams

The `java.io` package defines a large number of classes for reading and writing streaming, or sequential, data. The `InputStream` and `OutputStream` classes are for reading and writing streams of bytes, while the `Reader` and `Writer` classes are for reading and writing streams of characters. Streams can be nested, meaning you might read characters from a `FilterReader` object that reads and processes characters from an underlying `Reader` stream. This underlying `Reader` stream might read bytes from an `InputStream` and convert them to characters.

Reading Console Input

There are a number of common operations you can perform with streams. One is to read lines of input the user types at the console:

```
import java.io.*;

BufferedReader console = new BufferedReader(new InputStreamReader(System.in));
System.out.print("What is your name: ");
String name = null;
try {
  name = console.readLine();
```

```
}
catch (IOException e) { name = "<" + e + ">"; }  // This should never happen
System.out.println("Hello " + name);
```

Reading Lines from a Text File

Reading lines of text from a file is a similar operation. The following code reads an entire text file and quits when it reaches the end:

```
String filename = System.getProperty("user.home") + File.separator + ".cshrc";
try {
  BufferedReader in = new BufferedReader(new FileReader(filename));
  String line;
  while((line = in.readLine()) != null) {  // Read line, check for end-of-file
    System.out.println(line);              // Print the line
  }
  in.close();     // Always close a stream when you are done with it
}
catch (IOException e) {
  // Handle FileNotFoundException, etc. here
}
```

Writing Text to a File

Throughout this book, you've seen the use of the `System.out.println()` method to display text on the console. `System.out` simply refers to an output stream. You can print text to any output stream using similar techniques. The following code shows how to output text to a file:

```
try {
  File f = new File(homedir, ".config");
  PrintWriter out = new PrintWriter(new FileWriter(f));
  out.println("## Automatically generated config file. DO NOT EDIT!");
  out.close();  // We're done writing
}
catch (IOException e) { /* Handle exceptions */ }
```

Reading a Binary File

Not all files contain text, however. The following lines of code treat a file as a stream of bytes and read the bytes into a large array:

```
try {
  File f;                              // File to read; initialized elsewhere
  int filesize = (int) f.length();     // Figure out the file size
  byte[] data = new byte[filesize];    // Create an array that is big enough
  // Create a stream to read the file
  DataInputStream in = new DataInputStream(new FileInputStream(f));
  in.readFully(data);  // Read file contents into array
  in.close();
}
catch (IOException e) { /* Handle exceptions */ }
```

Compressing Data

Various other packages of the Java platform define specialized stream classes that operate on streaming data in some useful way. The following code shows how to use stream classes from `java.util.zip` to compute a checksum of data and then compress the data while writing it to a file:

```
import java.io.*;
import java.util.zip.*;

try {
  File f;                            // File to write to; initialized elsewhere
  byte[] data;                       // Data to write; initialized elsewhere
  Checksum check = new Adler32();    // An object to compute a simple checksum

  // Create a stream that writes bytes to the file f
  FileOutputStream fos = new FileOutputStream(f);
  // Create a stream that compresses bytes and writes them to fos
  GZIPOutputStream gzos = new GZIPOutputStream(fos);
  // Create a stream that computes a checksum on the bytes it writes to gzos
  CheckedOutputStream cos = new CheckedOutputStream(gzos, check);

  cos.write(data);              // Now write the data to the nested streams
  cos.close();                  // Close down the nested chain of streams
  long sum = check.getValue(); // Obtain the computed checksum
}
catch (IOException e) { /* Handle exceptions */ }
```

Reading ZIP Files

The `java.util.zip` package also contains a `ZipFile` class that gives you random access to the entries of a ZIP archive and allows you to read those entries through a stream:

```
import java.io.*;
import java.util.zip.*;

String filename;      // File to read; initialized elsewhere
String entryname;     // Entry to read from the ZIP file; initialized elsewhere
ZipFile zipfile = new ZipFile(filename);         // Open the ZIP file
ZipEntry entry = zipfile.getEntry(entryname);    // Get one entry
InputStream in = zipfile.getInputStream(entry); // A stream to read the entry
BufferedInputStream bis = new BufferedInputStream(in);  // Improves efficiency
// Now read bytes from bis...
// Print out contents of the ZIP file
for(java.util.Enumeration e = zipfile.entries(); e.hasMoreElements();) {
  ZipEntry zipentry = (ZipEntry) e.nextElement();
  System.out.println(zipentry.getName());
}
```

Computing Message Digests

If you need to compute a cryptographic-strength checksum (also knows as a message digest), use one of the stream classes of the `java.security` package. For example:

```
import java.io.*;
import java.security.*;
import java.util.*;

File f;             // File to read and compute digest on; initialized elsewhere
List text = new ArrayList();  // We'll store the lines of text here

// Get an object that can compute an SHA message digest
MessageDigest digester = MessageDigest.getInstance("SHA");
// A stream to read bytes from the file f
FileInputStream fis = new FileInputStream(f);
// A stream that reads bytes from fis and computes an SHA message digest
DigestInputStream dis = new DigestInputStream(fis, digester);
// A stream that reads bytes from dis and converts them to characters
InputStreamReader isr = new InputStreamReader(dis);
// A stream that can read a line at a time
BufferedReader br = new BufferedReader(isr);
// Now read lines from the stream
for(String line; (line = br.readLine()) != null; text.add(line)) ;
// Close the streams
br.close();
// Get the message digest
byte[] digest = digester.digest();
```

The Java Platform

Streaming Data to and from Arrays

So far, we've used a variety of stream classes to manipulate streaming data, but the data itself ultimately comes from a file or is written to the console. The `java.io` package defines other stream classes that can read data from and write data to arrays of bytes or strings of text:

```
import java.io.*;

// Set up a stream that uses a byte array as its destination
ByteArrayOutputStream baos = new ByteArrayOutputStream();
DataOutputStream out = new DataOutputStream(baos);
out.writeUTF("hello");             // Write some string data out as bytes
out.writeDouble(Math.PI);          // Write a floating-point value out as bytes
byte[] data = baos.toByteArray(); // Get the array of bytes we've written
out.close();                       // Close the streams

// Set up a stream to read characters from a string
Reader in = new StringReader("Now is the time!");
// Read characters from it until we reach the end
int c;
while((c = in.read()) != -1) System.out.print((char) c);
```

Other classes that operate this way include `ByteArrayInputStream`, `StringWriter`, `CharArrayReader`, and `CharArrayWriter`.

Thread Communication with Pipes

`PipedInputStream` and `PipedOutputStream` and their character-based counterparts, `PipedReader` and `PipedWriter`, are another interesting set of streams defined by `java.io`. These streams are used in pairs by two threads that want to communicate. One thread writes bytes to a `PipedOutputStream` or characters to a

PipedWriter, and another thread reads bytes or characters from the corresponding PipedInputStream or PipedReader:

```
// A pair of connected piped I/O streams forms a pipe. One thread writes
// bytes to the PipedOutputStream, and another thread reads them from the
// corresponding PipedInputStream. Or use PipedWriter/PipedReader for chars.
final PipedOutputStream writeEndOfPipe = new PipedOutputStream();
final PipedInputStream readEndOfPipe = new PipedInputStream(writeEndOfPipe);

// This thread reads bytes from the pipe and discards them
Thread devnull = new Thread(new Runnable() {
  public void run() {
    try { while(readEndOfPipe.read() != -1); }
    catch (IOException e) {}  // ignore it
  }
});
devnull.start();
```

Serialization

One of the most important features of the java.io package is the ability to *serialize* objects: to convert an object into a stream of bytes that can later be deserialized back into a copy of the original object. The following code shows how to use serialization to save an object to a file and later read it back:

```
Object o;  // The object we are serializing; it must implement Serializable
File f;    // The file we are saving it to

try {
  // Serialize the object
  ObjectOutputStream oos = new ObjectOutputStream(new FileOutputStream(f));
  oos.writeObject(o);
  oos.close();

  // Read the object back in
  ObjectInputStream ois = new ObjectInputStream(new FileInputStream(f));
  Object copy = ois.readObject();
  ois.close();
}
catch (IOException e) { /* Handle input/output exceptions */ }
catch (ClassNotFoundException cnfe) { /* readObject() can throw this */ }
```

The previous example serializes to a file, but remember, you can write serialized objects to any type of stream. Thus, you can write an object to a byte array, then read it back from the byte array, creating a deep copy of the object. You can write the object's bytes to a compression stream or even write the bytes to a stream connected across a network to another program!

JavaBeans Persistence

Java 1.4 introduces a new serialization mechanism intended for use with JavaBeans components. java.io serialization works by saving the state of the internal fields of an object. java.beans persistence, on the other hand, works by saving a bean's state as a sequence of calls to the public methods defined by the class. Since it is based on the public API rather than on the internal state, the

JavaBeans persistence mechanism allows interoperability between different implementations of the same API, handles version skew more robustly, and is suitable for longer-term storage of serialized objects.

A bean and any descendant beans or other objects serialized with `java.beans.XMLEncoder` and can be deserialized with `java.beans.XMLDecoder`. These classes write to and read from specified streams, but they are not stream classes themselves. Here is how you might encode a bean:

```
// Create a JavaBean, and set some properties on it
javax.swing.JFrame bean = new javax.swing.JFrame("PersistBean");
bean.setSize(300, 300);
// Now save its encoded form to the file bean.xml
BufferedOutputStream out =                   // Create an output stream
    new BufferedOutputStream(new FileOutputStream("bean.xml"));
XMLEncoder encoder = new XMLEncoder(out);  // Create encoder for stream
encoder.writeObject(bean);                   // Encode the bean
encoder.close();                             // Close encoder and stream
```

Here is the corresponding code to decode the bean from its serialized form:

```
BufferedInputStream in =                     // Create input stream
    new BufferedInputStream(new FileInputStream("bean.xml"));
XMLDecoder decoder = new XMLDecoder(in);   // Create decoder for stream
Object b = decoder.readObject();             // Decode a bean
decoder.close();                             // Close decoder and stream
bean = (javax.swing.JFrame) b;               // Cast bean to proper type
bean.setVisible(true);                       // Start using it
```


Networking

The `java.net` package defines a number of classes that make writing networked applications surprisingly easy. Various examples follow.

Networking with the URL Class

The easiest networking class to use is `URL`, which represents a uniform resource locator. Different Java implementations may support different sets of URL protocols, but, at a minimum, you can rely on support for the `http://`, `ftp://`, and `file://` protocols. In Java 1.4, secure HTTP is also supported with the `https://` protocol. Here are some ways you can use the `URL` class:

```
import java.net.*;
import java.io.*;

// Create some URL objects
URL url=null, url2=null, url3=null;
try {
  url = new URL("http://www.oreilly.com");         // An absolute URL
  url2 = new URL(url, "catalog/books/javanut4/"); // A relative URL
  url3 = new URL("http:", "www.oreilly.com", "index.html");
} catch (MalformedURLException e) { /* Ignore this exception */ }

// Read the content of a URL from an input stream
InputStream in = url.openStream();
```

```
// For more control over the reading process, get a URLConnection object
URLConnection conn = url.openConnection();

// Now get some information about the URL
String type = conn.getContentType();
String encoding = conn.getContentEncoding();
java.util.Date lastModified = new java.util.Date(conn.getLastModified());
int len = conn.getContentLength();

// If necessary, read the contents of the URL using this stream
InputStream in = conn.getInputStream();
```

Working with Sockets

Sometimes you need more control over your networked application than is possible with the URL class. In this case, you can use a Socket to communicate directly with a server. For example:

```
import java.net.*;
import java.io.*;

// Here's a simple client program that connects to a web server,
// requests a document, and reads the document from the server.
String hostname = "java.oreilly.com";  // The server to connect to
int port = 80;                         // Standard port for HTTP
String filename = "/index.html";       // The file to read from the server
Socket s = new Socket(hostname, port); // Connect to the server

// Get I/O streams we can use to talk to the server
InputStream sin = s.getInputStream();
BufferedReader fromServer = new BufferedReader(new InputStreamReader(sin));
OutputStream sout = s.getOutputStream();
PrintWriter toServer = new PrintWriter(new OutputStreamWriter(sout));

// Request the file from the server, using the HTTP protocol
toServer.print("GET " + filename + " HTTP/1.0\r\n\r\n");
toServer.flush();

// Now read the server's response, assume it is a text file, and print it out
for(String l = null; (l = fromServer.readLine()) != null; )
  System.out.println(l);

// Close everything down when we're done
toServer.close();
fromServer.close();
s.close();
```

Secure Sockets with SSL

In Java 1.4, the Java Secure Socket Extension, or JSSE, has been added to the core Java platform in the packages javax.net and javax.net.ssl.* This API enables encrypted network communication over sockets that use the SSL (Secure Sockets Layer, also known as TLS) protocol. SSL is widely used on the Internet: it is the

* An earlier version of JSSE using different package names is available as a separate download for use with Java 1.2 and Java 1.3. See *http://java.sun.com/products/jsse/*.

basis for secure web communication using the `https://` protocol. In Java 1.4 and later, you can use `https://` with the `URL` class as previously shown to securely download documents from web servers that support SSL.

Like all Java security APIs, JSSE is highly configurable and gives low-level control over all details of setting up and communicating over an SSL socket. The `javax.net` and `javax.net.ssl` packages are fairly complex, but in practice, there are only a few classes you need to use to securely communicate with a server. The following program is a variant on the preceding code that uses HTTPS instead of HTTP to securely transfer the contents of the requested URL:

```
import java.io.*;
import java.net.*;
import javax.net.ssl.*;
import java.security.cert.*;

/**
 * Get a document from a web server using HTTPS. Usage:
 *   java HttpsDownload <hostname> <filename>
 **/
public class HttpsDownload {
    public static void main(String[] args) throws IOException {
        // Get a SocketFactory object for creating SSL sockets
        SSLSocketFactory factory =
            (SSLSocketFactory) SSLSocketFactory.getDefault();

        // Use the factory to create a secure socket connected to the
        // HTTPS port of the specified web server.
        SSLSocket sslsock=(SSLSocket)factory.createSocket(args[0], // Hostname
                                                          443); // HTTPS port

        // Get the certificate presented by the web server
        SSLSession session = sslsock.getSession();
        X509Certificate cert;
        try { cert = (X509Certificate)session.getPeerCertificates()[0]; }
        catch(SSLPeerUnverifiedException e) { // If no or invalid certificate
            System.err.println(session.getPeerHost() +
                               " did not present a valid certificate.");
            return;
        }

        // Display details about the certificate
        System.out.println(session.getPeerHost() +
                           " has presented a certificate belonging to:");
        System.out.println("\t[" + cert.getSubjectDN().getName() + "]");
        System.out.println("The certificate bears the valid signature of:");
        System.out.println("\t[" + cert.getIssuerDN().getName() + "]");

        // If the user does not trust the certificate, abort
        System.out.print("Do you trust this certificate (y/n)? ");
        System.out.flush();
        BufferedReader console =
            new BufferedReader(new InputStreamReader(System.in));
        if (Character.toLowerCase(console.readLine().charAt(0)) != 'y') return;

        // Now use the secure socket just as you would use a regular socket
        // First, send a regular HTTP request over the SSL socket
        PrintWriter out = new PrintWriter(sslsock.getOutputStream());
```

```
            out.print("GET " + args[1] + " HTTP/1.0\r\n\r\n");
            out.flush();

            // Next, read the server's response and print it to the console
            BufferedReader in =
             new BufferedReader(new InputStreamReader(sslsock.getInputStream()));
            String line;
            while((line = in.readLine()) != null) System.out.println(line);

            // Finally, close the socket
            sslsock.close();
        }
    }
```

Servers

A client application uses a Socket to communicate with a server. The server does the same thing: it uses a Socket object to communicate with each of its clients. However, the server has an additional task, in that it must be able to recognize and accept client connection requests. This is done with the ServerSocket class. The following code shows how you might use a ServerSocket. The code implements a simple HTTP server that responds to all requests by sending back (or mirroring) the exact contents of the HTTP request. A dummy server like this is useful when debugging HTTP clients:

```
import java.io.*;
import java.net.*;

public class HttpMirror {
  public static void main(String[] args) {
    try {
      int port = Integer.parseInt(args[0]);          // The port to listen on
      ServerSocket ss = new ServerSocket(port);      // Create a socket to listen
      for(;;) {                                      // Loop forever
        Socket client = ss.accept();                 // Wait for a connection
        ClientThread t = new ClientThread(client);  // A thread to handle it
        t.start();                                   // Start the thread running
      }                                              // Loop again
    }
    catch (Exception e) {
      System.err.println(e.getMessage());
      System.err.println("Usage: java HttpMirror <port>;");
    }
  }

  static class ClientThread extends Thread {
    Socket client;
    ClientThread(Socket client) { this.client = client; }
    public void run() {
      try {
        // Get streams to talk to the client
        BufferedReader in =
          new BufferedReader(new InputStreamReader(client.getInputStream()));
        PrintWriter out =
          new PrintWriter(new OutputStreamWriter(client.getOutputStream()));

        // Send an HTTP response header to the client
        out.print("HTTP/1.0 200\r\nContent-Type: text/plain\r\n\r\n");
```

```
        // Read the HTTP request from the client and send it right back
        // Stop when we read the blank line from the client that marks
        // the end of the request and its headers.
        String line;
        while((line = in.readLine()) != null) {
          if (line.length() == 0) break;
          out.println(line);
        }

        out.close();
        in.close();
        client.close();
      }
      catch (IOException e) { /* Ignore exceptions */ }
    }
  }
}
```

This server code could be modified using JSSE to support SSL connections. Making a server secure is more complex than making a client secure, however, because a server must have a certificate it can present to the client. Therefore, server-side JSSE is not demonstrated here.

The Java Platform

Datagrams

Both URL and Socket perform networking on top of a stream-based network connection. Setting up and maintaining a stream across a network takes work at the network level, however. Sometimes you need a low-level way to speed a packet of data across a network, but you don't care about maintaining a stream. If, in addition, you don't need a guarantee that your data will get there or that the packets of data will arrive in the order you sent them, you may be interested in the DatagramSocket and DatagramPacket classes:

```
import java.net.*;

// Send a message to another computer via a datagram
try {
  String hostname = "host.example.com";     // The computer to send the data to
  InetAddress address =                     // Convert the DNS hostname
    InetAddress.getByName(hostname);        // to a lower-level IP address.
  int port = 1234;                          // The port to connect to
  String message = "The eagle has landed."; // The message to send
  byte[] data = message.getBytes();         // Convert string to bytes
  DatagramSocket s = new DatagramSocket();  // Socket to send message with
  DatagramPacket p =                        // Create the packet to send
    new DatagramPacket(data, data.length, address, port);
  s.send(p);                                // Now send it!
  s.close();                                // Always close sockets when done
}
catch (UnknownHostException e) {}  // Thrown by InetAddress.getByName()
catch (SocketException e) {}       // Thrown by new DatagramSocket()
catch (java.io.IOException e) {}   // Thrown by DatagramSocket.send()

// Here's how the other computer can receive the datagram
try {
  byte[] buffer = new byte[4096];               // Buffer to hold data
```

```
    DatagramSocket s = new DatagramSocket(1234);  // Socket that receives it
                                                  // through
    DatagramPacket p =
      new DatagramPacket(buffer, buffer.length);  // The packet that receives it
    s.receive(p);                                 // Wait for a packet to arrive
    String msg =                                  // Convert the bytes from the
      new String(buffer, 0, p.getLength());       // packet back to a string.
    s.close();                                    // Always close the socket
  }
  catch (SocketException e) {}       // Thrown by new DatagramSocket()
  catch (java.io.IOException e) {}   // Thrown by DatagramSocket.receive()
```

Properties and Preferences

java.util.Properties is a subclass of java.util.Hashtable, a legacy collections class that predates the Collections API of Java 1.2. A Properties object maintains a mapping between string keys and string values and defines methods that allow the mappings to be written to and read from a simply formatted text file. This makes the Properties class ideal for configuration and user preference files. The Properties class is also used for the system properties returned by System.getProperty():

```
import java.util.*;
import java.io.*;

// Note: many of these system properties calls throw a security exception if
// called from untrusted code such as applets.
String homedir = System.getProperty("user.home");  // Get a system property
Properties sysprops = System.getProperties();      // Get all system properties

// Print the names of all defined system properties
for(Enumeration e = sysprops.propertyNames(); e.hasMoreElements();)
  System.out.println(e.nextElement());

sysprops.list(System.out);  // Here's an even easier way to list the properties

// Read properties from a configuration file
Properties options = new Properties();              // Empty properties list
File configfile = new File(homedir, ".config");     // The configuration file
try {
  options.load(new FileInputStream(configfile));    // Load props from the file
} catch (IOException e) { /* Handle exception here */ }

// Query a property ("color"), specifying a default ("gray") if undefined
String color = options.getProperty("color", "gray");

// Set a property named "color" to the value "green"
options.setProperty("color", "green");

// Store the contents of the Properties object back into a file
try {
  options.store(new FileOutputStream(configfile),   // Output stream
                "MyApp Config File");               // File header comment text
} catch (IOException e) { /* Handle exception */ }
```

Preferences

Java 1.4 introduces a new Preferences API, which is specifically tailored for working with user and systemwide preferences and is more useful than Properties for this purpose. The Preferences API is defined by the java.util.prefs package. The key class in that package is Preferences. You can obtain a Preferences object that contains user-specific preferences with the static method Preferences.userNodeForPackage() and obtain a Preferences object that contains systemwide preferences with Preferences.systemNodeForPackage(). Both methods take a java.lang.Class object as their sole argument and return a Preferences object shared by all classes in that package. (This means that the preference names you use must be unique within the package.) Once you have a Preferences object, use the get() method to query the string value of a named preference, or use other type-specific methods such as getInt(), getBoolean(), and getByteArray(). Note that to query preference values, a default value must be passed for all methods. This default value is returned if no preference with the specified name has been registered or if the file or database that holds the preference data cannot be accessed. A typical use of Preferences is the following:

```
package com.davidflanagan.editor;
import java.util.prefs.Preferences;

public class TextEditor {
  // Fields to be initialized from preference values
  public int width;              // Screen width in columns
  public String dictionary;      // Dictionary name for spell checking

  public void initPrefs() {
    // Get Preferences objects for user and system preferences for this package
    Preferences userprefs = Preferences.userNodeForPackage(TextEditor.class);
    Preferences sysprefs = Preferences.systemNodeForPackage(TextEditor.class);

    // Look up preference values. Note that you always pass a default value.
    width = userprefs.getInt("width", 80);
    // Look up a user preference using a system preference as the default
    dictionary = userprefs.get("dictionary"
                               sysprefs.get("dictionary",
                                            "default_dictionary"));
  }
}
```

In addition to the get() methods for querying preference values, there are corresponding put() methods for setting the values of named preferences:

```
// User has indicated a new preference, so store it
userprefs.putBoolean("autosave", false);
```

If your application wants to be notified of user or system preference changes while the application is in progress, it may register a PreferenceChangeListener with addPreferenceChangeListener(). A Preferences object can export the names and values of its preferences as an XML file and can read preferences from such an XML file. (See importPreferences(), exportNode(), and exportSubtree() in java.util.pref.Preferences in Chapter 17.) Preferences objects exist in a hierarchy that typically corresponds to the hierarchy of package names. Methods for navigating this hierarchy exist but are not typically used by ordinary applications.

Logging

Another new feature of Java 1.4 is the Logging API, defined in the `java.util.logging` package. Typically, the application developer uses a `Logger` object with a name that corresponds to the class or package name of the application to generate log messages at any of seven severity levels (see the `Level` class in Chapter 17). These messages may report errors and warnings or provide informational messages about interesting events in the application's life cycle. They can include debugging information or even trace the execution of important methods within the program.

The system administrator or end user of the application is responsible for setting up a logging configuration file that specifies where log messages are directed (the console, a file, a network socket, or a combination of these), how they are formatted (as plain text or XML documents), and at what severity threshold they are logged (log messages with a severity below the specified threshold are discarded with very little overhead and should not significantly impact the performance of the application). The logging level severity threshold can be configured independently for each named `Logger`. This end-user configurability means that you can write programs to output diagnostic messages that are normally discarded but can be logged during program development or when a problem arises in a deployed application. Logging is particularly useful for applications such as servers that run unattended and do not have a graphical user interface.

For most applications, using the Logging API is quite simple. Obtain a named `Logger` object whenever necessary by calling the static `Logger.getLogger()` method, passing the class or package name of the application as the logger name. Then, use one of the many `Logger` instance methods to generate log messages. The easiest methods to use have names that correspond to severity levels, such as `severe()`, `warning()`, and `info()`:

```
import java.util.logging.*;

// Get a Logger object named after the current package
Logger logger = Logger.getLogger("com.davidflanagan.servers.pop");
logger.info("Starting server.");       // Log an informational message
ServerSocket ss;                       // Do some stuff
try { ss = new ServerSocket(110); }
catch(Exception e) {                   // Log exceptions
  logger.log(Level.SEVERE, "Can't bind port 110", e);  // Complex log message
  logger.warning("Exiting");                           // Simple warning
  return;
}
logger.fine("got server socket");  // Low-severity (fine-detail) debug message
```

The New I/O API

Java 1.4 introduces an entirely new API for high-performance, nonblocking I/O and networking. This API consists primarily of three new packages. `java.nio` defines `Buffer` classes that are used to store sequences of bytes or other primitive values. `java.nio.channels` defines *channels* through which data can be transferred between a buffer and a data source or sink, such as a file or a network socket. This package also contains important classes used for nonblocking I/O. Finally, the `java.nio.charset` package contains classes for efficiently converting buffers of bytes into buffers of characters. The subsections that follow contain examples of using all three of these packages, as well as examples of specific I/O tasks with the New I/O API.

Basic Buffer Operations

The `java.nio` package includes an abstract `Buffer` class, which defines generic operations on buffers. This package also defines type-specific subclasses such as `ByteBuffer`, `CharBuffer`, and `IntBuffer`. (See `Buffer` and `ByteBuffer` in Chapter 14 for details on these classes and their various methods.) The following code illustrates typical sequences of buffer operations on a `ByteBuffer`. The other type-specific buffer classes have similar methods.

```
import java.nio.*;

// Buffers don't have public constructors. They are allocated instead.
ByteBuffer b = ByteBuffer.allocate(4096);    // Create a buffer for 4,096 bytes
// Or do this to try to get an efficient buffer from the low-level OS
ByteBuffer buf2 = ByteBuffer.allocateDirect(65536);
// Here's another way to get a buffer: by "wrapping" an array
byte[] data;  // Assume this array is created and initialized elsewhere
ByteBuffer buf3 = ByteBuffer.wrap(data); // Create buffer that uses the array
// It is also possible to create a "view buffer" to view bytes as other types
buf3.order(ByteOrder.BIG_ENDIAN);        // Specify the byte order for the buffer
IntBuffer ib = buf3.asIntBuffer();       // View those bytes as integers

// Now store some data in the buffer
b.put(data);         // Copy bytes from array to buffer at current position
b.put((byte)42);     // Store another byte at the new current position
b.put(0, (byte)9);   // Overwrite first byte in buffer. Don't change position.
b.order(ByteOrder.BIG_ENDIAN);  // Set the byte order of the buffer
b.putChar('x');          // Store the two bytes of a Unicode character in buffer
b.putInt(0xcafebabe); // Store four bytes of an int into the buffer

// Here are methods for querying basic numbers about a buffer
int capacity = b.capacity();    // How many bytes can the buffer hold? (4,096)
int position = b.position();    // Where will the next byte be written or read?
// A buffer's limit specifies how many bytes of the buffer can be used.
// When writing into a buffer, this should be the capacity. When reading data
// from a buffer, it should be the number of bytes that were previously
// written.
int limit = b.limit();          // How many should be used?
int remaining = b.remaining(); // How many left? Return limit-position.
boolean more=b.hasRemaining(); // Test if there is still room in the buffer

// The position and limit can also be set with methods of the same name
```

```
// Suppose you want to read the bytes you've written into the buffer
b.limit(b.position());          // Set limit to current position
b.position(0);                  // Set limit to 0; start reading at beginning

// Instead of the two previous calls, you usually use a convenience method
b.flip();   // Set limit to position and position to 0; prepare for reading
b.rewind(); // Set position to 0; don't change limit; prepare for rereading
b.clear();  // Set position to 0 and limit to capacity; prepare for writing

// Assuming you've called flip(), you can start reading bytes from the buffer
buf2.put(b);          // Read all bytes from b and put them into buf2
b.rewind();           // Rewind b for rereading from the beginning
byte b0 = b.get();    // Read first byte; increment buffer position
byte b1 = b.get();    // Read second byte; increment buffer position
byte[] fourbytes = new byte[4];
b.get(fourbytes);     // Read next four bytes, add 4 to buffer position
byte b9 = b.get(9);   // Read 10th byte, without changing current position
int i = b.getInt();   // Read next four bytes as an integer; add 4 to position

// Discard bytes you've already read; shift the remaining ones to the beginning
// of the buffer; set position to new limit and limit to capacity, preparing
// the buffer for writing more bytes into it.
b.compact();
```

You may notice that many buffer methods return the object on which they operate. This is done so that method calls can be "chained" in code, as follows:

```
ByteBuffer bb=ByteBuffer.allocate(32).order(ByteOrder.BIG_ENDIAN).putInt(1234);
```

Many methods throughout `java.nio` and its subpackages return the current object to enable this kind of method chaining. Note that the use of this kind of chaining is a stylistic choice (which I have avoided in this chapter) and does not have any significant impact on efficiency.

`ByteBuffer` is the most important of the buffer classes. However, another commonly used class is `CharBuffer`. `CharBuffer` objects can be created by wrapping a string and can also be converted to strings. `CharBuffer` implements the new `java.lang.CharSequence` interface, which means that it can be used like a `String` or `StringBuffer` in certain applications, (e.g., for regular expression pattern matching.

```
// Create a read-only CharBuffer from a string
CharBuffer cb = CharBuffer.wrap("This string is the data for the CharBuffer");
String s = cb.toString();  // Convert to a String with toString() method
System.out.println(cb);    // or rely on an implicit call to toString().
char c = cb.charAt(0);     // Use CharSequence methods to get characters
char d = cb.get(1);        // or use a CharBuffer absolute read.
// A relative read that reads the char and increments the current position
// Note that only the characters between the position and limit are used when
// a CharBuffer is converted to a String or used as a CharSequence.
char e = cb.get();
```

Bytes in a `ByteBuffer` are commonly converted to characters in a `CharBuffer` and vice versa. We'll see how to do this when we consider the `java.nio.charset` package.

Basic Channel Operations

Buffers are not all that useful on their own—there isn't much point in storing bytes into a buffer only to read them out again. Instead, buffers are typically used with channels: your program stores bytes into a buffer, then passes the buffer to a channel, which reads the bytes out of the buffer and writes them to a file, network socket, or some other destination. Or, in the reverse, your program passes a buffer to a channel, which reads bytes from a file, socket, or other source, and stores those bytes into the buffer, where they can then be retrieved by your program. The `java.nio.channels` package defines several channel classes that represent files, sockets, datagrams, and pipes. (We'll see examples of these concrete classes later in this chapter.) The following code, however, is based on the capabilities of the various channel interfaces defined by `java.nio.channels` and should work with any `Channel` object:

```
Channel c;  // Object that implements Channel interface; initialized elsewhere
if (c.isOpen()) c.close();  // These are the only methods defined by Channel

// The read() and write() methods are defined by the
// ReadableByteChannel and WritableByteChannel interfaces.
ReadableByteChannel source;      // Initialized elsewhere
WritableByteChannel destination; // Initialized elsewhere
ByteBuffer buffer = ByteBuffer.allocateDirect(16384); // Low-level 16 KB buffer

// Here is the basic loop to use when reading bytes from a source channel
// and writing them to a destination channel until there are no more bytes to
// read from the source and no more buffered bytes to write to the destination.
while(source.read(buffer) != -1 || buffer.position() > 0) {
  // Flip buffer: set limit to position and position to 0. This prepares
  // the buffer for reading (which is done by a channel *write* operation).
  buffer.flip();
  // Write some or all of the bytes in the buffer to the destination
  destination.write(buffer);
  // Discard the bytes that were written, copying the remaining ones to
  // the start of the buffer. Set position to limit and limit to capacity,
  // preparing the buffer for writing (done by a channel *read* operation).
  buffer.compact();
}

// Don't forget to close the channels
source.close();
destination.close();
```

In addition to the `ReadableByteChannel` and `WritableByteChannel` interfaces illustrated in the preceding code, `java.nio.channels` defines several other channel interfaces. `ByteChannel` simply extends the readable and writable interfaces without adding any new methods. It is a useful shorthand for channels that support both reading and writing. `GatheringByteChannel` is an extension of `WritableByteChannel` that defines `write()` methods that *gather* bytes from more than one buffer and write them out. Similarly, `ScatteringByteChannel` is an extension of `ReadableByteChannel` that defines `read()` methods that read bytes from the channel and *scatter* or distribute them into more than one buffer. The gathering and scattering `write()` and `read()` methods can be useful when working with network protocols that use fixed-size headers that you want to store in a buffer separate from the rest of the transferred data.

One confusing point to be aware of is that a channel read operation involves writing (or putting) bytes into a buffer, and a channel write operation involves reading (or getting) bytes from a buffer. Thus, when I say that the `flip()` method prepares a buffer for reading, I mean that it prepares a buffer for use in a channel `write()` operation! The reverse is true for the buffer's `compact()` method.

Encoding and Decoding Text with Charsets

A `java.nio.charset.Charset` object represents a character set plus an encoding for that character set. `Charset` and its associated classes, `CharsetEncoder` and `CharsetDecoder`, define methods for encoding strings of characters into sequences of bytes and decoding sequences of bytes into strings of characters. Since these classes are part of the New I/O API, they use the `ByteBuffer` and `CharBuffer` classes:

```
// The simplest case. Use Charset convenience routines to convert.
Charset charset = Charset.forName("ISO-8859-1"); // Get Latin-1 Charset
CharBuffer cb = CharBuffer.wrap("Hello World");  // Characters to encode
// Encode the characters and store the bytes in a newly allocated ByteBuffer
ByteBuffer bb = charset.encode(cb);
// Decode these bytes into a newly allocated CharBuffer and print them out
System.out.println(charset.decode(bb));
```

Note the use of the ISO-8859-1 (a.k.a. "Latin-1") charset in this example. This 8-bit charset is suitable for most Western European languages, including English. Programmers who work only with English may also use the 7-bit "US-ASCII" charset. The `Charset` class does not do encoding and decoding itself, and the previous convenience routines create `CharsetEncoder` and `CharsetDecoder` classes internally. If you plan to encode or decode multiple times, it is more efficient to create these objects yourself:

```
Charset charset = Charset.forName("US-ASCII");     // Get the charset
CharsetEncoder encoder = charset.newEncoder();     // Create an encoder from it
CharBuffer cb = CharBuffer.wrap("Hello World!"); // Get a CharBuffer
WritableByteChannel destination;                   // Initialized elsewhere
destination.write(encoder.encode(cb));             // Encode chars and write
```

The preceding `CharsetEncoder.encode()` method must allocate a new `ByteBuffer` each time it is called. For maximum efficiency, there are lower-level methods you can call to do the encoding and decoding into an existing buffer:

```
ReadableByteChannel source;                        // Initialized elsewhere
Charset charset = Charset.forName("ISO-8859-1"); // Get the charset
CharsetDecoder decoder = charset.newDecoder();     // Create a decoder from it
ByteBuffer bb = ByteBuffer.allocateDirect(2048); // Buffer to hold bytes
CharBuffer cb = CharBuffer.allocate(2048);         // Buffer to hold characters

while(source.read(bb) != -1) {  // Read bytes from the channel until EOF
  bb.flip();                    // Flip byte buffer to prepare for decoding
  decoder.decode(bb, cb, true); // Decode bytes into characters
  cb.flip();                    // Flip char buffer to prepare for printing
  System.out.print(cb);         // Print the characters
  cb.clear();                   // Clear char buffer to prepare for decoding
  bb.clear();                   // Prepare byte buffer for next channel read
}
```

```
source.close();                    // Done with the channel, so close it
System.out.flush();                // Make sure all output characters appear
```

The preceding code relies on the fact that ISO-8895-1 is an 8-bit encoding charset and that there is one-to-one mapping between characters and bytes. For more complex charsets, such as the UTF-8 encoding of Unicode or the EUC-JP charset used with Japanese text, however, this does not hold, and more than one byte is required for some (or all) characters. When this is the case, there is no guarantee that all bytes in a buffer can be decoded at once (the end of the buffer may contain a partial character). Also, since a single character may encode to more than one byte, it can be tricky to know how many bytes a given string will encode into. The following code shows a loop you can use to decode bytes in a more general way:

```
ReadableByteChannel source;                          // Initialized elsewhere
Charset charset = Charset.forName("UTF-8");          // A Unicode encoding
CharsetDecoder decoder = charset.newDecoder();       // Create a decoder from it
ByteBuffer bb = ByteBuffer.allocateDirect(2048);     // Buffer to hold bytes
CharBuffer cb = CharBuffer.allocate(2048);           // Buffer to hold characters

// Tell the decoder to ignore errors that might result from bad bytes
decoder.onMalformedInput(CodingErrorAction.IGNORE);
decoder.onUnmappableCharacter(CodingErrorAction.IGNORE);

decoder.reset();                   // Reset decoder if it has been used before
while(source.read(bb) != -1) {     // Read bytes from the channel until EOF
  bb.flip();                       // Flip byte buffer to prepare for decoding
  decoder.decode(bb, cb, false);   // Decode bytes into characters
  cb.flip();                       // Flip char buffer to prepare for printing
  System.out.print(cb);            // Print the characters
  cb.clear();                      // Clear the character buffer
  bb.compact();                    // Discard already decoded bytes
}
source.close();                    // Done with the channel, so close it

// At this point, there may still be some bytes in the buffer to decode
bb.flip();                         // Prepare for decoding
decoder.decode(bb, cb, true);      // Pass true to indicate this is the last call
decoder.flush(cb);                 // Output any final characters
cb.flip();                         // Flip char buffer
System.out.print(cb);              // Print the final characters
```

Working with Files

FileChannel is a concrete Channel class that performs file I/O and implements ReadableByteChannel and WritableByteChannel (although its read() method works only if the underlying file is open for reading, and its write() method works only if the file is open for writing). Obtain a FileChannel object by using the java.io package to create a FileInputStream, a FileOutputStream, or a RandomAccessFile, and then call the getChannel() method (new in Java 1.4) of that object. As an example, you can use two FileChannel objects to copy a file with code such as the following:

```
String filename = "test";    // The name of the file to copy
// Create streams to read the original and write the copy
FileInputStream fin = new FileInputStream(filename);
```

The Java Platform

```
FileOutputStream fout = new FileOutputStream(filename + ".copy");
// Use the streams to create corresponding channel objects
FileChannel in = fin.getChannel();
FileChannel out = fout.getChannel();
// Allocate a low-level 8KB buffer for the copy
ByteBuffer buffer = ByteBuffer.allocateDirect(8192);
while(in.read(buffer) != -1 || buffer.position() > 0) {
  buffer.flip();      // Prepare to read from the buffer and write to the file
  out.write(buffer); // Write some or all buffer contents
  buffer.compact();   // Discard all bytes that were written and prepare to
}                     // read more from the file and store them in the buffer.
in.close();           // Always close channels and streams when done with them
out.close();
fin.close();          // Note that closing a FileChannel does not automatically
fout.close();         // close the underlying stream.
```

FileChannel has special transferTo() and transferFrom() methods that make it particularly easy (and on many operating systems, particularly efficient) to transfer a specified number of bytes from a FileChannel to some other specified channel, or from some other channel to a FileChannel. These methods allow us to simplify the preceding file-copying code to the following:

```
FileChannel in, out;               // Assume these are initialized as in the
                                   // preceding example.
long numbytes = in.size();         // Number of bytes in original file
in.transferTo(0, numbytes, out);  // Transfer that amount to output channel
```

This code could be equally well-written using transferFrom() instead of transferTo() (note that these two methods expect their arguments in different orders):

```
long numbytes = in.size();
out.transferFrom(in, 0, numbytes);
```

FileChannel also has other capabilities that are not shared by other channel classes. One of the most important is the ability to "memory map" a file or a portion of a file, i.e., to obtain a MappedByteBuffer (a subclass of ByteBuffer) that represents the contents of the file and allows you to read (and optionally write) file contents simply by reading from and writing to the buffer. Memory mapping a file is a somewhat expensive operation, so this technique is usually efficient only when you are working with a large file to which you need repeated access. Memory mapping offers you yet another way to perform the same file-copy operation shown previously:

```
long filesize = in.size();
ByteBuffer bb = in.map(FileChannel.MapMode.READ_ONLY, 0, filesize);
while(bb.hasRemaining()) out.write(bb);
```

The channel interfaces defined by java.nio.channels include ByteChannel but not CharChannel. The channel API is low-level and provides methods for reading bytes only. All of the previous examples have treated files as binary files. It is possible to use the CharsetEncoder and CharsetDecoder classes introduced earlier to convert between bytes and characters, but when you want to work with text files, the Reader and Writer classes of the java.io package are usually much easier to use than CharBuffer. Fortunately, the Channels class defines convenience methods that bridge between the new and old APIs. Here is code that wraps a Reader and a Writer object around input and output channels, reads lines of Latin-1 text from the input channel, and writes them back out to the output channel, with the encoding changed to UTF-8:

```
ReadableByteChannel in;      // Assume these are initialized elsewhere
WritableByteChannel out;
// Create a Reader and Writer from a FileChannel and charset name
BufferedReader reader=new BufferedReader(Channels.newReader(in, "ISO-8859-1"));
PrintWriter writer = new PrintWriter(Channels.newWriter(out, "UTF-8"));
String line;
while((line = reader.readLine()) != null) writer.println(line);
reader.close();
writer.close();
```

Unlike the `FileInputStream` and `FileOutputStream` classes, the `FileChannel` class allows random access to the contents of the file. The zero-argument `position()` method returns the *file pointer* (the position of the next byte to be read), and the one-argument `position()` method allows you to set this pointer to any value you want. This allows you to skip around in a file in the way that the `java.io.RandomAccessFile` does. Here is an example:

```
// Suppose you have a file that has data records scattered throughout, and the
// last 1,024 bytes of the file are an index that provides the position of
// those records. Here is code that reads the index of the file, looks up the
// position of the first record within the file, and then reads that record.
FileChannel in = new FileInputStream("test.data").getChannel();  // The channel
ByteBuffer index = ByteBuffer.allocate(1024);   // A buffer to hold the index
long size = in.size();                          // The size of the file
in.position(size - 1024);                       // Position at start of index
in.read(index);                                 // Read the index
int record0Position = index.getInt(0);          // Get first index entry
in.position(record0Position);                   // Position file at that point
ByteBuffer record0 = ByteBuffer.allocate(128);  // Get buffer to hold data
in.read(record0);                               // Finally, read the record
```

The final feature of `FileChannel` that we'll consider here is its ability to lock a file or a portion of a file against all concurrent access (an exclusive lock) or against concurrent writes (a shared lock). (Note that some operating systems strictly enforce all locks, while others only provide an advisory locking facility that requires programs to cooperate and to attempt to acquire a lock before reading or writing portions of a shared file.) In the previous random-access example, suppose we wanted to ensure that no other program was modifying the record data while we read it. We could acquire a shared lock on that portion of the file with the following code:

```
FileLock lock = in.lock(record0Position, // Start of locked region
                        128,         // Length of locked region
                        true);       // Shared lock: prevent concurrent updates
                                     // but allow concurrent reads.
in.position(record0Position);        // Move to start of index
in.read(record0);                    // Read the index data
lock.release();                      // You're done with the lock, so release it
```

The Java Platform

Client-Side Networking

The New I/O API includes networking capabilities as well as file-access capabilities. To communicate over the network, you can use the SocketChannel class. Create a SocketChannel with the static open() method, then read and write bytes from and to it as you would with any other channel object. The following code uses SocketChannel to send an HTTP request to a web server and saves the server's response (including all of the HTTP headers) to a file. Note the use of java.net.InetSocketAddress, a subclass of java.net.SocketAddress, to tell the SocketChannel what to connect to. These classes are also new in Java 1.4 and were introduced as part of the New I/O API.

```
import java.io.*;
import java.net.*;
import java.nio.*;
import java.nio.channels.*;
import java.nio.charset.*;

// Create a SocketChannel connected to the web server at www.oreilly.com
SocketChannel socket =
  SocketChannel.open(new InetSocketAddress("www.oreilly.com",80));
// A charset for encoding the HTTP request
Charset charset = Charset.forName("ISO-8859-1");
// Send an HTTP request to the server. Start with a string, wrap it to
// a CharBuffer, encode it to a ByteBuffer, then write it to the socket.
socket.write(charset.encode(CharBuffer.wrap("GET / HTTP/1.0\r\n\r\n")));
// Create a FileChannel to save the server's response to
FileOutputStream out = new FileOutputStream("oreilly.html");
FileChannel file = out.getChannel();
// Get a buffer for holding bytes while transferring from socket to file
ByteBuffer buffer = ByteBuffer.allocateDirect(8192);
// Now loop until all bytes are read from the socket and written to the file
while(socket.read(buffer) != -1 || buffer.position() > 0) {  // Are we done?
  buffer.flip();       // Prepare to read bytes from buffer and write to file
  file.write(buffer);  // Write some or all bytes to the file
  buffer.compact();    // Discard those that were written
}
socket.close();        // Close the socket channel
file.close();          // Close the file channel
out.close();           // Close the underlying file
```

Another way to create a SocketChannel is with the no-argument version of open(), which creates an unconnected channel. This allows you to call the socket() method to obtain the underlying socket, configure the socket as desired, and connect to the desired host with the connect method. For example:

```
SocketChannel sc = SocketChannel.open();  // Open an unconnected socket channel
Socket s = sc.socket();                   // Get underlying java.net.Socket
s.setSOTimeout(3000);                     // Time out after three seconds
// Now connect the socket channel to the desired host and port
sc.connect(new InetSocketAddress("www.davidflanagan.com", 80));

ByteBuffer buffer = ByteBuffer.allocate(8192);  // Create a buffer
try { sc.read(buffer); }                        // Try to read from socket
catch(SocketTimeoutException e) {               // Catch timeouts here
  System.out.println("The remote computer is not responding.");
  sc.close();
}
```

In addition to the SocketChannel class, the java.nio.channels package defines a DatagramChannel for networking with datagrams instead of sockets. Datagram-Channel is not demonstrated here, but you can read about it in Chapter 14.

One of the most powerful features of the New I/O API is that channels such as SocketChannel and DatagramChannel can be used in nonblocking mode. We'll see examples of this in later sections.

Server-Side Networking

The java.net package defines a Socket class for communication between a client and a server and defines a ServerSocket class used by the server to listen for and accept connections from clients. The java.nio.channels package is analogous: it defines a SocketChannel class for data transfer and a ServerSocketChannel class for accepting connections. ServerSocketChannel is an unusual channel because it does not implement ReadableByteChannel or WritableByteChannel. Instead of read() and write() methods, it has an accept() method for accepting client connections and obtaining a SocketChannel through which it communicates with the client. Here is the code for a simple, single-threaded server that listens for connections on port 8000 and reports the current time to any client that connects:

```
import java.nio.*;
import java.nio.channels.*;
import java.nio.charset.*;

public class DateServer {
    public static void main(String[] args) throws java.io.IOException {
        // Get a CharsetEncoder for encoding the text sent to the client
        CharsetEncoder encoder = Charset.forName("US-ASCII").newEncoder();

        // Create a new ServerSocketChannel and bind it to port 8000
        // Note that this must be done using the underlying ServerSocket
        ServerSocketChannel server = ServerSocketChannel.open();
        server.socket().bind(new java.net.InetSocketAddress(8000));

        for(;;) {  // This server runs forever
            // Wait for a client to connect
            SocketChannel client = server.accept();
            // Get the current date and time as a string
            String response = new java.util.Date().toString() + "\r\n";
            // Wrap, encode, and send the string to the client
            client.write(encoder.encode(CharBuffer.wrap(response)));
            // Disconnect from the client
            client.close();
        }
    }
}
```

The Java Platform

Nonblocking I/O

The preceding DateServer class is a simple network server. Because it does not maintain a connection with any client, it never needs to communicate with more than one at a time, and there is never more than one SocketChannel in use. More realistic servers must be able to communicate with more than one client at a time.

The java.io and java.net APIs allow only blocking I/O, so servers written using these APIs must use a separate thread for each client. For large-scale servers with many clients, this approach does not scale well. To solve this problem, the New I/O API allows most channels (but not FileChannel) to be used in nonblocking mode and allows a single thread to manage all pending connections. This is done with a Selector object, which keeps track of a set of registered channels and can block until one or more of those channels is ready for I/O, as the following code illustrates. This is a longer example than most in this chapter, but it is a complete working server class that manages a ServerSocketChannel and any number of SocketChannel connections to clients through a single Selector object.

```
import java.io.*;
import java.net.*;
import java.nio.*;
import java.nio.channels.*;
import java.nio.charset.*;
import java.util.*;           // For Set and Iterator

public class NonBlockingServer {
    public static void main(String[] args) throws IOException {

        // Get the character encoders and decoders you'll need
        Charset charset = Charset.forName("ISO-8859-1");
        CharsetEncoder encoder = charset.newEncoder();
        CharsetDecoder decoder = charset.newDecoder();

        // Allocate a buffer for communicating with clients
        ByteBuffer buffer = ByteBuffer.allocate(512);

        // All of the channels in this code will be in nonblocking mode.
        // So create a Selector object that will block while monitoring
        // all of the channels and stop blocking only when one or more
        // of the channels is ready for I/O of some sort.
        Selector selector = Selector.open();

        // Create a new ServerSocketChannel and bind it to port 8000
        // Note that this must be done using the underlying ServerSocket
        ServerSocketChannel server = ServerSocketChannel.open();
        server.socket().bind(new java.net.InetSocketAddress(8000));
        // Put the ServerSocketChannel into nonblocking mode
        server.configureBlocking(false);
        // Now register it with the Selector (note that register() is called
        // on the channel, not on the selector object, however).
        // The SelectionKey represents the registration of this channel with
        // this Selector.
        SelectionKey serverkey = server.register(selector,
                                                 SelectionKey.OP_ACCEPT);

        for(;;) {  // The main server loop. The server runs forever.
            // This call blocks until there is activity on one of the
            // registered channels. This is the key method in nonblocking
            // I/O.
            selector.select();

            // Get a java.util.Set containing the SelectionKey objects for
            // all channels that are ready for I/O.
            Set keys = selector.selectedKeys();
```

```
// Use a java.util.Iterator to loop through the selected keys
for(Iterator i = keys.iterator(); i.hasNext(); ) {
    // Get the next SelectionKey in the set, and remove it
    // from the set. It must be removed explicitly, or it will
    // be returned again by the next call to select().
    SelectionKey key = (SelectionKey) i.next();
    i.remove();

    // Check whether this key is the SelectionKey obtained when
    // you registered the ServerSocketChannel.
    if (key == serverkey) {
        // Activity on the ServerSocketChannel means a client
        // is trying to connect to the server.
        if (key.isAcceptable()) {
            // Accept the client connection and obtain a
            // SocketChannel to communicate with the client.
            SocketChannel client = server.accept();
            // Put the client channel in nonblocking mode
            client.configureBlocking(false);
            // Now register it with the Selector object,
            // telling it that you'd like to know when
            // there is data to be read from this channel.
            SelectionKey clientkey =
                client.register(selector,
                SelectionKey.OP_READ);
            // Attach some client state to the key. You'll
            // use this state when you talk to the client.
            clientkey.attach(new Integer(0));
        }
    }
    else {
        // If the key obtained from the Set of keys is not the
        // ServerSocketChannel key, then it must be a key
        // representing one of the client connections.
        // Get the channel from the key.
        SocketChannel client = (SocketChannel) key.channel();

        // If you are here, there should be data to read from
        // the channel, but double-check.
        if (!key.isReadable()) continue;

        // Now read bytes from the client. Assume that all the
        // client's bytes are in one read operation.
        int bytesread = client.read(buffer);

        // If read() returns -1, it indicates end-of-stream,
        // which means the client has disconnected, so
        // deregister the selection key and close the channel.
        if (bytesread == -1) {
            key.cancel();
            client.close();
            continue;
        }

        // Otherwise, decode the bytes to a request string
        buffer.flip();
        String request = decoder.decode(buffer).toString();
        buffer.clear();
        // Now reply to the client based on the request string
        if (request.trim().equals("quit")) {
```

The Java Platform

```
                            // If the request was "quit", send a final message
                            // Close the channel and deregister the
                            // SelectionKey
                            client.write(encoder.encode(CharBuffer.
                                wrap("Bye.")));
                            key.cancel();
                            client.close();
                        }
                        else {
                            // Otherwise, send a response string comprised of
                            // the sequence number of this request plus an
                            // uppercase version of the request string. Note
                            // that you keep track of the sequence number by
                            // "attaching" an Integer object to the
                            // SelectionKey and incrementing it each time.

                            // Get sequence number from SelectionKey
                            int num = ((Integer)key.attachment()).intValue();
                            // For response string

                            String response = num + ": " +
                                request.toUpperCase();
                            // Wrap, encode, and write the response string
                            client.write(encoder.encode(CharBuffer.
                                wrap(response)));
                            // Attach an incremented sequence nubmer to the key
                            key.attach(new Integer(num+1));
                        }
                    }
                }
            }
        }
    }
```

Nonblocking I/O is most useful for writing network servers. It is also useful in clients that have more than one network connection pending at the same time. For example, consider a web browser downloading a web page and the images referenced by that page at the same time. One other interesting use of nonblocking I/O is to perform nonblocking socket connection operations. The idea is that you can ask a `SocketChannel` to establish a connection to a remote host and then go do other stuff (such as build a GUI, for example) while the underlying OS is setting up the connection across the network. Later, you do a `select()` call to block until the connection has been established, if it hasn't been already. The code for a nonblocking connect looks like this:

```
// Create a new, unconnected SocketChannel. Put it in nonblocking
// mode, register it with a new Selector, and then tell it to connect.
// The connect call will return instead of waiting for the network
// connect to be fully established.
Selector selector = Selector.open();
SocketChannel channel = SocketChannel.open();
channel.configureBlocking(false);
channel.register(selector, SelectionKey.OP_CONNECT);
channel.connect(new InetSocketAddress(hostname, port));

// Now go do other stuff while the connection is set up
// For example, you can create a GUI here

// Now block if necessary until the SocketChannel is ready to connect.
```

```
// Since you've registered only one channel with this selector, you
// don't need to examine the key set; you know which channel is ready.
while(selector.select() == 0) /* empty loop */;

// This call is necessary to finish the nonblocking connections
channel.finishConnect();

// Finally, close the selector, which deregisters the channel from it
selector.close();
```

XML

JAXP, the Java API for XML Processing, was originally defined as an optional extension to the Java platform and was available as a separate download. In Java 1.4, however, JAXP has been made part of the core platform. It consists of the following packages (and their subpackages):

`javax.xml.parsers`
: This package provides high-level interfaces for instantiating SAX and DOM parsers; it is a "plugability layer" that allows the end user or system administrator to choose or even replace the default parser implementation with another.

`javax.xml.transform`
: This package and its subpackages define a Java API for transforming XML document content and representation using the XSLT standard. This package also provides a plugability layer that allows new XSLT engines to be "plugged in" and used in place of the default implementation.

`org.xml.sax`
: This package and its two subpackages define the de facto standard SAX (SAX stands for Simple API for XML) API. SAX is an event-driven, XML-parsing API: a SAX parser invokes methods of a specified `ContentHandler` object (as well as some other related handler objects) as it parses an XML document. The structure and content of the document are fully described by the method calls. This is a streaming API that does not build any permanent representation of the document. It is up to the `ContentHandler` implementation to store any state or perform any actions that are appropriate. This package includes classes for the SAX 2 API and deprecated classes for SAX 1.

`org.w3c.dom`
: This package defines interfaces that represent an XML document in tree form. The Document Object Model (DOM) is a recommendation (essentially a standard) of the World Wide Web Consortium (W3C). A DOM parser reads an XML document and converts it into a tree of nodes that represent the full content of the document. Once the tree representation of the document is created, a program can examine and manipulate it however it wants.

Examples of each of these packages are presented in the following subsections.

Parsing XML with SAX

The first step in parsing an XML document with SAX is to obtain a SAX parser. If you have a SAX parser implementation of your own, you can simply instantiate the appropriate parser class. It is usually simpler, however, to use the `javax.xml.parsers` package to instantiate whatever SAX parser is provided by the Java implementation. The code looks like this:

```
import javax.xml.parsers.*;

// Obtain a factory object for creating SAX parsers
SAXParserFactory parserFactory = SAXParserFactory.newInstance();

// Configure the factory object to specify attributes of the parsers it creates
parserFactory.setValidating(true);
parserFactory.setNamespaceAware(true);

// Now create a SAXParser object
SAXParser parser = parserFactory.newSAXParser();    // May throw exceptions
```

The `SAXParser` class is a simple wrapper around the `org.xml.sax.XMLReader` class. Once you have obtained one, as shown in the previous code, you can parse a document by simply calling one of the various `parse()` methods. Some of these methods use the deprecated SAX 1 `HandlerBase` class, and others use the current SAX 2 `org.xml.sax.helpers.DefaultHandler` class. The `DefaultHandler` class provides an empty implementation of all the methods of the `ContentHandler`, `ErrorHandler`, `DTDHandler`, and `EntityResolver` interfaces. These are all the methods that the SAX parser can call while parsing an XML document. By subclassing `DefaultHandler` and defining the methods you care about, you can perform whatever actions are necessary in response to the method calls generated by the parser. The following code shows a method that uses SAX to parse an XML file and determine the number of XML elements that appear in a document as well as the number of characters of plain text (possibly excluding "ignorable whitespace") that appear within those elements:

```
import java.io.*;
import javax.xml.parsers.*;
import org.xml.sax.*;
import org.xml.sax.helpers.*;

public class SAXCount {
    public static void main(String[] args)
         throws SAXException,IOException, ParserConfigurationException
    {
         // Create a parser factory and use it to create a parser
         SAXParserFactory parserFactory = SAXParserFactory.newInstance();
         SAXParser parser = parserFactory.newSAXParser();
         // This is the name of the file you're parsing
         String filename = args[0];
         // Instantiate a DefaultHandler subclass to do your counting for you
         CountHandler handler = new CountHandler();
         // Start the parser. It reads the file and calls methods of the
         // handler.
         parser.parse(new File(filename), handler);
         // When you're done, report the results stored by your handler object
         System.out.println(filename + " contains " + handler.numElements +
```

```
                                " elements and " + handler.numChars +
                                " other characters ");
    }

    // This inner class extends DefaultHandler to count elements and text in
    // the XML file and saves the results in public fields. There are many
    // other DefaultHandler methods you could override, but you need only
    // these.
    public static class CountHandler extends DefaultHandler {
        public int numElements = 0, numChars = 0;  // Save counts here
        // This method is invoked when the parser encounters the opening tag
        // of any XML element. Ignore the arguments but count the element.
        public void startElement(String uri, String localname, String qname,
                                 Attributes attributes) {
            numElements++;
        }

        // This method is called for any plain text within an element
        // Simply count the number of characters in that text


        public void characters(char[] text, int start, int length) {
            numChars += length;
        }
    }
}
```

The Java Platform

Parsing XML with DOM

The DOM API is much different from the SAX API. While SAX is an efficient way to scan an XML document, it is not well-suited for programs that want to modify documents. Instead of converting an XML document into a series of method calls, a DOM parser converts the document into an `org.w3c.dom.Document` object, which is a tree of `org.w3c.dom.Node` objects. The conversion of the complete XML document to tree form allows random access to the entire document but can consume substantial amounts of memory.

In the DOM API, each node in the document tree implements the `Node` interface and a type-specific subinterface. (The most common types of node in a DOM document are `Element` and `Text` nodes.) When the parser is done parsing the document, your program can examine and manipulate that tree using the various methods of `Node` and its subinterfaces. The following code uses JAXP to obtain a DOM parser (which, in JAXP parlance, is called a `DocumentBuilder`). It then parses an XML file and builds a document tree from it. Next, it examines the `Document` tree to search for `<sect1>` elements and prints the contents of the `<title>` of each.

```
import java.io.*;
import javax.xml.parsers.*;
import org.w3c.dom.*;

public class GetSectionTitles {
    public static void main(String[] args)
        throws IOException, ParserConfigurationException,
               org.xml.sax.SAXException
    {
        // Create a factory object for creating DOM parsers and configure it
        DocumentBuilderFactory factory = DocumentBuilderFactory.newInstance();
```

```
        factory.setIgnoringComments(true);  // We want to ignore comments
        factory.setCoalescing(true);        // Convert CDATA to Text nodes
        factory.setNamespaceAware(false);   // No namespaces: this is default
        factory.setValidating(false);       // Don't validate DTD: also default

        // Now use the factory to create a DOM parser, a.k.a. DocumentBuilder
        DocumentBuilder parser = factory.newDocumentBuilder();

        // Parse the file and build a Document tree to represent its content
        Document document = parser.parse(new File(args[0]));

        // Ask the document for a list of all <sect1> elements it contains
        NodeList sections = document.getElementsByTagName("sect1");
        // Loop through those <sect1> elements one at a time
        int numSections = sections.getLength();
        for(int i = 0; i < numSections; i++) {
            Element section = (Element)sections.item(i);  // A <sect1>
            // The first Element child of each <sect1> should be a <title>
            // element, but there may be some whitespace Text nodes first, so
            // loop through the children until you find the first element
            // child.
            Node title = section.getFirstChild();
            while(title != null && title.getNodeType() != Node.ELEMENT_NODE)
                title = title.getNextSibling();
            // Print the text contained in the Text node child of this element
            if (title != null)
                System.out.println(title.getFirstChild().getNodeValue());
        }
    }
}
```

Transforming XML Documents

The `javax.xml.transform` package defines a `TransformerFactory` class for creating `Transformer` objects. A `Transformer` can transform a document from its `Source` representation into a new `Result` representation and optionally apply an XSLT transformation to the document content in the process. Three subpackages define concrete implementations of the `Source` and `Result` interfaces, which allow documents to be transformed among three representations:

`javax.xml.transform.stream`
: Represents documents as streams of XML text

`javax.xml.transform.dom`
: Represents documents as DOM `Document` trees

`javax.xml.transform.sax`
: Represents documents as sequences of SAX method calls

The following code shows one use of these packages to transform the representation of a document from a DOM `Document` tree into a stream of XML text. An interesting feature of this code is that it does not create the `Document` tree by parsing a file; instead, it builds it up from scratch.

```
import javax.xml.transform.*;
import javax.xml.transform.dom.*;
import javax.xml.transform.stream.*;
```

```
import javax.xml.parsers.*;
import org.w3c.dom.*;

public class DOMToStream {
    public static void main(String[] args)
        throws ParserConfigurationException,
                TransformerConfigurationException,
                TransformerException
    {
        // Create a DocumentBuilderFactory and a DocumentBuilder
        DocumentBuilderFactory dbf = DocumentBuilderFactory.newInstance();
        DocumentBuilder db = dbf.newDocumentBuilder();
        // Instead of parsing an XML document, however, just create an empty
        // document that you can build up yourself.
        Document document = db.newDocument();

        // Now build a document tree using DOM methods
        Element book = document.createElement("book"); // Create new element
        book.setAttribute("id", "javanut4");           // Give it an attribute
        document.appendChild(book);                    // Add to the document
        for(int i = 1; i <= 3; i++) {                  // Add more elements
            Element chapter = document.createElement("chapter");
            Element title = document.createElement("title");
            title.appendChild(document.createTextNode("Chapter " + i));
            chapter.appendChild(title);
            chapter.appendChild(document.createElement("para"));
            book.appendChild(chapter);
        }

        // Now create a TransformerFactory and use it to create a Transformer
        // object to transform our DOM document into a stream of XML text.
        // No arguments to newTransformer() means no XSLT stylesheet
        TransformerFactory tf = TransformerFactory.newInstance();
        Transformer transformer = tf.newTransformer();

        // Create the Source and Result objects for the transformation
        DOMSource source = new DOMSource(document);          // DOM document
        StreamResult result = new StreamResult(System.out);  // to XML text

        // Finally, do the transformation
        transformer.transform(source, result);
    }
}
```

The most interesting uses of `javax.xml.transform` involve XSLT stylesheets. XSLT is a complex but powerful XML grammar that describes how XML document content should be converted to another form (e.g., XML, HTML, or plain text). A tutorial on XSLT stylesheets is beyond the scope of this book, but the following code (which contains only six key lines) shows how you can apply such a stylesheet (which is an XML document itself) to another XML document and write the resulting document to a stream:

```
import java.io.*;
import javax.xml.transform.*;
import javax.xml.transform.stream.*;
import javax.xml.parsers.*;
import org.w3c.dom.*;

public class Transform {
```

The Java Platform

```
    public static void main(String[] args)
        throws TransformerConfigurationException,
               TransformerException
    {
        // Get Source and Result objects for input, stylesheet, and output
        StreamSource input = new StreamSource(new File(args[0]));
        StreamSource stylesheet = new StreamSource(new File(args[1]));
        StreamResult output = new StreamResult(new File(args[2]));

        // Create a transformer and perform the transformation
        TransformerFactory tf = TransformerFactory.newInstance();
        Transformer transformer = tf.newTransformer(stylesheet);
        transformer.transform(input, output);
    }
}
```

Processes

Earlier in the chapter, we saw how easy it is to create and manipulate multiple threads of execution running within the same Java interpreter. Java also has a `java.lang.Process` class that represents a program running externally to the interpreter. A Java program can communicate with an external process using streams in the same way that it might communicate with a server running on some other computer on the network. Using a `Process` is always platform-dependent and is rarely portable, but it is sometimes a useful thing to do:

```
// Maximize portability by looking up the name of the command to execute
// in a configuration file.
java.util.Properties config;
String cmd = config.getProperty("sysloadcmd");
if (cmd != null) {
  // Execute the command; Process p represents the running command
  Process p = Runtime.getRuntime().exec(cmd);          // Start the command
  InputStream pin = p.getInputStream();                // Read bytes from it
  InputStreamReader cin = new InputStreamReader(pin); // Convert them to chars
  BufferedReader in = new BufferedReader(cin);         // Read lines of chars
  String load = in.readLine();                         // Get the command output
  in.close();                                          // Close the stream
}
```

Security

The `java.security` package defines quite a few classes related to the Java access-control architecture, which is discussed in more detail in Chapter 5. These classes allow Java programs to run untrusted code in a restricted environment from which it can do no harm. While these are important classes, you rarely need to use them. The more interesting classes are the ones used for authentication; examples of their use are shown below.

Message Digests

A *message digest* is a value, also known as cryptographic checksum or secure hash, that is computed over a sequence of bytes. The length of the digest is typically much smaller than the length of the data for which it is computed, but any change, no matter how small, in the input bytes, produces a change in the digest. When transmitting data (a message), you can transmit a message digest along with it. Then, the recipient of the message can recompute the message digest on the received data and, by comparing the computed digest to the received digest, determine whether the message or the digest was corrupted or tampered with during transmission. We saw a way to compute a message digest earlier in the chapter when we discussed streams. A similar technique can be used to compute a message digest for nonstreaming binary data:

```
import java.security.*;

// Obtain an object to compute message digests using the "Secure Hash
// Algorithm"; this method can throw a NoSuchAlgorithmException.
MessageDigest md = MessageDigest.getInstance("SHA");

byte[] data, data1, data2, secret;  // Some byte arrays initialized elsewhere

// Create a digest for a single array of bytes
byte[] digest = md.digest(data);

// Create a digest for several chunks of data
md.reset();             // Optional: automatically called by digest()
md.update(data1);       // Process the first chunk of data
md.update(data2);       // Process the second chunk of data
digest = md.digest();   // Compute the digest

// Create a keyed digest that can be verified if you know the secret bytes
md.update(data);              // The data to be transmitted with the digest
digest = md.digest(secret);   // Add the secret bytes and compute the digest

// Verify a digest like this
byte[] receivedData, receivedDigest;  // The data and the digest we received
byte[] verifyDigest = md.digest(receivedData);  // Digest the received data
// Compare computed digest to the received digest
boolean verified =  java.util.Arrays.equals(receivedDigest, verifyDigest);
```

Digital Signatures

A *digital signature* combines a message-digest algorithm with public-key cryptography. The sender of a message, Alice, can compute a digest for a message and then encrypt that digest with her private key. She then sends the message and the encrypted digest to a recipient, Bob. Bob knows Alice's public key (it is public, after all), so he can use it to decrypt the digest and verify that the message has not been tampered with. In performing this verification, Bob also learns that the digest was encrypted with Alice's private key, since he was able to decrypt the digest successfully using Alice's public key. As Alice is the only one who knows her private key, the message must have come from Alice. A digital signature is called such because, like a pen-and-paper signature, it serves to authenticate the origin of a document or message. Unlike a pen-and-paper signature, however, a digital signature is very difficult, if not impossible, to forge, and it cannot simply be cut and pasted onto another document.

Java makes creating digital signatures easy. In order to create a digital signature, however, you need a `java.security.PrivateKey` object. Assuming that a keystore exists on your system (see the *keytool* documentation in Chapter 8), you can get one with code like the following:

```
// Here is some basic data we need
File homedir = new File(System.getProperty("user.home"));
File keyfile = new File(homedir, ".keystore"); // Or read from config file
String filepass = "KeyStore password"       // Password for entire file
String signer = "david";                    // Read from config file
String password = "No one can guess this!";    // Better to prompt for this
PrivateKey key;  // This is the key we want to look up from the keystore

try {
  // Obtain a KeyStore object and then load data into it
  KeyStore keystore = KeyStore.getInstance(KeyStore.getDefaultType());
  keystore.load(new BufferedInputStream(new FileInputStream(keyfile)),
                filepass.toCharArray());
  // Now ask for the desired key
  key = (PrivateKey) keystore.getKey(signer, password.toCharArray());
}
catch (Exception e) { /* Handle various exception types here */ }
```

Once you have a `PrivateKey` object, you create a digital signature with a `java.security.Signature` object:

```
PrivateKey key;                 // Initialized as shown previously
byte[] data;                    // The data to be signed
Signature s =                   // Obtain object to create and verify signatures
  Signature.getInstance("SHA1withDSA");  // Can throw a
                                         // NoSuchAlgorithmException
s.initSign(key);                // Initialize it; can throw an InvalidKeyException
s.update(data);                 // Data to sign; can throw a SignatureException
/* s.update(data2); */          // Call multiple times to specify all data
byte[] signature = s.sign(); // Compute signature
```

A `Signature` object can verify a digital signature:

```
byte[] data;          // The signed data; initialized elsewhere
byte[] signature;     // The signature to be verified; initialized elsewhere
String signername;    // Who created the signature; initialized elsewhere
KeyStore keystore;    // Where certificates stored; initialize as shown earlier

// Look for a public-key certificate for the signer
java.security.cert.Certificate cert = keystore.getCertificate(signername);
PublicKey publickey = cert.getPublicKey();  // Get the public key from it

Signature s = Signature.getInstance("SHA1withDSA"); // Or some other algorithm
s.initVerify(publickey);                           // Setup for verification
s.update(data);                                    // Specify signed data
boolean verified = s.verify(signature);            // Verify signature data
```

Signed Objects

The `java.security.SignedObject` class is a convenient utility for wrapping a digital signature around an object. The `SignedObject` can then be serialized and transmitted to a recipient, who can deserialize it and use the `verify()` method to verify the signature:

```
Serializable o;  // The object to be signed; must be Serializable
PrivateKey k;    // The key to sign with; initialized elsewhere
Signature s = Signature.getInstance("SHA1withDSA"); // Signature "engine"
SignedObject so = new SignedObject(o, k, s);        // Create the SignedObject

// The SignedObject encapsulates the object o; it can now be serialized
// and transmitted to a recipient.

// Here's how the recipient verifies the SignedObject
SignedObject so;            // The deserialized SignedObject
Object o;                   // The original object to extract from it
PublicKey pk;               // The key to verify with
Signature s = Signature.getInstance("SHA1withDSA"); // Verification "engine"




if (so.verify(pk,s))        // If the signature is valid,
  o = so.getObject();       // retrieve the encapsulated object.
```

The Java Platform

Cryptography

The java.security package includes cryptography-based classes, but it does not contain classes for actual encryption and decryption. That is the job of the javax.crypto package. This package supports symmetric-key cryptography, in which the same key is used for both encryption and decryption and must be known by both the sender and the receiver of encrypted data.

Secret Keys

The SecretKey interface represents an encryption key; the first step of any cryptographic operation is to obtain an appropriate SecretKey. Unfortunately, the *keytool* program supplied with the Java SDK cannot generate and store secret keys, so a program must handle these tasks itself. Here is some code that shows various ways to work with SecretKey objects:

```
import javax.crypto.*;
import javax.crypto.spec.*;

// Generate encryption keys with a KeyGenerator object
KeyGenerator desGen = KeyGenerator.getInstance("DES");          // DES algorithm
SecretKey desKey = desGen.generateKey();                        // Generate a key
KeyGenerator desEdeGen = KeyGenerator.getInstance("DESede");    // Triple DES
SecretKey desEdeKey = desEdeGen.generateKey();                  // Generate a key

// SecretKey is an opaque representation of a key. Use SecretKeyFactory to
// convert to a transparent representation that can be manipulated: saved
// to a file, securely transmitted to a receiving party, etc.
SecretKeyFactory desFactory = SecretKeyFactory.getInstance("DES");
DESKeySpec desSpec = (DESKeySpec)
  desFactory.getKeySpec(desKey, javax.crypto.spec.DESKeySpec.class);
byte[] rawDesKey = desSpec.getKey();
// Do the same for a DESede key
SecretKeyFactory desEdeFactory = SecretKeyFactory.getInstance("DESede");
```

```
DESedeKeySpec desEdeSpec = (DESedeKeySpec)
  desEdeFactory.getKeySpec(desEdeKey, javax.crypto.spec.DESedeKeySpec.class);
byte[] rawDesEdeKey = desEdeSpec.getKey();

// Convert the raw bytes of a key back to a SecretKey object
DESedeKeySpec keyspec = new DESedeKeySpec(rawDesEdeKey);
SecretKey k = desEdeFactory.generateSecret(keyspec);

// For DES and DESede keys, there is an even easier way to create keys
// SecretKeySpec implements SecretKey, so use it to represent these keys
byte[] desKeyData = new byte[8];        // Read 8 bytes of data from a file
byte[] tripleDesKeyData = new byte[24]; // Read 24 bytes of data from a file
SecretKey myDesKey = new SecretKeySpec(desKeyData, "DES");
SecretKey myTripleDesKey = new SecretKeySpec(tripleDesKeyData, "DESede");
```

Encryption and Decryption with Cipher

Once you have obtained an appropriate `SecretKey` object, the central class for encryption and decryption is `Cipher`. Use it like this:

```
SecretKey key;     // Obtain a SecretKey as shown earlier
byte[] plaintext;  // The data to encrypt; initialized elsewhere

// Obtain an object to perform encryption or decryption
Cipher cipher = Cipher.getInstance("DESede");  // Triple-DES encryption
// Initialize the cipher object for encryption
cipher.init(Cipher.ENCRYPT_MODE, key);
// Now encrypt data
byte[] ciphertext = cipher.doFinal(plaintext);

// If we had multiple chunks of data to encrypt, we can do this
cipher.update(message1);
cipher.update(message2);
byte[] ciphertext = cipher.doFinal();

// We simply reverse things to decrypt
cipher.init(Cipher.DECRYPT_MODE, key);
byte[] decryptedMessage = cipher.doFinal(ciphertext);

// To decrypt multiple chunks of data
byte[] decrypted1 = cipher.update(ciphertext1);
byte[] decrypted2 = cipher.update(ciphertext2);
byte[] decrypted3 = cipher.doFinal(ciphertext3);
```

Encrypting and Decrypting Streams

The `Cipher` class can also be used with `CipherInputStream` or `CipherOutputStream` to encrypt or decrypt while reading or writing streaming data:

```
byte[] data;                              // The data to encrypt
SecretKey key;                            // Initialize as shown earlier
Cipher c = Cipher.getInstance("DESede");  // The object to perform encryption
c.init(Cipher.ENCRYPT_MODE, key);         // Initialize it

// Create a stream to write bytes to a file
FileOutputStream fos = new FileOutputStream("encrypted.data");

// Create a stream that encrypts bytes before sending them to that stream
```

```
// See also CipherInputStream to encrypt or decrypt while reading bytes
CipherOutputStream cos = new CipherOutputStream(fos, c);

cos.write(data);                          // Encrypt and write the data to the file
cos.close();                              // Always remember to close streams
java.util.Arrays.fill(data, (byte)0); // Erase the unencrypted data
```

Encrypted Objects

Finally, the `javax.crypto.SealedObject` class provides an especially easy way to perform encryption. This class serializes a specified object and encrypts the resulting stream of bytes. The `SealedObject` can then be serialized itself and transmitted to a recipient. The recipient is only able to retrieve the original object if she knows the required `SecretKey`:

```
Serializable o;           // The object to be encrypted; must be Serializable
SecretKey key;                                 // The key to encrypt it with
Cipher c = Cipher.getInstance("Blowfish");  // Object to perform encryption
c.init(Cipher.ENCRYPT_MODE, key);           // Initialize it with the key
SealedObject so = new SealedObject(o, c);   // Create the sealed object

// Object so is a wrapper around an encrypted form of the original object o;
// it can now be serialized and transmitted to another party.
// Here's how the recipient decrypts the original object
Object original = so.getObject(key);        // Must use the same SecretKey
```

CHAPTER 5

Java Security

Java programs can dynamically load Java classes from a variety of sources, including untrusted sources, such as web sites reached across an insecure network. The ability to create and work with such mobile code is one of the great strengths and features of Java. To make it work successfully, however, Java puts great emphasis on a security architecture that allows untrusted code to run safely, without fear of damage to the host system.

The need for a security system in Java is most acutely demonstrated by applets—miniature Java applications designed to be embedded in web pages.* When a user visits a web page (with a Java-enabled web browser) that contains an applet, the web browser downloads the Java class files that define that applet and runs them. In the absence of a security system, an applet could wreak havoc on the user's system by deleting files, installing a virus, stealing confidential information, and so on. Somewhat more subtly, an applet could take advantage of the user's system to forge email, generate spam, or launch hacking attempts on other systems.

Java's main line of defense against such malicious code is *access control*: untrusted code is simply not given access to certain sensitive portions of the core Java API. For example, an untrusted applet is not typically allowed to read, write, or delete files on the host system or connect over the network to any computer other than the web server from which it was downloaded. This chapter describes the Java access control architecture and a few other facets of the Java security system.

Security Risks

Java has been designed from the ground up with security in mind; this gives it a great advantage over many other existing systems and platforms. Nevertheless, no system can guarantee 100% security, and Java is no exception.

* Applets are documented in *Java Foundation Classes in a Nutshell* (O'Reilly) and are not covered in this book. Still, they serve as good examples here.

The Java security architecture was designed by security experts and has been studied and probed by many other security experts. The consensus is that the architecture itself is strong and robust, theoretically without any security holes (at least none that have been discovered yet). The implementation of the security architecture is another matter, however, and there is a long history of security flaws being found and patched in particular implementations of Java. For example, in April 1999, a flaw was found in Sun's implementation of the class verifier in Java 1.1. Patches for Java 1.1.6 and 1.1.7 were issued and the problem was fixed in Java 1.1.8. Even more recently, in August 1999, a severe flaw was found in Microsoft's Java Virtual Machine (which is used by the Internet Explorer 4.0 and 5.0 web browsers). The flaw was a particularly dangerous one because it allowed a malicious applet to gain unrestricted access to the underlying system. Microsoft has released a new version of their VM, and (as of this writing) there have not been any known attacks that took advantage of the flaw.

In all likelihood, security flaws will continue to be discovered (and patched) in Java VM implementations. Despite this, Java remains perhaps the most secure platform currently available. There have been few, if any, reported instances of malicious Java code exploiting security holes "in the wild." For practical purposes, the Java platform appears to be adequately secure, especially when contrasted with some of the insecure and virus-ridden alternatives.

Java VM Security and Class File Verification

The lowest level of the Java security architecture involves the design of the Java Virtual Machine and the byte codes it executes. The Java VM does not allow any kind of direct access to individual memory addresses of the underlying system, which prevents Java code from interfering with the native hardware and operating system. These intentional restrictions on the VM are reflected in the Java language itself, which does not support pointers or pointer arithmetic. The language does not allow an integer to be cast to an object reference or vice versa, and there is no way whatsoever to obtain an object's address in memory. Without capabilities like these, malicious code simply cannot gain a foothold.

In addition to the secure design of the Virtual Machine instruction set, the VM goes through a process known as *byte-code verification* whenever it loads an untrusted class. This process ensures that the byte codes of a class (and their operands) are all valid; that the code never underflows or overflows the VM stack; that local variables are not used before they are initialized; that field, method, and class access control modifiers are respected; and so on. The verification step is designed to prevent the VM from executing byte codes that might crash it or put it into an undefined and untested state where it might be vulnerable to other attacks by malicious code. Byte-code verification is a defense against malicious hand-crafted Java byte codes and untrusted Java compilers that might output invalid byte codes.

Authentication and Cryptography

In Java 1.1 and later, the `java.security` package (and its subpackages) provides classes and interfaces for *authentication*. As described in Chapter 4, this piece of the security architecture allows Java code to create and verify message digests and digital signatures. These technologies can ensure that any data (such as a Java class file) is authentic; that it originates from the person who claims to have originated it and has not been accidentally or maliciously modified in transit.

The Java Cryptography Extension, or JCE, consists of the `javax.crypto` package and its subpackages. These packages define classes for encryption and decryption of data. This is an important security-related feature for many applications, but is not directly relevant to the basic problem of preventing untrusted code from damaging the host system, so it is not discussed in this chapter.

Access Control

As I noted at the beginning of this chapter, the heart of the Java security architecture is access control: untrusted code simply must not be granted access to the sensitive parts of the Java API that would allow it to do malicious things. As we'll discuss in the following sections, the Java access-control model evolved significantly between Java 1.0 and Java 1.2. The Java 1.2 access-control model is relatively stable; it has not changed significantly in Java 1.3.

Java 1.0: The Sandbox

In this first release of Java, all Java code installed locally on the system is trusted implicitly. All code downloaded over the network, however, is untrusted and run in a restricted environment playfully called "the sandbox." The access-control policies of the sandbox are defined by the currently installed `java.lang.SecurityManager` object. When system code is about to perform a restricted operation, such as reading a file from the local filesystem, it first calls an appropriate method (such as `checkRead()`) of the currently installed `SecurityManager` object. If untrusted code is running, the `SecurityManager` throws a `SecurityException` that prevents the restricted operation from taking place.

The most common user of the `SecurityManager` class is a Java-enabled web browser, which installs a `SecurityManager` object to allow applets to run without damaging the host system. The precise details of the security policy are an implementation detail of the web browser, of course, but applets are typically restricted in the following ways:

- An applet cannot read, write, rename, or delete files. It cannot query the length or modification date of a file or even check whether a given file exists. Similarly, an applet cannot create, list, or delete a directory.
- An applet cannot connect to or accept a connection from any computer other than the one it was downloaded from. It cannot use any privileged ports (i.e., ports below and including port 1024).

- An applet cannot perform system-level functions, such as loading a native library, spawning a new process, or exiting the Java interpreter. An applet cannot manipulate any threads or thread groups, except for those it creates itself. In Java 1.1 and later, applets cannot use the Java Reflection API to obtain information about the nonpublic members of classes, except for classes that were downloaded with the applet.
- An applet cannot access certain graphics- and GUI-related facilities. It cannot initiate a print job or access the system clipboard or event queue. In addition, all windows created by an applet typically display a prominent visual indicator that they are "insecure," to prevent an applet from spoofing the appearance of some other application.
- An applet cannot read certain system properties, notably the `user.home` and `user.dir` properties, that specify the user's home directory and current working directory.
- An applet cannot circumvent these security restrictions by registering a new `SecurityManager` object.

How the sandbox works

Suppose that an applet (or some other untrusted code running in the sandbox) attempts to read the contents of the file */etc/passwd* by passing this filename to the `FileInputStream()` constructor. The programmers who wrote the `FileInputStream` class were aware that the class provides access to a system resource (a file), so use of the class should therefore be subject to access control. For this reason, they coded the `FileInputStream()` constructor to use the `SecurityManager` class.

Every time `FileInputStream()` is called, it checks to see if a `SecurityManager` object has been installed. If so, the constructor calls the `checkRead()` method of that `SecurityManager` object, passing the filename (*/etc/passwd*, in this case) as the sole argument. The `checkRead()` method has no return value; it either returns normally or throws a `SecurityException`. If the method returns, the `FileInputStream()` constructor simply proceeds with whatever initialization is necessary and returns. Otherwise, it allows the `SecurityException` to propagate to the caller. When this happens, no `FileInputStream` object is created, and the applet does not gain access to the */etc/passwd* file.

Java 1.1: Digitally Signed Classes

Java 1.1 retains the sandbox model of Java 1.0, but adds the `java.security` package and its digital signature capabilities. With these capabilities, Java classes can be digitally signed and verified. Thus, web browsers and other Java installations can be configured to trust downloaded code that bears a valid digital signature of a trusted entity. Such code is treated as if it were installed locally, so it is given full access to the Java APIs. In this release, the *javakey* program manages keys and digitally signs JAR files of Java code. Although Java 1.1 adds the important ability to trust digitally signed code that would otherwise be untrusted, it sticks to the basic sandbox model: trusted code gets full access and untrusted code gets totally restricted access.

Java 1.2: Permissions and Policies

Java 1.2 introduces major new access-control features into the Java security architecture. These features are implemented by new classes in the `java.security` package. The `Policy` class is one of the most important: it defines a Java security policy. A `Policy` object maps `CodeSource` objects to associated sets of `Permission` objects. A `CodeSource` object represents the source of a piece of Java code, which includes both the URL of the class file (and can be a local file) and a list of entities that have applied their digital signatures to the class file. The `Permission` objects associated with a `CodeSource` in the `Policy` define the permissions that are granted to code from a given source. Various Java APIs includes subclasses of `Permission` that represent different types of permissions. These include `java.lang.RuntimePermission`, `java.io.FilePermission`, and `java.net.SocketPermission`, for example.

Under this new access-control model, the `SecurityManager` class continues to be the central class; access-control requests are still made by invoking methods of a `SecurityManager`. However, the default `SecurityManager` implementation now delegates most of those requests to a new `AccessController` class that makes access decisions based on the `Permission` and `Policy` architecture.

The new Java 1.2 access-control architecture has several important features:

- Code from different sources can be given different sets of permissions. In other words, the new architecture supports fine-grained levels of trust. Even locally installed code can be treated as untrusted or partially untrusted. Under this new architecture, only system classes and standard extensions run as fully trusted.

- It is no longer necessary to define a custom subclass of `SecurityManager` to define a security policy. Policies can be configured by a system administrator by editing a text file or using the new *policytool* program.

- The new architecture is not limited to a fixed set of access control methods in the `SecurityManager` class. New `Permission` subclasses can be defined easily to govern access to new system resources (which might be exposed, for example, by new standard extensions that include native code).

How policies and permissions work

Let's return to the example of an applet that attempts to create a `FileInputStream` to read the file */etc/passwd*. In Java 1.2, the `FileInputStream()` constructor behaves exactly the same as it does in Java 1.0 and Java 1.1: it looks to see if a `SecurityManager` is installed and, if so, calls its `checkRead()` method, passing the name of the file to be read.

What's new in Java 1.2 is the default behavior of the `checkRead()` method. Unless a program has replaced the default security manager with one of its own, the default implementation creates a `FilePermission` object to represent the access being requested. This `FilePermission` object has a *target* of "/etc/passwd" and an *action* of "read". The `checkRead()` method passes this `FilePermission` object to the static `checkPermission()` method of the `java.security.AccessController` class.

It is the `AccessController` and its `checkPermission()` method that do the real work of access control in Java 1.2. The method determines the `CodeSource` of each calling method and uses the current `Policy` object to determine the `Permission` objects associated with it. With this information, the `AccessController` can determine whether read access to the */etc/passwd* file should be allowed.

The `Permission` class represents both the permissions granted by a `Policy` and the permissions requested by a method like the `FileInputStream()` constructor. When requesting a permission, Java typically uses a `FilePermission` (or other `Permission` subclass) with a very specific target, like "/etc/passwd". When granting a permission, however, a `Policy` commonly uses a `FilePermission` object with a wildcard target, such as "/etc/*", to represent many files. One of the key features of a `Permission` subclass such as `FilePermission` is that it defines an `implies()` method that can determine whether permission to read "/etc/*" implies permission to read "/etc/passwd".

Security for Everyone

Programmers, system administrators, and end users all have different security concerns and, thus, different roles to play in the Java 1.2 security architecture.

Security for System Programmers

System programmers are the people who define new Java APIs that allow access to sensitive system resources. These programmers are typically working with native methods that have unprotected access to the system. They need to use the Java access-control architecture to prevent untrusted code from executing those native methods. To do this, system programmers must carefully insert `SecurityManager` calls at appropriate places in their code. A system programmer may choose to use an existing `Permission` subclass to govern access to the system resources exposed by her API, or she may decide to define a specialized subclass of `Permission`.

The system programmer carries a tremendous security burden: if she does not perform appropriate access control checks in her code, she compromises the security of the entire Java platform. The details are complex and are beyond the scope of this book. Fortunately, however, system programming that involves native methods is rare in Java; almost all of us are application programmers who can simply rely on the existing APIs.

Security for Application Programmers

Programmers who use the core Java APIs and standard extensions, but do not define new extensions or write native methods, can simply rely on the security efforts of the system programmers who created those APIs. In other words, most of us Java programmers can simply use the Java APIs and need not worry about introducing security holes into the Java platform.

In fact, application programmers rarely have to use the access-control architecture. If you are writing Java code that may be run as untrusted code, you should be aware of the restrictions placed on untrusted code by typical security policies. Keep in mind that some methods (such as methods that read or write files) can throw `SecurityException` objects, but don't feel you must write your code to catch these exceptions. Often, the appropriate response to a `SecurityException` is to allow it to propagate uncaught, so that it terminates the application.

Sometimes, as an application programmer, you want to write an application (such as an applet viewer) that can load untrusted classes and run them subject to access-control checks. To do this in Java 1.2, you must first install a security manager:

```
System.setSecurityManager(new SecurityManager());
```

Then use `java.net.URLClassLoader` to load the untrusted classes. `URLClassLoader` assigns a default set of safe permissions to the classes it loads, but in some cases you may want to modify the permissions granted to the loaded code through the `Policy` and `PermissionCollection` classes.

Security for System Administrators

In Java 1.2 and later, system administrators are responsible for defining the default security policy for the computers at their site. The default policy is stored in the file *lib/security/java.policy* in the Java installation. A system administrator can edit this text file by hand or use the *policytool* program from Sun to edit the file graphically. *policytool* is the preferred way to define policies, so the syntax of the underlying policy file is not documented in this book.

The default *java.policy* file defines a policy that is much like the policy of Java 1.0 and Java 1.1: system classes and installed extensions are fully trusted, while all other code is untrusted and only allowed a few simple permissions. While this default policy is adequate for many purposes, it may not be appropriate for all sites. For example, at some organizations, it may be appropriate to grant extra permissions to code downloaded from a secure intranet.

In order to define secure and effective security policies, a system administrator must understand the various `Permission` subclasses of the Java platform, the target and action names they support, and the security implications of granting any particular permission. These topics are explained well in a document titled "Permissions in the Java 2 SDK," which is part of the Java 1.2 release and also available (at the time of this writing) online at: *http://java.sun.com/products/jdk/1.2/docs/guide/security/permissions.html.*

Security for End Users

Most end users do not have to think about security at all: their Java programs should simply run in a secure way with no intervention by them. Some sophisticated end users may want to define their own security policies, however. An end user can do this by running *policytool* himself to define personal policy files that augment the system policy. The default personal policy is stored in a file named *.java.policy* in the user's home directory. By default, Java loads this policy file and uses it to augment the system policy file.

In Java 1.2 and later, a user can specify an additional policy file to use when starting up the Java interpreter, by defining the java.security.policy property with the -D option. For example:

```
C:\> java -Djava.security.policy=policyfile UntrustedApp
```

This line runs the class UntrustedApp after augmenting the default system and user policies with the policy specified in the file or URL *policyfile*. To replace the system and user policies instead of augmenting them, use a double equals sign in the property specification:

```
C:\> java -Djava.security.policy==policyfile UntrustedApp
```

Note, however, that specifying a policy file is only useful if there is a SecurityManager installed. If a user doesn't trust an application, he presumably doesn't trust that application to voluntarily install its own security manager. In this case, he can define the java.security.manager system property:

```
C:\> java -Djava.security.manager -Djava.security.policy=policyfile UntrustedApp
```

The value of this property does not matter; simply defining it is enough to tell the Java interpreter to automatically install a default SecurityManager object that subjects an application to the access control policies described in the system, user, and java.security.policy policy files.

Permission Classes

Table 5-1 lists the various Permission subclasses defined by the core Java platform and summarizes the permissions they represent. See the reference section for more information on the individual classes. See *http://java.sun.com/j2se/1.4/docs/guide/security/permissions.html* for a detailed description of these permissions, along with their target and action names and a list of methods and the permissions they require (this document is also part of the standard documentation bundle that can be downloaded along with the JDK).

Table 5-1. Java permission classes

Permission class	*Description*
java.security.AllPermission	An instance of this special permission class implies all other permissions.
javax.sound.sampled.AudioPermission	Controls the ability to play and record sound.
javax.security.auth.AuthPermission	Controls access to authentication methods in javax.security.auth and its subpackages.

Table 5-1. Java permission classes (continued)

Permission class	*Description*
`java.awt.AWTPermission`	Controls access to sensitive methods in `java.awt` and its subpackages.
`java.io.FilePermission`	Governs access to the filesystem.
`java.net.NetPermission`	Governs access to networking-related resources such as stream handlers and HTTP authentication. See also `java.net.SocketPermission`.
`java.util.PropertyPermission`	Governs access to system properties.
`java.lang.reflect.ReflectPermission`	Governs access through the `java.lang.reflect` package to classes and class members that would normally be inaccessible.
`java.lang.RuntimePermission`	Governs access to a number of methods and resources. Many of the controlled methods are defined by `java.lang.System` and `java.lang.Runtime`.
`java.security.SecurityPermission`	Governs access to various security-related methods.
`java.io.SerializablePermission`	Governs access to serialization-related methods.
`java.net.SocketPermission`	Governs access to the network.
`java.sql.SQLPermission`	Governs the ability to specify logging streams in the `java.sql` JDBC API.

CHAPTER 6

JavaBeans

The JavaBeans API provides a framework for defining reusable, embeddable, modular software components. The JavaBeans specification includes the following definition of a bean: "a reusable software component that can be manipulated visually in a builder tool." As you can see, this is a rather loose definition; beans can take a variety of forms. The most common use of beans is for graphical user interface components, such as components of the `java.awt` and `javax.swing` packages, which are documented in *Java Foundation Classes in a Nutshell* (O'Reilly).* Although all beans can be manipulated visually, this does not mean every bean has its own visual representation. For example, the `javax.sql.RowSet` class (documented in *Java Enterprise in a Nutshell* (O'Reilly)) is a JavaBeans component that represents the data resulting from a database query. There are no limits on the simplicity or complexity of a JavaBeans component. The simplest beans are typically basic graphical interface components, such as a `java.awt.Button` object. But even complex systems, such as an embeddable spreadsheet application, can function as individual beans.

One of the goals of the JavaBeans model is interoperability with similar component frameworks. So, for example, a native Windows program can, with an appropriate bridge or wrapper object, use a JavaBeans component as if it were a COM or ActiveX component. The details of this sort of interoperability are beyond the scope of this chapter, however.

The JavaBeans component model consists of the `java.beans` and `java.beans.beancontext` packages and a number of important naming and API conventions to which conforming beans and bean-manipulation tools must adhere. Because JavaBeans is a framework for generic components, the JavaBeans conventions are, in many ways, more important than the actual API.

---

* JavaBeans are documented in this book instead of that one because the JavaBeans component model is not specific to AWT or Swing programming. Nevertheless, it is hardly possible to discuss beans without mentioning AWT and Swing components. You will probably get the most out of this chapter if you have some familiarity with GUI programming in Java using AWT or Swing.

Beans can be used at three levels by three different categories of programmers:

- If you are writing an application that uses beans developed by other programmers or using a beanbox tool* to combine those beans into an application, you need to be familiar with general JavaBeans concepts and terminology. You also need to read the documentation for the individual beans you use in your application, but you do not need to understand the JavaBeans API. This chapter begins with an overview of JavaBeans concepts that should be sufficient for programmers using beans at this level.
- If you are writing beans, you need to understand and follow various JavaBeans naming and packaging conventions. After the introduction to general bean concepts and terminology, this chapter describes the basic bean conventions bean developers must follow. Although a JavaBeans component can be implemented without using the JavaBeans API, most beans are distributed with various auxiliary classes that make them easier to use within beanbox tools. These auxiliary classes rely heavily on the JavaBeans API so that they can interoperate with beanbox tools.
- If you are developing a GUI editor, application builder, or other beanbox tool, you use the JavaBeans API to help you manipulate beans within the tool. You also need to be intimately familiar with all the various JavaBeans programming conventions. Although this chapter describes the most important conventions, you should also refer to the primary source, the JavaBeans specification (see *http://java.sun.com/beans/*).

Bean Basics

Any object that conforms to certain basic rules can be a bean; there is no `Bean` class all beans are required to subclass. Many beans are AWT components, but it is also quite possible, and often useful, to write "invisible" beans that do not have an onscreen appearance. (Just because a bean does not have an onscreen appearance in a finished application does not mean it cannot be visually manipulated by a beanbox tool, however.)

A bean is characterized by the properties, events, and methods it exports. It is these properties, events, and methods an application designer manipulates in a beanbox tool. A *property* is a piece of the bean's internal state that can be programmatically set and/or queried, usually through a standard pair of `get` and `set` accessor methods.

A bean communicates with the application in which it is embedded and with other beans by generating *events*. The JavaBeans API uses the same event model AWT and Swing components use. This model is based on the `java.util.EventObject` class and the `java.util.EventListener` interface; it is described in detail in *Java Foundation Classes in a Nutshell* (O'Reilly). In brief, the event model works like this:

* *beanbox* is the name of the sample bean-manipulation program provided by Sun in its Beans Development Kit (BDK). The term is a useful one, and I'll use it to describe any kind of graphical design tool or application builder that manipulates beans.

- A bean defines an event if it provides `add` and `remove` methods for registering and deregistering listener objects for that event.
- An application that wants to be notified when an event of that type occurs uses these methods to register an event listener object of the appropriate type.
- When the event occurs, the bean notifies all registered listeners by passing an event object that describes the event to a method defined by the event listener interface.

A *unicast event* is a rare kind of event for which there can be only a single registered listener object. The `add` registration method for a unicast event throws a `TooManyListenersException` if an attempt is made to register more than a single listener.

The *methods* exported by a bean are simply any `public` methods defined by the bean, excluding those methods that get and set property values and register and remove event listeners.

In addition to the regular sort of properties described earlier, the JavaBeans API also supports several specialized property subtypes. An *indexed property* is a property that has an array value, as well as getter and setter methods that access both individual elements of the array and the entire array. A *bound property* is one that sends a `PropertyChangeEvent` to any interested `PropertyChangeListener` objects whenever the value of the property changes. A *constrained property* is one that can have any changes vetoed by any interested listener. When the value of a constrained property of a bean changes, the bean must send out a `PropertyChangeEvent` to the list of interested `VetoableChangeListener` objects. If any of these objects throws a `PropertyVetoException`, the property value is not changed, and the `PropertyVetoException` is propagated back to the property setter method.

Because Java allows dynamic loading of classes, beanbox programs can load arbitrary beans. The beanbox tool uses a process called *introspection* to determine the properties, events, and methods exported by a bean. The introspection mechanism is implemented by the `java.beans.Introspector` class; it relies on both the `java.lang.reflect` reflection mechanism and a number of JavaBeans naming conventions. `Introspector` can determine the list of properties supported by a bean, for example, by scanning the class for methods that have the right names and signatures to be `get` and `set` property accessor methods.

The introspection mechanism does not rely on the reflection capabilities of Java alone, however. Any bean can define an auxiliary `BeanInfo` class that provides additional information about the bean and its properties, events, and methods. The `Introspector` automatically attempts to locate and load the `BeanInfo` class of a bean.

The `BeanInfo` class provides additional information about the bean primarily in the form of `FeatureDescriptor` objects, each one describing a single feature of the bean. Each `FeatureDescriptor` provides a name and brief description of the feature it documents. The beanbox tool can display the name and description to the user, making the bean essentially self-documenting and easier to use. Specific bean features, such as properties, events, and methods, are described by specific subclasses of FeatureDescriptor, such as PropertyDescriptor, EventSetDescriptor, and MethodDescriptor.

One of the primary tasks of a beanbox application is to allow the user to customize a bean by setting property values. A beanbox defines *property editors* for commonly used property types, such as numbers, strings, fonts, and colors. If a bean has a property of a more complicated type, however, it can define a PropertyEditor class that enables the beanbox to let the user set values for that property.

In addition, a complex bean may not be satisfied with the property-by-property customization mechanism provided by most beanbox tools. Such a bean can define a Customizer class to create a graphical interface that allows the user to configure a bean in some useful way. A particularly complex bean can even define customizers that serve as "wizards" that guide the user step by step through the customization process.

A *bean context* is a logical container (and often a visual container) for JavaBeans and, optionally, for other nested bean contexts. In practice, most JavaBeans are AWT or Swing components or containers. Beanbox tools recognize this and allow component beans to be nested within container beans. A bean context is a kind of heavyweight container that formalizes this nesting relationship. More importantly, however, a bean context can provide a set of services (e.g., printing services, debugging services, database connection services) to the beans it contains. Beans that are aware of their context can be written to query the context and take advantage of the services that are available. Bean contexts are implemented using the java.beans.beancontext API, which is new as of Java 1.2 and discussed in more detail later in this chapter.

Java 1.4 introduces a JavaBeans Persistence API, which allows a bean, or a tree of beans, to have their state written persistently to an XML file from which the bean or beans can later be restored. This is done with the XMLEncoder and XMLDecoder classes in java.beans. JavaBeans persistence is similar to the serialization mechanism of the java.io package, but is based entirely on the public API of the beans, and is thus more robust in the presence of multiple versions or multiple implementations of that public API. You'll see examples of this new JavaBeans Persistence API along with examples of the Serialization API in Chapter 4. And you'll find details about XMLEncoder, XMLDecoder, and related classes in Chapter 9.

JavaBeans Conventions

The JavaBeans component model relies on a number of rules and conventions bean developers must follow. These conventions are not part of the JavaBeans API itself, but in many ways, they are more important to bean developers than the API itself. The conventions are sometimes referred to as *design patterns*; they specify such things as method names and signatures for property accessor methods defined by a bean.

The reason for these design patterns is interoperability between beans and the beanbox programs that manipulate them. As we've seen, beanbox programs may rely on introspection to determine the list of properties, events, and methods a bean supports. In order for this to work, bean developers must use method names the beanbox can recognize. The JavaBeans framework facilitates this process by establishing naming conventions. One such convention, for example, is that the getter and setter accessor methods for a property should begin with `get` and `set`.

Not all the patterns are absolute requirements. If a bean has property accessor methods that do not follow the naming conventions, it is possible to use a `PropertyDescriptor` object (specified in a `BeanInfo` class) to indicate the accessor methods for the property. Although the `BeanInfo` class provides an alternative to the property-accessor-method naming convention, the property accessor method must still follow the conventions that specify the number and type of its parameters and its return value.

Beans

A bean itself must adhere to the following conventions:

Class name
: There are no restrictions on the class name of a bean.

Superclass
: A bean can extend any other class. Beans are often AWT or Swing components, but there are no restrictions.

Instantiation
: A bean must provide a no-parameter constructor or a file that contains a serialized instance the beanbox can deserialize for use as a prototype bean, so a beanbox can instantiate the bean. The file that contains the bean should have the same name as the bean, with an extension of *.ser*.

Bean name
: The name of a bean is the name of the class that implements it or the name of the file that holds the serialized instance of the bean (with the *.ser* extension removed and directory separator (/) characters converted to dot (.) characters).

JavaBeans

Properties

A bean defines a property *p* of type *T* if it has accessor methods that follow these patterns (if *T* is `boolean`, a special form of getter method is allowed):

Getter
: `public T getP()`

Boolean getter
: `public boolean isP()`

Setter

`public void setP(T)`

Exceptions

Property accessor methods can throw any type of checked or unchecked exceptions

Indexed Properties

An indexed property is a property of array type that provides accessor methods that get and set the entire array, as well as methods that get and set individual elements of the array. A bean defines an indexed property *p* of type *T*`[]` if it defines the following accessor methods:

Array getter

`public T[] getP()`

Element getter

`public T getP(int)`

Array setter

`public void setP(T[])`

Element setter

`public void setP(int,T)`

Exceptions

Indexed property accessor methods can throw any type of checked or unchecked exceptions. In particular, they should throw an `ArrayIndexOutOfBoundsException` if the supplied index is out of bounds.

Bound Properties

A bound property is one that generates a `PropertyChangeEvent` when its value changes. Here are the conventions for a bound property:

Accessor methods

The getter and setter methods for a bound property follow the same conventions as a regular property.

Introspection

A beanbox cannot distinguish a bound property from a nonbound property through introspection alone. Therefore, you may want to implement a `BeanInfo` class that returns a `PropertyDescriptor` object for the property. The `isBound()` method of this `PropertyDescriptor` should return `true`.

Listener registration

A bean that defines one or more bound properties must define a pair of methods for the registration of listeners that are notified when any bound property value change. The methods must have these signatures:

```
public void addPropertyChangeListener(PropertyChangeListener)
public void removePropertyChangeListener(PropertyChangeListener)
```

Named property listener registration

A bean can optionally provide additional methods that allow event listeners to be registered for changes to a single bound property value. These methods are passed the name of a property and have the following signatures:

```
public void addPropertyChangeListener(String, PropertyChangeListener)
public void removePropertyChangeListener(String, PropertyChangeListener)
```

Per-property listener registration

A bean can optionally provide additional event listener registration methods that are specific to a single property. For a property *p*, these methods have the following signatures:

```
public void addPListener(PropertyChangeListener)
public void removePListener(PropertyChangeListener)
```

Methods of this type allow a beanbox to distinguish a bound property from a nonbound property.

Notification

When the value of a bound property changes, the bean should update its internal state to reflect the change and then pass a `PropertyChangeEvent` to the `propertyChange()` method of every `PropertyChangeListener` object registered for the bean or the specific bound property.

Support

`java.beans.PropertyChangeSupport` is a helpful class for implementing bound properties.

Constrained Properties

A constrained property is one for which any changes can be vetoed by registered listeners. Most constrained properties are also bound properties. Here are the conventions for a constrained property:

Getter

The getter method for a constrained property is the same as the getter method for a regular property.

Setter

The setter method of a constrained property throws a `PropertyVetoException` if the property change is vetoed. For a property *p* of type *T*, the signature looks like this:

```
public void setP(T) throws PropertyVetoException
```

Listener registration

A bean that defines one or more constrained properties must define a pair of methods for the registration of listeners that are notified when any constrained property value changes. The methods must have these signatures:

```
public void addVetoableChangeListener(VetoableChangeListener)
public void removeVetoableChangeListener(VetoableChangeListener)
```

Named property listener registration

A bean can optionally provide additional methods that allow event listeners to be registered for changes to a single constrained property value. These methods are passed the name of a property and have the following signatures:

```
public void addVetoableChangeListener(String, VetoableChangeListener)
public void removeVetoableChangeListener(String, VetoableChangeListener)
```

Per-property listener registration

A bean can optionally provide additional listener registration methods that are specific to a single constrained property. For a property *p*, these methods have the following signatures:

```
public void addPListener(VetoableChangeListener)
public void removePListener(VetoableChangeListener)
```

Notification

When the setter method of a constrained property is invoked, the bean must generate a `PropertyChangeEvent` that describes the requested change and pass that event to the `vetoableChange()` method of every `VetoableChangeListener` object registered for the bean or the specific constrained property. If any listener vetoes the change by throwing a `PropertyVetoException`, the bean must send out another `PropertyChangeEvent` to revert the property to its original value, and then it should throw a `PropertyVetoException` itself. If, on the other hand, the property change is not vetoed, the bean should update its internal state to reflect the change. If the constrained property is also a bound property, the bean should notify `PropertyChangeListener` objects at this point.

Support

`java.beans.VetoableChangeSupport` is a helpful class for implementing constrained properties.

Events

In addition to `PropertyChangeEvent` events generated when bound and constrained properties are changed, a bean can generate other types of events. An event named *E* should follow these conventions:

Event class

The event class should directly or indirectly extend `java.util.EventObject` and should be named *E*`Event`.

Listener interface

The event must be associated with an event listener interface that extends `java.util.EventListener` and is named *E*`Listener`.

Listener methods

The event listener interface can define any number of methods that take a single argument of type *E*`Event` and return `void`.

Listener registration

The bean must define a pair of methods for registering event listeners that want to be notified when an *E* event occurs. The methods should have the following signatures:

```
public void addEListener(EListener)
public void removeEListener(EListener)
```

Unicast events

A unicast event allows only one listener object to be registered at a single time. If *E* is a unicast event, the listener registration method should have this signature:

```
public void addEListener(EListener) throws TooManyListenersException
```

Methods

A beanbox can expose the methods of a bean to application designers. The only formal convention is that these methods must be declared `public`. The following guidelines are also useful, however:

Method name

A method can have any name that does not conflict with the property- and event-naming conventions. The name should be as descriptive as possible.

Parameters

A method can have any number and type of parameters. However, beanbox programs may work best with no-parameter methods or methods that have simple primitive parameters.

Excluding methods

A bean can explicitly specify the list of methods it exports by providing a `BeanInfo` implementation.

Documentation

A bean can provide user-friendly, human-readable localized names and descriptions for methods through `MethodDescriptor` objects returned by a `BeanInfo` implementation.

Auxiliary Classes

A bean can provide the following auxiliary classes:

`BeanInfo`

To provide additional information about a bean *B*, implement the `BeanInfo` interface in a class named *B*`BeanInfo`.

Property editor for a specific type

To enable a beanbox to work with properties of type *T*, implement the `PropertyEditor` interface in a class named *T*`Editor`. The class must have a no-parameter constructor.

Property editor for a specific property

To customize the way a beanbox allows the user to enter values for a single property, define a class that implements the `PropertyEditor` interface and has a no-parameter constructor, and register that class with a `PropertyDescriptor` object returned by the `BeanInfo` class for the bean.

Customizers

To define a customizer, or wizard, for configuring a bean *B*, define an AWT or Swing component with a no-parameter constructor that does the customization. The class is commonly called *B*`Customizer`, but this is not required. Register the class with the `BeanDescriptor` object returned by the `BeanInfo` class for the bean.

Documentation

Define default documentation for a bean *B* in HTML 2.0 format and store that documentation in a file named *B*`.html`. Define localized translations of the documentation in files by the same name in locale-specific directories.

Bean Packaging and Distribution

Beans are distributed in JAR archive files that have the following:

Content

The class or classes that implement a bean should be included in the JAR file, along with auxiliary classes such as `BeanInfo` and `PropertyEditor` implementations. If the bean is instantiated from a serialized instance, that instance should be included in the JAR archive with a filename ending in *.ser*. The JAR file can contain HTML documentation for the bean and should also contain any resource files, such as images, required by the bean and its auxiliary classes. A single JAR file can contain more than one bean.

`Java-Bean` *attribute*

The manifest of the JAR file must mark any *.class* and *.ser* files that define a bean with the attribute:

```
Java-Bean: true
```

`Depends-On` *attribute*

The manifest of a JAR file can use the `Depends-On` attribute to specify all other files in the JAR archive on which the bean depends. A beanbox application can use this information when generating applications or repackaging beans. Each bean can have zero or more `Depends-On` attributes, each of which can list zero or more space-separated filenames. Within a JAR file, / is always used as the directory separator.

`Design-Time-Only` *attribute*

The manifest of a JAR file can optionally use the `Design-Time-Only` attribute to specify auxiliary files, such as `BeanInfo` implementations, that are used by a beanbox, but not used by applications that use the bean. The beanbox can use this information when repackaging beans for use in an application.

Bean Contexts and Services

The JavaBeans component model was introduced in Java 1.1. Java 1.2 extends that model by introducing a containment and services protocol, defined in the `java.beans.beancontext` package. A bean context is a `java.util.Collection` of beans that implements the `BeanContext` interface and provides a context for the beans it contains. Many bean contexts define one or more services, such as a printing service, that beans can query and use. These bean contexts implement the `BeanContextServices` interface. All bean contexts are also `BeanContextChild` implementations, so contexts can be nested within each other.

Many beans never need to know about the contexts that contain them. A bean that does want to take advantage of its context and the services it provides implements the `BeanContextChild` interface. When a bean context child is added to a bean context, the `setBeanContext()` method of the `BeanContextChild` interface is invoked by the bean context. The implementation of this method should store the reference to the bean context for future use. The `setBeanContext()` method is a bound and constrained property, so it must notify `VetoableChangeListener` and `PropertyChangeListener` objects. For this reason, many beans delegate these responsibilities to a `BeanContextChildSuport` object.

If a bean (or bean context) is nested within a bean context that implements `BeanContextServices`, the bean can use the services provided by the bean context. A service is identified by the Java class that defines it. So a printing service is identified by the `Class` object of the `java.awt.print.PrinterJob` class, for example, and the system clipboard service is represented by the `java.awt.datatransfer.Clipboard` class. A bean can call the `hasService()` method of its containing `BeanContextServices` object to determine whether a specified service is available. If so, it can use `getService()` to obtain an appropriate instance of the service class. If a bean context is nested within another context, it can pass these `hasService()` and `getService()` methods to its containing context.

In addition to `getService()` and `hasService()`, a `BeanContext` provides several other methods beans can rely on. `getResource()` and `getResourceAsStream()` replace the methods by the same name defined by `Class` and `ClassLoader`. The `isDesignTime()` method (from the `DesignMode` interface) allows a bean to determine whether it is being displayed within a beanbox or run in an application or applet. The `BeanContext` method is preferred to the static `Beans.isDesignTime()` method because it is context-specific rather than global.

`BeanContext` and `BeanContextServices` are large interfaces; implementations must adhere to fairly complex specifications that govern the ways they interact with the beans they contain and the contexts within which they are nested. For these reasons, bean developers do not often create custom bean contexts. Instead, they rely on the contexts provided by the vendor of their beanbox tool. Advanced bean developers who do need to create bean contexts can delegate many of their methods to the `BeanContextSupport` and `BeanContextServicesSupport` classes that implement the basic framework and protocols.

CHAPTER 7

Java Programming and Documentation Conventions

This chapter explains a number of important and useful Java programming conventions. If you follow these conventions, your Java code will be self-documenting, easier to read and maintain, and more portable.

Naming and Capitalization Conventions

The following widely adopted naming conventions apply to packages, classes, methods, fields, and constants in Java. Because these conventions are almost universally followed and because they affect the public API of the classes you define, they should be followed carefully:

Packages
: Ensure that your package names are unique by prefixing them with the inverted name of your Internet domain (e.g., `com.davidflanagan.utils`). All package names, or at least their unique prefixes, should be lowercase.

Classes
: A class name should begin with a capital letter and be written in mixed case (e.g., `String`). If a class name consists of more than one word, each word should begin with a capital letter (e.g., `StringBuffer`). If a class name, or one of the words of a class name, is an acronym, the acronym can be written in all capital letters (e.g., `URL`, `HTMLParser`).

  Since classes are designed to represent objects, you should choose class names that are nouns (e.g., `Thread`, `Teapot`, `FormatConverter`).

Interfaces
: Interface names follow the same capitalization conventions as class names. When an interface is used to provide additional information about the classes that implement it, it is common to choose an interface name that is an adjective (e.g., `Runnable`, `Cloneable`, `Serializable`, `DataInput`). When an interface works more like an abstract superclass, use a name that is a noun (e.g., `Document`, `FileNameMap`, `Collection`).

Methods

A method name always begins with a lowercase letter. If the name contains more than one word, every word after the first begins with a capital letter (e.g., `insert()`, `insertObject()`, `insertObjectAt()`). Method names are typically chosen so that the first word is a verb. Method names can be as long as is necessary to make their purpose clear, but choose succinct names where possible.

Fields and constants

Nonconstant field names follow the same capitalization conventions as method names. If a field is a `static final` constant, it should be written in uppercase. If the name of a constant includes more than one word, the words should be separated with underscores (e.g., `MAX_VALUE`). A field name should be chosen to best describe the purpose of the field or the value it holds.

Parameters

The names of method parameters appear in the documentation for a method, so you should choose names that make the purpose of the parameters as clear as possible. Try to keep parameter names to a single word and use them consistently. For example, if a `WidgetProcessor` class defines many methods that accept a `Widget` object as the first parameter, name this parameter `widget` or even `w` in each method.

Local variables

Local variable names are an implementation detail and never visible outside your class. Nevertheless, choosing good names makes your code easier to read, understand, and maintain. Variables are typically named following the same conventions as methods and fields.

In addition to the conventions for specific types of names, there are conventions regarding the characters you should use in your names. Java allows the `$` character in any identifier, but, by convention, its use is reserved for synthetic names generated by source-code processors. (It is used by the Java compiler, for example, to make inner classes work.) Also, Java allows names to use any alphanumeric characters from the entire Unicode character set. While this can be convenient for non-English-speaking programmers, the use of Unicode characters should typically be restricted to local variables, private methods and fields, and other names that are not part of the public API of a class.

Portability Conventions and Pure Java Rules

Sun's motto, or core value proposition, for Java is "Write once, run anywhere." Java makes it easy to write portable programs, but Java programs do not automatically run successfully on any Java platform. To ensure portability, you must follow a few fairly simple rules that can be summarized as follows:

Native methods

Portable Java code can use any methods in the core Java APIs, including methods implemented as `native` methods. However, portable code must not define its own native methods. By their very nature, native methods must be ported to each new platform, so they directly subvert the "Write once, run anywhere" promise of Java.

The `Runtime.exec()` *method*
: Calling the `Runtime.exec()` method to spawn a process and execute an external command on the native system is rarely allowed in portable code. This is because the native OS command to be executed is never guaranteed to exist or behave the same way on all platforms. The only time it is legal to use `Runtime.exec()` is when the user is allowed to specify the command to run, either by typing the command at runtime or by specifying the command in a configuration file or preferences dialog box.

The `System.getenv()` *method*
: Using `System.getenv()` is nonportable, without exception. The method has actually been deprecated for this reason.

Undocumented classes
: Portable Java code must use only classes and interfaces that are a documented part of the Java platform. Most Java implementations ship with additional undocumented public classes that are part of the implementation, but not of the Java platform specification. There is nothing to prevent a program from using and relying on these undocumented classes, but doing so is not portable because the classes are not guaranteed to exist in all Java implementations or on all platforms.

The `java.awt.peer` *package*
: The interfaces in the `java.awt.peer` package are part of the Java platform, but are documented for use by AWT implementors only. Applications that use these interfaces directly are not portable.

Implementation-specific features
: Portable code must not rely on features specific to a single implementation. For example, Microsoft distributed a version of the Java runtime system that included a number of additional methods that were not part of the Java platform as defined by Sun. Any program that depends on the Microsoft-specific extensions is obviously not portable to other platforms. Microsoft's proprietary extension of the Java platform resulted in legal action between Sun and Microsoft and ultimately caused Microsoft to discontinue ongoing support for Java.

Implementation-specific bugs
: Just as portable code must not depend on implementation-specific features, it must not depend on implementation-specific bugs. If a class or method behaves differently than the specification says it should, a portable program cannot rely on this behavior, which may be different on different platforms.

Implementation-specific behavior
: Sometimes different platforms and different implementations may present different behaviors, all of which are legal according to the Java specification. Portable code must not depend on any one specific behavior. For example, the Java specification does not specify whether threads of equal priority share the CPU or if one long-running thread can starve another thread at the same

priority. If an application assumes one behavior or the other, it may not run properly on all platforms.

Standard extensions
: Portable code can rely on standard extensions to the Java platform, but, if it does so, it should clearly specify which extensions it uses and exit cleanly with an appropriate error message when run on a system that does not have the extensions installed.

Complete programs
: Any portable Java program must be complete and self-contained: it must supply all the classes it uses, except core platform and standard extension classes.

Defining system classes
: Portable Java code never defines classes in any of the system or standard extension packages. Doing so violates the protection boundaries of those packages and exposes package-visible implementation details.

Hardcoded filenames
: A portable program contains no hardcoded file or directory names. This is because different platforms have significantly different filesystem organizations and use different directory separator characters. If you need to work with a file or directory, have the user specify the filename, or at least the base directory beneath which the file can be found. This specification can be done at runtime, in a configuration file, or as a command-line argument to the program. When concatenating a file or directory name to a directory name, use the `File()` constructor or the `File.separator` constant.

Line separators
: Different systems use different characters or sequences of characters as line separators. Do not hardcode "\n", "\r", or "\r\n" as the line separator in your program. Instead, use the `println()` method of `PrintStream` or `PrintWriter`, which automatically terminates a line with the line separator appropriate for the platform, or use the value of the `line.separator` system property.

Mixed event models
: The AWT event model changed dramatically between Java 1.0 and Java 1.1. Although it is often possible to mix these two event models in a program, doing so is not technically portable.

The previous rules are the focus of Sun's "100% Pure Java" portability certification program; you can find out more about this program and read more about the "Pure Java" requirements at *http://java.sun.com/100percent/*.

Java Documentation Comments

Most ordinary comments within Java code explain the implementation details of that code. In contrast, the Java language specification defines a special type of comment known as a doc comment that serves to document the API of your code. A doc comment is an ordinary multiline comment that begins with /** (instead of the usual /*) and ends with */. A doc comment appears immediately before a class, interface, method, or field definition and contains documentation for that class, interface, method, or field. The documentation can include simple HTML formatting tags and other special keywords that provide additional information. Doc comments are ignored by the compiler, but they can be extracted and automatically turned into online HTML documentation by the *javadoc* program. (See Chapter 8, for more information about *javadoc*.) Here is an example class that contains appropriate doc comments:

```
/**
 * This immutable class represents <i>complex
 * numbers</i>.
 *
 * @author David Flanagan
 * @version 1.0
 */
public class Complex {
  /**
   * Holds the real part of this complex number.
   * @see #y
   */
  protected double x;

  /**
   * Holds the imaginary part of this complex number.
   * @see #x
   */
  protected double y;

  /**
   * Creates a new Complex object that represents the complex number
   * x+yi.
   * @param x The real part of the complex number.
   * @param y The imaginary part of the complex number.
   */
  public Complex(double x, double y) {
    this.x = x;
    this.y = y;
  }

  /**
   * Adds two Complex objects and produces a third object that represents
   * their sum.
   * @param c1 A Complex object
   * @param c2 Another Complex object
   * @return  A new Complex object that represents the sum of
   *          <code>c1</code> and
   *          <code>c2</code>.
   * @exception java.lang.NullPointerException
   *            If either argument is <code>null</code>.
   */
  public static Complex add(Complex c1, Complex c2) {
    return new Complex(c1.x + c2.x, c1.y + c2.y);
  }
}
```

Structure of a Doc Comment

The body of a doc comment should begin with a one-sentence summary of the class, interface, method, or field being documented. This sentence may be displayed by itself, as summary documentation, so it should be written to stand on its own. The initial sentence can be followed by any number of other sentences and paragraphs that describe the class, interface, method, or field.

After the descriptive paragraphs, a doc comment can contain any number of other paragraphs, each of which begins with a special doc-comment tag, such as `@author`, `@param`, or `@returns`. These tagged paragraphs provide specific information about the class, interface, method, or field that the *javadoc* program displays in a standard way. The full set of doc-comment tags is listed in the next section.

The descriptive material in a doc comment can contain simple HTML markup tags, such as such as `<I>` for emphasis, `<CODE>` for class, method, and field names, and `<PRE>` for multiline code examples. It can also contain `<P>` tags to break the description into separate paragraphs and `<UL>`, `<LI>`, and related tags to display bulleted lists and similar structures. Remember, however, that the material you write is embedded within a larger, more complex HTML document. For this reason, doc comments should not contain major structural HTML tags, such as `<H2>` or `<HR>`, that might interfere with the structure of the larger document.

Avoid the use of the `<A>` tag to include hyperlinks or cross references in your doc comments. Instead, use the special `{@link}` doc-comment tag, which, unlike the other doc-comment tags, can appear anywhere within a doc comment. As described in the next section, the `{@link}` tag allows you to specify hyperlinks to other classes, interfaces, methods, and fields without knowing the HTML-structuring conventions and filenames used by *javadoc*.

If you want to include an image in a doc comment, place the image file in a *doc-files* subdirectory of the source code directory. Give the image the same name as the class, with an integer suffix. For example, the second image that appears in the doc comment for a class named `Circle` can be included with this HTML tag:

```
<IMG src="doc-files/Circle-2.gif">
```

Because the lines of a doc comment are embedded within a Java comment, any leading spaces and asterisks (*) are stripped from each line of the comment before processing. Thus, you don't need to worry about the asterisks appearing in the generated documentation or about the indentation of the comment affecting the indentation of code examples included within the comment with a `<PRE>` tag.

Conventions

Doc-Comment Tags

As mentioned earlier, *javadoc* recognizes a number of special tags, each of which begins with an @ character. These doc-comment tags allow you to encode specific information into your comments in a standardized way, and they allow *javadoc* to choose the appropriate output format for that information. For example, the `@param` tag lets you specify the name and meaning of a single parameter for a method. *javadoc* can extract this information and display it using an HTML `<DL>` list, an HTML `<TABLE>`, or however it sees fit.

The doc-comment tags recognized by *javadoc* are the following; a doc comment should typically use these tags in the order listed here:

`@author` *name*

Adds an "Author:" entry that contains the specified name. This tag should be used for every class or interface definition, but must not be used for individual methods and fields. If a class has multiple authors, use multiple `@author` tags on adjacent lines. For example:

```
@author David Flanagan
@author Paula Ferguson
```

List the authors in chronological order, with the original author first. If the author is unknown, you can use "unascribed". *javadoc* does not output authorship information unless the `-author` command-line argument is specified.

`@version` *text*

Inserts a "Version:" entry that contains the specified text. For example:

```
@version 1.32, 08/26/99
```

This tag should be included in every class and interface doc comment, but cannot be used for individual methods and fields. This tag is often used in conjunction with the automated version-numbering capabilities of a version-control system, such as SCCS, RCS, or CVS. *javadoc* does not output version information in its generated documentation unless the `-version` command-line argument is specified.

`@param` *parameter-name description*

Adds the specified parameter and its description to the "Parameters:" section of the current method. The doc comment for a method or constructor must contain one `@param` tag for each parameter the method expects. These tags should appear in the same order as the parameters specified by the method. The tag cannot be used in class, interface, or field doc comments. You are encouraged to use phrases and sentence fragments where possible, to keep the descriptions brief. However, if a parameter requires detailed documentation, the description can wrap onto multiple lines and include as much text as necessary. You can also use spaces to align the descriptions with each other. For example:

```
@param o      the object to insert
@param index  the position to insert it at
```

`@return` *description*

Inserts a "Returns:" section that contains the specified description. This tag should appear in every doc comment for a method, unless the method returns `void` or is a constructor. The tag must not appear in class, interface, or field doc comments. The description can be as long as necessary, but consider using a sentence fragment to keep it short. For example:

```
@return <code>true</code> if the insertion is successful, or
        <code>false</code> if the list already contains the
        specified object.
```

`@exception` *`full-classname description`*

Adds a "Throws:" entry that contains the specified exception name and description. A doc comment for a method or constructor should contain an `@exception` tag for every checked exception that appears in its `throws` clause. For example:

```
@exception java.io.FileNotFoundException
           If the specified file could not be found
```

The `@exception` tag can optionally be used to document unchecked exceptions (i.e., subclasses of `RuntimeException`) the method may throw, when these are exceptions that a user of the method may reasonably want to catch. If a method can throw more than one exception, use multiple `@exception` tags on adjacent lines and list the exceptions in alphabetical order. The description can be as short or as long as necessary to describe the significance of the exception. This doc-comment tag cannot be used in class, interface, or field comments. The `@throws` tag is a synonym for `@exception`.

`@throws` *`full-classname description`*

This tag is a synonym for `@exception`. It was introduced in Java 1.2.

`@see` *`reference`*

Adds a "See Also:" entry that contains the specified reference. This tag can appear in any kind of doc comment. *`reference`* can take three different forms. If it begins with a quote character, it is taken to be the name of a book or some other printed resource and is displayed as is. If *`reference`* begins with a < character, it is taken to be an arbitrary HTML hyperlink that uses the `<A>` tag and the hyperlink is inserted into the output documentation as is. This form of the `@see` tag can insert links to other online documents, such as a programmer's guide or user's manual.

If *`reference`* is not a quoted string or a hyperlink, the `@see` tag is expected to have the following form:

```
@see feature label
```

In this case, *javadoc* outputs the text specified by *`label`* and encodes it as a hyperlink to the specified *`feature`*. If *`label`* is omitted (as it usually is), *javadoc* uses the name of the specified *`feature`* instead.

`feature` can refer to a package, class, interface, method, constructor, or field, using one of the following forms:

`pkgname`

A reference to the named package. For example:

```
@see java.lang.reflect
```

`pkgname.classname`

A reference to a class or interface specified with its full package name. For example:

```
@see java.util.List
```

Conventions

classname

A reference to a class or interface specified without its package name. For example:

```
@see List
```

javadoc resolves this reference by searching the current package and the list of imported classes for a class with this name.

classname#methodname

A reference to a named method or constructor within the specified class. For example:

```
@see java.io.InputStream#reset
@see InputStream#close
```

If the class is specified without its package name, it is resolved as described for *classname*. This syntax is ambiguous if the method is overloaded or the class defines a field by the same name.

classname#methodname(paramtypes)

A reference to a method or constructor with the type of its parameters explicitly specified. This form of the @see tag is useful when cross-referencing an overloaded method. For example:

```
@see InputStream#read(byte[], int, int)
```

#methodname

A reference to a non-overloaded method or constructor in the current class or interface or one of the containing classes, superclasses, or superinterfaces of the current class or interface. Use this concise form to refer to other methods in the same class. For example:

```
@see #setBackgroundColor
```

#methodname(paramtypes)

A reference to a method or constructor in the current class or interface or one of its superclasses or containing classes. This form works with overloaded methods because it lists the types of the method parameters explicitly. For example:

```
@see #setPosition(int, int)
```

classname#fieldname

A reference to a named field within the specified class. For example:

```
@see java.io.BufferedInputStream#buf
```

If the class is specified without its package name, it is resolved as described for *classname*.

#fieldname

A reference to a field in the current class or interface or one of the containing classes, superclasses, or superinterfaces of the current class or interface. For example:

```
@see #x
```

`@deprecated` *explanation*

As of Java 1.1, this tag specifies that the following class, interface, method, or field has been deprecated and that its use should be avoided. *javadoc* adds a prominent "Deprecated" entry to the documentation and includes the specified *explanation* text. This text should specify when the class or member was deprecated and, if possible, suggest a replacement class or member and include a link to it. For example:

```
@deprecated As of Version 3.0, this method is replaced
            by {@link #setColor}.
```

Although the Java compiler ignores all comments, it does take note of the `@deprecated` tag in doc comments. When this tag appears, the compiler notes the deprecation in the class file it produces. This allows it to issue warnings for other classes that rely on the deprecated feature.

`@since` *version*

Specifies when the class, interface, method, or field was added to the API. This tag should be followed by a version number or other version specification. For example:

```
@since JNUT 3.0
```

Every class and interface doc comment should include an `@since` tag, and any methods or fields added after the initial release of the class or interface should have `@since` tags in their doc comments.

`@serial` *description*

Technically, the way a class is serialized is part of its public API, and if you are writing a class that you expect to be serialized, you should document its serialization format using `@serial` and the related tags listed later. `@serial` should appear in the doc comment for any field that is part of the serialized state of a `Serializable` class. For classes that use the default serialization mechanism, this means all fields that are not declared `transient`, including fields declared `private`. The *description* should be a brief description of the field and of its purpose within a serialized object.

In Java 1.4, you can also use the `@serial` tag at the class and package level to specify whether a "serialized form page" should be generated for the class or package. The syntax is:

```
@serial include
@serial exclude
```

`@serialField` *name type description*

A `Serializable` class can define its serialized format by declaring an array of `ObjectStreamField` objects in a field named `serialPersistentFields`. For such a class, the doc comment for `serialPersistentFields` should include

Conventions

an `@serialField` tag for each element of the array. Each tag specifies the name, type, and description for a particular field in the serialized state of the class.

`@serialData` *`description`*

A `Serializable` class can define a `writeObject()` method to write data other than that written by the default serialization mechanism. An `Externalizable` class defines a `writeExternal()` method responsible for writing the complete state of an object to the serialization stream. The `@serialData` tag should be used in the doc comments for these `writeObject()` and `writeExternal()` methods, and the *`description`* should document the serialization format used by the method.

`@beaninfo` *`info`*

This nonstandard tag provides information about JavaBeans components and their methods. This tag is not currently used by *javadoc* (although it is under consideration) but is used by a tool inside Sun that extracts information from `@beaninfo` tags for a class and outputs an appropriate `java.beans.BeanInfo` class. This tag appears in the source code of the Swing component classes in Java 1.2. A typical usage looks like this:

```
@beaninfo         bound: true
            description: the background color of this JavaBeans component
```

In addition to the preceding tags, *javadoc* also supports several *inline tags* that may appear anywhere that HTML text appears in a doc comment. Because these tags appear directly within the flow of HTML text, they require the use of curly braces as delimiters to separate the tagged text from the HTML text. The supported inline tags are the following:

`{@link` *`reference`*`}`

In Java 1.2 and later, the `@link` tag is like the `@see` tag except that, instead of placing a link to the specified *`reference`* in a special "See Also:" section, it inserts the link inline. A `@link` tag can appear anywhere that HTML text appears in a doc comment. In other words, it can appear in the initial description of the class, interface, method, or field and in the descriptions associated with the `@param`, `@returns`, `@exception`, and `@deprecated` tags. The *`reference`* for the `@link` tag uses the same syntax as the `@see` tag documented previously. For example:

```
@param regexp The regular expression to search for. This string
              argument must follow the syntax rules described for
              {@link RegExpParser}.
```

`{@linkplain` *`reference`*`}`

In Java 1.4 and later, the `{@linkplain}` tag is just like the `{@link}` tag, except that the text of the link is formatted using the normal font rather than the code font used by the `{@link}` tag. This is most useful when *`reference`* contains both a *`feature`* to link to and a *`label`* that specifies alternate text to be displayed in the link. See the `@see` tag earlier in this section for a discussion of the *`feature`* and *`label`* portions of the *`reference`* argument.

`{@inheritDoc}`

When a method overrides a method in a superclass or implements a method in an interface, you can omit a doc comment, and *javadoc* will automatically inherit the documentation from the overridden or implemented method. In Java 1.4, however, the `{@inheritDoc}` tag allows you to inherit only the text of individual tags. If you inherit the entire doc comment, it allows you to wrap that inherited text in text of your own. To inherit individual tags, use it like this:

```
@param index @{inheritDoc}
@return @{inheritDoc}
```

To inherit the entire doc comment, including your own text before and after it, use the tag like this:

```
This method overrides {@link java.langObject#toString}, documented as
follows:
<P>{@inheritDoc}
<P>This overridden version of the method returns a string of the form...
```

`{@docRoot}`

This inline tag takes no parameters and is replaced with a reference to the root directory of the generated documentation. It is useful in hyperlinks that refer to an external file, such as an image or a copyright statement:

```
<img src="{@docroot}/images/logo.gif">
This is <a href="{@docRoot}/legal.html">Copyrighted</a> material.
```

`{@docRoot}` was introduced in Java 1.3.

Doc Comments for Packages

Documentation comments for classes, interfaces, methods, constructors, and fields appear in Java source code immediately before the definitions of the features they document. *javadoc* can also read and display summary documentation for packages. Since a package is defined in a directory, not in a single file of source code, *javadoc* looks for the package documentation in a file named *package.html* in the directory that contains the source code for the classes of the package.

The *package.html* file should contain simple HTML documentation for the package. It can also contain `@see`, `@link`, `@deprecated`, and `@since` tags. Since *package.html* is not a file of Java source code, the documentation it contains should *not* be a Java comment (i.e., it should not be enclosed within `/**` and `*/` characters). Finally, any `@see` and `@link` tags that appear in *package.html* must use fully qualified class names.

In addition to defining a *package.html* file for each package, you can also provide high-level documentation for a group of packages by defining an *overview.html* file in the source tree for those packages. When *javadoc* is run over that source tree, it uses *overview.html* as the highest level overview it displays.

CHAPTER 8

Java Development Tools

Sun's implementation of Java includes a number of tools for Java developers. Chief among these are the Java interpreter and the Java compiler, of course, but there are a number of others as well. This chapter documents all the tools shipped with the Java 2 SDK (formerly known as the JDK), except for the RMI and IDL tools that are specific to enterprise programming. Those tools are documented in *Java Enterprise in a Nutshell* (O'Reilly).

The tools documented here are part of Sun's development kit; they are implementation details and not part of the Java specification itself. If you are using a Java development environment other than Sun's SDK (or a port of it), you should consult your vendor's tool documentation.

Some examples in this chapter use Unix conventions for file and path separators. If Windows is your development platform, change forward slashes in filenames to backward slashes, and colons in path specifications to semicolons.

appletviewer — JDK 1.0 and later

The Java Applet Viewer

Synopsis

```
appletviewer [ options ] url | file...
```

Description

appletviewer reads or downloads the one or more HTML documents specified by the filename or URL on the command line. Next, it downloads any applets specified in any of those files and runs each applet in a separate window. If the specified document or documents do not contain any applets, *appletviewer* does nothing.

appletviewer recognizes applets specified with the <APPLET> tag and, in Java 1.2 and later, the <OBJECT> and <EMBED> tags.

Options

appletviewer recognizes the following options:

-debug
: If this option is specified, *appletviewer* is started within *jdb* (the Java debugger). This allows you to debug the applets referenced by the document or documents.

-encoding *enc*
: This option specifies the character encoding that *appletviewer* should use when reading the contents of the specified files or URLs. It is used in the conversion of applet parameter values to Unicode. Java 1.1 and later.

-J*javaoption*
: This option passes the specified *javaoption* as a command-line argument to the Java interpreter. *javaoption* should not contain spaces. If a multiword option must be passed to the Java interpreter, multiple -J options should be used. See *java* for a list of valid Java interpreter options. Java 1.1 and later.

appletviewer also recognizes the -classic, -native, and -green options that the Java interpreter recognizes. See *java* for details on these options.

Commands

Each window displayed by *appletviewer* contains a single Applet menu, with the following commands available:

Restart
: Stops and destroys the current applet, then reinitializes and restarts it.

Reload
: Stops, destroys, and unloads the applet, then reloads, reinitializes, and restarts it.

Stop
: Stops the current applet. Java 1.1 and later.

Save
: Serializes the applet and saves the serialized applet in the file *Applet.ser* in the user's home directory. The applet should be stopped before selecting this option. Java 1.1 and later.

Start
: Restarts a stopped applet. Java 1.1 and later.

Clone
: Creates a new copy of the applet in a new *appletviewer* window.

Tag
: Pops up a dialog box that displays the <APPLET> tag and all associated <PARAM> tags that created the current applet.

Info
: Pops up a dialog box that contains information about the applet. This information is provided by the getAppletInfo() and getParameterInfo() methods implemented by the applet.

Edit
: This command is not implemented. The Edit menu item is disabled.

Character Encoding
: Displays the current character encoding in the status line. Java 1.1 and later.

Print
: Prints the applet. Java 1.1 and later.

Properties
: Displays a dialog that allows the user to set *appletviewer* preferences, including settings for firewall and caching proxy servers.

Close
: Closes the current *appletviewer* window.

Quit
: Quits *appletviewer*, closing all open windows.

Environment

CLASSPATH
: In Java 1.0 and Java 1.1, *appletviewer* uses the CLASSPATH environment variable in the same way the Java interpreter does. See *java* for details. In Java 1.2 and later, however, *appletviewer* ignores this environment variable to better simulate the action of a web browser.

Properties

When it starts up, *appletviewer* reads property definitions from the file *~/.hotjava/properties* (Unix) or *.hotjava\properties* relative to the HOME environment variable (Windows). These properties are stored in the system properties list and can specify the various error and status messages the applet viewer displays, as well as its security policies and use of proxy servers. The properties that affect security and proxies are described in the following sections. Most users of *appletviewer* do not need to use these properties.

Security properties

The following properties specify the security restrictions *appletviewer* places on untrusted applets:

acl.read
: A list of files and directories an untrusted applet is allowed to read. The elements of the list should be separated with colons on Unix systems and semicolons on Windows systems. On Unix systems, the ~ character is replaced with the home directory of the current user. If the plus sign appears as an element in the list, it is replaced by the value of the acl.read.default property. This provides an easy way to enable read access—by simply setting acl.read to "+". By default, untrusted applets are not allowed to read any files or directories.

acl.read.default
: A list of files and directories that are readable by untrusted applets if the acl.read property contains a plus sign.

acl.write
: A list of files and directories an untrusted applet is allowed to write to. The elements of the list should be separated with colons on Unix systems and semicolons on Windows systems. On Unix systems, the ~ character is replaced with the home directory of the current user. If the plus sign appears as an element in the list, it is replaced by the value of the acl.write.default property. This provides an easy way to enable write access—by simply setting acl.write to "+". By default, untrusted applets are not allowed to write to any files or directories.

acl.write.default
: A list of files and directories that are writable by untrusted applets if the acl.write property contains a plus sign.

appletviewer.security.mode
: Specifies the types of network access an untrusted applet is allowed to perform. If it is set to "none", the applet can perform no networking at all. The value "host" is the default; it specifies that the applet can connect only to the host from which it was loaded. The value "unrestricted" specifies that an applet can connect to any host without restrictions.

package.restrict.access.*package-prefix*
: Properties of this form can be set to true to prevent untrusted applets from using classes in any package that has the specified package name prefix as the first component of its name. For example, to prevent applets from using any of the Sun classes (such as the Java compiler and the applet viewer itself) that are shipped with the Java SDK, you can specify the following property:

```
package.restrict.access.sun=true
```

appletviewer sets this property to true by default for the sun.* and netscape.* packages.

package.restrict.definition.*package-prefix*
: Properties of this form can be set to true to prevent untrusted applets from defining classes in a package that has the specified package name prefix as the first component of its name. For example, to prevent an applet from defining classes in any of the standard Java packages, you can specify the following property:

```
package.restrict.definition.java=true
```

appletviewer sets this property to true by default for the java.*, sun.*, and netscape.* packages.

property.applet
: When a property of this form is set to true (as of Java 1.1), it specifies that an applet should be allowed to read the property named property from the system properties list. By default, applets are allowed to read only 10 standard system properties (as detailed in *Java Foundation Classes in a Nutshell* [O'Reilly]). For example, to allow an applet to read the user.home property, specify a property of the form:

```
user.home.applet=true
```

Proxy properties

appletviewer uses the following properties to configure its use of firewall and caching proxy servers:

firewallHost
: The firewall proxy host to connect to if firewallSet is true.

firewallPort
: The port of the firewall proxy host to connect to if firewallSet is true.

firewallSet
: Whether the applet viewer should use a firewall proxy. Values are true or false.

proxyHost
: The caching proxy host to connect to if proxySet is true.

proxyPort
: The port of the caching proxy host to connect to if proxySet is true.

proxySet
: Whether the applet viewer should use a caching proxy. Values are true or false.

See also
java, javac, jdb

extcheck — Java 2 SDK 1.2 and later

JAR Version Conflict Utility

Synopsis

```
extcheck [-verbose] jarfile
```

Description
extcheck checks to see if the extension contained in the specified *jarfile* (or a newer version of that extension) has already been installed on the system. It does this by reading the Specification-Title and Specification-Version manifest attributes from the specified *jarfile* and from all of the JAR files found in the system extensions directory.

extcheck is designed for use in automated installation scripts. Without the -verbose option, it does not print the results of its check. Instead, it sets its exit code to 0 if the specified extension does not conflict with any installed extensions and can be safely installed. It sets its exit code to a nonzero value if an extension with the same name is already installed and has a specification version number equal to or greater than the version of the specified file.

Options

-verbose
: Lists the installed extensions as they are checked and displays the results of the check.

See also
jar

jar — JDK 1.1 and later

Java Archive Tool

Synopsis

```
jar c|t|u|x[f][m][M][0][v] [jar-file] [manifest] [-C directory] [input-files]
jar -i [jar-file]
```

Description
jar is a tool that can create and manipulate Java Archive (JAR) files. A JAR file is a ZIP file that contains Java class files, auxiliary resource files required by those classes, and optional meta-information. This meta-information includes a manifest file that lists the contents of the JAR archive and provides auxiliary information about each file.

The *jar* command can create JAR files, list the contents of JAR files, and extract files from a JAR archive. In Java 1.2 and later, it can also add files to an existing archive or update the manifest file of an archive. In Java 1.3 and later, *jar* can also add an index entry to a JAR file.

Options
The syntax of the *jar* command is reminiscent of the Unix *tar* (tape archive) command. Most options to *jar* are specified as a block of concatenated letters passed as a single argument, rather than as individual command-line arguments. The first letter of the first argument specifies what action *jar* is to perform; it is required. Other letters are optional. The various file arguments depend on which letters are specified.

Command options
The first letter of the first option to *jar* specifies the basic operation *jar* is to perform. Here are the four possible options:

`c`
: Creates a new JAR archive. A list of input files and/or directories must be specified as the final arguments to *jar*. The newly created JAR file has a *META-INF/MANIFEST.MF* file as its first entry. This automatically created manifest lists the contents of the JAR file and contains a message digest for each file.

`t`
: Lists the contents of a JAR archive.

`u`
: Updates the contents of a JAR archive. Any files listed on the command line are added to the archive. When used with the `m` option, this adds the specified manifest information to the JAR file. Java 1.2 and later.

`x`
: Extracts the contents of a JAR archive. The files and directories specified on the command line are extracted and created in the current working directory. If no file or directory names are specified, all the files and directories in the JAR file are extracted.

Modifier options
Each of the four command specifier letters can be followed by additional letters that provide further detail about the operation to be performed:

`f`
: Indicates that *jar* is to operate on a JAR file whose name is specified on the command line. If this option is not present, *jar* reads a JAR file from standard input and/or writes a JAR file to standard output. If the `f` option is present, the command line must contain the name of the JAR file to operate on.

`m`
: When *jar* creates or updates a JAR file, it automatically creates (or updates) a manifest file named *META-INF/MANIFEST.MF* in the JAR archive. This default manifest simply lists the contents of the JAR file. Many JAR files require additional information to be specified in the manifest; the `m` option tells the *jar* command that a manifest template is specified on the command line. *jar* reads this manifest file and stores all the information it contains into the *META-INF/MANIFEST.MF* file it creates. This `m` option should be used only with the `c` or `u` commands, not with the `t` or `x` commands.

`M`
: Used with the `c` and `u` commands to tell *jar* not to create a default manifest file.

v
: Tells *jar* to produce verbose output.

0
: Used with the c and u commands to tell *jar* to store files in the JAR archive without compressing them. Note that this option is the digit zero, not the letter O.

Files
The first option to *jar* consists of an initial command letter and various option letters. This first option is followed by a list of files:

jar
: If the first option contains the letter f, that option must be followed by the name of the JAR file to create or manipulate.

manifest
: If the first option contains the letter m, that option must be followed by the name of the file that contains manifest information. If the first option contains both the letters f and m, the JAR and manifest files should be listed in the same order the f and m options appear. In other words, if f comes before m, the JAR filename should come before the manifest filename. Otherwise, if m comes before f, the manifest filename should be specified before the JAR filename.

files
: The list of one or more files and/or directories to be inserted into or extracted from the JAR archive.

Additional options
In addition to all the options listed previously, *jar* also supports the following:

-C *dir*
: Used within the list of files to process; it tells *jar* to change to the specified *dir* while processing the subsequent files and directories. The subsequent file and directory names are interpreted relative to *dir* and are inserted into the JAR archive without *dir* as a prefix. Any number of -C options can be used; each remains in effect until the next is encountered. The directory specified by a -C option is interpreted relative to the current working directory, not the directory specified by the previous -C option. Java 1.2 and later.

-i *jarfile*
: The -i option is used instead of the c, t, u, and x commands. It tells *jar* to produce an index of all JAR files referenced by the specified *jarfile*. The index is stored in a file named *META-INF/INDEX.LIST*; a Java interpreter or applet viewer can use the information in this index to optimize its class and resource lookup algorithm and avoid downloading unnecessary JAR files. Java 1.3 and later.

Examples
The *jar* command has a confusing array of options, but, in most cases, its use is quite simple. To create a simple JAR file that contains all the class files in the current directory and all files in a subdirectory called *images*, you can type:

```
% jar cf my.jar *.class images
```

To verbosely list the contents of a JAR archive:

```
% jar tvf your.jar
```

To extract the manifest file from a JAR file for examination or editing:

```
% jar xf the.jar META-INF/MANIFEST.MF
```

To update the manifest of a JAR file:

```
% jar ufm my.jar manifest.template
```

See also
jarsigner

jarsigner — Java 2 SDK 1.2 and later

JAR Signing and Verification Tool

Synopsis

```
jarsigner [options] jarfile signer
jarsigner -verify jarfile
```

Description
jarsigner adds a digital signature to the specified *jarfile*, or, if the -verify option is specified, it verifies the digital signature or signatures already attached to the JAR file. The specified *signer* is a case-insensitive nickname or alias for the entity whose signature is to be used. The specified *signer* name is used to look up the private key that generates the signature.

When you apply your digital signature to a JAR file, you are implicitly vouching for the contents of the archive. You are offering your personal word that the JAR file contains only nonmalicious code, files that do not violate copyright laws, and so forth. When you verify a digitally signed JAR file, you can determine who the signer or signers of the file are and (if the verification succeeds) that the contents of the JAR file have not been changed, corrupted, or tampered with since the signature or signatures were applied. Verifying a digital signature is entirely different from deciding whether or not you trust the person or organization whose signature you verified.

jarsigner and the related *keytool* program replace the *javakey* program of Java 1.1.

Options
jarsigner defines a number of options, many of which specify how a private key is to be found for the specified *signer*. Most of these options are unnecessary when using the -verify option to verify a signed JAR file:

-certs
: If this option is specified along with either the -verify or -verbose option, it causes *jarsigner* to display details of the public-key certificates associated with the signed JAR file.

-J*javaoption*
: Passes the specified *javaoption* directly to the Java interpreter.

-keypass *password*
: Specifies the password that encrypts the private key of the specified *signer*. If this option is not specified, *jarsigner* prompts you for the password.

-keystore *url*
: A *keystore* is a file that contains keys and certificates. This option specifies the filename or URL of the keystore in which the private- and public-key certificates of the specified *signer* are looked up. The default is the file named *.keystore* in the user's home directory (the value of the system property user.home). This is also the default location of the keystore managed by *keytool*.

-sigfile *basename*
: Specifies the base names of the *.SF* and *.DSA* files added to the *META-INF/* directory of the JAR file. If you leave this option unspecified, the base filename is chosen based on the *signer* name.

-signedjar *outputfile*
: Specifies the name for the signed JAR file created by *jarsigner*. If this option is not specified, *jarsigner* overwrites the *jarfile* specified on the command line.

-storepass *password*
: Specifies the password that verifies the integrity of the keystore (but does not encrypt the private key). If this option is omitted, *jarsigner* prompts you for the password.

-storetype *type*
: Specifies the type of keystore specified by the -keystore option. The default is the system-default keystore type, which on most systems is the Java Keystore type, known as "JKS". If you have the Java Cryptography Extension installed, you may want to use a "JCEKS" keystore instead.

-verbose
: Displays extra information about the signing or verification process.

-verify
: Specifies that *jarsigner* should verify the specified JAR file rather than sign it.

See also
jar, keytool, javakey

java — JDK 1.0 and later

The Java Interpreter

Synopsis

```
java [ interpreter-options ] classname [ program-arguments ]
java [ interpreter-options ] -jar jarfile [ program-arguments ]
```

Description

java is the Java byte-code interpreter; it runs Java programs. The program to be run is the class specified by classname. This must be a fully qualified name: it must include the package name of the class, but not the *.class* file extension. For example:

```
% java david.games.Checkers
% java Test
```

The specified class must define a main() method with exactly the following signature:

```
public static void main(String[] args)
```

This method serves as the program entry point: the interpreter begins execution here.

In Java 1.2 and later, a program can be packaged in an executable JAR file. To run a program packaged in this fashion, use the -jar option to specify the JAR file. The manifest of an executable JAR file must contain a Main-Class attribute that specifies which class within the JAR file contains the main() method at which the interpreter is to begin execution.

Any command-line options that precede the name of the class or JAR file to execute are options to the Java interpreter itself. Any options that follow the class name or JAR filename are options to the program; they are ignored by the Java interpreter and passed as an array of strings to the main() method of the program.

The Java interpreter runs until the `main()` method exits, and any threads (except for threads marked as daemon threads) created by the program have also exited.

Interpreter versions

The *java* program is the basic version of the Java interpreter. In addition to this program, however, there are several other versions of the Java interpreter. Each of these versions is similar to *java*, but has a specialized function. The various interpreter programs are the following:

java
: This is the basic version of the Java interpreter; it is usually the correct one to use. The behavior and set of supported options changed significantly between Java 1.1 and Java 1.2, and there have been minor changes between other releases

oldjava
: This version of the interpreter is included in Java 1.2 and Java 1.3 for compatibility with the Java 1.1 interpreter. It loads classes using the Java 1.1 class-loading scheme. Very few Java applications need to use this version of the interpreter, and it has been removed from Java 1.4.

javaw
: This version of the interpreter is included only on Windows platforms. Use *javaw* when you want to run a Java program (from a script, for example) without forcing a console window to appear. In Java 1.2 and Java 1.3, there is also an *oldjavaw* program that combines the features of *oldjava* and *javaw*.

java_g
: In Java 1.0 and Java 1.1, *java_g* is a debugging version of the Java interpreter. It includes a few specialized command-line options, but is rarely used. Windows platforms also define a *javaw_g* program. *java_g* is not included in Java 1.2 or later versions.

Client or Server VM
: Sun's "HotSpot" virtual machine comes in two versions: one is tuned for use with short-lived client applications and one for use with long-running server code. In Java 1.4, you can select the server version of the VM with the `-server` option. You can specify the "Client VM" (which is the default) with the `-client` option.

Classic VM
: In Java 1.3, you can use the `-classic` option to specify that you want to use the "Classic VM" (essentially the same as the Java 1.2 VM) instead of the HotSpot VM (which uses incremental compilation). This option has been removed in Java 1.4.

Just-in-time compiler
: In Java 1.2, and in Java 1.3 when you specify the `-classic` option, the Java interpreter uses a just-in-time compiler (if one is available for your platform). A JIT converts Java byte codes to native machine instructions at runtime and significantly speeds up the execution of a typical Java program. If you do not want to use the JIT, you can disable it by setting the `JAVA_COMPILER` environment variable to "NONE" or the `java.compiler` system property to "NONE" using the `-D` option:

```
% setenv JAVA_COMPILER NONE          // Unix csh syntax
% java -Djava.compiler=NONE MyProgram
```

If you want to use a different JIT compiler implementation, set the environment variable or system property to the name of the desired implementation. This environment variable and property are no longer used in Java 1.4, which uses the HotSpot VM, which includes efficient JIT technology.

Threading systems

On Solaris and related Unix platforms, you have a choice of the type of threads used by the Java 1.2 interpreter and the "Classic VM" of Java 1.3. To use native OS threads, specify `-native`. To use nonnative, or green, threads (the default), specify `-green`. In Java 1.3, the default "Client VM" uses native threads. Specifying `-green` or `-native` in Java 1.3 implicitly specifies `-classic` as well. These options are no longer supported (or necessary) in Java 1.4.

Options

`-classic`

Runs the "Classic VM" instead of the default high-performance "Client VM." Java 1.3 only.

`-classpath` *path*

Specifies the directories, JAR files, and ZIP files *java* searches when trying to load a class. In Java 1.0 and 1.1, and with the *oldjava* interpreter, this option specifies the location of system classes, extension classes, and application classes. In Java 1.2 and later, this option specifies only the location of application classes.

`-client`

Optimizes the incremental compilation of the HotSpot VM for typical client-side applications. Java 1.4 and later. See also the `-server` option.

`-cp`

A synonym for `-classpath`. Java 1.2 and later.

`-cs`, `-checksource`

Both options tell *java* to check the modification times on the specified class file and its corresponding source file. If the class file cannot be found or if it is out of date, it is automatically recompiled from the source. Java 1.0 and Java 1.1 only; these options are not available in Java 1.2 and later.

`-D`*propertyname*`=`*value*

Defines *propertyname* to equal *value* in the system properties list. Your Java program can then look up the specified value by its property name. You can specify any number of `-D` options. For example:

```
% java -Dawt.button.color=gray -Dmy.class.pointsize=14 my.class
```

`-d32`

Runs in 32-bit mode. This option is valid in Java 1.4 and later but is currently implemented only for Solaris platforms.

`-d64`

Runs in 64-bit mode. This option is valid in Java 1.4 and later but is currently implemented only for Solaris platforms.

`-da[:`*where*`]`

Disables assertions. See `-disableassertions`. Java 1.4 and later.

`-debug`

Causes *java* to start up in a way that allows the *jdb* debugger to attach itself to the interpreter session. In Java 1.2 and later, this option has been replaced with `-Xdebug`.

-disableassertions[:*where*]
: Disables assertions. It is new in Java 1.4 and can be abbreviated -da. Used alone, it disables all assertions (except those in the system classes), which is the default. To disable assertions in a single class, follow the option with a colon and the fully qualified class name. To disable assertions in an entire package (and all of its subpackages), follow this option with a colon, the name of the package, and three dots. See also -enableassertions and -disablesystemassertions.

-disablesystemassertions
: Disables assertions in all system classes (which is the default). This option is new in Java 1.4. It can be abbreviated -dsa and takes no options.

-dsa
: An abbreviation for -disablesystemassertions. Java 1.4 and later.

-ea[:*where*]
: Enables assertions. An abbreviation for -enableassertions. Java 1.4 and later.

-enableassertions[:*where*]
: Enables assertions. This option is new in Java 1.4 and can be abbreviated -ea. Used alone, it enables all assertions (except in system classes). To enable assertions in a single class, follow the option with a colon and the full class name. To enable assertions in an entire package (and all of its subpackages), follow the option with a colon, the name of the package, and three dots. See also -disableassertions and -enablesystemassertions.

-enablesystemassertions
: Enables assertions in all system classes. May be abbreviated -esa. Java 1.4 and later.

-esa
: An abbreviation for -enablesystemassertions. Java 1.4 and later.

-green
: Selects nonnative, or green, threads on operating systems such as Solaris and Linux that support multiple styles of threading. This is the default in Java 1.2. In Java 1.3, using this option also selects the -classic option. See also -native. Java 1.2 and 1.3 only.

-help, -?
: Prints a usage message and exits. See also -X.

-jar *jarfile*
: Runs the specified executable *jarfile*. The manifest of the specified *jarfile* must contain a Main-Class attribute that identifies the class with the main() method at which program execution is to begin. Java 1.2 and later.

-native
: Selects native threads, instead of the default green threads, on operating systems such as Solaris that support multiple styles of threading. Using native threads can be advantageous in some circumstances, such as when running on a multi-CPU computer. In Java 1.3, the default HotSpot virtual machine uses native threads. Java 1.2 and 1.3 only.

-showversion
: Works like the -version option, except that the interpreter continues running after printing the version information. Java 1.3 and later.

-verbose, -verbose:class
: Prints a message each time *java* loads a class. In Java 1.2 and later, you can use -verbose:class as a synonym.

-verbose:gc
: Prints a message when garbage collection occurs. Java 1.2 and later. Prior to Java 1.2, use -verbosegc.

-verbose:jni
: Prints a message when native methods are called. Java 1.2 and later.

-version
: Prints the version of the Java interpreter and exits.

-X
: Displays usage information for the nonstandard interpreter options (those beginning with -X) and exits. See also -help. Java 1.2 and later.

-Xbatch
: Tells the HotSpot VM to perform all just-in-time compilation in the foreground, regardless of the time required for compilation. Without this option, the VM compiles methods in the background while interpreting them in the foreground. Java 1.3 and later.

-Xbootclasspath:*path*
: Specifies a search path consisting of directories, ZIP files, and JAR files the *java* interpreter should use to look up system classes. Use of this option is very rare. Java 1.2 and later.

-Xbootclasspath/a:*path*
: Appends the specified *path* to the system classpath. Java 1.3 and later.

-Xbootclasspath/p:*path*
: Prepends the specified *path* to the system boot classpath. Java 1.3 and later.

-Xcheck:jni
: Performs additional checks when using Java Native Interface functions. Java 1.2 and later.

-Xdebug
: Starts the interpreter in a way that allows a debugger to communicate with it. Java 1.2 and later. Prior to Java 1.2, use -debug.

-Xfuture
: Strictly checks the format of all class files loaded. Without this option, *java* performs the same checks that were performed in Java 1.1. Java 1.2 and later.

-Xincgc
: Uses incremental garbage collection. In this mode the garbage collector runs continuously in the background, and a running program is rarely, if ever, subject to noticeable pauses while garbage collection occurs. Using this option typically results in a 10% decrease in overall performance, however. Java 1.3 and later.

-Xint
: Tells the HotSpot VM to operate in interpreted mode only, without performing any just-in-time compilation. Java 1.3 and later.

-Xloggc:*filename*
Logs garbage collection events with timestamps to the named file.

-Xmixed
Tells the HotSpot VM to perform just-in-time compilation on frequently used methods ("hotspots") and execute other methods in interpreted mode. This is the default behavior. Contrast with -Xbatch and -Xint. Java 1.3 and later.

-Xms *initmem*[k|m]
Specifies how much memory is allocated for the heap when the interpreter starts up. By default, *initmem* is specified in bytes. You can specify it in kilobytes by appending the letter k or in megabytes by appending the letter m. The default is 1 MB. For large or memory-intensive applications (such as the Java compiler), you can improve runtime performance by starting the interpreter with a larger amount of memory. You must specify an initial heap size of at least 1,000 bytes. Java 1.2 and later. Prior to Java 1.2, use -ms.

-Xmx*maxmem*[k|m]
Specifies the maximum heap size the interpreter uses for dynamically allocated objects and arrays. *maxmem* is specified in bytes by default. You can specify *maxmem* in kilobytes by appending the letter k and in megabytes by appending the letter m. The default is 16 MB. You cannot specify a heap size less than 1,000 bytes. Java 1.2 and later. Prior to Java 1.2, use -mx.

-Xnoclassgc
Does not garbage-collect classes. Java 1.2 and later. In Java 1.1, use -noclassgc.

-Xprof
Prints profiling output to standard output. Java 1.3 and later. In Java 1.2, or when using the -classic option, use -Xrunhprof. Prior to Java 1.2, use -prof.

-Xrs
Requests that the interpreter use fewer operating system signals. This option may improve performance on some systems. Java 1.2 and later.

-Xrunhprof:*suboptions*
Turns on CPU, heap, or monitor profiling. *suboptions* is a comma-separated list of name=value pairs. Use -Xrunhprof:help for a list of supported options and values. Java 1.2 and later. Prior to Java 1.2, rudimentary profiling support is available with the -prof option. In Java 1.3, this option is supported if -classic is used, but is not supported by the new HotSpot VM. See -Xprof.

-Xss*size*[k|m]
Sets the thread stack size in bytes, kilobytes, or megabytes. Java 1.3 and later.

Loading classes

The Java interpreter knows where to find the system classes that comprise the Java platform. In Java 1.2 and later, it also knows where to find the class files for all extensions installed in the system extensions directory. However, the interpreter must be told where to find the nonsystem classes that comprise the application to be run.

Class files are stored in directories that correspond to their package name. For example, the class com.davidflanagan.utils.Util is stored in a file *com/davidflanagan/utils/Util.class*. By default, the interpreter uses the current working directory as the root and looks for all classes in and beneath this directory.

The interpreter can also search for classes within ZIP and JAR files. To tell the interpreter where to look for classes, you specify a *classpath*: a list of directories and ZIP and JAR archives. When looking for a class, the interpreter searches each of the specified locations in the order in which they are specified.

The easiest way to specify a classpath is to set the CLASSPATH environment variable, which works much like the PATH variable used by a Unix shell or a Windows command-interpreter path. To specify a classpath in Unix, you might type a command like this:

```
% setenv CLASSPATH .:~/myclasses:/usr/lib/javautils.jar:/usr/lib/javaapps
```

On a Windows system, you might use a command like the following:

```
C:\> set CLASSPATH=.;c:\myclasses;c:\javatools\classes.zip;d:\javaapps
```

Note that Unix and Windows use different characters to separate directory and path components.

You can also specify a classpath with the -classpath or -cp options to the Java interpreter. A path specified with one of these options overrides any path specified by the CLASSPATH environment variable. In Java 1.2 and later, the -classpath option specifies only the search path for application and user classes. Prior to Java 1.2, or when using the *oldjava* interpreter, this option specifies the search path for all classes, including system classes and extension classes.

See also
javac, jdb

javac — JDK 1.0 and later

The Java Compiler

Synopsis

```
javac [ options ] files
oldjavac [ options ] files
```

Description
javac is the Java compiler; it compiles Java source code (in *.java* files) into Java byte codes (in *.class* files). The Java compiler is itself written in Java. The Java compiler has been completely rewritten in Java 1.3, and its performance has been substantially improved. Although the new *javac* is substantially compatible with previous versions of the compiler, the old version of the compiler is provided (in Java 1.3 only) as *oldjavac*.

javac can be passed any number of Java source files, whose names must all end with the *.java* extension. *javac* produces a separate *.class* class file for each class defined in the source files. Each source file can contain any number of classes, although only one can be a public top-level class. The name of the source file (minus the *.java* extension) must match the name of the public class it contains.

In Java 1.2 and later, if a filename specified on the command line begins with the character @, that file is taken not as a Java source file, but as a list of compiler options and Java source files. Thus, if you keep a list of Java source files for a particular project in a file named *project.list*, you can compile all those files at once with the command:

```
% javac @project.list
```

To compile a source file, *javac* must be able to find definitions of all classes used in the source file. It looks for definitions in both source-file and class-file form, automatically compiling any source files that have no corresponding class files or that have been modified since they were most recently compiled.

Options

-bootclasspath *path*
: Specifies the search *path* *javac* uses to look up system classes. This option is handy when you are using *javac* as a cross-compiler to compile classes against different versions of the Java API. For example, you might use the Java 1.3 compiler to compile classes against the Java 1.2 runtime environment. This option does not specify the system classes used to run the compiler itself, only the system classes read by the compiler. See also -extdirs and -target. Java 1.2 and later.

-classpath *path*
: Specifies the path *javac* uses to look up classes referenced in the specified source code. This option overrides any path specified by the CLASSPATH environment variable. The *path* specified is an ordered list of directories, ZIP files, and JAR archives, separated by colons on Unix systems or semicolons on Windows systems. If the -sourcepath option is not set, this option also specifies the search path for source files.

  Prior to Java 1.2, this option specifies the path to system and extension classes, as well as user and application classes, and must be used carefully. In Java 1.2 and later, it specifies only the search path for application classes. See the discussion of "Loading classes" in the documentation for the *java* command for further information.

-d *directory*
: Specifies the directory in which (or beneath which) class files should be stored. By default, *javac* stores the *.class* files it generates in the same directory as the *.java* files those classes were defined in. If the -d option is specified, however, the specified *directory* is treated as the root of the class hierarchy, and *.class* files are placed in this directory or the appropriate subdirectory below it, depending on the package name of the class. Thus, the following command:

```
% javac -d /java/classes Checkers.java
```

  places the file *Checkers.class* in the directory */java/classes* if the *Checkers.java* file has no package statement. On the other hand, if the source file specifies that it is in a package:

```
package com.davidflanagan.games;
```

  the *.class* file is stored in */java/classes/com/davidflanagan/games*. When the -d option is specified, *javac* automatically creates any directories it needs to store its class files in the appropriate place.

-depend
: Tells *javac* to recursively search for out-of-date class files in need of recompilation. This option forces a thorough compilation, but can slow the process down significantly. In Java 1.2 and later, this option has been renamed -Xdepend.

-deprecation
: Tells *javac* to issue a warning for every use of a deprecated API. By default, *javac* issues only a single warning for each source file that uses deprecated APIs. Java 1.1 and later.

-encoding *encoding-name*
: Specifies the name of the character encoding used by the source files if it differs from the default platform encoding.

-extdirs *path*
: Specifies a list of directories to search for extension JAR files. It is used along with -bootclasspath when doing cross-compilation for different versions of the Java runtime environment. Java 1.2 and later.

-g
: Tells *javac* to add line number, source file, and local variable information to the output class files, for use by debuggers. By default, *javac* generates only the line numbers.

-g:none
: Tells *javac* to include no debugging information in the output class files. Java 1.2 and later.

-g:*keyword-list*
: Tells *javac* to output the types of debugging information specified by the comma-separated *keyword-list*. The valid keywords are: source, which specifies source-file information; lines, which specifies line number information; and vars, which specifies local variable debugging information. Java 1.2 and later.

-help
: Prints a list of options.

-J*javaoption*
: Passes the argument *javaoption* directly through to the Java interpreter. For example: -J-Xmx32m. *javaoption* should not contain spaces; if multiple arguments must be passed to the interpreter, use multiple -J options. Java 1.1 and later.

-nowarn
: Tells *javac* not to print warning messages. Errors are still reported as usual.

-nowrite
: Tells *javac* not to create any class files. Source files are parsed as usual, but no output is written. This option is useful when you want to check that a file will compile without actually compiling it. Java 1.0 and Java 1.1 only; this option is not available in Java 1.2 and later.

-O
: Enables optimization of class files to improve their execution speed. Using this option can result in larger class files that are difficult to debug and cause longer compilation times. Prior to Java 1.2, this option is incompatible with -g; turning on -O implicitly turns off -g and turns on -depend.

-source *release-number*
: Specifies the version of Java the code is written in. Use -source 1.4 to compile code that uses the assert statement. This option also sets the -target option. Java 1.4 and later.

-sourcepath *path*
: Specifies the list of directories, ZIP files, and JAR archives that *javac* searches when looking for source files. The files found in this source path are compiled if no corresponding class files are found or if the source files are newer than the class files. By default, source files are searched for in the same places class files are searched for. Java 1.2 and later.

-target *version*
: Specifies the class-file-format version to use for the generated class files. The default *version* is 1.1, which generates class files that can be read and executed by Java 1.0 and later virtual machines. If you specify *version* as 1.2, *javac* increments the class file version number, producing a class file that does not run with a Java 1.0 or Java 1.1 interpreter. There have not been any actual changes to the Java class-file format; the new version number is simply a convenient way to prevent classes that depend on the many new features of Java 1.2 from being run on out-of-date interpreters.

-verbose
: Tells the compiler to display messages about what it is doing. In particular, it causes *javac* to list all the source files it compiles, including files that did not appear on the command line.

-X
: Tells the *javac* compiler to display usage information for its nonstandard options (all of which begin with -X). Java 1.2 and Java 1.4 and later.

-Xdepend
: Tells *javac* to recursively search for source files that need recompilation. This causes a very thorough but time-consuming compilation process. Java 1.2 only; this option was removed in Java 1.3.

-Xstdout
: Tells *javac* to send warning and error messages to the standard output stream instead of the standard error stream. Java 1.2 only.

-Xstdout *filename*
: Tells *javac* to send warning and error messages the specified file instead of writing them to the console. Java 1.4 and later.

-Xswitchcheck
: Warns about case clauses in switch statements that "fall through."

-Xverbosepath
: Displays verbose output explaining where various class files and source files were found. Java 1.2 only.

Environment

CLASSPATH
: Specifies an ordered list (colon-separated on Unix, semicolon-separated on Windows systems) of directories, ZIP files, and JAR archives in which *javac* should look for user class files and source files. This variable is overridden by the -classpath option.

See also

java, jdb

javadoc — JDK 1.0 and later

The Java Documentation Generator

Synopsis

javadoc [*options*] *@list package... sourcefiles...*

Description

javadoc generates API documentation, in HTML format (by default), for any number of packages and classes you specify. The *javadoc* command line can list any number of package names and any number of Java source files. For convenience, when working with a large number of command-line options, or a large number of package or class names, you can place them all in an auxiliary file and specify the name of that file on the command line, preceded by an @ character.

javadoc uses the *javac* compiler to process all the specified Java source files and all the Java source files in all the specified packages. It uses the information it gleans from this processing to generate detailed API documentation. Most importantly, the generated documentation includes the contents of all documentation comments included in the source files. See Chapter 7, for information about writing doc comments in your own Java code.

When you specify a Java source file for *javadoc* to process, you must specify the name of the file that contains the source, including a complete path to the file. It is more common, however, to use *javadoc* to create documentation for entire packages of classes. When you specify a package for *javadoc* to process, you specify the package name, not the directory that contains the source code for the package. In this case, you may need to specify the -sourcepath option so that *javadoc* can find your package source code correctly if it is not stored in a location already listed in your default classpath.

javadoc creates HTML documentation by default, but you can customize its behavior by defining a doclet class that generates documentation in whatever format you desire. You can write your own doclets using the doclet API defined by the com.sun.javadoc package. Documentation for this package is included in the standard documentation bundle for Java 1.2 and later.

javadoc has significant new functionality as of Java 1.2. This reference page documents the Java 1.2 and later versions of the program, but makes no attempt to distinguish new features of the Java 1.2 version from the features that existed in previous versions.

Options

javadoc defines a large number of options. Some are standard options that are always recognized by *javadoc*. Other options are defined by the doclet that produces the documentation. The options for the standard HTML doclet are included in the following list:

-1.1

Simulates the output style and directory structure of the Java 1.1 version of *javadoc*. This option exists in Java 1.2 and 1.3 only, and has been removed in Java 1.4

-author

Includes authorship information specified with @author in the generated documentation. Default doclet only.

-bootclasspath

Specifies the location of an alternate set of system classes. This can be useful when cross-compiling. See *javac* for more information on this option.

-bottom *text*

Displays *text* at the bottom of each generated HTML file. *text* can contain HTML tags. See also -footer. Default doclet only.

-breakiterator
: Uses the java.text.BreakIterator algorithm for determining the end of the summary sentence in doc comments. Default doclet only.

-charset *encoding*
: Specifies the character encoding for the output. This depends on the encoding used in the documentation comments of your source code, of course. The *encoding* value is used in a <META> tag in the HTML output. Default doclet only.

-classpath *path*
: Specifies a path *javadoc* uses to look up both class files and, if you do not specify the -sourcepath option, source files. Because *javadoc* uses the *javac* compiler, it needs to be able to locate class files for all classes referenced by the packages being documented. See *java* and *javac* for more information about this option and the default value provided by the CLASSPATH environment variable.

-d *directory*
: Specifies the directory in and beneath which *javadoc* should store the HTML files it generates. If this option is omitted, the current directory is used. Default doclet only.

-docencoding *encoding*
: Specifies the encoding to be used for output HTML documents. The name of the encoding specified here may not exactly match the name of the charset specified with the -charset option. Default doclet only.

-docfilessubdirs
: Recursively copies any subdirectories of a *doc-files* directory instead of simply copying the files contained directly within *doc-files*. Default doclet only.

-doclet *classname*
: Specifies the name of the doclet class to use to generate the documentation. If this option is not specified, *javadoc* generates documentation using the default HTML doclet.

-docletpath *classpath*
: Specifies a path from which the class specified by the -doclet tag can be loaded if it is not available from the default classpath.

-doctitle *text*
: Provides a title to display at the top of the documentation overview file. This file is often the first thing readers see when they browse the generated documentation. The title can contain HTML tags. Default doclet only.

-encoding *encoding-name*
: Specifies the character encoding of the input source files and the documentation comments they contain. This can be different from the desired output encoding specified by -docencoding. The default is the platform default encoding.

-exclude *packages*
: Excludes the named packages from the set of packages defined by a -subpackages option. *packages* is a colon-separated list of package names. Default doclet only.

-excludedocfilessubdir *dirs*
: Excludes the specified subdirectories of a *doc-files* directory when -docfilessubdirs is specified. This is useful for excluding version control directories, for example. *dirs* is a colon-separated list of directory names relative to the *doc-files* directory. Default doclet only.

Java Tools

-extdirs *dirlist*
: Specifies a list of directories to search for standard extensions. Only necessary when cross-compiling with -bootclasspath. See *javac* for details.

-footer *text*
: Specifies text to be displayed near the bottom of each file, to the right of the navigation bar. *text* can contain HTML tags. See also -bottom and -header. Default doclet only.

-group *title packagelist*
: *javadoc* generates a top-level overview page that lists all packages in the generated document. By default, these packages are listed in alphabetical order in a single table. You can break them into groups of related packages with this option, however. The *title* specifies the title of the package group, such as "Core Packages." The *packagelist* is a colon-separated list of package names, each of which can include a trailing * character as a wildcard. The *javadoc* command line can contain any number of -group options. For example:

```
javadoc -group "AWT Packages" java.awt*
        -group "Swing Packages" javax.accessibility:javax.swing*
```

-header *text*
: Specifies text to be displayed near the top of each file, to the right of the upper navigation bar. *text* can contain HTML tags. See also -footer, -doctitle, and -windowtitle. Default doclet only.

-help
: Displays a usage message for *javadoc.*

-helpfile *file*
: Specifies the name of an HTML file that contains help for using the generated documentation. *javadoc* includes links to this help file in all files it generates. If this option is not specified, *javadoc* creates a default help file. Default doclet only.

-J*javaoption*
: Passes the argument *javaoption* directly through to the Java interpreter. When processing a large number of packages, you may need to use this option to increase the amount of memory *javadoc* is allowed to use. For example:

```
% javadoc -J-Xmx64m
```

Note that because -J options are passed directly to the Java interpreter before *javadoc* starts up, they cannot be included in an external file specified on the command line with the @list syntax.

-link *url*
: Specifies an absolute or relative URL of the top-level directory of another *javadoc*-generated document. *javadoc* uses this URL as the base URL for links from the current document to packages, classes, methods, and fields that are not documented in the current document. For example, when using *javadoc* to produce documentation for your own packages, you can use this option to link your documentation to the *javadoc* documentation for the core Java APIs. Default doclet only.

The directory specified by *url* must contain a file named *package-list*, and *javadoc* must be able to read this file at runtime. This file is automatically generated by a previous run of *javadoc*; it contains a list of all packages documented at the *url*.

More than one -link option can be specified, although this does not work properly in early releases of Java 1.2. If no -link option is specified, references in the generated documentation to classes and members that are external to the documentation are not hyperlinked.

-linkoffline *url packagelist*
: Similar to the -link option, except that the *packagelist* file is explicitly specified on the command line. This is useful when the directory specified by *url* does not have a *package-list* file or when that file is not available when *javadoc* is run. Default doclet only.

-linksource
: Creates an HTML version of each source file read and includes links to it from the documentation pages. Default doclet only.

-locale *language_country_variant*
: Specifies the locale to use for generated documentation. This is used to look up a resource file that contains localized messages and text for the output files.

-nocomment
: Ignores all doc comments and generates documentation that includes only raw API information without any accompanying prose. Default doclet only.

-nodeprecated
: Tells *javadoc* to omit documentation for deprecated features. This option implies -nodeprecatedlist. Default doclet only.

-nodeprecatedlist
: Tells *javadoc* not to generate the *deprecated-list.html* file and not to output a link to it on the navigation bar. Default doclet only.

-nohelp
: Tells *javadoc* not to generate a help file or a link to it in the navigation bar. Default doclet only.

-noindex
: Tells *javadoc* not to generate index files. Default doclet only.

-nonavbar
: Tells *javadoc* to omit the navigation bars from the top and bottom of every file. Also omits the text specified by -header and -footer. This is useful when generating documentation to be printed. Default doclet only.

-noqualifier *packages* | all
: *javadoc* omits package names in its generated documentation for classes in the same package being documented. This option tells it to additionally omit package names for classes in the specified packages, or, if the all keyword is used, in all packages. *packages* is a colon-separated list of package names, which may include the * wildcard to indicate subpackages. For example, -noqualifier java.io:java.nio.* would exclude package names for all classes in the java.io package and in java.nio and its subpackages. Default doclet only.

-nosince
: Ignores @since tags in doc comments. Default doclet only.

-notree
: Tells *javadoc* not to generate the *tree.html* class hierarchy diagram or a link to it in the navigation bar. Default doclet only.

-overview *filename*
: Reads an overview doc comment from *filename* and uses that comment in the overview page. This file does not contain Java source code, so the doc comment should not actually appear between /** and */ delimiters.

-package
: Includes package-visible classes and members in the output, as well as public and protected classes and members.

-private
: Includes all classes and members, including private and package-visible classes and members, in the generated documentation.

-protected
: Includes public and protected classes and members in the generated output. This is the default.

-public
: Includes only public classes and members in the generated output. Omits protected, private, and package-visible classes and members.

-quiet
: Suppresses output except warnings and error messages.

-serialwarn
: Issues warnings about serializable classes that do not adequately document their serialization format with @serial and related doc-comment tags. Default doclet only.

-source 1.4
: Specifies this option when running *javadoc* over Java 1.4 code that uses the new assert statement.

-sourcepath *path*
: Specifies a search path for source files, typically set to a single root directory. *javadoc* uses this path when looking for the Java source files that implement a specified package.

-splitindex
: Generates multiple index files, one for each letter of the alphabet. Use this option when documenting large amounts of code. Otherwise, the single index file generated by *javadoc* will be too large to be useful. Default doclet only.

-stylesheetfile *file*
: Specifies a file to use as a CSS stylesheet for the generated HTML. *javadoc* inserts appropriate links to this file in the generated documentation. Default doclet only.

-subpackages *packages*
: Specifies that *javadoc* should process the specified packages and all of their subpackages. *packages* is a colon-separated list of package names or package name prefixes. Using this option is often easier than explicitly listing all desired package names. For example:

```
-subpackages java:javax
```

See also -exclude. Default doclet only.

-tag *tagname:where:header-text*
: Specifies that *javadoc* should handle a doc-comment tag named *tagname* by outputting the text *header-text* followed by whatever text follows the tag. This enables the use of simple custom tags (with the same syntax as @return and @author) in doc comments. *where* is a string of characters that specifies the types of doc comments in which this custom tag is allowed. The characters and their meanings are a (all: valid everywhere), p (packages), t (types: classes and interfaces), c (constructors), m (methods), and f (fields).

  A secondary purpose of the -tag option is to specify the order in which tags are processed and in which their output appears. You can include the names of standard tags after the -tag option to specify this ordering. Custom tags and taglets can be included within this list of standard -tag options. Default doclet only.

-taglet *classname*
: Specifies the classname of a "taglet" class to process a custom tag. Writing taglets is not covered here. -taglet tags may be interspersed with -tag tags to specify the order in which tags should be processed and output. Default doclet only.

-tagletpath *classpath*
: Specifies a colon-separated list of JAR files or directories that form the classpath to be searched for taglet classes. Default doclet only.

-use
: Generates and inserts links to an additional file for each class and package that lists the uses of the class or package.

-verbose
: Displays additional messages while processing source files.

-version
: Includes information from @version tags in the generated output. This option does *not* tell *javadoc* to print its own version number. Default doclet only.

-windowtitle *text*
: Specifies *text* to be output in the <TITLE> tag of each generated file. This title typically appears in the web-browser titlebar and its history and bookmarks lists. *text* should not contain HTML tags. See also -doctitle and -header. Default doclet only.

Environment

CLASSPATH
: This environment variable specifies the default classpath *javadoc* uses to find the class files and source files. It is overridden by the -classpath and -sourcepath options. See *java* and *javac* for further discussion of the classpath.

See also

java, javac

javah — JDK 1.0 and later

Native Method C Stub Generator

Synopsis

```
javah [ options ] classnames
```

Description

javah generates C header and source files (*.h* and *.c* files) that are used when implementing Java native methods in C. The preferred native method interface has changed between Java 1.0 and Java 1.1. In Java 1.1 and earlier, *javah* generates files for old-style native methods. In Java 1.1, the -jni option specifies that *javah* should generate new-style files. In Java 1.2 and later, this option becomes the default.

This reference page describes only how to use *javah*. A full description of how to implement Java native methods in C is beyond the scope of this book.

Options

-bootclasspath
: Specifies the path to search for system classes. See *javac* for further discussion. Java 1.2 and later.

-classpath *path*
: Specifies the path *javah* uses to look up the classes named on the command line. This option overrides any path specified by the CLASSPATH environment variable. Prior to Java 1.2, this option can specify the location of the system classes and extensions. In Java 1.2 and later, it specifies only the location of application classes. See -bootclasspath. See also *java* for further discussion of the classpath.

-d *directory*
: Specifies the directory into which *javah* stores the files it generates. By default, it stores them in the current directory. This option cannot be used with -o.

-force
: Causes *javah* to always write output files, even if they contain no useful content.

-help
: Causes *javah* to display a simple usage message and exit.

-jni
: Specifies that *javah* should output header files for use with the new Java Native Interface (JNI), rather than using the old JDK 1.0 native interface. This option is the default in Java 1.2 and later. See also -old. Java 1.1 and later.

-o *outputfile*
: Combines all output into a single file, *outputfile*, instead of creating separate files for each specified class.

-old
: Outputs files for Java 1.0-style native methods. Prior to Java 1.2, this was the default. See also -jni. Java 1.2 and later.

-stubs
: Generates *.c* stub files for the class or classes, instead of header files. This option is only for the Java 1.0 native methods interface. See -old.

-td *directory*
: Specifies the directory where *javah* should store temporary files. On Unix systems, the default is */tmp*.

-trace
: Specifies that *javah* should include tracing output commands in the stub files it generates. In Java 1.2 and later, this option is obsolete and has been removed. In its place, you can use the -verbose:jni option of the Java interpreter.

-v, -verbose
: Specifies verbose mode. Causes *javah* to print messages about what it is doing. In Java 1.2 and later, -verbose is a synonym.

-version
: Causes *javah* to display its version number.

Environment

CLASSPATH
: Specifies the default classpath *javah* searches to find the specified classes. See *java* for a further discussion of the classpath.

See also
java, *javac*

javap — JDK 1.0 and later

The Java Class Disassembler

Synopsis

```
javap [ options ] classnames
```

Description
javap reads the class files specified by the class names on the command line and prints a human-readable version of the API defined by those classes. *javap* can also disassemble the specified classes, displaying the Java VM byte codes for the methods they contain.

Options

-b
: Enables backward compatibility with the output of the Java 1.1 version of *javap*. This option exists for programs that depend on the precise output format of *javap*. Java 1.2 and later.

-bootclasspath *path*
: Specifies the search path for the system classes. See *javac* for information about this rarely used option. Java 1.2 and later.

-c
: Displays the code (i.e., Java VM byte codes) for each method of each specified class. This option always disassembles all methods, regardless of their visibility level.

-classpath *path*
: Specifies the path *javap* uses to look up the classes named on the command line. This option overrides the path specified by the CLASSPATH environment variable. Prior to Java 1.2, this argument specifies the path for all system classes, extensions, and application classes. In Java 1.2 and later, it specifies only the application classpath. See also -bootclasspath and -extdirs. See *java* and *javac* for more information on the classpath.

-extdirs *dirs*
: Specifies one or more directories that should be searched for extension classes. See *javac* for information about this rarely used option. Java 1.2 and later.

-l
: Displays tables of line numbers and local variables, if available in the class files. This option is typically useful when used only with -c. The *javac* compiler does not include local variable information in its class files by default. See -g and related options to *javac*.

-help
: Prints a usage message and exits.

-J*javaoption*
: Passes the specified *javaoption* directly to the Java interpreter.

-package
: Displays package-visible, protected, and public class members, but not private members. This is the default.

-private
: Displays all class members, including private members.

-protected
: Displays only protected and public members.

-public
: Displays only public members of the specified classes.

-s
: Outputs the class member declarations using the internal VM type and method signature format, instead of the more readable source-code format.

-verbose
: Specifies verbose mode. Outputs additional information (in the form of Java comments) about each member of each specified class.

-verify
: Causes *javap* to perform partial class verification on the specified class or classes and display the results. Java 1.0 and 1.1. only; this option has been removed in Java 1.2 and later because it does not perform a sufficiently thorough verification.

-version
: Causes *javap* to display its version number.

Environment

CLASSPATH
: Specifies the default search path for application classes. The -classpath option overrides this environment variable. See *java* for a discussion of the classpath.

See also

java, *javac*

jdb — JDK 1.0 and later

The Java Debugger

Synopsis

```
jdb [ options ] class [ program options ]
jdb connect options
```

Description

jdb is a debugger for Java classes. It is text-based, command-line-oriented, and has a command syntax like that of the Unix *dbx* or *gdb* debuggers used with C and C++ programs.

jdb is written in Java, so it runs within a Java interpreter. When *jdb* is invoked with the name of a Java class, it starts another copy of the *java* interpreter, using any interpreter options specified on the command line. The new interpreter is started with special options that enable it to communicate with *jdb*. The new interpreter loads the specified class file and then stops and waits for debugging commands before executing the first byte code.

jdb can also debug a program that is already running in another Java interpreter. Doing so requires special options be passed to both the *java* interpreter and to *jdb*. The Java debugging architecture has changed dramatically with the introduction of Java 1.3, and so have the *java* and *jdb* options used to allow *jdb* to connect to a running interpreter.

jdb expression syntax

jdb debugging commands such as `print`, `dump`, and `suspend` allow you to refer to classes, objects, methods, fields, and threads in the program being debugged. You can refer to classes by name, with or without their package names. You can also refer to `static` class members by name. You can refer to individual objects by object ID, which is an eight-digit hexadecimal integer. Or, when the classes you are debugging contain local variable information, you can often use local variable names to refer to objects. You can use normal Java syntax to refer to the fields of an object and the elements of an array; you can also use this syntax to write quite complex expressions. In Java 1.3, *jdb* even supports method invocation using standard Java syntax.

A number of *jdb* commands require you to specify a thread. Each thread is given an integer identifier and is named using the syntax `t@`*`n`*, where *`n`* is the thread ID.

Options

When invoking *jdb* with a specified class file, any of the *java* interpreter options can be specified. See the *java* reference page for an explanation of these options. In addition, *jdb* supports the following options:

`-attach [`*`host`*`:]`*`port`*

Specifies that *jdb* should connect to the Java "Client VM" that is already running on the specified host (or the local host, if unspecified) and listening for debugging connections on the specified port. Java 1.3 and later.

In order to use *jdb* to connect to a running VM in this way, the VM must have been started with a command line something like this:

```
% java -Xdebug -Xrunjdwp:transport=dt_socket,address=8000,server=y,suspend=n
```

The Java 1.3 *jdb* architecture allows a complex set of interpreter-to-debugger connection options, and *java* and *jdb* provide a complex set of options and suboptions to enable it. A detailed description of those options is beyond the scope of this book.

`-help`

Displays a usage message listing supported options.

`-host` *`hostname`*

In Java 1.2 and earlier, this option is used to connect to an already running interpreter. It specifies the name of the host upon which the desired interpreter session is running. If omitted, the default is the local host. This option must be used with `-password`. In Java 1.3, this option has been replaced by the `-attach` option.

-launch
: Starts the specified application when *jdb* starts. This avoids the need to explicitly use the run command to start it. Java 1.3 and later.

-password *password*
: In Java 1.2 and earlier, this option specifies a password that uniquely identifies a Java VM on a particular host. When used in conjunction with -hostname, this option enables *jdb* to connect to a running interpreter. The interpreter must have been started with the -debug or -Xdebug option, which causes it to display an appropriate *password* for use with this option. In Java 1.3, this option has been replaced by the -attach option.

-sourcepath *path*
: Specifies the locations *jdb* searches when attempting to find source files that correspond to the class files being debugged. If unspecified, *jdb* uses the classpath by default. Java 1.3 and later.

-tclassic
: Tells *jdb* to invoke the "Classic VM" instead of the "Client VM" (HotSpot), which is the default VM in Java 1.3. Java 1.3 and later.

-version
: Displays the *jdb* version number and exits.

Commands

jdb understands the following debugging commands:

? or help
: Lists all supported commands, with a short explanation of each.

!!
: A shorthand command that is replaced with the text of the last command entered. It can be followed with additional text that is appended to that previous command.

catch [*exception-class*]
: Causes a breakpoint whenever the specified exception is thrown. If no exception is specified, the command lists the exceptions currently being caught. Use ignore to stop these breakpoints from occurring.

classes
: Lists all classes that have been loaded.

clear
: Lists all currently set breakpoints.

clear *class.method* [(*param-type*...)]
: Clears the breakpoint set in the specified method of the specified class.

clear [*class:line*]
: Removes the breakpoint set at the specified line of the specified class.

cont
: Resumes execution. This command should be used when the current thread is stopped at a breakpoint.

down [*n*]
: Moves down *n* frames in the call stack of the current thread. If n is not specified, moves down one frame.

dump *id...*
: Prints the value of all fields of the specified object or objects. If you specify the name of a class, dump displays all class (static) methods and variables of the class, and also displays the superclass and list of implemented interfaces. Objects and classes can be specified by name or by their eight-digit hexadecimal ID numbers. Threads can also be specified with the shorthand t@*thread-number*.

exit or quit
: Quits *jdb*.

gc
: Runs the garbage collector to force unused objects to be reclaimed.

ignore *exception-class*
: Does not treat the specified exception as a breakpoint. This command turns off a catch command. This command does not cause the Java interpreter to ignore exceptions; it merely tells *jdb* to ignore them.

list [*line-number*]
: Lists the specified line of source code as well as several lines that appear before and after it. If no line number is specified, uses the line number of the current stack frame of the current thread. The lines listed are from the source file of the current stack frame of the current thread. Use the use command to tell *jdb* where to find source files.

list *method*
: Displays the source code of the specified method.

load *classname*
: Loads the specified class into *jdb*.

locals
: Displays a list of local variables for the current stack frame. Java code must be compiled with the -g option in order to contain local variable information.

memory
: Displays a summary of memory usage for the Java program being debugged.

methods *class*
: Lists all methods of the specified class. Use dump to list the instance variables of an object or the class (static) variables of a class.

print *id...*
: Prints the value of the specified item or items. Each item can be a class, object, field, or local variable, and can be specified by name or by eight-digit hexadecimal ID number. You can also refer to threads with the special syntax t@*thread-number*. The print command displays an object's value by invoking its toString() method.

next
: Executes the current line of source code, including any method calls it makes. See also step.

resume [*thread-id* . . .]
: Resumes execution of the specified thread or threads. If no threads are specified, all suspended threads are resumed. See also suspend.

run [*class*] [*args*]
: Runs the main() method of the specified class, passing the specified arguments to it. If no class or arguments are specified, uses the class and arguments specified on the *jdb* command line.

step
: Runs the current line of the current thread and stops again. If the line invokes a method, steps into that method and stops. See also next.

stepi
: Executes a single Java VM instruction.

step up
: Runs until the current method returns to its caller and stops again.

stop
: Lists current breakpoints.

stop at *class:line*
: Sets a breakpoint at the specified line of the specified class. Program execution stops when it reaches this line. Use clear to remove a breakpoint.

stop in *class.method* [(*param-type* . . .)]
: Sets a breakpoint at the beginning of the specified method of the specified class. Program execution stops when it enters the method. Use clear to remove a breakpoint.

suspend [*thread-id* . . .]
: Suspends the specified thread or threads. If no threads are specified, suspends all running threads. Use resume to restart them.

thread *thread-id*
: Sets the current thread to the specified thread. This thread is used implicitly by a number of other *jdb* commands. The thread can be specified by name or number.

threadgroup *name*
: Sets the current thread group.

threadgroups
: Lists all thread groups running in the Java interpreter session being debugged.

threads [*threadgroup*]
: Lists all threads in the named thread group. If no thread group is specified, lists all threads in the current thread group (specified by threadgroup).

up [*n*]
: Moves up *n* frames in the call stack of the current thread. If n is not specified, moves up one frame.

use [*source-file-path*]
: Sets the path used by *jdb* to look up source files for the classes being debugged. If no path is specified, displays the current source path.

where [*thread-id*] [all]
: Displays a stack trace for the specified thread. If no thread is specified, displays a stack trace for the current thread. If all is specified, displays a stack trace for all threads.

wherei [*thread-id* x]
: Displays a stack trace for the specified or current thread, including detailed program counter information.

Environment

CLASSPATH
: Specifies an ordered list (colon-separated on Unix, semicolon-separated on Windows systems) of directories, ZIP files, and JAR archives in which *jdb* should look for class definitions. When a path is specified with this environment variable, *jdb* always implicitly appends the location of the system classes to the end of the path. If this environment variable is not specified, the default path is the current directory and the system classes. This variable is overridden by the -classpath option.

See also

java

keytool — Java 2 SDK 1.2 and later

Key and Certificate Management Tool

Synopsis

```
keytool command options
```

Description

keytool manages and manipulates a *keystore*: a repository for public and private keys and public-key certificates. *keytool* defines various commands for generating keys, importing data into the keystore, and exporting and displaying keystore data. Keys and certificates are stored in a keystore using a case-insensitive name, or *alias*. *keytool* uses this alias to refer to a key or certificate.

The first option to *keytool* always specifies the basic command to be performed. Subsequent options provide details about how the command is to be performed. Only the command must be specified. If a command requires an option that does not have a default value, *keytool* prompts you interactively for the value.

Commands

-certreq
: Generates a certificate signing request in PKCS#10 format for the specified alias. The request is written to the specified file or to the standard output stream. The request should be sent to a certificate authority (CA), which authenticates the requestor and sends back a signed certificate authenticating the requestor's public key. This signed certificate can then be imported into the keystore with the -import command. This command uses the following options: -alias, -file, -keypass, -keystore, -sigalg, -storepass, -storetype, and -v.

-delete
: Deletes a specified alias from a specified keystore. This command uses the following options: -alias, -keystore, -storepass, -storetype, and -v.

-export
: Writes the certificate associated with the specified alias to the specified file or to standard output. This command uses the following options: -alias, -file, -keystore, -rfc, -storepass, -storetype, and -v.

Java Tools

-genkey
: Generates a public/private key pair and a self-signed X.509 certificate for the public key. Self-signed certificates are not often useful by themselves, so this command is often followed by -certreq. This command uses the following options: -alias, -dname, -keyalg, -keypass, -keysize, -keystore, -sigalg, -storepass, -storetype, -v, and -validity.

-help
: Lists all available *keytool* commands and their options. This command is not used with any other options.

-identitydb
: Reads keys and certificates from a Java 1.1 identity database managed with *javakey* and stores them into a keystore so they can be manipulated by *keytool*. The identity database is read from the specified file or from standard input if no file is specified. The keys and certificates are written into the specified keystore file, which is automatically created if it does not exist yet. This command uses the following options: -file, -keystore, -storepass, -storetype, and -v.

-import
: Reads a certificate or PKCS#7-formatted certificate chain from a specified file or from standard input and stores it as a trusted certificate in the keystore with the specified alias. This command uses the following options: -alias, -file, -keypass, -keystore, -noprompt, -storepass, -storetype, -trustcacerts, and -v.

-keyclone
: Duplicates the keystore entry of a specified alias and stores it in the keystore under a new alias. This command uses the following options: -alias, -dest, -keypass, -keystore, -new, -storepass, -storetype, and -v.

-keypasswd
: Changes the password that encrypts the private key associated with a specified alias. This command uses the following options: -alias, -keypass, -new, -storetype, and -v.

-list
: Displays (on standard output) the fingerprint of the certificate associated with the specified alias. With the -v option, prints certificate details in human-readable format. With -rfc, prints certificate contents in a machine-readable, printable-encoding format. This command uses the following options: -alias, -keystore, -rfc, -storepass, -storetype, and -v.

-printcert
: Displays the contents of a certificate read from the specified file or from standard input. Unlike most *keytool* commands, this one does not use a keystore. This command uses the following options: -file and -v.

-selfcert
: Creates a self-signed certificate for the public key associated with the specified alias and uses it to replace any certificate or certificate chain already associated with that alias. This command uses the following options: -alias, -dname, -keypass, -keystore, -sigalg, -storepass, -storetype, -v, and -validity.

-storepasswd
: Changes the password that protects the integrity of the keystore as a whole. The new password must be at least six characters long. This command uses the following options: -keystore, -new, -storepass, -storetype, and -v.

Options

The various *keytool* commands can be passed various options from the following list. Many of these options have reasonable default values. *keytool* interactively prompts for any unspecified options that do not have defaults:

-alias *name*
: Specifies the alias to be manipulated in the keystore. The default is "mykey".

-dest *newalias*
: Specifies the new alias name (the destination alias) for the -keyclone command. If not specified, *keytool* prompts for a value.

-dname *X.500-distinguished-name*
: Specifies the X.500 distinguished name to appear on the certificate generated by -selfcert or -genkey. A distinguished name is a highly qualified name intended to be globally unique. For example:

```
CN=David Flanagan, OU=Editorial, O=OReilly, L=Cambridge, S=Massachusetts, C=US
```

The -genkey command of *keytool* prompts for a distinguished name if none is specified. The -selfcert command uses the distinguished name of the current certificate if no replacement name is specified.

-file *file*
: Specifies the input or output file for many of the *keytool* commands. If left unspecified, *keytool* reads from the standard input or writes to the standard output.

-keyalg *algorithm-name*
: Used with -genkey to specify what type of cryptographic keys to generate. In the default Java implementation shipped from Sun, the only supported algorithm is "DSA"; this is the default if this option is omitted.

-keypass *password*
: Specifies the password that encrypts a private key in the keystore. If this option is unspecified, *keytool* first tries the -storepass password. If that does not work, it prompts for the appropriate password.

-keysize *size*
: Used with the -genkey command to specify the length in bits of the generated keys. If unspecified, the default is 1024.

-keystore *filename*
: Specifies the location of the keystore file. If unspecified, a file named *.keystore* in the user's home directory is used.

-new *new-password-or-alias*
: Used with the -keyclone command to specify the new alias name and with -keypasswd and -storepasswd to specify the new password. If unspecified, *keytool* prompts for the value of this option.

-noprompt
: Used with the -import command to disable interactive prompting of the user when a chain of trust cannot be established for an imported certificate. If this option is not specified, the -import command prompts the user.

-rfc
: Used with the -list and -export commands to specify that certificate output should be in the printable encoding format specified by RFC-1421. If this option is not specified, -export outputs the certificate in binary format, and -list lists only the

certificate fingerprint. This option cannot be combined with -v in the -list command.

-sigalg *algorithm-name*
: Specifies a digital signature algorithm that signs a certificate. If omitted, the default for this option depends on the type of underlying public key. If it is a DSA key, the default algorithm is "SHA1withDSA". If the key is an RSA key, the default signature algorithm is "MD5withRSA".

-storepass *password*
: Specifies a password that protects the integrity of the entire keystore file. This password also serves as a default password for any private keys that do not have their own -keypass specified. If -storepass is not specified, *keytool* prompts for it. The password must be at least six characters long.

-storetype *type*
: Specifies the type of the keystore to be used. If this option is not specified, the default is taken from the system security properties file. Often, the default is Sun's "JKS" Java Keystore type.

-trustcacerts
: Used with the -import command to specify that the self-signed certificate authority certificates contained in the keystore in the *jre/lib/security/cacerts* file should be considered trusted. If this option is omitted, *keytool* ignores that file.

-v
: Specifies verbose mode, if present, and makes many *keytool* commands produce additional output.

-validity *time*
: Used with the -genkey and -selfcert commands to specify the period of validity (in days) of the generated certificate. If unspecified, the default is 90 days.

See also

jarsigner, javakey, policytool

native2ascii — JDK 1.1 and later

Converts Java Source Code to ASCII

Synopsis

```
native2ascii [ options ] [ inputfile [ outputfile ]]
```

Description

javac can only process files encoded in the eight-bit Latin-1 encoding, with any other characters encoded using the \uxxxx Unicode notation. *native2ascii* is a simple program that reads a Java source file encoded using a local encoding and converts it to the Latin-1-plus-ASCII-encoded-Unicode form required by *javac.*

The *inputfile* and *outputfile* are optional. If unspecified, standard input and standard output are used, making *native2ascii* suitable for use in pipes.

Options

-encoding *encoding-name*
: Specifies the encoding used by source files. If this option is not specified, the encoding is taken from the file.encoding system property.

-reverse

Specifies that the conversion should be done in reverse—from encoded \uxxxx characters to characters in the native encoding.

See also

java.io.InputStreamReader, java.io.OutputStreamWriter

policytool — Java 2 SDK 1.2 and later

Policy File Creation and Management Tool

Synopsis

```
policytool
```

Description

policytool displays a Swing user interface that makes it easy to edit security policy configuration files. The Java security architecture is based on policy files, which specify sets of permissions to be granted to code from various sources. By default, the Java security policy is defined by a system policy file stored in the *jre/lib/security/java.policy* file and a user policy file stored in the *.java.policy* file in the user's home directory. System administrators and users can edit these files with a text editor, but the syntax of the file is somewhat complex, so it is usually easier to use *policytool* to define and edit security policies.

Selecting the policy file to edit

When *policytool* starts up, it opens the *.java.policy* file in the user's home directory by default. Use the New, Open, and Save commands in the File menu to create a new policy file, open an existing file, and save an edited file, respectively.

Editing the policy file

The main *policytool* window displays a list of the entries contained in the policy file. Each entry specifies a code source and the permissions that are to be granted to code from that source. The window also contains buttons that allow you to add a new entry, edit an existing entry, or delete an entry from the policy file. If you add or edit an entry, *policytool* opens a new window that displays the details of that policy entry.

With the addition of the JAAS API to the core Java platform in Java 1.4, *policytool* has been updated to allow the specification of a Principal to whom a set of permissions will be granted.

Every policy file has an associated keystore, from which it obtains the certificates it needs when verifying the digital signatures of Java code. You can usually rely on the default keystore, but if you need to specify the keystore explicitly for a policy file, use the Change Keystore command in the Edit menu of the main *policytool* window.

Adding or editing a policy entry

The policy entry editor window displays the code source for the policy entry and a list of permissions associated with that code source. It also contains buttons that allow you to add a new permission, delete a permission, or edit an existing permission.

When defining a new policy entry, the first step is to specify the code source. A code source is defined by a URL from which the code is downloaded and/or a list of digital signatures that must appear on the code. Specify one or both of these values by typing in a URL and/or a comma-separated list of aliases. These aliases identify trusted certificates in the keystore associated with the policy file.

After you have defined the code source for a policy entry, you must define the permissions to be granted to code from that source. Use the Add Permission and Edit Permission buttons to add and edit permissions. These buttons bring up yet another *policytool* window.

Defining a permission

To define a permission in the permission editor window, first select the desired permission type from the Permission drop-down menu. Then, select an appropriate target value from the Target Name menu. The choices in this menu are customized depending on the permission type you selected. For some types of permission, such as FilePermission, there is not a fixed set of possible targets, and you usually have to type in the specific target you want. For example, you might type "/tmp" to specify the directory */tmp*, "/tmp/*" to specify all the files in that directory, or "/tmp/-" to specify all the files in the directory, and, recursively, any subdirectories. See the documentation of the individual Permission classes for a description of the targets they support.

Depending on the type of permission you select, you may also have to select one or more action values from the Actions menu. When you have selected a permission and appropriate target and action values, click the Okay button to dismiss the window.

See also

jarsigner, *keytool*

serialver — JDK 1.1 and later

Class Version Number Generator

Synopsis

```
serialver [-show] classname...
```

Description

serialver displays the version number of a class or classes. This version number is used for the purposes of serialization: the version number must change each time the serialization format of the class changes.

If the specified class declares a long serialVersionUID constant, the value of that field is displayed. Otherwise, a unique version number is computed by applying the Secure Hash Algorithm (SHA) to the API defined by the class. This program is primarily useful for computing an initial unique version number for a class, which is then declared as a constant in the class. The output of *serialver* is a line of legal Java code, suitable for pasting into a class definition.

Options

-show

When the -show option is specified, *serialver* displays a simple graphical interface that allows the user to type in a single classname at a time and obtain its serialization UID. When using -show, no class names can be specified on the command line.

Environment

CLASSPATH

serialver is written in Java, so it is sensitive to the CLASSPATH environment variable in the same way the *java* interpreter is. The specified classes are looked up relative to this classpath.

See also

java.io.ObjectStreamClass

PART II

API Quick Reference

Part II is the real heart of this book: quick-reference material for the essential APIs of the Java platform. Please read the following section, *How To Use This Quick Reference*, to learn how to get the most out of this material.

How to Use This Quick Reference

The quick-reference section that follows packs a lot of information into a small space. This introduction explains how to get the most out of that information. It describes how the quick reference is organized and how to read the individual quick-reference entries.

Finding a Quick-Reference Entry

The quick reference is organized into chapters, each of which documents a single package of the Java platform or a group of related packages. Packages are listed alphabetically within and between chapters, so you never really need to know which chapter documents which package: you can simply search alphabetically, as you might do in a dictionary. The documentation for each package begins with a quick-reference entry for the package itself. This entry includes a short overview of the package and a listing of the classes and interfaces included in the package. In this listing of package contents, classes and interfaces are first grouped by general category (interfaces, classes, and exceptions, for example). Within each category, they are grouped by class hierarchy, with indentation to indicate the level of the hierarchy. Finally, classes and interfaces at the same hierarchy level are listed alphabetically.

Each package overview is followed by individual quick-reference entries for the classes and interfaces defined in the package. All the entries in this reference are organized alphabetically by class *and* package name, so related classes are grouped near each other. This means that to look up a quick-reference entry for a particular class, you must also know the name of the package that contains that class. Usually, the package name is obvious from the context, and you should have no trouble looking up the quick-reference entry you want. Use the tabs on the outside edge of the book and the dictionary-style headers on the upper corner of each page to help you quickly find the package and class you need.

Occasionally, you may need to look up a class for which you do not already know the package. In this case, refer to Chapter 25. This index allows you to look up a class by class name and find out what package it is part of.

Reading a Quick-Reference Entry

The quick-reference entries for classes and interfaces contain quite a bit of information. The sections that follow describe the structure of a quick-reference entry, explaining what information is available, where it is found, and what it means. While reading the descriptions that follow, you may find it helpful to flip through the reference section itself to find examples of the features being described.

Class Name, Package Name, Availability, and Flags

Each quick-reference entry begins with a four-part title that specifies the name, package name, and availability of the class, and may also specify various additional flags that describe the class. The class name appears in bold at the upper left of the title. The package name appears, in smaller print, in the lower left, below the class name.

The upper-right portion of the title indicates the availability of the class; it specifies the earliest release that contained the class. If a class was introduced in Java 1.1, for example, this portion of the title reads "Java 1.1". The availability section of the title is also used to indicate whether a class has been deprecated, and, if so, in what release. For example, it might read "Java 1.1; Deprecated in Java 1.2".

In the lower-right corner of the title you may find a list of flags that describe the class. The possible flags and their meanings are as follows:

checked
: The class is a checked exception, which means that it extends `java.lang.Exception`, but not `java.lang.RuntimeException`. In other words, it must be declared in the `throws` clause of any method that may throw it.

cloneable
: The class, or a superclass, implements `java.lang.Cloneable`.

collection
: The class, or a superclass, implements `java.util.Collection` or `java.util.Map`.

comparable
: The class, or a superclass, implements `java.lang.Comparable`.

error
: The class extends `java.lang.Error`.

event
: The class extends `java.util.EventObject`.

event adapter
: The class, or a superclass, implements `java.util.EventListener`, and the class name ends with "Adapter".

event listener
: The class, or a superclass, implements `java.util.EventListener`.

runnable
: The class, or a superclass, implements `java.lang.Runnable`.

serializable
: The class, or a superclass, implements `java.io.Serializable`.

unchecked
: The class is an unchecked exception, which means it extends `java.lang.RuntimeException` and therefore does not need to be declared in the `throws` clause of a method that may throw it.

Description

The title of each quick-reference entry is followed by a short description of the most important features of the class or interface. This description may be anywhere from a couple of sentences to several paragraphs long.

Hierarchy

If a class or interface has a nontrivial class hierarchy, the "Description" section is followed by a figure that illustrates the hierarchy and helps you understand the class in the context of that hierarchy. The name of each class or interface in the diagram appears in a box; classes appear in rectangles (except for abstract classes, which appear in skewed rectangles or parallelograms). Interfaces appear in rounded rectangles, in which the corners have been replaced by arcs. The current class—the one that is the subject of the diagram—appears in a box that is bolder than the others. The boxes are connected by lines: solid lines indicate an "extends" relationship, and dotted lines indicate an "implements" relationship. The superclass-to-subclass hierarchy reads from left to right in the top row (or only row) of boxes in the figure. Interfaces are usually positioned beneath the classes that implement them, although in simple cases an interface is sometimes positioned on the same line as the class that implements it, resulting in a more compact figure. Note that the hierarchy figure shows only the superclasses of a class. If a class has subclasses, those are listed in the cross-reference section at the end of the quick-reference entry for the class.

Synopsis

The most important part of every quick-reference entry is the class synopsis, which follows the title and description. The synopsis for a class looks a lot like the source code for the class, except that the method bodies are omitted and some additional annotations are added. If you know Java syntax, you know how to read the class synopsis.

The first line of the synopsis contains information about the class itself. It begins with a list of class modifiers, such as `public`, `abstract`, and `final`. These modifiers are followed by the `class` or `interface` keyword and then by the name of the class. The class name may be followed by an `extends` clause that specifies the superclass and an `implements` clause that specifies any interfaces the class implements.

The class definition line is followed by a list of the fields and methods that the class defines. Once again, if you understand basic Java syntax, you should have no trouble making sense of these lines. The listing for each member includes the modifiers, type, and name of the member. For methods, the synopsis also includes the type and name of each method parameter and an optional `throws` clause that lists the exceptions the method can throw. The member names are in boldface, so it is easy to scan the list of members looking for the one you want. The names of method parameters are in italics to indicate that they are not to be used literally. The member listings are printed on alternating gray and white backgrounds to keep them visually separate.

Member availability and flags

Each member listing is a single line that defines the API for that member. These listings use Java syntax, so their meaning is immediately clear to any Java programmer. There is some auxiliary information associated with each member synopsis, however, that requires explanation.

Recall that each quick-reference entry begins with a title section that includes the release in which the class was first defined. When a member is introduced into a class after the initial release of the class, the version in which the member was introduced appears, in small print, to the left of the member synopsis. For example, if a class was first introduced in Java 1.1, but had a new method added in Java 1.2 the title contains the string "Java 1.1", and the listing for the new member is preceded by the number "1.2". Furthermore, if a member has been deprecated, that fact is indicated with a hash mark (#) to the left of the member synopsis.

The area to the right of the member synopsis is used to display a variety of flags that provide additional information about the member. Some of these flags indicate additional specification details that do not appear in the member API itself. Other flags contain implementation-specific information. This information can be quite useful in understanding the class and in debugging your code, but be aware that it may differ between implementations. The implementation-specific flags displayed in this book are based on Sun's Linux implementation of Java.

The following flags may be displayed to the right of a member synopsis:

native
: An implementation-specific flag that indicates that a method is implemented in native code. Although `native` is a Java keyword and can appear in method signatures, it is part of the method implementation, not part of its specification. Therefore, this information is included with the member flags, rather than as part of the member listing. This flag is useful as a hint about the expected performance of a method.

synchronized
: An implementation-specific flag that indicates that a method implementation is declared `synchronized`, meaning that it obtains a lock on the object or class before executing. Like the `native` keyword, the `synchronized` keyword is part of the method implementation, not part of the specification, so it appears as a flag, not in the method synopsis itself. This flag is a useful hint that the method is probably implemented in a thread-safe manner.

Whether or not a method is thread-safe is part of the method specification, and this information *should* appear (although it often does not) in the method documentation. There are a number of different ways to make a method thread-safe, however, and declaring the method with the `synchronized` keyword is only one possible implementation. In other words, a method that does not bear the `synchronized` flag can still be thread-safe.

Overrides:
This flag indicates that a method overrides a method in one of its superclasses. The flag is followed by the name of the superclass that the method overrides. This is a specification detail, not an implementation detail. As we'll see in the next section, overriding methods are usually grouped together in their own section of the class synopsis. The `Overrides:` flag is only used when an overriding method is not grouped in that way.

Implements:
This flag indicates that a method implements a method in an interface. The flag is followed by the name of the interface that is implemented. This is a specification detail, not an implementation detail. As we'll see in the next section, methods that implement an interface are usually grouped into a special section of the class synopsis. The `Implements:` flag is only used for methods that are not grouped in this way.

empty
This flag indicates that the implementation of the method has an empty body. This can be a hint to the programmer that the method may need to be overridden in a subclass.

constant
An implementation-specific flag that indicates that a method has a trivial implementation. Only methods with a `void` return type can be truly empty. Any method declared to return a value must have at least a `return` statement. The "constant" flag indicates that the method implementation is empty except for a `return` statement that returns a constant value. Such a method might have a body like `return null;` or `return false;`. Like the "empty" flag, this flag may indicate that a method needs to be overridden.

default:
This flag is used with property accessor methods that read the value of a property (i.e., methods whose names begins with "get" and take no arguments). The flag is followed by the default value of the property. Strictly speaking, default property values are a specification detail. In practice, however, these defaults are not always documented, and care should be taken, because the default values may change between implementations.

Not all property accessors have a "default:" flag. A default value is determined by dynamically loading the class in question, instantiating it using a no-argument constructor, and then calling the method to find out what it returns. This technique can be used only on classes that can be dynamically loaded and instantiated and that have no-argument constructors, so default values are shown for those classes only. Furthermore, note that when a class is instantiated using a different constructor, the default values for its properties may be different.

=

For `static final` fields, this flag is followed by the constant value of the field. Only constants of primitive and `String` types and constants with the value `null` are displayed. Some constant values are specification details, while others are implementation details. The reason that symbolic constants are defined, however, is so you can write code that does not rely directly upon the constant value. Use this flag to help you understand the class, but do not rely upon the constant values in your own programs.

Functional grouping of members

Within a class synopsis, the members are not listed in strict alphabetical order. Instead, they are broken down into functional groups and listed alphabetically within each group. Constructors, methods, fields, and inner classes are all listed separately. Instance methods are kept separate from static (class) methods. Constants are separated from non-constant fields. Public members are listed separately from protected members. Grouping members by category breaks a class down into smaller, more comprehensible segments, making the class easier to understand. This grouping also makes it easier for you to find a desired member.

Functional groups are separated from each other in a class synopsis with Java comments, such as "// Public Constructors", "// Inner Classes", and "// Methods Implementing DataInput". The various functional categories are as follows (in the order in which they appear in a class synopsis):

Constructors
Displays the constructors for the class. Public constructors and protected constructors are displayed separately in subgroupings. If a class defines no constructor at all, the Java compiler adds a default no-argument constructor that is displayed here. If a class defines only private constructors, it cannot be instantiated, so a special, empty grouping entitled "No Constructor" indicates this fact. Constructors are listed first because the first thing you do with most classes is instantiate them by calling a constructor.

Constants
Displays all of the constants (i.e., fields that are declared `static` and `final`) defined by the class. Public and protected constants are displayed in separate subgroups. Constants are listed here, near the top of the class synopsis, because constant values are often used throughout the class as legal values for method parameters and return values.

Inner classes
Groups all of the inner classes and interfaces defined by the class or interface. For each inner class, there is a single-line synopsis. Each inner class also has its own quick-reference entry that includes a full class synopsis for the inner class. Like constants, inner classes are listed near the top of the class synopsis because they are often used by a number of other members of the class.

Static methods

Lists the static methods (class methods) of the class, broken down into subgroups for public static methods and protected static methods.

Event listener registration methods

Lists the public instance methods that register and deregister event listener objects with the class. The names of these methods begin with the words "add" and "remove" and end in "Listener". These methods are always passed a `java.util.EventListener` object. The methods are typically defined in pairs, so the pairs are listed together. The methods are listed alphabetically by event name rather than by method name.

Property accessor methods

Lists the public instance methods that set or query the value of a property or attribute of the class. The names of these methods begin with the words "set", "get", and "is", and their signatures follow the patterns set out in the JavaBeans specification. Although the naming conventions and method signature patterns are defined for JavaBeans, classes and interfaces throughout the Java platform define property accessor methods that follow these conventions and patterns. Looking at a class in terms of the properties it defines can be a powerful tool for understanding the class, so property methods are grouped together in this section. Property accessor methods are listed alphabetically by property name, not by method name. This means that the "set", "get", and "is" methods for a property all appear together.

Public instance methods

Contains all of the public instance methods that are not grouped elsewhere.

Implementing methods

Groups the methods that implement the same interface. There is one subgroup for each interface implemented by the class. Methods that are defined by the same interface are almost always related to each other, so this is a useful functional grouping of methods.

Note that if an interface method is also an event registration method or a property accessor method, it is listed both in this group and in the event or property group. This situation does not arise often, but when it does, all of the functional groupings are important and useful enough to warrant the duplicate listing. When an interface method is listed in the event or property group, it displays an "Implements:" flag that specifies the name of the interface of which it is part.

Overriding methods

Groups the methods that override methods of a superclass broken down into subgroups by superclass. This is typically a useful grouping, because it helps to make it clear how a class modifies the default behavior of its superclasses. In practice, it is also often true that methods that override the same superclass are functionally related to each other.

Sometimes a method that overrides a superclass is also a property accessor method or (more rarely) an event registration method. When this happens, the method is grouped with the property or event methods and displays a flag that indicates which superclass it overrides. The method is not listed with other overriding methods, however. Note that this is different from interface methods, which, because they are more strongly functionally related, may have duplicate listings in both groups.

Protected instance methods
: Contains all of the protected instance methods that are not grouped elsewhere.

Fields
: Lists all the non-constant fields of the class, breaking them down into subgroups for public and protected static fields and public and protected instance fields. Many classes do not define any publicly accessible fields. For those that do, many object-oriented programmers prefer not to use those fields directly, but instead to use accessor methods when such methods are available.

Deprecated members
: Deprecated methods and deprecated fields are grouped at the very bottom of the class synopsis. Use of these members is strongly discouraged.

Cross-References

The synopsis section of a quick-reference entry is followed by a number of optional cross-reference sections that indicate other, related classes and methods that may be of interest. These sections are the following:

Subclasses
: This section lists the subclasses of this class, if there are any.

Implementations
: This section lists classes that implement this interface.

Passed To
: This section lists all of the methods and constructors that are passed an object of this type as an argument. This is useful when you have an object of a given type and want to figure out what you can do with it.

Returned By
: This section lists all of the methods (but not constructors) that return an object of this type. This is useful when you know that you want to work with an object of this type, but don't know how to obtain one.

Thrown By
: For checked exception classes, this section lists all of the methods and constructors that throw exceptions of this type. This material helps you figure out when a given exception or error may be thrown. Note, however, that this section is based on the exception types listed in the `throws` clauses of methods and constructors. Subclasses of `RuntimeException` and `Error` do not have to be listed in `throws` clauses, so it is not possible to generate a complete cross reference of methods that throw these types of unchecked exceptions.

Type Of
: This section lists all of the fields and constants that are of this type, which can help you figure out how to obtain an object of this type.

A Note About Class Names

Throughout the quick reference, you'll notice that classes are sometimes referred to by class name alone and at other times referred to by class name and package name. If package names were always used, the class synopses would become long and hard to read. On the other hand, if package names were never used, it would sometimes be difficult to know what class was being referred to. The rules for including or omitting the package name are complex. They can be summarized approximately as follows, however:

- If the class name alone is ambiguous, the package name is always used.
- If the class is part of the `java.lang` package or is a very commonly used class, such as `java.io.Serializable`, the package name is omitted.
- If the class being referred to is part of the current package (and has a quick-reference entry in the current chapter), the package name is omitted.

CHAPTER 9

java.beans and java.beans.beancontext

This chapter covers the java.beans and java.beans.beancontext packages. java.beans defines core classes and interfaces for the JavaBeans component framework. java.beans.beancontext defines JavaBeans containers.

Package java.beans — Java 1.1

The java.beans package contains classes and interfaces related to JavaBeans components. Most of the classes and interfaces are used by tools that manipulate beans, rather than by the beans themselves. They are also used or implemented by auxiliary classes provided by bean implementors for the benefit of bean-manipulation tools.

The Beans class defines several generally useful static methods. Its instantiate() method is particularly important. The Introspector class is used to obtain information about a bean and the properties, events, and methods it exports. Most of this information is returned using the FeatureDescriptor class and its various subclasses. The java.beans package also defines the PropertyChangeEvent class and the PropertyChangeListener interface that are widely used by AWT and Swing to provide notification when a bound property of a GUI component changes.

Java 1.4 adds several new classes to support the JavaBeans persistence mechanism. See XMLEncoder for details.

See Chapter 6, for a complete introduction to the JavaBeans component model.

Interfaces:

public interface **AppletInitializer**;
public interface **BeanInfo**;
public interface **Customizer**;
public interface **DesignMode**;
public interface **ExceptionListener**;
public interface **PropertyEditor**;
public interface **Visibility**;

Events:

public class **PropertyChangeEvent** extends java.util.EventObject;

Event Listeners:

public interface **PropertyChangeListener** extends java.util.EventListener;
public interface **VetoableChangeListener** extends java.util.EventListener;

Other Classes:

public class **Beans**;
public class **Encoder**;
 └ public class **XMLEncoder** extends Encoder;
public class **EventHandler** implements java.lang.reflect.InvocationHandler;
public class **FeatureDescriptor**;
 └ public class **BeanDescriptor** extends FeatureDescriptor;
 └ public class **EventSetDescriptor** extends FeatureDescriptor;
 └ public class **MethodDescriptor** extends FeatureDescriptor;
 └ public class **ParameterDescriptor** extends FeatureDescriptor;
 └ public class **PropertyDescriptor** extends FeatureDescriptor;
  └ public class **IndexedPropertyDescriptor** extends PropertyDescriptor;
public class **Introspector**;
public abstract class **PersistenceDelegate**;
 └ public class **DefaultPersistenceDelegate** extends PersistenceDelegate;
public class **PropertyChangeListenerProxy** extends java.util.EventListenerProxy implements PropertyChangeListener;
public class **PropertyChangeSupport** implements Serializable;
public class **PropertyEditorManager**;
public class **PropertyEditorSupport** implements PropertyEditor;
public class **SimpleBeanInfo** implements BeanInfo;
public class **Statement**;
 └ public class **Expression** extends Statement;
public class **VetoableChangeListenerProxy** extends java.util.EventListenerProxy implements VetoableChangeListener;
public class **VetoableChangeSupport** implements Serializable;
public class **XMLDecoder**;

Exceptions:

public class **IntrospectionException** extends Exception;
public class **PropertyVetoException** extends Exception;

AppletInitializer — Java 1.2

java.beans

This interface defines general methods to initialize a newly instantiated Applet object. An AppletInitializer can be passed to the Beans.instantiate() method so that when a bean that is also an applet is created, it can be properly initialized. The initialize() method should associate the applet object with an appropriate AppletContext and AppletStub, place it within an appropriate Container, and call its init() method. The activate() method should make the applet active by calling its start() method. This interface is typically used by bean context implementors. Applications writers may need to use AppletInitializer objects, but should not usually have to invoke or implement the methods directly.

```
public interface AppletInitializer {
// Public Instance Methods
```

```
    public abstract void activate(java.applet.Applet newApplet);
    public abstract void initialize(java.applet.Applet newAppletBean, java.beans.beancontext.BeanContext bCtxt);
}
```

Passed To: Beans.instantiate()

BeanDescriptor — Java 1.1

java.beans

A BeanDescriptor object is a type of FeatureDescriptor that describes a JavaBeans component. The BeanInfo class for a bean optionally creates and initializes a BeanDescriptor object to describe the bean. Typically, only application builders and similar tools use the BeanDescriptor. To create a BeanDescriptor, you must specify the class of the bean and, optionally, the class of a Customizer for the bean. You can use the methods of FeatureDescriptor to provide additional information about the bean.

Object — FeatureDescriptor — BeanDescriptor

```
public class BeanDescriptor extends FeatureDescriptor {
// Public Constructors
    public BeanDescriptor(Class beanClass);
    public BeanDescriptor(Class beanClass, Class customizerClass);
// Public Instance Methods
    public Class getBeanClass();
    public Class getCustomizerClass();
}
```

Returned By: BeanInfo.getBeanDescriptor(), SimpleBeanInfo.getBeanDescriptor()

BeanInfo — Java 1.1

java.beans

The BeanInfo interface defines the methods a class must implement in order to export information about a JavaBeans component. The Introspector class knows how to obtain all the basic information required about a bean. A bean that wants to be more programmer-friendly can provide a class that implements this interface, and provide additional information about itself (such as an icon and description strings for each of its properties, events, and methods). Note that a bean developer defines a class that implements the methods of this interface. Typically, only builder applications and similar tools actually invoke the methods defined here.

The getBeanDescriptor(), getEventSetDescriptors(), getPropertyDescriptors(), and getMethodDescriptors() methods should return appropriate descriptor objects for the bean or null if the bean does not provide explicit bean, event set, property, or method descriptor objects. The getDefaultEventIndex() and getDefaultPropertyIndex() methods return values that specify the default event and property (i.e., those most likely to be of interest to a programmer using the bean). These methods should return –1 if there are no defaults. The getIcon() method should return an image object suitable for representing the bean in a palate or menu of available beans. The argument passed to this method is one of the four constants defined by the class; it specifies the type and size of icon requested. If the requested icon cannot be provided, getIcon() should return null.

A BeanInfo class is allowed to return null or –1 if it cannot provide the requested information. In this case, the Introspector class provides basic values for the omitted information from its own introspection of the bean. See SimpleBeanInfo for a trivial implementation of this interface suitable for convenient subclassing.

```
public interface BeanInfo {
// Public Constants
    public static final int ICON_COLOR_16x16;                                    =1
    public static final int ICON_COLOR_32x32;                                    =2
    public static final int ICON_MONO_16x16;                                     =3
    public static final int ICON_MONO_32x32;                                     =4
// Property Accessor Methods (by property name)
    public abstract BeanInfo[ ] getAdditionalBeanInfo();
    public abstract BeanDescriptor getBeanDescriptor();
    public abstract int getDefaultEventIndex();
    public abstract int getDefaultPropertyIndex();
    public abstract EventSetDescriptor[ ] getEventSetDescriptors();
    public abstract MethodDescriptor[ ] getMethodDescriptors();
    public abstract PropertyDescriptor[ ] getPropertyDescriptors();
// Public Instance Methods
    public abstract java.awt.Image getIcon(int iconKind);
}
```

Implementations: SimpleBeanInfo, java.beans.beancontext.BeanContextServiceProviderBeanInfo

Returned By: BeanInfo.getAdditionalBeanInfo(), Introspector.getBeanInfo(), SimpleBeanInfo.getAdditionalBeanInfo(), java.beans.beancontext.BeanContextServiceProviderBeanInfo.getServicesBeanInfo()

Beans — Java 1.1

java.beans

The Beans class is not meant to be instantiated; its static methods provide miscellaneous JavaBeans features. The instantiate() method creates an instance of a bean. The specified bean name represents either a serialized bean file or a bean class file; it is interpreted relative to the specified ClassLoader object.

The setDesignTime() and isDesignTime() methods can set and query a flag that indicates whether beans are being used in a application builder environment. Similarly, setGuiAvailable() and isGuiAvailable() set and query a flag that indicates whether the Java Virtual Machine is running in an environment in which a GUI is available. (Note that untrusted applet code cannot call setDesignTime() or setGuiAvailable().)

The isInstanceOf() method is a replacement for the Java instanceof operator to use with beans. Currently, it behaves like instanceof, but in the future it may work with beans that consist of a set of Java objects, each of which provides a different view of a bean. Similarly, the getInstanceOf() method is a replacement for the Java cast operator. This method converts a bean to a superclass or interface type, and currently, it behaves like a cast, but in the future, it will be compatible with multiclass beans.

```
public class Beans {
// Public Constructors
    public Beans();
// Public Class Methods
    public static Object getInstanceOf(Object bean, Class targetType);
    public static Object instantiate(ClassLoader cls, String beanName) throws java.io.IOException,
        ClassNotFoundException;
1.2 public static Object instantiate(ClassLoader cls, String beanName,
                                     java.beans.beancontext.BeanContext beanContext) throws java.io.IOException,
        ClassNotFoundException;
1.2 public static Object instantiate(ClassLoader cls, String beanName,
                                     java.beans.beancontext.BeanContext beanContext, AppletInitializer initializer)
        throws java.io.IOException, ClassNotFoundException;
```

```
    public static boolean isDesignTime();
    public static boolean isGuiAvailable();
    public static boolean isInstanceOf(Object bean, Class targetType);
    public static void setDesignTime(boolean isDesignTime) throws SecurityException;
    public static void setGuiAvailable(boolean isGuiAvailable) throws SecurityException;
}
```

Customizer — Java 1.1

java.beans

The Customizer interface specifies the methods that must be defined by any class designed to customize a JavaBeans component. In addition to implementing this interface, a customizer class must be a subclass of java.awt.Component and have a constructor that takes no arguments so it can be instantiated by an application builder.

Customizer classes are typically used by a complex bean to allow the user to easily configure the bean and provide an alternative to a simple list of properties and their values. If a customizer class is defined for a bean, it must be associated with the bean through a BeanDescriptor object returned by a BeanInfo class for the bean. Note that while a Customizer class is created by the author of a bean, that class is instantiated and used only by application builders and similar tools.

After a Customizer class is instantiated, its setObject() method is invoked once to specify the bean object to customize. The addPropertyChangeListener() and removePropertyChangeListener() methods can be called to register and deregister PropertyChangeListener objects. The Customizer should send a PropertyChangeEvent to all registered listeners any time it changes a property of the bean it is customizing.

```
public interface Customizer {
// Event Registration Methods (by event name)
    public abstract void addPropertyChangeListener(PropertyChangeListener listener);
    public abstract void removePropertyChangeListener(PropertyChangeListener listener);
// Public Instance Methods
    public abstract void setObject(Object bean);
}
```

DefaultPersistenceDelegate — Java 1.4

java.beans

This class is the persistence delegate used to encode instances of classes that do not have a built-in delegate, that do not have a delegate specified by their BeanInfo, and for which no custom delegate has been registered. The JavaBeans persistence mechanism will use the no-argument constructor to instantiate a DefaultPersistenceDelegate as needed for any such class. The resulting persistence delegate assumes that the class has a no-argument constructor, and that its state can be completely described using pairs of property accessor methods. These methods must follow the standard JavaBeans get/set naming convention. When working with conforming JavaBeans classes such as these, there is never any need for an application to instantiate a DefaultPersistenceDelegate because this is done automatically by the beans persistence mechanism.

Instances of this class can also serve as a persistence delegate for beans that do not have a no-argument constructor, and that instead pass the values of read-only properties to the constructor. In this case, simply instantiate a DefaultPersistenceDelegate by passing an array of strings listing the names of the read-only constructor arguments. The bean class must of course define property getter methods for these named properties. These getter methods must follow the normal JavaBeans naming conventions, or must be specified in a BeanInfo class. Consider the java.awt.Color class, for example. (Color is documented in *Java Foundation Classes in a Nutshell* [O'Reilly].) If the JavaBeans persistence mechanism did not already define a persistence delegate for this class, you could create one like this:

```
PersistenceDelegate delegate = new DefaultPersistenceDelegate(new String[]{"red", "green", "blue"});
```

This works because Color defines a three argument constructor whose three arguments correspond to the return values of the property getter methods getRed(), getGreen(), and getBlue().

Object → PersistenceDelegate → DefaultPersistenceDelegate

```
public class DefaultPersistenceDelegate extends PersistenceDelegate {
// Public Constructors
    public DefaultPersistenceDelegate();
    public DefaultPersistenceDelegate(String[ ] constructorPropertyNames);
// Protected Methods Overriding PersistenceDelegate
    protected void initialize(Class type, Object oldInstance, Object newInstance, Encoder out);
    protected Expression instantiate(Object oldInstance, Encoder out);
    protected boolean mutatesTo(Object oldInstance, Object newInstance);
}
```

DesignMode — Java 1.2

java.beans

This interface defines a single boolean designTime property that specifies whether a bean is running within an interactive design tool or a standalone application or applet. This interface is typically implemented by a bean container or bean context, so that children beans can query the designTime property.

```
public interface DesignMode {
// Public Constants
    public static final String PROPERTYNAME;                    =[quot ] designTime [quot ]
// Public Instance Methods
    public abstract boolean isDesignTime();
    public abstract void setDesignTime(boolean designTime);
}
```

Implementations: java.beans.beancontext.BeanContext

Encoder — Java 1.4

java.beans

This class provides the architectural underpinnings for the JavaBeans persistence mechanism; the job of an Encoder object is to encode and output the Expression and Statement objects produced by a PersistenceDelegate to describe a the state of a bean. Although Encoder is not technically an abstract class, it is never used directly, since it does not perform any useful encoding itself. See the XMLEncoder subclass for further details.

```
public class Encoder {
// Public Constructors
    public Encoder();
// Public Instance Methods
    public Object get(Object oldInstance);
    public ExceptionListener getExceptionListener();
    public PersistenceDelegate getPersistenceDelegate(Class type);
    public Object remove(Object oldInstance);
    public void setExceptionListener(ExceptionListener exceptionListener);
```

```
    public void setPersistenceDelegate(Class type, PersistenceDelegate persistenceDelegate);
    public void writeExpression(Expression oldExp);
    public void writeStatement(java.beans.Statement oldStm);
// Protected Instance Methods
    protected void writeObject(Object o);
}
```

Subclasses: XMLEncoder

Passed To: DefaultPersistenceDelegate.{initialize(), instantiate()}, PersistenceDelegate.{initialize(), instantiate(), writeObject()}

EventHandler — Java 1.4

java.beans

This class uses Proxy and other classes from the java.lang.reflect package to create objects that can serve as simple event listeners and can be easily serialized using the JavaBeans persistence mechanism in a way that event listeners implemented as anonymous classes cannot.

Applications do not typically work with EventHandler objects or the EventHandler() constructor directly. Instead, they use one of the static create() methods to obtain an object that implements the desired event listener interface. A listener created with EventHandler.create() performs a single method call when activated. You specify the name of the method to call, the object upon which the method is to be called, and an optional argument to pass to the method. This argument value may be the event object that triggered the listener, or it may be a property of that event object. The arguments to create() are the following:

listenerInterface
: The Class object that represents the EventListener to be returned. For example, PropertyChangeListener.class.

target
: The object upon which the resulting event listener should invoke a method.

action
: The name of the method to be invoked on *target*. This argument may also specify the name of a property of *target*, in which case a property setter method will be invoked. So instead of specifying the method name "setX()" as the *action* you could also specify the property name "x".

eventPropertyName
: This optional argument specifies the name of a property of the EventObject object (or whatever other object is passed to the listener method) whose value is to be passed to the *action* method of the *target* object. If you use the three-argument version of create(), or pass null for this argument, then EventHandler will either pass the event object itself as the argument to the *action* method, or will pass no argument at all.

  If *eventPropertyName* is "x", the EventHandler first looks for a no-argument property getter method named getX() in the object (typically an EventObject) passed to the listener method. If no such method exists, it then looks for a no-argument getter named "isX". If that method does not exist either, it then looks for a no-argument method named "x" and uses that method.

eventPropertyName may actually specify multiple levels of property lookups using dot-separated names. For example, a *eventPropertyName* of "propertyName.toLowerCase" would be translated into the calls getPropertyName().toLowerCase() on the event object. The value returned by these calls would then be passed to the *action* method.

listenerMethodName
: This argument specifies the name of the method in the *listenerInterface* which is to be implemented by the returned object. If you specify null or use the three- or four-argument version of create() then all methods of the returned object will invoke the *action* method of the *target* object.

Object — EventHandler ··· InvocationHandler

```
public class EventHandler implements java.lang.reflect.InvocationHandler {
// Public Constructors
   public EventHandler(Object target, String action, String eventPropertyName, String listenerMethodName);
// Public Class Methods
   public static Object create(Class listenerInterface, Object target, String action);
   public static Object create(Class listenerInterface, Object target, String action, String eventPropertyName);
   public static Object create(Class listenerInterface, Object target, String action, String eventPropertyName,
                               String listenerMethodName);
// Public Instance Methods
   public String getAction();
   public String getEventPropertyName();
   public String getListenerMethodName();
   public Object getTarget();
// Methods Implementing InvocationHandler
   public Object invoke(Object proxy, java.lang.reflect.Method method, Object[ ] arguments);
}
```

EventSetDescriptor **Java 1.1**

java.beans

An EventSetDescriptor object is a type of FeatureDescriptor that describes a single set of events supported by a JavaBeans component. A set of events corresponds to one or more methods supported by a single EventListener interface. The BeanInfo class for a bean optionally creates EventSetDescriptor objects to describe the event sets the bean supports. Typically, only application builders and similar tools use the get and is methods of EventSetDescriptor objects to obtain the event-set description information.

To create an EventSetDescriptor object, you must specify the class of the bean that supports the event set, the base name of the event set, the class of the EventListener interface that corresponds to the event set, and the methods within this interface that are invoked when particular events within the set occur. Optionally, you can also specify the methods of the bean class that add and remove EventListener objects. The various constructors allow you to specify methods by name, as java.lang.reflect.Method objects, or as MethodDescriptor objects. In Java 1.4 and later, you can also specify the "get listeners" method used to query the set of registered listener objects for a event set.

Once you have created an EventSetDescriptor, use setUnicast() to specify whether it represents a unicast event and setInDefaultEventSet() to specify whether the event set should be treated as the default event set by builder applications. The methods of the FeatureDescriptor superclass allow additional information about the property to be specified.

```
public class EventSetDescriptor extends FeatureDescriptor {
// Public Constructors
    public EventSetDescriptor(Class sourceClass, String eventSetName, Class listenerType,
                              String listenerMethodName) throws IntrospectionException;
    public EventSetDescriptor(String eventSetName, Class listenerType, java.lang.reflect.Method[ ] listenerMethods,
                              java.lang.reflect.Method addListenerMethod,
                              java.lang.reflect.Method removeListenerMethod) throws IntrospectionException;
    public EventSetDescriptor(String eventSetName, Class listenerType,
                              MethodDescriptor[ ] listenerMethodDescriptors,
                              java.lang.reflect.Method addListenerMethod,
                              java.lang.reflect.Method removeListenerMethod) throws IntrospectionException;
1.4 public EventSetDescriptor(String eventSetName, Class listenerType, java.lang.reflect.Method[ ] listenerMethods,
                              java.lang.reflect.Method addListenerMethod,
                              java.lang.reflect.Method removeListenerMethod,
                              java.lang.reflect.Method getListenerMethod) throws IntrospectionException;
    public EventSetDescriptor(Class sourceClass, String eventSetName, Class listenerType,
                              String[ ] listenerMethodNames, String addListenerMethodName,
                              String removeListenerMethodName) throws IntrospectionException;
1.4 public EventSetDescriptor(Class sourceClass, String eventSetName, Class listenerType,
                              String[ ] listenerMethodNames, String addListenerMethodName,
                              String removeListenerMethodName, String getListenerMethodName)
        throws IntrospectionException;
// Property Accessor Methods (by property name)
    public java.lang.reflect.Method getAddListenerMethod();
1.4 public java.lang.reflect.Method getGetListenerMethod();
    public boolean isInDefaultEventSet();
    public void setInDefaultEventSet(boolean inDefaultEventSet);
    public MethodDescriptor[ ] getListenerMethodDescriptors();
    public java.lang.reflect.Method[ ] getListenerMethods();
    public Class getListenerType();
    public java.lang.reflect.Method getRemoveListenerMethod();
    public boolean isUnicast();
    public void setUnicast(boolean unicast);
}
```

Returned By: BeanInfo.getEventSetDescriptors(), SimpleBeanInfo.getEventSetDescriptors()

ExceptionListener — Java 1.4

java.beans

This interface is implemented by objects that wish to be notified of exceptions that occur during the JavaBeans encoding or decoding process performed by the Encoder or XMLDecoder classes. The exceptionThrown() method will be invoked when an exception occurs.

```
public interface ExceptionListener {
// Public Instance Methods
    public abstract void exceptionThrown(Exception e);
}
```

Passed To: Encoder.setExceptionListener(), XMLDecoder.{setExceptionListener(), XMLDecoder()}

Returned By: Encoder.getExceptionListener(), XMLDecoder.getExceptionListener()

Expression **Java 1.4**

java.beans

This subclass of Statement represents a method call that has a return value. You do not use the inherited execute() method to invoke an Expression, but instead call getValue() to invoke the described method and return its return value. getValue() caches the resulting value, so that only the first call to getValue() actually results in an invocation of the underlying method. You can also specify the value by passing it to the four-argument constructor or to setValue(). This is sometimes done for efficiency when encoding a method call whose result you already know. See Statement for information about specifying the target object, the method name, and the array of method argument objects.

There are two special-case method names you can use with the Expression class. To invoke a constructor, use the Class object for the desired class as the target object, and use "new" as the method name. To access an element of an array, specify the array as the target object, use "get" as the method name, and pass an Integer containing the desired array index as the sole method argument.

Object — Statement — Expression

```
public class Expression extends java.beans.Statement {
// Public Constructors
   public Expression(Object target, String methodName, Object[ ] arguments);
   public Expression(Object value, Object target, String methodName, Object[ ] arguments);
// Public Instance Methods
   public Object getValue() throws Exception;
   public void setValue(Object value);
// Public Methods Overriding Statement
   public String toString();
}
```

Passed To: Encoder.writeExpression(), XMLEncoder.writeExpression()

Returned By: DefaultPersistenceDelegate.instantiate(), PersistenceDelegate.instantiate()

FeatureDescriptor **Java 1.1**

java.beans

The FeatureDescriptor class is the base class for MethodDescriptor and PropertyDescriptor, as well as other classes used by the JavaBeans introspection mechanism. It provides basic information about a feature (e.g., method, property, or event) of a bean. Typically, the methods that begin with get and is are used by application builders or other tools to query the features of a bean. The set methods, on the other hand, may be used by bean authors to define information about the bean.

setName() specifies the locale-independent, programmatic name of the feature; setDisplayName() specifies a localized, human-readable name; and setShortDescription() specifies a short localized string (about 40 characters) that describes the feature. Both the short description and the localized name default to the value of the programmatic name. setExpert() and setHidden() allow you to indicate that the feature is for use only by experts or by the builder tool and should be hidden from users of the builder. Finally, the setValue() method allows you to associate an arbitrary named value with the feature.

```
public class FeatureDescriptor {
// Public Constructors
   public FeatureDescriptor();
// Property Accessor Methods (by property name)
   public String getDisplayName();                                    default:null
```

```
    public void setDisplayName(String displayName);
    public boolean isExpert();                                              default:false
    public void setExpert(boolean expert);
    public boolean isHidden();                                              default:false
    public void setHidden(boolean hidden);
    public String getName();                                                default:null
    public void setName(String name);
1.2 public boolean isPreferred();                                           default:false
1.2 public void setPreferred(boolean preferred);
    public String getShortDescription();                                    default:null
    public void setShortDescription(String text);
// Public Instance Methods
    public java.util.Enumeration attributeNames();
    public Object getValue(String attributeName);
    public void setValue(String attributeName, Object value);
}
```

Subclasses: BeanDescriptor, EventSetDescriptor, MethodDescriptor, ParameterDescriptor, PropertyDescriptor

IndexedPropertyDescriptor **Java 1.1**

java.beans

An IndexedPropertyDescriptor object is a type of PropertyDescriptor that describes a bean property that is (or behaves like) an array. The BeanInfo class for a bean optionally creates and initializes IndexedPropertyDescriptor objects to describe the indexed properties the bean supports. Typically, only application builders and similar tools use the descriptor objects to obtain indexed property description information.

You create an IndexedPropertyDescriptor by specifying the name of the indexed property and the Class object for the bean. If you have not followed the standard design patterns for accessor method naming, you can also specify the accessor methods for the property, either as method names or as java.lang.reflect.Method objects. Once you have created an IndexedPropertyDescriptor object, you can use the methods of PropertyDescriptor and FeatureDescriptor to provide additional information about the indexed property.

Object ─ FeatureDescriptor ─ PropertyDescriptor ─ IndexedPropertyDescriptor

```
public class IndexedPropertyDescriptor extends PropertyDescriptor {
// Public Constructors
    public IndexedPropertyDescriptor(String propertyName, Class beanClass) throws IntrospectionException;
    public IndexedPropertyDescriptor(String propertyName, java.lang.reflect.Method getter,
                                     java.lang.reflect.Method setter, java.lang.reflect.Method indexedGetter,
                                     java.lang.reflect.Method indexedSetter) throws IntrospectionException;
    public IndexedPropertyDescriptor(String propertyName, Class beanClass, String getterName,
                                     String setterName, String indexedGetterName, String indexedSetterName)
        throws IntrospectionException;
// Public Instance Methods
    public Class getIndexedPropertyType();
    public java.lang.reflect.Method getIndexedReadMethod();
    public java.lang.reflect.Method getIndexedWriteMethod();
1.2 public void setIndexedReadMethod(java.lang.reflect.Method getter) throws IntrospectionException;
1.2 public void setIndexedWriteMethod(java.lang.reflect.Method setter) throws IntrospectionException;
// Public Methods Overriding PropertyDescriptor
1.4 public boolean equals(Object obj);
}
```

IntrospectionException — Java 1.1

java.beans — ***serializable checked***

An IntrospectionException signals that introspection on a JavaBeans component cannot be completed. Typically, this indicates a bug in the way the bean or its associated BeanInfo class is defined.

Object — Throwable — Exception — IntrospectionException
Throwable ⋯ Serializable

```
public class IntrospectionException extends Exception {
// Public Constructors
   public IntrospectionException(String mess);
}
```

Thrown By: Too many methods to list.

Introspector — Java 1.1

java.beans

The Introspector is a class that is never instantiated. Its static getBeanInfo() methods provide a way to obtain information about a JavaBeans component and are typically only invoked by application builders or similar tools. getBeanInfo() first looks for a BeanInfo class for the specified bean class. For a class named *x*, it looks for a BeanInfo class named *x*BeanInfo, first in the current package and then in each of the packages in the BeanInfo search path.

If no BeanInfo class is found, or if the BeanInfo class found does not provide complete information about the bean properties, events, and methods, getBeanInfo() introspects on the bean class by using the java.lang.reflect package to fill in the missing information. When explicit information is provided by a BeanInfo class, getBeanInfo() treats it as definitive. When determining information through introspection, however, it examines each of the bean's superclasses in turn, looking for a BeanInfo class at that level or using introspection. When calling getBeanInfo(), you may optionally specify a second class argument that specifies a superclass for which, and above which, getBeanInfo() does not introspect.

```
public class Introspector {
// No Constructor
// Public Constants
1.2 public static final int IGNORE_ALL_BEANINFO;                                        =3
1.2 public static final int IGNORE_IMMEDIATE_BEANINFO;                                  =2
1.2 public static final int USE_ALL_BEANINFO;                                           =1
// Public Class Methods
    public static String decapitalize(String name);
1.2 public static void flushCaches();
1.2 public static void flushFromCaches(Class clz);
    public static BeanInfo getBeanInfo(Class beanClass) throws IntrospectionException;
1.2 public static BeanInfo getBeanInfo(Class beanClass, int flags) throws IntrospectionException;
    public static BeanInfo getBeanInfo(Class beanClass, Class stopClass) throws IntrospectionException;
    public static String[ ] getBeanInfoSearchPath();                                    synchronized
    public static void setBeanInfoSearchPath(String[ ] path);                            synchronized
}
```

MethodDescriptor

Java 1.1

java.beans

A MethodDescriptor object is a type of FeatureDescriptor that describes a method supported by a JavaBeans component. The BeanInfo class for a bean optionally creates MethodDescriptor objects that describe the methods the bean exports. While a BeanInfo class creates and initializes MethodDescriptor objects, it is typically only application builders and similar tools that use these objects to obtain information about the methods supported by a bean.

To create a MethodDescriptor, you must specify the java.lang.reflect.Method object for the method and, optionally, an array of ParameterDescriptor objects that describe the parameters of the method. Once you have created a MethodDescriptor object, you can use FeatureDescriptor methods to provide additional information about each method.

Object — FeatureDescriptor — MethodDescriptor

```
public class MethodDescriptor extends FeatureDescriptor {
// Public Constructors
   public MethodDescriptor(java.lang.reflect.Method method);
   public MethodDescriptor(java.lang.reflect.Method method, ParameterDescriptor[ ] parameterDescriptors);
// Public Instance Methods
   public java.lang.reflect.Method getMethod();
   public ParameterDescriptor[ ] getParameterDescriptors();
}
```

Passed To: EventSetDescriptor.EventSetDescriptor()

Returned By: BeanInfo.getMethodDescriptors(), EventSetDescriptor.getListenerMethodDescriptors(), SimpleBeanInfo.getMethodDescriptors()

ParameterDescriptor

Java 1.1

java.beans

A ParameterDescriptor object is a type of FeatureDescriptor that describes an argument or parameter to a method of a JavaBeans component. The BeanInfo class for a JavaBeans component optionally creates ParameterDescriptor objects that describe the parameters of the methods the bean exports. While the BeanInfo class creates and initializes ParameterDescriptor objects, it is typically only application builders and similar tools that use these objects to obtain information about method parameters supported by the bean.

The ParameterDescriptor class is a trivial subclass of FeatureDescriptor and does not provide any new methods. Thus, you should use the methods of FeatureDescriptor to provide information about method parameters.

Object — FeatureDescriptor — ParameterDescriptor

```
public class ParameterDescriptor extends FeatureDescriptor {
// Public Constructors
   public ParameterDescriptor();
}
```

Passed To: MethodDescriptor.MethodDescriptor()

Returned By: MethodDescriptor.getParameterDescriptors()

PersistenceDelegate Java 1.4

java.beans

A PersistenceDelegate plays the central role in the JavaBeans persistence mechanism: it is responsible for determining the current state of a bean, and expressing that state in terms of the public API of the bean as a series of constructor and method calls (represented by Statement and Expression objects) that can serve to later recreate the bean and its state.

writeObject() is is the key method: an Encoder passes an object to the writeObject() method of the appropriate PersistenceDelegate. It is the delegate's responsibility to determine the sequence of constructor and method calls required to recreate the object, and to tell the Encoder what those methods calls are by passing Statement and Expression objects to the encoder's writeStatement() and writeExpression() methods. The Encoder can then encode the Statement and Expression objects into some output format, such as an XML document. Note that writeObject() is the only public method of the PersistenceDelegate class. It is implemented in terms of the three protected methods, which subclasses can override to create custom persistence behavior.

The JavaBeans persistence implementation provides working delegates for all AWT and Swing GUI components, and for all types (such as colors and fonts) used as properties of those components. The DefaultPersistenceDelegate class works for any bean that expresses its complete state in terms of constructor arguments and property getter and setter methods. If you want to use the JavaBeans persistence mechanism to serialize objects that do not conform to these JavaBeans design conventions, you may need to subclass PersistenceDelegate and override one or more of its three protected methods. A full tutorial on writing custom persistence delegates is beyond the scope of this book, but briefly, the instantiate() method is responsible for returning an Expression object that represents a call to a constructor or factory method to instantiate an object with the same state as the specified object. mutatesTo() is supposed to determine whether one instance of an object can be mutated so that it has the same state as another object. If this method returns true, then the PersistenceDelegate may call the initialize() method which must actually write out the Expression and Statement objects that represent the method calls required to perform that initialization.

If you need to use an instance of DefaultPersistenceDelegate or an instance of a custom PersistenceDelegate you have written yourself in order to persistently save the state of a bean or related object, you must first associate the delegate with the class for which it is responsible by calling the setPersistenceDelegate() method of your XMLEncoder object. (Note that this method is not defined by XMLEncoder, but is actually inherited from the Encoder superclass.) Alternatively, a JavaBean may specify its PersistenceDelegate by defining a BeanInfo class that returns a BeanDescriptor that returns the name of the persistence delegate class as the value of the attribute returned by getValue("persistenceDelegate").

```
public abstract class PersistenceDelegate {
// Public Constructors
   public PersistenceDelegate();
// Public Instance Methods
   public void writeObject(Object oldInstance, Encoder out);
// Protected Instance Methods
   protected void initialize(Class type, Object oldInstance, Object newInstance, Encoder out);
   protected abstract Expression instantiate(Object oldInstance, Encoder out);
   protected boolean mutatesTo(Object oldInstance, Object newInstance);
}
```

Subclasses: DefaultPersistenceDelegate

Passed To: Encoder.setPersistenceDelegate()

Returned By: Encoder.getPersistenceDelegate()

PropertyChangeEvent — Java 1.1

java.beans — ***serializable event***

PropertyChangeEvent is a subclass of java.util.EventObject. An event of this type is sent to interested PropertyChangeListener objects whenever a JavaBeans component changes a bound property or whenever a PropertyEditor or Customizer changes a property value. A PropertyChangeEvent is also sent to registered VetoableChangeListener objects when a bean attempts to change the value of a constrained property.

When creating a PropertyChangeEvent, you normally specify the bean that generated the event, the programmatic (locale-independent) name of the property that changed, and the old and new values of the property. If the values cannot be determined, null should be passed instead. If the event is a notification that more than one property value changed, the name should also be null. While JavaBeans must generate and send PropertyChangeEvent objects, it is typically only application builders and similar tools that are interested in receiving them.

Object — EventObject — PropertyChangeEvent
Serializable

```
public class PropertyChangeEvent extends java.util.EventObject {
// Public Constructors
   public PropertyChangeEvent(Object source, String propertyName, Object oldValue, Object newValue);
// Public Instance Methods
   public Object getNewValue();
   public Object getOldValue();
   public Object getPropagationId();
   public String getPropertyName();
   public void setPropagationId(Object propagationId);
}
```

Passed To: Too many methods to list.

Returned By: PropertyVetoException.getPropertyChangeEvent()

PropertyChangeListener — Java 1.1

java.beans — ***event listener***

This interface is an extension of java.util.EventListener; it defines the method a class must implement in order to be notified when property changes occur. A PropertyChangeEvent is sent to all registered PropertyChangeListener objects when a bean changes one of its bound properties or when a PropertyEditor or Customizer changes the value of a property.

EventListener ··· PropertyChangeListener

```
public interface PropertyChangeListener extends java.util.EventListener {
// Public Instance Methods
   public abstract void propertyChange(PropertyChangeEvent evt);
}
```

Implementations: Too many classes to list.

Passed To: Too many methods to list.

Returned By: Too many methods to list.

Type Of: javax.swing.plaf.basic.BasicColorChooserUI.propertyChangeListener, javax.swing.plaf.basic.BasicComboBoxUI.propertyChangeListener, javax.swing.plaf.basic.BasicComboPopup.propertyChangeListener, javax.swing.plaf.basic.BasicInternalFrameTitlePane.propertyChangeListener, javax.swing.plaf.basic.BasicInternalFrameUI.propertyChangeListener, javax.swing.plaf.basic.BasicListUI.propertyChangeListener, javax.swing.plaf.basic.BasicMenuUI.propertyChangeListener, javax.swing.plaf.basic.BasicOptionPaneUI.propertyChangeListener, javax.swing.plaf.basic.BasicScrollBarUI.propertyChangeListener, javax.swing.plaf.basic.BasicScrollPaneUI.spPropertyChangeListener, javax.swing.plaf.basic.BasicSliderUI.propertyChangeListener, javax.swing.plaf.basic.BasicSplitPaneUI.propertyChangeListener, javax.swing.plaf.basic.BasicTabbedPaneUI.propertyChangeListener, javax.swing.plaf.basic.BasicToolBarUI.propertyListener, javax.swing.plaf.metal.MetalToolBarUI.rolloverListener

PropertyChangeListenerProxy — Java 1.4

java.beans

This class implements PropertyChangeListener and serves as a wrapper around another PropertyChangeListener object. Beans that implement a two-argument addPropertyChangeListener() method to allow registration of a property change listener for a specific named property may return instances of this class from their getPropertyChangeListeners() method (if they implement one). Use getPropertyName() to determine the name of the property to which the listener applies. And use the inherited getListener() method to obtain the underlying PropertyChangeListener object.

Object — EventListenerProxy — PropertyChangeListenerProxy
EventListener | EventListener ··· PropertyChangeListener

```
public class PropertyChangeListenerProxy extends java.util.EventListenerProxy
        implements PropertyChangeListener {
// Public Constructors
    public PropertyChangeListenerProxy(String propertyName, PropertyChangeListener listener);
// Public Instance Methods
    public String getPropertyName();
// Methods Implementing PropertyChangeListener
    public void propertyChange(PropertyChangeEvent evt);
}
```

PropertyChangeSupport — Java 1.1

java.beans — *serializable*

The PropertyChangeSupport class is a convenience class that maintains a list of registered PropertyChangeListener objects and provides the firePropertyChange() method for sending a PropertyChangeEvent object to all registered listeners. Because there are some tricky thread-synchronization issues involved in doing this correctly, it is recommended that all JavaBeans that support bound properties either extend this class or, more commonly, create an instance of this class to which they can delegate their addProperty-

ChangeListener() and removePropertyChangeListener() methods. In Java 1.4, beans that define getPropertyChangeListeners() methods can also delegate that method to this object.

Object ┤ PropertyChangeSupport ··· Serializable

```
public class PropertyChangeSupport implements Serializable {
// Public Constructors
   public PropertyChangeSupport(Object sourceBean);
// Event Registration Methods (by event name)
   public void addPropertyChangeListener(PropertyChangeListener listener);                          synchronized
   public void removePropertyChangeListener(PropertyChangeListener listener);                       synchronized
// Public Instance Methods
1.2 public void addPropertyChangeListener(String propertyName, PropertyChangeListener listener);    synchronized
1.2 public void firePropertyChange(PropertyChangeEvent evt);
1.2 public void firePropertyChange(String propertyName, int oldValue, int newValue);
1.2 public void firePropertyChange(String propertyName, boolean oldValue, boolean newValue);
   public void firePropertyChange(String propertyName, Object oldValue, Object newValue);
1.4 public PropertyChangeListener[ ] getPropertyChangeListeners();                                  synchronized
1.4 public PropertyChangeListener[ ] getPropertyChangeListeners(String propertyName);              synchronized
1.2 public boolean hasListeners(String propertyName);                                               synchronized
1.2 public void removePropertyChangeListener(String propertyName,                                   synchronized
                                              PropertyChangeListener listener);
}
```

Subclasses: javax.swing.event.SwingPropertyChangeSupport

Type Of: java.awt.Toolkit.desktopPropsSupport, java.beans.beancontext.BeanContextChildSupport.pcSupport

PropertyDescriptor — Java 1.1

java.beans

A PropertyDescriptor object is a type of FeatureDescriptor that describes a single property of a JavaBeans component. The BeanInfo class for a bean optionally creates and initializes PropertyDescriptor objects to describe the properties the bean supports. Typically, only application builders and similar tools use the get and is methods to obtain this property description information.

You create a PropertyDescriptor by specifying the name of the property and the Class object for the bean. If you have not followed the standard design patterns for accessor-method naming, you can also specify the accessor methods for the property. Once a PropertyDescriptor is created, the setBound() and setConstrained() methods allow you to specify whether the property is bound and/or constrained. setPropertyEditorClass() allows you to specify a specific property editor that should edit the value of this property (this is useful, for example, when the property is an enumerated type with a specific list of supported values). The methods of the FeatureDescriptor superclass allow additional information about the property to be specified.

Object ┤ FeatureDescriptor ┤ PropertyDescriptor

```
public class PropertyDescriptor extends FeatureDescriptor {
// Public Constructors
   public PropertyDescriptor(String propertyName, Class beanClass) throws IntrospectionException;
   public PropertyDescriptor(String propertyName, java.lang.reflect.Method getter, java.lang.reflect.Method setter)
       throws IntrospectionException;
   public PropertyDescriptor(String propertyName, Class beanClass, String getterName, String setterName)
       throws IntrospectionException;
```

```
// Property Accessor Methods (by property name)
    public boolean isBound();
    public void setBound(boolean bound);
    public boolean isConstrained();
    public void setConstrained(boolean constrained);
    public Class getPropertyEditorClass();
    public void setPropertyEditorClass(Class propertyEditorClass);
    public Class getPropertyType();
    public java.lang.reflect.Method getReadMethod();
1.2 public void setReadMethod(java.lang.reflect.Method getter) throws IntrospectionException;
    public java.lang.reflect.Method getWriteMethod();
1.2 public void setWriteMethod(java.lang.reflect.Method setter) throws IntrospectionException;
// Public Methods Overriding Object
1.4 public boolean equals(Object obj);
}
```

Subclasses: IndexedPropertyDescriptor

Returned By: BeanInfo.getPropertyDescriptors(), SimpleBeanInfo.getPropertyDescriptors()

PropertyEditor — Java 1.1

java.beans

The PropertyEditor interface defines the methods that must be implemented by a JavaBeans property editor intended for use within an application builder or similar tool. PropertyEditor is a complex interface because it defines methods to support different ways of displaying property values to the user. It also defines methods to support different ways of allowing the user to edit the property value.

For a property of type *x*, the author of a bean typically implements a property editor of class *x*Editor. While the editor is implemented by the bean author, it is usually instantiated or used only by application builders or similar tools (or by a Customizer class for a bean). In addition to implementing the PropertyEditor interface, a property editor must have a constructor that expects no arguments, so that it can be easily be instantiated by an application builder. Also, it must accept registration and deregistration of PropertyChangeListener objects and send a PropertyChangeEvent to all registered listeners when it changes the value of the property being edited. The PropertyEditorSupport class is a trivial implementation of PropertyEditor, suitable for subclassing or for supporting a list of PropertyChangeListener objects.

```
public interface PropertyEditor {
// Event Registration Methods (by event name)
    public abstract void addPropertyChangeListener(PropertyChangeListener listener);
    public abstract void removePropertyChangeListener(PropertyChangeListener listener);
// Property Accessor Methods (by property name)
    public abstract String getAsText();
    public abstract void setAsText(String text) throws IllegalArgumentException;
    public abstract java.awt.Component getCustomEditor();
    public abstract String getJavaInitializationString();
    public abstract boolean isPaintable();
    public abstract String[ ] getTags();
    public abstract Object getValue();
    public abstract void setValue(Object value);
// Public Instance Methods
    public abstract void paintValue(java.awt.Graphics gfx, java.awt.Rectangle box);
```

```
    public abstract boolean supportsCustomEditor();
}
```

Implementations: PropertyEditorSupport

Returned By: PropertyEditorManager.findEditor()

PropertyEditorManager Java 1.1

java.beans

The PropertyEditorManager class is not meant to be instantiated; it defines static methods for registering and looking up PropertyEditor classes for a specified property type. A bean can specify a particular PropertyEditor class for a given property by specifying it in a PropertyDescriptor object for the property. If it does not do this, the PropertyEditorManager is used to register and look up editors. A bean or an application builder tool can call the registerEditor() method to register a PropertyEditor for properties of a specified type. Application builders and bean Customizer classes can call the findEditor() method to obtain a PropertyEditor for a given property type. If no editor has been registered for a given type, the PropertyEditorManager attempts to locate one. For a type x, it looks for a class *x*Editor first in the same package as *x*, and then in each package listed in the property editor search path.

```
public class PropertyEditorManager {
// Public Constructors
    public PropertyEditorManager();
// Public Class Methods
    public static PropertyEditor findEditor(Class targetType);                    synchronized
    public static String[ ] getEditorSearchPath();                                synchronized
    public static void registerEditor(Class targetType, Class editorClass);
    public static void setEditorSearchPath(String[ ] path);                      synchronized
}
```

PropertyEditorSupport Java 1.1

java.beans

The PropertyEditorSupport class is a trivial implementation of the PropertyEditor interface. It provides no-op default implementations of most methods, so you can define simple PropertyEditor subclasses that override only a few required methods. In addition, PropertyEditorSupport defines working versions of addPropertyChangeListener() and removePropertyChangeListener(), along with a firePropertyChange() method that sends a PropertyChangeEvent to all registered listeners. PropertyEditor classes may choose to instantiate a PropertyEditorSupport object simply to handle the job of managing the list of listeners. When used in this way, the PropertyEditorSupport object should be instantiated with a source object specified, so that the source object can be used in the PropertyChangeEvent objects that are sent.

Object — PropertyEditorSupport ··· PropertyEditor

```
public class PropertyEditorSupport implements PropertyEditor {
// Protected Constructors
    protected PropertyEditorSupport();
    protected PropertyEditorSupport(Object source);
// Event Registration Methods (by event name)
    public void addPropertyChangeListener(               Implements:PropertyEditor synchronized
                                PropertyChangeListener listener);
    public void removePropertyChangeListener(            Implements:PropertyEditor synchronized
                                PropertyChangeListener listener);
```

```
// Public Instance Methods
   public void firePropertyChange();
// Methods Implementing PropertyEditor
   public void addPropertyChangeListener(PropertyChangeListener listener);          synchronized
   public String getAsText();
   public java.awt.Component getCustomEditor();                                     constant
   public String getJavaInitializationString();
   public String[ ] getTags();                                                      constant
   public Object getValue();
   public boolean isPaintable();                                                    constant
   public void paintValue(java.awt.Graphics gfx, java.awt.Rectangle box);           empty
   public void removePropertyChangeListener(PropertyChangeListener listener);       synchronized
   public void setAsText(String text) throws IllegalArgumentException;
   public void setValue(Object value);
   public boolean supportsCustomEditor();                                           constant
}
```

PropertyVetoException — Java 1.1

java.beans — *serializable checked*

A PropertyVetoException signals that a VetoableChangeListener that received a PropertyChangeEvent for a constrained property of a bean has vetoed that proposed change. When this exception is received, the property in question should revert to its original value, and any VetoableChangeListener objects that have already been notified of the property change must be renotified to indicate that the property has reverted to its old value. The VetoableChangeSupport class handles this renotification automatically and rethrows the PropertyVetoException to notify its caller that the change was rejected.

Object — Throwable — Exception — PropertyVetoException
Throwable ··· Serializable

```
public class PropertyVetoException extends Exception {
// Public Constructors
   public PropertyVetoException(String mess, PropertyChangeEvent evt);
// Public Instance Methods
   public PropertyChangeEvent getPropertyChangeEvent();
}
```

Thrown By: Too many methods to list.

SimpleBeanInfo — Java 1.1

java.beans

The SimpleBeanInfo class is a trivial implementation of the BeanInfo interface. The methods of this class all return null or –1, indicating that no bean information is available. To use this class, you need to override only the method or methods that return the particular type of bean information you want to provide. In addition, SimpleBeanInfo provides a convenience method, loadImage(), that takes a resource name as an argument and returns an Image object. This method is useful when defining the getIcon() method.

Object — SimpleBeanInfo ··· BeanInfo

```
public class SimpleBeanInfo implements BeanInfo {
// Public Constructors
   public SimpleBeanInfo();
```

```
// Public Instance Methods
   public java.awt.Image loadImage(String resourceName);
// Methods Implementing BeanInfo
   public BeanInfo[ ] getAdditionalBeanInfo();                              constant default:null
   public BeanDescriptor getBeanDescriptor();                               constant default:null
   public int getDefaultEventIndex();                                       constant default:-1
   public int getDefaultPropertyIndex();                                    constant default:-1
   public EventSetDescriptor[ ] getEventSetDescriptors();                   constant default:null
   public java.awt.Image getIcon(int iconKind);                                        constant
   public MethodDescriptor[ ] getMethodDescriptors();                       constant default:null
   public PropertyDescriptor[ ] getPropertyDescriptors();                   constant default:null
}
```

Statement — Java 1.4

java.beans

This simple class represents the invocation of a method that has no return value. Within the framework of the JavaBeans persistence mechanism, Statement objects are generated by a PersistenceDelegate and translated to some textual form by an Encoder, such as the XMLEncoder class.

To create a Statement object, specify the target object upon which the method is to be called, the name of the method to invoke, and an array of arguments to pass to the method. If any of the method arguments are primitive values, use a corresponding wrapper object: use an Integer to represent an int value, for example. To invoke a static method, use the appropriate Class object as the target object. If the target object is an array, you can set an element of the array by using the method name "set", passing an Integer to specify the array index and an Object to specify the value to be stored at that index. execute() uses the java.lang.reflect package to invoke the named method on the specified target with the specified arguments. See also the subclass Expression which describes a method invocation with a return value.

```
public class Statement {
// Public Constructors
   public Statement(Object target, String methodName, Object[ ] arguments);
// Public Instance Methods
   public void execute() throws Exception;
   public Object[ ] getArguments();
   public String getMethodName();
   public Object getTarget();
// Public Methods Overriding Object
   public String toString();
}
```

Subclasses: Expression

Passed To: Encoder.writeStatement(), XMLEncoder.writeStatement()

VetoableChangeListener — Java 1.1

java.beans *event listener*

This interface is an extension of java.util.EventListener. It defines the method a class must implement in order to be notified when a Java bean makes a change to a constrained property. A PropertyChangeEvent is passed to the vetoableChange() method when such a change occurs. If the VetoableChangeListener wants to prevent the change from occurring, this method should throw a PropertyVetoException.


```
public interface VetoableChangeListener extends java.util.EventListener {
// Public Instance Methods
   public abstract void vetoableChange(PropertyChangeEvent evt) throws PropertyVetoException;
}
```

Implementations: VetoableChangeListenerProxy, java.beans.beancontext.BeanContextSupport

Passed To: java.awt.KeyboardFocusManager.{addVetoableChangeListener(), removeVetoableChangeListener()}, VetoableChangeListenerProxy.VetoableChangeListenerProxy(), VetoableChangeSupport.{addVetoableChangeListener(), removeVetoableChangeListener()}, java.beans.beancontext.BeanContextChild.{addVetoableChangeListener(), removeVetoableChangeListener()}, java.beans.beancontext.BeanContextChildSupport.{addVetoableChangeListener(), removeVetoableChangeListener()}, javax.swing.JComponent.{addVetoableChangeListener(), removeVetoableChangeListener()}

Returned By: java.awt.KeyboardFocusManager.getVetoableChangeListeners(), VetoableChangeSupport.getVetoableChangeListeners(), java.beans.beancontext.BeanContextSupport.getChildVetoableChangeListener(), javax.swing.JComponent.getVetoableChangeListeners()

VetoableChangeListenerProxy — Java 1.4

java.beans

This class implements VetoableChangeListener and serves as a wrapper around another VetoableChangeListener object. Beans that define a two-argument addVetoableChangeListener() method to allow registration of a listener for a specific named property may return instances of this class from their getVetoableChangeListeners() method (if they implement one). Use getPropertyName() to determine the name of the property to which the listener applies. And use the inherited getListener() method to obtain the underlying VetoableChangeListener object.

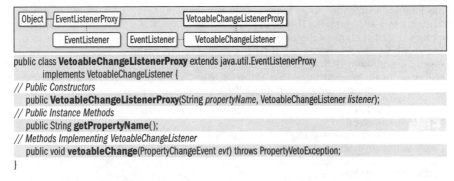

```
public class VetoableChangeListenerProxy extends java.util.EventListenerProxy
        implements VetoableChangeListener {
// Public Constructors
   public VetoableChangeListenerProxy(String propertyName, VetoableChangeListener listener);
// Public Instance Methods
   public String getPropertyName();
// Methods Implementing VetoableChangeListener
   public void vetoableChange(PropertyChangeEvent evt) throws PropertyVetoException;
}
```

VetoableChangeSupport — Java 1.1

java.beans — *serializable*

VetoableChangeSupport is a convenience class that maintains a list of registered VetoableChangeListener objects and provides a fireVetoableChange() method for sending a PropertyChangeEvent to all registered listeners. If any of the registered listeners veto the proposed change, fireVetoableChange() sends out another PropertyChangeEvent notifying previously notified listeners that the property has reverted to its original value. Because of the extra complexity of correctly handling veto-able changes and because of some tricky thread-synchronization issues involved in maintaining the list of listeners, it is recommended that all Java beans that support constrained events create a VetoableChangeSupport object to which they can delegate their addVetoableChangeListener() and removeVetoableChangeListener() methods. In Java 1.4, beans can also define a getVetoableChangeListeners() method and delegate it to a VetoableChangeSupport object.

Object — VetoableChangeSupport ··· Serializable

```
public class VetoableChangeSupport implements Serializable {
// Public Constructors
    public VetoableChangeSupport(Object sourceBean);
// Event Registration Methods (by event name)
    public void addVetoableChangeListener(VetoableChangeListener listener);                synchronized
    public void removeVetoableChangeListener(VetoableChangeListener listener);             synchronized
// Public Instance Methods
1.2 public void addVetoableChangeListener(String propertyName, VetoableChangeListener listener);   synchronized
1.2 public void fireVetoableChange(PropertyChangeEvent evt) throws PropertyVetoException;
1.2 public void fireVetoableChange(String propertyName, int oldValue, int newValue) throws PropertyVetoException;
    public void fireVetoableChange(String propertyName, Object oldValue, Object newValue)
        throws PropertyVetoException;
1.2 public void fireVetoableChange(String propertyName, boolean oldValue, boolean newValue)
        throws PropertyVetoException;
1.4 public VetoableChangeListener[ ] getVetoableChangeListeners();                      synchronized
1.4 public VetoableChangeListener[ ] getVetoableChangeListeners(String propertyName);   synchronized
1.2 public boolean hasListeners(String propertyName);                                    synchronized
1.2 public void removeVetoableChangeListener(String propertyName,                        synchronized
                                             VetoableChangeListener listener);
}
```

Type Of: java.beans.beancontext.BeanContextChildSupport.vcSupport

Visibility — Java 1.1

java.beans

This interface is intended to be implemented by advanced beans that can run both with and without a GUI present. The methods it defines allow a bean to specify whether it requires a GUI and allow the environment to notify the bean whether a GUI is available. If a bean absolutely requires a GUI, it should return true from needsGui(). If a bean is running without a GUI, it should return true from avoidingGui(). If no GUI is available, the bean can be notified through a call to dontUseGui(), and if a GUI is available, the bean can be notified through a call to okToUseGui().

```
public interface Visibility {
// Public Instance Methods
    public abstract boolean avoidingGui();
    public abstract void dontUseGui();
    public abstract boolean needsGui();
    public abstract void okToUseGui();
}
```

Implementations: java.beans.beancontext.BeanContext

Returned By: java.beans.beancontext.BeanContextSupport.getChildVisibility()

XMLDecoder Java 1.4

java.beans

This class recreates JavaBeans that were stored in XML format by an XMLEncoder. Create an XMLDecoder by specifying the java.io.InputStream that the XML-encoded serialized beans are to be read from. Then call readObject() one or more times to read encoded beans from that file. readObject() throws an ArrayIndexOutOfBoundsException when there are no more beans to read. Call close() to close the underlying stream when you are done with an XMLDecoder. Because the XMLEncoder encodes the state of a bean as a series of public method calls, the decoding process is relatively efficient, and there is no need for the decoding application to load, or even have access to, the various PersistenceDelegate classes that were used to encode the bean.

The bean decoding process is designed to be robust and tries to recover from any exceptions that are thrown whenever possible. Pass an ExceptionListener to the XMLDecoder() constructor if you want to receive notification of exceptions that occur during the decoding process. (An XMLDecoder begins decoding as soon as the constructor is called, so it is not useful to pass an ExceptionListener to setExceptionListener(): any such call is too late.)

If the stream you are decoding included a call to setOwner() when it was encoded, then you must pass an owner object to the XMLDecoder() constructor so that encoded method calls that use the owner object can be decoded. (There is a setOwner() method, but like setExceptionListener(), it is not useful.)

```
public class XMLDecoder {
// Public Constructors
   public XMLDecoder(java.io.InputStream in);
   public XMLDecoder(java.io.InputStream in, Object owner);
   public XMLDecoder(java.io.InputStream in, Object owner, ExceptionListener exceptionListener);
// Public Instance Methods
   public void close();
   public ExceptionListener getExceptionListener();
   public Object getOwner();
   public Object readObject();
   public void setExceptionListener(ExceptionListener exceptionListener);
   public void setOwner(Object owner);
}
```

XMLEncoder Java 1.4

java.beans

This class creates an XML-formatted description of a JavaBean or of a tree of beans and writes them to a stream. Specify the stream to be written to when you create the XMLEncoder. Then call the writeObject() method one or more times to serialize your JavaBeans using the XML persistence format. Note that writeObject() serializes the specified object, and, recursively, any objects it refers to in its public API. It is important to call close() when finished so that the XMLEncoder can flush its internal buffers, output a closing XML tag, and flush and close the stream. You can also flush() the encoder without closing it, if necessary. Use XMLDecoder to recreate any beans encoded with this class. Contrast this class with the java.io.ObjectOutputStream which performs serialization using a binary format.

The bean encoding process is designed to be robust and tries to recover from internal exceptions whenever possible. Use the inherited setExceptionListener() method if you want to register an ExceptionListener to receive notification of exceptions that occur and are handled during the encoding process.

The bean encoding process uses a PersistenceDelegate object internally. The DefaultPersistenceDelegate class is used for all conforming JavaBeans that have a no-argument constructor and whose entire state is encapsulated by properties that have public get and set accessor methods. The implementation also provides private persistence delegates for all java.awt.Component classes from the AWT and Swing packages (covered in the companion book *Java Foundation Classes in a Nutshell*), as well as all classes (such as java.awt.Font and java.awt.Color) that those components use as properties. If you want to encode a custom bean that does not strictly follow the JavaBeans constructor and property conventions, you need to create a custom PersistenceDelegate object and associate it with the Class object for the custom bean by calling the inherited setPersistenceDelegate() method. See PersistenceDelegate for details.

In addition to encoding the state of a bean, this class can also be used to encode arbitrary method calls with writeExpression() and writeStatement(). This is particularly useful when used with the setOwner() method. Use setOwner() to specify an object that is not to be serialized as part of the bean state. Then, encode method calls on this owner object with writeStatement(). When the XML archive is decoded with an XMLDecoder, you'll use a similar setOwner() method to specify the object on which those methods should be invoked. When the owner object represents the application backend, this is a powerful way to tie a serialized GUI to that backend by registering event listeners, or passing particular beans to the backend for manipulation.

Object ─ Encoder ─ XMLEncoder

```
public class XMLEncoder extends Encoder {
// Public Constructors
   public XMLEncoder(java.io.OutputStream out);
// Public Instance Methods
   public void close();
   public void flush();
   public Object getOwner();
   public void setOwner(Object owner);
// Public Methods Overriding Encoder
   public void writeExpression(Expression oldExp);
   public void writeObject(Object o);
   public void writeStatement(java.beans.Statement oldStm);
}
```

Package java.beans.beancontext — Java 1.2

The java.beans.beancontext package extends the JavaBeans component model to add the notion of a containment hierarchy. It also supports bean containers that provide an execution context for the beans they contain and that may also provide a set of services to those beans. This package is typically used by advanced bean developers and developers of bean-manipulation tools. Application programmers who are simply using beans do not typically use this package.

BeanContext is the central interface of this package. It is a container for beans and also defines several methods that specify context information for beans. BeanContextServices extends BeanContext to define methods that allow a contained bean to query and request available services. A bean that wishes to be told about its containing BeanContext implements the BeanContextChild interface. BeanContext is itself a BeanContextChild, which means that contexts can be nested within other contexts.

See Chapter 6 for more information on beans and bean contexts.

Interfaces:

public interface **BeanContextChild**;
public interface **BeanContextChildComponentProxy**;
public interface **BeanContextContainerProxy**;
public interface **BeanContextProxy**;
public interface **BeanContextServiceProvider**;
public interface **BeanContextServiceProviderBeanInfo** extends java.beans.BeanInfo;

Collections:

public interface **BeanContext** extends BeanContextChild, java.util.Collection,
    java.beans.DesignMode, java.beans.Visibility;
public class **BeanContextSupport** extends BeanContextChildSupport
    implements BeanContext, java.beans.PropertyChangeListener,
    Serializable, java.beans.VetoableChangeListener;
  └ public class **BeanContextServicesSupport** extends BeanContextSupport
      implements BeanContextServices;

Events:

public abstract class **BeanContextEvent** extends java.util.EventObject;
  └ public class **BeanContextMembershipEvent** extends BeanContextEvent;
  └ public class **BeanContextServiceAvailableEvent** extends BeanContextEvent;
  └ public class **BeanContextServiceRevokedEvent** extends BeanContextEvent;

Event Listeners:

public interface **BeanContextMembershipListener** extends java.util.EventListener;
public interface **BeanContextServiceRevokedListener** extends java.util.EventListener;
public interface **BeanContextServices** extends BeanContext, BeanContextServicesListener;
public interface **BeanContextServicesListener** extends BeanContextServiceRevokedListener;

Other Classes:

public class **BeanContextChildSupport**
    implements BeanContextChild, BeanContextServicesListener, Serializable;

Protected Inner Classes:

protected class **BeanContextServicesSupport.BCSSProxyServiceProvider**
    implements BeanContextServiceProvider, BeanContextServiceRevokedListener;
protected static class **BeanContextServicesSupport.BCSSServiceProvider** implements Serializable;
protected class **BeanContextSupport.BCSChild** implements Serializable;
  └ protected class **BeanContextServicesSupport.BCSSChild** extends BeanContextSupport.BCSChild;
protected static final class **BeanContextSupport.BCSIterator** implements java.util.Iterator;

BeanContext — Java 1.2

java.beans.beancontext — *collection*

This interface defines the methods that must be implemented by any class that wants to act as a logical container for JavaBeans components. Every BeanContext is also a BeanContextChild and can therefore be nested within a higher level bean context. BeanContext is extended by BeanContextServices; any bean context that wants to provide services to the beans it contains must implement this more specialized interface.

The BeanContext interface extends the java.util.Collection interface; the children it contains are accessed using the methods of that interface. In addition, BeanContext defines several important methods of its own. instantiateChild() instantiates a new bean, in the same manner as the standard Beans.instantiate() method, and then makes that new bean a child of the context. Calling this method is typically the same as calling the three-argument version of Beans.instantiate(). getResource() and getResourceAsStream() are the BeanContext versions of the java.lang.Class and java.lang.ClassLoader methods of the same name. Some bean-context implementations may provide special behavior for these methods; others may simply delegate to the Class or ClassLoader of the bean. The remaining two methods allow the registration and deregistration of event listeners that the BeanContext notifies when bean children are added or removed from the context.

Implementing a BeanContext is a more specialized task than developing a JavaBeans component. Many bean developers will never have to implement a bean context themselves. If you do implement a bean context, you'll probably find it easier to use BeanContextSupport, either by extending it or using an instance as a proxy.

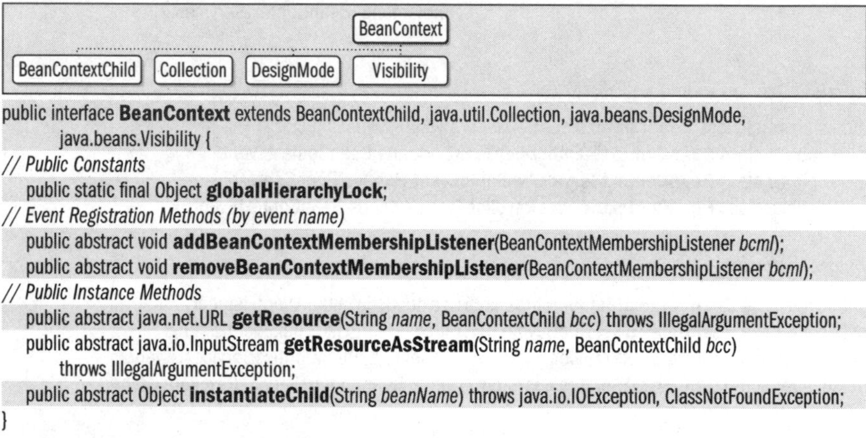


```
public interface BeanContext extends BeanContextChild, java.util.Collection, java.beans.DesignMode,
        java.beans.Visibility {
// Public Constants
    public static final Object globalHierarchyLock;
// Event Registration Methods (by event name)
    public abstract void addBeanContextMembershipListener(BeanContextMembershipListener bcml);
    public abstract void removeBeanContextMembershipListener(BeanContextMembershipListener bcml);
// Public Instance Methods
    public abstract java.net.URL getResource(String name, BeanContextChild bcc) throws IllegalArgumentException;
    public abstract java.io.InputStream getResourceAsStream(String name, BeanContextChild bcc)
        throws IllegalArgumentException;
    public abstract Object instantiateChild(String beanName) throws java.io.IOException, ClassNotFoundException;
}
```

Implementations: BeanContextServices, BeanContextSupport

Passed To: java.beans.AppletInitializer.initialize(), java.beans.Beans.instantiate(), BeanContextChild.setBeanContext(), BeanContextChildSupport.{setBeanContext(), validatePendingSetBeanContext()}, BeanContextEvent.{BeanContextEvent(), setPropagatedFrom()}, BeanContextMembershipEvent.BeanContextMembershipEvent(), BeanContextSupport.BeanContextSupport()

Returned By: BeanContextChild.getBeanContext(), BeanContextChildSupport.getBeanContext(), BeanContextEvent.{getBeanContext(), getPropagatedFrom()}, BeanContextSupport.getBeanContextPeer()

Type Of: BeanContextChildSupport.beanContext, BeanContextEvent.propagatedFrom

BeanContextChild — Java 1.2

java.beans.beancontext

JavaBeans components that are designed to be nested within a bean context and need to be aware of that context must implement this interface. BeanContextChild implements a single beanContext property that identifies the BeanContext within which the bean is contained. The beanContext property is bound and constrained, which means that it must fire PropertyChangeEvent events when setBeanContext() is called, and any call to setBeanContext() may result in a PropertyVetoException if one of the VetoableChangeListener objects vetoes the change. The setBeanContext() method is not intended for use by beans or by applications. When a bean is instantiated or deserialized, its containing bean context calls this method to introduce itself to the bean. The bean must store a reference to its BeanContext in a transient field so that the context is not serialized along with the bean itself.

Implementing a BeanContextChild from scratch can be somewhat tricky because you must correctly handle the VetoableChangeListener protocol and correctly implement important conventions, such as storing the BeanContext reference in a transient field. Therefore, most bean developers do not implement the interface directly, but instead use BeanContextSupport, either by subclassing it or by using an instance as a delegate.

```
public interface BeanContextChild {
// Public Instance Methods
   public abstract void addPropertyChangeListener(String name, java.beans.PropertyChangeListener pcl);
   public abstract void addVetoableChangeListener(String name, java.beans.VetoableChangeListener vcl);
   public abstract BeanContext getBeanContext();
   public abstract void removePropertyChangeListener(String name, java.beans.PropertyChangeListener pcl);
   public abstract void removeVetoableChangeListener(String name, java.beans.VetoableChangeListener vcl);
   public abstract void setBeanContext(BeanContext bc) throws java.beans.PropertyVetoException;
}
```

Implementations: BeanContext, BeanContextChildSupport

Passed To: BeanContext.{getResource(), getResourceAsStream()}, BeanContextChildSupport.BeanContextChildSupport(), BeanContextServices.{getService(), releaseService()}, BeanContextServicesSupport.{getService(), releaseService()}, BeanContextSupport.{getResource(), getResourceAsStream()}

Returned By: BeanContextChildSupport.getBeanContextChildPeer(), BeanContextProxy.getBeanContextProxy(), BeanContextSupport.getChildBeanContextChild()

Type Of: BeanContextChildSupport.beanContextChildPeer

BeanContextChildComponentProxy — Java 1.2

java.beans.beancontext

If a BeanContextChild is not a Component subclass but has an associated Component object to display its visual representation, it implements this interface to allow access to that component.

```
public interface BeanContextChildComponentProxy {
// Public Instance Methods
   public abstract java.awt.Component getComponent();
}
```

BeanContextChildSupport — Java 1.2

java.beans.beancontext — *serializable*

This class provides support for implementing the BeanContextChild interface in a way that correctly conforms to the details of the bean context specification. A subclass should implement initializeBeanContextResources() and releaseBeanContextResources() to obtain and release whatever resources the bean context child requires, such as service objects obtained from the containing BeanContext. These methods are called when the containing bean context introduces itself by calling setBeanContext(). Any resources obtained with these methods should be stored in transient fields so that they are not serialized along with the bean. A bean that wants a chance to approve any call to setBeanContext() before that call succeeds can implement validatePendingSetBeanContext(). If this method returns false, the setBeanContext() call that triggered it fails with a PropertyVetoException.

Many beans are AWT or Swing components and cannot subclass both Component and BeanContextChildSupport. Therefore, many bean developers find it useful to delegate to an internal instance of BeanContextChildSupport. One way to do this is to have your bean implement the BeanContextProxy interface and simply return an instance of BeanContextChildSupport from the getBeanContextProxy() method. Another technique is to actually implement the BeanContextChild interface in your bean, but provide dummy methods that call the corresponding methods of BeanContextChildSupport. If you do this, you should pass an instance of your bean to the BeanContextChildSupport() constructor. This makes the delegation transparent so events appear to come directly from your bean. In either case, you can instantiate BeanContextChildSupport directly. Often, however, you want to create a custom subclass (perhaps as an inner class) to implement methods such as initializeBeanContextResources().

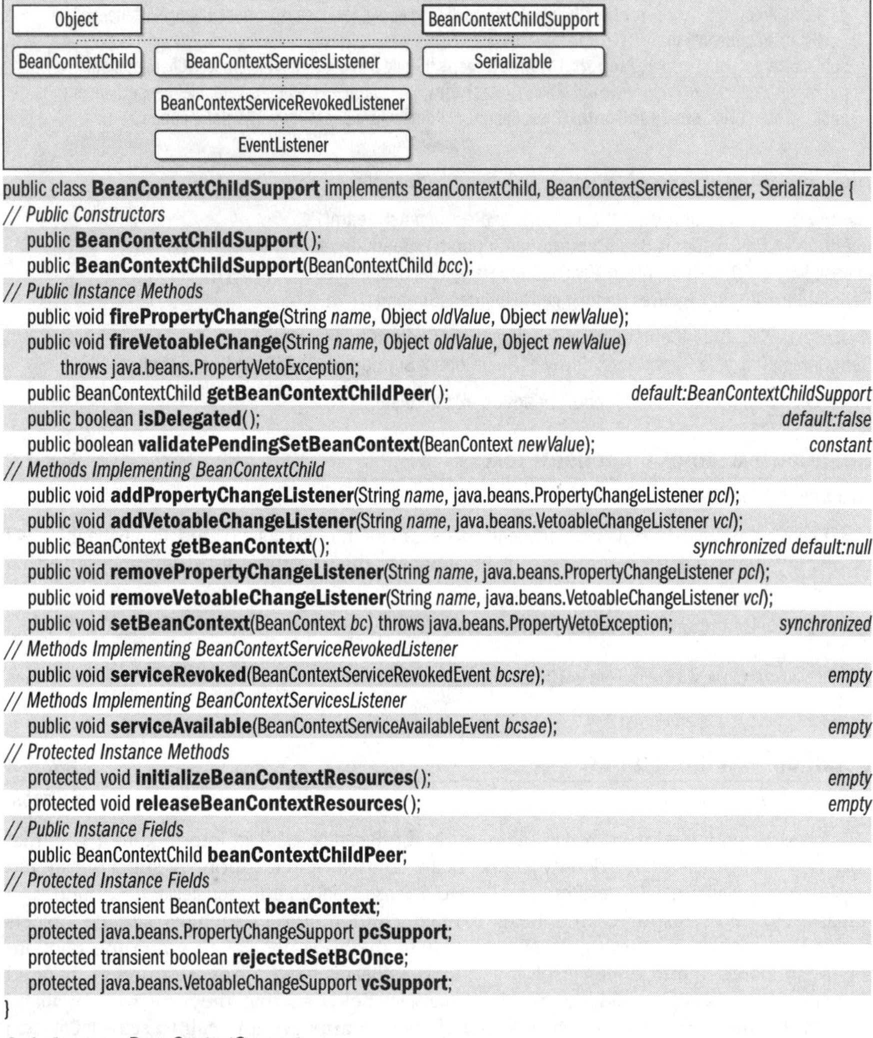


```
public class BeanContextChildSupport implements BeanContextChild, BeanContextServicesListener, Serializable {
// Public Constructors
   public BeanContextChildSupport();
   public BeanContextChildSupport(BeanContextChild bcc);
// Public Instance Methods
   public void firePropertyChange(String name, Object oldValue, Object newValue);
   public void fireVetoableChange(String name, Object oldValue, Object newValue)
      throws java.beans.PropertyVetoException;
   public BeanContextChild getBeanContextChildPeer();                  default:BeanContextChildSupport
   public boolean isDelegated();                                                          default:false
   public boolean validatePendingSetBeanContext(BeanContext newValue);                         constant
// Methods Implementing BeanContextChild
   public void addPropertyChangeListener(String name, java.beans.PropertyChangeListener pcl);
   public void addVetoableChangeListener(String name, java.beans.VetoableChangeListener vcl);
   public BeanContext getBeanContext();                                       synchronized default:null
   public void removePropertyChangeListener(String name, java.beans.PropertyChangeListener pcl);
   public void removeVetoableChangeListener(String name, java.beans.VetoableChangeListener vcl);
   public void setBeanContext(BeanContext bc) throws java.beans.PropertyVetoException;    synchronized
// Methods Implementing BeanContextServiceRevokedListener
   public void serviceRevoked(BeanContextServiceRevokedEvent bcsre);                              empty
// Methods Implementing BeanContextServicesListener
   public void serviceAvailable(BeanContextServiceAvailableEvent bcsae);                          empty
// Protected Instance Methods
   protected void initializeBeanContextResources();                                               empty
   protected void releaseBeanContextResources();                                                  empty
// Public Instance Fields
   public BeanContextChild beanContextChildPeer;
// Protected Instance Fields
   protected transient BeanContext beanContext;
   protected java.beans.PropertyChangeSupport pcSupport;
   protected transient boolean rejectedSetBCOnce;
   protected java.beans.VetoableChangeSupport vcSupport;
}
```

Subclasses: BeanContextSupport

BeanContextContainerProxy — Java 1.2

java.beans.beancontext

This interface is implemented by a BeanContext that has a java.awt.Container associated with it. The getContainer() method allows any interested parties to obtain a reference to the container associated with the bean context. It is a common practice for bean contexts to be associated with containers. Unfortunately, BeanContext implements java.util.Collection, which has method-name conflicts with java.awt.Container, so no Container subclass can implement the BeanContext interface. See also BeanContextProxy, which reverses the direction of the proxy relationship.

```
public interface BeanContextContainerProxy {
// Public Instance Methods
   public abstract java.awt.Container getContainer();
}
```

BeanContextEvent — Java 1.2

java.beans.beancontext — *serializable event*

This is the abstract superclass of all bean context-related events. getBeanContext() returns the source of the event. If isPropagated() returns true, the event has been propagated through a hierarchy of bean contexts, and getPropagatedFrom() returns the most recent bean context to propagate the event.

Object — EventObject — BeanContextEvent
Serializable

```
public abstract class BeanContextEvent extends java.util.EventObject {
// Protected Constructors
   protected BeanContextEvent(BeanContext bc);
// Public Instance Methods
   public BeanContext getBeanContext();
   public BeanContext getPropagatedFrom();                         synchronized
   public boolean isPropagated();                                  synchronized
   public void setPropagatedFrom(BeanContext bc);                  synchronized
// Protected Instance Fields
   protected BeanContext propagatedFrom;
}
```

Subclasses: BeanContextMembershipEvent, BeanContextServiceAvailableEvent, BeanContextServiceRevokedEvent

BeanContextMembershipEvent — Java 1.2

java.beans.beancontext — *serializable event*

An event of this type is generated by a BeanContext when beans are added to it or removed from it. The event object contains the list of children that were added or removed and allows access to that list in several ways. The size() method returns the number of affected children. The contains() method checks whether a specified object was one of the affected children. toArray() returns the list of affected children as an array, and iterator() returns the list in the form of a java.util.Iterator.

Object — EventObject — BeanContextEvent — BeanContextMembershipEvent
Serializable

```
public class BeanContextMembershipEvent extends BeanContextEvent {
// Public Constructors
   public BeanContextMembershipEvent(BeanContext bc, Object[ ] changes);
   public BeanContextMembershipEvent(BeanContext bc, java.util.Collection changes);
// Public Instance Methods
   public boolean contains(Object child);
   public java.util.Iterator iterator();
   public int size();
   public Object[ ] toArray();
// Protected Instance Fields
   protected java.util.Collection children;
}
```

Passed To: BeanContextMembershipListener.{childrenAdded(), childrenRemoved()}, BeanContextSupport.{fireChildrenAdded(), fireChildrenRemoved()}

BeanContextMembershipListener — Java 1.2

java.beans.beancontext — *event listener*

This interface should be implemented by any object that wants to be notified when children are added to or removed from a BeanContext.

EventListener ··· BeanContextMembershipListener

```
public interface BeanContextMembershipListener extends java.util.EventListener {
// Public Instance Methods
   public abstract void childrenAdded(BeanContextMembershipEvent bcme);
   public abstract void childrenRemoved(BeanContextMembershipEvent bcme);
}
```

Passed To: BeanContext.{addBeanContextMembershipListener(), removeBeanContextMembershipListener()}, BeanContextSupport.{addBeanContextMembershipListener(), removeBeanContextMembershipListener()}

Returned By: BeanContextSupport.getChildBeanContextMembershipListener()

BeanContextProxy — Java 1.2

java.beans.beancontext

This interface is implemented by a JavaBeans component (often, but not always, an AWT Component or Container object) that is not itself a BeanContext or BeanContextChild, but has a BeanContext or BeanContextChild object associated with it. The getBeanContextProxy() method returns the associated object. The return type of this method is BeanContextChild. Depending on the context in which you call this method, however, the returned object may actually be a BeanContext or BeanContextServices object. You should test for this using the instanceof operator before casting the object to these more specific types.

```
public interface BeanContextProxy {
// Public Instance Methods
   public abstract BeanContextChild getBeanContextProxy();
}
```

BeanContextServiceAvailableEvent **Java 1.2**

java.beans.beancontext ***serializable event***

An event of this type is generated to notify interested BeanContextServicesListener objects that a new class of service is available from a BeanContextServices object. getServiceClass() returns the class of the service, and getCurrentServiceSelectors() may return a set of additional arguments that can parameterize the service.

Object — EventObject — BeanContextEvent — BeanContextServiceAvailableEvent

Serializable

```
public class BeanContextServiceAvailableEvent extends BeanContextEvent {
// Public Constructors
   public BeanContextServiceAvailableEvent(BeanContextServices bcs, Class sc);
// Public Instance Methods
   public java.util.Iterator getCurrentServiceSelectors();
   public Class getServiceClass();
   public BeanContextServices getSourceAsBeanContextServices();
// Protected Instance Fields
   protected Class serviceClass;
}
```

Passed To: BeanContextChildSupport.serviceAvailable(), BeanContextServicesListener.serviceAvailable(), BeanContextServicesSupport.{fireServiceAdded(), serviceAvailable()}

BeanContextServiceProvider **Java 1.2**

java.beans.beancontext

This interface defines the methods that must be implemented by a factory class that wants to provide service objects to beans. To provide its service, a BeanContextServiceProvider is passed to the addService() method of a BeanContextServices object. This creates a mapping in the BeanContextServices object between a class of service (such as java.awt.print.PrinterJob) and a BeanContextServiceProvider that can return a suitable instance of that class to provide the service.

When a BeanContextChild requests a service of a particular class from its BeanContextServices container, the BeanContextServices object finds the appropriate BeanContextServiceProvider object and forwards the request to its getService() method. When the bean relinquishes the service, releaseService() is called. A getService() request may include an arbitrary object as an additional parameter or service selector. Service providers that use the service selector argument and that support a finite set of legal service selector values should implement the getCurrentServiceSelectors() method to allow the list of legal selector values to be queried.

Bean developers typically do not have to use or implement this interface. From the point of view of a bean context child, service objects are obtained from a BeanContextServices object. Developers creating BeanContextServices implementations, however, must implement appropriate BeanContextServiceProvider objects to provide the services.

```
public interface BeanContextServiceProvider {
// Public Instance Methods
   public abstract java.util.Iterator getCurrentServiceSelectors(BeanContextServices bcs, Class serviceClass);
   public abstract Object getService(BeanContextServices bcs, Object requestor, Class serviceClass,
                                     Object serviceSelector);
   public abstract void releaseService(BeanContextServices bcs, Object requestor, Object service);
}
```

Implementations: BeanContextServicesSupport.BCSSProxyServiceProvider

Passed To: BeanContextServices.{addService(), revokeService()}, BeanContextServicesSupport.{addService(), createBCSSServiceProvider(), revokeService()}

Returned By: BeanContextServicesSupport.BCSSServiceProvider.getServiceProvider()

Type Of: BeanContextServicesSupport.BCSSServiceProvider.serviceProvider

BeanContextServiceProviderBeanInfo — Java 1.2

java.beans.beancontext

A BeanContextServiceProvider that wishes to provide information to a GUI builder tool about the service or services it offers should implement this BeanInfo subinterface. Following the standard BeanInfo naming conventions, the implementing class should have the same name as the service provider class, with "BeanInfo" appended. This enables a design tool to look for and dynamically load the bean info class when necessary.

getServicesBeanInfo() should return an array of BeanInfo objects, one for each class of service offered by the BeanContextServiceProvider. These BeanInfo objects enable a design tool to allow the user to visually configure the service object. This can be quite useful, since service objects may be instances of existing classes that were not designed with the standard JavaBeans naming conventions in mind.

BeanInfo ··· BeanContextServiceProviderBeanInfo

```
public interface BeanContextServiceProviderBeanInfo extends java.beans.BeanInfo {
// Public Instance Methods
   public abstract java.beans.BeanInfo[ ] getServicesBeanInfo();
}
```

BeanContextServiceRevokedEvent — Java 1.2

java.beans.beancontext — *serializable event*

This event class provides details about a service revocation initiated by a BeanContextServices object. getServiceClass() specifies the class of service being revoked. isCurrentServiceInvalidNow() specifies whether the currently owned service object has become invalid. If this method returns true, the bean that receives this event must stop using the service object immediately. If the method returns false, the bean can continue to use the service object, but future requests for services of this class will fail.

Object — EventObject — BeanContextEvent — BeanContextServiceRevokedEvent
(EventObject ··· Serializable)

```
public class BeanContextServiceRevokedEvent extends BeanContextEvent {
// Public Constructors
   public BeanContextServiceRevokedEvent(BeanContextServices bcs, Class sc, boolean invalidate);
// Public Instance Methods
   public Class getServiceClass();
   public BeanContextServices getSourceAsBeanContextServices();
   public boolean isCurrentServiceInvalidNow();
   public boolean isServiceClass(Class service);
// Protected Instance Fields
   protected Class serviceClass;
}
```

Passed To: BeanContextChildSupport.serviceRevoked(), BeanContextServiceRevokedListener.serviceRevoked(),

BeanContextServicesSupport.{fireServiceRevoked(), serviceRevoked()}, BeanContextServicesSupport.BCSSProxyServiceProvider.serviceRevoked()

BeanContextServiceRevokedListener — Java 1.2

java.beans.beancontext — *event listener*

This interface defines a method that is invoked when a service object returned by a BeanContextServices object is forcibly revoked. Unlike other types of event listeners, the BeanContextServiceRevokedListener is not registered and deregistered with a pair of add and remove methods. Instead, an implementation of this interface must be passed to every getService() call on a BeanContextServices object. If the returned service is ever revoked by the granting BeanContextServiceProvider object before the bean has relinquished the service, the serviceRevoked() method of this interface is called.

When a service is revoked, it means that future requests for the service will not succeed. But it may also mean that current service objects have become invalid and must not be used anymore. The serviceRevoked() method should call the isCurrentServiceInvalidNow() method of the supplied event object to determine if this is the case. If so, it must immediately stop using the service object.

EventListener ··· BeanContextServiceRevokedListener

```
public interface BeanContextServiceRevokedListener extends java.util.EventListener {
// Public Instance Methods
   public abstract void serviceRevoked(BeanContextServiceRevokedEvent bcsre);
}
```

Implementations: BeanContextServicesListener, BeanContextServicesSupport.BCSSProxyServiceProvider

Passed To: BeanContextServices.getService(), BeanContextServicesSupport.getService()

BeanContextServices — Java 1.2

java.beans.beancontext — *collection event listener*

This interface defines additional methods a bean context class must implement if it wants to provide services to the beans it contains. A bean calls hasService() to determine if a service of a particular type is available from its bean context. It calls getService() to request an instance of the specified service class and then calls releaseService() when it no longer needs the service object. A bean that wants to find the complete list of available services can call getCurrentServiceClasses(). Some services allow (or require) a service selector object to be passed to the getService() method to provide additional information about the service object. If a service defines a fixed set of legal service selectors, getCurrentServiceSelectors() allows a bean to iterate through the set of selector objects. Beans that want to know when new services become available or when existing services are revoked should register a BeanContextServicesListener object with addBeanContextServicesListener().

If a BeanContextServices object does not provide a requested service, but is nested within another BeanContext, it should check whether any of its ancestor bean contexts can provide the service. The BeanContextServices interface extends BeanContextServicesListener. This means that every BeanContextServices object can be listening to the set of services available from its container.

The previous methods are the ones beans call to obtain services. BeanContextServices defines a different set of methods service providers use to deliver services. addService() defines a BeanContextServiceProvider for a specified Class of service. revokeService() removes this mapping between service class and service provider, and indicates that the specified service is no longer available. When a service is revoked, the BeanContextServices object must notify any beans that have been granted service objects (and have not released them yet) that the service has been revoked. It does this by notifying the BeanContextServiceRevokedListener objects passed to the getService() method.

Bean context developers may find it easier to use the BeanContextServicesSupport class, either by subclassing or by delegation, instead of implementing BeanContextServices from scratch.

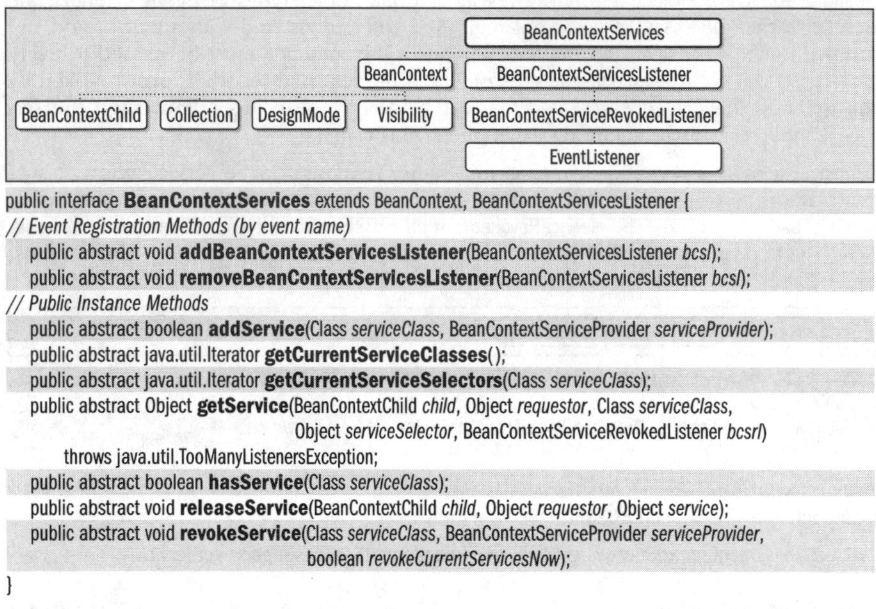


```
public interface BeanContextServices extends BeanContext, BeanContextServicesListener {
// Event Registration Methods (by event name)
   public abstract void addBeanContextServicesListener(BeanContextServicesListener bcsl);
   public abstract void removeBeanContextServicesListener(BeanContextServicesListener bcsl);
// Public Instance Methods
   public abstract boolean addService(Class serviceClass, BeanContextServiceProvider serviceProvider);
   public abstract java.util.Iterator getCurrentServiceClasses();
   public abstract java.util.Iterator getCurrentServiceSelectors(Class serviceClass);
   public abstract Object getService(BeanContextChild child, Object requestor, Class serviceClass,
                                     Object serviceSelector, BeanContextServiceRevokedListener bcsrl)
      throws java.util.TooManyListenersException;
   public abstract boolean hasService(Class serviceClass);
   public abstract void releaseService(BeanContextChild child, Object requestor, Object service);
   public abstract void revokeService(Class serviceClass, BeanContextServiceProvider serviceProvider,
                                      boolean revokeCurrentServicesNow);
}
```

Implementations: BeanContextServicesSupport

Passed To: BeanContextServiceAvailableEvent.BeanContextServiceAvailableEvent(), BeanContextServiceProvider.{getCurrentServiceSelectors(), getService(), releaseService()}, BeanContextServiceRevokedEvent.BeanContextServiceRevokedEvent(), BeanContextServicesSupport.BeanContextServicesSupport(), BeanContextServicesSupport.BCSSProxyServiceProvider.{getCurrentServiceSelectors(), getService(), releaseService()}

Returned By: BeanContextServiceAvailableEvent.getSourceAsBeanContextServices(), BeanContextServiceRevokedEvent.getSourceAsBeanContextServices(), BeanContextServicesSupport.getBeanContextServicesPeer()

BeanContextServicesListener — Java 1.2

java.beans.beancontext — *event listener*

This interface adds a serviceAvailable() method to the serviceRevoked() method of BeanContextServiceRevokedListener. Listeners of this type can be registered with a BeanContextServices object and are notified when a new class of service becomes available or when an existing class of service is revoked.

EventListener — BeanContextServiceRevokedListener — BeanContextServicesListener

```
public interface BeanContextServicesListener extends BeanContextServiceRevokedListener {
// Public Instance Methods
```

```
    public abstract void serviceAvailable(BeanContextServiceAvailableEvent bcsae);
}
```

Implementations: BeanContextChildSupport, BeanContextServices

Passed To: BeanContextServices.{addBeanContextServicesListener(), removeBeanContextServicesListener()}, BeanContextServicesSupport.{addBeanContextServicesListener(), removeBeanContextServicesListener()}

Returned By: BeanContextServicesSupport.getChildBeanContextServicesListener()

BeanContextServicesSupport — Java 1.2

java.beans.beancontext — ***serializable collection***

This class is a useful implementation of the BeanContextServices interface that correctly conforms to the bean context specifications and conventions. Most bean context implementors find it easier to subclass this class or delegate to an instance of this class rather than implement BeanContextServices from scratch. The most common technique is to implement the BeanContextProxy interface and return an instance of BeanContextServicesSupport from the getBeanContextProxy() method.

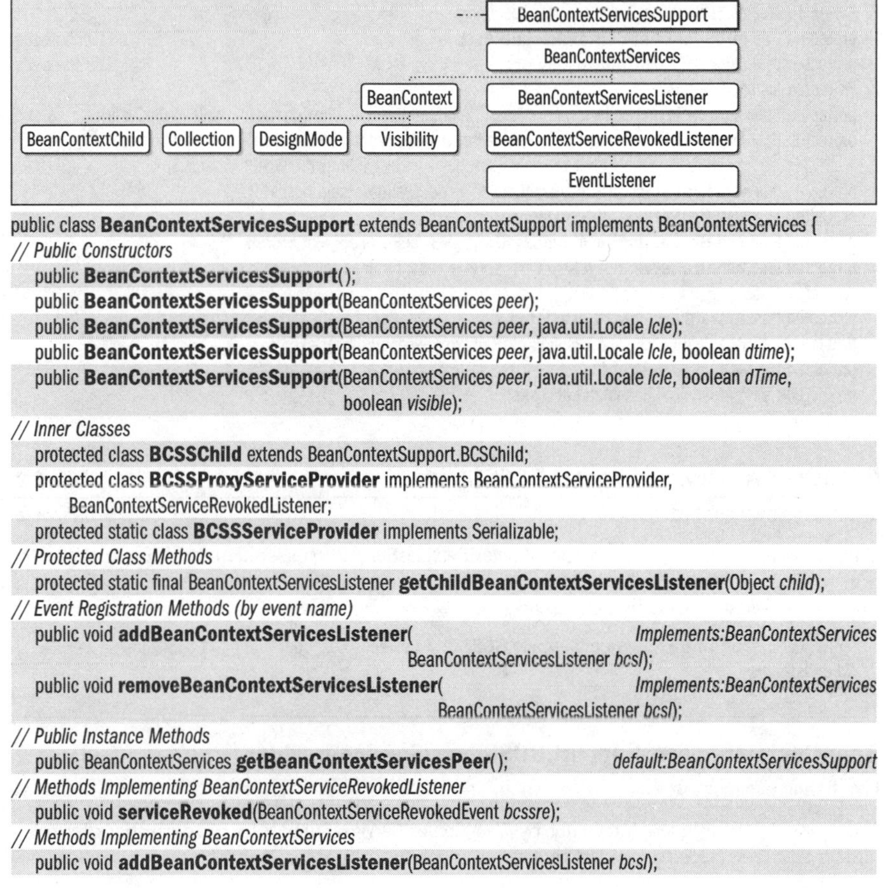


```
public class BeanContextServicesSupport extends BeanContextSupport implements BeanContextServices {
// Public Constructors
    public BeanContextServicesSupport();
    public BeanContextServicesSupport(BeanContextServices peer);
    public BeanContextServicesSupport(BeanContextServices peer, java.util.Locale lcle);
    public BeanContextServicesSupport(BeanContextServices peer, java.util.Locale lcle, boolean dtime);
    public BeanContextServicesSupport(BeanContextServices peer, java.util.Locale lcle, boolean dTime,
                                       boolean visible);
// Inner Classes
    protected class BCSSChild extends BeanContextSupport.BCSChild;
    protected class BCSSProxyServiceProvider implements BeanContextServiceProvider,
        BeanContextServiceRevokedListener;
    protected static class BCSSServiceProvider implements Serializable;
// Protected Class Methods
    protected static final BeanContextServicesListener getChildBeanContextServicesListener(Object child);
// Event Registration Methods (by event name)
    public void addBeanContextServicesListener(                      Implements:BeanContextServices
                                       BeanContextServicesListener bcsl);
    public void removeBeanContextServicesListener(                   Implements:BeanContextServices
                                       BeanContextServicesListener bcsl);
// Public Instance Methods
    public BeanContextServices getBeanContextServicesPeer();      default:BeanContextServicesSupport
// Methods Implementing BeanContextServiceRevokedListener
    public void serviceRevoked(BeanContextServiceRevokedEvent bcssre);
// Methods Implementing BeanContextServices
    public void addBeanContextServicesListener(BeanContextServicesListener bcsl);
```

```
    public boolean addService(Class serviceClass, BeanContextServiceProvider bcsp);
    public java.util.Iterator getCurrentServiceClasses();          default:BeanContextSupport.BCSIterator
    public java.util.Iterator getCurrentServiceSelectors(Class serviceClass);
    public Object getService(BeanContextChild child, Object requestor, Class serviceClass, Object serviceSelector,
                             BeanContextServiceRevokedListener bcsrl) throws java.util.TooManyListenersException;
    public boolean hasService(Class serviceClass);                                              synchronized
    public void releaseService(BeanContextChild child, Object requestor, Object service);
    public void removeBeanContextServicesListener(BeanContextServicesListener bcsl);
    public void revokeService(Class serviceClass, BeanContextServiceProvider bcsp,
                              boolean revokeCurrentServicesNow);
// Methods Implementing BeanContextServicesListener
    public void serviceAvailable(BeanContextServiceAvailableEvent bcssae);
// Public Methods Overriding BeanContextSupport
    public void initialize();
// Protected Methods Overriding BeanContextSupport
    protected void bcsPreDeserializationHook(java.io.ObjectInputStream ois)                     synchronized
        throws java.io.IOException, ClassNotFoundException;
    protected void bcsPreSerializationHook(java.io.ObjectOutputStream oos)                      synchronized
        throws java.io.IOException;
    protected void childJustRemovedHook(Object child, BeanContextSupport.BCSChild bcsc);
    protected BeanContextSupport.BCSChild createBCSChild(Object targetChild, Object peer);
// Protected Methods Overriding BeanContextChildSupport
    protected void initializeBeanContextResources();                                            synchronized
    protected void releaseBeanContextResources();                                               synchronized
// Protected Instance Methods
    protected boolean addService(Class serviceClass, BeanContextServiceProvider bcsp, boolean fireEvent);
    protected BeanContextServicesSupport.BCSSServiceProvider createBCSSServiceProvider(Class sc,
                                                              BeanContextServiceProvider bcsp);
    protected final void fireServiceAdded(BeanContextServiceAvailableEvent bcssae);
    protected final void fireServiceAdded(Class serviceClass);
    protected final void fireServiceRevoked(BeanContextServiceRevokedEvent bcsre);
    protected final void fireServiceRevoked(Class serviceClass, boolean revokeNow);
// Protected Instance Fields
    protected transient java.util.ArrayList bcsListeners;
    protected transient BeanContextServicesSupport.BCSSProxyServiceProvider proxy;
    protected transient int serializable;
    protected transient java.util.HashMap services;
}
```

BeanContextServicesSupport.BCSSChild — Java 1.2

java.beans.beancontext — *serializable*

This class is used internally by BeanContextServicesSupport to associate additional information with each child of the bean context. It has no public or protected method or fields, but may be customized by subclassing.

```
protected class BeanContextServicesSupport.BCSSChild extends BeanContextSupport.BCSChild {
// No Constructor
}
```

BeanContextServicesSupport.BCSSProxyServiceProvider — Java 1.2

java.beans.beancontext

This inner class is used internally by BeanContextServicesSupport to properly handle delegation to the services provided by containing bean contexts. It implements the BeanContextServiceProvider interface in terms of the methods of a containing BeanContextServices object.

```
protected class BeanContextServicesSupport.BCSSProxyServiceProvider
        implements BeanContextServiceProvider, BeanContextServiceRevokedListener {
// No Constructor
// Methods Implementing BeanContextServiceProvider
   public java.util.Iterator getCurrentServiceSelectors(BeanContextServices bcs, Class serviceClass);
   public Object getService(BeanContextServices bcs, Object requestor, Class serviceClass, Object serviceSelector);
   public void releaseService(BeanContextServices bcs, Object requestor, Object service);
// Methods Implementing BeanContextServiceRevokedListener
   public void serviceRevoked(BeanContextServiceRevokedEvent bcsre);
}
```

Type Of: BeanContextServicesSupport.proxy

BeanContextServicesSupport.BCSSServiceProvider — Java 1.2

java.beans.beancontext — *serializable*

This inner class is a trivial wrapper around a BeanContextServiceProvider object. Subclasses that want to associate additional information with each service provider can subclass this class and override the createBCSSServiceProvider() method of BeanContextServices-Support.

```
protected static class BeanContextServicesSupport.BCSSServiceProvider implements Serializable {
// No Constructor
// Protected Instance Methods
   protected BeanContextServiceProvider getServiceProvider();
// Protected Instance Fields
   protected BeanContextServiceProvider serviceProvider;
}
```

Returned By: BeanContextServicesSupport.createBCSSServiceProvider()

BeanContextSupport — Java 1.2

java.beans.beancontext — *serializable collection*

This class provides a simple, easily customizable implementation of BeanContext. Most bean context implementors find it easier to subclass BeanContextSupport or create a Bean-ContextSupport delegate object rather than implement the BeanContext interface from scratch.

Bean contexts are often AWT or Swing containers and cannot (because of a method-naming conflict) implement BeanContext. Therefore, a context object implements the BeanContextProxy interface and returns a BeanContext object from its getBeanContextProxy() method. A BeanContextSupport object is a suitable object to return from this method.

Some bean contexts require customized behavior, however, and BeanContextSupport is designed to be easily customized through subclassing. Protected methods such as child-JustAddedHook() and validatePendingAdd() are particularly useful when subclassing.

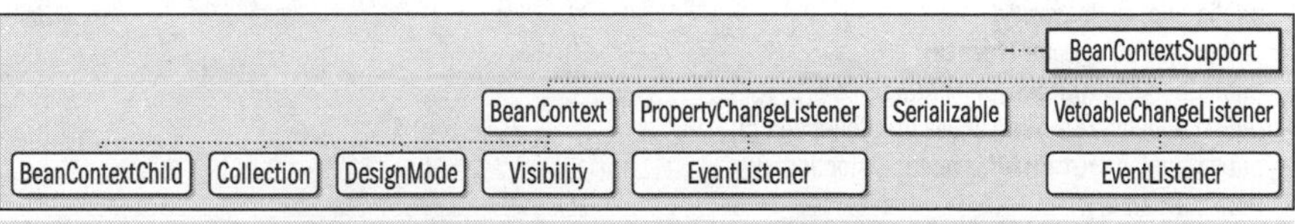


```
public class BeanContextSupport extends BeanContextChildSupport implements BeanContext,
        java.beans.PropertyChangeListener, Serializable, java.beans.VetoableChangeListener {
```

```
// Public Constructors
   public BeanContextSupport();
   public BeanContextSupport(BeanContext peer);
   public BeanContextSupport(BeanContext peer, java.util.Locale lcle);
   public BeanContextSupport(BeanContext peer, java.util.Locale lcle, boolean dtime);
   public BeanContextSupport(BeanContext peer, java.util.Locale lcle, boolean dTime, boolean visible);
// Inner Classes
   protected class BCSChild implements Serializable;
   protected static final class BCSIterator implements java.util.Iterator;
// Protected Class Methods
   protected static final boolean classEquals(Class first, Class second);
   protected static final BeanContextChild getChildBeanContextChild(Object child);
   protected static final BeanContextMembershipListener getChildBeanContextMembershipListener(
                                                         Object child);
   protected static final java.beans.PropertyChangeListener getChildPropertyChangeListener(Object child);
   protected static final Serializable getChildSerializable(Object child);
   protected static final java.beans.VetoableChangeListener getChildVetoableChangeListener(Object child);
   protected static final java.beans.Visibility getChildVisibility(Object child);
// Event Registration Methods (by event name)
   public void addBeanContextMembershipListener(                          Implements:BeanContext
                                                BeanContextMembershipListener bcml);
   public void removeBeanContextMembershipListener(                       Implements:BeanContext
                                                   BeanContextMembershipListener bcml);
// Property Accessor Methods (by property name)
   public BeanContext getBeanContextPeer();                          default:BeanContextSupport
   public boolean isDesignTime();              Implements:DesignMode synchronized default:false
   public void setDesignTime(boolean dTime);                Implements:DesignMode synchronized
   public boolean isEmpty();                                Implements:Collection default:true
   public java.util.Locale getLocale();                                           synchronized
   public void setLocale(java.util.Locale newLocale) throws java.beans.PropertyVetoException;  synchronized
   public boolean isSerializing();                                               default:false
// Public Instance Methods
   public boolean containsKey(Object o);
   public final void readChildren(java.io.ObjectInputStream ois) throws java.io.IOException, ClassNotFoundException;
   public final void writeChildren(java.io.ObjectOutputStream oos) throws java.io.IOException;
// Methods Implementing BeanContext
   public void addBeanContextMembershipListener(BeanContextMembershipListener bcml);
   public java.net.URL getResource(String name, BeanContextChild bcc);
   public java.io.InputStream getResourceAsStream(String name, BeanContextChild bcc);
   public Object instantiateChild(String beanName) throws java.io.IOException, ClassNotFoundException;
   public void removeBeanContextMembershipListener(BeanContextMembershipListener bcml);
// Methods Implementing Collection
   public boolean add(Object targetChild);
   public boolean addAll(java.util.Collection c);
   public void clear();
   public boolean contains(Object o);
   public boolean containsAll(java.util.Collection c);
   public boolean isEmpty();                                                      default:true
   public java.util.Iterator iterator();
   public boolean remove(Object targetChild);
   public boolean removeAll(java.util.Collection c);
   public boolean retainAll(java.util.Collection c);
   public int size();
   public Object[] toArray();
   public Object[] toArray(Object[] arry);
```

```
// Methods Implementing DesignMode
   public boolean isDesignTime();                                          synchronized default:false
   public void setDesignTime(boolean dTime);                                             synchronized
// Methods Implementing PropertyChangeListener
   public void propertyChange(java.beans.PropertyChangeEvent pce);
// Methods Implementing VetoableChangeListener
   public void vetoableChange(java.beans.PropertyChangeEvent pce) throws java.beans.PropertyVetoException;
// Methods Implementing Visibility
   public boolean avoidingGui();
   public void dontUseGui();                                                             synchronized
   public boolean needsGui();                                                            synchronized
   public void okToUseGui();                                                             synchronized
// Protected Instance Methods
   protected java.util.Iterator bcsChildren();
   protected void bcsPreDeserializationHook(java.io.ObjectInputStream ois) throws java.io.IOException,   empty
      ClassNotFoundException;
   protected void bcsPreSerializationHook(java.io.ObjectOutputStream oos) throws java.io.IOException;    empty
   protected void childDeserializedHook(Object child, BeanContextSupport.BCSChild bcsc);
   protected void childJustAddedHook(Object child, BeanContextSupport.BCSChild bcsc);                    empty
   protected void childJustRemovedHook(Object child, BeanContextSupport.BCSChild bcsc);                  empty
   protected final Object[ ] copyChildren();
   protected BeanContextSupport.BCSChild createBCSChild(Object targetChild, Object peer);
   protected final void deserialize(java.io.ObjectInputStream ois, java.util.Collection coll) throws java.io.IOException,
      ClassNotFoundException;
   protected final void fireChildrenAdded(BeanContextMembershipEvent bcme);
   protected final void fireChildrenRemoved(BeanContextMembershipEvent bcme);
   protected void initialize();                                                          synchronized
   protected boolean remove(Object targetChild, boolean callChildSetBC);
   protected final void serialize(java.io.ObjectOutputStream oos, java.util.Collection coll) throws java.io.IOException;
   protected boolean validatePendingAdd(Object targetChild);                                 constant
   protected boolean validatePendingRemove(Object targetChild);                              constant
// Protected Instance Fields
   protected transient java.util.ArrayList bcmListeners;
   protected transient java.util.HashMap children;
   protected boolean designTime;
   protected java.util.Locale locale;
   protected boolean okToUseGui;
}
```

Subclasses: BeanContextServicesSupport

BeanContextSupport.BCSChild — Java 1.2

java.beans.beancontext — *serializable*

This class is used internally by BeanContextSupport to keep track of additional information about its children. In particular, for children that implement the BeanContextProxy interface, it keeps track of the BeanContextChild object associated with the child. This class does not define any public or protected fields or methods. BeanContextSupport subclasses that want to associate additional information with each child can subclass this class and override the createBCSChild() method to instantiate the new subclass.

```
protected class BeanContextSupport.BCSChild implements Serializable {
// No Constructor
}
```

Subclasses: BeanContextServicesSupport.BCSSChild

Passed To: BeanContextServicesSupport.childJustRemovedHook(), BeanContextSupport.{childDeserializedHook(), childJustAddedHook(), childJustRemovedHook()}

Returned By: BeanContextServicesSupport.createBCSChild(), BeanContextSupport.createBCSChild()

BeanContextSupport.BCSIterator — Java 1.2

java.beans.beancontext

This class implements the java.util.Iterator interface. An instance of this class is returned by the iterator() method implemented by BeanContextSupport. The remove() method has an empty implementation and does not actually remove a child of the bean context.

```
protected static final class BeanContextSupport.BCSIterator implements java.util.Iterator {
// No Constructor
// Methods Implementing Iterator
   public boolean hasNext();
   public Object next();
   public void remove();                                                        empty
}
```

CHAPTER 10

java.io

Package java.io — Java 1.0

The java.io package is large, but most of the classes it contains fall into a well-structured hierarchy. Most of the package consists of byte streams—subclasses of InputStream or OutputStream and character streams—subclasses of Reader or Writer. Each of these stream subtypes has a specific purpose, and, despite its size, java.io is a straightforward package to understand and to use. In Java 1.4, the java.io package is complemented by a "New I/O API" defined in the java.nio package and its subpackages. The java.nio package is totally new, although it includes some compatibility with the classes in this package. It was designed for high-performance I/O, particularly for use in servers, and has a lower-level API than this package does. The I/O facilities of java.io are still quite adequate for most of the I/O required by typical client-side applications.

Before we consider the stream classes that comprise the bulk of this package, let's examine the important non-stream classes. File represents a file or directory name in a system-independent way and provides methods for listing directories, querying file attributes, and renaming and deleting files. FilenameFilter is an interface that defines a method that accepts or rejects specified filenames. It is used by File to specify what types of files should be included in directory listings. RandomAccessFile allows you to read from or write to arbitrary locations of a file. Often, though, you'll prefer sequential access to a file and should use one of the stream classes.

InputStream and OutputStream are abstract classes that define methods for reading and writing bytes. Their subclasses allow bytes to be read from and written to a variety of sources and sinks. FileInputStream and FileOutputStream read from and write to files. ByteArrayInputStream and ByteArrayOutputStream read from and write to an array of bytes in memory. PipedInputStream reads bytes from a PipedOutputStream, and PipedOutputStream writes bytes to a PipedInputStream. These classes work together to implement a *pipe* for communication between threads.

FilterInputStream and FilterOutputStream are special; they filter input and output bytes. When you create a FilterInputStream, you specify an InputStream for it to filter. When you call the read() method of a FilterInputStream, it calls the read() method of its InputStream, processes the bytes it reads, and returns the filtered bytes. Similarly, when you create a FilterOutputStream, you specify an OutputStream to be filtered. Calling the write() method of a FilterOutputStream causes it to process your bytes in some way and then pass those filtered bytes to the write() method of its OutputStream.

FilterInputStream and FilterOutputStream do not perform any filtering themselves; this is done by their subclasses. BufferedInputStream and BufferedOutputStream are filtered streams that provide input and output buffering and can increase I/O efficiency. DataInputStream reads raw bytes from a stream and interprets them in various binary formats. It has various methods to read primitive Java data types in their standard binary formats. DataOutputStream allows you to write Java primitive data types in binary format.

The byte streams I just described are complemented by an analogous set of character input and output streams. Reader is the superclass of all character input streams, and Writer is the superclass of all character output streams. Most of the Reader and Writer streams have obvious byte-stream analogs. BufferedReader is a commonly used stream; it provides buffering for efficiency and also has a readLine() method to read a line of text at a time. PrintWriter is another very common stream; its methods allow output of a textual representation of any primitive Java type or of any object (via the object's toString() method).

The ObjectInputStream and ObjectOutputStream classes are special. These byte-stream classes are used for serializing and deserializing the internal state of objects for storage or interprocess communication.

Interfaces:

public interface **DataInput**;
public interface **DataOutput**;
public interface **Externalizable** extends Serializable;
public interface **FileFilter**;
public interface **FilenameFilter**;
public interface **ObjectInput** extends DataInput;
public interface **ObjectInputValidation**;
public interface **ObjectOutput** extends DataOutput;
public interface **ObjectStreamConstants**;
public interface **Serializable**;

Classes:

public class **File** implements Comparable, Serializable;
public final class **FileDescriptor**;
public final class **FilePermission** extends java.security.Permission implements Serializable;
public abstract class **InputStream**;
    └ public class **ByteArrayInputStream** extends InputStream;
    └ public class **FileInputStream** extends InputStream;
    └ public class **FilterInputStream** extends InputStream;
        └ public class **BufferedInputStream** extends FilterInputStream;
        └ public class **DataInputStream** extends FilterInputStream implements DataInput;
        └ public class **LineNumberInputStream** extends FilterInputStream;
        └ public class **PushbackInputStream** extends FilterInputStream;
    └ public class **ObjectInputStream** extends InputStream
    implements ObjectInput, ObjectStreamConstants;
    └ public class **PipedInputStream** extends InputStream;
    └ public class **SequenceInputStream** extends InputStream;
    └ public class **StringBufferInputStream** extends InputStream;
public abstract static class **ObjectInputStream.GetField**;
public abstract static class **ObjectOutputStream.PutField**;

public class **ObjectStreamClass** implements Serializable;
public class **ObjectStreamField** implements Comparable;
public abstract class **OutputStream**;
  └ public class **ByteArrayOutputStream** extends OutputStream;
  └ public class **FileOutputStream** extends OutputStream;
  └ public class **FilterOutputStream** extends OutputStream;
    └ public class **BufferedOutputStream** extends FilterOutputStream;
    └ public class **DataOutputStream** extends FilterOutputStream implements DataOutput;
    └ public class **PrintStream** extends FilterOutputStream;
  └ public class **ObjectOutputStream** extends OutputStream
      implements ObjectOutput, ObjectStreamConstants;
  └ public class **PipedOutputStream** extends OutputStream;
public class **RandomAccessFile** implements DataInput, DataOutput;
public abstract class **Reader**;
  └ public class **BufferedReader** extends Reader;
    └ public class **LineNumberReader** extends BufferedReader;
  └ public class **CharArrayReader** extends Reader;
  └ public abstract class **FilterReader** extends Reader;
    └ public class **PushbackReader** extends FilterReader;
  └ public class **InputStreamReader** extends Reader;
    └ public class **FileReader** extends InputStreamReader;
  └ public class **PipedReader** extends Reader;
  └ public class **StringReader** extends Reader;
public final class **SerializablePermission** extends java.security.BasicPermission;
public class **StreamTokenizer**;
public abstract class **Writer**;
  └ public class **BufferedWriter** extends Writer;
  └ public class **CharArrayWriter** extends Writer;
  └ public abstract class **FilterWriter** extends Writer;
  └ public class **OutputStreamWriter** extends Writer;
    └ public class **FileWriter** extends OutputStreamWriter;
  └ public class **PipedWriter** extends Writer;
  └ public class **PrintWriter** extends Writer;
  └ public class **StringWriter** extends Writer;

Exceptions:

public class **IOException** extends Exception;
  └ public class **CharConversionException** extends IOException;
  └ public class **EOFException** extends IOException;
  └ public class **FileNotFoundException** extends IOException;
  └ public class **InterruptedIOException** extends IOException;
  └ public abstract class **ObjectStreamException** extends IOException;
    └ public class **InvalidClassException** extends ObjectStreamException;
    └ public class **InvalidObjectException** extends ObjectStreamException;
    └ public class **NotActiveException** extends ObjectStreamException;
    └ public class **NotSerializableException** extends ObjectStreamException;
    └ public class **OptionalDataException** extends ObjectStreamException;
    └ public class **StreamCorruptedException** extends ObjectStreamException;
    └ public class **WriteAbortedException** extends ObjectStreamException;
  └ public class **SyncFailedException** extends IOException;
  └ public class **UnsupportedEncodingException** extends IOException;
  └ public class **UTFDataFormatException** extends IOException;

BufferedInputStream **Java 1.0**

java.io

This class is a FilterInputStream that provides input data buffering; efficiency is increased by reading in a large amount of data and storing it in an internal buffer. When data is requested, it is usually available from the buffer. Thus, most calls to read data do not actually have to read data from a disk, network, or other slow source. Create a BufferedInputStream by specifying the InputStream that is to be buffered in the call to the constructor. See also BufferedReader.

Object ─ InputStream ─ FilterInputStream ─ BufferedInputStream

```
public class BufferedInputStream extends FilterInputStream {
// Public Constructors
    public BufferedInputStream(java.io.InputStream in);
    public BufferedInputStream(java.io.InputStream in, int size);
// Public Methods Overriding FilterInputStream
    public int available() throws IOException;                              synchronized
1.2 public void close() throws IOException;
    public void mark(int readlimit);                                        synchronized
    public boolean markSupported();                                         constant
    public int read() throws IOException;                                   synchronized
    public int read(byte[ ] b, int off, int len) throws IOException;        synchronized
    public void reset() throws IOException;                                 synchronized
    public long skip(long n) throws IOException;                            synchronized
// Protected Instance Fields
    protected byte[ ] buf;
    protected int count;
    protected int marklimit;
    protected int markpos;
    protected int pos;
}
```

BufferedOutputStream **Java 1.0**

java.io

This class is a FilterOutputStream that provides output data buffering; output efficiency is increased by storing values to be written in a buffer and actually writing them out only when the buffer fills up or when the flush() method is called. Create a BufferedOutputStream by specifying the OutputStream that is to be buffered in the call to the constructor. See also BufferedWriter.

Object ─ OutputStream ─ FilterOutputStream ─ BufferedOutputStream

```
public class BufferedOutputStream extends FilterOutputStream {
// Public Constructors
    public BufferedOutputStream(java.io.OutputStream out);
    public BufferedOutputStream(java.io.OutputStream out, int size);
// Public Methods Overriding FilterOutputStream
    public void flush() throws IOException;                                 synchronized
    public void write(int b) throws IOException;                            synchronized
    public void write(byte[ ] b, int off, int len) throws IOException;      synchronized
// Protected Instance Fields
    protected byte[ ] buf;
    protected int count;
}
```

BufferedReader **Java 1.1**

java.io

This class applies buffering to a character input stream, thereby improving the efficiency of character input. You create a BufferedReader by specifying some other character input stream from which it is to buffer input. (You can also specify a buffer size at this time, although the default size is usually fine.) Typically, you use this sort of buffering with a FileReader or InputStreamReader. BufferedReader defines the standard set of Reader methods and provides a readLine() method that reads a line of text (not including the line terminator) and returns it as a String. BufferedReader is the character-stream analog of BufferedInputStream. It also provides a replacement for the deprecated readLine() method of DataInputStream, which did not properly convert bytes into characters.

java.io

Object ─ Reader ─ BufferedReader

```
public class BufferedReader extends Reader {
// Public Constructors
   public BufferedReader(Reader in);
   public BufferedReader(Reader in, int sz);
// Public Instance Methods
   public String readLine() throws IOException;
// Public Methods Overriding Reader
   public void close() throws IOException;
   public void mark(int readAheadLimit) throws IOException;
   public boolean markSupported();                                   constant
   public int read() throws IOException;
   public int read(char[ ] cbuf, int off, int len) throws IOException;
   public boolean ready() throws IOException;
   public void reset() throws IOException;
   public long skip(long n) throws IOException;
}
```

Subclasses: LineNumberReader

BufferedWriter **Java 1.1**

java.io

This class applies buffering to a character output stream, improving output efficiency by coalescing many small write requests into a single larger request. You create a BufferedWriter by specifying some other character output stream to which it sends its buffered and coalesced output. (You can also specify a buffer size at this time, although the default size is usually satisfactory.) Typically, you use this sort of buffering with a FileWriter or OutputStreamWriter. BufferedWriter defines the standard write(), flush(), and close() methods all output streams define, but it adds a newLine() method that outputs the platform-dependent line separator (usually a newline character, a carriage-return character, or both) to the stream. BufferedWriter is the character-stream analog of BufferedOutputStream.

Object ─ Writer ─ BufferedWriter

```
public class BufferedWriter extends Writer {
// Public Constructors
   public BufferedWriter(Writer out);
   public BufferedWriter(Writer out, int sz);
// Public Instance Methods
   public void newLine() throws IOException;
```

```
// Public Methods Overriding Writer
   public void close() throws IOException;
   public void flush() throws IOException;
   public void write(int c) throws IOException;
   public void write(char[ ] cbuf, int off, int len) throws IOException;
   public void write(String s, int off, int len) throws IOException;
}
```

ByteArrayInputStream **Java 1.0**

java.io

This class is a subclass of InputStream in which input data comes from a specified array of byte values. This is useful when you want to read data in memory as if it were coming from a file, pipe, or socket. Note that the specified array of bytes is not copied when a ByteArrayInputStream is created. See also CharArrayReader.

Object — InputStream — ByteArrayInputStream

```
public class ByteArrayInputStream extends java.io.InputStream {
// Public Constructors
   public ByteArrayInputStream(byte[ ] buf);
   public ByteArrayInputStream(byte[ ] buf, int offset, int length);
// Public Methods Overriding InputStream
   public int available();                                   synchronized
1.2 public void close() throws IOException;                  empty
1.1 public void mark(int readAheadLimit);
1.1 public boolean markSupported();                          constant
   public int read();                                        synchronized
   public int read(byte[ ] b, int off, int len);             synchronized
   public void reset();                                      synchronized
   public long skip(long n);                                 synchronized
// Protected Instance Fields
   protected byte[ ] buf;
   protected int count;
1.1 protected int mark;
   protected int pos;
}
```

ByteArrayOutputStream **Java 1.0**

java.io

This class is a subclass of OutputStream in which output data is stored in an internal byte array. The internal array grows as necessary and can be retrieved with toByteArray() or toString(). The reset() method discards any data currently stored in the internal array and stores data from the beginning again. See also CharArrayWriter.

Object — OutputStream — ByteArrayOutputStream

```
public class ByteArrayOutputStream extends java.io.OutputStream {
// Public Constructors
   public ByteArrayOutputStream();
   public ByteArrayOutputStream(int size);
// Public Instance Methods
   public void reset();                                      synchronized
   public int size();
```

```
    public byte[ ] toByteArray();                                              synchronized
1.1 public String toString(String enc) throws UnsupportedEncodingException;
    public void writeTo(java.io.OutputStream out) throws IOException;          synchronized
// Public Methods Overriding OutputStream
1.2 public void close() throws IOException;                                    empty
    public void write(int b);                                                  synchronized
    public void write(byte[ ] b, int off, int len);                            synchronized
// Public Methods Overriding Object
    public String toString();
// Protected Instance Fields
    protected byte[ ] buf;
    protected int count;
// Deprecated Public Methods
#   public String toString(int hibyte);
}
```

CharArrayReader — Java 1.1

java.io

This class is a character input stream that uses a character array as the source of the characters it returns. You create a CharArrayReader by specifying the character array (or portion of an array) it is to read from. CharArrayReader defines the usual Reader methods and supports the mark() and reset() methods. Note that the character array you pass to the CharArrayReader() constructor is not copied. This means that changes you make to the elements of the array after you create the input stream affect the values read from the array. CharArrayReader is the character-array analog of ByteArrayInputStream and is similar to StringReader.

Object — Reader — CharArrayReader

```
public class CharArrayReader extends Reader {
// Public Constructors
    public CharArrayReader(char[ ] buf);
    public CharArrayReader(char[ ] buf, int offset, int length);
// Public Methods Overriding Reader
    public void close();
    public void mark(int readAheadLimit) throws IOException;
    public boolean markSupported();                                            constant
    public int read() throws IOException;
    public int read(char[ ] b, int off, int len) throws IOException;
    public boolean ready() throws IOException;
    public void reset() throws IOException;
    public long skip(long n) throws IOException;
// Protected Instance Fields
    protected char[ ] buf;
    protected int count;
    protected int markedPos;
    protected int pos;
}
```

CharArrayWriter — Java 1.1

java.io

This class is a character output stream that uses an internal character array as the destination of characters written to it. When you create a CharArrayWriter, you may optionally specify an initial size for the character array, but you do not specify the character array itself; this array is managed internally by the CharArrayWriter and grows as necessary to accommodate all the characters written to it. The toString() and toCharArray() methods return a copy of all characters written to the stream, as a string and an array of characters, respectively. CharArrayWriter defines the standard write(), flush(), and close() methods all Writer subclasses define. It also defines a few other useful methods. size() returns the number of characters that have been written to the stream. reset() resets the stream to its initial state, with an empty character array; this is more efficient than creating a new CharArrayWriter. Finally, writeTo() writes the contents of the internal character array to some other specified character stream. CharArrayWriter is the character-stream analog of ByteArrayOutputStream and is quite similar to StringWriter.

Object — Writer — CharArrayWriter

```
public class CharArrayWriter extends Writer {
// Public Constructors
   public CharArrayWriter();
   public CharArrayWriter(int initialSize);
// Public Instance Methods
   public void reset();
   public int size();
   public char[ ] toCharArray();
   public void writeTo(Writer out) throws IOException;
// Public Methods Overriding Writer
   public void close();                                    empty
   public void flush();                                    empty
   public void write(int c);
   public void write(char[ ] c, int off, int len);
   public void write(String str, int off, int len);
// Public Methods Overriding Object
   public String toString();
// Protected Instance Fields
   protected char[ ] buf;
   protected int count;
}
```

CharConversionException — Java 1.1

java.io — *serializable checked*

A CharConversionException signals an error when converting bytes to characters or vice versa.

Object — Throwable — Exception — IOException — CharConversionException
Serializable

```
public class CharConversionException extends IOException {
// Public Constructors
   public CharConversionException();
   public CharConversionException(String s);
}
```

DataInput — Java 1.0

java.io

This interface defines the methods required for streams that can read Java primitive data types in a machine-independent binary format. It is implemented by DataInputStream and RandomAccessFile. See DataInputStream for more information on the methods.

```
public interface DataInput {
// Public Instance Methods
    public abstract boolean readBoolean() throws IOException;
    public abstract byte readByte() throws IOException;
    public abstract char readChar() throws IOException;
    public abstract double readDouble() throws IOException;
    public abstract float readFloat() throws IOException;
    public abstract void readFully(byte[] b) throws IOException;
    public abstract void readFully(byte[] b, int off, int len) throws IOException;
    public abstract int readInt() throws IOException;
    public abstract String readLine() throws IOException;
    public abstract long readLong() throws IOException;
    public abstract short readShort() throws IOException;
    public abstract int readUnsignedByte() throws IOException;
    public abstract int readUnsignedShort() throws IOException;
    public abstract String readUTF() throws IOException;
    public abstract int skipBytes(int n) throws IOException;
}
```

Implementations: java.io.DataInputStream, ObjectInput, RandomAccessFile, javax.imageio.stream.ImageInputStream

Passed To: java.io.DataInputStream.readUTF(), java.rmi.server.UID.read()

DataInputStream — Java 1.0

java.io

This class is a type of FilterInputStream that allows you to read binary representations of Java primitive data types in a portable way. Create a DataInputStream by specifying the InputStream that is to be filtered in the call to the constructor. DataInputStream reads only primitive Java types; use ObjectInputStream to read object values.

Many of the methods read and return a single Java primitive type, in binary format, from the stream. readUnsignedByte() and readUnsignedShort() read unsigned values and return them as int values, since unsigned byte and short types are not supported in Java. read() reads data into an array of bytes, blocking until at least some data is available. By contrast, readFully() reads data into an array of bytes, but blocks until all requested data becomes available. skipBytes() blocks until the specified number of bytes have been read and discarded. readLine() reads characters from the stream until it encounters a newline, a carriage return, or a newline/carriage return pair. The returned string is not terminated with a newline or carriage return. This method is deprecated as of Java 1.1; see BufferedReader for an alternative. readUTF() reads a string of Unicode text encoded in a slightly modified version of the UTF-8 transformation format. UTF-8 is an ASCII-compatible encoding of Unicode characters that is often used for the transmission and storage of Unicode text. This class uses a modified UTF-8 encoding that never contains embedded null characters.

Object — InputStream — FilterInputStream — DataInputStream
DataInput

```
public class DataInputStream extends FilterInputStream implements DataInput {
// Public Constructors
    public DataInputStream(java.io.InputStream in);
// Public Class Methods
    public static final String readUTF(DataInput in) throws IOException;
```

```
// Methods Implementing DataInput
   public final boolean readBoolean() throws IOException;
   public final byte readByte() throws IOException;
   public final char readChar() throws IOException;
   public final double readDouble() throws IOException;
   public final float readFloat() throws IOException;
   public final void readFully(byte[ ] b) throws IOException;
   public final void readFully(byte[ ] b, int off, int len) throws IOException;
   public final int readInt() throws IOException;
   public final long readLong() throws IOException;
   public final short readShort() throws IOException;
   public final int readUnsignedByte() throws IOException;
   public final int readUnsignedShort() throws IOException;
   public final String readUTF() throws IOException;
   public final int skipBytes(int n) throws IOException;
// Public Methods Overriding FilterInputStream
   public final int read(byte[ ] b) throws IOException;
   public final int read(byte[ ] b, int off, int len) throws IOException;
// Deprecated Public Methods
#  public final String readLine() throws IOException;                    Implements:DataInput
}
```

Passed To: javax.swing.text.html.parser.DTD.read()

DataOutput   Java 1.0

java.io

This interface defines the methods required for streams that can write Java primitive data types in a machine-independent binary format. It is implemented by DataOutputStream and RandomAccessFile. See DataOutputStream for more information on the methods.

```
public interface DataOutput {
// Public Instance Methods
   public abstract void write(byte[ ] b) throws IOException;
   public abstract void write(int b) throws IOException;
   public abstract void write(byte[ ] b, int off, int len) throws IOException;
   public abstract void writeBoolean(boolean v) throws IOException;
   public abstract void writeByte(int v) throws IOException;
   public abstract void writeBytes(String s) throws IOException;
   public abstract void writeChar(int v) throws IOException;
   public abstract void writeChars(String s) throws IOException;
   public abstract void writeDouble(double v) throws IOException;
   public abstract void writeFloat(float v) throws IOException;
   public abstract void writeInt(int v) throws IOException;
   public abstract void writeLong(long v) throws IOException;
   public abstract void writeShort(int v) throws IOException;
   public abstract void writeUTF(String str) throws IOException;
}
```

Implementations: java.io.DataOutputStream, ObjectOutput, RandomAccessFile, javax.imageio.stream.ImageOutputStream

Passed To: java.rmi.server.UID.write()

DataOutputStream

Java 1.0

java.io

This class is a subclass of FilterOutputStream that allows you to write Java primitive data types in a portable binary format. Create a DataOutputStream by specifying the OutputStream that is to be filtered in the call to the constructor. DataOutputStream has methods that output only primitive types; use ObjectOutputStream to output object values.

Many of this class's methods write a single Java primitive type, in binary format, to the output stream. write() writes a single byte, an array, or a subarray of bytes. flush() forces any buffered data to be output. size() returns the number of bytes written so far. writeUTF() outputs a Java string of Unicode characters using a slightly modified version of the UTF-8 transformation format. UTF-8 is an ASCII-compatible encoding of Unicode characters that is often used for the transmission and storage of Unicode text. Except for the writeUTF() method, this class is used for binary output of data. Textual output should be done with PrintWriter (or PrintStream in Java 1.0).


```
public class DataOutputStream extends FilterOutputStream implements DataOutput {
// Public Constructors
   public DataOutputStream(java.io.OutputStream out);
// Public Instance Methods
   public final int size();
// Methods Implementing DataOutput
   public void write(int b) throws IOException;                          synchronized
   public void write(byte[ ] b, int off, int len) throws IOException;    synchronized
   public final void writeBoolean(boolean v) throws IOException;
   public final void writeByte(int v) throws IOException;
   public final void writeBytes(String s) throws IOException;
   public final void writeChar(int v) throws IOException;
   public final void writeChars(String s) throws IOException;
   public final void writeDouble(double v) throws IOException;
   public final void writeFloat(float v) throws IOException;
   public final void writeInt(int v) throws IOException;
   public final void writeLong(long v) throws IOException;
   public final void writeShort(int v) throws IOException;
   public final void writeUTF(String str) throws IOException;
// Public Methods Overriding FilterOutputStream
   public void flush() throws IOException;
// Protected Instance Fields
   protected int written;
}
```

EOFException

Java 1.0

java.io *serializable checked*

An EOFException is an IOException that signals the end of file.


```
public class EOFException extends IOException {
// Public Constructors
```

```
    public EOFException();
    public EOFException(String s);
}
```

Externalizable **Java 1.1**

java.io *serializable*

This interface defines the methods that must be implemented by an object that wants complete control over the way it is serialized. The writeExternal() and readExternal() methods should be implemented to write and read object data in some arbitrary format, using the methods of the DataOutput and DataInput interfaces. Externalizable objects must serialize their own fields and are also responsible for serializing the fields of their superclasses. Most objects do not need to define a custom output format and can use the Serializable interface instead of Externalizable for serialization.

Serializable ··· Externalizable

```
public interface Externalizable extends Serializable {
// Public Instance Methods
    public abstract void readExternal(ObjectInput in) throws IOException, ClassNotFoundException;
    public abstract void writeExternal(ObjectOutput out) throws IOException;
}
```

Implementations: java.awt.datatransfer.DataFlavor, java.rmi.server.RemoteRef

File **Java 1.0**

java.io *serializable comparable*

This class supports a platform-independent definition of file and directory names. It also provides methods to list the files in a directory; check the existence, readability, writability, type, size, and modification time of files and directories; make new directories; rename files and directories; delete files and directories; and create and delete temporary and lock files. The constants defined by this class are the platform-dependent directory and path-separator characters, available as a String and a char.

getName() returns the name of the File with any directory names omitted. getPath() returns the full name of the file, including the directory name. getParent() and getParentFile() return the directory that contains the File; the only difference between the two methods is that one returns a String, while the other returns a File. isAbsolute() tests whether the File is an absolute specification. If not, getAbsolutePath() returns an absolute filename created by appending the relative filename to the current working directory. getAbsoluteFile() returns the equivalent absolute File object. getCanonicalPath() and getCanonicalFile() are similar methods: they return an absolute filename or File object that has been converted to its system-dependent canonical form. This can be useful when comparing two File objects to see if they refer to the same file or directory. In Java 1.4 and later, the toURI() method returns a java.net.URI object that uses a file: scheme to name this file. This file-to-URI transformation can be reversed by passing a file: URI object to the File() constructor.

exists(), canWrite(), canRead(), isFile(), isDirectory(), and isHidden() perform the obvious tests on the specified File. length() returns the length of the file. lastModified() returns the modification time of the file (which should be used for comparison with other file times only and not interpreted as any particular time format). setLastModified() allows the modification time to be set; setReadOnly() makes a file or directory read-only.

list() returns the names of all entries in a directory that are not rejected by an optional FilenameFilter. listFiles() returns an array of File objects that represent all entries in a directory not rejected by an optional FilenameFilter or FileFilter. listRoots() returns an array of File objects representing all root directories on the system. On Unix systems, for example, there is typically only one root, */*. On Windows systems, however, there is a different root for each drive letter: *c:*, *d:*, and *e:*, for example.

mkdir() creates a directory, and mkdirs() creates all the directories in a File specification. renameTo() renames a file or directory; delete() deletes a file or directory. Prior to Java 1.2, the File class doesn't provide any way to create a file; that task is accomplished typically with FileOutputStream. As of Java 1.2, however, two special-purpose file creation methods have been added. The static createTempFile() method returns a File object that refers to a newly created empty file with a unique name that begins with the specified prefix (which must be at least three characters long) and ends with the specified suffix. One version of this method creates the file in a specified directory, and the other creates it in the system temporary directory. Applications can use temporary files for any purpose without worrying about overwriting files belonging to other applications. The other file-creation method of Java 1.2 is createNewFile(). This instance method attempts to create a new, empty file with the name specified by the File object. If it succeeds, it returns true. However, if the file already exists, it returns false. createNewFile() works atomically, and is therefore useful for file locking and other mutual-exclusion schemes. When working with createTempFile() or createNewFile(), consider using deleteOnExit() to request that the files be deleted when the Java VM exits normally.

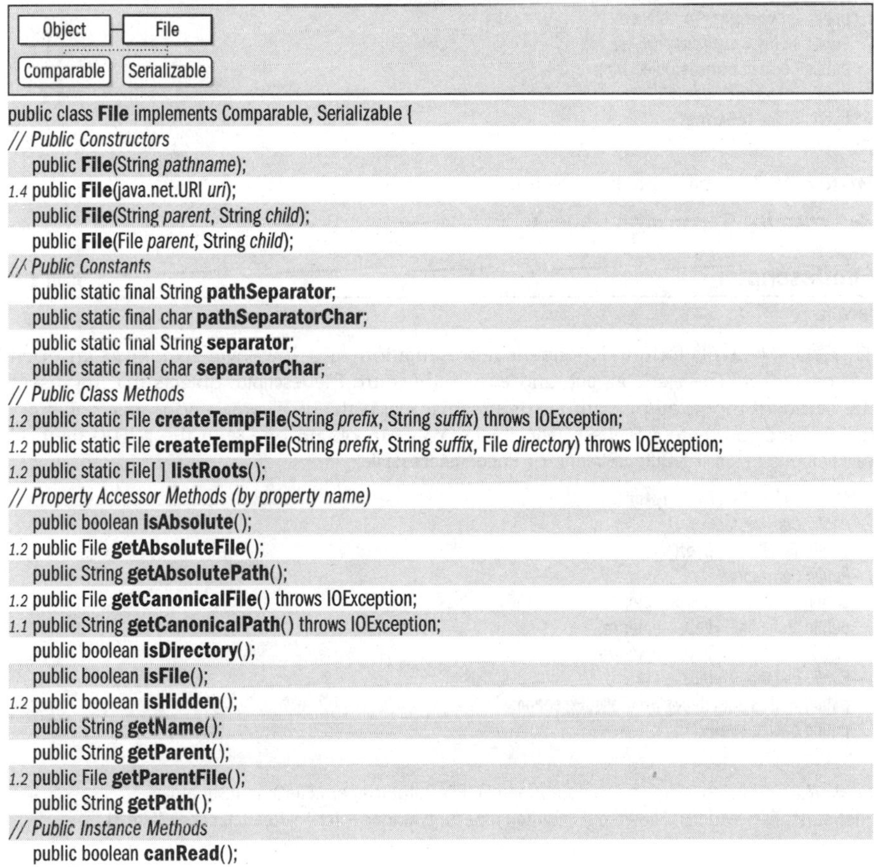


```
public class File implements Comparable, Serializable {
// Public Constructors
    public File(String pathname);
1.4 public File(java.net.URI uri);
    public File(String parent, String child);
    public File(File parent, String child);
// Public Constants
    public static final String pathSeparator;
    public static final char pathSeparatorChar;
    public static final String separator;
    public static final char separatorChar;
// Public Class Methods
1.2 public static File createTempFile(String prefix, String suffix) throws IOException;
1.2 public static File createTempFile(String prefix, String suffix, File directory) throws IOException;
1.2 public static File[ ] listRoots();
// Property Accessor Methods (by property name)
    public boolean isAbsolute();
1.2 public File getAbsoluteFile();
    public String getAbsolutePath();
1.2 public File getCanonicalFile() throws IOException;
1.1 public String getCanonicalPath() throws IOException;
    public boolean isDirectory();
    public boolean isFile();
1.2 public boolean isHidden();
    public String getName();
    public String getParent();
1.2 public File getParentFile();
    public String getPath();
// Public Instance Methods
    public boolean canRead();
```

```
   public boolean canWrite();
1.2 public int compareTo(File pathname);
1.2 public boolean createNewFile() throws IOException;
   public boolean delete();
1.2 public void deleteOnExit();
   public boolean exists();
   public long lastModified();
   public long length();
   public String[ ] list();
   public String[ ] list(FilenameFilter filter);
1.2 public File[ ] listFiles();
1.2 public File[ ] listFiles(FilenameFilter filter);
1.2 public File[ ] listFiles(java.io.FileFilter filter);
   public boolean mkdir();
   public boolean mkdirs();
   public boolean renameTo(File dest);
1.2 public boolean setLastModified(long time);
1.2 public boolean setReadOnly();
1.4 public java.net.URI toURI();
1.2 public java.net.URL toURL() throws java.net.MalformedURLException;
// Methods Implementing Comparable
1.2 public int compareTo(Object o);
// Public Methods Overriding Object
   public boolean equals(Object obj);
   public int hashCode();
   public String toString();
}
```

Passed To: Too many methods to list.

Returned By: Too many methods to list.

FileDescriptor — Java 1.0

java.io

This class is a platform-independent representation of a low-level handle to an open file or socket. The static in, out, and err variables are FileDescriptor objects that represent the standard input, output, and error streams, respectively. There is no public constructor method to create a FileDescriptor object. You can obtain one with the getFD() method of FileInputStream, FileOutputStream, or RandomAccessFile.

```
public final class FileDescriptor {
// Public Constructors
   public FileDescriptor();
// Public Constants
   public static final FileDescriptor err;
   public static final FileDescriptor in;
   public static final FileDescriptor out;
// Public Instance Methods
1.1 public void sync() throws SyncFailedException;                    native
   public boolean valid();
}
```

Passed To: FileInputStream.FileInputStream(), FileOutputStream.FileOutputStream(), FileReader.FileReader(), FileWriter.FileWriter(), SecurityManager.{checkRead(), checkWrite()}

Returned By: FileInputStream.getFD(), FileOutputStream.getFD(), RandomAccessFile.getFD(), java.net.DatagramSocketImpl.getFileDescriptor(), java.net.SocketImpl.getFileDescriptor()

Type Of: FileDescriptor.{err, in, out}, java.net.DatagramSocketImpl.fd, java.net.SocketImpl.fd

FileFilter — Java 1.2

java.io

This interface defines an accept() method that filters a list of files. You can list the contents of a directory by calling the listFiles() method of the File object that represents the desired directory. If you want a filtered listing, such as a listing of files but not subdirectories or a listing of files whose names end in *.class*, you can pass a FileFilter object to listFiles(). For each entry in the directory, a File object is passed to the accept() method. If accept() returns true, that File is included in the return value of listFiles(). If accept() returns false, that entry is not included in the listing. FileFilter is new in Java 1.2. Use FilenameFilter if compatibility with previous releases of Java is required or if you prefer to filter filenames (i.e., String objects) rather than File objects.

```
public interface FileFilter {
// Public Instance Methods
   public abstract boolean accept(File pathname);
}
```

Passed To: File.listFiles()

FileInputStream — Java 1.0

java.io

This class is a subclass of InputStream that reads bytes from a file specified by name or by a File or FileDescriptor object. read() reads a byte or array of bytes from the file. It returns –1 when the end-of-file has been reached. To read binary data, you typically use this class in conjunction with a BufferedInputStream and DataInputStream. To read text, you typically use it with an InputStreamReader and BufferedReader. Call close() to close the file when input is no longer needed.

In Java 1.4 and later, use getChannel() to obtain a FileChannel object for reading from the underlying file using the New I/O API of java.nio and its subpackages.

Object — InputStream — FileInputStream

```
public class FileInputStream extends java.io.InputStream {
// Public Constructors
   public FileInputStream(String name) throws FileNotFoundException;
   public FileInputStream(File file) throws FileNotFoundException;
   public FileInputStream(FileDescriptor fdObj);
// Public Instance Methods
1.4 public java.nio.channels.FileChannel getChannel();
   public final FileDescriptor getFD() throws IOException;
// Public Methods Overriding InputStream
   public int available() throws IOException;                              native
   public void close() throws IOException;
   public int read() throws IOException;                                   native
   public int read(byte[ ] b) throws IOException;
   public int read(byte[ ] b, int off, int len) throws IOException;
   public long skip(long n) throws IOException;                            native
```

```
// Protected Methods Overriding Object
   protected void finalize() throws IOException;
}
```

FilenameFilter — Java 1.0

java.io

This interface defines the accept() method that must be implemented by any object that filters filenames (i.e., selects a subset of filenames from a list of filenames). There are no standard FilenameFilter classes implemented by Java, but objects that implement this interface are used by the java.awt.FileDialog object and the File.list() method. A typical FilenameFilter object might check that the specified File represents a file (not a directory), is readable (and possibly writable as well), and that its name ends with some desired extension.

```
public interface FilenameFilter {
// Public Instance Methods
   public abstract boolean accept(File dir, String name);
}
```

Passed To: java.awt.FileDialog.setFilenameFilter(), java.awt.peer.FileDialogPeer.setFilenameFilter(), File.{list(), listFiles()}

Returned By: java.awt.FileDialog.getFilenameFilter()

FileNotFoundException — Java 1.0

java.io — *serializable checked*

A FileNotFoundException is an IOException that signals that a specified file cannot be found.

Object — Throwable — Exception — IOException — FileNotFoundException
Serializable

```
public class FileNotFoundException extends IOException {
// Public Constructors
   public FileNotFoundException();
   public FileNotFoundException(String s);
}
```

Thrown By: FileInputStream.FileInputStream(), FileOutputStream.FileOutputStream(), FileReader.FileReader(), RandomAccessFile.RandomAccessFile(), javax.imageio.stream.FileImageInputStream.FileImageInputStream(), javax.imageio.stream.FileImageOutputStream.FileImageOutputStream()

FileOutputStream — Java 1.0

java.io

This class is a subclass of OutputStream that writes data to a file specified by name or by a File or FileDescriptor object. If the specified file already exists, a FileOutputStream can be configured to overwrite or append to the existing file. write() writes a byte or array of bytes to the file. To write binary data, you typically use this class in conjunction with a BufferedOutputStream and a DataOutputStream. To write text, you typically use it with a PrintWriter, BufferedWriter and an OutputStreamWriter (or you use the convenience class FileWriter). Use close() to close a FileOutputStream when no further output will be written to it.

In Java 1.4 and later, use getChannel() to obtain a FileChannel object for writing to the underlying file using the New I/O API of java.nio and its subpackages.

Object — OutputStream — FileOutputStream

```
public class FileOutputStream extends java.io.OutputStream {
// Public Constructors
    public FileOutputStream(FileDescriptor fdObj);
    public FileOutputStream(File file) throws FileNotFoundException;
    public FileOutputStream(String name) throws FileNotFoundException;
1.1 public FileOutputStream(String name, boolean append) throws FileNotFoundException;
1.4 public FileOutputStream(File file, boolean append) throws FileNotFoundException;
// Public Instance Methods
1.4 public java.nio.channels.FileChannel getChannel();
    public final FileDescriptor getFD() throws IOException;
// Public Methods Overriding OutputStream
    public void close() throws IOException;
    public void write(int b) throws IOException;                                    native
    public void write(byte[ ] b) throws IOException;
    public void write(byte[ ] b, int off, int len) throws IOException;
// Protected Methods Overriding Object
    protected void finalize() throws IOException;
}
```

FilePermission — Java 1.2

java.io — *serializable permission*

This class is a java.security.Permission that governs access to the local filesystem. A FilePermission has a name, or target, which specifies what file or files it pertains to, and a comma-separated list of actions that may be performed on the file or files. The supported actions are read, write, delete, and execute. Read and write permission are required by any methods that read or write a file. Delete permission is required by File.delete(), and execute permission is required by Runtime.exec().

The name of a FilePermission may be as simple as a file or directory name. FilePermission also supports the use of certain wildcards, however, to specify a permission that applies to more than one file. If the name of the FilePermission is a directory name followed by /* (* on Windows platforms), it specifies all files in the named directory. If the name is a directory name followed by /- (\- on Windows), it specifies all files in the directory, and, recursively, all files in all subdirectories. A * alone specifies all files in the current directory, and a - alone specifies all files in or beneath the current directory. Finally, the special name <<ALL FILES>> matches all files anywhere in the filesystem.

Applications do not need to use this class directly. Programmers writing system-level code and system administrators configuring security policies may need to use it, however. Be very careful when granting any types of FilePermission. Restricting access (especially write access) to files is one of the cornerstones of the Java security model with regard to untrusted code.

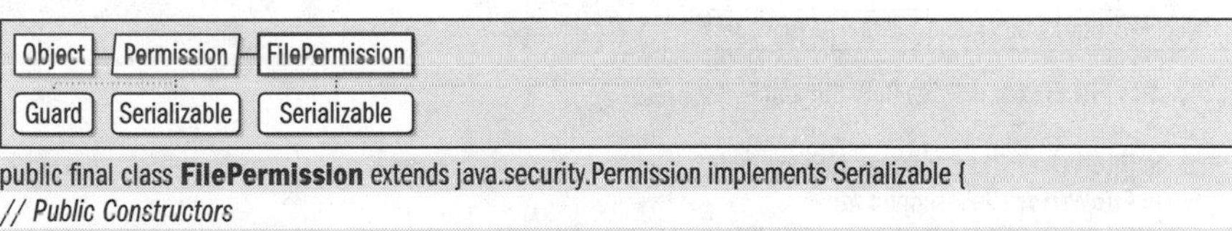


```
public final class FilePermission extends java.security.Permission implements Serializable {
// Public Constructors
    public FilePermission(String path, String actions);
// Public Methods Overriding Permission
```

```
    public boolean equals(Object obj);
    public String getActions();
    public int hashCode();
    public boolean implies(java.security.Permission p);
    public java.security.PermissionCollection newPermissionCollection();
}
```

FileReader — Java 1.1

java.io

FileReader is a convenience subclass of InputStreamReader that is useful when you want to read text (as opposed to binary data) from a file. You create a FileReader by specifying the file to be read in any of three possible forms. The FileReader constructor internally creates a FileInputStream to read bytes from the specified file and uses the functionality of its superclass, InputStreamReader, to convert those bytes from characters in the local encoding to the Unicode characters used by Java. Because FileReader is a trivial subclass of InputStreamReader, it does not define any read() methods or other methods of its own. Instead, it inherits all its methods from its superclass. If you want to read Unicode characters from a file that uses some encoding other than the default encoding for the locale, you must explicitly create your own InputStreamReader to perform the byte-to-character conversion.

Object — Reader — InputStreamReader — FileReader

```
public class FileReader extends InputStreamReader {
// Public Constructors
    public FileReader(FileDescriptor fd);
    public FileReader(File file) throws FileNotFoundException;
    public FileReader(String fileName) throws FileNotFoundException;
}
```

FileWriter — Java 1.1

java.io

FileWriter is a convenience subclass of OutputStreamWriter that is useful when you want to write text (as opposed to binary data) to a file. You create a FileWriter by specifying the file to be written to and, optionally, whether the data should be appended to the end of an existing file instead of overwriting that file. The FileWriter class creates an internal FileOutputStream to write bytes to the specified file and uses the functionality of its superclass, OutputStreamWriter, to convert the Unicode characters written to the stream into bytes using the default encoding of the default locale. (If you want to use an encoding other than the default, you cannot use FileWriter; in that case you must create your own OutputStreamWriter and FileOutputStream.) Because FileWriter is a trivial subclass of OutputStreamWriter, it does not define any methods of its own, but simply inherits them from its superclass.

Object — Writer — OutputStreamWriter — FileWriter

```
public class FileWriter extends OutputStreamWriter {
// Public Constructors
    public FileWriter(File file) throws IOException;
    public FileWriter(FileDescriptor fd);
    public FileWriter(String fileName) throws IOException;
1.4 public FileWriter(File file, boolean append) throws IOException;
```

```
    public FileWriter(String fileName, boolean append) throws IOException;
}
```

FilterInputStream — Java 1.0

java.io

This class provides method definitions required to filter data obtained from the InputStream specified when the FilterInputStream is created. It must be subclassed to perform some sort of filtering operation and cannot be instantiated directly. See the subclasses BufferedInputStream, DataInputStream, and PushbackInputStream.

Object — InputStream — FilterInputStream

```
public class FilterInputStream extends java.io.InputStream {
// Protected Constructors
    protected FilterInputStream(java.io.InputStream in);
// Public Methods Overriding InputStream
    public int available() throws IOException;
    public void close() throws IOException;
    public void mark(int readlimit);                                    synchronized
    public boolean markSupported();
    public int read() throws IOException;
    public int read(byte[ ] b) throws IOException;
    public int read(byte[ ] b, int off, int len) throws IOException;
    public void reset() throws IOException;                             synchronized
    public long skip(long n) throws IOException;
// Protected Instance Fields
    protected java.io.InputStream in;
}
```

Subclasses: BufferedInputStream, java.io.DataInputStream, LineNumberInputStream, PushbackInputStream, java.security.DigestInputStream, java.util.zip.CheckedInputStream, java.util.zip.InflaterInputStream, javax.crypto.CipherInputStream, javax.swing.ProgressMonitorInputStream

FilterOutputStream — Java 1.0

java.io

This class provides method definitions required to filter the data to be written to the OutputStream specified when the FilterOutputStream is created. It must be subclassed to perform some sort of filtering operation and may not be instantiated directly. See the subclasses BufferedOutputStream and DataOutputStream.

Object — OutputStream — FilterOutputStream

```
public class FilterOutputStream extends java.io.OutputStream {
// Public Constructors
    public FilterOutputStream(java.io.OutputStream out);
// Public Methods Overriding OutputStream
    public void close() throws IOException;
    public void flush() throws IOException;
    public void write(int b) throws IOException;
    public void write(byte[ ] b) throws IOException;
    public void write(byte[ ] b, int off, int len) throws IOException;
// Protected Instance Fields
```

```
    protected java.io.OutputStream out;
}
```

Subclasses: BufferedOutputStream, java.io.DataOutputStream, PrintStream, java.security.DigestOutputStream, java.util.zip.CheckedOutputStream, java.util.zip.DeflaterOutputStream, javax.crypto.CipherOutputStream

FilterReader — Java 1.1

java.io

This abstract class is intended to act as a superclass for character input streams that read data from some other character input stream, filter it in some way, and then return the filtered data when a read() method is called. FilterReader is declared abstract so that it cannot be instantiated. But none of its methods are themselves abstract: they all simply call the requested operation on the input stream passed to the FilterReader() constructor. If you were allowed to instantiate a FilterReader, you'd find that it is a null filter (i.e., it simply reads characters from the specified input stream and returns them without any kind of filtering).

Because FilterReader implements a null filter, it is an ideal superclass for classes that want to implement simple filters but do not want to override all the methods of Reader. In order to create your own filtered character input stream, you should subclass FilterReader and override both its read() methods to perform the desired filtering operation. Note that you can implement one of the read() methods in terms of the other, and thus only implement the filtration once. Recall that the other read() methods defined by Reader are implemented in terms of these methods, so you do not need to override those. In some cases, you may need to override other methods of FilterReader and provide methods or constructors that are specific to your subclass. FilterReader is the character stream analog to FilterInputStream.

Object — Reader — FilterReader

```
public abstract class FilterReader extends Reader {
// Protected Constructors
    protected FilterReader(Reader in);
// Public Methods Overriding Reader
    public void close() throws IOException;
    public void mark(int readAheadLimit) throws IOException;
    public boolean markSupported();
    public int read() throws IOException;
    public int read(char[ ] cbuf, int off, int len) throws IOException;
    public boolean ready() throws IOException;
    public void reset() throws IOException;
    public long skip(long n) throws IOException;
// Protected Instance Fields
    protected Reader in;
}
```

Subclasses: PushbackReader

FilterWriter — Java 1.1

java.io

This abstract class is intended to act as a superclass for character output streams that filter the data written to them before writing it to some other character output stream. FilterWriter is declared abstract so that it cannot be instantiated. But none of its methods are themselves abstract: they all simply invoke the corresponding method on the output stream that was passed to the FilterWriter constructor. If you were allowed to instantiate a FilterWriter object, you'd find that it acts as a null filter (i.e., it simply passes the characters written to it along, without any filtration).

Because FilterWriter implements a null filter, it is an ideal superclass for classes that want to implement simple filters without having to override all of the methods of Writer. In order to create your own filtered character output stream, you should subclass FilterWriter and override all its write() methods to perform the desired filtering operation. Note that you can implement two of the write() methods in terms of the third and thus implement your filtering algorithm only once. In some cases, you may want to override other Writer methods and add other methods or constructors that are specific to your subclass. FilterWriter is the character-stream analog of FilterOutputStream.

Object — Writer — FilterWriter

```
public abstract class FilterWriter extends Writer {
// Protected Constructors
   protected FilterWriter(Writer out);
// Public Methods Overriding Writer
   public void close() throws IOException;
   public void flush() throws IOException;
   public void write(int c) throws IOException;
   public void write(char[ ] cbuf, int off, int len) throws IOException;
   public void write(String str, int off, int len) throws IOException;
// Protected Instance Fields
   protected Writer out;
}
```

InputStream Java 1.0

java.io

This abstract class is the superclass of all input streams. It defines the basic input methods all input stream classes provide. read() reads a single byte or an array (or subarray) of bytes. It returns the byte read, the number of bytes read, or –1 if the end-of-file has been reached. skip() skips a specified number of bytes of input. available() returns the number of bytes that can be read without blocking. close() closes the input stream and frees up any system resources associated with it. The stream should not be used after close() has been called.

If markSupported() returns true for a given InputStream, that stream supports mark() and reset() methods. mark() marks the current position in the input stream so that reset() can return to that position (as long as no more than the specified number of bytes have been read between the calls to mark() and reset()). See also Reader.

```
public abstract class InputStream {
// Public Constructors
   public InputStream();
// Public Instance Methods
   public int available() throws IOException;                          constant
   public void close() throws IOException;                                empty
   public void mark(int readlimit);                          synchronized empty
   public boolean markSupported();                                     constant
   public abstract int read() throws IOException;
```

```
    public int read(byte[ ] b) throws IOException;
    public int read(byte[ ] b, int off, int len) throws IOException;
    public void reset() throws IOException;                                    synchronized
    public long skip(long n) throws IOException;
}
```

Subclasses: ByteArrayInputStream, FileInputStream, FilterInputStream, ObjectInputStream, PipedInputStream, SequenceInputStream, StringBufferInputStream, javax.sound.sampled.AudioInputStream, org.omg.CORBA.portable.InputStream

Passed To: Too many methods to list.

Returned By: Too many methods to list.

Type Of: FilterInputStream.in, System.in

InputStreamReader — Java 1.1

java.io

This class is a character input stream that uses a byte input stream as its data source. It reads bytes from a specified InputStream and translates them into Unicode characters according to a particular platform- and locale-dependent character encoding. This is an important internationalization feature in Java 1.1 and later. InputStreamReader supports the standard Reader methods. It also has a getEncoding() method that returns the name of the encoding being used to convert bytes to characters.

When you create an InputStreamReader, you specify an InputStream from which the InputStreamReader is to read bytes and, optionally, the name of the character encoding used by those bytes. If you do not specify an encoding name, the InputStreamReader uses the default encoding for the default locale, which is usually the correct thing to do. In Java 1.4 and later, this class uses the charset conversion facilities of the java.nio.charset package, and allows you to explicitly specify the Charset or CharsetDecoder to be used. Prior to Java 1.4, the class allows you to specify on the name of the desired charset encoding.

Object — Reader — InputStreamReader

```
public class InputStreamReader extends Reader {
// Public Constructors
    public InputStreamReader(java.io.InputStream in);
    public InputStreamReader(java.io.InputStream in, String charsetName) throws UnsupportedEncodingException;
1.4 public InputStreamReader(java.io.InputStream in, java.nio.charset.Charset cs);
1.4 public InputStreamReader(java.io.InputStream in, java.nio.charset.CharsetDecoder dec);
// Public Instance Methods
    public String getEncoding();
// Public Methods Overriding Reader
    public void close() throws IOException;
    public int read() throws IOException;
    public int read(char[ ] cbuf, int offset, int length) throws IOException;
    public boolean ready() throws IOException;
}
```

Subclasses: FileReader

InterruptedIOException — Java 1.0

java.io — *serializable checked*

An InterruptedIOEException is an IOException that signals that an input or output operation was interrupted. The bytesTransferred field contains the number of bytes read or written before the operation was interrupted.

Object — Throwable — Exception — IOException — InterruptedIOException
Serializable

```
public class InterruptedIOException extends IOException {
// Public Constructors
   public InterruptedIOException();
   public InterruptedIOException(String s);
// Public Instance Fields
   public int bytesTransferred;
}
```

Subclasses: java.net.SocketTimeoutException

InvalidClassException — Java 1.1

java.io — *serializable checked*

An InvalidClassException signals that the serialization mechanism has encountered one of several possible problems with the class of an object that is being serialized or deserialized. The classname field should contain the name of the class in question, and the getMessage() method is overridden to return this class name with the message.

Object — Throwable — Exception — IOException — ObjectStreamException — InvalidClassException
Serializable

```
public class InvalidClassException extends ObjectStreamException {
// Public Constructors
   public InvalidClassException(String reason);
   public InvalidClassException(String cname, String reason);
// Public Methods Overriding Throwable
   public String getMessage();
// Public Instance Fields
   public String classname;
}
```

InvalidObjectException — Java 1.1

java.io — *serializable checked*

This exception should be thrown by the validateObject() method of an object that implements the ObjectInputValidation interface when a deserialized object fails an input validation test for any reason.

Object — Throwable — Exception — IOException — ObjectStreamException — InvalidObjectException
Serializable

```
public class InvalidObjectException extends ObjectStreamException {
// Public Constructors
   public InvalidObjectException(String reason);
}
```

Thrown By: java.awt.font.TextAttribute.readResolve(), ObjectInputStream.registerValidation(), ObjectInputValidation.validateObject(), java.text.AttributedCharacterIterator.Attribute.readResolve(), java.text.DateFormat.Field.readResolve(), java.text.MessageFormat.Field.readResolve(), java.text.NumberFormat.Field.readResolve()

IOException — Java 1.0

java.io — *serializable checked*

An IOException signals that an exceptional condition has occurred during input or output. This class has several more specific subclasses. See EOFException, FileNotFoundException, InterruptedIOException, and UTFDataFormatException.

Object — Throwable — Exception — IOException
Throwable ⋮ Serializable

```
public class IOException extends Exception {
// Public Constructors
   public IOException();
   public IOException(String s);
}
```

Subclasses: Too many classes to list.

Passed To: java.awt.print.PrinterIOException.PrinterIOException()

Returned By: java.awt.print.PrinterIOException.getIOException()

Thrown By: Too many methods to list.

LineNumberInputStream — Java 1.0; Deprecated in Java 1.1

java.io

This class is a FilterInputStream that keeps track of the number of lines of data that have been read. getLineNumber() returns the current line number; setLineNumber() sets the line number of the current line. Subsequent lines are numbered starting from that number. This class is deprecated as of Java 1.1 because it does not properly convert bytes to characters. Use LineNumberReader instead.

Object — InputStream — FilterInputStream — LineNumberInputStream

```
public class LineNumberInputStream extends FilterInputStream {
// Public Constructors
   public LineNumberInputStream(java.io.InputStream in);
// Public Instance Methods
   public int getLineNumber();
   public void setLineNumber(int lineNumber);
// Public Methods Overriding FilterInputStream
   public int available() throws IOException;
   public void mark(int readlimit);
   public int read() throws IOException;
   public int read(byte[ ] b, int off, int len) throws IOException;
   public void reset() throws IOException;
   public long skip(long n) throws IOException;
}
```

LineNumberReader **Java 1.1**

java.io

This class is a character input stream that keeps track of the number of lines of text that have been read from it. It supports the usual Reader methods and also the readLine() method introduced by its superclass. In addition to these methods, you can call getLineNumber() to query the number of lines set so far. You can also call setLineNumber() to set the line number for the current line. Subsequent lines are numbered sequentially from this specified starting point. This class is a character-stream analog to LineNumberInputStream, which has been deprecated as of Java 1.1.

Object — Reader — BufferedReader — LineNumberReader

```
public class LineNumberReader extends BufferedReader {
// Public Constructors
   public LineNumberReader(Reader in);
   public LineNumberReader(Reader in, int sz);
// Public Instance Methods
   public int getLineNumber();
   public void setLineNumber(int lineNumber);
// Public Methods Overriding BufferedReader
   public void mark(int readAheadLimit) throws IOException;
   public int read() throws IOException;
   public int read(char[ ] cbuf, int off, int len) throws IOException;
   public String readLine() throws IOException;
   public void reset() throws IOException;
   public long skip(long n) throws IOException;
}
```

NotActiveException **Java 1.1**

java.io *serializable checked*

This exception is thrown in several circumstances. It indicates that the invoked method was not invoked at the right time or in the correct context. Typically, it means that an ObjectOutputStream or ObjectInputStream is not currently active and therefore the requested operation cannot be performed.

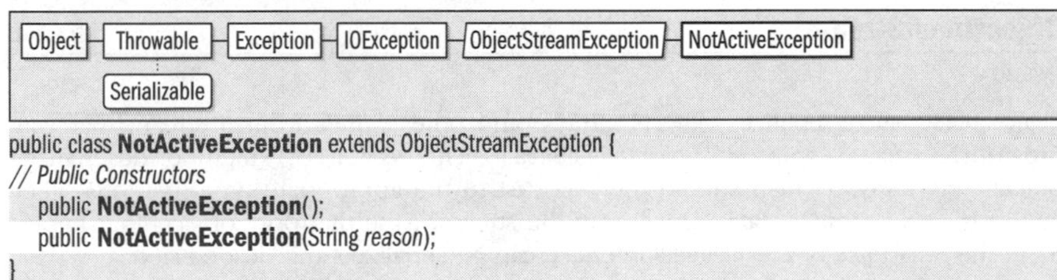


```
public class NotActiveException extends ObjectStreamException {
// Public Constructors
   public NotActiveException();
   public NotActiveException(String reason);
}
```

Thrown By: ObjectInputStream.registerValidation()

NotSerializableException **Java 1.1**

java.io *serializable checked*

This exception signals that an object cannot be serialized. It is thrown when serialization is attempted on an instance of a class that does not implement the Serializable interface. Note that it is also thrown when an attempt is made to serialize a Serializable object that refers to (or contains) an object that is not Serializable. A subclass of a class that is

Serializable can prevent itself from being serialized by throwing this exception from its writeObject() and/or readObject() methods.

Object ─ Throwable ─ Exception ─ IOException ─ ObjectStreamException ─ NotSerializableException
Serializable

```
public class NotSerializableException extends ObjectStreamException {
// Public Constructors
   public NotSerializableException();
   public NotSerializableException(String classname);
}
```

ObjectInput **Java 1.1**

java.io

This interface extends the DataInput interface and adds methods for deserializing objects and reading bytes and arrays of bytes.

DataInput ··· ObjectInput

```
public interface ObjectInput extends DataInput {
// Public Instance Methods
   public abstract int available() throws IOException;
   public abstract void close() throws IOException;
   public abstract int read() throws IOException;
   public abstract int read(byte[ ] b) throws IOException;
   public abstract int read(byte[ ] b, int off, int len) throws IOException;
   public abstract Object readObject() throws ClassNotFoundException, IOException;
   public abstract long skip(long n) throws IOException;
}
```

Implementations: ObjectInputStream

Passed To: java.awt.datatransfer.DataFlavor.readExternal(), Externalizable.readExternal(), java.rmi.server.ObjID.read()

Returned By: java.rmi.server.RemoteCall.getInputStream()

ObjectInputStream **Java 1.1**

java.io

ObjectInputStream deserializes objects, arrays, and other values from a stream that was previously created with an ObjectOutputStream. The readObject() method deserializes objects and arrays (which should then be cast to the appropriate type); various other methods read primitive data values from the stream. Note that only objects that implement the Serializable or Externalizable interface can be serialized and deserialized.

A class may implement its own private readObject(ObjectInputStream) method to customize the way it is deserialized. If you define such a method, there are several ObjectInputStream methods you can use to help you deserialize the object. defaultReadObject() is the easiest. It reads the content of the object just as an ObjectInputStream would normally do. If you wrote additional data before or after the default object contents, you should read that data before or after calling defaultReadObject(). When working with multiple versions or implementations of a class, you may have to deserialize a set of fields that do not match the fields of your class. In this case, give your class a static field named serialPersistentFields whose value is an array of ObjectStreamField objects that describe the fields to be deserialized. If you do this, your readObject() method can call readFields() to read the specified fields from the stream and return them in a ObjectInputStream.GetField object.

See ObjectStreamField and ObjectInputStream.GetField for more details. Finally, you can call registerValidation() from a custom readObject() method. This method registers an ObjectInputValidation object (typically the object being deserialized) to be notified when a complete tree of objects has been deserialized, and the original call to the readObject() method of the ObjectInputStream is about to return to its caller.

The remaining methods include miscellaneous stream-manipulation methods and several protected methods for use by subclasses that want to customize the deserialization behavior of ObjectInputStream.

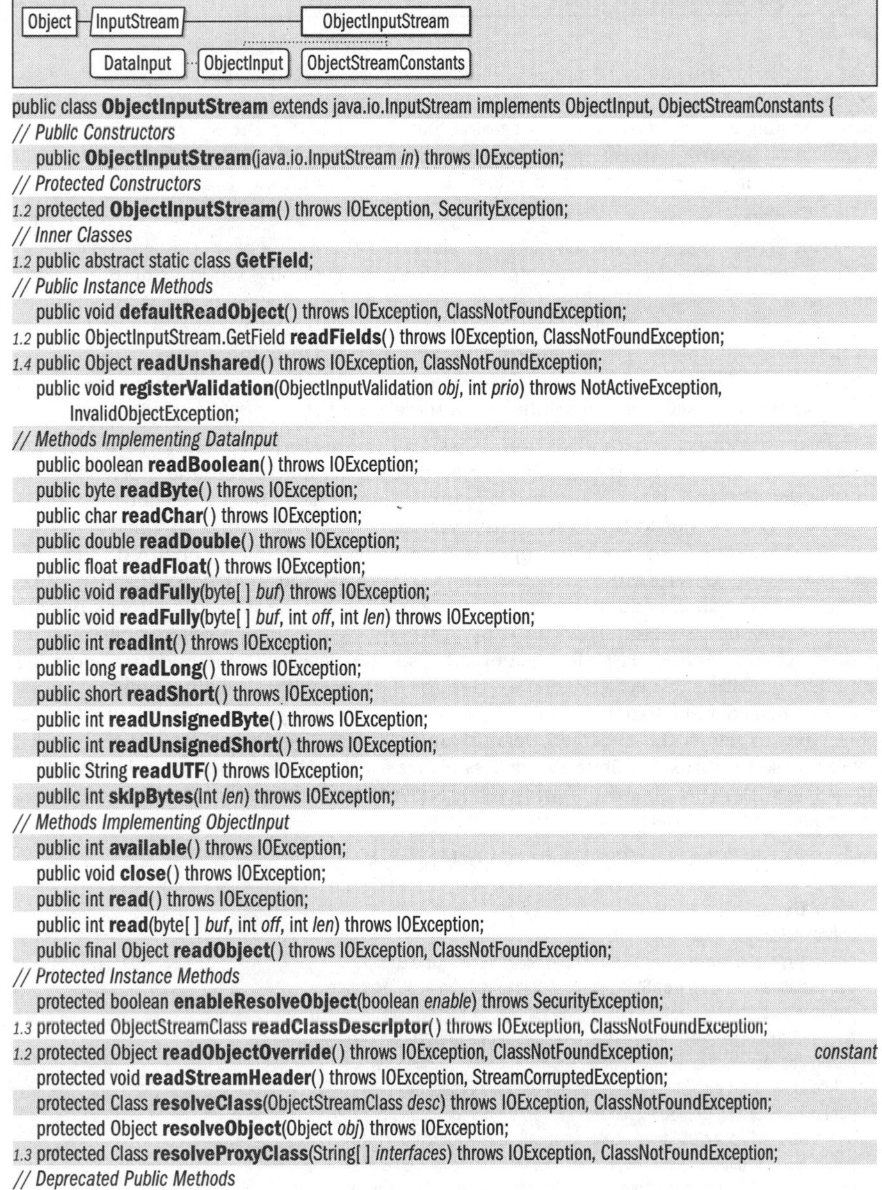


```
public class ObjectInputStream extends java.io.InputStream implements ObjectInput, ObjectStreamConstants {
// Public Constructors
    public ObjectInputStream(java.io.InputStream in) throws IOException;
// Protected Constructors
1.2 protected ObjectInputStream() throws IOException, SecurityException;
// Inner Classes
1.2 public abstract static class GetField;
// Public Instance Methods
    public void defaultReadObject() throws IOException, ClassNotFoundException;
1.2 public ObjectInputStream.GetField readFields() throws IOException, ClassNotFoundException;
1.4 public Object readUnshared() throws IOException, ClassNotFoundException;
    public void registerValidation(ObjectInputValidation obj, int prio) throws NotActiveException,
        InvalidObjectException;
// Methods Implementing DataInput
    public boolean readBoolean() throws IOException;
    public byte readByte() throws IOException;
    public char readChar() throws IOException;
    public double readDouble() throws IOException;
    public float readFloat() throws IOException;
    public void readFully(byte[ ] buf) throws IOException;
    public void readFully(byte[ ] buf, int off, int len) throws IOException;
    public int readInt() throws IOException;
    public long readLong() throws IOException;
    public short readShort() throws IOException;
    public int readUnsignedByte() throws IOException;
    public int readUnsignedShort() throws IOException;
    public String readUTF() throws IOException;
    public int skipBytes(int len) throws IOException;
// Methods Implementing ObjectInput
    public int available() throws IOException;
    public void close() throws IOException;
    public int read() throws IOException;
    public int read(byte[ ] buf, int off, int len) throws IOException;
    public final Object readObject() throws IOException, ClassNotFoundException;
// Protected Instance Methods
    protected boolean enableResolveObject(boolean enable) throws SecurityException;
1.3 protected ObjectStreamClass readClassDescriptor() throws IOException, ClassNotFoundException;
1.2 protected Object readObjectOverride() throws IOException, ClassNotFoundException;        constant
    protected void readStreamHeader() throws IOException, StreamCorruptedException;
    protected Class resolveClass(ObjectStreamClass desc) throws IOException, ClassNotFoundException;
    protected Object resolveObject(Object obj) throws IOException;
1.3 protected Class resolveProxyClass(String[ ] interfaces) throws IOException, ClassNotFoundException;
// Deprecated Public Methods
```

```
# public String readLine() throws IOException;                    Implements:DataInput
}
```

Passed To: java.beans.beancontext.BeanContextServicesSupport.bcsPreDeserializationHook(), java.beans.beancontext.BeanContextSupport.{bcsPreDeserializationHook(), deserialize(), readChildren()}, javax.rmi.CORBA.StubDelegate.readObject(), javax.swing.text.StyleContext.{readAttributes(), readAttributeSet()}

ObjectInputStream.GetField **Java 1.2**

java.io

This class holds the values of named fields read by an ObjectInputStream. It gives the programmer precise control over the deserialization process and is typically used when implementing an object with a set of fields that do not match the set of fields (and the serialization stream format) of the original implementation of the object. This class allows the implementation of a class to change without breaking serialization compatibility.

In order to use the GetField class, your class must implement a private readObject() method that is responsible for custom deserialization. Typically, when using the GetField class, you have also specified an array of ObjectStreamField objects as the value of a private static field named serialPersistentFields. This array specifies the names and types of all fields expected to be found when reading from a serialization stream. If there is no serialPersistentField field, the array of ObjectStreamField objects is created from the actual fields (excluding static and transient fields) of the class.

Within the readObject() method of your class, call the readFields() method of ObjectInputStream(). This method reads the values of all fields from the stream and stores them in an ObjectInputStream.GetField object that it returns. This GetField object is essentially a mapping from field names to field values, and you can extract the values of whatever fields you need in order to restore the proper state of the object being deserialized. The various get() methods return the values of named fields of specified types. Each method takes a default value as an argument, in case no value for the named field was present in the serialization stream. (This can happen when deserializing an object written by an earlier version of the class, for example.) Use the defaulted() method to determine whether the GetField object contains a value for the named field. If this method returns true, the named field had no value in the stream, so the get() method of the GetField object has to return the specified default value. The getObjectStreamClass() method of a GetField object returns the ObjectStreamClass object for the object being deserialized. This ObjectStreamClass can obtain the array of ObjectStreamField objects for the class. See also ObjectOutputStream.PutField.

```
public abstract static class ObjectInputStream.GetField {
// Public Constructors
   public GetField();
// Public Instance Methods
   public abstract boolean defaulted(String name) throws IOException;
   public abstract boolean get(String name, boolean val) throws IOException;
   public abstract byte get(String name, byte val) throws IOException;
   public abstract char get(String name, char val) throws IOException;
   public abstract short get(String name, short val) throws IOException;
   public abstract int get(String name, int val) throws IOException;
   public abstract long get(String name, long val) throws IOException;
   public abstract float get(String name, float val) throws IOException;
   public abstract double get(String name, double val) throws IOException;
   public abstract Object get(String name, Object val) throws IOException;
```

```
    public abstract ObjectStreamClass getObjectStreamClass();
}
```

Returned By: ObjectInputStream.readFields()

ObjectInputValidation **Java 1.1**

java.io

A class implements this interface and defines the validateObject() method in order to validate itself when it and all the objects it depends on have been completely deserialized from an ObjectInputStream. The validateObject() method is only invoked, however, if the object is passed to ObjectInputStream.registerValidation(); this must be done from the readObject() method of the object. Note that if an object is deserialized as part of a larger object graph, its validateObject() method is not invoked until the entire graph is read, and the original call to ObjectInputStream.readObject() is about to return. validateObject() should throw an InvalidObjectException if the object fails validation. This stops object serialization, and the original call to ObjectInputStream.readObject() terminates with the InvalidObjectException exception.

```
public interface ObjectInputValidation {
// Public Instance Methods
    public abstract void validateObject() throws InvalidObjectException;
}
```

Passed To: ObjectInputStream.registerValidation()

ObjectOutput **Java 1.1**

java.io

This interface extends the DataOutput interface and adds methods for serializing objects and writing bytes and arrays of bytes.

DataOutput ··· ObjectOutput

```
public interface ObjectOutput extends DataOutput {
// Public Instance Methods
    public abstract void close() throws IOException;
    public abstract void flush() throws IOException;
    public abstract void write(byte[ ] b) throws IOException;
    public abstract void write(int b) throws IOException;
    public abstract void write(byte[ ] b, int off, int len) throws IOException;
    public abstract void writeObject(Object obj) throws IOException;
}
```

Implementations: ObjectOutputStream

Passed To: java.awt.datatransfer.DataFlavor.writeExternal(), Externalizable.writeExternal(), ObjectOutputStream.PutField.write(), java.rmi.server.ObjID.write(), java.rmi.server.RemoteRef.getRefClass()

Returned By: java.rmi.server.RemoteCall.{getOutputStream(), getResultStream()}

ObjectOutputStream **Java 1.1**

java.io

The ObjectOutputStream serializes objects, arrays, and other values to a stream. The writeObject() method serializes an object or array, and various other methods write primitive data values to the stream. Note that only objects that implement the Serializable or Externalizable interface can be serialized.

A class that wants to customize the way instances are serialized should declare a private writeObject(ObjectOutputStream) method. This method is invoked when an object is being serialized and can use several additional methods of ObjectOutputStream. defaultWriteObject() performs the same serialization that would happen if no writeObject() method existed. An object can call this method to serialize itself and then use other methods of ObjectOutputStream to write additional data to the serialization stream. The class must define a matching readObject() method to read that additional data, of course. When working with multiple versions or implementations of a class, you may have to serialize a set of fields that do not precisely match the fields of your class. In this case, give your class a static field named serialPersistentFields whose value is an array of ObjectStreamField objects that describe the fields to be serialized. In your writeObject() method, call putFields() to obtain an ObjectOutputStream.PutField object. Store field names and values into this object, and then call writeFields() to write them out to the serialization stream. See ObjectStreamField and ObjectOutputStream.PutField for further details.

The remaining methods of ObjectOutputStream are miscellaneous stream-manipulation methods and protected methods for use by subclasses that want to customize its serialization behavior.

```
public class ObjectOutputStream extends java.io.OutputStream implements ObjectOutput, ObjectStreamConstants {
// Public Constructors
    public ObjectOutputStream(java.io.OutputStream out) throws IOException;
// Protected Constructors
1.2 protected ObjectOutputStream() throws IOException, SecurityException;
// Inner Classes
1.2 public abstract static class PutField;
// Public Instance Methods
    public void defaultWriteObject() throws IOException;
1.2 public ObjectOutputStream.PutField putFields() throws IOException;
    public void reset() throws IOException;
1.2 public void useProtocolVersion(int version) throws IOException;
1.2 public void writeFields() throws IOException;
1.4 public void writeUnshared(Object obj) throws IOException;
// Methods Implementing DataOutput
    public void writeBoolean(boolean val) throws IOException;
    public void writeByte(int val) throws IOException;
    public void writeBytes(String str) throws IOException;
    public void writeChar(int val) throws IOException;
    public void writeChars(String str) throws IOException;
    public void writeDouble(double val) throws IOException;
    public void writeFloat(float val) throws IOException;
    public void writeInt(int val) throws IOException;
    public void writeLong(long val) throws IOException;
    public void writeShort(int val) throws IOException;
    public void writeUTF(String str) throws IOException;
// Methods Implementing ObjectOutput
    public void close() throws IOException;
```

```
    public void flush() throws IOException;
    public void write(int val) throws IOException;
    public void write(byte[ ] buf) throws IOException;
    public void write(byte[ ] buf, int off, int len) throws IOException;
    public final void writeObject(Object obj) throws IOException;
// Protected Instance Methods
    protected void annotateClass(Class cl) throws IOException;                                  empty
1.3 protected void annotateProxyClass(Class cl) throws IOException;                             empty
    protected void drain() throws IOException;
    protected boolean enableReplaceObject(boolean enable) throws SecurityException;
    protected Object replaceObject(Object obj) throws IOException;
1.3 protected void writeClassDescriptor(ObjectStreamClass desc) throws IOException;
1.2 protected void writeObjectOverride(Object obj) throws IOException;                          empty
    protected void writeStreamHeader() throws IOException;
}
```

Passed To: java.awt.AWTEventMulticaster.{save(), saveInternal()}, java.beans.beancontext.BeanContextServicesSupport.bcsPreSerializationHook(), java.beans.beancontext.BeanContextSupport.{bcsPreSerializationHook(), serialize(), writeChildren()}, javax.rmi.CORBA.StubDelegate.writeObject(), javax.swing.text.StyleContext.{writeAttributes(), writeAttributeSet()}

ObjectOutputStream.PutField — Java 1.2

java.io

This class holds values of named fields and allows them to be written to an ObjectOutputStream during the process of object serialization. It gives the programmer precise control over the serialization process and is typically used when the set of fields defined by a class do not match the set of fields (and the serialization stream format) defined by the original implementation of the class. In other words, ObjectOutputStream.PutField allows the implementation of a class to change without breaking serialization compatibility.

To use the PutField class, you typically define a private static serialPersistentFields field that refers to an array of ObjectStreamField objects. This array defines the set of fields written to the ObjectOutputStream, and therefore defines the serialization format. If you do not declare a serialPersistentFields field, the set of fields is all fields of the class, excluding static and transient fields.

In addition to the serialPersistentFields field, your class must also define a private writeObject() method that is responsible for the custom serialization of your class. In this method, call the putFields() method of ObjectOutputStream to obtain an ObjectOutputStream.PutField object. Once you have this object, use its various put() methods to specify the names and values of the field to be written out. The set of named fields should match those specified by serialPersistentFields. You may specify the fields in any order; the PutField class is responsible for writing them out in the correct order. Once you have specified the values of all fields, call the write() method of your PutField object in order to write the field values out to the serialization stream.

To reverse this custom serialization process, see ObjectInputStream.GetField.

```
public abstract static class ObjectOutputStream.PutField {
// Public Constructors
    public PutField();
```

```
// Public Instance Methods
   public abstract void put(String name, long val);
   public abstract void put(String name, int val);
   public abstract void put(String name, float val);
   public abstract void put(String name, Object val);
   public abstract void put(String name, double val);
   public abstract void put(String name, byte val);
   public abstract void put(String name, boolean val);
   public abstract void put(String name, short val);
   public abstract void put(String name, char val);
// Deprecated Public Methods
#  public abstract void write(ObjectOutput out) throws IOException;
}
```

Returned By: ObjectOutputStream.putFields()

ObjectStreamClass **Java 1.1**

java.io ***serializable***

This class represents a class that is being serialized. An ObjectStreamClass object contains the name of a class, its unique version identifier, and the name and type of the fields that constitute the serialization format for the class. getSerialVersionUID() returns a unique version identifier for the class. It returns either the value of the private serialVersionUID field of the class or a computed value that is based upon the public API of the class. In Java 1.2 and later, getFields() returns an array of ObjectStreamField objects that represent the names and types of the fields of the class to be serialized. getField() returns a single ObjectStreamField object that represents a single named field. By default, these methods use all the fields of a class except those that are static or transient. However, this default set of fields can be overridden by declaring a private serialPersistentFields field in the class. The value of this field should be the desired array of ObjectStreamField objects.

ObjectStreamClass class does not have a constructor; you should use the static lookup() method to obtain an ObjectStreamClass object for a given Class object. The forClass() instance method performs the opposite operation; it returns the Class object that corresponds to a given ObjectStreamClass. Most applications never need to use this class.

Object — ObjectStreamClass ··· Serializable

```
public class ObjectStreamClass implements Serializable {
// No Constructor
// Public Constants
1.2 public static final ObjectStreamField[ ] NO_FIELDS;
// Public Class Methods
   public static ObjectStreamClass lookup(Class cl);
// Public Instance Methods
   public Class forClass();
1.2 public ObjectStreamField getField(String name);
1.2 public ObjectStreamField[ ] getFields();
   public String getName();
   public long getSerialVersionUID();
// Public Methods Overriding Object
   public String toString();
}
```

Passed To: ObjectInputStream.resolveClass(), ObjectOutputStream.writeClassDescriptor()

Returned By: ObjectInputStream.readClassDescriptor(), ObjectInputStream.GetField.getObjectStreamClass(), ObjectStreamClass.lookup()

ObjectStreamConstants **Java 1.2**

java.io

This interface defines various constants used by the Java object-serialization mechanism. Two important constants are PROTOCOL_VERSION_1 and PROTOCOL_VERSION_2, which specify the version of the serialization protocol to use. In Java 1.2, you can pass either of these values to the useProtocolVersion() method of an ObjectOutputStream. By default, Java 1.2 uses Version 2 of the protocol, and Java 1.1 uses Version 1 when serializing objects. Java 1.2 can deserialize objects written using either version of the protocol, as can Java 1.1.7 and later. If you want to serialize an object so that it can be read by versions of Java prior to Java 1.1.7, use PROTOCOL_VERSION_1.

The other constants defined by this interface are low-level values used by the serialization protocol. You do not need to use them unless you are reimplementing the serialization mechanism yourself.

```
public interface ObjectStreamConstants {
// Public Constants
    public static final int baseWireHandle;                               =8257536
    public static final int PROTOCOL_VERSION_1;                           =1
    public static final int PROTOCOL_VERSION_2;                           =2
    public static final byte SC_BLOCK_DATA;                               =8
    public static final byte SC_EXTERNALIZABLE;                           =4
    public static final byte SC_SERIALIZABLE;                             =2
    public static final byte SC_WRITE_METHOD;                             =1
    public static final short STREAM_MAGIC;                               =-21267
    public static final short STREAM_VERSION;                             =5
    public static final SerializablePermission SUBCLASS_IMPLEMENTATION_PERMISSION;
    public static final SerializablePermission SUBSTITUTION_PERMISSION;
    public static final byte TC_ARRAY;                                    =117
    public static final byte TC_BASE;                                     =112
    public static final byte TC_BLOCKDATA;                                =119
    public static final byte TC_BLOCKDATALONG;                            =122
    public static final byte TC_CLASS;                                    =118
    public static final byte TC_CLASSDESC;                                =114
    public static final byte TC_ENDBLOCKDATA;                             =120
    public static final byte TC_EXCEPTION;                                =123
1.3 public static final byte TC_LONGSTRING;                               =124
    public static final byte TC_MAX;                                      =125
    public static final byte TC_NULL;                                     =112
    public static final byte TC_OBJECT;                                   =115
1.3 public static final byte TC_PROXYCLASSDESC;                           =125
    public static final byte TC_REFERENCE;                                =113
    public static final byte TC_RESET;                                    =121
    public static final byte TC_STRING;                                   =116
}
```

Implementations: ObjectInputStream, ObjectOutputStream

ObjectStreamException Java 1.1

java.io *serializable checked*

This class is the superclass of a number of more specific exception types that may be raised in the process of serializing and deserializing objects with the ObjectOutputStream and ObjectInputStream classes.

Object — Throwable — Exception — IOException — ObjectStreamException
Throwable ⋯ Serializable

```
public abstract class ObjectStreamException extends IOException {
// Protected Constructors
   protected ObjectStreamException();
   protected ObjectStreamException(String classname);
}
```

Subclasses: InvalidClassException, InvalidObjectException, NotActiveException, NotSerializableException, OptionalDataException, StreamCorruptedException, WriteAbortedException

Thrown By: java.awt.AWTKeyStroke.readResolve(), java.awt.color.ICC_Profile.readResolve(), java.security.cert.Certificate.writeReplace(), java.security.cert.Certificate.CertificateRep.readResolve(), java.security.cert.CertPath.writeReplace(), java.security.cert.CertPath.CertPathRep.readResolve(), javax.print.attribute.EnumSyntax.readResolve()

ObjectStreamField Java 1.2

java.io *comparable*

This class represents a named field of a specified type (i.e., a specified Class). When a class serializes itself by writing a set of fields that are different from the fields it uses in its own implementation, it defines the set of fields to be written with an array of ObjectStreamField objects. This array should be the value of a private static field named serialPersistentFields. The methods of this class are used internally by the serialization mechanism and are not typically used elsewhere. See also ObjectOutputStream.PutField and ObjectInputStream.GetField.

Object — ObjectStreamField ⋯ Comparable

```
public class ObjectStreamField implements Comparable {
// Public Constructors
    public ObjectStreamField(String name, Class type);
1.4 public ObjectStreamField(String name, Class type, boolean unshared);
// Property Accessor Methods (by property name)
    public String getName();
    public int getOffset();
    public boolean isPrimitive();
    public Class getType();
    public char getTypeCode();
    public String getTypeString();
1.4 public boolean isUnshared();
// Methods Implementing Comparable
    public int compareTo(Object obj);
// Public Methods Overriding Object
    public String toString();
// Protected Instance Methods
    protected void setOffset(int offset);
}
```

Returned By: ObjectStreamClass.{getField(), getFields()}

Type Of: ObjectStreamClass.NO_FIELDS

OptionalDataException — Java 1.1

java.io — *serializable checked*

Thrown by the readObject() method of an ObjectInputStream when it encounters primitive type data where it expects object data. Despite the exception name, this data is not optional, and object deserialization is stopped.

Object — Throwable — Exception — IOException — ObjectStreamException — OptionalDataException
Throwable: Serializable

```
public class OptionalDataException extends ObjectStreamException {
// No Constructor
// Public Instance Fields
   public boolean eof;
   public int length;
}
```

OutputStream — Java 1.0

java.io

This abstract class is the superclass of all output streams. It defines the basic output methods all output stream classes provide. write() writes a single byte or an array (or subarray) of bytes. flush() forces any buffered output to be written. close() closes the stream and frees up any system resources associated with it. The stream may not be used once close() has been called. See also Writer.

```
public abstract class OutputStream {
// Public Constructors
   public OutputStream();
// Public Instance Methods
   public void close() throws IOException;                                    empty
   public void flush() throws IOException;                                    empty
   public abstract void write(int b) throws IOException;
   public void write(byte[ ] b) throws IOException;
   public void write(byte[ ] b, int off, int len) throws IOException;
}
```

Subclasses: ByteArrayOutputStream, FileOutputStream, FilterOutputStream, ObjectOutputStream, PipedOutputStream, org.omg.CORBA.portable.OutputStream

Passed To: Too many methods to list.

Returned By: Process.getOutputStream(), Runtime.getLocalizedOutputStream(), java.net.Socket.getOutputStream(), java.net.SocketImpl.getOutputStream(), java.net.URLConnection.getOutputStream(), java.nio.channels.Channels.newOutputStream(), java.rmi.server.LogStream.getOutputStream(), java.sql.Blob.setBinaryStream(), java.sql.Clob.setAsciiStream(), javax.print.StreamPrintService.getOutputStream(), javax.xml.transform.stream.StreamResult.getOutputStream()

Type Of: FilterOutputStream.out

OutputStreamWriter Java 1.1

java.io

This class is a character output stream that uses a byte output stream as the destination for its data. When characters are written to an OutputStreamWriter, it translates them into bytes according to a particular locale- and/or platform-specific character encoding and writes those bytes to the specified OutputStream. This is an important internationalization feature in Java 1.1 and later. OutputStreamWriter supports the usual Writer methods. It also has a getEncoding() method that returns the name of the encoding being used to convert characters to bytes.

When you create an OutputStreamWriter, specify the OutputStream to which it writes bytes and, optionally, the name of the character encoding that should be used to convert characters to bytes. If you do not specify an encoding name, the OutputStreamWriter uses the default encoding of the default locale, which is usually the correct thing to do. In Java 1.4 and later, this class uses the charset conversion facilities of the java.nio.charset package, and allows you to explicitly specify the Charset or CharsetEncoder to be used. Prior to Java 1.4, the class allows you to specify on the name of the desired charset encoding.

Object — Writer — OutputStreamWriter

```
public class OutputStreamWriter extends Writer {
// Public Constructors
   public OutputStreamWriter(java.io.OutputStream out);
   public OutputStreamWriter(java.io.OutputStream out, String charsetName)
       throws UnsupportedEncodingException;
1.4 public OutputStreamWriter(java.io.OutputStream out, java.nio.charset.CharsetEncoder enc);
1.4 public OutputStreamWriter(java.io.OutputStream out, java.nio.charset.Charset cs);
// Public Instance Methods
   public String getEncoding();
// Public Methods Overriding Writer
   public void close() throws IOException;
   public void flush() throws IOException;
   public void write(int c) throws IOException;
   public void write(char[ ] cbuf, int off, int len) throws IOException;
   public void write(String str, int off, int len) throws IOException;
}
```

Subclasses: FileWriter

PipedInputStream Java 1.0

java.io

This class is an InputStream that implements one half of a pipe and is useful for communication between threads. A PipedInputStream must be connected to a PipedOutputStream object, which may be specified when the PipedInputStream is created or with the connect() method. Data read from a PipedInputStream object is received from the PipedOutputStream to which it is connected. See InputStream for information on the low-level methods for reading data from a PipedInputStream. A FilterInputStream can provide a higher-level interface for reading data from a PipedInputStream.

Object — InputStream — PipedInputStream

```
public class PipedInputStream extends java.io.InputStream {
// Public Constructors
   public PipedInputStream();
```

```
    public PipedInputStream(PipedOutputStream src) throws IOException;
// Protected Constants
1.1 protected static final int PIPE_SIZE;                                    =1024
// Public Instance Methods
    public void connect(PipedOutputStream src) throws IOException;
// Public Methods Overriding InputStream
    public int available() throws IOException;                         synchronized
    public void close() throws IOException;
    public int read() throws IOException;                              synchronized
    public int read(byte[] b, int off, int len) throws IOException;    synchronized
// Protected Instance Methods
1.1 protected void receive(int b) throws IOException;                  synchronized
// Protected Instance Fields
1.1 protected byte[] buffer;
1.1 protected int in;
1.1 protected int out;
}
```

Passed To: PipedOutputStream.{connect(), PipedOutputStream()}

PipedOutputStream — Java 1.0

java.io

This class is an OutputStream that implements one half of a pipe and is useful for communication between threads. A PipedOutputStream must be connected to a PipedInput-Stream, which may be specified when the PipedOutputStream is created or with the connect() method. Data written to the PipedOutputStream is available for reading on the PipedInputStream. See OutputStream for information on the low-level methods for writing data to a PipedOutputStream. A FilterOutputStream can provide a higher-level interface for writing data to a PipedOutputStream.

Object — OutputStream — PipedOutputStream

```
public class PipedOutputStream extends java.io.OutputStream {
// Public Constructors
    public PipedOutputStream();
    public PipedOutputStream(PipedInputStream snk) throws IOException;
// Public Instance Methods
    public void connect(PipedInputStream snk) throws IOException;      synchronized
// Public Methods Overriding OutputStream
    public void close() throws IOException;
    public void flush() throws IOException;                            synchronized
    public void write(int b) throws IOException;
    public void write(byte[] b, int off, int len) throws IOException;
}
```

Passed To: PipedInputStream.{connect(), PipedInputStream()}

PipedReader — Java 1.1

java.io

PipedReader is a character input stream that reads characters from a PipedWriter character output stream to which it is connected. PipedReader implements one half of a pipe and is useful for communication between two threads of an application. A PipedReader can not be used until it is connected to a PipedWriter object, which may be passed to the PipedReader() constructor or to the connect() method. PipedReader inherits most of the methods of its superclass. See Reader for more information. PipedReader is the character-stream analog of PipedInputStream.

Object — Reader — PipedReader

```
public class PipedReader extends Reader {
// Public Constructors
    public PipedReader();
    public PipedReader(PipedWriter src) throws IOException;
// Public Instance Methods
    public void connect(PipedWriter src) throws IOException;
// Public Methods Overriding Reader
    public void close() throws IOException;
1.2 public int read() throws IOException;                                         synchronized
    public int read(char[ ] cbuf, int off, int len) throws IOException;           synchronized
1.2 public boolean ready() throws IOException;                                    synchronized
}
```

Passed To: PipedWriter.{connect(), PipedWriter()}

PipedWriter — Java 1.1

java.io

PipedWriter is a character output stream that writes characters to the PipedReader character input stream to which it is connected. PipedWriter implements one half of a pipe and is useful for communication between two threads of an application. A PipedWriter cannot be used until it is connected to a PipedReader object, which may be passed to the PipedWriter() constructor, or to the connect() method. PipedWriter inherits most of the methods of its superclass. See Writer for more information. PipedWriter is the character stream analog of PipedOutputStream.

Object — Writer — PipedWriter

```
public class PipedWriter extends Writer {
// Public Constructors
    public PipedWriter();
    public PipedWriter(PipedReader snk) throws IOException;
// Public Instance Methods
    public void connect(PipedReader snk) throws IOException;                      synchronized
// Public Methods Overriding Writer
    public void close() throws IOException;
    public void flush() throws IOException;                                       synchronized
1.2 public void write(int c) throws IOException;
    public void write(char[ ] cbuf, int off, int len) throws IOException;
}
```

Passed To: PipedReader.{connect(), PipedReader()}

PrintStream — Java 1.0

java.io

This class is a FilterOutputStream that implements a number of methods for displaying textual representations of Java primitive data types. The print() methods output standard textual representations of each data type. The println() methods do the same and follow the representations with newlines. Each method converts a Java primitive type to a String representation and outputs the resulting string. When an Object is passed to a print() or println(), it is converted to a String by calling its toString() method. PrintStream is the OutputStream type that makes it easiest to output text. As such, it is the most commonly used of the output streams. The System.out variable is a PrintStream.

Note that in Java 1.0 this class does not handle Unicode characters correctly; it discards the top 8 bits of all 16-bit characters and thus works only with Latin-1 (ISO8859-1) characters. Although this problem has been fixed as of Java 1.1, PrintStream has been superseded by PrintWriter as of Java 1.1. The constructors of this class have been deprecated, but the class itself has not, because it is still used by the System.out and System.err standard output streams.

PrintStream, and its PrintWriter replacement, output textual representations of Java data types. Use DataOutputStream to output binary representations of data.

Object — OutputStream — FilterOutputStream — PrintStream

```
public class PrintStream extends FilterOutputStream {
// Public Constructors
   public PrintStream(java.io.OutputStream out);
   public PrintStream(java.io.OutputStream out, boolean autoFlush);
1.4 public PrintStream(java.io.OutputStream out, boolean autoFlush, String encoding)
       throws UnsupportedEncodingException;
// Public Instance Methods
   public boolean checkError();
   public void print(float f);
   public void print(long l);
   public void print(int i);
   public void print(double d);
   public void print(char[ ] s);
   public void print(String s);
   public void print(Object obj);
   public void print(char c);
   public void print(boolean b);
   public void println();
   public void println(float x);
   public void println(long x);
   public void println(int x);
   public void println(String x);
   public void println(Object x);
   public void println(double x);
   public void println(char[ ] x);
   public void println(char x);
   public void println(boolean x);
// Public Methods Overriding FilterOutputStream
   public void close();
   public void flush();
   public void write(int b);
   public void write(byte[ ] buf, int off, int len);
// Protected Instance Methods
1.1 protected void setError();
}
```

Subclasses: java.rmi.server.LogStream

Passed To: Too many methods to list.

Returned By: java.rmi.server.LogStream.getDefaultStream(), java.rmi.server.RemoteServer.getLog(), java.sql.DriverManager.getLogStream(), javax.swing.DebugGraphics.logStream()

Type Of: System.{err, out}

PrintWriter **Java 1.1**

java.io

This class is a character output stream that implements a number of print() and println() methods that output textual representations of primitive values and objects. When you create a PrintWriter object, you specify a character or byte output stream that it should write its characters to and, optionally, whether the PrintWriter stream should be automatically flushed whenever println() is called. If you specify a byte output stream as the destination, the PrintWriter() constructor automatically creates the necessary OutputStreamWriter object to convert characters to bytes using the default encoding.

PrintWriter implements the normal write(), flush(), and close() methods all Writer subclasses define. It is more common to use the higher-level print() and println() methods, each of which converts its argument to a string before outputting it. println() can also terminate the line (and optionally flush the buffer) after printing its argument.

The methods of PrintWriter never throw exceptions. Instead, when errors occur, they set an internal flag you can check by calling checkError(). checkError() first flushes the internal stream and then returns true if any exception has occurred while writing values to that stream. Once an error has occurred on a PrintWriter object, all subsequent calls to checkError() return true; there is no way to reset the error flag.

PrintWriter is the character stream analog to PrintStream, which it supersedes. You can usually trivially replace any PrintStream objects in a program with PrintWriter objects. This is particularly important for internationalized programs. The only valid remaining use for the PrintStream class is for the System.out and System.err standard output streams. See PrintStream for details.

Object — Writer — PrintWriter

```
public class PrintWriter extends Writer {
// Public Constructors
    public PrintWriter(java.io.OutputStream out);
    public PrintWriter(Writer out);
    public PrintWriter(java.io.OutputStream out, boolean autoFlush);
    public PrintWriter(Writer out, boolean autoFlush);
// Public Instance Methods
    public boolean checkError();
    public void print(int i);
    public void print(long l);
    public void print(char c);
    public void print(boolean b);
    public void print(float f);
    public void print(double d);
    public void print(char[ ] s);
    public void print(Object obj);
    public void print(String s);
    public void println();
    public void println(int x);
    public void println(long x);
    public void println(boolean x);
    public void println(char x);
    public void println(String x);
    public void println(Object x);
    public void println(char[ ] x);
    public void println(float x);
    public void println(double x);
```

```
// Public Methods Overriding Writer
   public void close();
   public void flush();
   public void write(char[ ] buf);
   public void write(String s);
   public void write(int c);
   public void write(String s, int off, int len);
   public void write(char[ ] buf, int off, int len);
// Protected Instance Methods
   protected void setError();
// Protected Instance Fields
1.2 protected Writer out;
}
```

Passed To: java.awt.Component.list(), java.awt.Container.list(), Throwable.printStackTrace(), java.security.cert.CertPathBuilderException.printStackTrace(), java.security.cert.CertPathValidatorException.printStackTrace(), java.security.cert.CertStoreException.printStackTrace(), java.sql.DriverManager.setLogWriter(), java.util.Properties.list(), javax.naming.NamingException.printStackTrace(), javax.sql.ConnectionPoolDataSource.setLogWriter(), javax.sql.DataSource.setLogWriter(), javax.sql.XADataSource.setLogWriter(), javax.xml.transform.TransformerException.printStackTrace()

Returned By: java.sql.DriverManager.getLogWriter(), javax.sql.ConnectionPoolDataSource.getLogWriter(), javax.sql.DataSource.getLogWriter(), javax.sql.XADataSource.getLogWriter()

PushbackInputStream — Java 1.0

java.io

This class is a FilterInputStream that implements a one-byte pushback buffer or, as of Java 1.1, a pushback buffer of a specified length. The unread() methods push bytes back into the stream; these bytes are the first ones read by the next call to a read() method. This class is sometimes useful when writing parsers. See also PushbackReader.

Object — InputStream — FilterInputStream — PushbackInputStream

```
public class PushbackInputStream extends FilterInputStream {
// Public Constructors
   public PushbackInputStream(java.io.InputStream in);
1.1 public PushbackInputStream(java.io.InputStream in, int size);
// Public Instance Methods
   public void unread(int b) throws IOException;
1.1 public void unread(byte[ ] b) throws IOException;
1.1 public void unread(byte[ ] b, int off, int len) throws IOException;
// Public Methods Overriding FilterInputStream
   public int available() throws IOException;
1.2 public void close() throws IOException;                    synchronized
   public boolean markSupported();                             constant
   public int read() throws IOException;
   public int read(byte[ ] b, int off, int len) throws IOException;
1.2 public long skip(long n) throws IOException;
// Protected Instance Fields
1.1 protected byte[ ] buf;
1.1 protected int pos;
}
```

PushbackReader **Java 1.1**

java.io

This class is a character input stream that uses another input stream as its input source and adds the ability to push characters back onto the stream. This feature is often useful when writing parsers. When you create a PushbackReader stream, you specify the stream to be read from and, optionally, the size of the pushback buffer (i.e., the number of characters that may be pushed back onto the stream or unread). If you do not specify a size for this buffer, the default size is one character. PushbackReader inherits or overrides all standard Reader methods and adds three unread() methods that push a single character, an array of characters, or a portion of an array of characters back onto the stream. This class is the character stream analog of PushbackInputStream.

Object → Reader → FilterReader → PushbackReader

```
public class PushbackReader extends FilterReader {
// Public Constructors
    public PushbackReader(Reader in);
    public PushbackReader(Reader in, int size);
// Public Instance Methods
    public void unread(int c) throws IOException;
    public void unread(char[ ] cbuf) throws IOException;
    public void unread(char[ ] cbuf, int off, int len) throws IOException;
// Public Methods Overriding FilterReader
    public void close() throws IOException;
1.2 public void mark(int readAheadLimit) throws IOException;
    public boolean markSupported();                                    constant
    public int read() throws IOException;
    public int read(char[ ] cbuf, int off, int len) throws IOException;
    public boolean ready() throws IOException;
1.2 public void reset() throws IOException;
}
```

RandomAccessFile **Java 1.0**

java.io

This class allows you to read and write arbitrary bytes, text, and primitive Java data types from or to any specified location in a file. Because this class provides random, rather than sequential, access to files, it is neither a subclass of InputStream nor of OutputStream, but provides an entirely independent method for reading and writing data from or to files. RandomAccessFile implements the same interfaces as DataInputStream and DataOutputStream, and thus defines the same methods for reading and writing data as those classes do.

The seek() method provides random access to the file; it is used to select the position in the file where data should be read or written. The various read and write methods update this file position so that a sequence of read or write operations can be performed on a contiguous portion of the file without having to call the seek() method before each read or write.

The *mode* argument to the constructor methods should be "r" for a file that will be read-only or "rw" for a file that will be written (and perhaps read as well). In Java 1.4 and later, two other values for the *mode* argument are allowed as well. A mode of "rwd" opens the file for reading and writing and requires that, if the file resides on a local filesystem, every update to the file content be written synchronously to the underlying file. The "rws" mode is similar but requires synchronous updates to both the file's content and its "metadata" (which includes things such as file access times). Using "rws" mode may require that the file metadata be modified every time the file is read.

In Java 1.4 and later, use the getChannel() method to obtain a FileChannel object that you can use to access the file using the New I/O API of java.nio and its subpackages. If the RandomAccessFile was opened with a mode of "r", then the FileChannel will allow only reading. Otherwise, it will allow both reading and writing.

Object ─ RandomAccessFile
DataInput   DataOutput

```
public class RandomAccessFile implements DataInput, DataOutput {
// Public Constructors
    public RandomAccessFile(File file, String mode) throws FileNotFoundException;
    public RandomAccessFile(String name, String mode) throws FileNotFoundException;
// Public Instance Methods
    public void close() throws IOException;                                      native
1.4 public final java.nio.channels.FileChannel getChannel();
    public final FileDescriptor getFD() throws IOException;
    public long getFilePointer() throws IOException;                             native
    public long length() throws IOException;                                     native
    public int read() throws IOException;                                        native
    public int read(byte[ ] b) throws IOException;
    public int read(byte[ ] b, int off, int len) throws IOException;
    public void seek(long pos) throws IOException;                               native
1.2 public void setLength(long newLength) throws IOException;                    native
// Methods Implementing DataInput
    public final boolean readBoolean() throws IOException;
    public final byte readByte() throws IOException;
    public final char readChar() throws IOException;
    public final double readDouble() throws IOException;
    public final float readFloat() throws IOException;
    public final void readFully(byte[ ] b) throws IOException;
    public final void readFully(byte[ ] b, int off, int len) throws IOException;
    public final int readInt() throws IOException;
    public final String readLine() throws IOException;
    public final long readLong() throws IOException;
    public final short readShort() throws IOException;
    public final int readUnsignedByte() throws IOException;
    public final int readUnsignedShort() throws IOException;
    public final String readUTF() throws IOException;
    public int skipBytes(int n) throws IOException;
// Methods Implementing DataOutput
    public void write(int b) throws IOException;                                 native
    public void write(byte[ ] b) throws IOException;
    public void write(byte[ ] b, int off, int len) throws IOException;
    public final void writeBoolean(boolean v) throws IOException;
    public final void writeByte(int v) throws IOException;
    public final void writeBytes(String s) throws IOException;
    public final void writeChar(int v) throws IOException;
    public final void writeChars(String s) throws IOException;
    public final void writeDouble(double v) throws IOException;
    public final void writeFloat(float v) throws IOException;
    public final void writeInt(int v) throws IOException;
    public final void writeLong(long v) throws IOException;
    public final void writeShort(int v) throws IOException;
```

```
    public final void writeUTF(String str) throws IOException;
}
```

Passed To: javax.imageio.stream.FileImageInputStream.FileImageInputStream(), javax.imageio.stream.FileImageOutputStream.FileImageOutputStream()

Reader **Java 1.1**

java.io

This abstract class is the superclass of all character input streams. It is an analog to InputStream, which is the superclass of all byte input streams. Reader defines the basic methods that all character output streams provide. read() returns a single character or an array (or subarray) of characters, blocking if necessary; it returns –1 if the end of the stream has been reached. ready() returns true if there are characters available for reading. If ready() returns true, the next call to read() is guaranteed not to block. close() closes the character input stream. skip() skips a specified number of characters in the input stream. If markSupported() returns true, mark() marks a position in the stream and, if necessary, creates a look-ahead buffer of the specified size. Future calls to reset() restore the stream to the marked position if they occur within the specified look-ahead limit. Note that not all stream types support this mark-and-reset functionality. To create a subclass of Reader, you need only implement the three-argument version of read() and the close() method. Most subclasses implement additional methods, however.

```
public abstract class Reader {
// Protected Constructors
    protected Reader();
    protected Reader(Object lock);
// Public Instance Methods
    public abstract void close() throws IOException;
    public void mark(int readAheadLimit) throws IOException;
    public boolean markSupported();                                    constant
    public int read() throws IOException;
    public int read(char[ ] cbuf) throws IOException;
    public abstract int read(char[ ] cbuf, int off, int len) throws IOException;
    public boolean ready() throws IOException;                         constant
    public void reset() throws IOException;
    public long skip(long n) throws IOException;
// Protected Instance Fields
    protected Object lock;
}
```

Subclasses: BufferedReader, CharArrayReader, FilterReader, InputStreamReader, PipedReader, StringReader

Passed To: Too many methods to list.

Returned By: java.awt.datatransfer.DataFlavor.getReaderForText(), java.nio.channels.Channels.newReader(), java.sql.Clob.getCharacterStream(), java.sql.ResultSet.getCharacterStream(), java.sql.SQLInput.readCharacterStream(), javax.print.Doc.getReaderForText(), javax.print.SimpleDoc.getReaderForText(), javax.xml.transform.stream.StreamSource.getReader(), org.xml.sax.InputSource.getCharacterStream()

Type Of: FilterReader.in

SequenceInputStream **Java 1.0**

java.io

This class provides a way of seamlessly concatenating the data from two or more input streams. It provides an InputStream interface to a sequence of InputStream objects. Data is read from the streams in the order in which the streams are specified. When the end of one stream is reached, data is automatically read from the next stream. This class might be useful, for example, when implementing an include file facility for a parser of some sort.

Object — InputStream — SequenceInputStream


```
public class SequenceInputStream extends java.io.InputStream {
// Public Constructors
   public SequenceInputStream(java.util.Enumeration e);
   public SequenceInputStream(java.io.InputStream s1, java.io.InputStream s2);
// Public Methods Overriding InputStream
1.1 public int available() throws IOException;
   public void close() throws IOException;
   public int read() throws IOException;
   public int read(byte[ ] b, int off, int len) throws IOException;
}
```

Serializable **Java 1.1**

java.io *serializable*

The Serializable interface defines no methods or constants. A class should implement this interface simply to indicate that it allows itself to be serialized and deserialized with ObjectOutputStream.writeObject() and ObjectInputStream.readObject().

Objects that need special handling during serialization or deserialization may implement one or both of the following methods. Note, however, that these methods are not part of the Serializable interface:

```
private void writeObject(java.io.ObjectOutputStream out) throws IOException;
private void readObject(java.io.ObjectInputStream in) throws IOException, ClassNotFoundException;
```

Typically, the writeObject() method performs any necessary cleanup or preparation for serialization, invokes the defaultWriteObject() method of the ObjectOutputStream to serialize the nontransient fields of the class, and optionally writes any additional data that is required. Similarly, the readObject() method typically invokes the defaultReadObject() method of the ObjectInputStream, reads any additional data written by the corresponding writeObject() method, and performs any extra initialization required by the object. The readObject() method may also register an ObjectInputValidation object to validate the object once it is completely deserialized.

```
public interface Serializable {
}
```

Implementations: Too many classes to list.

Passed To: Too many methods to list.

Returned By: Too many methods to list.

Type Of: org.omg.CORBA.ValueBaseHolder.value

SerializablePermission — Java 1.2

java.io — *serializable permission*

This class is a java.security.Permission that governs the use of certain sensitive features of serialization. SerializablePermission objects have a name, or target, but do not have an action list. The name "enableSubclassImplementation" represents permission to serialize and deserialize objects using subclasses of ObjectOutputStream and ObjectInputStream. This capability is protected by a permission because malicious code can define object stream subclasses that incorrectly serialize and deserialize objects.

The only other name supported by SerializablePermission is "enableSubstitution", which represents permission for one object to be substituted for another during serialization or deserialization. The ObjectOutputStream.enableReplaceObject() and ObjectInput-Stream.enableResolveObject() methods require a permission of this type.

Applications never need to use this class. Programmers writing system-level code may use it, and system administrators configuring security policies should be familiar with it.

Object — Permission — BasicPermission — SerializablePermission
Guard, Serializable, Serializable

```
public final class SerializablePermission extends java.security.BasicPermission {
// Public Constructors
   public SerializablePermission(String name);
   public SerializablePermission(String name, String actions);
}
```

Type Of: ObjectStreamConstants.{SUBCLASS_IMPLEMENTATION_PERMISSION, SUBSTITUTION_PERMISSION}

StreamCorruptedException — Java 1.1

java.io — *serializable checked*

This exception signals that the data stream being read by an ObjectInputStream has been corrupted and does not contain valid serialized object data.

Object — Throwable — Exception — IOException — ObjectStreamException — StreamCorruptedException
Serializable

```
public class StreamCorruptedException extends ObjectStreamException {
// Public Constructors
   public StreamCorruptedException();
   public StreamCorruptedException(String reason);
}
```

Thrown By: ObjectInputStream.readStreamHeader(), java.rmi.server.RemoteCall.getResultStream()

StreamTokenizer — Java 1.0

java.io

This class performs lexical analysis of a specified input stream and breaks the input into tokens. It can be extremely useful when writing simple parsers. nextToken() returns the next token in the stream; this is either one of the constants defined by the class (which represent end-of-file, end-of-line, a parsed floating-point number, and a parsed word) or a character value. pushBack() pushes the token back onto the stream, so that it is returned by the next call to nextToken(). The public variables sval and nval contain the string and numeric values (if applicable) of the most recently read token. They are applicable when the returned token is TT_WORD or TT_NUMBER. lineno() returns the current line number.

The remaining methods allow you to specify how tokens are recognized. wordChars() specifies a range of characters that should be treated as parts of words. whitespaceChars() specifies a range of characters that serve to delimit tokens. ordinaryChars() and ordinaryChar() specify characters that are never part of tokens and should be returned as-is. resetSyntax() makes all characters ordinary. eolIsSignificant() specifies whether end-of-line is significant. If so, the TT_EOL constant is returned for end-of-lines; otherwise, they are treated as whitespace. commentChar() specifies a character that begins a comment that lasts until the end of the line. No characters in the comment are returned. slashStarComments() and slashSlashComments() specify whether the StreamTokenizer should recognize C- and C++-style comments. If so, no part of the comment is returned as a token. quoteChar() specifies a character used to delimit strings. When a string token is parsed, the quote character is returned as the token value, and the body of the string is stored in the sval variable. lowerCaseMode() specifies whether TT_WORD tokens should be converted to all lowercase characters before being stored in sval. parseNumbers() specifies that the StreamTokenizer should recognize and return double-precision, floating-point number tokens.


```
public class StreamTokenizer {
// Public Constructors
#   public StreamTokenizer(java.io.InputStream is);
1.1 public StreamTokenizer(Reader r);
// Public Constants
    public static final int TT_EOF;                                   =-1
    public static final int TT_EOL;                                   =10
    public static final int TT_NUMBER;                                =-2
    public static final int TT_WORD;                                  =-3
// Public Instance Methods
    public void commentChar(int ch);
    public void eolIsSignificant(boolean flag);
    public int lineno();
    public void lowerCaseMode(boolean fl);
    public int nextToken() throws IOException;
    public void ordinaryChar(int ch);
    public void ordinaryChars(int low, int hi);
    public void parseNumbers();
    public void pushBack();
    public void quoteChar(int ch);
    public void resetSyntax();
    public void slashSlashComments(boolean flag);
    public void slashStarComments(boolean flag);
    public void whitespaceChars(int low, int hi);
    public void wordChars(int low, int hi);
// Public Methods Overriding Object
    public String toString();
// Public Instance Fields
    public double nval;
    public String sval;
    public int ttype;
}
```

StringBufferInputStream

Java 1.0; Deprecated in Java 1.1

java.io

This class is a subclass of InputStream in which input bytes come from the characters of a specified String object. This class does not correctly convert the characters of a StringBuffer into bytes and is deprecated as of Java 1.1. Use StringReader instead to convert characters into bytes or use ByteArrayInputStream to read bytes from an array of bytes.

Object — InputStream — StringBufferInputStream

```
public class StringBufferInputStream extends java.io.InputStream {
// Public Constructors
   public StringBufferInputStream(String s);
// Public Methods Overriding InputStream
   public int available();                                    synchronized
   public int read();                                         synchronized
   public int read(byte[ ] b, int off, int len);              synchronized
   public void reset();                                       synchronized
   public long skip(long n);                                  synchronized
// Protected Instance Fields
   protected String buffer;
   protected int count;
   protected int pos;
}
```

StringReader

Java 1.1

java.io

This class is a character input stream that uses a String object as the source of the characters it returns. When you create a StringReader, you must specify the String to read from. StringReader defines the normal Reader methods and supports mark() and reset(). If reset() is called before mark() has been called, the stream is reset to the beginning of the specified string. StringReader is a character stream analog to StringBufferInputStream, which is deprecated as of Java 1.1. StringReader is also similar to CharArrayReader.

Object — Reader — StringReader

```
public class StringReader extends Reader {
// Public Constructors
   public StringReader(String s);
// Public Methods Overriding Reader
   public void close();
   public void mark(int readAheadLimit) throws IOException;
   public boolean markSupported();                            constant
   public int read() throws IOException;
   public int read(char[ ] cbuf, int off, int len) throws IOException;
   public boolean ready() throws IOException;
   public void reset() throws IOException;
   public long skip(long ns) throws IOException;
}
```

StringWriter

Java 1.1

java.io

This class is a character output stream that uses an internal StringBuffer object as the destination of the characters written to the stream. When you create a StringWriter, you may optionally specify an initial size for the StringBuffer, but you do not specify the StringBuffer itself; it is managed internally by the StringWriter and grows as necessary to accommodate the characters written to it. StringWriter defines the standard write(), flush(), and close() methods all Writer subclasses define, as well as two methods to obtain the characters that have been written to the streaM's internal buffer. toString() returns the contents of the internal buffer as a String, and getBuffer() returns the buffer itself. Note that getBuffer() returns a reference to the actual internal buffer, not a copy of it, so any changes you make to the buffer are reflected in subsequent calls to toString(). StringWriter is quite similar to CharArrayWriter, but does not have a byte-stream analog.

Object — Writer — StringWriter

```
public class StringWriter extends Writer {
// Public Constructors
   public StringWriter();
   public StringWriter(int initialSize);
// Public Instance Methods
   public StringBuffer getBuffer();
// Public Methods Overriding Writer
   public void close() throws IOException;                    empty
   public void flush();                                       empty
   public void write(int c);
   public void write(String str);
   public void write(String str, int off, int len);
   public void write(char[ ] cbuf, int off, int len);
// Public Methods Overriding Object
   public String toString();
}
```

SyncFailedException — Java 1.1

java.io — *serializable checked*

This exception signals that a call to FileDescriptor.sync() did not complete successfully.

Object — Throwable — Exception — IOException — SyncFailedException
Throwable ⋮ Serializable

```
public class SyncFailedException extends IOException {
// Public Constructors
   public SyncFailedException(String desc);
}
```

Thrown By: FileDescriptor.sync()

UnsupportedEncodingException — Java 1.1

java.io — *serializable checked*

This exception signals that a requested character encoding is not supported by the current Java Virtual Machine.

Object — Throwable — Exception — IOException — UnsupportedEncodingException
Throwable ⋮ Serializable

```
public class UnsupportedEncodingException extends IOException {
// Public Constructors
   public UnsupportedEncodingException();
```

```
    public UnsupportedEncodingException(String s);
}
```

Thrown By: ByteArrayOutputStream.toString(), InputStreamReader.InputStreamReader(), OutputStreamWriter.OutputStreamWriter(), PrintStream.PrintStream(), String.{getBytes(), String()}, java.net.URLDecoder.decode(), java.net.URLEncoder.encode(), java.util.logging.Handler.setEncoding(), java.util.logging.StreamHandler.setEncoding()

UTFDataFormatException — Java 1.0

java.io — *serializable checked*

This exception is an IOException that signals that a malformed UTF-8 string has been encountered by a class that implements the DataInput interface. UTF-8 is an ASCII-compatible transformation format for Unicode characters that is often used to store and transmit Unicode text.

Object — Throwable — Exception — IOException — UTFDataFormatException
(Throwable ⋯ Serializable)

```
public class UTFDataFormatException extends IOException {
// Public Constructors
    public UTFDataFormatException();
    public UTFDataFormatException(String s);
}
```

WriteAbortedException — Java 1.1

java.io — *serializable checked*

This exception is thrown when reading a stream of data that is incomplete because an exception was thrown while it was being written. The detail field may contain the exception that terminated the output stream. In Java 1.4 and later, this exception can also be obtained with the standard Throwable getCause() method. The getMessage() method has been overridden to include the message of this detail exception, if any.

Object — Throwable — Exception — IOException — ObjectStreamException — WriteAbortedException
(Throwable ⋯ Serializable)

```
public class WriteAbortedException extends ObjectStreamException {
// Public Constructors
    public WriteAbortedException(String s, Exception ex);
// Public Methods Overriding Throwable
1.4 public Throwable getCause();
    public String getMessage();
// Public Instance Fields
    public Exception detail;
}
```

Writer — Java 1.1

java.io

This abstract class is the superclass of all character output streams. It is an analog to OutputStream, which is the superclass of all byte output streams. Writer defines the basic write(), flush(), and close() methods all character output streams provide. The five versions of the write() method write a single character, a character array or subarray, or a string or substring to the destination of the stream. The most general version of this method—the one that writes a specified portion of a character array—is abstract and must be implemented by all subclasses. By default, the other write() methods are implemented in terms of this abstract one. The flush() method is another abstract method all subclasses must implement. It should force any output buffered by the stream to be written to its destination. If that destination is itself a character or byte output stream, it should invoke the flush() method of the destination stream as well. The close() method is also abstract. A subclass must implement this method so that it flushes and then closes the current stream and also closes whatever destination stream it is connected to. Once the stream is closed, any future calls to write() or flush() should throw an IOException.


```
public abstract class Writer {
// Protected Constructors
   protected Writer();
   protected Writer(Object lock);
// Public Instance Methods
   public abstract void close() throws IOException;
   public abstract void flush() throws IOException;
   public void write(String str) throws IOException;
   public void write(char[ ] cbuf) throws IOException;
   public void write(int c) throws IOException;
   public void write(String str, int off, int len) throws IOException;
   public abstract void write(char[ ] cbuf, int off, int len) throws IOException;
// Protected Instance Fields
   protected Object lock;
}
```

Subclasses: BufferedWriter, CharArrayWriter, FilterWriter, OutputStreamWriter, PipedWriter, PrintWriter, StringWriter

Passed To: Too many methods to list.

Returned By: java.nio.channels.Channels.newWriter(), java.sql.Clob.setCharacterStream(), javax.swing.text.AbstractWriter.getWriter(), javax.xml.transform.stream.StreamResult.getWriter()

Type Of: FilterWriter.out, PrintWriter.out

CHAPTER 11

java.lang, java.lang.ref, and java.lang.reflect

This chapter covers the java.lang package, which defines the core classes and interfaces that are indispensable to the Java platform and the Java programming language. It also covers two specialized subpackages. java.lang.ref defines "reference" classes that refer to objects without preventing the garbage collector from reclaiming those objects. java.lang.reflect allows Java to examine the members of arbitrary classes, invoking methods and querying and setting the value of fields.

Package java.lang — Java 1.0

The java.lang package contains the classes that are most central to the Java language. Object is the ultimate superclass of all Java classes and is therefore at the top of all class hierarchies. Class is a class that describes a Java class. There is one Class object for each class that is loaded into Java.

Boolean, Character, Byte, Short, Integer, Long, Float, and Double are immutable class wrappers around each of the primitive Java data types. These classes are useful when you need to manipulate primitive types as objects. They also contain useful conversion and utility methods. Void is a related class that defines a representation for the void method return type, but that defines no methods. String and StringBuffer are objects that represent strings. String is an immutable type, while StringBuffer can have its string changed in place. In Java 1.4, both String and StringBuffer implement the CharSequence interface which allows instances of both classes to be manipulated through a simple shared API. String and the various primitive type wrapper classes all implement the Comparable interface which defines an ordering for instances of those classes and enables sorting and searching algorithms (such as those of java.util.Arrays and java.util.Collections, for example). Cloneable is an important marker interface that specifies that the Object.clone() method is allowed to make copies of an object.

The Math class (and, in Java 1.3, the StrictMath class) defines static methods for various floating-point mathematical functions.

The Thread class provides support for multiple threads of control running within the same Java interpreter. The Runnable interface is implemented by objects that have a run() method that can serve as the body of a thread.

System provides low-level system methods. Runtime provides similar low-level methods, including an exec() method that, along with the Process class, defines a platform-dependent API for running external processes.

Throwable is the root class of the exception and error hierarchy. Throwable objects are used with the Java throw and catch statements. java.lang defines quite a few subclasses of Throwable. Exception and Error are the superclasses of all exceptions and errors. RuntimeException defines a special class or "unchecked exceptions" that do not need to be declared in a method's throws clause. The Throwable class was overhauled in Java 1.4, adding the ability to "chain" exceptions, and the ability to obtain the stack trace of an exception as an array of StackTraceElement objects.

Interfaces:

public interface **CharSequence**;
public interface **Cloneable**;
public interface **Comparable**;
public interface **Runnable**;

Classes:

public class **Object**;
  └ public final class **Boolean** implements Serializable;
  └ public final class **Character** implements Comparable, Serializable;
  └ public static class **Character.Subset**;
    └ public static final class **Character.UnicodeBlock** extends Character.Subset;
  └ public final class **Class** implements Serializable;
  └ public abstract class **ClassLoader**;
  └ public final class **Compiler**;
  └ public final class **Math**;
  └ public abstract class **Number** implements Serializable;
    └ public final class **Byte** extends Number implements Comparable;
    └ public final class **Double** extends Number implements Comparable;
    └ public final class **Float** extends Number implements Comparable;
    └ public final class **Integer** extends Number implements Comparable;
    └ public final class **Long** extends Number implements Comparable;
    └ public final class **Short** extends Number implements Comparable;
  └ public class **Package**;
  └ public abstract class **Process**;
  └ public class **Runtime**;
  └ public class **SecurityManager**;
  └ public final class **StackTraceElement** implements Serializable;
  └ public final class **StrictMath**;
  └ public final class **String** implements CharSequence, Comparable, Serializable;
  └ public final class **StringBuffer** implements CharSequence, Serializable;
  └ public final class **System**;
  └ public class **Thread** implements Runnable;
  └ public class **ThreadGroup**;

└ public class **ThreadLocal**;
　└ public class **InheritableThreadLocal** extends ThreadLocal;
└ public class **Throwable** implements Serializable;
└ public final class **Void**;
public final class **RuntimePermission** extends java.security.BasicPermission;

Exceptions:

public class **Exception** extends Throwable;
└ public class **ClassNotFoundException** extends Exception;
└ public class **CloneNotSupportedException** extends Exception;
└ public class **IllegalAccessException** extends Exception;
└ public class **InstantiationException** extends Exception;
└ public class **InterruptedException** extends Exception;
└ public class **NoSuchFieldException** extends Exception;
└ public class **NoSuchMethodException** extends Exception;
└ public class **RuntimeException** extends Exception;
　└ public class **ArithmeticException** extends RuntimeException;
　└ public class **ArrayStoreException** extends RuntimeException;
　└ public class **ClassCastException** extends RuntimeException;
　└ public class **IllegalArgumentException** extends RuntimeException;
　　└ public class **IllegalThreadStateException** extends IllegalArgumentException;
　　└ public class **NumberFormatException** extends IllegalArgumentException;
　└ public class **IllegalMonitorStateException** extends RuntimeException;
　└ public class **IllegalStateException** extends RuntimeException;
　└ public class **IndexOutOfBoundsException** extends RuntimeException;
　　└ public class **ArrayIndexOutOfBoundsException** extends IndexOutOfBoundsException;
　　└ public class **StringIndexOutOfBoundsException** extends IndexOutOfBoundsException;
　└ public class **NegativeArraySizeException** extends RuntimeException;
　└ public class **NullPointerException** extends RuntimeException;
　└ public class **SecurityException** extends RuntimeException;
　└ public class **UnsupportedOperationException** extends RuntimeException;

Errors:

public class **Error** extends Throwable;
└ public class **AssertionError** extends Error;
└ public class **LinkageError** extends Error;
　└ public class **ClassCircularityError** extends LinkageError;
　└ public class **ClassFormatError** extends LinkageError;
　　└ public class **UnsupportedClassVersionError** extends ClassFormatError;
　└ public class **ExceptionInInitializerError** extends LinkageError;
　└ public class **IncompatibleClassChangeError** extends LinkageError;
　　└ public class **AbstractMethodError** extends IncompatibleClassChangeError;
　　└ public class **IllegalAccessError** extends IncompatibleClassChangeError;
　　└ public class **InstantiationError** extends IncompatibleClassChangeError;
　　└ public class **NoSuchFieldError** extends IncompatibleClassChangeError;
　　└ public class **NoSuchMethodError** extends IncompatibleClassChangeError;
　└ public class **NoClassDefFoundError** extends LinkageError;
　└ public class **UnsatisfiedLinkError** extends LinkageError;
　└ public class **VerifyError** extends LinkageError;
└ public class **ThreadDeath** extends Error;
└ public abstract class **VirtualMachineError** extends Error;

```
└ public class InternalError extends VirtualMachineError;
└ public class OutOfMemoryError extends VirtualMachineError;
└ public class StackOverflowError extends VirtualMachineError;
└ public class UnknownError extends VirtualMachineError;
```

AbstractMethodError — Java 1.0

java.lang — *serializable error*

This error signals an attempt to invoke an abstract method.

Object ─ Throwable ─ Error ─ LinkageError ─ IncompatibleClassChangeError ─ AbstractMethodError
Throwable ⋮ Serializable

```
public class AbstractMethodError extends IncompatibleClassChangeError {
// Public Constructors
   public AbstractMethodError();
   public AbstractMethodError(String s);
}
```

ArithmeticException — Java 1.0

java.lang — *serializable unchecked*

This RuntimeException signals an exceptional arithmetic condition, such as integer division by zero.

Object ─ Throwable ─ Exception ─ RuntimeException ─ ArithmeticException
Throwable ⋮ Serializable

```
public class ArithmeticException extends RuntimeException {
// Public Constructors
   public ArithmeticException();
   public ArithmeticException(String s);
}
```

ArrayIndexOutOfBoundsException — Java 1.0

java.lang — *serializable unchecked*

This exception signals that an array index less than zero or greater than or equal to the array size has been used.

Object ─ Throwable ─ Exception ─ RuntimeException ─ IndexOutOfBoundsException ─ ArrayIndexOutOfBoundsException
Throwable ⋮ Serializable

```
public class ArrayIndexOutOfBoundsException extends IndexOutOfBoundsException {
// Public Constructors
   public ArrayIndexOutOfBoundsException();
   public ArrayIndexOutOfBoundsException(String s);
   public ArrayIndexOutOfBoundsException(int index);
}
```

Thrown By: Too many methods to list.

ArrayStoreException — Java 1.0

java.lang — *serializable unchecked*

This exception signals an attempt to store the wrong type of object into an array.

Object — Throwable — Exception — RuntimeException — ArrayStoreException
Serializable

```
public class ArrayStoreException extends RuntimeException {
// Public Constructors
    public ArrayStoreException();
    public ArrayStoreException(String s);
}
```

AssertionError — Java 1.4

java.lang — *serializable error*

An instance of this class is thrown if when an assertion fails. This happens when assertions are enabled and the expression following an assert statement does not evaluate to true. If an assertion fails, and the assert statement has a second expression separated from the first by a colon, then the second expression is evaluated and the resulting value is passed to the AssertionError() constructor, where it is converted to a string and used as the error message.

Object — Throwable — Error — AssertionError
Serializable

```
public class AssertionError extends Error {
// Public Constructors
    public AssertionError();
    public AssertionError(long detailMessage);
    public AssertionError(float detailMessage);
    public AssertionError(double detailMessage);
    public AssertionError(int detailMessage);
    public AssertionError(Object detailMessage);
    public AssertionError(boolean detailMessage);
    public AssertionError(char detailMessage);
}
```

Boolean — Java 1.0

java.lang — *serializable*

This class provides an immutable object wrapper around the boolean primitive type. Note that the TRUE and FALSE constants are Boolean objects; they are not the same as the true and false boolean values. As of Java 1.1, this class defines a Class constant that represents the boolean type. booleanValue() returns the boolean value of a Boolean object. The class method getBoolean() retrieves the boolean value of a named property from the system property list. The class method valueOf() parses a string and returns the Boolean object it represents. In Java 1.4, two new class methods convert primitive boolean values to Boolean and String objects.

Object — Boolean ··· Serializable

```
public final class Boolean implements Serializable {
// Public Constructors
```

```
   public Boolean(String s);
   public Boolean(boolean value);
// Public Constants
   public static final Boolean FALSE;
   public static final Boolean TRUE;
1.1 public static final Class TYPE;
// Public Class Methods
   public static boolean getBoolean(String name);
1.4 public static String toString(boolean b);
1.4 public static Boolean valueOf(boolean b);
   public static Boolean valueOf(String s);
// Public Instance Methods
   public boolean booleanValue();
// Public Methods Overriding Object
   public boolean equals(Object obj);
   public int hashCode();
   public String toString();
}
```


Passed To: javax.swing.DefaultDesktopManager.setWasIcon()

Returned By: Boolean.valueOf(), javax.swing.filechooser.FileSystemView.isTraversable(), javax.swing.filechooser.FileView.isTraversable(), javax.swing.plaf.basic.BasicFileChooserUI.BasicFileView.isHidden()

Type Of: java.awt.font.TextAttribute.{RUN_DIRECTION_LTR, RUN_DIRECTION_RTL, STRIKETHROUGH_ON, SWAP_COLORS_ON}, Boolean.{FALSE, TRUE}

Byte — Java 1.1

java.lang — *serializable comparable*

This class provides an object wrapper around the byte primitive type. It defines useful constants for the minimum and maximum values that can be stored by the byte type and a Class object constant that represents the byte type. It also provides various methods for converting Byte values to and from strings and other numeric types.

Most of the static methods of this class can convert a String to a Byte object or a byte value: the four parseByte() and valueOf() methods parse a number from the specified string using an optionally specified radix and return it in one of these two forms. The decode() method parses a byte specified in base 10, base 8, or base 16 and returns it as a Byte. If the string begins with "0x" or "#", it is interpreted as a hexadecimal number. If it begins with "0", it is interpreted as an octal number. Otherwise, it is interpreted as a decimal number.

Note that this class has two toString() methods. One is static and converts a byte primitive value to a string; the other is the usual toString() method that converts a Byte object to a string. Most of the remaining methods convert a Byte to various primitive numeric types.

Object — Number — Byte
Serializable (Number) · Comparable (Byte)

```
public final class Byte extends Number implements Comparable {
// Public Constructors
   public Byte(byte value);
   public Byte(String s) throws NumberFormatException;
// Public Constants
   public static final byte MAX_VALUE;                                   =127
```

```
    public static final byte MIN_VALUE;                                    =-128
    public static final Class TYPE;
// Public Class Methods
    public static Byte decode(String nm) throws NumberFormatException;
    public static byte parseByte(String s) throws NumberFormatException;
    public static byte parseByte(String s, int radix) throws NumberFormatException;
    public static String toString(byte b);
    public static Byte valueOf(String s) throws NumberFormatException;
    public static Byte valueOf(String s, int radix) throws NumberFormatException;
// Public Instance Methods
1.2 public int compareTo(Byte anotherByte);
// Methods Implementing Comparable
1.2 public int compareTo(Object o);
// Public Methods Overriding Number
    public byte byteValue();
    public double doubleValue();
    public float floatValue();
    public int intValue();
    public long longValue();
    public short shortValue();
// Public Methods Overriding Object
    public boolean equals(Object obj);
    public int hashCode();
    public String toString();
}
```

Passed To: Byte.compareTo()

Returned By: Byte.{decode(), valueOf()}

Character — Java 1.0

java.lang — *serializable comparable*

This class provides an immutable object wrapper around the primitive char data type. charValue() returns the char value of a Character object. The compareTo() method implements the Comparable interface so that Character objects can be ordered and sorted. The static methods are the most interesting thing about this class, however: they categorize char values based on the categories defined by the Unicode standard. (And some of the methods are useful only if you have a detailed understanding of that standard). Static methods beginning with "is" test whether a character is in a given category. isDigit(), isLetter(), isWhitespace(), isUpperCase(), and isLowerCase() are some of the most useful. Note that these methods work for any Unicode character, not just with the familiar Latin letters and Arabic numbers of the ASCII character set. getType() returns a constant that identifies the category of a character. getDirectionality() returns a separate DIRECTIONALITY_ constant that specifies the "directionality category" of a character.

In addition to testing the category of a character, this class also defines static methods for converting characters. toUpperCase() returns the uppercase equivalent of the specified character (or returns the character itself if the character is uppercase or has no uppercase equivalent). toLowerCase() converts instead to lowercase. digit() returns the integer equivalent of a given character in a given radix (or base; for example, use 16 for hexadecimal). It works with any Unicode digit character and, for sufficiently large radix values, with the ASCII letters a-z and A-Z. forDigit() returns the ASCII character that corresponds to the specified value (0–35) for the specified radix. getNumericValue() is similar but also works with any Unicode character including those that represent numbers but are not decimal digits, such as Roman numerals. Finally, the static toString() method returns a String of length 1 that contains the specified char value.

Object — Character

Comparable Serializable

```
public final class Character implements Comparable, Serializable {
// Public Constructors
    public Character(char value);
// Public Constants
1.1 public static final byte COMBINING_SPACING_MARK;                                   =8
1.1 public static final byte CONNECTOR_PUNCTUATION;                                    =23
1.1 public static final byte CONTROL;                                                  =15
1.1 public static final byte CURRENCY_SYMBOL;                                          =26
1.1 public static final byte DASH_PUNCTUATION;                                         =20
1.1 public static final byte DECIMAL_DIGIT_NUMBER;                                     =9
1.1 public static final byte ENCLOSING_MARK;                                           =7
1.1 public static final byte END_PUNCTUATION;                                          =22
1.4 public static final byte FINAL_QUOTE_PUNCTUATION;                                  =30
1.1 public static final byte FORMAT;                                                   =16
1.4 public static final byte INITIAL_QUOTE_PUNCTUATION;                                =29
1.1 public static final byte LETTER_NUMBER;                                            =10
1.1 public static final byte LINE_SEPARATOR;                                           =13
1.1 public static final byte LOWERCASE_LETTER;                                         =2
1.1 public static final byte MATH_SYMBOL;                                              =25
    public static final int MAX_RADIX;                                                 =36
    public static final char MAX_VALUE;                                      ='[bsol ]uFFFF'
    public static final int MIN_RADIX;                                                 =2
    public static final char MIN_VALUE;                                      ='[bsol ]u0000'
1.1 public static final byte MODIFIER_LETTER;                                          =4
1.1 public static final byte MODIFIER_SYMBOL;                                          =27
1.1 public static final byte NON_SPACING_MARK;                                         =6
1.1 public static final byte OTHER_LETTER;                                             =5
1.1 public static final byte OTHER_NUMBER;                                             =11
1.1 public static final byte OTHER_PUNCTUATION;                                        =24
1.1 public static final byte OTHER_SYMBOL;                                             =28
1.1 public static final byte PARAGRAPH_SEPARATOR;                                      =14
1.1 public static final byte PRIVATE_USE;                                              =18
1.1 public static final byte SPACE_SEPARATOR;                                          =12
1.1 public static final byte START_PUNCTUATION;                                        =21
1.1 public static final byte SURROGATE;                                                =19
1.1 public static final byte TITLECASE_LETTER;                                         =3
1.1 public static final Class TYPE;
1.1 public static final byte UNASSIGNED;                                               =0
1.1 public static final byte UPPERCASE_LETTER;                                         =1
1.4 public static final byte DIRECTIONALITY_ARABIC_NUMBER;                             =6
1.4 public static final byte DIRECTIONALITY_BOUNDARY_NEUTRAL;                          =9
1.4 public static final byte DIRECTIONALITY_COMMON_NUMBER_SEPARATOR;                   =7
1.4 public static final byte DIRECTIONALITY_EUROPEAN_NUMBER;                           =3
1.4 public static final byte DIRECTIONALITY_EUROPEAN_NUMBER_SEPARATOR;                 =4
1.4 public static final byte DIRECTIONALITY_EUROPEAN_NUMBER_TERMINATOR;                =5
1.4 public static final byte DIRECTIONALITY_LEFT_TO_RIGHT;                             =0
1.4 public static final byte DIRECTIONALITY_LEFT_TO_RIGHT_EMBEDDING;                   =14
1.4 public static final byte DIRECTIONALITY_LEFT_TO_RIGHT_OVERRIDE;                    =15
1.4 public static final byte DIRECTIONALITY_NONSPACING_MARK;                           =8
1.4 public static final byte DIRECTIONALITY_OTHER_NEUTRALS;                            =13
```

```
1.4 public static final byte DIRECTIONALITY_PARAGRAPH_SEPARATOR;              =10
1.4 public static final byte DIRECTIONALITY_POP_DIRECTIONAL_FORMAT;           =18
1.4 public static final byte DIRECTIONALITY_RIGHT_TO_LEFT;                    =1
1.4 public static final byte DIRECTIONALITY_RIGHT_TO_LEFT_ARABIC;             =2
1.4 public static final byte DIRECTIONALITY_RIGHT_TO_LEFT_EMBEDDING;          =16
1.4 public static final byte DIRECTIONALITY_RIGHT_TO_LEFT_OVERRIDE;           =17
1.4 public static final byte DIRECTIONALITY_SEGMENT_SEPARATOR;                =11
1.4 public static final byte DIRECTIONALITY_UNDEFINED;                        =-1
1.4 public static final byte DIRECTIONALITY_WHITESPACE;                       =12
// Inner Classes
1.2 public static class Subset;
1.2 public static final class UnicodeBlock extends Character.Subset;
// Public Class Methods
    public static int digit(char ch, int radix);
    public static char forDigit(int digit, int radix);
1.4 public static byte getDirectionality(char c);
1.1 public static int getNumericValue(char ch);
1.1 public static int getType(char ch);
    public static boolean isDefined(char ch);
    public static boolean isDigit(char ch);
1.1 public static boolean isIdentifierIgnorable(char ch);
1.1 public static boolean isISOControl(char ch);
1.1 public static boolean isJavaIdentifierPart(char ch);
1.1 public static boolean isJavaIdentifierStart(char ch);
    public static boolean isLetter(char ch);
    public static boolean isLetterOrDigit(char ch);
    public static boolean isLowerCase(char ch);
1.4 public static boolean isMirrored(char c);
1.1 public static boolean isSpaceChar(char ch);
    public static boolean isTitleCase(char ch);
1.1 public static boolean isUnicodeIdentifierPart(char ch);
1.1 public static boolean isUnicodeIdentifierStart(char ch);
    public static boolean isUpperCase(char ch);
1.1 public static boolean isWhitespace(char ch);
    public static char toLowerCase(char ch);
1.4 public static String toString(char c);
    public static char toTitleCase(char ch);
    public static char toUpperCase(char ch);
// Public Instance Methods
    public char charValue();
1.2 public int compareTo(Character anotherCharacter);
// Methods Implementing Comparable
1.2 public int compareTo(Object o);
// Public Methods Overriding Object
    public boolean equals(Object obj);
    public int hashCode();
    public String toString();
// Deprecated Public Methods
#   public static boolean isJavaLetter(char ch);
#   public static boolean isJavaLetterOrDigit(char ch);
#   public static boolean isSpace(char ch);
}
```

Passed To: java.awt.AWTKeyStroke.getAWTKeyStroke(), Character.compareTo(), javax.swing.KeyStroke.getKeyStroke()

Character.Subset — Java 1.2

java.lang

This class represents a named subset of the Unicode character set. The toString() method returns the name of the subset. This is a base class intended for further subclassing. Note, in particular, that it does not provide a way to list the members of the subset, nor a way to test for membership in the subset. See Character.UnicodeBlock.

```
public static class Character.Subset {
// Protected Constructors
   protected Subset(String name);
// Public Methods Overriding Object
   public final boolean equals(Object obj);
   public final int hashCode();
   public final String toString();
}
```

Subclasses: java.awt.im.InputSubset, Character.UnicodeBlock

Passed To: java.awt.im.InputContext.setCharacterSubsets(), java.awt.im.spi.InputMethod.setCharacterSubsets()

Character.UnicodeBlock — Java 1.2

java.lang

This subclass of Character.Subset defines a number of constants that represent named subsets of the Unicode character set. The subsets and their names are the character blocks defined by the Unicode specification (see *http://www.unicode.org/*). Java 1.4 updates this class to a new version of the Unicode standard and defines a number of new block constants. The static method of() takes a character and returns the Character.UnicodeBlock to which it belongs, or null if it is not part of any defined block. When presented with an unknown Unicode character, this method provides a useful way to determine what alphabet it belongs to.

```
public static final class Character.UnicodeBlock extends Character.Subset {
// No Constructor
// Public Constants
    public static final Character.UnicodeBlock ALPHABETIC_PRESENTATION_FORMS;
    public static final Character.UnicodeBlock ARABIC;
    public static final Character.UnicodeBlock ARABIC_PRESENTATION_FORMS_A;
    public static final Character.UnicodeBlock ARABIC_PRESENTATION_FORMS_B;
    public static final Character.UnicodeBlock ARMENIAN;
    public static final Character.UnicodeBlock ARROWS;
    public static final Character.UnicodeBlock BASIC_LATIN;
    public static final Character.UnicodeBlock BENGALI;
    public static final Character.UnicodeBlock BLOCK_ELEMENTS;
    public static final Character.UnicodeBlock BOPOMOFO;
1.4 public static final Character.UnicodeBlock BOPOMOFO_EXTENDED;
    public static final Character.UnicodeBlock BOX_DRAWING;
1.4 public static final Character.UnicodeBlock BRAILLE_PATTERNS;
1.4 public static final Character.UnicodeBlock CHEROKEE;
    public static final Character.UnicodeBlock CJK_COMPATIBILITY;
    public static final Character.UnicodeBlock CJK_COMPATIBILITY_FORMS;
    public static final Character.UnicodeBlock CJK_COMPATIBILITY_IDEOGRAPHS;
1.4 public static final Character.UnicodeBlock CJK_RADICALS_SUPPLEMENT;
    public static final Character.UnicodeBlock CJK_SYMBOLS_AND_PUNCTUATION;
    public static final Character.UnicodeBlock CJK_UNIFIED_IDEOGRAPHS;
```

```
1.4 public static final Character.UnicodeBlock CJK_UNIFIED_IDEOGRAPHS_EXTENSION_A;
    public static final Character.UnicodeBlock COMBINING_DIACRITICAL_MARKS;
    public static final Character.UnicodeBlock COMBINING_HALF_MARKS;
    public static final Character.UnicodeBlock COMBINING_MARKS_FOR_SYMBOLS;
    public static final Character.UnicodeBlock CONTROL_PICTURES;
    public static final Character.UnicodeBlock CURRENCY_SYMBOLS;
    public static final Character.UnicodeBlock CYRILLIC;
    public static final Character.UnicodeBlock DEVANAGARI;
    public static final Character.UnicodeBlock DINGBATS;
    public static final Character.UnicodeBlock ENCLOSED_ALPHANUMERICS;
    public static final Character.UnicodeBlock ENCLOSED_CJK_LETTERS_AND_MONTHS;
1.4 public static final Character.UnicodeBlock ETHIOPIC;
    public static final Character.UnicodeBlock GENERAL_PUNCTUATION;
    public static final Character.UnicodeBlock GEOMETRIC_SHAPES;
    public static final Character.UnicodeBlock GEORGIAN;
    public static final Character.UnicodeBlock GREEK;
    public static final Character.UnicodeBlock GREEK_EXTENDED;
    public static final Character.UnicodeBlock GUJARATI;
    public static final Character.UnicodeBlock GURMUKHI;
    public static final Character.UnicodeBlock HALFWIDTH_AND_FULLWIDTH_FORMS;
    public static final Character.UnicodeBlock HANGUL_COMPATIBILITY_JAMO;
    public static final Character.UnicodeBlock HANGUL_JAMO;
    public static final Character.UnicodeBlock HANGUL_SYLLABLES;
    public static final Character.UnicodeBlock HEBREW;
    public static final Character.UnicodeBlock HIRAGANA;
1.4 public static final Character.UnicodeBlock IDEOGRAPHIC_DESCRIPTION_CHARACTERS;
    public static final Character.UnicodeBlock IPA_EXTENSIONS;
    public static final Character.UnicodeBlock KANBUN;
1.4 public static final Character.UnicodeBlock KANGXI_RADICALS;
    public static final Character.UnicodeBlock KANNADA;
    public static final Character.UnicodeBlock KATAKANA;
1.4 public static final Character.UnicodeBlock KHMER;
    public static final Character.UnicodeBlock LAO;
    public static final Character.UnicodeBlock LATIN_1_SUPPLEMENT;
    public static final Character.UnicodeBlock LATIN_EXTENDED_A;
    public static final Character.UnicodeBlock LATIN_EXTENDED_ADDITIONAL;
    public static final Character.UnicodeBlock LATIN_EXTENDED_B;
    public static final Character.UnicodeBlock LETTERLIKE_SYMBOLS;
    public static final Character.UnicodeBlock MALAYALAM;
    public static final Character.UnicodeBlock MATHEMATICAL_OPERATORS;
    public static final Character.UnicodeBlock MISCELLANEOUS_SYMBOLS;
    public static final Character.UnicodeBlock MISCELLANEOUS_TECHNICAL;
1.4 public static final Character.UnicodeBlock MONGOLIAN;
1.4 public static final Character.UnicodeBlock MYANMAR;
    public static final Character.UnicodeBlock NUMBER_FORMS;
1.4 public static final Character.UnicodeBlock OGHAM;
    public static final Character.UnicodeBlock OPTICAL_CHARACTER_RECOGNITION;
    public static final Character.UnicodeBlock ORIYA;
    public static final Character.UnicodeBlock PRIVATE_USE_AREA;
1.4 public static final Character.UnicodeBlock RUNIC;
1.4 public static final Character.UnicodeBlock SINHALA;
    public static final Character.UnicodeBlock SMALL_FORM_VARIANTS;
    public static final Character.UnicodeBlock SPACING_MODIFIER_LETTERS;
    public static final Character.UnicodeBlock SPECIALS;
    public static final Character.UnicodeBlock SUPERSCRIPTS_AND_SUBSCRIPTS;
```

```
     public static final Character.UnicodeBlock SURROGATES_AREA;
1.4  public static final Character.UnicodeBlock SYRIAC;
     public static final Character.UnicodeBlock TAMIL;
     public static final Character.UnicodeBlock TELUGU;
1.4  public static final Character.UnicodeBlock THAANA;
     public static final Character.UnicodeBlock THAI;
     public static final Character.UnicodeBlock TIBETAN;
1.4  public static final Character.UnicodeBlock UNIFIED_CANADIAN_ABORIGINAL_SYLLABICS;
1.4  public static final Character.UnicodeBlock YI_RADICALS;
1.4  public static final Character.UnicodeBlock YI_SYLLABLES;
// Public Class Methods
     public static Character.UnicodeBlock of(char c);
}
```

Returned By: Character.UnicodeBlock.of()

Type Of: Too many fields to list.

CharSequence — Java 1.4

java.lang

This interface defines a simple API for read-only access to sequences of characters. In the core platform it is implemented by the String, StringBuffer, and java.nio.CharBuffer classes. charAt() returns the character at a specified position in the sequence. length() returns the number of characters in the sequence. subSequence() returns a CharSequence that consists of the characters starting at, and including, the specified *start* index, and continuing up to, but not including, the specified *end* index. Finally, toString() returns a String version of the sequence.

Note that CharSequence implementations do not typically have interoperable equals() or hashCode() methods, and it is not usually possible to compare two CharSequence objects or use multiple sequences in a set or hashtable unless they are instances of the same implementing class.

```
public interface CharSequence {
// Public Instance Methods
     public abstract char charAt(int index);
     public abstract int length();
     public abstract CharSequence subSequence(int start, int end);
     public abstract String toString();
}
```

Implementations: String, StringBuffer, java.nio.CharBuffer

Passed To: java.nio.CharBuffer.wrap(), java.nio.charset.CharsetEncoder.canEncode(), java.util.regex.Matcher.reset(), java.util.regex.Pattern.{matcher(), matches(), split()}

Returned By: CharSequence.subSequence(), String.subSequence(), StringBuffer.subSequence(), java.nio.CharBuffer.subSequence()

Class — Java 1.0

java.lang — *serializable*

This class represents a Java class or interface, or, as of Java 1.1, any Java type. There is one Class object for each class that is loaded into the Java Virtual Machine, and, as of Java 1.1, there are special Class objects that represent the Java primitive types. The TYPE constants defined by Boolean, Integer, and the other primitive wrapper classes hold these special Class objects. Array types are also represented by Class objects in Java 1.1.

There is no constructor for this class. You can obtain a Class object by calling the getClass() method of any instance of the desired class. In Java 1.1 and later, you can also refer to a Class object by appending .class to the name of a class. Finally, and most interestingly, a class can be dynamically loaded by passing its fully qualified name (i.e., package name plus class name) to the static Class.forName() method. This method loads the named class (if it is not already loaded) into the Java interpreter and returns a Class object for it. Classes can also be loaded with a ClassLoader object.

The newInstance() method creates an instance of a given class; this allows you to create instances of dynamically loaded classes for which you cannot use the new keyword. Note that this method only works when the target class has a no-argument constructor. See newInstance() in java.lang.reflect.Constructor for a more powerful way to instantiate dynamically loaded classes.

getName() returns the name of the class. getSuperclass() returns its superclass. isInterface() tests whether the Class object represents an interface, and getInterfaces() returns an array of the interfaces that this class implements. In Java 1.2 and later, getPackage() returns a Package object that represents the package containing the class. getProtectionDomain() returns the java.security.ProtectionDomain to which this class belongs. The various other get() and is() methods return other information about the represented class; they form part of the Java Reflection API, along with the classes in java.lang.reflect.

Object — Class ··· Serializable

```
public final class Class implements Serializable {
// No Constructor
// Public Class Methods
    public static Class forName(String className) throws ClassNotFoundException;
1.2 public static Class forName(String name, boolean initialize, ClassLoader loader) throws ClassNotFoundException;
// Property Accessor Methods (by property name)
1.1 public boolean isArray();                                                        native
1.1 public Class[ ] getClasses();
    public ClassLoader getClassLoader();
1.1 public Class getComponentType();                                                 native
1.1 public java.lang.reflect.Constructor[ ] getConstructors() throws SecurityException;
1.1 public Class[ ] getDeclaredClasses() throws SecurityException;
1.1 public java.lang.reflect.Constructor[ ] getDeclaredConstructors() throws SecurityException;
1.1 public java.lang.reflect.Field[ ] getDeclaredFields() throws SecurityException;
1.1 public java.lang.reflect.Method[ ] getDeclaredMethods() throws SecurityException;
1.1 public Class getDeclaringClass();                                                native
1.1 public java.lang.reflect.Field[ ] getFields() throws SecurityException;
    public boolean isInterface();                                                    native
    public Class[ ] getInterfaces();                                                 native
1.1 public java.lang.reflect.Method[ ] getMethods() throws SecurityException;
1.1 public int getModifiers();                                                       native
    public String getName();                                                         native
1.2 public Package getPackage();
1.1 public boolean isPrimitive();                                                    native
1.2 public java.security.ProtectionDomain getProtectionDomain();
1.1 public Object[ ] getSigners();                                                   native
    public Class getSuperclass();                                                    native
// Public Instance Methods
1.4 public boolean desiredAssertionStatus();
1.1 public java.lang.reflect.Constructor getConstructor(Class[ ] parameterTypes) throws NoSuchMethodException,
        SecurityException;
1.1 public java.lang.reflect.Constructor getDeclaredConstructor(Class[ ] parameterTypes)
        throws NoSuchMethodException, SecurityException;
```

```
1.1 public java.lang.reflect.Field getDeclaredField(String name) throws NoSuchFieldException, SecurityException;
1.1 public java.lang.reflect.Method getDeclaredMethod(String name, Class[ ] parameterTypes)
        throws NoSuchMethodException, SecurityException;
1.1 public java.lang.reflect.Field getField(String name) throws NoSuchFieldException, SecurityException;
1.1 public java.lang.reflect.Method getMethod(String name, Class[ ] parameterTypes) throws NoSuchMethodException,
        SecurityException;
1.1 public java.net.URL getResource(String name);
1.1 public java.io.InputStream getResourceAsStream(String name);
1.1 public boolean isAssignableFrom(Class cls);                                    native
1.1 public boolean isInstance(Object obj);                                        native
    public Object newInstance( ) throws InstantiationException, IllegalAccessException;
// Public Methods Overriding Object
    public String toString( );
}
```

Passed To: Too many methods to list.

Returned By: Too many methods to list.

Type Of: Too many fields to list.

ClassCastException — Java 1.0

java.lang — *serializable unchecked*

This exception signals an invalid cast of an object to a type of which it is not an instance.

Object — Throwable — Exception — RuntimeException — ClassCastException
(Throwable implements Serializable)

```
public class ClassCastException extends RuntimeException {
// Public Constructors
    public ClassCastException( );
    public ClassCastException(String s);
}
```

Thrown By: javax.rmi.PortableRemoteObject.narrow(), javax.rmi.CORBA.PortableRemoteObjectDelegate.narrow(), org.xml.sax.helpers.ParserFactory.makeParser()

ClassCircularityError — Java 1.0

java.lang — *serializable error*

This error signals that a circular dependency has been detected while performing initialization for a class.

Object — Throwable — Error — LinkageError — ClassCircularityError
(Throwable implements Serializable)

```
public class ClassCircularityError extends LinkageError {
// Public Constructors
    public ClassCircularityError( );
    public ClassCircularityError(String s);
}
```

ClassFormatError — Java 1.0

java.lang — *serializable error*

This error signals an error in the binary format of a class file.

Object → Throwable → Error → LinkageError → ClassFormatError (Throwable implements Serializable)

```
public class ClassFormatError extends LinkageError {
// Public Constructors
   public ClassFormatError();
   public ClassFormatError(String s);
}
```

Subclasses: UnsupportedClassVersionError

Thrown By: ClassLoader.defineClass()

ClassLoader — Java 1.0

java.lang

This class is the abstract superclass of objects that know how to load Java classes into a Java VM. Given a ClassLoader object, you can dynamically load a class by calling the public loadClass() method, specifying the full name of the desired class. You can obtain a resource associated with a class by calling getResource(), getResources(), and getResourceAsStream(). Many applications do not need to use ClassLoader directly; these applications use the Class.forName() and Class.getResource() methods to dynamically load classes and resources using the ClassLoader object that loaded the application itself.

In order to load classes over the network or from any source other than the class path, you must use a custom ClassLoader object that knows how to obtain data from that source. A java.net.URLClassLoader is suitable for this purpose for almost all applications. Only rarely should an application need to define a ClassLoader subclass of its own. When this is necessary, the subclass should typically extend java.security.SecureClassLoader and override the findClass() method. This method must find the bytes that comprise the named class, then pass them to the defineClass() method and return the resulting Class object. In Java 1.2 and later, the findClass() method must also define the Package object associated with the class, if it has not already been defined. It can use getPackage() and definePackage() for this purpose. Custom subclasses of ClassLoader should also override findResource() and findResources() to enable the public getResource() and getResources() methods.

In Java 1.4 and later you can specify whether the classes loaded through a ClassLoader should have assertions (assert statements) enabled. setDefaultAssertionStatus() enables or disables assertions for all loaded classes. setPackageAssertionStatus() and setClassAssertionStatus() allow you to override the default assertion status for a named package or a named class. Finally, clearAssertionStatus() sets the default status to false and discards the assertions status for any named packages and classes.

```
public abstract class ClassLoader {
// Protected Constructors
    protected ClassLoader();
1.2 protected ClassLoader(ClassLoader parent);
// Public Class Methods
1.2 public static ClassLoader getSystemClassLoader();
1.1 public static java.net.URL getSystemResource(String name);
1.1 public static java.io.InputStream getSystemResourceAsStream(String name);
```

```
1.2 public static java.util.Enumeration getSystemResources(String name) throws java.io.IOException;
// Public Instance Methods
1.4 public void clearAssertionStatus();                                                      synchronized
1.2 public final ClassLoader getParent();
1.1 public java.net.URL getResource(String name);
1.1 public java.io.InputStream getResourceAsStream(String name);
1.2 public final java.util.Enumeration getResources(String name) throws java.io.IOException;
1.1 public Class loadClass(String name) throws ClassNotFoundException;
1.4 public void setClassAssertionStatus(String className, boolean enabled);                  synchronized
1.4 public void setDefaultAssertionStatus(boolean enabled);                                  synchronized
1.4 public void setPackageAssertionStatus(String packageName, boolean enabled);              synchronized
// Protected Instance Methods
1.1 protected final Class defineClass(String name, byte[ ] b, int off, int len) throws ClassFormatError;
1.2 protected final Class defineClass(String name, byte[ ] b, int off, int len,
                  java.security.ProtectionDomain protectionDomain) throws ClassFormatError;
1.2 protected Package definePackage(String name, String specTitle, String specVersion, String specVendor,
                  String implTitle, String implVersion, String implVendor, java.net.URL sealBase)
        throws IllegalArgumentException;
1.2 protected Class findClass(String name) throws ClassNotFoundException;
1.2 protected String findLibrary(String libname);                                            constant
1.1 protected final Class findLoadedClass(String name);                                      native
1.2 protected java.net.URL findResource(String name);                                        constant
1.2 protected java.util.Enumeration findResources(String name) throws java.io.IOException;
    protected final Class findSystemClass(String name) throws ClassNotFoundException;
1.2 protected Package getPackage(String name);
1.2 protected Package[ ] getPackages();
    protected Class loadClass(String name, boolean resolve) throws ClassNotFoundException;   synchronized
    protected final void resolveClass(Class c);
1.1 protected final void setSigners(Class c, Object[ ] signers);
// Deprecated Protected Methods
#   protected final Class defineClass(byte[ ] b, int off, int len) throws ClassFormatError;
}
```

Subclasses: java.security.SecureClassLoader

Passed To: Too many methods to list.

Returned By: Class.getClassLoader(), ClassLoader.{getParent(), getSystemClassLoader()}, SecurityManager.currentClassLoader(), Thread.getContextClassLoader(), java.rmi.server.RMIClassLoader.getClassLoader(), java.rmi.server.RMIClassLoaderSpi.getClassLoader(), java.security.ProtectionDomain.getClassLoader()

ClassNotFoundException — Java 1.0

java.lang — *serializable checked*

This exception signals that a class to be loaded cannot be found. If an exception of this type was caused by some underlying exception, you can query that lower-level exception with getException(), or with the newer, more general getCause().

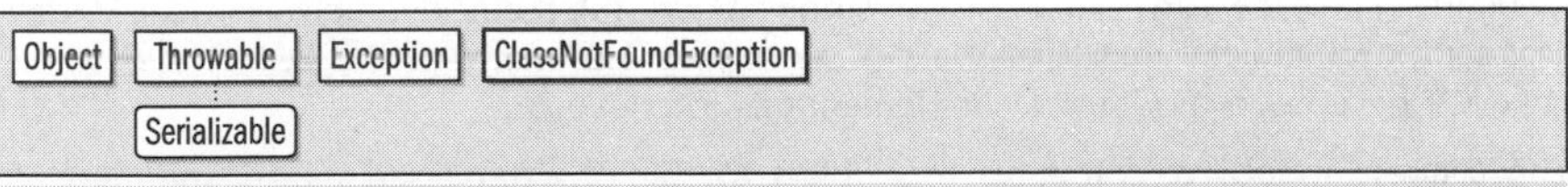


```
public class ClassNotFoundException extends Exception {
// Public Constructors
    public ClassNotFoundException();
    public ClassNotFoundException(String s);
```

```
1.2 public ClassNotFoundException(String s, Throwable ex);
// Public Instance Methods
1.2 public Throwable getException();                                    default:null
// Public Methods Overriding Throwable
1.4 public Throwable getCause();                                        default:null
}
```

Thrown By: Too many methods to list.

Cloneable — Java 1.0

java.lang — *cloneable*

This interface defines no methods or variables, but indicates that the class that implements it may be cloned (i.e., copied) by calling the Object method clone(). Calling clone() for an object that does not implement this interface (and does not override clone() with its own implementation) causes a CloneNotSupportedException to be thrown.

```
public interface Cloneable {
}
```

Implementations: Too many classes to list.

CloneNotSupportedException — Java 1.0

java.lang — *serializable checked*

This exception signals that the clone() method has been called for an object of a class that does not implement the Cloneable interface.

Object — Throwable — Exception — CloneNotSupportedException
Throwable ⋯ Serializable

```
public class CloneNotSupportedException extends Exception {
// Public Constructors
   public CloneNotSupportedException();
   public CloneNotSupportedException(String s);
}
```

Subclasses: java.rmi.server.ServerCloneException

Thrown By: Too many methods to list.

Comparable — Java 1.2

java.lang — *comparable*

This interface defines a single method, compareTo(), that is responsible for comparing one object to another and determining their relative order, according to some natural ordering for that class of objects. Any general-purpose class that represents a value that can be sorted or ordered should implement this interface. Any class that does implement this interface can make use of various powerful methods such as java.util.Collections.sort() and java.util.Arrays.binarySearch(). As of Java 1.2, many of the key classes in the Java API have been modified to implement this interface.

The compareTo() object compares this object to the object passed as an argument. It should assume that the supplied object is of the appropriate type; if it is not, it should throw a ClassCastException. If this object is less than the supplied object or should appear before the supplied object in a sorted list, compareTo() should return a negative number. If this object is greater than the supplied object or should come after the supplied object in a sorted list, compareTo() should return a positive integer. If the two objects are equivalent, and their relative order in a sorted list does not matter, compareTo() should return 0. If compareTo() returns 0 for two objects, the equals() method should typically return true. If this is not the case, the Comparable objects are not suitable for use in java.util.TreeSet and java.util.TreeMap classes.

See java.util.Comparator for a way to define an ordering for objects that do not implement Comparable or to define an ordering other than the natural ordering defined by a Comparable class.

```
public interface Comparable {
// Public Instance Methods
   public abstract int compareTo(Object o);
}
```

Implementations: Too many classes to list.

Passed To: javax.imageio.metadata.IIOMetadataFormatImpl.addObjectValue(), javax.swing.SpinnerDateModel.{setEnd(), setStart(), SpinnerDateModel()}, javax.swing.SpinnerNumberModel.{setMaximum(), setMinimum(), SpinnerNumberModel()}, javax.swing.text.InternationalFormatter.{setMaximum(), setMinimum()}

Returned By: javax.imageio.metadata.IIOMetadataFormat.{getObjectMaxValue(), getObjectMinValue()}, javax.imageio.metadata.IIOMetadataFormatImpl.{getObjectMaxValue(), getObjectMinValue()}, javax.swing.SpinnerDateModel.{getEnd(), getStart()}, javax.swing.SpinnerNumberModel.{getMaximum(), getMinimum()}, javax.swing.text.InternationalFormatter.{getMaximum(), getMinimum()}

Compiler — Java 1.0

java.lang

The static methods of this class provide an interface to the just-in-time (JIT) byte-code-to-native code compiler in use by the Java interpreter. If no JIT compiler is in use by the VM, these methods do nothing. compileClass() asks the JIT compiler to compile the specified class. compileClasses() asks the JIT compiler to compile all classes that match the specified name. These methods return true if the compilation was successful, or false if it failed or if there is no JIT compiler on the system. enable() and disable() turn just-in-time compilation on and off. command() asks the JIT compiler to perform some compiler-specific operation; this is a hook for vendor extensions. No standard operations have been defined.

```
public final class Compiler {
// No Constructor
// Public Class Methods
   public static Object command(Object any);                    native
   public static boolean compileClass(Class clazz);             native
   public static boolean compileClasses(String string);         native
   public static void disable();                                native
   public static void enable();                                 native
}
```

Double — Java 1.0

java.lang — *serializable comparable*

This class provides an immutable object wrapper around the double primitive data type. doubleValue() returns the primitive double value of a Double object, and there are other methods (which override Number methods and whose names all end in "Value") for returning a the wrapped double value as a variety of other primitive types.

This class also provides some useful constants and static methods for testing double values. MIN_VALUE and MAX_VALUE are the smallest (closest to zero) and largest representable double values. POSITIVE_INFINITY and NEGATIVE_INFINITY are the double representations of infinity and negative infinity, and NaN is special double "not-a-number" value. isInfinite() in class and instance method forms tests whether a double or a Double has an infinite value. Similarly, isNaN() tests whether a double or Double is not-a-number; this is a comparison that cannot be done directly because the NaN constant never equals any other value, including itself.

The static parseDouble() method converts a String to a double. The static valueOf() converts a String to a Double and is basically equivalent to the Double() constructor that takes a String argument. The static and instance toString() methods perform the opposite conversion: they convert a double or a Double to a String. See also java.text.NumberFormat for more flexible number parsing and formatting.

The compareTo() method makes the Double object Comparable, which is useful for ordering and sorting. The static compare() method is similar (its return values have the same meaning as those of Comparable.compareTo()) but works on primitive values rather than on objects and is useful when ordering and sorting arrays of double values.

doubleToLongBits(), doubleToRawLongBits(), and longBitsToDouble() allow you to manipulate the bit representation (defined by IEEE 754) of a double directly (which is not something that most applications ever need to do).

Object — Number — Double
Serializable (Number), Comparable (Double)

```
public final class Double extends Number implements Comparable {
// Public Constructors
    public Double(String s) throws NumberFormatException;
    public Double(double value);
// Public Constants
    public static final double MAX_VALUE;                              =1.7976931348623157E308
    public static final double MIN_VALUE;                              =4.9E-324
    public static final double NaN;                                    =NaN
    public static final double NEGATIVE_INFINITY;                      =-Infinity
    public static final double POSITIVE_INFINITY;                      =Infinity
1.1 public static final Class TYPE;
// Public Class Methods
1.4 public static int compare(double d1, double d2);
    public static long doubleToLongBits(double value);                 native
1.3 public static long doubleToRawLongBits(double value);              native
    public static boolean isInfinite(double v);
    public static boolean isNaN(double v);
    public static double longBitsToDouble(long bits);                  native
1.2 public static double parseDouble(String s) throws NumberFormatException;
    public static String toString(double d);
    public static Double valueOf(String s) throws NumberFormatException;
// Public Instance Methods
1.2 public int compareTo(Double anotherDouble);
    public boolean isInfinite();
    public boolean isNaN();
// Methods Implementing Comparable
1.2 public int compareTo(Object o);
// Public Methods Overriding Number
1.1 public byte byteValue();
    public double doubleValue();
```

```
    public float floatValue();
    public int intValue();
    public long longValue();
1.1 public short shortValue();
// Public Methods Overriding Object
    public boolean equals(Object obj);
    public int hashCode();
    public String toString();
}
```

Passed To: Double.compareTo()

Returned By: Double.valueOf()

Error **Java 1.0**

java.lang *serializable error*

This class forms the root of the error hierarchy in Java. Subclasses of Error, unlike subclasses of Exception, should not be caught and generally cause termination of the program. Subclasses of Error need not be declared in the throws clause of a method definition. This class inherits methods from Throwable but declares none of its own. Each of its constructors simply invokes the corresponding Throwable() constructor. See Throwable for details.

Object — Throwable — Error
Serializable

```
public class Error extends Throwable {
// Public Constructors
    public Error();
1.4 public Error(Throwable cause);
    public Error(String message);
1.4 public Error(String message, Throwable cause);
}
```

Subclasses: java.awt.AWTError, AssertionError, LinkageError, ThreadDeath, VirtualMachineError, java.nio.charset.CoderMalfunctionError, javax.xml.parsers.FactoryConfigurationError, javax.xml.transform.TransformerFactoryConfigurationError

Passed To: java.rmi.ServerError.ServerError()

Exception **Java 1.0**

java.lang *serializable checked*

This class forms the root of the exception hierarchy in Java. An Exception signals an abnormal condition that must be specially handled to prevent program termination. Exceptions may be caught and handled. An exception that is not a subclass of RuntimeException must be declared in the throws clause of any method that can throw it. This class inherits methods from Throwable but declares none of its own. Each of its constructors simply invokes the corresponding Throwable() constructor. See Throwable for details.

Object — Throwable — Exception
Serializable

```
public class Exception extends Throwable {
// Public Constructors
```

```
    public Exception();
1.4 public Exception(Throwable cause);
    public Exception(String message);
1.4 public Exception(String message, Throwable cause);
}
```

Subclasses: Too many classes to list.

Passed To: Too many methods to list.

Returned By: java.awt.event.InvocationEvent.getException(), java.security.PrivilegedActionException.getException(), javax.xml.parsers.FactoryConfigurationError.getException(), javax.xml.transform.TransformerFactoryConfigurationError.getException(), org.omg.CORBA.Environment.exception(), org.xml.sax.SAXException.getException()

Thrown By: java.awt.im.spi.InputMethodDescriptor.createInputMethod(), java.beans.Expression.getValue(), java.beans.Statement.execute(), java.rmi.server.RemoteCall.executeCall(), java.rmi.server.RemoteRef.invoke(), java.rmi.server.Skeleton.dispatch(), java.security.PrivilegedExceptionAction.run(), javax.naming.spi.DirectoryManager.getObjectInstance(), javax.naming.spi.DirObjectFactory.getObjectInstance(), javax.naming.spi.NamingManager.getObjectInstance(), javax.naming.spi.ObjectFactory.getObjectInstance()

Type Of: java.io.WriteAbortedException.detail, java.rmi.server.ServerCloneException.detail

ExceptionInInitializerError — Java 1.1

java.lang — ***serializable error***

This error is thrown by the Java Virtual Machine when an exception occurs in the static initializer of a class. You can use the getException() method to obtain the Throwable object that was thrown from the initializer. In Java 1.4 and later, getException() has been superseded by the more general getCause() method of the Throwable class.

Object — Throwable — Error — LinkageError — ExceptionInInitializerError
(Throwable implements Serializable)

```
public class ExceptionInInitializerError extends LinkageError {
// Public Constructors
    public ExceptionInInitializerError();
    public ExceptionInInitializerError(String s);
    public ExceptionInInitializerError(Throwable thrown);
// Public Instance Methods
    public Throwable getException();                    default:null
// Public Methods Overriding Throwable
1.4 public Throwable getCause();                        default:null
}
```

Float — Java 1.0

java.lang — ***serializable comparable***

This class provides an immutable object wrapper around a primitive float value. floatValue() returns the primitive float value of a Float object, and there are methods for returning the value of a Float as a variety of other primitive types. This class is very similar to Double, and defines the same set of useful methods and constants as that class does. See Double for details.


```
public final class Float extends Number implements Comparable {
// Public Constructors
    public Float(String s) throws NumberFormatException;
    public Float(float value);
    public Float(double value);
// Public Constants
    public static final float MAX_VALUE;                                   =3.4028235E38
    public static final float MIN_VALUE;                                   =1.4E-45
    public static final float NaN;                                         =NaN
    public static final float NEGATIVE_INFINITY;                           =-Infinity
    public static final float POSITIVE_INFINITY;                           =Infinity
1.1 public static final Class TYPE;
// Public Class Methods
1.4 public static int compare(float f1, float f2);
    public static int floatToIntBits(float value);                         native
1.3 public static int floatToRawIntBits(float value);                      native
    public static float intBitsToFloat(int bits);                          native
    public static boolean isInfinite(float v);
    public static boolean isNaN(float v);
1.2 public static float parseFloat(String s) throws NumberFormatException;
    public static String toString(float f);
    public static Float valueOf(String s) throws NumberFormatException;
// Public Instance Methods
1.2 public int compareTo(Float anotherFloat);
    public boolean isInfinite();
    public boolean isNaN();
// Methods Implementing Comparable
1.2 public int compareTo(Object o);
// Public Methods Overriding Number
1.1 public byte byteValue();
    public double doubleValue();
    public float floatValue();
    public int intValue();
    public long longValue();
1.1 public short shortValue();
// Public Methods Overriding Object
    public boolean equals(Object obj);
    public int hashCode();
    public String toString();
}
```

Passed To: Float.compareTo()

Returned By: Float.valueOf()

Type Of: Too many fields to list.

IllegalAccessError — Java 1.0

java.lang — *serializable error*

This error signals an attempted use of a class, method, or field that is not accessible.

Object — Throwable — Error — LinkageError — IncompatibleClassChangeError — IllegalAccessError
Serializable

```
public class IllegalAccessError extends IncompatibleClassChangeError {
// Public Constructors
   public IllegalAccessError();
   public IllegalAccessError(String s);
}
```

IllegalAccessException — Java 1.0

java.lang — *serializable checked*

This exception signals that a class or initializer is not accessible. It is thrown by Class.newInstance().

Object — Throwable — Exception — IllegalAccessException
Serializable

```
public class IllegalAccessException extends Exception {
// Public Constructors
   public IllegalAccessException();
   public IllegalAccessException(String s);
}
```

Thrown By: Too many methods to list.

IllegalArgumentException — Java 1.0

java.lang — *serializable unchecked*

This exception signals an illegal argument to a method. See subclasses IllegalThreadStateException and NumberFormatException.

Object — Throwable — Exception — RuntimeException — IllegalArgumentException
Serializable

```
public class IllegalArgumentException extends RuntimeException {
// Public Constructors
   public IllegalArgumentException();
   public IllegalArgumentException(String s);
}
```

Subclasses: IllegalThreadStateException, NumberFormatException, java.nio.channels.IllegalSelectorException, java.nio.channels.UnresolvedAddressException, java.nio.channels.UnsupportedAddressTypeException, java.nio.charset.IllegalCharsetNameException, java.nio.charset.UnsupportedCharsetException, java.security.InvalidParameterException, java.util.regex.PatternSyntaxException

Thrown By: Too many methods to list.

IllegalMonitorStateException **Java 1.0**

java.lang ***serializable unchecked***

This exception signals an illegal monitor state. It is thrown by the Object notify() and wait() methods used for thread synchronization.

Object ─ Throwable ─ Exception ─ RuntimeException ─ IllegalMonitorStateException
Serializable

```
public class IllegalMonitorStateException extends RuntimeException {
// Public Constructors
   public IllegalMonitorStateException();
   public IllegalMonitorStateException(String s);
}
```

IllegalStateException **Java 1.1**

java.lang ***serializable unchecked***

This exception signals that a method has been invoked on an object that is not in an appropriate state to perform the requested operation.

Object ─ Throwable ─ Exception ─ RuntimeException ─ IllegalStateException
Serializable

```
public class IllegalStateException extends RuntimeException {
// Public Constructors
   public IllegalStateException();
   public IllegalStateException(String s);
}
```

Subclasses: java.awt.IllegalComponentStateException, java.awt.dnd.InvalidDnDOperationException, java.nio.InvalidMarkException, java.nio.channels.AlreadyConnectedException, java.nio.channels.CancelledKeyException, java.nio.channels.ClosedSelectorException, java.nio.channels.ConnectionPendingException, java.nio.channels.IllegalBlockingModeException, java.nio.channels.NoConnectionPendingException, java.nio.channels.NonReadableChannelException, java.nio.channels.NonWritableChannelException, java.nio.channels.NotYetBoundException, java.nio.channels.NotYetConnectedException, java.nio.channels.OverlappingFileLockException

Thrown By: Too many methods to list.

IllegalThreadStateException **Java 1.0**

java.lang ***serializable unchecked***

This exception signals that a thread is not in the appropriate state for an attempted operation to succeed.

Object ─ Throwable ─ Exception ─ RuntimeException ─ IllegalArgumentException ─ IllegalThreadStateException
Serializable

```
public class IllegalThreadStateException extends IllegalArgumentException {
// Public Constructors
   public IllegalThreadStateException();
   public IllegalThreadStateException(String s);
}
```

IncompatibleClassChangeError — Java 1.0

java.lang — *serializable error*

This is the superclass of a group of related error types. It signals some kind of illegal use of a legal class.

Object — Throwable — Error — LinkageError — IncompatibleClassChangeError
Serializable

```
public class IncompatibleClassChangeError extends LinkageError {
// Public Constructors
   public IncompatibleClassChangeError();
   public IncompatibleClassChangeError(String s);
}
```

Subclasses: AbstractMethodError, IllegalAccessError, InstantiationError, NoSuchFieldError, NoSuchMethodError

IndexOutOfBoundsException — Java 1.0

java.lang — *serializable unchecked*

This exception signals that an index is out of bounds. See the subclasses ArrayIndexOutOfBoundsException and StringIndexOutOfBoundsException.

Object — Throwable — Exception — RuntimeException — IndexOutOfBoundsException
Serializable

```
public class IndexOutOfBoundsException extends RuntimeException {
// Public Constructors
   public IndexOutOfBoundsException();
   public IndexOutOfBoundsException(String s);
}
```

Subclasses: ArrayIndexOutOfBoundsException, StringIndexOutOfBoundsException

Thrown By: java.awt.Toolkit.createCustomCursor(), java.awt.print.Book.{getPageFormat(), getPrintable(), setPage()}, java.awt.print.Pageable.{getPageFormat(), getPrintable()}

InheritableThreadLocal — Java 1.2

java.lang

This class holds a thread-local value that is inherited by child threads. See ThreadLocal for a discussion of thread-local values. Note that the inheritance referred to in the name of this class is not superclass-to-subclass inheritance; instead, it is parent-thread-to-child-thread inheritance.

This class is best understood by example. Suppose that an application has defined an InheritableThreadLocal object and that a certain thread (the parent thread) has a thread-local value stored in that object. Whenever that thread creates a new thread (a child thread), the InheritableThreadLocal object is automatically updated so that the new child thread has the same value associated with it as the parent thread. Note that the value associated with the child thread is independent from the value associated with the parent thread. If the child thread subsequently alters its value by calling the set() method of the InheritableThreadLocal, the value associated with the parent thread does not change.

By default, a child thread inherits a parent's values unmodified. By overriding the childValue() method, however, you can create a subclass of InheritableThreadLocal in which the child thread inherits some arbitrary function of the parent thread's value.

Object ─ ThreadLocal ─ InheritableThreadLocal

```
public class InheritableThreadLocal extends ThreadLocal {
// Public Constructors
   public InheritableThreadLocal();
// Protected Instance Methods
   protected Object childValue(Object parentValue);
}
```

InstantiationError — Java 1.0

java.lang — *serializable error*

This error signals an attempt to instantiate an interface or abstract class.

Object ─ Throwable ─ Error ─ LinkageError ─ IncompatibleClassChangeError ─ InstantiationError
(Throwable implements Serializable)

```
public class InstantiationError extends IncompatibleClassChangeError {
// Public Constructors
   public InstantiationError();
   public InstantiationError(String s);
}
```

InstantiationException — Java 1.0

java.lang — *serializable checked*

This exception signals an attempt to instantiate an interface or an abstract class.

Object ─ Throwable ─ Exception ─ InstantiationException
(Throwable implements Serializable)

```
public class InstantiationException extends Exception {
// Public Constructors
   public InstantiationException();
   public InstantiationException(String s);
}
```

Thrown By: Class.newInstance(), java.lang.reflect.Constructor.newInstance(), javax.swing.UIManager.setLookAndFeel(), org.xml.sax.helpers.ParserFactory.makeParser()

Integer — Java 1.0

java.lang — *serializable comparable*

This class provides an immutable object wrapper around the int primitive data type. This class also contains useful minimum and maximum constants and useful conversion methods. parseInt() and valueOf() convert a string to an int or to an Integer, respectively. Each can take a radix argument to specify the base the value is represented in. decode() also converts a String to an Integer. It assumes a hexadecimal number if the string begins with "0X" or "0x", or an octal number if the string begins with "0". Otherwise, a decimal number is assumed. toString() converts in the other direction, and the static version takes a radix argument. toBinaryString(), toOctalString(), and toHexString() convert an int to a string using base 2, base 8, and base 16. These methods treat the integer as an unsigned value. Other routines return the value of an Integer as various primitive types, and, finally, the getInteger() methods return the integer value of a named property from the system property list, or the specified default value.

Object — Number — Integer
Serializable Comparable

```
public final class Integer extends Number implements Comparable {
// Public Constructors
   public Integer(int value);
   public Integer(String s) throws NumberFormatException;
// Public Constants
   public static final int MAX_VALUE;                                    =2147483647
   public static final int MIN_VALUE;                                    =-2147483648
1.1 public static final Class TYPE;
// Public Class Methods
1.1 public static Integer decode(String nm) throws NumberFormatException;
   public static Integer getInteger(String nm);
   public static Integer getInteger(String nm, int val);
   public static Integer getInteger(String nm, Integer val);
   public static int parseInt(String s) throws NumberFormatException;
   public static int parseInt(String s, int radix) throws NumberFormatException;
   public static String toBinaryString(int i);
   public static String toHexString(int i);
   public static String toOctalString(int i);
   public static String toString(int i);
   public static String toString(int i, int radix);
   public static Integer valueOf(String s) throws NumberFormatException;
   public static Integer valueOf(String s, int radix) throws NumberFormatException;
// Public Instance Methods
1.2 public int compareTo(Integer anotherInteger);
// Methods Implementing Comparable
1.2 public int compareTo(Object o);
// Public Methods Overriding Number
1.1 public byte byteValue();
   public double doubleValue();
   public float floatValue();
   public int intValue();
   public long longValue();
1.1 public short shortValue();
// Public Methods Overriding Object
   public boolean equals(Object obj);
   public int hashCode();
   public String toString();
}
```

Passed To: Integer.{compareTo(), getInteger()}, javax.swing.JInternalFrame.setLayer()

Returned By: Integer.{decode(), getInteger(), valueOf()}, javax.swing.JLayeredPane.getObjectForLayer()

Type Of: java.awt.font.TextAttribute.{SUPERSCRIPT_SUB, SUPERSCRIPT_SUPER, UNDERLINE_LOW_DASHED, UNDERLINE_LOW_DOTTED, UNDERLINE_LOW_GRAY, UNDERLINE_LOW_ONE_PIXEL, UNDERLINE_LOW_TWO_PIXEL, UNDERLINE_ON}, javax.swing.JLayeredPane.{DEFAULT_LAYER, DRAG_LAYER, FRAME_CONTENT_LAYER, MODAL_LAYER, PALETTE_LAYER, POPUP_LAYER}

InternalError — Java 1.0

java.lang — *serializable error*

This error signals an internal error in the Java interpreter.

Object ─ Throwable ─ Error ─ VirtualMachineError ─ InternalError
Serializable

```
public class InternalError extends VirtualMachineError {
// Public Constructors
   public InternalError();
   public InternalError(String s);
}
```

InterruptedException — Java 1.0

java.lang — *serializable checked*

This exception signals that the thread has been interrupted.

Object ─ Throwable ─ Exception ─ InterruptedException
Serializable

```
public class InterruptedException extends Exception {
// Public Constructors
   public InterruptedException();
   public InterruptedException(String s);
}
```

Thrown By: Too many methods to list.

LinkageError — Java 1.0

java.lang — *serializable error*

This is the superclass of a group of errors that signal problems linking a class or resolving dependencies between classes.

Object ─ Throwable ─ Error ─ LinkageError
Serializable

```
public class LinkageError extends Error {
// Public Constructors
   public LinkageError();
   public LinkageError(String s);
}
```

Subclasses: ClassCircularityError, ClassFormatError, ExceptionInInitializerError, IncompatibleClassChangeError, NoClassDefFoundError, UnsatisfiedLinkError, VerifyError

Long — Java 1.0

java.lang — *serializable comparable*

This class provides an immutable object wrapper around the long primitive data type. This class also contains useful minimum and maximum constants and useful conversion methods. parseLong() and valueOf() convert a string to a long or to a Long, respectively.

Each can take a radix argument to specify the base the value is represented in. toString() converts in the other direction and may also take a radix argument. toBinaryString(), toOctalString(), and toHexString() convert a long to a string using base 2, base 8, and base 16. These methods treat the long as an unsigned value. Other routines return the value of a Long as various primitive types, and, finally, the getLong() methods return the long value of a named property or the value of the specified default.

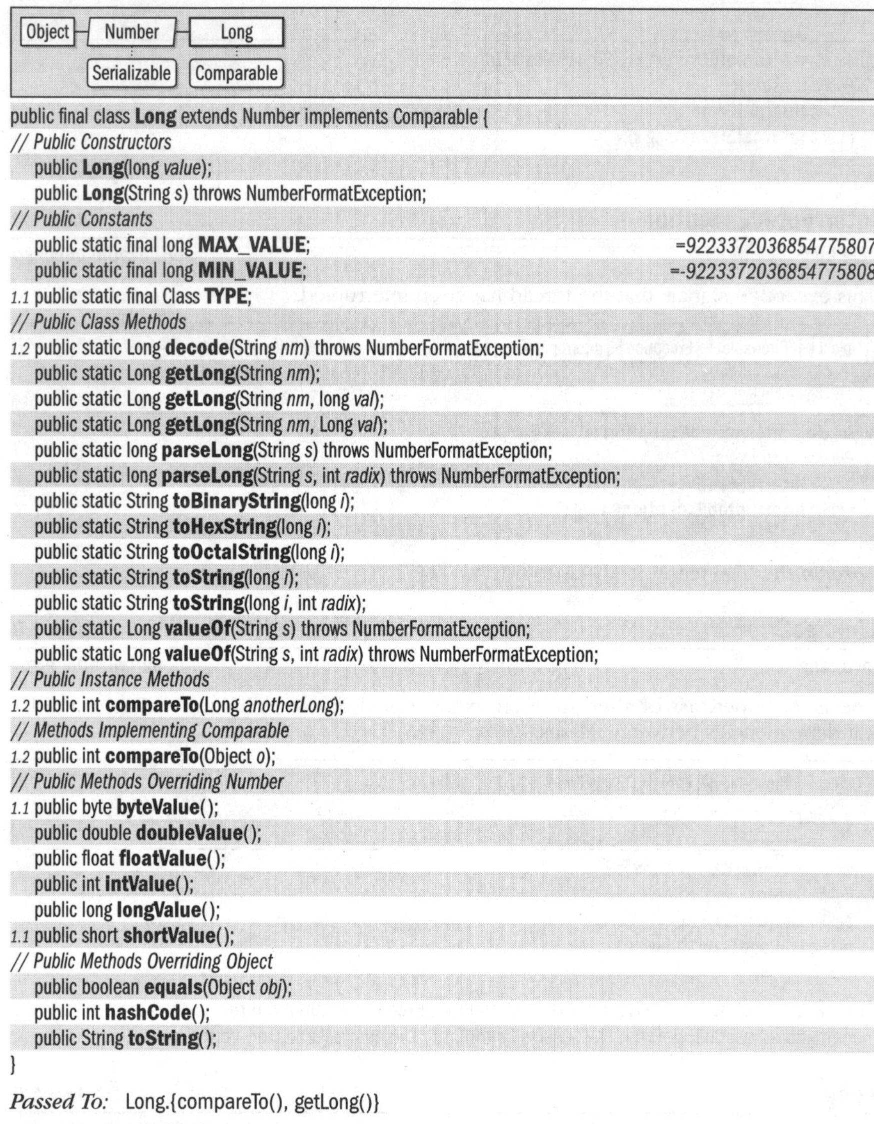


```
public final class Long extends Number implements Comparable {
// Public Constructors
   public Long(long value);
   public Long(String s) throws NumberFormatException;
// Public Constants
   public static final long MAX_VALUE;                          =9223372036854775807
   public static final long MIN_VALUE;                          =-9223372036854775808
1.1 public static final Class TYPE;
// Public Class Methods
1.2 public static Long decode(String nm) throws NumberFormatException;
   public static Long getLong(String nm);
   public static Long getLong(String nm, long val);
   public static Long getLong(String nm, Long val);
   public static long parseLong(String s) throws NumberFormatException;
   public static long parseLong(String s, int radix) throws NumberFormatException;
   public static String toBinaryString(long i);
   public static String toHexString(long i);
   public static String toOctalString(long i);
   public static String toString(long i);
   public static String toString(long i, int radix);
   public static Long valueOf(String s) throws NumberFormatException;
   public static Long valueOf(String s, int radix) throws NumberFormatException;
// Public Instance Methods
1.2 public int compareTo(Long anotherLong);
// Methods Implementing Comparable
1.2 public int compareTo(Object o);
// Public Methods Overriding Number
1.1 public byte byteValue();
   public double doubleValue();
   public float floatValue();
   public int intValue();
   public long longValue();
1.1 public short shortValue();
// Public Methods Overriding Object
   public boolean equals(Object obj);
   public int hashCode();
   public String toString();
}
```

Passed To: Long.{compareTo(), getLong()}

Returned By: Long.{decode(), getLong(), valueOf()}

Math **Java 1.0**

java.lang

This class defines constants for the mathematical values *e* and π and defines static methods for floating-point trigonometry, exponentiation, and other operations. It is the equivalent of the C <*math.h*> functions. It also contains methods for computing minimum and maximum values and for generating pseudo-random numbers.

Most methods of Math operate on float and double floating-point values. Remember that these values are only approximations of actual real numbers. To allow implementations to take full advantage of the floating-point capabilities of a native platform, the methods of Math are not required to return exactly the same values on all platforms. In other words, the results returned by different implementations may differ slightly in the least-significant bits. In Java 1.3, applications that require strict platform-independence of results should use StrictMath instead.

```
public final class Math {
// No Constructor
// Public Constants
   public static final double E;                                        =2.718281828459045
   public static final double PI;                                       =3.141592653589793
// Public Class Methods
   public static int abs(int a);                                                 strictfp
   public static long abs(long a);                                               strictfp
   public static float abs(float a);                                             strictfp
   public static double abs(double a);                                           strictfp
   public static double acos(double a);                                          strictfp
   public static double asin(double a);                                          strictfp
   public static double atan(double a);                                          strictfp
   public static double atan2(double y, double x);                               strictfp
   public static double ceil(double a);                                          strictfp
   public static double cos(double a);                                           strictfp
   public static double exp(double a);                                           strictfp
   public static double floor(double a);                                         strictfp
   public static double IEEEremainder(double f1, double f2);                     strictfp
   public static double log(double a);                                           strictfp
   public static int max(int a, int b);                                          strictfp
   public static long max(long a, long b);                                       strictfp
   public static float max(float a, float b);                                    strictfp
   public static double max(double a, double b);                                 strictfp
   public static int min(int a, int b);                                          strictfp
   public static long min(long a, long b);                                       strictfp
   public static float min(float a, float b);                                    strictfp
   public static double min(double a, double b);                                 strictfp
   public static double pow(double a, double b);                                 strictfp
   public static double random();                                                strictfp
   public static double rint(double a);                                          strictfp
   public static int round(float a);                                             strictfp
   public static long round(double a);                                           strictfp
   public static double sin(double a);                                           strictfp
   public static double sqrt(double a);                                          strictfp
   public static double tan(double a);                                           strictfp
1.2 public static double toDegrees(double angrad);                               strictfp
1.2 public static double toRadians(double angdeg);                               strictfp
}
```

NegativeArraySizeException — Java 1.0

java.lang — ***serializable unchecked***

This exception signals an attempt to allocate an array with fewer than zero elements.

Object ─ Throwable ─ Exception ─ RuntimeException ─ NegativeArraySizeException
Throwable ⋮ Serializable

```
public class NegativeArraySizeException extends RuntimeException {
// Public Constructors
   public NegativeArraySizeException();
   public NegativeArraySizeException(String s);
}
```

Thrown By: java.lang.reflect.Array.newInstance()

NoClassDefFoundError — Java 1.0

java.lang — ***serializable error***

This error signals that the definition of a specified class cannot be found.

Object ─ Throwable ─ Error ─ LinkageError ─ NoClassDefFoundError
Throwable ⋮ Serializable

```
public class NoClassDefFoundError extends LinkageError {
// Public Constructors
   public NoClassDefFoundError();
   public NoClassDefFoundError(String s);
}
```

NoSuchFieldError — Java 1.0

java.lang — ***serializable error***

This error signals that a specified field cannot be found.

Object ─ Throwable ─ Error ─ LinkageError ─ IncompatibleClassChangeError ─ NoSuchFieldError
Throwable ⋮ Serializable

```
public class NoSuchFieldError extends IncompatibleClassChangeError {
// Public Constructors
   public NoSuchFieldError();
   public NoSuchFieldError(String s);
}
```

NoSuchFieldException — Java 1.1

java.lang — ***serializable checked***

This exception signals that the specified field does not exist in the specified class.

Object ─ Throwable ─ Exception ─ NoSuchFieldException
Throwable ⋮ Serializable

```
public class NoSuchFieldException extends Exception {
// Public Constructors
    public NoSuchFieldException();
    public NoSuchFieldException(String s);
}
```

Thrown By: Class.{getDeclaredField(), getField()}

NoSuchMethodError — Java 1.0

java.lang — *serializable error*

This error signals that a specified method cannot be found.

Object → Throwable → Error → LinkageError → IncompatibleClassChangeError → NoSuchMethodError (Throwable implements Serializable)

```
public class NoSuchMethodError extends IncompatibleClassChangeError {
// Public Constructors
    public NoSuchMethodError();
    public NoSuchMethodError(String s);
}
```

NoSuchMethodException — Java 1.0

java.lang — *serializable checked*

This exception signals that the specified method does not exist in the specified class.

Object → Throwable → Exception → NoSuchMethodException (Throwable implements Serializable)

```
public class NoSuchMethodException extends Exception {
// Public Constructors
    public NoSuchMethodException();
    public NoSuchMethodException(String s);
}
```

Thrown By: Class.{getConstructor(), getDeclaredConstructor(), getDeclaredMethod(), getMethod()}

NullPointerException — Java 1.0

java.lang — *serializable unchecked*

This exception signals an attempt to access a field or invoke a method of a null object.

Object → Throwable → Exception → RuntimeException → NullPointerException (Throwable implements Serializable)

```
public class NullPointerException extends RuntimeException {
// Public Constructors
    public NullPointerException();
    public NullPointerException(String s);
}
```

Thrown By: java.awt.print.PrinterJob.setPageable(), org.xml.sax.helpers.ParserFactory.makeParser()

Number

Java 1.0

java.lang *serializable*

This is an abstract class that is the superclass of Byte, Short, Integer, Long, Float, and Double. It defines the conversion functions those types implement.

Object — Number ··· Serializable

```
public abstract class Number implements Serializable {
// Public Constructors
   public Number();
// Public Instance Methods
1.1 public byte byteValue();
   public abstract double doubleValue();
   public abstract float floatValue();
   public abstract int intValue();
   public abstract long longValue();
1.1 public short shortValue();
}
```

Subclasses: Byte, Double, Float, Integer, Long, Short, java.math.BigDecimal, java.math.BigInteger

Passed To: Too many methods to list.

Returned By: Too many methods to list.

NumberFormatException

Java 1.0

java.lang *serializable unchecked*

This exception signals an illegal number format.

Object — Throwable — Exception — RuntimeException — IllegalArgumentException — NumberFormatException

Serializable

```
public class NumberFormatException extends IllegalArgumentException {
// Public Constructors
   public NumberFormatException();
   public NumberFormatException(String s);
}
```

Thrown By: Too many methods to list.

Object

Java 1.0

java.lang

This is the root class in Java. All classes are subclasses of Object, and thus all objects can invoke the public and protected methods of this class. For classes that implement the Cloneable interface, clone() makes a byte-for-byte copy of an Object. getClass() returns the Class object associated with any Object, and the notify(), notifyAll(), and wait() methods are used for thread synchronization on a given Object.

A number of these Object methods should be overridden by subclasses of Object. For example, a subclass should provide its own definition of the toString() method so that it can be used with the string concatenation operator and with the PrintWriter.println() methods. Defining the toString() method for all objects also helps with debugging.

The default implementation of the equals() method simply uses the == operator to test whether this object reference and the specified object reference refer to the same object. Many subclasses override this method to compare the individual fields of two distinct objects (i.e., they override the method to test for the equivalence of distinct objects rather than the equality of object references). Some classes, particularly those that override equals(), may also want to override the hashCode() method to provide an appropriate hashcode to be used when storing instances in a Hashtable data structure.

A class that allocates system resources other than memory (such as file descriptors or windowing system graphic contexts) should override the finalize() method to release these resources when the object is no longer referred to and is about to be garbage collected.

```
public class Object {
// Public Constructors
   public Object();                                                          empty
// Public Instance Methods
   public boolean equals(Object obj);
   public final Class getClass();                                             native
   public int hashCode();                                                    native
   public final void notify();                                               native
   public final void notifyAll();                                            native
   public String toString();
   public final void wait() throws InterruptedException;
   public final void wait(long timeout) throws InterruptedException;         native
   public final void wait(long timeout, int nanos) throws InterruptedException;
// Protected Instance Methods
   protected Object clone() throws CloneNotSupportedException;               native
   protected void finalize() throws Throwable;                               empty
}
```

Subclasses: Too many classes to list.

Passed To: Too many methods to list.

Returned By: Too many methods to list.

Type Of: Too many fields to list.

OutOfMemoryError — Java 1.0

java.lang — *serializable error*

This error signals that the interpreter has run out of memory (and that garbage collection is unable to free any memory).

Object — Throwable — Error — VirtualMachineError — OutOfMemoryError
Serializable

```
public class OutOfMemoryError extends VirtualMachineError {
// Public Constructors
   public OutOfMemoryError();
   public OutOfMemoryError(String s);
}
```

Package — Java 1.2

java.lang

This class represents a Java package. You can obtain the Package object for a given Class by calling the getPackage() method of the Class object. The static Package.getPackage() method returns a Package object for the named package, if any such package has been loaded by the current class loader. Similarly, the static Package.getPackages() returns all Package objects that have been loaded by the current class loader. Note that a Package object is not defined unless at least one class has been loaded from that package. Although you can obtain the Package of a given Class, you cannot obtain an array of Class objects contained in a specified Package.

If the classes that comprise a package are contained in a JAR file that has the appropriate attributes set in its manifest file, the Package object allows you to query the title, vendor, and version of both the package specification and the package implementation; all six values are strings. The specification version string has a special format. It consists of one or more integers, separated from each other by periods. Each integer can have leading zeros, but is not considered an octal digit. Increasing numbers indicate later versions. The isCompatibleWith() method calls getSpecificationVersion() to obtain the specification version and compares it with the version string supplied as an argument. If the package-specification version is the same as or greater than the specified string, isCompatibleWith() returns true. This allows you to test whether the version of a package (typically a standard extension) is new enough for the purposes of your application.

Packages may be sealed, which means that all classes in the package must come from the same JAR file. If a package is sealed, the no-argument version of isSealed() returns true. The one-argument version of isSealed() returns true if the specified URL represents the JAR file from which the package is loaded.

```
public class Package {
// No Constructor
// Public Class Methods
   public static Package getPackage(String name);
   public static Package[ ] getPackages();
// Property Accessor Methods (by property name)
   public String getImplementationTitle();
   public String getImplementationVendor();
   public String getImplementationVersion();
   public String getName();
   public boolean isSealed();
   public boolean isSealed(java.net.URL url);
   public String getSpecificationTitle();
   public String getSpecificationVendor();
   public String getSpecificationVersion();
// Public Instance Methods
   public boolean isCompatibleWith(String desired) throws NumberFormatException;
// Public Methods Overriding Object
   public int hashCode();
   public String toString();
}
```

Returned By: Class.getPackage(), ClassLoader.{definePackage(), getPackage(), getPackages()}, Package.{getPackage(), getPackages()}, java.net.URLClassLoader.definePackage()

Process — Java 1.0

java.lang

This class describes a process that is running externally to the Java interpreter. Note that a Process is very different from a Thread; the Process class is abstract and cannot be instantiated. Call one of the Runtime.exec() methods to start a process and return a corresponding Process object.

waitFor() blocks until the process exits. exitValue() returns the exit code of the process. destroy() kills the process. getErrorStream() returns an InputStream from which you can read any bytes the process sends to its standard error stream. getInputStream() returns an InputStream from which you can read any bytes the process sends to its standard output stream. getOutputStream() returns an OutputStream you can use to send bytes to the standard input stream of the process.

```
public abstract class Process {
// Public Constructors
   public Process();
// Property Accessor Methods (by property name)
   public abstract java.io.InputStream getErrorStream();
   public abstract java.io.InputStream getInputStream();
   public abstract java.io.OutputStream getOutputStream();
// Public Instance Methods
   public abstract void destroy();
   public abstract int exitValue();
   public abstract int waitFor() throws InterruptedException;
}
```

Returned By: Runtime.exec()

Runnable — Java 1.0

java.lang — *runnable*

This interface specifies the run() method that is required to use with the Thread class. Any class that implements this interface can provide the body of a thread. See Thread for more information.

```
public interface Runnable {
// Public Instance Methods
   public abstract void run();
}
```

Implementations: java.awt.image.renderable.RenderableImageProducer, Thread, java.util.TimerTask, javax.swing.text.AsyncBoxView.ChildState

Passed To: java.awt.EventQueue.{invokeAndWait(), invokeLater()}, java.awt.event.InvocationEvent.InvocationEvent(), Thread.Thread(), javax.swing.SwingUtilities.{invokeAndWait(), invokeLater()}, javax.swing.text.AbstractDocument.render(), javax.swing.text.Document.render(), javax.swing.text.LayoutQueue.addTask()

Returned By: javax.swing.text.LayoutQueue.waitForWork()

Type Of: java.awt.event.InvocationEvent.runnable

Runtime — Java 1.0

java.lang

This class encapsulates a number of platform-dependent system functions. The static method getRuntime() returns the Runtime object for the current platform; this object can perform system functions in a platform-independent way.

exit() causes the Java interpreter to exit and return a specified return code. This method is usually invoked through System.exit(). In Java 1.3, addShutdownHook() registers an unstarted Thread object that is run when the virtual machine shuts down, either through a call to exit() or through a user interrupt (a Ctrl-C, for example). The purpose of a shutdown hook is to perform necessary cleanup, such as shutting down network connections, deleting temporary files, and so on. Any number of hooks can be registered with addShutdownHook(). Before the interpreter exits, it starts all registered shutdown-hook threads and lets them run concurrently. Any hooks you write should perform their cleanup operation and exit promptly so they do not delay the shutdown process. To remove a shutdown hook before it is run, call removeShutdownHook(). To force an immediate exit that does not invoke the shutdown hooks, call halt().

exec() starts a new process running externally to the interpreter. Note that any processes run outside of Java may be system-dependent.

freeMemory() returns the approximate amount of free memory. totalMemory() returns the total amount of memory available to the Java interpreter. gc() forces the garbage collector to run synchronously, which may free up more memory. Similarly, runFinalization() forces the finalize() methods of unreferenced objects to be run immediately. This may free up system resources those objects were holding.

load() loads a dynamic library with a fully specified pathname. loadLibrary() loads a dynamic library with only the library name specified; it looks in platform-dependent locations for the specified library. These libraries generally contain native code definitions for native methods.

traceInstructions() and traceMethodCalls() enable and disable tracing by the interpreter. These methods are used for debugging or profiling an application. It is not specified how the VM emits the trace information, and VMs are not even required to support this feature.

Note that some of the Runtime methods are more commonly called via the static methods of the System class.

```
public class Runtime {
// No Constructor
// Public Class Methods
    public static Runtime getRuntime();
// Public Instance Methods
1.3 public void addShutdownHook(Thread hook);
1.4 public int availableProcessors();                                    native
    public Process exec(String[ ] cmdarray) throws java.io.IOException;
    public Process exec(String command) throws java.io.IOException;
    public Process exec(String cmd, String[ ] envp) throws java.io.IOException;
    public Process exec(String[ ] cmdarray, String[ ] envp) throws java.io.IOException;
1.3 public Process exec(String[ ] cmdarray, String[ ] envp, java.io.File dir) throws java.io.IOException;
1.3 public Process exec(String command, String[ ] envp, java.io.File dir) throws java.io.IOException;
    public void exit(int status);
    public long freeMemory();                                            native
    public void gc();                                                    native
1.3 public void halt(int status);
    public void load(String filename);
    public void loadLibrary(String libname);
1.4 public long maxMemory();                                             native
1.3 public boolean removeShutdownHook(Thread hook);
    public void runFinalization();
    public long totalMemory();                                           native
    public void traceInstructions(boolean on);                           native
    public void traceMethodCalls(boolean on);                            native
// Deprecated Public Methods
#   public java.io.InputStream getLocalizedInputStream(java.io.InputStream in);
#   public java.io.OutputStream getLocalizedOutputStream(java.io.OutputStream out);
1.1# public static void runFinalizersOnExit(boolean value);
}
```

Returned By: Runtime.getRuntime()

RuntimeException — Java 1.0

java.lang — *serializable unchecked*

This exception type is not used directly, but serves as a superclass of a group of runtime exceptions that need not be declared in the throws clause of a method definition.

These exceptions need not be declared because they are runtime conditions that can generally occur in any Java method. Thus, declaring them would be unduly burdensome, and Java does not require it.

This class inherits methods from Throwable but declares none of its own. Each of the RuntimeException constructors simply invokes the corresponding Exception() and Throwable() constructor. See Throwable for details.

```
Object ─ Throwable ─ Exception ─ RuntimeException
         Serializable
```

```
public class RuntimeException extends Exception {
// Public Constructors
    public RuntimeException();
1.4 public RuntimeException(Throwable cause);
    public RuntimeException(String message);
1.4 public RuntimeException(String message, Throwable cause);
}
```

Subclasses: Too many classes to list.

RuntimePermission — Java 1.2

java.lang — ***serializable permission***

This class is a java.security.Permission that represents access to various important system facilities. A RuntimePermission has a name, or target, that represents the facility for which permission is being sought or granted. The name "exitVM" represents permission to call System.exit(), and the name "accessClassInPackage.java.lang" represents permission to read classes from the java.lang package. The name of a RuntimePermission may use a ".*" suffix as a wildcard. For example, the name "accessClassInPackage.java.*" represents permission to read classes from any package whose name begins with "java.". RuntimePermission does not use action list strings as some Permission classes do; the name of the permission alone is enough.

Supported RuntimePermssion names are: "accessClassInPackage.*package*", "accessDeclaredMembers", "createClassLoader", "createSecurityManager", "defineClassInPackage.*package*", "exitVM", "getClassLoader", "getProtectionDomain", "loadLibrary.*library_name*", "modifyThread", "modifyThreadGroup", "queuePrintJob", "readFileDescriptor", "set-ContextClassLoader", "setFactory", "setIO", "setSecurityManager", "stopThread", and "writeFileDescriptor".

System administrators configuring security policies should be familiar with these permission names, the operations they govern access to, and with the risks inherent in granting any of them. Although system programmers may need to work with this class, application programmers should never need to use RuntimePermssion directly.

```
Object ─ Permission ─ BasicPermission ─ RuntimePermission
Guard    Serializable  Serializable
```

```
public final class RuntimePermission extends java.security.BasicPermission {
// Public Constructors
    public RuntimePermission(String name);
    public RuntimePermission(String name, String actions);
}
```

SecurityException — Java 1.0

java.lang — *serializable unchecked*

This exception signals that an operation is not permitted for security reasons.

Object ─ Throwable ─ Exception ─ RuntimeException ─ SecurityException
Serializable

```
public class SecurityException extends RuntimeException {
// Public Constructors
   public SecurityException();
   public SecurityException(String s);
}
```

Subclasses: java.rmi.RMISecurityException, java.security.AccessControlException

Thrown By: Too many methods to list.

SecurityManager — Java 1.0

java.lang

This class defines the methods necessary to implement a security policy for the safe execution of untrusted code. Before performing potentially sensitive operations, Java calls methods of the SecurityManager object currently in effect to determine whether the operations are permitted. These methods throw a SecurityException if the operation is not permitted. Typical applications do not need to use or subclass SecurityManager. It is typically used only by web browsers, applet viewers, and other programs that need to run untrusted code in a controlled environment.

Prior to Java 1.2, this class is abstract, and the default implementation of each check() method throws a SecurityException unconditionally. The Java security mechanism has been overhauled as of Java 1.2. As part of the overhaul, this class is no longer abstract and its methods have useful default implementations, so there is rarely a need to subclass it. If so, the method returns silently; if not, it throws a SecurityException. checkPermission() operates by invoking the checkPermission() method of the system java.security.AccessController object. In Java 1.2 and later, all other check() methods of SecurityManager are now implemented on top of checkPermission().

```
public class SecurityManager {
// Public Constructors
   public SecurityManager();
// Property Accessor Methods (by property name)
   public Object getSecurityContext();                    default:AccessControlContext
1.1 public ThreadGroup getThreadGroup();
// Public Instance Methods
   public void checkAccept(String host, int port);
   public void checkAccess(ThreadGroup g);
   public void checkAccess(Thread t);
1.1 public void checkAwtEventQueueAccess();
   public void checkConnect(String host, int port);
   public void checkConnect(String host, int port, Object context);
   public void checkCreateClassLoader();
   public void checkDelete(String file);
   public void checkExec(String cmd);
   public void checkExit(int status);
   public void checkLink(String lib);
   public void checkListen(int port);
```

```
1.1 public void checkMemberAccess(Class clazz, int which);
1.1 public void checkMulticast(java.net.InetAddress maddr);
    public void checkPackageAccess(String pkg);
    public void checkPackageDefinition(String pkg);
1.2 public void checkPermission(java.security.Permission perm);
1.2 public void checkPermission(java.security.Permission perm, Object context);
1.1 public void checkPrintJobAccess();
    public void checkPropertiesAccess();
    public void checkPropertyAccess(String key);
    public void checkRead(String file);
    public void checkRead(java.io.FileDescriptor fd);
    public void checkRead(String file, Object context);
1.1 public void checkSecurityAccess(String target);
    public void checkSetFactory();
1.1 public void checkSystemClipboardAccess();
    public boolean checkTopLevelWindow(Object window);
    public void checkWrite(java.io.FileDescriptor fd);
    public void checkWrite(String file);
// Protected Instance Methods
    protected Class[ ] getClassContext();                                    native
// Deprecated Public Methods
1.1# public void checkMulticast(java.net.InetAddress maddr, byte ttl);
#   public boolean getInCheck();                                       default:false
// Deprecated Protected Methods
#   protected int classDepth(String name);                                   native
#   protected int classLoaderDepth();
#   protected ClassLoader currentClassLoader();
1.1# protected Class currentLoadedClass();
#   protected boolean inClass(String name);
#   protected boolean inClassLoader();
// Deprecated Protected Fields
#   protected boolean inCheck;
}
```

Subclasses: java.rmi.RMISecurityManager

Passed To: System.setSecurityManager()

Returned By: System.getSecurityManager()

Short — Java 1.1

java.lang — ***serializable comparable***

This class provides an object wrapper around the short primitive type. It defines useful constants for the minimum and maximum values that can be stored by the short type, and also a Class object constant that represents the short type. It also provides various methods for converting Short values to and from strings and other numeric types.

Most of the static methods of this class can convert a String to a Short object or a short value; the four parseShort() and valueOf() methods parse a number from the specified string using an optionally specified radix and return it in one of these two forms. The decode() method parses a number specified in base 10, base 8, or base 16 and returns it as a Short. If the string begins with "0x" or "#", it is interpreted as a hexadecimal number; if it begins with "0", it is interpreted as an octal number. Otherwise, it is interpreted as a decimal number.

Note that this class has two different toString() methods. One is static and converts a short primitive value to a string. The other is the usual toString() method that converts a

Short object to a string. Most of the remaining methods convert a Short to various primitive numeric types.


```
public final class Short extends Number implements Comparable {
// Public Constructors
    public Short(short value);
    public Short(String s) throws NumberFormatException;
// Public Constants
    public static final short MAX_VALUE;                                    =32767
    public static final short MIN_VALUE;                                    =-32768
    public static final Class TYPE;
// Public Class Methods
    public static Short decode(String nm) throws NumberFormatException;
    public static short parseShort(String s) throws NumberFormatException;
    public static short parseShort(String s, int radix) throws NumberFormatException;
    public static String toString(short s);
    public static Short valueOf(String s) throws NumberFormatException;
    public static Short valueOf(String s, int radix) throws NumberFormatException;
// Public Instance Methods
1.2 public int compareTo(Short anotherShort);
// Methods Implementing Comparable
1.2 public int compareTo(Object o);
// Public Methods Overriding Number
    public byte byteValue();
    public double doubleValue();
    public float floatValue();
    public int intValue();
    public long longValue();
    public short shortValue();
// Public Methods Overriding Object
    public boolean equals(Object obj);
    public int hashCode();
    public String toString();
}
```

Passed To: Short.compareTo()

Returned By: Short.{decode(), valueOf()}

StackOverflowError — Java 1.0

java.lang — *serializable error*

This error signals that a stack overflow has occurred within the Java interpreter.


```
public class StackOverflowError extends VirtualMachineError {
// Public Constructors
    public StackOverflowError();
    public StackOverflowError(String s);
}
```

StackTraceElement — Java 1.4

java.lang — *serializable*

Instances of this class are returned in an array by Throwable.getStackTrace(). Each instance represents one frame in the stack trace associated with an exception or error. getClassName() and getMethodName() return the name of the class (including package name) and method that contain the point of execution that the stack frame represents. If the class file contains sufficient information, getFileName() and getLineNumber() return the source file and line number associated with the frame. getFileName() returns null and getLineNumber() returns a negative value if source or line number information is not available. isNativeMethod() returns true if the named method is a native method (and therefore, does not have a meaningful source file or line number).

Object ─ StackTraceElement ··· Serializable

```
public final class StackTraceElement implements Serializable {
// No Constructor
// Property Accessor Methods (by property name)
   public String getClassName();
   public String getFileName();
   public int getLineNumber();
   public String getMethodName();
   public boolean isNativeMethod();
// Public Methods Overriding Object
   public boolean equals(Object obj);
   public int hashCode();
   public String toString();
}
```

Passed To: Throwable.setStackTrace()

Returned By: Throwable.getStackTrace()

StrictMath — Java 1.3

java.lang

This class is identical to the Math class, but additionally requires that its methods strictly adhere to the behavior of certain published algorithms. The methods of StrictMath are intended to operate identically, down to the least significant bit, for all possible arguments. When strict platform independence of floating-point results is not required, use the Math class for better performance.

```
public final class StrictMath {
// No Constructor
// Public Constants
   public static final double E;                                   =2.718281828459045
   public static final double PI;                                  =3.141592653589793
// Public Class Methods
   public static int abs(int a);                                             strictfp
   public static long abs(long a);                                           strictfp
   public static float abs(float a);                                         strictfp
   public static double abs(double a);                                       strictfp
   public static double acos(double a);                               native strictfp
   public static double asin(double a);                               native strictfp
   public static double atan(double a);                               native strictfp
   public static double atan2(double y, double x);                    native strictfp
   public static double ceil(double a);                               native strictfp
```

```
    public static double cos(double a);                                    native strictfp
    public static double exp(double a);                                    native strictfp
    public static double floor(double a);                                  native strictfp
    public static double IEEEremainder(double f1, double f2);              native strictfp
    public static double log(double a);                                    native strictfp
    public static int max(int a, int b);                                          strictfp
    public static long max(long a, long b);                                       strictfp
    public static float max(float a, float b);                                    strictfp
    public static double max(double a, double b);                                 strictfp
    public static int min(int a, int b);                                          strictfp
    public static long min(long a, long b);                                       strictfp
    public static float min(float a, float b);                                    strictfp
    public static double min(double a, double b);                                 strictfp
    public static double pow(double a, double b);                          native strictfp
    public static double random();                                                strictfp
    public static double rint(double a);                                   native strictfp
    public static int round(float a);                                             strictfp
    public static long round(double a);                                           strictfp
    public static double sin(double a);                                    native strictfp
    public static double sqrt(double a);                                   native strictfp
    public static double tan(double a);                                    native strictfp
    public static double toDegrees(double angrad);                                strictfp
    public static double toRadians(double angdeg);                                strictfp
}
```

String — Java 1.0

java.lang — *serializable comparable*

The String class represents a read-only string of characters. A String object is created by the Java compiler whenever it encounters a string in double quotes; typically, this method of creation is simpler than using a constructor. The static valueOf() factory methods create new String objects that hold the textual representation of various Java primitive types. There are also valueOf() methods, copyValueOf() methods, and String() constructors for creating a String object that holds a copy of the text contained in a char array or subarray. All three variants perform an identical function. You can also use the String() constructor to create a String object from an array or subarray of bytes. If you do this, you may explicitly specify the name of the charset (or character encoding) to be used to decode the bytes into characters, or you can rely on the default charset for your platform. (See java.nio.charset.Charset for more on charset names.)

length() returns the number of characters in a string. charAt() extracts a character from a string. You can use these two methods to iterate through the characters of a string. You can obtain a char array that holds the characters of a string with toCharArray() or use getChars() to copy only a selected region of the string into an existing array. Use getBytes() to obtain an array of bytes that contains the encoded form of the characters in a string, using either the platform's default encoding or a named encoding.

This class defines many methods for comparing strings and substrings. equals() returns true if two String objects contain the same text, and equalsIgnoreCase() returns true if two strings are equal when uppercase and lowercase differences are ignored. In Java 1.4, the contentEquals() method compares a string to a specified StringBuffer object, returning true if they contain the same text. startsWith() and endsWith() return true if a string starts with the specified prefix string or ends with the specified suffix string. There is a two-argument version of startsWith() that allows you to specify a position within this string where the prefix comparison will be done. The regionMatches() method is a generalized version of this startsWith() method. It returns true if the specified region of the specified string matches the characters that begin at a specified position within the string. The five-argument version of this method allows you to perform this comparison ignoring the cases of the characters being compared. The final string comparison method is matches(), which, as described later, compares a string to a regular expression pattern.

compareTo() is another string comparison method, but it is used for comparing the order of two strings, rather than simply comparing them for equality. compareTo() implements the Comparable interface and enables sorting of lists and arrays of String objects. See Comparable for more information. compareToIgnoreCase() is like compareTo() but ignores the case of the two strings when doing the comparison. The CASE_INSENSITIVE_ORDER constant is a Comparator for sorting strings in a way that ignores the case of their characters. (The java.util.Comparator interface is similar to the Comparable interface but allows the definition of object orderings that are different than the default ordering defined by Comparable.) The compareTo() and compareToIgnoreCase() methods and the CASE_INSENSITIVE_ORDER Comparator object order strings based only on the numeric ordering of the Unicode encoding of their characters. This is not always the preferred "alphabetical ordering" in some languages. See java.text.Collator for a more general technique for collating strings.

indexOf() and lastIndexOf() search forward and backward in a string for a specified character or substring. They return the position of the match, or –1 if there is no match. The one-argument versions of these methods start at the beginning or end of the string, and the two-argument versions start searching from a specified character position.

substring() returns a string that consists of the characters from (and including) the specified start position to (but not including) the specified end position. There is also a one-argument version that returns all characters from (and including) the specified start position to the end of the string. In Java 1.4, the String class implements the CharSequence interface and defines the subSequence() methods, which works just like the two-argument version of substring() but returns the specified characters as a CharSequence rather than as a String.

Several methods return new strings that contain modified versions of the text held by the original string (the original string remains unchanged). replace() creates a new string with all occurrences of one character replaced by another. More general methods, replaceAll() and replaceFirst(), use regular expression pattern matching; they are described later. toUpperCase() and toLowerCase() return a new string in which all characters have been converted to upper- or lowercase. These case-conversion methods take an optional Locale argument to perform locale-specific case conversion. trim() is a utility method that returns a new string in which all leading and trailing whitespace has been removed. concat() returns the new string formed by concatenating or appending the specified string to this string. String concatenation is more commonly done, however, with the + operator.

Note that String objects are immutable; there is no setCharAt() method to change the contents. The methods that return a String do not modify the string on which they are invoked but instead return a new String object that holds a modified copy of the text of the original. Use a StringBuffer if you want to manipulate the contents of a string or call toCharArray() or getChars() to convert a string to an array of char values.

Java 1.4 introduces support for pattern matching with regular expressions. matches() returns true if this string exactly matches the pattern specified by the regular expression argument. replaceAll() and replaceFirst() create a new string in which all occurrences or the first occurrence of a substring that matches the specified regular expression is replaced with the specified replacement string. And the split() methods return an array of substrings of this string, formed by splitting this string at positions that match the specified regular expression. These regular expression methods are all convenience methods that simply call methods of the same name in the java.util.regex package. See the Pattern and Matcher classes in that package for further details.

Many programs use strings as often as they use Java primitive values. Because the String type is an object rather than a primitive value, however, you cannot generally use the == operator to compare two strings for equality. Even though strings are immutable, you must instead use the more expensive equals() method. For programs that perform a lot of string comparison, the intern() provides a way to speed up those comparisons. The String class maintains a set of String objects that includes all double-quoted string literals and all compile-time constant strings defined in a Java program. The set is guaranteed not to contain duplicates and ensures that duplicate String objects are not created unnecessarily. The intern() method looks up a string in or adds a new string to this set of unique strings. It searches the set for a string that contains exactly the same characters as the string you invoked the method on. If such a string is found, intern() returns it. If no matching string is found, the string you invoked intern() on is itself stored in the set ("interned") and becomes the return value of the method. What this means is that you can safely compare any strings returned by the intern() method using the == and != operators instead of equals(). You can also successfully compare any string returned by intern() to any string constant with == and !=.

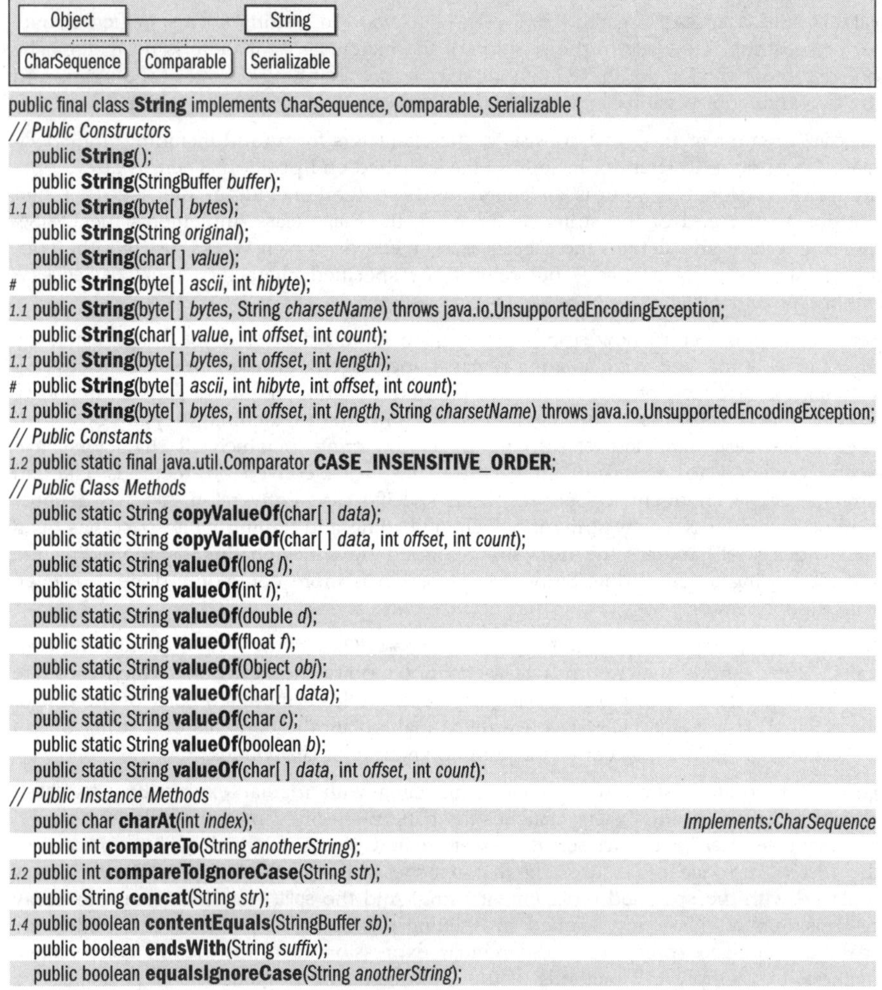


```
public final class String implements CharSequence, Comparable, Serializable {
// Public Constructors
    public String();
    public String(StringBuffer buffer);
1.1 public String(byte[ ] bytes);
    public String(String original);
    public String(char[ ] value);
#   public String(byte[ ] ascii, int hibyte);
1.1 public String(byte[ ] bytes, String charsetName) throws java.io.UnsupportedEncodingException;
    public String(char[ ] value, int offset, int count);
1.1 public String(byte[ ] bytes, int offset, int length);
#   public String(byte[ ] ascii, int hibyte, int offset, int count);
1.1 public String(byte[ ] bytes, int offset, int length, String charsetName) throws java.io.UnsupportedEncodingException;
// Public Constants
1.2 public static final java.util.Comparator CASE_INSENSITIVE_ORDER;
// Public Class Methods
    public static String copyValueOf(char[ ] data);
    public static String copyValueOf(char[ ] data, int offset, int count);
    public static String valueOf(long l);
    public static String valueOf(int i);
    public static String valueOf(double d);
    public static String valueOf(float f);
    public static String valueOf(Object obj);
    public static String valueOf(char[ ] data);
    public static String valueOf(char c);
    public static String valueOf(boolean b);
    public static String valueOf(char[ ] data, int offset, int count);
// Public Instance Methods
    public char charAt(int index);                                    Implements:CharSequence
    public int compareTo(String anotherString);
1.2 public int compareToIgnoreCase(String str);
    public String concat(String str);
1.4 public boolean contentEquals(StringBuffer sb);
    public boolean endsWith(String suffix);
    public boolean equalsIgnoreCase(String anotherString);
```

```
1.1 public byte[ ] getBytes();
1.1 public byte[ ] getBytes(String charsetName) throws java.io.UnsupportedEncodingException;
    public void getChars(int srcBegin, int srcEnd, char[ ] dst, int dstBegin);
    public int indexOf(String str);
    public int indexOf(int ch);
    public int indexOf(String str, int fromIndex);
    public int indexOf(int ch, int fromIndex);
    public String intern();                                              native
    public int lastIndexOf(String str);
    public int lastIndexOf(int ch);
    public int lastIndexOf(String str, int fromIndex);
    public int lastIndexOf(int ch, int fromIndex);
    public int length();                                  Implements:CharSequence
1.4 public boolean matches(String regex);
    public boolean regionMatches(int toffset, String other, int ooffset, int len);
    public boolean regionMatches(boolean ignoreCase, int toffset, String other, int ooffset, int len);
    public String replace(char oldChar, char newChar);
1.4 public String replaceAll(String regex, String replacement);
1.4 public String replaceFirst(String regex, String replacement);
1.4 public String[ ] split(String regex);
1.4 public String[ ] split(String regex, int limit);
    public boolean startsWith(String prefix);
    public boolean startsWith(String prefix, int toffset);
    public String substring(int beginIndex);
    public String substring(int beginIndex, int endIndex);
    public char[ ] toCharArray();
    public String toLowerCase();
1.1 public String toLowerCase(java.util.Locale locale);
    public String toString();                             Implements:CharSequence
    public String toUpperCase();
1.1 public String toUpperCase(java.util.Locale locale);
    public String trim();
// Methods Implementing CharSequence
    public char charAt(int index);
    public int length();
1.4 public CharSequence subSequence(int beginIndex, int endIndex);
    public String toString();
// Methods Implementing Comparable
1.2 public int compareTo(Object o);
// Public Methods Overriding Object
    public boolean equals(Object anObject);
    public int hashCode();
// Deprecated Public Methods
#   public void getBytes(int srcBegin, int srcEnd, byte[ ] dst, int dstBegin);
}
```

Passed To: Too many methods to list.

Returned By: Too many methods to list.

Type Of: Too many fields to list.

StringBuffer — Java 1.0

java.lang — *serializable*

This class represents a mutable string of characters that can grow or shrink as necessary. Its mutability makes it suitable for processing text in place, which is not possible with the immutable String class. Its resizability and the various methods it implements make it easier to use than a char[]. Create a StringBuffer with the StringBuffer() constructor. You may pass a String that contains the initial text for the buffer to this constructor, but if you do not, the buffer will start out empty. You may also specify the initial capacity for the buffer if you can estimate the number of characters the buffer will eventually hold.

Query the character stored at a given index with charAt() and set or delete that character with setCharAt() or deleteCharAt(). Use length() to return the length of the buffer and setLength() to set the length of the buffer by truncating it or filling it with null characters ("\u0000") as necessary. capacity() returns the number of characters a StringBuffer can hold before its internal buffer will need to be reallocated. If you expect a StringBuffer to grow substantially and can approximate its eventual size, you can use ensureCapacity() to preallocate sufficient internal storage.

Use the various append() methods to append text to the end of the buffer. Use insert() to insert text at a specified position within the buffer. Note that in addition to strings, primitive values, and character arrays, arbitrary objects may be passed to append() and insert(). These values are converted to strings before they are appended or inserted. Use delete() to delete a range of characters from the buffer and use replace() to replace a range of characters with a specified String.

Call substring() to convert a portion of a StringBuffer to a String. The two versions of this method work just like the same-named methods of String. In Java 1.4, StringBuffer implements CharSequence, and therefore defines a subSequence() method that is like substring() but returns its value as a CharSequence. Also new in Java 1.4 is the addition of indexOf() and lastIndexOf() methods, which search forward or backward (from the optionally specified index) in a StringBuffer for a sequence of characters that matches the specified String. These methods return the index of the matching string or –1 if no match was found. See also the same-named methods of String after which these methods are modeled.

Call toString() to obtain the contents of a StringBuffer as a String object or use getChars() to extract the specified range of characters from the StringBuffer and store them into the specified character array starting at the specified index of that array.

String concatenation in Java is performed with the + operator and implemented using the append() method of a StringBuffer. After a string is processed in a StringBuffer object, it can be efficiently converted to a String object for subsequent use. The StringBuffer.toString() method is typically implemented so that it does not copy the internal array of characters. Instead, it shares that array with the new String object, making a new copy for itself only if and when further modifications are made to the StringBuffer object.

Object — StringBuffer

CharSequence | Serializable

```
public final class StringBuffer implements CharSequence, Serializable {
// Public Constructors
    public StringBuffer();
    public StringBuffer(int length);
    public StringBuffer(String str);
// Public Instance Methods
    public StringBuffer append(Object obj);                    synchronized
    public StringBuffer append(boolean b);
    public StringBuffer append(char c);                        synchronized
    public StringBuffer append(char[ ] str);                   synchronized
1.4 public StringBuffer append(StringBuffer sb);               synchronized
    public StringBuffer append(String str);                    synchronized
```

```
   public StringBuffer append(float f);
   public StringBuffer append(long l);
   public StringBuffer append(int i);
   public StringBuffer append(double d);
   public StringBuffer append(char[ ] str, int offset, int len);                        synchronized
   public int capacity( );                                                              synchronized
   public char charAt(int index);                              Implements:CharSequence synchronized
1.2 public StringBuffer delete(int start, int end);                                     synchronized
1.2 public StringBuffer deleteCharAt(int index);                                        synchronized
   public void ensureCapacity(int minimumCapacity);                                     synchronized
   public void getChars(int srcBegin, int srcEnd, char[ ] dst, int dstBegin);           synchronized
1.4 public int indexOf(String str);
1.4 public int indexOf(String str, int fromIndex);                                      synchronized
   public StringBuffer insert(int offset, boolean b);
   public StringBuffer insert(int offset, char[ ] str);                                 synchronized
   public StringBuffer insert(int offset, Object obj);                                  synchronized
   public StringBuffer insert(int offset, String str);                                  synchronized
   public StringBuffer insert(int offset, char c);                                      synchronized
   public StringBuffer insert(int offset, float f);
   public StringBuffer insert(int offset, double d);
   public StringBuffer insert(int offset, int i);
   public StringBuffer insert(int offset, long l);
1.2 public StringBuffer insert(int index, char[ ] str, int offset, int len);            synchronized
1.4 public int lastIndexOf(String str);                                                 synchronized
1.4 public int lastIndexOf(String str, int fromIndex);                                  synchronized
   public int length( );                                       Implements:CharSequence synchronized
1.2 public StringBuffer replace(int start, int end, String str);                        synchronized
   public StringBuffer reverse( );                                                      synchronized
   public void setCharAt(int index, char ch);                                           synchronized
   public void setLength(int newLength);                                                synchronized
1.2 public String substring(int start);                                                 synchronized
1.2 public String substring(int start, int end);                                        synchronized
   public String toString( );                                             Implements:CharSequence
// Methods Implementing CharSequence
   public char charAt(int index);                                                       synchronized
   public int length( );                                                                synchronized
1.4 public CharSequence subSequence(int start, int end);
   public String toString( );
}
```

Passed To: Too many methods to list.

Returned By: Too many methods to list.

StringIndexOutOfBoundsException — Java 1.0

java.lang — *serializable unchecked*

This exception signals that the index used to access a character of a String or StringBuffer is less than zero or is too large.

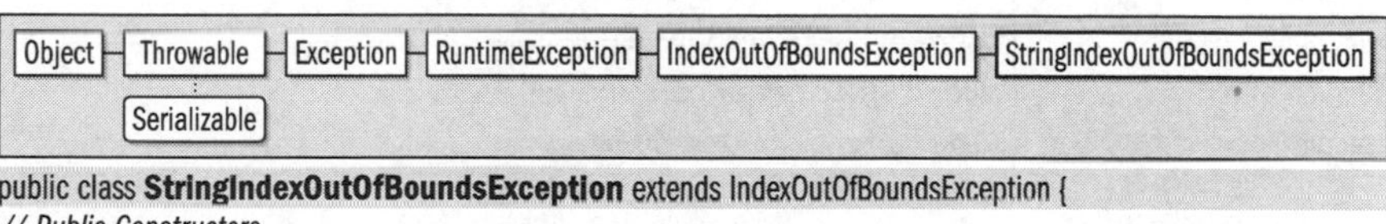


```
public class StringIndexOutOfBoundsException extends IndexOutOfBoundsException {
// Public Constructors
   public StringIndexOutOfBoundsException( );
```

```
    public StringIndexOutOfBoundsException(int index);
    public StringIndexOutOfBoundsException(String s);
}
```

System — Java 1.0

java.lang

This class defines a platform-independent interface to system facilities, including system properties and system input and output streams. All methods and variables of this class are static, and the class cannot be instantiated. Because the methods defined by this class are low-level system methods, most require special permissions and cannot be executed by untrusted code.

getProperty() looks up a named property on the system-properties list, returning the optionally specified default value if no property definition is found. getProperties() returns the entire properties list. setProperties() sets a Properties object on the properties list. In Java 1.2 and later, setProperty() sets the value of a system property. The following table lists system properties that are always defined. Untrusted code may be unable to read some or all of these properties. Additional properties can be defined using the -D option when invoking the Java interpreter.

Property name	*Description*
java.home	The directory Java is installed in
java.class.path	Where classes are loaded from
java.specification.version	Version of the Java API specification (Java 1.2)
java.specification.vendor	Vendor of the Java API specification (Java 1.2)
java.specification.name	Name of the Java API specification (Java 1.2)
java.version	Version of the Java API implementation
java.vendor	Vendor of this Java API implementation
java.vendor.url	URL of the vendor of this Java API implementation
java.vm.specification.version	Version of the Java VM specification (Java 1.2)
java.vm.specification.vendor	Vendor of the Java VM specification (Java 1.2)
java.vm.specification.name	Name of the Java VM specification (Java 1.2)
java.vm.version	Version of the Java VM implementation (Java 1.2)
java.vm.vendor	Vendor of the Java VM implementation (Java 1.2)
java.vm.name	Name of the Java VM implementation (Java 1.2)
java.class.version	Version of the Java class file format
os.name	Name of the host operating system
os.arch	Host operating system architecture
os.version	Version of the host operating system
file.separator	Platform directory separator character
path.separator	Platform path separator character
line.separator	Platform line separator character(s)
user.name	Current user's account name
user.home	Home directory of current user
user.dir	The current working directory

The in, out, and err fields hold the standard input, output, and error streams for the system. These fields are frequently used in calls such as System.out.println(). In Java 1.1, setIn(), setOut(), and setErr() allow these streams to be redirected.

System also defines various other useful static methods. exit() causes the Java VM to exit. arraycopy() efficiently copies an array or a portion of an array into a destination array. currentTimeMillis() returns the current time in milliseconds since midnight GMT, January 1, 1970 GMT. gc() requests that the garbage collector perform a thorough garbage-collection pass, and runFinalization() requests that the garbage collector finalize all objects that are ready for finalization. Applications do not typically need to call these garbage-collection methods, but they can be useful when benchmarking code with currentTimeMillis(). identityHashCode() computes the hashcode for an object in the same way that the default Object.hashCode() method does. It does this regardless of whether or how the hashCode() method has been overridden. load() and loadLibrary() can read libraries of native code into the system. mapLibraryName() converts a system-independent library name into a system-dependent library filename. Finally, getSecurityManager() and setSecurityManager() get and set the system SecurityManager object responsible for the system security policy.

See also Runtime, which defines several other methods that provide low-level access to system facilities.


```
public final class System {
// No Constructor
// Public Constants
    public static final java.io.PrintStream err;
    public static final java.io.InputStream in;
    public static final java.io.PrintStream out;
// Public Class Methods
    public static void arraycopy(Object src, int srcPos, Object dest, int destPos, int length);   native
    public static long currentTimeMillis();                                                       native
    public static void exit(int status);
    public static void gc();
    public static java.util.Properties getProperties();
    public static String getProperty(String key);
    public static String getProperty(String key, String def);
    public static SecurityManager getSecurityManager();
1.1 public static int identityHashCode(Object x);                                                 native
    public static void load(String filename);
    public static void loadLibrary(String libname);
1.2 public static String mapLibraryName(String libname);                                          native
    public static void runFinalization();
1.1 public static void setErr(java.io.PrintStream err);
1.1 public static void setIn(java.io.InputStream in);
1.1 public static void setOut(java.io.PrintStream out);
    public static void setProperties(java.util.Properties props);
1.2 public static String setProperty(String key, String value);
    public static void setSecurityManager(SecurityManager s);
// Deprecated Public Methods
#   public static String getenv(String name);
1.1# public static void runFinalizersOnExit(boolean value);
}
```

Thread — Java 1.0

java.lang — *runnable*

This class encapsulates all information about a single thread of control running on the Java interpreter. To create a thread, you must either pass a Runnable object (i.e., an object that implements the Runnable interface by defining a run() method) to the Thread constructor or subclass Thread so that it defines its own run() method. The run() method of the Thread or of the specified Runnable object is the body of the thread. It begins executing when the start() method of the Thread object is called. The thread runs until the run() method returns. isAlive() returns true if a thread has been started, and the run() method has not yet exited.

The static methods of this class operate on the currently running thread. currentThread() returns the Thread object of the currently running code. sleep() makes the current thread stop for a specified amount of time. yield() makes the current thread give up control to any other threads of equal priority that are waiting to run. holdsLock() tests whether the current thread holds a lock (through a synchronized method or statement) on the specified object; this Java 1.4 method is often useful with an assert statement.

The instance methods may be called by one thread to operate on a different thread. checkAccess() checks whether the running thread has permission to modify a Thread object and throws a SecurityException if it does not. join() waits for a thread to die. interrupt() wakes up a waiting or sleeping thread (with an InterruptedException) or sets an interrupted flag on a nonsleeping thread. A thread can test its own interrupted flag with the static interrupted() method or can test the flag of another thread with isInterrupted(). Calling interrupted() implicitly clears the interrupted flag, but calling isInterrupted() does not. Methods related to sleep() and interrupt() are the wait() and notify() methods defined by the Object class. Calling wait() causes the current thread to block until the object's notify() method is called by another thread.

setName() sets the name of a thread, which is purely optional. setPriority() sets the priority of the thread. Higher priority threads run before lower-priority threads. Java does not specify what happens to multiple threads of equal priority; some systems perform time-slicing and share the CPU between such threads. On other systems, one compute-bound thread that does not call yield() may starve another thread of the same priority. setDaemon() sets a boolean flag that specifies whether this thread is a daemon or not. The Java VM keeps running as long as at least one non-daemon thread is running. Call getThreadGroup() to obtain the ThreadGroup of which a thread is part. In Java 1.2 and later, use setContextClassLoader() to specify the ClassLoader to be used to load any classes required by the thread.

suspend(), resume(), and stop() suspend, resume, and stop a given thread, respectively, but all three methods are deprecated because they are inherently unsafe and can cause deadlock. If a thread must be stoppable, have it periodically check a flag and exit if the flag is set.

In Java 1.4 and later, the four-argument Thread() constructor allows you to specify the "stack size" parameter for the thread. Typically larger stack sizes allow threads to reduce more deeply before running out of stack space. And smaller stack sizes reduce the fixed per-thread memory requirements, and may allow more threads to exist concurrently. The meaning of this argument is implementation dependent, and implementations may even ignore it.

Object — Thread ··· Runnable

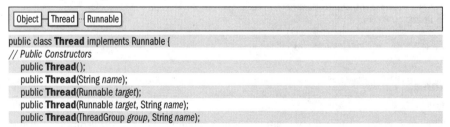

```
public class Thread implements Runnable {
// Public Constructors
    public Thread();
    public Thread(String name);
    public Thread(Runnable target);
    public Thread(Runnable target, String name);
    public Thread(ThreadGroup group, String name);
```

```
    public Thread(ThreadGroup group, Runnable target);
    public Thread(ThreadGroup group, Runnable target, String name);
1.4 public Thread(ThreadGroup group, Runnable target, String name, long stackSize);
// Public Constants
    public static final int MAX_PRIORITY;                                          =10
    public static final int MIN_PRIORITY;                                          =1
    public static final int NORM_PRIORITY;                                         =5
// Public Class Methods
    public static int activeCount();
    public static Thread currentThread();                                          native
    public static void dumpStack();
    public static int enumerate(Thread[ ] tarray);
1.4 public static boolean holdsLock(Object obj);                                   native
    public static boolean interrupted();
    public static void sleep(long millis) throws InterruptedException;             native
    public static void sleep(long millis, int nanos) throws InterruptedException;
    public static void yield();                                                    native
// Property Accessor Methods (by property name)
    public final boolean isAlive();                                   native default:false
1.2 public ClassLoader getContextClassLoader();
1.2 public void setContextClassLoader(ClassLoader cl);
    public final boolean isDaemon();                                         default:false
    public final void setDaemon(boolean on);
    public boolean isInterrupted();                                          default:false
    public final String getName();                    default: [quot ] Thread-1 [quot ]
    public final void setName(String name);
    public final int getPriority();                                              default:5
    public final void setPriority(int newPriority);
    public final ThreadGroup getThreadGroup();
// Public Instance Methods
    public final void checkAccess();
    public void destroy();
    public void interrupt();
    public final void join() throws InterruptedException;
    public final void join(long millis) throws InterruptedException;          synchronized
    public final void join(long millis, int nanos) throws InterruptedException; synchronized
    public void start();                                               native synchronized
// Methods Implementing Runnable
    public void run();
// Public Methods Overriding Object
    public String toString();
// Deprecated Public Methods
#   public int countStackFrames();                                                 native
#   public final void resume();
#   public final void stop();
#   public final void stop(Throwable obj);                                   synchronized
#   public final void suspend();
}
```

Passed To: Runtime.{addShutdownHook(), removeShutdownHook()}, SecurityManager.checkAccess(), Thread.enumerate(), ThreadGroup.{enumerate(), uncaughtException()}

Returned By: Thread.currentThread(), javax.swing.text.AbstractDocument.getCurrentWriter()

ThreadDeath — Java 1.0

java.lang — *serializable error*

This error signals that a thread should terminate. It is thrown in a thread when the Thread.stop() method is called for that thread. This is an unusual Error type that simply causes a thread to be terminated, but does not print an error message or cause the interpreter to exit. You can catch ThreadDeath errors to do any necessary cleanup for a thread, but if you do, you must rethrow the error so that the thread actually terminates.

Object — Throwable — Error — ThreadDeath
Serializable

```
public class ThreadDeath extends Error {
// Public Constructors
   public ThreadDeath();
}
```

ThreadGroup — Java 1.0

java.lang

This class represents a group of threads and allows that group to be manipulated as a whole. A ThreadGroup can contain Thread objects, as well as other child ThreadGroup objects. All ThreadGroup objects are created as children of some other ThreadGroup, and thus there is a parent/child hierarchy of ThreadGroup objects. Use getParent() to obtain the parent ThreadGroup, and use activeCount(), activeGroupCount(), and the various enumerate() methods to list the child Thread and ThreadGroup objects. Most applications can simply rely on the default system thread group. System-level code and applications such as servers that need to create a large number of threads may find it convenient to create their own ThreadGroup objects, however.

interrupt() interrupts all threads in the group at once. setMaxPriority() specifies the maximum priority any thread in the group can have. checkAccess() checks whether the calling thread has permission to modify the given thread group. The method throws a SecurityException if the current thread does not have access. uncaughtException() contains the code that is run when a thread terminates because of an uncaught exception or error. You can customize this method by subclassing ThreadGroup.

```
public class ThreadGroup {
// Public Constructors
   public ThreadGroup(String name);
   public ThreadGroup(ThreadGroup parent, String name);
// Property Accessor Methods (by property name)
   public final boolean isDaemon();
   public final void setDaemon(boolean daemon);
1.1 public boolean isDestroyed();                                    synchronized
   public final int getMaxPriority();
   public final void setMaxPriority(int pri);
   public final String getName();
   public final ThreadGroup getParent();
// Public Instance Methods
   public int activeCount();
   public int activeGroupCount();
   public final void checkAccess();
   public final void destroy();
   public int enumerate(ThreadGroup[ ] list);
   public int enumerate(Thread[ ] list);
```

```
    public int enumerate(Thread[ ] list, boolean recurse);
    public int enumerate(ThreadGroup[ ] list, boolean recurse);
1.2 public final void interrupt();
    public void list();
    public final boolean parentOf(ThreadGroup g);
    public void uncaughtException(Thread t, Throwable e);
// Public Methods Overriding Object
    public String toString();
// Deprecated Public Methods
1.1# public boolean allowThreadSuspension(boolean b);
#   public final void resume();
#   public final void stop();
#   public final void suspend();
}
```

Passed To: SecurityManager.checkAccess(), Thread.Thread(), ThreadGroup.{enumerate(), parentOf(), ThreadGroup()}

Returned By: SecurityManager.getThreadGroup(), Thread.getThreadGroup(), ThreadGroup.getParent()

ThreadLocal — Java 1.2

java.lang

This class provides a convenient way to create thread-local variables. When you declare a static field in a class, there is only one value for that field, shared by all objects of the class. When you declare a nonstatic instance field in a class, every object of the class has its own separate copy of that variable. ThreadLocal provides an option between these two extremes. If you declare a static field to hold a ThreadLocal object, that ThreadLocal holds a different value for each thread. Objects running in the same thread see the same value when they call the get() method of the ThreadLocal object. Objects running in different threads obtain different values from get(), however.

The set() method sets the value held by the ThreadLocal object for the currently running thread. get() returns the value held for the currently running thread. Note that there is no way to obtain the value of the ThreadLocal object for any thread other than the one that calls get(). To understand the ThreadLocal class, you may find it helpful to think of a ThreadLocal object as a hashtable or java.util.Map that maps from Thread objects to arbitrary values. Calling set() creates an association between the current Thread (Thread.currentThread()) and the specified value. Calling get() first looks up the current thread, then uses the hashtable to look up the value associated with that current thread.

If a thread calls get() for the first time without having first called set() to establish a thread-local value, get() calls the protected initialValue() method to obtain the initial value to return. The default implementation of initialValue() simply returns null, but subclasses can override this if they desire.

See also InheritableThreadLocal, which allows thread-local values to be inherited from parent threads by child threads.

```
public class ThreadLocal {
// Public Constructors
    public ThreadLocal();
// Public Instance Methods
    public Object get();
    public void set(Object value);
```

```
// Protected Instance Methods
   protected Object initialValue();                                      constant
}
```

Subclasses: InheritableThreadLocal

Throwable — Java 1.0

java.lang — *serializable*

This is the root class of the Java exception and error hierarchy. All exceptions and errors are subclasses of Throwable. The getMessage() method retrieves any error message associated with the exception or error. The default implementation of getLocalizedMessage() simply calls getMessage(), but subclasses may override this method to return an error message that has been localized for the default locale.

It is often the case that an Exception or Error is generated as a direct result of some other exception or error, perhaps one thrown by a lower-level API. In Java 1.4 and later, all Throwable objects may have a "cause" object that specifies the Throwable that caused them. If there is a cause, pass it to the Throwable() constructor or to the initCause() method. When you catch a Throwable object, you can obtain the Throwable that caused it, if any, with getCause().

Every Throwable object has information about the execution stack associated with it. This information is initialized when the Throwable object is created. If the object will be thrown somewhere other than where it was created, or if it was caught and will be re-thrown, you can use fillInStackTrace() to capture the current execution stack before throwing it. printStackTrace() prints a textual representation of the stack to the specified PrintWriter, PrintStream, or to the System.err stream. In Java 1.4, you can also obtain this information with getStackTrace(), which returns an array of StackTraceElement objects describing the execution stack.

Object — Throwable ··· Serializable

```
public class Throwable implements Serializable {
// Public Constructors
    public Throwable();
    public Throwable(String message);
1.4 public Throwable(Throwable cause);
1.4 public Throwable(String message, Throwable cause);
// Property Accessor Methods (by property name)
1.4 public Throwable getCause();                                         default:null
1.1 public String getLocalizedMessage();                                 default:null
    public String getMessage();                                          default:null
1.4 public StackTraceElement[ ] getStackTrace();
1.4 public void setStackTrace(StackTraceElement[ ] stackTrace);
// Public Instance Methods
    public Throwable fillInStackTrace();                     native synchronized
1.4 public Throwable initCause(Throwable cause);                         synchronized
    public void printStackTrace();
    public void printStackTrace(java.io.PrintStream s);
1.1 public void printStackTrace(java.io.PrintWriter s);
// Public Methods Overriding Object
    public String toString();
}
```

Subclasses: Error, Exception

Passed To: Too many methods to list.

Returned By: Too many methods to list.

Thrown By: java.awt.Cursor.finalize(), java.awt.Font.finalize(), java.awt.Frame.finalize(), java.awt.Window.finalize(), Object.finalize(), java.lang.reflect.InvocationHandler.invoke(), javax.imageio.spi.ServiceRegistry.finalize(), javax.imageio.stream.ImageInputStreamImpl.finalize(), javax.swing.text.AbstractDocument.AbstractElement.finalize()

Type Of: java.rmi.RemoteException.detail, java.rmi.activation.ActivationException.detail, javax.naming.NamingException.rootException, org.omg.CORBA.portable.UnknownException.originalEx

UnknownError — Java 1.0

java.lang — *serializable error*

This error signals that an unknown error has occurred at the level of the Java VM.

Object — Throwable — Error — VirtualMachineError — UnknownError
Serializable

```
public class UnknownError extends VirtualMachineError {
// Public Constructors
   public UnknownError();
   public UnknownError(String s);
}
```

UnsatisfiedLinkError — Java 1.0

java.lang — *serializable error*

This error signals that Java cannot satisfy all the links in a class that it has loaded.

Object — Throwable — Error — LinkageError — UnsatisfiedLinkError
Serializable

```
public class UnsatisfiedLinkError extends LinkageError {
// Public Constructors
   public UnsatisfiedLinkError();
   public UnsatisfiedLinkError(String s);
}
```

UnsupportedClassVersionError — Java 1.2

java.lang — *serializable error*

Every Java class file contains a version number that specifies the version of the class file format. This error is thrown when the Java VM attempts to read a class file with a version number it does not support.

Object — Throwable — Error — LinkageError — ClassFormatError — UnsupportedClassVersionError
Serializable

```
public class UnsupportedClassVersionError extends ClassFormatError {
// Public Constructors
   public UnsupportedClassVersionError();
   public UnsupportedClassVersionError(String s);
}
```

UnsupportedOperationException — Java 1.2

java.lang — *serializable unchecked*

This exception signals that a method you have called is not supported, and its implementation does not do anything (except throw this exception). This exception is used most often by the Java collection framework of java.util. Immutable or unmodifiable collections throw this exception when a modification method, such as add() or delete(), is called.

Object — Throwable — Exception — RuntimeException — UnsupportedOperationException
Serializable

```
public class UnsupportedOperationException extends RuntimeException {
// Public Constructors
   public UnsupportedOperationException();
   public UnsupportedOperationException(String message);
}
```

Subclasses: java.awt.HeadlessException, java.nio.ReadOnlyBufferException

Thrown By: java.awt.Toolkit.{getLockingKeyState(), setLockingKeyState()}, javax.imageio.ImageReadParam.setSourceRenderSize()

VerifyError — Java 1.0

java.lang — *serializable error*

This error signals that a class has not passed the byte-code verification procedures.

Object — Throwable — Error — LinkageError — VerifyError
Serializable

```
public class VerifyError extends LinkageError {
// Public Constructors
   public VerifyError();
   public VerifyError(String s);
}
```

VirtualMachineError — Java 1.0

java.lang — *serializable error*

This is an abstract error type that serves as superclass for a group of errors related to the Java Virtual Machine. See InternalError, UnknownError, OutOfMemoryError, and StackOverflowError.

Object — Throwable — Error — VirtualMachineError
Serializable

```
public abstract class VirtualMachineError extends Error {
// Public Constructors
   public VirtualMachineError();
   public VirtualMachineError(String s);
}
```

Subclasses: InternalError, OutOfMemoryError, StackOverflowError, UnknownError

Void — Java 1.1

java.lang

The Void class cannot be instantiated and serves merely as a placeholder for its static TYPE field, which is a Class object constant that represents the void type.

```
public final class Void {
// No Constructor
// Public Constants
   public static final Class TYPE;
}
```

Package java.lang.ref — Java 1.2

The java.lang.ref package defines classes that allow Java programs to interact with the Java garbage collector. A Reference represents an indirect reference to an arbitrary object, known as the *referent*. SoftReference, WeakReference, and PhantomReference are three concrete subclasses of Reference that interact with the garbage collector in different ways, as explained in the individual class descriptions that follow. ReferenceQueue represents a linked list of Reference objects. Any Reference object may have a ReferenceQueue associated with it. A Reference object is *enqueued* on its ReferenceQueue at some point after the garbage collector determines that the referent object has become appropriately unreachable. (The exact level of unreachability depends on the type of Reference being used.) An application can monitor a ReferenceQueue to determine when referent objects enter a new reachability status.

Using the mechanisms defined in this package, you can implement a cache that grows and shrinks in size according to the amount of available system memory. Or, you can implement a hashtable that associates auxiliary information with arbitrary objects, but does not prevent those objects from being garbage-collected if they are otherwise unused. The mechanisms provided by this package are low-level ones, however, and typical applications do not use java.lang.ref directly. Instead, they rely on higher-level utilities built on top of the package. See java.util.WeakHashMap for one example.

Classes:

```
public abstract class Reference;
   └ public class PhantomReference extends Reference;
   └ public class SoftReference extends Reference;
   └ public class WeakReference extends Reference;
public class ReferenceQueue;
```

PhantomReference — Java 1.2

java.lang.ref

This class represents a reference to an object that does not prevent the referent object from being finalized by the garbage collector. When (or at some point after) the garbage collector determines that there are no more hard (direct) references to the referent object, that there are no SoftReference or WeakReference objects that refer to the referent, and that the referent has been finalized, it enqueues the PhantomReference object on the ReferenceQueue specified when the PhantomReference was created. This serves as notification that the object has been finalized and provides one last opportunity for any required cleanup code to be run.

To prevent a PhantomReference object from resurrecting its referent object, its get() method always returns null, both before and after the PhantomReference is enqueued. Nevertheless, a PhantomReference is not automatically cleared when it is enqueued, so when you remove a PhantomReference from a ReferenceQueue, you must call its clear() method or allow the PhantomReference object itself to be garbage collected.

This class provides a more flexible mechanism for object cleanup than the finalize() method does. Note that in order to take advantage of it, it is necessary to subclass PhantomReference and define a method to perform the desired cleanup. Furthermore, since the get() method of a PhantomReference always returns null, such a subclass must also store whatever data is required for the cleanup operation.

Object — Reference — PhantomReference

```
public class PhantomReference extends java.lang.ref.Reference {
// Public Constructors
   public PhantomReference(Object referent, ReferenceQueue q);
// Public Methods Overriding Reference
   public Object get();                                          constant
}
```

Reference — Java 1.2

java.lang.ref

This abstract class represents some type of indirect reference to a referent. get() returns the referent if the reference has not been explicitly cleared by the clear() method or implicitly cleared by the garbage collector. There are three concrete subclasses of Reference. The garbage collector handles these subclasses differently and clears their references under different circumstances.

Each of the subclasses of Reference defines a constructor that allows a ReferenceQueue to be associated with the Reference object. The garbage collector places Reference objects onto their associated ReferenceQueue objects to provide notification about the state of the referent object. isEnqueued() tests whether a Reference has been placed on the associated queue, and enqueue() explicitly places it on the queue. enqueue() returns false if the Reference object does not have an associated ReferenceQueue, or if it has already been enqueued.

```
public abstract class Reference {
// No Constructor
// Public Instance Methods
   public void clear();
   public boolean enqueue();
   public Object get();
   public boolean isEnqueued();
}
```

Subclasses: PhantomReference, SoftReference, WeakReference

Returned By: ReferenceQueue.{poll(), remove()}

ReferenceQueue — Java 1.2

java.lang.ref

This class represents a queue (or linked list) of Reference objects that have been enqueued because the garbage collector has determined that the referent objects to which they refer are no longer adequately reachable. It serves as a notification system for object-reachability changes. Use poll() to return the first Reference object on the queue; the method returns null if the queue is empty. Use remove() to return the first element on the queue, or, if the queue is empty, to wait for a Reference object to be enqueued. You can create as many ReferenceQueue objects as needed. Specify a ReferenceQueue for a Reference object by passing it to the SoftReference(), WeakReference(), or PhantomReference() constructor.

A ReferenceQueue is required to use PhantomReference objects. It is optional with SoftReference and WeakReference objects; for these classes, the get() method returns null if the referent object is no longer adequately reachable.

```
public class ReferenceQueue {
// Public Constructors
   public ReferenceQueue();
// Public Instance Methods
   public java.lang.ref.Reference poll();
   public java.lang.ref.Reference remove() throws InterruptedException;
   public java.lang.ref.Reference remove(long timeout) throws IllegalArgumentException, InterruptedException;
}
```

Passed To: PhantomReference.PhantomReference(), SoftReference.SoftReference(), WeakReference.WeakReference()

SoftReference — Java 1.2

java.lang.ref

This class represents a soft reference to an object. A SoftReference is not cleared while there are any remaining hard (direct) references to the referent. Once the referent is no longer in use (i.e., there are no remaining hard references to it), the garbage collector may clear the SoftReference to the referent at any time. However, the garbage collector does not clear a SoftReference until it determines that system memory is running low. In particular, the Java VM never throws an OutOfMemoryError without first clearing all soft references and reclaiming the memory of the referents. The VM may (but is not required to) clear soft references according to a least-recently-used ordering.

If a SoftReference has an associated ReferenceQueue, the garbage collector enqueues the SoftReference at some time after it clears the reference.

SoftReference is particularly useful for implementing object-caching systems that do not have a fixed size, but grow and shrink as available memory allows.

Object — Reference — SoftReference

```
public class SoftReference extends java.lang.ref.Reference {
// Public Constructors
   public SoftReference(Object referent);
   public SoftReference(Object referent, ReferenceQueue q);
// Public Methods Overriding Reference
   public Object get();
}
```

WeakReference — Java 1.2

java.lang.ref

This class refers to an object in a way that does not prevent that referent object from being finalized and reclaimed by the garbage collector. When the garbage collector determines that there are no more hard (direct) references to the object, and that there are no SoftReference objects that refer to the object, it clears the WeakReference and marks the referent object for finalization. At some point after this, it also enqueues the WeakReference on its associated ReferenceQueue, if there is one, in order to provide notification that the referent has been reclaimed.

WeakReference is used by java.util.WeakHashMap to implement a hashtable that does not prevent the hashtable key object from being garbage-collected. WeakHashMap is useful when you want to associate auxiliary information with an object but do not want to prevent the object from being reclaimed.

Object ─ Reference ─ WeakReference

```
public class WeakReference extends java.lang.ref.Reference {
// Public Constructors
   public WeakReference(Object referent);
   public WeakReference(Object referent, ReferenceQueue q);
}
```

Package java.lang.reflect

Java 1.1

The java.lang.reflect package contains the classes and interfaces that, along with java.lang.Class, comprise the Java Reflection API.

The Constructor, Field, and Method classes represent the constructors, fields, and methods of a class. Because these types all represent members of a class, they each implement the Member interface, which defines a simple set of methods that can be invoked for any class member. These classes allow information about the class members to be obtained, methods and constructors to be invoked, and fields to be queried and set.

Class member modifiers are represented as integers that specify a number of bit flags. The Modifier class defines static methods that help interpret the meanings of these flags. The Array class defines static methods for creating arrays, and reading and writing array elements.

In Java 1.3, the Proxy class allows the dynamic creation of new Java classes that implement a specified set of interfaces. When an interface method is invoked on an instance of such a proxy class, the invocation is delegated to an InvocationHandler object.

Interfaces:

public interface **InvocationHandler**;
public interface **Member**;

Classes:

public class **AccessibleObject**;
   └ public final class **Constructor** extends AccessibleObject implements Member;
   └ public final class **Field** extends AccessibleObject implements Member;
   └ public final class **Method** extends AccessibleObject implements Member;
public final class **Array**;
public class **Modifier**;
public class **Proxy** implements Serializable;
public final class **ReflectPermission** extends java.security.BasicPermission;

Exceptions:

public class **InvocationTargetException** extends Exception;
public class **UndeclaredThrowableException** extends RuntimeException;

AccessibleObject **Java 1.2**

java.lang.reflect

This class is the superclass of the Method, Constructor, and Field classes; its methods provide a mechanism for trusted applications to work with private, protected, and default visibility members that would otherwise not be accessible through the Reflection API. This class is new as of Java 1.2; in Java 1.1, the Method, Constructor, and Field classes extended Object directly.

To use the java.lang.reflect package to access a member to which your code would not normally have access, pass true to the setAccessible() method. If your code has an appropriate ReflectPermission ("suppressAccessChecks"), this allows access to the member as if it were declared public. The static version of setAccessible() is a convenience method that sets the accessible flag for an array of members, but performs only a single security check.

```
public class AccessibleObject {
// Protected Constructors
   protected AccessibleObject();
// Public Class Methods
   public static void setAccessible(AccessibleObject[ ] array, boolean flag) throws SecurityException;
// Public Instance Methods
   public boolean isAccessible();
   public void setAccessible(boolean flag) throws SecurityException;
}
```

Subclasses: Constructor, Field, Method

Passed To: AccessibleObject.setAccessible()

Array **Java 1.1**

java.lang.reflect

This class contains methods that allow you to set and query the values of array elements, to determine the length of an array, and to create new instances of arrays. Note that the Array class can manipulate only array values, not array types; Java data types, including array types, are represented by java.lang.Class. Since the Array class represents a Java value, unlike the Field, Method, and Constructor classes, which represent class members, the Array class is significantly different (despite some surface similarities) from those other classes in this package. Most notably, all the methods of Array are static and apply to all array values, not just a specific field, method, or constructor.

The get() method returns the value of the specified element of the specified array as an Object. If the array elements are of a primitive type, the value is converted to a wrapper object before being returned. You can also use getInt() and related methods to query array elements and return them as specific primitive types. The set() method and its primitive type variants perform the opposite operation. Also, the getLength() method returns the length of the array.

The newInstance() methods create new arrays. One version of this method is passed the number of elements in the array and the type of those elements. The other version of this method creates multidimensional arrays. Besides specifying the component type of the array, it is passed an array of numbers. The length of this array specifies the number of dimensions for the array to be created, and the values of each of the array elements specify the size of each dimension of the created array.

```
public final class Array {
// No Constructor
```

```
// Public Class Methods
   public static Object get(Object array, int index) throws IllegalArgumentException,          native
       ArrayIndexOutOfBoundsException;
   public static boolean getBoolean(Object array, int index) throws IllegalArgumentException,  native
       ArrayIndexOutOfBoundsException;
   public static byte getByte(Object array, int index) throws IllegalArgumentException,        native
       ArrayIndexOutOfBoundsException;
   public static char getChar(Object array, int index) throws IllegalArgumentException,        native
       ArrayIndexOutOfBoundsException;
   public static double getDouble(Object array, int index) throws IllegalArgumentException,    native
       ArrayIndexOutOfBoundsException;
   public static float getFloat(Object array, int index) throws IllegalArgumentException,      native
       ArrayIndexOutOfBoundsException;
   public static int getInt(Object array, int index) throws IllegalArgumentException,          native
       ArrayIndexOutOfBoundsException;
   public static int getLength(Object array) throws IllegalArgumentException;                  native
   public static long getLong(Object array, int index) throws IllegalArgumentException,        native
       ArrayIndexOutOfBoundsException;
   public static short getShort(Object array, int index) throws IllegalArgumentException,      native
       ArrayIndexOutOfBoundsException;
   public static Object newInstance(Class componentType, int length) throws NegativeArraySizeException;
   public static Object newInstance(Class componentType, int[ ] dimensions) throws IllegalArgumentException,
       NegativeArraySizeException;
   public static void set(Object array, int index, Object value) throws IllegalArgumentException,  native
       ArrayIndexOutOfBoundsException;
   public static void setBoolean(Object array, int index, boolean z) throws IllegalArgumentException,  native
       ArrayIndexOutOfBoundsException;
   public static void setByte(Object array, int index, byte b) throws IllegalArgumentException,  native
       ArrayIndexOutOfBoundsException;
   public static void setChar(Object array, int index, char c) throws IllegalArgumentException,  native
       ArrayIndexOutOfBoundsException;
   public static void setDouble(Object array, int index, double d) throws IllegalArgumentException,  native
       ArrayIndexOutOfBoundsException;
   public static void setFloat(Object array, int index, float f) throws IllegalArgumentException,  native
       ArrayIndexOutOfBoundsException;
   public static void setInt(Object array, int index, int i) throws IllegalArgumentException,  native
       ArrayIndexOutOfBoundsException;
   public static void setLong(Object array, int index, long l) throws IllegalArgumentException,  native
       ArrayIndexOutOfBoundsException;
   public static void setShort(Object array, int index, short s) throws IllegalArgumentException,  native
       ArrayIndexOutOfBoundsException;
}
```

Constructor — Java 1.1

java.lang.reflect

This class represents a constructor method of a class. Instances of Constructor are obtained by calling getConstructor() and related methods of java.lang.Class. Constructor implements the Member interface, so you can use the methods of that interface to obtain the constructor name, modifiers, and declaring class. In addition, getParameterTypes() and getExceptionTypes() also return important information about the represented constructor.

In addition to these methods that return information about the constructor, the newInstance() method allows the constructor to be invoked with an array of arguments in order to create a new instance of the class that declares the constructor. If any of the arguments to the constructor are of primitive types, they must be converted to their corresponding wrapper object types to be passed to newInstance(). If the constructor causes an exception, the Throwable object it throws is wrapped within the InvocationTargetException that is thrown by newInstance(). Note that newInstance() is much more useful than the newInstance() method of java.lang.Class because it can pass arguments to the constructor.

Object – AccessibleObject – Constructor
Member

```
public final class Constructor extends AccessibleObject implements Member {
// No Constructor
// Public Instance Methods
   public Class[ ] getExceptionTypes();
   public Class[ ] getParameterTypes();
   public Object newInstance(Object[ ] initargs) throws InstantiationException, IllegalAccessException,
       IllegalArgumentException, InvocationTargetException;
// Methods Implementing Member
   public Class getDeclaringClass();
   public int getModifiers();
   public String getName();
// Public Methods Overriding Object
   public boolean equals(Object obj);
   public int hashCode();
   public String toString();
}
```

Returned By: Class.{getConstructor(), getConstructors(), getDeclaredConstructor(), getDeclaredConstructors()}

Field — Java 1.1

java.lang.reflect

This class represents a field of a class. Instances of Field are obtained by calling the getField() and related methods of java.lang.Class. Field implements the Member interface, so once you have obtained a Field object, you can use getName(), getModifiers(), and getDeclaringClass() to determine the name, modifiers, and class of the field. Additionally, getType() returns the type of the field.

The set() method sets the value of the represented field for a specified object. (If the represented field is static, no object need be specified, of course.) If the field is of a primitive type, its value can be specified using a wrapper object of type Boolean, Integer, and so on, or it can be set using the setBoolean(), setInt(), and related methods. Similarly, the get() method queries the value of the represented field for a specified object and returns the field value as an Object. Various other methods query the field value and return it as various primitive types.

Object – AccessibleObject – Field
Member

```
public final class Field extends AccessibleObject implements Member {
// No Constructor
// Public Instance Methods
   public Object get(Object obj) throws IllegalArgumentException, IllegalAccessException;
   public boolean getBoolean(Object obj) throws IllegalArgumentException, IllegalAccessException;
   public byte getByte(Object obj) throws IllegalArgumentException, IllegalAccessException;
   public char getChar(Object obj) throws IllegalArgumentException, IllegalAccessException;
```

```
    public double getDouble(Object obj) throws IllegalArgumentException, IllegalAccessException;
    public float getFloat(Object obj) throws IllegalArgumentException, IllegalAccessException;
    public int getInt(Object obj) throws IllegalArgumentException, IllegalAccessException;
    public long getLong(Object obj) throws IllegalArgumentException, IllegalAccessException;
    public short getShort(Object obj) throws IllegalArgumentException, IllegalAccessException;
    public Class getType();
    public void set(Object obj, Object value) throws IllegalArgumentException, IllegalAccessException;
    public void setBoolean(Object obj, boolean z) throws IllegalArgumentException, IllegalAccessException;
    public void setByte(Object obj, byte b) throws IllegalArgumentException, IllegalAccessException;
    public void setChar(Object obj, char c) throws IllegalArgumentException, IllegalAccessException;
    public void setDouble(Object obj, double d) throws IllegalArgumentException, IllegalAccessException;
    public void setFloat(Object obj, float f) throws IllegalArgumentException, IllegalAccessException;
    public void setInt(Object obj, int i) throws IllegalArgumentException, IllegalAccessException;
    public void setLong(Object obj, long l) throws IllegalArgumentException, IllegalAccessException;
    public void setShort(Object obj, short s) throws IllegalArgumentException, IllegalAccessException;
// Methods Implementing Member
    public Class getDeclaringClass();
    public int getModifiers();
    public String getName();
// Public Methods Overriding Object
    public boolean equals(Object obj);
    public int hashCode();
    public String toString();
}
```

Returned By: Class.{getDeclaredField(), getDeclaredFields(), getField(), getFields()}

InvocationHandler — Java 1.3

java.lang.reflect

This interface defines a single invoke() method that is called whenever a method is invoked on a dynamically created Proxy object. Every Proxy object has an associated InvocationHandler object that is specified when the Proxy is instantiated. All method invocations on the proxy object are translated into calls to the invoke() method of the InvocationHandler.

The first argument to invoke() is the Proxy object through which the method was invoked. The second argument is a Method object that represents the method that was invoked. Call the getDeclaringClass() method of this Method object to determine the interface in which the method was declared. This may be a superinterface of one of the specified interfaces or even java.lang.Object when the method invoked is toString(), hashCode(), or one of the other Object methods. The third argument to invoke() is the array of method arguments. Any primitive type arguments are wrapped in their corresponding object wrappers (e.g., Boolean, Integer, Double).

The value returned by invoke() becomes the return value of the proxy object method invocation and must be of an appropriate type. If the proxy object method returns a primitive type, invoke() should return an instance of the corresponding wrapper class. invoke() can throw any unchecked (i.e., runtime) exceptions or any checked exceptions declared by the proxy object method. If invoke() throws a checked exception that is not declared by the proxy object, that exception is wrapped within an unchecked UndeclaredThrowableException that is thrown in its place.

```
public interface InvocationHandler {
// Public Instance Methods
   public abstract Object invoke(Object proxy, Method method, Object[ ] args) throws Throwable;
}
```

Implementations: java.beans.EventHandler

Passed To: Proxy.{newProxyInstance(), Proxy()}

Returned By: Proxy.getInvocationHandler()

Type Of: Proxy.h

InvocationTargetException — Java 1.1

java.lang.reflect — *serializable checked*

An object of this class is thrown by Method.invoke() and Constructor.newInstance() when an exception is thrown by the method or constructor invoked through those methods. The InvocationTargetException class serves as a wrapper around the object that was thrown; that object can be retrieved with the getTargetException() method. In Java 1.4 and later, all exceptions can be "chained" in this way, and getTargetException() is superseded by the more general getCause() method.

Object — Throwable — Exception — InvocationTargetException
Serializable

```
public class InvocationTargetException extends Exception {
// Public Constructors
   public InvocationTargetException(Throwable target);
   public InvocationTargetException(Throwable target, String s);
// Protected Constructors
   protected InvocationTargetException();
// Public Instance Methods
   public Throwable getTargetException();
// Public Methods Overriding Throwable
1.4 public Throwable getCause();
}
```

Thrown By: java.awt.EventQueue.invokeAndWait(), Constructor.newInstance(), Method.invoke(), javax.swing.SwingUtilities.invokeAndWait()

Member — Java 1.1

java.lang.reflect

This interface defines the methods shared by all members (fields, methods, and constructors) of a class. getName() returns the name of the member, getModifiers() returns its modifiers, and getDeclaringClass() returns the Class object that represents the class of which the member is a part.

```
public interface Member {
// Public Constants
   public static final int DECLARED;                                            =1
   public static final int PUBLIC;                                              =0
// Public Instance Methods
   public abstract Class getDeclaringClass();
   public abstract int getModifiers();
```

```
    public abstract String getName();
}
```

Implementations: Constructor, Field, Method

Method **Java 1.1**

java.lang.reflect

This class represents a method. Instances of Method are obtained by calling the getMethod() and related methods of java.lang.Class. Method implements the Member interface, so you can use the methods of that interface to obtain the method name, modifiers, and declaring class. In addition, getReturnType(), getParameterTypes(), and getExceptionTypes() also return important information about the represented method.

Perhaps most importantly, the invoke() method allows the method represented by the Method object to be invoked with a specified array of argument values. If any of the arguments are of primitive types, they must be converted to their corresponding wrapper object types in order to be passed to invoke(). If the represented method is an instance method (i.e., if it is not static), the instance on which it should be invoked must also be passed to invoke(). The return value of the represented method is returned by invoke(). If the return value is a primitive value, it is first converted to the corresponding wrapper type. If the invoked method causes an exception, the Throwable object it throws is wrapped within the InvocationTargetException that is thrown by invoke().

Object — AccessibleObject — Method
Member

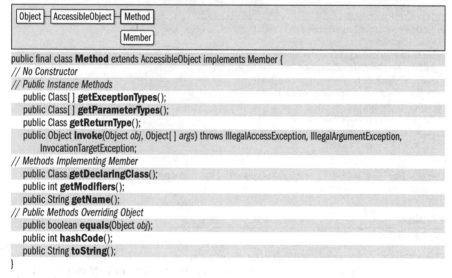

```
public final class Method extends AccessibleObject implements Member {
// No Constructor
// Public Instance Methods
    public Class[ ] getExceptionTypes();
    public Class[ ] getParameterTypes();
    public Class getReturnType();
    public Object invoke(Object obj, Object[ ] args) throws IllegalAccessException, IllegalArgumentException,
        InvocationTargetException;
// Methods Implementing Member
    public Class getDeclaringClass();
    public int getModifiers();
    public String getName();
// Public Methods Overriding Object
    public boolean equals(Object obj);
    public int hashCode();
    public String toString();
}
```

Passed To: Too many methods to list.

Returned By: java.beans.EventSetDescriptor.{getAddListenerMethod(), getGetListenerMethod(), getListenerMethods(), getRemoveListenerMethod()}, java.beans.IndexedPropertyDescriptor.{getIndexedReadMethod(), getIndexedWriteMethod()}, java.beans.MethodDescriptor.getMethod(), java.beans.PropertyDescriptor.{getReadMethod(), getWriteMethod()}, Class.{getDeclaredMethod(), getDeclaredMethods(), getMethod(), getMethods()}

Modifier — Java 1.1

java.lang.reflect

This class defines a number of constants and static methods that can interpret the integer values returned by the getModifiers() methods of the Field, Method, and Constructor classes. The isPublic(), isAbstract(), and related methods return true if the modifier value includes the specified modifier; otherwise, they return false. The constants defined by this class specify the various bit flags used in the modifiers value. You can use these constants to test for modifiers if you want to perform your own Boolean algebra.

```
public class Modifier {
// Public Constructors
    public Modifier();
// Public Constants
    public static final int ABSTRACT;                    =1024
    public static final int FINAL;                       =16
    public static final int INTERFACE;                   =512
    public static final int NATIVE;                      =256
    public static final int PRIVATE;                     =2
    public static final int PROTECTED;                   =4
    public static final int PUBLIC;                      =1
    public static final int STATIC;                      =8
1.2 public static final int STRICT;                      =2048
    public static final int SYNCHRONIZED;                =32
    public static final int TRANSIENT;                   =128
    public static final int VOLATILE;                    =64
// Public Class Methods
    public static boolean isAbstract(int mod);
    public static boolean isFinal(int mod);
    public static boolean isInterface(int mod);
    public static boolean isNative(int mod);
    public static boolean isPrivate(int mod);
    public static boolean isProtected(int mod);
    public static boolean isPublic(int mod);
    public static boolean isStatic(int mod);
1.2 public static boolean isStrict(int mod);
    public static boolean isSynchronized(int mod);
    public static boolean isTransient(int mod);
    public static boolean isVolatile(int mod);
    public static String toString(int mod);
}
```

Proxy — Java 1.3

java.lang.reflect — *serializable*

This class defines a simple but powerful API for dynamically generating a *proxy class*. A proxy class implements a specified list of interfaces and delegates invocations of the methods defined by those interfaces to a separate invocation handler object.

The static getProxyClass() method dynamically creates a new Class object that implements each of the interfaces specified in the supplied Class[] array. The newly created class is defined in the context of the specified ClassLoader. The Class returned by getProxyClass() is a subclass of Proxy. Every class that is dynamically generated by getProxyClass() has a single public constructor, which expects a single argument of type InvocationHandler. You can create an instance of the dynamic proxy class by using the Constructor class to invoke this constructor. Or, more simply, you can combine the call to getProxyClass()

with the constructor call by calling the static newProxyInstance() method, which both defines and instantiates a proxy class.

Every instance of a dynamic proxy class has an associated InvocationHandler object. All method calls made on a proxy class are translated into calls to the invoke() method of this InvocationHandler object, which can handle the call in any way it sees fit. The static getInvocationHandler() method returns the InvocationHandler object for a given proxy object. The static isProxyClass() method returns true if a specified Class object is a dynamically generated proxy class.

Object — Proxy ··· Serializable

```
public class Proxy implements Serializable {
// Protected Constructors
   protected Proxy(InvocationHandler h);
// Public Class Methods
   public static InvocationHandler getInvocationHandler(Object proxy) throws IllegalArgumentException;
   public static Class getProxyClass(ClassLoader loader, Class[ ] interfaces) throws IllegalArgumentException;
   public static boolean isProxyClass(Class cl);
   public static Object newProxyInstance(ClassLoader loader, Class[ ] interfaces, InvocationHandler h)
       throws IllegalArgumentException;
// Protected Instance Fields
   protected InvocationHandler h;
}
```

ReflectPermission — Java 1.2

java.lang.reflect — ***serializable permission***

This class is a java.security.Permission that governs access to private, protected, and default-visibility methods, constructors, and fields through the Java Reflection API. In Java 1.2, the only defined name, or target, for ReflectPermission is "suppressAccessChecks". This permission is required to call the setAccessible() method of AccessibleObject. Unlike some Permission subclasses, ReflectPermission does not use a list of actions. See also AccessibleObject.

System administrators configuring security policies should be familiar with this class, but application programmers should never need to use it directly.

Object — Permission — BasicPermission — ReflectPermission

Guard, Serializable (Permission); Serializable (BasicPermission)

```
public final class ReflectPermission extends java.security.BasicPermission {
// Public Constructors
   public ReflectPermission(String name);
   public ReflectPermission(String name, String actions);
}
```

UndeclaredThrowableException — Java 1.3

java.lang.reflect — ***serializable unchecked***

This exception is thrown by a method of a Proxy object if the invoke() method of the proxy's InvocationHandler throws a checked exception not declared by the original method. This class serves as an unchecked exception wrapper around the checked exception. Use getUndeclaredThrowable() to obtain the checked exception thrown by invoke(). In Java 1.4 and later, all exceptions can be "chained" in this way, and getUndeclaredThrowable() is superseded by the more general getCause() method.


```
public class UndeclaredThrowableException extends RuntimeException {
// Public Constructors
   public UndeclaredThrowableException(Throwable undeclaredThrowable);
   public UndeclaredThrowableException(Throwable undeclaredThrowable, String s);
// Public Instance Methods
   public Throwable getUndeclaredThrowable();
// Public Methods Overriding Throwable
1.4 public Throwable getCause();
}
```

CHAPTER 12

java.math

Package java.math **Java 1.1**

The java.math package, new as of Java 1.1, contains classes for arbitrary-precision integer and floating-point arithmetic. Arbitrary-length integers are required for cryptography, and arbitrary-precision floating-point values are useful for financial applications that need to be careful about rounding errors.

Classes:

public class **BigDecimal** extends Number implements Comparable;
public class **BigInteger** extends Number implements Comparable;

BigDecimal **Java 1.1**

java.math *serializable comparable*

This subclass of java.lang.Number represents a floating-point number of arbitrary size and precision. Its methods duplicate the functionality of the standard Java arithmetic operators. The compareTo() method compares the value of two BigDecimal objects and returns –1, 0, or 1 to indicate the result of the comparison.

A BigDecimal object is represented as an integer of arbitrary size and an integer scale that specifies the number of decimal places in the value. When working with BigDecimal values, you can explicitly specify the amount of precision (i.e., the number of decimal places) you are interested in. Also, whenever a BigDecimal method can discard precision (e.g., in a division operation), you are required to specify what sort of rounding should be performed on the digit to the left of the discarded digit or digits. The eight constants defined by this class specify the available rounding modes. Because the BigDecimal class provides arbitrary precision and gives you explicit control over rounding and the number of decimal places you are interested in, it can be useful when dealing with quantities that represent money or in other circumstances where the tolerance for rounding errors is low.


```
public class BigDecimal extends Number implements Comparable {
// Public Constructors
   public BigDecimal(BigInteger val);
   public BigDecimal(String val);
   public BigDecimal(double val);
   public BigDecimal(BigInteger unscaledVal, int scale);
// Public Constants
   public static final int ROUND_CEILING;                         =2
   public static final int ROUND_DOWN;                            =1
   public static final int ROUND_FLOOR;                           =3
   public static final int ROUND_HALF_DOWN;                       =5
   public static final int ROUND_HALF_EVEN;                       =6
   public static final int ROUND_HALF_UP;                         =4
   public static final int ROUND_UNNECESSARY;                     =7
   public static final int ROUND_UP;                              =0
// Public Class Methods
   public static BigDecimal valueOf(long val);
   public static BigDecimal valueOf(long unscaledVal, int scale);
// Public Instance Methods
   public BigDecimal abs();
   public BigDecimal add(BigDecimal val);
   public int compareTo(BigDecimal val);
   public BigDecimal divide(BigDecimal val, int roundingMode);
   public BigDecimal divide(BigDecimal val, int scale, int roundingMode);
   public BigDecimal max(BigDecimal val);
   public BigDecimal min(BigDecimal val);
   public BigDecimal movePointLeft(int n);
   public BigDecimal movePointRight(int n);
   public BigDecimal multiply(BigDecimal val);
   public BigDecimal negate();
   public int scale();
   public BigDecimal setScale(int scale);
   public BigDecimal setScale(int scale, int roundingMode);
   public int signum();
   public BigDecimal subtract(BigDecimal val);
   public BigInteger toBigInteger();
1.2 public BigInteger unscaledValue();
// Methods Implementing Comparable
1.2 public int compareTo(Object o);
// Public Methods Overriding Number
   public double doubleValue();
   public float floatValue();
   public int intValue();
   public long longValue();
// Public Methods Overriding Object
   public boolean equals(Object x);
   public int hashCode();
   public String toString();
}
```

Passed To: Too many methods to list.

Returned By: Too many methods to list.

Type Of: org.omg.CORBA.FixedHolder.value

BigInteger **Java 1.1**

java.math ***serializable comparable***

This subclass of java.lang.Number represents integers that can be arbitrarily large (i.e., integers that are not limited to the 64 bits available with the long data type). BigInteger defines methods that duplicate the functionality of the standard Java arithmetic and bit-manipulation operators. The compareTo() method compares two BigInteger objects and returns –1, 0, or 1 to indicate the result of the comparison. The gcd(), modPow(), modInverse(), and isProbablePrime() methods perform advanced operations and are used primarily in cryptographic and related algorithms.

Object — Number — BigInteger
Serializable (Number) · Comparable (BigInteger)

```
public class BigInteger extends Number implements Comparable {
// Public Constructors
    public BigInteger(byte[ ] val);
    public BigInteger(String val);
    public BigInteger(String val, int radix);
    public BigInteger(int signum, byte[ ] magnitude);
    public BigInteger(int numBits, java.util.Random rnd);
    public BigInteger(int bitLength, int certainty, java.util.Random rnd);
// Public Constants
1.2 public static final BigInteger ONE;
1.2 public static final BigInteger ZERO;
// Public Class Methods
1.4 public static BigInteger probablePrime(int bitLength, java.util.Random rnd);
    public static BigInteger valueOf(long val);
// Public Instance Methods
    public BigInteger abs();
    public BigInteger add(BigInteger val);
    public BigInteger and(BigInteger val);
    public BigInteger andNot(BigInteger val);
    public int bitCount();
    public int bitLength();
    public BigInteger clearBit(int n);
    public int compareTo(BigInteger val);
    public BigInteger divide(BigInteger val);
    public BigInteger[ ] divideAndRemainder(BigInteger val);
    public BigInteger flipBit(int n);
    public BigInteger gcd(BigInteger val);
    public int getLowestSetBit();
    public boolean isProbablePrime(int certainty);
    public BigInteger max(BigInteger val);
    public BigInteger min(BigInteger val);
    public BigInteger mod(BigInteger m);
    public BigInteger modInverse(BigInteger m);
    public BigInteger modPow(BigInteger exponent, BigInteger m);
    public BigInteger multiply(BigInteger val);
    public BigInteger negate();
```

```
    public BigInteger not();
    public BigInteger or(BigInteger val);
    public BigInteger pow(int exponent);
    public BigInteger remainder(BigInteger val);
    public BigInteger setBit(int n);
    public BigInteger shiftLeft(int n);
    public BigInteger shiftRight(int n);
    public int signum();
    public BigInteger subtract(BigInteger val);
    public boolean testBit(int n);
    public byte[] toByteArray();
    public String toString(int radix);
    public BigInteger xor(BigInteger val);
// Methods Implementing Comparable
1.2 public int compareTo(Object o);
// Public Methods Overriding Number
    public double doubleValue();
    public float floatValue();
    public int intValue();
    public long longValue();
// Public Methods Overriding Object
    public boolean equals(Object x);
    public int hashCode();
    public String toString();
}
```

Passed To: Too many methods to list.

Returned By: Too many methods to list.

Type Of: BigInteger.{ONE, ZERO}, java.security.spec.RSAKeyGenParameterSpec.{F0, F4}

CHAPTER 13

java.net

Package java.net — Java 1.0

The java.net package provides a powerful and flexible infrastructure for networking. The most common classes are briefly described in the following sections. Note that as of Java 1.4, the New I/O API of java.nio and java.nio.channels can be used for high-performance non-blocking networking. See also the javax.net.ssl package for classes for secure networking using SSL.

The URL class represents an Internet uniform resource locator (URL). It provides a very simple interface to networking: the object referred to by the URL can be downloaded with a single call, or streams may be opened to read from or write to the object. At a slightly more complex level, a URLConnection object can be obtained from a given URL object. The URLConnection class provides additional methods that allow you to work with URLs in more sophisticated ways. Java 1.4 introduces the URI class; it provides a powerful API for manipulating URI and URL strings, but does not have any networking capabilities itself.

If you want to do more than simply download an object referenced by a URL, you can do your own networking with the Socket class. This class allows you to connect to a specified port on a specified Internet host and read and write data using the InputStream and OutputStream classes of the java.io package. If you want to implement a server to accept connections from clients, you can use the related ServerSocket class. Both Socket and ServerSocket use the InetAddress address class, which represents an Internet address. In Java 1.4, Inet4Address and Inet6Address are subclasses that represent the addresses used by Versions 4 and 6 of the IP protocol. Java 1.4 also introduces the SocketAddress class as a high-level representation of a network address that is not tied to a specific networking protocol. There is also an IP-specific InetSocketAddress subclass that encapsulates an InetAddress and a port number.

The java.net package allows you to do low-level networking with DatagramPacket objects, which may be sent and received over the network through a DatagramSocket object. MulticastSocket extends DatagramSocket to support multicast networking.

Interfaces:

public interface **ContentHandlerFactory**;
public interface **DatagramSocketImplFactory**;
public interface **FileNameMap**;
public interface **SocketImplFactory**;
public interface **SocketOptions**;
public interface **URLStreamHandlerFactory**;

Classes:

public abstract class **Authenticator**;
public abstract class **ContentHandler**;
public final class **DatagramPacket**;
public class **DatagramSocket**;
　└ public class **MulticastSocket** extends DatagramSocket;
public abstract class **DatagramSocketImpl** implements SocketOptions;
public class **InetAddress** implements Serializable;
　└ public final class **Inet4Address** extends InetAddress;
　└ public final class **Inet6Address** extends InetAddress;
public final class **NetPermission** extends java.security.BasicPermission;
public final class **NetworkInterface**;
public final class **PasswordAuthentication**;
public class **ServerSocket**;
public class **Socket**;
public abstract class **SocketAddress** implements Serializable;
　└ public class **InetSocketAddress** extends SocketAddress;
public abstract class **SocketImpl** implements SocketOptions;
public final class **SocketPermission** extends java.security.Permission implements Serializable;
public final class **URI** implements Comparable, Serializable;
public final class **URL** implements Serializable;
public class **URLClassLoader** extends java.security.SecureClassLoader;
public abstract class **URLConnection**;
　└ public abstract class **HttpURLConnection** extends URLConnection;
　└ public abstract class **JarURLConnection** extends URLConnection;
public class **URLDecoder**;
public class **URLEncoder**;
public abstract class **URLStreamHandler**;

Exceptions:

public class **MalformedURLException** extends java.io.IOException;
public class **ProtocolException** extends java.io.IOException;
public class **SocketException** extends java.io.IOException;
　└ public class **BindException** extends SocketException;
　└ public class **ConnectException** extends SocketException;
　└ public class **NoRouteToHostException** extends SocketException;
　└ public class **PortUnreachableException** extends SocketException;
public class **SocketTimeoutException** extends java.io.InterruptedIOException;
public class **UnknownHostException** extends java.io.IOException;
public class **UnknownServiceException** extends java.io.IOException;
public class **URISyntaxException** extends Exception;

Authenticator **Java 1.2**

java.net

This abstract class defines a customizable mechanism for requesting and performing password authentication when required in URL-based networking. The static setDefault() method establishes the systemwide Authenticator. An Authenticator implementation can obtain the required authentication information from the user however it wants (e.g., through a text- or a GUI-based interface). setDefault() can be called only once; subsequent calls are ignored. Calling setDefault() requires an appropriate NetPermission.

When an application or the Java runtime system requires password authentication (to read the contents of a specified URL, for example), it calls the static requestPasswordAuthentication() method, passing arguments that specify the host and port for which the password is required and a prompt that may be displayed to the user. This method looks up the default Authenticator for the system and calls its getPasswordAuthentication() method. Calling requestPasswordAuthentication() requires an appropriate NetPermission.

Authenticator is an abstract class; its default implementation of getPasswordAuthentication() always returns null. To create an Authenticator, you must override this method so that it prompts the user to enter a username and password and returns that information in the form of a PasswordAuthentication object. Your implementation of getPasswordAuthentication() may call the various getRequesting() methods to find who is requesting the password and what the recommended user prompt is. In Java 1.4, a new version of the static request-PasswordAuthentication() method has been defined to allow specification of the requesting hostname. A corresponding getRequestingHost() instance method has also been added.

```
public abstract class Authenticator {
// Public Constructors
   public Authenticator();
// Public Class Methods
   public static PasswordAuthentication requestPasswordAuthentication(InetAddress addr, int port,
                                         String protocol, String prompt, String scheme);
1.4 public static PasswordAuthentication requestPasswordAuthentication(String host, InetAddress addr, int port,
                                         String protocol, String prompt, String scheme);
   public static void setDefault(Authenticator a);                           synchronized
// Protected Instance Methods
   protected PasswordAuthentication getPasswordAuthentication();             constant
1.4 protected final String getRequestingHost();
   protected final int getRequestingPort();
   protected final String getRequestingPrompt();
   protected final String getRequestingProtocol();
   protected final String getRequestingScheme();
   protected final InetAddress getRequestingSite();
}
```

Passed To: Authenticator.setDefault()

BindException **Java 1.1**

java.net *serializable checked*

This exception signals that a socket cannot be bound to a local address and port. This often means that the port is already in use.

Object — Throwable — Exception — IOException — SocketException — BindException
Serializable

```
public class BindException extends SocketException {
// Public Constructors
   public BindException();
   public BindException(String msg);
}
```

ConnectException — Java 1.1

java.net — *serializable checked*

This exception signals that a socket cannot be connected to a remote address and port. This means that the remote host can be reached, but is not responding, perhaps because there is no process on that host that is listening on the specified port.

Object — Throwable — Exception — IOException — SocketException — ConnectException

Serializable

```
public class ConnectException extends SocketException {
// Public Constructors
   public ConnectException();
   public ConnectException(String msg);
}
```

ContentHandler — Java 1.0

java.net

This abstract class defines a method that reads data from a URLConnection and returns an object that represents that data. Each subclass that implements this method is responsible for handling a different type of content (i.e., a different MIME type). Applications never create ContentHandler objects directly; they are created, when necessary, by the registered ContentHandlerFactory object. Applications should also never call ContentHandler methods directly; they should call URL.getContent() or URLConnection.getContent() instead. You need to subclass ContentHandler only if you are writing a web browser or similar application that needs to parse and understand some new content type.

```
public abstract class ContentHandler {
// Public Constructors
   public ContentHandler();
// Public Instance Methods
   public abstract Object getContent(URLConnection urlc) throws java.io.IOException;
1.3 public Object getContent(URLConnection urlc, Class[ ] classes) throws java.io.IOException;
}
```

Returned By: ContentHandlerFactory.createContentHandler()

ContentHandlerFactory — Java 1.0

java.net

This interface defines a method that creates and returns an appropriate ContentHandler object for a specified MIME type. A systemwide ContentHandlerFactory interface may be specified using the URLConnection.setContentHandlerFactory() method. Normal applications never need to use or implement this interface.

```
public interface ContentHandlerFactory {
// Public Instance Methods
   public abstract java.net.ContentHandler createContentHandler(String mimetype);
}
```

Passed To: URLConnection.setContentHandlerFactory()

DatagramPacket — Java 1.0

java.net

This class implements a packet of data that may be sent or received over the network through a DatagramSocket. Create a DatagramPacket to be sent over the network with one of the constructor methods that includes a network address. Create a DatagramPacket into which data can be received using one of the constructors that does not include a network address argument. The receive() method of DatagramSocket waits for data and stores it in a DatagramPacket created in this way. The contents and sender of a received packet can be queried with the DatagramPacket instance methods.

New constructors and methods were added to this class in Java 1.4 to support the SocketAddress abstraction of a network address.

```
public final class DatagramPacket {
// Public Constructors
    public DatagramPacket(byte[ ] buf, int length);
1.4 public DatagramPacket(byte[ ] buf, int length, SocketAddress address) throws SocketException;
1.2 public DatagramPacket(byte[ ] buf, int offset, int length);
    public DatagramPacket(byte[ ] buf, int length, InetAddress address, int port);
1.4 public DatagramPacket(byte[ ] buf, int offset, int length, SocketAddress address) throws SocketException;
1.2 public DatagramPacket(byte[ ] buf, int offset, int length, InetAddress address, int port);
// Property Accessor Methods (by property name)
    public InetAddress getAddress();                                          synchronized
1.1 public void setAddress(InetAddress iaddr);                                synchronized
    public byte[ ] getData();                                                 synchronized
1.1 public void setData(byte[ ] buf);                                         synchronized
1.2 public void setData(byte[ ] buf, int offset, int length);                 synchronized
    public int getLength();                                                   synchronized
1.1 public void setLength(int length);                                        synchronized
1.2 public int getOffset();                                                   synchronized
    public int getPort();                                                     synchronized
1.1 public void setPort(int iport);                                           synchronized
1.4 public SocketAddress getSocketAddress();                                  synchronized
1.4 public void setSocketAddress(SocketAddress address);                      synchronized
}
```

Passed To: DatagramSocket.{receive(), send()}, DatagramSocketImpl.{peekData(), receive(), send()}, MulticastSocket.send()

DatagramSocket — Java 1.0

java.net

This class defines a socket that can receive and send unreliable datagram packets over the network using the UDP protocol. A *datagram* is a very low-level networking interface: it is simply an array of bytes sent over the network. A datagram does not implement any kind of stream-based communication protocol, and there is no connection established between the sender and the receiver. Datagram packets are called unreliable because the protocol does not make any attempt to ensure they arrive or to resend them if they don't. Thus, packets sent through a DatagramSocket are not guaranteed to arrive in the order sent or even to arrive at all. On the other hand, this low-overhead protocol makes datagram transmission very fast. See Socket and URL for higher-level interfaces to networking. This class was introduced in Java 1.0, and was enhanced in Java 1.4 to allow local and remote addresses to be specified using the protocol-independent SocketAddress class.

send() sends a DatagramPacket through the socket. The packet must contain the destination address to which it should be sent. receive() waits for data to arrive at the socket and stores it, along with the address of the sender, in the specified DatagramPacket. close() closes the socket and frees the local port for reuse. Once close() has been called, the DatagramSocket should not be used again, except to call the isClosed() method, which returns true if the socket has been closed.

Each time a packet is sent or received, the system must perform a security check to ensure that the calling code has permission to send data to or receive data from the specified host. In Java 1.2 and later, if you are sending multiple packets to or receiving multiple packets from a single host, use connect() to specify the host with which you are communicating. This causes the security check to be done a single time but does not allow the socket to communicate with any other host until disconnect() is called. Use getRemoteSocketAddress(), or getInetAddress() and getPort(), to obtain the network address, if any, that the socket is connected to. Use isConnected() to determine if the socket is currently connected in this way.

By default, a DatagramSocket sends data through a local address assigned by the system. If desired, however, you can *bind* the socket to a specified local address. Do this by using one of the constructors other than the no-arg constructor or by binding the DatagramSocket to a local SocketAddress with the bind() method. You can determine whether a DatagramSocket is bound with isBound() and obtain the local address of the socket with getLocalSocketAddress() or with getLocalAddress() and getLocalPort().

This class defines a number of get/set method pairs for setting and querying a variety of "socket options" for datagram transmission. setSoTimeout() specifies the number of milliseconds that receive() waits for a packet to arrive before throwing an InterruptedIOException. Specify 0 milliseconds to wait forever. setSendBufferSize() and setReceiveBufferSize() set hints as to the underlying size of the networking buffers. setBroadcast(), setReuseAddress(), and setTrafficClass() set more complex socket options; use of these options requires a sophisticated understanding of low-level network protocols, and an explanation of them is beyond the scope of this reference.

In Java 1.4 and later, getChannel() returns a java.nio.channels.DatagramChannel associated with this DatagramSocket. Sockets created with one of the DatagramSocket() constructors always return null from this method. getChannel() returns only a useful value for sockets that were created by and belong to a DatagramChannel.

```
public class DatagramSocket {
// Public Constructors
    public DatagramSocket() throws SocketException;
1.4 public DatagramSocket(SocketAddress bindaddr) throws SocketException;
    public DatagramSocket(int port) throws SocketException;
1.1 public DatagramSocket(int port, InetAddress laddr) throws SocketException;
// Protected Constructors
1.4 protected DatagramSocket(DatagramSocketImpl impl);
// Public Class Methods
1.3 public static void setDatagramSocketImplFactory(DatagramSocketImplFactory fac)        synchronized
        throws java.io.IOException;
// Property Accessor Methods (by property name)
1.4 public boolean isBound();                                                            default:true
1.4 public boolean getBroadcast() throws SocketException;                   synchronized default:true
```

```
1.4 public void setBroadcast(boolean on) throws SocketException;                          synchronized
1.4 public java.nio.channels.DatagramChannel getChannel();                        constant default:null
1.4 public boolean isClosed();                                                             default:false
1.4 public boolean isConnected();                                                          default:false
1.2 public InetAddress getInetAddress();                                                    default:null
1.1 public InetAddress getLocalAddress();                                           default:Inet4Address
    public int getLocalPort();
1.4 public SocketAddress getLocalSocketAddress();                              default:InetSocketAddress
1.2 public int getPort();                                                                     default:-1
1.2 public int getReceiveBufferSize() throws SocketException;             synchronized default:32767
1.2 public void setReceiveBufferSize(int size) throws SocketException;                  synchronized
1.4 public SocketAddress getRemoteSocketAddress();                                          default:null
1.4 public boolean getReuseAddress() throws SocketException;              synchronized default:false
1.4 public void setReuseAddress(boolean on) throws SocketException;                     synchronized
1.2 public int getSendBufferSize() throws SocketException;                synchronized default:32767
1.2 public void setSendBufferSize(int size) throws SocketException;                     synchronized
1.1 public int getSoTimeout() throws SocketException;                         synchronized default:0
1.1 public void setSoTimeout(int timeout) throws SocketException;                       synchronized
1.4 public int getTrafficClass() throws SocketException;                      synchronized default:0
1.4 public void setTrafficClass(int tc) throws SocketException;                         synchronized
// Public Instance Methods
1.4 public void bind(SocketAddress addr) throws SocketException;                        synchronized
    public void close();
1.4 public void connect(SocketAddress addr) throws SocketException;
1.2 public void connect(InetAddress address, int port);
1.2 public void disconnect();
    public void receive(DatagramPacket p) throws java.io.IOException;                  synchronized
    public void send(DatagramPacket p) throws java.io.IOException;
}
```

Subclasses: MulticastSocket

Returned By: java.nio.channels.DatagramChannel.socket()

DatagramSocketImpl — Java 1.1

java.net

This abstract class defines the methods necessary to implement communication through datagram and multicast sockets. System programmers may create subclasses of this class when they need to implement datagram or multicast sockets in a nonstandard network environment, such as behind a firewall or on a network that uses a nonstandard transport protocol. Normal applications never need to use or subclass this class.

Object — DatagramSocketImpl ··· SocketOptions

```
public abstract class DatagramSocketImpl implements SocketOptions {
// Public Constructors
    public DatagramSocketImpl();
// Protected Instance Methods
    protected abstract void bind(int lport, InetAddress laddr) throws SocketException;
    protected abstract void close();
1.4 protected void connect(InetAddress address, int port) throws SocketException;             empty
    protected abstract void create() throws SocketException;
1.4 protected void disconnect();                                                                empty
    protected java.io.FileDescriptor getFileDescriptor();
    protected int getLocalPort();
```

```
1.2 protected abstract int getTimeToLive() throws java.io.IOException;
    protected abstract void join(InetAddress inetaddr) throws java.io.IOException;
1.4 protected abstract void joinGroup(SocketAddress mcastaddr, NetworkInterface netIf) throws java.io.IOException;
    protected abstract void leave(InetAddress inetaddr) throws java.io.IOException;
1.4 protected abstract void leaveGroup(SocketAddress mcastaddr, NetworkInterface netIf) throws java.io.IOException;
    protected abstract int peek(InetAddress i) throws java.io.IOException;
1.4 protected abstract int peekData(DatagramPacket p) throws java.io.IOException;
    protected abstract void receive(DatagramPacket p) throws java.io.IOException;
    protected abstract void send(DatagramPacket p) throws java.io.IOException;
1.2 protected abstract void setTimeToLive(int ttl) throws java.io.IOException;
// Protected Instance Fields
    protected java.io.FileDescriptor fd;
    protected int localPort;
// Deprecated Protected Methods
#   protected abstract byte getTTL() throws java.io.IOException;
#   protected abstract void setTTL(byte ttl) throws java.io.IOException;
}
```

Passed To: DatagramSocket.DatagramSocket()

Returned By: DatagramSocketImplFactory.createDatagramSocketImpl()

DatagramSocketImplFactory — Java 1.3

java.net

This interface defines a method that creates DatagramSocketImpl objects. You can register an instance of this factory interface with the static setDatagramSocketImplFactory() method of DatagramSocket. Application-level code never needs to use or implement this interface.

```
public interface DatagramSocketImplFactory {
// Public Instance Methods
    public abstract DatagramSocketImpl createDatagramSocketImpl();
}
```

Passed To: DatagramSocket.setDatagramSocketImplFactory()

FileNameMap — Java 1.1

java.net

This interface defines a single method that is called to obtain the MIME type of a file based on the name of the file. The fileNameMap field of the URLConnection class refers to an object that implements this interface. The filename-to-file-type map it implements is used by the static URLConnection.guessContentTypeFromName() method.

```
public interface FileNameMap {
// Public Instance Methods
    public abstract String getContentTypeFor(String fileName);
}
```

Passed To: URLConnection.setFileNameMap()

Returned By: URLConnection.getFileNameMap()

HttpURLConnection — Java 1.1

java.net

This class is a specialization of URLConnection. An instance of this class is returned when the openConnection() method is called for a URL object that uses the HTTP protocol. The many constants defined by this class are the status codes returned by HTTP servers. setRequestMethod() specifies what kind of HTTP request is made. The contents of this request must be sent through the OutputStream returned by the getOutputStream() method of the superclass. Once an HTTP request has been sent, getResponseCode() returns the HTTP server's response code as an integer, and getResponseMessage() returns the server's response message. The disconnect() method closes the connection. The static setFollowRedirects() specifies whether URL connections that use the HTTP protocol should automatically follow redirect responses sent by HTTP servers. In order to successfully use this class, you need to understand the details of the HTTP protocol.

Object — URLConnection — HttpURLConnection

```
public abstract class HttpURLConnection extends URLConnection {
// Protected Constructors
   protected HttpURLConnection(URL u);
// Public Constants
   public static final int HTTP_ACCEPTED;                                =202
   public static final int HTTP_BAD_GATEWAY;                             =502
   public static final int HTTP_BAD_METHOD;                              =405
   public static final int HTTP_BAD_REQUEST;                             =400
   public static final int HTTP_CLIENT_TIMEOUT;                          =408
   public static final int HTTP_CONFLICT;                                =409
   public static final int HTTP_CREATED;                                 =201
   public static final int HTTP_ENTITY_TOO_LARGE;                        =413
   public static final int HTTP_FORBIDDEN;                               =403
   public static final int HTTP_GATEWAY_TIMEOUT;                         =504
   public static final int HTTP_GONE;                                    =410
   public static final int HTTP_INTERNAL_ERROR;                          =500
   public static final int HTTP_LENGTH_REQUIRED;                         =411
   public static final int HTTP_MOVED_PERM;                              =301
   public static final int HTTP_MOVED_TEMP;                              =302
   public static final int HTTP_MULT_CHOICE;                             =300
   public static final int HTTP_NO_CONTENT;                              =204
   public static final int HTTP_NOT_ACCEPTABLE;                          =406
   public static final int HTTP_NOT_AUTHORITATIVE;                       =203
   public static final int HTTP_NOT_FOUND;                               =404
1.3 public static final int HTTP_NOT_IMPLEMENTED;                        =501
   public static final int HTTP_NOT_MODIFIED;                            =304
   public static final int HTTP_OK;                                      =200
   public static final int HTTP_PARTIAL;                                 =206
   public static final int HTTP_PAYMENT_REQUIRED;                        =402
   public static final int HTTP_PRECON_FAILED;                           =412
   public static final int HTTP_PROXY_AUTH;                              =407
   public static final int HTTP_REQ_TOO_LONG;                            =414
   public static final int HTTP_RESET;                                   =205
   public static final int HTTP_SEE_OTHER;                               =303
   public static final int HTTP_UNAUTHORIZED;                            =401
   public static final int HTTP_UNAVAILABLE;                             =503
   public static final int HTTP_UNSUPPORTED_TYPE;                        =415
   public static final int HTTP_USE_PROXY;                               =305
   public static final int HTTP_VERSION;                                 =505
// Public Class Methods
   public static boolean getFollowRedirects();
   public static void setFollowRedirects(boolean set);
// Property Accessor Methods (by property name)
1.2 public java.io.InputStream getErrorStream();                         constant
```

```
1.3 public boolean getInstanceFollowRedirects();
1.3 public void setInstanceFollowRedirects(boolean followRedirects);
1.2 public java.security.Permission getPermission() throws java.io.IOException;     Overrides:URLConnection
    public String getRequestMethod();
    public void setRequestMethod(String method) throws ProtocolException;
    public int getResponseCode() throws java.io.IOException;                       constant
    public String getResponseMessage() throws java.io.IOException;
// Public Instance Methods
    public abstract void disconnect();
    public abstract boolean usingProxy();
// Public Methods Overriding URLConnection
1.3 public long getHeaderFieldDate(String name, long Default);
// Protected Instance Fields
1.3 protected boolean instanceFollowRedirects;
    protected String method;
    protected int responseCode;
    protected String responseMessage;
// Deprecated Public Fields
#   public static final int HTTP_SERVER_ERROR;                                     =500
}
```

Subclasses: javax.net.ssl.HttpsURLConnection

Inet4Address — Java 1.4

java.net — *serializable*

Inet4Address implements methods defined by its superclass to make them specific to Internet Protocol version 4 (IPv4) Internet addresses. Inet4Address does not have a constructor. Create instances with the static methods of InetAddress, which return instances of Inet4Address or Inet6Address as appropriate.

Object — InetAddress — Inet4Address
Serializable

```
public final class Inet4Address extends InetAddress {
// No Constructor
// Public Methods Overriding InetAddress
    public boolean equals(Object obj);
    public byte[ ] getAddress();
    public String getHostAddress();
    public int hashCode();
    public boolean isAnyLocalAddress();
    public boolean isLinkLocalAddress();
    public boolean isLoopbackAddress();
    public boolean isMCGlobal();
    public boolean isMCLinkLocal();
    public boolean isMCNodeLocal();                                                constant
    public boolean isMCOrgLocal();
    public boolean isMCSiteLocal();
    public boolean isMulticastAddress();
    public boolean isSiteLocalAddress();
}
```

Inet6Address — Java 1.4

java.net — *serializable*

Inet4Address implements methods defined by its superclass to make them specific to Internet Protocol version 6 (IPv6) Internet addresses. See RFC 2373 for complete details about Internet addresses of this type. Inet6Address does not have a constructor. Create instances with the static methods of InetAddress, which return instances of Inet4Address or Inet6Address as appropriate.

Object — InetAddress — Inet6Address
Serializable

```
public final class Inet6Address extends InetAddress {
// No Constructor
// Public Instance Methods
   public boolean isIPv4CompatibleAddress();
// Public Methods Overriding InetAddress
   public boolean equals(Object obj);
   public byte[ ] getAddress();
   public String getHostAddress();
   public int hashCode();
   public boolean isAnyLocalAddress();
   public boolean isLinkLocalAddress();
   public boolean isLoopbackAddress();
   public boolean isMCGlobal();
   public boolean isMCLinkLocal();
   public boolean isMCNodeLocal();
   public boolean isMCOrgLocal();
   public boolean isMCSiteLocal();
   public boolean isMulticastAddress();
   public boolean isSiteLocalAddress();
}
```

InetAddress — Java 1.0

java.net — *serializable*

This class represents an Internet Protocol (IP) address. The class does not have a public constructor but instead supports static factory methods for obtaining InetAddress objects. getLocalHost() returns the InetAddress of the local computer. getByName() returns the InetAddress of a host specified by name. getAllByName() returns an array of InetAddress objects that represents all the available addresses for a host specified by name. getByAddress() returns an InetAddress that represents the IP address defined by the specified array of bytes.

Once you have obtained an InetAddress object, its instance methods provide various sorts of information about it. Two of the most important are getHostName(), which returns the hostname, and getAddress(), which returns the Internet IP address as an array of bytes, with the highest-order byte as the first element of the array. getHostAddress() returns the IP address formatted as a string rather than as an array of bytes. The various methods whose names begin with "is" determine whether the address falls into any of the named categories. The "isMC" methods are all related to multicast addresses.

This class was originally defined in Java 1.0, but many of its methods were added in Java 1.4. Java 1.4 also defines two subclasses, Inet4Address and Inet6Address, representing IPv4 and IPv6 (Versions 4 and 6) addresses.

Object — InetAddress ··· Serializable

```
public class InetAddress implements Serializable {
// No Constructor
// Public Class Methods
    public static InetAddress[ ] getAllByName(String host) throws java.net.UnknownHostException;
1.4 public static InetAddress getByAddress(byte[ ] addr) throws java.net.UnknownHostException;
1.4 public static InetAddress getByAddress(String host, byte[ ] addr) throws java.net.UnknownHostException;
    public static InetAddress getByName(String host) throws java.net.UnknownHostException;
    public static InetAddress getLocalHost() throws java.net.UnknownHostException;     synchronized
// Property Accessor Methods (by property name)
    public byte[ ] getAddress();                                                        constant
1.4 public boolean isAnyLocalAddress();                                                 constant
1.4 public String getCanonicalHostName();
    public String getHostAddress();                                                     constant
    public String getHostName();
1.4 public boolean isLinkLocalAddress();                                                constant
1.4 public boolean IsLoopbackAddress();                                                 constant
1.4 public boolean isMCGlobal();                                                        constant
1.4 public boolean isMCLinkLocal();                                                     constant
1.4 public boolean isMCNodeLocal();                                                     constant
1.4 public boolean isMCOrgLocal();                                                      constant
1.4 public boolean isMCSiteLocal();                                                     constant
1.1 public boolean isMulticastAddress();                                                constant
1.4 public boolean isSiteLocalAddress();                                                constant
// Public Methods Overriding Object
    public boolean equals(Object obj);                                                  constant
    public int hashCode();                                                              constant
    public String toString();
}
```

Subclasses: Inet4Address, Inet6Address

Passed To: Too many methods to list.

Returned By: Too many methods to list.

Type Of: SocketImpl.address

InetSocketAddress — Java 1.4

java.net — *serializable*

InetSocketAddress represents the combination of an Internet Protocol (IP) address and a port number. The constructors allow you to specify the IP address as an InetAddress or as a hostname and also allow you to omit the IP address, in which case the wildcard address is used (this is useful for server sockets).

Object — SocketAddress — InetSocketAddress
Serializable

```
public class InetSocketAddress extends SocketAddress {
// Public Constructors
    public InetSocketAddress(int port);
    public InetSocketAddress(InetAddress addr, int port);
```

```
    public InetSocketAddress(String hostname, int port);
// Public Instance Methods
    public final InetAddress getAddress();
    public final String getHostName();
    public final int getPort();
    public final boolean isUnresolved();
// Public Methods Overriding Object
    public final boolean equals(Object obj);
    public final int hashCode();
    public String toString();
}
```

JarURLConnection — Java 1.2

java.net

This class is a specialized URLConnection that represents a connection to a jar: URL. A jar: URL is a compound URL that includes the URL of a JAR archive and, optionally, a reference to a file or directory within the JAR archive. The jar: URL syntax uses the ! character to separate the pathname of the JAR archive from the filename within the JAR archive. Note that a jar: URL contains a subprotocol that specifies the protocol that retrieves the JAR file itself. For example:

```
jar:http://my.jar.com/my.jar!/                          // The whole archive
jar:file:/usr/java/lib/my.jar!/com/jar/                 // A directory of the archive
jar:ftp://ftp.jar.com/pub/my.jar!/com/jar/Jar.class  // A file in the archive
```

To obtain a JarURLConnection, define a URL object for a jar: URL, open a connection to it with openConnection(), and cast the returned URLConnection object to a JarURLConnection. The various methods defined by JarURLConnection allow you to read the manifest file of the JAR archive and look up attributes from that manifest for the archive as a whole or for individual entries in the archive. These methods make use of various classes from the java.util.jar package.

Object — URLConnection — JarURLConnection

```
public abstract class JarURLConnection extends URLConnection {
// Protected Constructors
    protected JarURLConnection(URL url) throws MalformedURLException;
// Property Accessor Methods (by property name)
    public java.util.jar.Attributes getAttributes() throws java.io.IOException;
    public java.security.cert.Certificate[ ] getCertificates() throws java.io.IOException;
    public String getEntryName();
    public java.util.jar.JarEntry getJarEntry() throws java.io.IOException;
    public abstract java.util.jar.JarFile getJarFile() throws java.io.IOException;
    public URL getJarFileURL();
    public java.util.jar.Attributes getMainAttributes() throws java.io.IOException;
    public java.util.jar.Manifest getManifest() throws java.io.IOException;
// Protected Instance Fields
    protected URLConnection jarFileURLConnection;
}
```

MalformedURLException **Java 1.0**

java.net ***serializable checked***

This exception signals that an unparseable URL specification has been passed to a method.

Object — Throwable — Exception — IOException — MalformedURLException
Serializable

```
public class MalformedURLException extends java.io.IOException {
// Public Constructors
   public MalformedURLException();
   public MalformedURLException(String msg);
}
```

Thrown By: Too many methods to list.

MulticastSocket **Java 1.1**

java.net

This subclass of DatagramSocket can send and receive multicast UDP packets. It extends DatagramSocket by adding joinGroup() and leaveGroup() methods to join and leave multicast groups. You do not have to join a group to send a packet to a multicast address, but you must join the group to receive packets sent to that address. Note that the use of a MulticastSocket is governed by a security manager.

Use setTimeToLive() to set a time-to-live value for any packets sent through a MulticastSocket. This constrains the number of network hops a packet can take and controls the scope of a multicast. Use setInterface() or setNetworkInterface() to specify the InetAddress or the NetworkInterface that outgoing multicast packets should use: this is useful for servers or other computers that have more than one Internet address or network interface. setLoopbackMode() specifies whether a multicast packet sent through this socket should be sent back to this socket or not. This method should really be named "setLoopbackModeDisabled()": passing an argument of true requests (but does not require) that the system disable loopback packets.

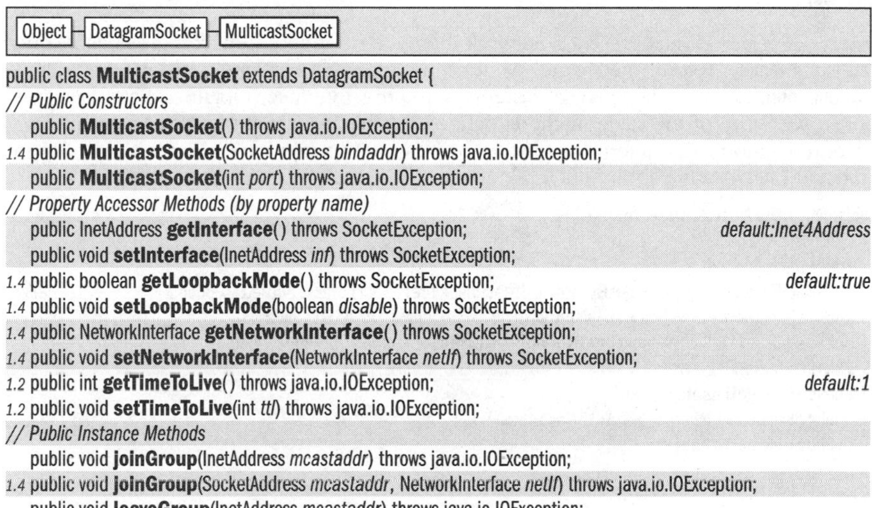


```
public class MulticastSocket extends DatagramSocket {
// Public Constructors
    public MulticastSocket() throws java.io.IOException;
1.4 public MulticastSocket(SocketAddress bindaddr) throws java.io.IOException;
    public MulticastSocket(int port) throws java.io.IOException;
// Property Accessor Methods (by property name)
    public InetAddress getInterface() throws SocketException;                    default:Inet4Address
    public void setInterface(InetAddress inf) throws SocketException;
1.4 public boolean getLoopbackMode() throws SocketException;                        default:true
1.4 public void setLoopbackMode(boolean disable) throws SocketException;
1.4 public NetworkInterface getNetworkInterface() throws SocketException;
1.4 public void setNetworkInterface(NetworkInterface netIf) throws SocketException;
1.2 public int getTimeToLive() throws java.io.IOException;                          default:1
1.2 public void setTimeToLive(int ttl) throws java.io.IOException;
// Public Instance Methods
    public void joinGroup(InetAddress mcastaddr) throws java.io.IOException;
1.4 public void joinGroup(SocketAddress mcastaddr, NetworkInterface netIf) throws java.io.IOException;
    public void leaveGroup(InetAddress mcastaddr) throws java.io.IOException;
```

```
1.4 public void leaveGroup(SocketAddress mcastaddr, NetworkInterface netIf) throws java.io.IOException;
// Deprecated Public Methods
#  public byte getTTL() throws java.io.IOException;                                    default:1
#  public void send(DatagramPacket p, byte ttl) throws java.io.IOException;
#  public void setTTL(byte ttl) throws java.io.IOException;
}
```

NetPermission — Java 1.2

java.net — *serializable permission*

This class is a java.security.Permission that represents various permissions required for Java's URL-based networking system. See also SocketPermission, which represents permissions to perform lower-level networking operations. A NetPermission is defined solely by its name; no actions list is required or supported. As of Java 1.2, there are three NetPermission targets defined: "setDefaultAuthenticator" is required to call Authenticator.setDefault(); "requestPasswordAuthentication" to call Authenticator.requestPasswordAuthentication(); and "specifyStreamHandler" to explicitly pass a URLStreamHandler object to the URL() constructor. The target "*" is a wildcard that represents all defined NetPermission targets.

System administrators configuring security policies must be familiar with this class and the permissions it represents. System programmers may use this class, but application programmers never need to use it explicitly.

Object — Permission — BasicPermission — NetPermission
Guard, Serializable (Permission); Serializable (BasicPermission)

```
public final class NetPermission extends java.security.BasicPermission {
// Public Constructors
   public NetPermission(String name);
   public NetPermission(String name, String actions);
}
```

NetworkInterface — Java 1.4

java.net

Instances of this class represent a network interface on the local machine. getName() and getDisplayName() return the name of the interface, and getInetAddresses() returns a java.util.Enumeration of the Internet addresses for the interface. Obtain a NetworkInterface object with one of the static methods defined by this class. getNetworkInterfaces() returns an enumeration of all interfaces for the local host. Typically, this class is used only in advanced networking applications.

```
public final class NetworkInterface {
// No Constructor
// Public Class Methods
   public static NetworkInterface getByInetAddress(InetAddress addr) throws SocketException;     native
   public static NetworkInterface getByName(String name) throws SocketException;                native
   public static java.util.Enumeration getNetworkInterfaces() throws SocketException;
// Public Instance Methods
   public String getDisplayName();
   public java.util.Enumeration getInetAddresses();
   public String getName();
```

```
// Public Methods Overriding Object
   public boolean equals(Object obj);
   public int hashCode();
   public String toString();
}
```

Passed To: DatagramSocketImpl.{joinGroup(), leaveGroup()}, MulticastSocket.{joinGroup(), leaveGroup(), setNetworkInterface()}

Returned By: MulticastSocket.getNetworkInterface(), NetworkInterface.{getByInetAddress(), getByName()}

NoRouteToHostException — Java 1.1

java.net — *serializable checked*

This exception signals that a socket cannot be connected to a remote host because the host cannot be contacted. Typically, this means that some link in the network between the local machine and the remote host is down or that the host is behind a firewall.

Object — Throwable — Exception — IOException — SocketException — NoRouteToHostException
Serializable

```
public class NoRouteToHostException extends SocketException {
// Public Constructors
   public NoRouteToHostException();
   public NoRouteToHostException(String msg);
}
```

PasswordAuthentication — Java 1.2

java.net

This simple immutable class encapsulates a username and a password. The password is stored as a character array rather than as a String object so that the caller can erase the contents of the array after use for increased security. Note that the PasswordAuthentication() constructor clones the specified password character array, but getPassword() returns a reference to the object's internal array.

Application programmers defining an Authenticator object for their application need to create and return a PasswordAuthentication object from the getPasswordAuthentication() method of that object. System programmers writing URLStreamHandler implementations or otherwise interacting with a network server that requests password authentication may obtain a PasswordAuthentication object representing the user's name and password by calling the static Authenticator.requestPasswordAuthentication() method.

```
public final class PasswordAuthentication {
// Public Constructors
   public PasswordAuthentication(String userName, char[ ] password);
// Public Instance Methods
   public char[ ] getPassword();
   public String getUserName();
}
```

Returned By: Authenticator.{getPasswordAuthentication(), requestPasswordAuthentication()}

PortUnreachableException **Java 1.4**

java.net ***serializable checked***

An exception of this type may be thrown by a send() or receive() call on a DatagramSocket if the connect() method of that socket has been called and if the connection attempt resulted in an ICMP "port unreachable" message.

Object — Throwable — Exception — IOException — SocketException — PortUnreachableException
Throwable ⋯ Serializable

```
public class PortUnreachableException extends SocketException {
// Public Constructors
   public PortUnreachableException();
   public PortUnreachableException(String msg);
}
```

ProtocolException **Java 1.0**

java.net ***serializable checked***

This exception signals a protocol error in the Socket class.

Object — Throwable — Exception — IOException — ProtocolException
Throwable ⋯ Serializable

```
public class ProtocolException extends java.io.IOException {
// Public Constructors
   public ProtocolException();
   public ProtocolException(String host);
}
```

Thrown By: HttpURLConnection.setRequestMethod()

ServerSocket **Java 1.0**

java.net

This class is used by servers to listen for connection requests from clients. Before you can use a ServerSocket, it must be *bound* to the local network address on which it will listen. All of the ServerSocket() constructors, except for the no-argument constructor, create a server socket and bind it to the specified local port, optionally specifying a "connection backlog" value: the number of client connection attempts that may be queued before subsequent connection attempts are rejected.

In Java 1.4 and later, the no-argument ServerSocket() constructor allows you to create an unbound socket. Doing this allows you to bind the socket using the bind() method, which uses a SocketAddress object rather than a port number. It also allows you to call setReuseAddress(), which is useful only when done before the socket is bound. Call isBound() to determine whether a server socket has been bound. If it has, use getLocalSocketAddress(), or getLocalPort() and getInetAddress(), to obtain the local address it is bound to.

Once a ServerSocket has been bound, you can call the accept() method to listen on the specified port and block until the client requests a connection on the port. When this happens, accept() accepts the connection, creating and returning a Socket the server can use to communicate with the client. A typical server starts a new thread to handle the communication with the client and calls accept() again to listen for another connection.

ServerSocket defines several methods for setting socket options that affect the socket's behavior. setSoTimeout() specifies the number of milliseconds that accept() should block before throwing an InterruptedIOException. A value of 0 means that it should block forever. setReceiveBufferSize() is an advanced option that suggests the desired size for the internal receive buffer of the Socket objects returned by accept(). This is only a hint and may be ignored by the system. setReuseAddress() is another advanced option; it specifies that a bind() operation should succeed even if the local bind address is still nominally in use by a socket that is in the process of shutting down.

Like all sockets, a ServerSocket should be closed with the close() method when it is no longer needed. Once closed, a ServerSocket should not be used, except to call the isClosed() method, which returns true if it has been closed.

The getChannel() method is a link between this ServerSocket class and the New I/O java.nio.channels.ServerSocketChannel class. It returns the ServerSocketChannel associated with this ServerSocket, if there is one. Note, however, that this method always returns null for sockets created with any of the ServerSocket() constructors. If you create a ServerSocketChannel object, and obtain a ServerSocket from it, however, then the getChannel() method provides a way to link back to the parent channel.

```
public class ServerSocket {
// Public Constructors
1.4 public ServerSocket() throws java.io.IOException;
    public ServerSocket(int port) throws java.io.IOException;
    public ServerSocket(int port, int backlog) throws java.io.IOException;
1.1 public ServerSocket(int port, int backlog, InetAddress bindAddr) throws java.io.IOException;
// Public Class Methods
    public static void setSocketFactory(SocketImplFactory fac) throws java.io.IOException;     synchronized
// Property Accessor Methods (by property name)
1.4 public boolean isBound();                                                                  default:false
1.4 public java.nio.channels.ServerSocketChannel getChannel();                         constant default:null
1.4 public boolean isClosed();                                                                 default:false
    public InetAddress getInetAddress();                                                        default:null
    public int getLocalPort();                                                                    default:-1
1.4 public SocketAddress getLocalSocketAddress();                                               default:null
1.4 public int getReceiveBufferSize() throws SocketException;                  synchronized default:32767
1.4 public void setReceiveBufferSize(int size) throws SocketException;                         synchronized
1.4 public boolean getReuseAddress() throws SocketException;                                     default:true
1.4 public void setReuseAddress(boolean on) throws SocketException;
1.1 public int getSoTimeout() throws java.io.IOException;                          synchronized default:0
1.1 public void setSoTimeout(int timeout) throws SocketException;                               synchronized
// Public Instance Methods
    public Socket accept() throws java.io.IOException;
1.4 public void bind(SocketAddress endpoint) throws java.io.IOException;
1.4 public void bind(SocketAddress endpoint, int backlog) throws java.io.IOException;
    public void close() throws java.io.IOException;
// Public Methods Overriding Object
    public String toString();
// Protected Instance Methods
1.1 protected final void implAccept(Socket s) throws java.io.IOException;
}
```

Subclasses: javax.net.ssl.SSLServerSocket

Returned By: java.nio.channels.ServerSocketChannel.socket(), java.rmi.server.RMIServerSocketFactory.createServerSocket(), java.rmi.server.RMISocketFactory.createServerSocket(), javax.net.ServerSocketFactory.createServerSocket()

Socket Java 1.0

java.net

This class implements a socket for stream-based communication over the network. See URL for a higher-level interface to networking and DatagramSocket for a lower-level interface.

Before you can use a socket for communication, it must be *bound* to a local address and *connected* to a remote address. Binding and connection are done automatically when you call any of the Socket() constructors, except the no-argument constructor. These constructors allow you to specify either the name or the InetAddress of the computer to connect to and require you to specify the port number to connect to. Two of these constructors also allow you to specify the local InetAddress and port number to bind the socket to. Most applications do not need to specify a local address and can simply use one of the two-argument versions of Socket() and allow the constructor to choose an ephemeral local port to bind the socket to.

The no-argument Socket() constructor is different from the others; it creates an unbound and unconnected socket. In Java 1.4 and later, you can explicitly call bind() and connect() to bind and connect the socket. It can be useful to do this when you want to set a socket option (described later) that must be set before binding or connection. bind() uses a SocketAddress object to describe the local address to bind to, and connect() uses a SocketAddress to specify the remote address to connect to. There is also a version of connect() that takes a timeout value in milliseconds: if the connection attempt takes longer than the specified amount of time, connect() throws an IOException. See ServerSocket for a description of how to write server code that accepts socket connection requests from client code.

Use isBound() and isConnected() to determine whether a Socket is bound and connected. Use getInetAddress() and getPort() to determine the IP address and port number that the socket is connected to. In Java 1.4, use getRemoteSocketAddress() to obtain the remote address as a SocketAddress object. Similarly, use getLocalAddress() and getLocalPort(), or getLocalSocketAddress(), to find the address a socket is bound to.

Once you have a Socket object that is bound and connected, use getInputStream() and getOutputStream() to obtain InputStream and OutputStream objects you can use to communicate with the remote host. Use these streams just as you would similar streams for file input and output. When you are done with a Socket, use close() to close it. Once a socket has been closed, it is not possible to call connect() again to reuse it, and you should not call any of its methods except isClosed(). Because networking code can throw many exceptions, it is common practice to close() a socket in the finally clause of a try/catch statement to ensure that the socket always gets closed. Note, however, that the close() method itself can throw an IOException, and you may need to put it in its own try block. In Java 1.3 and later, shutdownInput() and shutdownOutput() allow you to close the input and output communication channels individually without closing the entire socket. In Java 1.4, isInputShutdown() and isOutputShutdown() allow you to test for this.

The Socket class defines a number of methods that allow you to set (and query) "socket options" that affect the low-level networking behavior of the socket. setSendBufferSize() and setReceiveBufferSize() provide hints to the underlying networking system as to what buffer size is best to use with this socket. setSoTimeout() specifies the number of milliseconds a read() call on the input stream returned by getInputStream() waits for data before throwing an InterruptedIOException. The default value of 0 specifies that the stream blocks indefinitely. setSoLinger() specifies what to do when a socket is closed while there is still data waiting to be transmitted. If lingering is turned on, the close() call blocks for up to the specified number of seconds while attempting to transmit the remaining data. Calling setTcpNoDelay() with an argument of true causes data to be sent through the socket as soon as it is available, instead of waiting for the TCP packet to fill up more before sending it. In Java 1.3, use setKeepAlive() to enable or disable the periodic exchange of control messages across an idle socket connection. The keepalive protocol enables a client to determine if its server has crashed without closing the socket and vice versa. In Java 1.4, pass true to setOOBInline() if you want to receive "out of band" data sent to this socket "inline" on the input stream of the socket (by default, such data is simply discarded). This can be used to receive bytes sent with sendUrgentData(). Java 1.4 also adds setReuseAddress(), which you can use before binding the socket to specify that the socket should be allowed to bind to a port that is still nominally in use by another socket in the process of shutting down. setTrafficClass() is also new in Java 1.4; it sets the "traffic class" field for the socket and requires an understanding of the low-level details of the IP protocol.

The getChannel() method is a link between this Socket class and the New I/O java.nio.channels.SocketChannel class. It returns the SocketChannel associated with this Socket if there is one. Note, however, that this method always returns null for sockets created with any of the Socket() constructors. If you create a SocketChannel object, and obtain a Socket from it, then the getChannel() method provides a way to link back to the parent channel.

```
public class Socket {
// Public Constructors
1.1 public Socket();
    public Socket(InetAddress address, int port) throws java.io.IOException;
    public Socket(String host, int port) throws java.net.UnknownHostException, java.io.IOException;
#   public Socket(InetAddress host, int port, boolean stream) throws java.io.IOException;
#   public Socket(String host, int port, boolean stream) throws java.io.IOException;
1.1 public Socket(InetAddress address, int port, InetAddress localAddr, int localPort) throws java.io.IOException;
1.1 public Socket(String host, int port, InetAddress localAddr, int localPort) throws java.io.IOException;
// Protected Constructors
1.1 protected Socket(SocketImpl impl) throws SocketException;
// Public Class Methods
    public static void setSocketImplFactory(SocketImplFactory fac) throws java.io.IOException;    synchronized
// Property Accessor Methods (by property name)
1.4 public boolean isBound();                                                      default:false
1.4 public java.nio.channels.SocketChannel getChannel();                   constant default:null
1.4 public boolean isClosed();                                                     default:false
1.4 public boolean isConnected();                                                  default:false
    public InetAddress getInetAddress();                                           default:null
1.4 public boolean isInputShutdown();                                              default:false
    public java.io.InputStream getInputStream() throws java.io.IOException;
1.3 public boolean getKeepAlive() throws SocketException;                          default:false
1.3 public void setKeepAlive(boolean on) throws SocketException;
1.1 public InetAddress getLocalAddress();                                   default:Inet4Address
    public int getLocalPort();                                                     default:-1
1.4 public SocketAddress getLocalSocketAddress();                                  default:null
1.4 public boolean getOOBInline() throws SocketException;                          default:false
1.4 public void setOOBInline(boolean on) throws SocketException;
1.4 public boolean isOutputShutdown();                                             default:false
    public java.io.OutputStream getOutputStream() throws java.io.IOException;
    public int getPort();                                                          default:0
1.2 public int getReceiveBufferSize() throws SocketException;         synchronized default:32767
1.2 public void setReceiveBufferSize(int size) throws SocketException;              synchronized
```

```
1.4 public SocketAddress getRemoteSocketAddress();                                          default:null
1.4 public boolean getReuseAddress() throws SocketException;                               default:false
1.4 public void setReuseAddress(boolean on) throws SocketException;
1.2 public int getSendBufferSize() throws SocketException;               synchronized default:32767
1.2 public void setSendBufferSize(int size) throws SocketException;                    synchronized
1.1 public int getSoLinger() throws SocketException;                                          default:-1
1.1 public int getSoTimeout() throws SocketException;                        synchronized default:0
1.1 public void setSoTimeout(int timeout) throws SocketException;                      synchronized
1.1 public boolean getTcpNoDelay() throws SocketException;                                 default:false
1.1 public void setTcpNoDelay(boolean on) throws SocketException;
1.4 public int getTrafficClass() throws SocketException;                                       default:0
1.4 public void setTrafficClass(int tc) throws SocketException;
// Public Instance Methods
1.4 public void bind(SocketAddress bindpoint) throws java.io.IOException;
    public void close() throws java.io.IOException;                                       synchronized
1.4 public void connect(SocketAddress endpoint) throws java.io.IOException;
1.4 public void connect(SocketAddress endpoint, int timeout) throws java.io.IOException;
1.4 public void sendUrgentData(int data) throws java.io.IOException;
1.1 public void setSoLinger(boolean on, int linger) throws SocketException;
1.3 public void shutdownInput() throws java.io.IOException;
1.3 public void shutdownOutput() throws java.io.IOException;
// Public Methods Overriding Object
    public String toString();
}
```

Subclasses: javax.net.ssl.SSLSocket

Passed To: ServerSocket.implAccept(), javax.net.ssl.SSLSocketFactory.createSocket(), javax.net.ssl.X509KeyManager.{chooseClientAlias(), chooseServerAlias()}

Returned By: ServerSocket.accept(), java.nio.channels.SocketChannel.socket(), java.rmi.server.RMIClientSocketFactory.createSocket(), java.rmi.server.RMISocketFactory.createSocket(), javax.net.SocketFactory.createSocket(), javax.net.ssl.SSLSocketFactory.createSocket()

SocketAddress — Java 1.4

java.net — *serializable*

Instances of this abstract class are opaque representations of network socket addresses. The only concrete subclass in the core Java platform is InetSocketAddress, which represents an Internet address and port number. See InetSocketAddress.

Object — SocketAddress ··· Serializable

```
public abstract class SocketAddress implements Serializable {
// Public Constructors
    public SocketAddress();
}
```

Subclasses: InetSocketAddress

Passed To: Too many methods to list.

Returned By: DatagramPacket.getSocketAddress(), DatagramSocket.{getLocalSocketAddress(), getRemoteSocketAddress()}, ServerSocket.getLocalSocketAddress(), Socket.{getLocalSocketAddress(), getRemoteSocketAddress()}, java.nio.channels.DatagramChannel.receive()

SocketException **Java 1.0**

java.net *serializable checked*

This exception signals an exceptional condition while using a socket.

Object — Throwable — Exception — IOException — SocketException
Serializable

```
public class SocketException extends java.io.IOException {
// Public Constructors
   public SocketException();
   public SocketException(String msg);
}
```

Subclasses: BindException, java.net.ConnectException, NoRouteToHostException, PortUnreachableException

Thrown By: Too many methods to list.

SocketImpl **Java 1.0**

java.net

This abstract class defines the methods necessary to implement communication through sockets. Different subclasses of this class may provide different implementations suitable in different environments (such as behind firewalls). These socket implementations are used by the Socket and ServerSocket classes. Normal applications never need to use or subclass this class.

Object — SocketImpl ··· SocketOptions

```
public abstract class SocketImpl implements SocketOptions {
// Public Constructors
   public SocketImpl();
// Public Methods Overriding Object
   public String toString();
// Protected Instance Methods
   protected abstract void accept(SocketImpl s) throws java.io.IOException;
   protected abstract int available() throws java.io.IOException;
   protected abstract void bind(InetAddress host, int port) throws java.io.IOException;
   protected abstract void close() throws java.io.IOException;
   protected abstract void connect(String host, int port) throws java.io.IOException;
   protected abstract void connect(InetAddress address, int port) throws java.io.IOException;
1.4 protected abstract void connect(SocketAddress address, int timeout) throws java.io.IOException;
   protected abstract void create(boolean stream) throws java.io.IOException;
   protected java.io.FileDescriptor getFileDescriptor();
   protected InetAddress getInetAddress();
   protected abstract java.io.InputStream getInputStream() throws java.io.IOException;
   protected int getLocalPort();
   protected abstract java.io.OutputStream getOutputStream() throws java.io.IOException;
   protected int getPort();
   protected abstract void listen(int backlog) throws java.io.IOException;
1.4 protected abstract void sendUrgentData(int data) throws java.io.IOException;
1.3 protected void shutdownInput() throws java.io.IOException;
1.3 protected void shutdownOutput() throws java.io.IOException;
1.4 protected boolean supportsUrgentData();                                constant
```

```
// Protected Instance Fields
   protected InetAddress address;
   protected java.io.FileDescriptor fd;
   protected int localport;
   protected int port;
}
```

Passed To: Socket.Socket(), SocketImpl.accept()

Returned By: SocketImplFactory.createSocketImpl()

SocketImplFactory — Java 1.0

java.net

This interface defines a method that creates SocketImpl objects. SocketImplFactory objects may be registered to create SocketImpl objects for the Socket and ServerSocket classes. Normal applications never need to use or implement this interface.

```
public interface SocketImplFactory {
// Public Instance Methods
   public abstract SocketImpl createSocketImpl();
}
```

Passed To: ServerSocket.setSocketFactory(), Socket.setSocketImplFactory()

SocketOptions — Java 1.2

java.net

This interface defines constants that represent low-level BSD Unix-style socket options and methods that set and query the value of those options. In Java 1.2, SocketImpl and DatagramSocketImpl implement this interface. Any custom socket implementations you define should also provide meaningful implementations for the getOption() and setOption() methods. Your implementation may support options other than those defined here. Only custom socket implementations need to use this interface. All other code can use methods defined by Socket, ServerSocket, DatagramSocket, and MulticastSocket to set specific socket options for those socket types.

```
public interface SocketOptions {
// Public Constants
    public static final int IP_MULTICAST_IF;                                =16
1.4 public static final int IP_MULTICAST_IF2;                               =31
1.4 public static final int IP_MULTICAST_LOOP;                              =18
1.4 public static final int IP_TOS;                                         =3
    public static final int SO_BINDADDR;                                    =15
1.4 public static final int SO_BROADCAST;                                   =32
1.3 public static final int SO_KEEPALIVE;                                   =8
    public static final int SO_LINGER;                                      =128
1.4 public static final int SO_OOBINLINE;                                   =4099
    public static final int SO_RCVBUF;                                      =4098
    public static final int SO_REUSEADDR;                                   =4
    public static final int SO_SNDBUF;                                      =4097
    public static final int SO_TIMEOUT;                                     =4102
    public static final int TCP_NODELAY;                                    =1
// Public Instance Methods
    public abstract Object getOption(int optID) throws SocketException;
```

```
    public abstract void setOption(int optID, Object value) throws SocketException;
}
```

Implementations: DatagramSocketImpl, SocketImpl

SocketPermission **Java 1.2**

java.net *serializable permission*

This class is a java.security.Permission that governs all networking operations performed with sockets. Like all permissions, a SocketPermission consists of a name, or target, and a list of actions that may be performed on that target. The target of a SocketPermission is the host and, optionally, the port or ports for which permission is being granted or requested. The target consists of a hostname optionally followed by a colon and a port specification. The host may be a DNS domain name, a numerical IP address, or the string "localhost". If you specify a host domain name, you may use * as a wildcard as the leftmost portion of the hostname. The port specification, if present, must be a single port number or a range of port numbers in the form n1-n2. If n1 is omitted, it is taken to be 0, and if n2 is omitted, it is taken to be 65535. If no port is specified, the socket permission applies to all ports of the specified host. Here are some legal SocketPermission targets:

```
java.sun.com:80
*.sun.com:1024-2000
*:1024-
localhost:-1023
```

In addition to a target, each SocketPermission must have a comma-separated list of actions, which specify the operations that may be performed on the specified host(s) and port(s). The available actions are "connect", "accept", "listen", and "resolve". "connect" represents permission to connect to the specified target. "accept" indicates permission to accept connections from the specified target. "listen" represents permission to listen on the specified ports for connection requests. This action is only valid when used for ports on "localhost". Finally, the "resolve" action indicates permission to use the DNS name service to resolve domain names into IP addresses. This action is required for and implied by all other actions.

System administrators configuring security policies must be familiar with this class and understand the risks of granting the various permissions it represents. System programmers writing new low-level networking libraries or connecting to native code that performs networking may need to use this class. Application programmers, however, should never need to use it directly.

Object — Permission — SocketPermission
Guard | Serializable | Serializable

```
public final class SocketPermission extends java.security.Permission implements Serializable {
// Public Constructors
    public SocketPermission(String host, String action);
// Public Methods Overriding Permission
    public boolean equals(Object obj);
    public String getActions();
    public int hashCode();
    public boolean implies(java.security.Permission p);
    public java.security.PermissionCollection newPermissionCollection();
}
```

SocketTimeoutException — Java 1.4

java.net — *serializable checked*

This exception signals that a timeout value was exceeded for a socket read or accept operation. See the setSoTimeout() method of Socket.

Object — Throwable — Exception — IOException — InterruptedIOException — SocketTimeoutException
(Throwable implements Serializable)

```
public class SocketTimeoutException extends java.io.InterruptedIOException {
// Public Constructors
   public SocketTimeoutException();
   public SocketTimeoutException(String msg);
}
```

UnknownHostException — Java 1.0

java.net — *serializable checked*

This exception signals that the name of a specified host could not be resolved.

Object — Throwable — Exception — IOException — UnknownHostException
(Throwable implements Serializable)

```
public class UnknownHostException extends java.io.IOException {
// Public Constructors
   public UnknownHostException();
   public UnknownHostException(String host);
}
```

Thrown By: InetAddress.{getAllByName(), getByAddress(), getByName(), getLocalHost()}, Socket.Socket(), javax.net.SocketFactory.createSocket(), javax.net.ssl.SSLSocket.SSLSocket()

UnknownServiceException — Java 1.0

java.net — *serializable checked*

This exception signals an attempt to use an unsupported service of a network connection.

Object — Throwable — Exception — IOException — UnknownServiceException
(Throwable implements Serializable)

```
public class UnknownServiceException extends java.io.IOException {
// Public Constructors
   public UnknownServiceException();
   public UnknownServiceException(String msg);
}
```

URI — Java 1.4

java.net — *serializable comparable*

The URI class is an immutable representation of a Uniform Resource Identifier (URI). A URI is a generalization of the Uniform Resource Locators (URLs) used on the World Wide Web. The URI supports parsing and textual manipulation of URI strings but does not have any direct networking capabilities the way that the URL class does. The advantages of the URI class over the URL class are that the URI class provides more general facilities for parsing and manipulating URLs than the URL class; it can represent relative

URIs, which do not include a scheme (or protocol); and it can manipulate URIs that include unsupported or even unknown schemes.

Obtain a URI with one of the constructors, which allow a URI to be parsed from a single string, or allow the specification of the individual components of a URI. These constructors can throw URISyntaxException, which is a checked exception. When using hard-coded URIs (rather than URIs based on user input), you may prefer to use the static create() method, which does not throw any checked exceptions.

Once you have created a URI object, you can use the various get methods to query the various portions of the URI. The getRaw() methods are like the get() methods, except that they do not decode hexadecimal escape sequences of the form %xx that appear in the URI. normalize() returns a new URI object that has "." and unnecessary ".." sequences removed from its path component. resolve() interprets its URI (or string) argument relative to this URI and returns the result. relativize() performs the reverse operation. It returns a new URI that represents the same resource as the specified URI argument but is relative to this URI. Finally, the toURL() method converts an absolute URI object to the equivalent URL. Since the URI class provides superior textual manipulation capabilities for URLs, it can be useful to use the URI class to resolve relative URLs (for example) and then convert those URI objects to URL objects when they are ready for networking.

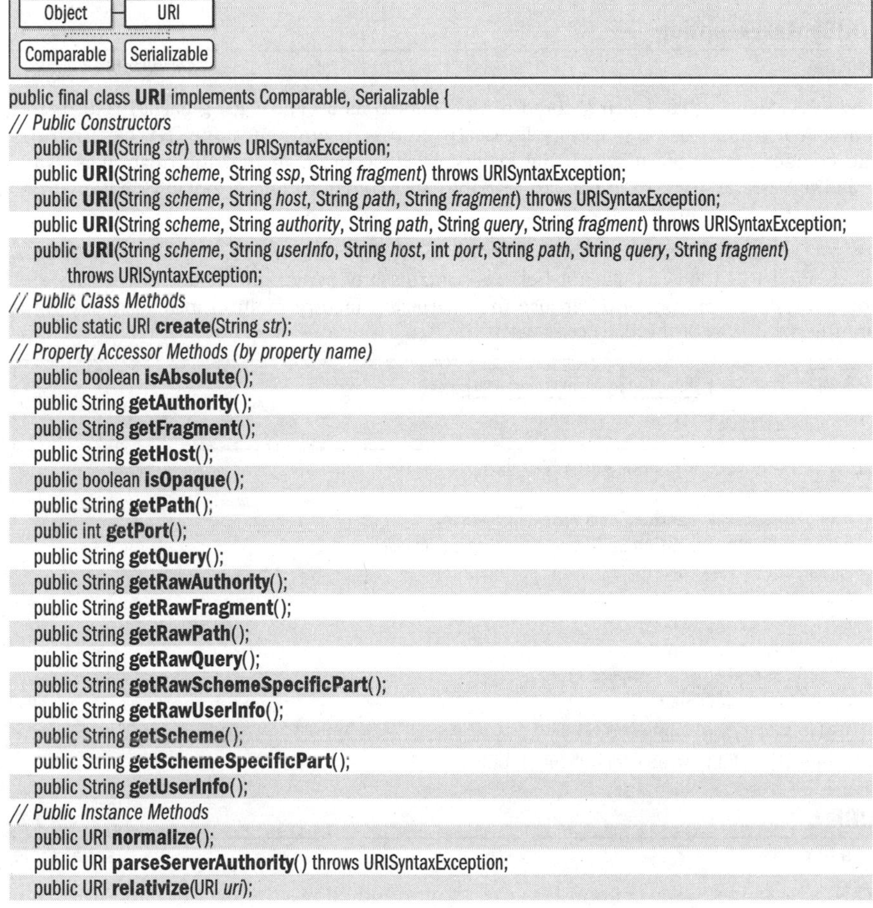


```
public final class URI implements Comparable, Serializable {
// Public Constructors
   public URI(String str) throws URISyntaxException;
   public URI(String scheme, String ssp, String fragment) throws URISyntaxException;
   public URI(String scheme, String host, String path, String fragment) throws URISyntaxException;
   public URI(String scheme, String authority, String path, String query, String fragment) throws URISyntaxException;
   public URI(String scheme, String userInfo, String host, int port, String path, String query, String fragment)
        throws URISyntaxException;
// Public Class Methods
   public static URI create(String str);
// Property Accessor Methods (by property name)
   public boolean isAbsolute();
   public String getAuthority();
   public String getFragment();
   public String getHost();
   public boolean isOpaque();
   public String getPath();
   public int getPort();
   public String getQuery();
   public String getRawAuthority();
   public String getRawFragment();
   public String getRawPath();
   public String getRawQuery();
   public String getRawSchemeSpecificPart();
   public String getRawUserInfo();
   public String getScheme();
   public String getSchemeSpecificPart();
   public String getUserInfo();
// Public Instance Methods
   public URI normalize();
   public URI parseServerAuthority() throws URISyntaxException;
   public URI relativize(URI uri);
```

```
    public URI resolve(URI uri);
    public URI resolve(String str);
    public String toASCIIString();
    public URL toURL() throws MalformedURLException;
// Methods Implementing Comparable
    public int compareTo(Object ob);
// Public Methods Overriding Object
    public boolean equals(Object ob);
    public int hashCode();
    public String toString();
}
```

Passed To: java.io.File.File(), URI.{relativize(), resolve()}, javax.print.attribute.URISyntax.URISyntax(), javax.print.attribute.standard.Destination.Destination(), javax.print.attribute.standard.PrinterMoreInfo.PrinterMoreInfo(), javax.print.attribute.standard.PrinterMoreInfoManufacturer.PrinterMoreInfoManufacturer(), javax.print.attribute.standard.PrinterURI.PrinterURI()

Returned By: java.io.File.toURI(), URI.{create(), normalize(), parseServerAuthority(), relativize(), resolve()}, javax.print.URIException.getUnsupportedURI(), javax.print.attribute.URISyntax.getURI()

URISyntaxException — Java 1.4

java.net — *serializable checked*

This class signals that a string could not be parsed as a valid URI. getInput() returns the string that could not be parsed. getReason() returns an error message. getIndex() returns the character position at which the syntax error occurred, if that information is available. getMessage() returns a human-readable string that includes the information from each of the other three methods.

This is a checked exception thrown by all the URI() constructors. If you are parsing a hardcoded URI that you do not believe contains any syntax errors and wish to avoid the checked exception, you can use the URI.create() factory method instead of the one-argument version of the URI() constructor.

Object — Throwable — Exception — URISyntaxException
Serializable

```
public class URISyntaxException extends Exception {
// Public Constructors
    public URISyntaxException(String input, String reason);
    public URISyntaxException(String input, String reason, int index);
// Public Instance Methods
    public int getIndex();
    public String getInput();
    public String getReason();
// Public Methods Overriding Throwable
    public String getMessage();
}
```

Thrown By: URI.{parseServerAuthority(), URI()}

URL — Java 1.0

java.net — *serializable*

This class represents a uniform resource locator and allows the data referred to by the URL to be downloaded. A URL can be specified as a single string or with separate protocol, host, port, and file specifications. Relative URLs can also be specified with a String and the URL object to which it is relative. getFile(), getHost(), getProtocol() and related methods return the various portions of the URL specified by a URL object. sameFile() determines whether a URL object refers to the same file as this one. getDefaultPort() returns the default port number for the protocol of the URL object; it may differ from the number returned by getPort(). Use openConnection() to obtain a URLConnection object with which you can download the content of the URL. For simple cases, however, the URL class defines shortcut methods that create and invoke methods on a URLConnection internally. getContent() downloads the URL data and parses it into an appropriate Java object (such as a string or image) if an appropriate ContentHandler can be found. In Java 1.3 and later, you can pass an array of Class objects that specify the type of objects that you are willing to accept as the return value of this method. If you wish to parse the URL content yourself, call openStream() to obtain an InputStream from which you can read the data.

Object — URL ··· Serializable

```
public final class URL implements Serializable {
// Public Constructors
    public URL(String spec) throws MalformedURLException;
    public URL(URL context, String spec) throws MalformedURLException;
    public URL(String protocol, String host, String file) throws MalformedURLException;
1.2 public URL(URL context, String spec, URLStreamHandler handler) throws MalformedURLException;
    public URL(String protocol, String host, int port, String file) throws MalformedURLException;
1.2 public URL(String protocol, String host, int port, String file, URLStreamHandler handler)
        throws MalformedURLException;
// Public Class Methods
    public static void setURLStreamHandlerFactory(URLStreamHandlerFactory fac);
// Property Accessor Methods (by property name)
1.3 public String getAuthority();
    public final Object getContent() throws java.io.IOException;
1.3 public final Object getContent(Class[ ] classes) throws java.io.IOException;
1.4 public int getDefaultPort();
    public String getFile();
    public String getHost();
1.3 public String getPath();
    public int getPort();
    public String getProtocol();
1.3 public String getQuery();
    public String getRef();
1.3 public String getUserInfo();
// Public Instance Methods
    public URLConnection openConnection() throws java.io.IOException;
    public final java.io.InputStream openStream() throws java.io.IOException;
    public boolean sameFile(URL other);
    public String toExternalForm();
// Public Methods Overriding Object
    public boolean equals(Object obj);
    public int hashCode();                                              synchronized
    public String toString();
// Protected Instance Methods
    protected void set(String protocol, String host, int port, String file, String ref);
1.3 protected void set(String protocol, String host, int port, String authority, String userInfo, String path, String query,
                    String ref);
}
```

java.net

Passed To: Too many methods to list.

Returned By: Too many methods to list.

Type Of: URLConnection.url

URLClassLoader — Java 1.2

java.net

This ClassLoader provides a useful way to load untrusted Java code from a search path of arbitrary URLs, where each URL represents a directory or JAR file to search. Use the inherited loadClass() method to load a named class with a URLClassLoader. Classes loaded by a URLClassLoader have whatever permissions are granted to their java.security.CodeSource by the system java.security.Policy, plus they have one additional permission that allows the class loader to read any resource files associated with the class. If the class is loaded from a local file: URL that represents a directory, the class is given permission to read all files and directories below that directory. If the class is loaded from a local file: URL that represents a JAR file, the class is given permission to read that JAR file. If the class is loaded from a URL that represents a resource on another host, that class is given permission to connect to and accept network connections from that host. Note, however, that loaded classes are not granted this additional permission if the code that created the URLClassLoader in the first place would not have had that permission.

You can obtain a URLClassLoader by calling one of the URLClassLoader() constructors or one of the static newInstance() methods. If you call newInstance(), the loadClass() method of the returned URLClassLoader performs an additional check to ensure that the caller has permission to access the specified package.

Object — ClassLoader — SecureClassLoader — URLClassLoader

```
public class URLClassLoader extends java.security.SecureClassLoader {
// Public Constructors
   public URLClassLoader(URL[ ] urls);
   public URLClassLoader(URL[ ] urls, ClassLoader parent);
   public URLClassLoader(URL[ ] urls, ClassLoader parent, URLStreamHandlerFactory factory);
// Public Class Methods
   public static URLClassLoader newInstance(URL[ ] urls);
   public static URLClassLoader newInstance(URL[ ] urls, ClassLoader parent);
// Public Instance Methods
   public URL[ ] getURLs();
// Protected Methods Overriding SecureClassLoader
   protected java.security.PermissionCollection getPermissions(java.security.CodeSource codesource);
// Public Methods Overriding ClassLoader
   public URL findResource(String name);
   public java.util.Enumeration findResources(String name) throws java.io.IOException;
// Protected Methods Overriding ClassLoader
   protected Class findClass(String name) throws ClassNotFoundException;
// Protected Instance Methods
   protected void addURL(URL url);
   protected Package definePackage(String name, java.util.jar.Manifest man, URL url)
       throws IllegalArgumentException;
}
```

Returned By: URLClassLoader.newInstance()

URLConnection **Java 1.0**

java.net

This abstract class defines a network connection to an object specified by a URL. URL.openConnection() returns a URLConnection instance. You should use a URLConnection object when you want more control over the downloading of data than is available through the simpler URL methods. connect() actually establishes the network connection. Some methods must be called before the connection is made, and others depend on being connected. The methods that depend on being connected call connect() themselves if no connection exists yet, so you never need to call this method explicitly. The getContent() methods are just like the same-named methods of the URL class; they download the data referred to by the URL and parse it into an appropriate type of object (such as a string or an image). In Java 1.3 and later, there is a version of getContent() that allows you to specify the types of parsed objects you are willing to accept by passing an array of Class objects. If you prefer to parse the URL content yourself instead of calling getContent(), you can call getInputStream() (and getOutputStream() if the URL protocol supports writing) to obtain a stream through which you can read (or write) data from (or to) the resource identified by the URL.

Before a connection is established, you may want to set request fields (such as HTTP request headers) to refine the URL request. Use setRequestProperty() to set a new value for a named header. In Java 1.4 and later, you can use addRequestProperty() to add a new comma-separated item to an existing header. Java 1.4 also adds getRequestProperties(), which returns the current set of request properties in the form of an unmodifiable Map object that maps request header names to List objects that contain the string value or values for the named header.

Once a connection has been established, there are a number of methods you can call to obtain information from the "response headers" of the URL. getContentLength(), getContentType(), getContentEncoding(), getExpiration(), getDate(), and getLastModified() return the appropriate information about the object referred to by the URL, if that information can be determined (e.g., from HTTP header fields). getHeaderField() returns an HTTP header field specified by name or by number. getHeaderFieldInt() and getHeaderFieldDate() return the value of a named header field parsed as an integer or a date. In Java 1.4 and later, getHeaderFields() returns an unmodifiable Map object that maps response header names to an unmodifiable List that contains the string value or values for the named header.

There are a number of options you can specify to control how the URLConnection behaves. These options are set with the various set() methods and may be queried with corresponding get() methods. The options must be set before the connect() method is called. setDoInput() and setDoOutput() allow you to specify whether you are using the URLConnection for input and/or output (input-only by default). setAllowUserInteraction() specifies whether user interaction (such as typing a password) is allowed during the data transfer (false by default). setDefaultAllowUserInteraction() is a class method that allows you to change the default value for user interaction. setUseCaches() allows you to specify whether a cached version of the URL can be used. You can set this to false to force a URL to be reloaded. setDefaultUseCaches() sets the default value for setUseCaches(). setIfModifiedSince() allows you to specify that a URL should not be fetched unless it has been modified since a specified time (if it is possible to determine its modification date).

```
public abstract class URLConnection {
// Protected Constructors
   protected URLConnection(URL url);
// Public Class Methods
   public static boolean getDefaultAllowUserInteraction();
```

```
1.1 public static FileNameMap getFileNameMap();                              synchronized
    public static String guessContentTypeFromName(String fname);
    public static String guessContentTypeFromStream(java.io.InputStream is) throws java.io.IOException;
    public static void setContentHandlerFactory(ContentHandlerFactory fac);     synchronized
    public static void setDefaultAllowUserInteraction(boolean defaultallowuserinteraction);
1.1 public static void setFileNameMap(FileNameMap map);
// Property Accessor Methods (by property name)
    public boolean getAllowUserInteraction();
    public void setAllowUserInteraction(boolean allowuserinteraction);
    public Object getContent() throws java.io.IOException;
1.3 public Object getContent(Class[ ] classes) throws java.io.IOException;
    public String getContentEncoding();
    public int getContentLength();
    public String getContentType();
    public long getDate();
    public boolean getDefaultUseCaches();
    public void setDefaultUseCaches(boolean defaultusecaches);
    public boolean getDoInput();
    public void setDoInput(boolean doinput);
    public boolean getDoOutput();
    public void setDoOutput(boolean dooutput);
    public long getExpiration();
1.4 public java.util.Map getHeaderFields();
    public long getIfModifiedSince();
    public void setIfModifiedSince(long ifmodifiedsince);
    public java.io.InputStream getInputStream() throws java.io.IOException;
    public long getLastModified();
    public java.io.OutputStream getOutputStream() throws java.io.IOException;
1.2 public java.security.Permission getPermission() throws java.io.IOException;
1.4 public java.util.Map getRequestProperties();
    public URL getURL();
    public boolean getUseCaches();
    public void setUseCaches(boolean usecaches);
// Public Instance Methods
1.4 public void addRequestProperty(String key, String value);
    public abstract void connect() throws java.io.IOException;
    public String getHeaderField(String name);                                 constant
    public String getHeaderField(int n);                                       constant
    public long getHeaderFieldDate(String name, long Default);
    public int getHeaderFieldInt(String name, int Default);
    public String getHeaderFieldKey(int n);                                    constant
    public String getRequestProperty(String key);
    public void setRequestProperty(String key, String value);
// Public Methods Overriding Object
    public String toString();
// Protected Instance Fields
    protected boolean allowUserInteraction;
    protected boolean connected;
    protected boolean doInput;
    protected boolean doOutput;
    protected long ifModifiedSince;
    protected URL url;
    protected boolean useCaches;
// Deprecated Public Methods
#   public static String getDefaultRequestProperty(String key);                constant
```

```
#   public static void setDefaultRequestProperty(String key, String value);          empty
}
```

Subclasses: HttpURLConnection, JarURLConnection

Passed To: java.net.ContentHandler.getContent()

Returned By: URL.openConnection(), URLStreamHandler.openConnection()

Type Of: JarURLConnection.jarFileURLConnection

URLDecoder **Java 1.2**

java.net

This class defines a static decode() method that reverses the encoding performed by URLEncoder.encode(). It decodes 8-bit text with the MIME type "x-www-form-urlencoded", which is a standard encoding used by web browsers to submit form contents to CGI scripts and other server-side programs.

```
public class URLDecoder {
// Public Constructors
   public URLDecoder();
// Public Class Methods
1.4 public static String decode(String s, String enc) throws java.io.UnsupportedEncodingException;
// Deprecated Public Methods
#   public static String decode(String s);
}
```

URLEncoder **Java 1.0**

java.net

This class defines a single static method that converts a string to its URL-encoded form. That is, spaces are converted to +, and nonalphanumeric characters other than underscore are output as two hexadecimal digits following a percent sign. Note that this technique works only for 8-bit characters. This method canonicalizes a URL specification so that it uses only characters from an extremely portable subset of ASCII that can be correctly handled by computers around the world.

```
public class URLEncoder {
// No Constructor
// Public Class Methods
1.4 public static String encode(String s, String enc) throws java.io.UnsupportedEncodingException;
// Deprecated Public Methods
#   public static String encode(String s);
}
```

URLStreamHandler **Java 1.0**

java.net

This abstract class defines the openConnection() method that creates a URLConnection for a given URL. A separate subclass of this class may be defined for various URL protocol types. A URLStreamHandler is created by a URLStreamHandlerFactory. Normal applications never need to use or subclass this class.

```
public abstract class URLStreamHandler {
// Public Constructors
   public URLStreamHandler();
// Protected Instance Methods
```

```
1.3 protected boolean equals(URL u1, URL u2);
1.3 protected int getDefaultPort();                                                       constant
1.3 protected InetAddress getHostAddress(URL u);                                      synchronized
1.3 protected int hashCode(URL u);
1.3 protected boolean hostsEqual(URL u1, URL u2);
    protected abstract URLConnection openConnection(URL u) throws java.io.IOException;
    protected void parseURL(URL u, String spec, int start, int limit);
1.3 protected boolean sameFile(URL u1, URL u2);
1.3 protected void setURL(URL u, String protocol, String host, int port, String authority, String userInfo, String path,
                          String query, String ref);
    protected String toExternalForm(URL u);
// Deprecated Protected Methods
#   protected void setURL(URL u, String protocol, String host, int port, String file, String ref);
}
```

Passed To: URL.URL()

Returned By: URLStreamHandlerFactory.createURLStreamHandler()

URLStreamHandlerFactory — Java 1.0

java.net

This interface defines a method that creates a URLStreamHandler object for a specified protocol. Normal applications never need to use or implement this interface.

```
public interface URLStreamHandlerFactory {
// Public Instance Methods
    public abstract URLStreamHandler createURLStreamHandler(String protocol);
}
```

Passed To: URL.setURLStreamHandlerFactory(), URLClassLoader.URLClassLoader()

CHAPTER 14

java.nio and Subpackages

This chapter documents the New I/O API defined by the java.nio package and its subpackages. It covers:

java.nio
: Defines the Buffer class and type-specific subclasses, most notably the ByteBuffer class that is often used for I/O in the java.nio.channels package.

java.nio.channels
: Defines the Channel abstraction for high-performance I/O and implements channels for file and network I/O. Also allows nonblocking I/O with the Selector class.

java.nio.channels.spi
: The service provider interface for channel and selector implementations.

java.nio.charset
: Defines classes for encoding sequences of characters into bytes and decoding sequences of bytes into characters, according to the encoding rules of a named charset.

java.nio.charset.spi
: The service provider interface for charset implementations.

Package java.nio — Java 1.4

This package defines buffer classes that are fundamental to the java.nio API. See Buffer for an overview of buffers and ByteBuffer (the most important of the buffer classes) for full documentation of byte buffers. The other type-specific buffer classes are close analogs to ByteBuffer and are documented in terms of that class. See the java.nio.channels package for classes that perform I/O operations on buffers.

Classes:

public abstract class **Buffer**;
└ public abstract class **ByteBuffer** extends Buffer implements Comparable;
  └ public abstract class **MappedByteBuffer** extends ByteBuffer;
└ public abstract class **CharBuffer** extends Buffer implements CharSequence, Comparable;
└ public abstract class **DoubleBuffer** extends Buffer implements Comparable;
└ public abstract class **FloatBuffer** extends Buffer implements Comparable;
└ public abstract class **IntBuffer** extends Buffer implements Comparable;
└ public abstract class **LongBuffer** extends Buffer implements Comparable;
└ public abstract class **ShortBuffer** extends Buffer implements Comparable;
public final class **ByteOrder**;

Exceptions:

public class **BufferOverflowException** extends RuntimeException;
public class **BufferUnderflowException** extends RuntimeException;
public class **InvalidMarkException** extends IllegalStateException;
public class **ReadOnlyBufferException** extends UnsupportedOperationException;

Buffer — Java 1.4

java.nio

This class is the abstract superclass of all buffer classes in the java.nio API. A buffer is a linear (finite) sequence of primitive values. The java.nio package defines a Buffer subclass for each primitive type in Java except for boolean. Buffer itself defines the common, type-independent features of all buffers. Buffer and its subclasses are intended for use by a single thread at a time and contain no synchronization code to make them thread-safe.

The purpose of a buffer is to store data, and buffer classes must define methods for reading data from a buffer and writing data into a buffer. Because each Buffer subclass stores data of a different primitive type, however, the get() and put() methods that read and write data must be defined by each of the individual subclasses. See ByteBuffer (the most important subclass) for documentation of these methods; all the other subclasses define similar methods that differ only in the datatype of the values being read or written.

Each buffer has four numbers associated with it:

Capacity
: A buffer's capacity is its maximum size; it can hold this many values. The capacity is specified when a buffer is created and cannot be changed. It can be queried with the capacity() method.

Limit
: A buffer's limit is its current size, or the index of the first element that does not contain valid data. Data cannot be read from or written into a buffer beyond the limit. When data is written into a buffer, the limit is usually the same as the capacity. When data is read from a buffer, the limit may be less than the capacity and indicate the amount of valid data contained in the buffer. Two limit() methods exist: one to query a buffer's limit and one to set it.

Position

A buffer's position is the index of the element in the buffer at which data is read or written. It is used and updated by the relative get() and put() methods defined by ByteBuffer and the other Buffer subclasses. Two position() methods exist to query and set the current position of the buffer. A buffer's position is always greater than or equal to 0 and less than or equal to the buffer's limit. The remaining() method returns the number of elements between the position and the limit, and hasRemaining() returns true if this number is greater than 0.

Mark

A buffer's mark is a temporarily saved position. Call mark() to set the mark to the current position. Call reset() to restore the buffer's position to the marked position.

Buffer defines several methods that perform important operations on a buffer:

clear()

This method does not actually clear the contents of the buffer but sets the position to 0, sets the limit to the capacity, and discards any saved mark. This prepares the buffer to have new data written into it.

flip()

This method sets the limit to the position, sets the position to 0, and discards any saved mark. After data has been written into a buffer, this method "flips" the purpose of the buffer and prepares it for reading.

rewind()

This method sets the position to 0 and discards any saved mark. It does not alter the limit and can be used to restart a read operation at the beginning of the buffer.

Buffer objects may be read-only, in which case, any attempt to store data in the buffer results in a ReadOnlyBufferException. The isReadOnly() method returns true if a buffer is read-only.

```
public abstract class Buffer {
// No Constructor
// Public Instance Methods
   public final int capacity();
   public final Buffer clear();
   public final Buffer flip();
   public final boolean hasRemaining();
   public abstract boolean isReadOnly();
   public final int limit();
   public final Buffer limit(int newLimit);
   public final Buffer mark();
   public final int position();
   public final Buffer position(int newPosition);
   public final int remaining();
   public final Buffer reset();
   public final Buffer rewind();
}
```

Subclasses: ByteBuffer, CharBuffer, DoubleBuffer, FloatBuffer, IntBuffer, LongBuffer, ShortBuffer

Returned By: Buffer.{clear(), flip(), limit(), mark(), position(), reset(), rewind()}

BufferOverflowException **Java 1.4**

java.nio *serializable unchecked*

This exception signals that a relative put() operation on a buffer could not be completed because the number of elements that need to be written exceeds the number of remaining elements between the buffer's position and its limit.

Object ─ Throwable ─ Exception ─ RuntimeException ─ BufferOverflowException
Throwable ⋮ Serializable

```
public class BufferOverflowException extends RuntimeException {
// Public Constructors
   public BufferOverflowException();
}
```

BufferUnderflowException **Java 1.4**

java.nio *serializable unchecked*

This exception signals that a relative get() operation on a buffer could not be completed because the number of elements that need to be read exceeds the number of remaining elements between the buffer's position and its limit.

Object ─ Throwable ─ Exception ─ RuntimeException ─ BufferUnderflowException
Throwable ⋮ Serializable

```
public class BufferUnderflowException extends RuntimeException {
// Public Constructors
   public BufferUnderflowException();
}
```

ByteBuffer **Java 1.4**

java.nio *comparable*

ByteBuffer holds a sequence of bytes for use in an I/O operation. ByteBuffer is an abstract class, so you cannot instantiate one by calling a constructor. Instead, you must use allocate(), allocateDirect(), or wrap().

allocate() returns a ByteBuffer with the specified capacity. The position of this new buffer is 0, and its limit is set to its capacity. allocateDirect() is like allocate() except that it attempts to allocate a buffer that the underlying operating system can use directly. Such direct buffers may be substantially more efficient than normal buffers for low-level I/O operations but may also have significantly larger allocation costs.

If you have already allocated an array of bytes, you can use the wrap() method to create a ByteBuffer that uses the byte array to store it. In the one-argument version of wrap(), you specify only the array; the buffer capacity and limit are set to the array length, and the position is set to 0. In the other form of wrap(), you specify the array as well as an offset and length that specify a portion of that array. The capacity of the resulting ByteBuffer is again set to the total array length, but its position is set to the specified offset, and its limit is set to the offset plus length.

Once you have obtained a ByteBuffer, you can use the various get() and put() methods to read data from it or write data into it. Several versions of these methods exist to read and write single bytes or arrays of bytes. The single-byte methods come in two forms. Relative get() and put() methods query or set the byte at the current position and then increment the position. The absolute forms of the methods take an additional argument that specifies the buffer element that will be read or written and do not affect the buffer position. Two other relative forms of the get() method exist to read a sequence of bytes (starting at and incrementing the buffer's position) into a specified byte array or a specified subarray. These methods throw a BufferUnderflowException if there are not enough bytes left in the buffer. Two relative forms of the put() method copy bytes from a specified array or subarray into the buffer (starting at and incrementing the buffer's position). They throw a BufferOverflowException if there is not enough room left in the buffer to hold the bytes. One final form of the put() method transfers all the remaining bytes from one ByteBuffer into this buffer, incrementing the positions of both buffers.

In addition to the get() and put() methods, ByteBuffer also defines another operation that affects the buffer's content. compact() discards any bytes before the buffer position and copies all bytes between the position and limit to the beginning of the buffer. The position is then set to the new limit, and the limit is set to the capacity. This method compacts a buffer by discarding elements that have already been read, and then prepares the buffer for appending new elements to those that remain.

All Buffer subclasses, such as CharBuffer, IntBuffer, and FloatBuffer, have analogous methods that are just like the get() and put() methods except that they operate on different data types. ByteBuffer is unique among Buffer subclasses in that it has additional methods for reading and writing values of other primitive types from and into the byte buffer. These methods have names such as getInt() and putChar(), and there are methods for all primitive types except byte and boolean. Each method reads or writes a single primitive value. Like the get() and put() methods, they come in relative and absolute variations. The relative methods start with the byte at the buffer's position and increment the position by the appropriate number of bytes (two bytes for a char, four bytes for an int, eight bytes for a double, etc.). The absolute methods take a buffer index (a byte index that is not multiplied by the size of the primitive value) as an argument and do not modify the buffer position. The encoding of multibyte primitive values into a byte buffer can be done most-significant byte to least-significant byte (big-endian byte order) or the reverse (little-endian byte order). The byte order used by these primitive-type get() and put() methods is specified by a ByteOrder object. The byte order for a ByteBuffer can be queried and set with the two forms of the order() method. The default byte order for all newly created ByteBuffer objects is ByteOrder.BIG_ENDIAN.

Other methods unique to ByteBuffer() are a set methods that allow a buffer of bytes to be viewed as a buffer of other primitive types. asCharBuffer(), asIntBuffer() and related methods return "view buffers" that allow the bytes between the position and the limit of the underlying ByteBuffer to be viewed as a sequence of characters, integers, or other primitive values. The returned buffers have position, limit, and mark values that are independent of those of the underlying buffer. The initial position of the returned buffer is 0, and the limit and capacity are the number of bytes between the position and limit of the original buffer divided by the size in bytes of the relevant primitive type (two for char and short, four for int and float, and eight for long and double). Note that the returned view buffer is a view of the bytes between the position and limit of the byte buffer. Subsequent changes to the position and limit of the byte buffer do not change the size of the view buffer, but changes to the bytes themselves do change the values that are viewed through the view buffer. View buffers use the byte ordering that was current in the byte buffer when they were created; subsequent changes to the byte order of the byte buffer do not affect the view buffer. If the underlying byte buffer is direct, then the returned buffer is also direct; this is important because ByteBuffer is the only buffer class with an allocateDirect() method.

ByteBuffer defines some additional methods, which, like the get() and put() methods, have analogs in all Buffer subclasses. duplicate() returns a new buffer that shares the content with the original buffer. The two buffers have independent position, limit, and mark values, although the duplicate buffer starts off with the same values as the original buffer. The duplicate buffer is direct if the original is direct and is read-only if the original is read-only. The buffers share content, and content changes made to either buffer are visible through the other. asReadOnlyBuffer() is like duplicate() except that the re turned buffer is read-only, and all of its put() and related methods throw a ReadOnlyBufferException. slice() is also somewhat like duplicate() except that the returned buffer represents only the content between the current position and limit. The returned buffer has a position of 0, a limit and capacity equal to the number of remaining elements in this buffer, and an undefined mark. isDirect() is a simple method that returns true if a buffer is a direct buffer and false otherwise. If this buffer has a backing array and is not a read-only buffer (e.g., if it was created with the allocate() or wrap() methods), then hasArray() returns true, array() returns the backing array, and arrayOffset() returns the offset within that array of the first element of the buffer. If hasArray() returns false, then array() and arrayOffset() may throw an UnsupportedOperationException or a ReadOnlyBufferException.

Finally, ByteBuffer and other Buffer subclasses override several standard object methods. The equals() method compares the elements between the position and limit of two buffers and returns true only if there are the same number and have the same value. Note that elements before the position of the buffer are not considered. The hashCode() method is implemented to match the equals() method: the hashcode is based upon only the elements between the position and limit of the buffer. This means that the hashcode changes if either the contents or position of the buffer changes. This means that instances of ByteBuffer and other Buffer subclasses are not usually useful as keys for hashtables or java.util.Map objects. toString() returns a string summary of the buffer, but the precise contents of the string are unspecified. ByteBuffer and each of the other Buffer subclasses also implement the Comparable interface and define a compareTo() method that performs an element-by-element comparison operation on the buffer elements between the position and the limit of the buffer.

Object — Buffer — ByteBuffer
Comparable

```
public abstract class ByteBuffer extends Buffer implements Comparable {
// No Constructor
// Public Class Methods
   public static ByteBuffer allocate(int capacity);
   public static ByteBuffer allocateDirect(int capacity);
   public static ByteBuffer wrap(byte[ ] array);
   public static ByteBuffer wrap(byte[ ] array, int offset, int length);
// Property Accessor Methods (by property name)
   public abstract char getChar();
   public abstract char getChar(int index);
   public abstract boolean isDirect();
   public abstract double getDouble();
   public abstract double getDouble(int index);
   public abstract float getFloat();
   public abstract float getFloat(int index);
   public abstract int getInt();
   public abstract int getInt(int index);
   public abstract long getLong();
   public abstract long getLong(int index);
   public abstract short getShort();
   public abstract short getShort(int index);
// Public Instance Methods
   public final byte[ ] array();
   public final int arrayOffset();
   public abstract CharBuffer asCharBuffer();
```

```
    public abstract DoubleBuffer asDoubleBuffer();
    public abstract FloatBuffer asFloatBuffer();
    public abstract IntBuffer asIntBuffer();
    public abstract LongBuffer asLongBuffer();
    public abstract ByteBuffer asReadOnlyBuffer();
    public abstract ShortBuffer asShortBuffer();
    public abstract ByteBuffer compact();
    public abstract ByteBuffer duplicate();
    public abstract byte get();
    public abstract byte get(int index);
    public ByteBuffer get(byte[ ] dst);
    public ByteBuffer get(byte[ ] dst, int offset, int length);
    public final boolean hasArray();
    public final ByteOrder order();
    public final ByteBuffer order(ByteOrder bo);
    public ByteBuffer put(ByteBuffer src);
    public abstract ByteBuffer put(byte b);
    public final ByteBuffer put(byte[ ] src);
    public abstract ByteBuffer put(int index, byte b);
    public ByteBuffer put(byte[ ] src, int offset, int length);
    public abstract ByteBuffer putChar(char value);
    public abstract ByteBuffer putChar(int index, char value);
    public abstract ByteBuffer putDouble(double value);
    public abstract ByteBuffer putDouble(int index, double value);
    public abstract ByteBuffer putFloat(float value);
    public abstract ByteBuffer putFloat(int index, float value);
    public abstract ByteBuffer putInt(int value);
    public abstract ByteBuffer putInt(int index, int value);
    public abstract ByteBuffer putLong(long value);
    public abstract ByteBuffer putLong(int index, long value);
    public abstract ByteBuffer putShort(short value);
    public abstract ByteBuffer putShort(int index, short value);
    public abstract ByteBuffer slice();
// Methods Implementing Comparable
    public int compareTo(Object ob);
// Public Methods Overriding Object
    public boolean equals(Object ob);
    public int hashCode();
    public String toString();
}
```

Subclasses: MappedByteBuffer

Passed To: Too many methods to list.

Returned By: Too many methods to list.

ByteOrder — Java 1.4

java.nio

This class is a type-safe enumeration of byte orders used by the ByteBuffer class. The two constant fields define the two legal byte order values. BIG_ENDIAN byte order means most-significant byte first. LITTLE_ENDIAN means least-significant byte first. The static nativeOrder() method returns whichever of these two constants represents the native byte order of the underlying operating system and hardware. Finally, the toString() method returns the string "BIG_ENDIAN" or "LITTLE_ENDIAN".

```
public final class ByteOrder {
// No Constructor
// Public Constants
    public static final ByteOrder BIG_ENDIAN;
    public static final ByteOrder LITTLE_ENDIAN;
// Public Class Methods
    public static ByteOrder nativeOrder();
// Public Methods Overriding Object
    public String toString();
}
```

Passed To: ByteBuffer.order(), javax.imageio.stream.ImageInputStream.setByteOrder(), javax.imageio.stream.ImageInputStreamImpl.setByteOrder()

Returned By: ByteBuffer.order(), ByteOrder.nativeOrder(), CharBuffer.order(), DoubleBuffer.order(), FloatBuffer.order(), IntBuffer.order(), LongBuffer.order(), ShortBuffer.order(), javax.imageio.stream.ImageInputStream.getByteOrder(), javax.imageio.stream.ImageInputStreamImpl.getByteOrder()

Type Of: ByteOrder.{BIG_ENDIAN, LITTLE_ENDIAN}, javax.imageio.stream.ImageInputStreamImpl.byteOrder

CharBuffer — Java 1.4

java.nio — *comparable*

CharBuffer holds a sequence of Unicode character values for use in an I/O operation. Most of this class's methods are directly analogous to methods defined by ByteBuffer except that they use char and char[] argument and return values instead of byte and byte[] values. See ByteBuffer for details.

In addition to the ByteBuffer analogs, this class also implements the java.lang.CharSequence interface so it can be used with java.util.regex regular expression operations or anywhere else a CharSequence is expected.

Note that CharBuffer is an abstract class and does not define a constructor. There are three ways to obtain a CharBuffer:

- By calling the static allocate() method. Note that there is no allocateDirect() method as there is for ByteBuffer.
- By calling one of the static wrap() methods to create a CharBuffer that uses the specified char array or CharSequence for its content. Note that wrapping a CharSequence results in a read-only CharBuffer.
- By calling the asCharBuffer() method of a ByteBuffer to obtain a CharBuffer view of the underlying bytes. If the underlying ByteBuffer is direct, then the CharBuffer view will also be direct.

Note that this class holds a sequence of 16-bit Unicode characters and does not represent text in any other encoding. Classes in the java.nio.charset package can be used to encode a CharBuffer of Unicode characters into a ByteBuffer or decode the bytes in a ByteBuffer into a CharBuffer of Unicode text.

```
public abstract class CharBuffer extends Buffer implements CharSequence, Comparable {
// No Constructor
```

```
// Public Class Methods
   public static CharBuffer allocate(int capacity);
   public static CharBuffer wrap(CharSequence csq);
   public static CharBuffer wrap(char[ ] array);
   public static CharBuffer wrap(char[ ] array, int offset, int length);
   public static CharBuffer wrap(CharSequence csq, int start, int end);
// Public Instance Methods
   public final char[ ] array();
   public final int arrayOffset();
   public abstract CharBuffer asReadOnlyBuffer();
   public abstract CharBuffer compact();
   public abstract CharBuffer duplicate();
   public abstract char get();
   public abstract char get(int index);
   public CharBuffer get(char[ ] dst);
   public CharBuffer get(char[ ] dst, int offset, int length);
   public final boolean hasArray();
   public abstract boolean isDirect();
   public abstract ByteOrder order();
   public final CharBuffer put(String src);
   public abstract CharBuffer put(char c);
   public CharBuffer put(CharBuffer src);
   public final CharBuffer put(char[ ] src);
   public abstract CharBuffer put(int index, char c);
   public CharBuffer put(char[ ] src, int offset, int length);
   public CharBuffer put(String src, int start, int end);
   public abstract CharBuffer slice();
// Methods Implementing CharSequence
   public final char charAt(int index);
   public final int length();
   public abstract CharSequence subSequence(int start, int end);
   public String toString();
// Methods Implementing Comparable
   public int compareTo(Object ob);
// Public Methods Overriding Object
   public boolean equals(Object ob);
   public int hashCode();
}
```

Passed To: CharBuffer.put(), java.nio.charset.Charset.encode(), java.nio.charset.CharsetDecoder.{decode(), decodeLoop(), flush(), implFlush()}, java.nio.charset.CharsetEncoder.{encode(), encodeLoop()}

Returned By: Too many methods to list.

DoubleBuffer — Java 1.4

java.nio — *comparable*

DoubleBuffer holds a sequence of double values for use in an I/O operation. Most of this class's methods are directly analogous to methods defined by ByteBuffer except that they use double and double[] argument and return values instead of byte and byte[] values. See ByteBuffer for details.

java.nio.*

DoubleBuffer is abstract and has no constructor. Create one by calling the static allocate() or wrap() methods, which are also analogs of ByteBuffer methods, or create a view DoubleBuffer by calling the asDoubleBuffer() method of an underlying ByteBuffer.


```
public abstract class DoubleBuffer extends Buffer implements Comparable {
// No Constructor
// Public Class Methods
   public static DoubleBuffer allocate(int capacity);
   public static DoubleBuffer wrap(double[ ] array);
   public static DoubleBuffer wrap(double[ ] array, int offset, int length);
// Public Instance Methods
   public final double[ ] array();
   public final int arrayOffset();
   public abstract DoubleBuffer asReadOnlyBuffer();
   public abstract DoubleBuffer compact();
   public abstract DoubleBuffer duplicate();
   public abstract double get();
   public abstract double get(int index);
   public DoubleBuffer get(double[ ] dst);
   public DoubleBuffer get(double[ ] dst, int offset, int length);
   public final boolean hasArray();
   public abstract boolean isDirect();
   public abstract ByteOrder order();
   public DoubleBuffer put(DoubleBuffer src);
   public abstract DoubleBuffer put(double d);
   public final DoubleBuffer put(double[ ] src);
   public abstract DoubleBuffer put(int index, double d);
   public DoubleBuffer put(double[ ] src, int offset, int length);
   public abstract DoubleBuffer slice();
// Methods Implementing Comparable
   public int compareTo(Object ob);
// Public Methods Overriding Object
   public boolean equals(Object ob);
   public int hashCode();
   public String toString();
}
```

Passed To: DoubleBuffer.put()

Returned By: ByteBuffer.asDoubleBuffer(), DoubleBuffer.{allocate(), asReadOnlyBuffer(), compact(), duplicate(), get(), put(), slice(), wrap()}

FloatBuffer — Java 1.4

java.nio — *comparable*

FloatBuffer holds a sequence of float values for use in an I/O operation. Most of the methods of this class are directly analogous to methods defined by ByteBuffer except that they use float and float[] argument and return values instead of byte and byte[] values. See ByteBuffer for details.

FloatBuffer is abstract and has no constructor. Create one by calling the static allocate() or wrap() methods, which are also analogs of ByteBuffer methods, or create a view FloatBuffer by calling the asFloatBuffer() method of an underlying ByteBuffer.

Object — Buffer — FloatBuffer
Comparable

```
public abstract class FloatBuffer extends Buffer implements Comparable {
// No Constructor
// Public Class Methods
   public static FloatBuffer allocate(int capacity);
   public static FloatBuffer wrap(float[ ] array);
   public static FloatBuffer wrap(float[ ] array, int offset, int length);
// Public Instance Methods
   public final float[ ] array();
   public final int arrayOffset();
   public abstract FloatBuffer asReadOnlyBuffer();
   public abstract FloatBuffer compact();
   public abstract FloatBuffer duplicate();
   public abstract float get();
   public abstract float get(int index);
   public FloatBuffer get(float[ ] dst);
   public FloatBuffer get(float[ ] dst, int offset, int length);
   public final boolean hasArray();
   public abstract boolean isDirect();
   public abstract ByteOrder order();
   public FloatBuffer put(FloatBuffer src);
   public abstract FloatBuffer put(float f);
   public final FloatBuffer put(float[ ] src);
   public abstract FloatBuffer put(int index, float f);
   public FloatBuffer put(float[ ] src, int offset, int length);
   public abstract FloatBuffer slice();
// Methods Implementing Comparable
   public int compareTo(Object ob);
// Public Methods Overriding Object
   public boolean equals(Object ob);
   public int hashCode();
   public String toString();
}
```

Passed To: FloatBuffer.put()

Returned By: ByteBuffer.asFloatBuffer(), FloatBuffer.{allocate(), asReadOnlyBuffer(), compact(), duplicate(), get(), put(), slice(), wrap()}

IntBuffer — Java 1.4

java.nio — *comparable*

IntBuffer holds a sequence of int values for use in an I/O operation. Most of the methods of this class are directly analogous to methods defined by ByteBuffer except that they use int and int[] argument and return values instead of byte and byte[] values. See ByteBuffer for details.

IntBuffer is abstract and has no constructor. Create one by calling the static allocate() or wrap() methods, which are also analogs of ByteBuffer methods, or create a view IntBuffer by calling the asIntBuffer() method of an underlying ByteBuffer.

Object — Buffer — IntBuffer
Comparable

```
public abstract class IntBuffer extends Buffer implements Comparable {
// No Constructor
// Public Class Methods
    public static IntBuffer allocate(int capacity);
    public static IntBuffer wrap(int[ ] array);
    public static IntBuffer wrap(int[ ] array, int offset, int length);
// Public Instance Methods
    public final int[ ] array();
    public final int arrayOffset();
    public abstract IntBuffer asReadOnlyBuffer();
    public abstract IntBuffer compact();
    public abstract IntBuffer duplicate();
    public abstract int get();
    public abstract int get(int index);
    public IntBuffer get(int[ ] dst);
    public IntBuffer get(int[ ] dst, int offset, int length);
    public final boolean hasArray();
    public abstract boolean isDirect();
    public abstract ByteOrder order();
    public IntBuffer put(IntBuffer src);
    public abstract IntBuffer put(int i);
    public final IntBuffer put(int[ ] src);
    public abstract IntBuffer put(int index, int i);
    public IntBuffer put(int[ ] src, int offset, int length);
    public abstract IntBuffer slice();
// Methods Implementing Comparable
    public int compareTo(Object ob);
// Public Methods Overriding Object
    public boolean equals(Object ob);
    public int hashCode();
    public String toString();
}
```

Passed To: IntBuffer.put()

Returned By: ByteBuffer.asIntBuffer(), IntBuffer.{allocate(), asReadOnlyBuffer(), compact(), duplicate(), get(), put(), slice(), wrap()}

InvalidMarkException — Java 1.4

java.nio — *serializable unchecked*

This exception signals that a buffer's position cannot be reset() because there is no mark defined.

Object — Throwable — Exception — RuntimeException — IllegalStateException — InvalidMarkException
Serializable

```
public class InvalidMarkException extends IllegalStateException {
// Public Constructors
```

```
    public InvalidMarkException();
}
```

LongBuffer — Java 1.4

java.nio — *comparable*

LongBuffer holds a sequence of long values for use in an I/O operation. Most of the methods of this class are directly analogous to methods defined by ByteBuffer except that they use long and long[] argument and return values instead of byte and byte[] values. See ByteBuffer for details.

LongBuffer is abstract and has no constructor. Create one by calling the static allocate() or wrap() methods, which are also analogs of ByteBuffer methods, or create a "view" LongBuffer by calling the asLongBuffer() method of an underlying ByteBuffer.

Object — Buffer — LongBuffer (Comparable)

```
public abstract class LongBuffer extends Buffer implements Comparable {
// No Constructor
// Public Class Methods
    public static LongBuffer allocate(int capacity);
    public static LongBuffer wrap(long[ ] array);
    public static LongBuffer wrap(long[ ] array, int offset, int length);
// Public Instance Methods
    public final long[ ] array();
    public final int arrayOffset();
    public abstract LongBuffer asReadOnlyBuffer();
    public abstract LongBuffer compact();
    public abstract LongBuffer duplicate();
    public abstract long get();
    public abstract long get(int index);
    public LongBuffer get(long[ ] dst);
    public LongBuffer get(long[ ] dst, int offset, int length);
    public final boolean hasArray();
    public abstract boolean isDirect();
    public abstract ByteOrder order();
    public LongBuffer put(LongBuffer src);
    public abstract LongBuffer put(long l);
    public final LongBuffer put(long[ ] src);
    public abstract LongBuffer put(int index, long l);
    public LongBuffer put(long[ ] src, int offset, int length);
    public abstract LongBuffer slice();
// Methods Implementing Comparable
    public int compareTo(Object ob);
// Public Methods Overriding Object
    public boolean equals(Object ob);
    public int hashCode();
    public String toString();
}
```

Passed To: LongBuffer.put()

Returned By: ByteBuffer.asLongBuffer(), LongBuffer.{allocate(), asReadOnlyBuffer(), compact(), duplicate(), get(), put(), slice(), wrap()}

MappedByteBuffer Java 1.4

java.nio *comparable*

This class is a ByteBuffer that represents a memory-mapped portion of a file. Create a MappedByteBuffer by calling the map() method of a java.nio.channels.FileChannel. All MappedByteBuffer buffers are direct buffers.

isLoaded() returns a hint as to whether the contents of the buffer are currently in primary memory (as opposed to resident on disk). If it returns true, then operations on the buffer will probably execute quickly. The load() method requests, but does not require, that the operating system load the buffer contents into primary memory. It is not guaranteed to succeed. For buffers mapped in read/write mode, the force() method outputs any changes that have been made to the buffer contents to the underlying file. If the file is on a local device, then it is guaranteed to be updated before force() returns. No such guarantees can be made for mapped network files.

Note that the underlying file of a MappedByteBuffer may be shared, which means that the contents of such a buffer can change asynchronously if the contents of the file are modified by another thread or another process (such asynchronous changes to the underlying file may or may not be visible through the buffer; this is platform-dependent, and should not be relied on). Furthermore, if another thread or process truncates the file, some or all of the elements of the buffer may no longer map to any content of the file. An attempt to read or write such an inaccessible element of the buffer will cause an implementation-defined exception, either immediately or at some later time.

Object — Buffer — ByteBuffer — MappedByteBuffer
ByteBuffer ⋮ Comparable

```
public abstract class MappedByteBuffer extends ByteBuffer {
// No Constructor
// Public Instance Methods
   public final MappedByteBuffer force();
   public final boolean isLoaded();
   public final MappedByteBuffer load();
}
```

Returned By: MappedByteBuffer.{force(), load()}, java.nio.channels.FileChannel.map()

ReadOnlyBufferException Java 1.4

java.nio *serializable unchecked*

This exception signals that a buffer is read-only and that its put() or compact() methods are not allowed to modify the buffer contents.

Object — Throwable — Exception — RuntimeException — UnsupportedOperationException — ReadOnlyBufferException
Throwable ⋮ Serializable

```
public class ReadOnlyBufferException extends UnsupportedOperationException {
// Public Constructors
   public ReadOnlyBufferException();
}
```

ShortBuffer Java 1.4

java.nio *comparable*

ShortBuffer holds a sequence of short values for use in an I/O operation. Most of the methods of this class are directly analogous to methods defined by ByteBuffer except that they use short and short[] argument and return values instead of byte and byte[] values. See ByteBuffer for details.

ShortBuffer is abstract and has no constructor. Create one by calling the static allocate() or wrap() methods, which are also analogs of ByteBuffer methods. Or, create a "view" ShortBuffer by calling the asShortBuffer() method of an underlying ByteBuffer.

Object — Buffer — ShortBuffer
Comparable

```
public abstract class ShortBuffer extends Buffer implements Comparable {
// No Constructor
// Public Class Methods
   public static ShortBuffer allocate(int capacity);
   public static ShortBuffer wrap(short[ ] array);
   public static ShortBuffer wrap(short[ ] array, int offset, int length);
// Public Instance Methods
   public final short[ ] array();
   public final int arrayOffset();
   public abstract ShortBuffer asReadOnlyBuffer();
   public abstract ShortBuffer compact();
   public abstract ShortBuffer duplicate();
   public abstract short get();
   public abstract short get(int index);
   public ShortBuffer get(short[ ] dst);
   public ShortBuffer get(short[ ] dst, int offset, int length);
   public final boolean hasArray();
   public abstract boolean isDirect();
   public abstract ByteOrder order();
   public ShortBuffer put(ShortBuffer src);
   public abstract ShortBuffer put(short s);
   public final ShortBuffer put(short[ ] src);
   public abstract ShortBuffer put(int index, short s);
   public ShortBuffer put(short[ ] src, int offset, int length);
   public abstract ShortBuffer slice();
// Methods Implementing Comparable
   public int compareTo(Object ob);
// Public Methods Overriding Object
   public boolean equals(Object ob);
   public int hashCode();
   public String toString();
}
```

Passed To: ShortBuffer.put()

Returned By: ByteBuffer.asShortBuffer(), ShortBuffer.{allocate(), asReadOnlyBuffer(), compact(), duplicate(), get(), put(), slice(), wrap()}

Package java.nio.channels — Java 1.4

This package is at the heart of the NIO API. A *channel* is a communication channel for transferring bytes from or to a java.nio.ByteBuffer. Channels serve a similar purpose in the InputStream and OutputStream classes of the java.io package but are completely unrelated to those classes and provide important features not available with the java.io API. The Channels class defines methods that bridge the java.io and java.nio.channels APIs by returning channels based on streams and streams based on channels.

java.nio.

The Channel interface simply defines methods for testing whether a channel is open and for closing a channel. The other interfaces in the package extend Channel and define read() and write() methods for reading bytes from the channel into one or more byte buffers and for writing bytes from one or more byte buffers to the channel.

The FileChannel class defines a channel-based API for reading and writing from files and provides other important file functionality, such as file locking and memory mapping, that is not available through the java.io package. SocketChannel, ServerSocketChannel, and DatagramChannel are channels for communication over a network. Pipe defines two inner classes that use the channel abstraction for communication between threads.

The network and pipe channels are all subclasses of the SelectableChannel class and may be put into nonblocking mode, in which calls to read() and write() return immediately, even if the channel is not ready for reading or writing. Nonblocking I/O and networking are not possible using the stream abstraction of the java.io and java.net packages and are perhaps the most important new features of the java.nio API. The Selector class is crucial in the efficient use of nonblocking channels; it allows a program interested in I/O operations to register on several different channels at once. A call to the select() method of a Selector will block until one of those channels becomes ready for I/O, and will then wake up. This technique is important for writing scalable, high-performance network servers. See Selector and SelectionKey for details.

Finally, this package allows for fine-grained error handling by defining a large number of exception classes, several of which may be thrown by only a single method within the java.nio API.

Interfaces:

```
public interface ByteChannel extends ReadableByteChannel, WritableByteChannel;
public interface Channel;
public interface GatheringByteChannel extends WritableByteChannel;
public interface InterruptibleChannel extends Channel;
public interface ReadableByteChannel extends Channel;
public interface ScatteringByteChannel extends ReadableByteChannel;
public interface WritableByteChannel extends Channel;
```

Classes:

```
public final class Channels;
public abstract class DatagramChannel extends java.nio.channels.spi.AbstractSelectableChannel
        implements ByteChannel, GatheringByteChannel, ScatteringByteChannel;
public abstract class FileChannel extends java.nio.channels.spi.AbstractInterruptibleChannel
        implements ByteChannel, GatheringByteChannel, ScatteringByteChannel;
public static class FileChannel.MapMode;
public abstract class FileLock;
public abstract class Pipe;
public abstract static class Pipe.SinkChannel extends java.nio.channels.spi.AbstractSelectableChannel
        implements GatheringByteChannel, WritableByteChannel;
public abstract static class Pipe.SourceChannel
        extends java.nio.channels.spi.AbstractSelectableChannel
        implements ReadableByteChannel, ScatteringByteChannel;
public abstract class SelectableChannel extends java.nio.channels.spi.AbstractInterruptibleChannel
        implements Channel;
public abstract class SelectionKey;
public abstract class Selector;
public abstract class ServerSocketChannel extends java.nio.channels.spi.AbstractSelectableChannel;
```

public abstract class **SocketChannel** extends java.nio.channels.spi.AbstractSelectableChannel
    implements ByteChannel, GatheringByteChannel, ScatteringByteChannel;

Exceptions:

public class **AlreadyConnectedException** extends IllegalStateException;
public class **CancelledKeyException** extends IllegalStateException;
public class **ClosedChannelException** extends java.io.IOException;
  └ public class **AsynchronousCloseException** extends ClosedChannelException;
    └ public class **ClosedByInterruptException** extends AsynchronousCloseException;
public class **ClosedSelectorException** extends IllegalStateException;
public class **ConnectionPendingException** extends IllegalStateException;
public class **FileLockInterruptionException** extends java.io.IOException;
public class **IllegalBlockingModeException** extends IllegalStateException;
public class **IllegalSelectorException** extends IllegalArgumentException;
public class **NoConnectionPendingException** extends IllegalStateException;
public class **NonReadableChannelException** extends IllegalStateException;
public class **NonWritableChannelException** extends IllegalStateException;
public class **NotYetBoundException** extends IllegalStateException;
public class **NotYetConnectedException** extends IllegalStateException;
public class **OverlappingFileLockException** extends IllegalStateException;
public class **UnresolvedAddressException** extends IllegalArgumentException;
public class **UnsupportedAddressTypeException** extends IllegalArgumentException;

AlreadyConnectedException — Java 1.4

java.nio.channels — *serializable unchecked*

This exception is thrown by a call to connect() on a SocketChannel that is already connected.

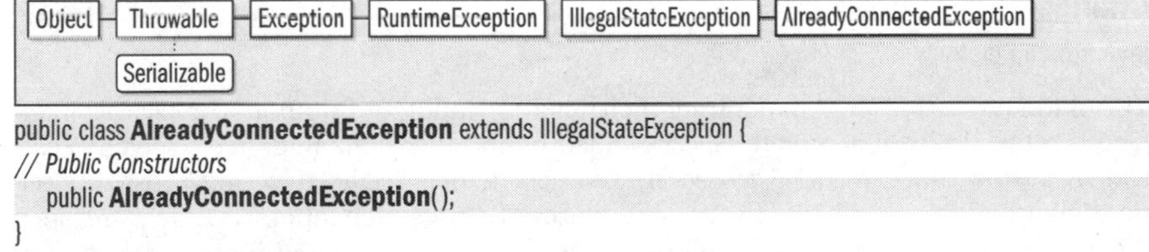


```
public class AlreadyConnectedException extends IllegalStateException {
// Public Constructors
   public AlreadyConnectedException();
}
```

AsynchronousCloseException — Java 1.4

java.nio.channels — *serializable checked*

This exception signals the termination of a blocked I/O operation because another thread closed the channel asynchronously. See also ClosedByInterruptException.

Object — Throwable — Exception — IOException — ClosedChannelException — AsynchronousCloseException
Serializable

```
public class AsynchronousCloseException extends ClosedChannelException {
// Public Constructors
   public AsynchronousCloseException();
}
```

Subclasses: ClosedByInterruptException

Thrown By: java.nio.channels.spi.AbstractInterruptibleChannel.end()

ByteChannel — Java 1.4

java.nio.channels

This interface extends ReadableByteChannel and WritableByteChannel but adds no methods or constants of its own. It exists simply as a convenient way to unify the two interfaces.

Channel — ReadableByteChannel — Channel — WritableByteChannel — ByteChannel

```
public interface ByteChannel extends ReadableByteChannel, WritableByteChannel {
}
```

Implementations: DatagramChannel, FileChannel, SocketChannel

CancelledKeyException — Java 1.4

java.nio.channels — *serializable unchecked*

This exception signals an attempt to use a SelectionKey with a cancel() method that has previously been called.

Object — Throwable — Exception — RuntimeException — IllegalStateException — CancelledKeyException
Serializable

```
public class CancelledKeyException extends IllegalStateException {
// Public Constructors
   public CancelledKeyException();
}
```

Channel — Java 1.4

java.nio.channels

This interface defines a communication channel for input and output. The Channel interface is a high-level generic interface extended by more specific interfaces, such as ReadableByteChannel and WritableByteChannel. Channel defines only two methods: isOpen() determines whether a channel is open, and close() closes a channel. Channels are open when they are first created. Once closed, a channel remains closed forever, and no further I/O operations may go through it.

Many channel implementations are interruptible and asynchronously closeable and implement the InterruptibleChannel interface to advertise this fact. See InterruptibleChannel for details.

```
public interface Channel {
// Public Instance Methods
   public abstract void close() throws java.io.IOException;
   public abstract boolean isOpen();
}
```

Implementations: InterruptibleChannel, ReadableByteChannel, SelectableChannel, WritableByteChannel, java.nio.channels.spi.AbstractInterruptibleChannel

Channels **Java 1.4**

java.nio.channels

This class defines static methods that provide a bridge between the byte stream and character stream classes of the java.io package and the channel classes of java.nio.channels. Channels is never intended to be instantiated; it serves solely as a placeholder for static methods. These methods create byte channels based on java.io byte streams and java.io byte streams based on byte channels. Note that the channel objects returned by the newChannel() methods may not implement InterruptibleChannel, and so may not be asynchronously closeable and interruptible like other channel classes in this package. Channels also defines methods that create character streams (java.io.Reader and java.io.Writer) based on the combination of a byte channel and a character encoding. The encoding may be specified by charset name, or with a CharsetDecoder or CharsetEncoder. See java.nio.charset.

```
public final class Channels {
// No Constructor
// Public Class Methods
   public static ReadableByteChannel newChannel(java.io.InputStream in);
   public static WritableByteChannel newChannel(java.io.OutputStream out);
   public static java.io.InputStream newInputStream(ReadableByteChannel ch);
   public static java.io.OutputStream newOutputStream(WritableByteChannel ch);
   public static java.io.Reader newReader(ReadableByteChannel ch, String csName);
   public static java.io.Reader newReader(ReadableByteChannel ch, java.nio.charset.CharsetDecoder dec,
                                          int minBufferCap);
   public static java.io.Writer newWriter(WritableByteChannel ch, String csName);
   public static java.io.Writer newWriter(WritableByteChannel ch, java.nio.charset.CharsetEncoder enc,
                                          int minBufferCap);
}
```

ClosedByInterruptException **Java 1.4**

java.nio.channels *serializable checked*

An exception of this type is thrown by a thread blocked in an I/O operation on a channel when another thread calls its interrupt() method. This exception is a subclass of AsynchronousCloseException, and the channel will be closed as a side effect of the thread interruption.

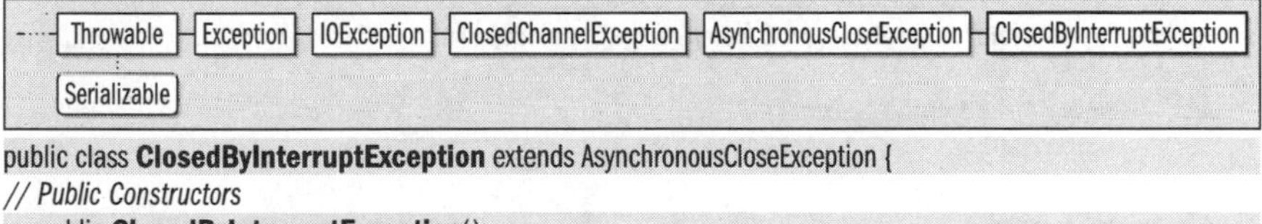


```
public class ClosedByInterruptException extends AsynchronousCloseException {
// Public Constructors
   public ClosedByInterruptException();
}
```

ClosedChannelException **Java 1.4**

java.nio.channels *serializable checked*

This exception signals an attempt to perform I/O on a channel that was closed with the close() method or closed for a particular type of I/O operation. (For example, a SocketChannel may have its read and write halves shut down independently.) Channels may be closed asynchronously, and threads blocking to complete an I/O operation will throw a subclass of this exception type. See AsynchronousCloseException and ClosedByInterruptException.

Object ─ Throwable ─ Exception ─ IOException ─ ClosedChannelException
Serializable

```
public class ClosedChannelException extends java.io.IOException {
// Public Constructors
   public ClosedChannelException();
}
```

Subclasses: AsynchronousCloseException

Thrown By: SelectableChannel.register(), java.nio.channels.spi.AbstractSelectableChannel.register()

ClosedSelectorException Java 1.4

java.nio.channels *serializable unchecked*

This exception signals an attempt to use a Selector object with close() method that has been called.

Object ─ Throwable ─ Exception ─ RuntimeException ─ IllegalStateException ─ ClosedSelectorException
Serializable

```
public class ClosedSelectorException extends IllegalStateException {
// Public Constructors
   public ClosedSelectorException();
}
```

ConnectionPendingException Java 1.4

java.nio.channels *serializable unchecked*

This exception signals a call to the connect() method of a SocketChannel when there is already a connection pending for that channel. See SocketChannel.isConnectionPending().

Object ─ Throwable ─ Exception ─ RuntimeException ─ IllegalStateException ─ ConnectionPendingException
Serializable

```
public class ConnectionPendingException extends IllegalStateException {
// Public Constructors
   public ConnectionPendingException();
}
```

DatagramChannel Java 1.4

java.nio.channels

This class implements a communication channel based on network datagrams. Obtain a DatagramChannel by calling the static open() method. Call socket() to obtain the java.net.DatagramSocket object on which the channel is based if you need to set any socket options to control low-level networking details.

The send() method sends the remaining bytes of the specified ByteBuffer to the host and port specified in the java.net.SocketAddress in the form of a datagram. receive() does the opposite: it receives a datagram, stores its content into the specified buffer (discarding any bytes that do not fit), and returns a SocketAddress that specifies the sender of the datagram (or returns null if the channel was in nonblocking mode and no datagram was waiting).

Typically, the send() and receive() methods must perform security checks on each invocation to see if the application has permissions to communicate with the remote host. If your application will be using a DatagramChannel to exchange datagrams with a single remote host and port, use the connect() method to connect to a specified SocketAddress. The connect() method performs the required security checks once and allows future communication with the specified address without the overhead. Once a DatagramChannel is connected, you can use the standard read() and write() methods defined by the ReadableByteChannel, WritableByteChannel, GatheringByteChannel, and ScatteringByteChannel interfaces. Like the receive() method, the read() methods silently discard any received bytes that do not fit in the specified ByteBuffer. The read() and write() methods throw a NotYetConnectedException if connect() has not been called.

DatagramChannel is a SelectableChannel; its validOps() method specifies that read and write operations may be selected. DatagramChannel objects are thread-safe. Read and write operations may proceed concurrently, but the class ensures that only one thread may read and one thread write at a time.

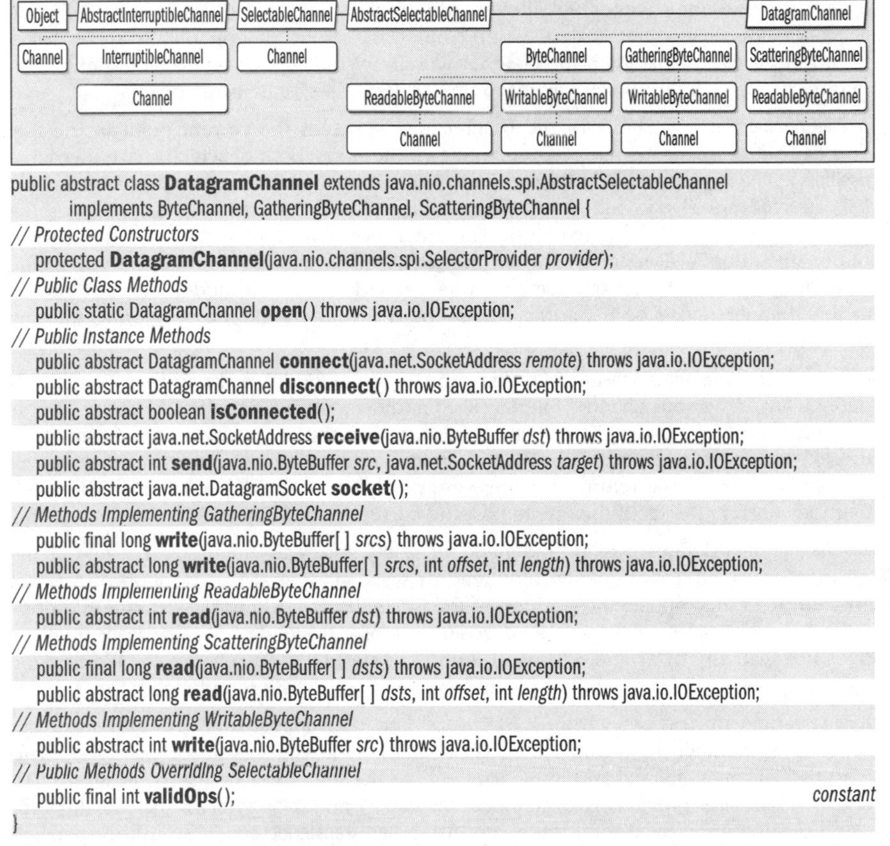


```
public abstract class DatagramChannel extends java.nio.channels.spi.AbstractSelectableChannel
        implements ByteChannel, GatheringByteChannel, ScatteringByteChannel {
// Protected Constructors
    protected DatagramChannel(java.nio.channels.spi.SelectorProvider provider);
// Public Class Methods
    public static DatagramChannel open() throws java.io.IOException;
// Public Instance Methods
    public abstract DatagramChannel connect(java.net.SocketAddress remote) throws java.io.IOException;
    public abstract DatagramChannel disconnect() throws java.io.IOException;
    public abstract boolean isConnected();
    public abstract java.net.SocketAddress receive(java.nio.ByteBuffer dst) throws java.io.IOException;
    public abstract int send(java.nio.ByteBuffer src, java.net.SocketAddress target) throws java.io.IOException;
    public abstract java.net.DatagramSocket socket();
// Methods Implementing GatheringByteChannel
    public final long write(java.nio.ByteBuffer[ ] srcs) throws java.io.IOException;
    public abstract long write(java.nio.ByteBuffer[ ] srcs, int offset, int length) throws java.io.IOException;
// Methods Implementing ReadableByteChannel
    public abstract int read(java.nio.ByteBuffer dst) throws java.io.IOException;
// Methods Implementing ScatteringByteChannel
    public final long read(java.nio.ByteBuffer[ ] dsts) throws java.io.IOException;
    public abstract long read(java.nio.ByteBuffer[ ] dsts, int offset, int length) throws java.io.IOException;
// Methods Implementing WritableByteChannel
    public abstract int write(java.nio.ByteBuffer src) throws java.io.IOException;
// Public Methods Overriding SelectableChannel
    public final int validOps();                                                          constant
}
```

Returned By: java.net.DatagramSocket.getChannel(), DatagramChannel.{connect(), disconnect(), open()}, java.nio.channels.spi.SelectorProvider.openDatagramChannel()

FileChannel **Java 1.4**

java.nio.channels

This class implements a communication channel for efficiently reading and writing files. It implements the standard read() and write() methods of the ReadableByteChannel, WritableByteChannel, GatheringByteChannel and ScatteringByteChannel methods. In addition, FileChannel provides methods for random access to the file, efficient transfer of bytes between the file and another channel, file locking, memory mapping, querying and setting the file size, and forcing buffered updates to be written to disk. (These important features are described in further detail later.) Note that since file operations do not typically block for extended periods the way network operations can, FileChannel does not subclass SelectableChannel (it is the only channel class that does not) and cannot be used with Selector objects.

FileChannel has no public constructor and no static factory methods. To obtain a FileChannel, first create a FileInputStream, FileOutputStream, or RandomAccessFile object (see the java.io package) and then call the getChannel() method of that object. If you use a FileInputStream, the resulting channel will allow reading but not writing, and if you use a FileOutputStream, the channel will allow writing but not reading. If you obtain a FileChannel from a RandomAccessFile, then the channel will allow reading, or both reading and writing, depending on the *mode* argument to the RandomAccessFile constructor.

A FileChannel has a position, or file pointer, that specifies the current point in the file. You can set or query the file position with two methods, both of which share the name position(). The position of a FileChannel and of the stream or RandomAccessFile from which it is derived are always the same; changing the position of the channel changes the position of the stream, and vice versa. The initial position of a FileChannel is the position of the stream or RandomAccessFile when the getChannel() method was called. If you create a FileChannel from a FileOutputStream that was opened in append mode, then any output to the channel always occurs at the end of the file and sets the file position to the end of the file.

Once you have a FileChannel object, you can use the standard read() and write() methods defined by the various channel interfaces. In addition to updating the buffer position as they read and write bytes, these methods also update the file position to or from which those bytes are written or read. These standard read() methods return the number of bytes actually read and return –1 if there are no bytes left in the file to read. The write() methods enlarge the file if they write past the current end-of-file.

FileChannel also defines position-independent read() and write() methods that take a file position as an explicit argument; they read or write starting at that position of the file, and although they update the position of the ByteBuffer, they do not update the file position of the FileChannel. If the specified position is past the end-of-file, the read() method does not read any bytes and returns –1, and the write() method enlarges the file, leaving any bytes between the old end-of-file and the specified position undefined.

It is common to read bytes from a FileChannel and then immediately write them out to some other channel (such as a SocketChannel: think of a web server, for example), or to read bytes from a channel and immediately write them to a FileChannel (consider an FTP client). FileChannel provides two methods, transferTo() and transferFrom(), that do this efficiently, without the need for a temporary ByteBuffer. transferTo() reads up to the specified number of bytes starting at the specified location from this FileChannel and writes them to the specified channel. It does not alter the file position of the FileChannel and returns the number of bytes actually transferred. transferFrom() does the reverse: it reads up to the specified number of available bytes from the specified channel, writes them to this

FileChannel at the specified location without altering the file position of this channel, and returns the actual number of bytes transferred. For both methods, if the destination or source channel is a FileChannel, then the file position of that channel is updated.

The size() method returns the size (in bytes) of the underlying file. truncate() reduces the file size to the specified value, discarding any file content that exceeds that size. If the specified size is greater than or equal to the current file size, the file is unchanged. If the file position is greater than the new size of the file, the position is changed to the new size.

Use the force() method to force any buffered modifications to the file that will be written to the underlying storage device. If the file resides on a local device (as opposed to a network filesystem, for example), then force() guarantees that any changes to the file made since the channel was opened or since a previous call to force() were written to the device. The argument to this method is a hint as to whether file metadata (such as last modification time) will be forced out with file content. If this argument is true, the system will force out content and metadata. If false, the system may omit updates to metadata. Note that force() is required only to output changes made directly through the FileChannel. File updates made through a MappedByteBuffer returned by the map() method (described later) should be forced out with the force() method of MappedByteBuffer.

FileChannel defines two blocking lock() methods and two nonblocking tryLock() methods for locking a file or a region of a file against concurrent access by another program. (These methods are not suitable for preventing concurrent access to a file by two threads within the same Java virtual machine.) The no-argument versions of these methods attempt to acquire an exclusive lock on the entire file. The three-argument versions of these methods attempt to lock a specified region of the file and may acquire shared locks in addition to exclusive locks. (A shared lock prevents any other process from acquiring an exclusive lock but does not prevent other shared locks. Typically, you acquire a shared lock when reading a file that should not be concurrently updated and an exclusive lock before writing file content to ensure that no one else is trying to read it at the same time.) The tryLock() methods return a FileLock object, or null if there was already a conflicting lock on the file. The lock() methods block if there is already a conflicting lock and never return null. (See FileLock for more information about locks.) The FileChannel file-locking mechanism uses whatever locking capability is provided by the underlying platform. Some operating systems enforce file locking: if one process holds a lock, other processes are prevented by the operating system from accessing the file. Other operating systems merely prevent other processes from acquiring a conflicting lock; in this case, successful file locking requires the cooperation of all processes. Some operating systems do not support shared locks; on these systems, an exclusive lock is returned even when a shared lock is requested.

The map() method returns a MappedByteBuffer that represents the specified region of the file. File contents can be read directly from the buffer, and bytes placed in the buffer will be written to the file (if the mapping is done in read/write mode). The mapping represented by a MappedByteBuffer remains valid until the buffer is garbage collected; the buffer continues to function even if the FileChannel from which it was created is closed. File mappings can be done in three different modes that specify whether bytes can be written into the buffer and what happens when this is done. See FileChannel.MapMode for a description of these three modes.

The map() method relies on the memory-mapping facilities provided by the underlying operating system. This means that a number of details may vary from implementation to implementation. In particular, it is not specified whether changes to the underlying file made after the call to map() are visible through the MappedByteBuffer. Typically, a mapped file is more efficient than an unmapped file, but only when the file is large.

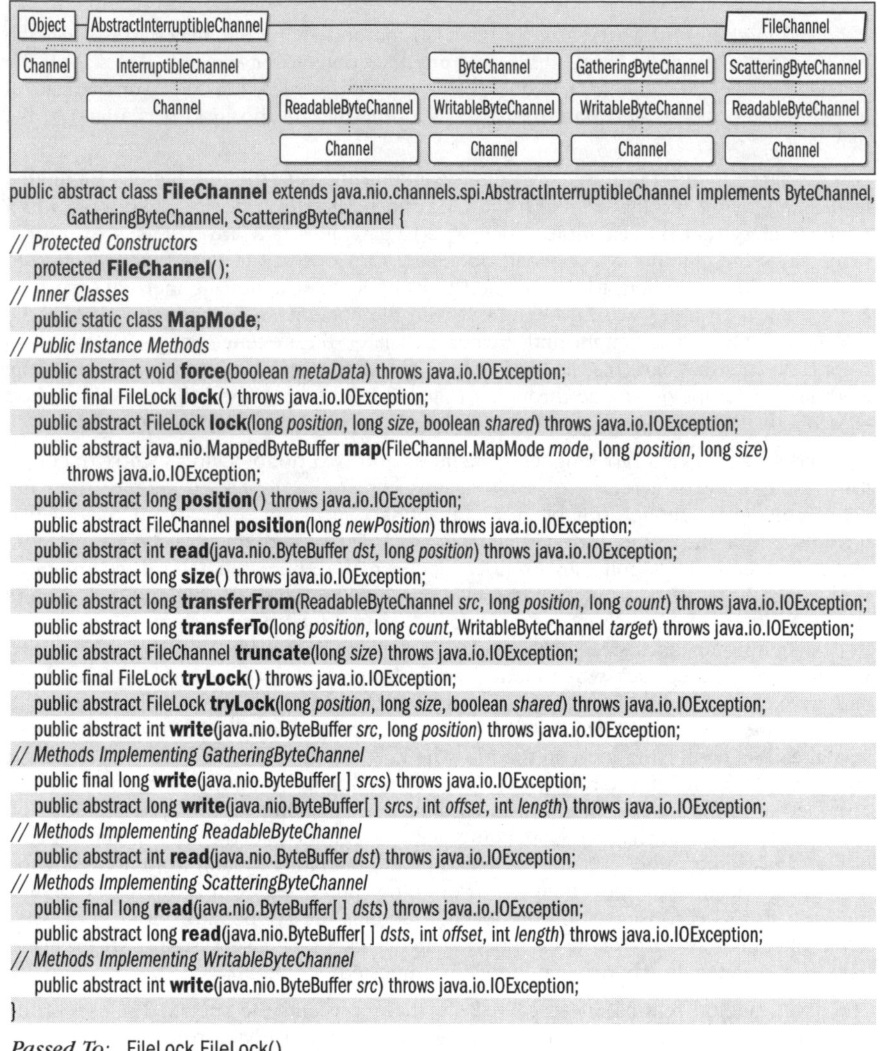


```
public abstract class FileChannel extends java.nio.channels.spi.AbstractInterruptibleChannel implements ByteChannel,
        GatheringByteChannel, ScatteringByteChannel {
// Protected Constructors
   protected FileChannel();
// Inner Classes
   public static class MapMode;
// Public Instance Methods
   public abstract void force(boolean metaData) throws java.io.IOException;
   public final FileLock lock() throws java.io.IOException;
   public abstract FileLock lock(long position, long size, boolean shared) throws java.io.IOException;
   public abstract java.nio.MappedByteBuffer map(FileChannel.MapMode mode, long position, long size)
        throws java.io.IOException;
   public abstract long position() throws java.io.IOException;
   public abstract FileChannel position(long newPosition) throws java.io.IOException;
   public abstract int read(java.nio.ByteBuffer dst, long position) throws java.io.IOException;
   public abstract long size() throws java.io.IOException;
   public abstract long transferFrom(ReadableByteChannel src, long position, long count) throws java.io.IOException;
   public abstract long transferTo(long position, long count, WritableByteChannel target) throws java.io.IOException;
   public abstract FileChannel truncate(long size) throws java.io.IOException;
   public final FileLock tryLock() throws java.io.IOException;
   public abstract FileLock tryLock(long position, long size, boolean shared) throws java.io.IOException;
   public abstract int write(java.nio.ByteBuffer src, long position) throws java.io.IOException;
// Methods Implementing GatheringByteChannel
   public final long write(java.nio.ByteBuffer[ ] srcs) throws java.io.IOException;
   public abstract long write(java.nio.ByteBuffer[ ] srcs, int offset, int length) throws java.io.IOException;
// Methods Implementing ReadableByteChannel
   public abstract int read(java.nio.ByteBuffer dst) throws java.io.IOException;
// Methods Implementing ScatteringByteChannel
   public final long read(java.nio.ByteBuffer[ ] dsts) throws java.io.IOException;
   public abstract long read(java.nio.ByteBuffer[ ] dsts, int offset, int length) throws java.io.IOException;
// Methods Implementing WritableByteChannel
   public abstract int write(java.nio.ByteBuffer src) throws java.io.IOException;
}
```

Passed To: FileLock.FileLock()

Returned By: java.io.FileInputStream.getChannel(), java.io.FileOutputStream.getChannel(), java.io.RandomAccessFile.getChannel(), FileChannel.{position(), truncate()}, FileLock.channel()

FileChannel.MapMode — Java 1.4

java.nio.channels

This class defines three constants that define the legal values of the *mode* argument to the map() method of the FileChannel class:

READ_ONLY
: The memory mapping is read-only. The contents of the MappedByteBuffer returned by the map() method may be read but not modified.

READ_WRITE

The memory mapping is bidirectional: the contents of the returned buffer can be modified, and any modifications will eventually be written to the underlying file. The FileChannel must have been created from a java.io.RandomAccessFile opened in read/write mode.

PRIVATE

The returned buffer may be modified, but any such changes are private to the buffer and are never written to the underlying file. This mapping mode is also known as "copy-on-write".

```
public static class FileChannel.MapMode {
// No Constructor
// Public Constants
   public static final FileChannel.MapMode PRIVATE;
   public static final FileChannel.MapMode READ_ONLY;
   public static final FileChannel.MapMode READ_WRITE;
// Public Methods Overriding Object
   public String toString();
}
```

Passed To: FileChannel.map()

Type Of: FileChannel.MapMode.{PRIVATE, READ_ONLY, READ_WRITE}

FileLock — Java 1.4

java.nio.channels

A FileLock object is returned by the lock() and tryLock() methods of FileChannel and represents a lock on a file or a region of a file. (See FileChannel for more information on file locking with those methods.) When a lock is no longer required, it should be released with the release() method. A lock will also be released if the channel is closed, or when the virtual machine terminates. isValid() returns true if the lock has not yet been released and returns false if it has been released.

The channel(), position(), size(), and isShared() methods return basic information about the lock: the FileChannel that was locked, the region of the file that was locked, and whether the lock is shared or exclusive. If the entire file is locked, then the size() method returns a value (Long.MAX_VALUE) that is much greater than the actual file size. If the underlying operating system does not support shared locks, then isShared() may return false even if a shared lock was requested. overlaps() is a convenience method that returns true if the position and size of this lock overlap the specified position and size.

```
public abstract class FileLock {
// Protected Constructors
   protected FileLock(FileChannel channel, long position, long size, boolean shared);
// Public Instance Methods
   public final FileChannel channel();
   public final boolean isShared();
   public abstract boolean isValid();
   public final boolean overlaps(long position, long size);
   public final long position();
   public abstract void release() throws java.io.IOException;
   public final long size();
// Public Methods Overriding Object
   public final String toString();
}
```

Returned By: FileChannel.{lock(), tryLock()}

FileLockInterruptionException — Java 1.4

java.nio.channels — *serializable checked*

This exception signals that the interrupt() method of a blocked thread that was waiting to acquire a file lock was called. See FileChannel.lock().

Object ─ Throwable ─ Exception ─ IOException ─ FileLockInterruptionException
Serializable

```
public class FileLockInterruptionException extends java.io.IOException {
// Public Constructors
   public FileLockInterruptionException();
}
```

GatheringByteChannel — Java 1.4

java.nio.channels

This interface extends WritableByteChannel and adds two additional write() methods that can gather bytes from one or more buffers and write them out to the channel. These methods are passed an array of ByteBuffer objects and, optionally, an offset and length that define the relevant subarray to be used. The write() method attempts to write all the remaining bytes from all the specified buffers (in the order in which they appear in the buffer array) to the channel. The return value of the method is the number of bytes actually written. See WritableByteChannel for a discussion of exceptions and thread safety that apply to these write() methods.

Channel ··· WritableByteChannel ··· GatheringByteChannel

```
public interface GatheringByteChannel extends WritableByteChannel {
// Public Instance Methods
   public abstract long write(java.nio.ByteBuffer[ ] srcs) throws java.io.IOException;
   public abstract long write(java.nio.ByteBuffer[ ] srcs, int offset, int length) throws java.io.IOException;
}
```

Implementations: DatagramChannel, FileChannel, Pipe.SinkChannel, SocketChannel

IllegalBlockingModeException — Java 1.4

java.nio.channels — *serializable unchecked*

This exception signals an attempt to use a channel in the wrong blocking mode. An exception of this type is thrown by SelectableChannel.register() if the channel is not in nonblocking mode.

Object ─ Throwable ─ Exception ─ RuntimeException ─ IllegalStateException ─ IllegalBlockingModeException
Serializable

```
public class IllegalBlockingModeException extends IllegalStateException {
// Public Constructors
   public IllegalBlockingModeException();
}
```

IllegalSelectorException — Java 1.4

java.nio.channels — *serializable unchecked*

This exception signals an attempt to register a SelectableChannel with a Selector when the channel and the selector were not created by the same java.nio.channels.spi.SelectorProvider.

Object ─ Throwable ─ Exception ─ RuntimeException ─ IllegalArgumentException ─ IllegalSelectorException
Throwable ⋯ Serializable

```
public class IllegalSelectorException extends IllegalArgumentException {
// Public Constructors
   public IllegalSelectorException();
}
```

InterruptibleChannel — Java 1.4

java.nio.channels

Channels that implement this marker interface have two important properties that are relevant to multithreaded programs: they are asynchronously closeable and interruptible. When the close() method of an InterruptibleChannel is called, any other thread that is blocked while waiting for an I/O operation to complete on that channel will stop blocking and receive an AsynchronousCloseException. Furthermore, if a thread is blocked while waiting for an I/O operation to complete on an InterruptibleChannel, then another thread may call the interrupt() method of the blocked thread. This sets the interrupt status of the blocked thread and causes the thread to wake up and receive a ClosedByInterruptException (a subclass of AsynchronousCloseException). As the name of this interrupt implies, the channel that the thread was blocked on is closed as a side effect of the thread interruption. There is no way to interrupt a blocked thread without closing the channel upon which it is blocked. This ability to interrupt a blocked thread is particularly noteworthy because it has never worked reliably with the older java.io API.

All the concrete channel implementations that are part of this package implement InterruptibleChannel. Note, however, that methods such as Channels.newChannel() may return channel objects that are not interruptible. You can use the instanceof to determine whether an unknown channel object implements this interface.

Channel ⋯ InterruptibleChannel

```
public interface InterruptibleChannel extends Channel {
// Public Instance Methods
   public abstract void close() throws java.io.IOException;
}
```

Implementations: java.nio.channels.spi.AbstractInterruptibleChannel

NoConnectionPendingException — Java 1.4

java.nio.channels — *serializable unchecked*

This exception signals that SocketChannel.finishConnect() was called without a previous call to SocketChannel.connect().

Object ─ Throwable ─ Exception ─ RuntimeException ─ IllegalStateException ─ NoConnectionPendingException
Throwable ⋯ Serializable

```
public class NoConnectionPendingException extends IllegalStateException {
// Public Constructors
   public NoConnectionPendingException();
}
```

NonReadableChannelException — Java 1.4

java.nio.channels — *serializable unchecked*

This exception signals a call to the read() method of a readable channel that is not open for reading, such as a FileChannel created from a FileOutputStream.

Object — Throwable — Exception — RuntimeException — IllegalStateException — NonReadableChannelException
Throwable ⋮ Serializable

```
public class NonReadableChannelException extends IllegalStateException {
// Public Constructors
   public NonReadableChannelException();
}
```

NonWritableChannelException — Java 1.4

java.nio.channels — *serializable unchecked*

This exception signals a call to a write() method of a writable channel that is not open for writing, such as a FileChannel created from a FileInputStream.

Object — Throwable — Exception — RuntimeException — IllegalStateException — NonWritableChannelException
Throwable ⋮ Serializable

```
public class NonWritableChannelException extends IllegalStateException {
// Public Constructors
   public NonWritableChannelException();
}
```

NotYetBoundException — Java 1.4

java.nio.channels — *serializable unchecked*

This exception signals a call to ServerSocketChannel.accept() before the underlying server socket has been bound to a local port. Call socket().bind() to bind the java.net.ServerSocket that underlies the ServerSocketChannel.

Object — Throwable — Exception — RuntimeException — IllegalStateException — NotYetBoundException
Throwable ⋮ Serializable

```
public class NotYetBoundException extends IllegalStateException {
// Public Constructors
   public NotYetBoundException();
}
```

NotYetConnectedException **Java 1.4**

java.nio.channels ***serializable unchecked***

This exception signals an attempt to read() or write() on a SocketChannel that is not yet connected to a remote host. See SocketChannel.connect().

Object ─ Throwable ─ Exception ─ RuntimeException ─ IllegalStateException ─ NotYetConnectedException
Serializable

```
public class NotYetConnectedException extends IllegalStateException {
// Public Constructors
    public NotYetConnectedException();
}
```

OverlappingFileLockException **Java 1.4**

java.nio.channels ***serializable unchecked***

This exception is thrown by the lock() and tryLock() methods of FileChannel if the requested lock region overlaps a file lock already held by a thread in this JVM, or if there is already a thread in this JVM waiting to lock an overlapping region of the same file. The FileChannel file-locking mechanism is designed to lock files against concurrent access by two separate processes. Two threads within the same JVM should not attempt to acquire a lock on overlapping regions of the same file—any attempt to do so causes an exception of this type to be thrown.

Object ─ Throwable ─ Exception ─ RuntimeException ─ IllegalStateException ─ OverlappingFileLockException
Serializable

```
public class OverlappingFileLockException extends IllegalStateException {
// Public Constructors
    public OverlappingFileLockException();
}
```

Pipe **Java 1.4**

java.nio.channels

A pipe is an abstraction that allows the one-way transfer of bytes from one thread to another. A pipe has a "read end" and a "write end," which are represented by objects that implement the ReadableByteChannel and WritableByteChannel interfaces. Create a new pipe with the static Pipe.open() method. Call the sink() method to obtain the Pipe.SinkChannel object that represents the write end of the pipe, and call the source() method to obtain the Pipe.SourceChannel object that represents the read end of the pipe.

Programmers familiar with only Unix-style pipes may find the names and return values of the sink() and source() methods confusing. A Unix pipe is an interprocess communication mechanism tied to two specific processes: a source of bytes and a destination, or sink, for those bytes. With this conceptual model of a pipe, you would expect the source to obtain the channel it writes to with the source() method and the sink to obtain the channel it reads from with the sink() method.

This Pipe class is not a Unix-style pipe, however. While it can be used for communication between two threads, the ends of the pipe are not tied to those threads, and a single source thread and a single sink thread are not necessary. Therefore, in the Pipe API, it is the pipe itself that serves as the source and sink of bytes: bytes are read from the source end of the pipe and written to the sink end.

```
public abstract class Pipe {
// Protected Constructors
    protected Pipe();
// Inner Classes
    public abstract static class SinkChannel extends java.nio.channels.spi.AbstractSelectableChannel implements
        GatheringByteChannel, WritableByteChannel;
    public abstract static class SourceChannel extends java.nio.channels.spi.AbstractSelectableChannel implements
        ReadableByteChannel, ScatteringByteChannel;
// Public Class Methods
    public static Pipe open() throws java.io.IOException;
// Public Instance Methods
    public abstract Pipe.SinkChannel sink();
    public abstract Pipe.SourceChannel source();
}
```

Returned By: Pipe.open(), java.nio.channels.spi.SelectorProvider.openPipe()

Pipe.SinkChannel Java 1.4

java.nio.channels

This public inner class represents the write end of a pipe. Bytes written to a Pipe.SinkChannel become available on the corresponding Pipe.SourceChannel of the pipe. Obtain a Pipe.SinkChannel by creating a Pipe object with Pipe.open() and calling the sink() method of that object. See also the containing Pipe class.

Pipe.SinkChannel implements WritableByteChannel and GatheringByteChannel and defines the write() methods of those interfaces. This class subclasses SelectableChannel so it can be used with a Selector. It overrides the abstract validOps() method of SelectableChannel to return SelectionKey.OP_WRITE but defines no new methods of its own.

```
public abstract static class Pipe.SinkChannel extends java.nio.channels.spi.AbstractSelectableChannel
        implements GatheringByteChannel, WritableByteChannel {
// Protected Constructors
    protected SinkChannel(java.nio.channels.spi.SelectorProvider provider);
// Public Methods Overriding SelectableChannel
    public final int validOps();                                                    constant
}
```

Returned By: Pipe.sink()

Pipe.SourceChannel Java 1.4

java.nio.channels

This public inner class represents the read end of a pipe. Bytes written to the corresponding write end of the pipe (see Pipe.SinkChannel) become available for reading through this channel. Obtain a Pipe.SourceChannel by creating a Pipe object with Pipe.open() and then calling the source() method of that object. See also the containing Pipe class.

Pipe.SourceChannel implements ReadableByteChannel and ScatteringByteChannel and defines the read() methods of those interfaces. This class subclasses SelectableChannel so it can be used with a Selector. It overrides the abstract validOps() method of SelectableChannel to return SelectionKey.OP_READ but defines no new methods of its own.

```
public abstract static class Pipe.SourceChannel extends java.nio.channels.spi.AbstractSelectableChannel
        implements ReadableByteChannel, ScatteringByteChannel {
// Protected Constructors
```

```
    protected SourceChannel(java.nio.channels.spi.SelectorProvider provider);
// Public Methods Overriding SelectableChannel
    public final int validOps( );                                    constant
}
```

Returned By: Pipe.source()

ReadableByteChannel — Java 1.4

java.nio.channels

This subinterface of Channel defines a single-key read() method that reads bytes from the channel and stores them in the specified ByteBuffer, updating the buffer position as it does so. read() attempts to read as many bytes as will fit in the specified buffer (see Buffer.remaining()) but may read fewer than this. For example, if the channel is a nonblocking channel, read() will return immediately, even if there are no bytes available to be read. read() returns the number of bytes actually read (which may be zero in the nonblocking case) or –1 if there are no more bytes to be read in the channel (for example, if the end of a file has been reached, or the other end of a socket has been closed).

read() is declared to throw an IOException. More specifically, it may throw a ClosedChannelException if the channel is closed. If the channel is closed asynchronously, or if a blocked thread is interrupted, the read() method may terminate with an AsynchronousCloseException or a ClosedByInterruptException. read() may also throw an unchecked NonReadableChannelException if it is called on a channel that was not opened or configured to allow reading.

ReadableByteChannel implementations are required to be thread-safe: only one thread may perform a read operation on a channel at a time. If a read operation is in progress, then any call to read() will block until the operation is completed. Some channel implementations may allow read and write operations to proceed concurrently, but none will allow two read operations to proceed at the same time.

Channel ··· ReadableByteChannel

```
public interface ReadableByteChannel extends Channel {
// Public Instance Methods
    public abstract int read(java.nio.ByteBuffer dst) throws java.io.IOException;
}
```

Implementations: ByteChannel, Pipe.SourceChannel, ScatteringByteChannel

Passed To: Channels.{newInputStream(), newReader()}, FileChannel.transferFrom()

Returned By: Channels.newChannel()

ScatteringByteChannel — Java 1.4

java.nio.channels

This interface extends ReadableByteChannel and adds two additional read() methods that read bytes for a channel and scatter them to an array (or subarray) of buffers. These methods are passed an array of ByteBuffer objects and, optionally, an offset and length that define the region of the array to be used. The read() method attempts to read enough bytes from the channel to fill each of the specified buffers in the order in which they appear in the buffer array (the scattering process is actually much more orderly and linear than the name implies). The return value of the method is the number of bytes actually read, which may be different than the sum of the remaining bytes in the buffers. See ReadableByteChannel for a discussion of exceptions and thread safety that applies to these read() methods as well.

```
Channel ··· ReadableByteChannel ··· ScatteringByteChannel
```

```
public interface ScatteringByteChannel extends ReadableByteChannel {
// Public Instance Methods
   public abstract long read(java.nio.ByteBuffer[ ] dsts) throws java.io.IOException;
   public abstract long read(java.nio.ByteBuffer[ ] dsts, int offset, int length) throws java.io.IOException;
}
```

Implementations: DatagramChannel, FileChannel, Pipe.SourceChannel, SocketChannel

SelectableChannel — Java 1.4

java.nio.channels

This abstract class defines the API for channels that can be used with a Selector object to allow a thread to block while waiting for activity on any of a group of channels. All channel classes in the java.nio.channels package except for FileChannel are subclasses of SelectableChannel.

A selectable channel may be registered only with a Selector if it is nonblocking, so this class defines the configureBlocking() method—pass false to this method to put a channel into nonblocking mode, or pass true to make calls to its read() and/or write() methods block. Use isBlocking() to determine the current blocking mode of a selectable channel.

Register a SelectableChannel with a Selector by calling the register() method of the channel (not of the selector). There are two versions of this method; both take a Selector object and a bitmask that specifies the set of channel operations that will be selected on that channel. (See SelectionKey for the constants that can be OR-ed together to form this bitmask). Both methods return a SelectionKey object that represents the registration of the channel with the selector. One version of the register() method also takes an arbitrary object argument that serves as an attachment to the SelectionKey and allows you to associate arbitrary data with it. The validOps() method returns a bitmask that specifies the set of operations that a particular channel object allows to be selected. The bitmask passed to register() may contain only bits that are set in this validOps() value.

Note that SelectableChannel does not define a deregister() method. Instead, to remove a channel from the set of channels monitored by a Selector, you must call the cancel() method of the SelectionKey returned by register().

Call isRegistered() to determine whether a SelectableChannel is registered with any Selector. (Note that a single channel may be registered with more than one Selector.) If you did not keep track of the SelectionKey returned by a call to register(), you can query it with the keyFor() method.

See Selector and SelectionKey for further details on multiplexing selectable channels.

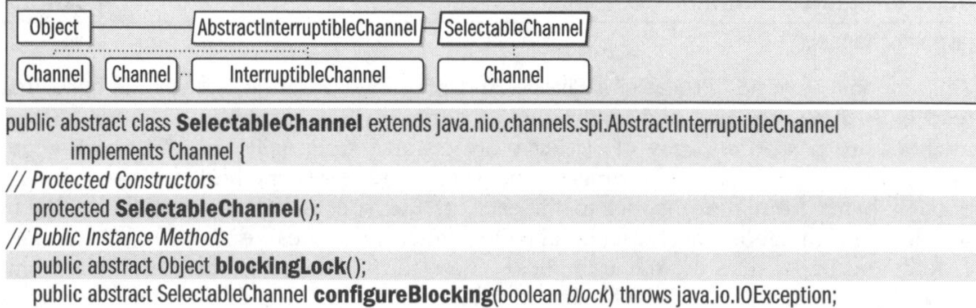


```
public abstract class SelectableChannel extends java.nio.channels.spi.AbstractInterruptibleChannel
       implements Channel {
// Protected Constructors
   protected SelectableChannel();
// Public Instance Methods
   public abstract Object blockingLock();
   public abstract SelectableChannel configureBlocking(boolean block) throws java.io.IOException;
```

```
    public abstract boolean isBlocking();
    public abstract boolean isRegistered();
    public abstract SelectionKey keyFor(Selector sel);
    public abstract java.nio.channels.spi.SelectorProvider provider();
    public final SelectionKey register(Selector sel, int ops) throws ClosedChannelException;
    public abstract SelectionKey register(Selector sel, int ops, Object att) throws ClosedChannelException;
    public abstract int validOps();
}
```

Subclasses: java.nio.channels.spi.AbstractSelectableChannel

Returned By: SelectableChannel.configureBlocking(), SelectionKey.channel(), java.nio.channels.spi.AbstractSelectableChannel.configureBlocking()

SelectionKey — Java 1.4

java.nio.channels

A SelectionKey represents the registration of a SelectableChannel with a Selector and identifies a selected channel and the operations that are ready to be performed on that channel. After a call to the select() method of a selector, the selectedKeys() method of the selector returns a Set of SelectionKey objects to identify the channel or channels that are ready for reading, for writing, or for another operation.

Create a SelectionKey by passing a Selector object to the register() method of a SelectableChannel. The channel() and selector() methods of the returned SelectionKey return the SelectableChannel and Selector objects associated with that key.

When you no longer want the channel to be registered with the selector, call the cancel() method of the SelectionKey. isValid() determines whether a SelectionKey is still valid—it returns true unless the cancel() method has been called, the channel has been closed, or the selector has been closed.

The main purpose of a SelectionKey is to hold the "interest set" of channel operations that the selector should monitor for the channel and the "ready set" of operations that the selector has determined are ready to proceed on the channel. Both sets are represented as integer bitmasks (not as java.util.Set objects) formed by OR-ing together any of the OP_ constants defined by this class. Those constants are:

OP_READ
: In the interest set, this bit specifies an interest in read operations. In the ready set, this bit specifies that the channel has bytes available for reading, has reached the end-of-stream, has been remotely closed, or that an error has occurred.

OP_WRITE
: In the interest set, this bit specifies an interest in write operations. In the ready set, this bit specifies that the channel is ready to have bytes written, has been closed, or that an error has occurred.

OP_CONNECT
: In the interest set, this bit specifies an interest in socket connection operations. In the ready set, it indicates that a socket channel is ready to connect or that an error has occurred.

OP_ACCEPT
: In the interest set, this bit specifies an interest in server socket accept operations. In the ready set, it indicates that a server socket channel is ready to accept a connection or that an error has occurred.

The no-argument version of the interestOps() method allows you to query the interest set. The initial value of the interest set is the bitmask that was passed to the register() method of the channel. It can be changed, however, by passing a new bitmask to the one-argument version of interestOps(). (Note that the same method name is used to both query and set the interest set.) The current state of the ready set can be queried with readyOps(). You can also use the convenience methods isReadable(), isWritable(), isConnectable(), and isAcceptable() to test whether individual operation bits are set in the ready set bitmask. There is no way to explicitly set the state of the ready set—each call to the select() method updates the ready set for you. Note, however, that you must remove a SelectionKey object from the Set returned by Selector.selectedKeys() for the bits of the ready set that will be cleared at the start of the next selection operation. If you never remove the SelectionKey from the set of selected keys, the Selector assumes that none of the I/O readiness conditions represented by the ready set have been handled yet, and leaves their bits set.

Use attach() to associate an arbitrary object with a SelectionKey and call attachment() to query that object. This ability to associate data with a selection key is often useful when using a Selector with multiple channels: it can provide the context necessary to process a SelectionKey that has selected.

```
public abstract class SelectionKey {
// Protected Constructors
   protected SelectionKey();
// Public Constants
   public static final int OP_ACCEPT;                                    =16
   public static final int OP_CONNECT;                                   =8
   public static final int OP_READ;                                      =1
   public static final int OP_WRITE;                                     =4
// Property Accessor Methods (by property name)
   public final boolean isAcceptable();
   public final boolean isConnectable();
   public final boolean isReadable();
   public abstract boolean isValid();
   public final boolean isWritable();
// Public Instance Methods
   public final Object attach(Object ob);
   public final Object attachment();
   public abstract void cancel();
   public abstract SelectableChannel channel();
   public abstract int interestOps();
   public abstract SelectionKey interestOps(int ops);
   public abstract int readyOps();
   public abstract Selector selector();
}
```

Subclasses: java.nio.channels.spi.AbstractSelectionKey

Returned By: SelectableChannel.{keyFor(), register()}, SelectionKey.interestOps(), java.nio.channels.spi.AbstractSelectableChannel.{keyFor(), register()}, java.nio.channels.spi.AbstractSelector.register()

Selector — Java 1.4

java.nio.channels

A Selector is an object that monitors multiple nonblocking SelectableChannel objects and selects the channel or channels (after blocking, if necessary) ready for I/O. Create a new Selector with the static open() method. Next, register the channels that it will monitor; a channel is registered by passing the Selector to the register() method of the channel (register() is defined by the abstract SelectableChannel class). In addition to the Selector, you must pass a bitmask that specifies which I/O operations (reading, writing, connecting, or accepting) that the Selector will monitor for that channel. Each call to this register() method returns a SelectionKey object. (The SelectionKey class also defines the constants used to form the bitmask of I/O operations.) Note that before a SelectableChannel can be registered, it must be in nonblocking mode, which can be accomplished with the configureBlocking() method of SelectableChannel.

Once the channels are registered with the Selector, call select() to block until one or more of the channels is ready for I/O. One version of select() takes a timeout value and returns if the specified number of milliseconds elapses without any channels becoming ready for I/O. These methods also return if any of the channels are closed, if an error occurs on any channel, if the wakeup() method of the Selector is called, or if the interrupt() method of the blocked thread is called. There is also a selectNow() method similar to select(): it does not block but simply polls each of the channels and determines which are ready for I/O. The return value of selectNow() and of both select() methods is the number of channels ready for I/O. It is possible for this return value to be 0.

The select() and selectNow() methods return the number of channels ready for I/O; they do not return the channels themselves. To obtain this information, you must call the selectedKeys() method, which returns a java.util.Set containing SelectionKey objects. After calling select() and selectedKeys(), applications typically obtain a java.util.Iterator for the Set and use it to loop through the SelectionKey objects that represent the channels ready for I/O. Use the channel() method of the SelectionKey to determine which channel is ready and call readyOps(), isReadable(), isWritable(), or related methods of the SelectionKey to determine the kind of I/O operation that is ready on the channel. SelectionKey objects remain in the selectedKeys() set until explicitly removed, so after performing the I/O operation for a given SelectionKey, remove that key from the Set returned by selectedKeys() (use the remove() method of the Set of its Iterator).

In addition to the selectedKeys() method, Selector defines a keys() method, which also returns a Set of SelectionKey objects. This set represents the complete set of channels that are monitored by the Selector and may not be modified, except by closing or deregistering the channel by calling the cancel() method of the associated SelectionKey. Canceled keys are removed from the keys() set on the next call to select() or selectNow().

Call wakeup() to have another thread blocked in a call to select() wake up and return immediately. If wakeup() is called, but no thread is currently blocked in a select() call, then the next call to select() or selectNow() will return immediately.

When a Selector object is no longer needed, close it by calling close(). If any thread is blocked in a select() call, it will return immediately as if wakeup() had been called. After calling close(), you should not call any other methods of a Selector. isOpen() returns true if a Selector is still open and false if it has been closed.

The Selector class is thread-safe. Note, however, that the Set object returned by selectedKeys() is not; it should be used by only one thread at a time.

```
public abstract class Selector {
// Protected Constructors
   protected Selector();
// Public Class Methods
   public static Selector open() throws java.io.IOException;
// Public Instance Methods
   public abstract void close() throws java.io.IOException;
   public abstract boolean isOpen();
   public abstract java.util.Set keys();
   public abstract java.nio.channels.spi.SelectorProvider provider();
```

```
    public abstract int select() throws java.io.IOException;
    public abstract int select(long timeout) throws java.io.IOException;
    public abstract java.util.Set selectedKeys();
    public abstract int selectNow() throws java.io.IOException;
    public abstract Selector wakeup();
}
```

Subclasses: java.nio.channels.spi.AbstractSelector

Passed To: SelectableChannel.{keyFor(), register()}, java.nio.channels.spi.AbstractSelectableChannel.{keyFor(), register()}

Returned By: SelectionKey.selector(), Selector.{open(), wakeup()}

ServerSocketChannel — Java 1.4

java.nio.channels

This class is the java.nio version of java.net.ServerSocket. It is a selectable channel that can be used by servers to accept connections from clients. Unlike other channel classes in this package, this class cannot be used for reading or writing bytes; it does not implement any of the ByteChannel interfaces and exists only to accept and establish connections with clients, not to communicate with those clients. ServerSocketChannel differs from java.net.ServerSocket in two important ways: it can be put into nonblocking mode and used with a Selector, and its accept() method returns a SocketChannel rather than a Socket, so communication with the client whose connection was just accepted can be done with the java.nio APIs.

Create a new ServerSocketChannel with the static open() method. Next, call socket() to obtain the associated ServerSocket object and use its bind() method to bind the server socket to a specific port on the local host. You can also call any other ServerSocket methods to configure other socket options at this point.

To accept a new connection through this ServerSocketChannel, simply call accept(). If the channel is in blocking mode, this method will block until a client connects and will then return a SocketChannel connected to the client. In nonblocking mode (see the inherited configureBlocking() method), accept() returns a SocketChannel only if a client is currently waiting to connect; otherwise, it immediately returns null. To be notified when a client is waiting to connect, use the inherited register() method to register a nonblocking ServerSocketChannel with a Selector and specify an interest in accept operations with the SelectionKey.OP_ACCEPT constant. See Selector and SelectionKey for further details.

Note that the SocketChannel object returned by the accept() method is always in nonblocking mode, regardless of the blocking mode of the ServerSocketChannel.

ServerSocketChannel is thread-safe; only one thread may call the accept() method at a time. When a ServerSocketChannel is no longer required, close it with the inherited close() method.

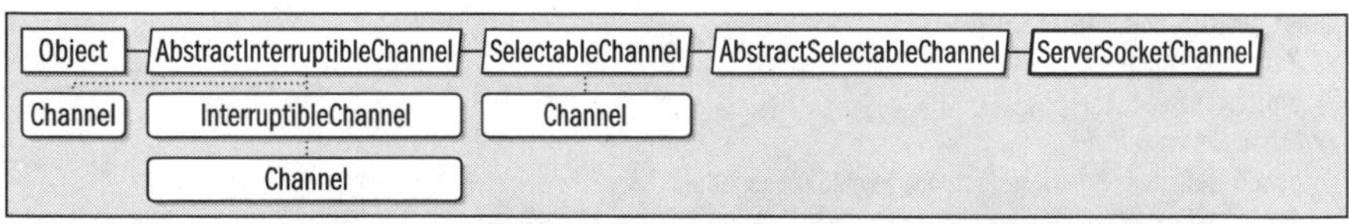


```
public abstract class ServerSocketChannel extends java.nio.channels.spi.AbstractSelectableChannel {
// Protected Constructors
    protected ServerSocketChannel(java.nio.channels.spi.SelectorProvider provider);
```

```
// Public Class Methods
    public static ServerSocketChannel open() throws java.io.IOException;
// Public Instance Methods
    public abstract SocketChannel accept() throws java.io.IOException;
    public abstract java.net.ServerSocket socket();
// Public Methods Overriding SelectableChannel
    public final int validOps();
}
```

Returned By: java.net.ServerSocket.getChannel(), ServerSocketChannel.open(), java.nio.channels.spi.SelectorProvider.openServerSocketChannel()

SocketChannel — Java 1.4

java.nio.channels

This class is a channel for communicating over a java.net.Socket. It implements ReadableByteChannel and WritableByteChannel, as well as GatheringByteChannel and ScatteringByteChannel. It is a subclass of SelectableChannel and can be used with a Selector.

Create a new SocketChannel with one of the static open() methods. The no-argument version of open() creates a new SocketChannel but does not connect it to a remote host. The other version of open() opens a new channel and connects it to the specified java.net.SocketAddress. If you create an unconnected socket, you can explicitly connect it with the connect() method. The main reason to open the channel and connect to the remote host in separate steps is if you want to do a nonblocking connect. To do this, first put the channel into nonblocking mode with the inherited configureBlocking() method. Next, call connect(); it will return immediately, without waiting for the connection to be established. Then register the channel with a Selector, specifying that you are interested in SelectionKey.OP_CONNECT operations. When you are notified that your channel is ready to connect (see Selector and SelectionKey for details), simply call the nonblocking finishConnect() method to complete the connection. isConnected() returns true once a connection is established, and false otherwise. isConnectionPending() returns true if connect() has been called in blocking mode and has not yet returned, or if connect() has been called in nonblocking mode, but finishConnect() has not been called yet.

Once you have opened and connected a SocketChannel, you can read and write bytes to it with the various read() and write() methods. SocketChannel is thread-safe: read and write operations may proceed concurrently, but SocketChannel will not allow more than one read operation and more than one write operation to proceed at the same time. If you put a SocketChannel into nonblocking mode, you can register it with a Selector using the SelectionKey constants OP_READ and OP_WRITE, which will have the Selector tell you when the channel is ready for reading or writing.

The socket() method returns the java.net.Socket associated with the SocketChannel. You can use this Socket object to configure socket options, bind the socket to a specific local address, close the socket, or shut down its input or output sides. (See java.net.Socket.) Note that although all SocketChannel objects have associated Socket objects, the reverse is not true: you cannot obtain a SocketChannel from a Socket unless the Socket was created with the SocketChannel by a call to SocketChannel.open().

When you are done with a SocketChannel, close it with the close() method. You can also independently shut down the read and write portions of the channel with socket().shutdownInput() and socket().shutdownOutput(). When the input is shut down, any future reads (and any blocked read operation) will return –1 to indicate that the end-of-stream has been reached. When the output is shut down, any future writes throw a ClosedChannelException, and any write operation that was blocked at the time of shutdown throws a AsynchronousCloseException.

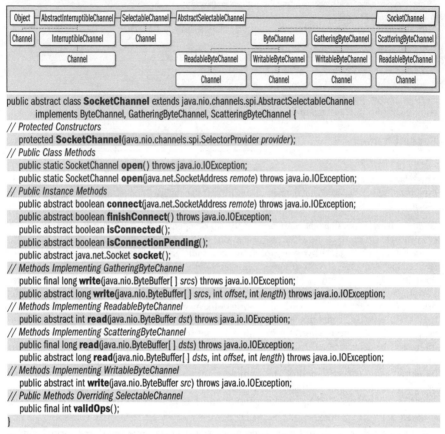

```
public abstract class SocketChannel extends java.nio.channels.spi.AbstractSelectableChannel
        implements ByteChannel, GatheringByteChannel, ScatteringByteChannel {
// Protected Constructors
    protected SocketChannel(java.nio.channels.spi.SelectorProvider provider);
// Public Class Methods
    public static SocketChannel open() throws java.io.IOException;
    public static SocketChannel open(java.net.SocketAddress remote) throws java.io.IOException;
// Public Instance Methods
    public abstract boolean connect(java.net.SocketAddress remote) throws java.io.IOException;
    public abstract boolean finishConnect() throws java.io.IOException;
    public abstract boolean isConnected();
    public abstract boolean isConnectionPending();
    public abstract java.net.Socket socket();
// Methods Implementing GatheringByteChannel
    public final long write(java.nio.ByteBuffer[ ] srcs) throws java.io.IOException;
    public abstract long write(java.nio.ByteBuffer[ ] srcs, int offset, int length) throws java.io.IOException;
// Methods Implementing ReadableByteChannel
    public abstract int read(java.nio.ByteBuffer dst) throws java.io.IOException;
// Methods Implementing ScatteringByteChannel
    public final long read(java.nio.ByteBuffer[ ] dsts) throws java.io.IOException;
    public abstract long read(java.nio.ByteBuffer[ ] dsts, int offset, int length) throws java.io.IOException;
// Methods Implementing WritableByteChannel
    public abstract int write(java.nio.ByteBuffer src) throws java.io.IOException;
// Public Methods Overriding SelectableChannel
    public final int validOps();
}
```

Returned By: java.net.Socket.getChannel(), ServerSocketChannel.accept(), SocketChannel.open(), java.nio.channels.spi.SelectorProvider.openSocketChannel()

UnresolvedAddressException **Java 1.4**

java.nio.channels ***serializable unchecked***

This exception signals the use of a java.net.SocketAddress that could not be resolved—for example, a java.net.InetSocketAddress that contains an unknown hostname.

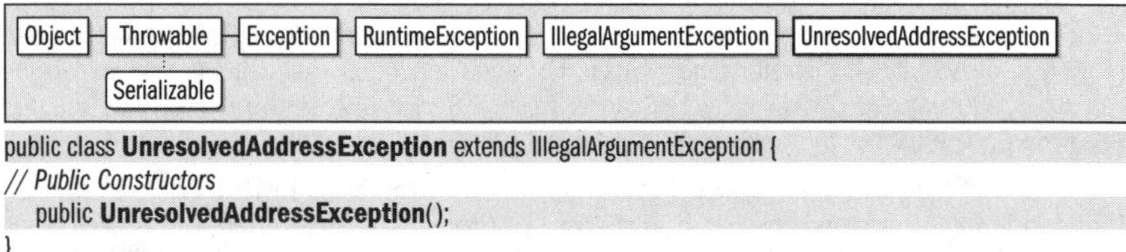


```
public class UnresolvedAddressException extends IllegalArgumentException {
// Public Constructors
    public UnresolvedAddressException();
}
```

UnsupportedAddressTypeException — Java 1.4

java.nio.channels — *serializable unchecked*

This exception signals the use of a java.net.SocketAddress subclass unknown to or not supported by the implementation. It is safe to assume that addresses of the type java.net.InetSocketAddress are universally supported.

Object ─ Throwable ─ Exception ─ RuntimeException ─ IllegalArgumentException ─ UnsupportedAddressTypeException
Serializable

```
public class UnsupportedAddressTypeException extends IllegalArgumentException {
// Public Constructors
   public UnsupportedAddressTypeException();
}
```

WritableByteChannel — Java 1.4

java.nio.channels

This subinterface of Channel defines a single-key write() method which writes bytes from a specified ByteBuffer to the channel, updating the buffer position as it goes. If possible, it writes all remaining bytes in the buffer (see Buffer.remaining()). This is not always possible (with nonblocking channels, for example), so the write() method returns the number of bytes it was actually able to write to the channel.

write() is declared to throw an IOException. More specifically, it may throw a ClosedChannelException if the channel is closed. If the channel is closed asynchronously, or if a blocked thread is interrupted, the write() method may terminate with an AsynchronousCloseException or a ClosedByInterruptException. write() may also throw an unchecked NonWritableChannelException if it is called on a channel that was not opened or configured to allow writing (such as a FileChannel).

WritableByteChannel implementations are required to be thread-safe: only one thread may perform a write operation on a channel at a time. If a write operation is in progress, then any call to write() will block until the operation is completed. Some channel implementations may allow read and write operations to proceed concurrently; some may not.

Channel ··· WritableByteChannel

```
public interface WritableByteChannel extends Channel {
// Public Instance Methods
   public abstract int write(java.nio.ByteBuffer src) throws java.io.IOException;
}
```

Implementations: ByteChannel, GatheringByteChannel, Pipe.SinkChannel

Passed To: Channels.{newOutputStream(), newWriter()}, FileChannel.transferTo()

Returned By: Channels.newChannel()

Package java.nio.channels.spi — Java 1.4

This package defines four classes used by implementors of channels and selector classes of java.nio.channels. It also defines the SelectorProvider class, which allows a custom implementation of channels and selectors to be specified instead of the default implementation. Application programmers should never need to use this package, except in rare circumstances to explicitly install a SelectorProvider implementation with the Selector-Provider.provider() method.

Classes:

public abstract class **AbstractInterruptibleChannel** implements java.nio.channels.Channel, java.nio.channels.InterruptibleChannel;
public abstract class **AbstractSelectableChannel** extends java.nio.channels.SelectableChannel;
public abstract class **AbstractSelectionKey** extends java.nio.channels.SelectionKey;
public abstract class **AbstractSelector** extends java.nio.channels.Selector;
public abstract class **SelectorProvider**;

AbstractInterruptibleChannel — Java 1.4

java.nio.channels.spi

This class exists as a convenience for implementors of new channel classes. Application programmers should never need to use or subclass it.

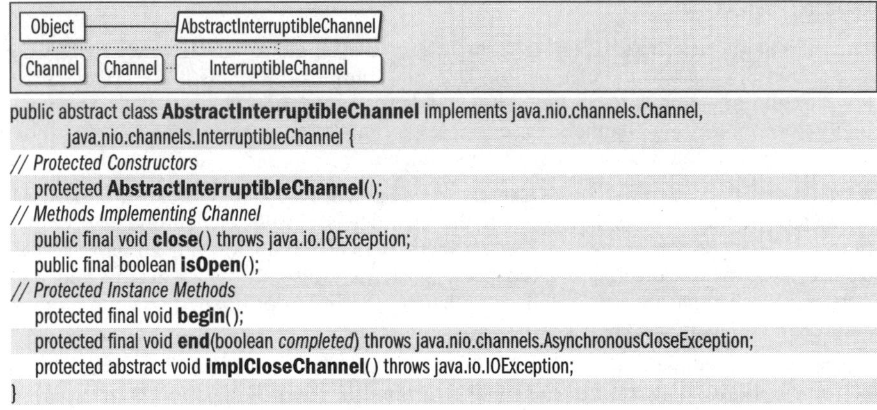


```
public abstract class AbstractInterruptibleChannel implements java.nio.channels.Channel,
        java.nio.channels.InterruptibleChannel {
// Protected Constructors
   protected AbstractInterruptibleChannel();
// Methods Implementing Channel
   public final void close() throws java.io.IOException;
   public final boolean isOpen();
// Protected Instance Methods
   protected final void begin();
   protected final void end(boolean completed) throws java.nio.channels.AsynchronousCloseException;
   protected abstract void implCloseChannel() throws java.io.IOException;
}
```

Subclasses: java.nio.channels.FileChannel, java.nio.channels.SelectableChannel

AbstractSelectableChannel — Java 1.4

java.nio.channels.spi

This class exists as a convenience for implementors of new selectable channel classes. It defines common methods of SelectableChannel in terms of protected methods with names that begin with impl. Application programmers should never need to use or subclass this class.

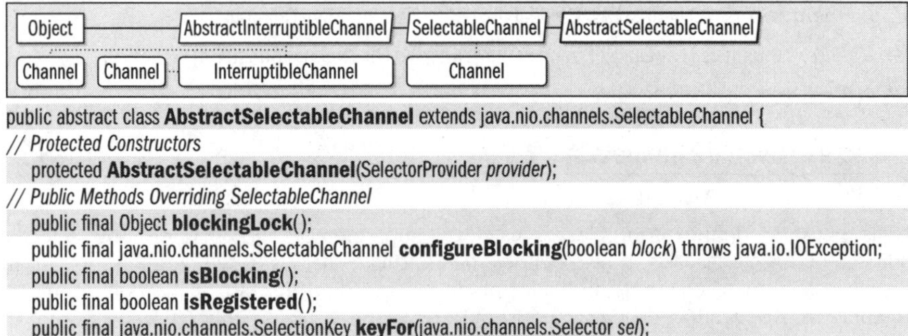


```
public abstract class AbstractSelectableChannel extends java.nio.channels.SelectableChannel {
// Protected Constructors
   protected AbstractSelectableChannel(SelectorProvider provider);
// Public Methods Overriding SelectableChannel
   public final Object blockingLock();
   public final java.nio.channels.SelectableChannel configureBlocking(boolean block) throws java.io.IOException;
   public final boolean isBlocking();
   public final boolean isRegistered();
   public final java.nio.channels.SelectionKey keyFor(java.nio.channels.Selector sel);
```

```
    public final SelectorProvider provider();
    public final java.nio.channels.SelectionKey register(java.nio.channels.Selector sel, int ops, Object att)
        throws java.nio.channels.ClosedChannelException;
// Protected Methods Overriding AbstractInterruptibleChannel
    protected final void implCloseChannel() throws java.io.IOException;
// Protected Instance Methods
    protected abstract void implCloseSelectableChannel() throws java.io.IOException;
    protected abstract void implConfigureBlocking(boolean block) throws java.io.IOException;
}
```

Subclasses: java.nio.channels.DatagramChannel, java.nio.channels.Pipe.SinkChannel, java.nio.channels.Pipe.SourceChannel, java.nio.channels.ServerSocketChannel, java.nio.channels.SocketChannel

Passed To: AbstractSelector.register()

AbstractSelectionKey **Java 1.4**

java.nio.channels.spi

This class exists as a convenience for implementors of new SelectionKey classes. Application programmers should never need to use or subclass this class.

Object — SelectionKey — AbstractSelectionKey

```
public abstract class AbstractSelectionKey extends java.nio.channels.SelectionKey {
// Protected Constructors
    protected AbstractSelectionKey();
// Public Methods Overriding SelectionKey
    public final void cancel();
    public final boolean isValid();
}
```

Passed To: AbstractSelector.deregister()

AbstractSelector **Java 1.4**

java.nio.channels.spi

This class exists as a convenience for implementors of new Selector classes. Application programmers should never need to use or subclass this class.

Object — Selector — AbstractSelector

```
public abstract class AbstractSelector extends java.nio.channels.Selector {
// Protected Constructors
    protected AbstractSelector(SelectorProvider provider);
// Public Methods Overriding Selector
    public final void close() throws java.io.IOException;
    public final boolean isOpen();
    public final SelectorProvider provider();
// Protected Instance Methods
    protected final void begin();
    protected final java.util.Set cancelledKeys();
    protected final void deregister(AbstractSelectionKey key);
    protected final void end();
    protected abstract void implCloseSelector() throws java.io.IOException;
    protected abstract java.nio.channels.SelectionKey register(AbstractSelectableChannel ch, int ops, Object att);
}
```

Returned By: SelectorProvider.openSelector()

SelectorProvider **Java 1.4**

java.nio.channels.spi

This class is the central service-provider class for the channels and selectors of the java.nio.channels API. A concrete subclass of SelectorProvider implements factory methods that return open socket channels, server socket channels, datagram channels, pipes (with their two internal channels), and Selector objects. There is one default SelectorProvider object per JVM; this object can be obtained with the static SelectorProvider.provider() method.

You can specify a custom SelectorProvider implementation by setting its class name as the value of the system property java.nio.channels.spi.SelectorProvider. Or you can put the class name in a file called *META-INF/services/java.nio.channels.spi.SelectorProvider* in your application's JAR file. The provider() method first looks for the system property then looks for the JAR file entry. If it finds neither, it instantiates the implementation's default SelectorProvider.

Applications are not required to use the default SelectorProvider exclusively. It is legal to instantiate other SelectorProvider objects and explicitly invoke their open() methods to create channels in this way.

```
public abstract class SelectorProvider {
// Protected Constructors
   protected SelectorProvider();
// Public Class Methods
   public static SelectorProvider provider();
// Public Instance Methods
   public abstract java.nio.channels.DatagramChannel openDatagramChannel() throws java.io.IOException;
   public abstract java.nio.channels.Pipe openPipe() throws java.io.IOException;
   public abstract AbstractSelector openSelector() throws java.io.IOException;
   public abstract java.nio.channels.ServerSocketChannel openServerSocketChannel() throws java.io.IOException;
   public abstract java.nio.channels.SocketChannel openSocketChannel() throws java.io.IOException;
}
```

Passed To: java.nio.channels.DatagramChannel.DatagramChannel(), java.nio.channels.Pipe.SinkChannel.SinkChannel(), java.nio.channels.Pipe.SourceChannel.SourceChannel(), java.nio.channels.ServerSocketChannel.ServerSocketChannel(), java.nio.channels.SocketChannel.SocketChannel(), AbstractSelectableChannel.AbstractSelectableChannel(), AbstractSelector.AbstractSelector()

Returned By: java.nio.channels.SelectableChannel.provider(), java.nio.channels.Selector.provider(), AbstractSelectableChannel.provider(), AbstractSelector.provider(), SelectorProvider.provider()

Package java.nio.charset **Java 1.4**

This package contains classes that represent character sets or encodings and defines methods that encode characters into bytes and decode bytes into characters. The key class is Charset. You can obtain a Charset object for a named character encoding with the static forName() method. Charset defines encode() and decode() convenience methods, but for full control over the encoding and decoding process, you can also obtain a CharsetEncoder or CharsetDecoder object from the Charset.

The Java platform has had a character encoding and decoding facility since Java 1.1 and defines a number of classes and methods that perform character encoding or decoding. Some of these classes and methods are specified to use the default charset for the locale; others take the name of a charset as a method or constructor argument. (For example, see the String(), java.io.InputStreamReader(), and java.io.OutputStreamWriter() constructors.) In Java 1.4, the java.nio.charset package defines a public API for the character encoding and decoding facility and allows applications to work with it explicitly. Most applications will not have to do this, however, and can simply continue to rely on the default charset or can continue to supply charset names where needed. Even applications that use the java.nio.channels package can avoid explicit character encoding and decoding by passing the name of a desired charset to the newReader() and newWriter() methods of java.nio.channels.Channels.

Classes:

public abstract class **Charset** implements Comparable;
public abstract class **CharsetDecoder**;
public abstract class **CharsetEncoder**;
public class **CoderResult**;
public class **CodingErrorAction**;

Exceptions:

public class **CharacterCodingException** extends java.io.IOException;
　└ public class **MalformedInputException** extends CharacterCodingException;
　└ public class **UnmappableCharacterException** extends CharacterCodingException;
public class **IllegalCharsetNameException** extends IllegalArgumentException;
public class **UnsupportedCharsetException** extends IllegalArgumentException;

Errors:

public class **CoderMalfunctionError** extends Error;

CharacterCodingException — Java 1.4

java.nio.charset — *serializable checked*

This class signals a problem encoding or decoding characters or bytes. It is a generic superclass for more specific exception types. Note that the one-argument versions of CharsetEncoder.encode() and CharsetDecoder.decode() may throw an exception of this type, but that the three-argument versions of the same method report encoding problems through their CoderResult return value. Also note that the encode() and decode() convenience methods of Charset do not throw this exception because they specify that malformed input and unmappable characters or bytes should be replaced. See CodingErrorAction.

Object — Throwable — Exception — IOException — CharacterCodingException
Serializable

```
public class CharacterCodingException extends java.io.IOException {
// Public Constructors
   public CharacterCodingException();
}
```

Subclasses: MalformedInputException, UnmappableCharacterException

Thrown By: CharsetDecoder.decode(), CharsetEncoder.encode(), CoderResult.throwException()

java.nio.*

Charset **Java 1.4**

java.nio.charset *comparable*

A Charset represents a character set or encoding. Each Charset has a canonical name, returned by name(), and a set of aliases, returned by aliases(). You can look up a Charset by name or alias with the static method Charset.forName() method, which throws an UnsupportedCharsetException if the named charset is not installed on the system. Check whether a charset specified by name or alias is supported with the static isSupported(). Obtain the complete set of installed charsets with availableCharsets(), which returns a sorted map from canonical names to Charset objects. Note that charset names are not case-sensitive, and you can use any capitalization for charset names you pass to isSupported() and forName(). Also note that there are a number of classes and methods in the Java platform that specify charsets by name rather than by Charset object. (For example, see java.io.InputStreamReader, java.io.OutputStreamWriter, String.getBytes(), and java.nio.channels.Channels.newWriter().) When working with classes and methods such as these, there is no need to use a Charset object.

All implementations of Java are required to support at least the following six charsets:

Canonical name	*Description*
US-ASCII	7-bit ASCII.
ISO-8859-1	The 8-bit superset of ASCII that includes the characters used in most Western European languages. Also known as ISO-LATIN-1.
UTF-8	An 8-bit encoding of Unicode characters that is compatible with US-ASCII.
UTF-16BE	A 16-bit encoding of Unicode characters, using big-endian byte order.
UTF-16LE	A 16-bit encoding of Unicode characters, using little-endian byte order.
UTF-16	A 16-bit encoding of Unicode characters with byte order specified by a "byte order mark" character. Assumes big-endian when decoding if there is no byte order mark. Encodes using big-endian byte order and outputs an appropriate byte order mark.

Once you have obtained a Charset with forName() or availableCharsets(), you can use the encode() method to encode a String or CharBuffer of text into a ByteBuffer or use the decode() method to convert the bytes in a ByteBuffer into characters in a CharBuffer. These convenience methods create a new CharsetEncoder or CharsetDecoder, specify that malformed input or unmappable characters or bytes should be replaced with the default replacement string or bytes, and then invoke the encode() or decode() method of the encoder or decoder. For full control over the encoding and decoding process, you may want to obtain your own CharsetEncoder or CharsetDecoder object with newEncoder() or newDecoder(). See CharsetDecoder for details.

Instead of using a Charset, CharsetEncoder, or CharsetDecoder directly, you may also pass an encoder or decoder to the static methods of java.nio.channels.Channels to obtain a java.io.Reader or java.io.Writer that you can use to read or write characters from or to a byte-oriented Channel.

Note that not all Charset objects support encoding ("auto-detect" charsets can determine the source charset when decoding but have no way to encode). Use canEncode() to determine whether a given Charset can encode.

Charset also defines, implements, or overrides various other methods. displayName() returns a localized name for the charset or returns the canonical name if there is no localization. toString() returns an implementation-dependent textual representation of the charset. The equals() method compares two charsets by comparing their canonical names. Charset implements Comparable, and its compareTo() method orders charsets by their canonical name. contains() returns true if a specified charset is "contained in" this charset, that is, if every character that can be represented in the specified charset can also be represented in this charset. Note that these representations need not be the same, however. isRegistered() returns true if the charset is registered with the IANA charset registry (see *http://www.iana.org/assignments/character-sets*).

Object — Charset ··· Comparable

```
public abstract class Charset implements Comparable {
// Protected Constructors
   protected Charset(String canonicalName, String[ ] aliases);
// Public Class Methods
   public static java.util.SortedMap availableCharsets();
   public static Charset forName(String charsetName);
   public static boolean isSupported(String charsetName);
// Public Instance Methods
   public final java.util.Set aliases();
   public boolean canEncode();                                        constant
   public abstract boolean contains(Charset cs);
   public final java.nio.CharBuffer decode(java.nio.ByteBuffer bb);
   public String displayName();
   public String displayName(java.util.Locale locale);
   public final java.nio.ByteBuffer encode(java.nio.CharBuffer cb);
   public final java.nio.ByteBuffer encode(String str);
   public final boolean isRegistered();
   public final String name();
   public abstract CharsetDecoder newDecoder();
   public abstract CharsetEncoder newEncoder();
// Methods Implementing Comparable
   public final int compareTo(Object ob);
// Public Methods Overriding Object
   public final boolean equals(Object ob);
   public final int hashCode();
   public final String toString();
}
```

Passed To: java.io.InputStreamReader.InputStreamReader(), java.io.OutputStreamWriter.OutputStreamWriter(), Charset.contains(), CharsetDecoder.CharsetDecoder(), CharsetEncoder.CharsetEncoder()

Returned By: Charset.forName(), CharsetDecoder.{charset(), detectedCharset()}, CharsetEncoder.charset(), java.nio.charset.spi.CharsetProvider.charsetForName()

CharsetDecoder — Java 1.4

java.nio.charset

A CharsetDecoder is a "decoding engine" that converts a sequence of bytes into a sequence of characters based on the encoding of a charset. Obtain a CharsetDecoder from the Charset that represents the charset to be decoded. If you have a complete sequence of bytes to be decoded in a ByteBuffer, you can pass that buffer to the one-argument version of decode(). This convenience method decodes the bytes and stores the resulting characters into a newly allocated CharBuffer, resetting and flushing the decoder as necessary. It throws an exception if there are problems with the bytes that will be decoded.

Typically, however, the three-argument version of decode() is used in a three-step decoding process:

1. Call the reset() method, unless this is the first time the CharsetDecoder has been used.
2. Call the three-argument version of decode() one or more times. The third argument should be true on, and only on, the last invocation of the method. The first argument to decode() is a ByteBuffer that contains bytes to be decoded. The second argument is a CharBuffer into which the resulting characters are stored. The return value of the method is a CoderResult object that specifies the state of the ongoing decoding operation. (The possible CoderResult return values are detailed later.) In a typical case, however, decode() returns after it has decoded all of the bytes in the input buffer. In this case, you would then fill the input buffer with more bytes to be decoded and read characters from the output buffer, calling its compact() method to make room for more. If an unexpected problem arises in the CharsetDecoder implementation, decode() throws a CoderMalfunctionError.
3. Pass the output CharBuffer to the flush() method to allow any remaining characters to be output.

The decode() method returns a CoderResult that indicates the state of the decoding operation. If the return value is CoderResult.UNDERFLOW, this means that decode() returned because all bytes from the input buffer have been read, and more input is required. If the return value is CoderResult.OVERFLOW, this means that decode() returned because the output CharBuffer is full, and no more characters can be decoded into it. Otherwise, the return value is a CoderResult with an isError() method that returns true. There are two basic types of decoding errors. If isMalformed() returns true, then the input included bytes that are not legal for the charset. These bytes start at the position of the input buffer and continue for length() bytes. Otherwise, if isUnmappable() returns true, then the input bytes include a character for which there is no representation in Unicode. The relevant bytes start at the position of the input buffer and continue for length() bytes.

By default, a CharsetDecoder reports all malformed input and unmappable character errors by returning a CoderResult object, as described previously. This behavior can be altered, however, by passing a CodingErrorAction to onMalformedInput() and onUnmappableCharacter(). (Query the current action for these types of errors with malformedInputAction() and unmappableCharacterAction().) CodingErrorAction defines three constants that represent the three possible actions. The default action is REPORT. The IGNORE action tells the CharsetDecoder to ignore (i.e., skip) malformed input and unmappable characters. The REPLACE action tells the CharsetDecoder to replace malformed input and unmappable characters with the replacement string. This replacement string can be set with replaceWith() and queried with replacement().

averageCharsPerByte() and maxCharsPerByte() return the average and maximum number of characters produced by this decoder per decoded byte. These values can help you choose the size of the CharBuffer to allocate for decoding.

CharsetDecoder is not a thread-safe class; only one thread should use an instance at a time.

CharsetDecoder is an abstract class. Implementors defining new charsets will need to subclass CharsetDecoder and define the abstract decodeLoop() method, which is invoked by decode().

```
public abstract class CharsetDecoder {
// Protected Constructors
   protected CharsetDecoder(Charset cs, float averageCharsPerByte, float maxCharsPerByte);
```

```
// Public Instance Methods
    public final float averageCharsPerByte();
    public final Charset charset();
    public final java.nio.CharBuffer decode(java.nio.ByteBuffer in) throws CharacterCodingException;
    public final CoderResult decode(java.nio.ByteBuffer in, java.nio.CharBuffer out, boolean endOfInput);
    public Charset detectedCharset();
    public final CoderResult flush(java.nio.CharBuffer out);
    public boolean isAutoDetecting();                                                    constant
    public boolean isCharsetDetected();
    public CodingErrorAction malformedInputAction();
    public final float maxCharsPerByte();
    public final CharsetDecoder onMalformedInput(CodingErrorAction newAction);
    public final CharsetDecoder onUnmappableCharacter(CodingErrorAction newAction);
    public final String replacement();
    public final CharsetDecoder replaceWith(String newReplacement);
    public final CharsetDecoder reset();
    public CodingErrorAction unmappableCharacterAction();
// Protected Instance Methods
    protected abstract CoderResult decodeLoop(java.nio.ByteBuffer in, java.nio.CharBuffer out);
    protected CoderResult implFlush(java.nio.CharBuffer out);
    protected void implOnMalformedInput(CodingErrorAction newAction);                    empty
    protected void implOnUnmappableCharacter(CodingErrorAction newAction);               empty
    protected void implReplaceWith(String newReplacement);                               empty
    protected void implReset();                                                          empty
}
```

Passed To: java.io.InputStreamReader.InputStreamReader(), java.nio.channels.Channels.newReader()

Returned By: Charset.newDecoder(), CharsetDecoder.{onMalformedInput(), onUnmappableCharacter(), replaceWith(), reset()}

CharsetEncoder — Java 1.4

java.nio.charset

A CharsetEncoder is an "encoding engine" that converts a sequence of characters into a sequence of bytes using character encoding. Obtain a CharsetEncoder with the newEncoder() method of the Charset that represents the desired encoding.

A CharsetEncoder works like a CharsetDecoder in reverse. Use the encode() method to encode characters read from a CharBuffer into bytes stored in a ByteBuffer. See CharsetDecoder, which documents this process in detail.

```
public abstract class CharsetEncoder {
// Protected Constructors
    protected CharsetEncoder(Charset cs, float averageBytesPerChar, float maxBytesPerChar);
    protected CharsetEncoder(Charset cs, float averageBytesPerChar, float maxBytesPerChar, byte[ ] replacement);
// Public Instance Methods
    public final float averageBytesPerChar();
    public boolean canEncode(CharSequence cs);
    public boolean canEncode(char c);
    public final Charset charset();
    public final java.nio.ByteBuffer encode(java.nio.CharBuffer in) throws CharacterCodingException;
    public final CoderResult encode(java.nio.CharBuffer in, java.nio.ByteBuffer out, boolean endOfInput);
    public final CoderResult flush(java.nio.ByteBuffer out);
    public boolean isLegalReplacement(byte[ ] repl);
    public CodingErrorAction malformedInputAction();
    public final float maxBytesPerChar();
```

```
    public final CharsetEncoder onMalformedInput(CodingErrorAction newAction);
    public final CharsetEncoder onUnmappableCharacter(CodingErrorAction newAction);
    public final byte[ ] replacement( );
    public final CharsetEncoder replaceWith(byte[ ] newReplacement);
    public final CharsetEncoder reset( );
    public CodingErrorAction unmappableCharacterAction( );
// Protected Instance Methods
    protected abstract CoderResult encodeLoop(java.nio.CharBuffer in, java.nio.ByteBuffer out);
    protected CoderResult implFlush(java.nio.ByteBuffer out);
    protected void implOnMalformedInput(CodingErrorAction newAction);                    empty
    protected void implOnUnmappableCharacter(CodingErrorAction newAction);               empty
    protected void implReplaceWith(byte[ ] newReplacement);                               empty
    protected void implReset( );                                                          empty
}
```

Passed To: java.io.OutputStreamWriter.OutputStreamWriter(), java.nio.channels.Channels.newWriter()

Returned By: Charset.newEncoder(), CharsetEncoder.{onMalformedInput(), onUnmappableCharacter(), replaceWith(), reset()}

CoderMalfunctionError — Java 1.4

java.nio.charset — *serializable error*

This signals a malfunction—typically, an unknown and unrecoverable error—in a CharsetEncoder or CharsetDecoder. An error of this type is thrown by the encode() and decode() methods when the protected encodeLoop() or decodeLoop() methods upon which they are implemented throw an exception of an unexpected type.

Object — Throwable — Error — CoderMalfunctionError

Serializable

```
public class CoderMalfunctionError extends Error {
// Public Constructors
    public CoderMalfunctionError(Exception cause);
}
```

CoderResult — Java 1.4

java.nio.charset

A CoderResult object specifies the results of a call to CharsetDecoder.decode() or CharsetEncoder.encode(). There are four possible reasons why a call to the decode() or encode() would return:

- If all the bytes have been decoded or all the characters have been encoded, and the input buffer is empty, then the return value is the constant object CoderResult.UNDERFLOW, indicating that coding stopped because there was no more data to code. Calling the isUnderflow() method on the returned object returns true, and calling isError() returns false. This is a normal return value.
- If there is more data to be coded but no more room in the output buffer to store the coded data, then the return value is the constant object CoderResult.OVERFLOW. Calling isOverflow() on the returned object returns true, and calling isError() returns false. This is a normal return value.
- If the input data was malformed, containing characters or bytes that are not legal for the charset, and the CharsetEncoder or CharsetDecoder has not specified that malformed input should be ignored or replaced, then the returned value is a

CoderResult object with isError() and isMalformed() methods that both return true. The position of the input buffer is at the first malformed character or byte, and the length() method of the returned object specifies the number of characters or bytes that are malformed.

If the input was well-formed but contained characters or bytes that were unmappable—that cannot be encoded or decoded in the specified charset—and if the CharsetEncoder or CharsetDecoder has not specified that unmappable characters should be ignored or replaced, then the returned value is a CoderResult object with isError() and isUnmappable() methods that both return true. The input buffer is positioned at the first unmappable character or byte, and the length() method of the CoderResult specifies the number of unmappable characters or bytes.

```
public class CoderResult {
// No Constructor
// Public Constants
   public static final CoderResult OVERFLOW;
   public static final CoderResult UNDERFLOW;
// Public Class Methods
   public static CoderResult malformedForLength(int length);
   public static CoderResult unmappableForLength(int length);
// Property Accessor Methods (by property name)
   public boolean isError();
   public boolean isMalformed();
   public boolean isOverflow();
   public boolean isUnderflow();
   public boolean isUnmappable();
// Public Instance Methods
   public int length();
   public void throwException() throws CharacterCodingException;
// Public Methods Overriding Object
   public String toString();
}
```

Returned By: CharsetDecoder.{decode(), decodeLoop(), flush(), implFlush()}, CharsetEncoder.{encode(), encodeLoop(), flush(), implFlush()}, CoderResult.{malformedForLength(), unmappableForLength()}

Type Of: CoderResult.{OVERFLOW, UNDERFLOW}

java.nio.*

CodingErrorAction — Java 1.4

java.nio.charset

This class is a typesafe enumeration that defines three constants that serve as the legal argument values to the onMalformedInput() and onUnmappableCharacter() methods of CharsetDecoder and CharsetEncoder. These constants specify how malformed input and unmappable error conditions should be handled. The values are:

CodingErrorAction.REPORT
: Specifies that the error should be reported. This is done by returning a CoderResult object from the three-argument version of decode() or encode() or by throwing a MalformedInputException or UnmappableCharacterException from the one-argument version of decode() or encode(). This is the default action for both error types for CharsetDecoder and CharsetEncoder.

CodingErrorAction.IGNORE
: Specifies that the malformed input or unmappable input character should simply be skipped, with no output.

CodingErrorAction.REPLACE
: Specifies that the malformed input or unmappable character should be skipped and the replacement string or replacement bytes should be appended to the output.

See CharsetDecoder for more information.

```
public class CodingErrorAction {
// No Constructor
// Public Constants
   public static final CodingErrorAction IGNORE;
   public static final CodingErrorAction REPLACE;
   public static final CodingErrorAction REPORT;
// Public Methods Overriding Object
   public String toString();
}
```

Passed To: CharsetDecoder.{implOnMalformedInput(), implOnUnmappableCharacter(), onMalformedInput(), onUnmappableCharacter()}, CharsetEncoder.{implOnMalformedInput(), implOnUnmappableCharacter(), onMalformedInput(), onUnmappableCharacter()}

Returned By: CharsetDecoder.{malformedInputAction(), unmappableCharacterAction()}, CharsetEncoder.{malformedInputAction(), unmappableCharacterAction()}

Type Of: CodingErrorAction.{IGNORE, REPLACE, REPORT}

IllegalCharsetNameException **Java 1.4**

java.nio.charset *serializable unchecked*

This signals that a charset name is illegal (for example, one passed to Charset.forName() or Charset.isSupported()). Charset names may contain only the characters A–Z (upper- and lowercase), the digits 0–9, hyphens, underscores, colons, and periods. They must begin with a letter or a digit, not with a punctuation character.

Object — Throwable — Exception — RuntimeException — IllegalArgumentException — IllegalCharsetNameException
Serializable

```
public class IllegalCharsetNameException extends IllegalArgumentException {
// Public Constructors
   public IllegalCharsetNameException(String charsetName);
// Public Instance Methods
   public String getCharsetName();
}
```

MalformedInputException **Java 1.4**

java.nio.charset *serializable checked*

This signals that input to the CharsetDecoder.decode() or CharsetEncoder.encode() method was malformed.

Object — Throwable — Exception — IOException — CharacterCodingException — MalformedInputException
Serializable

```
public class MalformedInputException extends CharacterCodingException {
// Public Constructors
    public MalformedInputException(int inputLength);
// Public Instance Methods
    public int getInputLength();
// Public Methods Overriding Throwable
    public String getMessage();
}
```

UnmappableCharacterException — Java 1.4

java.nio.charset — *serializable checked*

This signals that input to the CharsetDecoder.decode() or CharsetEncoder.encode() method contained a character or byte sequence that is not mappable in the specified charset.

Object — Throwable — Exception — IOException — CharacterCodingException — UnmappableCharacterException

Serializable

```
public class UnmappableCharacterException extends CharacterCodingException {
// Public Constructors
    public UnmappableCharacterException(int inputLength);
// Public Instance Methods
    public int getInputLength();
// Public Methods Overriding Throwable
    public String getMessage();
}
```

UnsupportedCharsetException — Java 1.4

java.nio.charset — *serializable unchecked*

This signals that the requested charset is not supported on the current platform. This exception is thrown by Charset.forName() when no Charset object can be obtained for the named charset. See also Charset.isSupported().

Object — Throwable — Exception — RuntimeException — IllegalArgumentException — UnsupportedCharsetException

Serializable

```
public class UnsupportedCharsetException extends IllegalArgumentException {
// Public Constructors
    public UnsupportedCharsetException(String charsetName);
// Public Instance Methods
    public String getCharsetName();
}
```

Package java.nio.charset.spi — Java 1.4

This package defines a "provider" class for system developers who are defining new Charset implementations and want to make them available to the system. Application programmers never need to use this package or the class it defines.

Classes:

public abstract class **CharsetProvider**;

CharsetProvider **Java 1.4**

java.nio.charset.spi

System programmers developing new Charset implementations should implement this class to make these charsets available to the system. charsetForName() should return a Charset instance for the given name. charsets() should return a java.util.Iterator that allows the caller to iterate through the set of Charset objects defined by the provider.

A CharsetProvider and its associated Charset implementations should be packaged in a JAR file and made available to the system in the *jre/lib/ext/* extensions directory (or in another extensions location). The JAR file should contain a file named *META-INF/services/java.nio.charset.spi.CharsetProvider*, which contains the class name of the CharsetProvider implementation.

```
public abstract class CharsetProvider {
// Protected Constructors
   protected CharsetProvider();
// Public Instance Methods
   public abstract java.nio.charset.Charset charsetForName(String charsetName);
   public abstract java.util.Iterator charsets();
}
```

CHAPTER 15

java.security and Subpackages

This chapter documents the java.security package and its subpackages. Those packages are:

java.security
: This large package contains much of Java's security infrastructure, including a group of classes that provide access control through policies and permissions, and another group that provides authentication-related services such as digital signatures.

java.security.acl
: This package implements an infrastructure for Access Control Lists. It is not used by the Java security mechanism and has been superseded by classes in java.security.

java.security.cert
: This package defines classes and interfaces for working with public key certificates, certificate revocation lists (CRLs) and, in Java 1.4 and later, certificate chains (or certificate paths). It defines generic classes that should work with any type of certificate and type-specific subclasses for X.509 certificates and CRLs.

java.security.interfaces
: This package defines interfaces for algorithm-specific types of cryptographic keys. Providers that support those algorithms must implement these interfaces.

java.security.spec
: This package defines classes that define a transparent, portable representation of algorithm specific objects such as cryptographic keys. Instances of these classes can be used with any security provider.

Package java.security — Java 1.1

The java.security package contains the classes and interfaces that implement the Java security architecture. These classes can be divided into two broad categories. First, there are classes that implement access control and prevent untrusted code from performing sensitive operations. Second, there are authentication classes that implement message digests and digital signatures and can authenticate Java classes and other objects.

The central access control class is AccessController; it uses the currently installed Policy object to decide whether a given class has Permission to access a given system resource. The Permissions and ProtectionDomain classes are also important pieces of the Java access control architecture.

The key classes for authentication are MessageDigest and Signature; they compute and verify cryptographic message digests and digital signatures. These classes use public-key cryptography techniques and rely on the PublicKey and PrivateKey interfaces. They also rely on an infrastructure of related classes, such as SecureRandom for producing cryptographic-strength pseudo-random numbers, KeyPairGenerator for generating pairs of public and private keys, and KeyStore for managing a collection of keys and certificates. (This package defines a Certificate interface, but it is deprecated; see the java.security.cert package for the preferred Certificate class.)

The CodeSource class unites the authentication classes with the access control classes. It represents the source of a Java class as a URL and a set of java.security.cert.Certificate objects that contain the digital signatures of the code. The AccessController and Policy classes look at the CodeSource of a class when making access control decisions.

All the cryptographic-authentication features of this package are provider-based, which means they are implemented by security provider modules that can be plugged easily into any Java 1.2 (or later) installation. Thus, in addition to defining a security API, this package also defines a service provider interface (SPI). Various classes with names that end in Spi are part of this SPI. Security provider implementations must subclass these Spi classes, but applications never need to use them. Each security provider is represented by a Provider class, and the Security class allows new providers to be dynamically installed.

The java.security package contains several useful utility classes. For example, DigestInputStream and DigestOutputStream make it easy to compute message digests. GuardedObject provides customizable access control for an individual object. SignedObject protects the integrity of an arbitrary Java object by attaching a digital signature, making it easy to detect any tampering with the object. Although the java.security package contains cryptographic classes for authentication, it does not contain classes for encryption or decryption. Instead, this functionality is part of the Java Cryptography Extension or JCE which defines the javax.crypto package and its sub-packages. The JCE is part of the core platform in Java 1.4 and later, and is available as a standard extension to Java 1.2 and Java 1.3.

Interfaces:

public interface **Certificate**;
public interface **DomainCombiner**;
public interface **Guard**;
public interface **Key** extends Serializable;
public interface **Principal**;
public interface **PrivateKey** extends Key;
public interface **PrivilegedAction**;
public interface **PrivilegedExceptionAction**;
public interface **PublicKey** extends Key;

Collections:

public abstract class **Provider** extends java.util.Properties;

Other Classes:

public final class **AccessControlContext**;
public final class **AccessController**;
public class **AlgorithmParameterGenerator**;
public abstract class **AlgorithmParameterGeneratorSpi**;
public class **AlgorithmParameters**;
public abstract class **AlgorithmParametersSpi**;
public class **CodeSource** implements Serializable;
public class **DigestInputStream** extends java.io.FilterInputStream;
public class **DigestOutputStream** extends java.io.FilterOutputStream;
public class **GuardedObject** implements Serializable;
public abstract class **Identity** implements Principal, Serializable;
└ public abstract class **IdentityScope** extends Identity;
└ public abstract class **Signer** extends Identity;
public class **KeyFactory**;
public abstract class **KeyFactorySpi**;
public final class **KeyPair** implements Serializable;
public abstract class **KeyPairGeneratorSpi**;
└ public abstract class **KeyPairGenerator** extends KeyPairGeneratorSpi;
public class **KeyStore**;
public abstract class **KeyStoreSpi**;
public abstract class **MessageDigestSpi**;
└ public abstract class **MessageDigest** extends MessageDigestSpi;
public abstract class **Permission** implements Guard, Serializable;
└ public final class **AllPermission** extends Permission;
└ public abstract class **BasicPermission** extends Permission implements Serializable;
  └ public final class **SecurityPermission** extends BasicPermission;
└ public final class **UnresolvedPermission** extends Permission implements Serializable;
public abstract class **PermissionCollection** implements Serializable;
└ public final class **Permissions** extends PermissionCollection implements Serializable;
public abstract class **Policy**;
public class **ProtectionDomain**;
public class **SecureClassLoader** extends ClassLoader;
public class **SecureRandom** extends java.util.Random;
public abstract class **SecureRandomSpi** implements Serializable;
public final class **Security**;
public abstract class **SignatureSpi**;
└ public abstract class **Signature** extends SignatureSpi;
public final class **SignedObject** implements Serializable;

Exceptions:

public class **AccessControlException** extends SecurityException;
public class **GeneralSecurityException** extends Exception;
└ public class **DigestException** extends GeneralSecurityException;
└ public class **InvalidAlgorithmParameterException** extends GeneralSecurityException;
└ public class **KeyException** extends GeneralSecurityException;
  └ public class **InvalidKeyException** extends KeyException;
  └ public class **KeyManagementException** extends KeyException;

```
  └ public class KeyStoreException extends GeneralSecurityException;
  └ public class NoSuchAlgorithmException extends GeneralSecurityException;
  └ public class NoSuchProviderException extends GeneralSecurityException;
  └ public class SignatureException extends GeneralSecurityException;
  └ public class UnrecoverableKeyException extends GeneralSecurityException;
public class InvalidParameterException extends IllegalArgumentException;
public class PrivilegedActionException extends Exception;
public class ProviderException extends RuntimeException;
```

AccessControlContext **Java 1.2**

java.security

This class encapsulates the state of a call stack. The checkPermission() method can make access-control decisions based on the saved state of the call stack. Access-control checks are usually performed by the AccessController.checkPermission() method, which checks that the current call stack has the required permissions. Sometimes, however, it is necessary to make access-control decisions based on a previous state of the call stack. Call AccessController.getContext() to create an AccessControlContext for a particular call stack. In Java 1.3, this class has constructors that specify a custom context in the form of an array of ProtectionDomain objects and that associate a DomainCombiner object with an existing AccessControlContext. This class is used only by system-level code; typical applications rarely need to use it.

```
public final class AccessControlContext {
// Public Constructors
    public AccessControlContext(ProtectionDomain[ ] context);
1.3 public AccessControlContext(AccessControlContext acc, DomainCombiner combiner);
// Public Instance Methods
    public void checkPermission(java.security.Permission perm) throws AccessControlException;
1.3 public DomainCombiner getDomainCombiner();
// Public Methods Overriding Object
    public boolean equals(Object obj);
    public int hashCode();
}
```

Passed To: AccessControlContext.AccessControlContext(), AccessController.doPrivileged(), javax.security.auth.Subject.{doAsPrivileged(), getSubject()}

Returned By: AccessController.getContext()

AccessControlException **Java 1.2**

java.security ***serializable unchecked***

This is thrown by AccessController to signal that an access request has been denied. getPermission() returns the Permission object, if any, that was involved in the denied request.

Object — Throwable — Exception — RuntimeException — SecurityException — AccessControlException
Serializable

```
public class AccessControlException extends SecurityException {
// Public Constructors
    public AccessControlException(String s);
    public AccessControlException(String s, java.security.Permission p);
```

```
// Public Instance Methods
   public java.security.Permission getPermission();
}
```

Thrown By: AccessControlContext.checkPermission(), AccessController.checkPermission()

AccessController — Java 1.2

java.security

The static methods of this class implement the default access-control mechanism as of Java 1.2. checkPermission() traverses the call stack of the current thread and checks whether all classes in the call stack have the requested permission. If so, checkPermission() returns, and the operation can proceed. If not, checkPermission() throws an AccessControlException. As of Java 1.2, the checkPermission() method of the default java.lang.SecurityManager calls AccessController.checkPermission(). System-level code that needs to perform an access check should invoke the SecurityManager method rather than calling the AccessController method directly. Unless you are writing system-level code that must control access to system resources, you never need to use this class or the SecurityManager.checkPermission() method.

The various doPrivileged() methods run blocks of privileged code encapsulated in a PrivilegedAction or PrivilegedExceptionAction object. When checkPermission() is traversing the call stack of a thread, it stops if it reaches a privileged block that was executed with doPrivileged(). This means that privileged code can run with a full set of privileges, even if it was invoked by untrusted or lower-privileged code. See PrivilegedAction for more details.

The getContext() method returns an AccessControlContext that represents the current security context of the caller. Such a context might be saved and passed to a future call (perhaps a call made from a different thread). Use the two-argument version of doPrivileged() to force permission checks to check the AccessControlContext as well.

```
public final class AccessController {
// No Constructor
// Public Class Methods
   public static void checkPermission(java.security.Permission perm) throws AccessControlException;
   public static Object doPrivileged(PrivilegedExceptionAction action) throws PrivilegedActionException;      native
   public static Object doPrivileged(PrivilegedAction action);                                                native
   public static Object doPrivileged(PrivilegedExceptionAction action, AccessControlContext context)          native
       throws PrivilegedActionException;
   public static Object doPrivileged(PrivilegedAction action, AccessControlContext context);                  native
   public static AccessControlContext getContext();
}
```

AlgorithmParameterGenerator — Java 1.2

java.security

This class defines a generic API for generating parameters for a cryptographic algorithm, typically a Signature or a javax.crypto.Cipher. Create an AlgorithmParameterGenerator by calling one of the static getInstance() factory methods and specifying the name of the algorithm and, optionally, the name or Provider object of the desired provider. The default "SUN" provider supports the "DSA" algorithm. The "SunJCE" provider shipped with the JCE supports "DiffieHellman". Once you have obtained a generator, initialize it by calling the init() method and specifying an algorithm-independent parameter size (in bits) or an algorithm-dependent AlgorithmParameterSpec object. You may also specify a SecureRandom source of randomness when you call init(). Once you have created and initialized the AlgorithmParameterGenerator, call generateParameters() to generate an AlgorithmParameters object.

```
public class AlgorithmParameterGenerator {
// Protected Constructors
   protected AlgorithmParameterGenerator(AlgorithmParameterGeneratorSpi paramGenSpi, Provider provider,
                                         String algorithm);
// Public Class Methods
   public static AlgorithmParameterGenerator getInstance(String algorithm) throws NoSuchAlgorithmException;
1.4 public static AlgorithmParameterGenerator getInstance(String algorithm, Provider provider)
        throws NoSuchAlgorithmException;
   public static AlgorithmParameterGenerator getInstance(String algorithm, String provider)
        throws NoSuchAlgorithmException, NoSuchProviderException;
// Public Instance Methods
   public final AlgorithmParameters generateParameters();
   public final String getAlgorithm();
   public final Provider getProvider();
   public final void init(java.security.spec.AlgorithmParameterSpec genParamSpec)
        throws InvalidAlgorithmParameterException;
   public final void init(int size);
   public final void init(java.security.spec.AlgorithmParameterSpec genParamSpec, SecureRandom random)
        throws InvalidAlgorithmParameterException;
   public final void init(int size, SecureRandom random);
}
```

Returned By: AlgorithmParameterGenerator.getInstance()

AlgorithmParameterGeneratorSpi — Java 1.2

java.security

This abstract class defines the service-provider interface for algorithm-parameter generation. A security provider must implement a concrete subclass of this class for each algorithm it supports. Applications never need to use or subclass this class.

```
public abstract class AlgorithmParameterGeneratorSpi {
// Public Constructors
   public AlgorithmParameterGeneratorSpi();
// Protected Instance Methods
   protected abstract AlgorithmParameters engineGenerateParameters();
   protected abstract void engineInit(java.security.spec.AlgorithmParameterSpec genParamSpec,
                                      SecureRandom random) throws InvalidAlgorithmParameterException;
   protected abstract void engineInit(int size, SecureRandom random);
}
```

Passed To: AlgorithmParameterGenerator.AlgorithmParameterGenerator()

AlgorithmParameters — Java 1.2

java.security

This class is a generic, opaque representation of the parameters used by some cryptographic algorithm. You can create an instance of the class with one of the static getInstance() factory methods, specifying the desired algorithm and, optionally, the desired provider. The default "SUN" provider supports the "DSA" algorithm. The "SunJCE" provider shipped with the JCE supports "DES", "DESede", "PBE", "Blowfish", and "DiffieHellman". Once you have obtained an AlgorithmParameters object, initialize it by passing an algorithm-specific java.security.spec.AlgorithmParameterSpec object or the encoded parameter values as a byte array to the init() method. You can also create an AlgorithmParameters object with an AlgorithmParameterGenerator. getEncoded() returns the initialized algorithm parameters as a byte array, using either the algorithm-specific default encoding or the named encoding format you specified.

```
public class AlgorithmParameters {
// Protected Constructors
   protected AlgorithmParameters(AlgorithmParametersSpi paramSpi, Provider provider, String algorithm);
// Public Class Methods
   public static AlgorithmParameters getInstance(String algorithm) throws NoSuchAlgorithmException;
   public static AlgorithmParameters getInstance(String algorithm, String provider) throws NoSuchAlgorithmException,
        NoSuchProviderException;
1.4 public static AlgorithmParameters getInstance(String algorithm, Provider provider)
        throws NoSuchAlgorithmException;
// Public Instance Methods
   public final String getAlgorithm();
   public final byte[ ] getEncoded() throws java.io.IOException;
   public final byte[ ] getEncoded(String format) throws java.io.IOException;
   public final java.security.spec.AlgorithmParameterSpec getParameterSpec(Class paramSpec)
        throws java.security.spec.InvalidParameterSpecException;
   public final Provider getProvider();
   public final void init(java.security.spec.AlgorithmParameterSpec paramSpec)
        throws java.security.spec.InvalidParameterSpecException;
   public final void init(byte[ ] params) throws java.io.IOException;
   public final void init(byte[ ] params, String format) throws java.io.IOException;
// Public Methods Overriding Object
   public final String toString();
}
```

Passed To: javax.crypto.Cipher.init(), javax.crypto.CipherSpi.engineInit(), javax.crypto.EncryptedPrivateKeyInfo.EncryptedPrivateKeyInfo(), javax.crypto.ExemptionMechanism.init(), javax.crypto.ExemptionMechanismSpi.engineInit()

Returned By: AlgorithmParameterGenerator.generateParameters(), AlgorithmParameterGeneratorSpi.engineGenerateParameters(), AlgorithmParameters.getInstance(), Signature.getParameters(), SignatureSpi.engineGetParameters(), javax.crypto.Cipher.getParameters(), javax.crypto.CipherSpi.engineGetParameters(), javax.crypto.EncryptedPrivateKeyInfo.getAlgParameters()

AlgorithmParametersSpi — Java 1.2

java.security

This abstract class defines the service-provider interface for AlgorithmParameters. A security provider must implement a concrete subclass of this class for each cryptographic algorithm it supports. Applications never need to use or subclass this class.

```
public abstract class AlgorithmParametersSpi {
// Public Constructors
   public AlgorithmParametersSpi();
// Protected Instance Methods
   protected abstract byte[ ] engineGetEncoded() throws java.io.IOException;
   protected abstract byte[ ] engineGetEncoded(String format) throws java.io.IOException;
   protected abstract java.security.spec.AlgorithmParameterSpec engineGetParameterSpec(Class paramSpec)
        throws java.security.spec.InvalidParameterSpecException;
   protected abstract void engineInit(java.security.spec.AlgorithmParameterSpec paramSpec)
        throws java.security.spec.InvalidParameterSpecException;
   protected abstract void engineInit(byte[ ] params) throws java.io.IOException;
   protected abstract void engineInit(byte[ ] params, String format) throws java.io.IOException;
   protected abstract String engineToString();
}
```

Passed To: AlgorithmParameters.AlgorithmParameters()

AllPermission **Java 1.2**

java.security ***serializable permission***

This class is a Permission subclass whose implies() method always returns true. This means that code that has been granted AllPermission is granted all other possible permissions. This class exists to provide a convenient way to grant all permissions to completely trusted code. It should be used with care. Applications typically do not need to work directly with Permission objects.

```
public final class AllPermission extends java.security.Permission {
// Public Constructors
   public AllPermission();
   public AllPermission(String name, String actions);
// Public Methods Overriding Permission
   public boolean equals(Object obj);
   public String getActions();                          default: [quot ] <all actions> [quot ]
   public int hashCode();                                                             constant
   public boolean implies(java.security.Permission p);                                constant
   public PermissionCollection newPermissionCollection();
}
```

BasicPermission **Java 1.2**

java.security ***serializable permission***

This Permission class is the abstract superclass for a number of simple permission types. BasicPermission is typically subclassed to implement named permissions that have a name, or target, string, but do not support actions. The implies() method of BasicPermission defines a simple wildcarding capability. The target "*" implies permission for any target. The target "x.*" implies permission for any target that begins with "x.". Applications typically do not need to work directly with Permission objects.

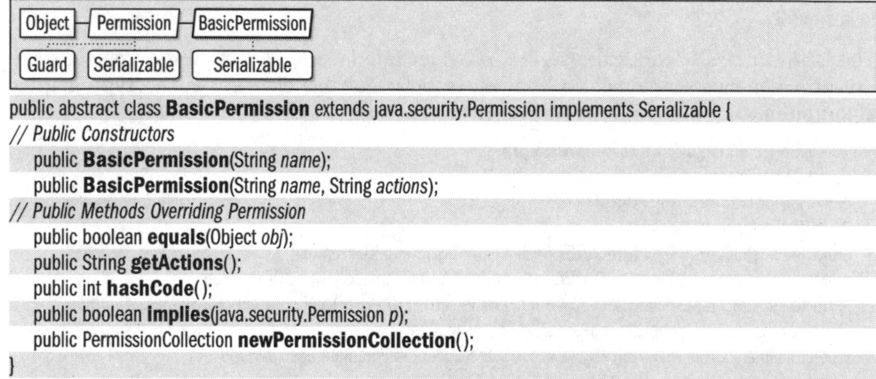


```
public abstract class BasicPermission extends java.security.Permission implements Serializable {
// Public Constructors
   public BasicPermission(String name);
   public BasicPermission(String name, String actions);
// Public Methods Overriding Permission
   public boolean equals(Object obj);
   public String getActions();
   public int hashCode();
   public boolean implies(java.security.Permission p);
   public PermissionCollection newPermissionCollection();
}
```

Subclasses: java.awt.AWTPermission, java.io.SerializablePermission, RuntimePermission, java.lang.reflect.ReflectPermission, java.net.NetPermission, SecurityPermission, java.sql.SQLPermission, java.util.PropertyPermission, java.util.logging.LoggingPermission, javax.net.ssl.SSLPermission, javax.security.auth.AuthPermission, javax.security.auth.kerberos.DelegationPermission, javax.sound.sampled.AudioPermission

Certificate

Java 1.1; Deprecated in Java 1.2

java.security

This interface was used in Java 1.1 to represent an identity certificate. It has been deprecated as of Java 1.2 in favor of the java.security.cert package. See also java.security.cert.Certificate.

```
public interface Certificate {
// Public Instance Methods
   public abstract void decode(java.io.InputStream stream) throws KeyException, java.io.IOException;
   public abstract void encode(java.io.OutputStream stream) throws KeyException, java.io.IOException;
   public abstract String getFormat();
   public abstract java.security.Principal getGuarantor();
   public abstract java.security.Principal getPrincipal();
   public abstract PublicKey getPublicKey();
   public abstract String toString(boolean detailed);
}
```

Passed To: Identity.{addCertificate(), removeCertificate()}

Returned By: Identity.certificates()

CodeSource

Java 1.2

java.security

serializable

This class represents the source of a Java class, as defined by the URL from which the class was loaded and the set of digital signatures attached to the class. A CodeSource object is created by specifying a java.net.URL and an array of java.security.cert.Certificate objects. Only applications that create custom ClassLoader objects should ever need to use or subclass this class.

When a CodeSource represents a specific piece of Java code, it includes a fully qualified URL and the actual set of certificates used to sign the code. When a CodeSource object defines a ProtectionDomain, however, the URL may include wildcards, and the array of certificates is a minimum required set of signatures. The implies() method of such a CodeSource tests whether a particular Java class comes from a matching URL and has the required set of signatures.

Object ─ CodeSource ··· Serializable

```
public class CodeSource implements Serializable {
// Public Constructors
   public CodeSource(java.net.URL url, java.security.cert.Certificate[ ] certs);
// Public Instance Methods
   public final java.security.cert.Certificate[ ] getCertificates();
   public final java.net.URL getLocation();
   public boolean implies(CodeSource codesource);
// Public Methods Overriding Object
   public boolean equals(Object obj);
   public int hashCode();
   public String toString();
}
```

Passed To: java.net.URLClassLoader.getPermissions(), CodeSource.implies(), java.security.Policy.getPermissions(), ProtectionDomain.ProtectionDomain(), SecureClassLoader.{defineClass(), getPermissions()}, javax.security.auth.Policy.getPermissions()

Returned By: ProtectionDomain.getCodeSource()

DigestException — Java 1.1

java.security — ***serializable checked***

This exception signals a problem creating a message digest.

Object → Throwable → Exception → GeneralSecurityException → DigestException
(Throwable implements Serializable)

```
public class DigestException extends GeneralSecurityException {
// Public Constructors
   public DigestException();
   public DigestException(String msg);
}
```

Thrown By: MessageDigest.digest(), MessageDigestSpi.engineDigest()

DigestInputStream — Java 1.1

java.security

This class is a byte input stream with an associated MessageDigest object. When bytes are read with any of the read() methods, those bytes are automatically passed to the update() method of the MessageDigest. When you have finished reading bytes, you can call the digest() method of the MessageDigest to obtain a message digest. If you want to compute a digest just for some of the bytes read from the stream, use on() to turn the digesting function on and off. Digesting is on by default; call on(false) to turn it off. See also DigestOutputStream and MessageDigest.

Object → InputStream → FilterInputStream → DigestInputStream

```
public class DigestInputStream extends java.io.FilterInputStream {
// Public Constructors
   public DigestInputStream(java.io.InputStream stream, MessageDigest digest);
// Public Instance Methods
   public MessageDigest getMessageDigest();
   public void on(boolean on);
   public void setMessageDigest(MessageDigest digest);
// Public Methods Overriding FilterInputStream
   public int read() throws java.io.IOException;
   public int read(byte[ ] b, int off, int len) throws java.io.IOException;
// Public Methods Overriding Object
   public String toString();
// Protected Instance Fields
   protected MessageDigest digest;
}
```

DigestOutputStream — Java 1.1

java.security

This class is a byte output stream with an associated MessageDigest object. When bytes are written to the stream with any of the write() methods, those bytes are automatically passed to the update() method of the MessageDigest. When you have finished writing bytes, you can call the digest() method of the MessageDigest to obtain a message digest. If you want to compute a digest just for some of the bytes written to the stream, use on()

to turn the digesting function on and off. Digesting is on by default; call on(false) to turn it off. See also DigestInputStream and MessageDigest.

Object — OutputStream — FilterOutputStream — DigestOutputStream

```
public class DigestOutputStream extends java.io.FilterOutputStream {
// Public Constructors
   public DigestOutputStream(java.io.OutputStream stream, MessageDigest digest);
// Public Instance Methods
   public MessageDigest getMessageDigest();
   public void on(boolean on);
   public void setMessageDigest(MessageDigest digest);
// Public Methods Overriding FilterOutputStream
   public void write(int b) throws java.io.IOException;
   public void write(byte[ ] b, int off, int len) throws java.io.IOException;
// Public Methods Overriding Object
   public String toString();
// Protected Instance Fields
   protected MessageDigest digest;
}
```

DomainCombiner **Java 1.3**

java.security

This interface defines a single combine() method that combines two arrays of ProtectionDomain objects into a single equivalent (and perhaps optimized) array. You can associate a DomainCombiner with an existing AccessControlContext by calling the two-argument AccessControlContext() constructor. Then, when the checkPermission() method of the AccessControlContext is called or when the AccessControlContext is passed to a doPrivileged() method of AccessController, the specified DomainCombiner merges the protection domains of the current stack frame with the protection domains encapsulated in the AccessControlContext. This class is used only by system-level code; typical applications rarely need to use it.

```
public interface DomainCombiner {
// Public Instance Methods
   public abstract ProtectionDomain[ ] combine(ProtectionDomain[ ] currentDomains,
                                               ProtectionDomain[ ] assignedDomains);
}
```

Implementations: javax.security.auth.SubjectDomainCombiner

Passed To: AccessControlContext.AccessControlContext()

Returned By: AccessControlContext.getDomainCombiner()

GeneralSecurityException **Java 1.2**

java.security ***serializable checked***

This class is the superclass of most of the exceptions defined by the java.security package.

Object — Throwable — Exception — GeneralSecurityException
Throwable ⋯ Serializable

```
public class GeneralSecurityException extends Exception {
// Public Constructors
   public GeneralSecurityException();
```

```
    public GeneralSecurityException(String msg);
}
```

Subclasses: Too many classes to list.

Guard **Java 1.2**

java.security

This interface guards access to an object. The checkGuard() method is passed an object to which access has been requested. If access should be granted, checkGuard() should return silently. Otherwise, if access is denied, checkGuard() should throw a java.lang.SecurityException. The Guard object is used primarily by the GuardedObject class. Note that all Permission objects implement the Guard interface.

```
public interface Guard {
// Public Instance Methods
    public abstract void checkGuard(Object object) throws SecurityException;
}
```

Implementations: java.security.Permission

Passed To: GuardedObject.GuardedObject()

GuardedObject **Java 1.2**

java.security *serializable*

This class uses a Guard object to guard against unauthorized access to an arbitrary encapsulated object. Create a GuardedObject by specifying an object and a Guard for it. The getObject() method calls the checkGuard() method of the Guard to determine whether access to the object should be allowed. If access is allowed, getObject() returns the encapsulated object. Otherwise, it throws a java.lang.SecurityException.

The Guard object used by a GuardedObject is often a Permission. In this case, access to the guarded object is granted only if the calling code is granted the specified permission by the current security policy.

Object — GuardedObject ··· Serializable

```
public class GuardedObject implements Serializable {
// Public Constructors
    public GuardedObject(Object object, Guard guard);
// Public Instance Methods
    public Object getObject() throws SecurityException;
}
```

Identity **Java 1.1; Deprecated in Java 1.2**

java.security *serializable*

This deprecated class was used in Java 1.1 to represent an entity or Principal with an associated PublicKey object. In Java 1.1, the public key for a named entity could be retrieved from the system keystore with a line such as the following:

```
IdentityScope.getSystemScope().getIdentity(name).getPublicKey()
```

As of Java 1.2, the Identity class and the related IdentityScope and Signer classes have been deprecated in favor of KeyStore and java.security.cert.Certificate.

Object — Identity
Principal Serializable

```
public abstract class Identity implements java.security.Principal, Serializable {
// Public Constructors
   public Identity(String name);
   public Identity(String name, IdentityScope scope) throws KeyManagementException;
// Protected Constructors
   protected Identity();
// Property Accessor Methods (by property name)
   public String getInfo();
   public void setInfo(String info);
   public final String getName();                                          Implements:Principal
   public PublicKey getPublicKey();
   public void setPublicKey(PublicKey key) throws KeyManagementException;
   public final IdentityScope getScope();
// Public Instance Methods
   public void addCertificate(java.security.Certificate certificate) throws KeyManagementException;
   public java.security.Certificate[ ] certificates();
   public void removeCertificate(java.security.Certificate certificate) throws KeyManagementException;
   public String toString(boolean detailed);
// Methods Implementing Principal
   public final boolean equals(Object identity);
   public final String getName();
   public int hashCode();
   public String toString();
// Protected Instance Methods
   protected boolean identityEquals(Identity identity);
}
```

Subclasses: IdentityScope, Signer

Passed To: Identity.identityEquals(), IdentityScope.{addIdentity(), removeIdentity()}

Returned By: IdentityScope.getIdentity()

IdentityScope — Java 1.1; Deprecated in Java 1.2

java.security — *serializable*

This deprecated class was used in Java 1.1 to represent a group of Identity and Signer objects and their associated PublicKey and PrivateKey objects. As of Java 1.2, it has been replaced by the KeyStore class.

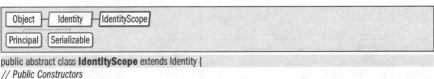

Object — Identity — IdentityScope
Principal Serializable

```
public abstract class IdentityScope extends Identity {
// Public Constructors
   public IdentityScope(String name);
   public IdentityScope(String name, IdentityScope scope) throws KeyManagementException;
```

java.security.*

```
// Protected Constructors
   protected IdentityScope();
// Public Class Methods
   public static IdentityScope getSystemScope();
// Protected Class Methods
   protected static void setSystemScope(IdentityScope scope);
// Public Instance Methods
   public abstract void addIdentity(Identity identity) throws KeyManagementException;
   public abstract Identity getIdentity(String name);
   public Identity getIdentity(java.security.Principal principal);
   public abstract Identity getIdentity(PublicKey key);
   public abstract java.util.Enumeration identities();
   public abstract void removeIdentity(Identity identity) throws KeyManagementException;
   public abstract int size();
// Public Methods Overriding Identity
   public String toString();
}
```

Passed To: Identity.Identity(), IdentityScope.{IdentityScope(), setSystemScope()}, Signer.Signer()

Returned By: Identity.getScope(), IdentityScope.getSystemScope()

InvalidAlgorithmParameterException — Java 1.2

java.security — *serializable checked*

This exception signals that one or more algorithm parameters (usually specified by a java.security.spec.AlgorithmParameterSpec object) are not valid.

Object — Throwable — Exception — GeneralSecurityException — InvalidAlgorithmParameterException
Throwable ⋮ Serializable

```
public class InvalidAlgorithmParameterException extends GeneralSecurityException {
// Public Constructors
   public InvalidAlgorithmParameterException();
   public InvalidAlgorithmParameterException(String msg);
}
```

Thrown By: Too many methods to list.

InvalidKeyException — Java 1.1

java.security — *serializable checked*

This exception signals that a Key is not valid.

Object — Throwable — Exception — GeneralSecurityException — KeyException — InvalidKeyException
Throwable ⋮ Serializable

```
public class InvalidKeyException extends KeyException {
// Public Constructors
   public InvalidKeyException();
   public InvalidKeyException(String msg);
}
```

Thrown By: Too many methods to list.

InvalidParameterException **Java 1.1**

java.security ***serializable unchecked***

This subclass of java.lang.IllegalArgumentException signals that a parameter passed to a security method is not valid. This exception type is not widely used.

Object — Throwable — Exception — RuntimeException — IllegalArgumentException — InvalidParameterException
Serializable

```
public class InvalidParameterException extends IllegalArgumentException {
// Public Constructors
   public InvalidParameterException();
   public InvalidParameterException(String msg);
}
```

Thrown By: Signature.{getParameter(), setParameter()}, SignatureSpi.{engineGetParameter(), engineSetParameter()}, Signer.setKeyPair(), java.security.interfaces.DSAKeyPairGenerator.initialize()

Key **Java 1.1**

java.security ***serializable***

This interface defines the high-level characteristics of all cryptographic keys. getAlgorithm() returns the name of the cryptographic algorithm (such as RSA) used with the key. getFormat() return the name of the external encoding (such as X.509) used with the key. getEncoded() returns the key as an array of bytes, encoded using the format specified by getFormat().

Serializable ··· Key

```
public interface Key extends Serializable {
// Public Constants
1.2 public static final long serialVersionUID;                 =6603384152749567654
// Public Instance Methods
   public abstract String getAlgorithm();
   public abstract byte[ ] getEncoded();
   public abstract String getFormat();
}
```

Implementations: PrivateKey, PublicKey, javax.crypto.SecretKey

Passed To: Too many methods to list.

Returned By: KeyFactory.translateKey(), KeyFactorySpi.engineTranslateKey(), KeyStore.getKey(), KeyStoreSpi.engineGetKey(), javax.crypto.Cipher.unwrap(), javax.crypto.CipherSpi.engineUnwrap(), javax.crypto.KeyAgreement.doPhase(), javax.crypto.KeyAgreementSpi.engineDoPhase()

java.security.*

KeyException **Java 1.1**

java.security ***serializable checked***

This exception signals that something is wrong with a key. See also the subclasses InvalidKeyException and KeyManagementException.

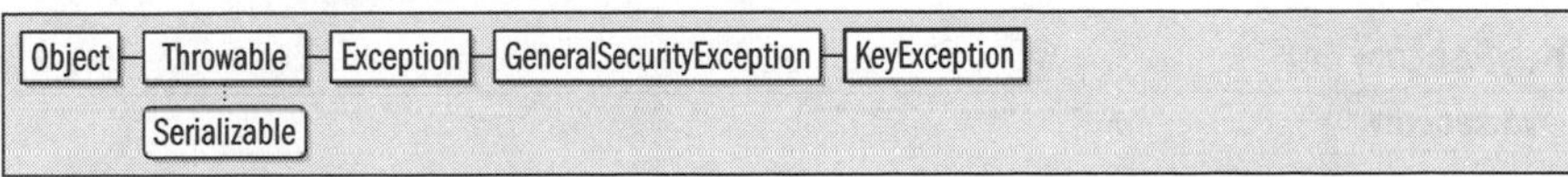


```
public class KeyException extends GeneralSecurityException {
// Public Constructors
```

```
    public KeyException();
    public KeyException(String msg);
}
```

Subclasses: InvalidKeyException, KeyManagementException

Thrown By: java.security.Certificate.{decode(), encode()}, Signer.setKeyPair()

KeyFactory — Java 1.2

java.security

This class translates asymmetric cryptographic keys between the two representations used by the Java Security API. java.security.Key is the opaque, algorithm-independent representation of a key used by most of the Security API. java.security.spec.KeySpec is a marker interface implemented by transparent, algorithm-specific representations of keys. KeyFactory is used with public and private keys; see javax.crypto.SecretKeyFactory if you are working with symmetric or secret keys.

To convert a Key to a KeySpec or vice versa, create a KeyFactory by calling one of the static getInstance() factory methods specifying the name of the key algorithm (e.g., DSA or RSA) and optionally specifying the name or Provider object for the desired provider. Then, use generatePublic() or generatePrivate() to create a PublicKey or PrivateKey object from a corresponding KeySpec. Or use getKeySpec() to obtain a KeySpec for a given Key. Because there can be more than one KeySpec implementation used by a particular cryptographic algorithm, you must also specify the Class of the KeySpec you desire.

If you do not need to transport keys portably between applications and/or systems, you can use a KeyStore to store and retrieve keys and certificates, avoiding KeySpec and KeyFactory altogether.

```
public class KeyFactory {
// Protected Constructors
    protected KeyFactory(KeyFactorySpi keyFacSpi, Provider provider, String algorithm);
// Public Class Methods
    public static KeyFactory getInstance(String algorithm) throws NoSuchAlgorithmException;
    public static KeyFactory getInstance(String algorithm, String provider) throws NoSuchAlgorithmException,
        NoSuchProviderException;
1.4 public static KeyFactory getInstance(String algorithm, Provider provider) throws NoSuchAlgorithmException;
// Public Instance Methods
    public final PrivateKey generatePrivate(java.security.spec.KeySpec keySpec)
        throws java.security.spec.InvalidKeySpecException;
    public final PublicKey generatePublic(java.security.spec.KeySpec keySpec)
        throws java.security.spec.InvalidKeySpecException;
    public final String getAlgorithm();
    public final java.security.spec.KeySpec getKeySpec(Key key, Class keySpec)
        throws java.security.spec.InvalidKeySpecException;
    public final Provider getProvider();
    public final Key translateKey(Key key) throws InvalidKeyException;
}
```

Returned By: KeyFactory.getInstance()

KeyFactorySpi — Java 1.2

java.security

This abstract class defines the service-provider interface for KeyFactory. A security provider must implement a concrete subclass of this class for each cryptographic algorithm it supports. Applications never need to use or subclass this class.

```
public abstract class KeyFactorySpi {
// Public Constructors
   public KeyFactorySpi();
// Protected Instance Methods
   protected abstract PrivateKey engineGeneratePrivate(java.security.spec.KeySpec keySpec)
        throws java.security.spec.InvalidKeySpecException;
   protected abstract PublicKey engineGeneratePublic(java.security.spec.KeySpec keySpec)
        throws java.security.spec.InvalidKeySpecException;
   protected abstract java.security.spec.KeySpec engineGetKeySpec(Key key, Class keySpec)
        throws java.security.spec.InvalidKeySpecException;
   protected abstract Key engineTranslateKey(Key key) throws InvalidKeyException;
}
```

Passed To: KeyFactory.KeyFactory()

KeyManagementException — Java 1.1

java.security — *serializable checked*

This exception signals an exception in a key management operation. In Java 1.2, this exception is thrown only by deprecated methods.

Object ─ Throwable ─ Exception ─ GeneralSecurityException ─ KeyException ─ KeyManagementException
Throwable ··· Serializable

```
public class KeyManagementException extends KeyException {
// Public Constructors
   public KeyManagementException();
   public KeyManagementException(String msg);
}
```

Thrown By: Identity.{addCertificate(), Identity(), removeCertificate(), setPublicKey()}, IdentityScope.{addIdentity(), IdentityScope(), removeIdentity()}, Signer.Signer(), javax.net.ssl.SSLContext.init(), javax.net.ssl.SSLContextSpi.engineInit()

KeyPair — Java 1.1

java.security — *serializable*

This class is a simple container for a PublicKey and a PrivateKey object. Because a KeyPair contains an unprotected private key, it must be used with as much caution as a PrivateKey object.

Object ─ KeyPair ··· Serializable

```
public final class KeyPair implements Serializable {
// Public Constructors
   public KeyPair(PublicKey publicKey, PrivateKey privateKey);
// Public Instance Methods
   public PrivateKey getPrivate();
   public PublicKey getPublic();
}
```

Passed To: Signer.setKeyPair()

Returned By: KeyPairGenerator.{generateKeyPair(), genKeyPair()}, KeyPairGeneratorSpi.generateKeyPair()

KeyPairGenerator — Java 1.1

java.security

This class generates a public/private key pair for a specified cryptographic algorithm. To create a KeyPairGenerator, call one of the static getInstance() methods, specifying the name of the algorithm and, optionally, the name or Provider object of the security provider to use. The default "SUN" provider shipped with Java 1.2 supports only the "DSA" algorithm. The "SunJCE" provider of the Java Cryptography Extension (JCE) additionally supports the "DiffieHellman" algorithm.

Once you have created a KeyPairGenerator, initialize it by calling initialize(). You can perform an algorithm-independent initialization by simply specifying the desired key size in bits. Alternatively, you can do an algorithm-dependent initialization by providing an appropriate AlgorithmParameterSpec object for the key-generation algorithm. In either case, you may optionally provide your own source of randomness in the guise of a SecureRandom object. Once you have created and initialized a KeyPairGenerator, call genKeyPair() to create a KeyPair object. Remember that the KeyPair contains a PrivateKey that *must* be kept private.

For historical reasons, KeyPairGenerator extends KeyPairGeneratorSpi. Applications should not use any methods inherited from that class.

Object — KeyPairGeneratorSpi — KeyPairGenerator

```
public abstract class KeyPairGenerator extends KeyPairGeneratorSpi {
// Protected Constructors
    protected KeyPairGenerator(String algorithm);
// Public Class Methods
    public static KeyPairGenerator getInstance(String algorithm) throws NoSuchAlgorithmException;
1.4 public static KeyPairGenerator getInstance(String algorithm, Provider provider) throws NoSuchAlgorithmException;
    public static KeyPairGenerator getInstance(String algorithm, String provider) throws NoSuchAlgorithmException,
        NoSuchProviderException;
// Public Instance Methods
1.2 public final KeyPair genKeyPair();
    public String getAlgorithm();
1.2 public final Provider getProvider();
1.2 public void initialize(java.security.spec.AlgorithmParameterSpec params)
        throws InvalidAlgorithmParameterException;
    public void initialize(int keysize);
// Public Methods Overriding KeyPairGeneratorSpi
    public KeyPair generateKeyPair();                                                          constant
1.2 public void initialize(java.security.spec.AlgorithmParameterSpec params, SecureRandom random)  empty
        throws InvalidAlgorithmParameterException;
    public void initialize(int keysize, SecureRandom random);                                  empty
}
```

Returned By: KeyPairGenerator.getInstance()

KeyPairGeneratorSpi — Java 1.2

java.security

This abstract class defines the service-provider interface for KeyPairGenerator. A security provider must implement a concrete subclass of this class for each cryptographic algorithm for which it can generate key pairs. Applications never need to use or subclass this class.

```
public abstract class KeyPairGeneratorSpi {
// Public Constructors
   public KeyPairGeneratorSpi();
// Public Instance Methods
   public abstract KeyPair generateKeyPair();
   public void initialize(java.security.spec.AlgorithmParameterSpec params, SecureRandom random)
      throws InvalidAlgorithmParameterException;
   public abstract void initialize(int keysize, SecureRandom random);
}
```

Subclasses: KeyPairGenerator

KeyStore — Java 1.2

java.security

This class represents a mapping of names, or aliases, to Key and java.security.cert.Certificate objects. Obtain a KeyStore object by calling one of the static getInstance() methods, specifying the desired key store type and, optionally, the desired provider. Use "JKS" to specify the "Java Key Store" type defined by Sun. Because of U.S. export regulations, this default KeyStore supports only weak encryption of private keys. If you have the Java Cryptography Extension installed, use the type "JCEKS" and provider "SunJCE" to obtain a KeyStore implementation that offers much stronger password-based encryption of keys. Once you have created a KeyStore, use load() to read its contents from a stream, supplying an optional password that verifies the integrity of the stream data. Keystores are typically read from a file named *.keystore* in the user's home directory.

A KeyStore may contain both public and private key entries. A public key entry is represented by a Certificate object. Use getCertificate() to look up a named public key certificate and setCertificateEntry() to add a new public key certificate to the keystore. A private key entry in the keystore contains both a password-protected Key and an array of Certificate objects that represent the certificate chain for the public key that corresponds to the private key. Use getKey() and getCertificateChain() to look up the key and certificate chain. Use setKeyEntry() to create a new private key entry. You must provide a password when reading or writing a private key from the keystore; this password encrypts the key data, and each private key entry should have a different password. If you are using the JCE, you may also store javax.crypto.SecretKey objects in a KeyStore. Secret keys are stored like private keys, except that they do not have a certificate chain associated with them.

To delete an entry from a KeyStore, use deleteEntry(). If you modify the contents of a KeyStore, use store() to save the keystore to a specified stream. You may specify a password that is used to validate the integrity of the data, but it is not used to encrypt the keystore.

```
public class KeyStore {
// Protected Constructors
   protected KeyStore(KeyStoreSpi keyStoreSpi, Provider provider, String type);
// Public Class Methods
   public static final String getDefaultType();
   public static KeyStore getInstance(String type) throws KeyStoreException;
   public static KeyStore getInstance(String type, String provider) throws KeyStoreException,
      NoSuchProviderException;
1.4 public static KeyStore getInstance(String type, Provider provider) throws KeyStoreException;
// Public Instance Methods
   public final java.util.Enumeration aliases() throws KeyStoreException;
   public final boolean containsAlias(String alias) throws KeyStoreException;
   public final void deleteEntry(String alias) throws KeyStoreException;
```

```
    public final java.security.cert.Certificate getCertificate(String alias) throws KeyStoreException;
    public final String getCertificateAlias(java.security.cert.Certificate cert) throws KeyStoreException;
    public final java.security.cert.Certificate[ ] getCertificateChain(String alias) throws KeyStoreException;
    public final java.util.Date getCreationDate(String alias) throws KeyStoreException;
    public final Key getKey(String alias, char[ ] password) throws KeyStoreException, NoSuchAlgorithmException,
        UnrecoverableKeyException;
    public final Provider getProvider();
    public final String getType();
    public final boolean isCertificateEntry(String alias) throws KeyStoreException;
    public final boolean isKeyEntry(String alias) throws KeyStoreException;
    public final void load(java.io.InputStream stream, char[ ] password) throws java.io.IOException,
        NoSuchAlgorithmException, java.security.cert.CertificateException;
    public final void setCertificateEntry(String alias, java.security.cert.Certificate cert) throws KeyStoreException;
    public final void setKeyEntry(String alias, byte[ ] key, java.security.cert.Certificate[ ] chain)
        throws KeyStoreException;
    public final void setKeyEntry(String alias, Key key, char[ ] password, java.security.cert.Certificate[ ] chain)
        throws KeyStoreException;
    public final int size() throws KeyStoreException;
    public final void store(java.io.OutputStream stream, char[ ] password) throws KeyStoreException,
        java.io.IOException, NoSuchAlgorithmException, java.security.cert.CertificateException;
}
```

Passed To: java.security.cert.PKIXBuilderParameters.PKIXBuilderParameters(), java.security.cert.PKIXParameters.PKIXParameters(), javax.net.ssl.KeyManagerFactory.init(), javax.net.ssl.KeyManagerFactorySpi.engineInit(), javax.net.ssl.TrustManagerFactory.init(), javax.net.ssl.TrustManagerFactorySpi.engineInit()

Returned By: KeyStore.getInstance()

KeyStoreException — Java 1.2

java.security — *serializable checked*

This exception signals a problem with a KeyStore.

Object — Throwable — Exception — GeneralSecurityException — KeyStoreException
(Throwable implements Serializable)

```
public class KeyStoreException extends GeneralSecurityException {
// Public Constructors
    public KeyStoreException();
    public KeyStoreException(String msg);
}
```

Thrown By: Too many methods to list.

KeyStoreSpi — Java 1.2

java.security

This abstract class defines the service-provider interface for KeyStore. A security provider must implement a concrete subclass of this class for each KeyStore type it supports. Applications never need to use or subclass this class.

```
public abstract class KeyStoreSpi {
// Public Constructors
    public KeyStoreSpi();
// Public Instance Methods
```

```
    public abstract java.util.Enumeration engineAliases();
    public abstract boolean engineContainsAlias(String alias);
    public abstract void engineDeleteEntry(String alias) throws KeyStoreException;
    public abstract java.security.cert.Certificate engineGetCertificate(String alias);
    public abstract String engineGetCertificateAlias(java.security.cert.Certificate cert);
    public abstract java.security.cert.Certificate[ ] engineGetCertificateChain(String alias);
    public abstract java.util.Date engineGetCreationDate(String alias);
    public abstract Key engineGetKey(String alias, char[ ] password) throws NoSuchAlgorithmException,
        UnrecoverableKeyException;
    public abstract boolean engineIsCertificateEntry(String alias);
    public abstract boolean engineIsKeyEntry(String alias);
    public abstract void engineLoad(java.io.InputStream stream, char[ ] password) throws java.io.IOException,
        NoSuchAlgorithmException, java.security.cert.CertificateException;
    public abstract void engineSetCertificateEntry(String alias, java.security.cert.Certificate cert)
        throws KeyStoreException;
    public abstract void engineSetKeyEntry(String alias, byte[ ] key, java.security.cert.Certificate[ ] chain)
        throws KeyStoreException;
    public abstract void engineSetKeyEntry(String alias, Key key, char[ ] password,
                                           java.security.cert.Certificate[ ] chain) throws KeyStoreException;
    public abstract int engineSize();
    public abstract void engineStore(java.io.OutputStream stream, char[ ] password) throws java.io.IOException,
        NoSuchAlgorithmException, java.security.cert.CertificateException;
}
```

Passed To: KeyStore.KeyStore()

MessageDigest — Java 1.1

java.security

This class computes a message digest (also known as a cryptographic checksum) for an arbitrary sequence of bytes. Obtain a MessageDigest object by calling one of the static getInstance() factory methods and specifying the desired algorithm (e.g., SHA or MD5) and, optionally, the desired provider. Next, specify the data to be digested by calling any of the update() methods one or more times. Finally, call digest(), which computes the message digest and returns it as an array of bytes. If you have only one array of bytes to be digested, you can pass it directly to digest() and skip the update() step. When you call digest(), the MessageDigest() object is reset and is then ready to compute a new digest. You can also explicitly reset a MessageDigest without computing the digest by calling reset(). To compute a digest for part of a message without resetting the MessageDigest, clone the MessageDigest and call digest() on the cloned copy. Note that not all implementations are cloneable, so the clone() method may throw an exception.

The MessageDigest class is often used in conjunction with DigestInputStream and DigestOutputStream, which automate the update() calls for you.

Object — MessageDigestSpi — MessageDigest

```
public abstract class MessageDigest extends MessageDigestSpi {
// Protected Constructors
    protected MessageDigest(String algorithm);
// Public Class Methods
    public static MessageDigest getInstance(String algorithm) throws NoSuchAlgorithmException;
```

```
1.4 public static MessageDigest getInstance(String algorithm, Provider provider) throws NoSuchAlgorithmException;
    public static MessageDigest getInstance(String algorithm, String provider) throws NoSuchAlgorithmException,
        NoSuchProviderException;
    public static boolean isEqual(byte[ ] digesta, byte[ ] digestb);
// Public Instance Methods
    public byte[ ] digest();
    public byte[ ] digest(byte[ ] input);
1.2 public int digest(byte[ ] buf, int offset, int len) throws DigestException;
    public final String getAlgorithm();
1.2 public final int getDigestLength();
1.2 public final Provider getProvider();
    public void reset();
    public void update(byte[ ] input);
    public void update(byte input);
    public void update(byte[ ] input, int offset, int len);
// Public Methods Overriding MessageDigestSpi
    public Object clone() throws CloneNotSupportedException;
// Public Methods Overriding Object
    public String toString();
}
```

Passed To: DigestInputStream.{DigestInputStream(), setMessageDigest()}, DigestOutputStream.{DigestOutputStream(), setMessageDigest()}

Returned By: DigestInputStream.getMessageDigest(), DigestOutputStream.getMessageDigest(), MessageDigest.getInstance()

Type Of: DigestInputStream.digest, DigestOutputStream.digest

MessageDigestSpi — Java 1.2

java.security

This abstract class defines the service-provider interface for MessageDigest. A security provider must implement a concrete subclass of this class for each message-digest algorithm it supports. Applications never need to use or subclass this class.

```
public abstract class MessageDigestSpi {
// Public Constructors
    public MessageDigestSpi();
// Public Methods Overriding Object
    public Object clone() throws CloneNotSupportedException;
// Protected Instance Methods
    protected abstract byte[ ] engineDigest();
    protected int engineDigest(byte[ ] buf, int offset, int len) throws DigestException;
    protected int engineGetDigestLength();                                    constant
    protected abstract void engineReset();
    protected abstract void engineUpdate(byte input);
    protected abstract void engineUpdate(byte[ ] input, int offset, int len);
}
```

Subclasses: MessageDigest

NoSuchAlgorithmException — Java 1.1

java.security — *serializable checked*

This signals that a requested cryptographic algorithm is not available. It is thrown by getInstance() factory methods throughout the java.security package.

```
Object ─ Throwable ─ Exception ─ GeneralSecurityException ─ NoSuchAlgorithmException
         Serializable
```

```
public class NoSuchAlgorithmException extends GeneralSecurityException {
// Public Constructors
   public NoSuchAlgorithmException();
   public NoSuchAlgorithmException(String msg);
}
```

Thrown By: Too many methods to list.

NoSuchProviderException — Java 1.1

java.security — *serializable checked*

This signals that a requested cryptographic service provider is not available. It is thrown by getInstance() factory methods throughout the java.security package.

```
Object ─ Throwable ─ Exception ─ GeneralSecurityException ─ NoSuchProviderException
         Serializable
```

```
public class NoSuchProviderException extends GeneralSecurityException {
// Public Constructors
   public NoSuchProviderException();
   public NoSuchProviderException(String msg);
}
```

Thrown By: Too many methods to list.

Permission — Java 1.2

java.security — *serializable permission*

This abstract class represents a system resource, such as a file in the filesystem, or a system capability, such as the ability to accept network connections. Concrete subclasses of Permission, such as java.io.FilePermission and java.net.SocketPermission, represent specific types of resources. Permission objects are used by system code that is requesting access to a resource. They are also used by Policy objects that grant access to resources. The AccessController.checkPermission() method considers the source of the currently running Java code, determines the set of permissions that are granted to that code by the current Policy, and then checks to see whether a specified Permission object is included in that set. With the introduction of Java 1.2, this is the fundamental Java access-control mechanism.

Each permission has a name (sometimes called the *target*) and, optionally, a comma-separated list of actions. For example, the name of a FilePermission is the name of the file or directory for which permission is being granted. The actions associated with this permission might be "read"; "write"; or "read,write". The interpretation of the name and action strings is entirely up to the implementation of Permission. A number of implementations support the use of wildcards; for example, a FilePermission can have a name of "/tmp/*", which represents access to any files in a */tmp* directory. Permission objects must be immutable, so an implementation must never define a setName() or setActions() method.

One of the most important abstract methods defined by Permission is implies(). This method must return true if this Permission implies another Permission. For example, if an application requests a FilePermission with name "/tmp/test" and action "read", and the current security Policy grants a FilePermission with name "/tmp/*" and actions "read,write", the request is granted because the requested permission is implied by the granted one.

In general, only system-level code needs to work directly with Permission and its concrete subclasses. System administrators who are configuring security policies need to understand the various Permission subclasses. Applications that want to extend the Java access-control mechanism to provide customized access control to their own resources should subclass Permission to define custom permission types.

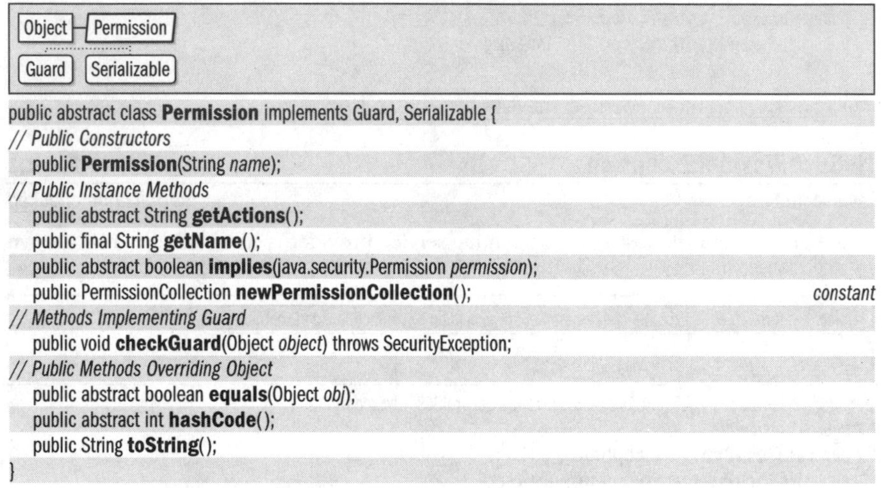


```
public abstract class Permission implements Guard, Serializable {
// Public Constructors
   public Permission(String name);
// Public Instance Methods
   public abstract String getActions();
   public final String getName();
   public abstract boolean implies(java.security.Permission permission);
   public PermissionCollection newPermissionCollection();                constant
// Methods Implementing Guard
   public void checkGuard(Object object) throws SecurityException;
// Public Methods Overriding Object
   public abstract boolean equals(Object obj);
   public abstract int hashCode();
   public String toString();
}
```

Subclasses: java.io.FilePermission, java.net.SocketPermission, AllPermission, BasicPermission, UnresolvedPermission, javax.security.auth.PrivateCredentialPermission, javax.security.auth.kerberos.ServicePermission

Passed To: Too many methods to list.

Returned By: java.net.HttpURLConnection.getPermission(), java.net.URLConnection.getPermission(), AccessControlException.getPermission()

PermissionCollection — Java 1.2

java.security — *serializable*

This class is used by Permissions to store a collection of Permission objects that are all the same type. Like the Permission class itself, PermissionCollection defines an implies() method that can determine whether a requested Permission is implied by any of the Permission objects in the collection. Some Permission types may require a custom PermissionCollection type in order to correctly implement the implies() method. In this case, the Permission subclass should override newPermissionCollection() to return a Permission of the appropriate type. PermissionCollection is used by system code that manages security policies. Applications rarely need to use it.

Object — PermissionCollection ··· Serializable

```
public abstract class PermissionCollection implements Serializable {
// Public Constructors
   public PermissionCollection();
```

```
// Public Instance Methods
    public abstract void add(java.security.Permission permission);
    public abstract java.util.Enumeration elements();
    public abstract boolean implies(java.security.Permission permission);
    public boolean isReadOnly();
    public void setReadOnly();
// Public Methods Overriding Object
    public String toString();
}
```

Subclasses: Permissions

Passed To: ProtectionDomain.ProtectionDomain()

Returned By: Too many methods to list.

Permissions — Java 1.2

java.security — *serializable*

This class stores an arbitrary collection of Permission objects. When Permission objects are added with the add() method, they are grouped into an internal set of PermissionCollection objects that contain only a single type of Permission. Use the elements() method to obtain an Enumeration of the Permission objects in the collection. Use implies() to determine if a specified Permission is implied by any of the Permission objects in the collection. Permissions is used by system code that manages security policies. Applications rarely need to use it.

Object — PermissionCollection — Permissions
Serializable   Serializable

```
public final class Permissions extends PermissionCollection implements Serializable {
// Public Constructors
    public Permissions();
// Public Methods Overriding PermissionCollection
    public void add(java.security.Permission permission);
    public java.util.Enumeration elements();
    public boolean implies(java.security.Permission permission);
}
```

Policy — Java 1.2

java.security

This class represents a security policy that determines the permissions granted to code based on its source and signers, and, in Java 1.4 and later, based on the user on whose behalf that code is running. There is only a single Policy in effect at any one time. Obtain the system policy by calling the static getPolicy() method. Code that has appropriate permissions can specify a new system policy by calling setPolicy(). The refresh() method is a request to a Policy object to update its state (for example, by rereading its configuration file). The Policy class is used primarily by system-level code. Applications should not need to use this class unless they implement some kind of custom access control mechanism.

Prior to Java 1.4, this class provides a mapping from CodeSource objects to PermissionCollection objects. getPermissions() is the central Policy method; it evaluates the Policy for a given CodeSource and returns an appropriate PermissionCollection representing the static set of permissions available to code from that source.

In Java 1.4, you can use a ProtectionDomain object to encapsulate a CodeSource and a set of users on whose behalf the code is running. In this release, there is a new getPermissions() method that returns a PermissionsCollection appropriate for the specified ProtectionDomain. In addition, there is a new implies() method that dynamically queries the Policy to see if the specified permission is granted to the specific ProtectionDomain.

```
public abstract class Policy {
// Public Constructors
   public Policy();
// Public Class Methods
   public static java.security.Policy getPolicy();
   public static void setPolicy(java.security.Policy policy);
// Public Instance Methods
   public abstract PermissionCollection getPermissions(CodeSource codesource);
1.4 public PermissionCollection getPermissions(ProtectionDomain domain);
1.4 public boolean implies(ProtectionDomain domain, java.security.Permission permission);
   public abstract void refresh();
}
```

Passed To: java.security.Policy.setPolicy()

Returned By: java.security.Policy.getPolicy()

Principal — Java 1.1

java.security

This interface represents any entity that may serve as a principal in a cryptographic transaction of any kind. A Principal may represent an individual, a computer, or an organization, for example.

```
public interface Principal {
// Public Instance Methods
   public abstract boolean equals(Object another);
   public abstract String getName();
   public abstract int hashCode();
   public abstract String toString();
}
```

Implementations: Identity, java.security.acl.Group, javax.security.auth.kerberos.KerberosPrincipal, javax.security.auth.x500.X500Principal

Passed To: Too many methods to list.

Returned By: java.security.Certificate.{getGuarantor(), getPrincipal()}, ProtectionDomain.getPrincipals(), java.security.acl.AclEntry.getPrincipal(), java.security.cert.X509Certificate.{getIssuerDN(), getSubjectDN()}, java.security.cert.X509CRL.getIssuerDN(), javax.security.cert.X509Certificate.{getIssuerDN(), getSubjectDN()}

PrivateKey — Java 1.1

java.security — *serializable*

This interface represents a private cryptographic key. It extends the Key interface, but does not add any new methods. The interface exists in order to create a strong distinction between private and public keys. See also PublicKey.

```
Serializable ··· Key ··· PrivateKey
```

```
public interface PrivateKey extends Key {
// Public Constants
1.2 public static final long serialVersionUID;                                    =6034044314589513430
}
```

Implementations: java.security.interfaces.DSAPrivateKey, java.security.interfaces.RSAPrivateKey, javax.crypto.interfaces.DHPrivateKey

Passed To: KeyPair.KeyPair(), Signature.initSign(), SignatureSpi.engineInitSign(), SignedObject.SignedObject(), javax.security.auth.x500.X500PrivateCredential.X500PrivateCredential()

Returned By: KeyFactory.generatePrivate(), KeyFactorySpi.engineGeneratePrivate(), KeyPair.getPrivate(), Signer.getPrivateKey(), javax.net.ssl.X509KeyManager.getPrivateKey(), javax.security.auth.x500.X500PrivateCredential.getPrivateKey()

PrivilegedAction — Java 1.2

java.security

This interface defines a block of code (the run() method) that is to be executed as privileged code by the AccessController.doPrivileged() method. When privileged code is run in this way, the AccessController looks only at the permissions of the immediate caller, not the permissions of the entire call stack. The immediate caller is typically fully trusted system code that has a full set of permissions, and therefore the privileged code runs with that full set of permissions, even if the system code is invoked by untrusted code with no permissions whatsoever.

Privileged code is typically required only when you are writing a trusted system library (such as a Java extension package) that must read local files or perform other restricted actions, even when called by untrusted code. For example, a class that must call System.loadLibrary() to load native methods should make the call to loadLibrary() within the run() method of a PrivilegedAction. If your privileged code may throw a checked exception, implement it in the run() method of a PrivilegedExceptionAction instead.

Be very careful when implementing this interface. To minimize the possibility of security holes, keep the body of the run() method as short as possible.

```
public interface PrivilegedAction {
// Public Instance Methods
   public abstract Object run();
}
```

Passed To: AccessController.doPrivileged(), javax.security.auth.Subject.{doAs(), doAsPrivileged()}

PrivilegedActionException — Java 1.2

java.security — *serializable checked*

This exception class is a wrapper around an arbitrary Exception thrown by a PrivilegedExceptionAction executed by the AccessController.doPrivileged() method. Use getException() to obtain the wrapped Exception object. Or, in Java 1.4 and later, use the more general getCause() method.

```
public class PrivilegedActionException extends Exception {
// Public Constructors
   public PrivilegedActionException(Exception exception);
```

*java.security.**

```
// Public Instance Methods
   public Exception getException();
// Public Methods Overriding Throwable
1.4 public Throwable getCause();
1.3 public String toString();
}
```

Thrown By: AccessController.doPrivileged(), javax.security.auth.Subject.{doAs(), doAsPrivileged()}

PrivilegedExceptionAction — Java 1.2

java.security

This interface is like PrivilegedAction, except that its run() method may throw an exception. See PrivilegedAction for details.

```
public interface PrivilegedExceptionAction {
// Public Instance Methods
   public abstract Object run() throws Exception;
}
```

Passed To: AccessController.doPrivileged(), javax.security.auth.Subject.{doAs(), doAsPrivileged()}

ProtectionDomain — Java 1.2

java.security

This class represents a "protection domain": the set of permissions associated with code based on its source, and optionally, the identities of the users on whose behalf? the code is running. Use the getProtectionDomain() of a Class object to obtain the ProtectionDomain that the class is part of.

Prior to Java 1.4, a ProtectionDomain simply associates a CodeSource with the PermissionCollection granted to code from that source by a Policy. The set of permissions is static, and the implies() method checks to see whether the specified Permission is implied by any of the permissions granted to this ProtectionDomain.

In Java 1.4 and later, a ProtectionDomain can also be created with the four-argument constructor, which associates a PermissionCollection with a ClassLoader and an array of Principal objects in addition to a CodeSource. A ProtectionDomain of this sort represents permissions granted to code loaded from a specified source, through a specified class loader, and running under the auspices of one or more specified principals. When a ProtectionDomain is instantiated with this four-argument constructor, the PermissionCollection is not static, and the implies() method calls the implies() method of the current Policy object before checking the specified collection of permissions. This allows security policies to be updated (to add new permissions for specific users, for example) without having to restart long-running programs such as servers.

```
public class ProtectionDomain {
// Public Constructors
   public ProtectionDomain(CodeSource codesource, PermissionCollection permissions);
1.4 public ProtectionDomain(CodeSource codesource, PermissionCollection permissions, ClassLoader classloader,
                            java.security.Principal[ ] principals);
// Public Instance Methods
1.4 public final ClassLoader getClassLoader();
   public final CodeSource getCodeSource();
   public final PermissionCollection getPermissions();
1.4 public final java.security.Principal[ ] getPrincipals();
   public boolean implies(java.security.Permission permission);
```

```
// Public Methods Overriding Object
    public String toString();
}
```

Passed To: ClassLoader.defineClass(), AccessControlContext.AccessControlContext(), DomainCombiner.combine(), java.security.Policy.{getPermissions(), implies()}, javax.security.auth.SubjectDomainCombiner.combine()

Returned By: Class.getProtectionDomain(), DomainCombiner.combine(), javax.security.auth.SubjectDomainCombiner.combine()

Provider — Java 1.1

java.security — *cloneable serializable collection*

This class represents a security provider. It specifies class names for implementations of one or more algorithms for message digests, digital signatures, key generation, key conversion, key management, secure random number generation, certificate conversion, and algorithm parameter management. The getName(), getVersion(), and getInfo() methods return information about the provider. Provider inherits from Properties and maintains a mapping of property names to property values. These name/value pairs specify the capabilities of the Provider implementation. Each property name has the form:

service_type.algorithm_name

The corresponding property value is the name of the class that implements the named algorithm. For example, say a Provider defines properties named "Signature.DSA", "MessageDigest.MD5", and "KeyStore.JKS". The values of these properties are the class names of SignatureSpi, MessageDigestSpi, and KeyStoreSpi implementations. Other properties defined by a Provider are used to provide aliases for algorithm names. For example, the property Alg.Alias.MessageDigest.SHA1 might have the value "SHA", meaning that the algorithm name "SHA1" is an alias for "SHA".

Security providers are installed for a Java system in an implementation-dependent way. For Sun's implementation, the *${java.home}/lib/security/java.security* file specifies the class names of all installed Provider implementations. An application can also install its own custom Provider with the addProvider() and insertProviderAt() methods of the Security class. Most applications do not need to use the Provider class directly. Typically, only security-provider implementors need to use the Provider class. Some applications may explicitly specify the name of a desired Provider when calling a static getInstance() factory method, however. Only applications with the most demanding cryptographic needs need to install custom providers.

Object — Dictionary — Hashtable — Properties — Provider
Cloneable, Map, Serializable

```
public abstract class Provider extends java.util.Properties {
// Protected Constructors
    protected Provider(String name, double version, String info);
// Public Instance Methods
    public String getInfo();
    public String getName();
    public double getVersion();
// Public Methods Overriding Properties
1.2 public void load(java.io.InputStream inStream) throws java.io.IOException;     synchronized
// Public Methods Overriding Hashtable
1.2 public void clear();     synchronized
```

```
1.2 public java.util.Set entrySet();                                    synchronized
1.2 public java.util.Set keySet();
1.2 public Object put(Object key, Object value);                        synchronized
1.2 public void putAll(java.util.Map t);                                synchronized
1.2 public Object remove(Object key);                                   synchronized
    public String toString();
1.2 public java.util.Collection values();
}
```

Passed To: Too many methods to list.

Returned By: Too many methods to list.

ProviderException — Java 1.1

java.security — *serializable unchecked*

This signals that an exception has occurred inside a cryptographic service provider. Note that ProviderException extends RuntimeException and is therefore an unchecked exception that may be thrown from any method without being declared.

Object → Throwable → Exception → RuntimeException → ProviderException; Throwable ⋯ Serializable

```
public class ProviderException extends RuntimeException {
// Public Constructors
    public ProviderException();
    public ProviderException(String s);
}
```

PublicKey — Java 1.1

java.security — *serializable*

This interface represents a public cryptographic key. It extends the Key interface, but does not add any new methods. The interface exists in order to create a strong distinction between public and private keys. See also PrivateKey.

Serializable ⋯ Key ⋯ PublicKey

```
public interface PublicKey extends Key {
// Public Constants
1.2 public static final long serialVersionUID;                  =7187392471159151072
}
```

Implementations: java.security.interfaces.DSAPublicKey, java.security.interfaces.RSAPublicKey, javax.crypto.interfaces.DHPublicKey

Passed To: Too many methods to list.

Returned By: java.security.Certificate.getPublicKey(), Identity.getPublicKey(), KeyFactory.generatePublic(), KeyFactorySpi.engineGeneratePublic(), KeyPair.getPublic(), java.security.cert.Certificate.getPublicKey(), java.security.cert.PKIXCertPathValidatorResult.getPublicKey(), java.security.cert.TrustAnchor.getCAPublicKey(), java.security.cert.X509CertSelector.getSubjectPublicKey(), javax.security.cert.Certificate.getPublicKey()

SecureClassLoader — Java 1.2

java.security

This class adds two protected methods to those defined by ClassLoader. The defineClass() method is passed a CodeSource object that represents the source of the class being loaded. It calls the getPermissions() method to obtain a PermissionCollection for that CodeSource. It then uses the CodeSource and PermissionCollection to create a ProtectionDomain, which is passed to the defineClass() method of its superclass.

The default implementation of the getPermissions() method uses the default Policy to determine the appropriate set of permissions for a given code source. The value of SecureClassLoader is that subclasses can use its defineClass() method to load classes without having to work explicitly with the ProtectionDomain and Policy classes. A subclass of SecureClassLoader can define its own security policy by overriding getPermissions(). In Java 1.2 and later, any application that implements a custom class loader should do so by extending SecureClassLoader, instead of subclassing ClassLoader directly. Most applications can use java.net.URLClassLoader, however, and never have to subclass this class.

Object — ClassLoader — SecureClassLoader

```
public class SecureClassLoader extends ClassLoader {
// Protected Constructors
   protected SecureClassLoader();
   protected SecureClassLoader(ClassLoader parent);
// Protected Instance Methods
   protected final Class defineClass(String name, byte[ ] b, int off, int len, CodeSource cs);
   protected PermissionCollection getPermissions(CodeSource codesource);
}
```

Subclasses: java.net.URLClassLoader

SecureRandom — Java 1.1

java.security — *serializable*

This class generates cryptographic-quality pseudo-random bytes. Although SecureRandom defines public constructors, the preferred technique for obtaining a SecureRandom object is to call one of the static getInstance() factory methods, specifying the desired pseudo-random number-generation algorithm, and, optionally, the desired provider of that algorithm. Sun's implementation of Java ships with an algorithm named "SHA1PRNG" in the "SUN" provider.

Once you have obtained a SecureRandom object, call nextBytes() to fill an array with pseudo-random bytes. You can also call any of the methods defined by the Random superclass to obtain random numbers. The first time one of these methods is called, the SecureRandom() method uses its generateSeed() method to seed itself. If you have a source of random or very high-quality pseudo-random bytes, you may provide your own seed by calling setSeed(). Repeated calls to setSeed() augment the existing seed instead of replacing it. You can also call generateSeed() to generate seeds for use with other pseudo-random generators. generateSeed() may use a different algorithm than nextBytes() and may produce higher-quality randomness, usually at the expense of increased computation time.

```
public class SecureRandom extends java.util.Random {
// Public Constructors
   public SecureRandom();
   public SecureRandom(byte[] seed);
// Protected Constructors
1.2 protected SecureRandom(SecureRandomSpi secureRandomSpi, Provider provider);
// Public Class Methods
1.2 public static SecureRandom getInstance(String algorithm) throws NoSuchAlgorithmException;
1.2 public static SecureRandom getInstance(String algorithm, String provider) throws NoSuchAlgorithmException,
        NoSuchProviderException;
1.4 public static SecureRandom getInstance(String algorithm, Provider provider) throws NoSuchAlgorithmException;
   public static byte[] getSeed(int numBytes);
// Public Instance Methods
1.2 public byte[] generateSeed(int numBytes);
1.2 public final Provider getProvider();                                        default:Sun
   public void setSeed(byte[] seed);                                           synchronized
// Public Methods Overriding Random
   public void nextBytes(byte[] bytes);                                        synchronized
   public void setSeed(long seed);
// Protected Methods Overriding Random
   protected final int next(int numBits);
}
```

Passed To: Too many methods to list.

Returned By: SecureRandom.getInstance()

Type Of: SignatureSpi.appRandom

SecureRandomSpi — Java 1.2

java.security — *serializable*

This abstract class defines the service-provider interface for SecureRandom. A security provider must implement a concrete subclass of this class for each pseudo-random number-generation algorithm it supports. Applications never need to use or subclass this class.

Object — SecureRandomSpi ··· Serializable

```
public abstract class SecureRandomSpi implements Serializable {
// Public Constructors
   public SecureRandomSpi();
// Protected Instance Methods
   protected abstract byte[] engineGenerateSeed(int numBytes);
   protected abstract void engineNextBytes(byte[] bytes);
   protected abstract void engineSetSeed(byte[] seed);
}
```

Passed To: SecureRandom.SecureRandom()

Security — Java 1.1

java.security

This class defines static methods both for managing the list of installed security providers and for reading and setting the values of various properties used by the Java security system. It is essentially an interface to the *${java.home}/lib/security/java.security* properties file that is included in Sun's implementation of Java. Use getProperty() and setProperty() to query or set the value of security properties whose default values are stored in that file.

One of the important features of the *java.security* properties file is that it specifies a set of security provider implementations and a preference order in which they are to be used. getProviders() returns an array of Provider objects, in the order they are specified in the file. In Java 1.3 and later, versions of this method that return only providers that implement the algorithm or algorithms specified in a String or Map object exist. You can also look up a single named Provider object by name with getProvider(). Note that a provider name is the string returned by getName() method of the Provider class, not the class name of the Provider.

You can alter the set of providers installed by default from the java.security file. Use addProvider() to add a new Provider object to the list, placing it at the end of the list, with a lower preference than all other providers. Use insertProviderAt() to insert a provider into the list at a specified position. Note that provider preference positions are 1-based. Specify a position of 1 to make the provider the most preferred one. Finally, use removeProvider() to remove a named provider.

In Java 1.4 and later, the getAlgorithms method returns a Set that includes the names of all supported algorithms (from any installed provider) for the specified service. A service name specifies the category of security service you are querying. It is a case-insensitive value that has the same name as one of the key service classes from this package or security-related packages; for example, "Signature", "MessageDigest", and "KeyStore" (from this package), or "Cipher" (from the javax.crypto package).

```
public final class Security {
// No Constructor
// Public Class Methods
    public static int addProvider(Provider provider);
1.4 public static java.util.Set getAlgorithms(String serviceName);
    public static String getProperty(String key);
    public static Provider getProvider(String name);                                  synchronized
    public static Provider[ ] getProviders( );                                         synchronized
1.3 public static Provider[ ] getProviders(java.util.Map filter);
1.3 public static Provider[ ] getProviders(String filter);
    public static int insertProviderAt(Provider provider, int position);              synchronized
    public static void removeProvider(String name);                                   synchronized
    public static void setProperty(String key, String datum);
// Deprecated Public Methods
#   public static String getAlgorithmProperty(String algName, String propName);
}
```

SecurityPermission — Java 1.2

java.security — *serializable permission*

This class is a Permission subclass that represents access to various methods of the Policy, Security, Provider, Signer, and Identity objects. SecurityPermission objects are defined by a name only; they do not use a list of actions. Important SecurityPermission names are "getPolicy" and "setPolicy", which represent the ability query and set the system security policy by invoking the Policy.getPolicy() and Policy.setPolicy() methods. Applications do not typically need to use this class.

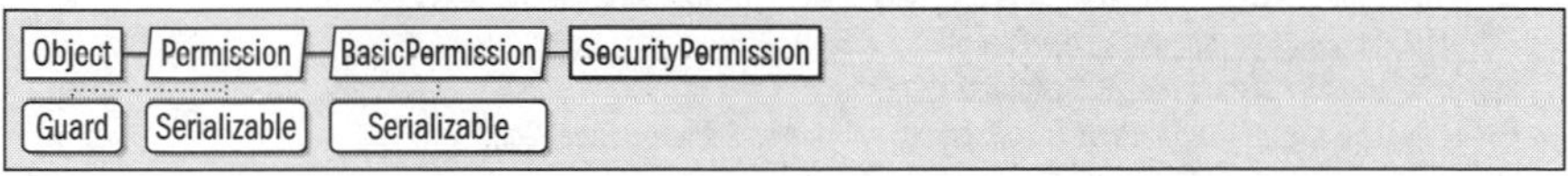

```
public final class SecurityPermission extends BasicPermission {
// Public Constructors
   public SecurityPermission(String name);
   public SecurityPermission(String name, String actions);
}
```

Signature — Java 1.1

java.security

This class computes or verifies a digital signature. Obtain a Signature object by calling one of the static getInstance() factory methods and specifying the desired digital signature algorithm and, optionally, the desired provider of that algorithm. A *digital signature* is essentially a message digest encrypted by a public-key encryption algorithm. Thus, to specify a digital signature algorithm, you must specify both the digest algorithm and the encryption algorithm. The only algorithm supported by the default "SUN" provider is "SHA1withDSA".

Once you have obtained a Signature object, you must initialize it before you can create or verify a digital signature. To initialize a digital signature for creation, call initSign() and specify the private key to be used to create the signature. To initialize a signature for verification, call initVerify() and specify the public key of the signer. Once the Signature object has been initialized, call update() one or more times to specify the bytes to be signed or verified. Finally, to create a digital signature, call sign(), passing a byte array into which the signature is stored. Or, pass the bytes of the digital signature to verify(), which returns true if the signature is valid or false otherwise. After calling either sign() or verify(), the Signature object is reset internally and can be used to create or verify another signature.

Object — SignatureSpi — Signature

```
public abstract class Signature extends SignatureSpi {
// Protected Constructors
   protected Signature(String algorithm);
// Protected Constants
   protected static final int SIGN;                                         =2
   protected static final int UNINITIALIZED;                                =0
   protected static final int VERIFY;                                       =3
// Public Class Methods
   public static Signature getInstance(String algorithm) throws NoSuchAlgorithmException;
1.4 public static Signature getInstance(String algorithm, Provider provider) throws NoSuchAlgorithmException;
   public static Signature getInstance(String algorithm, String provider) throws NoSuchAlgorithmException,
       NoSuchProviderException;
// Public Instance Methods
   public final String getAlgorithm();
1.4 public final AlgorithmParameters getParameters();
1.2 public final Provider getProvider();
   public final void initSign(PrivateKey privateKey) throws InvalidKeyException;
1.2 public final void initSign(PrivateKey privateKey, SecureRandom random) throws InvalidKeyException;
1.3 public final void initVerify(java.security.cert.Certificate certificate) throws InvalidKeyException;
   public final void initVerify(PublicKey publicKey) throws InvalidKeyException;
1.2 public final void setParameter(java.security.spec.AlgorithmParameterSpec params)
       throws InvalidAlgorithmParameterException;
   public final byte[ ] sign() throws SignatureException;
1.2 public final int sign(byte[ ] outbuf, int offset, int len) throws SignatureException;
   public final void update(byte[ ] data) throws SignatureException;
```

```
    public final void update(byte b) throws SignatureException;
    public final void update(byte[ ] data, int off, int len) throws SignatureException;
    public final boolean verify(byte[ ] signature) throws SignatureException;
1.4 public final boolean verify(byte[ ] signature, int offset, int length) throws SignatureException;
// Public Methods Overriding SignatureSpi
    public Object clone() throws CloneNotSupportedException;
// Public Methods Overriding Object
    public String toString();
// Protected Instance Fields
    protected int state;
// Deprecated Public Methods
#   public final Object getParameter(String param) throws InvalidParameterException;
#   public final void setParameter(String param, Object value) throws InvalidParameterException;
}
```

Passed To: SignedObject.{SignedObject(), verify()}

Returned By: Signature.getInstance()

SignatureException — Java 1.1

java.security — *serializable checked*

This signals a problem while creating or verifying a digital signature.

Object — Throwable — Exception — GeneralSecurityException — SignatureException
Serializable

```
public class SignatureException extends GeneralSecurityException {
// Public Constructors
    public SignatureException();
    public SignatureException(String msg);
}
```

Thrown By: Too many methods to list.

SignatureSpi — Java 1.2

java.security

This abstract class defines the service-provider interface for Signature. A security provider must implement a concrete subclass of this class for each digital signature algorithm it supports. Applications never need to use or subclass this class.

```
public abstract class SignatureSpi {
// Public Constructors
    public SignatureSpi();
// Public Methods Overriding Object
    public Object clone() throws CloneNotSupportedException;
// Protected Instance Methods
1.4 protected AlgorithmParameters engineGetParameters();
    protected abstract void engineInitSign(PrivateKey privateKey) throws InvalidKeyException;
    protected void engineInitSign(PrivateKey privateKey, SecureRandom random) throws InvalidKeyException;
    protected abstract void engineInitVerify(PublicKey publicKey) throws InvalidKeyException;
    protected void engineSetParameter(java.security.spec.AlgorithmParameterSpec params)
        throws InvalidAlgorithmParameterException;
    protected abstract byte[ ] engineSign() throws SignatureException;
    protected int engineSign(byte[ ] outbuf, int offset, int len) throws SignatureException;
```

```
    protected abstract void engineUpdate(byte b) throws SignatureException;
    protected abstract void engineUpdate(byte[ ] b, int off, int len) throws SignatureException;
    protected abstract boolean engineVerify(byte[ ] sigBytes) throws SignatureException;
1.4 protected boolean engineVerify(byte[ ] sigBytes, int offset, int length) throws SignatureException;
// Protected Instance Fields
    protected SecureRandom appRandom;
// Deprecated Protected Methods
#   protected abstract Object engineGetParameter(String param) throws InvalidParameterException;
#   protected abstract void engineSetParameter(String param, Object value) throws InvalidParameterException;
}
```

Subclasses: Signature

SignedObject — Java 1.2

java.security — *serializable*

This class applies a digital signature to any serializable Java object. Create a SignedObject by specifying the object to be signed, the PrivateKey to use for the signature, and the Signature object to create the signature. The SignedObject() constructor serializes the specified object into an array of bytes and creates a digital signature for those bytes.

After creation, a SignedObject is itself typically serialized for storage or transmission to another Java thread or process. Once the SignedObject is reconstituted, the integrity of the object it contains can be verified by calling verify() and supplying the PublicKey of the signer and a Signature that performs the verification. Whether or not verification is performed or is successful, getObject() can be called to deserialize and return the wrapped object.

Object — SignedObject ··· Serializable

```
public final class SignedObject implements Serializable {
// Public Constructors
    public SignedObject(Serializable object, PrivateKey signingKey, Signature signingEngine)
        throws java.io.IOException, InvalidKeyException, SignatureException;
// Public Instance Methods
    public String getAlgorithm();
    public Object getObject() throws java.io.IOException, ClassNotFoundException;
    public byte[ ] getSignature();
    public boolean verify(PublicKey verificationKey, Signature verificationEngine) throws InvalidKeyException,
        SignatureException;
}
```

Signer — Java 1.1; Deprecated in Java 1.2

java.security — *serializable*

This deprecated class was used in Java 1.1 to represent an entity or Principal that has an associated PrivateKey that enables it to create digital signatures. As of Java 1.2, this class and the related Identity and IdentityScope classes have been replaced by KeyStore and java.security.cert.Certificate. See also Identity.

Object — Identity — Signer
Principal Serializable

```
public abstract class Signer extends Identity {
// Public Constructors
```

```
    public Signer(String name);
    public Signer(String name, IdentityScope scope) throws KeyManagementException;
// Protected Constructors
    protected Signer();
// Public Instance Methods
    public PrivateKey getPrivateKey();
    public final void setKeyPair(KeyPair pair) throws InvalidParameterException, KeyException;
// Public Methods Overriding Identity
    public String toString();
}
```

UnrecoverableKeyException — Java 1.2

java.security — *serializable checked*

This exception is thrown if a Key cannot be retrieved from a KeyStore. This often occurs when an incorrect password is used.

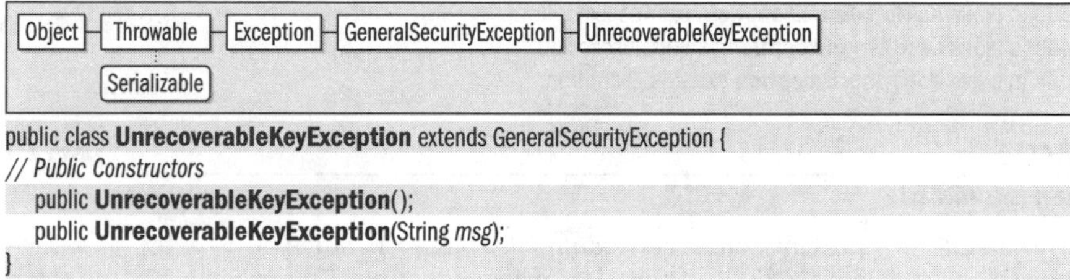


```
public class UnrecoverableKeyException extends GeneralSecurityException {
// Public Constructors
    public UnrecoverableKeyException();
    public UnrecoverableKeyException(String msg);
}
```

Thrown By: KeyStore.getKey(), KeyStoreSpi.engineGetKey(), javax.net.ssl.KeyManagerFactory.init(), javax.net.ssl.KeyManagerFactorySpi.engineInit()

UnresolvedPermission — Java 1.2

java.security — *serializable permission*

This class is used internally to provide a mechanism for delayed resolution of permissions. An UnresolvedPermission holds a textual representation of a Permission object that can later be used to create the actual Permission object. Applications never need to use this class.

Object — Permission — UnresolvedPermission
Guard | Serializable | Serializable

```
public final class UnresolvedPermission extends java.security.Permission implements Serializable {
// Public Constructors
    public UnresolvedPermission(String type, String name, String actions, java.security.cert.Certificate[ ] certs);
// Public Methods Overriding Permission
    public boolean equals(Object obj);
    public String getActions();
    public int hashCode();
    public boolean implies(java.security.Permission p);                    constant
    public PermissionCollection newPermissionCollection();
    public String toString();
}
```

Package java.security.acl — Java 1.1

The java.security.acl package defines, but does not implement, an incomplete framework for working with access control lists (ACLs). This package was added in Java 1.1, but has been superseded in Java 1.2 by the access-control mechanisms of the java.security package. In particular, see the Permission and Policy classes of that package. The use of this package is not recommended.

Interfaces:

```
public interface Acl extends Owner;
public interface AclEntry extends Cloneable;
public interface Group extends java.security.Principal;
public interface Owner;
public interface Permission;
```

Exceptions:

```
public class AclNotFoundException extends Exception;
public class LastOwnerException extends Exception;
public class NotOwnerException extends Exception;
```

Acl — Java 1.1

java.security.acl

This interface represents an *access control list*, or ACL. An ACL is a list of AclEntry objects; most of the methods of this class manage that list. The exception is the checkPermission() method that tests whether this ACL grants a specified java.security.acl.Permission to a specified java.security.Principal. Note that Acl extends Owner. The methods of the Owner interface maintain a list of ACL owners. Only owners are allowed to modify an ACL.

```
public interface Acl extends Owner {
// Public Instance Methods
   public abstract boolean addEntry(java.security.Principal caller, AclEntry entry) throws NotOwnerException;
   public abstract boolean checkPermission(java.security.Principal principal,
                                           java.security.acl.Permission permission);
   public abstract java.util.Enumeration entries();
   public abstract String getName();
   public abstract java.util.Enumeration getPermissions(java.security.Principal user);
   public abstract boolean removeEntry(java.security.Principal caller, AclEntry entry) throws NotOwnerException;
   public abstract void setName(java.security.Principal caller, String name) throws NotOwnerException;
   public abstract String toString();
}
```

AclEntry — Java 1.1

java.security.acl — *cloneable*

This interface defines a single entry of an ACL. Each AclEntry represents a set of java.security.acl.Permission objects either granted or denied to a given java.security.Principal. By default, an AclEntry represents permissions granted to the principal. Call setNegativePermissions() if you want the AclEntry to represent a set of permissions to be denied.

Cloneable ··· AclEntry

```
public interface AclEntry extends Cloneable {
// Public Instance Methods
   public abstract boolean addPermission(java.security.acl.Permission permission);
   public abstract boolean checkPermission(java.security.acl.Permission permission);
   public abstract Object clone();
   public abstract java.security.Principal getPrincipal();
   public abstract boolean isNegative();
   public abstract java.util.Enumeration permissions();
   public abstract boolean removePermission(java.security.acl.Permission permission);
   public abstract void setNegativePermissions();
   public abstract boolean setPrincipal(java.security.Principal user);
   public abstract String toString();
}
```

Passed To: Acl.{addEntry(), removeEntry()}

AclNotFoundException — Java 1.1

java.security.acl — *serializable checked*

This signals that the specified Acl could not be found. Note that none of the interfaces in java.security.acl throw this exception; it is provided for the benefit of Acl implementations.

Object — Throwable — Exception — AclNotFoundException
Serializable

```
public class AclNotFoundException extends Exception {
// Public Constructors
   public AclNotFoundException();
}
```

Group — Java 1.1

java.security.acl

This interface represents a set, or group, of java.security.Principal objects. The methods of the interface serve to manage the membership of the group. Note that Group extends the Principal interface, and, therefore, you can use a Group object wherever you would use a Principal object in this package.

Principal ··· Group

```
public interface Group extends java.security.Principal {
// Public Instance Methods
   public abstract boolean addMember(java.security.Principal user);
   public abstract boolean isMember(java.security.Principal member);
   public abstract java.util.Enumeration members();
   public abstract boolean removeMember(java.security.Principal user);
}
```

LastOwnerException

Java 1.1

java.security.acl *serializable checked*

This signals that an Acl or Owner has only one Principal remaining in its ownership list and that this single owner cannot be removed.

Object — Throwable — Exception — LastOwnerException
Serializable

```
public class LastOwnerException extends Exception {
// Public Constructors
    public LastOwnerException();
}
```

Thrown By: Owner.deleteOwner()

NotOwnerException

Java 1.1

java.security.acl *serializable checked*

This exception is thrown by various methods of Acl and Owner when they are called by a Principal that is not an owner.

Object — Throwable — Exception — NotOwnerException
Serializable

```
public class NotOwnerException extends Exception {
// Public Constructors
    public NotOwnerException();
}
```

Thrown By: Acl.{addEntry(), removeEntry(), setName()}, Owner.{addOwner(), deleteOwner()}

Owner

Java 1.1

java.security.acl

This interface represents the owner or owners of an ACL. The interface defines methods for managing and checking membership in the list of owners.

```
public interface Owner {
// Public Instance Methods
    public abstract boolean addOwner(java.security.Principal caller, java.security.Principal owner)
        throws NotOwnerException;
    public abstract boolean deleteOwner(java.security.Principal caller, java.security.Principal owner)
        throws NotOwnerException, LastOwnerException;
    public abstract boolean isOwner(java.security.Principal owner);
}
```

Implementations: Acl

Permission

Java 1.1

java.security.acl

This interface represents a permission. The meaning of the permission is entirely up to the implementation. Do not confuse this interface with the newer java.security.Permission class. Also note that this interface does not have the implies() method of java.security.Permission and is therefore significantly less versatile.

```
public interface Permission {
// Public Instance Methods
    public abstract boolean equals(Object another);
    public abstract String toString();
}
```

Passed To: Acl.checkPermission(), AclEntry.{addPermission(), checkPermission(), removePermission()}

Package java.security.cert — Java 1.2

The java.security.cert package contains classes for working with identity certificates, certificate chains (also known as certification paths), and certificate revocation lists (CRLs). It defines generic Certificate and CRL classes as well as X509Certificate and X509CRL classes that provide full support for standard X.509 certificates and CRLs. The CertPath class represents a certificate chain, and CertPathValidator provides the ability to validate a certificate chain. The CertificateFactory class serves as a certificate parser, providing the ability to convert a stream of bytes (or the base64 encoding of those bytes) into a Certificate, a CertPath, or a CRL object. In addition to the algorithm-independent API of CertificateFactory, this package also defines low-level, algorithm-specific classes for working with certificate chains using the PKIX standards.

This package replaces the deprecated java.security.Certificate interface and the deprecated javax.security.cert package used by early versions of the JAAS API before javax.security.auth and its subpackages were added to the core Java platform.

Interfaces:

public interface **CertPathBuilderResult** extends Cloneable;
public interface **CertPathParameters** extends Cloneable;
public interface **CertPathValidatorResult** extends Cloneable;
public interface **CertSelector** extends Cloneable;
public interface **CertStoreParameters** extends Cloneable;
public interface **CRLSelector** extends Cloneable;
public interface **PolicyNode**;
public interface **X509Extension**;

Classes:

public abstract class **Certificate** implements Serializable;
    └ public abstract class **X509Certificate** extends Certificate implements X509Extension;
public class **CertificateFactory**;
public abstract class **CertificateFactorySpi**;
public abstract class **CertPath** implements Serializable;
public class **CertPathBuilder**;
public abstract class **CertPathBuilderSpi**;
public class **CertPathValidator**;
public abstract class **CertPathValidatorSpi**;
public class **CertStore**;
public abstract class **CertStoreSpi**;
public class **CollectionCertStoreParameters** implements CertStoreParameters;
public abstract class **CRL**;
    └ public abstract class **X509CRL** extends CRL implements X509Extension;

public class **LDAPCertStoreParameters** implements CertStoreParameters;
public abstract class **PKIXCertPathChecker** implements Cloneable;
public class **PKIXCertPathValidatorResult** implements CertPathValidatorResult;
　└ public class **PKIXCertPathBuilderResult** extends PKIXCertPathValidatorResult implements CertPathBuilderResult;
public class **PKIXParameters** implements CertPathParameters;
　└ public class **PKIXBuilderParameters** extends PKIXParameters;
public final class **PolicyQualifierInfo**;
public class **TrustAnchor**;
public class **X509CertSelector** implements CertSelector;
public abstract class **X509CRLEntry** implements X509Extension;
public class **X509CRLSelector** implements CRLSelector;

Protected Inner Classes:

protected static class **Certificate.CertificateRep** implements Serializable;
protected static class **CertPath.CertPathRep** implements Serializable;

Exceptions:

public class **CertificateException** extends java.security.GeneralSecurityException;
　└ public class **CertificateEncodingException** extends CertificateException;
　└ public class **CertificateExpiredException** extends CertificateException;
　└ public class **CertificateNotYetValidException** extends CertificateException;
　└ public class **CertificateParsingException** extends CertificateException;
public class **CertPathBuilderException** extends java.security.GeneralSecurityException;
public class **CertPathValidatorException** extends java.security.GeneralSecurityException;
public class **CertStoreException** extends java.security.GeneralSecurityException;
public class **CRLException** extends java.security.GeneralSecurityException;

Certificate — Java 1.2

java.security.cert — *serializable*

n

This abstract class represents an public-key (or identity) certificate. A *certificate* is an object that contains the name of an entity and a public key for that entity. Certificates are issued by, and bear the digital signature of, a (presumably trusted) third party, typically a *certificate authority* (CA). By issuing and signing the certificate, the CA is certifying that, based on their research, the entity named on the certificate really is who they say they are and that the public key in the certificate really does belong to that entity. Sometimes the signer of a certificate is not a trusted CA, and the certificate is accompanied by the signer's certificate which may be signed by a CA, or by another untrusted intermediary who provides his or her own certificate. A chain of such certificates is known as a certification path. See CertPath for further details.

Use a CertificateFactory to parse a stream of bytes into a Certificate object; getEncoded() reverses this process. Use verify() to verify the digital signature of the entity that issued the certificate. If the signature cannot be verified, the certificate should not be trusted. Call getPublicKey() to obtain the java.security.PublicKey of the subject of the certificate. Note that this class does not define a method for obtaining the Principal that is associated with the PublicKey. That functionality is dependent on the type of the certificate. See X509Certificate.getSubjectDN(), for example.

Do not confuse this class with the java.security.Certificate interface defined in Java 1.1 and deprecated in Java 1.2.

Object — Certificate ··· Serializable

```
public abstract class Certificate implements Serializable {
// Protected Constructors
   protected Certificate(String type);
// Inner Classes
1.3 protected static class CertificateRep implements Serializable;
// Public Instance Methods
   public abstract byte[ ] getEncoded( ) throws java.security.cert.CertificateEncodingException;
   public abstract java.security.PublicKey getPublicKey( );
   public final String getType( );
   public abstract void verify(java.security.PublicKey key) throws java.security.cert.CertificateException,
        java.security.NoSuchAlgorithmException, java.security.InvalidKeyException,
        java.security.NoSuchProviderException, java.security.SignatureException;
   public abstract void verify(java.security.PublicKey key, String sigProvider)
        throws java.security.cert.CertificateException, java.security.NoSuchAlgorithmException,
        java.security.InvalidKeyException, java.security.NoSuchProviderException, java.security.SignatureException;
// Public Methods Overriding Object
   public boolean equals(Object other);
   public int hashCode( );
   public abstract String toString( );
// Protected Instance Methods
1.3 protected Object writeReplace( ) throws java.io.ObjectStreamException;
}
```

Subclasses: java.security.cert.X509Certificate

Passed To: Too many methods to list.

Returned By: java.net.JarURLConnection.getCertificates(), java.security.CodeSource.getCertificates(), java.security.KeyStore.{getCertificate(), getCertificateChain()}, java.security.KeyStoreSpi.{engineGetCertificate(), engineGetCertificateChain()}, CertificateFactory.generateCertificate(), CertificateFactorySpi.engineGenerateCertificate(), java.util.jar.JarEntry.getCertificates(), javax.net.ssl.HandshakeCompletedEvent.{getLocalCertificates(), getPeerCertificates()}, javax.net.ssl.HttpsURLConnection.{getLocalCertificates(), getServerCertificates()}, javax.net.ssl.SSLSession.{getLocalCertificates(), getPeerCertificates()}

Certificate.CertificateRep — Java 1.3

java.security.cert — *serializable*

This protected inner class provides an alternate representation of a certificate that can be used for serialization purposes by the writeReplace() method of some Certificate implementations. Applications do not typically need this class.

```
protected static class Certificate.CertificateRep implements Serializable {
// Protected Constructors
   protected CertificateRep(String type, byte[ ] data);
// Protected Instance Methods
   protected Object readResolve( ) throws java.io.ObjectStreamException;
}
```

CertificateEncodingException **Java 1.2**

java.security.cert ***serializable checked***

This signals an error while attempting to encode a certificate.

Object ─ Throwable ─ Exception ─ GeneralSecurityException ─ CertificateException ─ CertificateEncodingException
Serializable

```
public class CertificateEncodingException extends java.security.cert.CertificateException {
// Public Constructors
   public CertificateEncodingException();
   public CertificateEncodingException(String message);
}
```

Thrown By: java.security.cert.Certificate.getEncoded(), CertPath.getEncoded(), java.security.cert.X509Certificate.getTBSCertificate()

CertificateException **Java 1.2**

java.security.cert ***serializable checked***

This class is the superclass of several more specific exception types that may be thrown when working with certificates.

Object ─ Throwable ─ Exception ─ GeneralSecurityException ─ CertificateException
Serializable

```
public class CertificateException extends java.security.GeneralSecurityException {
// Public Constructors
   public CertificateException();
   public CertificateException(String msg);
}
```

Subclasses: java.security.cert.CertificateEncodingException, java.security.cert.CertificateExpiredException, java.security.cert.CertificateNotYetValidException, java.security.cert.CertificateParsingException

Thrown By: Too many methods to list.

CertificateExpiredException **Java 1.2**

java.security.cert ***serializable checked***

This signals that a certificate has expired or will have expired by a specified date.

Object ─ Throwable ─ Exception ─ GeneralSecurityException ─ CertificateException ─ CertificateExpiredException
Serializable

```
public class CertificateExpiredException extends java.security.cert.CertificateException {
// Public Constructors
   public CertificateExpiredException();
   public CertificateExpiredException(String message);
}
```

Thrown By: java.security.cert.X509Certificate.checkValidity()

CertificateFactory **Java 1.2**

java.security.cert

This class defines methods for parsing certificates, certificate chains (certification paths) and certificate revocation lists (CRLs) from byte streams. Obtain a CertificateFactory by calling one of the static getInstance() factory methods and specifying the type of certificate or CRL to be parsed, and, optionally, the desired service provider to perform the parsing. The default "SUN" provider defines only a single "X.509" certificate type, so you typically obtain a CertificateFactory with this code:

```
CertificateFactory certFactory = CertificateFactory.getInstance("X.509");
```

Once you have obtained a CertificateFactory for the desired type of certificate, call generateCertificate() to parse a Certificate from a specified byte stream, or call generateCertificates() to parse a group of unrelated certificates (i.e., certificates that do not form a certificate chain) from a stream and return them as a Collection of Certificate objects. Similarly, call generateCRL() to parse a single CRL object from a stream, and call generateCRLs() to parse a Collection of CRL objects from the stream. These CertificateFactory methods read to the end of the specified stream. If the stream supports mark() and reset(), however, the CertificateFactory resets the stream to the position after the end of the last certificate or CRL read. If you specified a certificate type of "X.509", the Certificate and CRL objects returned by a CertificateFactory can be cast safely to X509Certificate and X509CRL. A certificate factory for X.509 certificates can parse certificates encoded in binary or printable hexadecimal form. If the certificate is in hexadecimal form, it must begin with the string "-----BEGIN CERTIFICATE-----" and end with the string "-----END CERTIFICATE-----".

The generateCertPath() methods return a CertPath object representing a certificate chain. These methods can create a CertPath object from a List of Certificate objects or by reading the chained certificates from a stream. Specify the encoding of the certificate chain by passing the name of the encoding standard to generateCertPath(). The default "SUN" provider supports the "PKCS7" and "PkiPath" encodings. getCertPathEncodings() returns an Iterator of the encodings supported by the current provider. The first encoding returned by the iterator is the default used when no encoding is explicitly specified.

```
public class CertificateFactory {
// Protected Constructors
    protected CertificateFactory(CertificateFactorySpi certFacSpi, java.security.Provider provider, String type);
// Public Class Methods
    public static final CertificateFactory getInstance(String type) throws java.security.cert.CertificateException;
1.4 public static final CertificateFactory getInstance(String type, java.security.Provider provider)
        throws java.security.cert.CertificateException;
    public static final CertificateFactory getInstance(String type, String provider)
        throws java.security.cert.CertificateException, java.security.NoSuchProviderException;
// Public Instance Methods
    public final java.security.cert.Certificate generateCertificate(java.io.InputStream inStream)
        throws java.security.cert.CertificateException;
    public final java.util.Collection generateCertificates(java.io.InputStream inStream)
        throws java.security.cert.CertificateException;
1.4 public final CertPath generateCertPath(java.util.List certificates) throws java.security.cert.CertificateException;
1.4 public final CertPath generateCertPath(java.io.InputStream inStream)
        throws java.security.cert.CertificateException;
1.4 public final CertPath generateCertPath(java.io.InputStream inStream, String encoding)
        throws java.security.cert.CertificateException;
```

java.security.*

```
    public final CRL generateCRL(java.io.InputStream inStream) throws CRLException;
    public final java.util.Collection generateCRLs(java.io.InputStream inStream) throws CRLException;
1.4 public final java.util.Iterator getCertPathEncodings();
    public final java.security.Provider getProvider();
    public final String getType();
}
```

Returned By: CertificateFactory.getInstance()

CertificateFactorySpi — Java 1.2

java.security.cert

This abstract class defines the service provider interface, or SPI, for the CertificateFactory class. A security provider must implement this class for each type of certificate it wishes to support. Applications never need to use or subclass this class.

```
public abstract class CertificateFactorySpi {
// Public Constructors
    public CertificateFactorySpi();
// Public Instance Methods
    public abstract java.security.cert.Certificate engineGenerateCertificate(java.io.InputStream inStream)
        throws java.security.cert.CertificateException;
    public abstract java.util.Collection engineGenerateCertificates(java.io.InputStream inStream)
        throws java.security.cert.CertificateException;
1.4 public CertPath engineGenerateCertPath(java.util.List certificates) throws java.security.cert.CertificateException;
1.4 public CertPath engineGenerateCertPath(java.io.InputStream inStream)
        throws java.security.cert.CertificateException;
1.4 public CertPath engineGenerateCertPath(java.io.InputStream inStream, String encoding)
        throws java.security.cert.CertificateException;
    public abstract CRL engineGenerateCRL(java.io.InputStream inStream) throws CRLException;
    public abstract java.util.Collection engineGenerateCRLs(java.io.InputStream inStream) throws CRLException;
1.4 public java.util.Iterator engineGetCertPathEncodings();
}
```

Passed To: CertificateFactory.CertificateFactory()

CertificateNotYetValidException — Java 1.2

java.security.cert — *serializable checked*

This signals that a certificate is not yet valid or will not yet be valid on a specified date.

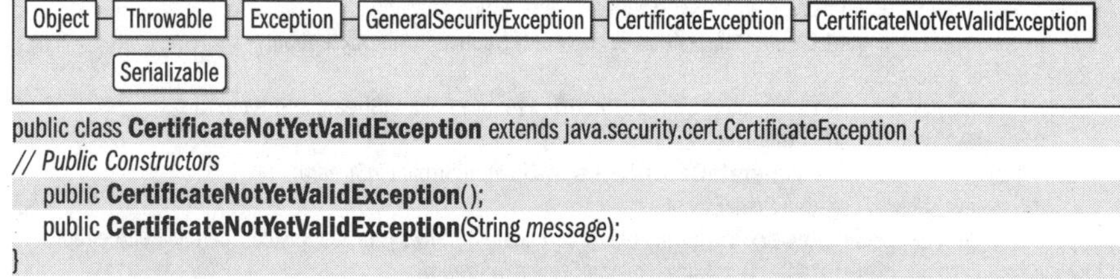


```
public class CertificateNotYetValidException extends java.security.cert.CertificateException {
// Public Constructors
    public CertificateNotYetValidException();
    public CertificateNotYetValidException(String message);
}
```

Thrown By: java.security.cert.X509Certificate.checkValidity()

CertificateParsingException — Java 1.2

java.security.cert — *serializable checked*

This signals an error or other problem while parsing a certificate.

Object → Throwable → Exception → GeneralSecurityException → CertificateException → CertificateParsingException
(Throwable implements Serializable)

```
public class CertificateParsingException extends java.security.cert.CertificateException {
// Public Constructors
   public CertificateParsingException();
   public CertificateParsingException(String message);
}
```

Thrown By: java.security.cert.X509Certificate.{getExtendedKeyUsage(), getIssuerAlternativeNames(), getSubjectAlternativeNames()}

CertPath — Java 1.4

java.security.cert — *serializable*

A CertPath is a immutable sequence or chain of certificates that establishes a "certification path" from an unknown "end entity" to a known and trusted Certificate Authority or "trust anchor". Use a CertPathValidator to validate a certificate chain and establish trust in the public key presented in the certificate of the end entity.

getType() returns the type of the certificates in the CertPath. For X.509 certificate chains (the only type supported by the default "SUN" provider) this method returns "X.509". getCertificates() returns a java.util.List object that contains the Certificate objects that comprise the chain. For X.509 chains, the list contains X509Certificate objects. Also, for X.509 certificate paths, the List returned by getCertificates() starts with the certificate of of the end entity, and ends with a certificate signed by the trust anchor. The signer of any certificate but the last must be the subject of the next certificate in the List. If the end entity presents a certificate that is directly signed by a trust anchor (which is a not uncommon occurrence) then the List returned by getCertificates() consists of only that single certificate. Note that the list of certificates does not include the certificate of the trust anchor. The public keys of trusted CAs must be known by the system in advance. In Sun's JDK implementation, the public-key certificates of trusted CAs are stored in the file *jre/lib/security/cacerts*.

CertPath objects can be created with a CertificateFactory, or at a lower level with a CertPathBuilder object. A CertificateFactory can parse or decode a CertPath object from a binary stream. The getEncoded() methods reverse the process and encode a CertPath into an array of bytes. getEncodings() returns the encodings supported for a CertPath. The first returned encoding name is the default one, but you can use any supported encoding by using the one-argument version of getEncoded(). The default "SUN" provider supports encodings named "PKCS7" and "PkiPath".

CertPath objects are immutable as is the List object returned by getCertificates() and the Certificate objects contained in the list. Furthermore, all CertPath methods are thread-safe.

Object → CertPath ··· Serializable

```
public abstract class CertPath implements Serializable {
// Protected Constructors
   protected CertPath(String type);
// Inner Classes
   protected static class CertPathRep implements Serializable;
```

```
// Public Instance Methods
   public abstract java.util.List getCertificates();
   public abstract byte[ ] getEncoded() throws java.security.cert.CertificateEncodingException;
   public abstract byte[ ] getEncoded(String encoding) throws java.security.cert.CertificateEncodingException;
   public abstract java.util.Iterator getEncodings();
   public String getType();
// Public Methods Overriding Object
   public boolean equals(Object other);
   public int hashCode();
   public String toString();
// Protected Instance Methods
   protected Object writeReplace() throws java.io.ObjectStreamException;
}
```

Passed To: CertPathValidator.validate(), CertPathValidatorException.CertPathValidatorException(), CertPathValidatorSpi.engineValidate(), PKIXCertPathBuilderResult.PKIXCertPathBuilderResult()

Returned By: CertificateFactory.generateCertPath(), CertificateFactorySpi.engineGenerateCertPath(), CertPathBuilderResult.getCertPath(), CertPathValidatorException.getCertPath(), PKIXCertPathBuilderResult.getCertPath()

CertPath.CertPathRep — Java 1.4

java.security.cert — *serializable*

This protected inner class defines an implementation-independent representation of a CertPath for serialization purposes. Applications never need to use this class.

```
protected static class CertPath.CertPathRep implements Serializable {
// Protected Constructors
   protected CertPathRep(String type, byte[ ] data);
// Protected Instance Methods
   protected Object readResolve() throws java.io.ObjectStreamException;
}
```

CertPathBuilder — Java 1.4

java.security.cert

CertPathBuilder attempts to build a certification path from a specified certificate to a trust anchor. Unlike the CertificateFactory.generateCertPath() method, which might be used by a server to parse a certificate chain presented to it by a client, this class is used to create a new certificate chain, and might be used by a client that needs to send a certificate chain to a server. The CertPathBuilder API is provider-based and algorithm-independent, although the use of any algorithms other than the "PKIX" standards (which work with X.509 certificate chains) require appropriate external implementations of CertPathParameters and CertPathBuilderResult.

Obtain a CertPathBuilder object by calling one of the static getInstance() methods, specifying the desired algorithm and, optionally, the desired provider. The "PKIX" algorithm is the only one supported by the default "SUN" provider, and is the only one that has the required algorithm-specific classes defined by this package. Once you have a CertPathBuilder, you create a CertPath object by passing a CertPathParameters object to the build() method. CertPathParameters is a marker interfaces that defines no method of its own, so you must use an algorithm-specific implementation such as PKIXBuilderParameters to supply the information required to build a CertPath. The build() method returns a CertPathBuilderResult object. Use the getCertPath() method of this returned object to obtain the CertPath that was built. The algorithm-specific implementation PKIXCertPathBuilderResult has additional methods that return further algorithm-specific results.

```
public class CertPathBuilder {
// Protected Constructors
    protected CertPathBuilder(CertPathBuilderSpi builderSpi, java.security.Provider provider, String algorithm);
// Public Class Methods
    public static final String getDefaultType();
    public static CertPathBuilder getInstance(String algorithm) throws java.security.NoSuchAlgorithmException;
    public static CertPathBuilder getInstance(String algorithm, String provider)
        throws java.security.NoSuchAlgorithmException, java.security.NoSuchProviderException;
    public static CertPathBuilder getInstance(String algorithm, java.security.Provider provider)
        throws java.security.NoSuchAlgorithmException;
// Public Instance Methods
    public final CertPathBuilderResult build(CertPathParameters params) throws CertPathBuilderException,
        java.security.InvalidAlgorithmParameterException;
    public final String getAlgorithm();
    public final java.security.Provider getProvider();
}
```

Returned By: CertPathBuilder.getInstance()

CertPathBuilderException — Java 1.4

java.security.cert — ***serializable checked***

This signals a problem while building a certification path with CertPathBuilder.

Object — Throwable — Exception — GeneralSecurityException — CertPathBuilderException
Serializable

```
public class CertPathBuilderException extends java.security.GeneralSecurityException {
// Public Constructors
    public CertPathBuilderException();
    public CertPathBuilderException(Throwable cause);
    public CertPathBuilderException(String msg);
    public CertPathBuilderException(String msg, Throwable cause);
// Public Methods Overriding Throwable
    public Throwable getCause();                                      default:null
    public String getMessage();                                       default:null
    public void printStackTrace();
    public void printStackTrace(java.io.PrintWriter pw);
    public void printStackTrace(java.io.PrintStream ps);
    public String toString();
}
```

Thrown By: CertPathBuilder.build(), CertPathBuilderSpi.engineBuild()

CertPathBuilderResult — Java 1.4

java.security.cert — ***cloneable***

An object of this type is returned by the build() method of a CertPathBuilder. The getCertPath() method returns the CertPath object that was built; this method will never return null. The algorithm-specific PKIXCertPathBuilderResult implementation defines other methods to return additional information about the path that was built.

Cloneable — CertPathBuilderResult

```
public interface CertPathBuilderResult extends Cloneable {
// Public Instance Methods
```


java.security.*

```
    public abstract Object clone();
    public abstract CertPath getCertPath();
}
```

Implementations: PKIXCertPathBuilderResult

Returned By: CertPathBuilder.build(), CertPathBuilderSpi.engineBuild()

CertPathBuilderSpi — Java 1.4

java.security.cert

This abstract class defines the Service Provider Interface for the CertPathBuilder. Security providers must implement this interface, but applications never need to use it.

```
public abstract class CertPathBuilderSpi {
// Public Constructors
    public CertPathBuilderSpi();
// Public Instance Methods
    public abstract CertPathBuilderResult engineBuild(CertPathParameters params) throws CertPathBuilderException,
        java.security.InvalidAlgorithmParameterException;
}
```

Passed To: CertPathBuilder.CertPathBuilder()

CertPathParameters — Java 1.4

java.security.cert — *cloneable*

CertPathParameters is a marker interface for objects that hold parameters (such as the set of trust anchors) for validating or building a certification path with CertPathValidator and CertPathBuilder. It defines no methods of its own, but requires that all implementations include a working clone() method. You must use an algorithm-specific implementation of this interface, such as PKIXParameters or PKIXBuilderParameters when validating or building a CertPath, and it is rarely useful to work with this interface directly.

Cloneable ··· CertPathParameters

```
public interface CertPathParameters extends Cloneable {
// Public Instance Methods
    public abstract Object clone();
}
```

Implementations: PKIXParameters

Passed To: CertPathBuilder.build(), CertPathBuilderSpi.engineBuild(), CertPathValidator.validate(), CertPathValidatorSpi.engineValidate()

CertPathValidator — Java 1.4

java.security.cert

This class validates certificate chains, establishing a chain of trust from the end entity to a trust anchor, and thereby establishing the validity of the public key presented in the end entity's certificate. The CertPathValidator is provider-based and algorithm-independent. To obtain a CertPathValidator instance, call one of the static getInstance() methods specifying the name of the desired validation algorithm and, optionally, the provider to use. The "PKIX" algorithm for validating X.509 certificates is the only one supported by the default "SUN" provider.

Once you have a CertPathValidator object, you can use it to validate certificate chains by passing the CertPath object to be validated to the validate() method along with a

CertPathParameters object that specifies valid trust anchors and other validation parameters. CertPathParameters is simply a marker interface, and you must use an application-specific implementation such as PKIXParameters. If validation fails, the validate() method throws a CertPathValidatorException which may include the index in the chain of the certificate that failed to validate. Otherwise, if validation is successful, the validate() method returns a CertPathValidatorResult. If you are interested in the details of the validation (such as the trust anchor that was used or the public key of the end entity), you may cast this returned value to an algorithm-specific subtype such as PKIXCertPathValidatorResult and use its methods to find out more about the result.

```
public class CertPathValidator {
// Protected Constructors
   protected CertPathValidator(CertPathValidatorSpi validatorSpi, java.security.Provider provider, String algorithm);
// Public Class Methods
   public static final String getDefaultType();
   public static CertPathValidator getInstance(String algorithm) throws java.security.NoSuchAlgorithmException;
   public static CertPathValidator getInstance(String algorithm, String provider)
       throws java.security.NoSuchAlgorithmException, java.security.NoSuchProviderException;
   public static CertPathValidator getInstance(String algorithm, java.security.Provider provider)
       throws java.security.NoSuchAlgorithmException;
// Public Instance Methods
   public final String getAlgorithm();
   public final java.security.Provider getProvider();
   public final CertPathValidatorResult validate(CertPath certPath, CertPathParameters params)
       throws CertPathValidatorException, java.security.InvalidAlgorithmParameterException;
}
```

Returned By: CertPathValidator.getInstance()

CertPathValidatorException — Java 1.4

java.security.cert — ***serializable checked***

This signals a problem while validating a certificate chain with a CertPathValidator. getCertPath() returns the CertPath object that was being validated, and getIndex() returns the index within the path of the certificate that caused the exception (or –1 if that information is not available).

Object → Throwable → Exception → GeneralSecurityException → CertPathValidatorException
Throwable ⋯ Serializable

```
public class CertPathValidatorException extends java.security.GeneralSecurityException {
// Public Constructors
   public CertPathValidatorException();
   public CertPathValidatorException(Throwable cause);
   public CertPathValidatorException(String msg);
   public CertPathValidatorException(String msg, Throwable cause);
   public CertPathValidatorException(String msg, Throwable cause, CertPath certPath, int index);
// Public Instance Methods
   public CertPath getCertPath();                                         default:null
   public int getIndex();                                                  default:-1
// Public Methods Overriding Throwable
   public Throwable getCause();                                           default:null
   public String getMessage();                                            default:null
   public void printStackTrace();
   public void printStackTrace(java.io.PrintStream ps);
   public void printStackTrace(java.io.PrintWriter pw);
```

java.security.*

```
    public String toString();
}
```

Thrown By: CertPathValidator.validate(), CertPathValidatorSpi.engineValidate(), PKIXCertPathChecker.{check(), init()}

CertPathValidatorResult — Java 1.4

java.security.cert — *cloneable*

This marker interface defines the type of the object returned by the validate() method of a CertPathValidator, but does not define any of the contents of that object, other to specify that it must be Cloneable. If you want any details about the results of validating a CertPath, you must cast the return value of validate() to an algorithm-specific types implementation of this interface, such as PKIXCertPathValidatorResult.

Cloneable ··· CertPathValidatorResult

```
public interface CertPathValidatorResult extends Cloneable {
// Public Instance Methods
    public abstract Object clone();
}
```

Implementations: PKIXCertPathValidatorResult

Returned By: CertPathValidator.validate(), CertPathValidatorSpi.engineValidate()

CertPathValidatorSpi — Java 1.4

java.security.cert

This abstract class defines the Service Provider Interface for the CertPathValidator class. Security providers must implement this interface, but applications never need to use it.

```
public abstract class CertPathValidatorSpi {
// Public Constructors
    public CertPathValidatorSpi();
// Public Instance Methods
    public abstract CertPathValidatorResult engineValidate(CertPath certPath, CertPathParameters params)
        throws CertPathValidatorException, java.security.InvalidAlgorithmParameterException;
}
```

Passed To: CertPathValidator.CertPathValidator()

CertSelector — Java 1.4

java.security.cert — *cloneable*

This interface defines an API for determining whether a Certificate meets some criteria. Implementations are used to specify criteria by which a certificate or certificates should be selected from a CertStore object. The match() method should examine the Certificate it is passed and return true if it "matches" based on whatever criteria the implementation defines. See X509CertSelector for an implementation that works with X.509 certificates. See CRLSelector for a similar interface for use when selecting CRL objects from a CertStore.

Cloneable ··· CertSelector

```
public interface CertSelector extends Cloneable {
// Public Instance Methods
    public abstract Object clone();
```

```
    public abstract boolean match(java.security.cert.Certificate cert);
}
```

Implementations: X509CertSelector

Passed To: CertStore.getCertificates(), CertStoreSpi.engineGetCertificates(), PKIXBuilderParameters.PKIXBuilderParameters(), PKIXParameters.setTargetCertConstraints()

Returned By: PKIXParameters.getTargetCertConstraints()

CertStore — Java 1.4

java.security.cert

A CertStore object is a repository for Certificate and CRL objects. You may query a CertStore for a java.util.Collection of Certificate or CRL objects that match specified criteria by passing a CertSelector or CRLSelector to getCertificates() or getCRLs(). A CertStore is conceptually similar to a java.security.KeyStore, but there are significant differences in how the two classes are intended to be used. A KeyStore is designed to store a relatively small local collection of private keys and trusted certificates. A CertStore, however, may represent a large public database (in the form of an LDAP server, for example) of untrusted certificates.

Obtain a CertStore object by calling a getInstance() method and specifying the name of the desired CertStore type and a CertStoreParameters object that is specific to that type. Optionally, you may also specify the desired provider of your CertStore object. The default "SUN" provider defines two CertStore types, named "LDAP" and "Collection", which you should use with LDAPCertStoreParameters and CollectionCertStoreParameters objects, respectively. The "LDAP" type obtains certificates and CRLs from a network LDAP server, and the "Collection" type obtains them from a a specified Collection object.

The CertStore class may be directly useful to applications that want to query a LDAP server for certificates. It is also used by PKIXParameters.addCertStore() and PKIXParameters.setCertStores() to specify a source of certificates to by used by the CertPathBuilder and CertPathValidator classes.

All public methods of CertStore are thread-safe.

```
public class CertStore {
// Protected Constructors
    protected CertStore(CertStoreSpi storeSpi, java.security.Provider provider, String type,
                        CertStoreParameters params);
// Public Class Methods
    public static final String getDefaultType();
    public static CertStore getInstance(String type, CertStoreParameters params)
        throws java.security.InvalidAlgorithmParameterException, java.security.NoSuchAlgorithmException;
    public static CertStore getInstance(String type, CertStoreParameters params, String provider)
        throws java.security.InvalidAlgorithmParameterException, java.security.NoSuchAlgorithmException,
        java.security.NoSuchProviderException;
    public static CertStore getInstance(String type, CertStoreParameters params, java.security.Provider provider)
        throws java.security.NoSuchAlgorithmException, java.security.InvalidAlgorithmParameterException;
// Public Instance Methods
    public final java.util.Collection getCertificates(CertSelector selector) throws CertStoreException;
    public final CertStoreParameters getCertStoreParameters();
    public final java.util.Collection getCRLs(CRLSelector selector) throws CertStoreException;
    public final java.security.Provider getProvider();
    public final String getType();
}
```

Passed To: PKIXParameters.addCertStore()

Returned By: CertStore.getInstance()

CertStoreException — Java 1.4

java.security.cert — *serializable checked*

This signals a problem while querying a CertStore for certificates or CRLs.

Object → Throwable → Exception → GeneralSecurityException → CertStoreException; Throwable ··· Serializable

```
public class CertStoreException extends java.security.GeneralSecurityException {
// Public Constructors
    public CertStoreException();
    public CertStoreException(Throwable cause);
    public CertStoreException(String msg);
    public CertStoreException(String msg, Throwable cause);
// Public Methods Overriding Throwable
    public Throwable getCause();                                  default:null
    public String getMessage();                                   default:null
    public void printStackTrace();
    public void printStackTrace(java.io.PrintWriter pw);
    public void printStackTrace(java.io.PrintStream ps);
    public String toString();
}
```

Thrown By: CertStore.{getCertificates(), getCRLs()}, CertStoreSpi.{engineGetCertificates(), engineGetCRLs()}

CertStoreParameters — Java 1.4

java.security.cert — *cloneable*

This marker interface defines the type, but not the content, of the parameters object that is passed to the CertStore.getInstance() methods. It does not define any methods of its own and simply requires that all implementing classes be cloneable. Use one of the concrete implementations of this class for CertStore objects of type "LDAP" and "Collection".

Cloneable ··· CertStoreParameters

```
public interface CertStoreParameters extends Cloneable {
// Public Instance Methods
    public abstract Object clone();
}
```

Implementations: CollectionCertStoreParameters, LDAPCertStoreParameters

Passed To: CertStore.{CertStore(), getInstance()}, CertStoreSpi.CertStoreSpi()

Returned By: CertStore.getCertStoreParameters()

CertStoreSpi — Java 1.4

java.security.cert

This abstract class defines the Service Provider Interface for the CertStore class. Security providers must implement this interface, but applications never need to use it.

```
public abstract class CertStoreSpi {
// Public Constructors
```

```
    public CertStoreSpi(CertStoreParameters params) throws java.security.InvalidAlgorithmParameterException;
// Public Instance Methods
    public abstract java.util.Collection engineGetCertificates(CertSelector selector) throws CertStoreException;
    public abstract java.util.Collection engineGetCRLs(CRLSelector selector) throws CertStoreException;
}
```

Passed To: CertStore.CertStore()

CollectionCertStoreParameters — Java 1.4

java.security.cert — *cloneable*

This concrete implementation of CertStoreParameters is used when creating a CertStore object of type "Collection". Pass the Collection of Certificate and CRL objects that will be searched by the CertStore to the constructor method.

Object — CollectionCertStoreParameters
Cloneable — CertStoreParameters

```
public class CollectionCertStoreParameters implements CertStoreParameters {
// Public Constructors
    public CollectionCertStoreParameters();
    public CollectionCertStoreParameters(java.util.Collection collection);
// Public Instance Methods
    public java.util.Collection getCollection();
// Methods Implementing CertStoreParameters
    public Object clone();
// Public Methods Overriding Object
    public String toString();
}
```

CRL — Java 1.2

java.security.cert

This abstract class represents a *certificate revocation list* (CRL). A CRL is an object issued by a certificate authority (or other certificate signer) that lists certificates that have been revoked, meaning that they are now invalid and should be rejected. Use a CertificateFactory to parse a CRL from a byte stream. Use the isRevoked() method to test whether a specified Certificate is listed on the CRL. Note that type-specific CRL subclasses, such as X509CRL, may provide access to substantially more information about the revocation list.

```
public abstract class CRL {
// Protected Constructors
    protected CRL(String type);
// Public Instance Methods
    public final String getType();
    public abstract boolean isRevoked(java.security.cert.Certificate cert);
// Public Methods Overriding Object
    public abstract String toString();
}
```

Subclasses: X509CRL

Passed To: CRLSelector.match(), X509CRLSelector.match()

Returned By: CertificateFactory.generateCRL(), CertificateFactorySpi.engineGenerateCRL()

CRLException — Java 1.2

java.security.cert — *serializable checked*

This signals an error or other problem while working with a CRL.

Object ─ Throwable ─ Exception ─ GeneralSecurityException ─ CRLException
Serializable

```
public class CRLException extends java.security.GeneralSecurityException {
// Public Constructors
   public CRLException();
   public CRLException(String message);
}
```

Thrown By: CertificateFactory.{generateCRL(), generateCRLs()}, CertificateFactorySpi.{engineGenerateCRL(), engineGenerateCRLs()}, X509CRL.{getEncoded(), getTBSCertList(), verify()}, X509CRLEntry.getEncoded()

CRLSelector — Java 1.4

java.security.cert — *cloneable*

This interface defines an API for determining whether a CRL object meets some criteria. Implementations are used to specify criteria by which a CRL objects should be selected from a CertStore. The match() method should examine the CRL it is passed and return true if it "matches" based on whatever criteria the implementation defines. See X509CRLSelector for an implementation that works with X.509 certificates. See CertSelector for a similar interface for use when selecting Certificate objects from a CertStore.

Cloneable ··· CRLSelector

```
public interface CRLSelector extends Cloneable {
// Public Instance Methods
   public abstract Object clone();
   public abstract boolean match(CRL crl);
}
```

Implementations: X509CRLSelector

Passed To: CertStore.getCRLs(), CertStoreSpi.engineGetCRLs()

LDAPCertStoreParameters — Java 1.4

java.security.cert — *cloneable*

This concrete implementation of CertStoreParameters is used when creating a CertStore object of type "LDAP". It specifies the hostname of the LDAP server to connect to and, optionally, the port to connect on.

Object ─ LDAPCertStoreParameters
Cloneable ··· CertStoreParameters

```
public class LDAPCertStoreParameters implements CertStoreParameters {
// Public Constructors
   public LDAPCertStoreParameters();
   public LDAPCertStoreParameters(String serverName);
   public LDAPCertStoreParameters(String serverName, int port);
// Public Instance Methods
```

```
   public int getPort();                                                    default:389
   public String getServerName();                          default: [quot ] localhost [quot ]
// Methods Implementing CertStoreParameters
   public Object clone();
// Public Methods Overriding Object
   public String toString();
}
```

PKIXBuilderParameters — Java 1.4

java.security.cert — *cloneable*

Instances of this class are used to specify parameters to the build() method of a CertPathBuilder object. These parameters must include the two mandatory ones passed to the constructors. The first is a source of trust anchors, which may be supplied as a Set of TrustAnchor objects or as a java.security.KeyStore object. The second required parameter is a CertSelector object (typically, an X509CertSelector) that specifies the selection criteria for the certificate that is to have the certification path built. In addition to these parameters that are passed to the constructor, this class also inherits a number of methods for setting other parameters, and defines setMaxPathLength() for specifying the maximum length of the certificate chain that is built.

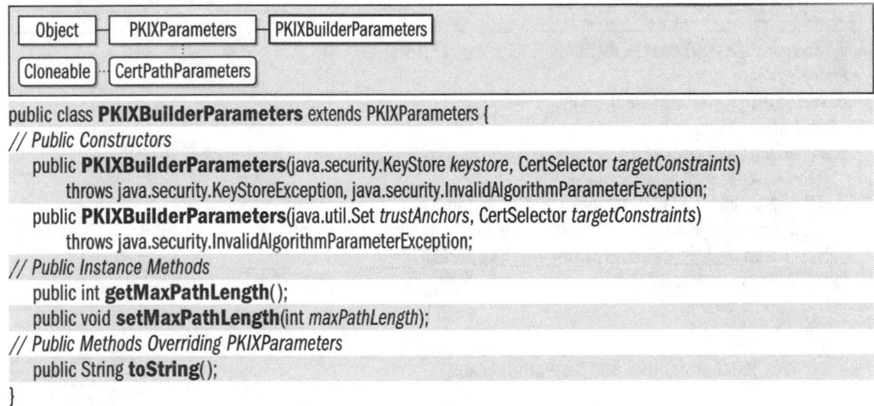


```
public class PKIXBuilderParameters extends PKIXParameters {
// Public Constructors
   public PKIXBuilderParameters(java.security.KeyStore keystore, CertSelector targetConstraints)
       throws java.security.KeyStoreException, java.security.InvalidAlgorithmParameterException;
   public PKIXBuilderParameters(java.util.Set trustAnchors, CertSelector targetConstraints)
       throws java.security.InvalidAlgorithmParameterException;
// Public Instance Methods
   public int getMaxPathLength();
   public void setMaxPathLength(int maxPathLength);
// Public Methods Overriding PKIXParameters
   public String toString();
}
```

PKIXCertPathBuilderResult — Java 1.4

java.security.cert — *cloneable*

An instance of this class is returned by the build() method of a CertPathBuilder created for the "PKIX" algorithm. getCertPath() returns the CertPath object that was built, and methods inherited from the superclass return additional information such as the public key of the subject of the certificate chain and the trust anchor that terminates the chain.

Object — PKIXCertPathValidatorResult — PKIXCertPathBuilderResult
Cloneable … CertPathValidatorResult; Cloneable … CertPathBuilderResult

```
public class PKIXCertPathBuilderResult extends PKIXCertPathValidatorResult implements CertPathBuilderResult {
// Public Constructors
   public PKIXCertPathBuilderResult(CertPath certPath, TrustAnchor trustAnchor, PolicyNode policyTree,
                                    java.security.PublicKey subjectPublicKey);
// Methods Implementing CertPathBuilderResult
   public CertPath getCertPath();
```

```
// Public Methods Overriding PKIXCertPathValidatorResult
    public String toString();
}
```

PKIXCertPathChecker — Java 1.4

java.security.cert — *cloneable*

This abstract class defines an extension mechanism for the PKIX certification path building and validation algorithms. Most applications will never need to use this class. You may pass one or more PKIXCertPathChecker objects to the setCertPathCheckers() or addCertPathChecker() methods of the PKIXParameters or PKIXBuilderParameters object that is passed to the build() or validate() methods of a CertPathBuilder or CertPathValidator. The check() method of all PKIXCertPathChecker objects registered in this way will be invoked for each certificate considered in the building or validation algorithms. check() should throw a CertPathValidatorException if a certificate does not the implemented test. The init() method is invoked to tell the checker to reset its internal state and to notify it of the direction in which certificates will be presented. Checkers are not required to support the forward direction, and should return false from isForwardCheckingSupported() if they do not.

Object — PKIXCertPathChecker ··· Cloneable

```
public abstract class PKIXCertPathChecker implements Cloneable {
// Protected Constructors
    protected PKIXCertPathChecker();
// Public Instance Methods
    public abstract void check(java.security.cert.Certificate cert, java.util.Collection unresolvedCritExts)
        throws CertPathValidatorException;
    public abstract java.util.Set getSupportedExtensions();
    public abstract void init(boolean forward) throws CertPathValidatorException;
    public abstract boolean isForwardCheckingSupported();
// Public Methods Overriding Object
    public Object clone();
}
```

Passed To: PKIXParameters.addCertPathChecker()

PKIXCertPathValidatorResult — Java 1.4

java.security.cert — *cloneable*

An instance of this class is returned upon successful validation by the validate() method of a CertPathValidator created for the "PKIX" algorithm. getPublicKey() returns the validated public key of the subject of the certificate chain. getTrustAnchor() returns the TrustAnchor that anchors the chain.

Object — PKIXCertPathValidatorResult
Cloneable ··· CertPathValidatorResult

```
public class PKIXCertPathValidatorResult implements CertPathValidatorResult {
// Public Constructors
    public PKIXCertPathValidatorResult(TrustAnchor trustAnchor, PolicyNode policyTree,
                                       java.security.PublicKey subjectPublicKey);
// Public Instance Methods
    public PolicyNode getPolicyTree();
    public java.security.PublicKey getPublicKey();
```

```
    public TrustAnchor getTrustAnchor();
// Methods Implementing CertPathValidatorResult
    public Object clone();
// Public Methods Overriding Object
    public String toString();
}
```

Subclasses: PKIXCertPathBuilderResult

PKIXParameters — Java 1.4

java.security.cert — *cloneable*

This implementation of CertPathParameters defines parameters that are passed to the validate() method of a PKIX CertPathValidator and defines a subset of the parameters that are passed to the build() method of a PKIX CertPathBuilder. A full understanding of this class requires a detailed discussion of the PKIX certification path building and validation algorithms, which is beyond the scope of this book. However, some of the more important parameters are described here.

When you create a PKIXParameters object, you must specify which trust anchors are to be used. You can do this by passing a Set of TrustAnchor objects to the constructor, or by passing a KeyStore containing trust anchor keys to the constructor. Once a PKIXParameters object is created, you can modify the set of TrustAnchor objects with setTrustAnchors(). Specify a Set of CertStore objects to be searched for certificates with setCertStores() or add a single CertStore to the set with addCertStore(). If certificate validity is to be checked for some date and time other than the current time, use setDate() to specify this date.

Object — PKIXParameters
Cloneable ··· CertPathParameters

```
public class PKIXParameters implements CertPathParameters {
// Public Constructors
    public PKIXParameters(java.security.KeyStore keystore) throws java.security.KeyStoreException,
        java.security.InvalidAlgorithmParameterException;
    public PKIXParameters(java.util.Set trustAnchors) throws java.security.InvalidAlgorithmParameterException;
// Property Accessor Methods (by property name)
    public boolean isAnyPolicyInhibited();
    public void setAnyPolicyInhibited(boolean val);
    public java.util.List getCertPathCheckers();
    public void setCertPathCheckers(java.util.List checkers);
    public java.util.List getCertStores();
    public void setCertStores(java.util.List stores);
    public java.util.Date getDate();
    public void setDate(java.util.Date date);
    public boolean isExplicitPolicyRequired();
    public void setExplicitPolicyRequired(boolean val);
    public java.util.Set getInitialPolicies();
    public void setInitialPolicies(java.util.Set initialPolicies);
    public boolean isPolicyMappingInhibited();
    public void setPolicyMappingInhibited(boolean val);
    public boolean getPolicyQualifiersRejected();
    public void setPolicyQualifiersRejected(boolean qualifiersRejected);
    public boolean isRevocationEnabled();
    public void setRevocationEnabled(boolean val);
    public String getSigProvider();
```

```
    public void setSigProvider(String sigProvider);
    public CertSelector getTargetCertConstraints();
    public void setTargetCertConstraints(CertSelector selector);
    public java.util.Set getTrustAnchors();
    public void setTrustAnchors(java.util.Set trustAnchors) throws java.security.InvalidAlgorithmParameterException;
// Public Instance Methods
    public void addCertPathChecker(PKIXCertPathChecker checker);
    public void addCertStore(CertStore store);
// Methods Implementing CertPathParameters
    public Object clone();
// Public Methods Overriding Object
    public String toString();
}
```

Subclasses: PKIXBuilderParameters

PolicyNode — Java 1.4

java.security.cert

This class represents a node in the policy tree created by the PKIX certification path validation algorithm. A discussion of X.509 policy extensions and their use in the PKIX certification path algorithms is beyond the scope of this reference.

```
public interface PolicyNode {
// Property Accessor Methods (by property name)
    public abstract java.util.Iterator getChildren();
    public abstract boolean isCritical();
    public abstract int getDepth();
    public abstract java.util.Set getExpectedPolicies();
    public abstract PolicyNode getParent();
    public abstract java.util.Set getPolicyQualifiers();
    public abstract String getValidPolicy();
}
```

Passed To: PKIXCertPathBuilderResult.PKIXCertPathBuilderResult(), PKIXCertPathValidatorResult.PKIXCertPathValidatorResult()

Returned By: PKIXCertPathValidatorResult.getPolicyTree(), PolicyNode.getParent()

PolicyQualifierInfo — Java 1.4

java.security.cert

This class is a low-level representation of a policy qualifier information from a X.509 certificate extension. A discussion of X.509 policy extensions and their use in the PKIX certification path algorithms is beyond the scope of this reference.

```
public final class PolicyQualifierInfo {
// Public Constructors
    public PolicyQualifierInfo(byte[ ] encoded) throws java.io.IOException;
// Public Instance Methods
    public byte[ ] getEncoded();
    public byte[ ] getPolicyQualifier();
    public String getPolicyQualifierId();
// Public Methods Overriding Object
    public String toString();
}
```

TrustAnchor **Java 1.4**

java.security.cert

A TrustAnchor represents a certificate authority that is trusted to "anchor" a certificate chain. A TrustAnchor object includes the X.500 distinguished name of the CA and the public key of the CA. You may specify these values explicitly or by passing an X509Certificate to the TrustAnchor() constructor. Both forms of the TrustAnchor() constructor also allow you to specify a byte array containing a binary representation of a "Name Constraints" extension. The format and meaning of such name constraints is beyond the scope of this reference, and most applications can simply specify null for this constructor argument.

```
public class TrustAnchor {
// Public Constructors
   public TrustAnchor(java.security.cert.X509Certificate trustedCert, byte[ ] nameConstraints);
   public TrustAnchor(String caName, java.security.PublicKey pubKey, byte[ ] nameConstraints);
// Public Instance Methods
   public final String getCAName();
   public final java.security.PublicKey getCAPublicKey();
   public final byte[ ] getNameConstraints();
   public final java.security.cert.X509Certificate getTrustedCert();
// Public Methods Overriding Object
   public String toString();
}
```

Passed To: PKIXCertPathBuilderResult.PKIXCertPathBuilderResult(), PKIXCertPathValidatorResult.PKIXCertPathValidatorResult()

Returned By: PKIXCertPathValidatorResult.getTrustAnchor()

X509Certificate **Java 1.2**

java.security.cert *serializable*

This class represents an X.509 certificate. Its various methods provide complete access to the contents of the certificate. A full understanding of this class requires detailed knowledge of the X.509 standard which is beyond the scope of this reference. Some of the more important methods are described here, however. getSubjectDN() returns the Principal to whom this certificate applies, and the inherited getPublicKey() method returns the PublicKey that the certificate associates with that Principal. getIssuerDN() returns a Principal that represents the issuer of the certificate, and if you know the public key for that Principal, you can pass it to the verify() method to check the digital signature of the issuer and ensure that the certificate is not forged. checkValidity() checks whether the certificate has expired or has not yet gone into effect. Note that verify() and getPublicKey() are inherited from Certificate.

Obtain an X509Certificate object by creating a CertificateFactory for certificate type "X.509" and then using generateCertificate() to parse an X.509 certificate from a stream of bytes. Finally, cast the Certificate returned by this method to an X509Certificate.

Object — Certificate — X509Certificate
Serializable   X509Extension

```
public abstract class X509Certificate extends java.security.cert.Certificate implements X509Extension {
// Protected Constructors
   protected X509Certificate();
// Property Accessor Methods (by property name)
   public abstract int getBasicConstraints();
```

java.security.*

```
1.4 public java.util.List getExtendedKeyUsage() throws java.security.cert.CertificateParsingException;
1.4 public java.util.Collection getIssuerAlternativeNames() throws java.security.cert.CertificateParsingException;
    public abstract java.security.Principal getIssuerDN();
    public abstract boolean[ ] getIssuerUniqueID();
1.4 public javax.security.auth.x500.X500Principal getIssuerX500Principal();
    public abstract boolean[ ] getKeyUsage();
    public abstract java.util.Date getNotAfter();
    public abstract java.util.Date getNotBefore();
    public abstract java.math.BigInteger getSerialNumber();
    public abstract String getSigAlgName();
    public abstract String getSigAlgOID();
    public abstract byte[ ] getSigAlgParams();
    public abstract byte[ ] getSignature();
1.4 public java.util.Collection getSubjectAlternativeNames() throws java.security.cert.CertificateParsingException;
    public abstract java.security.Principal getSubjectDN();
    public abstract boolean[ ] getSubjectUniqueID();
1.4 public javax.security.auth.x500.X500Principal getSubjectX500Principal();
    public abstract byte[ ] getTBSCertificate() throws java.security.cert.CertificateEncodingException;
    public abstract int getVersion();
// Public Instance Methods
    public abstract void checkValidity() throws java.security.cert.CertificateExpiredException,
        java.security.cert.CertificateNotYetValidException;
    public abstract void checkValidity(java.util.Date date) throws java.security.cert.CertificateExpiredException,
        java.security.cert.CertificateNotYetValidException;
}
```

Passed To: TrustAnchor.TrustAnchor(), X509CertSelector.setCertificate(), X509CRLSelector.setCertificateChecking(), javax.net.ssl.X509TrustManager.{checkClientTrusted(), checkServerTrusted()}, javax.security.auth.x500.X500PrivateCredential.X500PrivateCredential()

Returned By: TrustAnchor.getTrustedCert(), X509CertSelector.getCertificate(), X509CRLSelector.getCertificateChecking(), javax.net.ssl.X509KeyManager.getCertificateChain(), javax.net.ssl.X509TrustManager.getAcceptedIssuers(), javax.security.auth.x500.X500PrivateCredential.getCertificate()

X509CertSelector — Java 1.4

java.security.cert — *cloneable*

This class is a CertSelector for X.509 certificates. Its various set methods allow you to specify values for various certificate fields and extensions. The match() method will return true only for certificates that have the specified values for those fields and extensions. A full understanding of this class requires detailed knowledge of the X.509 standard, which is beyond the scope of this reference. Some of the more important methods are described here, however.

When you want to match exactly one specific certificate, simply pass the desired X509Certificate to setCertificate(). Constrain the subject of the certificate with setSubject(), setSubjectAlternativeNames(), or addSubjectAlternativeName(); constrain the issuer of the certificate with setIssuer(); constrain the public key of the certificate with setPublicKey(); constrain the certificate to be valid on a given date with setCertificateValid(); and specify a specific issuer's serial number for the certificate with setSerialNumber().

Object — X509CertSelector
Cloneable ··· CertSelector

```
public class X509CertSelector implements CertSelector {
// Public Constructors
    public X509CertSelector();
// Property Accessor Methods (by property name)
    public byte[ ] getAuthorityKeyIdentifier();                                       default:null
    public void setAuthorityKeyIdentifier(byte[ ] authorityKeyID);
    public int getBasicConstraints();                                                 default:-1
    public void setBasicConstraints(int minMaxPathLen);
    public java.security.cert.X509Certificate getCertificate();                        default:null
    public void setCertificate(java.security.cert.X509Certificate cert);
    public java.util.Date getCertificateValid();                                      default:null
    public void setCertificateValid(java.util.Date certValid);
    public java.util.Set getExtendedKeyUsage();                                       default:null
    public void setExtendedKeyUsage(java.util.Set keyPurposeSet) throws java.io.IOException;
    public byte[ ] getIssuerAsBytes() throws java.io.IOException;                     default:null
    public String getIssuerAsString();                                                default:null
    public boolean[ ] getKeyUsage();                                                  default:null
    public void setKeyUsage(boolean[ ] keyUsage);
    public boolean getMatchAllSubjectAltNames();                                      default:true
    public void setMatchAllSubjectAltNames(boolean matchAllNames);
    public byte[ ] getNameConstraints();                                              default:null
    public void setNameConstraints(byte[ ] bytes) throws java.io.IOException;
    public java.util.Collection getPathToNames();                                     default:null
    public void setPathToNames(java.util.Collection names) throws java.io.IOException;
    public java.util.Set getPolicy();                                                 default:null
    public void setPolicy(java.util.Set certPolicySet) throws java.io.IOException;
    public java.util.Date getPrivateKeyValid();                                       default:null
    public void setPrivateKeyValid(java.util.Date privateKeyValid);
    public java.math.BigInteger getSerialNumber();                                    default:null
    public void setSerialNumber(java.math.BigInteger serial);
    public java.util.Collection getSubjectAlternativeNames();                         default:null
    public void setSubjectAlternativeNames(java.util.Collection names) throws java.io.IOException;
    public byte[ ] getSubjectAsBytes() throws java.io.IOException;                    default:null
    public String getSubjectAsString();                                               default:null
    public byte[ ] getSubjectKeyIdentifier();                                         default:null
    public void setSubjectKeyIdentifier(byte[ ] subjectKeyID);
    public java.security.PublicKey getSubjectPublicKey();                             default:null
    public void setSubjectPublicKey(java.security.PublicKey key);
    public void setSubjectPublicKey(byte[ ] key) throws java.io.IOException;
    public String getSubjectPublicKeyAlgID();                                         default:null
    public void setSubjectPublicKeyAlgID(String oid) throws java.io.IOException;
// Public Instance Methods
    public void addPathToName(int type, String name) throws java.io.IOException;
    public void addPathToName(int type, byte[ ] name) throws java.io.IOException;
    public void addSubjectAlternativeName(int type, String name) throws java.io.IOException;
    public void addSubjectAlternativeName(int type, byte[ ] name) throws java.io.IOException;
    public void setIssuer(String issuerDN) throws java.io.IOException;
    public void setIssuer(byte[ ] issuerDN) throws java.io.IOException;
    public void setSubject(byte[ ] subjectDN) throws java.io.IOException;
    public void setSubject(String subjectDN) throws java.io.IOException;
// Methods Implementing CertSelector
    public Object clone();
    public boolean match(java.security.cert.Certificate cert);
```

```
// Public Methods Overriding Object
   public String toString();
}
```

X509CRL   Java 1.2

java.security.cert

This class represents an X.509 CRL, which consists primarily of a set of X509CRLEntry objects. The various methods of this class provide access to the full details of the CRL, and require a complete understanding of the X.509 standard, which is beyond the scope of this reference. Use verify() to check the digital signature of the CRL to ensure that it does indeed originate from the the source it specifies. Use the inherited isRevoked() method to determine whether a given certificate has been revoked. If you are curious about the revocation date for a revoked certificate, obtain the X509CRLEntry for that certificate by calling getRevokedCertificate(). Call getThisUpdate() to obtain the date when this CRL was issued. Use getNextUpdate() to find if the CRL has been superseded by a newer version. Use getRevokedCertificates() to obtain a Set of all X509CRLEntry objects from this CRL.

Obtain an X509CRL object by creating a CertificateFactory for certificate type "X.509" and then using the generateCRL() to parse an X.509 CRL from a stream of bytes. Finally, cast the CRL returned by this method to an X509CRL.

Object — CRL — X509CRL
X509Extension

```
public abstract class X509CRL extends CRL implements X509Extension {
// Protected Constructors
   protected X509CRL();
// Property Accessor Methods (by property name)
   public abstract byte[ ] getEncoded() throws CRLException;
   public abstract java.security.Principal getIssuerDN();
1.4 public javax.security.auth.x500.X500Principal getIssuerX500Principal();
   public abstract java.util.Date getNextUpdate();
   public abstract java.util.Set getRevokedCertificates();
   public abstract String getSigAlgName();
   public abstract String getSigAlgOID();
   public abstract byte[ ] getSigAlgParams();
   public abstract byte[ ] getSignature();
   public abstract byte[ ] getTBSCertList() throws CRLException;
   public abstract java.util.Date getThisUpdate();
   public abstract int getVersion();
// Public Instance Methods
   public abstract X509CRLEntry getRevokedCertificate(java.math.BigInteger serialNumber);
   public abstract void verify(java.security.PublicKey key) throws CRLException, java.security.NoSuchAlgorithmException,
        java.security.InvalidKeyException, java.security.NoSuchProviderException, java.security.SignatureException;
   public abstract void verify(java.security.PublicKey key, String sigProvider) throws CRLException,
        java.security.NoSuchAlgorithmException, java.security.InvalidKeyException,
        java.security.NoSuchProviderException, java.security.SignatureException;
// Public Methods Overriding Object
   public boolean equals(Object other);
   public int hashCode();
}
```

X509CRLEntry — Java 1.2

java.security.cert

This class represents a single entry in an X509CRL. It contains the serial number and revocation date for a revoked certificate.

Object ─ X509CRLEntry ··· X509Extension

```
public abstract class X509CRLEntry implements X509Extension {
// Public Constructors
   public X509CRLEntry();
// Property Accessor Methods (by property name)
   public abstract byte[ ] getEncoded() throws CRLException;
   public abstract java.util.Date getRevocationDate();
   public abstract java.math.BigInteger getSerialNumber();
// Public Instance Methods
   public abstract boolean hasExtensions();
// Public Methods Overriding Object
   public boolean equals(Object other);
   public int hashCode();
   public abstract String toString();
}
```

Returned By: X509CRL.getRevokedCertificate()

X509CRLSelector — Java 1.4

java.security.cert — *cloneable*

This class is a CRLSelector implementation for X.509 CRLs. The various set methods allow you to specify criteria that the match() method will use to accept or reject CRL objects. Use addIssuerName() to specify the distinguished name of an acceptable issuer for the CRL, or use setIssuerNames() to specify a Collection of valid issuer names. Use setDateAndTime() to specify a Date for which the CRL must be valid. Use setMinCRLNumber() and setMaxCRLNumber() to set bounds on the sequence number of the CRL. If you are selecting a CRL to check for revocation of a particular X509Certificate, pass that certificate to setCertificateChecking(). This method does not actually constrain the returned CRL objects, but it may help a CertStore optimize its search for a relevant CRL.

Object ─ X509CRLSelector
Cloneable ··· CRLSelector

```
public class X509CRLSelector implements CRLSelector {
// Public Constructors
   public X509CRLSelector();
// Property Accessor Methods (by property name)
   public java.security.cert.X509Certificate getCertificateChecking();      default:null
   public void setCertificateChecking(java.security.cert.X509Certificate cert);
   public java.util.Date getDateAndTime();                                   default:null
   public void setDateAndTime(java.util.Date dateAndTime);
   public java.util.Collection getIssuerNames();                             default:null
   public void setIssuerNames(java.util.Collection names) throws java.io.IOException;
   public java.math.BigInteger getMaxCRL();                                  default:null
   public java.math.BigInteger getMinCRL();                                  default:null
// Public Instance Methods
   public void addIssuerName(String name) throws java.io.IOException;
   public void addIssuerName(byte[ ] name) throws java.io.IOException;
```

java.security.*

```
    public void setMaxCRLNumber(java.math.BigInteger maxCRL);
    public void setMinCRLNumber(java.math.BigInteger minCRL);
// Methods Implementing CRLSelector
    public Object clone();
    public boolean match(CRL crl);
// Public Methods Overriding Object
    public String toString();
}
```

X509Extension — Java 1.2

java.security.cert

This interface defines methods for handling a set of extensions to X.509 certificates and CRLs. Each extension has a name, or OID (object identifier), that identifies the type of the extension. An extension may be marked critical or noncritical. Noncritical extensions whose OIDs are not recognized can safely be ignored. However, if a critical exception is not recognized, the Certificate or CRL should be rejected. Each extension in the set has a byte array of data as its value. The interpretation of these bytes depends on the OID of the extension, of course. Specific extensions are defined by the X.509 and related standards and their details are beyond the scope of this reference.

```
public interface X509Extension {
// Public Instance Methods
    public abstract java.util.Set getCriticalExtensionOIDs();
    public abstract byte[ ] getExtensionValue(String oid);
    public abstract java.util.Set getNonCriticalExtensionOIDs();
    public abstract boolean hasUnsupportedCriticalExtension();
}
```

Implementations: java.security.cert.X509Certificate, X509CRL, X509CRLEntry

Package java.security.interfaces — Java 1.1

As its name implies, the java.security.interfaces package contains only interfaces. These interfaces define methods that provide algorithm-specific information (such as key values and initialization parameter values) about DSA and RSA public and private keys. If you are using the RSA algorithm, for example, and working with a java.security.PublicKey object, you can cast that PublicKey to an RSAPublicKey object and use the RSA-specific methods defined by RSAPublicKey to query the key value directly.

The java.security.interfaces package was introduced in Java 1.1. In Java 1.2, the java.security.spec package is the preferred way for obtaining algorithm-specific information about keys and algorithm parameters. This package remains useful in Java 1.2, however, for identifying the type of a given PublicKey or PrivateKey object.

The interfaces in this package are typically of interest only to programmers who are implementing a security provider or who want to implement cryptographic algorithms themselves. Typically, using this package requires some familiarity with the mathematics underlying DSA and RSA public-key cryptography.

Interfaces:

```
public interface DSAKey;
public interface DSAKeyPairGenerator;
```

```
public interface DSAParams;
public interface DSAPrivateKey extends DSAKey, java.security.PrivateKey;
public interface DSAPublicKey extends DSAKey, java.security.PublicKey;
public interface RSAKey;
public interface RSAMultiPrimePrivateCrtKey extends RSAPrivateKey;
public interface RSAPrivateCrtKey extends RSAPrivateKey;
public interface RSAPrivateKey extends java.security.PrivateKey, RSAKey;
public interface RSAPublicKey extends java.security.PublicKey, RSAKey;
```

DSAKey — Java 1.1

java.security.interfaces

This interface defines a method that must be implemented by both public and private DSA keys.

```
public interface DSAKey {
// Public Instance Methods
    public abstract DSAParams getParams();
}
```

Implementations: DSAPrivateKey, DSAPublicKey

DSAKeyPairGenerator — Java 1.1

java.security.interfaces

This interface defines algorithm-specific KeyPairGenerator initialization methods for DSA keys. To generate a pair of DSA keys, use the static getInstance() factory method of java.security.KeyPairGenerator and specify "DSA" as the desired algorithm name. If you wish to perform DSA-specific initialization, cast the returned KeyPairGenerator to a DSAKeyPairGenerator and call one of the initialize() methods defined by this interface. Finally, generate the keys by calling generateKeyPair() on the KeyPairGenerator.

```
public interface DSAKeyPairGenerator {
// Public Instance Methods
    public abstract void initialize(DSAParams params, java.security.SecureRandom random)
        throws java.security.InvalidParameterException;
    public abstract void initialize(int modlen, boolean genParams, java.security.SecureRandom random)
        throws java.security.InvalidParameterException;
}
```

DSAParams — Java 1.1

java.security.interfaces

This interface defines methods for obtaining the DSA parameters g, p, and q. These methods are useful only if you wish to perform cryptographic computation yourself. Using these methods requires a detailed understanding of the mathematics underlying DSA public-key cryptography.

```
public interface DSAParams {
// Public Instance Methods
    public abstract java.math.BigInteger getG();
    public abstract java.math.BigInteger getP();
    public abstract java.math.BigInteger getQ();
}
```

Implementations: java.security.spec.DSAParameterSpec

Passed To: DSAKeyPairGenerator.initialize()

Returned By: DSAKey.getParams()

DSAPrivateKey — Java 1.1

java.security.interfaces — *serializable*

This interface represents a DSA private key and provides direct access to the underlying key value. If you are working with a private key you know is a DSA key, you can cast the PrivateKey to a DSAPrivateKey.


```
public interface DSAPrivateKey extends DSAKey, java.security.PrivateKey {
// Public Constants
1.2 public static final long serialVersionUID;                    =7776497482533790279
// Public Instance Methods
   public abstract java.math.BigInteger getX();
}
```

DSAPublicKey — Java 1.1

java.security.interfaces — *serializable*

This interface represents a DSA public key and provides direct access to the underlying key value. If you are working with a public key you know is a DSA key, you can cast the PublicKey to a DSAPublicKey.


```
public interface DSAPublicKey extends DSAKey, java.security.PublicKey {
// Public Constants
1.2 public static final long serialVersionUID;                    =1234526332779022332
// Public Instance Methods
   public abstract java.math.BigInteger getY();
}
```

RSAKey — Java 1.3

java.security.interfaces

This is a superinterface for RSAPublicKey and RSAPrivateKey; it defines a method shared by both classes. Prior to Java 1.3, the getModulus() method was defined independently by RSAPublicKey and RSAPrivateKey.

```
public interface RSAKey {
// Public Instance Methods
   public abstract java.math.BigInteger getModulus();
}
```

Implementations: RSAPrivateKey, RSAPublicKey

RSAMultiPrimePrivateCrtKey — Java 1.4

java.security.interfaces — *serializable*

This interface extends RSAPrivateKey and provides a decomposition of the private key into the various numbers used to create it. This interface is similar to RSAPrivateCrtKey, except that it is used to represent RSA private keys that are based on more than two prime factors, and it implements the additional getOtherPrimeInfo() method to return information about these additional prime numbers.

Serializable · Key · PrivateKey · RSAKey · RSAPrivateKey · RSAMultiPrimePrivateCrtKey

```
public interface RSAMultiPrimePrivateCrtKey extends RSAPrivateKey {
// Property Accessor Methods (by property name)
   public abstract java.math.BigInteger getCrtCoefficient();
   public abstract java.security.spec.RSAOtherPrimeInfo[ ] getOtherPrimeInfo();
   public abstract java.math.BigInteger getPrimeExponentP();
   public abstract java.math.BigInteger getPrimeExponentQ();
   public abstract java.math.BigInteger getPrimeP();
   public abstract java.math.BigInteger getPrimeQ();
   public abstract java.math.BigInteger getPublicExponent();
}
```

RSAPrivateCrtKey — Java 1.2

java.security.interfaces — *serializable*

This interface extends RSAPrivateKey and provides a decomposition (based on the Chinese remainder theorem) of the private-key value into the various pieces that comprise it. This interface is useful only if you plan to implement your own cryptographic algorithms. To use this interface, you must have a detailed understanding of the mathematics underlying RSA public-key cryptography. Given a java.security.PrivateKey object, you can use the instanceof operator to determine whether you can safely cast it to an RSAPrivateCrtKey.

Serializable · Key · PrivateKey · RSAKey · RSAPrivateKey · RSAPrivateCrtKey

```
public interface RSAPrivateCrtKey extends RSAPrivateKey {
// Property Accessor Methods (by property name)
   public abstract java.math.BigInteger getCrtCoefficient();
   public abstract java.math.BigInteger getPrimeExponentP();
   public abstract java.math.BigInteger getPrimeExponentQ();
   public abstract java.math.BigInteger getPrimeP();
   public abstract java.math.BigInteger getPrimeQ();
   public abstract java.math.BigInteger getPublicExponent();
}
```

RSAPrivateKey — Java 1.2

java.security.interfaces — *serializable*

This interface represents an RSA private key and provides direct access to the underlying key values. If you are working with a private key you know is an RSA key, you can cast the PrivateKey to an RSAPrivateKey.

Serializable · Key · PrivateKey · RSAKey · RSAPrivateKey

```
public interface RSAPrivateKey extends java.security.PrivateKey, RSAKey {
// Public Instance Methods
   public abstract java.math.BigInteger getPrivateExponent();
}
```

Implementations: RSAMultiPrimePrivateCrtKey, RSAPrivateCrtKey

RSAPublicKey — Java 1.2

java.security.interfaces — *serializable*

This interface represents an RSA public key and provides direct access to the underlying key values. If you are working with a public key you know is an RSA key, you can cast the PublicKey to an RSAPublicKey.

Serializable --- Key --- PublicKey --- RSAPublicKey; RSAKey --- RSAPublicKey

```
public interface RSAPublicKey extends java.security.PublicKey, RSAKey {
// Public Instance Methods
   public abstract java.math.BigInteger getPublicExponent();
}
```

Package java.security.spec — Java 1.2

The java.security.spec package contains classes that define transparent representations for DSA and RSA public and private keys and for X.509 and PKCS#8 encodings of those keys. It also defines a transparent representation for DSA algorithm parameters. The classes in this package are used in conjunction with java.security.KeyFactory and java.security.AlgorithmParameters for converting opaque Key and AlgorithmParameters objects to and from transparent representations.

This package is not frequently used. To make use of it, you must be somewhat familiar with the mathematics that underlies DSA and RSA public-key encryption and the encoding standards that specify how keys are encoded as byte streams.

Interfaces:

```
public interface AlgorithmParameterSpec;
public interface KeySpec;
```

Classes:

```
public class DSAParameterSpec implements AlgorithmParameterSpec,
      java.security.interfaces.DSAParams;
public class DSAPrivateKeySpec implements KeySpec;
public class DSAPublicKeySpec implements KeySpec;
public abstract class EncodedKeySpec implements KeySpec;
   └ public class PKCS8EncodedKeySpec extends EncodedKeySpec;
   └ public class X509EncodedKeySpec extends EncodedKeySpec;
public class PSSParameterSpec implements AlgorithmParameterSpec;
public class RSAKeyGenParameterSpec implements AlgorithmParameterSpec;
public class RSAOtherPrimeInfo;
public class RSAPrivateKeySpec implements KeySpec;
   └ public class RSAMultiPrimePrivateCrtKeySpec extends RSAPrivateKeySpec;
```

```
    └ public class RSAPrivateCrtKeySpec extends RSAPrivateKeySpec;
public class RSAPublicKeySpec implements KeySpec;
```

Exceptions:

```
public class InvalidKeySpecException extends java.security.GeneralSecurityException;
public class InvalidParameterSpecException extends java.security.GeneralSecurityException;
```

AlgorithmParameterSpec — Java 1.2

java.security.spec

This interface defines no methods; it marks classes that define a transparent representation of cryptographic parameters. You can use an AlgorithmParameterSpec object to initialize an opaque java.security.AlgorithmParameters object.

```
public interface AlgorithmParameterSpec {
}
```

Implementations: DSAParameterSpec, PSSParameterSpec, RSAKeyGenParameterSpec, javax.crypto.spec.DHGenParameterSpec, javax.crypto.spec.DHParameterSpec, javax.crypto.spec.IvParameterSpec, javax.crypto.spec.PBEParameterSpec, javax.crypto.spec.RC2ParameterSpec, javax.crypto.spec.RC5ParameterSpec

Passed To: Too many methods to list.

Returned By: java.security.AlgorithmParameters.getParameterSpec(), java.security.AlgorithmParametersSpi.engineGetParameterSpec()

DSAParameterSpec — Java 1.2

java.security.spec

This class represents algorithm parameters used with DSA public-key cryptography.

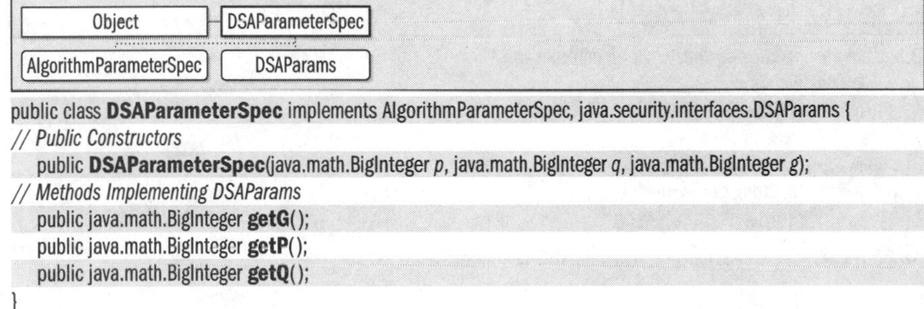


```
public class DSAParameterSpec implements AlgorithmParameterSpec, java.security.interfaces.DSAParams {
// Public Constructors
    public DSAParameterSpec(java.math.BigInteger p, java.math.BigInteger q, java.math.BigInteger g);
// Methods Implementing DSAParams
    public java.math.BigInteger getG();
    public java.math.BigInteger getP();
    public java.math.BigInteger getQ();
}
```

DSAPrivateKeySpec — Java 1.2

java.security.spec

This class is a transparent representation of a DSA private key.

Object — DSAPrivateKeySpec ··· KeySpec

```
public class DSAPrivateKeySpec implements KeySpec {
// Public Constructors
    public DSAPrivateKeySpec(java.math.BigInteger x, java.math.BigInteger p, java.math.BigInteger q,
                              java.math.BigInteger g);
// Public Instance Methods
```

```
    public java.math.BigInteger getG();
    public java.math.BigInteger getP();
    public java.math.BigInteger getQ();
    public java.math.BigInteger getX();
}
```

DSAPublicKeySpec — Java 1.2

java.security.spec

This class is a transparent representation of a DSA public key.

Object ─ DSAPublicKeySpec ··· KeySpec

```
public class DSAPublicKeySpec implements KeySpec {
// Public Constructors
    public DSAPublicKeySpec(java.math.BigInteger y, java.math.BigInteger p, java.math.BigInteger q,
                            java.math.BigInteger g);
// Public Instance Methods
    public java.math.BigInteger getG();
    public java.math.BigInteger getP();
    public java.math.BigInteger getQ();
    public java.math.BigInteger getY();
}
```

EncodedKeySpec — Java 1.2

java.security.spec

This abstract class represents a public or private key in an encoded format. It serves as the superclass for encoding-specific classes.

Object ─ EncodedKeySpec ··· KeySpec

```
public abstract class EncodedKeySpec implements KeySpec {
// Public Constructors
    public EncodedKeySpec(byte[ ] encodedKey);
// Public Instance Methods
    public byte[ ] getEncoded();
    public abstract String getFormat();
}
```

Subclasses: PKCS8EncodedKeySpec, X509EncodedKeySpec

InvalidKeySpecException — Java 1.2

java.security.spec — *serializable checked*

This exception signals a problem with a KeySpec.

Object ─ Throwable ─ Exception ─ GeneralSecurityException ─ InvalidKeySpecException
Throwable ··· Serializable

```
public class InvalidKeySpecException extends java.security.GeneralSecurityException {
// Public Constructors
    public InvalidKeySpecException();
    public InvalidKeySpecException(String msg);
}
```

Thrown By: java.security.KeyFactory.{generatePrivate(), generatePublic(), getKeySpec()}, java.security.KeyFactorySpi.{engineGeneratePrivate(), engineGeneratePublic(), engineGetKeySpec()}, javax.crypto.EncryptedPrivateKeyInfo.getKeySpec(), javax.crypto.SecretKeyFactory.{generateSecret(), getKeySpec()}, javax.crypto.SecretKeyFactorySpi.{engineGenerateSecret(), engineGetKeySpec()}

InvalidParameterSpecException **Java 1.2**

java.security.spec ***serializable checked***

This exception signals a problem with an AlgorithmParameterSpec.

Object — Throwable — Exception — GeneralSecurityException — InvalidParameterSpecException
Serializable

```
public class InvalidParameterSpecException extends java.security.GeneralSecurityException {
// Public Constructors
    public InvalidParameterSpecException();
    public InvalidParameterSpecException(String msg);
}
```

Thrown By: java.security.AlgorithmParameters.{getParameterSpec(), init()}, java.security.AlgorithmParametersSpi.{engineGetParameterSpec(), engineInit()}

KeySpec **Java 1.2**

java.security.spec

This interface defines no methods; it marks classes that define a transparent representation of a cryptographic key. Use a java.security.KeyFactory to convert a KeySpec to and from an opaque java.security.Key.

```
public interface KeySpec {
}
```

Implementations: DSAPrivateKeySpec, DSAPublicKeySpec, EncodedKeySpec, RSAPrivateKeySpec, RSAPublicKeySpec, javax.crypto.spec.DESedeKeySpec, javax.crypto.spec.DESKeySpec, javax.crypto.spec.DHPrivateKeySpec, javax.crypto.spec.DHPublicKeySpec, javax.crypto.spec.PBEKeySpec, javax.crypto.spec.SecretKeySpec

Passed To: java.security.KeyFactory.{generatePrivate(), generatePublic()}, java.security.KeyFactorySpi.{engineGeneratePrivate(), engineGeneratePublic()}, javax.crypto.SecretKeyFactory.generateSecret(), javax.crypto.SecretKeyFactorySpi.engineGenerateSecret()

Returned By: java.security.KeyFactory.getKeySpec(), java.security.KeyFactorySpi.engineGetKeySpec(), javax.crypto.SecretKeyFactory.getKeySpec(), javax.crypto.SecretKeyFactorySpi.engineGetKeySpec()

PKCS8EncodedKeySpec **Java 1.2**

java.security.spec

This class represents a private key, encoded according to the PKCS#8 standard.

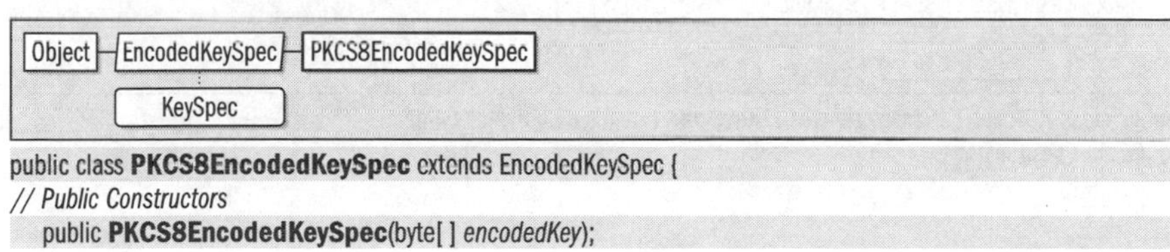


```
public class PKCS8EncodedKeySpec extends EncodedKeySpec {
// Public Constructors
    public PKCS8EncodedKeySpec(byte[ ] encodedKey);
```

```
// Public Methods Overriding EncodedKeySpec
   public byte[ ] getEncoded();
   public final String getFormat();
}
```

Returned By: javax.crypto.EncryptedPrivateKeyInfo.getKeySpec()

PSSParameterSpec — Java 1.4

java.security.spec

This class represents algorithm parameters used with the RSA PSS encoding scheme, which is defined by version 2.1 of the RSA standard PKCS#1.

Object — PSSParameterSpec ··· AlgorithmParameterSpec

```
public class PSSParameterSpec implements AlgorithmParameterSpec {
// Public Constructors
   public PSSParameterSpec(int saltLen);
// Public Instance Methods
   public int getSaltLength();
}
```

RSAKeyGenParameterSpec — Java 1.3

java.security.spec

This class represents parameters that generate public/private key pairs for RSA cryptography.

Object — RSAKeyGenParameterSpec ··· AlgorithmParameterSpec

```
public class RSAKeyGenParameterSpec implements AlgorithmParameterSpec {
// Public Constructors
   public RSAKeyGenParameterSpec(int keysize, java.math.BigInteger publicExponent);
// Public Constants
   public static final java.math.BigInteger F0;
   public static final java.math.BigInteger F4;
// Public Instance Methods
   public int getKeysize();
   public java.math.BigInteger getPublicExponent();
}
```

RSAMultiPrimePrivateCrtKeySpec — Java 1.4

java.security.spec

This class is a transparent representation of a multi-prime RSA private key. It is very similar to RSAPrivateCrtKeySpec, but adds an additional method for obtaining information about the other primes associated with the key.

Object — RSAPrivateKeySpec — RSAMultiPrimePrivateCrtKeySpec
RSAPrivateKeySpec ··· KeySpec

```
public class RSAMultiPrimePrivateCrtKeySpec extends RSAPrivateKeySpec {
// Public Constructors
```

```
    public RSAMultiPrimePrivateCrtKeySpec(java.math.BigInteger modulus, java.math.BigInteger publicExponent,
                                          java.math.BigInteger privateExponent, java.math.BigInteger primeP,
                                          java.math.BigInteger primeQ, java.math.BigInteger primeExponentP,
                                          java.math.BigInteger primeExponentQ,
                                          java.math.BigInteger crtCoefficient,
                                          RSAOtherPrimeInfo[ ] otherPrimeInfo);
// Property Accessor Methods (by property name)
    public java.math.BigInteger getCrtCoefficient();
    public RSAOtherPrimeInfo[ ] getOtherPrimeInfo();
    public java.math.BigInteger getPrimeExponentP();
    public java.math.BigInteger getPrimeExponentQ();
    public java.math.BigInteger getPrimeP();
    public java.math.BigInteger getPrimeQ();
    public java.math.BigInteger getPublicExponent();
}
```

RSAOtherPrimeInfo — Java 1.4

java.security.spec

This class represents the triplet (prime, exponent, coefficient) that constitutes an "OtherPrimeInfo" structure used with RSA multi-prime private keys, as defined in Version 2.1 of the PKCS#1 standard.

```
public class RSAOtherPrimeInfo {
// Public Constructors
    public RSAOtherPrimeInfo(java.math.BigInteger prime, java.math.BigInteger primeExponent,
                             java.math.BigInteger crtCoefficient);
// Public Instance Methods
    public final java.math.BigInteger getCrtCoefficient();
    public final java.math.BigInteger getExponent();
    public final java.math.BigInteger getPrime();
}
```

Passed To: RSAMultiPrimePrivateCrtKeySpec.RSAMultiPrimePrivateCrtKeySpec()

Returned By: java.security.interfaces.RSAMultiPrimePrivateCrtKey.getOtherPrimeInfo(), RSAMultiPrimePrivateCrtKeySpec.getOtherPrimeInfo()

RSAPrivateCrtKeySpec — Java 1.2

java.security.spec

This class is a transparent representation of an RSA private key including, for convenience, the Chinese remainder theorem values associated with the key.

Object — RSAPrivateKeySpec — RSAPrivateCrtKeySpec
KeySpec

```
public class RSAPrivateCrtKeySpec extends RSAPrivateKeySpec {
// Public Constructors
    public RSAPrivateCrtKeySpec(java.math.BigInteger modulus, java.math.BigInteger publicExponent,
                                java.math.BigInteger privateExponent, java.math.BigInteger primeP,
                                java.math.BigInteger primeQ, java.math.BigInteger primeExponentP,
                                java.math.BigInteger primeExponentQ, java.math.BigInteger crtCoefficient);
// Property Accessor Methods (by property name)
    public java.math.BigInteger getCrtCoefficient();
    public java.math.BigInteger getPrimeExponentP();
```

```
    public java.math.BigInteger getPrimeExponentQ();
    public java.math.BigInteger getPrimeP();
    public java.math.BigInteger getPrimeQ();
    public java.math.BigInteger getPublicExponent();
}
```

RSAPrivateKeySpec — Java 1.2

java.security.spec

This class is a transparent representation of an RSA private key.

Object — RSAPrivateKeySpec ··· KeySpec

```
public class RSAPrivateKeySpec implements KeySpec {
// Public Constructors
    public RSAPrivateKeySpec(java.math.BigInteger modulus, java.math.BigInteger privateExponent);
// Public Instance Methods
    public java.math.BigInteger getModulus();
    public java.math.BigInteger getPrivateExponent();
}
```

Subclasses: RSAMultiPrimePrivateCrtKeySpec, RSAPrivateCrtKeySpec

RSAPublicKeySpec — Java 1.2

java.security.spec

This class is a transparent representation of an RSA public key.

Object — RSAPublicKeySpec ··· KeySpec

```
public class RSAPublicKeySpec implements KeySpec {
// Public Constructors
    public RSAPublicKeySpec(java.math.BigInteger modulus, java.math.BigInteger publicExponent);
// Public Instance Methods
    public java.math.BigInteger getModulus();
    public java.math.BigInteger getPublicExponent();
}
```

X509EncodedKeySpec — Java 1.2

java.security.spec

This class represents a public or private key encoded according to the X.509 standard.

Object — EncodedKeySpec — X509EncodedKeySpec
EncodedKeySpec ··· KeySpec

```
public class X509EncodedKeySpec extends EncodedKeySpec {
// Public Constructors
    public X509EncodedKeySpec(byte[ ] encodedKey);
// Public Methods Overriding EncodedKeySpec
    public byte[ ] getEncoded();
    public final String getFormat();
}
```

CHAPTER 16

java.text

Package java.text — Java 1.1

The java.text package consists of classes and interfaces that are useful for writing internationalized programs that handle local customs, such as date and time formatting and string alphabetization, correctly.

The NumberFormat class formats numbers, monetary quantities, and percentages as appropriate for the default or specified locale. DateFormat formats dates and times in a locale-specific way. The concrete DecimalFormat and SimpleDateFormat subclasses of these classes can be used for customized number, date, and time formatting. MessageFormat allows substitution of dynamic values, including formatted numbers and dates, into static message strings. ChoiceFormat formats a number using an enumerated set of string values. See the Format superclass for a general description of formatting and parsing strings with these classes. Collator compares strings according to the customary sorting order for a locale. BreakIterator scans text to find word, line, and sentence boundaries following locale-specific rules. The Bidi class of Java 1.4 implements the Unicode "bidirectional" algorithm for working with languages such as Arabic and Hebrew that display text right to left but display numbers left to right.

Interfaces:

public interface **AttributedCharacterIterator** extends CharacterIterator;
public interface **CharacterIterator** extends Cloneable;

Classes:

public class **Annotation**;
public static class **AttributedCharacterIterator.Attribute** implements Serializable;
 └ public static class **Format.Field** extends AttributedCharacterIterator.Attribute;
  └ public static class **DateFormat.Field** extends Format.Field;
  └ public static class **MessageFormat.Field** extends Format.Field;
  └ public static class **NumberFormat.Field** extends Format.Field;
public class **AttributedString**;

```
public final class Bidi;
public abstract class BreakIterator implements Cloneable;
public class CharSet.Enumeration implements java.util.Enumeration;
public final class CollationElementIterator;
public final class CollationKey implements Comparable;
public abstract class Collator implements Cloneable, java.util.Comparator;
   └ public class RuleBasedCollator extends Collator;
public class DateFormatSymbols implements Cloneable, Serializable;
public final class DecimalFormatSymbols implements Cloneable, Serializable;
public class FieldPosition;
public abstract class Format implements Cloneable, Serializable;
   └ public abstract class DateFormat extends Format;
      └ public class SimpleDateFormat extends DateFormat;
   └ public class MessageFormat extends Format;
   └ public abstract class NumberFormat extends Format;
      └ public class ChoiceFormat extends NumberFormat;
      └ public class DecimalFormat extends NumberFormat;
public class ParsePosition;
public final class StringCharacterIterator implements CharacterIterator;
```

Exceptions:

```
public class ParseException extends Exception;
```

Annotation — Java 1.2

java.text

This class is a wrapper for a the value of a text attribute that represents an annotation. Annotations differ from other types of text attributes in two ways. First, annotations are linked to the text they are applied to, so changing the text invalidates or corrupts the meaning of the annotation. Second, annotations cannot be merged with adjacent annotations, even if they have the same value. Putting an annotation value in an Annotation wrapper serves to indicate these special characteristics. Note that two of the attribute keys defined by AttributedCharacterIterator.Attribute, READING and INPUT_METHOD_SEGMENT, must be used with Annotation objects.

```
public class Annotation {
// Public Constructors
   public Annotation(Object value);
// Public Instance Methods
   public Object getValue();
// Public Methods Overriding Object
   public String toString();
}
```

AttributedCharacterIterator — Java 1.2

java.text — *cloneable*

This interface extends CharacterIterator for working with text that is marked up with attributes in some way. It defines an inner class, AttributedCharacterIterator.Attribute, that represents attribute keys. AttributedCharacterIterator defines methods for querying the attribute keys, values, and runs for the text being iterated over. getAllAttributeKeys() returns the Set of all attribute keys that appear anywhere in the text. getAttributes() returns a Map that contains the attribute keys and values that apply to the current character. getAttribute() returns the value associated with the specified attribute key for the current character.

getRunStart() and getRunLimit() return the index of the first and last characters in a run. A *run* is a string of adjacent characters for which an attribute has the same value or is undefined (i.e., has a value of null). A run can also be defined for a set of attributes, in which case it is a set of adjacent characters for which all attributes in the set hold a constant value (which may include null). Programs that process or display attributed text must usually work with it one run at a time. The no-argument versions of getRunStart() and getRunLimit() return the start and end of the run that includes the current character and all attributes that are applied to the current character. The other versions of these methods return the start and end of the run of the specified attribute or set of attributes that includes the current character.

The AttributedString class provides a simple way to define short strings of attributed text and obtain an AttributedCharacterIterator over them. Most applications that process attributed text are working with attributed text from specialized data sources, stored in some specialized data format, so they need to define a custom implementation of AttributedCharacterIterator.

Cloneable ··· CharacterIterator ··· AttributedCharacterIterator

```
public interface AttributedCharacterIterator extends CharacterIterator {
// Inner Classes
   public static class Attribute implements Serializable;
// Public Instance Methods
   public abstract java.util.Set getAllAttributeKeys();
   public abstract Object getAttribute(AttributedCharacterIterator.Attribute attribute);
   public abstract java.util.Map getAttributes();
   public abstract int getRunLimit();
   public abstract int getRunLimit(java.util.Set attributes);
   public abstract int getRunLimit(AttributedCharacterIterator.Attribute attribute);
   public abstract int getRunStart();
   public abstract int getRunStart(AttributedCharacterIterator.Attribute attribute);
   public abstract int getRunStart(java.util.Set attributes);
}
```

Passed To: Too many methods to list.

Returned By: java.awt.event.InputMethodEvent.getText(), java.awt.im.InputMethodRequests.{cancelLatestCommittedText(), getCommittedText(), getSelectedText()}, AttributedString.getIterator(), DecimalFormat.formatToCharacterIterator(), Format.formatToCharacterIterator(), MessageFormat.formatToCharacterIterator(), SimpleDateFormat.formatToCharacterIterator()

AttributedCharacterIterator.Attribute — Java 1.2

java.text — *serializable*

This class defines the types of the attribute keys used with AttributedCharacterIterator and AttributedString. It defines several constant Attribute keys that are commonly used with multilingual text and input methods. The LANGUAGE key represents the language of the underlying text. The value of this key should be a Locale object. The READING key represents arbitrary reading information associated with text. The value must be an Annotation object. The INPUT_METHOD_SEGMENT key serves to define text segments (usually words) that an input method operates on. The value of this attribute should be an Annotation object that contains null. Other classes may subclass this class and define other attribute keys that are useful in other circumstances or problem domains. See, for example, java.awt.font.TextAttribute in *Java Foundation Classes in a Nutshell* (O'Reilly).

```
public static class AttributedCharacterIterator.Attribute implements Serializable {
// Protected Constructors
    protected Attribute(String name);
// Public Constants
    public static final AttributedCharacterIterator.Attribute INPUT_METHOD_SEGMENT;
    public static final AttributedCharacterIterator.Attribute LANGUAGE;
    public static final AttributedCharacterIterator.Attribute READING;
// Public Methods Overriding Object
    public final boolean equals(Object obj);
    public final int hashCode();
    public String toString();
// Protected Instance Methods
    protected String getName();
    protected Object readResolve() throws java.io.InvalidObjectException;
}
```

Subclasses: java.awt.font.TextAttribute, Format.Field

Passed To: java.awt.im.InputMethodRequests.{cancelLatestCommittedText(), getCommittedText(), getSelectedText()}, AttributedCharacterIterator.{getAttribute(), getRunLimit(), getRunStart()}, AttributedString.{addAttribute(), AttributedString(), getIterator()}

Returned By: java.awt.Font.getAvailableAttributes()

Type Of: AttributedCharacterIterator.Attribute.{INPUT_METHOD_SEGMENT, LANGUAGE, READING}

AttributedString **Java 1.2**

java.text

This class represents text and associated attributes. An AttributedString can be defined in terms of an underlying AttributedCharacterIterator or an underlying String. Additional attributes can be specified with the addAttribute() and addAttributes() methods. getIterator() returns an AttributedCharacterIterator over the AttributedString or over a specified portion of the string. Note that two of the getIterator() methods take an array of Attribute keys as an argument. These methods return an AttributedCharacterIterator that ignores all attributes that are not in the specified array. If the array argument is null, however, the returned iterator contains all attributes.

```
public class AttributedString {
// Public Constructors
    public AttributedString(String text);
    public AttributedString(AttributedCharacterIterator text);
    public AttributedString(String text, java.util.Map attributes);
    public AttributedString(AttributedCharacterIterator text, int beginIndex, int endIndex);
    public AttributedString(AttributedCharacterIterator text, int beginIndex, int endIndex,
                            AttributedCharacterIterator.Attribute[ ] attributes);
// Public Instance Methods
    public void addAttribute(AttributedCharacterIterator.Attribute attribute, Object value);
    public void addAttribute(AttributedCharacterIterator.Attribute attribute, Object value, int beginIndex, int endIndex);
    public void addAttributes(java.util.Map attributes, int beginIndex, int endIndex);
    public AttributedCharacterIterator getIterator();
    public AttributedCharacterIterator getIterator(AttributedCharacterIterator.Attribute[ ] attributes);
    public AttributedCharacterIterator getIterator(AttributedCharacterIterator.Attribute[ ] attributes, int beginIndex,
                                                   int endIndex);
}
```

Bidi **Java 1.4**

java.text

The Bidi class implements the "Unicode Version 3.0 Bidirectional Algorithm" for working with Arabic and Hebrew text in which letters run right-to-left and numbers run left-to-right. It is named after the first four letters of "bidirectional." A full description of the bidirectional text handling and the bidirectional algorithm is beyond the scope of this book, but the simplest case for this class is outlined here. Create a Bidi object by passing an AttributedCharacterIterator or a String and one of the DIRECTION constants (to indicate the base direction of the text) to the Bidi() constructor. Or use createLineBidi() to return a "substring" of an existing Bidi object (this is usually done when formatting a paragraph of text to fit on individual lines).

Once you have a Bidi object, use isLeftToRight() and isRightToLeft() to determine whether all the text has the same direction. If both of these methods return false (which is the same as isMixed() returning true), then you cannot treat the text as a single run of unidirectional text. In this case, you must break it into two or more runs of unidirectional text. getRunCount() returns the number of distinct runs of text. For each such numbered run, getRunStart() returns the index of the first character of the run, and getRunLimit() returns the index of the first character past the end of the run. getRunLevel() returns the *level* of the text, which is an integer that represents the direction and nesting level of the text. Even levels represent left-to-right text, and odd levels represent right-to-left text. The level divided by two is the nesting level of the text. For example, left-to-right text embedded within right-to-left text has a level of 2.

```
public final class Bidi {
// Public Constructors
   public Bidi(AttributedCharacterIterator paragraph);
   public Bidi(String paragraph, int flags);
   public Bidi(char[ ] text, int textStart, byte[ ] embeddings, int embStart, int paragraphLength, int flags);
// Public Constants
   public static final int DIRECTION_DEFAULT_LEFT_TO_RIGHT;                    =-2
   public static final int DIRECTION_DEFAULT_RIGHT_TO_LEFT;                    =-1
   public static final int DIRECTION_LEFT_TO_RIGHT;                            =0
   public static final int DIRECTION_RIGHT_TO_LEFT;                            =1
// Public Class Methods
   public static void reorderVisually(byte[ ] levels, int levelStart, Object[ ] objects, int objectStart, int count);
   public static boolean requiresBidi(char[ ] text, int start, int limit);
// Property Accessor Methods (by property name)
   public int getBaseLevel();
   public boolean isLeftToRight();
   public int getLength();
   public boolean isMixed();
   public boolean isRightToLeft();
   public int getRunCount();
// Public Instance Methods
   public boolean baseIsLeftToRight();
   public Bidi createLineBidi(int lineStart, int lineLimit);
   public int getLevelAt(int offset);
   public int getRunLevel(int run);
   public int getRunLimit(int run);
   public int getRunStart(int run);
// Public Methods Overriding Object
   public String toString();
}
```

Returned By: Bidi.createLineBidi()

BreakIterator **Java 1.1**

java.text ***cloneable***

This class determines character, word, sentence, and line breaks in a block of text in a way that is independent of locale and text encoding. As an abstract class, BreakIterator cannot be instantiated directly. Instead, you must use one of the class methods getCharacterInstance(), getWordInstance(), getSentenceInstance(), or getLineInstance() to return an instance of a nonabstract subclass of BreakIterator. These various factory methods return a BreakIterator object that is configured to locate the requested boundary types and is localized to work for the optionally specified locale.

Once you have obtained an appropriate BreakIterator object, use setText() to specify the text in which to locate boundaries. To locate boundaries in a Java String object, simply specify the string. To locate boundaries in text that uses some other encoding, you must specify a CharacterIterator object for that text so that the BreakIterator object can locate the individual characters of the text. Having set the text to be searched, you can determine the character positions of characters, words, sentences, or line breaks with the first(), last(), next(), previous(), current(), and following() methods, which perform the obvious functions. Note that these methods do not return text itself, but merely the position of the appropriate word, sentence, or line break.

Object — BreakIterator ··· Cloneable

```
public abstract class BreakIterator implements Cloneable {
// Protected Constructors
   protected BreakIterator();
// Public Constants
   public static final int DONE;                                                        =-1
// Public Class Methods
   public static java.util.Locale[ ] getAvailableLocales();                   synchronized
   public static BreakIterator getCharacterInstance();
   public static BreakIterator getCharacterInstance(java.util.Locale where);
   public static BreakIterator getLineInstance();
   public static BreakIterator getLineInstance(java.util.Locale where);
   public static BreakIterator getSentenceInstance();
   public static BreakIterator getSentenceInstance(java.util.Locale where);
   public static BreakIterator getWordInstance();
   public static BreakIterator getWordInstance(java.util.Locale where);
// Public Instance Methods
   public abstract int current();
   public abstract int first();
   public abstract int following(int offset);
   public abstract CharacterIterator getText();
1.2 public boolean isBoundary(int offset);
   public abstract int last();
   public abstract int next();
   public abstract int next(int n);
1.2 public int preceding(int offset);
   public abstract int previous();
   public abstract void setText(CharacterIterator newText);
   public void setText(String newText);
// Public Methods Overriding Object
   public Object clone();
}
```

Passed To: java.awt.font.LineBreakMeasurer.LineBreakMeasurer()

Returned By: BreakIterator.{getCharacterInstance(), getLineInstance(), getSentenceInstance(), getWordInstance()}

CharacterIterator **Java 1.1**

java.text *cloneable*

This interface defines an API for portably iterating through the characters that make up a string of text, regardless of the encoding of that text. Such an API is necessary because the number of bytes per character is different for different encodings, and some encodings even use variable-width characters within the same string of text. In addition to allowing iteration, a class that implements the CharacterIterator interface for non-Unicode text also performs translation of characters from their native encoding to standard Java Unicode characters.

CharacterIterator is similar to java.util.Enumeration, but is somewhat more complex than that interface. The first() and last() methods return the first and last characters in the text, and the next() and previous() methods allow you to loop forward or backwards through the characters of the text. These methods return the DONE constant when they go beyond the first or last character in the text; a test for this constant can be used to terminate a loop. The CharacterIterator interface also allows random access to the characters in a string of text. The getBeginIndex() and getEndIndex() methods return the character positions for the start and end of the string, and setIndex() sets the current position. getIndex() returns the index of the current position, and current() returns the character at that position.

Cloneable ··· CharacterIterator

```
public interface CharacterIterator extends Cloneable {
// Public Constants
   public static final char DONE;                                ='[bsol ]uFFFF'
// Public Instance Methods
   public abstract Object clone();
   public abstract char current();
   public abstract char first();
   public abstract int getBeginIndex();
   public abstract int getEndIndex();
   public abstract int getIndex();
   public abstract char last();
   public abstract char next();
   public abstract char previous();
   public abstract char setIndex(int position);
}
```

Implementations: AttributedCharacterIterator, StringCharacterIterator, javax.swing.text.Segment

Passed To: java.awt.Font.{canDisplayUpTo(), createGlyphVector(), getLineMetrics(), getStringBounds()}, java.awt.FontMetrics.{getLineMetrics(), getStringBounds()}, BreakIterator.setText(), CollationElementIterator.setText(), RuleBasedCollator.getCollationElementIterator()

Returned By: BreakIterator.getText()

ChoiceFormat **Java 1.1**

java.text *cloneable serializable*

This class is a subclass of Format that converts a number to a String in a way reminiscent of a switch statement or an enumerated type. Each ChoiceFormat object has an array of doubles known as its *limits* and an array of strings known as its *formats*. When the format() method is called to format a number x, the ChoiceFormat finds an index i such that:

```
limits[i] <= x < limits[i+1]
```

If x is less than the first element of the array, the first element is used, and if it is greater than the last, the last element is used. Once the index i has been determined, it is used as the index into the array of strings, and the indexed string is returned as the result of the format() method.

A ChoiceFormat object may also be created by encoding its limits and formats into a single string known as its *pattern*. A typical pattern looks like the one below, used to return the singular or plural form of a word based on the numeric value passed to the format() method:

```
ChoiceFormat cf = new ChoiceFormat("0#errors|1#error|2#errors");
```

A ChoiceFormat object created in this way returns the string "errors" when it formats the number 0 or any number greater than or equal to 2. It returns "error" when it formats the number 1. In the syntax shown here, note the pound sign (#) used to separate the limit number from the string that corresponds to that case and the vertical bar (|) used to separate the individual cases. You can use the applyPattern() method to change the pattern used by a ChoiceFormat object; use toPattern() to query the pattern it uses.

Object — Format — NumberFormat — ChoiceFormat
Cloneable Serializable

```
public class ChoiceFormat extends NumberFormat {
// Public Constructors
   public ChoiceFormat(String newPattern);
   public ChoiceFormat(double[ ] limits, String[ ] formats);
// Public Class Methods
   public static final double nextDouble(double d);
   public static double nextDouble(double d, boolean positive);
   public static final double previousDouble(double d);
// Public Instance Methods
   public void applyPattern(String newPattern);
   public Object[ ] getFormats();
   public double[ ] getLimits();
   public void setChoices(double[ ] limits, String[ ] formats);
   public String toPattern();
// Public Methods Overriding NumberFormat
   public Object clone();
   public boolean equals(Object obj);
   public StringBuffer format(long number, StringBuffer toAppendTo, FieldPosition status);
   public StringBuffer format(double number, StringBuffer toAppendTo, FieldPosition status);
   public int hashCode();
   public Number parse(String text, ParsePosition status);
}
```

CollationElementIterator — Java 1.1

java.text

A CollationElementIterator object is returned by the getCollationElementIterator() method of the RuleBasedCollator object. The purpose of this class is to allow a program to iterate (with the next() method) through the characters of a string, returning ordering values for each of the collation keys in the string. Note that collation keys are not exactly the same as characters. In the traditional Spanish collation order, for example, the two-character sequence "ch" is treated as a single collation key that comes alphabetically between the letters "c" and "d". The value returned by the next() method is the collation order of the next collation key in the string. This numeric value can be directly compared to the value returned by next() for other CollationElementIterator objects. The value returned by next() can also be decomposed into primary, secondary, and tertiary ordering values with the static methods of this class. This class is used by RuleBasedCollator to implement its compare() method and to create CollationKey objects. Few applications ever need to use it directly.

```
public final class CollationElementIterator {
// No Constructor
// Public Constants
   public static final int NULLORDER;                                    =-1
// Public Class Methods
   public static final int primaryOrder(int order);
   public static final short secondaryOrder(int order);
   public static final short tertiaryOrder(int order);
// Public Instance Methods
1.2 public int getMaxExpansion(int order);
1.2 public int getOffset();
   public int next();
1.2 public int previous();
   public void reset();
1.2 public void setOffset(int newOffset);
1.2 public void setText(String source);
1.2 public void setText(CharacterIterator source);
}
```

Returned By: RuleBasedCollator.getCollationElementIterator()

CollationKey — Java 1.1

java.text — *comparable*

CollationKey objects compare strings more quickly than is possible with Collation.compare(). Objects of this class are returned by Collation.getCollationKey(). To compare two CollationKey objects, invoke the compareTo() method of key A, passing the key B as an argument (both CollationKey objects must be created through the same Collation object). The return value of this method is less than zero if the key A is collated before the key B, equal to zero if they are equivalent for the purposes of collation, or greater than zero if the key A is collated after the key B. Use getSourceString() to obtain the string represented by a CollationKey.

Object — CollationKey ··· Comparable

```
public final class CollationKey implements Comparable {
// No Constructor
// Public Instance Methods
   public int compareTo(CollationKey target);
   public String getSourceString();
   public byte[] toByteArray();
// Methods Implementing Comparable
1.2 public int compareTo(Object o);
// Public Methods Overriding Object
   public boolean equals(Object target);
   public int hashCode();
}
```

java.text

Passed To: CollationKey.compareTo()

Returned By: Collator.getCollationKey(), RuleBasedCollator.getCollationKey()

Collator — Java 1.1

java.text — *cloneable*

This class compares, orders, and sorts strings in a way appropriate for the default locale or some other specified locale. Because it is an abstract class, it cannot be instantiated directly. Instead, you must use the static getInstance() method to obtain an instance of a Collator subclass that is appropriate for the default or specified locale. You can use getAvailableLocales() to determine whether a Collator object is available for a desired locale.

Once an appropriate Collator object has been obtained, you can use the compare() method to compare strings. The possible return values of this method are –1, 0, and 1, which indicate, respectively, that the first string is collated before the second, that the two are equivalent for collation purposes, and that the first string is collated after the second. The equals() method is a convenient shortcut for testing two strings for collation equivalence.

When sorting an array of strings, each string in the array is typically compared more than once. Using the compare() method in this case is inefficient. A more efficient method for comparing strings multiple times is to use getCollationKey() for each string to create CollationKey objects. These objects can then be compared to each other more quickly than the strings themselves can be compared.

You can customize the way the Collator object performs comparisons by calling setStrength(). If you pass the constant PRIMARY to this method, the comparison looks only at primary differences in the strings; it compares letters but ignores accents and case differences. If you pass the constant SECONDARY, it ignores case differences but does not ignore accents. And if you pass TERTIARY (the default), the Collator object takes both accents and case differences into account in its comparison.

Object — Collator

Cloneable, Comparator

```
public abstract class Collator implements Cloneable, java.util.Comparator {
// Protected Constructors
   protected Collator();
// Public Constants
   public static final int CANONICAL_DECOMPOSITION;                          =1
   public static final int FULL_DECOMPOSITION;                               =2
   public static final int IDENTICAL;                                        =3
   public static final int NO_DECOMPOSITION;                                 =0
   public static final int PRIMARY;                                          =0
   public static final int SECONDARY;                                        =1
   public static final int TERTIARY;                                         =2
// Public Class Methods
   public static java.util.Locale[ ] getAvailableLocales();        synchronized
   public static Collator getInstance();                           synchronized
   public static Collator getInstance(java.util.Locale desiredLocale); synchronized
// Public Instance Methods
   public abstract int compare(String source, String target);
   public boolean equals(Object that);                   Implements:Comparator
   public boolean equals(String source, String target);
   public abstract CollationKey getCollationKey(String source);
```

```
    public int getDecomposition();                                    synchronized
    public int getStrength();                                         synchronized
    public void setDecomposition(int decompositionMode);              synchronized
    public void setStrength(int newStrength);                         synchronized
// Methods Implementing Comparator
1.2 public int compare(Object o1, Object o2);
    public boolean equals(Object that);
// Public Methods Overriding Object
    public Object clone();
    public abstract int hashCode();
}
```

Subclasses: RuleBasedCollator

Returned By: Collator.getInstance()

DateFormat — Java 1.1

java.text — *cloneable serializable*

This class formats and parses dates and times in a locale-specific way. As an abstract class, it cannot be instantiated directly, but it provides a number of static methods that return instances of a concrete subclass you can use to format dates in a variety of ways. The getDateInstance() methods return a DateFormat object suitable for formatting dates in either the default locale or a specified locale. A formatting style may also optionally be specified; the constants FULL, LONG, MEDIUM, SHORT, and DEFAULT specify this style. Similarly, the getTimeInstance() methods return a DateFormat object that formats and parses times, and the getDateTimeInstance() methods return a DateFormat object that formats both dates and times. These methods also optionally take a format style constant and a Locale. Finally, getInstance() returns a default DateFormat object that formats both dates and times in the SHORT format.

Once you have created a DateFormat object, you can use the setCalendar() and setTimeZone() methods if you want to format the date using a calendar or time zone other than the default. The various format() methods convert java.util.Date objects to strings using whatever format is encapsulated in the DateFormat object. The parse() and parseObject() methods perform the reverse operation; they parse a string formatted according to the rules of the DateFormat object and convert it into to a Date object. The DEFAULT, FULL, MEDIUM, LONG, and SHORT constants specify how verbose or compact the formatted date or time should be. The remaining constants, which all end with _FIELD, specify various fields of formatted dates and times and are used with the FieldPosition object that is optionally passed to format().

Object — Format — DateFormat
Cloneable, Serializable

```
public abstract class DateFormat extends Format {
// Protected Constructors
    protected DateFormat();
// Public Constants
    public static final int AM_PM_FIELD;                                   =14
    public static final int DATE_FIELD;                                    =3
    public static final int DAY_OF_WEEK_FIELD;                             =9
    public static final int DAY_OF_WEEK_IN_MONTH_FIELD;                    =11
    public static final int DAY_OF_YEAR_FIELD;                             =10
    public static final int DEFAULT;                                       =2
```

```
public static final int ERA_FIELD;                                    =0
public static final int FULL;                                         =0
public static final int HOUR0_FIELD;                                  =16
public static final int HOUR1_FIELD;                                  =15
public static final int HOUR_OF_DAY0_FIELD;                           =5
public static final int HOUR_OF_DAY1_FIELD;                           =4
public static final int LONG;                                         =1
public static final int MEDIUM;                                       =2
public static final int MILLISECOND_FIELD;                            =8
public static final int MINUTE_FIELD;                                 =6
public static final int MONTH_FIELD;                                  =2
public static final int SECOND_FIELD;                                 =7
public static final int SHORT;                                        =3
public static final int TIMEZONE_FIELD;                               =17
public static final int WEEK_OF_MONTH_FIELD;                          =13
public static final int WEEK_OF_YEAR_FIELD;                           =12
public static final int YEAR_FIELD;                                   =1
// Inner Classes
1.4 public static class Field extends Format.Field;
// Public Class Methods
public static java.util.Locale[ ] getAvailableLocales( );
public static final DateFormat getDateInstance( );
public static final DateFormat getDateInstance(int style);
public static final DateFormat getDateInstance(int style, java.util.Locale aLocale);
public static final DateFormat getDateTimeInstance( );
public static final DateFormat getDateTimeInstance(int dateStyle, int timeStyle);
public static final DateFormat getDateTimeInstance(int dateStyle, int timeStyle, java.util.Locale aLocale);
public static final DateFormat getInstance( );
public static final DateFormat getTimeInstance( );
public static final DateFormat getTimeInstance(int style);
public static final DateFormat getTimeInstance(int style, java.util.Locale aLocale);
// Property Accessor Methods (by property name)
public java.util.Calendar getCalendar( );
public void setCalendar(java.util.Calendar newCalendar);
public boolean isLenient( );
public void setLenient(boolean lenient);
public NumberFormat getNumberFormat( );
public void setNumberFormat(NumberFormat newNumberFormat);
public java.util.TimeZone getTimeZone( );
public void setTimeZone(java.util.TimeZone zone);
// Public Instance Methods
public final String format(java.util.Date date);
public abstract StringBuffer format(java.util.Date date, StringBuffer toAppendTo, FieldPosition fieldPosition);
public java.util.Date parse(String source) throws ParseException;
public abstract java.util.Date parse(String source, ParsePosition pos);
// Public Methods Overriding Format
public Object clone( );
public final StringBuffer format(Object obj, StringBuffer toAppendTo, FieldPosition fieldPosition);
public Object parseObject(String source, ParsePosition pos);
// Public Methods Overriding Object
public boolean equals(Object obj);
public int hashCode( );
// Protected Instance Fields
protected java.util.Calendar calendar;
```

```
    protected NumberFormat numberFormat;
}
```

Subclasses: SimpleDateFormat

Passed To: javax.swing.text.DateFormatter.{DateFormatter(), setFormat()}

Returned By: DateFormat.{getDateInstance(), getDateTimeInstance(), getInstance(), getTimeInstance()}

DateFormat.Field — Java 1.4

java.text — *serializable*

This class defines a typesafe enumeration of AttributedCharacterIterator.Attribute objects that may be used by the AttributedCharacterIterator returned by the formatToCharacterIterator() inherited from Format, or that may be used when creating a FieldPosition object with which to obtain the bounds of a specific date field in formatted output. Note that the constants defined by this class correspond closely to the integer constants defined by java.util.Calendar, and that this class defines methods for converting between the two sets of constants.

```
public static class DateFormat.Field extends Format.Field {
// Protected Constructors
    protected Field(String name, int calendarField);
// Public Constants
    public static final DateFormat.Field AM_PM;
    public static final DateFormat.Field DAY_OF_MONTH;
    public static final DateFormat.Field DAY_OF_WEEK;
    public static final DateFormat.Field DAY_OF_WEEK_IN_MONTH;
    public static final DateFormat.Field DAY_OF_YEAR;
    public static final DateFormat.Field ERA;
    public static final DateFormat.Field HOUR0;
    public static final DateFormat.Field HOUR1;
    public static final DateFormat.Field HOUR_OF_DAY0;
    public static final DateFormat.Field HOUR_OF_DAY1;
    public static final DateFormat.Field MILLISECOND;
    public static final DateFormat.Field MINUTE;
    public static final DateFormat.Field MONTH;
    public static final DateFormat.Field SECOND;
    public static final DateFormat.Field TIME_ZONE;
    public static final DateFormat.Field WEEK_OF_MONTH;
    public static final DateFormat.Field WEEK_OF_YEAR;
    public static final DateFormat.Field YEAR;
// Public Class Methods
    public static DateFormat.Field ofCalendarField(int calendarField);
// Public Instance Methods
    public int getCalendarField();
// Protected Methods Overriding AttributedCharacterIterator.Attribute
    protected Object readResolve() throws java.io.InvalidObjectException;
}
```

Returned By: DateFormat.Field.ofCalendarField()

Type Of: Too many fields to list.

DateFormatSymbols **Java 1.1**

java.text ***cloneable serializable***

This class defines accessor methods for the various pieces of data, such as names of months and days, used by SimpleDateFormat to format and parse dates and times. You do not typically need to use this class unless you are formatting dates for an unsupported locale or in some highly customized way.

Object — DateFormatSymbols
Cloneable, Serializable

```
public class DateFormatSymbols implements Cloneable, Serializable {
// Public Constructors
   public DateFormatSymbols();
   public DateFormatSymbols(java.util.Locale locale);
// Property Accessor Methods (by property name)
   public String[ ] getAmPmStrings();
   public void setAmPmStrings(String[ ] newAmpms);
   public String[ ] getEras();
   public void setEras(String[ ] newEras);
   public String getLocalPatternChars();
   public void setLocalPatternChars(String newLocalPatternChars);
   public String[ ] getMonths();
   public void setMonths(String[ ] newMonths);
   public String[ ] getShortMonths();
   public void setShortMonths(String[ ] newShortMonths);
   public String[ ] getShortWeekdays();
   public void setShortWeekdays(String[ ] newShortWeekdays);
   public String[ ] getWeekdays();
   public void setWeekdays(String[ ] newWeekdays);
   public String[ ][ ] getZoneStrings();
   public void setZoneStrings(String[ ][ ] newZoneStrings);
// Public Methods Overriding Object
   public Object clone();
   public boolean equals(Object obj);
   public int hashCode();
}
```

Passed To: SimpleDateFormat.{setDateFormatSymbols(), SimpleDateFormat()}

Returned By: SimpleDateFormat.getDateFormatSymbols()

DecimalFormat **Java 1.1**

java.text ***cloneable serializable***

This is the concrete Format class used by NumberFormat for all locales that use base 10 numbers. Most applications do not need to use this class directly; they can use the static methods of NumberFormat to obtain a default NumberFormat object for a desired locale and then perform minor locale-independent customizations on that object.

Applications that require highly customized number formatting and parsing may create custom DecimalFormat objects by passing a suitable pattern to the DecimalFormat() constructor method. The applyPattern() method can change this pattern. A pattern consists of a string of characters from the following table. For example:

```
"$#,##0.00;($#,##0.00)"
```

Character	*Meaning*
#	A digit; zeros show as absent
0	A digit; zeros show as 0
.	The locale-specific decimal separator
,	The locale-specific grouping separator (comma)
-	The locale-specific negative prefix
%	Shows value as a percentage
;	Separates positive number format (on left) from optional negative number format (on right)
'	Quotes a reserved character, so it appears literally in the output (apostrophe)
other	Appears literally in output

A DecimalFormatSymbols object can be specified optionally when creating a DecimalFormat object. If one is not specified, a DecimalFormatSymbols object suitable for the default locale is used.

Object — Format — NumberFormat — DecimalFormat
Cloneable Serializable

```
public class DecimalFormat extends NumberFormat {
// Public Constructors
   public DecimalFormat();
   public DecimalFormat(String pattern);
   public DecimalFormat(String pattern, DecimalFormatSymbols symbols);
// Property Accessor Methods (by property name)
1.4 public java.util.Currency getCurrency();                              Overrides:NumberFormat
1.4 public void setCurrency(java.util.Currency currency);                 Overrides:NumberFormat
   public DecimalFormatSymbols getDecimalFormatSymbols();
   public void setDecimalFormatSymbols(DecimalFormatSymbols newSymbols);
   public boolean isDecimalSeparatorAlwaysShown();                        default:false
   public void setDecimalSeparatorAlwaysShown(boolean newValue);
   public int getGroupingSize();                                          default:3
   public void setGroupingSize(int newValue);
1.2 public void setMaximumFractionDigits(int newValue);                   Overrides:NumberFormat
1.2 public void setMaximumIntegerDigits(int newValue);                    Overrides:NumberFormat
1.2 public void setMinimumFractionDigits(int newValue);                   Overrides:NumberFormat
1.2 public void setMinimumIntegerDigits(int newValue);                    Overrides:NumberFormat
   public int getMultiplier();                                            default:1
   public void setMultiplier(int newValue);
   public String getNegativePrefix();                                     default: [quot ] - [quot ]
   public void setNegativePrefix(String newValue);
   public String getNegativeSuffix();                                     default: [quot ] [quot ]
   public void setNegativeSuffix(String newValue);
   public String getPositivePrefix();                                     default: [quot ] [quot ]
   public void setPositivePrefix(String newValue);
   public String getPositiveSuffix();                                     default: [quot ] [quot ]
   public void setPositiveSuffix(String newValue);
// Public Instance Methods
   public void applyLocalizedPattern(String pattern);
   public void applyPattern(String pattern);
   public String toLocalizedPattern();
   public String toPattern();
// Public Methods Overriding NumberFormat
```

java.text

```
   public Object clone();
   public boolean equals(Object obj);
   public StringBuffer format(double number, StringBuffer result, FieldPosition fieldPosition);
   public StringBuffer format(long number, StringBuffer result, FieldPosition fieldPosition);
   public int hashCode();
   public Number parse(String text, ParsePosition pos);
// Public Methods Overriding Format
1.4 public AttributedCharacterIterator formatToCharacterIterator(Object obj);
}
```

Returned By: javax.swing.JSpinner.NumberEditor.getFormat()

DecimalFormatSymbols — Java 1.1

java.text — *cloneable serializable*

This class defines the various characters and strings, such as the decimal point, percent sign, and thousands separator, used by DecimalFormat when formatting numbers. You do not typically use this class directly unless you are formatting dates for an unsupported locale or in some highly customized way.

Object — DecimalFormatSymbols
Cloneable   Serializable

```
public final class DecimalFormatSymbols implements Cloneable, Serializable {
// Public Constructors
   public DecimalFormatSymbols();
   public DecimalFormatSymbols(java.util.Locale locale);
// Property Accessor Methods (by property name)
1.4 public java.util.Currency getCurrency();
1.4 public void setCurrency(java.util.Currency currency);
1.2 public String getCurrencySymbol();                                  default: [quot ] $ [quot ]
1.2 public void setCurrencySymbol(String currency);
   public char getDecimalSeparator();                                   default:.
   public void setDecimalSeparator(char decimalSeparator);
   public char getDigit();                                              default:#
   public void setDigit(char digit);
   public char getGroupingSeparator();                                  default:,
   public void setGroupingSeparator(char groupingSeparator);
   public String getInfinity();                      default: [quot ] [bsol ] u221E [quot ]
   public void setInfinity(String infinity);
1.2 public String getInternationalCurrencySymbol();               default: [quot ] USD [quot ]
1.2 public void setInternationalCurrencySymbol(String currencyCode);
   public char getMinusSign();                                          default:-
   public void setMinusSign(char minusSign);
1.2 public char getMonetaryDecimalSeparator();                          default:.
1.2 public void setMonetaryDecimalSeparator(char sep);
   public String getNaN();                           default: [quot ] [bsol ] uFFFD [quot ]
   public void setNaN(String NaN);
   public char getPatternSeparator();                                   default:;
   public void setPatternSeparator(char patternSeparator);
   public char getPercent();                                            default:%
   public void setPercent(char percent);
   public char getPerMill();                                     default: [bsol ] u2030
   public void setPerMill(char perMill);
   public char getZeroDigit();                                          default:0
```

```
    public void setZeroDigit(char zeroDigit);
// Public Methods Overriding Object
    public Object clone();
    public boolean equals(Object obj);
    public int hashCode();
}
```

Passed To: DecimalFormat.{DecimalFormat(), setDecimalFormatSymbols()}

Returned By: DecimalFormat.getDecimalFormatSymbols()

FieldPosition — Java 1.1

java.text

FieldPosition objects are optionally passed to the format() methods of the Format class and its subclasses to return information about the start and end positions of a specific part or "field" of the formatted string. This kind of information is often useful for aligning formatted strings in columns—for example, aligning the decimal points in a column of numbers.

The field of interest is specified when the FieldPosition() constructor is called. The NumberFormat and DateFormat classes define various integer constants (which end with the string _FIELD) that can be used here. In Java 1.4 and later, you can also construct a FieldPosition by specifying the Format.Field object that identifies the field. See DateFormat.Field, MessageFormat.Field, and NumberFormat.Field for constant Field instances.

After a FieldPosition has been created and passed to a format() method, use getBeginIndex() and getEndIndex() methods of this class to obtain the starting and ending character positions of the desired field of the formatted string.

```
public class FieldPosition {
// Public Constructors
1.4 public FieldPosition(Format.Field attribute);
    public FieldPosition(int field);
1.4 public FieldPosition(Format.Field attribute, int fieldID);
// Public Instance Methods
    public int getBeginIndex();
    public int getEndIndex();
    public int getField();
1.4 public Format.Field getFieldAttribute();
1.2 public void setBeginIndex(int bi);
1.2 public void setEndIndex(int ei);
// Public Methods Overriding Object
1.2 public boolean equals(Object obj);
1.2 public int hashCode();
1.2 public String toString();
}
```

Passed To: ChoiceFormat.format(), DateFormat.format(), DecimalFormat.format(), Format.format(), MessageFormat.format(), NumberFormat.format(), SimpleDateFormat.format()

Format — Java 1.1

java.text — *cloneable serializable*

This abstract class is the base class for all number, date, and string formatting classes in the java.text package. It defines the key formatting and parsing methods that are implemented by all subclasses. format() converts an object to a string using the formatting rules encapsulated by the Format subclass and optionally appends the resulting string to an existing StringBuffer. parseObject() performs the reverse operation; it parses a formatted string and returns the corresponding object. Status information for these two operations is returned in FieldPosition and ParsePosition objects.

Java 1.4 defines a variant on the format() method. formatToCharacterIterator() performs the same formatting operation as format() but returns the result as an AttributedCharacterIterator, which uses attributes to identify the various parts (such the integer part, the decimal separator, and the fractional part of a formatted number) of the formatted string. The attribute keys are all instances of the Format.Field inner class. Each of the Format subclasses define a Field subclass that defines a set of Field constants (such as NumberFormat.Field.DECIMAL_SEPARATOR) for use by the character iterator returned by this method. See ChoiceFormat, DateFormat, MessageFormat, and NumberFormat for subclasses that perform specific types of formatting.

Object — Format
Cloneable Serializable

```
public abstract class Format implements Cloneable, Serializable {
// Public Constructors
    public Format();
// Inner Classes
1.4 public static class Field extends AttributedCharacterIterator.Attribute;
// Public Instance Methods
    public final String format(Object obj);
    public abstract StringBuffer format(Object obj, StringBuffer toAppendTo, FieldPosition pos);
1.4 public AttributedCharacterIterator formatToCharacterIterator(Object obj);
    public Object parseObject(String source) throws ParseException;
    public abstract Object parseObject(String source, ParsePosition pos);
// Public Methods Overriding Object
    public Object clone();
}
```

Subclasses: DateFormat, MessageFormat, NumberFormat

Passed To: MessageFormat.{setFormat(), setFormatByArgumentIndex(), setFormats(), setFormatsByArgumentIndex()}, javax.swing.JFormattedTextField.JFormattedTextField(), javax.swing.text.InternationalFormatter.{InternationalFormatter(), setFormat()}, javax.swing.text.NumberFormatter.setFormat()

Returned By: MessageFormat.{getFormats(), getFormatsByArgumentIndex()}, javax.swing.text.InternationalFormatter.getFormat()

Format.Field — Java 1.4

java.text — *serializable*

This inner class extends AttributedCharacterIterator.Attribute and serves as the common superclass for DateFormat.Field, MessageFormat.Field, and NumberFormat.Field. See those specific subclasses for details.

```
public static class Format.Field extends AttributedCharacterIterator.Attribute {
// Protected Constructors
    protected Field(String name);
}
```

Subclasses: DateFormat.Field, MessageFormat.Field, NumberFormat.Field

Passed To: FieldPosition.FieldPosition()

Returned By: FieldPosition.getFieldAttribute(), javax.swing.text.InternationalFormatter.getFields()

MessageFormat **Java 1.1**

java.text ***cloneable serializable***

This class formats and substitutes objects into specified positions in a message string (also known as the pattern string). It provides the closest Java equivalent to the printf() function of the C programming language. If a message is to be displayed only a single time, the simplest way to use the MessageFormat class is through the static format() method. This method is passed a message or pattern string and an array of argument objects to be formatted and substituted into the string. If the message is to be displayed several times, it makes more sense to create a MessageFormat object, supplying the pattern string, and then call the format() instance method of this object, supplying the array of objects to be formatted into the message.

The message or pattern string used by the MessageFormat contains digits enclosed in curly braces to indicate where each argument should be substituted. The sequence "{0}" indicates that the first object should be converted to a string (if necessary) and inserted at that point, while the sequence "{3}" indicates that the fourth object should be inserted. If the object to be inserted is not a string, MessageFormat checks to see if it is a Date or a subclass of Number. If so, it uses a default DateFormat or NumberFormat object to convert the value to a string. If not, it simply invokes the object's toString() method to convert it.

A digit within curly braces in a pattern string may be followed optionally by a comma, and one of the words "date", "time", "number", or "choice", to indicate that the corresponding argument should be formatted as a date, time, number, or choice before being substituted into the pattern string. Any of these keywords can additionally be followed by a comma and additional pattern information to be used in formatting the date, time, number, or choice. (See SimpleDateFormat, DecimalFormat, and ChoiceFormat for more information.)

You can pass a Locale to the constructor or call setLocale() to specify a nondefault locale that the MessageFormat should use when obtaining DateFormat and NumberFormat objects to format dates, times, and numbers inserted into the pattern. You can change the Format object used at a particular position in the pattern with the setFormat() method, or change all Format objects with setFormats(). Both of these methods depend on the order in which arguments are displayed in the pattern string. The pattern string is often subjected to localization, and the arguments may appear in different orders in different localizations of the pattern. Therefore, in Java 1.4 and later, it is usually more convenient to use the "ByArgumentIndex" versions of the setFormat(), setFormats(), and getFormats() methods.

You can set a new pattern for the MessageFormat object by calling applyPattern() and obtain a string that represents the current formatting pattern by calling toPattern(). MessageFormat also supports a parse() method that can parse an array of objects out of a specified string, according to the specified pattern.

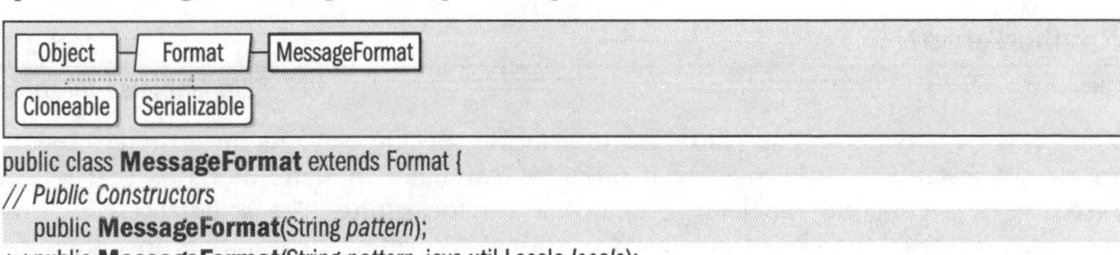


```
public class MessageFormat extends Format {
// Public Constructors
   public MessageFormat(String pattern);
1.4 public MessageFormat(String pattern, java.util.Locale locale);
// Inner Classes
```

```
1.4 public static class Field extends Format.Field;
// Public Class Methods
   public static String format(String pattern, Object[ ] arguments);
// Public Instance Methods
   public void applyPattern(String pattern);
   public final StringBuffer format(Object[ ] arguments, StringBuffer result, FieldPosition pos);
   public Format[ ] getFormats();
1.4 public Format[ ] getFormatsByArgumentIndex();
   public java.util.Locale getLocale();
   public Object[ ] parse(String source) throws ParseException;
   public Object[ ] parse(String source, ParsePosition pos);
   public void setFormat(int formatElementIndex, Format newFormat);
1.4 public void setFormatByArgumentIndex(int argumentIndex, Format newFormat);
   public void setFormats(Format[ ] newFormats);
1.4 public void setFormatsByArgumentIndex(Format[ ] newFormats);
   public void setLocale(java.util.Locale locale);
   public String toPattern();
// Public Methods Overriding Format
   public Object clone();
   public final StringBuffer format(Object arguments, StringBuffer result, FieldPosition pos);
1.4 public AttributedCharacterIterator formatToCharacterIterator(Object arguments);
   public Object parseObject(String source, ParsePosition pos);
// Public Methods Overriding Object
   public boolean equals(Object obj);
   public int hashCode();
}
```

MessageFormat.Field — Java 1.4

java.text — *serializable*

This class defines an ARGUMENT AttributedCharacterIterator.Attribute constant that can be used by the AttributedCharacterIterator returned by MessageFormat.formatToCharacterIterator() to identify portions of the formatted message derived from the arguments passed to formatToCharacterIterator(). The value associated with this ARGUMENT attribute will be an Integer specifying the argument number.

```
public static class MessageFormat.Field extends Format.Field {
// Protected Constructors
   protected Field(String name);
// Public Constants
   public static final MessageFormat.Field ARGUMENT;
// Protected Methods Overriding AttributedCharacterIterator.Attribute
   protected Object readResolve() throws java.io.InvalidObjectException;
}
```

Type Of: MessageFormat.Field.ARGUMENT

NumberFormat — Java 1.1

java.text — *cloneable serializable*

This class formats and parses numbers in a locale-specific way. As an abstract class, it cannot be instantiated directly, but it provides a number of static methods that return instances of a concrete subclass you can use for formatting. The getInstance() method returns a NumberFormat object suitable for normal formatting of numbers in either the default locale or in a specified locale. getIntegerInstance(), getCurrencyInstance() and getPercentInstance() return NumberFormat objects for formatting numbers that are integers, or represent monetary amounts or percentages. These methods return a NumberFormat suitable for the default locale, or for the specified Locale object. getAvailableLocales() returns an array of locales for which NumberFormat objects are available. In Java 1.4, use setCurrency() to provide a java.util.Currency object when formatting monetary values. Note that the NumberFormat class is not intended for the display of very large or very small numbers that require exponential notation, and it might not gracefully handle infinite or NaN (not-a-number) values.

Once you have created a suitable NumberFormat object, you can customize its locale-independent behavior with setMaximumFractionDigits(), setGroupingUsed(), and similar set methods. In order to customize the locale-dependent behavior, you can use instanceof to test if the NumberFormat object is an instance of DecimalFormat, and, if so, cast it to that type. The DecimalFormat class provides complete control over number formatting. Note, however, that a NumberFormat customized in this way may no longer be appropriate for the desired locale.

After creating and customizing a NumberFormat object, you can use the various format() methods to convert numbers to strings or string buffers, and you can use the parse() or parseObject() methods to convert strings to numbers. You can also use the formatToCharacterIterator() method inherited from Format (and overridden by DecimalFormat) in place of format(). The constants defined by this class are to be used by the FieldPosition object.

```
public abstract class NumberFormat extends Format {
// Public Constructors
    public NumberFormat();
// Public Constants
    public static final int FRACTION_FIELD;                                   =1
    public static final int INTEGER_FIELD;                                    =0
// Inner Classes
1.4 public static class Field extends Format.Field;
// Public Class Methods
    public static java.util.Locale[ ] getAvailableLocales();
    public static final NumberFormat getCurrencyInstance();
    public static NumberFormat getCurrencyInstance(java.util.Locale inLocale);
    public static final NumberFormat getInstance();
    public static NumberFormat getInstance(java.util.Locale inLocale);
1.4 public static final NumberFormat getIntegerInstance();
1.4 public static NumberFormat getIntegerInstance(java.util.Locale inLocale);
    public static final NumberFormat getNumberInstance();
    public static NumberFormat getNumberInstance(java.util.Locale inLocale);
    public static final NumberFormat getPercentInstance();
    public static NumberFormat getPercentInstance(java.util.Locale inLocale);
// Property Accessor Methods (by property name)
1.4 public java.util.Currency getCurrency();
1.4 public void setCurrency(java.util.Currency currency);
    public boolean isGroupingUsed();
    public void setGroupingUsed(boolean newValue);
    public int getMaximumFractionDigits();
    public void setMaximumFractionDigits(int newValue);
    public int getMaximumIntegerDigits();
    public void setMaximumIntegerDigits(int newValue);
    public int getMinimumFractionDigits();
    public void setMinimumFractionDigits(int newValue);
```

```
    public int getMinimumIntegerDigits();
    public void setMinimumIntegerDigits(int newValue);
    public boolean isParseIntegerOnly();
    public void setParseIntegerOnly(boolean value);
// Public Instance Methods
    public final String format(long number);
    public final String format(double number);
    public abstract StringBuffer format(long number, StringBuffer toAppendTo, FieldPosition pos);
    public abstract StringBuffer format(double number, StringBuffer toAppendTo, FieldPosition pos);
    public Number parse(String source) throws ParseException;
    public abstract Number parse(String source, ParsePosition parsePosition);
// Public Methods Overriding Format
    public Object clone();
    public final StringBuffer format(Object number, StringBuffer toAppendTo, FieldPosition pos);
    public final Object parseObject(String source, ParsePosition pos);
// Public Methods Overriding Object
    public boolean equals(Object obj);
    public int hashCode();
}
```

Subclasses: ChoiceFormat, DecimalFormat

Passed To: DateFormat.setNumberFormat(), javax.swing.text.NumberFormatter.NumberFormatter()

Returned By: DateFormat.getNumberFormat(), NumberFormat.{getCurrencyInstance(), getInstance(), getIntegerInstance(), getNumberInstance(), getPercentInstance()}

Type Of: DateFormat.numberFormat

NumberFormat.Field — Java 1.4

java.text — *serializable*

This class defines a typesafe enumeration of AttributedCharacterIterator.Attribute objects that may be used by the AttributedCharacterIterator returned by the formatToCharacterIterator() method inherited from the Format class, or that may be used when creating a FieldPosition object to pass to format() in order to obtain the bounds of a specific number field (such as the decimal point for aligning numbers) in formatted output.

```
public static class NumberFormat.Field extends Format.Field {
// Protected Constructors
    protected Field(String name);
// Public Constants
    public static final NumberFormat.Field CURRENCY;
    public static final NumberFormat.Field DECIMAL_SEPARATOR;
    public static final NumberFormat.Field EXPONENT;
    public static final NumberFormat.Field EXPONENT_SIGN;
    public static final NumberFormat.Field EXPONENT_SYMBOL;
    public static final NumberFormat.Field FRACTION;
    public static final NumberFormat.Field GROUPING_SEPARATOR;
    public static final NumberFormat.Field INTEGER;
    public static final NumberFormat.Field PERCENT;
    public static final NumberFormat.Field PERMILLE;
    public static final NumberFormat.Field SIGN;
// Protected Methods Overriding AttributedCharacterIterator.Attribute
    protected Object readResolve() throws java.io.InvalidObjectException;
}
```

Type Of: NumberFormat.Field.{CURRENCY, DECIMAL_SEPARATOR, EXPONENT, EXPONENT_SIGN, EXPONENT_SYMBOL, FRACTION, GROUPING_SEPARATOR, INTEGER, PERCENT, PERMILLE, SIGN}

ParseException — Java 1.1

java.text — *serializable checked*

This signals that a string has an incorrect format and cannot be parsed. It is typically thrown by the parse() or parseObject() methods of Format and its subclasses, but is also thrown by certain methods in the java.text package that are passed patterns or other rules in string form. The getErrorOffset() method of this class returns the character position at which the parsing error occurred in the offending string.

Object — Throwable — Exception — ParseException
Serializable

```
public class ParseException extends Exception {
// Public Constructors
    public ParseException(String s, int errorOffset);
// Public Instance Methods
    public int getErrorOffset();
}
```

Thrown By: Too many methods to list.

ParsePosition — Java 1.1

java.text

ParsePosition objects are passed to the parse() and parseObject() methods of Format and its subclasses. The ParsePosition class represents the position in a string at which parsing should begin or at which parsing stopped. Before calling a parse() method, you can specify the starting position of parsing by passing the desired index to the ParsePosition() constructor or by calling the setIndex() of an existing ParsePosition object. When parse() returns, you can determine where parsing ended by calling getIndex(). When parsing multiple objects or values from a string, a single ParsePosition object can be used sequentially.

```
public class ParsePosition {
// Public Constructors
    public ParsePosition(int index);
// Public Instance Methods
1.2 public int getErrorIndex();
    public int getIndex();
1.2 public void setErrorIndex(int ei);
    public void setIndex(int index);
// Public Methods Overriding Object
1.2 public boolean equals(Object obj);
1.2 public int hashCode();
1.2 public String toString();
}
```

Passed To: ChoiceFormat.parse(), DateFormat.{parse(), parseObject()}, DecimalFormat.parse(), Format.parseObject(), MessageFormat.{parse(), parseObject()}, NumberFormat.{parse(), parseObject()}, SimpleDateFormat.parse()

RuleBasedCollator **Java 1.1**

java.text *cloneable*

This class is a concrete subclass of the abstract Collator class. It performs collations using a table of rules that are specified in textual form. Most applications do not use this class directly; instead they call Collator.getInstance() to obtain a Collator object (typically, a RuleBasedCollator object) that implements the default collation order for a specified or default locale. You should need to use this class only if you are collating strings for a locale that is not supported by default or if you need to implement a highly customized collation order.


```
public class RuleBasedCollator extends Collator {
// Public Constructors
   public RuleBasedCollator(String rules) throws ParseException;
// Public Instance Methods
1.2 public CollationElementIterator getCollationElementIterator(CharacterIterator source);
   public CollationElementIterator getCollationElementIterator(String source);
   public String getRules();
// Public Methods Overriding Collator
   public Object clone();
   public int compare(String source, String target);                synchronized
   public boolean equals(Object obj);
   public CollationKey getCollationKey(String source);               synchronized
   public int hashCode();
}
```

SimpleDateFormat **Java 1.1**

java.text *cloneable serializable*

This is the concrete Format subclass used by DateFormat to handle the formatting and parsing of dates. Most applications should not use this class directly; instead, they should obtain a localized DateFormat object by calling one of the static methods of DateFormat.

SimpleDateFormat formats dates and times according to a pattern, which specifies the positions of the various fields of the date, and a DateFormatSymbols object, which specifies important auxiliary data, such as the names of months. Applications that require highly customized date or time formatting can create a custom SimpleDateFormat object by specifying the desired pattern. This creates a SimpleDateFormat object that uses the DateFormatSymbols object for the default locale. You may also specify an locale explicitly, to use the DateFormatSymbols object for that locale. You can even provide an explicit DateFormatSymbols object of your own if you need to format dates and times for an unsupported locale.

You can use the applyPattern() method of a SimpleDateFormat to change the formatting pattern used by the object. The syntax of this pattern is described in the following table. Any characters in the format string that do not appear in this table appear literally in the formatted date.

Field	Full form	Short form
Year	yyyy (four digits)	yy (two digits)
Month	MMM (name)	MM (two digits), M (one or two digits)
Day of week	EEEE	EE
Day of month	dd (two digits)	d (one or two digits)
Hour (1–12)	hh (two digits)	h (one or two digits)
Hour (0–23)	HH (two digits)	H (one or two digits)
Hour (0–11)	KK	K
Hour (1–24)	kk	k
Minute	mm	
Second	ss	
Millisecond	SSS	
AM/PM	a	
Time zone	zzzz	zz
Day of week in month	F (e.g., 3rd Thursday)	
Day in year	DDD (three digits)	D (one, two, or three digits)
Week in year	ww	
Era (e.g., BC/AD)	G	

Object — Format — DateFormat — SimpleDateFormat
Cloneable, Serializable

```
public class SimpleDateFormat extends DateFormat {
// Public Constructors
   public SimpleDateFormat();
   public SimpleDateFormat(String pattern);
   public SimpleDateFormat(String pattern, java.util.Locale locale);
   public SimpleDateFormat(String pattern, DateFormatSymbols formatSymbols);
// Public Instance Methods
   public void applyLocalizedPattern(String pattern);
   public void applyPattern(String pattern);
1.2 public java.util.Date get2DigitYearStart();
   public DateFormatSymbols getDateFormatSymbols();
1.2 public void set2DigitYearStart(java.util.Date startDate);
   public void setDateFormatSymbols(DateFormatSymbols newFormatSymbols);
   public String toLocalizedPattern();
   public String toPattern();
// Public Methods Overriding DateFormat
   public Object clone();
   public boolean equals(Object obj);
   public StringBuffer format(java.util.Date date, StringBuffer toAppendTo, FieldPosition pos);
   public int hashCode();
   public java.util.Date parse(String text, ParsePosition pos);
// Public Methods Overriding Format
1.4 public AttributedCharacterIterator formatToCharacterIterator(Object obj);
}
```

Returned By: javax.swing.JSpinner.DateEditor.getFormat()

StringCharacterIterator — Java 1.1

java.text — *cloneable*

This class is a trivial implementation of the CharacterIterator interface that works for text stored in Java String objects. See CharacterIterator for details.

Object — StringCharacterIterator
Cloneable ··· CharacterIterator

```
public final class StringCharacterIterator implements CharacterIterator {
// Public Constructors
   public StringCharacterIterator(String text);
   public StringCharacterIterator(String text, int pos);
   public StringCharacterIterator(String text, int begin, int end, int pos);
// Public Instance Methods
1.2 public void setText(String text);
// Methods Implementing CharacterIterator
   public Object clone();
   public char current();
   public char first();
   public int getBeginIndex();
   public int getEndIndex();
   public int getIndex();
   public char last();
   public char next();
   public char previous();
   public char setIndex(int p);
// Public Methods Overriding Object
   public boolean equals(Object obj);
   public int hashCode();
}
```

CHAPTER 17

java.util and Subpackages

This chapter documents the java.util package and each of its subpackages. Those packages are:

java.util
: This package defines many commonly used utility classes, the most important of which are the various Collection, Set, List, and Map implementations.

java.util.jar
: This package defines classes for reading and writing JAR (Java ARchive) files, which are based on the classes of the java.util.zip package.

java.util.logging
: This package defines a powerful and flexible logging API for Java applications.

java.util.prefs
: This package allows applications to set and query persistent values for user-specific preferences or system-wide configuration parameters.

java.util.regex
: This package defines an API for textual pattern matching using regular expressions.

java.util.zip
: This package defines classes for reading and writing ZIP files and for compressing and uncompressing data using the "gzip" format.

Package java.util — Java 1.0

The java.util package defines a number of useful classes, primarily collections classes that are useful for working with groups of objects. This package should not be considered merely a utility package that is separate from the rest of the language; it is an integral and frequently used part of the Java platform.

The most important classes in java.util are the collections classes. Prior to Java 1.2, these were Vector, a growable list of objects, and Hashtable, a mapping between arbitrary key and value objects. Java 1.2 adds an entire collections framework consisting of the Collection, Map, Set, List, SortedMap, and SortedSet interfaces and the classes that implement them. Other important classes and interfaces of the collections framework are Comparator, Collections, Arrays, Iterator, and ListIterator. Java 1.4 extends the Collections framework with the addition of new Map and Set implementations, and a new RandomAccess marker interface used by List implementations. BitSet is a related class that is not actually part of the Collections framework (and is not even a set). It provides a very compact representation of an arbitrary-size array or list of boolean values or bits. Its API was substantially enhanced in Java 1.4.

The other classes of the package are also quite useful. Date, Calendar, and TimeZone work with dates and times. Currency represents a national currency. Locale represents the language and related text formatting conventions of a country, region, or culture. ResourceBundle and its subclasses represent a bundle of localized resources that are read in by an internationalized program at runtime. Random generates and returns pseudo-random numbers in a variety of forms. StringTokenizer is a simple but surprisingly useful parser that breaks a string into tokens. In Java 1.3 and later, Timer and TimerTask provide a powerful API for scheduling code to be run by a background thread, once or repetitively, at a specified time in the future.

Interfaces:

public interface **Comparator**;
public interface **Enumeration**;
public interface **Iterator**;
public interface **ListIterator** extends Iterator;
public static interface **Map.Entry**;
public interface **Observer**;
public interface **RandomAccess**;

Collections:

public abstract class **AbstractCollection** implements Collection;
  └ public abstract class **AbstractList** extends AbstractCollection implements List;
    └ public abstract class **AbstractSequentialList** extends AbstractList;
      └ public class **LinkedList** extends AbstractSequentialList
          implements Cloneable, List, Serializable;
    └ public class **ArrayList** extends AbstractList
        implements Cloneable, List, RandomAccess, Serializable;
    └ public class **Vector** extends AbstractList
        implements Cloneable, List, RandomAccess, Serializable;
      └ public class **Stack** extends Vector;
  └ public abstract class **AbstractSet** extends AbstractCollection implements Set;
    └ public class **HashSet** extends AbstractSet implements Cloneable, Serializable, Set;
      └ public class **LinkedHashSet** extends HashSet implements Cloneable, Serializable, Set;
    └ public class **TreeSet** extends AbstractSet implements Cloneable, Serializable, SortedSet;
public abstract class **AbstractMap** implements Map;
  └ public class **HashMap** extends AbstractMap implements Cloneable, Map, Serializable;
    └ public class **LinkedHashMap** extends HashMap;
  └ public class **IdentityHashMap** extends AbstractMap implements Cloneable, Map, Serializable;
  └ public class **TreeMap** extends AbstractMap implements Cloneable, Serializable, SortedMap;
  └ public class **WeakHashMap** extends AbstractMap implements Map;
public interface **Collection**;
public class **Hashtable** extends Dictionary implements Cloneable, Map, Serializable;
  └ public class **Properties** extends Hashtable;

public interface **List** extends Collection;
public interface **Map**;
public interface **Set** extends Collection;
public interface **SortedMap** extends Map;
public interface **SortedSet** extends Set;

Events:

public class **EventObject** implements Serializable;

Event Listeners:

public interface **EventListener**;

Other Classes:

public class **Arrays**;
public class **BitSet** implements Cloneable, Serializable;
public abstract class **Calendar** implements Cloneable, Serializable;
 └ public class **GregorianCalendar** extends Calendar;
public class **Collections**;
public final class **Currency** implements Serializable;
public class **Date** implements Cloneable, Comparable, Serializable;
public abstract class **Dictionary**;
public abstract class **EventListenerProxy** implements EventListener;
public final class **Locale** implements Cloneable, Serializable;
public class **Observable**;
public final class **PropertyPermission** extends java.security.BasicPermission;
public class **Random** implements Serializable;
public abstract class **ResourceBundle**;
 └ public abstract class **ListResourceBundle** extends ResourceBundle;
 └ public class **PropertyResourceBundle** extends ResourceBundle;
public class **StringTokenizer** implements Enumeration;
public class **Timer**;
public abstract class **TimerTask** implements Runnable;
public abstract class **TimeZone** implements Cloneable, Serializable;
 └ public class **SimpleTimeZone** extends TimeZone;

Exceptions:

public class **ConcurrentModificationException** extends RuntimeException;
public class **EmptyStackException** extends RuntimeException;
public class **MissingResourceException** extends RuntimeException;
public class **NoSuchElementException** extends RuntimeException;
public class **TooManyListenersException** extends Exception;

AbstractCollection **Java 1.2**

java.util *collection*

This abstract class is a partial implementation of Collection that makes it easy to define custom Collection implementations. To create an unmodifiable collection, simply override size() and iterator(). The Iterator object returned by iterator() has to support only the hasNext() and next() methods. To define a modifiable collection, you must additionally override the add() method of AbstractCollection and make sure the Iterator returned by iterator() supports the remove() method. Some subclasses may choose to override other methods to tune performance. In addition, it is conventional that all subclasses provide two constructors: one that takes no arguments and one that accepts a Collection argument that specifies the initial contents of the collection.

Note that if you subclass AbstractCollection directly, you are implementing a *bag*—an unordered collection that allows duplicate elements. If your add() method rejects duplicate elements, you should subclass AbstractSet instead. See also AbstractList.

Object — AbstractCollection ··· Collection

```
public abstract class AbstractCollection implements Collection {
// Protected Constructors
   protected AbstractCollection();
// Methods Implementing Collection
   public boolean add(Object o);
   public boolean addAll(Collection c);
   public void clear();
   public boolean contains(Object o);
   public boolean containsAll(Collection c);
   public boolean isEmpty();
   public abstract Iterator iterator();
   public boolean remove(Object o);
   public boolean removeAll(Collection c);
   public boolean retainAll(Collection c);
   public abstract int size();
   public Object[ ] toArray();
   public Object[ ] toArray(Object[ ] a);
// Public Methods Overriding Object
   public String toString();
}
```

Subclasses: AbstractList, AbstractSet

AbstractList — Java 1.2

java.util — *collection*

This abstract class is a partial implementation of the List interface that makes it easy to define custom List implementations based on random-access list elements (such as objects stored in an array). If you want to base a List implementation on a sequential-access data model (such as a linked list), subclass AbstractSequentialList instead.

To create an unmodifiable List, simply subclass AbstractList and override the (inherited) size() and get() methods. To create a modifiable list, you must also override set() and, optionally, add() and remove(). These three methods are optional, so unless you override them, they simply throw an UnsupportedOperationException. All other methods of the List interface are implemented in terms of size(), get(), set(), add(), and remove(). In some cases, you may want to override these other methods to improve performance. By convention, all List implementations should define two constructors: one that accepts no arguments and another that accepts a Collection of initial elements for the list.

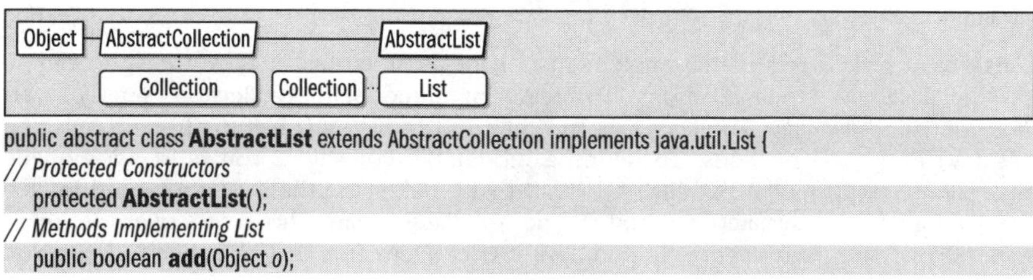


```
public abstract class AbstractList extends AbstractCollection implements java.util.List {
// Protected Constructors
   protected AbstractList();
// Methods Implementing List
   public boolean add(Object o);
```

```
    public void add(int index, Object element);
    public boolean addAll(int index, Collection c);
    public void clear();
    public boolean equals(Object o);
    public abstract Object get(int index);
    public int hashCode();
    public int indexOf(Object o);
    public Iterator iterator();
    public int lastIndexOf(Object o);
    public ListIterator listIterator();
    public ListIterator listIterator(int index);
    public Object remove(int index);
    public Object set(int index, Object element);
    public java.util.List subList(int fromIndex, int toIndex);
// Protected Instance Methods
    protected void removeRange(int fromIndex, int toIndex);
// Protected Instance Fields
    protected transient int modCount;
}
```

Subclasses: AbstractSequentialList, ArrayList, Vector

AbstractMap — Java 1.2

java.util — *collection*

This abstract class is a partial implementation of the Map interface that makes it easy to define simple custom Map implementations. To define an unmodifiable map, subclass AbstractMap and override the entrySet() method so that it returns a set of Map.Entry objects. (Note that you must also implement Map.Entry, of course.) The returned set should not support add() or remove(), and its iterator should not support remove(). In order to define a modifiable Map, you must additionally override the put() method and provide support for the remove() method of the iterator returned by entrySet().iterator(). In addition, it is conventional that all Map implementations define two constructors: one that accepts no arguments and another that accepts a Map of initial mappings.

AbstractMap defines all Map methods in terms of its entrySet() and put() methods and the remove() method of the entry set iterator. Note, however, that the implementation is based on a linear search of the Set returned by entrySet() and is not efficient when the Map contains more than a handful of entries. Some subclasses may want to override additional AbstractMap methods to improve performance. HashMap and TreeMap use different algorithms are are substantially more efficient.

Object — AbstractMap ··· Map

```
public abstract class AbstractMap implements Map {
// Protected Constructors
    protected AbstractMap();
// Methods Implementing Map
    public void clear();
    public boolean containsKey(Object key);
    public boolean containsValue(Object value);
    public abstract Set entrySet();
    public boolean equals(Object o);
    public Object get(Object key);
    public int hashCode();
    public boolean isEmpty();
```

```
    public Set keySet();
    public Object put(Object key, Object value);
    public void putAll(Map t);
    public Object remove(Object key);
    public int size();
    public Collection values();
// Public Methods Overriding Object
    public String toString();
// Protected Methods Overriding Object
1.4 protected Object clone() throws CloneNotSupportedException;
}
```

Subclasses: HashMap, IdentityHashMap, TreeMap, WeakHashMap

AbstractSequentialList — Java 1.2

java.util — *collection*

This abstract class is a partial implementation of the List interface that makes it easy to define List implementations based on a sequential-access data model, as is the case with the LinkedList subclass. To implement a List based on an array or other random-access model, subclass AbstractList instead.

To implement an unmodifiable list, subclass this class and override the size() and listIterator() methods. listIterator() must return a ListIterator that defines the hasNext(), hasPrevious(), next(), previous(), and index() methods. If you want to allow the list to be modified, the ListIterator should also support the set() method and, optionally, the add() and remove() methods. AbstractSequentialList implements all other List methods in terms of these methods. Some subclasses may want to override additional methods to improve performance. In addition, it is conventional that all List implementations define two constructors: one that accepts no arguments and another that accepts a Collection of initial elements for the list.

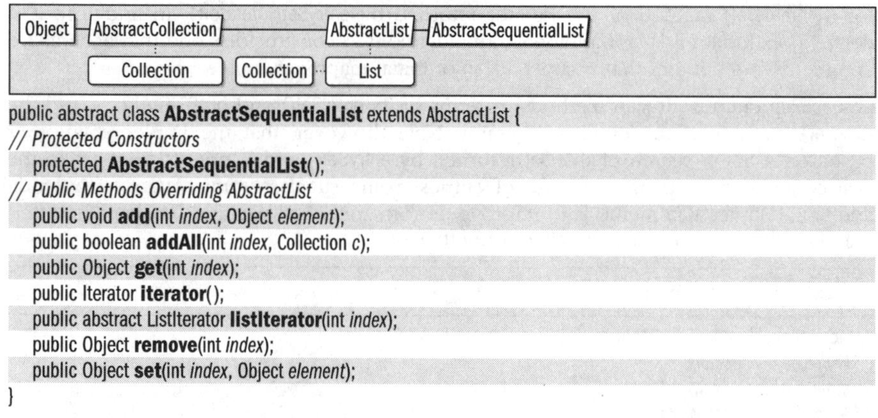


```
public abstract class AbstractSequentialList extends AbstractList {
// Protected Constructors
    protected AbstractSequentialList();
// Public Methods Overriding AbstractList
    public void add(int index, Object element);
    public boolean addAll(int index, Collection c);
    public Object get(int index);
    public Iterator iterator();
    public abstract ListIterator listIterator(int index);
    public Object remove(int index);
    public Object set(int index, Object element);
}
```

Subclasses: LinkedList

AbstractSet — Java 1.2

java.util — *collection*

This abstract class is a partial implementation of the Set interface that makes it easy to create custom Set implementations. Since Set defines the same methods as Collection, you can subclass AbstractSet exactly as you would subclass AbstractCollection. See

AbstractCollection for details. Note, however, that when subclassing AbstractSet, you should be sure that your add() method and your constructors do not allow duplicate elements to be added to the set. See also AbstractList.

```
public abstract class AbstractSet extends AbstractCollection implements Set {
// Protected Constructors
   protected AbstractSet();
// Methods Implementing Set
   public boolean equals(Object o);
   public int hashCode();
1.3 public boolean removeAll(Collection c);
}
```

Subclasses: HashSet, TreeSet

ArrayList **Java 1.2**

java.util ***cloneable serializable collection***

This class is a List implementation based on an array (that is recreated as necessary as the list grows or shrinks). ArrayList implements all optional List and Collection methods and allows list elements of any type (including null). Because ArrayList is based on an array, the get() and set() methods are very efficient. (This is not the case for the LinkedList implementation, for example.) ArrayList is a general-purpose implementation of List and is quite commonly used. ArrayList is very much like the Vector class, except that its methods are not synchronized. If you are using an ArrayList in a multithreaded environment, you should explicitly synchronize any modifications to the list, or wrap the list with Collections.synchronizedList(). See List and Collection for details on the methods of ArrayList. See also LinkedList.

An ArrayList has a *capacity*, which is the number of elements in the internal array that contains the elements of the list. When the number of elements exceeds the capacity, a new array, with a larger capacity, must be created. In addition to the List and Collection methods, ArrayList defines a couple of methods that help you manage this capacity. If you know in advance how many elements an ArrayList will contain, you can call ensureCapacity(), which can increase efficiency by avoiding incremental reallocation of the internal array. You can also pass an initial capacity value to the ArrayList() constructor. Finally, if an ArrayList has reached its final size and will not change in the future, you can call trimToSize() to reallocate the internal array with a capacity that matches the list size exactly. When the ArrayList will have a long lifetime, this can be a useful technique to reduce memory usage.

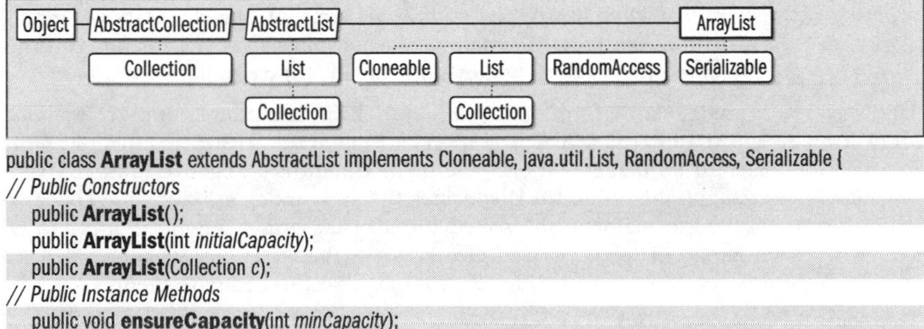


```
public class ArrayList extends AbstractList implements Cloneable, java.util.List, RandomAccess, Serializable {
// Public Constructors
   public ArrayList();
   public ArrayList(int initialCapacity);
   public ArrayList(Collection c);
// Public Instance Methods
   public void ensureCapacity(int minCapacity);
```

```
    public void trimToSize();
// Methods Implementing List
    public boolean add(Object o);
    public void add(int index, Object element);
    public boolean addAll(Collection c);
    public boolean addAll(int index, Collection c);
    public void clear();
    public boolean contains(Object elem);
    public Object get(int index);
    public int indexOf(Object elem);
    public boolean isEmpty();                                          default:true
    public int lastIndexOf(Object elem);
    public Object remove(int index);
    public Object set(int index, Object element);
    public int size();
    public Object[ ] toArray();
    public Object[ ] toArray(Object[ ] a);
// Protected Methods Overriding AbstractList
    protected void removeRange(int fromIndex, int toIndex);
// Public Methods Overriding Object
    public Object clone();
}
```

Returned By: Collections.list()

Type Of: java.awt.dnd.DragGestureRecognizer.events, java.beans.beancontext.BeanContextServicesSupport.bcsListeners, java.beans.beancontext.BeanContextSupport.bcmListeners

Arrays — Java 1.2

java.util

This class defines static methods for sorting, searching, and performing other useful operations on arrays. It also defines the asList() method, which returns a List wrapper around a specified array of objects. Any changes made to the List are also made to the underlying array. This is a powerful method that allows any array of objects to be manipulated in any of the ways a List can be manipulated. It provides a link between arrays and the Java collections framework.

The various sort() methods sort an array (or a specified portion of an array) in place. Variants of the method are defined for arrays of each primitive type and for arrays of Object. For arrays of primitive types, the sorting is done according to the natural ordering of the type. For arrays of objects, the sorting is done according to the specified Comparator, or, if the array contains only java.lang.Comparable objects, according to the ordering defined by that interface. When sorting an array of objects, a stable sorting algorithm is used so that the relative ordering of equal objects is not disturbed. (This allows repeated sorts to order objects by key and subkey, for example.)

The binarySearch() methods perform an efficient search (in logarithmic time) of a sorted array for a specified value. If a match is found in the array, binarySearch() returns the index of the match. If no match is found, the method returns a negative number. For a negative return value r, the index -(r+1) specifies the array index at which the specified value can be inserted to maintain the sorted order of the array. When the array to be searched is an array of objects, the elements of the array must all implement java.lang.Comparable, or you must provide a Comparator object to compare them.

The equals() methods test whether two arrays are equal. Two arrays of primitive type are equal if they contain the same number of elements and if corresponding pairs of elements are equal according to the == operator. Two arrays of objects are equal if they contain the same number of elements and if corresponding pairs of elements are equal according to the equals() method defined by those objects. The fill() methods fill an array or a specified range of an array with the specified value.

```
public class Arrays {
// No Constructor
// Public Class Methods
   public static java.util.List asList(Object[ ] a);
   public static int binarySearch(double[ ] a, double key);
   public static int binarySearch(byte[ ] a, byte key);
   public static int binarySearch(Object[ ] a, Object key);
   public static int binarySearch(float[ ] a, float key);
   public static int binarySearch(int[ ] a, int key);
   public static int binarySearch(long[ ] a, long key);
   public static int binarySearch(char[ ] a, char key);
   public static int binarySearch(short[ ] a, short key);
   public static int binarySearch(Object[ ] a, Object key, Comparator c);
   public static boolean equals(double[ ] a, double[ ] a2);
   public static boolean equals(boolean[ ] a, boolean[ ] a2);
   public static boolean equals(Object[ ] a, Object[ ] a2);
   public static boolean equals(float[ ] a, float[ ] a2);
   public static boolean equals(byte[ ] a, byte[ ] a2);
   public static boolean equals(int[ ] a, int[ ] a2);
   public static boolean equals(long[ ] a, long[ ] a2);
   public static boolean equals(char[ ] a, char[ ] a2);
   public static boolean equals(short[ ] a, short[ ] a2);
   public static void fill(short[ ] a, short val);
   public static void fill(char[ ] a, char val);
   public static void fill(long[ ] a, long val);
   public static void fill(int[ ] a, int val);
   public static void fill(byte[ ] a, byte val);
   public static void fill(float[ ] a, float val);
   public static void fill(Object[ ] a, Object val);
   public static void fill(boolean[ ] a, boolean val);
   public static void fill(double[ ] a, double val);
   public static void fill(short[ ] a, int fromIndex, int toIndex, short val);
   public static void fill(char[ ] a, int fromIndex, int toIndex, char val);
   public static void fill(long[ ] a, int fromIndex, int toIndex, long val);
   public static void fill(int[ ] a, int fromIndex, int toIndex, int val);
   public static void fill(byte[ ] a, int fromIndex, int toIndex, byte val);
   public static void fill(float[ ] a, int fromIndex, int toIndex, float val);
   public static void fill(Object[ ] a, int fromIndex, int toIndex, Object val);
   public static void fill(boolean[ ] a, int fromIndex, int toIndex, boolean val);
   public static void fill(double[ ] a, int fromIndex, int toIndex, double val);
   public static void sort(Object[ ] a);
   public static void sort(short[ ] a);
   public static void sort(char[ ] a);
   public static void sort(long[ ] a);
   public static void sort(byte[ ] a);
   public static void sort(float[ ] a);
   public static void sort(int[ ] a);
   public static void sort(double[ ] a);
   public static void sort(Object[ ] a, Comparator c);
   public static void sort(long[ ] a, int fromIndex, int toIndex);
   public static void sort(byte[ ] a, int fromIndex, int toIndex);
   public static void sort(char[ ] a, int fromIndex, int toIndex);
```

```
    public static void sort(float[ ] a, int fromIndex, int toIndex);
    public static void sort(int[ ] a, int fromIndex, int toIndex);
    public static void sort(double[ ] a, int fromIndex, int toIndex);
    public static void sort(Object[ ] a, int fromIndex, int toIndex);
    public static void sort(short[ ] a, int fromIndex, int toIndex);
    public static void sort(Object[ ] a, int fromIndex, int toIndex, Comparator c);
}
```

BitSet — Java 1.0

java.util — *cloneable serializable*

This class implements an array or list of boolean values and stores them using a compact representation that requires only about 1 bit per value stored. It implements methods for setting, querying, and flipping the values stored at any given position within the list; for counting the number of true values stored in the list; and for finding the next true or false value in the list. It also defines a number of methods that perform bitwise boolean operations on two BitSet objects. Despite its name, BitSet does not implement the Set interface, nor does it have the behavior associated with a set; it is a list or vector for boolean values but is not related to the List interface or Vector class. This class was introduced in Java 1.0 but was substantially enhanced in Java 1.4; note that many of the following methods are available only in Java 1.4 and later.

Create a BitSet with the BitSet() constructor. You may optionally specify a size (the number of bits) for the BitSet, but this merely provides an optimization since a BitSet will grow as needed to accommodate any number of boolean values. BitSet does not define a precise notion of the size of a "set". The size() method returns the number of boolean values that can be stored before more internal storage needs to be allocated. The length() method returns one more than the highest index of a set bit (i.e., a true value). This means that a BitSet that contains all false values will have a length() of 0. If your code needs to remember the index of the highest value stored in a BitSet, regardless of whether that value was true or false, then you should maintain that length information separately from the BitSet.

Set values in a BitSet with the set() method. There are four versions of this method. Two set the value at a specific index, and two set values for a range of indexes. Two of the set() methods do not take a value argument to set; they "set" the specified bit or range of bites, which means they store the value true. The other two methods take a boolean argument, allowing you to set the specified value or range of values to true (a set bit) or false (a clear bit). There are also two clear() methods that "clear" (or set to false) the value at the specified index or range of indexes. The flip() methods flip, or toggle (change true to false and false to true), the value or values at the specified index or range. The set(), clear(), and flip() methods, as well as all other BitSet methods that operate on a range of values, specify the range with two index values. They define the range as the values starting from, and including, the value stored at the first specified index up to, *but not including*, the value stored at the second specified index. (A number of methods of String and related classes follow the same convention for specifying a range of characters.)

To test the value stored at a specified location, use get(), which returns true if the specified bit is set, or false if it is not. There is also a get() method that specifies a range of bits and returns their state in the form of a BitSet; this get() method is analogous to the substring() method of a String. Because a BitSet does not define a maximum index, it is legal to pass any nonnegative value to get(). If the index you specify is greater than or equal to the value returned by length(), then the returned value will always be false.

cardinality() returns the number of true values (or of set bits) stored in a BitSet. isEmpty() returns true if a BitSet has no true values stored in it (in this case, both length() and cardinality() return 0). nextSetBit() returns the first index at or after the specified index at which a true value is stored (or at which the bit is set). You can use this method in a loop to iterate through the indexes of true values. nextClearBit() is similar but searches the BitSet for false values (clear bits) instead. The intersects() method returns true if the target BitSet and the argument BitSet intersect, i.e., if there is at least one index at which both BitSet objects have a true value.

BitSet defines several methods that perform bitwise Boolean operations. These methods combine the BitSet on which they are invoked (called the "target" BitSet) with the BitSet passed as an argument and store the result in the target BitSet. If you want to perform a Boolean operation without altering the original BitSet, you should first make a copy of the original with the clone() method and invoke the method on the copy. The and() method performs a bitwise Boolean AND operation, much like the & does when applied to integer arguments. A value in the target BitSet will be true only if it was originally true and the value at the same index of the argument BitSet is also true. For all false values in the argument BitSet, and() sets the corresponding value in the target BitSet to false, leaving other values unchanged. The andNot() method combines a Boolean AND operation with a Boolean NOT operation on the argument BitSet (it does not alter the contents of that argument BitSet, however). The result is that for all true values in the argument BitSet, the corresponding values in the target BitSet are set to false.

The or() method performs a bitwise Boolean OR operation like the | operator: a value in the BitSet will be set to true if its original value was true or the corresponding value in the argument BitSet was true. For all true values in the argument BitSet, the or() method sets the corresponding value in the target BitSet to true, leaving the other values unchanged. The xor() method performs an "exclusive OR" operation: it sets a value in the target BitSet to true if it was originally true or if the corresponding value in the argument BitSet was true. If both values were false, or if both values were true, however, it sets the value to false.

Finally, the toString() method returns a String representation of a BitSet that consists of a list within curly braces of the indexes at which true values are stored.

The BitSet class is not thread-safe.

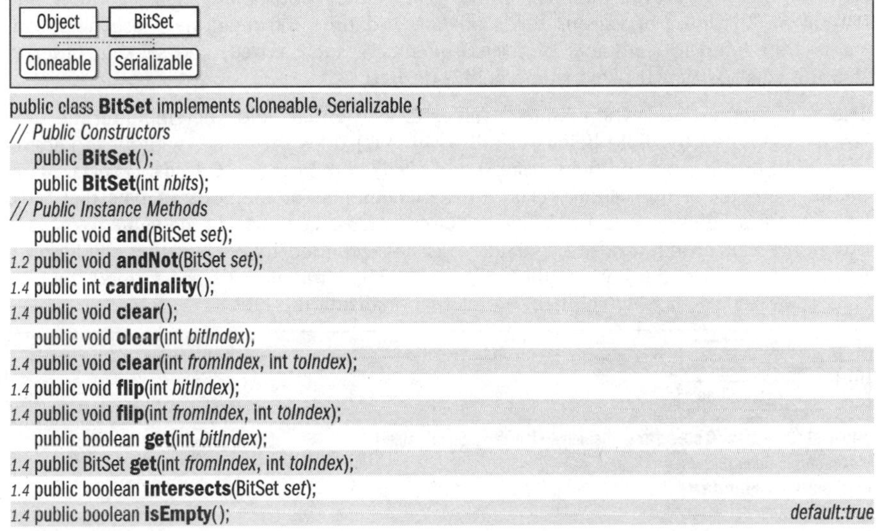


```
public class BitSet implements Cloneable, Serializable {
// Public Constructors
    public BitSet();
    public BitSet(int nbits);
// Public Instance Methods
    public void and(BitSet set);
1.2 public void andNot(BitSet set);
1.4 public int cardinality();
1.4 public void clear();
    public void clear(int bitIndex);
1.4 public void clear(int fromIndex, int toIndex);
1.4 public void flip(int bitIndex);
1.4 public void flip(int fromIndex, int toIndex);
    public boolean get(int bitIndex);
1.4 public BitSet get(int fromIndex, int toIndex);
1.4 public boolean intersects(BitSet set);
1.4 public boolean isEmpty();                                    default:true
```

```
1.2 public int length();
1.4 public int nextClearBit(int fromIndex);
1.4 public int nextSetBit(int fromIndex);
    public void or(BitSet set);
    public void set(int bitIndex);
1.4 public void set(int bitIndex, boolean value);
1.4 public void set(int fromIndex, int toIndex);
1.4 public void set(int fromIndex, int toIndex, boolean value);
    public int size();
    public void xor(BitSet set);
// Public Methods Overriding Object
    public Object clone();
    public boolean equals(Object obj);
    public int hashCode();
    public String toString();
}
```

Passed To: BitSet.{and(), andNot(), intersects(), or(), xor()}, javax.swing.text.html.parser.DTD.defineElement()

Returned By: BitSet.get()

Type Of: javax.swing.text.html.parser.Element.{exclusions, inclusions}

Calendar — Java 1.1

java.util — *cloneable serializable*

This abstract class defines methods that perform date and time arithmetic. It also includes methods that convert dates and times to and from the machine-usable millisecond format used by the Date class and units such as minutes, hours, days, weeks, months, and years that are more useful to humans. As an abstract class, Calendar cannot be directly instantiated. Instead, it provides static getInstance() methods that return instances of a Calendar subclass suitable for use in a specified or default locale with a specified or default time zone. See also Date, DateFormat, and TimeZone.

Calendar defines a number of useful constants. Some of these are values that represent days of the week and months of the year. Other constants, such as HOUR and DAY_OF_WEEK, represent various fields of date and time information. These field constants are passed to a number of Calendar methods, such as get() and set(), in order to indicate what particular date or time field is desired.

The add() method adds (or subtracts) values to a calendar field, incrementing the next larger field when the field being set rolls over. roll() does the same, without modifying anything but the specified field. before() and after() compare two Calendar objects. Many of the methods of the Calendar class are replacements for methods of Date that have been deprecated as of Java 1.1. While the Calendar class converts a time value to its various hour, day, month, and other fields, it is not intended to present those fields in a form suitable for display to the end user. That function is performed by the java.text.DateFormat class, which handles internationalization issues.

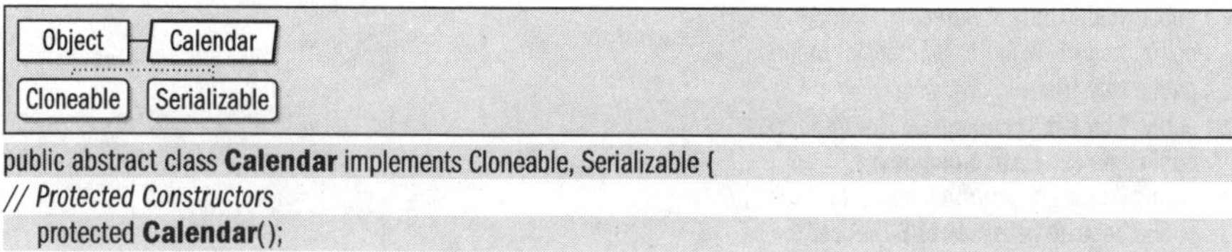


```
public abstract class Calendar implements Cloneable, Serializable {
// Protected Constructors
    protected Calendar();
```

```
    protected Calendar(TimeZone zone, Locale aLocale);
// Public Constants
    public static final int AM;                                          =0
    public static final int AM_PM;                                       =9
    public static final int APRIL;                                       =3
    public static final int AUGUST;                                      =7
    public static final int DATE;                                        =5
    public static final int DAY_OF_MONTH;                                =5
    public static final int DAY_OF_WEEK;                                 =7
    public static final int DAY_OF_WEEK_IN_MONTH;                        =8
    public static final int DAY_OF_YEAR;                                 =6
    public static final int DECEMBER;                                    =11
    public static final int DST_OFFSET;                                  =16
    public static final int ERA;                                         =0
    public static final int FEBRUARY;                                    =1
    public static final int FIELD_COUNT;                                 =17
    public static final int FRIDAY;                                      =6
    public static final int HOUR;                                        =10
    public static final int HOUR_OF_DAY;                                 =11
    public static final int JANUARY;                                     =0
    public static final int JULY;                                        =6
    public static final int JUNE;                                        =5
    public static final int MARCH;                                       =2
    public static final int MAY;                                         =4
    public static final int MILLISECOND;                                 =14
    public static final int MINUTE;                                      =12
    public static final int MONDAY;                                      =2
    public static final int MONTH;                                       =2
    public static final int NOVEMBER;                                    =10
    public static final int OCTOBER;                                     =9
    public static final int PM;                                          =1
    public static final int SATURDAY;                                    =7
    public static final int SECOND;                                      =13
    public static final int SEPTEMBER;                                   =8
    public static final int SUNDAY;                                      =1
    public static final int THURSDAY;                                    =5
    public static final int TUESDAY;                                     =3
    public static final int UNDECIMBER;                                  =12
    public static final int WEDNESDAY;                                   =4
    public static final int WEEK_OF_MONTH;                               =4
    public static final int WEEK_OF_YEAR;                                =3
    public static final int YEAR;                                        =1
    public static final int ZONE_OFFSET;                                 =15
// Public Class Methods
    public static Locale[ ] getAvailableLocales();                       synchronized
    public static Calendar getInstance();
    public static Calendar getInstance(TimeZone zone);
    public static Calendar getInstance(Locale aLocale);
    public static Calendar getInstance(TimeZone zone, Locale aLocale);
// Property Accessor Methods (by property name)
    public int getFirstDayOfWeek();
    public void setFirstDayOfWeek(int value);
    public boolean isLenient();
    public void setLenient(boolean lenient);
    public int getMinimalDaysInFirstWeek();
```

```
    public void setMinimalDaysInFirstWeek(int value);
    public final java.util.Date getTime();
    public final void setTime(java.util.Date date);
    public long getTimeInMillis();
    public void setTimeInMillis(long millis);
    public TimeZone getTimeZone();
    public void setTimeZone(TimeZone value);
// Public Instance Methods
    public abstract void add(int field, int amount);
    public boolean after(Object when);
    public boolean before(Object when);
    public final void clear();
    public final void clear(int field);
    public int get(int field);
1.2 public int getActualMaximum(int field);
1.2 public int getActualMinimum(int field);
    public abstract int getGreatestMinimum(int field);
    public abstract int getLeastMaximum(int field);
    public abstract int getMaximum(int field);
    public abstract int getMinimum(int field);
    public final boolean isSet(int field);
    public abstract void roll(int field, boolean up);
1.2 public void roll(int field, int amount);
    public void set(int field, int value);
    public final void set(int year, int month, int date);
    public final void set(int year, int month, int date, int hour, int minute);
    public final void set(int year, int month, int date, int hour, int minute, int second);
// Public Methods Overriding Object
    public Object clone();
    public boolean equals(Object obj);
1.2 public int hashCode();
    public String toString();
// Protected Instance Methods
    protected void complete();
    protected abstract void computeFields();
    protected abstract void computeTime();
    protected final int internalGet(int field);
// Protected Instance Fields
    protected boolean areFieldsSet;
    protected int[ ] fields;
    protected boolean[ ] isSet;
    protected boolean isTimeSet;
    protected long time;
}
```

Subclasses: GregorianCalendar

Passed To: Too many methods to list.

Returned By: java.text.DateFormat.getCalendar(), Calendar.getInstance()

Type Of: java.text.DateFormat.calendar

Collection — Java 1.2

java.util — *collection*

This interface represents a group, or collection, of objects. The objects may or may not be ordered, and the collection may or may not contain duplicate objects. Collection is not often implemented directly. Instead, most collection classes implement one of the more specific subinterfaces: Set, an unordered collection that does not allow duplicates, or List, an ordered collection that does allow duplicates.

The Collection type provides a general way to refer to any set, list, or other collection of objects; it defines generic methods that work with any collection. contains() and containsAll() test whether the Collection contains a specified object or all the objects in a given collection. isEmpty() returns true if the Collection has no elements, or false otherwise. size() returns the number of elements in the Collection. iterator() returns an Iterator object that allows you to iterate through the objects in the collection. toArray() returns the objects in the Collection in a new array of type Object. Another version of toArray() takes an array as an argument and stores all elements of the Collection (which must all be compatible with the array) into that array. If the array is not big enough, the method allocates a new, larger array of the same type. If the array is too big, the method stores null into the first empty element of the array. This version of toArray() returns the array that was passed in or the new array, if one was allocated.

The previous methods all query or extract the contents of a collection. The Collection interface also defines methods for modifying the contents of the collection. add() and addAll() add an object or a collection of objects to a Collection. remove() and removeAll() remove an object or collection. retainAll() is a variant that removes all objects except those in a specified Collection. clear() removes all objects from the collection. All these modification methods except clear() return true if the collection was modified as a result of the call. An interface cannot specify constructors, but it is conventional that all implementations of Collection provide at least two standard constructors: one that takes no arguments and creates an empty collection, and a copy constructor that accepts a Collection object that specifies the initial contents of the new Collection.

Implementations of Collection and its subinterfaces are not required to support all operations defined by the Collection interface. All modification methods listed above are optional; an implementation (such as an immutable Set implementation) that does not support them simply throws java.lang.UnsupportedOperationException for these methods. Furthermore, implementations are free to impose restrictions on the types of objects that can be members of a collection. Some implementations might require elements to be of a particular type, for example, and others might not allow null as an element.

See also Set, List, Map, and Collections.

```
public interface Collection {
// Public Instance Methods
   public abstract boolean add(Object o);
   public abstract boolean addAll(Collection c);
   public abstract void clear();
   public abstract boolean contains(Object o);
   public abstract boolean containsAll(Collection c);
   public abstract boolean equals(Object o);
   public abstract int hashCode();
   public abstract boolean isEmpty();
   public abstract Iterator iterator();
   public abstract boolean remove(Object o);
   public abstract boolean removeAll(Collection c);
   public abstract boolean retainAll(Collection c);
```

```
    public abstract int size();
    public abstract Object[ ] toArray();
    public abstract Object[ ] toArray(Object[ ] a);
}
```

Implementations: java.beans.beancontext.BeanContext, AbstractCollection, java.util.List, Set

Passed To: Too many methods to list.

Returned By: Too many methods to list.

Type Of: java.beans.beancontext.BeanContextMembershipEvent.children

Collections **Java 1.2**

java.util

This class defines static methods and constants that are useful for working with collections and maps. One of the most commonly used methods is sort(), which sorts a List in place (the list cannot be immutable, of course). The sorting algorithm is stable, which means that equal elements retain the same relative order. One version of sort() uses a specified Comparator to perform the sort; the other relies on the natural ordering of the list elements and requires all the elements to implement java.lang.Comparable. reverseOrder() returns a convenient predefined Comparator object that can order Comparable objects into the reverse of their natural ordering.

A related method is binarySearch(). It efficiently (in logarithmic time) searches a sorted List for a specified object and returns the index at which a matching object is found. If no match is found, it returns a negative number. For a negative return value r, the value -(r+1) specifies the index at which the specified object can be inserted into the list to maintain the sorted order of the list. As with sort(), binarySearch() can be passed a Comparator that defines the order of the sorted list. If no Comparator is specified, the list elements must all implement Comparable, and the list is assumed to be sorted according to the natural ordering defined by this interface.

See Arrays for methods that perform sorting and searching operations on arrays instead of collections.

The various methods with names beginning with synchronized return a thread-safe collection object wrapped around the specified collection. Vector and Hashtable are the only two collection objects that are thread-safe by default. Use these methods to obtain a synchronized wrapper object if you are using any other type of Collection or Map in a multithreaded environment where more than one thread can modify it.

The various methods whose names begin with unmodifiable function like synchronized methods. They return a Collection or Map object wrapped around the specified collection. The returned object is unmodifiable, however, so its add(), remove(), set(), put(), etc., methods all throw java.lang.UnsupportedOperationException.

In addition to the "synchronized" and "unmodifiable" methods, Collections defines a number of other methods that return special-purpose collections or maps. singleton() returns an unmodifiable set that contains only the specified object. singletonList() and singletonMap() return an immutable list and an immutable map, respectively, each of which contains only a single entry. The Collections class also defines related constants—EMPTY_LIST, EMPTY_SET, and EMPTY_MAP—which are immutable List, Set, and Map objects that contain no elements or mappings. nCopies() creates a new immutable List that contains a specified number of copies of a specified object. list() returns a List object that represents the elements of the specified Enumeration object. enumeration() does the reverse: it returns an Enumeration for a Collection, which is useful when working with code that uses the old Enumeration interface instead of the newer Iterator interface.

The Collections class also defines methods that mutate a collection. These methods throw an UnsupportedOperationException if the target collection does not allow mutation. copy() copies elements of a source list into a destination list. fill() replaces all elements of the specified list with the specified object. swap() swaps the elements at two specified indexes of a List. replaceAll() replaces all elements in a List that are equal to (using the equals() method) with another object and returns true if any replacements were done. reverse() reverses the order of the elements in a list. rotate() "rotates" a list, adding the specified number to the index of each element and wrapping elements from the end of the list back to the front of the list. (Specifying a negative rotation rotates the list in the other direction.) shuffle() randomizes the order of elements in a list, using either an internal source of randomness or the Random pseudo-random number generator that you provide.

Finally, Collections defines methods (in addition to the binarySearch() methods described earlier) that search the elements of a collection; min() and max() methods search an unordered Collection for the minimum and maximum elements, according to either a specified Comparator or to the natural order defined by the Comparable elements themselves. indexOfSubList() and lastIndexOfSubList() search a specified list forward or backward for a subsequence of elements that match (using equals()) the elements of a second specified list. They return the start index of any such matching sublist, or return –1 if no match was found. These methods are like the indexOf() and lastIndexOf() methods of String and do not require the List to be sorted, as the binarySearch() methods do.

```
public class Collections {
// No Constructor
// Public Constants
    public static final java.util.List EMPTY_LIST;
1.3 public static final Map EMPTY_MAP;
    public static final Set EMPTY_SET;
// Public Class Methods
    public static int binarySearch(java.util.List list, Object key);
    public static int binarySearch(java.util.List list, Object key, Comparator c);
    public static void copy(java.util.List dest, java.util.List src);
    public static Enumeration enumeration(Collection c);
    public static void fill(java.util.List list, Object obj);
1.4 public static int indexOfSubList(java.util.List source, java.util.List target);
1.4 public static int lastIndexOfSubList(java.util.List source, java.util.List target);
1.4 public static ArrayList list(Enumeration e);
    public static Object max(Collection coll);
    public static Object max(Collection coll, Comparator comp);
    public static Object min(Collection coll);
    public static Object min(Collection coll, Comparator comp);
    public static java.util.List nCopies(int n, Object o);
1.4 public static boolean replaceAll(java.util.List list, Object oldVal, Object newVal);
    public static void reverse(java.util.List list);
    public static Comparator reverseOrder();
1.4 public static void rotate(java.util.List list, int distance);
    public static void shuffle(java.util.List list);
    public static void shuffle(java.util.List list, Random rnd);
    public static Set singleton(Object o);
1.3 public static java.util.List singletonList(Object o);
1.3 public static Map singletonMap(Object key, Object value);
    public static void sort(java.util.List list);
    public static void sort(java.util.List list, Comparator c);
1.4 public static void swap(java.util.List list, int i, int j);
    public static Collection synchronizedCollection(Collection c);
```

```
   public static java.util.List synchronizedList(java.util.List list);
   public static Map synchronizedMap(Map m);
   public static Set synchronizedSet(Set s);
   public static SortedMap synchronizedSortedMap(SortedMap m);
   public static SortedSet synchronizedSortedSet(SortedSet s);
   public static Collection unmodifiableCollection(Collection c);
   public static java.util.List unmodifiableList(java.util.List list);
   public static Map unmodifiableMap(Map m);
   public static Set unmodifiableSet(Set s);
   public static SortedMap unmodifiableSortedMap(SortedMap m);
   public static SortedSet unmodifiableSortedSet(SortedSet s);
}
```

Comparator — Java 1.2

java.util

This interface defines a compare() method that specifies a total ordering for a set of objects, allowing those objects to be sorted. The Comparator is used when the objects to be ordered do not have a natural ordering defined by the Comparable interface, or when you want to order them using something other than their natural ordering.

The compare() method is passed two objects. If the first argument is less than the second argument or should be placed before the second argument in a sorted list, compare() should return a negative integer. If the first argument is greater than the second argument or should be placed after the second argument in a sorted list, compare() should return a positive integer. If the two objects are equivalent or if their relative position in a sorted list does not matter, compare() should return 0. Comparator implementations may assume that both Object arguments are of appropriate types and cast them as desired. If either argument is not of the expected type, the compare() method throws a ClassCastException.

Note that the magnitude of the numbers returned by compare() does not matter, only whether they are less than, equal to, or greater than zero. In most cases, you should implement a Comparator so that compare(o1,o2) returns 0 if and only if o1.equals(o2) returns true. This is particularly important when using a Comparator to impose an ordering on a TreeSet or a TreeMap.

See Collections and Arrays for various methods that use Comparator objects for sorting and searching. See also the related java.lang.Comparable interface.

```
public interface Comparator {
// Public Instance Methods
   public abstract int compare(Object o1, Object o2);
   public abstract boolean equals(Object obj);
}
```

Implementations: java.text.Collator

Passed To: Arrays.{binarySearch(), sort()}, Collections.{binarySearch(), max(), min(), sort()}, TreeMap.TreeMap(), TreeSet.TreeSet(), javax.swing.SortingFocusTraversalPolicy.{setComparator(), SortingFocusTraversalPolicy()}

Returned By: Collections.reverseOrder(), SortedMap.comparator(), SortedSet.comparator(), TreeMap.comparator(), TreeSet.comparator(), javax.swing.SortingFocusTraversalPolicy.getComparator()

Type Of: String.CASE_INSENSITIVE_ORDER

ConcurrentModificationException — Java 1.2

java.util — *serializable unchecked*

This exception signals that a modification has been made to a data structure at the same time some other operation is in progress and that, as a result, the correctness of the ongoing operation cannot be guaranteed. It is typically thrown by an Iterator or ListIterator object to stop an iteration if it detects that the underlying collection has been modified while the iteration is in progress.

Object — Throwable — Exception — RuntimeException — ConcurrentModificationException
Serializable

```
public class ConcurrentModificationException extends RuntimeException {
// Public Constructors
    public ConcurrentModificationException();
    public ConcurrentModificationException(String message);
}
```

Currency — Java 1.4

java.util — *serializable*

Instances of this class represent a currency. Obtain a Currency object by passing a "currency code," such as "USD" for U.S. dollars or "EUR" for Euros, to getInstance(). Once you have a Currency object, use getSymbol() to obtain the currency symbol (which is often different from the currency code) for the default locale or for a specified Locale. For example, the symbol for a USD would be "$" in a U.S locale but might be "US$" in other locales. If no symbol is known, this method returns the currency code.

Use getDefaultFractionDigits() to determine how many fractional digits are conventionally used with the currency. This method returns 2 for the U.S. dollar and other currencies that are divided into hundredths but returns 3 for the Jordanian Dinar (JOD) and other currencies that are traditionally divided into thousandths. It returns 0 for the Japanese Yen (JPY) and other currencies that have a small unit value and are not usually divided into fractional parts at all. Currency codes are standardized by the ISO 4217 standard. For a complete list of currencies and currency codes, see the web site of the maintenance agency for this standard at *http://www.bsi-global.com/Technical+Information/Publications/_Publications/tig90.xalter*.

Object — Currency ··· Serializable

```
public final class Currency implements Serializable {
// No Constructor
// Public Class Methods
    public static Currency getInstance(String currencyCode);
    public static Currency getInstance(Locale locale);
// Public Instance Methods
    public String getCurrencyCode();
    public int getDefaultFractionDigits();
    public String getSymbol();
    public String getSymbol(Locale locale);
// Public Methods Overriding Object
    public String toString();
}
```

Passed To: java.text.DecimalFormat.setCurrency(), java.text.DecimalFormatSymbols.setCurrency(), java.text.NumberFormat.setCurrency()

Returned By: java.text.DecimalFormat.getCurrency(), java.text.DecimalFormatSymbols.getCurrency(), java.text.NumberFormat.getCurrency(), Currency.getInstance()

Date **Java 1.0**

java.util ***cloneable serializable comparable***

This class represents dates and times and lets you work with them in a system-independent way. You can create a Date by specifying the number of milliseconds from the epoch (midnight GMT, January 1st, 1970) or the year, month, date, and, optionally, the hour, minute, and second. Years are specified as the number of years since 1900. If you call the Date constructor with no arguments, the Date is initialized to the current time and date. The instance methods of the class allow you to get and set the various date and time fields, to compare dates and times, and to convert dates to and from string representations. As of Java 1.1, many of the date methods have been deprecated in favor of the methods of the Calendar class.

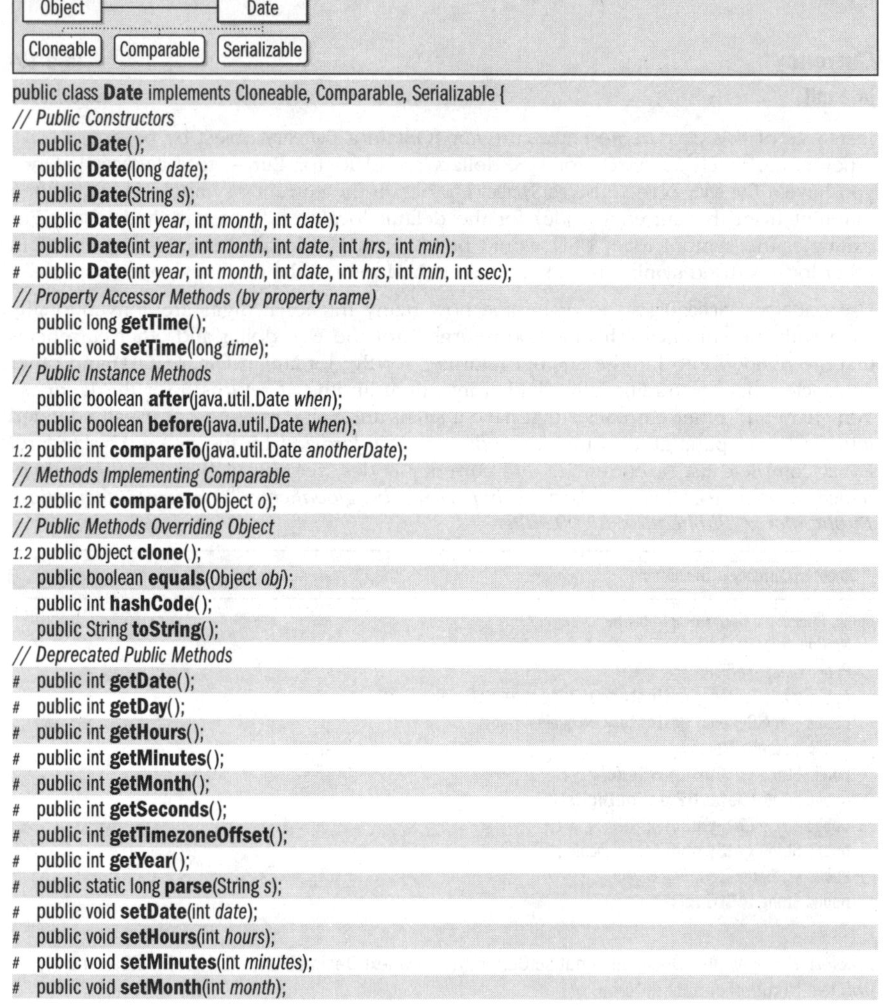


```
public class Date implements Cloneable, Comparable, Serializable {
// Public Constructors
   public Date();
   public Date(long date);
#  public Date(String s);
#  public Date(int year, int month, int date);
#  public Date(int year, int month, int date, int hrs, int min);
#  public Date(int year, int month, int date, int hrs, int min, int sec);
// Property Accessor Methods (by property name)
   public long getTime();
   public void setTime(long time);
// Public Instance Methods
   public boolean after(java.util.Date when);
   public boolean before(java.util.Date when);
1.2 public int compareTo(java.util.Date anotherDate);
// Methods Implementing Comparable
1.2 public int compareTo(Object o);
// Public Methods Overriding Object
1.2 public Object clone();
   public boolean equals(Object obj);
   public int hashCode();
   public String toString();
// Deprecated Public Methods
#  public int getDate();
#  public int getDay();
#  public int getHours();
#  public int getMinutes();
#  public int getMonth();
#  public int getSeconds();
#  public int getTimezoneOffset();
#  public int getYear();
#  public static long parse(String s);
#  public void setDate(int date);
#  public void setHours(int hours);
#  public void setMinutes(int minutes);
#  public void setMonth(int month);
```

```
# public void setSeconds(int seconds);
# public void setYear(int year);
# public String toGMTString();
# public String toLocaleString();
# public static long UTC(int year, int month, int date, int hrs, int min, int sec);
}
```

Subclasses: java.sql.Date, java.sql.Time, java.sql.Timestamp

Passed To: Too many methods to list.

Returned By: Too many methods to list.

Dictionary — Java 1.0

java.util

This abstract class is the superclass of Hashtable. Other hashtable-like data structures might also extend this class. See Hashtable for more information. In Java 1.2, the Map interface replaces the functionality of this class.

```
public abstract class Dictionary {
// Public Constructors
   public Dictionary();
// Public Instance Methods
   public abstract Enumeration elements();
   public abstract Object get(Object key);
   public abstract boolean isEmpty();
   public abstract Enumeration keys();
   public abstract Object put(Object key, Object value);
   public abstract Object remove(Object key);
   public abstract int size();
}
```

Subclasses: Hashtable

Passed To: javax.swing.JSlider.setLabelTable(), javax.swing.text.AbstractDocument.setDocumentProperties()

Returned By: javax.swing.JSlider.getLabelTable(), javax.swing.text.AbstractDocument.getDocumentProperties()

EmptyStackException — Java 1.0

java.util — *serializable unchecked*

This exception signals that a Stack object is empty.

Object — Throwable — Exception — RuntimeException — EmptyStackException
Throwable ⋯ Serializable

```
public class EmptyStackException extends RuntimeException {
// Public Constructors
   public EmptyStackException();
}
```

Thrown By: java.awt.EventQueue.pop()

Enumeration — Java 1.0

java.util

This interface defines the methods necessary to enumerate, or iterate, through a set of values, such as the set of values contained in a hashtable or binary tree. It is particularly useful for data structures, like hashtables, for which elements cannot simply be looked up by index, as they can in arrays. An Enumeration is usually not instantiated directly, but instead is created by the object that is to have its values enumerated. A number of classes, such as Vector and Hashtable, have methods that return Enumeration objects. In Java 1.2, the new Iterator interface is preferred over Enumeration.

To use an Enumeration object, you use its two methods in a loop. hasMoreElements() returns true if there are more values to be enumerated and can determine whether a loop should continue. Within a loop, a call to nextElement() returns a value from the enumeration. An Enumeration makes no guarantees about the order in which the values are returned. The values in an Enumeration can be iterated through only once; there is no way to reset it to the beginning.

```
public interface Enumeration {
// Public Instance Methods
   public abstract boolean hasMoreElements();
   public abstract Object nextElement();
}
```

Implementations: java.text.CharSet.Enumeration, StringTokenizer, javax.naming.NamingEnumeration

Passed To: java.io.SequenceInputStream.SequenceInputStream(), Collections.list(), javax.naming.CompositeName.CompositeName(), javax.naming.CompoundName.CompoundName(), javax.swing.JTree.removeDescendantToggledPaths(), javax.swing.text.AbstractDocument.AbstractElement.removeAttributes(), javax.swing.text.AbstractDocument.AttributeContext.removeAttributes(), javax.swing.text.MutableAttributeSet.removeAttributes(), javax.swing.text.SimpleAttributeSet.removeAttributes(), javax.swing.text.StyleContext.removeAttributes(), javax.swing.text.StyleContext.NamedStyle.removeAttributes(), javax.swing.text.html.StyleSheet.removeAttributes()

Returned By: Too many methods to list.

Type Of: javax.swing.tree.DefaultMutableTreeNode.EMPTY_ENUMERATION

EventListener — Java 1.1

java.util — *event listener*

EventListener is a base interface for the event model that is used by AWT and Swing in Java 1.1 and later. This interface defines no methods or constants; it serves simply as a tag that identifies objects that act as event listeners. The event listener interfaces in the java.awt.event, java.beans, and javax.swing.event packages extend this interface.

```
public interface EventListener {
}
```

Implementations: Too many classes to list.

Passed To: java.awt.AWTEventMulticaster.{addInternal(), AWTEventMulticaster(), getListeners(), remove(), removeInternal(), save()}, EventListenerProxy.EventListenerProxy(), javax.swing.event.EventListenerList.{add(), remove()}

Returned By: Too many methods to list.

Type Of: java.awt.AWTEventMulticaster.{a, b}

EventListenerProxy **Java 1.4**

java.util

This abstract class serves as the superclass for event listener proxy objects. Subclasses of this class implement an event listener interface and serve as a wrapper around an event listener of that type, defining methods that provide additional information about the listener. See java.beans.PropertyChangeListenerProxy for an explanation of how event listener proxy objects are used.

Object — EventListenerProxy ··· EventListener

```
public abstract class EventListenerProxy implements java.util.EventListener {
// Public Constructors
   public EventListenerProxy(java.util.EventListener listener);
// Public Instance Methods
   public java.util.EventListener getListener();
}
```

Subclasses: java.awt.event.AWTEventListenerProxy, java.beans.PropertyChangeListenerProxy, java.beans.VetoableChangeListenerProxy

EventObject **Java 1.1**

java.util *serializable event*

EventObject serves as the superclass for all event objects used by the event model introduced in Java 1.1 for AWT and JavaBeans and also used by Swing in Java 1.2. This class defines a generic type of event; it is extended by the more specific event classes in the java.awt, java.awt.event, java.beans, and javax.swing.event packages. The only common feature shared by all events is a source object, which is the object that, in some way, generated the event. The source object is passed to the EventObject() constructor and is returned by the getSource() method.

Object — EventObject ··· Serializable

```
public class EventObject implements Serializable {
// Public Constructors
   public EventObject(Object source);
// Public Instance Methods
   public Object getSource();
// Public Methods Overriding Object
   public String toString();
// Protected Instance Fields
   protected transient Object source;
}
```

Subclasses: Too many classes to list.

Passed To: javax.swing.AbstractCellEditor.{isCellEditable(), shouldSelectCell()}, javax.swing.CellEditor.{isCellEditable(), shouldSelectCell()}, javax.swing.DefaultCellEditor.{isCellEditable(), shouldSelectCell()}, javax.swing.DefaultCellEditor.EditorDelegate.{isCellEditable(), shouldSelectCell(), startCellEditing()}, javax.swing.JTable.editCellAt(), javax.swing.tree.DefaultTreeCellEditor.{canEditImmediately(), isCellEditable(), shouldSelectCell(), shouldStartEditingTimer()}

GregorianCalendar — Java 1.1

java.util — *cloneable serializable*

This concrete subclass of Calendar implements the standard solar calendar with years numbered from the birth of Christ that is used is most locales throughout the world. You do not typically use this class directly, but instead obtain a Calendar object suitable for the default locale by calling Calendar.getInstance(). See Calendar for details on working with Calendar objects. There is a discontinuity in the Gregorian calendar that represents the historical switch from the Julian calendar to the Gregorian calendar. By default, GregorianCalendar assumes that this switch occurs on October 15, 1582. Most programs need not be concerned with the switch.

Object — Calendar — GregorianCalendar
Cloneable, Serializable

```
public class GregorianCalendar extends Calendar {
// Public Constructors
    public GregorianCalendar();
    public GregorianCalendar(TimeZone zone);
    public GregorianCalendar(Locale aLocale);
    public GregorianCalendar(TimeZone zone, Locale aLocale);
    public GregorianCalendar(int year, int month, int date);
    public GregorianCalendar(int year, int month, int date, int hour, int minute);
    public GregorianCalendar(int year, int month, int date, int hour, int minute, int second);
// Public Constants
    public static final int AD;                                                        =1
    public static final int BC;                                                        =0
// Public Instance Methods
    public final java.util.Date getGregorianChange();
    public boolean isLeapYear(int year);
    public void setGregorianChange(java.util.Date date);
// Public Methods Overriding Calendar
    public void add(int field, int amount);
    public boolean equals(Object obj);
1.2 public int getActualMaximum(int field);
1.2 public int getActualMinimum(int field);
    public int getGreatestMinimum(int field);
    public int getLeastMaximum(int field);
    public int getMaximum(int field);
    public int getMinimum(int field);
    public int hashCode();
1.2 public void roll(int field, int amount);
    public void roll(int field, boolean up);
// Protected Methods Overriding Calendar
    protected void computeFields();
    protected void computeTime();
}
```

HashMap — Java 1.2

java.util — *cloneable serializable collection*

This class implements the Map interface using an internal hashtable. It supports all optional Map methods, allows key and value objects of any types, and allows null to be used as a key or a value. Because HashMap is based on a hashtable data structure, the get() and put() methods are very efficient. HashMap is much like the Hashtable class, except that the HashMap methods are not synchronized (and are therefore faster), and

HashMap allows null to be used as a key or a value. If you are working in a multithreaded environment, or if compatibility with previous versions of Java is a concern, use Hashtable. Otherwise, use HashMap.

If you know in advance approximately how many mappings a HashMap will contain, you can improve efficiency by specifying *initialCapacity* when you call the HashMap() constructor. The *initialCapacity* argument times the *loadFactor* argument should be greater than the number of mappings the HashMap will contain. A good value for *loadFactor* is 0.75; this is also the default value. See Map for details on the methods of HashMap. See also TreeMap and HashSet.


```
public class HashMap extends AbstractMap implements Cloneable, Map, Serializable {
// Public Constructors
   public HashMap();
   public HashMap(int initialCapacity);
   public HashMap(Map m);
   public HashMap(int initialCapacity, float loadFactor);
// Methods Implementing Map
   public void clear();
   public boolean containsKey(Object key);
   public boolean containsValue(Object value);
   public Set entrySet();
   public Object get(Object key);
   public boolean isEmpty();                                   default:true
   public Set keySet();
   public Object put(Object key, Object value);
   public void putAll(Map t);
   public Object remove(Object key);
   public int size();
   public Collection values();
// Public Methods Overriding AbstractMap
   public Object clone();
}
```

Subclasses: LinkedHashMap, javax.print.attribute.standard.PrinterStateReasons

Type Of: java.beans.beancontext.BeanContextServicesSupport.services, java.beans.beancontext.BeanContextSupport.children

HashSet — Java 1.2

java.util — *cloneable serializable collection*

This class implements Set using an internal hashtable. It supports all optional Set and Collection methods and allows any type of object or null to be a member of the set. Because HashSet is based on a hashtable, the basic add(), remove(), and contains() methods are all quite efficient. HashSet makes no guarantee about the order in which the set elements are enumerated by the Iterator returned by iterator(). The methods of HashSet are not synchronized. If you are using it in a multithreaded environment, you must explicitly synchronize all code that modifies the set or obtain a synchronized wrapper for it by calling Collections.synchronizedSet().

If you know in advance approximately how many mappings a HashSet will contain, you can improve efficiency by specifying *initialCapacity* when you call the HashSet() constructor. The *initialCapacity* argument times the *loadFactor* argument should be greater than the number of mappings the HashSet will contain. A good value for *loadFactor* is 0.75; this is also the default value. See Set and Collection for details on the methods of HashSet. See also TreeSet and HashMap.

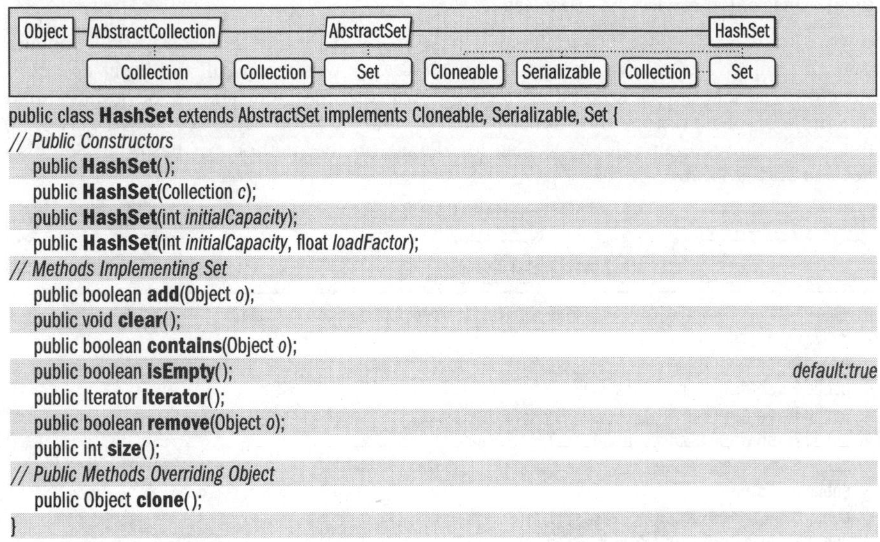


```
public class HashSet extends AbstractSet implements Cloneable, Serializable, Set {
// Public Constructors
   public HashSet();
   public HashSet(Collection c);
   public HashSet(int initialCapacity);
   public HashSet(int initialCapacity, float loadFactor);
// Methods Implementing Set
   public boolean add(Object o);
   public void clear();
   public boolean contains(Object o);
   public boolean isEmpty();                                        default:true
   public Iterator iterator();
   public boolean remove(Object o);
   public int size();
// Public Methods Overriding Object
   public Object clone();
}
```

Subclasses: LinkedHashSet, javax.print.attribute.standard.JobStateReasons

Hashtable **Java 1.0**

java.util ***cloneable serializable collection***

This class implements a hashtable data structure, which maps key objects to value objects and allows the efficient lookup of the value associated with a given key. put() associates a value with a key in a Hashtable. get() retrieves a value for a specified key. remove() deletes a key/value association. keys() and elements() return Enumeration objects that allow you to iterate through the complete set of keys and values stored in the table. Objects used as keys in a Hashtable must have valid equals() and hashCode() methods (the versions inherited from Object are okay). null is not legal as a key or value in a Hashtable.

Hashtable is a commonly used class and has been a part of the Java API since Java 1.0. In Java 1.2, it has been enhanced to implement the Map interface, which defines some functionality in addition to the Java 1.0 Hashtable methods. Hashtable is very similar to the HashMap class, but has synchronized methods, which make it thread-safe but increase the overhead associated with it. If you need thread safety or require compatibility with Java 1.0 or Java 1.1, use Hashtable. Otherwise, use HashMap.

Object — Dictionary — Hashtable

Cloneable | Map | Serializable

```
public class Hashtable extends Dictionary implements Cloneable, Map, Serializable {
// Public Constructors
    public Hashtable();
1.2 public Hashtable(Map t);
    public Hashtable(int initialCapacity);
    public Hashtable(int initialCapacity, float loadFactor);
// Public Instance Methods
    public void clear();                                Implements:Map synchronized
```

```
    public boolean contains(Object value);                                          synchronized
    public boolean containsKey(Object key);                          Implements:Map synchronized
    public Object get(Object key);                                   Implements:Map synchronized
    public boolean isEmpty();                           Implements:Map synchronized default:true
    public Object put(Object key, Object value);                     Implements:Map synchronized
    public Object remove(Object key);                                Implements:Map synchronized
    public int size();                                               Implements:Map synchronized
// Methods Implementing Map
    public void clear();                                                            synchronized
    public boolean containsKey(Object key);                                         synchronized
1.2 public boolean containsValue(Object value);
1.2 public Set entrySet();
1.2 public boolean equals(Object o);                                                synchronized
    public Object get(Object key);                                                  synchronized
1.2 public int hashCode();                                                          synchronized
    public boolean isEmpty();                                       synchronized default:true
1.2 public Set keySet();
    public Object put(Object key, Object value);                                    synchronized
1.2 public void putAll(Map t);                                                      synchronized
    public Object remove(Object key);                                               synchronized
    public int size();                                                              synchronized
1.2 public Collection values();
// Public Methods Overriding Dictionary
    public Enumeration elements();                                                  synchronized
    public Enumeration keys();                                                      synchronized
// Public Methods Overriding Object
    public Object clone();                                                          synchronized
    public String toString();                                                       synchronized
// Protected Instance Methods
    protected void rehash();
}
```

Subclasses: Properties, javax.swing.UIDefaults

Passed To: Too many methods to list.

Returned By: javax.naming.CannotProceedException.getEnvironment(), javax.naming.Context.getEnvironment(), javax.naming.InitialContext.getEnvironment(), javax.swing.JLayeredPane.getComponentToLayer(), javax.swing.JSlider.createStandardLabels()

Type Of: java.awt.GridBagLayout.comptable, java.text.RuleBasedBreakIterator.Builder.expressions, javax.naming.CannotProceedException.environment, javax.naming.InitialContext.myProps, javax.swing.JTable.{defaultEditorsByColumnClass, defaultRenderersByColumnClass}, javax.swing.plaf.basic.BasicFileChooserUI.BasicFileView.iconCache, javax.swing.plaf.basic.BasicTreeUI.drawingCache, javax.swing.text.html.parser.DTD.{elementHash, entityHash}, javax.swing.undo.StateEdit.{postState, preState}

IdentityHashMap — Java 1.4

java.util — ***cloneable serializable collection***

This Map implementation has an API similar to HashMap and uses an internal hashtable, as HashMap does. However, it behaves differently from HashMap in one very important way. When testing two keys to see if they are equal, HashMap, LinkedHashMap, and TreeMap use the equals() method to determine whether the two objects are indistinguishable in terms of their content or state. IdentityHashMap is different: it uses the == operator to determine whether the two key objects are identical—i.e., whether they are exactly the same object. This one difference in how key equality is tested has profound ramifications for the behavior of the Map. In most cases, the equality testing of a HashMap, LinkedHashMap, or TreeMap is the appropriate behavior, and you should use one of those classes. For certain purposes, however, the identity testing of IdentityHashMap is required.

Object — AbstractMap — IdentityHashMap
Map | Cloneable | Map | Serializable

```
public class IdentityHashMap extends AbstractMap implements Cloneable, Map, Serializable {
// Public Constructors
   public IdentityHashMap();
   public IdentityHashMap(int expectedMaxSize);
   public IdentityHashMap(Map m);
// Methods Implementing Map
   public void clear();
   public boolean containsKey(Object key);
   public boolean containsValue(Object value);
   public Set entrySet();
   public boolean equals(Object o);
   public Object get(Object key);
   public int hashCode();
   public boolean isEmpty();                                    default:true
   public Set keySet();
   public Object put(Object key, Object value);
   public void putAll(Map t);
   public Object remove(Object key);
   public int size();
   public Collection values();
// Public Methods Overriding AbstractMap
   public Object clone();
}
```

Iterator — Java 1.2

java.util

This interface defines methods for iterating, or enumerating, the elements of a collection. The hasNext() method returns true if there are more elements to be enumerated or false if all elements have already been returned. The next() method returns the next element. These two methods make it easy to loop through an iterator with code such as the following:

```
for(Iterator i = c.iterator(); i.hasNext(); )
   processObject(i.next());
```

The Iterator interface is much like the Enumeration interface. In Java 1.2, Iterator is preferred over Enumeration because it provides a well-defined way to safely remove elements from a collection while the iteration is in progress. The remove() method removes the object most recently returned by next() from the collection that is being iterated through. Note, however, that support for remove() is optional; if an Iterator does not support remove(), it throws a java.lang.UnsupportedOperationException when you call it. While you are iterating through a collection, you are allowed to modify the collection only by calling the remove() method of the Iterator. If the collection is modified in any other way while an iteration is ongoing, the Iterator may fail to operate correctly, or it may throw a ConcurrentModificationException.

```
public interface Iterator {
// Public Instance Methods
   public abstract boolean hasNext();
   public abstract Object next();
   public abstract void remove();
}
```

Implementations: java.beans.beancontext.BeanContextSupport.BCSIterator, ListIterator

Passed To: javax.imageio.ImageReader.{getDestination(), readAll()}, javax.imageio.spi.ServiceRegistry.{registerServiceProviders(), ServiceRegistry()}

Returned By: Too many methods to list.

LinkedHashMap — Java 1.4

java.util — *cloneable serializable collection*

This class is a Map implementation based on a hashtable, just like its superclass HashMap. It defines no new public methods, and can be used exactly as HashMap is used. What is unique about this Map is that in addition to the hashtable data structure, it also uses a doubly-linked list to connect the keys of the Map into an internal list which defines a predictable iteration order.

You can iterate through the keys or values of a LinkedHashMap by calling entrySet(), keySet(), or values() and then obtaining an Iterator for the returned collection, just as you would for a HashMap. When you do this, however, the keys and/or values are returned in a well-defined order rather than the essentially random order provided by a HashMap. The default ordering for LinkedHashMap is the insertion order of the key: the first key inserted into the Map is enumerated first (as is the value associated with it), and the last entry inserted is enumerated last. Note that this order is not affect by re-insertions. That is, if a LinkedHashMap contains a mapping from a key *k* to a value *v1*, and you call the put() method to map from *k* to a new value *v2*, this does not change the insertion order, or the iteration order of the key *k*. The iteration order of a value in the map is the iteration order of the key with which it is associated.

Insertion order is the default iteration order for this class, but if you instantiate a LinkedHashMap with the three-argument constructor, and pass true for the third argument, then the iteration order will be based on access order: the first key returned by an iterator is the one that was least-recently used in a get() or put() operation. The last key returned is the one that has been most-recently used. As with insertion order, the values() collection is iterated in the order defined by the keys with which those values are associated.

"Access ordering" is particularly useful for implementing LRU caches from which the Least-Recently Used elements are periodically purged. To facilitate this use, LinkedHashMap defines the protected removeEldestEntry() method. Each time the put() method is called (or for each mapping added by putAll()) the LinkedHashMap calls removeEldestEntry() and passes the least-recently used (or first inserted if insertion order is being used) Map.Entry object. If the method returns true, then that entry will be removed from the map. In LinkedHashMap, removeEldestEntry() always returns false, and old entries are never automatically removed, but you can override this behavior in a subclass. The decision to remove an old entry might be based on the content of the entry itself, or might more simply be based on the size() of the LinkedHashMap. Note that removeEldestEntry() need simply return true or false; it should not remove the entry itself.

Object — AbstractMap — HashMap — LinkedHashMap
Map Cloneable Map Serializable

```
public class LinkedHashMap extends HashMap {
// Public Constructors
   public LinkedHashMap();
   public LinkedHashMap(int initialCapacity);
   public LinkedHashMap(Map m);
   public LinkedHashMap(int initialCapacity, float loadFactor);
   public LinkedHashMap(int initialCapacity, float loadFactor, boolean accessOrder);
// Public Methods Overriding HashMap
   public void clear();
   public boolean containsValue(Object value);
   public Object get(Object key);
// Protected Instance Methods
   protected boolean removeEldestEntry(Map.Entry eldest);                constant
}
```

LinkedHashSet — Java 1.4

java.util — ***cloneable serializable collection***

This subclass of HashSet is a Set implementation based on a hashtable. It defines no new methods and is used just like a HashSet. What makes LinkedHashSet unique is that in addition to the hashtable data structure, it uses a doubly linked list to connect the elements of the set into an internal list in the order in which they were inserted. This means that the Iterator returned by the inherited iterator() method always enumerates the elements of the set in the order in which they were inserted. By contrast, the elements of a HashSet are enumerated in an essentially random order. Note that the iteration order is not affected by reinsertion of set elements. That is, if you attempt to add an element that already exists in the set, the iteration order of the set is not modified. If you delete an element and then reinsert it, the insertion order, and therefore the iteration order, does change.

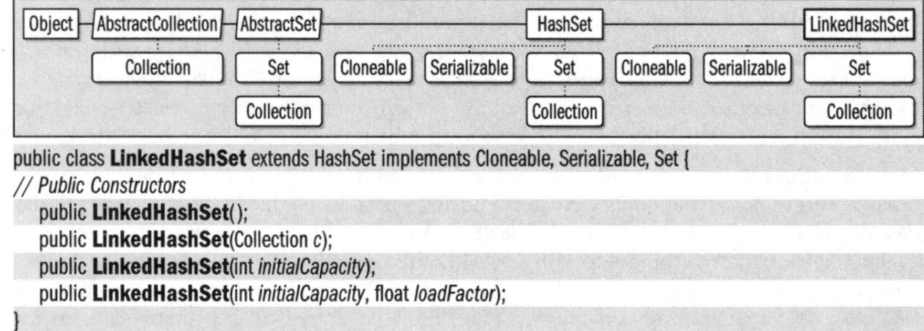


```
public class LinkedHashSet extends HashSet implements Cloneable, Serializable, Set {
// Public Constructors
   public LinkedHashSet();
   public LinkedHashSet(Collection c);
   public LinkedHashSet(int initialCapacity);
   public LinkedHashSet(int initialCapacity, float loadFactor);
}
```

LinkedList — Java 1.2

java.util — ***cloneable serializable collection***

This class implements the List interface in terms of a doubly linked list. It supports all optional methods of List and Collection and allows list elements of any type, including null. Because LinkedList is implemented with a linked list data structure, the get() and set() methods are substantially less efficient than the same methods for an ArrayList. However, a LinkedList may be more efficient when the add() and remove() methods are used frequently. The methods of LinkedList are not synchronized. If you are using a LinkedList in a multithreaded environment, you must explicitly synchronize any code that modifies the list or obtain a synchronized wrapper object with Collections.synchronizedList().

In addition to the methods defined by the List interface, LinkedList defines methods to get the first and last elements of the list, to add an element to the beginning or end of the list, and to remove the first or last element of the list. These convenient and efficient methods make LinkedList well-suited for use as a stack or queue. See List and Collection for details on the methods of LinkedList. See also ArrayList.

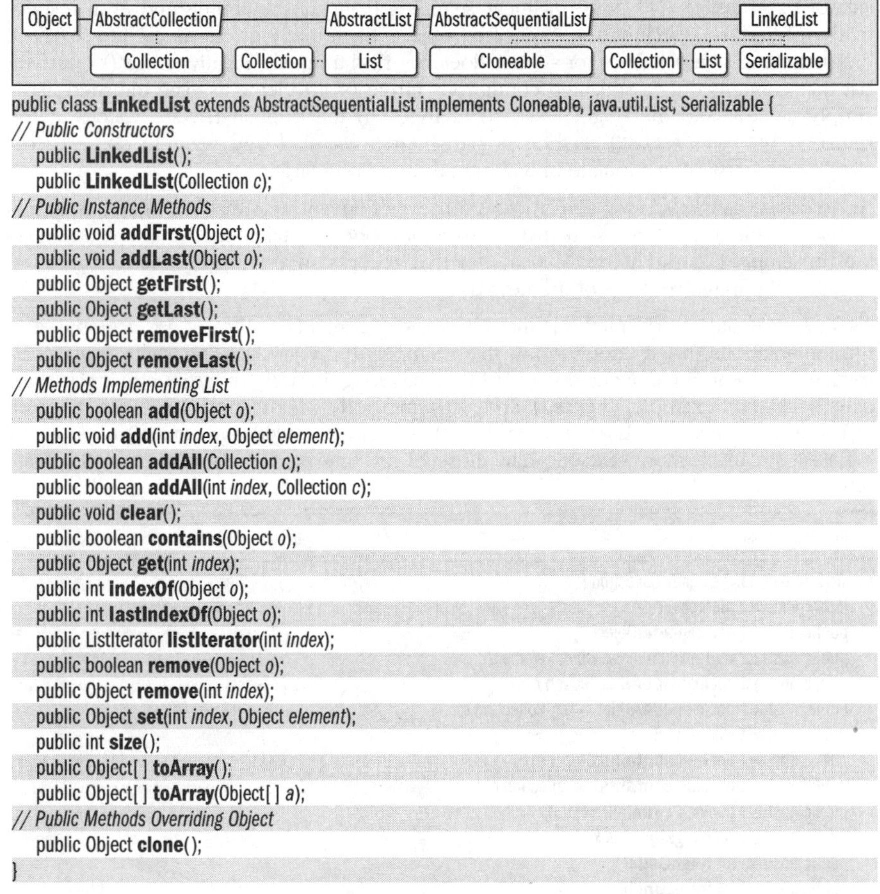


```
public class LinkedList extends AbstractSequentialList implements Cloneable, java.util.List, Serializable {
// Public Constructors
   public LinkedList();
   public LinkedList(Collection c);
// Public Instance Methods
   public void addFirst(Object o);
   public void addLast(Object o);
   public Object getFirst();
   public Object getLast();
   public Object removeFirst();
   public Object removeLast();
// Methods Implementing List
   public boolean add(Object o);
   public void add(int index, Object element);
   public boolean addAll(Collection c);
   public boolean addAll(int index, Collection c);
   public void clear();
   public boolean contains(Object o);
   public Object get(int index);
   public int indexOf(Object o);
   public int lastIndexOf(Object o);
   public ListIterator listIterator(int index);
   public boolean remove(Object o);
   public Object remove(int index);
   public Object set(int index, Object element);
   public int size();
   public Object[ ] toArray();
   public Object[ ] toArray(Object[ ] a);
// Public Methods Overriding Object
   public Object clone();
}
```

List **Java 1.2**

java.util *collection*

This interface represents an ordered collection of objects. Each element in a List has an index, or position, in the list, and elements can be inserted, queried, and removed by index. The first element of a List has an index of 0. The last element in a list has index size()-1.

In addition to the methods defined by the superinterface, Collection, List defines a number of methods for working with its indexed elements. get() and set() query and set the object at a particular index, respectively. Versions of add() and addAll() that take an *index* argument insert an object or Collection of objects at a specified index. The versions of add() and addAll() that do not take an *index* argument insert an object or collection of objects at the end of the list. List defines a version of remove() that removes the object at a specified index.

The iterator() method is just like the iterator() method of Collection, except that the Iterator it returns is guaranteed to enumerate the elements of the List in order. listIterator() returns a ListIterator object, which is more powerful than a regular Iterator and allows the list to be modified while iteration proceeds. listIterator() can take an index argument to specify where in the list iteration should begin.

indexOf() and lastIndexOf() perform linear searches from the beginning and end, respectively, of the list, searching for a specified object. Each method returns the index of the first matching object it finds, or –1 if it does not find a match. Finally, subList() returns a List that contains only a specified contiguous range of list elements. The returned list is simply a view into the original list, so changes in the original List are visible in the returned List. This subList() method is particularly useful if you want to sort, search, clear(), or otherwise manipulate only a partial range of a larger list.

An interface cannot specify constructors, but it is conventional that all implementations of List provide at least two standard constructors: one that takes no arguments and creates an empty list, and a copy constructor that accepts an arbitrary Collection object that specifies the initial contents of the new List.

As with Collection, all List methods that change the contents of the list are optional, and implementations that do not support them simply throw java.lang.UnsupportedOperationException. Different implementations of List may have significantly different efficiency characteristics. For example, the get() and set() methods of an ArrayList are much more efficient than those of a LinkedList. On the other hand, the add() and remove() methods of a LinkedList can be more efficient than those of an ArrayList. See also Collection, Set, Map, ArrayList, and LinkedList.

Collection ··· List

```
public interface List extends Collection {
// Public Instance Methods
    public abstract boolean add(Object o);
    public abstract void add(int index, Object element);
    public abstract boolean addAll(Collection c);
    public abstract boolean addAll(int index, Collection c);
    public abstract void clear();
    public abstract boolean contains(Object o);
    public abstract boolean containsAll(Collection c);
    public abstract boolean equals(Object o);
    public abstract Object get(int index);
    public abstract int hashCode();
    public abstract int indexOf(Object o);
    public abstract boolean isEmpty();
    public abstract Iterator iterator();
    public abstract int lastIndexOf(Object o);
    public abstract ListIterator listIterator();
    public abstract ListIterator listIterator(int index);
    public abstract boolean remove(Object o);
    public abstract Object remove(int index);
    public abstract boolean removeAll(Collection c);
    public abstract boolean retainAll(Collection c);
    public abstract Object set(int index, Object element);
```

```
    public abstract int size();
    public abstract java.util.List subList(int fromIndex, int toIndex);
    public abstract Object[ ] toArray();
    public abstract Object[ ] toArray(Object[ ] a);
}
```

Implementations: AbstractList, ArrayList, LinkedList, Vector

Passed To: Too many methods to list.

Returned By: Too many methods to list.

Type Of: Collections.EMPTY_LIST, javax.imageio.IIOImage.thumbnails, javax.imageio.ImageReader.{progressListeners, updateListeners, warningListeners, warningLocales}, javax.imageio.ImageWriter.{progressListeners, warningListeners, warningLocales}

ListIterator — Java 1.2

java.util

This interface is an extension of Iterator for use with ordered collections, or lists. It defines methods to iterate forward and backward through a list, to determine the list index of the elements being iterated, and, for mutable lists, to safely insert, delete, and edit elements in the list while the iteration is in progress. For some lists, notably LinkedList, using an iterator to enumerate the list's elements may be substantially more efficient than looping through the list by index and calling get() repeatedly.

hasNext() and next() are the most commonly used methods of ListIterator; they iterate forward through the list. See Iterator for details. In addition to these two methods, however, ListIterator also defines hasPrevious() and previous() that allow you to iterate backward through the list. previous() returns the previous element on the list or throws a NoSuchElementException if there is no previous element. hasPrevious() returns true if a subsequent call to previous() returns an object. nextIndex() and previousIndex() return the index of the object that would be returned by a subsequent call to next() or previous(). If next() or previous() throw a NoSuchElementException, nextIndex() returns the size of the list, and previousIndex() returns –1.

ListIterator defines three optionally supported methods that provide a safe way to modify the contents of the underlying list while the iteration is in progress. add() inserts a new object into the list, immediately before the object that would be returned by a subsequent call to next(). Calling add() does not affect the value that is returned by next(), however. If you call previous() immediately after calling add(), the method returns the object you just added. remove() deletes from the list the object most recently returned by next() or previous(). You can only call remove() once per call to next() or previous(). If you have called add(), you must call next() or previous() again before calling remove(). set() replaces the object most recently returned by next() or previous() with the specified object. If you have called add() or remove(), you must call next() or previous() again before calling set(). Remember that support for the add(), remove(), and set() methods is optional. Iterators for immutable lists never support them, of course. An unsupported method throws a java.lang.UnsupportedOperationException when called. Also, when an iterator is in use, all modifications should be made through the iterator rather than to the list itself. If the underlying list is modified while an iteration is ongoing, the ListIterator may fail to operate correctly or may throw a ConcurrentModificationException.

Iterator — ListIterator

```
public interface ListIterator extends Iterator {
// Public Instance Methods
```

```
    public abstract void add(Object o);
    public abstract boolean hasNext();
    public abstract boolean hasPrevious();
    public abstract Object next();
    public abstract int nextIndex();
    public abstract Object previous();
    public abstract int previousIndex();
    public abstract void remove();
    public abstract void set(Object o);
}
```

Returned By: AbstractList.listIterator(), AbstractSequentialList.listIterator(), LinkedList.listIterator(), java.util.List.listIterator()

ListResourceBundle — Java 1.1

java.util

This abstract class provides a simple way to define a ResourceBundle. You may find it easier to subclass ListResourceBundle than to subclass ResourceBundle directly. ListResourceBundle provides implementations for the abstract handleGetObject() and getKeys() methods defined by ResourceBundle and adds its own abstract getContents() method a subclass must override. getContents() returns an Object[][]—an array of arrays of objects. This array can have any number of elements. Each element of this array must itself be an array with two elements: the first element of each subarray should be a String that specifies the name of a resource, and the corresponding second element should be the value of that resource; this value can be an Object of any desired type. See also ResourceBundle and PropertyResourceBundle.

Object — ResourceBundle — ListResourceBundle

```
public abstract class ListResourceBundle extends ResourceBundle {
// Public Constructors
    public ListResourceBundle();
// Public Methods Overriding ResourceBundle
    public Enumeration getKeys();
    public final Object handleGetObject(String key);
// Protected Instance Methods
    protected abstract Object[ ][ ] getContents();
}
```

Subclasses: javax.accessibility.AccessibleResourceBundle

Locale — Java 1.1

java.util — *cloneable serializable*

The Locale class represents a locale: a political, geographical, or cultural region that typically has a distinct language and distinct customs and conventions for such things as formatting dates, times, and numbers. The Locale class defines a number of constants that represent commonly used locales. Locale also defines a static getDefault() method that returns the default Locale object, which represents a locale value inherited from the host system. getAvailableLocales() returns the list of all locales supported by the underlying system. If none of these methods for obtaining a Locale object are suitable, you can explicitly create your own Locale object. To do this, you must specify a language code and optionally a country code and variant string. getISOCountries() and getISOLanguages() return the list of supported country codes and language codes.

The Locale class does not implement any internationalization behavior itself; it merely serves as a locale identifier for those classes that can localize their behavior. Given a Locale object, you can invoke the various getDisplay methods to obtain a description of the locale suitable for display to a user. These methods may themselves take a Locale argument, so the names of languages and countries can be localized as appropriate.

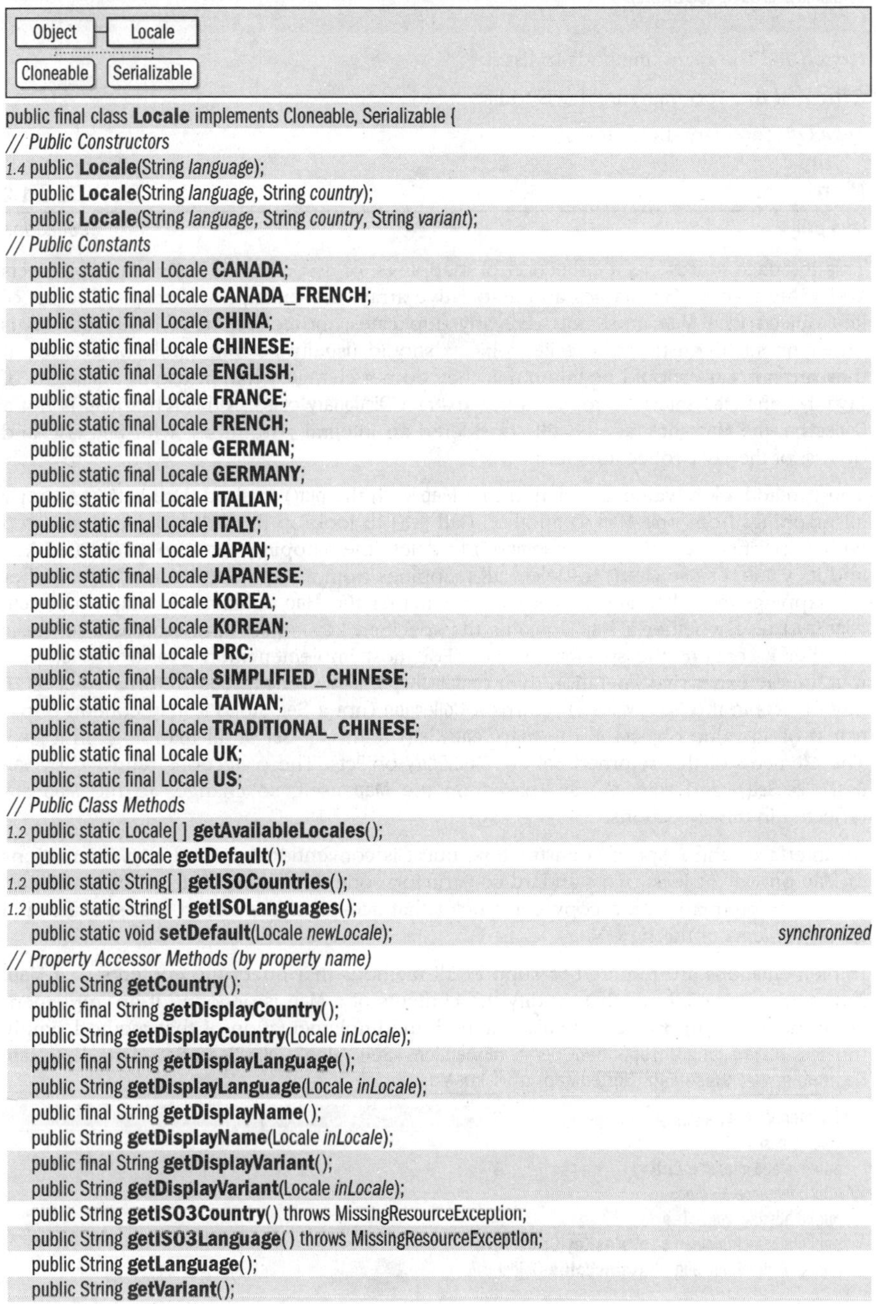


```
public final class Locale implements Cloneable, Serializable {
// Public Constructors
1.4 public Locale(String language);
    public Locale(String language, String country);
    public Locale(String language, String country, String variant);
// Public Constants
    public static final Locale CANADA;
    public static final Locale CANADA_FRENCH;
    public static final Locale CHINA;
    public static final Locale CHINESE;
    public static final Locale ENGLISH;
    public static final Locale FRANCE;
    public static final Locale FRENCH;
    public static final Locale GERMAN;
    public static final Locale GERMANY;
    public static final Locale ITALIAN;
    public static final Locale ITALY;
    public static final Locale JAPAN;
    public static final Locale JAPANESE;
    public static final Locale KOREA;
    public static final Locale KOREAN;
    public static final Locale PRC;
    public static final Locale SIMPLIFIED_CHINESE;
    public static final Locale TAIWAN;
    public static final Locale TRADITIONAL_CHINESE;
    public static final Locale UK;
    public static final Locale US;
// Public Class Methods
1.2 public static Locale[ ] getAvailableLocales();
    public static Locale getDefault();
1.2 public static String[ ] getISOCountries();
1.2 public static String[ ] getISOLanguages();
    public static void setDefault(Locale newLocale);                                   synchronized
// Property Accessor Methods (by property name)
    public String getCountry();
    public final String getDisplayCountry();
    public String getDisplayCountry(Locale inLocale);
    public final String getDisplayLanguage();
    public String getDisplayLanguage(Locale inLocale);
    public final String getDisplayName();
    public String getDisplayName(Locale inLocale);
    public final String getDisplayVariant();
    public String getDisplayVariant(Locale inLocale);
    public String getISO3Country() throws MissingResourceException;
    public String getISO3Language() throws MissingResourceException;
    public String getLanguage();
    public String getVariant();
```

```
// Public Methods Overriding Object
   public Object clone();
   public boolean equals(Object obj);
   public int hashCode();                                              synchronized
   public final String toString();
}
```

Passed To: Too many methods to list.

Returned By: Too many methods to list.

Type Of: Too many fields to list.

Map — Java 1.2

java.util — *collection*

This interface represents a collection of mappings, or associations, between key objects and value objects. Hashtables and associative arrays are examples of maps. The set of key objects in a Map must not have any duplicates; the collection of value objects is under no such constraint. The key objects should usually be immutable objects, or, if they are not, care should be taken that they do not change while in use in a Map. As of Java 1.2, the Map interface replaces the abstract Dictionary class. Although a Map is not a Collection, the Map interface is still considered an integral part, along with Set, List, and others, of the Java collections framework.

You can add a key/value association to a Map with the put() method. Use putAll() to copy all mappings from one Map to another. Call get() to look up the value object associated with a specified key object. Use remove() to delete the mapping between a specified key and its value, or use clear() to delete all mappings from a Map. size() returns the number of mappings in a Map, and isEmpty() tests whether the Map contains no mappings. containsKey() tests whether a Map contains the specified key object, and containsValue() tests whether it contains the specified value. (For most implementations, containsValue() is a much more expensive operation than containsKey(), however.) keySet() returns a Set of all key objects in the Map. values() returns a Collection (not a Set, since it may contain duplicates) of all value objects in the map. entrySet() returns a Set of all mappings in a Map. The elements of this returned Set are Map.Entry objects. The collections returned by values(), keySet(), and entrySet() are based on the Map itself, so changes to the Map are reflected in the collections.

An interface cannot specify constructors, but it is conventional that all implementations of Map provide at least two standard constructors: one that takes no arguments and creates an empty map, and a copy constructor that accepts a Map object that specifies the initial contents of the new Map.

Implementations are required to support all methods that query the contents of a Map, but support for methods that modify the contents of a Map is optional. If an implementation does not support a particular method, the implementation of that method simply throws a java.lang.UnsupportedOperationException. See also Collection, Set, List, HashMap, Hashtable, WeakHashMap, SortedMap, and TreeMap.

```
public interface Map {
// Inner Classes
   public static interface Entry;
// Public Instance Methods
   public abstract void clear();
   public abstract boolean containsKey(Object key);
   public abstract boolean containsValue(Object value);
```

```
    public abstract Set entrySet();
    public abstract boolean equals(Object o);
    public abstract Object get(Object key);
    public abstract int hashCode();
    public abstract boolean isEmpty();
    public abstract Set keySet();
    public abstract Object put(Object key, Object value);
    public abstract void putAll(Map t);
    public abstract Object remove(Object key);
    public abstract int size();
    public abstract Collection values();
}
```

Implementations: java.awt.RenderingHints, AbstractMap, HashMap, Hashtable, IdentityHashMap, SortedMap, WeakHashMap, java.util.jar.Attributes

Passed To: Too many methods to list.

Returned By: Too many methods to list.

Type Of: java.awt.Toolkit.desktopProperties, Collections.EMPTY_MAP, java.util.jar.Attributes.map

Map.Entry — Java 1.2

java.util

This interface represents a single mapping, or association, between a key object and a value object in a Map. The entrySet() method of a Map returns a Set of Map.Entry objects that represent the set of mappings in the map. Use the iterator() method of that Set to enumerate these Map.Entry objects. Use getKey() and getValue() to obtain the key and value objects for the entry. Use the optionally supported setValue() method to change the value of an entry. This method throws a java.lang.UnsupportedOperationException if it is not supported by the implementation.

```
public static interface Map.Entry {
// Public Instance Methods
    public abstract boolean equals(Object o);
    public abstract Object getKey();
    public abstract Object getValue();
    public abstract int hashCode();
    public abstract Object setValue(Object value);
}
```

Passed To: LinkedHashMap.removeEldestEntry()

MissingResourceException — Java 1.1

java.util — *serializable unchecked*

This signals that no ResourceBundle can be located for the desired locale or that a named resource cannot be found within a given ResourceBundle. getClassName() returns the name of the ResourceBundle class in question, and getKey() returns the name of the resource that cannot be located.

Object — Throwable — Exception — RuntimeException — MissingResourceException

Serializable

```
public class MissingResourceException extends RuntimeException {
// Public Constructors
```

```
    public MissingResourceException(String s, String className, String key);
// Public Instance Methods
    public String getClassName();
    public String getKey();
}
```

Thrown By: Locale.{getISO3Country(), getISO3Language()}

NoSuchElementException — Java 1.0

java.util — *serializable unchecked*

This signals that there are no elements in an object (such as a Vector) or that there are no more elements in an object (such as an Enumeration).

Object — Throwable — Exception — RuntimeException — NoSuchElementException

Serializable

```
public class NoSuchElementException extends RuntimeException {
// Public Constructors
    public NoSuchElementException();
    public NoSuchElementException(String s);
}
```

Observable — Java 1.0

java.util

This class is the superclass for classes that want to provide notifications of state changes to interested Observer objects. Register an Observer to be notified by passing it to the addObserver() method of an Observable and deregister it by passing it to the deleteObserver() method. You can delete all observers registered for an Observable with deleteObservers() and find out how many observers have been added with countObservers(). Note that there is not a method to enumerate the particular Observer objects that have been added.

An Observable subclass should call the protected method setChanged() when its state has changed in some way. This sets a "state changed" flag. After an operation or series of operations that may have caused the state to change, the Observable subclass should call notifyObservers(), optionally passing an arbitrary Object argument. If the state changed flag is set, this notifyObservers() calls the update() method of each registered Observer (in some arbitrary order), passing the Observable object and the optional argument, if any. Once the update() method of each Observable has been called, notifyObservers() calls clearChanged() to clear the state changed flag. If notifyObservers() is called when the state changed flag is not set, it does not do anything. You can use hasChanged() to query the current state of the changed flag.

The Observable class and Observer interface are not commonly used. Most applications prefer the event-based notification model defined by the JavaBeans component framework and by the EventObject class and EventListener interface of this package.

```
public class Observable {
// Public Constructors
    public Observable();
// Public Instance Methods
    public void addObserver(Observer o);                    synchronized
    public int countObservers();                            synchronized
    public void deleteObserver(Observer o);                 synchronized
```

```
    public void deleteObservers();                                  synchronized
    public boolean hasChanged();                                    synchronized
    public void notifyObservers();
    public void notifyObservers(Object arg);
// Protected Instance Methods
    protected void clearChanged();                                  synchronized
    protected void setChanged();                                    synchronized
}
```

Passed To: Observer.update()

Observer — Java 1.0

java.util

This interface defines the update() method required for an object to observe subclasses of Observable. An Observer registers interest in an Observable object by calling the addObserver() method of Observable. Observer objects that have been registered in this way have their update() methods invoked by the Observable when that object has changed.

This interface is conceptually similar to, but less commonly used than, the EventListener interface and its various event-specific subinterfaces.

```
public interface Observer {
// Public Instance Methods
    public abstract void update(Observable o, Object arg);
}
```

Passed To: Observable.{addObserver(), deleteObserver()}

Properties — Java 1.0

java.util — *cloneable serializable collection*

This class is an extension of Hashtable that allows key/value pairs to be read from and written to a stream. The Properties class implements the system properties list, which supports user customization by allowing programs to look up the values of named resources. Because the load() and store() methods provide an easy way to read and write properties from and to a text stream, this class provides a convenient way to implement an application configuration file.

When you create a Properties object, you may specify another Properties object that contains default values. Keys (property names) and values are associated in a Properties object with the Hashtable method put(). Values are looked up with getProperty(); if this method does not find the key in the current Properties object, it looks in the default Properties object that was passed to the constructor method. A default value can also be specified, in case the key is not found at all. Use setProperty() to add a property name/value pair to the Properties object. This Java 1.2 method is preferred over the inherited put() method because it enforces the constraint that property names and values be strings.

propertyNames() returns an enumeration of all property names (keys) stored in the Properties object and (recursively) all property names stored in the default Properties object associated with it. list() prints the properties stored in a Properties object, which can be useful for debugging. store() writes a Properties object to a stream, writing one property per line, in name=value format. As of Java 1.2, store() is preferred over the deprecated save() method, which writes properties in the same way but suppresses any I/O exceptions that may be thrown in the process. The second argument to both store() and save() is a comment that is written out at the beginning of the property file. Finally, load()

reads key/value pairs from a stream and stores them in a Properties object. It is suitable for reading both properties written with store() and hand-edited properties files.

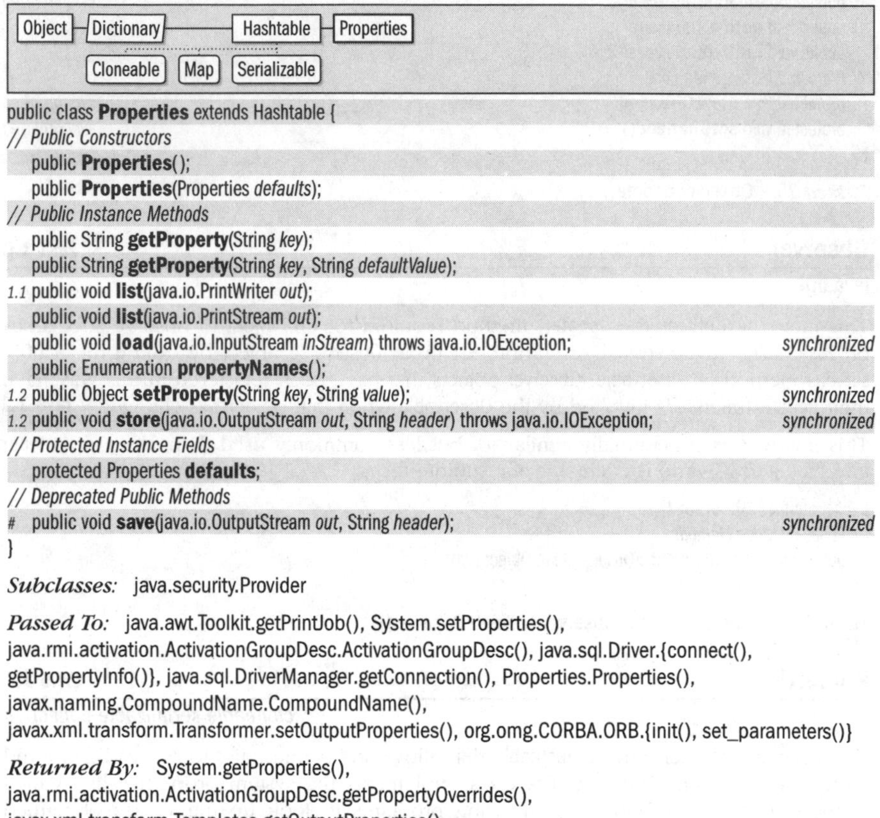


```
public class Properties extends Hashtable {
// Public Constructors
   public Properties();
   public Properties(Properties defaults);
// Public Instance Methods
   public String getProperty(String key);
   public String getProperty(String key, String defaultValue);
1.1 public void list(java.io.PrintWriter out);
   public void list(java.io.PrintStream out);
   public void load(java.io.InputStream inStream) throws java.io.IOException;            synchronized
   public Enumeration propertyNames();
1.2 public Object setProperty(String key, String value);                                  synchronized
1.2 public void store(java.io.OutputStream out, String header) throws java.io.IOException; synchronized
// Protected Instance Fields
   protected Properties defaults;
// Deprecated Public Methods
#  public void save(java.io.OutputStream out, String header);                             synchronized
}
```

Subclasses: java.security.Provider

Passed To: java.awt.Toolkit.getPrintJob(), System.setProperties(), java.rmi.activation.ActivationGroupDesc.ActivationGroupDesc(), java.sql.Driver.{connect(), getPropertyInfo()}, java.sql.DriverManager.getConnection(), Properties.Properties(), javax.naming.CompoundName.CompoundName(), javax.xml.transform.Transformer.setOutputProperties(), org.omg.CORBA.ORB.{init(), set_parameters()}

Returned By: System.getProperties(), java.rmi.activation.ActivationGroupDesc.getPropertyOverrides(), javax.xml.transform.Templates.getOutputProperties(), javax.xml.transform.Transformer.getOutputProperties()

Type Of: Properties.defaults, javax.naming.CompoundName.mySyntax

PropertyPermission — Java 1.2

java.util — ***serializable permission***

This class is a java.security.Permission that governs read and write access to system properties with System.getProperty() and System.setProperty(). A PropertyPermission object has a name, or target, and a comma-separated list of actions. The name of the permission is the name of the property of interest. The action string can be "read" for getProperty() access, "write" for setProperty() access, or "read,write" for both types of access. PropertyPermission extends java.security.BasicPermission, so the name of the property supports simple wildcards. The name "*" represents any property name. If a name ends with ".*", it represents any property names that share the specified prefix. For example, the name "java.*" represents "java.version", "java.vendor", "java.vendor.url", and all other properties that begin with "java".

Granting access to system properties is not overtly dangerous, but caution is still necessary. Some properties, such as "user.home", reveal details about the host system that malicious code can use to mount an attack. Programmers writing system-level code and system administrators configuring security policies may need to use this class, but applications never need to use it.

Object — Permission — BasicPermission — PropertyPermission
Guard, Serializable, Serializable

```
public final class PropertyPermission extends java.security.BasicPermission {
// Public Constructors
   public PropertyPermission(String name, String actions);
// Public Methods Overriding BasicPermission
   public boolean equals(Object obj);
   public String getActions();
   public int hashCode();
   public boolean implies(java.security.Permission p);
   public java.security.PermissionCollection newPermissionCollection();
}
```

PropertyResourceBundle — Java 1.1

java.util

This class is a concrete subclass of ResourceBundle. It reads a Properties file from a specified InputStream and implements the ResourceBundle API for looking up named resources from the resulting Properties object. A Properties file contains lines of the form:

name=value

Each such line defines a named property with the specified String value. Although you can instantiate a PropertyResourceBundle yourself, it is more common to simply define a Properties file and then allow ResourceBundle.getBundle() to look up that file and return the necessary PropertyResourceBundle object. See also Properties and ResourceBundle.

Object — ResourceBundle — PropertyResourceBundle

```
public class PropertyResourceBundle extends ResourceBundle {
// Public Constructors
   public PropertyResourceBundle(java.io.InputStream stream) throws java.io.IOException;
// Public Methods Overriding ResourceBundle
   public Enumeration getKeys();
   public Object handleGetObject(String key);
}
```

Random — Java 1.0

java.util — *serializable*

This class implements a pseudo-random number generator suitable for games and similar applications. If you need a cryptographic-strength source of pseudo-randomness, see java.security.SecureRandom. nextDouble() and nextFloat() return a value between 0.0 and 1.0. nextLong() and the no-argument version of nextInt() return long and int values distributed across the range of those data types. In Java 1.2, if you pass an argument to nextInt(), it returns a value between zero (inclusive) and the specified number (exclusive). nextGaussian() returns pseudo-random floating-point values with a Gaussian distribution; the mean of the values is 0.0 and the standard deviation is 1.0. nextBoolean() returns a pseudo-random boolean value, and nextBytes() fills in the specified byte array with pseudo-random bytes. You can use the setSeed() method or the optional constructor argument to initialize the pseudo-random number generator with some variable seed value other than the current time (the default) or with a constant to ensure a repeatable sequence of pseudo-randomness.

Object ─ Random ··· Serializable

```
public class Random implements Serializable {
// Public Constructors
    public Random();
    public Random(long seed);
// Public Instance Methods
1.2 public boolean nextBoolean();
1.1 public void nextBytes(byte[ ] bytes);
    public double nextDouble();
    public float nextFloat();
    public double nextGaussian();                      synchronized
    public int nextInt();
1.2 public int nextInt(int n);
    public long nextLong();
    public void setSeed(long seed);                    synchronized
// Protected Instance Methods
1.1 protected int next(int bits);                      synchronized
}
```

Subclasses: java.security.SecureRandom

Passed To: java.math.BigInteger.{BigInteger(), probablePrime()}, Collections.shuffle()

RandomAccess — Java 1.4

java.util

This marker interface is implemented by List implementations to advertise that they provide efficient random access (usually constant time) to all list elements. ArrayList and Vector implement this interface, but LinkedList does not. Classes that manipulate generic List objects may want to test for this interface with instanceof and use different algorithms for lists that provide efficient random access than they use for lists that are most efficiently accessed sequentially.

```
public interface RandomAccess {
}
```

Implementations: ArrayList, Vector

ResourceBundle — Java 1.1

java.util

This abstract class allows subclasses to define sets of localized resources that can then be dynamically loaded as needed by internationalized programs. Such resources may include user-visible text and images that appear in an application, as well as more complex things such as Menu objects. Use getBundle() to load a ResourceBundle subclass that is appropriate for the default or specified locale. Use getObject(), getString(), and getStringArray() to look up a named resource in a bundle. To define a bundle, provide implementations of handleGetObject() and getKeys(). It is often easier, however, to subclass ListResourceBundle or provide a Properties file that is used by PropertyResourceBundle. The name of any localized ResourceBundle class you define should include the locale language code, and, optionally, the locale country code.

```
public abstract class ResourceBundle {
// Public Constructors
```

```
  public ResourceBundle();
// Public Class Methods
  public static final ResourceBundle getBundle(String baseName);
  public static final ResourceBundle getBundle(String baseName, Locale locale);
1.2 public static ResourceBundle getBundle(String baseName, Locale locale, ClassLoader loader);
// Public Instance Methods
  public abstract Enumeration getKeys();
1.2 public Locale getLocale();
  public final Object getObject(String key);
  public final String getString(String key);
  public final String[ ] getStringArray(String key);
// Protected Instance Methods
  protected abstract Object handleGetObject(String key);
  protected void setParent(ResourceBundle parent);
// Protected Instance Fields
  protected ResourceBundle parent;
}
```

Subclasses: ListResourceBundle, PropertyResourceBundle

Passed To: java.awt.ComponentOrientation.getOrientation(), java.awt.Window.applyResourceBundle(), ResourceBundle.setParent(), java.util.logging.LogRecord.setResourceBundle()

Returned By: ResourceBundle.getBundle(), java.util.logging.Logger.getResourceBundle(), java.util.logging.LogRecord.getResourceBundle()

Type Of: ResourceBundle.parent

Set — Java 1.2

java.util — *collection*

This interface represents an unordered Collection of objects that contains no duplicate elements. That is, a Set cannot contain two elements e1 and e2 where e1.equals(e2), and it can contain at most one null element. The Set interface defines the same methods as its superinterface, Collection. It constrains the add() and addAll() methods from adding duplicate elements to the Set.

An interface cannot specify constructors, but it is conventional that all implementations of Set provide at least two standard constructors: one that takes no arguments and creates an empty set, and a copy constructor that accepts a Collection object that specifies the initial contents of the new Set. This copy constructor must ensure that duplicate elements are not added to the Set, of course.

As with Collection, the Set methods that modify the contents of the set are optional, and implementations that do not support these methods simply throw java.lang.UnsupportedOperationException. See also Collection, List, Map, SortedSet, HashSet, and TreeSet.

Collection — Set

```
public interface Set extends Collection {
// Public Instance Methods
  public abstract boolean add(Object o);
  public abstract boolean addAll(Collection c);
  public abstract void clear();
  public abstract boolean contains(Object o);
  public abstract boolean containsAll(Collection c);
  public abstract boolean equals(Object o);
  public abstract int hashCode();
```

```
    public abstract boolean isEmpty();
    public abstract Iterator iterator();
    public abstract boolean remove(Object o);
    public abstract boolean removeAll(Collection c);
    public abstract boolean retainAll(Collection c);
    public abstract int size();
    public abstract Object[ ] toArray();
    public abstract Object[ ] toArray(Object[ ] a);
}
```

Implementations: AbstractSet, HashSet, LinkedHashSet, SortedSet

Passed To: Too many methods to list.

Returned By: Too many methods to list.

Type Of: Collections.EMPTY_SET

SimpleTimeZone — Java 1.1

java.util — ***cloneable serializable***

This concrete subclass of TimeZone is a simple implementation of that abstract class that is suitable for use in locales that use the Gregorian calendar. Programs do not normally need to instantiate this class directly; instead, they use one of the static factory methods of TimeZone to obtain a suitable TimeZone subclass. The only reason to instantiate this class directly is if you need to support a time zone with non-standard-daylight-savings-time rules. In that case, you can call setStartRule() and setEndRule() to specify the starting and ending dates of daylight-savings time for the time zone.

Object — TimeZone — SimpleTimeZone

Cloneable, Serializable

```
public class SimpleTimeZone extends TimeZone {
// Public Constructors
    public SimpleTimeZone(int rawOffset, String ID);
    public SimpleTimeZone(int rawOffset, String ID, int startMonth, int startDay, int startDayOfWeek, int startTime,
                          int endMonth, int endDay, int endDayOfWeek, int endTime);
1.2 public SimpleTimeZone(int rawOffset, String ID, int startMonth, int startDay, int startDayOfWeek, int startTime,
                          int endMonth, int endDay, int endDayOfWeek, int endTime, int dstSavings);
1.4 public SimpleTimeZone(int rawOffset, String ID, int startMonth, int startDay, int startDayOfWeek, int startTime,
                          int startTimeMode, int endMonth, int endDay, int endDayOfWeek, int endTime,
                          int endTimeMode, int dstSavings);
// Public Constants
1.4 public static final int STANDARD_TIME;                                                              =1
1.4 public static final int UTC_TIME;                                                                   =2
1.4 public static final int WALL_TIME;                                                                  =0
// Public Instance Methods
1.2 public void setDSTSavings(int millisSavedDuringDST);
1.2 public void setEndRule(int endMonth, int endDay, int endTime);
    public void setEndRule(int endMonth, int endDay, int endDayOfWeek, int endTime);
1.2 public void setEndRule(int endMonth, int endDay, int endDayOfWeek, int endTime, boolean after);
1.2 public void setStartRule(int startMonth, int startDay, int startTime);
    public void setStartRule(int startMonth, int startDay, int startDayOfWeek, int startTime);
1.2 public void setStartRule(int startMonth, int startDay, int startDayOfWeek, int startTime, boolean after);
    public void setStartYear(int year);
// Public Methods Overriding TimeZone
```

```
    public Object clone();
1.2 public int getDSTSavings();
1.4 public int getOffset(long date);
    public int getOffset(int era, int year, int month, int day, int dayOfWeek, int millis);
    public int getRawOffset();
1.2 public boolean hasSameRules(TimeZone other);
    public boolean inDaylightTime(java.util.Date date);
    public void setRawOffset(int offsetMillis);
    public boolean useDaylightTime();
// Public Methods Overriding Object
    public boolean equals(Object obj);
    public int hashCode();                                                    synchronized
    public String toString();
}
```

SortedMap **Java 1.2**

java.util *collection*

This interface represents a Map object that keeps its set of key objects in sorted order. As with Map, it is conventional that all implementations of this interface define a no-argument constructor to create an empty map and a copy constructor that accepts a Map object that specifies the initial contents of the SortedMap. Furthermore, when creating a SortedMap, there should be a way to specify a Comparator object to sort the key objects of the map. If no Comparator is specified, all key objects must implement the java.lang.Comparable interface so they can be sorted in their natural order. See also Map, TreeMap, and SortedSet.

The inherited keySet(), values(), and entrySet() methods return collections that can be iterated in the sorted order. firstKey() and lastKey() return the lowest and highest key values in the SortedMap. subMap() returns a SortedMap that contains only mappings for keys from (and including) the first specified key up to (but not including) the second specified key. headMap() returns a SortedMap that contains mappings whose keys are less than (but not equal to) the specified key. tailMap() returns a SortedMap that contains mappings whose keys are greater than or equal to the specified key. subMap(), headMap(), and tailMap() return SortedMap objects that are simply views of the original SortedMap; any changes in the original map are reflected in the returned map and vice versa.

Map ··· SortedMap

```
public interface SortedMap extends Map {
// Public Instance Methods
    public abstract Comparator comparator();
    public abstract Object firstKey();
    public abstract SortedMap headMap(Object toKey);
    public abstract Object lastKey();
    public abstract SortedMap subMap(Object fromKey, Object toKey);
    public abstract SortedMap tailMap(Object fromKey);
}
```

Implementations: TreeMap

Passed To: Collections.{synchronizedSortedMap(), unmodifiableSortedMap()}, TreeMap.TreeMap()

Returned By: java.nio.charset.Charset.availableCharsets(), Collections.{synchronizedSortedMap(), unmodifiableSortedMap()}, SortedMap.{headMap(), subMap(), tailMap()}, TreeMap.{headMap(), subMap(), tailMap()}

SortedSet — Java 1.2

java.util — *collection*

This interface is a Set that sorts its elements and guarantees that its iterator() method returns an Iterator that enumerates the elements of the set in sorted order. As with the Set interface, it is conventional for all implementations of SortedSet to provide a no-argument constructor that creates an empty set and a copy constructor that expects a Collection object specifying the initial (unsorted) contents of the set. Furthermore, when creating a SortedSet, there should be a way to specify a Comparator object that compares and sorts the elements of the set. If no Comparator is specified, the elements of the set must all implement java.lang.Comparable so they can be sorted in their natural order. See also Set, TreeSet, and SortedMap.

SortedSet defines a few methods in addition to those it inherits from the Set interface. first() and last() return the lowest and highest objects in the set. headSet() returns all elements from the beginning of the set up to (but not including) the specified element. tailSet() returns all elements between (and including) the specified element and the end of the set. subSet() returns all elements of the set from (and including) the first specified element up to (but excluding) the second specified element. Note that all three methods return a SortedSet that is implemented as a view onto the original SortedSet. Changes in the original set are visible through the returned set and vice versa.

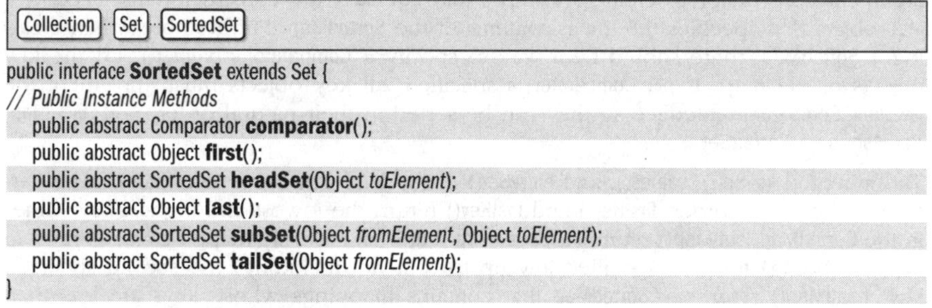


```
public interface SortedSet extends Set {
// Public Instance Methods
    public abstract Comparator comparator();
    public abstract Object first();
    public abstract SortedSet headSet(Object toElement);
    public abstract Object last();
    public abstract SortedSet subSet(Object fromElement, Object toElement);
    public abstract SortedSet tailSet(Object fromElement);
}
```

Implementations: TreeSet

Passed To: Collections.{synchronizedSortedSet(), unmodifiableSortedSet()}, TreeSet.TreeSet()

Returned By: Collections.{synchronizedSortedSet(), unmodifiableSortedSet()}, SortedSet.{headSet(), subSet(), tailSet()}, TreeSet.{headSet(), subSet(), tailSet()}

Stack — Java 1.0

java.util — *cloneable serializable collection*

This class implements a last-in-first-out (LIFO) stack of objects. push() puts an object on the top of the stack. pop() removes and returns the top object from the stack. peek() returns the top object without removing it. In Java 1.2, you can instead use a LinkedList as a stack.

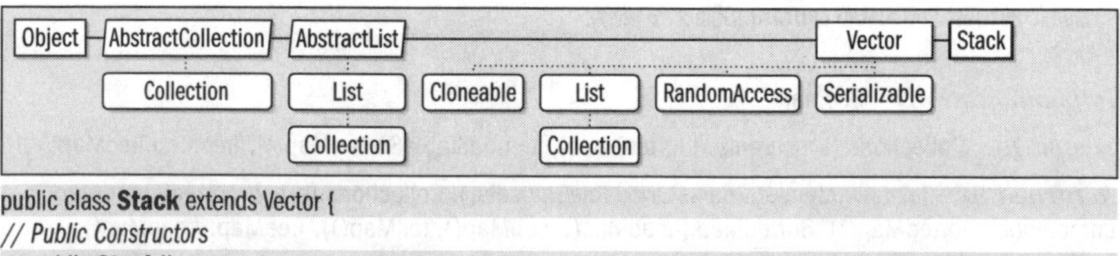


```
public class Stack extends Vector {
// Public Constructors
    public Stack();
```

```
// Public Instance Methods
   public boolean empty();
   public Object peek();                                          synchronized
   public Object pop();                                           synchronized
   public Object push(Object item);
   public int search(Object o);                                   synchronized
}
```

Type Of: java.text.RuleBasedBreakIterator.Builder.decisionPointStack

StringTokenizer — Java 1.0

java.util

When a StringTokenizer is instantiated with a String, it breaks the string up into tokens separated by any of the characters in the specified string of delimiters. (For example, words separated by space and tab characters are tokens.) The hasMoreTokens() and nextToken() methods obtain the tokens in order. countTokens() returns the number of tokens in the string. StringTokenizer implements the Enumeration interface, so you may also access the tokens with the familiar hasMoreElements() and nextElement() methods. When you create a StringTokenizer, you can specify a string of delimiter characters to use for the entire string, or you can rely on the default whitespace delimiters. You can also specify whether the delimiters themselves should be returned as tokens. Finally, you can optionally specify a new string of delimiter characters when you call nextToken().

Object — StringTokenizer ··· Enumeration

```
public class StringTokenizer implements Enumeration {
// Public Constructors
   public StringTokenizer(String str);
   public StringTokenizer(String str, String delim);
   public StringTokenizer(String str, String delim, boolean returnDelims);
// Public Instance Methods
   public int countTokens();
   public boolean hasMoreTokens();
   public String nextToken();
   public String nextToken(String delim);
// Methods Implementing Enumeration
   public boolean hasMoreElements();
   public Object nextElement();
}
```

Timer — Java 1.3

java.util

This class implements a timer: its methods allow you to schedule one or more runnable TimerTask objects to be executed (once or repetitively) by a background thread at a specified time in the future. You can create a timer with the Timer() constructor. The no-argument version of this constructor creates a regular non-daemon background thread, which means that the Java VM will not terminate while the timer thread is running. Pass true to the constructor if you want the background thread to be a daemon thread.

Once you have created a Timer, you can schedule TimerTask objects to be run in the future with the various schedule() and scheduleAtFixedRate() methods. To schedule a task for a single execution, use one of the two-argument schedule() methods and specify the desired execution time either as a number of milliseconds in the future or as an absolute Date. If the number of milliseconds is 0, or if the Date object represents a time already passed, the task is scheduled for immediate execution.

To schedule a repeating task, use one of the three-argument versions of schedule() or scheduleAtFixedRate(). These methods are passed an argument that specifies the time (either as a number of milliseconds or as a Date object) of the first execution of the task and another argument, *period*, that specifies the number of milliseconds between repeated executions of the task. The schedule() methods schedule the task for *fixed-interval* execution. That is, each execution is scheduled for *period* milliseconds after the previous execution *ends*. Use schedule() for tasks such as animation, where it is important to have a relatively constant interval between executions. The scheduleAtFixedRate() methods, on the other hand, schedule tasks for *fixed-rate* execution. That is, each repetition of the task is scheduled for *period* milliseconds after the previous execution begins. Use scheduleAtFixedRate() for tasks, such as updating a clock display, that must occur at specific absolute times rather than at fixed intervals.

A single Timer object can comfortably schedule many TimerTask objects. Note, however, that all tasks scheduled by a single Timer share a single thread. If you are scheduling many rapidly repeating tasks, or if some tasks take a long time to execute, other tasks may have their scheduled executions delayed.

When you are done with a Timer, call cancel() to stop its associated thread from running. This is particularly important when you are using a timer whose associated thread is not a daemon thread, because otherwise the timer thread can prevent the Java VM from exiting. To cancel the execution of a particular task, use the cancel() method of TimerTask.

```
public class Timer {
// Public Constructors
   public Timer();
   public Timer(boolean isDaemon);
// Public Instance Methods
   public void cancel();
   public void schedule(TimerTask task, long delay);
   public void schedule(TimerTask task, java.util.Date time);
   public void schedule(TimerTask task, java.util.Date firstTime, long period);
   public void schedule(TimerTask task, long delay, long period);
   public void scheduleAtFixedRate(TimerTask task, java.util.Date firstTime, long period);
   public void scheduleAtFixedRate(TimerTask task, long delay, long period);
}
```

TimerTask — Java 1.3

java.util — *runnable*

This abstract Runnable class represents a task that is scheduled with a Timer object for one-time or repeated execution in the future. You can define a task by subclassing TimerTask and implementing the abstract run() method. Schedule the task for future execution by passing an instance of your subclass to one of the schedule() or scheduleAtFixedRate() methods of Timer. The Timer object will then invoke the run() method at the scheduled time or times.

Call cancel() to cancel the one-time or repeated execution of a TimerTask(). This method returns true if a pending execution was actually canceled. It returns false if the task has already been canceled, was never scheduled, or was scheduled for one-time execution and has already been executed. scheduledExecutionTime() returns the time in milliseconds at which the most recent execution of the TimerTask was scheduled to occur. When the host system is heavily loaded, the run() method may not be invoked exactly when scheduled. Some tasks may choose to do nothing if they are not invoked on time. The run() method can compare the return values of scheduledExecutionTime() and

System.currentTimeMillis() to determine whether the current invocation is sufficiently timely.

Object — TimerTask ··· Runnable

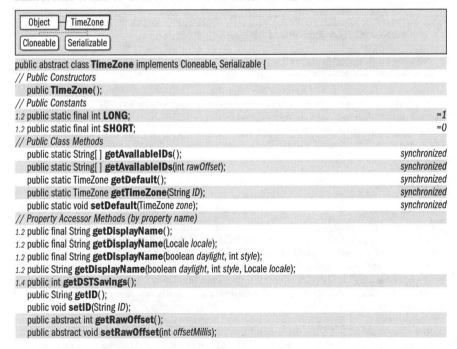

```
public abstract class TimerTask implements Runnable {
// Protected Constructors
   protected TimerTask();
// Public Instance Methods
   public boolean cancel();
   public long scheduledExecutionTime();
// Methods Implementing Runnable
   public abstract void run();
}
```

Passed To: java.util.Timer.{schedule(), scheduleAtFixedRate()}

TimeZone — Java 1.1

java.util — *cloneable serializable*

The TimeZone class represents a time zone; it is used with the Calendar and DateFormat classes. As an abstract class, TimeZone cannot be directly instantiated. Instead, you should call the static getDefault() method to obtain a TimeZone object that represents the time zone inherited from the host operating system. Or you can call the static getTimeZone() method with the name of the desired zone. You can obtain a list of the supported time-zone names by calling the static getAvailableIDs() method.

Once you have a TimeZone object, you can call inDaylightTime() to determine whether, for a given Date, daylight-savings time is in effect for that time zone. Call getID() to obtain the name of the time zone. Call getOffset() for a given date to determine the number of milliseconds to add to GMT to convert to the time zone.

Object — TimeZone
Cloneable, Serializable

```
public abstract class TimeZone implements Cloneable, Serializable {
// Public Constructors
   public TimeZone();
// Public Constants
1.2 public static final int LONG;                                                  =1
1.2 public static final int SHORT;                                                 =0
// Public Class Methods
   public static String[ ] getAvailableIDs();                                      synchronized
   public static String[ ] getAvailableIDs(int rawOffset);                         synchronized
   public static TimeZone getDefault();                                            synchronized
   public static TimeZone getTimeZone(String ID);                                  synchronized
   public static void setDefault(TimeZone zone);                                   synchronized
// Property Accessor Methods (by property name)
1.2 public final String getDisplayName();
1.2 public final String getDisplayName(Locale locale);
1.2 public final String getDisplayName(boolean daylight, int style);
1.2 public String getDisplayName(boolean daylight, int style, Locale locale);
1.4 public int getDSTSavings();
   public String getID();
   public void setID(String ID);
   public abstract int getRawOffset();
   public abstract void setRawOffset(int offsetMillis);
```

```
// Public Instance Methods
1.4 public int getOffset(long date);
    public abstract int getOffset(int era, int year, int month, int day, int dayOfWeek, int milliseconds);
1.2 public boolean hasSameRules(TimeZone other);
    public abstract boolean inDaylightTime(java.util.Date date);
    public abstract boolean useDaylightTime();
// Public Methods Overriding Object
    public Object clone();
}
```

Subclasses: SimpleTimeZone

Passed To: java.text.DateFormat.setTimeZone(), Calendar.{Calendar(), getInstance(), setTimeZone()}, GregorianCalendar.GregorianCalendar(), SimpleTimeZone.hasSameRules(), TimeZone.{hasSameRules(), setDefault()}

Returned By: java.text.DateFormat.getTimeZone(), Calendar.getTimeZone(), TimeZone.{getDefault(), getTimeZone()}

TooManyListenersException — Java 1.1

java.util — *serializable checked*

This exception signals that an AWT component, JavaBeans component, or Swing component can have only one EventListener object registered for some specific type of event. That is, it signals that a particular event is a unicast event rather than a multicast event. This exception type serves a formal purpose in the Java event model; its presence in the throws clause of an EventListener registration method (even if the method never actually throws the exception) signals that an event is a unicast event.

Object — Throwable — Exception — TooManyListenersException
Serializable

```
public class TooManyListenersException extends Exception {
// Public Constructors
    public TooManyListenersException();
    public TooManyListenersException(String s);
}
```

Thrown By: java.awt.dnd.DragGestureRecognizer.addDragGestureListener(), java.awt.dnd.DragSourceContext.addDragSourceListener(), java.awt.dnd.DropTarget.addDropTargetListener(), java.beans.beancontext.BeanContextServices.getService(), java.beans.beancontext.BeanContextServicesSupport.getService()

TreeMap — Java 1.2

java.util — *cloneable serializable collection*

This class implements the SortedMap interface using an internal Red-Black tree data structure and guarantees that the keys and values of the mapping can be enumerated in ascending order of keys. TreeMap supports all optional Map methods. The objects used as keys in a TreeMap must all be mutually Comparable, or an appropriate Comparator must be provided when the TreeMap is created. Because TreeMap is based on a binary tree data structure, the get(), put(), remove(), and containsKey() methods operate in relatively efficient logarithmic time. If you do not need the sorting capability of TreeMap, however, use HashMap instead, as it is even more efficient. See Map and SortedMap for details on the methods of TreeMap. See also the related TreeSet class.

In order for a TreeMap to work correctly, the comparison method from the Comparable or Comparator interface must be consistent with the equals() method. That is, the equals() method must compare two objects as equal if and only if the comparison method also indicates those two objects are equal.

The methods of TreeMap are not synchronized. If you are working in a multithreaded environment, you must explicitly synchronize all code that modifies the TreeMap, or obtain a synchronized wrapper with Collections.synchronizedMap().

Object — AbstractMap — TreeMap
Map | Cloneable | Serializable | Map ··· SortedMap

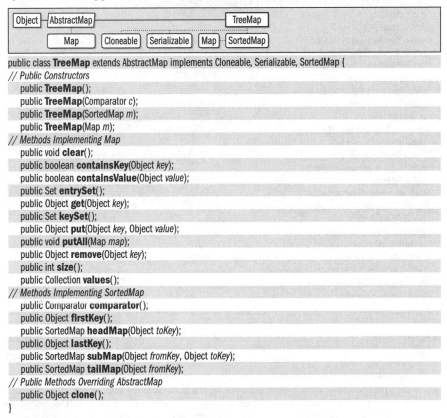

```
public class TreeMap extends AbstractMap implements Cloneable, Serializable, SortedMap {
// Public Constructors
   public TreeMap();
   public TreeMap(Comparator c);
   public TreeMap(SortedMap m);
   public TreeMap(Map m);
// Methods Implementing Map
   public void clear();
   public boolean containsKey(Object key);
   public boolean containsValue(Object value);
   public Set entrySet();
   public Object get(Object key);
   public Set keySet();
   public Object put(Object key, Object value);
   public void putAll(Map map);
   public Object remove(Object key);
   public int size();
   public Collection values();
// Methods Implementing SortedMap
   public Comparator comparator();
   public Object firstKey();
   public SortedMap headMap(Object toKey);
   public Object lastKey();
   public SortedMap subMap(Object fromKey, Object toKey);
   public SortedMap tailMap(Object fromKey);
// Public Methods Overriding AbstractMap
   public Object clone();
}
```

TreeSet — Java 1.2

java.util — *cloneable serializable collection*

This class implements SortedSet, provides support for all optional methods, and guarantees that the elements of the set can be enumerated in ascending order. In order to be sorted, the elements of the set must all be mutually Comparable objects, or they must all be compatible with a Comparator object that is specified when the TreeSet is created. TreeSet is implemented on top of a TreeMap, so its add(), remove(), and contains() methods all operate in relatively efficient logarithmic time. If you do not need the sorting capability of TreeSet, however, use HashSet instead, as it is significantly more efficient. See Set, SortedSet, and Collection for details on the methods of TreeSet.

For a TreeSet to operate correctly, the Comparable or Comparator comparison method must be consistent with the equals() method. That is, the equals() method must compare two objects as equal if and only if the comparison method also indicates those two objects are equal.

The methods of TreeSet are not synchronized. If you are working in a multithreaded environment, you must explicitly synchronize code that modifies the contents of the set, or obtain a synchronized wrapper with Collections.synchronizedSet().

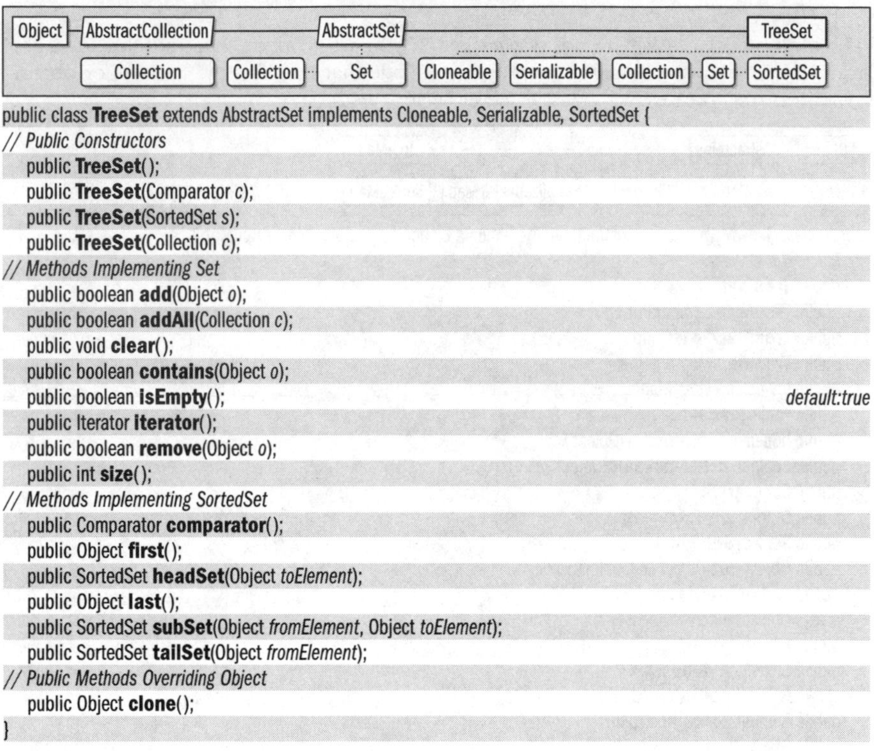


```
public class TreeSet extends AbstractSet implements Cloneable, Serializable, SortedSet {
// Public Constructors
   public TreeSet();
   public TreeSet(Comparator c);
   public TreeSet(SortedSet s);
   public TreeSet(Collection c);
// Methods Implementing Set
   public boolean add(Object o);
   public boolean addAll(Collection c);
   public void clear();
   public boolean contains(Object o);
   public boolean isEmpty();                                              default:true
   public Iterator iterator();
   public boolean remove(Object o);
   public int size();
// Methods Implementing SortedSet
   public Comparator comparator();
   public Object first();
   public SortedSet headSet(Object toElement);
   public Object last();
   public SortedSet subSet(Object fromElement, Object toElement);
   public SortedSet tailSet(Object fromElement);
// Public Methods Overriding Object
   public Object clone();
}
```

Vector **Java 1.0**

java.util ***cloneable serializable collection***

This class implements an ordered collection—essentially an array—of objects that can grow or shrink as necessary. Vector is useful when you need to keep track of a number of objects, but do not know in advance how many there will be. Use setElementAt() to set the object at a given index of a Vector. Use elementAt() to retrieve the object stored at a specified index. Note that you typically must cast the Object returned by elementAt() to the desired type. Call add() to append an object to the end of the Vector or to insert an object at any specified position. Use removeElementAt() to delete the element at a specified index or removeElement() to remove a specified object from the vector. size() returns the number of objects currently in the Vector. elements() returns an Enumeration that allows you to iterate through those objects. capacity() is not the same as size(); it returns the maximum number of objects a Vector can hold before its internal storage must be resized. Vector automatically resizes its internal storage for you, but if you know in advance how many objects a Vector will contain, you can increase its efficiency by pre-allocating this many elements with ensureCapacity().

Vector has been part of the java.util package since Java 1.0, but in Java 1.2 it has been enhanced to implement the List interface. List defines new names for many of the methods already present in Vector; see List for details on those methods. Vector is quite similar to the ArrayList class, except that the methods of Vector are synchronized, which makes them thread-safe but increases the overhead of calling them. If you need thread safety or need to be compatible with Java 1.0 or Java 1.1, use Vector; otherwise, use ArrayList.

Object — AbstractCollection — AbstractList — Vector
Collection | List | Cloneable | List | RandomAccess | Serializable
Collection | Collection

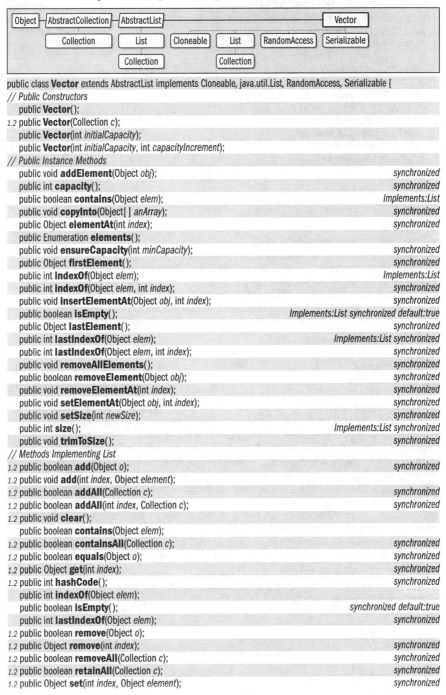

```
public class Vector extends AbstractList implements Cloneable, java.util.List, RandomAccess, Serializable {
// Public Constructors
    public Vector();
1.2 public Vector(Collection c);
    public Vector(int initialCapacity);
    public Vector(int initialCapacity, int capacityIncrement);
// Public Instance Methods
    public void addElement(Object obj);                                  synchronized
    public int capacity();                                               synchronized
    public boolean contains(Object elem);                                Implements:List
    public void copyInto(Object[ ] anArray);                             synchronized
    public Object elementAt(int index);                                  synchronized
    public Enumeration elements();
    public void ensureCapacity(int minCapacity);                         synchronized
    public Object firstElement();                                        synchronized
    public int indexOf(Object elem);                                     Implements:List
    public int indexOf(Object elem, int index);                          synchronized
    public void insertElementAt(Object obj, int index);                  synchronized
    public boolean isEmpty();                Implements:List synchronized default:true
    public Object lastElement();                                         synchronized
    public int lastIndexOf(Object elem);                 Implements:List synchronized
    public int lastIndexOf(Object elem, int index);                      synchronized
    public void removeAllElements();                                     synchronized
    public boolean removeElement(Object obj);                            synchronized
    public void removeElementAt(int index);                              synchronized
    public void setElementAt(Object obj, int index);                     synchronized
    public void setSize(int newSize);                                    synchronized
    public int size();                                   Implements:List synchronized
    public void trimToSize();                                            synchronized
// Methods Implementing List
1.2 public boolean add(Object o);                                        synchronized
1.2 public void add(int index, Object element);
1.2 public boolean addAll(Collection c);                                 synchronized
1.2 public boolean addAll(int index, Collection c);                      synchronized
1.2 public void clear();
    public boolean contains(Object elem);
1.2 public boolean containsAll(Collection c);                            synchronized
1.2 public boolean equals(Object o);                                     synchronized
1.2 public Object get(int index);                                        synchronized
1.2 public int hashCode();                                               synchronized
    public int indexOf(Object elem);
    public boolean isEmpty();                            synchronized default:true
    public int lastIndexOf(Object elem);                                 synchronized
1.2 public boolean remove(Object o);
1.2 public Object remove(int index);                                     synchronized
1.2 public boolean removeAll(Collection c);                              synchronized
1.2 public boolean retainAll(Collection c);                              synchronized
1.2 public Object set(int index, Object element);                        synchronized
```

```
   public int size();                                                    synchronized
1.2 public java.util.List subList(int fromIndex, int toIndex);           synchronized
1.2 public Object[ ] toArray();                                          synchronized
1.2 public Object[ ] toArray(Object[ ] a);                               synchronized
// Protected Methods Overriding AbstractList
1.2 protected void removeRange(int fromIndex, int toIndex);
// Public Methods Overriding AbstractCollection
   public String toString();                                             synchronized
// Public Methods Overriding Object
   public Object clone();                                                synchronized
// Protected Instance Fields
   protected int capacityIncrement;
   protected int elementCount;
   protected Object[ ] elementData;
}
```

Subclasses: Stack

Passed To: Too many methods to list.

Returned By: java.awt.image.BufferedImage.getSources(), java.awt.image.RenderedImage.getSources(), java.awt.image.renderable.ParameterBlock.{getParameters(), getSources()}, java.awt.image.renderable.RenderableImage.getSources(), java.awt.image.renderable.RenderableImageOp.getSources(), javax.swing.plaf.basic.BasicDirectoryModel.{getDirectories(), getFiles()}, javax.swing.table.DefaultTableModel.{convertToVector(), getDataVector()}, javax.swing.text.GapContent.getPositionsInRange(), javax.swing.text.StringContent.getPositionsInRange()

Type Of: Too many fields to list.

WeakHashMap — Java 1.2

java.util — *collection*

This class implements Map using an internal hashtable. It is similar in features and performance to HashMap, except that it uses the capabilities of the java.lang.ref package, so that the key-to-value mappings it maintains do not prevent the key objects from being reclaimed by the garbage collector. When there are no more references to a key object except for the weak reference maintained by the WeakHashMap, the garbage collector reclaims the object, and the WeakHashMap deletes the mapping between the reclaimed key and its associated value. If there are no references to the value object except for the one maintained by the WeakHashMap, the value object also becomes available for garbage collection. Thus, you can use a WeakHashMap to associate an auxiliary value with an object without preventing either the object (the key) or the auxiliary value from being reclaimed. See HashMap for a discussion of the implementation features of this class. See Map for a description of the methods it defines.

WeakHashMap is primarily useful with objects whose equals() methods use the == operator for comparison. It is less useful with key objects of type String, for example, because there can be multiple String objects that are equal to one another and, even if the original key value has been reclaimed by the garbage collector, it is always possible to pass a String with the same value to the get() method.


```
public class WeakHashMap extends AbstractMap implements Map {
// Public Constructors
    public WeakHashMap();
    public WeakHashMap(int initialCapacity);
1.3 public WeakHashMap(Map t);
    public WeakHashMap(int initialCapacity, float loadFactor);
// Methods Implementing Map
    public void clear();
    public boolean containsKey(Object key);
1.4 public boolean containsValue(Object value);
    public Set entrySet();
    public Object get(Object key);
    public boolean isEmpty();                                  default:true
1.4 public Set keySet();
    public Object put(Object key, Object value);
1.4 public void putAll(Map t);
    public Object remove(Object key);
    public int size();
1.4 public Collection values();
}
```

Package java.util.jar — Java 1.2

The java.util.jar package contains classes for reading and writing JAR (Java ARchive) files. It is based on the java.util.zip package. A JAR file is nothing more than a ZIP file whose first entry is a specially named manifest file that contains attributes and digital signatures for the ZIP file entries that follow it. Many of the classes in this package are relatively simple extensions of classes from the java.util.zip package.

The easiest way to read a JAR file is with the random-access JarFile class. This class allows you to obtain the JarEntry that describes any named file within the JAR archive. It also allows you to obtain an enumeration of all entries in the archive and an InputStream for reading the bytes of a specific JarEntry. Each JarEntry describes a single entry in the archive and allows access to the Attributes and the digital signatures associated with the entry. The JarFile also provides access to the Manifest object for the JAR archive; this object contains Attributes for all entries in the JAR file. Attributes is a mapping of attribute name/value pairs, of course, and the inner class Attributes.Name defines constants for various standard attribute names.

You can also read a JAR file with JarInputStream. This class requires to you read each entry of the file sequentially, however. JarOutputStream allows you to write out a JAR file sequentially. Finally, you can also read an entry within a JAR file and manifest attributes for that entry with a java.net.JarURLConnection object.

Collections:

```
public class Attributes implements Cloneable, java.util.Map;
```

Other Classes:

public static class **Attributes.Name**;
public class **JarEntry** extends java.util.zip.ZipEntry;
public class **JarFile** extends java.util.zip.ZipFile;
public class **JarInputStream** extends java.util.zip.ZipInputStream;
public class **JarOutputStream** extends java.util.zip.ZipOutputStream;
public class **Manifest** implements Cloneable;

Exception:

public class **JarException** extends java.util.zip.ZipException;

Attributes — Java 1.2

java.util.jar — ***cloneable collection***

This class is a java.util.Map that maps the attribute names of a JAR file manifest to arbitrary string values. The JAR manifest format specifies that attribute names can contain only the ASCII characters A to Z (uppercase and lowercase), the digits 0 through 9, and the hyphen and underscore characters. Thus, this class uses Attributes.Name as the type of attribute names, in addition to the more general String class. Although you can create your own Attributes objects, you more commonly obtain Attributes objects from a Manifest.

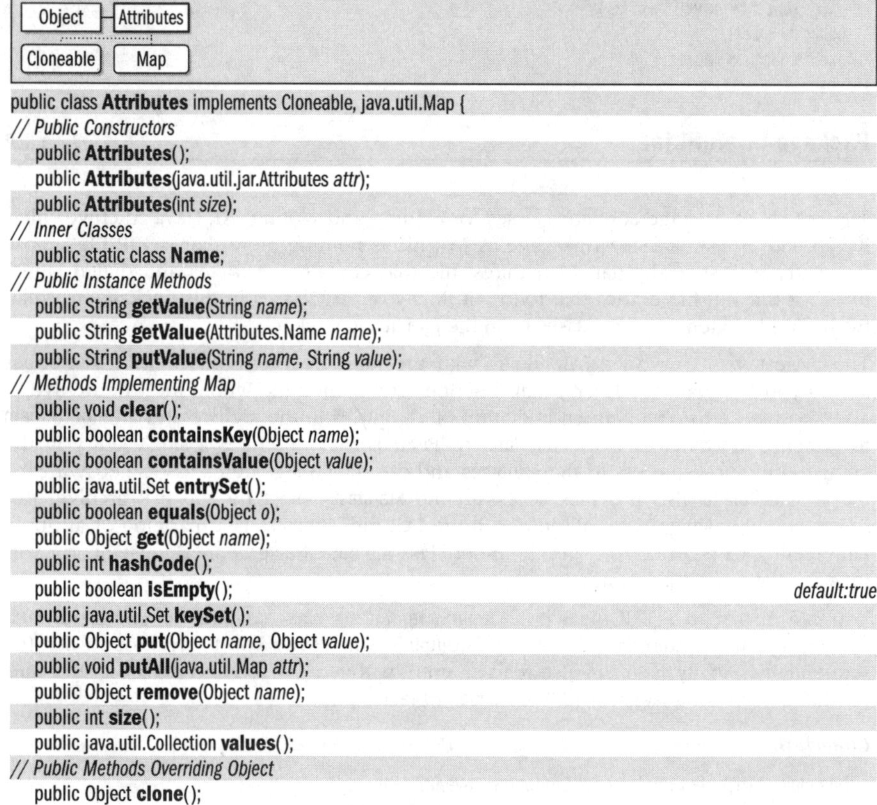


```
public class Attributes implements Cloneable, java.util.Map {
// Public Constructors
   public Attributes();
   public Attributes(java.util.jar.Attributes attr);
   public Attributes(int size);
// Inner Classes
   public static class Name;
// Public Instance Methods
   public String getValue(String name);
   public String getValue(Attributes.Name name);
   public String putValue(String name, String value);
// Methods Implementing Map
   public void clear();
   public boolean containsKey(Object name);
   public boolean containsValue(Object value);
   public java.util.Set entrySet();
   public boolean equals(Object o);
   public Object get(Object name);
   public int hashCode();
   public boolean isEmpty();                                   default:true
   public java.util.Set keySet();
   public Object put(Object name, Object value);
   public void putAll(java.util.Map attr);
   public Object remove(Object name);
   public int size();
   public java.util.Collection values();
// Public Methods Overriding Object
   public Object clone();
```

```
// Protected Instance Fields
   protected java.util.Map map;
}
```

Passed To: java.util.jar.Attributes.Attributes()

Returned By: java.net.JarURLConnection.{getAttributes(), getMainAttributes()}, JarEntry.getAttributes(), Manifest.{getAttributes(), getMainAttributes()}

Attributes.Name — Java 1.2

java.util.jar

This class represents the name of an attribute in an Attributes object. It defines constants for the various standard attribute names used in JAR file manifests. Attribute names can contain only ASCII letters, digits, and the hyphen and underscore characters. Any other Unicode characters are illegal.

```
public static class Attributes.Name {
// Public Constructors
   public Name(String name);
// Public Constants
   public static final Attributes.Name CLASS_PATH;
   public static final Attributes.Name CONTENT_TYPE;
1.3 public static final Attributes.Name EXTENSION_INSTALLATION;
1.3 public static final Attributes.Name EXTENSION_LIST;
1.3 public static final Attributes.Name EXTENSION_NAME;
   public static final Attributes.Name IMPLEMENTATION_TITLE;
1.3 public static final Attributes.Name IMPLEMENTATION_URL;
   public static final Attributes.Name IMPLEMENTATION_VENDOR;
1.3 public static final Attributes.Name IMPLEMENTATION_VENDOR_ID;
   public static final Attributes.Name IMPLEMENTATION_VERSION;
   public static final Attributes.Name MAIN_CLASS;
   public static final Attributes.Name MANIFEST_VERSION;
   public static final Attributes.Name SEALED;
   public static final Attributes.Name SIGNATURE_VERSION;
   public static final Attributes.Name SPECIFICATION_TITLE;
   public static final Attributes.Name SPECIFICATION_VENDOR;
   public static final Attributes.Name SPECIFICATION_VERSION;
// Public Methods Overriding Object
   public boolean equals(Object o);
   public int hashCode();
   public String toString();
}
```

Passed To: java.util.jar.Attributes.getValue()

Type Of: Too many fields to list.

JarEntry — Java 1.2

java.util.jar — *cloneable*

This class extends java.util.zip.ZipEntry; it represents a single file in a JAR archive and the manifest attributes and digital signatures associated with that file. JarEntry objects can be read from a JAR file with JarFile or JarInputStream, and they can be written to a JAR file with JarOutputStream. Use getAttributes() to obtain the Attributes for the entry. Use getCertificates() to obtain a java.security.cert.Certificate array that contains the certificate chains for all digital signatures associated with the file.

Object — ZipEntry — JarEntry
Cloneable, ZipConstants

```
public class JarEntry extends java.util.zip.ZipEntry {
// Public Constructors
   public JarEntry(JarEntry je);
   public JarEntry(String name);
   public JarEntry(java.util.zip.ZipEntry ze);
// Public Instance Methods
   public java.util.jar.Attributes getAttributes() throws java.io.IOException;
   public java.security.cert.Certificate[ ] getCertificates();
}
```

Passed To: JarEntry.JarEntry()

Returned By: java.net.JarURLConnection.getJarEntry(), JarFile.getJarEntry(), JarInputStream.getNextJarEntry()

JarException — Java 1.2

java.util.jar — *serializable checked*

This exception signals an error while reading or writing a JAR file.

Object — Throwable — Exception — IOException — ZipException — JarException
Serializable

```
public class JarException extends java.util.zip.ZipException {
// Public Constructors
   public JarException();
   public JarException(String s);
}
```

JarFile — Java 1.2

java.util.jar

This class represents a JAR file and allows the manifest, file list, and individual files to be read from the JAR file. It extends java.util.zip.ZipFile, and its use is similar to that of its superclass. Create a JarFile by specifying a filename or File object. If you do not want JarFile to attempt to verify any digital signatures contained in the JarFile, pass an optional boolean argument of false to the JarFile() constructor. In Java 1.3, temporary JAR files can be automatically deleted when they are closed. To take advantage of this feature, pass ZipFile.OPEN_READ|ZipFile.OPEN_DELETE as the *mode* argument to the JarFile() constructor.

Once you have created a JarFile object, obtain the JAR Manifest with getManifest(). Obtain an enumeration of the java.util.zip.ZipEntry objects in the file with entries(). Get the JarEntry for a specified file in the JAR file with getJarEntry(). To read the contents of a specific entry in the JAR file, obtain the JarEntry or ZipEntry object that represents that entry, pass it to getInputStream(), and then read until the end of that stream. JarFile does not support the creation of new JAR files or the modification of existing files.

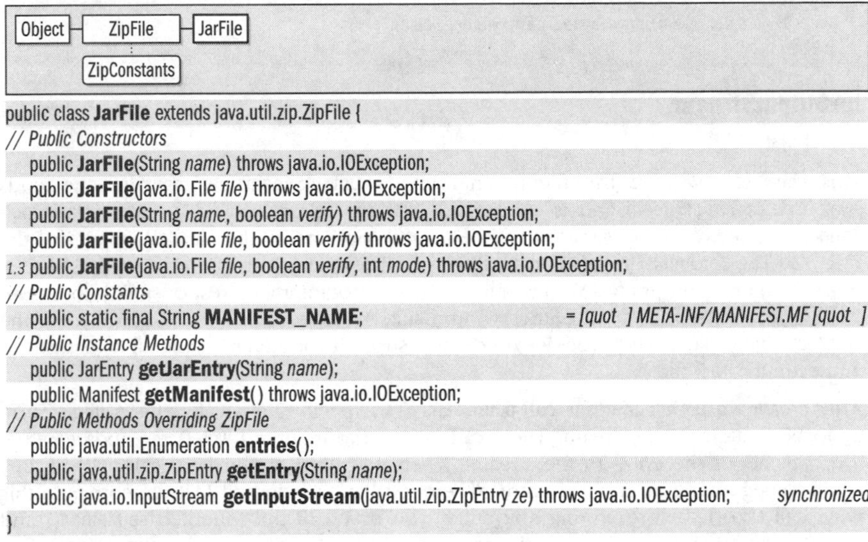


```
public class JarFile extends java.util.zip.ZipFile {
// Public Constructors
   public JarFile(String name) throws java.io.IOException;
   public JarFile(java.io.File file) throws java.io.IOException;
   public JarFile(String name, boolean verify) throws java.io.IOException;
   public JarFile(java.io.File file, boolean verify) throws java.io.IOException;
1.3 public JarFile(java.io.File file, boolean verify, int mode) throws java.io.IOException;
// Public Constants
   public static final String MANIFEST_NAME;                    = [quot ] META-INF/MANIFEST.MF [quot ]
// Public Instance Methods
   public JarEntry getJarEntry(String name);
   public Manifest getManifest() throws java.io.IOException;
// Public Methods Overriding ZipFile
   public java.util.Enumeration entries();
   public java.util.zip.ZipEntry getEntry(String name);
   public java.io.InputStream getInputStream(java.util.zip.ZipEntry ze) throws java.io.IOException;    synchronized
}
```

Returned By: java.net.JarURLConnection.getJarFile()

JarInputStream — Java 1.2

java.util.jar

This class allows a JAR file to be read from an input stream. It extends java.util.ZipInputStream and is used much like that class is used. To create a JarInputStream, simply specify the InputStream from which to read. If you do not want the JarInputStream to attempt to verify any digital signatures contained in the JAR file, pass false as the second argument to the JarInputStream() constructor. The JarInputStream() constructor first reads the JAR manifest entry, if one exists. The manifest must be the first entry in the JAR file. getManifest() returns the Manifest object for the JAR file.

Once you have created a JarInputStream, call getNextJarEntry() or getNextEntry() to obtain the JarEntry or java.util.zip.ZipEntry object that describes the next entry in the JAR file. Then, call a read() method (including the inherited versions) to read the contents of that entry. When the stream reaches the end of file, call getNextJarEntry() again to start reading the next entry in the file. When all entries have been read from the JAR file, getNextJarEntry() and getNextEntry() return null.

Object – InputStream – FilterInputStream – InflaterInputStream – ZipInputStream – JarInputStream; ZipConstants

```
public class JarInputStream extends java.util.zip.ZipInputStream {
// Public Constructors
   public JarInputStream(java.io.InputStream in) throws java.io.IOException;
   public JarInputStream(java.io.InputStream in, boolean verify) throws java.io.IOException;
// Public Instance Methods
   public Manifest getManifest();
   public JarEntry getNextJarEntry() throws java.io.IOException;
// Public Methods Overriding ZipInputStream
   public java.util.zip.ZipEntry getNextEntry() throws java.io.IOException;
```

```
    public int read(byte[ ] b, int off, int len) throws java.io.IOException;
// Protected Methods Overriding ZipInputStream
    protected java.util.zip.ZipEntry createZipEntry(String name);
}
```

JarOutputStream — Java 1.2

java.util.jar

This class can write a JAR file to an arbitrary OutputStream. JarOutputStream extends java.util.zip.ZipOutputStream and is used much like that class is used. Create a JarOutputStream by specifying the stream to write to and, optionally, the Manifest object for the JAR file. The JarOutputStream() constructor starts by writing the contents of the Manifest object into an appropriate JAR file entry. It is the programmer's responsibility to ensure that the contents of the JAR entries written subsequently match those specified in the Manifest object. This class provides no explicit support for attaching digital signatures to entries in the JAR file.

After creating a JarOutputStream, call putNextEntry() to specify the JarEntry or java.util.zip.ZipEntry to be written to the stream. Then, call any of the inherited write() methods to write the contents of the entry to the stream. When that entry is finished, call putNextEntry() again to begin writing the next entry. When you have written all JAR file entries in this way, call close(). Before writing any entry, you may call the inherited setMethod() and setLevel() methods to specify how the entry should be compressed. See java.util.zip.ZipOutputStream.

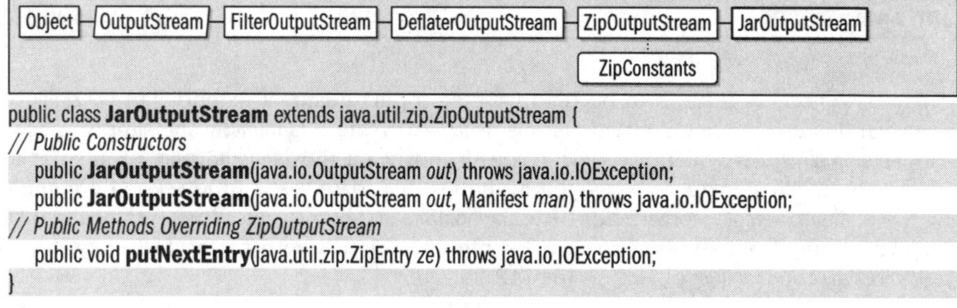


```
public class JarOutputStream extends java.util.zip.ZipOutputStream {
// Public Constructors
    public JarOutputStream(java.io.OutputStream out) throws java.io.IOException;
    public JarOutputStream(java.io.OutputStream out, Manifest man) throws java.io.IOException;
// Public Methods Overriding ZipOutputStream
    public void putNextEntry(java.util.zip.ZipEntry ze) throws java.io.IOException;
}
```

Manifest — Java 1.2

java.util.jar — *cloneable*

This class represents the manifest entry of a JAR file. getMainAttributes() returns an Attributes object that represents the manifest attributes that apply to the entire JAR file. getAttributes() returns an Attributes object that represents the manifest attributes specified for a single file in the JAR file. getEntries() returns a java.util.Map that maps the names of entries in the JAR file to the Attributes objects associated with those entries. getEntries() returns the Map object used internally by the Manifest. You can edit the contents of the Manifest by adding, deleting, or editing entries in the Map. read() reads manifest entries from an input stream, merging them into the current set of entries. write() writes the Manifest out to the specified output stream.

Object — Manifest ··· Cloneable

```
public class Manifest implements Cloneable {
// Public Constructors
```

```
    public Manifest();
    public Manifest(Manifest man);
    public Manifest(java.io.InputStream is) throws java.io.IOException;
// Public Instance Methods
    public void clear();
    public java.util.jar.Attributes getAttributes(String name);
    public java.util.Map getEntries();                                   default:HashMap
    public java.util.jar.Attributes getMainAttributes();
    public void read(java.io.InputStream is) throws java.io.IOException;
    public void write(java.io.OutputStream out) throws java.io.IOException;
// Public Methods Overriding Object
    public Object clone();
    public boolean equals(Object o);
    public int hashCode();
}
```

Passed To: java.net.URLClassLoader.definePackage(), JarOutputStream.JarOutputStream(), Manifest.Manifest()

Returned By: java.net.JarURLConnection.getManifest(), JarFile.getManifest(), JarInputStream.getManifest()

Package java.util.logging — Java 1.4

The java.util.logging package defines a sophisticated and highly configurable logging facility that Java applications can use to emit, filter, format, and output warning, diagnostic, tracing, and debugging messages. An application generates log messages by calling various methods of a Logger object. The content of a log message (with other pertinent details such as the time and sequence number) is encapsulated in a LogRecord object generated by the Logger. A Handler object represents a destination for LogRecord objects. Concrete subclasses of Handler support destinations such as files and sockets. Most Handler objects have an associated Formatter that converts a LogRecord object into the actual text that is logged. The subclasses SimpleFormatter and XMLFormatter produce simple plain-text log messages and detailed XML logs respectively.

Each log message has an associated severity level. The Level class defines a type-safe enumeration of defined levels. Logger and Handler objects both have an associated Level, and discard any log messages whose severity is less than that specified level. In addition to this level-based filtering, Logger and Handler objects may also have an associated Filter object which may be implemented to filter log messages based on any desired criteria.

Applications that desire complete control over the logs they generate can create a Logger object, along with Handler, Formatter and Filter objects that control the destination, content, and appearance of the log. Simpler applications need only to create a Logger for themselves, and can leave the rest to the LogManager class. LogManager reads a system-wide configuration file (or a configuration class) and automatically directs log messages to a standard destination (or destinations) for the system.

Interfaces:

```
public interface Filter;
```

Classes:

```
public class ErrorManager;
public abstract class Formatter;
    └ public class SimpleFormatter extends Formatter;
    └ public class XMLFormatter extends Formatter;
public abstract class Handler;
    └ public class MemoryHandler extends Handler;
    └ public class StreamHandler extends Handler;
        └ public class ConsoleHandler extends StreamHandler;
        └ public class FileHandler extends StreamHandler;
        └ public class SocketHandler extends StreamHandler;
public class Level implements Serializable;
public class Logger;
public final class LoggingPermission extends java.security.BasicPermission;
public class LogManager;
public class LogRecord implements Serializable;
```

ConsoleHandler — Java 1.4

java.util.logging

This Handler subclass formats LogRecord objects and outputs the resulting string to the System.err output stream. When a ConsoleHandler is created, the various properties inherited from Handler are initialized using system-wide defaults obtained by querying named values with LogManager.getProperty(). The following table lists these properties: the value passed to getProperty() and the default value used if getProperty() returns null. See Handler for further details.

Handler property	*LogManager property name*	*Default*
level	java.util.logging.ConsoleHandler.level	Level.INFO
filter	java.util.logging.ConsoleHandler.filter	null
formatter	java.util.logging.ConsoleHandler.formatter	SimpleFormatter
encoding	java.util.logging.ConsoleHandler.encoding	platform default

Object — Handler — StreamHandler — ConsoleHandler

```
public class ConsoleHandler extends StreamHandler {
// Public Constructors
    public ConsoleHandler();
// Public Methods Overriding StreamHandler
    public void close();
    public void publish(LogRecord record);
}
```

ErrorManager — Java 1.4

java.util.logging

An important feature of the Logging API is that the logging methods called by applications never throw exceptions: it is not reasonable to expect programmers to nest all their logging calls within try/catch blocks, and even if they did, there is no useful way for an application to recover from an exception in the logging subsystem. Since handler classes such as FileHandler are inherently subject to I/O exceptions, the ErrorManager provides a way for a handler to report an exception instead of simply discarding it.

All Handler objects have an instance of ErrorManager associated with them. If an exception occurs in the handler, it passes the exception, along with a message and one of the error code constants defined by ErrorManager to the error() method. error() writes a message describing the exception to System.err, but does so only the first time it is called: the expectation is that a Handler that throws an exception once will continue to throw the same exception with each subsequent log message, and it is not useful to flood System.err with repeated error messages. You can of course define subclasses of ErrorManager that override error() to provide some other reporting mechanism. If you do this, register an instance of your custom ErrorManager by calling the setErrorManager() method of your Handler.

```
public class ErrorManager {
// Public Constructors
   public ErrorManager();
// Public Constants
   public static final int CLOSE_FAILURE;                                    =3
   public static final int FLUSH_FAILURE;                                    =2
   public static final int FORMAT_FAILURE;                                   =5
   public static final int GENERIC_FAILURE;                                  =0
   public static final int OPEN_FAILURE;                                     =4
   public static final int WRITE_FAILURE;                                    =1
// Public Instance Methods
   public void error(String msg, Exception ex, int code);          synchronized
}
```

Passed To: Handler.setErrorManager()

Returned By: Handler.getErrorManager()

FileHandler — Java 1.4

java.util.logging

This Handler subclass formats LogRecord objects and outputs the resulting strings to a file or to a rotating set of files. Arguments passed to the FileHandler() constructor specify which file or files are used, and how they are used. The arguments are optional, and if they are not specified, defaults are obtained through LogManager.getProperty(), as described later. The constructor arguments are:

pattern
: A string containing substitution characters that describes one or more files to use. The substitutions performed to convert this pattern to a filename are described below.

limit
: An approximate maximum file size for the log file, or 0 for no limit. If *count* is set to greater than one, then when a log file reaches this maximum, FileHandler closes it, renames it, and then starts a new log with the original filename.

count
: When *limit* is set to be nonzero, this argument specifies the number of old log files to retain.

append
: true if the FileHandler should append to log messages already in the named file, or false if it should overwrite the file.

The *pattern* argument is the most important of these; it specifies which file or files the FileHandler will write to. FileHandler performs the following substitutions on the specified pattern to convert it to a filename.

For	*Substitute*
/	The directory separator character for the platform. This means that you can always use a forward slash in your patterns, even on Windows filesystems that use backward slashes.
%%	A single literal percent sign.
%h	The user's home directory: the value of the system property "user.home".
%t	The temporary directory for the system.
%u	A unique number to be used to distinguish this log file from other log files with the same pattern (this may be necessary when multiple Java programs are creating logs at the same time).
%g	The "generation number" of old log files when the *limit* argument is nonzero and the *count* argument is greater than 1. FileHandler always writes log records into a file in which %g is replaced by 0. But when that file fills up, it is closed and renamed with the 0 replaced by a 1. Older files are similarly renamed, with their generation number incremented. When the number of log files reaches the number specified by *count*, then the oldest file is deleted to make room for the new one.

When a FileHandler is created, the LogManager.getProperty() method is used to obtain defaults for any unspecified constructor arguments, and also to obtain initial values for the various properties inherited from Handler. The table below lists these arguments and properties, the value passed to getProperty(), and the default value used if getProperty() returns null. See Handler for further details.

Property or argument	*LogManager property name*	*Default*
level	java.util.logging.FileHandler.level	Level.ALL
filter	java.util.logging.FileHandler.filter	null
formatter	java.util.logging.FileHandler.formatter	XMLFormatter
encoding	java.util.logging.FileHandler.encoding	platform default
pattern	java.util.logging.FileHandler.pattern	%h/java%u.log
limit	java.util.logging.FileHandler.limit	0 (no limit)
count	java.util.logging.FileHandler.count	1
append	java.util.logging.FileHandler.append	false

Object — Handler — StreamHandler — FileHandler

```
public class FileHandler extends StreamHandler {
// Public Constructors
   public FileHandler() throws java.io.IOException, SecurityException;
   public FileHandler(String pattern) throws java.io.IOException, SecurityException;
   public FileHandler(String pattern, boolean append) throws java.io.IOException, SecurityException;
   public FileHandler(String pattern, int limit, int count) throws java.io.IOException, SecurityException;
   public FileHandler(String pattern, int limit, int count, boolean append) throws java.io.IOException,
        SecurityException;
// Public Methods Overriding StreamHandler
   public void close() throws SecurityException;                                    synchronized
   public void publish(LogRecord record);                                           synchronized
}
```

Filter — Java 1.4

java.util.logging

This interface defines the method that a class must implement if it wants to filter log messages for a Logger or Handler class. isLoggable() should return true if the specified LogRecord contains information that should be logged. It should return false if the LogRecord should be filtered out not appear in any destination log. Note that both Logger and Handler provide built-in filtering based on the severity level of the LogRecord. This Filter interface exists to provide a customized filtering capability.

```
public interface Filter {
// Public Instance Methods
    public abstract boolean isLoggable(LogRecord record);
}
```

Passed To: Handler.setFilter(), Logger.setFilter()

Returned By: Handler.getFilter(), Logger.getFilter()

Formatter — Java 1.4

java.util.logging

A Formatter object is used by a Handler to convert a LogRecord to a String prior to logging it. Most applications can simply use one one of the predefined concrete subclasses: SimpleFormatter or XMLFormatter. Applications requiring custom formatting of log messages will need to subclass this class and define the format() method to perform the desired conversion. Such subclasses may find the formatMessage() method useful; it performs localization using java.util.ResourceBundle and formatting using the facilities of the java.text package. getHead() and getTail() return a prefix and suffix (such as opening and closing XML tags) for a log file.

```
public abstract class Formatter {
// Protected Constructors
    protected Formatter();
// Public Instance Methods
    public abstract String format(LogRecord record);
    public String formatMessage(LogRecord record);                synchronized
    public String getHead(Handler h);
    public String getTail(Handler h);
}
```

Subclasses: SimpleFormatter, XMLFormatter

Passed To: Handler.setFormatter(), StreamHandler.StreamHandler()

Returned By: Handler.getFormatter()

Handler — Java 1.4

java.util.logging

A Handler takes LogRecord objects from a Logger and, if their severity level is high enough, formats and publishes them to some destination (a file or socket, for example). The subclasses of this abstract class support various destinations, and implement destination-specific publish(), flush() and close() methods.

In addition to the destination-specific abstract methods, this class also defines concrete methods used by most Handler subclasses. These are property getter and setter methods to specify the severity Level of logging messages to be handled, an optional Filter, a Formatter to convert log messages from LogRecord objects to text, a text encoding for the output text, and an ErrorManager to handle any exceptions that arise during log output.

Subclass-specific defaults for each of these properties are typically defined as properties of LogManager and are read from a system-wide logging configuration file.

In the simplest uses of the Logging API, a Logger sends it log messages to one or more handlers defined by the LogManager class for its "root logger". In this case there is no need for the application to ever instantiate or use a Handler directly. Applications that want custom control over the destination of their logs create and configure an instance of a Handler subclass, but never need to call its publish(), flush() or close() methods directly: that is done by the Logger.

```
public abstract class Handler {
// Protected Constructors
   protected Handler();
// Property Accessor Methods (by property name)
   public String getEncoding();
   public void setEncoding(String encoding) throws SecurityException, java.io.UnsupportedEncodingException;
   public ErrorManager getErrorManager();
   public void setErrorManager(ErrorManager em);
   public Filter getFilter();
   public void setFilter(Filter newFilter) throws SecurityException;
   public Formatter getFormatter();
   public void setFormatter(Formatter newFormatter) throws SecurityException;
   public Level getLevel();                                                    synchronized
   public void setLevel(Level newLevel) throws SecurityException;              synchronized
// Public Instance Methods
   public abstract void close() throws SecurityException;
   public abstract void flush();
   public boolean isLoggable(LogRecord record);
   public abstract void publish(LogRecord record);
// Protected Instance Methods
   protected void reportError(String msg, Exception ex, int code);
}
```

Subclasses: MemoryHandler, StreamHandler

Passed To: Formatter.{getHead(), getTail()}, Logger.{addHandler(), removeHandler()}, MemoryHandler.MemoryHandler(), XMLFormatter.{getHead(), getTail()}

Returned By: Logger.getHandlers()

Level — Java 1.4

java.util.logging — *serializable*

This class defines constants that represent the seven standard severity levels for log messages plus constants that turn logging off and enable logging at any level. When logging is enabled at one severity level, it is also enabled at all higher levels. The seven level constants, in order from most severe to least severe are: SEVERE, WARNING, INFO, CONFIG, FINE, FINER, and FINEST. The constant ALL enable logging of any message, regardless of its level. The constant OFF disables logging entirely. Note that these constants are all Level objects, rather than integers. This provides type safety.

Application code should rarely, if ever, need to use any of the methods of this class. Instead, they can simply use the constants it defines.

Object — Level ··· Serializable

```
public class Level implements Serializable {
// Protected Constructors
   protected Level(String name, int value);
   protected Level(String name, int value, String resourceBundleName);
// Public Constants
   public static final Level ALL;
   public static final Level CONFIG;
   public static final Level FINE;
   public static final Level FINER;
   public static final Level FINEST;
   public static final Level INFO;
   public static final Level OFF;
   public static final Level SEVERE;
   public static final Level WARNING;
// Public Class Methods
   public static Level parse(String name) throws IllegalArgumentException;          synchronized
// Public Instance Methods
   public String getLocalizedName();
   public String getName();
   public String getResourceBundleName();
   public final int intValue();
// Public Methods Overriding Object
   public boolean equals(Object ox);
   public int hashCode();
   public final String toString();
}
```

Passed To: Too many methods to list.

Returned By: Handler.getLevel(), Level.parse(), Logger.getLevel(), LogRecord.getLevel(), MemoryHandler.getPushLevel()

Type Of: Level.{ALL, CONFIG, FINE, FINER, FINEST, INFO, OFF, SEVERE, WARNING}

Logger — Java 1.4

java.util.logging

A Logger object is used to emit log messages. Logger does not have a public constructor, but there are several ways to obtain a Logger object to use in your code:

- Typically, applications call the static getLogger() method to create or lookup a named Logger within a hierarchy of named loggers. Loggers have dot-separated hierarchical names, which should be based on the name of the class or package that uses them. Loggers obtained in this way inherit their logging level, resource bundle (for localization) and Handler objects from their ancestors in the hierarchy and ultimately from the root Logger defined by the global LogManager.

- Applets that require a Logger with no security restrictions should use the static getAnonymousLogger() method to create an unnamed Logger that is not part of the hierarchy of named Logger objects managed by the LogManager. A Logger created by this method has the LogManager root logger as its parent, and inherits the logging level and handlers of that root logger.

- Finally, the static Logger.global field refers to a predefined Logger named "global"; programmers may find this predefined Logger convenient during the early stages of application development, but it should not be used in production code.

Once a suitable Logger has been obtained, there are a variety of methods that can be used to create a log message:

- The log() methods log a specified message at the specified level, with optional parameters that can be used in message localization. These methods examine the call stack and make an attempt to determine the class and method name from which the method is emitted. Because of code optimization and just-in-time compilation techniques, however, they may not always be able to determine this information.
- The logp() ("log precise") methods are like the log() methods but allow you to explicitly specify the name of the class and method that are emitting the log message.
- The logrb() methods are like the logp() methods, but additionally take the name of a resource bundle to use for localizing the message.
- entering(), exiting(), and throwing() are convenience methods for emitting log messages that trace the execution of a program. These methods use a logging level of Level.FINER. Note that there are variants of entering() and exiting() that allow specification of method arguments and return values.
- Finally, Logger defines a set of easy-to-use convenience methods for logging a simple message at a specific logging level. These methods have the same names as the logging levels: severe(), warning(), info(), config(), fine(), finer(), and finest().

A Logger has an associated logging Level, and discards any log messages with a severity lower than this. The severity level is initialized from the system configuration file, which is usually the desired behavior. You can explicitly override this setting with setLevel(). You might want to do this if you created the Logger with getAnonymousLogger() and have read the desired logging level from a configuration file of your own. If level-based filtering of log messages is not sufficient, you can associate a Filter with your Logger by calling setFilter. If you do this, any log messages rejected by the Filter will be discarded.

A Logger sends its log messages to any Handler objects that have been registered with addHandler(). Call getHandlers() to obtain an array of all registered handlers, and call removeHandler() to de-register a handler. By default, all log messages are also sent to the handlers of the parent logger and any other ancestor loggers. Since all named and anonymous loggers have the LogManager root logger as a parent or ancestor, all loggers by default send their log messages to the handlers defined in the system logging configuration file. See LogManager for details. If you do not want a Logger to use the handlers of its ancestors, pass false to setUseParentHandlers().

getLogger() and getAnonymousLogger() allow you to specify the name of a java.util.ResourceBundle for use in localizing log messages, and logrb() allows you to specify the name of a resource bundle to use to localize a specific log message. If a resource bundle is specified for the Logger or for a specific log message, then the message argument to the various logging methods is treated not as a literal message but instead as a localization key for which a localized version is to be looked up in the resource bundle. As part of the localization, any parameters, such as those specified by the *param1* and *params* arguments to the log() method are substituted into the localized message string as per java.text.MessageFormat. (Note, however that this localization and formatting is not performed by the Logger itself: instead, it simply stores the ResourceBundle and parameters in the LogRecord. It is the Formatter associated with the output Handler object that actually performs the localization.)

All the methods of this class are thread-safe and do not require external synchronization.

```
public class Logger {
// Protected Constructors
   protected Logger(String name, String resourceBundleName);
// Public Constants
   public static final Logger global;
// Public Class Methods
   public static Logger getAnonymousLogger();                                    synchronized
   public static Logger getAnonymousLogger(String resourceBundleName);           synchronized
   public static Logger getLogger(String name);                                  synchronized
   public static Logger getLogger(String name, String resourceBundleName);       synchronized
// Property Accessor Methods (by property name)
   public Filter getFilter();
   public void setFilter(Filter newFilter) throws SecurityException;
   public Handler[ ] getHandlers();                                              synchronized
   public Level getLevel();
   public void setLevel(Level newLevel) throws SecurityException;
   public String getName();
   public Logger getParent();
   public void setParent(Logger parent);
   public java.util.ResourceBundle getResourceBundle();
   public String getResourceBundleName();
   public boolean getUseParentHandlers();                                        synchronized
   public void setUseParentHandlers(boolean useParentHandlers);                  synchronized
// Public Instance Methods
   public void addHandler(Handler handler) throws SecurityException;             synchronized
   public void config(String msg);
   public void entering(String sourceClass, String sourceMethod);
   public void entering(String sourceClass, String sourceMethod, Object param1);
   public void entering(String sourceClass, String sourceMethod, Object[ ] params);
   public void exiting(String sourceClass, String sourceMethod);
   public void exiting(String sourceClass, String sourceMethod, Object result);
   public void fine(String msg);
   public void finer(String msg);
   public void finest(String msg);
   public void info(String msg);
   public boolean isLoggable(Level level);
   public void log(LogRecord record);
   public void log(Level level, String msg);
   public void log(Level level, String msg, Throwable thrown);
   public void log(Level level, String msg, Object param1);
   public void log(Level level, String msg, Object[ ] params);
   public void logp(Level level, String sourceClass, String sourceMethod, String msg);
   public void logp(Level level, String sourceClass, String sourceMethod, String msg, Object param1);
   public void logp(Level level, String sourceClass, String sourceMethod, String msg, Object[ ] params);
   public void logp(Level level, String sourceClass, String sourceMethod, String msg, Throwable thrown);
   public void logrb(Level level, String sourceClass, String sourceMethod, String bundleName, String msg);
   public void logrb(Level level, String sourceClass, String sourceMethod, String bundleName, String msg,
                     Object param1);
   public void logrb(Level level, String sourceClass, String sourceMethod, String bundleName, String msg,
                     Throwable thrown);
   public void logrb(Level level, String sourceClass, String sourceMethod, String bundleName, String msg,
                     Object[ ] params);
   public void removeHandler(Handler handler) throws SecurityException;          synchronized
   public void severe(String msg);
   public void throwing(String sourceClass, String sourceMethod, Throwable thrown);
```

```
    public void warning(String msg);
}
```

Passed To: Logger.setParent(), LogManager.addLogger()

Returned By: Logger.{getAnonymousLogger(), getLogger(), getParent()}, LogManager.getLogger()

Type Of: Logger.global

LoggingPermission — Java 1.4

java.util.logging — ***serializable permission***

This class is a java.security.Permission that governs the use of security-sensitive logging methods. The single defined name (or target) for LoggingPermission is "control", which represents permission to invoke various logging control methods such as Logger.setLevel() and LogManager.readConfiguration(). The methods in this package that throw SecurityException all require a LoggingPermission named "control" in order to run. Application programmers never need to use this class. System administrators configuring security policies may need to be familiar with it.

Object — Permission — BasicPermission — LoggingPermission
Guard, Serializable (Permission); Serializable (BasicPermission)

```
public final class LoggingPermission extends java.security.BasicPermission {
// Public Constructors
    public LoggingPermission(String name, String actions) throws IllegalArgumentException;
}
```

LogManager — Java 1.4

java.util.logging

As its name implies, this class is the manager for the java.util.logging API. It has three specific purposes:

1. To read a logging configuration file and create the default Handler objects specified in that file
2. To manage a set of Logger objects, arranging them into a tree based on their hierarchical names
3. To create and manage the unnamed Logger object that serves as the parent or ancestor of every other Logger

This class handles the important behind-the-scenes details that makes the Logging API work. Typical applications can make use of logging without ever having to use this class explicitly. Although its API is not commonly used by application programmers, it is still useful to understand the LogManager class, so it is described in detail here.

There is a single global instance of LogManager, which is obtained with the static getLogManager() method. By default, this global log manager object is an instance of the LogManager class itself. You may instead instantiate an instance of a subclass of LogManager by specifying the full class name of the subclass as the value of the system property java.util.logging.manager.

One of the primary purposes of the LogManager class is to read a java.util.Properties file that specifies the default logging configuration for the system. By default, this file is named *logging.properties* and is stored in the *jre/lib* directory of the Java installation. If you want to run a Java application using a different logging configuration, you can edit the default configuration file, but it is typically easier to create a new configuration file and tell the JVM about it by setting the system property java.util.logging.config.file to the name of your customized configuration file.

The most important purpose of the configuration file is to specify a set of Handler objects to which all log messages are sent. This is done by setting the handlers property in the file to a space-separated list of Handler class names. The LogManager will load the specified classes and instantiate each one using the default no-arg constructor, then register those Handler objects on the root Logger, where they are inherited by all other loggers. (You'll learn more about the root logger later.) Each of these Handler objects further configures itself by reading additional properties from the configuration file, as described in the documentation for each handler class.

The configuration file may also contain property name that are formed by appending ".level" to the name of a logger. The value of any such property is taken as the name of a logging Level for the named Logger. When the named logger is created and registered with the LogManager (described below) its logging level is automatically set to the specified level.

An application or any custom Handler or Formatter subclass or Filter implementation can read its own properties from the logging configuration file with the getProperty() method of LogManager. This is a useful way to provide customizability for logging-related classes.

In addition to managing the configuration file properties, a second purpose of LogManager is to maintain a tree of Logger objects organized into a hierarchy based on their dot-separated hierarchical names. The addLogger() method registers a new Logger object with the LogManager and inserts it into the tree. This method is called automatically by the Logger.getLogger() factory method, however, so you never need to call it yourself. The getLogger() method of LogManager finds and returns a named Logger object within the tree. Use getLoggerNames() to obtain an Enumeration of the names of all registered loggers.

At the root of the tree is a root logger, created by the LogManager, and initialized with default Handler objects specified in the logging configuration file as described above. This root logger has no name, and you can obtain a reference to it by passing the empty string to the getLogger() method. Except for this root logger and anonymous loggers (see Logger.getAnonymousLogger()), all loggers have names, and they are typically named after the package or class for which they provide logging. When a named logger is registered with the LogManager, the LogManager examines its name and inserts it into the tree of loggers at the appropriate place: a logger named "java.util.logging" would be inserted as the child of a logger named "java.util", if any such logger existed, or as a child of a logger named "java", or, if no logger with that name existed either, it would be inserted as a child of the root logger named "". When the LogManager determines the position of a logger within the tree of loggers, it calls the setParent() method of the newly-registered Logger to tell it who its parent is. This is important because, by default, loggers inherit their logging level and handlers from their parent. Although the Logger.setParent() method is public, it is intended for use only by the LogManager class.

Anonymous loggers created with Logger.getAnonymousLogger() do not have names, and are not part of the logger tree. When they are created, however, their parent is set to the root logger of the LogManager. For this reason, anonymous loggers inherit the default handlers specified in the logging configuration file.

The readConfiguration() methods are used to force the LogManager to re-read the system configuration file, or to read a new configuration file from the specified stream. Both versions of the method generate a java.beans.PropertyChangeEvent and use it to notify any listeners that have been registered with addPropertyChangeListener. Both methods also first invoke the reset() method which discards the properties of the current configuration file, removes and closes all handlers for all loggers, and sets the logging level of all loggers to null, except for the root logger's logging level, which it sets to Level.INFO. It is unlikely that you would ever want to invoke reset() yourself. A number of LogManager methods throw a SecurityException if the caller does not have appropriate permissions. You can use checkAccess() to test whether the current calling context has the required LoggingPermission named "control".

All LogManager methods can be safely used by multiple threads.

```
public class LogManager {
// Protected Constructors
   protected LogManager();
// Public Class Methods
   public static LogManager getLogManager();
// Event Registration Methods (by event name)
   public void addPropertyChangeListener(java.beans.PropertyChangeListener l) throws SecurityException;
   public void removePropertyChangeListener(java.beans.PropertyChangeListener l) throws SecurityException;
// Public Instance Methods
   public boolean addLogger(Logger logger);                                              synchronized
   public void checkAccess() throws SecurityException;
   public Logger getLogger(String name);                                                 synchronized
   public java.util.Enumeration getLoggerNames();                                        synchronized
   public String getProperty(String name);
   public void readConfiguration() throws java.io.IOException, SecurityException;
   public void readConfiguration(java.io.InputStream ins) throws java.io.IOException, SecurityException;
   public void reset() throws SecurityException;
}
```

Returned By: LogManager.getLogManager()

LogRecord — Java 1.4

java.util.logging — *serializable*

Instances of this class are used to represent log messages as they are passed between Logger, Handler, Filter and Formatter objects. LogRecord defines a number of JavaBeans-type property getter and setter methods. The values of the various properties encapsulate all details of the log message. The LogRecord() constructor takes arguments for the two most important properties: the log level and the log message (or localization key). The constructor also initializes the millis property to the current time, the sequenceNumber property to a unique (within the VM) value that can be used to compare the order of two log messages, and the threadID property to a unique identifier for the current thread. All other properties of the LogRecord are left uninitialized with their default null values.

Object — LogRecord ··· Serializable

```
public class LogRecord implements Serializable {
// Public Constructors
   public LogRecord(Level level, String msg);
// Property Accessor Methods (by property name)
   public Level getLevel();
   public void setLevel(Level level);
   public String getLoggerName();
   public void setLoggerName(String name);
   public String getMessage();
   public void setMessage(String message);
   public long getMillis();
   public void setMillis(long millis);
   public Object[] getParameters();
   public void setParameters(Object[] parameters);
```

```
    public java.util.ResourceBundle getResourceBundle();
    public void setResourceBundle(java.util.ResourceBundle bundle);
    public String getResourceBundleName();
    public void setResourceBundleName(String name);
    public long getSequenceNumber();
    public void setSequenceNumber(long seq);
    public String getSourceClassName();
    public void setSourceClassName(String sourceClassName);
    public String getSourceMethodName();
    public void setSourceMethodName(String sourceMethodName);
    public int getThreadID();
    public void setThreadID(int threadID);
    public Throwable getThrown();
    public void setThrown(Throwable thrown);
}
```

Passed To: ConsoleHandler.publish(), FileHandler.publish(), Filter.isLoggable(), Formatter.{format(), formatMessage()}, Handler.{isLoggable(), publish()}, Logger.log(), MemoryHandler.{isLoggable(), publish()}, SimpleFormatter.format(), SocketHandler.publish(), StreamHandler.{isLoggable(), publish()}, XMLFormatter.format()

MemoryHandler **Java 1.4**

java.util.logging

A MemoryHandler stores LogRecord objects in a fixed-sized buffer in memory. When the buffer fills up, it discards the oldest record one each time a new record arrives. It maintains a reference to another Handler object, and whenever the push() method is called, or whenever a LogRecord arrives with a level at or higher than the pushLevel threshold, it "pushes" all of buffered LogRecord objects to that other Handler object, which typically formats and outputs them to some appropriate destination. Because MemoryHandler never outputs log records itself, it does not use the formatter or encoding properties inherited from its superclass.

When you create a MemoryHandler, you can specify the target Handler object, the size of the in-memory buffer, and the value of the pushLevel property, or you can omit these constructor arguments and rely on system-wide defaults obtained with LogManager.getProperty(). MemoryHandler also uses LogManager.getProperty() to obtain initial values for the level and filter properties inherited from Handler. The following table lists these properties, as well as the *target*, *size*, and *pushLevel* constructor arguments, the value passed to getProperty(), and the default value used if getProperty() returns null. See Handler for further details.

Property or argument	*LogManager property name*	*Default*
level	java.util.logging.MemoryHandler.level	Level.ALL
filter	java.util.logging.MemoryHandler.filter	null
target	java.util.logging.MemoryHandler.target	No default
size	java.util.logging.MemoryHandler.size	1,000 log records
pushLevel	java.util.logging.MemoryHandler.push	Level.SEVERE

Object — Handler — MemoryHandler

```
public class MemoryHandler extends Handler {
// Public Constructors
```

```
    public MemoryHandler();
    public MemoryHandler(Handler target, int size, Level pushLevel);
// Public Instance Methods
    public Level getPushLevel();                                                synchronized
    public void push();                                                         synchronized
    public void setPushLevel(Level newLevel) throws SecurityException;
// Public Methods Overriding Handler
    public void close() throws SecurityException;
    public void flush();
    public boolean isLoggable(LogRecord record);
    public void publish(LogRecord record);                                      synchronized
}
```

SimpleFormatter — Java 1.4

java.util.logging

This Formatter subclass converts a LogRecord object to a human-readable log message that is typically one or two lines long. See also XMLFormatter.

Object — Formatter — SimpleFormatter

```
public class SimpleFormatter extends Formatter {
// Public Constructors
    public SimpleFormatter();
// Public Methods Overriding Formatter
    public String format(LogRecord record);                                     synchronized
}
```

SocketHandler — Java 1.4

java.util.logging

This Handler subclass formats LogRecord objects and outputs the resulting strings to a network socket. When you create a SocketHandler, you can pass the hostname and port of the socket to the constructor or you can rely on system-wide defaults obtained with LogManager.getProperty(). SocketHandler also uses LogManager.getProperty() to obtain initial values for the properties inherited from Handler. The following table lists these properties, as well as the host and port arguments, the value passed to getProperty(), and the default value used if getProperty() returns null. See Handler for further details.

Handler property	*LogManager property name*	*Default*
level	java.util.logging.SocketHandler.level	Level.ALL
filter	java.util.logging.SocketHandler.filter	null
formatter	java.util.logging.SocketHandler.formatter	XMLFormatter
encoding	java.util.logging.SocketHandler.encoding	Platform default
hostname	java.util.logging.SocketHandler.host	No default
port	java.util.logging.SocketHandler.port	No default

Object — Handler — StreamHandler — SocketHandler

```
public class SocketHandler extends StreamHandler {
// Public Constructors
    public SocketHandler() throws java.io.IOException;
```

```
    public SocketHandler(String host, int port) throws java.io.IOException;
// Public Methods Overriding StreamHandler
    public void close() throws SecurityException;                                    synchronized
    public void publish(LogRecord record);                                           synchronized
}
```

StreamHandler **Java 1.4**

java.util.logging

This Handler subclass sends log messages to an arbitrary java.io.OutputStream. It exists primarily to serve as the common superclass of ConsoleHandler, FileHandler, and SocketHandler.

Object ─ Handler ─ StreamHandler

```
public class StreamHandler extends Handler {
// Public Constructors
    public StreamHandler();
    public StreamHandler(java.io.OutputStream out, Formatter formatter);
// Public Methods Overriding Handler
    public void close() throws SecurityException;                                    synchronized
    public void flush();                                                             synchronized
    public boolean isLoggable(LogRecord record);
    public void publish(LogRecord record);                                           synchronized
    public void setEncoding(String encoding) throws SecurityException, java.io.UnsupportedEncodingException;
// Protected Instance Methods
    protected void setOutputStream(java.io.OutputStream out) throws SecurityException;    synchronized
}
```

Subclasses: ConsoleHandler, FileHandler, SocketHandler

XMLFormatter **Java 1.4**

java.util.logging

This Formatter subclass converts a LogRecord to an XML-formatted string. The format() method returns a <record> element, which always contains <date>, <millis>, <sequence>, <level> and <message> tags, and may also contain <logger>, <class>, <method>, <thread>, <key>, <catalog>, <param>, and <exception> tags. See *http://java.sun.com/dtd/logger.dtd* for the DTD of the output document.

The getHead() and getTail() methods are overridden to return opening and closing <log> and </log> tags to surround all output <record> tags. Note however, that if an application terminates abnormally, the logging facility may be unable to terminate the log file with the closing <log> tag.

Object ─ Formatter ─ XMLFormatter

```
public class XMLFormatter extends Formatter {
// Public Constructors
    public XMLFormatter();
// Public Methods Overriding Formatter
    public String format(LogRecord record);
    public String getHead(Handler h);
    public String getTail(Handler h);
}
```

Package java.util.prefs

Java 1.4

The java.util.prefs package contains classes and interfaces for managing persistent user and system-wide preferences for Java applications and classes. Most applications will use only the Preferences class itself. Some will also use the event objects and listener interfaces defined by this package, and some may need to explicitly catch the types of exceptions defined by this package. Application programmers never need to use the PreferencesFactory interface or the AbstractPreferences class, which are intended for Preferences implementors only.

To use the Preferences class, first use a static method to obtain an appropriate Preferences object or objects, and then use a get() method to query a preference value or a put() method to set a preference value. The following code shows a typical usage. See the Preferences class for details.

```
import java.util.prefs.Preferences;

public class TextEditor {
  // Some constants that define default values for preferences
  public static final int WIDTH_DEFAULT = 80;
  public static final String DICTIONARY_DEFAULT = "";

  // Fields to be initialized from preference values
  public int width;              // Screen width in columns
  public String dictionary;   // Dictionary name for spell checking

  public void initPrefs() {
    // Get Preferences objects for user and system preferences for this package
    Preferences userprefs = Preferences.userNodeForPackage(TextEditor.class);
    Preferences sysprefs = Preferences.systemNodeForPackage(TextEditor.class);

    // Look up preference values.  Note that you always pass a default value.
    width = userprefs.getInt("width", WIDTH_DEFAULT);
    // Look up a user preference using a system preference as the default
    dictionary = userprefs.get("dictionary",
                               sysprefs.get("dictionary",
                                            DICTIONARY_DEFAULT));
  }
}
```

Interface:

public interface **PreferencesFactory**;

Events:

public class **NodeChangeEvent** extends java.util.EventObject;
public class **PreferenceChangeEvent** extends java.util.EventObject;

Event Listeners:

public interface **NodeChangeListener** extends java.util.EventListener;
public interface **PreferenceChangeListener** extends java.util.EventListener;

Other Classes:

public abstract class **Preferences**;
└ public abstract class **AbstractPreferences** extends Preferences;

Exceptions:

public class **BackingStoreException** extends Exception;
public class **InvalidPreferencesFormatException** extends Exception;

AbstractPreferences — Java 1.4

java.util.prefs

This class implements all the abstract methods of Preferences on top of a smaller set of abstract methods. Programmers creating a Preferences implementation (or "service provider") can subclass this class and need define only the nine methods whose names end in "Spi". Application programmers never need to use this class.

Object — Preferences — AbstractPreferences

```
public abstract class AbstractPreferences extends Preferences {
// Protected Constructors
   protected AbstractPreferences(AbstractPreferences parent, String name);
// Event Registration Methods (by event name)
   public void addNodeChangeListener(NodeChangeListener ncl);                    Overrides:Preferences
   public void removeNodeChangeListener(NodeChangeListener ncl);                 Overrides:Preferences
   public void addPreferenceChangeListener(PreferenceChangeListener pcl);        Overrides:Preferences
   public void removePreferenceChangeListener(PreferenceChangeListener pcl);     Overrides:Preferences
// Public Methods Overriding Preferences
   public String absolutePath();
   public String[ ] childrenNames() throws BackingStoreException;
   public void clear() throws BackingStoreException;
   public void exportNode(java.io.OutputStream os) throws java.io.IOException, BackingStoreException;
   public void exportSubtree(java.io.OutputStream os) throws java.io.IOException, BackingStoreException;
   public void flush() throws BackingStoreException;
   public String get(String key, String def);
   public boolean getBoolean(String key, boolean def);
   public byte[ ] getByteArray(String key, byte[ ] def);
   public double getDouble(String key, double def);
   public float getFloat(String key, float def);
   public int getInt(String key, int def);
   public long getLong(String key, long def);
   public boolean isUserNode();
   public String[ ] keys() throws BackingStoreException;
   public String name();
   public Preferences node(String path);
   public boolean nodeExists(String path) throws BackingStoreException;
   public Preferences parent();
   public void put(String key, String value);
   public void putBoolean(String key, boolean value);
   public void putByteArray(String key, byte[ ] value);
```

```
    public void putDouble(String key, double value);
    public void putFloat(String key, float value);
    public void putInt(String key, int value);
    public void putLong(String key, long value);
    public void remove(String key);
    public void removeNode() throws BackingStoreException;
    public void sync() throws BackingStoreException;
    public String toString();
// Protected Instance Methods
    protected final AbstractPreferences[ ] cachedChildren();
    protected abstract String[ ] childrenNamesSpi() throws BackingStoreException;
    protected abstract AbstractPreferences childSpi(String name);
    protected abstract void flushSpi() throws BackingStoreException;
    protected AbstractPreferences getChild(String nodeName) throws BackingStoreException;
    protected abstract String getSpi(String key);
    protected boolean isRemoved();
    protected abstract String[ ] keysSpi() throws BackingStoreException;
    protected abstract void putSpi(String key, String value);
    protected abstract void removeNodeSpi() throws BackingStoreException;
    protected abstract void removeSpi(String key);
    protected abstract void syncSpi() throws BackingStoreException;
// Protected Instance Fields
    protected final Object lock;
    protected boolean newNode;
}
```

Passed To: AbstractPreferences.AbstractPreferences()

Returned By: AbstractPreferences.{cachedChildren(), childSpi(), getChild()}

BackingStoreException — Java 1.4

java.util.prefs — *serializable checked*

This exception signals that a Preferences method could not complete because of an implementation-specific problem with the preferences database. The most commonly used methods of the Preferences class do not throw this exception, and are guaranteed to succeed even if the implementation's preferences data is not available. Note that although this class inherits the Serializable interface, implementations are not actually required to be serializable.

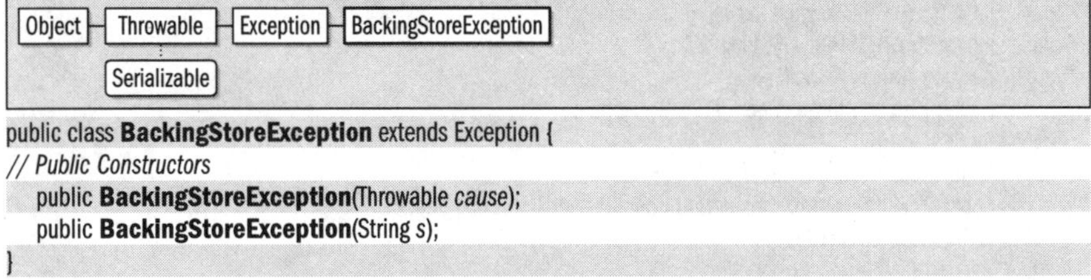


```
public class BackingStoreException extends Exception {
// Public Constructors
    public BackingStoreException(Throwable cause);
    public BackingStoreException(String s);
}
```

Thrown By: Too many methods to list.

InvalidPreferencesFormatException — Java 1.4

java.util.prefs — *serializable checked*

This exception signals a syntax error in XML preference data. Note that although this class inherits the Serializable interface, implementations are not actually required to be serializable.


```
public class InvalidPreferencesFormatException extends Exception {
// Public Constructors
   public InvalidPreferencesFormatException(String message);
   public InvalidPreferencesFormatException(Throwable cause);
   public InvalidPreferencesFormatException(String message, Throwable cause);
}
```

Thrown By: Preferences.importPreferences()

NodeChangeEvent — Java 1.4

java.util.prefs — *serializable event*

A NodeChangeEvent object is passed to the methods of any NodeChangeListener objects registered on a Preferences object when a child Preferences node is added or removed. getChild() returns the Preferences object that was added or removed. getParent() returns the parent Preferences node from which the child was added or removed. This parent Preferences object is the one on which the NodeChangeListener was registered.

Although this class inherits the Serializable interface, it is not actually serializable.


```
public class NodeChangeEvent extends java.util.EventObject {
// Public Constructors
   public NodeChangeEvent(Preferences parent, Preferences child);
// Public Instance Methods
   public Preferences getChild();
   public Preferences getParent();
}
```

Passed To: NodeChangeListener.{childAdded(), childRemoved()}

NodeChangeListener — Java 1.4

java.util.prefs — *event listener*

This interface defines the methods that an object must implement if it wants to be notified when a child preferences node is added to or removed from a Preferences object. When such an addition or removal occurs, the parent Preferences object passes a NodeChangeEvent object to the appropriate method of any NodeChangeListener objects that have been registered through the Preferences.addNodeChangeListener() method.


```
public interface NodeChangeListener extends java.util.EventListener {
// Public Instance Methods
```

```
    public abstract void childAdded(NodeChangeEvent evt);
    public abstract void childRemoved(NodeChangeEvent evt);
}
```

Passed To: AbstractPreferences.{addNodeChangeListener(), removeNodeChangeListener()}, Preferences.{addNodeChangeListener(), removeNodeChangeListener()}

PreferenceChangeEvent — Java 1.4

java.util.prefs — *serializable event*

A PreferenceChangeEvent object is passed to the preferenceChange() method of any PreferenceChangeListener objects registered on a Preferences object whenever a preferences value is added to, removed from, or modified in that Preferences node. getNode() returns the affected Preferences object. getKey() returns name of the modified preference. If the preference value was added or modified, getNewValue() returns that value. If a preference was deleted, getNewValue() returns null.

Although this class inherits the Serializable interface, it is not actually serializable.

Object — EventObject — PreferenceChangeEvent
Serializable

```
public class PreferenceChangeEvent extends java.util.EventObject {
// Public Constructors
    public PreferenceChangeEvent(Preferences node, String key, String newValue);
// Public Instance Methods
    public String getKey();
    public String getNewValue();
    public Preferences getNode();
}
```

Passed To: PreferenceChangeListener.preferenceChange()

PreferenceChangeListener — Java 1.4

java.util.prefs — *event listener*

This interface defines the method that an object must implement if it wants to be notified when a preference key/value pair is added to, removed from, or changed in a Preferences object. After any such change, the Preferences object passes a PreferenceChangeEvent object describing the change to the preferenceChange() method of any PreferenceChangeListener objects that have been registered through the Preferences.addPreferenceChangeListener() method.

EventListener ··· PreferenceChangeListener

```
public interface PreferenceChangeListener extends java.util.EventListener {
// Public Instance Methods
    public abstract void preferenceChange(PreferenceChangeEvent evt);
}
```

Passed To: AbstractPreferences.{addPreferenceChangeListener(), removePreferenceChangeListener()}, Preferences.{addPreferenceChangeListener(), removePreferenceChangeListener()}

Preferences **Java 1.4**

java.util.prefs

A Preferences object represents a mapping between preference names, which are case-sensitive strings, and corresponding preference values. get() allows you to query the string value of a named preference, and put() allows you to set a string value for a named preference. Although all preference values are stored as strings, various convenience methods whose names begin with "get" and "put" exist to convert preference values of type boolean byte[], double, float, int, and long to and from strings.

The remove() method allows you to delete a named preference altogether, and clear() deletes all preference values stored in a Preferences object. The keys() method returns an array of strings that specify the names of all preferences in the Preferences object.

Preference values are stored in some implementation-dependent back-end which may be a file, a LDAP directory server, the Windows Registry, or any other persistent "backing store." Note that all the get() methods of this class require a default value to be specified. They return this default if no value has been stored for the named preference, or if the backing store is unavailable for any reason. The Preferences class is completely independent of the underlying implementation, except that it enforces an 80-character limit for preference names and Preference node names (see the following) and a 8,192-character limit on preference value strings.

Preferences does not have a public constructor. To obtain a Preferences object for use in your application, you must must use one of the static methods described below. Each Preferences object is a node in a hierarchy of Preferences nodes. There are two distinct hierarchies: one stores user-specific preferences, and one stores system-wide preferences. All Preferences nodes (in either hierarchy) have a unique name and use the same naming convention that Unix filesystems use. Applications (and classes) may store their preferences in a Preferences node with any name, but the convention is to use a node name that corresponds to the package name of the application or class, with all "." characters in the package name converted to "/" characters. For example, the preferences node used by java.lang.System would be "/java/lang".

Preferences defines static methods that you can use to obtain the Preferences objects your application requires. Pass a Class object to systemNodeForPackage() and userNodeForPackage() to obtain the system and user Preferences objects that are specific to the package of that class. If you want a Preferences node specific to a single class rather than to the package, you can pass the class name to the node() method of the package-specific node returned by systemNodeForPackage() or userNodeForPackage(). If you want to navigate the entire tree of preferences nodes (which most applications never need to do) call systemRoot() and userRoot() to obtain the root node of the two hierarchies, and then use the node() method to look up child nodes of those roots.

Various Preferences methods allow you to traverse the preferences hierarchies. parent() returns the parent Preferences node. childrenNames() returns an array of the relative names of all children of a Preferences node. node() returns a named Preferences object from the hierarchy. If the specified node name begins with a slash, it is an absolute name and is interpreted relative to the root of the hierarchy. Otherwise, it is a relative name and is interpreted relative to the Preferences object on which node() was called. nodeExists() allows you to test whether a named node exists. removeNode() allows you to delete an entire Preferences node from the hierarchy (useful when uninstalling an application). name() returns the simple name of a Preferences node, relative to its parent. absoutePath() returns the full, absolute name of the node, relative to the root of the hierarchy. Finally, isUserNode() allows you to determine whether a Preferences object is part of the user or system hierarchies.

Many applications will simply read their preference values once at startup. Long-lived applications or applications that want to respond dynamically to modifications to preferences (such as applications that are tightly integrated with a graphical desktop) may use addPreferenceChangeListener() to register a PreferenceChangeListener to receive notifications of preference changes (in the form of PreferenceChangeEvent objects). Applications that are interested in changes to the Preferences hierarchy itself can register a NodeChangeListener.

put() and the various type-specific put...() convenience methods may return asynchronously, before the new preference value is stored persistently within the backing store. Call flush() to force any preference changes to this Preferences node (and any of its descendants in the hierarchy) to be stored persistently. Note that it is not necessary to call flush() before an application terminates; all preferences will eventually be made persistent. More than one application (within more than one Java virtual machine) may set preference values in the same Preferences node at the same time. Call sync() to ensure that future calls to get() and its related convenience methods retrieve current preference values set by this or other virtual machines. Note that the flush() and sync() operations are typically much more expensive than get() and put() operations, and applications do not often need to use them.

Preferences implementations ensure that all the methods of this class are thread safe. If multiple threads or multiple VMs write store the same preferences concurrently, their values may overwrite one another, but the preference data will not be corrupted. Note that, for simplicity, Preferences does not define any way to set multiple preferences in a single atomic transaction. If you need to ensure atomicity for multiple preference values, define a data format that allows you to store all the requisite values in a single string, and set and query those values with a single call to put() or get().

The contents of a Preferences node, or of a node and all of its descendants may be exported as an XML file with exportNode() and exportSubtree(). The static importPreferences() method reads an exported XML file back into the preferences hierarchy. These methods allow backups to be made of preference data, and allow preferences to be transferred between systems or between users.

Prior to Java 1.4, application preferences were sometimes managed with the java.util.Properties object.

```
public abstract class Preferences {
// Protected Constructors
   protected Preferences();
// Public Constants
   public static final int MAX_KEY_LENGTH;                                        =80
   public static final int MAX_NAME_LENGTH;                                       =80
   public static final int MAX_VALUE_LENGTH;                                      =8192
// Public Class Methods
   public static void importPreferences(java.io.InputStream is) throws java.io.IOException,
        InvalidPreferencesFormatException;
   public static Preferences systemNodeForPackage(Class c);
   public static Preferences systemRoot();
   public static Preferences userNodeForPackage(Class c);
   public static Preferences userRoot();
// Event Registration Methods (by event name)
   public abstract void addNodeChangeListener(NodeChangeListener ncl);
   public abstract void removeNodeChangeListener(NodeChangeListener ncl);
   public abstract void addPreferenceChangeListener(PreferenceChangeListener pcl);
   public abstract void removePreferenceChangeListener(PreferenceChangeListener pcl);
// Public Instance Methods
```

```
   public abstract String absolutePath();
   public abstract String[] childrenNames() throws BackingStoreException;
   public abstract void clear() throws BackingStoreException;
   public abstract void exportNode(java.io.OutputStream os) throws java.io.IOException, BackingStoreException;
   public abstract void exportSubtree(java.io.OutputStream os) throws java.io.IOException, BackingStoreException;
   public abstract void flush() throws BackingStoreException;
   public abstract String get(String key, String def);
   public abstract boolean getBoolean(String key, boolean def);
   public abstract byte[] getByteArray(String key, byte[] def);
   public abstract double getDouble(String key, double def);
   public abstract float getFloat(String key, float def);
   public abstract int getInt(String key, int def);
   public abstract long getLong(String key, long def);
   public abstract boolean isUserNode();
   public abstract String[] keys() throws BackingStoreException;
   public abstract String name();
   public abstract Preferences node(String pathName);
   public abstract boolean nodeExists(String pathName) throws BackingStoreException;
   public abstract Preferences parent();
   public abstract void put(String key, String value);
   public abstract void putBoolean(String key, boolean value);
   public abstract void putByteArray(String key, byte[] value);
   public abstract void putDouble(String key, double value);
   public abstract void putFloat(String key, float value);
   public abstract void putInt(String key, int value);
   public abstract void putLong(String key, long value);
   public abstract void remove(String key);
   public abstract void removeNode() throws BackingStoreException;
   public abstract void sync() throws BackingStoreException;
// Public Methods Overriding Object
   public abstract String toString();
}
```

Subclasses: AbstractPreferences

Passed To: NodeChangeEvent.NodeChangeEvent(), PreferenceChangeEvent.PreferenceChangeEvent()

Returned By: AbstractPreferences.{node(), parent()}, NodeChangeEvent.{getChild(), getParent()}, PreferenceChangeEvent.getNode(), Preferences.{node(), parent(), systemNodeForPackage(), systemRoot(), userNodeForPackage(), userRoot()}, PreferencesFactory.{systemRoot(), userRoot()}

PreferencesFactory — Java 1.4

java.util.prefs

The PreferencesFactory interface defines the factory methods used by the static methods of the Preferences class to obtain the root Preferences nodes for user-specific and system-wide preferences hierarchies. Application programmers never need to use this interface.

An implementation of the preferences API for a specific back-end data store must include an implementation of this interface that works with that data store. Sun's implementation of Java includes a default filesystem-based implementation, which you can override by specifying the name of a PreferencesFactory implementation as the value of the java.util.prefs.PreferencesFactory system property.

```
public interface PreferencesFactory {
// Public Instance Methods
   public abstract Preferences systemRoot();
```

```
    public abstract Preferences userRoot();
}
```

Package java.util.regex — Java 1.4

This small package provides a facility for textual pattern matching with regular expressions. Pattern objects represent regular expressions, which are specified using a syntax very close to the one used by the Perl programming language. The Matcher class encapsulates a Pattern and a string of text, and defines various methods for matching the pattern to the text. The methods of the Pattern and Matcher classes that specify text to be matched all specify that text in the form of a java.lang.CharSequence. The CharSequence interface is new in Java 1.4. It is implemented by the String and StringBuffer classes, and also by the java.nio.CharBuffer class of the New I/O API.

In addition to the pattern matching methods defined in this package, the java.lang.String class has been augmented in Java 1.4 with a number of convenience methods for matching strings against regular expressions that are specified in their text form as strings, rather than in their compiled form as Pattern objects. Applications with simple pattern matching needs can use these convenience methods and may never have to directly use the Pattern or Matcher classes.

Classes:

public final class **Matcher**;
public final class **Pattern** implements Serializable;

Exceptions:

public class **PatternSyntaxException** extends IllegalArgumentException;

Matcher — Java 1.4

java.util.regex

A Matcher object encapsulates a regular expression and a string of text (a Pattern and a java.lang.CharSequence) and defines methods for matching the pattern to the text in several different ways, for obtaining details about pattern matches, and for doing search-and-replace operations on the text. Matcher has no public constructor. Obtain a Matcher by passing the character sequence to be matched to the matcher() method of the desired Pattern object. You can also reuse an existing Matcher object with a new character sequence (but the same Pattern) by passing a new CharSequence to the matcher's reset() method.

Once you have created or reset a Matcher, there are several types of comparisons you can perform between the regular expression and the character sequence. The simplest comparison is the matches() method. It returns true if the pattern matches the complete character sequence, and returns false otherwise. The lookingAt() method is similar: it returns true if the pattern matches the complete sequence, or if it matches some subsequence at the beginning of the text. If the pattern does not match the start of the text, lookingAt() returns false. matches() requires the pattern to match both the beginning and ending of the text, and lookingAt() requires the pattern to match the beginning. The find() method, on the other hand, has neither of these requirements: it returns true if the pattern matches any part of the text. As will be described below, find() has some special behavior that allows it to be used in a loop to find all matches in the text.

If matches(), lookingAt(), or find() return true, then several other Matcher methods can be used to obtain details about the matched text. The no-argument start() method returns the index of the first character that matched the pattern (for matches() and lookingAt() this must be zero, of course.) The no-argument end() method returns the index of the last character that matched plus one (or the index of the first character following the matched text). Some regular expressions can match the empty string. If this occurs, then end() returns the same value as start().

Regular expressions may include subexpressions grouped within parentheses, which are also known as "capturing groups". When working with regular expressions, it is often useful to obtain information about the text that matches these groups. The one-argument versions of the start() and end() methods take a group number and return the index of the first character that matched that group and the index of the first character following the text that matched that group. Similarly, the group() method takes a group number and returns a String that contains the text that matched that group. (The no-argument version of group() returns the text that matched the entire regular expression.) Groups are numbered from 1 (group 0 is the entire regular expression) and are ordered from left-to-right within the regular expression. When there are nested groups, their ordering is based on the position of the opening left parenthesis that begins the group.

The no-argument version of find() has special behavior that makes it suitable for use in a loop to find all matches of a pattern within a string. The first time find() is called after a Matcher is created or after the reset() method is called, it starts it search at the beginning of the string. If it finds a match, it stores the start and end position of the matched text. If reset() is not called in the meantime, then the next call to find() searches again but starts the search at the first character after the match: at the position returned by end(). (If the previous call to find() matched the empty string, then the next call begins at end()+1 instead.) In this way, it is possible to find all matches of a pattern within a string simply by calling find() repeatedly until it returns false indicating that no match was found. After each repeated call to find() you can use the start(), end() and group() methods to obtain more information about the text that matched the pattern and any of its subpatterns.

Matcher also defines methods that perform search-and-replace operations. replaceFirst() searches the character sequence for the first subsequence that matches the pattern. It then returns a string that is the character sequence with the matched text replaced with the specified replacement string. replaceAll() is similar, but replaces all matching subsequences within the character sequence instead of just replacing the first. The replacement string passed to replaceFirst() and replaceAll() is not always replaced literally. If the replacement contains a dollar sign followed by an integer that is a valid group number, then the dollar sign and the number are replaced by the text that matched the numbered group. If you want to include a literal dollar sign in the replacement string, precede it with a backslash.

replaceFirst() and replaceAll() are convenience methods that cover the most common search-and-replace cases. However, Matcher also defines lower-level methods that you can use to do a custom search-and-replace operation in conjunction with calls to find(), and build up a modified string in a StringBuffer. In order to understand this search-and-replace procedure, you must know that a Matcher maintains a "append position", which starts at zero when the Matcher is created, and is restored to zero by the reset() method. The appendReplacement() method is designed to be used after a successful call to find(). It copies all the text between the append position and the character before the start() position for the last match into the specified string buffer. Then it appends the specified replacement text to that string buffer (performing the same substitutions that replaceAll() does). Finally, it sets the append position to the end() of the last match, so that a subsequent call to appendReplacement() starts at a new character. appendReplacement() is intended for use after a call to find() that returns true. When find() cannot find another match and returns false, you should complete the replacement operation by calling appendTail(): this method copies all text between the end() position of the last match and the end of the character sequence into the specified StringBuffer.

The reset() method has been mentioned several times. It erases any saved information about the last match, and restores the Matcher to its initial state so that subsequent calls to find() and appendReplacement() start at the beginning of the character sequence. The one-argument version of reset() also allows you to specify an entirely new character sequence to match against. It is important to understand that several other Matcher methods call reset() themselves before they perform their operation. They are: matches(), lookingAt(), the one-argument version of find(), replaceAll(), and replaceFirst().

Matcher is not thread-safe, and should not be used by more than one thread concurrently.

```
public final class Matcher {
// No Constructor
// Public Instance Methods
    public Matcher appendReplacement(StringBuffer sb, String replacement);
    public StringBuffer appendTail(StringBuffer sb);
    public int end();
    public int end(int group);
    public boolean find();
    public boolean find(int start);
    public String group();
    public String group(int group);
    public int groupCount();
    public boolean lookingAt();
    public boolean matches();
    public Pattern pattern();
    public String replaceAll(String replacement);
    public String replaceFirst(String replacement);
    public Matcher reset();
    public Matcher reset(CharSequence input);
    public int start();
    public int start(int group);
}
```

Returned By: Matcher.{appendReplacement(), reset()}, Pattern.matcher()

Pattern — Java 1.4

java.util.regex — *serializable*

This class represents a regular expression. It has no public constructor; obtain a Pattern by calling one of the static compile() methods, passing the string representation of the regular expression, and an optional bitmask of flags that modify the behavior of the regex. pattern() and flags() return the string form of the regular expression and the bitmask that were passed to compile().

If you want to perform only a single match operation with a regular expression, and don't need to use any of the flags, you don't have to create a Pattern object: simply pass the string representation of the pattern and the CharSequence to be matched to the static matches() method: the method returns true if the specified pattern matches the complete specified text, or returns false otherwise.

Pattern represents a regular expression, but does not actually define any primitive methods for matching regular expressions to text. To do that, you must create a Matcher object that encapsulates a pattern and the text it is to be compared with. Do this by calling the matcher() method and specifying the CharSequence you want to match against. See Matcher for a description of what you can do with it.

The split() methods are the exception to the rule that you must obtain a Matcher in order to be able to do anything with a Pattern (although they create and use a Matcher internally). They take a CharSequence as input, and split it into substrings, using text that matches the regular expression as the delimiter, returning the substrings as a String[]. The two-argument version of split() takes an integer argument that specifies the maximum number of substrings to break the input into.

Pattern defines the following flags that control various aspects of how regular expression matching is performed. The flags are the following:

CANON_EQ
: The Unicode standard sometimes allows more than one way to specify the same character. If this flag is set, characters are compared by comparing their full canonical decompositions, so that characters will match even if expressed in different ways. Enabling this flag typically slows down performance. Unlike all the other flags, there is no way to temporarily enable this flag within a pattern.

CASE_INSENSITIVE
: Match letters without regard to case. By default this flag only affects the comparisons of ASCII letters. Also set the UNICODE_CASE flag if you want to ignore the case of all Unicode characters. You can enable this flag within a pattern with (?i).

COMMENTS
: If this flag is set, then whitespace and comments within a pattern are ignored. Comments are all characters between a # and end of line. You can enable this flag within a pattern with (?x)

DOTALL
: If this flag is set, then the . expression matches any character. If it is not set, then it does not match line terminator characters. This is also known as single-line mode, and you can enable it within a pattern with (?s).

MULTILINE
: If this flag is set, then the ^ and $ anchors match not only at the beginning and end of the input string, but also at the beginning and end of any lines within that string. Within a pattern you can enable this flag with (?m).

UNICODE_CASE
: If this flag is set along with the CASE_INSENSITIVE flag, then case-insensitive comparison is done for all Unicode letters, rather than just for ASCII letters. You can enable both flags within a pattern with (?iu)

UNIX_LINES
: If this flag is set, then only the newline character is considered a line terminator for the purposes of ., ^, and $. If the flag is not set, then newlines (\n), carriage returns (\r), and carriage return newline sequences (\r\n) are all considered line terminators, as are the Unicode characters, \u0085 ("next line"), \u2028 ("line separator"), and \u2029 ("paragraph separator"). You can turn this flag on within a pattern with (?d).

Although the API for the Pattern class is quite simple, the syntax for the text representation of regular expressions is fairly complex. A complete tutorial on regular expressions is beyond the scope of this book. Table 17-1 is a quick reference for regular expression syntax. It is very similar to the syntax used in Perl. Note that many of the syntax elements of a regular expression include a backslash character, such as \d to match one of the digits 0–9. Because Java strings also use the backslash character as an escape, you must double the backslashes when expressing a regular expression as a string literal: "\\d". For complete details on regular expressions, see *Programming Perl* or *Mastering Regular Expressions* (both by O'Reilly).

Table 17-1. Java regular expression quick reference

Syntax	*Matches*
Single characters	
x	The character *x*, as long as *x* is not a punctuation character with special meaning in the regular expression syntax.
p	The punctuation character *p*.
\\\\	The backslash character.
\n	The newline character \u000A.
\t	The tab character \u0009.
\r	The carriage return character \u000D.
\f	The form feed character \u000C.
\e	The escape character \u001B.
\a	The bell (alert) character \u0007.
\u*xxxx*	The Unicode character with hexadecimal code *xxxx*.
\x*xx*	The character with hexadecimal code *xx*.
\0*n*	The character with octal code *n*.
\0*nn*	The character with octal code *nn*.
\0*nnn*	Character with octal code *nnn*, in which *nnn* <= 377.
\c*x*	The control character ^*x*.
Character classes	
[...]	One of the characters between the brackets. Characters may be specified literally, and the syntax also allows the specification of character ranges, with intersection, union and subtraction operators. See specific examples that follow.
[^...]	Any one character not between the brackets.
[a-z0-9]	The character range: a character between (inclusive) a and z or 0 and 9.
[0-9[a-fA-F]]	The union of classes: same as [0-9a-fA-F].
[a-z&&[aeiou]]	The intersection of classes: same as [aeiou].

Table 17-1. Java regular expression quick reference (continued)

Syntax	*Matches*
[a-z&&[^aeiou]]	Subtraction: the characters a through z, except for the vowels.
.	Any character, except a line terminator. If the DOTALL flag is set, it matches any character, including line terminators.
\d	An ASCII digit: [0-9].
\D	Anything but an ASCII digit: [^\d].
\s	ASCII whitespace: [\t\n\f\r\x0B].
\S	Anything but ASCII whitespace: [^\s].
\w	An ASCII word character: [a-zA-Z0-9_].
\W	Anything but an ASCII word character: [^\w].
\p{*group*}	Any character in the named group. See the following group names. Many of the group names are from POSIX, which is why p is used for this character class.
\P{*group*}	Any character not in the named group.
\p{Lower}	An ASCII lowercase letter: [a-z].
\p{Upper}	An ASCII uppercase letter: [A-Z].
\p{ASCII}	Any ASCII character: [\x00-\x7f].
\p{Alpha}	An ASCII letter: [a-zA-Z].
\p{Digit}	An ASCII digit: [0-9]
\p{XDigit}	A hexadecimal digit: [0-9a-fA-F].
\p{Alnum}	ASCII letter or digit: [\p{Alpha}\p{Digit}].
\p{Punct}	ASCII punctuation: one of !"#$%&'()*+,-./:;<=>?@[\]^_`{|}~.
\p{Graph}	A visible ASCII character: [\p{Alnum}\p{Punct}].
\p{Print}	A visible ASCII character: same as \p{Graph}.
\p{Blank}	An ASCII space or tab: [\t].
\p{Space}	ASCII whitespace: [\t\n\f\r\x0b].
\p{Cntrl}	An ASCII control character: [\x00-\x1f\x7f].
\p{*category*}	Any character in the named Unicode category. Category names are one- or two-letter codes defined by the Unicode standard. One-letter codes include L for letter, N for number, S for symbol, Z for separator, and P for punctuation. Two-letter codes represent subcategories, such as Lu for uppercase letter, Nd for decimal digit, Sc for currency symbol, Sm for math symbol, and Zs for space separator. See java.lang.Character for a set of constants that correspond to these subcategories, and note that the full set of one- and two-letter codes is not documented in this book.

Table 17-1. Java regular expression quick reference (continued)

Syntax	Matches
\p{*block*}	Any character in the named Unicode block. In Java regular expressions, block names begin with "In", followed by mixed-case capitalization of the Unicode block name, without spaces or underscores. For example: \p{InOgham} or \p{InMathematicalOperators}. See java.lang.Character.UnicodeBlock for a list of Unicode block names.
Sequences, alternatives, groups, and references	
xy	Match *x* followed by *y*.
x|*y*	Match *x* or *y*.
(...)	Grouping. Group subexpression within parentheses into a single unit that can be used with *, +, ?, |, and so on. Also "capture" the characters that match this group for later use.
(?:...)	Grouping only. Group subexpression as with (), but do not capture the text that matched.
n	Match the same characters that were matched when capturing group number *n* was first matched. Be careful when *n* is followed by another digit: the largest number that is a valid group number will be used.
Repetition[a]	
x?	Zero or one occurrence of *x*; i.e., *x* is optional.
*x**	Zero or more occurrences of *x*.
x+	One or more occurrences of *x*.
x{*n*}	Exactly *n* occurrences of *x*.
x{*n*,}	*n* or more occurrences of *x*.
x{*n*,*m*}	At least *n*, and at most *m* occurrences of *x*.
Anchors[b]	
^	The beginning of the input string or, if the MULTILINE flag is specified, the beginning of the string or of any new line.
$	The end of the input string or, if the MULTILINE flag is specified, the end of the string or of line within the string.
\b	A word boundary: a position in the string between a word and a non-word character.
\B	A position in the string that is not a word boundary.
\A	The beginning of the input string. Like ^, but never matches the beginning of a new line, regardless of what flags are set.
\Z	The end of the input string, ignoring any trailing line terminator.

Table 17-1. Java regular expression quick reference (continued)

Syntax	*Matches*
\z	The end of the input string, including any line terminator.
\G	The end of the previous match.
(?=*x*)	A positive look-ahead assertion. Require that the following characters match *x*, but do not include those characters in the match.
(?!*x*)	A negative look-ahead assertion. Require that the following characters do not match the pattern *x*.
(?<=*x*)	A positive look-behind assertion. Require that the characters immediately before the position match *x*, but do not include those characters in the match. *x* must be a pattern with a fixed number of characters.
(?<!*x*)	A negative look-behind assertion. Require that the characters immediately before the position do not match *x*. *x* must be a pattern with a fixed number of characters.
Miscellaneous	
(?>*x*)	Match *x* independently of the rest of the expression, without considering whether the match causes the rest of the expression to fail to match. Useful to optimize certain complex regular expressions. A group of this form does not capture the matched text.
(?*onflags-offflags*)	Don't match anything, but turn on the flags specified by *onflags*, and turn off the flags specified by *offflags*. These two strings are combinations in any order of the following letters and correspond to the following Pattern constants: i (CASE_INSENSITIVE), d (UNIX_LINES), m (MULTILINE), s (DOTALL), u (UNICODE_CASE), and x (COMMENTS). Flag settings specified in this way take effect at the point that they appear in the expression and persist until the end of the expression, or until the end of the parenthesized group of which they are a part, or until overridden by another flag setting expression.
(?*onflags-offflags*:*x*)	Match *x*, applying the specified flags to this subexpression only. This is a noncapturing group, such as (?:...), with the addition of flags.
\Q	Don't match anything, but quote all subsequent pattern text until \E. All characters within such a quoted section are interpreted as literal characters to match, and none (except \E) have special meanings.
\E	Don't match anything; terminate a quote started with \Q.

Table 17-1. Java regular expression quick reference (continued)

Syntax	*Matches*
#comment	If the COMMENT flag is set, pattern text between a # and the end of the line is considered a comment and is ignored.

[a] These repetition characters are known as greedy quantifiers because they match as many occurrences of *x* as possible while still allowing the rest of the regular expression to match. If you want a "reluctant quantifier," which matches as few occurrences as possible while still allowing the rest of the regular expression to match, follow the previous quantifiers with a question mark. For example, use *? instead of *, and {2,}? instead of {2,}. Or, if you follow a quantifier with a plus sign instead of a question mark, then you specify a "possessive quantifier," which matches as many occurrences as possible, even if it means that the rest of the regular expression will not match. Possessive quantifiers can be useful when you are sure that they will not adversely affect the rest of the match, because they can be implemented more efficiently than regular greedy quantifiers.

[b] Anchors do not match characters but instead match the zero-width positions between characters, "anchoring" the match to a position at which a specific condition holds.

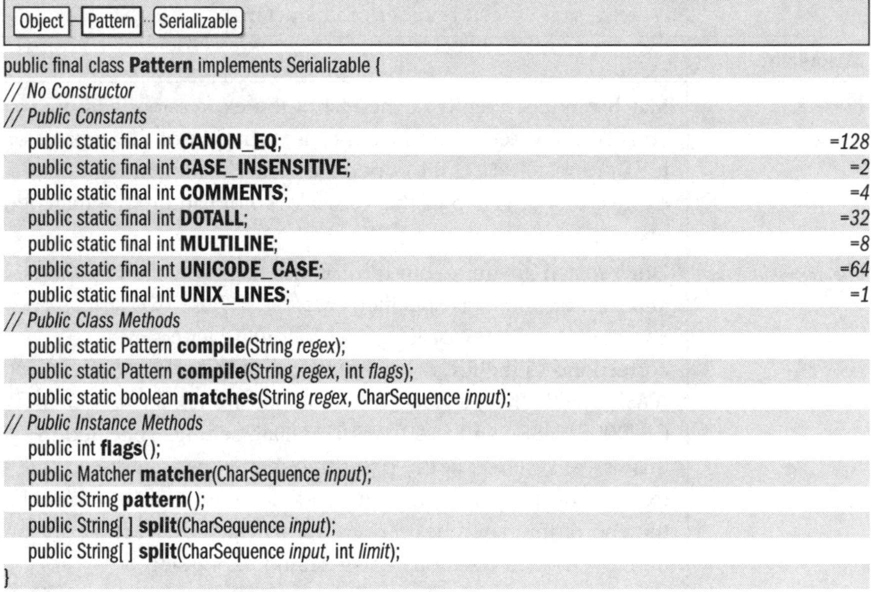

Object — Pattern ··· Serializable

```
public final class Pattern implements Serializable {
// No Constructor
// Public Constants
   public static final int CANON_EQ;                                    =128
   public static final int CASE_INSENSITIVE;                            =2
   public static final int COMMENTS;                                    =4
   public static final int DOTALL;                                      =32
   public static final int MULTILINE;                                   =8
   public static final int UNICODE_CASE;                                =64
   public static final int UNIX_LINES;                                  =1
// Public Class Methods
   public static Pattern compile(String regex);
   public static Pattern compile(String regex, int flags);
   public static boolean matches(String regex, CharSequence input);
// Public Instance Methods
   public int flags();
   public Matcher matcher(CharSequence input);
   public String pattern();
   public String[ ] split(CharSequence input);
   public String[ ] split(CharSequence input, int limit);
}
```

Returned By: Matcher.pattern(), Pattern.compile()

PatternSyntaxException **Java 1.4**

java.util.regex ***serializable unchecked***

This exception signals a syntax error in the text representation of a regular expression. An exception of this type may be thrown by the Pattern.compile() and Pattern.matches() methods, and also by the String matches(), replaceFirst(), replaceAll() and split() methods which call those Pattern methods.

getPattern() returns the text that contained the syntax error, and getIndex() returns the approximate location of the error within that text, or –1, if the location is not known.

getDescription() returns an error message that provides further detail about the error. The inherited getMessage() method combines the information provided by these other three methods into a single multiline message.


```
public class PatternSyntaxException extends IllegalArgumentException {
// Public Constructors
   public PatternSyntaxException(String desc, String regex, int index);
// Public Instance Methods
   public String getDescription();
   public int getIndex();
   public String getPattern();
// Public Methods Overriding Throwable
   public String getMessage();
}
```

Package java.util.zip — Java 1.1

The java.util.zip package contains classes for data compression and decompression. The Deflater and Inflater classes perform data compression and decompression. DeflaterOutputStream and InflaterInputStream apply that functionality to byte streams; the subclasses of these streams implement both the GZIP and ZIP compression formats. The Adler32 and CRC32 classes implement the Checksum interface and compute the checksums required for data compression.

Interfaces:

```
public interface Checksum;
```

Classes:

```
public class Adler32 implements Checksum;
public class CheckedInputStream extends java.io.FilterInputStream;
public class CheckedOutputStream extends java.io.FilterOutputStream;
public class CRC32 implements Checksum;
public class Deflater;
public class DeflaterOutputStream extends java.io.FilterOutputStream;
   └ public class GZIPOutputStream extends DeflaterOutputStream;
   └ public class ZipOutputStream extends DeflaterOutputStream;
public class Inflater;
public class InflaterInputStream extends java.io.FilterInputStream;
   └ public class GZIPInputStream extends InflaterInputStream;
   └ public class ZipInputStream extends InflaterInputStream;
public class ZipEntry implements Cloneable;
public class ZipFile;
```

Exceptions:

```
public class DataFormatException extends Exception;
public class ZipException extends java.io.IOException;
```

Adler32 — Java 1.1

java.util.zip

This class implements the Checksum interface and computes a checksum on a stream of data using the Adler-32 algorithm. This algorithm is significantly faster than the CRC-32 algorithm and is almost as reliable. The CheckedInputStream and CheckedOutputStream classes provide a higher-level interface to computing checksums on streams of data.

Object — Adler32 ··· Checksum

```
public class Adler32 implements Checksum {
// Public Constructors
   public Adler32();
// Public Instance Methods
   public void update(byte[ ] b);
// Methods Implementing Checksum
   public long getValue();                                    default:1
   public void reset();
   public void update(int b);
   public void update(byte[ ] b, int off, int len);
}
```

CheckedInputStream — Java 1.1

java.util.zip

This class is a subclass of java.io.FilterInputStream; it allows a stream to be read and a checksum computed on its contents at the same time. This is useful when you want to check the integrity of a stream of data against a published checksum value. To create a CheckedInputStream, you must specify both the stream it should read and a Checksum object, such as CRC32, that implements the particular checksum algorithm you desire. The read() and skip() methods are the same as those of other input streams. As bytes are read, they are incorporated into the checksum that is being computed. The getChecksum() method does not return the checksum value itself, but rather the Checksum object. You must call the getValue() method of this object to obtain the checksum value.

Object — InputStream — FilterInputStream — CheckedInputStream

```
public class CheckedInputStream extends java.io.FilterInputStream {
// Public Constructors
   public CheckedInputStream(java.io.InputStream in, Checksum cksum);
// Public Instance Methods
   public Checksum getChecksum();
// Public Methods Overriding FilterInputStream
   public int read() throws java.io.IOException;
   public int read(byte[ ] buf, int off, int len) throws java.io.IOException;
   public long skip(long n) throws java.io.IOException;
}
```

CheckedOutputStream — Java 1.1

java.util.zip

This class is a subclass of java.io.FilterOutputStream that allows data to be written to a stream and a checksum computed on that data at the same time. To create a CheckedOutputStream, you must specify both the output stream to write its data to and a Checksum object, such as an instance of Adler32, that implements the particular checksum algorithm you desire. The write() methods are similar to those of other OutputStream classes.

The getChecksum() method returns the Checksum object. You must call getValue() on this object in order to obtain the actual checksum value.

Object — OutputStream — FilterOutputStream — CheckedOutputStream

```
public class CheckedOutputStream extends java.io.FilterOutputStream {
// Public Constructors
   public CheckedOutputStream(java.io.OutputStream out, Checksum cksum);
// Public Instance Methods
   public Checksum getChecksum();
// Public Methods Overriding FilterOutputStream
   public void write(int b) throws java.io.IOException;
   public void write(byte[ ] b, int off, int len) throws java.io.IOException;
}
```

Checksum — Java 1.1

java.util.zip

This interface defines the methods required to compute a checksum on a stream of data. The checksum is computed based on the bytes of data supplied by the update() methods; the current value of the checksum can be obtained at any time with the getValue() method. reset() resets the checksum to its default value; use this method before beginning a new stream of data. The checksum value computed by a Checksum object and returned through the getValue() method must fit into a long value. Therefore, this interface is not suitable for the cryptographic checksum algorithms used in cryptography and security. The classes CheckedInputStream and CheckedOutputStream provide a higher-level API for computing a checksum on a stream of data. See also java.security.MessageDigest.

```
public interface Checksum {
// Public Instance Methods
   public abstract long getValue();
   public abstract void reset();
   public abstract void update(int b);
   public abstract void update(byte[ ] b, int off, int len);
}
```

Implementations: Adler32, CRC32

Passed To: CheckedInputStream.CheckedInputStream(), CheckedOutputStream.CheckedOutputStream()

Returned By: CheckedInputStream.getChecksum(), CheckedOutputStream.getChecksum()

CRC32 — Java 1.1

java.util.zip

This class implements the Checksum interface and computes a checksum on a stream of data using the CRC-32 algorithm. The CheckedInputStream and CheckedOutputStream classes provide a higher-level interface to computing checksums on streams of data.

Object — CRC32 ··· Checksum

```
public class CRC32 implements Checksum {
// Public Constructors
   public CRC32();
// Public Instance Methods
   public void update(byte[ ] b);
```

```
// Methods Implementing Checksum
   public long getValue();                                                   default:0
   public void reset();
   public void update(int b);
   public void update(byte[ ] b, int off, int len);
}
```

Type Of: GZIPInputStream.crc, GZIPOutputStream.crc

DataFormatException — Java 1.1

java.util.zip — *serializable checked*

Signals that invalid or corrupt data has been encountered while uncompressing data.

```
Object ─ Throwable ─ Exception ─ DataFormatException
            ⋮
        Serializable
```

```
public class DataFormatException extends Exception {
// Public Constructors
   public DataFormatException();
   public DataFormatException(String s);
}
```

Thrown By: Inflater.inflate()

Deflater — Java 1.1

java.util.zip

This class implements the general ZLIB data-compression algorithm used by the *gzip* and *PKZip* compression programs. The constants defined by this class are used to specify the compression strategy and the compression speed/strength tradeoff level to be used. If you set the *nowrap* argument to the constructor to true, the ZLIB header and checksum data are omitted from the compressed output, which is the format both *gzip* and *PKZip* use.

The important methods of this class are setInput(), which specifies input data to be compressed, and deflate(), which compresses the data and returns the compressed output. The remaining methods exist so that Deflater can be used for stream-based compression, as it is in higher-level classes, such as GZIPOutputStream and ZipOutputStream. These stream classes are sufficient in most cases. Most applications do not need to use Deflater directly. The Inflater class uncompresses data compressed with a Deflater object.

```
public class Deflater {
// Public Constructors
   public Deflater();
   public Deflater(int level);
   public Deflater(int level, boolean nowrap);
// Public Constants
   public static final int BEST_COMPRESSION;                                 =9
   public static final int BEST_SPEED;                                       =1
   public static final int DEFAULT_COMPRESSION;                              =-1
   public static final int DEFAULT_STRATEGY;                                 =0
   public static final int DEFLATED;                                         =8
   public static final int FILTERED;                                         =1
   public static final int HUFFMAN_ONLY;                                     =2
   public static final int NO_COMPRESSION;                                   =0
```

```
// Property Accessor Methods (by property name)
   public int getAdler();                                             synchronized default:1
   public int getTotalIn();                                           synchronized default:0
   public int getTotalOut();                                          synchronized default:0
// Public Instance Methods
   public int deflate(byte[ ] b);
   public int deflate(byte[ ] b, int off, int len);                   synchronized
   public void end();                                                 synchronized
   public void finish();                                              synchronized
   public boolean finished();                                         synchronized
   public boolean needsInput();
   public void reset();                                               synchronized
   public void setDictionary(byte[ ] b);
   public void setDictionary(byte[ ] b, int off, int len);            synchronized
   public void setInput(byte[ ] b);
   public void setInput(byte[ ] b, int off, int len);                 synchronized
   public void setLevel(int level);                                   synchronized
   public void setStrategy(int strategy);                             synchronized
// Protected Methods Overriding Object
   protected void finalize();
}
```

Passed To: DeflaterOutputStream.DeflaterOutputStream()

Type Of: DeflaterOutputStream.def

DeflaterOutputStream — Java 1.1

java.util.zip

This class is a subclass of java.io.FilterOutputStream; it filters a stream of data by compressing (deflating) it and then writing the compressed data to another output stream. To create a DeflaterOutputStream, you must specify both the stream it is to write to and a Deflater object to perform the compression. You can set various options on the Deflater object to specify just what type of compression is to be performed. Once a DeflaterOutputStream is created, its write() and close() methods are the same as those of other output streams. The InflaterInputStream class can read data written with a DeflaterOutputStream. A DeflaterOutputStream writes raw compressed data; applications often prefer one of its subclasses, GZIPOutputStream or ZipOutputStream, that wraps the raw compressed data within a standard file format.

Object — OutputStream — FilterOutputStream — DeflaterOutputStream

```
public class DeflaterOutputStream extends java.io.FilterOutputStream {
// Public Constructors
   public DeflaterOutputStream(java.io.OutputStream out);
   public DeflaterOutputStream(java.io.OutputStream out, Deflater def);
   public DeflaterOutputStream(java.io.OutputStream out, Deflater def, int size);
// Public Instance Methods
   public void finish() throws java.io.IOException;
// Public Methods Overriding FilterOutputStream
   public void close() throws java.io.IOException;
   public void write(int b) throws java.io.IOException;
   public void write(byte[ ] b, int off, int len) throws java.io.IOException;
// Protected Instance Methods
   protected void deflate() throws java.io.IOException;
// Protected Instance Fields
```

```
    protected byte[ ] buf;
    protected Deflater def;
}
```

Subclasses: GZIPOutputStream, ZipOutputStream

GZIPInputStream — Java 1.1

java.util.zip

This class is a subclass of InflaterInputStream that reads and uncompresses data compressed in *gzip* format. To create a GZIPInputStream, simply specify the InputStream to read compressed data from and, optionally, a buffer size for the internal decompression buffer. Once a GZIPInputStream is created, you can use the read() and close() methods as you would with any input stream.

Object ─ InputStream ─ FilterInputStream ─ InflaterInputStream ─ GZIPInputStream

```
public class GZIPInputStream extends InflaterInputStream {
// Public Constructors
    public GZIPInputStream(java.io.InputStream in) throws java.io.IOException;
    public GZIPInputStream(java.io.InputStream in, int size) throws java.io.IOException;
// Public Constants
    public static final int GZIP_MAGIC;                                    =35615
// Public Methods Overriding InflaterInputStream
    public void close() throws java.io.IOException;
    public int read(byte[ ] buf, int off, int len) throws java.io.IOException;
// Protected Instance Fields
    protected CRC32 crc;
    protected boolean eos;
}
```

GZIPOutputStream — Java 1.1

java.util.zip

This class is a subclass of DeflaterOutputStream that compresses and writes data using the *gzip* file format. To create a GZIPOutputStream, specify the OutputStream to write to and, optionally, a size for the internal compression buffer. Once the GZIPOutputStream is created, you can use the write() and close() methods as you would any output stream.

Object ─ OutputStream ─ FilterOutputStream ─ DeflaterOutputStream ─ GZIPOutputStream

```
public class GZIPOutputStream extends DeflaterOutputStream {
// Public Constructors
    public GZIPOutputStream(java.io.OutputStream out) throws java.io.IOException;
    public GZIPOutputStream(java.io.OutputStream out, int size) throws java.io.IOException;
// Public Methods Overriding DeflaterOutputStream
    public void finish() throws java.io.IOException;
    public void write(byte[ ] buf, int off, int len) throws java.io.IOException;      synchronized
// Protected Instance Fields
    protected CRC32 crc;
}
```

Inflater **Java 1.1**

java.util.zip

This class implements the general ZLIB data-decompression algorithm used by *gzip*, *PKZip*, and other data-compression applications. It decompresses or inflates data compressed through the Deflater class. The important methods of this class are setInput(), which specifies input data to be decompressed, and inflate(), which decompresses the input data into an output buffer. A number of other methods exist so that this class can be used for stream-based decompression, as it is in the higher-level classes, such as GZIPInputStream and ZipInputStream. These stream-based classes are sufficient in most cases. Most applications do not need to use Inflater directly.

```
public class Inflater {
// Public Constructors
   public Inflater();
   public Inflater(boolean nowrap);
// Property Accessor Methods (by property name)
   public int getAdler();                                           synchronized default:1
   public int getRemaining();                                       synchronized default:0
   public int getTotalIn();                                         synchronized default:0
   public int getTotalOut();                                        synchronized default:0
// Public Instance Methods
   public void end();                                               synchronized
   public boolean finished();                                       synchronized
   public int inflate(byte[ ] b) throws DataFormatException;
   public int inflate(byte[ ] b, int off, int len) throws DataFormatException;   synchronized
   public boolean needsDictionary();                                synchronized
   public boolean needsInput();                                     synchronized
   public void reset();                                             synchronized
   public void setDictionary(byte[ ] b);
   public void setDictionary(byte[ ] b, int off, int len);          synchronized
   public void setInput(byte[ ] b);
   public void setInput(byte[ ] b, int off, int len);               synchronized
// Protected Methods Overriding Object
   protected void finalize();
}
```

Passed To: InflaterInputStream.InflaterInputStream()

Type Of: InflaterInputStream.inf

InflaterInputStream **Java 1.1**

java.util.zip

This class is a subclass of java.io.FilterInputStream; it reads a specified stream of compressed input data (typically, one that was written with DeflaterOutputStream or a subclass) and filters that data by uncompressing (inflating) it. To create an InflaterInputStream, specify both the input stream to read from and an Inflater object to perform the decompression. Once an InflaterInputStream is created, the read() and skip() methods are the same as those of other input streams. The InflaterInputStream uncompresses raw data. Applications often prefer one of its subclasses, GZIPInputStream or ZipInputStream, that work with compressed data written in the standard *gzip* and *PKZip* file formats.

Object — InputStream — FilterInputStream — InflaterInputStream

```
public class InflaterInputStream extends java.io.FilterInputStream {
// Public Constructors
   public InflaterInputStream(java.io.InputStream in);
   public InflaterInputStream(java.io.InputStream in, Inflater inf);
   public InflaterInputStream(java.io.InputStream in, Inflater inf, int size);
// Public Methods Overriding FilterInputStream
1.2 public int available() throws java.io.IOException;
1.2 public void close() throws java.io.IOException;
   public int read() throws java.io.IOException;
   public int read(byte[ ] b, int off, int len) throws java.io.IOException;
   public long skip(long n) throws java.io.IOException;
// Protected Instance Methods
   protected void fill() throws java.io.IOException;
// Protected Instance Fields
   protected byte[ ] buf;
   protected Inflater inf;
   protected int len;
}
```

Subclasses: GZIPInputStream, ZipInputStream

ZipEntry — Java 1.1

java.util.zip — ***cloneable***

This class describes a single entry (typically a compressed file) stored within a ZIP file. The various methods get and set various pieces of information about the entry. The ZipEntry class is used by ZipFile and ZipInputStream, which read ZIP files, and by ZipOutputStream, which writes ZIP files.

When you are reading a ZIP file, a ZipEntry object returned by ZipFile or ZipInputStream contains the name, size, modification time, and other information about an entry in the file. When writing a ZIP file, on the other hand, you must create your own ZipEntry objects and initialize them to contain the entry name and other appropriate information before writing the contents of the entry.

Object — ZipEntry
Cloneable, ZipConstants

```
public class ZipEntry implements Cloneable {
// Public Constructors
   public ZipEntry(String name);
1.2 public ZipEntry(ZipEntry e);
// Public Constants
   public static final int DEFLATED;                                  =8
   public static final int STORED;                                    =0
// Property Accessor Methods (by property name)
   public String getComment();
   public void setComment(String comment);
   public long getCompressedSize();
1.2 public void setCompressedSize(long csize);
   public long getCrc();
   public void setCrc(long crc);
   public boolean isDirectory();
   public byte[ ] getExtra();
   public void setExtra(byte[ ] extra);
```

```
    public int getMethod();
    public void setMethod(int method);
    public String getName();
    public long getSize();
    public void setSize(long size);
    public long getTime();
    public void setTime(long time);
// Public Methods Overriding Object
1.2 public Object clone();
1.2 public int hashCode();
    public String toString();
}
```

Subclasses: java.util.jar.JarEntry

Passed To: java.util.jar.JarEntry.JarEntry(), java.util.jar.JarFile.getInputStream(), java.util.jar.JarOutputStream.putNextEntry(), ZipEntry.ZipEntry(), ZipFile.getInputStream(), ZipOutputStream.putNextEntry()

Returned By: java.util.jar.JarFile.getEntry(), java.util.jar.JarInputStream.{createZipEntry(), getNextEntry()}, ZipFile.getEntry(), ZipInputStream.{createZipEntry(), getNextEntry()}

ZipException — Java 1.1

java.util.zip — *serializable checked*

Signals that an error has occurred in reading or writing a ZIP file.

Object ─ Throwable ─ Exception ─ IOException ─ ZipException
Throwable ⋮ Serializable

```
public class ZipException extends java.io.IOException {
// Public Constructors
    public ZipException();
    public ZipException(String s);
}
```

Subclasses: java.util.jar.JarException

Thrown By: ZipFile.ZipFile()

ZipFile — Java 1.1

java.util.zip

This class reads the contents of ZIP files. It uses a random-access file internally so that the entries of the ZIP file do not have to be read sequentially, as they do with the ZipInputStream class. A ZipFile object can be created by specifying the ZIP file to be read either as a String filename or as a File object. In Java 1.3, temporary ZIP files can be marked for automatic deletion when they are closed. To take advantage of this feature, pass ZipFile.OPEN_READ|ZipFile.OPEN_DELETE as the *mode* argument to the ZipFile() constructor.

Once a ZipFile is created, the getEntry() method returns a ZipEntry object for a named entry, and the entries() method returns an Enumeration object that allows you to loop through all the ZipEntry objects for the file. To read the contents of a specific ZipEntry within the ZIP file, pass the ZipEntry to getInputStream(); this returns an InputStream object from which you can read the entry's contents.

Object — ZipFile ··· ZipConstants

```
public class ZipFile {
// Public Constructors
    public ZipFile(String name) throws java.io.IOException;
    public ZipFile(java.io.File file) throws ZipException, java.io.IOException;
1.3 public ZipFile(java.io.File file, int mode) throws java.io.IOException;
// Public Constants
1.3 public static final int OPEN_DELETE;                                          =4
1.3 public static final int OPEN_READ;                                            =1
// Public Instance Methods
    public void close() throws java.io.IOException;
    public java.util.Enumeration entries();
    public ZipEntry getEntry(String name);
    public java.io.InputStream getInputStream(ZipEntry entry) throws java.io.IOException;
    public String getName();
1.2 public int size();
// Protected Methods Overriding Object
1.3 protected void finalize() throws java.io.IOException;
}
```

Subclasses: java.util.jar.JarFile

ZipInputStream — Java 1.1

java.util.zip

This class is a subclass of InflaterInputStream that reads the entries of a ZIP file in sequential order. Create a ZipInputStream by specifying the InputStream from which it is to read the contents of the ZIP file. Once the ZipInputStream is created, you can use getNextEntry() to begin reading data from the next entry in the ZIP file. This method must be called before read() is called to begin reading the first entry. getNextEntry() returns a ZipEntry object that describes the entry being read, or null when there are no more entries to be read from the ZIP file.

The read() methods of ZipInputStream read until the end of the current entry and then return –1, indicating that there is no more data to read. To continue with the next entry in the ZIP file, you must call getNextEntry() again. Similarly, the skip() method only skips bytes within the current entry. closeEntry() can be called to skip the remaining data in the current entry, but it is usually easier simply to call getNextEntry() to begin the next entry.

Object — InputStream — FilterInputStream — InflaterInputStream — ZipInputStream ··· ZipConstants

```
public class ZipInputStream extends InflaterInputStream {
// Public Constructors
    public ZipInputStream(java.io.InputStream in);
// Public Instance Methods
    public void closeEntry() throws java.io.IOException;
    public ZipEntry getNextEntry() throws java.io.IOException;
// Public Methods Overriding InflaterInputStream
1.2 public int available() throws java.io.IOException;
    public void close() throws java.io.IOException;
```

```
   public int read(byte[ ] b, int off, int len) throws java.io.IOException;
   public long skip(long n) throws java.io.IOException;
// Protected Instance Methods
1.2 protected ZipEntry createZipEntry(String name);
}
```

Subclasses: java.util.jar.JarInputStream

ZipOutputStream — Java 1.1

java.util.zip

This class is a subclass of DeflaterOutputStream that writes data in ZIP file format to an output stream. Before writing any data to the ZipOutputStream, you must begin an entry within the ZIP file with putNextEntry(). The ZipEntry object passed to this method should specify at least a name for the entry. Once you have begun an entry with putNextEntry(), you can write the contents of that entry with the write() methods. When you reach the end of an entry, you can begin a new one by calling putNextEntry() again, you can close the current entry with closeEntry(), or you can close the stream itself with close().

Before beginning an entry with putNextEntry(), you can set the compression method and level with setMethod() and setLevel(). The constants DEFLATED and STORED are the two legal values for setMethod(). If you use STORED, the entry is stored in the ZIP file without any compression. If you use DEFLATED, you can also specify the compression speed/strength tradeoff by passing a number from 1 to 9 to setLevel(), in which 9 gives the strongest and slowest level of compression. You can also use the constants Deflater.BEST_SPEED, Deflater.BEST_COMPRESSION, and Deflater.DEFAULT_COMPRESSION with the setLevel() method.

If you are storing an entry without compression, the ZIP file format requires that you specify, in advance, the entry size and CRC-32 checksum in the ZipEntry object for the entry. An exception is thrown if these values are not specified or specified incorrectly.

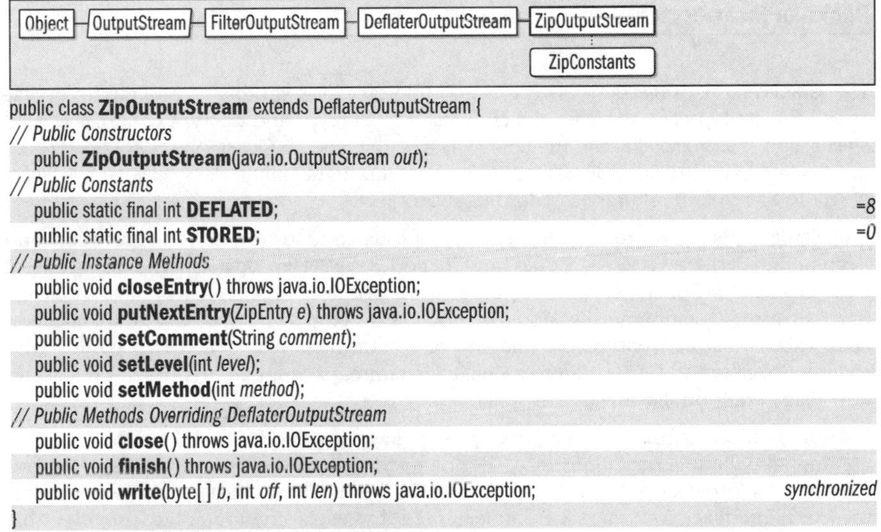


```
public class ZipOutputStream extends DeflaterOutputStream {
// Public Constructors
   public ZipOutputStream(java.io.OutputStream out);
// Public Constants
   public static final int DEFLATED;                                      =8
   public static final int STORED;                                        =0
// Public Instance Methods
   public void closeEntry() throws java.io.IOException;
   public void putNextEntry(ZipEntry e) throws java.io.IOException;
   public void setComment(String comment);
   public void setLevel(int level);
   public void setMethod(int method);
// Public Methods Overriding DeflaterOutputStream
   public void close() throws java.io.IOException;
   public void finish() throws java.io.IOException;
   public void write(byte[ ] b, int off, int len) throws java.io.IOException;   synchronized
}
```

Subclasses: java.util.jar.JarOutputStream

CHAPTER 18

javax.crypto and Subpackages

This chapter documents the cryptographic features (including encryption and decryption) of the javax.crypto package and its subpackages. These packages were originally part of the Java Cryptography Extension (JCE) before being integrated into Java 1.4, which is why they have the "javax" extension prefix. All of the commonly used cryptography classes are in the javax.crypto package itself. The javax.crypto.interfaces subpackage defines algorithm-specific interfaces for certain type of cryptographic keys. The javax.crypto.spec subpackage defines classes that provide a transparent, portable, and provider-independent representation of cryptographic keys and related objects.

Package javax.crypto — Java 1.4

The javax.crypto package defines classes and interfaces for various cryptographic operations. The central class is Cipher, which is used to encrypt and decrypt data. CipherInputStream and CipherOutputStream are utility classes that use a Cipher object to encrypt or decrypt streaming data. SealedObject is another important utility class that uses a Cipher object to encrypt an arbitrary serializable Java object.

The KeyGenerator class creates the SecretKey objects used by Cipher for encryption and decryption. SecretKeyFactory encodes and decodes SecretKey objects. The KeyAgreement class enables two or more parties to agree on a SecretKey in such a way that an eavesdropper cannot determine the key. The Mac class computes a message authentication code (MAC) that can ensure the integrity of a transmission between two parties who share a SecretKey. A MAC is akin to a digital signature, except that it is based on a secret key instead of a public/private key pair.

Like the java.security package, the javax.crypto package is provider-based, so that arbitrary cryptographic implementations may be plugged into any Java installation. Various classes in this package have names that end in Spi. These classes define a service-provider interface and must be implemented by each cryptographic provider that wishes to provide an implementation of a particular cryptographic service or algorithm.

This package was originally shipped as part of the Java Cryptography Extension (JCE), but it has been added to the core platform in Java 1.4. A version of the JCE is still available (see *http://java.sun.com/security/*) as a standard extension for Java 1.2 and Java 1.3. This package is distributed with a cryptographic provider named "SunJCE" that includes a robust set of implementations for Cipher, KeyAgreement, Mac, and other classes. This provider is installed by the default java.security properties in Java 1.4 distributions.

A full tutorial on cryptography is beyond the scope of this chapter and of this book. In order to use this package, you need to have a basic understanding of cryptographic algorithms such as DES. In order to take full advantage of this package, you also need to have a detailed understanding of things like feedback modes, padding schemes, the Diffie-Hellman key-agreement protocol, and so on. For a good introduction to modern cryptography in Java, see *Java Cryptography* (O'Reilly). For more in-depth coverage, not specific to Java, see *Applied Cryptography* (Wiley).

Interface:

public interface **SecretKey** extends java.security.Key;

Classes:

public class **Cipher**;
  └ public class **NullCipher** extends Cipher;
public class **CipherInputStream** extends java.io.FilterInputStream;
public class **CipherOutputStream** extends java.io.FilterOutputStream;
public abstract class **CipherSpi**;
public class **EncryptedPrivateKeyInfo**;
public class **ExemptionMechanism**;
public abstract class **ExemptionMechanismSpi**;
public class **KeyAgreement**;
public abstract class **KeyAgreementSpi**;
public class **KeyGenerator**;
public abstract class **KeyGeneratorSpi**;
public class **Mac** implements Cloneable;
public abstract class **MacSpi**;
public class **SealedObject** implements Serializable;
public class **SecretKeyFactory**;
public abstract class **SecretKeyFactorySpi**;

Exceptions:

public class **BadPaddingException** extends java.security.GeneralSecurityException;
public class **ExemptionMechanismException** extends java.security.GeneralSecurityException;
public class **IllegalBlockSizeException** extends java.security.GeneralSecurityException;
public class **NoSuchPaddingException** extends java.security.GeneralSecurityException;
public class **ShortBufferException** extends java.security.GeneralSecurityException;

BadPaddingException — Java 1.4

javax.crypto — *serializable checked*

This exception signals that input data to a Cipher is not padded correctly.

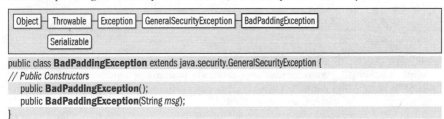

Object ─ Throwable ─ Exception ─ GeneralSecurityException ─ BadPaddingException
Serializable

```
public class BadPaddingException extends java.security.GeneralSecurityException {
// Public Constructors
   public BadPaddingException();
   public BadPaddingException(String msg);
}
```

Thrown By: Cipher.doFinal(), CipherSpi.engineDoFinal(), SealedObject.getObject()

Cipher **Java 1.4**

javax.crypto

This class performs encryption and decryption of byte arrays. Cipher is provider-based, so to obtain a Cipher object, you must call the static getInstance() factory method. The arguments to this method are a string that describes the type of encryption desired and, optionally, the name of the provider whose implementation should be used. To specify the desired type of encryption, you can simply specify the name of an encryption algorithm, such as "DES". Or you can specify a three-part name that includes the encryption algorithm, the algorithm operating mode, and the padding scheme. These three parts are separated by slash characters, as in "DES/CBC/PKCS5Padding". Finally, if you are requesting a block cipher algorithm in a stream mode, you can specify the number of bits to be processed at a time by following the name of the feedback mode with a number of bits. For example: "DES/CFB8/NoPadding".

The "SunJCE" provider supports the following cryptographic algorithms:

"DES"
: The Digital Encryption Standard.

"DESede"
: Triple DES encryption, also known as "TripleDES".

"Blowfish"
: The Blowfish block cipher designed by Bruce Schneier.

"PBEWithMD5AndDES"
: A password-based encryption scheme specified in PKCS#5. This algorithm implicitly uses "CBC" mode and the "PKCS5Padding" padding; it cannot be used with other modes or padding schemes.

"PBEWithMD5AndTripleDES"
: A password-based encryption similar to "PBEWithMD5AndDES", but uses DESede instead of DES.

SunJCE supports the following operating modes:

"ECB"
: Electronic Codebook mode

"CBC"
: Cipher Block Chaining mode

"CFB"
: Cipher Feedback mode

"OFB"
: Output Feedback mode

"PCBC"
: Plaintext Cipher Block Chaining mode

Finally, the "SunJCE" provider also supports two padding schemes: "NoPadding" and "PKCS5Padding". The name "SSL3Padding" is reserved, but this padding scheme is not implemented in the current release of "SunJCE".

Once you have obtained a Cipher object for the desired cryptographic algorithm, mode, and padding scheme, you must initialize it by calling one of the init() methods. The first argument to init() is one of the constants ENCRYPT_MODE or DECRYPT_MODE. The second argument is a java.security.Key object that performs the encryption or decryption. If you use one of the symmetric (i.e., non-public key) encryption algorithms supported by the "SunJCE" provider, this Key object is a SecretKey implementation. You can optionally pass a java.security.SecureRandom object to init() to provide a source of randomness. If you do not, the Cipher implementation provides its own pseudo-random number generator.

Some cryptographic algorithms require additional initialization parameters; these can be passed to init() as a java.security.AlgorithmParameters object or as a java.security.spec.AlgorithmParameterSpec object. When encrypting, you can omit these parameters, and the Cipher implementation uses default values or generates appropriate random parameters for you. In this case, you should call getParameters() after performing encryption to obtain the AlgorithmParameters used to encrypt. These parameters are required in order to decrypt, and must therefore be saved or transferred along with the encrypted data. Of the algorithms supported by the "SunJCE" provider, the block ciphers "DES", "DESede", and "Blowfish" all require an initialization vector when they are used in "CBC", "CFB", "OFB", or "PCBC" mode. You can represent an initialization vector with a javax.crypto.spec.IvParameterSpec object and obtain the raw bytes of the initialization vector used by a Cipher with the getIV() method. The "PBEWithMD5AndDES" algorithm requires a salt and iteration count as parameters. These can be specified with a javax.crypto.spec.PBEParameterSpec object.

Once you have obtained and initialized a Cipher object, you are ready to use it for encryption or decryption. If you have only a single array of bytes to encrypt or decrypt, pass that input array to one of the doFinal() methods. Some versions of this method return the encrypted or decrypted bytes as the return value of the function. Other versions store the encrypted or decrypted bytes to another byte array you specify. If you choose to use one of these latter methods, you should first call getOutputSize() to determine the required size of the output array. If you want to encrypt or decrypt data from a streaming source or have more than one array of data, pass the data to one of the update() methods, calling it as many times as necessary. Then pass the last array of data to one of the doFinal() methods. If you are working with streaming data, consider using the CipherInputStream and CipherOutputStream classes instead.

```
public class Cipher {
// Protected Constructors
   protected Cipher(CipherSpi cipherSpi, java.security.Provider provider, String transformation);
// Public Constants
   public static final int DECRYPT_MODE;                                                    =2
   public static final int ENCRYPT_MODE;                                                    =1
   public static final int PRIVATE_KEY;                                                     =2
   public static final int PUBLIC_KEY;                                                      =1
   public static final int SECRET_KEY;                                                      =3
   public static final int UNWRAP_MODE;                                                     =4
   public static final int WRAP_MODE;                                                       =3
// Public Class Methods
   public static final Cipher getInstance(String transformation) throws java.security.NoSuchAlgorithmException,
        NoSuchPaddingException;
   public static final Cipher getInstance(String transformation, String provider)
        throws java.security.NoSuchAlgorithmException, java.security.NoSuchProviderException,
        NoSuchPaddingException;
   public static final Cipher getInstance(String transformation, java.security.Provider provider)
        throws java.security.NoSuchAlgorithmException, NoSuchPaddingException;
// Property Accessor Methods (by property name)
   public final String getAlgorithm();
   public final int getBlockSize();
```

```
    public final ExemptionMechanism getExemptionMechanism();
    public final byte[] getIV();
    public final java.security.AlgorithmParameters getParameters();
    public final java.security.Provider getProvider();
// Public Instance Methods
    public final byte[] doFinal() throws IllegalStateException, IllegalBlockSizeException, BadPaddingException;
    public final byte[] doFinal(byte[] input) throws IllegalStateException, IllegalBlockSizeException,
        BadPaddingException;
    public final int doFinal(byte[] output, int outputOffset) throws IllegalStateException, IllegalBlockSizeException,
        ShortBufferException, BadPaddingException;
    public final byte[] doFinal(byte[] input, int inputOffset, int inputLen) throws IllegalStateException,
        IllegalBlockSizeException, BadPaddingException;
    public final int doFinal(byte[] input, int inputOffset, int inputLen, byte[] output) throws IllegalStateException,
        ShortBufferException, IllegalBlockSizeException, BadPaddingException;
    public final int doFinal(byte[] input, int inputOffset, int inputLen, byte[] output, int outputOffset)
        throws IllegalStateException, ShortBufferException, IllegalBlockSizeException, BadPaddingException;
    public final int getOutputSize(int inputLen) throws IllegalStateException;
    public final void init(int opmode, java.security.cert.Certificate certificate) throws java.security.InvalidKeyException;
    public final void init(int opmode, java.security.Key key) throws java.security.InvalidKeyException;
    public final void init(int opmode, java.security.cert.Certificate certificate, java.security.SecureRandom random)
        throws java.security.InvalidKeyException;
    public final void init(int opmode, java.security.Key key, java.security.AlgorithmParameters params)
        throws java.security.InvalidKeyException, java.security.InvalidAlgorithmParameterException;
    public final void init(int opmode, java.security.Key key, java.security.SecureRandom random)
        throws java.security.InvalidKeyException;
    public final void init(int opmode, java.security.Key key, java.security.spec.AlgorithmParameterSpec params)
        throws java.security.InvalidKeyException, java.security.InvalidAlgorithmParameterException;
    public final void init(int opmode, java.security.Key key, java.security.spec.AlgorithmParameterSpec params,
                           java.security.SecureRandom random) throws java.security.InvalidKeyException,
        java.security.InvalidAlgorithmParameterException;
    public final void init(int opmode, java.security.Key key, java.security.AlgorithmParameters params,
                           java.security.SecureRandom random) throws java.security.InvalidKeyException,
        java.security.InvalidAlgorithmParameterException;
    public final java.security.Key unwrap(byte[] wrappedKey, String wrappedKeyAlgorithm, int wrappedKeyType)
        throws IllegalStateException, java.security.InvalidKeyException, java.security.NoSuchAlgorithmException;
    public final byte[] update(byte[] input) throws IllegalStateException;
    public final byte[] update(byte[] input, int inputOffset, int inputLen) throws IllegalStateException;
    public final int update(byte[] input, int inputOffset, int inputLen, byte[] output) throws IllegalStateException,
        ShortBufferException;
    public final int update(byte[] input, int inputOffset, int inputLen, byte[] output, int outputOffset)
        throws IllegalStateException, ShortBufferException;
    public final byte[] wrap(java.security.Key key) throws IllegalStateException, IllegalBlockSizeException,
        java.security.InvalidKeyException;
}
```

Subclasses: NullCipher

Passed To: CipherInputStream.CipherInputStream(), CipherOutputStream.CipherOutputStream(), EncryptedPrivateKeyInfo.getKeySpec(), SealedObject.{getObject(), SealedObject()}

Returned By: Cipher.getInstance()

CipherInputStream — Java 1.4

javax.crypto

This class is an input stream that uses a Cipher object to encrypt or decrypt the bytes it reads from another stream. You must initialize the Cipher object before passing it to the CipherInputStream() constructor.

Object → InputStream → FilterInputStream → CipherInputStream

```
public class CipherInputStream extends java.io.FilterInputStream {
// Public Constructors
   public CipherInputStream(java.io.InputStream is, Cipher c);
// Protected Constructors
   protected CipherInputStream(java.io.InputStream is);
// Public Methods Overriding FilterInputStream
   public int available() throws java.io.IOException;
   public void close() throws java.io.IOException;
   public boolean markSupported();                                  constant
   public int read() throws java.io.IOException;
   public int read(byte[ ] b) throws java.io.IOException;
   public int read(byte[ ] b, int off, int len) throws java.io.IOException;
   public long skip(long n) throws java.io.IOException;
}
```

CipherOutputStream — Java 1.4

javax.crypto

This class is an output stream that uses a Cipher object to encrypt or decrypt bytes before passing them to another output stream. You must initialize the Cipher object before passing it to the CipherOutputStream() constructor. If you are using a Cipher with any kind of padding, you must not call flush() until you are done writing all data to the stream; otherwise decryption fails.

Object → OutputStream → FilterOutputStream → CipherOutputStream

```
public class CipherOutputStream extends java.io.FilterOutputStream {
// Public Constructors
   public CipherOutputStream(java.io.OutputStream os, Cipher c);
// Protected Constructors
   protected CipherOutputStream(java.io.OutputStream os);
// Public Methods Overriding FilterOutputStream
   public void close() throws java.io.IOException;
   public void flush() throws java.io.IOException;
   public void write(int b) throws java.io.IOException;
   public void write(byte[ ] b) throws java.io.IOException;
   public void write(byte[ ] b, int off, int len) throws java.io.IOException;
}
```

CipherSpi — Java 1.4

javax.crypto

This abstract class defines the service-provider interface for Cipher. A cryptographic provider must implement a concrete subclass of this class for each encryption algorithm it supports. A provider can implement a separate class for each combination of algorithm, mode, and padding scheme it supports or implement more general classes and leave the mode and/or padding scheme to be specified in calls to engineSetMode() and engineSetPadding(). Applications never need to use or subclass this class.

```
public abstract class CipherSpi {
// Public Constructors
   public CipherSpi();
// Protected Instance Methods
   protected abstract byte[ ] engineDoFinal(byte[ ] input, int inputOffset, int inputLen)
      throws IllegalBlockSizeException, BadPaddingException;
   protected abstract int engineDoFinal(byte[ ] input, int inputOffset, int inputLen, byte[ ] output, int outputOffset)
      throws ShortBufferException, IllegalBlockSizeException, BadPaddingException;
   protected abstract int engineGetBlockSize();
   protected abstract byte[ ] engineGetIV();
   protected int engineGetKeySize(java.security.Key key) throws java.security.InvalidKeyException;
   protected abstract int engineGetOutputSize(int inputLen);
   protected abstract java.security.AlgorithmParameters engineGetParameters();
   protected abstract void engineInit(int opmode, java.security.Key key, java.security.SecureRandom random)
      throws java.security.InvalidKeyException;
   protected abstract void engineInit(int opmode, java.security.Key key, java.security.AlgorithmParameters params,
                                   java.security.SecureRandom random) throws java.security.InvalidKeyException,
      java.security.InvalidAlgorithmParameterException;
   protected abstract void engineInit(int opmode, java.security.Key key,
                                   java.security.spec.AlgorithmParameterSpec params,
                                   java.security.SecureRandom random) throws java.security.InvalidKeyException,
      java.security.InvalidAlgorithmParameterException;
   protected abstract void engineSetMode(String mode) throws java.security.NoSuchAlgorithmException;
   protected abstract void engineSetPadding(String padding) throws NoSuchPaddingException;
   protected java.security.Key engineUnwrap(byte[ ] wrappedKey, String wrappedKeyAlgorithm, int wrappedKeyType)
      throws java.security.InvalidKeyException, java.security.NoSuchAlgorithmException;
   protected abstract byte[ ] engineUpdate(byte[ ] input, int inputOffset, int inputLen);
   protected abstract int engineUpdate(byte[ ] input, int inputOffset, int inputLen, byte[ ] output, int outputOffset)
      throws ShortBufferException;
   protected byte[ ] engineWrap(java.security.Key key) throws IllegalBlockSizeException,
      java.security.InvalidKeyException;
}
```

Passed To: Cipher.Cipher()

EncryptedPrivateKeyInfo **Java 1.4**

javax.crypto

This class represents an encrypted private key. getEncryptedData() returns the encrypted bytes. getAlgName() and getAlgParameters() return the algorithm name and parameters used to encrypt it. Pass a Cipher object to getKeySpec() to decrypt the key.

```
public class EncryptedPrivateKeyInfo {
// Public Constructors
   public EncryptedPrivateKeyInfo(byte[ ] encoded) throws java.io.IOException;
   public EncryptedPrivateKeyInfo(java.security.AlgorithmParameters algParams, byte[ ] encryptedData)
      throws java.security.NoSuchAlgorithmException;
   public EncryptedPrivateKeyInfo(String algName, byte[ ] encryptedData)
      throws java.security.NoSuchAlgorithmException;
// Public Instance Methods
   public String getAlgName();
   public java.security.AlgorithmParameters getAlgParameters();
```

```
    public byte[] getEncoded() throws java.io.IOException;
    public byte[] getEncryptedData();
    public java.security.spec.PKCS8EncodedKeySpec getKeySpec(Cipher c)
        throws java.security.spec.InvalidKeySpecException;
}
```

ExemptionMechanism — Java 1.4

javax.crypto

Some countries place legal restrictions on the use of cryptographic algorithms. In some cases, a program may be exempt from these restrictions if it implements an "exemption mechanism" such as key recovery, key escrow, or key weakening. This class defines a general API to such mechanism. This class is rarely used and is not supported in the default implementation provided by Sun. Using this class successfully is quite complex and is beyond the scope of this reference. For details, see the discussion "How to Make Applicaions 'Exempt' from Cryptographic Restrictions" in the *JCE Reference Guide*, which is part of the standard bundle of documentation shipped by Sun with the JDK.

```
public class ExemptionMechanism {
// Protected Constructors
    protected ExemptionMechanism(ExemptionMechanismSpi exmechSpi, java.security.Provider provider,
                                 String mechanism);
// Public Class Methods
    public static final ExemptionMechanism getInstance(String mechanism)
        throws java.security.NoSuchAlgorithmException;
    public static final ExemptionMechanism getInstance(String mechanism, String provider)
        throws java.security.NoSuchAlgorithmException, java.security.NoSuchProviderException;
    public static final ExemptionMechanism getInstance(String mechanism, java.security.Provider provider)
        throws java.security.NoSuchAlgorithmException;
// Public Instance Methods
    public final byte[] genExemptionBlob() throws IllegalStateException, ExemptionMechanismException;
    public final int genExemptionBlob(byte[] output) throws IllegalStateException, ShortBufferException,
        ExemptionMechanismException;
    public final int genExemptionBlob(byte[] output, int outputOffset) throws IllegalStateException,
        ShortBufferException, ExemptionMechanismException;
    public final String getName();
    public final int getOutputSize(int inputLen) throws IllegalStateException;
    public final java.security.Provider getProvider();
    public final void init(java.security.Key key) throws java.security.InvalidKeyException, ExemptionMechanismException;
    public final void init(java.security.Key key, java.security.spec.AlgorithmParameterSpec params)
        throws java.security.InvalidKeyException, java.security.InvalidAlgorithmParameterException,
        ExemptionMechanismException;
    public final void init(java.security.Key key, java.security.AlgorithmParameters params)
        throws java.security.InvalidKeyException, java.security.InvalidAlgorithmParameterException,
        ExemptionMechanismException;
    public final boolean isCryptoAllowed(java.security.Key key) throws ExemptionMechanismException;
// Protected Methods Overriding Object
    protected void finalize();
}
```

Returned By: Cipher.getExemptionMechanism(), ExemptionMechanism.getInstance()

ExemptionMechanismException — Java 1.4

javax.crypto — *serializable checked*

This exception signals a problem in one of the ExemptionMechanism methods.

Object ─ Throwable ─ Exception ─ GeneralSecurityException ─ ExemptionMechanismException
Throwable ⋯ Serializable

```
public class ExemptionMechanismException extends java.security.GeneralSecurityException {
// Public Constructors
   public ExemptionMechanismException();
   public ExemptionMechanismException(String msg);
}
```

Thrown By: ExemptionMechanism.{genExemptionBlob(), init(), isCryptoAllowed()}, ExemptionMechanismSpi.{engineGenExemptionBlob(), engineInit()}

ExemptionMechanismSpi — Java 1.4

javax.crypto

This abstract class defines the Service Provider Interface for ExemptionMechanism. Security providers may implement this interface, but applications never need to use it. Note that the default "SunJCE" provider does not provide an implementation.

```
public abstract class ExemptionMechanismSpi {
// Public Constructors
   public ExemptionMechanismSpi();
// Protected Instance Methods
   protected abstract byte[ ] engineGenExemptionBlob() throws ExemptionMechanismException;
   protected abstract int engineGenExemptionBlob(byte[ ] output, int outputOffset) throws ShortBufferException,
        ExemptionMechanismException;
   protected abstract int engineGetOutputSize(int inputLen);
   protected abstract void engineInit(java.security.Key key) throws java.security.InvalidKeyException,
        ExemptionMechanismException;
   protected abstract void engineInit(java.security.Key key, java.security.AlgorithmParameters params)
        throws java.security.InvalidKeyException, java.security.InvalidAlgorithmParameterException,
        ExemptionMechanismException;
   protected abstract void engineInit(java.security.Key key, java.security.spec.AlgorithmParameterSpec params)
        throws java.security.InvalidKeyException, java.security.InvalidAlgorithmParameterException,
        ExemptionMechanismException;
}
```

Passed To: ExemptionMechanism.ExemptionMechanism()

IllegalBlockSizeException — Java 1.4

javax.crypto — *serializable checked*

This exception signals that the length of data provided to a block cipher (as implemented, for example, by Cipher and SealedObject) does not match the block size for the cipher.

Object ─ Throwable ─ Exception ─ GeneralSecurityException ─ IllegalBlockSizeException
Throwable ⋯ Serializable

```
public class IllegalBlockSizeException extends java.security.GeneralSecurityException {
// Public Constructors
```

```
    public IllegalBlockSizeException();
    public IllegalBlockSizeException(String msg);
}
```

Thrown By: Cipher.{doFinal(), wrap()}, CipherSpi.{engineDoFinal(), engineWrap()}, SealedObject.{getObject(), SealedObject()}

KeyAgreement Java 1.4

javax.crypto

This class provides an API to a key-agreement protocol that allows two or more parties to agree on a secret key without exchanging any secrets and in such a way that an eavesdropper listening in on the communication between those parties cannot determine the secret key. The KeyAgreement class is algorithm-independent and provider-based, so you must obtain a KeyAgreement object by calling one of the static getInstance() factory methods and specifying the name of the desired key agreement algorithm and, optionally, the name of the desired provider of that algorithm. The "SunJCE" provider implements a single key-agreement algorithm named "DiffieHellman".

To use a KeyAgreement object, each party first calls the init() method and supplies a Key object of its own. Then, each party obtains a Key object from one of the other parties to the agreement and calls doPhase(). Each party obtains an intermediate Key object as the return value of doPhase(), and these keys are again exchanged and passed to doPhase(). This process typically repeats n–1 times, where n is the number of parties, but the actual number of repetitions is algorithm-dependent. When doPhase() is called the last time, the second argument must be true to indicate that it is the last phase of the agreement. After all calls to doPhase() have been made, each party calls generateSecret() to obtain an array of bytes or a SecretKey object for a named algorithm type. All parties obtain the same bytes or SecretKey from this method. The KeyAgreement class is not responsible for the transfer of Key objects between parties or for mutual authentication among the parties. These tasks must be accomplished through some external mechanism.

The most common type of key agreement is "DiffieHellman" key agreement between two parties. It proceeds as follows. First, both parties obtain a java.security.KeyPairGenerator for the "DiffieHellman" algorithm and use it to generate a java.security.KeyPair of Diffie-Hellman public and private keys. Each party passes its private key to the init() method of its KeyAgreement object. (The init() method can be passed a java.security.spec.AlgorithmParameterSpec object, but the Diffie-Hellman protocol does not require any additional parameters.) Next, the two parties exchange public keys, typically through some kind of networking mechanism (the KeyAgreement class is not responsible for the actual exchange of keys). Each party passes the public key of the other party to the doPhase() method of its KeyAgreement object. There are only two parties to this agreement, so only one phase is required, and the second argument to doPhase() is true. At this point, both parties call generateSecret() to obtain the shared secret key.

A three-party Diffie-Hellman key agreement requires two phases and is slightly more complicated. Let's call the three parties Alice, Bob, and Carol. Each generates a key pair and uses its private key to initialize its KeyAgreement object, as before. Then Alice passes her public key to Bob, Bob passes his to Carol, and Carol passes hers to Alice. Each party passes this public key to doPhase(). Since this is not the final doPhase(), the second argument is false, and doPhase() returns an intermediate Key object. The three parties exchange these intermediate keys again in the same way: Alice to Bob, Bob to Carol, and Carol to Alice. Now each party passes the intermediate key it has received to doPhase() a second time, passing true to indicate that this is the final phase. Finally, all three can call generateSecret() to obtain a shared key to encrypt future communication.

```
public class KeyAgreement {
// Protected Constructors
   protected KeyAgreement(KeyAgreementSpi keyAgreeSpi, java.security.Provider provider, String algorithm);
// Public Class Methods
   public static final KeyAgreement getInstance(String algorithm) throws java.security.NoSuchAlgorithmException;
   public static final KeyAgreement getInstance(String algorithm, String provider)
       throws java.security.NoSuchAlgorithmException, java.security.NoSuchProviderException;
   public static final KeyAgreement getInstance(String algorithm, java.security.Provider provider)
       throws java.security.NoSuchAlgorithmException;
// Public Instance Methods
   public final java.security.Key doPhase(java.security.Key key, boolean lastPhase)
       throws java.security.InvalidKeyException, IllegalStateException;
   public final byte[ ] generateSecret( ) throws IllegalStateException;
   public final SecretKey generateSecret(String algorithm) throws IllegalStateException,
       java.security.NoSuchAlgorithmException, java.security.InvalidKeyException;
   public final int generateSecret(byte[ ] sharedSecret, int offset) throws IllegalStateException, ShortBufferException;
   public final String getAlgorithm( );
   public final java.security.Provider getProvider( );
   public final void init(java.security.Key key) throws java.security.InvalidKeyException;
   public final void init(java.security.Key key, java.security.SecureRandom random)
       throws java.security.InvalidKeyException;
   public final void init(java.security.Key key, java.security.spec.AlgorithmParameterSpec params)
       throws java.security.InvalidKeyException, java.security.InvalidAlgorithmParameterException;
   public final void init(java.security.Key key, java.security.spec.AlgorithmParameterSpec params,
                          java.security.SecureRandom random) throws java.security.InvalidKeyException,
       java.security.InvalidAlgorithmParameterException;
}
```

Returned By: KeyAgreement.getInstance()

KeyAgreementSpi — Java 1.4

javax.crypto

This abstract class defines the service-provider interface for KeyAgreement. A cryptographic provider must implement a concrete subclass of this class for each encryption algorithm it supports. Applications never need to use or subclass this class.

```
public abstract class KeyAgreementSpi {
// Public Constructors
   public KeyAgreementSpi( );
// Protected Instance Methods
   protected abstract java.security.Key engineDoPhase(java.security.Key key, boolean lastPhase)
       throws java.security.InvalidKeyException, IllegalStateException;
   protected abstract byte[ ] engineGenerateSecret( ) throws IllegalStateException;
   protected abstract SecretKey engineGenerateSecret(String algorithm) throws IllegalStateException,
       java.security.NoSuchAlgorithmException, java.security.InvalidKeyException;
   protected abstract int engineGenerateSecret(byte[ ] sharedSecret, int offset) throws IllegalStateException,
       ShortBufferException;
   protected abstract void engineInit(java.security.Key key, java.security.SecureRandom random)
       throws java.security.InvalidKeyException;
   protected abstract void engineInit(java.security.Key key, java.security.spec.AlgorithmParameterSpec params,
                                      java.security.SecureRandom random) throws java.security.InvalidKeyException,
       java.security.InvalidAlgorithmParameterException;
}
```

Passed To: KeyAgreement.KeyAgreement()

KeyGenerator **Java 1.4**

javax.crypto

This class provides an API for generating secret keys for symmetric cryptography. It is similar to java.security.KeyPairGenerator, which generates public/private key pairs for asymmetric or public-key cryptography. KeyGenerator is algorithm-independent and provider-based, so you must obtain a KeyGenerator instance by calling one of the static getInstance() factory methods and specifying the name of the cryptographic algorithm for which a key is desired and, optionally, the name of the security provider whose key-generation implementation is to be used. The "SunJCE" provider includes KeyGenerator implementations for the "DES", "DESede", and "Blowfish" encryption algorithms, and also for the "HmacMD5" and "HmacSHA1" message authentication (MAC) algorithms.

Once you have obtained a KeyGenerator, you initialize it with the init() method. You can provide a java.security.spec.AlgorithmParameterSpec object to provide algorithm-specific initialization parameters or simply specify the desired size (in bits) of the key to be generated. In either case, you can also specify a source of randomness in the form of a SecureRandom object. If you do not specify a SecureRandom, the KeyGenerator instantiates one of its own. None of the algorithms supported by the "SunJCE" provider require algorithm-specific parameters.

After calling getInstance() to obtain a KeyGenerator and init() to initialize it, simply call generateKey() to create a new SecretKey. Remember that the SecretKey must be kept secret. Take precautions when storing or transmitting the key, so that it does not fall into the wrong hands. You may want to use a java.security.KeyStore object to store the key in a password-protected form.

```
public class KeyGenerator {
// Protected Constructors
   protected KeyGenerator(KeyGeneratorSpi keyGenSpi, java.security.Provider provider, String algorithm);
// Public Class Methods
   public static final KeyGenerator getInstance(String algorithm) throws java.security.NoSuchAlgorithmException;
   public static final KeyGenerator getInstance(String algorithm, java.security.Provider provider)
       throws java.security.NoSuchAlgorithmException;
   public static final KeyGenerator getInstance(String algorithm, String provider)
       throws java.security.NoSuchAlgorithmException, java.security.NoSuchProviderException;
// Public Instance Methods
   public final SecretKey generateKey();
   public final String getAlgorithm();
   public final java.security.Provider getProvider();
   public final void init(int keysize);
   public final void init(java.security.spec.AlgorithmParameterSpec params)
       throws java.security.InvalidAlgorithmParameterException;
   public final void init(java.security.SecureRandom random);
   public final void init(int keysize, java.security.SecureRandom random);
   public final void init(java.security.spec.AlgorithmParameterSpec params, java.security.SecureRandom random)
       throws java.security.InvalidAlgorithmParameterException;
}
```

Returned By: KeyGenerator.getInstance()

KeyGeneratorSpi **Java 1.4**

javax.crypto

This abstract class defines the service-provider interface for KeyGenerator. A cryptographic provider must implement a concrete subclass of this class for each key-generation algorithm it supports. Applications never need to use or subclass this class.

```
public abstract class KeyGeneratorSpi {
// Public Constructors
   public KeyGeneratorSpi();
// Protected Instance Methods
   protected abstract SecretKey engineGenerateKey();
   protected abstract void engineInit(java.security.SecureRandom random);
   protected abstract void engineInit(int keysize, java.security.SecureRandom random);
   protected abstract void engineInit(java.security.spec.AlgorithmParameterSpec params,
                                      java.security.SecureRandom random)
      throws java.security.InvalidAlgorithmParameterException;
}
```

Passed To: KeyGenerator.KeyGenerator()

Mac — Java 1.4

javax.crypto — *cloneable*

This class defines an API for computing a *message authentication code* (MAC) that can check the integrity of information transmitted between two parties that share a secret key. A MAC is similar to a digital signature, except that it is generated with a secret key rather than with a public/private key pair. The Mac class is algorithm-independent and provider-based. Obtain a Mac object by calling one of the static getInstance() factory methods and specifying the name of the desired MAC algorithm and, optionally, the name of the provider of the desired implementation. The "SunJCE" provider implements two algorithms: "HmacMD5" and "HmacSHA1". These are MAC algorithms based on the MD5 and SHA-1 cryptographic hash functions.

After obtaining a Mac object, initialize it by calling the init() method and specifying a SecretKey and, optionally, a java.security.spec.AlgorithmParameterSpec object. The "HmacMD5" and "HmacSHA1" algorithms can use any kind of SecretKey; they are not restricted to a particular cryptographic algorithm. And neither algorithm requires an AlgorithmParameterSpec object.

After obtaining and initializing a Mac object, specify the data for which the MAC is to be computed. If the data is contained in a single byte array, simply pass it to doFinal(). If the data is streaming or is stored in various locations, you can supply the data in multiple calls to update(). End the series of update() calls with a single call to doFinal(). Note that some versions of doFinal() return the MAC data as the function return value. Another version stores the MAC data in a byte array you supply. If you use this version of doFinal(), be sure to call getMacLength() to instantiate an array of the correct length.

A call to doFinal() resets the internal state of a Mac object. If you want to compute a MAC for part of your data and then proceed to compute the MAC for the full data, you should clone() the Mac object before calling doFinal(). Note, however, that Mac implementations are not required to implement Cloneable.

Object — Mac ··· Cloneable

```
public class Mac implements Cloneable {
// Protected Constructors
   protected Mac(MacSpi macSpi, java.security.Provider provider, String algorithm);
// Public Class Methods
   public static final Mac getInstance(String algorithm) throws java.security.NoSuchAlgorithmException;
   public static final Mac getInstance(String algorithm, String provider)
      throws java.security.NoSuchAlgorithmException, java.security.NoSuchProviderException;
   public static final Mac getInstance(String algorithm, java.security.Provider provider)
      throws java.security.NoSuchAlgorithmException;
```

```
// Public Instance Methods
    public final byte[ ] doFinal() throws IllegalStateException;
    public final byte[ ] doFinal(byte[ ] input) throws IllegalStateException;
    public final void doFinal(byte[ ] output, int outOffset) throws ShortBufferException, IllegalStateException;
    public final String getAlgorithm();
    public final int getMacLength();
    public final java.security.Provider getProvider();
    public final void init(java.security.Key key) throws java.security.InvalidKeyException;
    public final void init(java.security.Key key, java.security.spec.AlgorithmParameterSpec params)
        throws java.security.InvalidKeyException, java.security.InvalidAlgorithmParameterException;
    public final void reset();
    public final void update(byte[ ] input) throws IllegalStateException;
    public final void update(byte input) throws IllegalStateException;
    public final void update(byte[ ] input, int offset, int len) throws IllegalStateException;
// Public Methods Overriding Object
    public final Object clone() throws CloneNotSupportedException;
}
```

Returned By: Mac.getInstance()

MacSpi — Java 1.4

javax.crypto

This abstract class defines the service-provider interface for Mac. A cryptographic provider must implement a concrete subclass of this class for each MAC algorithm it supports. Applications never need to use or subclass this class.

```
public abstract class MacSpi {
// Public Constructors
    public MacSpi();
// Public Methods Overriding Object
    public Object clone() throws CloneNotSupportedException;
// Protected Instance Methods
    protected abstract byte[ ] engineDoFinal();
    protected abstract int engineGetMacLength();
    protected abstract void engineInit(java.security.Key key, java.security.spec.AlgorithmParameterSpec params)
        throws java.security.InvalidKeyException, java.security.InvalidAlgorithmParameterException;
    protected abstract void engineReset();
    protected abstract void engineUpdate(byte input);
    protected abstract void engineUpdate(byte[ ] input, int offset, int len);
}
```

Passed To: Mac.Mac()

NoSuchPaddingException — Java 1.4

javax.crypto — *serializable checked*

This exception signals that no implementation of the requested padding scheme can be found.

Object — Throwable — Exception — GeneralSecurityException — NoSuchPaddingException
Throwable ⋯ Serializable

```
public class NoSuchPaddingException extends java.security.GeneralSecurityException {
// Public Constructors
    public NoSuchPaddingException();
```

```
    public NoSuchPaddingException(String msg);
}
```

Thrown By: Cipher.getInstance(), CipherSpi.engineSetPadding()

NullCipher — Java 1.4

javax.crypto

This trivial subclass of Cipher implements an identity cipher that does not transform plain text in any way. Unlike Cipher objects returned by Cipher.getInstance(), a NullCipher must be created with the NullCipher() constructor.

Object ─ Cipher ─ NullCipher

```
public class NullCipher extends Cipher {
// Public Constructors
    public NullCipher();
}
```

SealedObject — Java 1.4

javax.crypto — *serializable*

This class is a wrapper around a serializable object. It serializes the object and encrypts the resulting data stream, thereby protecting the confidentiality of the object. Create a SealedObject by specifying the object to be sealed and a Cipher object to perform the encryption. Retrieve the sealed object by calling getObject() and specifying the Cipher or java.security.Key to use for decryption. The SealedObject keeps track of the encryption algorithm and parameters so that a Key object alone can decrypt the object.

Object ─ SealedObject ··· Serializable

```
public class SealedObject implements Serializable {
// Public Constructors
    public SealedObject(Serializable object, Cipher c) throws java.io.IOException, IllegalBlockSizeException;
// Protected Constructors
    protected SealedObject(SealedObject so);
// Public Instance Methods
    public final String getAlgorithm();
    public final Object getObject(java.security.Key key) throws java.io.IOException, ClassNotFoundException,
        java.security.NoSuchAlgorithmException, java.security.InvalidKeyException;
    public final Object getObject(Cipher c) throws java.io.IOException, ClassNotFoundException,
        IllegalBlockSizeException, BadPaddingException;
    public final Object getObject(java.security.Key key, String provider) throws java.io.IOException,
        ClassNotFoundException, java.security.NoSuchAlgorithmException, java.security.NoSuchProviderException,
        java.security.InvalidKeyException;
// Protected Instance Fields
    protected byte[ ] encodedParams;
}
```

Passed To: SealedObject.SealedObject()

SecretKey — Java 1.4

javax.crypto — *serializable*

This interface represents a secret key used for symmetric cryptographic algorithms that depend on both the sender and receiver knowing the same secret. SecretKey extends the java.security.Key interface, but does not add any new methods. The interface exists in order to keep secret keys distinct from the public and private keys used in public-key, or asymmetric, cryptography. See also java.security.PublicKey and java.security.PrivateKey.

A secret key is nothing more than arrays of bytes and does not require a specialized encoding format. Therefore, an implementation of this interface should return the format name "RAW" from getFormat() and should return the bytes of the key from getEncoded(). (These two methods are defined by the java.security.Key interface that SecretKey extends.)

Serializable — Key — SecretKey

```
public interface SecretKey extends java.security.Key {
}
```

Implementations: javax.crypto.interfaces.PBEKey, javax.crypto.spec.SecretKeySpec, javax.security.auth.kerberos.KerberosKey

Passed To: SecretKeyFactory.{getKeySpec(), translateKey()}, SecretKeyFactorySpi.{engineGetKeySpec(), engineTranslateKey()}

Returned By: KeyAgreement.generateSecret(), KeyAgreementSpi.engineGenerateSecret(), KeyGenerator.generateKey(), KeyGeneratorSpi.engineGenerateKey(), SecretKeyFactory.{generateSecret(), translateKey()}, SecretKeyFactorySpi.{engineGenerateSecret(), engineTranslateKey()}, javax.security.auth.kerberos.KerberosTicket.getSessionKey()

SecretKeyFactory Java 1.4

javax.crypto

This class defines an API for translating a secret key between its opaque SecretKey representation and its transparent javax.crypto.SecretKeySpec representation. It is much like java.security.KeyFactory, except that it works with secret (or symmetric) keys rather than with public and private (asymmetric) keys. SecretKeyFactory is algorithm independent and provider-based, so you must obtain a SecretKeyFactory object by calling one of the static getInstance() factory methods and specifying the name of the desired secret-key algorithm and, optionally, the name of the provider whose implementation is desired. The "SunJCE" provider provides SecretKeyFactory implementations for the "DES", "DESede", and "PBEWithMD5AndDES" algorithms.

Once you have obtained a SecretKeyFactory, use generateSecret() to create a SecretKey from a java.security.spec.KeySpec (or its subclass, javax.crypto.spec.SecretKeySpec) or call getKeySpec() to obtain a KeySpec for a Key object. Because there can be more than one suitable type of KeySpec, getKeySpec() requires a Class object to specify the type of the KeySpec to be created. See also DESKeySpec, DESedeKeySpec, and PBEKeySpec in the javax.crypto.spec package.

```
public class SecretKeyFactory {
// Protected Constructors
   protected SecretKeyFactory(SecretKeyFactorySpi keyFacSpi, java.security.Provider provider, String algorithm);
// Public Class Methods
   public static final SecretKeyFactory getInstance(String algorithm) throws java.security.NoSuchAlgorithmException;
   public static final SecretKeyFactory getInstance(String algorithm, java.security.Provider provider)
        throws java.security.NoSuchAlgorithmException;
   public static final SecretKeyFactory getInstance(String algorithm, String provider)
        throws java.security.NoSuchAlgorithmException, java.security.NoSuchProviderException;
// Public Instance Methods
   public final SecretKey generateSecret(java.security.spec.KeySpec keySpec)
        throws java.security.spec.InvalidKeySpecException;
```

```
    public final String getAlgorithm();
    public final java.security.spec.KeySpec getKeySpec(SecretKey key, Class keySpec)
        throws java.security.spec.InvalidKeySpecException;
    public final java.security.Provider getProvider();
    public final SecretKey translateKey(SecretKey key) throws java.security.InvalidKeyException;
}
```

Returned By: SecretKeyFactory.getInstance()

SecretKeyFactorySpi — Java 1.4

javax.crypto

This abstract class defines the service-provider interface for SecretKeyFactory. A cryptographic provider must implement a concrete subclass of this class for each type of secret key it supports. Applications never need to use or subclass this class.

```
public abstract class SecretKeyFactorySpi {
// Public Constructors
    public SecretKeyFactorySpi();
// Protected Instance Methods
    protected abstract SecretKey engineGenerateSecret(java.security.spec.KeySpec keySpec)
        throws java.security.spec.InvalidKeySpecException;
    protected abstract java.security.spec.KeySpec engineGetKeySpec(SecretKey key, Class keySpec)
        throws java.security.spec.InvalidKeySpecException;
    protected abstract SecretKey engineTranslateKey(SecretKey key) throws java.security.InvalidKeyException;
}
```

Passed To: SecretKeyFactory.SecretKeyFactory()

ShortBufferException — Java 1.4

javax.crypto — *serializable checked*

This signals that an output buffer is too short to hold the results of an operation.

Object — Throwable — Exception — GeneralSecurityException — ShortBufferException
Serializable

```
public class ShortBufferException extends java.security.GeneralSecurityException {
// Public Constructors
    public ShortBufferException();
    public ShortBufferException(String msg);
}
```

Thrown By: Cipher.{doFinal(), update()}, CipherSpi.{engineDoFinal(), engineUpdate()}, ExemptionMechanism.genExemptionBlob(), ExemptionMechanismSpi.engineGenExemptionBlob(), KeyAgreement.generateSecret(), KeyAgreementSpi.engineGenerateSecret(), Mac.doFinal()

Package javax.crypto.interfaces — Java 1.4

The interfaces in the javax.crypto.interfaces package define the public methods that must be supported by various types of encryption keys. The "DH" interfaces represent Diffie-Hellman public/private key pairs used in the Diffie-Hellman key-agreement protocol. The "PBE" interface is for Password-Based Encryption. These interfaces are typically of interest only to programmers who are implementing a cryptographic provider or who want to implement cryptographic algorithms themselves. Use of this package requires basic familiarity with the encryption algorithms and the mathematics that underlie them. Note that the javax.crypto.spec package contains classes that provide algorithm-specific details about encryption keys.

Interfaces:

```
public interface DHKey;
public interface DHPrivateKey extends DHKey, java.security.PrivateKey;
public interface DHPublicKey extends DHKey, java.security.PublicKey;
public interface PBEKey extends javax.crypto.SecretKey;
```

DHKey — Java 1.4

javax.crypto.interfaces

This interface represents a Diffie-Hellman key. The javax.crypto.spec.DHParameterSpec returned by getParams() specifies the parameters that generate the key; they define a key family. See the subinterfaces DHPublicKey and DHPrivateKey for the actual key values.

```
public interface DHKey {
// Public Instance Methods
   public abstract javax.crypto.spec.DHParameterSpec getParams();
}
```

Implementations: DHPrivateKey, DHPublicKey

DHPrivateKey — Java 1.4

javax.crypto.interfaces — *serializable*

This interface represents a Diffie-Hellman private key. Note that it extends two interfaces: DHKey and java.security.PrivateKey. getX() returns the private-key value. If you are working with a PrivateKey you know is a Diffie-Hellman key, you can cast your PrivateKey to a DHPrivateKey.

DHPrivateKey
DHKey | Serializable | Key | PrivateKey

```
public interface DHPrivateKey extends DHKey, java.security.PrivateKey {
// Public Instance Methods
   public abstract java.math.BigInteger getX();
}
```

DHPublicKey — Java 1.4

javax.crypto.interfaces — *serializable*

This interface represents a Diffie-Hellman public key. Note that it extends two interfaces: DHKey and java.security.PublicKey. getY() returns the public-key value. If you are working with a PublicKey you know is a Diffie-Hellman key, you can cast your PublicKey to a DHPublicKey.

DHPublicKey
DHKey | Serializable | Key | PublicKey

```
public interface DHPublicKey extends DHKey, java.security.PublicKey {
// Public Instance Methods
```

```
    public abstract java.math.BigInteger getY();
}
```

PBEKey Java 1.4

javax.crypto.interfaces *serializable*

This interface represents a key for password-based encryption. If you are working with a SecretKey that you know is a password-based key, you can cast it to a PBEKey.

Serializable ··· Key ··· SecretKey ··· PBEKey

```
public interface PBEKey extends javax.crypto.SecretKey {
// Public Instance Methods
    public abstract int getIterationCount();
    public abstract char[ ] getPassword();
    public abstract byte[ ] getSalt();
}
```

Package javax.crypto.spec Java 1.4

The javax.crypto.spec package contains classes that define transparent java.security.spec.KeySpec and java.security.spec.AlgorithmParameterSpec representations of secret keys, Diffie-Hellman public and private keys, and parameters used by various cryptographic algorithms. The classes in this package are used in conjunction with java.security.KeyFactory, javax.crypto.SecretKeyFactory and java.security.AlgorithmParameters for converting opaque Key, and AlgorithmParameters objects to and from transparent representations. In order to make good use of this package, you must be familiar with the specifications of the various cryptographic algorithms it supports and the basic mathematics that underlie those algorithms.

Classes:

```
public class DESedeKeySpec implements java.security.spec.KeySpec;
public class DESKeySpec implements java.security.spec.KeySpec;
public class DHGenParameterSpec implements java.security.spec.AlgorithmParameterSpec;
public class DHParameterSpec implements java.security.spec.AlgorithmParameterSpec;
public class DHPrivateKeySpec implements java.security.spec.KeySpec;
public class DHPublicKeySpec implements java.security.spec.KeySpec;
public class IvParameterSpec implements java.security.spec.AlgorithmParameterSpec;
public class PBEKeySpec implements java.security.spec.KeySpec;
public class PBEParameterSpec implements java.security.spec.AlgorithmParameterSpec;
public class RC2ParameterSpec implements java.security.spec.AlgorithmParameterSpec;
public class RC5ParameterSpec implements java.security.spec.AlgorithmParameterSpec;
public class SecretKeySpec implements java.security.spec.KeySpec, javax.crypto.SecretKey;
```

DESedeKeySpec Java 1.4

javax.crypto.spec

This class is a transparent representation of a DESede (triple-DES) key. The key is 24 bytes long.

Object — DESedeKeySpec ··· KeySpec

```
public class DESedeKeySpec implements java.security.spec.KeySpec {
// Public Constructors
   public DESedeKeySpec(byte[ ] key) throws java.security.InvalidKeyException;
   public DESedeKeySpec(byte[ ] key, int offset) throws java.security.InvalidKeyException;
// Public Constants
   public static final int DES_EDE_KEY_LEN;                                              =24
// Public Class Methods
   public static boolean isParityAdjusted(byte[ ] key, int offset) throws java.security.InvalidKeyException;
// Public Instance Methods
   public byte[ ] getKey();
}
```

DESKeySpec — Java 1.4

javax.crypto.spec

This class is a transparent representation of a DES key. The key is 8 bytes long.

Object — DESKeySpec ··· KeySpec

```
public class DESKeySpec implements java.security.spec.KeySpec {
// Public Constructors
   public DESKeySpec(byte[ ] key) throws java.security.InvalidKeyException;
   public DESKeySpec(byte[ ] key, int offset) throws java.security.InvalidKeyException;
// Public Constants
   public static final int DES_KEY_LEN;                                                   =8
// Public Class Methods
   public static boolean isParityAdjusted(byte[ ] key, int offset) throws java.security.InvalidKeyException;
   public static boolean isWeak(byte[ ] key, int offset) throws java.security.InvalidKeyException;
// Public Instance Methods
   public byte[ ] getKey();
}
```

DHGenParameterSpec — Java 1.4

javax.crypto.spec

This class is a transparent representation of the values needed to generate a set of Diffie-Hellman parameters (see DHParameterSpec). An instance of this class can be passed to the init() method of a java.security.AlgorithmParameterGenerator that computes Diffie-Hellman parameters.

Object — DHGenParameterSpec ··· AlgorithmParameterSpec

```
public class DHGenParameterSpec implements java.security.spec.AlgorithmParameterSpec {
// Public Constructors
   public DHGenParameterSpec(int primeSize, int exponentSize);
// Public Instance Methods
   public int getExponentSize();
   public int getPrimeSize();
}
```

DHParameterSpec — Java 1.4

javax.crypto.spec

This class is a transparent representation of the set of parameters required by the Diffie-Hellman key-agreement algorithm. All parties to the key agreement must share these parameters and use them to generate a Diffie-Hellman public/private key pair.

Object — DHParameterSpec ··· AlgorithmParameterSpec

```
public class DHParameterSpec implements java.security.spec.AlgorithmParameterSpec {
// Public Constructors
   public DHParameterSpec(java.math.BigInteger p, java.math.BigInteger g);
   public DHParameterSpec(java.math.BigInteger p, java.math.BigInteger g, int l);
// Public Instance Methods
   public java.math.BigInteger getG();
   public int getL();
   public java.math.BigInteger getP();
}
```

Returned By: javax.crypto.interfaces.DHKey.getParams()

DHPrivateKeySpec — Java 1.4

javax.crypto.spec

This java.security.spec.KeySpec is a transparent representation of a Diffie-Hellman private key.

Object — DHPrivateKeySpec ··· KeySpec

```
public class DHPrivateKeySpec implements java.security.spec.KeySpec {
// Public Constructors
   public DHPrivateKeySpec(java.math.BigInteger x, java.math.BigInteger p, java.math.BigInteger g);
// Public Instance Methods
   public java.math.BigInteger getG();
   public java.math.BigInteger getP();
   public java.math.BigInteger getX();
}
```

DHPublicKeySpec — Java 1.4

javax.crypto.spec

This java.security.spec.KeySpec is a transparent representation of a Diffie-Hellman public key.

Object — DHPublicKeySpec ··· KeySpec

```
public class DHPublicKeySpec implements java.security.spec.KeySpec {
// Public Constructors
   public DHPublicKeySpec(java.math.BigInteger y, java.math.BigInteger p, java.math.BigInteger g);
// Public Instance Methods
   public java.math.BigInteger getG();
   public java.math.BigInteger getP();
   public java.math.BigInteger getY();
}
```

IvParameterSpec **Java 1.4**

javax.crypto.spec

This java.security.spec.AlgorithmParameterSpec is a transparent representation of an initialization vector, or IV. An IV is required for block ciphers used in feedback mode, such as DES in CBC mode.

Object — IvParameterSpec ··· AlgorithmParameterSpec

```
public class IvParameterSpec implements java.security.spec.AlgorithmParameterSpec {
// Public Constructors
   public IvParameterSpec(byte[ ] iv);
   public IvParameterSpec(byte[ ] iv, int offset, int len);
// Public Instance Methods
   public byte[ ] getIV();
}
```

PBEKeySpec **Java 1.4**

javax.crypto.spec

This class is a transparent representation of a password used in password-based encryption (PBE). The password is stored as a char array rather than as a String so that the characters of the password can be overwritten when they are no longer needed (for increased security).

Object — PBEKeySpec ··· KeySpec

```
public class PBEKeySpec implements java.security.spec.KeySpec {
// Public Constructors
   public PBEKeySpec(char[ ] password);
   public PBEKeySpec(char[ ] password, byte[ ] salt, int iterationCount);
   public PBEKeySpec(char[ ] password, byte[ ] salt, int iterationCount, int keyLength);
// Public Instance Methods
   public final void clearPassword();
   public final int getIterationCount();
   public final int getKeyLength();
   public final char[ ] getPassword();
   public final byte[ ] getSalt();
}
```

PBEParameterSpec **Java 1.4**

javax.crypto.spec

This class is a transparent representation of the parameters used with the password-based encryption algorithm defined by PKCS#5.

Object — PBEParameterSpec ··· AlgorithmParameterSpec

```
public class PBEParameterSpec implements java.security.spec.AlgorithmParameterSpec {
// Public Constructors
   public PBEParameterSpec(byte[ ] salt, int iterationCount);
// Public Instance Methods
   public int getIterationCount();
   public byte[ ] getSalt();
}
```

RC2ParameterSpec **Java 1.4**

javax.crypto.spec

This class is a transparent representation of the parameters used by the RC2 encryption algorithm. An object of this class initializes a Cipher object that implements RC2. Note that the "SunJCE" provider supplied by Sun does not implement RC2.

Object — RC2ParameterSpec ··· AlgorithmParameterSpec

```
public class RC2ParameterSpec implements java.security.spec.AlgorithmParameterSpec {
// Public Constructors
   public RC2ParameterSpec(int effectiveKeyBits);
   public RC2ParameterSpec(int effectiveKeyBits, byte[ ] iv);
   public RC2ParameterSpec(int effectiveKeyBits, byte[ ] iv, int offset);
// Public Instance Methods
   public int getEffectiveKeyBits();
   public byte[ ] getIV();
// Public Methods Overriding Object
   public boolean equals(Object obj);
   public int hashCode();
}
```

RC5ParameterSpec **Java 1.4**

javax.crypto.spec

This class is a transparent representation of the parameters used by the RC5 encryption algorithm. An object of this class initializes a Cipher object that implements RC5. Note that the "SunJCE" provider supplied by Sun does not implement RC5.

Object — RC5ParameterSpec ··· AlgorithmParameterSpec

```
public class RC5ParameterSpec implements java.security.spec.AlgorithmParameterSpec {
// Public Constructors
   public RC5ParameterSpec(int version, int rounds, int wordSize);
   public RC5ParameterSpec(int version, int rounds, int wordSize, byte[ ] iv);
   public RC5ParameterSpec(int version, int rounds, int wordSize, byte[ ] iv, int offset);
// Public Instance Methods
   public byte[ ] getIV();
   public int getRounds();
   public int getVersion();
   public int getWordSize();
// Public Methods Overriding Object
   public boolean equals(Object obj);
   public int hashCode();
}
```

SecretKeySpec **Java 1.4**

javax.crypto.spec *serializable*

This class is a transparent and algorithm-independent representation of a secret key. This class is useful only for encryption algorithms (such as DES and DESede) whose secret keys can be represented as arbitrary byte arrays and do not require auxiliary parameters. Note that SecretKeySpec implements the javax.crypto.SecretKey interface directly, so no algorithm-specific javax.crypto.SecretKeyFactory object is required.

Object — SecretKeySpec
KeySpec | Serializable | Key | SecretKey


```
public class SecretKeySpec implements java.security.spec.KeySpec, javax.crypto.SecretKey {
// Public Constructors
    public SecretKeySpec(byte[ ] key, String algorithm);
    public SecretKeySpec(byte[ ] key, int offset, int len, String algorithm);
// Methods Implementing Key
    public String getAlgorithm();
    public byte[ ] getEncoded();
    public String getFormat();
// Public Methods Overriding Object
    public boolean equals(Object obj);
    public int hashCode();
}
```

CHAPTER 19

javax.net and javax.net.ssl

This chapter documents the javax.net package and, more importantly, its subpackage javax.net.ssl. These packages were originally defined by the Java Secure Sockets Extension (JSSE) before they were integrated into Java 1.4, which is why they have a "javax" prefix.

javax.net is a small package that simply defines abstract factory classes for creating network sockets and servers sockets. javax.net.ssl provides subclasses of these factory classes that have the specific purpose of creating sockets and server sockets that enable secure network communication through the SSL protocol and the closely related TLS protocol.

Package javax.net — Java 1.4

This small package defines factory classes for creating socket and server sockets. These factory classes can be used to create regular java.net.Socket and java.net.ServerSocket objects. More importantly, however, these factory classes can be subclassed to serve as factories for other types of sockets such as the SSL-enabled sockets of the javax.net.ssl package.

Classes:

public abstract class **ServerSocketFactory**;
public abstract class **SocketFactory**;

ServerSocketFactory — Java 1.4

javax.net

This abstract class defines a factory API for creating server socket objects. Use the static getDefault() method to obtain a default ServerSocketFactory object that is suitable for creating regular java.net.ServerSocket sockets. Once you have a ServerSocketFactory object, call one of the createServerSocket() methods to create a new socket and optionally bind it to a local port and specify the allowed backlog of queued connections. See javax.net.ssl.SSLServerSocketFactory for a socket factory that can create secure javax.net.ssl.SSLServerSocket objects.

```
public abstract class ServerSocketFactory {
// Protected Constructors
   protected ServerSocketFactory();
// Public Class Methods
   public static ServerSocketFactory getDefault();
// Public Instance Methods
   public java.net.ServerSocket createServerSocket() throws java.io.IOException;
   public abstract java.net.ServerSocket createServerSocket(int port) throws java.io.IOException;
   public abstract java.net.ServerSocket createServerSocket(int port, int backlog) throws java.io.IOException;
   public abstract java.net.ServerSocket createServerSocket(int port, int backlog, java.net.InetAddress ifAddress)
       throws java.io.IOException;
}
```

Subclasses: javax.net.ssl.SSLServerSocketFactory

Returned By: ServerSocketFactory.getDefault(), javax.net.ssl.SSLServerSocketFactory.getDefault()

SocketFactory — Java 1.4

javax.net

This abstract class defines a factory API for creating socket objects. Use the static getDefault() method to obtain a default SocketFactory object that is suitable for creating regular java.net.Socket sockets. (This default SocketFactory is the one used by the Socket() constructor, which usually provides an easier way to create normal sockets.) Once you have a SocketFactory object, call one of the createSocket() methods to create a new socket and optionally connect it to a remote host and optionally bind it to a local address and port. See javax.net.ssl.SSLSocketFactory for a socket factory that can create secure javax.net.ssl.SSLSocket objects.

```
public abstract class SocketFactory {
// Protected Constructors
   protected SocketFactory();
// Public Class Methods
   public static SocketFactory getDefault();
// Public Instance Methods
   public java.net.Socket createSocket() throws java.io.IOException;
   public abstract java.net.Socket createSocket(String host, int port) throws java.io.IOException,
       java.net.UnknownHostException;
   public abstract java.net.Socket createSocket(java.net.InetAddress host, int port) throws java.io.IOException;
   public abstract java.net.Socket createSocket(java.net.InetAddress address, int port,
                                                java.net.InetAddress localAddress, int localPort)
       throws java.io.IOException;
   public abstract java.net.Socket createSocket(String host, int port, java.net.InetAddress localHost, int localPort)
       throws java.io.IOException, java.net.UnknownHostException;
}
```

Subclasses: javax.net.ssl.SSLSocketFactory

Returned By: SocketFactory.getDefault(), javax.net.ssl.SSLSocketFactory.getDefault()

Package javax.net.ssl — Java 1.4

This package defines an API for secure network sockets using the Secure Sockets Layer (SSL) protocol or the closely related Transport Layer Security (TLS) protocol. It defines the SSLSocket and SSLServerSocket subclasses of the java.net socket and server socket classes. And it defines SSLSocketFactory and SSLServerSocketFactory subclasses of the javax.net factory classes to create those SSL-enabled sockets and server sockets. Clients that want to perform simple SSL-enabled networking can create an SSLSocket with code such as the following:

```
SSLSocketFactory factory = SSLSocketFactory.getDefault();
SSLSocket securesock = (SSLSocket)factory.getSocket(hostname, 443);    // https port
```

Once an SSLSocket has been created, it can be used just like a normal java.net.Socket. Once a connection is established over an SSLSocket, you can use the getSession() method to obtain an SSLSession object that provides information about the connection. Note that despite the name of this package and of its key classes, it supports the TLS protocol in addition to the SSL. (The default provider in Sun's implementation supports SSL 3.0 and TLS 1.0.) The TLS protocol is closely related to SSL, and we'll simply use the term SSL here.

The SSLSocket class allows you to do arbitrary networking with an SSL-enabled peer. The most common use of SSL today is with the https: protocol on the web. The addition of this package to the core Java platform enables support for https: URLs in the java.net.URL class, which allows you to securely transfer data over the web without having to directly use this package at all. When you call openConnection() on a https: URL, the URLConnection object that is returned can be cast to an HttpsURLConnection object, which defines some SSL-specific methods. See java.net.URL and java.net.URLConnection for more information about networking with URLs.

Although the code shown above to create a SSLSocket is quite simple, this package is much more complex because it exposes a lot of SSL infrastructure so that applications with advanced networking needs can configure it as needed. Also, like all security-related packages, this one is provider-based and algorithm-independent, which adds a layer of complexity. If you want to explore this package beyond the two socket classes, the two factory classes, and the HttpsURLConnection class, start with SSLContext. This class is a factory for socket factories, and as such is the central class of the API. To customize the way SSL networking is done, you create an SSLContext optionally specifying the desired provider of the implementation. Next, you initialize the SSLContext by providing a custom KeyManager as a source of authentication information to be supplied to the remote host if required, a custom TrustManager as a verifier for the authentication information (if any) presented by the remote host, and a custom java.security.SecureRandom object as a source of randomness. Once the SSLContext is initialized in this way, you can use it to create SSLSocketFactory and SSLServerSocketFactory objects that use the KeyManager and TrustManager objects you supplied.

The contents of this package are known as the Java Secure Sockets Extension or JSSE. Prior to being incorporated into Java 1.4, JSSE was a standard extension and JSSE Version 1.0.2 is available as a separate download for use with Java 1.2 and Java 1.3. Note, however, that there are some API differences between JSSE Version 1.0.2 and the updated version that is now part of Java 1.4.

Interfaces:

public interface **HostnameVerifier**;
public interface **KeyManager**;
public interface **ManagerFactoryParameters**;
public interface **SSLSession**;
public interface **SSLSessionContext**;
public interface **TrustManager**;
public interface **X509KeyManager** extends KeyManager;
public interface **X509TrustManager** extends TrustManager;

Events:

public class **HandshakeCompletedEvent** extends java.util.EventObject;
public class **SSLSessionBindingEvent** extends java.util.EventObject;

Event Listeners:

public interface **HandshakeCompletedListener** extends java.util.EventListener;
public interface **SSLSessionBindingListener** extends java.util.EventListener;

Other Classes:

public abstract class **HttpsURLConnection** extends java.net.HttpURLConnection;
public class **KeyManagerFactory**;
public abstract class **KeyManagerFactorySpi**;
public class **SSLContext**;
public abstract class **SSLContextSpi**;
public final class **SSLPermission** extends java.security.BasicPermission;
public abstract class **SSLServerSocket** extends java.net.ServerSocket;
public abstract class **SSLServerSocketFactory** extends javax.net.ServerSocketFactory;
public abstract class **SSLSocket** extends java.net.Socket;
public abstract class **SSLSocketFactory** extends javax.net.SocketFactory;
public class **TrustManagerFactory**;
public abstract class **TrustManagerFactorySpi**;

Exceptions:

public class **SSLException** extends java.io.IOException;
  └ public class **SSLHandshakeException** extends SSLException;
  └ public class **SSLKeyException** extends SSLException;
  └ public class **SSLPeerUnverifiedException** extends SSLException;
  └ public class **SSLProtocolException** extends SSLException;

HandshakeCompletedEvent — Java 1.4

javax.net.ssl — ***serializable event***

An instance of this class is passed to the handshakeCompleted() method of any registered HandshakeCompletedListener objects by an SSLSocket when that socket completes the handshake phase of establishing a connection. The various methods of a HandshakeCompletedEvent return information (such as the name of the cipher suite in use and the certificate chain of the remote host) that was determined during that handshake.

Note that the getPeerCertificateChain() method returns an object from the javax.security.cert package, which is not documented in this book. The method and package exist only for backward compatibility with earlier versions of the JSSE API, and should be considered deprecated. Use getPeerCertificates(), which uses java.security.cert instead.

```
public class HandshakeCompletedEvent extends java.util.EventObject {
// Public Constructors
   public HandshakeCompletedEvent(SSLSocket sock, SSLSession s);
// Property Accessor Methods (by property name)
   public String getCipherSuite();
   public java.security.cert.Certificate[ ] getLocalCertificates();
```

```
    public javax.security.cert.X509Certificate[ ] getPeerCertificateChain() throws SSLPeerUnverifiedException;
    public java.security.cert.Certificate[ ] getPeerCertificates() throws SSLPeerUnverifiedException;
    public SSLSession getSession();
    public SSLSocket getSocket();
}
```

Passed To: HandshakeCompletedListener.handshakeCompleted()

HandshakeCompletedListener — Java 1.4

javax.net.ssl — *event listener*

This interface is implemented by any class that wants to receive notifications (in the form of a call to handshakeCompleted() method) when an SSLSocket completes the SSL handshake. Register a HandshakeCompletedListener for an SSLSocket by passing it to the addHandshakeCompletedListener() method of the socket. When the socket completes the handshake phase of connection, it will call the handshakeCompleted() method of all registered listeners, passing in a HandshakeCompletedEvent object.

EventListener ··· HandshakeCompletedListener

```
public interface HandshakeCompletedListener extends java.util.EventListener {
// Public Instance Methods
    public abstract void handshakeCompleted(HandshakeCompletedEvent event);
}
```

Passed To: SSLSocket.{addHandshakeCompletedListener(), removeHandshakeCompletedListener()}

HostnameVerifier — Java 1.4

javax.net.ssl

An object that implements this interface may be used with an HttpsURLConnection object to handle the case in which the hostname that appears in the URL does not match the hostname obtained during the SSL handshake with the server. This occurs, for example, when a web site uses the secure certificate of its parent web hosting company, for example. In this situation, the verify() method of the HostnameVerifier is called to determine whether the connection should proceed or not. verify() should return true to allow the connection to proceed, and should return false to cause the connection to fail. The *hostname* argument to verify() specifies the hostname that appeared in the URL. The *session* argument specifies the SSLSession object that was established during the handshake. Call getPeerHost() on this object to determine the hostname reported during server authentication. If no HostnameVerifier is registered with a HttpsURLConnection object, and no default verifier is registered with the HttpsURLConnection class, then hostname mismatches will always cause the connection to fail. In user-driven applications such as web browsers, a HostnameVerifier can be used to ask if the user wants to proceed or not.

```
public interface HostnameVerifier {
// Public Instance Methods
    public abstract boolean verify(String hostname, SSLSession session);
}
```

Passed To: javax.naming.ldap.StartTlsResponse.setHostnameVerifier(), HttpsURLConnection.{setDefaultHostnameVerifier(), setHostnameVerifier()}

Returned By: HttpsURLConnection.{getDefaultHostnameVerifier(), getHostnameVerifier()}

Type Of: HttpsURLConnection.hostnameVerifier

HttpsURLConnection — Java 1.4

javax.net.ssl

This class is a java.net.URLConnection for a URL that uses the https: protocol. It extends java.net.HttpURLConnection and, in addition to inheriting the methods of its superclasses, it defines methods for specifying the SSLSocketFactory and HostnameVerifier to use when establishing the connection. Static versions of these methods allow you to specify a default factory and verifier objects for use with all HttpsURLConnection objects. After the connection has been established, several other methods exist to obtain information (such as the cipher suite and the server certificates) about the connection itself.

Obtain a HttpsURLConnection object by calling the openConnection() method of a URL that uses the https:// protocol specifier, and casting the returned value to this type. The HttpsURLConnection object is unconnected at this point, and you can call setHostnameVerifier() and setSSLSocketFactory() to customize the way the connection is made. (If you do not specify a HostnameVerifier for the instance, or a default one for the class, then hostname mismatches will always cause the connection to fail. If you do not specify an SSLSocketFactory for the instance or class, then a default one will be used.) To connect, call the inherited connect() method, and then call the inherited getContent() to retrieve the content of the URL as an object, or use the inherited getInputStream() to obtain a java.io.InputStream with which you can read the content of the URL.

Object — URLConnection — HttpURLConnection — HttpsURLConnection

```
public abstract class HttpsURLConnection extends java.net.HttpURLConnection {
// Protected Constructors
   protected HttpsURLConnection(java.net.URL url) throws java.io.IOException;
// Public Class Methods
   public static HostnameVerifier getDefaultHostnameVerifier();
   public static SSLSocketFactory getDefaultSSLSocketFactory();
   public static void setDefaultHostnameVerifier(HostnameVerifier v);
   public static void setDefaultSSLSocketFactory(SSLSocketFactory sf);
// Property Accessor Methods (by property name)
   public abstract String getCipherSuite();
   public HostnameVerifier getHostnameVerifier();
   public void setHostnameVerifier(HostnameVerifier v);
   public abstract java.security.cert.Certificate[ ] getLocalCertificates();
   public abstract java.security.cert.Certificate[ ] getServerCertificates() throws SSLPeerUnverifiedException;
   public SSLSocketFactory getSSLSocketFactory();
   public void setSSLSocketFactory(SSLSocketFactory sf);
// Protected Instance Fields
   protected HostnameVerifier hostnameVerifier;
}
```

KeyManager — Java 1.4

javax.net.ssl

This is a marker interface to identify key manager objects. A key manager is responsible for obtaining and managing authentication credentials (such as a certificate chain and an associated private key) that the local host can use to authenticate itself to the remote host. It is usually used on the server-side of an SSL connection, but can be used on the client side as well.

Use a KeyManagerFactory to obtain KeyManager objects. KeyManager objects returned by a KeyManagerFactory can always be cast to a sub-interface specific to a particular type of authentication credentials. See X509KeyManager, for example.

```
public interface KeyManager {
}
```

Implementations: X509KeyManager

Passed To: SSLContext.init(), SSLContextSpi.engineInit()

Returned By: KeyManagerFactory.getKeyManagers(), KeyManagerFactorySpi.engineGetKeyManagers()

KeyManagerFactory **Java 1.4**

javax.net.ssl

A KeyManagerFactory is responsible for creating KeyManager objects for a specific key management algorithm. Obtain a KeyManagerFactory object by calling one of the getInstance() methods and specifying the desired algorithm and, optionally, the desired provider. In Java 1.4, the "SunX509" algorithm is the only one supported by the default "SunJSSE" provider. After calling getInstance(), you initialize the factory object with init(). For the "SunX509" algorithm, you always use the two-argument version of init() passing in a KeyStore object that contains the private keys and certificates required by X509KeyManager objects, and also specifying the password used to protect the private keys in that KeyStore. Once a KeyManagerFactory has been created and initialized, use it to create a KeyManager by calling getKeyManagers(). This method returns an array of KeyManager objects because some key management algorithms may handle more than one type of key. The "SunX509" algorithm manages only X509 keys, and always returns an array with an X509KeyManager object as its single element. This returned array is typically passed to the init() method of an SSLContext object.

If a KeyStore and password are not passed to the init() method of the KeyManagerFactory for the "SunX509" algorithm, then the factory uses attempts to read a KeyStore from the file specified by the javax.net.ssl.keyStore system property using the password specified by the javax.net.ssl.keyStorePassword. The type of the keystore is specified by javax.net.ssl.keyStoreType.

```
public class KeyManagerFactory {
// Protected Constructors
   protected KeyManagerFactory(KeyManagerFactorySpi factorySpi, java.security.Provider provider,
                               String algorithm);
// Public Class Methods
   public static final String getDefaultAlgorithm();
   public static final KeyManagerFactory getInstance(String algorithm)
      throws java.security.NoSuchAlgorithmException;
   public static final KeyManagerFactory getInstance(String algorithm, java.security.Provider provider)
      throws java.security.NoSuchAlgorithmException;
   public static final KeyManagerFactory getInstance(String algorithm, String provider)
      throws java.security.NoSuchAlgorithmException, java.security.NoSuchProviderException;
// Public Instance Methods
   public final String getAlgorithm();
   public final KeyManager[ ] getKeyManagers();
   public final java.security.Provider getProvider();
   public final void init(ManagerFactoryParameters spec) throws java.security.InvalidAlgorithmParameterException;
   public final void init(java.security.KeyStore ks, char[ ] password) throws java.security.KeyStoreException,
      java.security.NoSuchAlgorithmException, java.security.UnrecoverableKeyException;
}
```

Returned By: KeyManagerFactory.getInstance()

KeyManagerFactorySpi — Java 1.4

javax.net.ssl

This abstract class defines the Service Provider Interface for KeyManagerFactory. Security providers must implement this interface, but applications never need to use it.

```
public abstract class KeyManagerFactorySpi {
// Public Constructors
   public KeyManagerFactorySpi();
// Protected Instance Methods
   protected abstract KeyManager[ ] engineGetKeyManagers();
   protected abstract void engineInit(ManagerFactoryParameters spec)
       throws java.security.InvalidAlgorithmParameterException;
   protected abstract void engineInit(java.security.KeyStore ks, char[ ] password)
       throws java.security.KeyStoreException, java.security.NoSuchAlgorithmException,
       java.security.UnrecoverableKeyException;
}
```

Passed To: KeyManagerFactory.KeyManagerFactory()

ManagerFactoryParameters — Java 1.4

javax.net.ssl

This marker interface identifies objects that provide algorithm-specific or provider-specific initialization parameters for KeyManagerFactory and TrustManagerFactory objects. In the default "SunJSSE" provider shipped by Sun, the only supported type for these factory classes is "SunX509". Factories of these types need to be initialized with a KeyStore object but do not require any specialized ManagerFactoryParameters object. Therefore, the javax.net.ssl package does not define any sub-interfaces of this interface, and it is never used with the default provider. Third-party or future providers may use it, however.

```
public interface ManagerFactoryParameters {
}
```

Passed To: KeyManagerFactory.init(), KeyManagerFactorySpi.engineInit(), TrustManagerFactory.init(), TrustManagerFactorySpi.engineInit()

SSLContext — Java 1.4

javax.net.ssl

This class is a factory for socket and server socket factories. Although most applications do not need to use this class directly, it is the central class of the javax.net.ssl package. Most applications use the default SSLSocketFactory and SSLServerSocketFactory objects returned by the static getDefault() methods of those classes. Applications that want to perform SSL networking using a security provider other than the default provider, or that want to customize key management or trust management for the SSL connection should use custom socket factories created from a custom SSLContext.

Create an SSLContext by passing the name of the desired secure socket protocol and, optionally, the desired provider to getInstance(). The default "SunJSSE" provider supports protocol strings "SSL", "SSLv2", "SSLv3", "TLS", and "TLSv1". Once you have created an SSLContext object, call its init() method to supply the KeyManager, TrustManager and SecureRandom objects it requires. If any of the init() arguments is null, a default value will be used. Finally, obtain a SSLSocketFactory and SSLServerSocketFactory by calling getSocketFactory() and getServerSocketFactory().

```
public class SSLContext {
// Protected Constructors
```

```
    protected SSLContext(SSLContextSpi contextSpi, java.security.Provider provider, String protocol);
// Public Class Methods
    public static SSLContext getInstance(String protocol) throws java.security.NoSuchAlgorithmException;
    public static SSLContext getInstance(String protocol, java.security.Provider provider)
        throws java.security.NoSuchAlgorithmException;
    public static SSLContext getInstance(String protocol, String provider)
        throws java.security.NoSuchAlgorithmException, java.security.NoSuchProviderException;
// Property Accessor Methods (by property name)
    public final SSLSessionContext getClientSessionContext();
    public final String getProtocol();
    public final java.security.Provider getProvider();
    public final SSLSessionContext getServerSessionContext();
    public final SSLServerSocketFactory getServerSocketFactory();
    public final SSLSocketFactory getSocketFactory();
// Public Instance Methods
    public final void init(KeyManager[ ] km, TrustManager[ ] tm, java.security.SecureRandom random)
        throws java.security.KeyManagementException;
}
```

Returned By: SSLContext.getInstance()

SSLContextSpi — Java 1.4

javax.net.ssl

This abstract class defines the Service Provider Interface for SSLContext. Security providers must implement this interface, but applications never need to use it.

```
public abstract class SSLContextSpi {
// Public Constructors
    public SSLContextSpi();
// Protected Instance Methods
    protected abstract SSLSessionContext engineGetClientSessionContext();
    protected abstract SSLSessionContext engineGetServerSessionContext();
    protected abstract SSLServerSocketFactory engineGetServerSocketFactory();
    protected abstract SSLSocketFactory engineGetSocketFactory();
    protected abstract void engineInit(KeyManager[ ] km, TrustManager[ ] tm, java.security.SecureRandom sr)
        throws java.security.KeyManagementException;
}
```

Passed To: SSLContext.SSLContext()

SSLException — Java 1.4

javax.net.ssl — *serializable checked*

This exception signals an SSL-related problem. This class serves as the common superclass of more specific SSL exception subclasses.

Object — Throwable — Exception — IOException — SSLException
Serializable

```
public class SSLException extends java.io.IOException {
// Public Constructors
    public SSLException(String reason);
}
```

Subclasses: SSLHandshakeException, SSLKeyException, SSLPeerUnverifiedException, SSLProtocolException

SSLHandshakeException

Java 1.4

javax.net.ssl

serializable checked

This exception signals that the SSL handshake failed for some reason other than failed authentication (see SSLPeerUnverifiedException). For example, it may be thrown because the client and server count not agree on a mutually-acceptable cipher suite. When this exception is thrown, the SSLSocket object is no longer usable.

Object — Throwable — Exception — IOException — SSLException — SSLHandshakeException
(Throwable implements Serializable)

```
public class SSLHandshakeException extends SSLException {
// Public Constructors
   public SSLHandshakeException(String reason);
}
```

SSLKeyException

Java 1.4

javax.net.ssl

serializable checked

This exception signals a problem with the public key certificate and private key used by a server (or client) for authentication.

Object — Throwable — Exception — IOException — SSLException — SSLKeyException
(Throwable implements Serializable)

```
public class SSLKeyException extends SSLException {
// Public Constructors
   public SSLKeyException(String reason);
}
```

SSLPeerUnverifiedException

Java 1.4

javax.net.ssl

serializable checked

This exception signals that authentication of the remote host was not successfully completed.

Object — Throwable — Exception — IOException — SSLException — SSLPeerUnverifiedException
(Throwable implements Serializable)

```
public class SSLPeerUnverifiedException extends SSLException {
// Public Constructors
   public SSLPeerUnverifiedException(String reason);
}
```

Thrown By: HandshakeCompletedEvent.{getPeerCertificateChain(), getPeerCertificates()}, HttpsURLConnection.getServerCertificates(), SSLSession.{getPeerCertificateChain(), getPeerCertificates()}

SSLPermission

Java 1.4

javax.net.ssl

serializable permission

This Permission class controls access to sensitive methods in the javax.net.ssl package. The two defined target names are "setHostnameVerifier" and "getSSLSessionContext". The first is required in order to call HttpURLConnection.setHostnameVerifier() and HttpURLConnection.setDefaultHostnameVerifier(). The second permission target is required in order to call SSLSession.getSessionContext().

Object — Permission — BasicPermission — SSLPermission
Guard · Serializable · Serializable

```
public final class SSLPermission extends java.security.BasicPermission {
// Public Constructors
    public SSLPermission(String name);
    public SSLPermission(String name, String actions);
}
```

SSLProtocolException — Java 1.4

javax.net.ssl — *serializable checked*

This signals a problem at the SSL protocol level. An exception of this type usually indicates that there is a bug in the SSL implementation being used locally or on the remote host.

Object — Throwable — Exception — IOException — SSLException — SSLProtocolException
Serializable

```
public class SSLProtocolException extends SSLException {
// Public Constructors
    public SSLProtocolException(String reason);
}
```

SSLServerSocket — Java 1.4

javax.net.ssl

This class is an SSL-enabled subclass of java.net.ServerSocket that is used to listen for and accept connections from clients and to create SSLSocket objects for communicating with those clients. Create an SSLServerSocket and bind it to a local port by calling one of the inherited createServerSocket() methods of an SSLServerSocketFactory. Once a SSLServerSocket is created, use it as you would a regular ServerSocket: call the inherited accept() method to wait for and accept a connection from a client, returning a Socket object. With SSLServerSocket, the Socket returned by accept() can always be cast to an instance of SSLSocket.

SSLServerSocket defines methods for setting the enabled protocols and cipher suites, and for querying the full set of supported protocols and suites. See SSLSocket, which has methods with the same names, for details. If your server desires or requires authentication by its clients, call setWantClientAuth() or setNeedClientAuth(). These methods cause the SSLSocket objects returned by accept() to be configured to request or require client authentication.

In typical SSL networking scenarios, the client requires the server to provide authentication information. When you create an SSLServerSocket using the default SSLServerSocketFactory, the authentication information required is an X.509 public key certificate and the corresponding private key. The default SSLServerSocketFactory uses an X509KeyManager to obtain this information. The default X509KeyManager attempts to read this information from the java.security.KeyStore file specified by the system property javax.net.ssl.keyStore. It uses the value of the the javax.net.ssl.keyStorePassword as the keystore password, and uses the value of the javax.net.ssl.keyStoreType system property to specify the keystore type. The key store should only contain valid keys and certificate chains that identify the server; the X509KeyManager automatically chooses a key and certificate chain that are appropriate for the client.

Object — ServerSocket — SSLServerSocket

```
public abstract class SSLServerSocket extends java.net.ServerSocket {
// Protected Constructors
   protected SSLServerSocket() throws java.io.IOException;
   protected SSLServerSocket(int port) throws java.io.IOException;
   protected SSLServerSocket(int port, int backlog) throws java.io.IOException;
   protected SSLServerSocket(int port, int backlog, java.net.InetAddress address) throws java.io.IOException;
// Property Accessor Methods (by property name)
   public abstract String[ ] getEnabledCipherSuites();
   public abstract void setEnabledCipherSuites(String[ ] suites);
   public abstract String[ ] getEnabledProtocols();
   public abstract void setEnabledProtocols(String[ ] protocols);
   public abstract boolean getEnableSessionCreation();
   public abstract void setEnableSessionCreation(boolean flag);
   public abstract boolean getNeedClientAuth();
   public abstract void setNeedClientAuth(boolean flag);
   public abstract String[ ] getSupportedCipherSuites();
   public abstract String[ ] getSupportedProtocols();
   public abstract boolean getUseClientMode();
   public abstract void setUseClientMode(boolean flag);
   public abstract boolean getWantClientAuth();
   public abstract void setWantClientAuth(boolean flag);
}
```

SSLServerSocketFactory — Java 1.4

javax.net.ssl

This class is a javax.net.ServerSocketFactory for creating SSLServerSocket objects. Most applications use the default SSLServerSocketFactory returned by the static getDefault() method. Once this SSLServerSocketFactory has been obtained, they use one of the inherited createServerSocket() methods to create and optionally bind a new SSLServerSocket. The return value of the createServerSocket() methods is a java.net.ServerSocket object, but you can safely cast this object to a SSLServerSocket if you need to.

Applications that need to customize the SSL configuration and cannot use the default server socket factory may obtain a custom SSLServerSocketFactory from an SSLContext, which is essentially a factory for socket factories. See SSLContext for details.

Object — ServerSocketFactory — SSLServerSocketFactory

```
public abstract class SSLServerSocketFactory extends javax.net.ServerSocketFactory {
// Protected Constructors
   protected SSLServerSocketFactory();
// Public Class Methods
   public static javax.net.ServerSocketFactory getDefault();                  synchronized
// Public Instance Methods
   public abstract String[ ] getDefaultCipherSuites();
   public abstract String[ ] getSupportedCipherSuites();
}
```

Returned By: SSLContext.getServerSocketFactory(), SSLContextSpi.engineGetServerSocketFactory()

SSLSession — Java 1.4

javax.net.ssl

A SSLSession object contains information about the SSL connection established through an SSLSocket. Use the the getSession() method of a SSLSocket to obtain the SSLSession object for that socket. Many of the SSLSession methods return information that was obtained during the handshake phase of the connection. getProtocol() returns the specific version of the SSL or TLS protocol in use. getCipherSuite() returns the name of the cipher suite negotiated for the connection. getPeerHost() returns the name of the remote host, and getPeerCertificates() returns the certificate chain, if any, that was received from the remote host during authentication.

The invalidate() method ends the session. It does not affect any current connections, but all future connections and any renegotiations of existing connections will need to establish a new SSLSession.

Multiple SSL connections between two hosts may share the same SSLSession as long as they are using the same protocol version and cipher suite. There is no way to enumerate the SSLSocket objects that share a session, but these sockets can exchange information by using putValue() to bind a shared object to some well-known name that can be looked up by other sockets with getValue(). removeValue() removes such a binding, and getValueNames() returns an array of all names that have objects bound to them in this session. Objects bound and unbound with putValue() and removeValue() may implement SSLSessionBindingListener to be notified when they are bound and unbound.

Note that the getPeerCertificateChain() method returns an object from the javax.security.cert package, which is not documented in this book. The method and package exist only for backward compatibility with earlier versions of the JSSE API, and should be considered deprecated. Use getPeerCertificates(), which uses java.security.cert instead.

```
public interface SSLSession {
// Property Accessor Methods (by property name)
   public abstract String getCipherSuite();
   public abstract long getCreationTime();
   public abstract byte[] getId();
   public abstract long getLastAccessedTime();
   public abstract java.security.cert.Certificate[] getLocalCertificates();
   public abstract javax.security.cert.X509Certificate[] getPeerCertificateChain() throws
        SSLPeerUnverifiedException;
   public abstract java.security.cert.Certificate[] getPeerCertificates() throws SSLPeerUnverifiedException;
   public abstract String getPeerHost();
   public abstract String getProtocol();
   public abstract SSLSessionContext getSessionContext();
   public abstract String[] getValueNames();
// Public Instance Methods
   public abstract Object getValue(String name);
   public abstract void invalidate();
   public abstract void putValue(String name, Object value);
   public abstract void removeValue(String name);
}
```

Passed To: HandshakeCompletedEvent.HandshakeCompletedEvent(), HostnameVerifier.verify(), SSLSessionBindingEvent.SSLSessionBindingEvent()

Returned By: javax.naming.ldap.StartTlsResponse.negotiate(), HandshakeCompletedEvent.getSession(), SSLSessionBindingEvent.getSession(), SSLSessionContext.getSession(), SSLSocket.getSession()

SSLSessionBindingEvent

Java 1.4

javax.net.ssl ***serializable event***

An object of this type is passed to the valueBound() and valueUnbound() methods of and object that implements SSLSessionBindingListener when that object is bound or unbound in a SSLSession with the putValue() or removeValue() methods of SSLSession. getName() returns the name to which the object was bound or unbound, and getSession() returns the SSLSession object in which the binding was created or removed.

Object ─ EventObject ─ SSLSessionBindingEvent
Serializable

```
public class SSLSessionBindingEvent extends java.util.EventObject {
// Public Constructors
    public SSLSessionBindingEvent(SSLSession session, String name);
// Public Instance Methods
    public String getName();
    public SSLSession getSession();
}
```

Passed To: SSLSessionBindingListener.{valueBound(), valueUnbound()}

SSLSessionBindingListener

Java 1.4

javax.net.ssl ***event listener***

This interface is implemented by an object that want to be notified when it is bound or unbound in an SSLSession object. If the object passed to the putValue() method of a SSLSession implements this interface, then its valueBound() method will be called by putValue(), and its valueUnbound() method will be called when that object is removed from the SSLSession with removeValue() or when it is replaced with a new object by putValue(). The argument to both methods of this interface is a SSLSessionBindingEvent, which specifies both the name to which the object was bound or unbound, and the SSLSession within which it was bound or unbound.

EventListener ··· SSLSessionBindingListener

```
public interface SSLSessionBindingListener extends java.util.EventListener {
// Public Instance Methods
    public abstract void valueBound(SSLSessionBindingEvent event);
    public abstract void valueUnbound(SSLSessionBindingEvent event);
}
```

SSLSessionContext

Java 1.4

javax.net.ssl

A SSLSessionContext groups and controls SSLSession objects. It is a low-level interface and is not commonly used in application code. getIds() returns an Enumeration of session IDs, and getSession() returns the SSLSession object associated with one of those IDs. setSessionCacheSize() specifies the total number of concurrent sessions allowed in the group, and setSessionTimeout() specifies the timeout length for those sessions. An SSLSessionContext can serve as a cache for SSLSession objects, facilitating reuse of those objects for multiple connections between the same two hosts.

Providers are not required to support this interface. Those that do return an implementing object from the getSessionContext() method of an SSLSession object, and also return implementing objects from the getClientSessionContext() and getServerSessionContext() methods of an SSLContext object, providing separate control over client and server SSL connections.

```
public interface SSLSessionContext {
// Public Instance Methods
    public abstract java.util.Enumeration getIds();
    public abstract SSLSession getSession(byte[ ] sessionId);
    public abstract int getSessionCacheSize();
    public abstract int getSessionTimeout();
    public abstract void setSessionCacheSize(int size) throws IllegalArgumentException;
    public abstract void setSessionTimeout(int seconds) throws IllegalArgumentException;
}
```

Returned By: SSLContext.{getClientSessionContext(), getServerSessionContext()}, SSLContextSpi.{engineGetClientSessionContext(), engineGetServerSessionContext()}, SSLSession.getSessionContext()

SSLSocket — Java 1.4

javax.net.ssl

An SSLSocket is a "secure socket" subclass of java.net.Socket that implements the SSL or TLS protocols, which are commonly used to authenticate a server to a client and to encrypt the data transferred between the two. Create a SSLSocket for connecting to a SSL-enabled server by calling one of the createSocket() methods of a SSLSocketFactory object. See SSLSocketFactory for details. If you are writing server code, then you will obtain a SSLSocket for communicating with an SSL-enabled client from the inherited accept() method of an SSLServerSocket. See SSLServerSocket for details.

SSLSocket inherits all of the standard socket method of its superclass, and can be used for networking just like an ordinary java.net.Socket object. In addition, however, it also defines methods that control how the secure connection is established. These methods may be called before the SSL "handshake" occurs. The handshake does not occur when the socket is first created and connected, so that you can configure various SSL parameters that control how the handshake occurs. Calling startHandshake(), getSession(), or reading or writing data on the socket trigger a handshake, so you must configure the socket before doing any of these things. If you want to be notified when the handshake occurs, call addHandshakeCompletedListener() to register a listener object to receive the notification.

getSupportedProtocols() returns a list of secure socket protocols that are supported by the socket implementation. setEnabledProtocols() allows you to specify the name or names of the supported protocols that you are willing to use for this socket. getSupportedCipherSuites() returns the full set of cipher suites supported by the underlying security provider. setEnabledCipherSuites() specifies a list of one or more cipher suites that you are willing to use for the connection. Note that not all supported cipher suites are enabled by default: only suites that provide encryption and require the server to authenticate itself to the client are enabled. If you want to allow the server to remain anonymous, you can use setEnabledCipherSuites() to enable a nonauthenticating suite. Specific protocols and cipher suites are not described here because using them correctly requires a detailed understanding of cryptography, which is beyond the scope of this reference. Most applications can simply rely on the default set of enabled protocols and cipher suites.

If you are writing a server and have obtained an SSLSocket by accepting a connection on an SSLServerSocket, then you may call setWantClientAuth() to request that the client authenticate itself to you, and you may call setNeedClientAuth() to require that the client authenticate itself during the handshake. Note, however, that it is usually more efficient to request or require client authentication on the server socket than it is to call these methods on each SSLSocket it creates.

The configuration methods described above must be called before the SSL handshake occurs. Call getSession() to obtain an SSLSession object that you can query for for information about the handshake, such as the protocol and cipher suite in use, and the identity of the server. Note that a call to getSession() will cause the handshake to occur if it has not already occurred, so you can call this method at any time.

Object ─ Socket ─ SSLSocket


```
public abstract class SSLSocket extends java.net.Socket {
// Protected Constructors
   protected SSLSocket();
   protected SSLSocket(String host, int port) throws java.io.IOException, java.net.UnknownHostException;
   protected SSLSocket(java.net.InetAddress address, int port) throws java.io.IOException,
        java.net.UnknownHostException;
   protected SSLSocket(String host, int port, java.net.InetAddress clientAddress, int clientPort)
        throws java.io.IOException, java.net.UnknownHostException;
   protected SSLSocket(java.net.InetAddress address, int port, java.net.InetAddress clientAddress, int clientPort)
        throws java.io.IOException, java.net.UnknownHostException;
// Event Registration Methods (by event name)
   public abstract void addHandshakeCompletedListener(HandshakeCompletedListener listener);
   public abstract void removeHandshakeCompletedListener(HandshakeCompletedListener listener);
// Property Accessor Methods (by property name)
   public abstract String[ ] getEnabledCipherSuites();
   public abstract void setEnabledCipherSuites(String[ ] suites);
   public abstract String[ ] getEnabledProtocols();
   public abstract void setEnabledProtocols(String[ ] protocols);
   public abstract boolean getEnableSessionCreation();
   public abstract void setEnableSessionCreation(boolean flag);
   public abstract boolean getNeedClientAuth();
   public abstract void setNeedClientAuth(boolean need);
   public abstract SSLSession getSession();
   public abstract String[ ] getSupportedCipherSuites();
   public abstract String[ ] getSupportedProtocols();
   public abstract boolean getUseClientMode();
   public abstract void setUseClientMode(boolean mode);
   public abstract boolean getWantClientAuth();
   public abstract void setWantClientAuth(boolean want);
// Public Instance Methods
   public abstract void startHandshake() throws java.io.IOException;
}
```

Passed To: HandshakeCompletedEvent.HandshakeCompletedEvent()

Returned By: HandshakeCompletedEvent.getSocket()

SSLSocketFactory — Java 1.4

javax.net.ssl

This class is a javax.net.SocketFactory for creating SSLSocket objects. Most applications use the default SSLSocketFactory returned by the static getDefault() method. Once this SSLSocketFactory has been obtained, they use one of the inherited createSocket() methods to create, and optionally connect and bind, a new SSLSocket. The return value of the createSocket() methods is a java.net.Socket object, but you can safely cast this object to a SSLSocket if you need to. SSLSocketFactory defines one new version of createSocket() in addition to the ones it inherits from its superclass. This version of the method creates an SSLSocket that is layered over an existing Socket object rather than creating a new socket entirely from scratch.

Applications that need to customize the SSL configuration and cannot use the default socket factory may obtain a custom SSLSocketFactory from an SSLContext, which is essentially a factory for socket factories. See SSLContext for details.

Object — SocketFactory — SSLSocketFactory

```
public abstract class SSLSocketFactory extends javax.net.SocketFactory {
// Public Constructors
   public SSLSocketFactory();
// Public Class Methods
   public static javax.net.SocketFactory getDefault();                    synchronized
// Public Instance Methods
   public abstract java.net.Socket createSocket(java.net.Socket s, String host, int port, boolean autoClose)
        throws java.io.IOException;
   public abstract String[ ] getDefaultCipherSuites();
   public abstract String[ ] getSupportedCipherSuites();
}
```

Passed To: javax.naming.ldap.StartTlsResponse.negotiate(), HttpsURLConnection.{setDefaultSSLSocketFactory(), setSSLSocketFactory()}

Returned By: HttpsURLConnection.{getDefaultSSLSocketFactory(), getSSLSocketFactory()}, SSLContext.getSocketFactory(), SSLContextSpi.engineGetSocketFactory()

TrustManager — Java 1.4

javax.net.ssl

This is a marker interface to identify trust manager objects. A trust manager is responsible for examining the authentication credentials (such as a certificate chain) presented by the remote host and deciding whether to trust those credentials and accept them. A TrustManager is usually used an SSL client to decide whether the SSL server is authentic, but may also be used by an SSL server when client authentication is also required.

Use a TrustManagerFactory to obtain TrustManager objects. TrustManager objects returned by a TrustManagerFactory can always be cast to a sub-interface specific to a specific type of keys. See X509TrustManager, for example.

```
public interface TrustManager {
}
```

Implementations: X509TrustManager

Passed To: SSLContext.init(), SSLContextSpi.engineInit()

Returned By: TrustManagerFactory.getTrustManagers(), TrustManagerFactorySpi.engineGetTrustManagers()

TrustManagerFactory — Java 1.4

javax.net.ssl

A TrustManagerFactory is responsible for creating TrustManager objects for a specific trust management algorithm. Obtain a TrustManagerFactory object by calling one of the getInstance() methods and specifying the desired algorithm and, optionally, the desired provider. In Java 1.4, the "SunX509" algorithm is the only one supported by the default "SunJSSE" provider. After calling getInstance(), you initialize the factory object with init(). For the "SunX509" algorithm, you pass a KeyStore object to init(). This KeyStore should contain the public keys of trusted CAs (certification authorities). Once a TrustManagerFactory has been created and initialized, use it to create a TrustManager by calling getTrustManagers(). This method returns an array of TrustManager objects because some trust management algorithms may handle more than one type of key or certificate. The "SunX509" algorithm manages only X.509 keys, and always returns an array with an X509TrustManager object as its single element. This returned array is typically passed to the init() method of an SSLContext object.

If no KeyStore is passed to the init() method of the TrustManagerFactory for the "SunX509" algorithm, then the factory uses a KeyStore created from the file named by the system property javax.net.ssl.trustStore if that property is defined. (It also uses the key store type and password specified by the properties javax.net.ssl.trustStoreType and javax.net.ssl.trustStorePassword.) Otherwise, it uses the file *jre/lib/security/jssecacerts* in the Java distribution, if it exists. Otherwise it uses the file *jre/lib/security/cacerts* which is part of Sun's Java distribution. Sun ships a default *cacerts* file that contains certificates for several well-known and reputable CAs. You can use the *keytool* program to edit the *cacerts* keystore (the default password is "changeit").


```
public class TrustManagerFactory {
// Protected Constructors
   protected TrustManagerFactory(TrustManagerFactorySpi factorySpi, java.security.Provider provider,
                                 String algorithm);
// Public Class Methods
   public static final String getDefaultAlgorithm();
   public static final TrustManagerFactory getInstance(String algorithm)
       throws java.security.NoSuchAlgorithmException;
   public static final TrustManagerFactory getInstance(String algorithm, java.security.Provider provider)
       throws java.security.NoSuchAlgorithmException;
   public static final TrustManagerFactory getInstance(String algorithm, String provider)
       throws java.security.NoSuchAlgorithmException, java.security.NoSuchProviderException;
// Public Instance Methods
   public final String getAlgorithm();
   public final java.security.Provider getProvider();
   public final TrustManager[] getTrustManagers();
   public final void init(ManagerFactoryParameters spec) throws java.security.InvalidAlgorithmParameterException;
   public final void init(java.security.KeyStore ks) throws java.security.KeyStoreException;
}
```

Returned By: TrustManagerFactory.getInstance()

TrustManagerFactorySpi — Java 1.4

javax.net.ssl

This abstract class defines the Service Provider Interface for TrustManagerFactory. Security providers must implement this interface, but applications never need to use it.

```
public abstract class TrustManagerFactorySpi {
// Public Constructors
   public TrustManagerFactorySpi();
// Protected Instance Methods
   protected abstract TrustManager[] engineGetTrustManagers();
   protected abstract void engineInit(ManagerFactoryParameters spec)
       throws java.security.InvalidAlgorithmParameterException;
   protected abstract void engineInit(java.security.KeyStore ks) throws java.security.KeyStoreException;
}
```

Passed To: TrustManagerFactory.TrustManagerFactory()

X509KeyManager — Java 1.4

javax.net.ssl

This interface is a KeyManager for working with X.509 certificates. An X509KeyManager is used during the SSL handshake by a peer that authenticates itself by providing an X.509 certificate chain to the remote host. This is usually done on the server side of the SSL connection, and can be done on the client-side as well, although that is uncommon. Obtain an X509KeyManager object either by implementing your own or from a KeyManagerFactory created with an algorithm of "SunX509". Applications do not call the methods of an X509KeyManager themselves. Instead, they simply supply an appropriate X509KeyManager object to the SSLContext object that is responsible for setting up SSL connections. When the system needs to authenticate itself during an SSL handshake, it calls various methods of the key manager object to obtain the information in needs.

An X509KeyManager retrieves keys and certificate chains from the KeyStore object that was passed to the init() method of the KeyManagerFactory object from which it was created. getPrivateKey() and getCertificateChain() return the private key and the certificate chain for a specified alias. The other methods are called to list all aliases in the keystore or to choose one alias from the keystore that matches the specified keytype and certificate authority criteria. In this way, a X509KeyManager can choose a certificate chain (and its corresponding key) based on the types of keys and the list of certificate authorities recognized by the remote host.

KeyManager — X509KeyManager

```
public interface X509KeyManager extends KeyManager {
// Public Instance Methods
   public abstract String chooseClientAlias(String[ ] keyType, java.security.Principal[ ] issuers,
                                            java.net.Socket socket);
   public abstract String chooseServerAlias(String keyType, java.security.Principal[ ] issuers, java.net.Socket socket);
   public abstract java.security.cert.X509Certificate[ ] getCertificateChain(String alias);
   public abstract String[ ] getClientAliases(String keyType, java.security.Principal[ ] issuers);
   public abstract java.security.PrivateKey getPrivateKey(String alias);
   public abstract String[ ] getServerAliases(String keyType, java.security.Principal[ ] issuers);
}
```

X509TrustManager — Java 1.4

javax.net.ssl

This interface is a TrustManager for working with X.509 certificates. Trust managers are used during the handshake phase of SSL connection to determine whether the authentication credentials presented by the remote host are trusted. This is usually done on the client-side of an SSL connection, but may also be done on the server side. Obtain an X509TrustManager either by implementing your own or from a TrustManagerFactory that was created to use the "SunX509" algorithm. Applications do call the methods of this interface themselves; instead, they simply provide an appropriate X509TrustManager object to the SSLContext object that is responsible for setting up SSL connections. When the system needs to determine whether the authentication credentials presented by the remote host are trusted, it calls the methods of the trust manager.

TrustManager — X509TrustManager

```
public interface X509TrustManager extends TrustManager {
// Public Instance Methods
   public abstract void checkClientTrusted(java.security.cert.X509Certificate[ ] chain, String authType)
       throws java.security.cert.CertificateException;
```

```
    public abstract void checkServerTrusted(java.security.cert.X509Certificate[ ] chain, String authType)
        throws java.security.cert.CertificateException;
    public abstract java.security.cert.X509Certificate[ ] getAcceptedIssuers( );
}
```

CHAPTER 20

javax.security.auth and Subpackages

This chapter documents the javax.security.auth package and its sub-packages, which, together, form the Java Authentication and Authorization Service, or JAAS. Before being integrated into Java 1.4, JAAS was available as a standard extension, which is why these packages have the "javax" prefix. The individual packages are the following:

javax.security.auth
: This top-level package defines the Subject class that is central to JAAS.

javax.security.auth.callback
: This package defines a callback API to enable communication (such as the exchange of a username and password) between a low-level login module and the end user.

javax.security.auth.kerberos
: This package contains JAAS classes related to the Kerberos network authentication protocol.

javax.security.auth.login
: This package defines the LoginContext class and related classes used by applications to perform a JAAS login.

javax.security.auth.spi
: This package defines the "service provider interface" for JAAS.

javax.security.auth.x500
: This package includes JAAS classes related to X.500 principals.

Package javax.security.auth — Java 1.4

This is the top-level package of the Java Authentication and Authorization Service (JAAS). The key class is Subject, which represents an authenticated user, and defines static methods that allow Java code be run "as" (i.e., using the permissions of) a specified Subject. The remaining classes and interfaces in this package are important parts of the JAAS infrastructure, but are not commonly used in application code. Applications do not create Subject objects directly, but typically obtain them from a javax.security.auth.login.LoginContext constructed with a javax.security.auth.callback.Callback-Handler.

Interfaces:

public interface **Destroyable**;
public interface **Refreshable**;

Classes:

public final class **AuthPermission** extends java.security.BasicPermission;
public abstract class **Policy**;
public final class **PrivateCredentialPermission** extends java.security.Permission;
public final class **Subject** implements Serializable;
public class **SubjectDomainCombiner** implements java.security.DomainCombiner;

Exceptions:

public class **DestroyFailedException** extends Exception;
public class **RefreshFailedException** extends Exception;

AuthPermission — Java 1.4

javax.security.auth — *serializable permission*

This java.security.Permission class governs the use of various methods in this package and its subpackages. The target name of the permission specifies which methods are allowed; AuthPermission objects have no actions list. Application programmers never need to use this class directly. System implementors may need to use it, and system administrators who configure security policies may need to be familiar with the following table of target names and the permissions they represent.

Target name	*Gives permission to*
doAs	Invoke Subject.doAs() methods.
doAsPrivileged	Invoke Subject.doAsPrivileged() methods.
getSubject	Invoke Subject.getSubject().
getSubjectFromDomainCombiner	Invoke SubjectDomainCombiner.getSubject().
setReadOnly	Invoke Subject.setReadOnly().
modifyPrincipals	Modify the Set of principals associated with a Subject.
modifyPublicCredentials	Modify the Set of public credentials associated with a Subject.
modifyPrivateCredentials	Modify the Set of private credentials associated with a Subject.
refreshCredential	Invoke the refresh() method of a Refreshable credential class.
destroyCredential	Invoke the destroy() method of a Destroyable credential class.
createLoginContext.*name*	Instantiate a LoginContext with the specified *name*. If *name* is "*", it allows a LoginContext of any name to be created.
getLoginConfiguration	Invoke the getConfiguration() method of javax.security.auth.login.Configuration.

Target name	*Gives permission to*
setLoginConfiguration	Invoke the setConfiguration() method of javax.security.auth.login.Configuration.
refreshLoginConfiguration	Invoke the refresh() method of javax.security.auth.login.Configuration.

Object — Permission — BasicPermission — AuthPermission
Guard, Serializable, Serializable

```
public final class AuthPermission extends java.security.BasicPermission {
// Public Constructors
   public AuthPermission(String name);
   public AuthPermission(String name, String actions);
}
```

Destroyable Java 1.4

javax.security.auth

Classes that encapsulate sensitive information, such as security credentials, may implement this interface to provide an API that allows the sensitive information to be destroyed or erased. The destroy() method erases or clears the sensitive information. It may throw a DestroyFailedException if the information cannot be erased for any reason. It may also throw a SecurityException if the caller does not have whatever permissions are required. Once destroy() has been called on an object, the isDestroyed() method returns true. Once an object has been destroyed, any other methods it defines may throw an IllegalStateException.

```
public interface Destroyable {
// Public Instance Methods
   public abstract void destroy() throws DestroyFailedException;
   public abstract boolean isDestroyed();
}
```

Implementations: javax.security.auth.kerberos.KerberosKey, javax.security.auth.kerberos.KerberosTicket, javax.security.auth.x500.X500PrivateCredential

DestroyFailedException Java 1.4

javax.security.auth *serializable checked*

This exception signals that the destroy() method of a Destroyable object did not succeed.

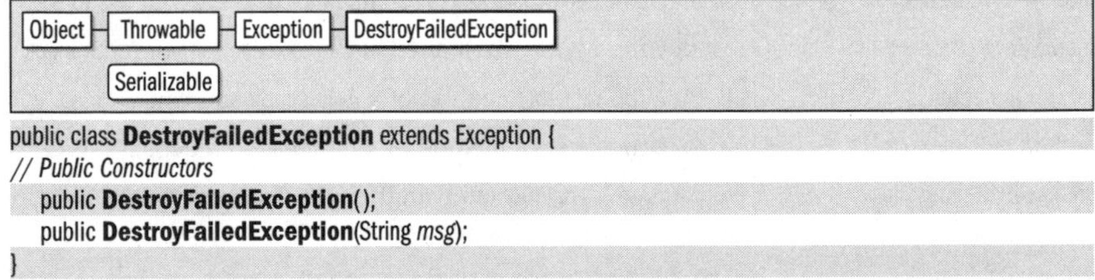


```
public class DestroyFailedException extends Exception {
// Public Constructors
   public DestroyFailedException();
   public DestroyFailedException(String msg);
}
```

Thrown By: Destroyable.destroy(), javax.security.auth.kerberos.KerberosKey.destroy(), javax.security.auth.kerberos.KerberosTicket.destroy()

Policy — Java 1.4; Deprecated in Java 1.4

javax.security.auth

This deprecated class represents a Subject-based security policy. It Because the JAAS API (this package and its sub-packages) were introduced as an extension to the core Java platform, this class was required to augment the java.security.Policy class which, prior to Java 1.4, had no provisions for Subject-based authorization. In Java 1.4, however, java.security.Policy has been extended to represent security policies based on code origin, code signers, and subjects. Thus, this class is no longer required and has been deprecated.

```
public abstract class Policy {
// Protected Constructors
   protected Policy();
// Public Class Methods
   public static javax.security.auth.Policy getPolicy();
   public static void setPolicy(javax.security.auth.Policy policy);
// Public Instance Methods
   public abstract java.security.PermissionCollection getPermissions(Subject subject, java.security.CodeSource cs);
   public abstract void refresh();
}
```

Passed To: javax.security.auth.Policy.setPolicy()

Returned By: javax.security.auth.Policy.getPolicy()

PrivateCredentialPermission — Java 1.4

javax.security.auth — *serializable permission*

This Permission class protects access to private credential objects belonging to a Subject (as specified by a set of one or more Principal objects). Application programmers rarely need to use it. System programmers implementing new private credentials classes may need to use it, and system administrators configuring security policy files should be familiar with it.

The only defined action for PrivateCredentialPermission is "read". The target name for this permission has a complex syntax and specifies the name of the credential class and a list of one or more principals. Each principal is specified as the name of the Principal class followed by the principal name in quotes. For example, a security policy file might contain a statement such as the following to allow permission to read the private KerberosKey credentials of a KerberosPrincipal named "david":

```
permission javax.security.auth.PrivateCredentialPermission
  "javax.security.auth.kerberos.KerberosKey javax.security.auth.kerberos.KerberosPrincipal \"david\"", "read";
```

The target name syntax for PrivateCredentialPermission also allows the use of the "*" wildcard in place of the credential class name or in place of the Principal class name and/or name.

Object — Permission — PrivateCredentialPermission
Guard, Serializable

```
public final class PrivateCredentialPermission extends java.security.Permission {
// Public Constructors
   public PrivateCredentialPermission(String name, String actions);
// Public Instance Methods
   public String getCredentialClass();
   public String[ ][ ] getPrincipals();
```

```
// Public Methods Overriding Permission
   public boolean equals(Object obj);
   public String getActions();
   public int hashCode();
   public boolean implies(java.security.Permission p);
   public java.security.PermissionCollection newPermissionCollection();          constant
}
```

Refreshable — Java 1.4

javax.security.auth

A class implements this interface if its instances that have a limited period of validity (as some security credentials do) and need to be periodically "refreshed" in order to remain valid. isCurrent() returns true if the object is currently valid, and false if it has expired and needs to be refreshed. refresh() attempts to revalidate or extend the validity of the object. It throws a RefreshFailedException if it does not succeed (and may also throw a SecurityException if the caller does not have the requisite permissions).

```
public interface Refreshable {
// Public Instance Methods
   public abstract boolean isCurrent();
   public abstract void refresh() throws RefreshFailedException;
}
```

Implementations: javax.security.auth.kerberos.KerberosTicket

RefreshFailedException — Java 1.4

javax.security.auth — *serializable checked*

This exception signals that the refresh() method of a Refreshable object failed.

Object — Throwable — Exception — RefreshFailedException
Serializable

```
public class RefreshFailedException extends Exception {
// Public Constructors
   public RefreshFailedException();
   public RefreshFailedException(String msg);
}
```

Thrown By: Refreshable.refresh(), javax.security.auth.kerberos.KerberosTicket.refresh()

Subject — Java 1.4

javax.security.auth — *serializable*

The Subject class is the key abstraction of the JAAS API. It represents a person or other entity and consists of:

- A java.util.Set of Principal objects that specify the identity (or identities) of the Subject.
- A Set of objects that specify the public credentials, such as the public key certificates of the Subject.
- A Set of objects that specify the private credentials, such as the private keys and Kerberos tickets of the Subject.

Subject defines methods that allow you to retrieve each of these three sets, or to retrieve a subset of each set that contains only objects of a specified Class. Unless the Subject is read-only, you can use the methods of java.util.Set to modify each of the three sets. Once setReadOnly() has been called, however, the sets become immutable and their contents may not be modified.

Application code does not typically create Subject objects itself. Instead, it obtains a Subject that represents the authenticated user of the application by calling the login() and getSubject() methods of a javax.security.auth.login.LoginContext object.

Once an authenticated Subject has been obtained from a LoginContext, an application can call the doAs() method to run code using the permissions granted to that Subject combined with the permissions granted to the code itself. doAs() runs the code defined in the run() method of a PrivilegedAction or PrivilegedExceptionAction object. doAsPrivileged() is a similar method but executes the specified run() method using the Subject's permissions only, unconstrained by unprivileged code in the call stack.

Note that many of the methods of this class throw a SecurityException if the caller has not been granted the requisite AuthPermission.

Object — Subject ··· Serializable

```
public final class Subject implements Serializable {
// Public Constructors
   public Subject();
   public Subject(boolean readOnly, java.util.Set principals, java.util.Set pubCredentials, java.util.Set privCredentials);
// Public Class Methods
   public static Object doAs(Subject subject, java.security.PrivilegedExceptionAction action)
       throws java.security.PrivilegedActionException;
   public static Object doAs(Subject subject, java.security.PrivilegedAction action);
   public static Object doAsPrivileged(Subject subject, java.security.PrivilegedExceptionAction action,
                                       java.security.AccessControlContext acc)
       throws java.security.PrivilegedActionException;
   public static Object doAsPrivileged(Subject subject, java.security.PrivilegedAction action,
                                       java.security.AccessControlContext acc);
   public static Subject getSubject(java.security.AccessControlContext acc);
// Property Accessor Methods (by property name)
   public java.util.Set getPrincipals();
   public java.util.Set getPrincipals(Class c);
   public java.util.Set getPrivateCredentials();
   public java.util.Set getPrivateCredentials(Class c);
   public java.util.Set getPublicCredentials();
   public java.util.Set getPublicCredentials(Class c);
   public boolean isReadOnly();                                                     default:false
// Public Instance Methods
   public void setReadOnly();
// Public Methods Overriding Object
   public boolean equals(Object o);
   public int hashCode();
   public String toString();
}
```

Passed To: javax.security.auth.Policy.getPermissions(), Subject.{doAs(), doAsPrivileged()}, SubjectDomainCombiner.SubjectDomainCombiner(), javax.security.auth.login.LoginContext.LoginContext(), javax.security.auth.spi.LoginModule.initialize()

Returned By: Subject.getSubject(), SubjectDomainCombiner.getSubject(), javax.security.auth.login.LoginContext.getSubject()

SubjectDomainCombiner Java 1.4

javax.security.auth

This class implements the DomainCombiner interface. It is used to merge permissions based on code source and code signers with permissions granted to the specified Subject. A SubjectDomainCombiner is created by the Subject.doAs() and Subject.doAsPrivileged() methods for use in by the AccessControlContext.

Object ─ SubjectDomainCombiner ··· DomainCombiner

```
public class SubjectDomainCombiner implements java.security.DomainCombiner {
// Public Constructors
   public SubjectDomainCombiner(Subject subject);
// Public Instance Methods
   public Subject getSubject();
// Methods Implementing DomainCombiner
   public java.security.ProtectionDomain[ ] combine(java.security.ProtectionDomain[ ] currentDomains,
                                                     java.security.ProtectionDomain[ ] assignedDomains);
}
```

Package javax.security.auth.callback Java 1.4

This package defines a mechanism that allows the low-level code of a javax.security.auth.spi.LoginModule to interact with the end user of an application to obtain a username, password, or other authentication-related information. The LoginModule sends messages and requests for information in the form of objects that implement the Callback interface. An application that wants to authenticate a user provides (via a javax.security.auth.login.LoginContext) a CallbackHandler object to convert these Callback objects into text or GUI-based interactions with the user. An application that want to provide a customized login interface must implement its own CallbackHandler. The CallbackHandler API consists of only a single method, but the implementation of that method can require a substantial amount of code. See the various Callback classes for directions on how a CallbackHandler should handle them.

Sun's J2SE SDK for Java 1.4 ships with two implementations of CallbackHandler, both in the package com.sun.security.auth.callback. Although these classes are not guaranteed to exist in all distributions, text-based applications may use the TextCallbackHandler, and GUI-based applications may use the DialogCallbackHandler. Programmers wanting to write a custom CallbackHandler may also find it useful to study the source code of these two existing handlers.

Interfaces:

```
public interface Callback;
public interface CallbackHandler;
```

Classes:

```
public class ChoiceCallback implements Callback, Serializable;
public class ConfirmationCallback implements Callback, Serializable;
public class LanguageCallback implements Callback, Serializable;
public class NameCallback implements Callback, Serializable;
public class PasswordCallback implements Callback, Serializable;
public class TextInputCallback implements Callback, Serializable;
public class TextOutputCallback implements Callback, Serializable;
```

Exception:

public class **UnsupportedCallbackException** extends Exception;

Callback **Java 1.4**

javax.security.auth.callback

This interface defines no methods but serves as a "marker interface" to identify the type of objects that can be passed to the handle() method of a CallbackHandler. All of the classes in this package, with the exception of UnsupportedCallbackException implement this interface.

```
public interface Callback {
}
```

Implementations: ChoiceCallback, ConfirmationCallback, LanguageCallback, NameCallback, PasswordCallback, TextInputCallback, TextOutputCallback

Passed To: CallbackHandler.handle(), UnsupportedCallbackException.UnsupportedCallbackException()

Returned By: UnsupportedCallbackException.getCallback()

JAAS

CallbackHandler **Java 1.4**

javax.security.auth.callback

A CallbackHandler is responsible for communication between the end-user of an application and the javax.security.auth.spi.LoginModule that is performing authentication of that user on behalf of the javax.security.auth.login.LoginContext instantiated by the application. When an application needs to authenticate a user, it creates a LoginContext and specifies a CallbackHandler object for that context. The underlying LoginModule uses the CallbackHandler to communicate with the end user—for example, prompting them to enter a name and password.

The LoginModule passes an array of objects that implement the Callback interface to the handle() method of CallbackHandler. The handle() method must determine the type of Callback object, and display the information and/or prompt for the input it represents. Different Callback classes have different purposes and must be handled differently. NameCallback and PasswordCallback are two of the most commonly used: they represent requests for the user's name and password. TextOutputCallback is also common: it represents a request to display a message (such as "Authentication Failed") to the user. See the descriptions of the individual Callback classes for information on how a CallbackHandler should handle them. CallbackHandler implementations are not required to support every type of Callback and my throw an UnsupportedCallbackException if passed a Callback object of a type they do not recognize or do not support.

The handle() method is passed an array of Callback objects. A CallbackHandler (such as a typical console-based handler) may choose to handle the Callback objects one at a time, prompting for and returning the user's input before moving on to the next. Or (for example in GUI-based handlers) it may choose to present all of the callbacks in a single unified "login dialog box". LoginModule implementations may, of course, call the handle() method more than once. Note, finally, that if a CallbackHandler implementation has knowledge of the user from some other source, it is allowed to handle certain callbacks automatically, such as automatically providing the user's name for a NameCallback.

Java installations may have a default CallbackHandler registered by setting the auth.login.defaultCallbackHandler security property to the name of the implementing class.

No such default is defined by the default security policy that ships with Sun's distribution of Java 1.4. Sun's Java 1.4 SDK does include CallbackHandler implementations to perform text-based and GUI-based communication in the classes TextCallbackHandler and DialogCallbackHandler in the com.sun.security.auth.callback package. Note that these are part of Sun's implementation, and are not part of the specification; they are not guaranteed to exist in all releases.

```
public interface CallbackHandler {
// Public Instance Methods
   public abstract void handle(Callback[ ] callbacks) throws java.io.IOException, UnsupportedCallbackException;
}
```

Passed To: javax.security.auth.login.LoginContext.LoginContext(), javax.security.auth.spi.LoginModule.initialize()

ChoiceCallback — Java 1.4

javax.security.auth.callback — *serializable*

A Callback of this type represents a request to display set of text choices and allow the user to select one or more of them. A CallbackHandler, should display the prompt returned by getPrompt() and also the strings returned by getChoices(). If allowMultipleSelections() is true, then it should allow the user to select zero or more; otherwise, it should only allow the user to select a single one. In either case, the CallbackHandler should also call getDefaultChoice() and make the choice at the returned index the default choice. When the user has made her selection, the CallbackHandler should pass the index of a single selection to setSelectedIndex(), or the indexes of multiple selections to setSelectedIndexes().

Object — ChoiceCallback
Callback, Serializable

```
public class ChoiceCallback implements Callback, Serializable {
// Public Constructors
   public ChoiceCallback(String prompt, String[ ] choices, int defaultChoice, boolean multipleSelectionsAllowed);
// Property Accessor Methods (by property name)
   public String[ ] getChoices();
   public int getDefaultChoice();
   public String getPrompt();
   public int[ ] getSelectedIndexes();
   public void setSelectedIndexes(int[ ] selections);
// Public Instance Methods
   public boolean allowMultipleSelections();
   public void setSelectedIndex(int selection);
}
```

ConfirmationCallback — Java 1.4

javax.security.auth.callback — *serializable*

A Callback of this type represents a request to ask the user a yes/no or multiple-choice question. A CallbackHandler should first call getPrompt() to obtain the text of the question. It should also call getMessageType() to determine the message type (INFORMATION, WARNING, or ERROR) and present the question to the user in a suitable manner based on that type.

Next, the CallbackHandler must determine the appropriate set of responses to the question. It does this by calling getOptionType(). The return values have the following meanings:

YES_NO_OPTION
: The CallbackHandler should allow the user to respond to the question with a "yes" or a "no" (or their localized equivalents).

YES_NO_CANCEL_OPTION
: The CallbackHandler should allow "yes", "no", and "cancel" (or their localized equivalents) responses.

OK_CANCEL_OPTION
: The CallbackHandler should allow "ok" and "cancel" (or their localized equivalents) responses.

UNSPECIFIED_OPTION
: The CallbackHandler should call getOptions() and use present all strings it returns as possible responses.

In each of these cases, the CallbackHandler should also call getDefaultOption() to determine which response should be presented as the default response. If getOptionType() returned UNSPECIFIED_OPTION, then getDefaultOption() returns an index into the array of options returned by getOptions(). Otherwise getDefaultOption() returns one of the constants YES, NO, OK, or CANCEL.

When the user has selected a response to the callback, the CallbackHandler should pass that response to setSelectedIndex(). The response value should be one of the constants YES, NO, OK, or CANCEL, or an index into the array of options returned by getOptions().

Object — ConfirmationCallback

Callback   Serializable

```
public class ConfirmationCallback implements Callback, Serializable {
// Public Constructors
   public ConfirmationCallback(int messageType, String[ ] options, int defaultOption);
   public ConfirmationCallback(int messageType, int optionType, int defaultOption);
   public ConfirmationCallback(String prompt, int messageType, String[ ] options, int defaultOption);
   public ConfirmationCallback(String prompt, int messageType, int optionType, int defaultOption);
// Public Constants
   public static final int CANCEL;                                   =2
   public static final int ERROR;                                    =2
   public static final int INFORMATION;                              =0
   public static final int NO;                                       =1
   public static final int OK;                                       =3
   public static final int OK_CANCEL_OPTION;                         =2
   public static final int UNSPECIFIED_OPTION;                       =-1
   public static final int WARNING;                                  =1
   public static final int YES;                                      =0
   public static final int YES_NO_CANCEL_OPTION;                     =1
   public static final int YES_NO_OPTION;                            =0
// Property Accessor Methods (by property name)
   public int getDefaultOption();
   public int getMessageType();
   public String[ ] getOptions();
   public int getOptionType();
   public String getPrompt();
```

```
    public int getSelectedIndex();
    public void setSelectedIndex(int selection);
}
```

LanguageCallback Java 1.4

javax.security.auth.callback *serializable*

This Callback class represents a request for the user's preferred language (as represented by a Locale object), which a LoginModule can use to localize things such as prompts and error messages in subsequent Callback objects. If a CallbackHandler already has knowledge of the user's preferred langauge, it is not required to prompt the user for this information and can simply pass an appropriate Locale object to setLocale().

Object — LanguageCallback
Callback, Serializable

```
public class LanguageCallback implements Callback, Serializable {
// Public Constructors
    public LanguageCallback();
// Public Instance Methods
    public java.util.Locale getLocale();                              default:null
    public void setLocale(java.util.Locale locale);
}
```

NameCallback Java 1.4

javax.security.auth.callback *serializable*

This Callback class represents a request for the username or other text that identifies the user to be authenticated. An interactive CallbackHandler should call getPrompt() and getDefaultName() and should display the returned prompt and optionally, the returned default name to the user. When the user has entered a name (or accepted the default name), the handler should pass the user's input to setName().

Object — NameCallback
Callback, Serializable

```
public class NameCallback implements Callback, Serializable {
// Public Constructors
    public NameCallback(String prompt);
    public NameCallback(String prompt, String defaultName);
// Public Instance Methods
    public String getDefaultName();
    public String getName();
    public String getPrompt();
    public void setName(String name);
}
```

PasswordCallback Java 1.4

javax.security.auth.callback *serializable*

This Callback class represents a request for a password. A CallbackHandler should handle it by displaying the prompt returned by getPrompt() and then allowing the user the enter a password. When the user has entered the password, it should pass the entered text to setPassword(). If isEchoOn() returns true, then the Handler should display the password as the user types it.

Object — PasswordCallback
Callback — Serializable

```
public class PasswordCallback implements Callback, Serializable {
// Public Constructors
   public PasswordCallback(String prompt, boolean echoOn);
// Public Instance Methods
   public void clearPassword();
   public char[ ] getPassword();
   public String getPrompt();
   public boolean isEchoOn();
   public void setPassword(char[ ] password);
}
```


TextInputCallback — Java 1.4

javax.security.auth.callback — *serializable*

A Callback of this type is a request to prompt the user for text input; it is essentially a generic version of NameCallback. A CallbackHandler should call getPrompt() and should display the returned prompt text to the user. It should then allow the user to enter text, and provide the option of selecting the default text returned by getDefaultText(). When the user has entered text (or selected the default text) it should pass the user's input to setText().

Object — TextInputCallback
Callback — Serializable

```
public class TextInputCallback implements Callback, Serializable {
// Public Constructors
   public TextInputCallback(String prompt);
   public TextInputCallback(String prompt, String defaultText);
// Public Instance Methods
   public String getDefaultText();
   public String getPrompt();
   public String getText();
   public void setText(String text);
}
```

TextOutputCallback — Java 1.4

javax.security.auth.callback — *serializable*

A Callback of this type represents a request to display text to the user. A callback handler should call getMessage() and display the returned string to the user. It should also call getMessageType() and use the returned value (which is one of the constants defined by the class) to indicate the type or severity of the information.

Object — TextOutputCallback
Callback — Serializable

```
public class TextOutputCallback implements Callback, Serializable {
// Public Constructors
```

```
    public TextOutputCallback(int messageType, String message);
// Public Constants
    public static final int ERROR;                                         =2
    public static final int INFORMATION;                                   =0
    public static final int WARNING;                                       =1
// Public Instance Methods
    public String getMessage();
    public int getMessageType();
}
```

UnsupportedCallbackException — Java 1.4

javax.security.auth.callback — *serializable checked*

CallbackHandler implementations may throw exceptions of this type from their handle() method if a Callback object passed to that method is of an unrecognized or unsupported type. Note that the offending Callback object must be passed to the constructor method.


```
public class UnsupportedCallbackException extends Exception {
// Public Constructors
    public UnsupportedCallbackException(Callback callback);
    public UnsupportedCallbackException(Callback callback, String msg);
// Public Instance Methods
    public Callback getCallback();
}
```

Thrown By: CallbackHandler.handle()

Package javax.security.auth.kerberos — Java 1.4

This package defines classes for use with Kerberos: a secure network authentication protocol. They are primarily of interest to system-level programmers writing Kerberos-based javax.security.auth.spi.LoginModule implementations. Developers writing Kerberos-enabled applications should use the org.ietf.jgss package. A full description of Kerberos is beyond the scope of this book; it is assumed that the reader is familiar with Kerberos authentication.

Classes:

```
public final class DelegationPermission extends java.security.BasicPermission implements Serializable;
public class KerberosKey implements javax.security.auth.Destroyable, javax.crypto.SecretKey;
public final class KerberosPrincipal implements java.security.Principal, Serializable;
public class KerberosTicket implements javax.security.auth.Destroyable,
                                       javax.security.auth.Refreshable, Serializable;
public final class ServicePermission extends java.security.Permission implements Serializable;
```

DelegationPermission — Java 1.4

javax.security.auth.kerberos — *serializable permission*

This java.security.Permission class governs the delegation of Kerberos tickets from a Kerberos principal to a Kerberos service for use on behalf of the original principal. The target name of a DelegationPermission consists of the principal names of two Kerberos services. The first specifies the service that is being delegated to, and the second specifies the service that is to be used by the first on behalf of the original Kerberos principal.


```
public final class DelegationPermission extends java.security.BasicPermission implements Serializable {
// Public Constructors
   public DelegationPermission(String principals);
   public DelegationPermission(String principals, String actions);
// Public Methods Overriding BasicPermission
   public boolean equals(Object obj);
   public int hashCode();
   public boolean implies(java.security.Permission p);
   public java.security.PermissionCollection newPermissionCollection();
}
```


KerberosKey — Java 1.4

javax.security.auth.kerberos — *serializable*

This class is a javax.crypto.SecretKey implementation that represents the secret key of a Kerberos principal. A Kerberos-based javax.security.auth.spi.LoginModule implementation instantiates a KerberosKey object and stores it in the private credential set of the authenticated Subject it creates.


```
public class KerberosKey implements javax.security.auth.Destroyable, javax.crypto.SecretKey {
// Public Constructors
   public KerberosKey(KerberosPrincipal principal, char[ ] password, String algorithm);
   public KerberosKey(KerberosPrincipal principal, byte[ ] keyBytes, int keyType, int versionNum);
// Public Instance Methods
   public final int getKeyType();
   public final KerberosPrincipal getPrincipal();
   public final int getVersionNumber();
// Methods Implementing Destroyable
   public void destroy() throws javax.security.auth.DestroyFailedException;
   public boolean isDestroyed();
// Methods Implementing Key
   public final String getAlgorithm();
   public final byte[ ] getEncoded();
   public final String getFormat();
// Public Methods Overriding Object
   public String toString();
}
```

KerberosPrincipal — Java 1.4

javax.security.auth.kerberos — *serializable*

This class represents a Kerberos principal, specified as a principal name with an optional realm. If no realm is specified in the name, the default realm (from the *krb5.conf* configuration file or from the java.security.krb5.realm system property) is used.

Object — KerberosPrincipal
Principal, Serializable

```
public final class KerberosPrincipal implements java.security.Principal, Serializable {
// Public Constructors
   public KerberosPrincipal(String name);
   public KerberosPrincipal(String name, int nameType);
// Public Constants
   public static final int KRB_NT_PRINCIPAL;                                  =1
   public static final int KRB_NT_SRV_HST;                                    =3
   public static final int KRB_NT_SRV_INST;                                   =2
   public static final int KRB_NT_SRV_XHST;                                   =4
   public static final int KRB_NT_UID;                                        =5
   public static final int KRB_NT_UNKNOWN;                                    =0
// Public Instance Methods
   public int getNameType();
   public String getRealm();
// Methods Implementing Principal
   public boolean equals(Object other);
   public String getName();
   public int hashCode();
   public String toString();
}
```

Passed To: KerberosKey.KerberosKey(), KerberosTicket.KerberosTicket()

Returned By: KerberosKey.getPrincipal(), KerberosTicket.{getClient(), getServer()}

KerberosTicket — Java 1.4

javax.security.auth.kerberos — *serializable*

This class represents a Kerberos ticket: a credential used to authenticate a Kerberos principal to some Kerberos-enabled network service. A Kerberos-based javax.security.auth.spi.LoginModule implementation will instantiate a KerberosTicket object and store it in the private credential set of the authenticated Subject it creates.

Object — KerberosTicket
Destroyable, Refreshable, Serializable

```
public class KerberosTicket implements javax.security.auth.Destroyable, javax.security.auth.Refreshable, Serializable {
// Public Constructors
   public KerberosTicket(byte[ ] asn1Encoding, KerberosPrincipal client, KerberosPrincipal server, byte[ ] sessionKey,
                         int keyType, boolean[ ] flags, java.util.Date authTime, java.util.Date startTime,
                         java.util.Date endTime, java.util.Date renewTill, java.net.InetAddress[ ] clientAddresses);
// Property Accessor Methods (by property name)
   public final java.util.Date getAuthTime();
   public final KerberosPrincipal getClient();
   public final java.net.InetAddress[ ] getClientAddresses();
   public boolean isCurrent();                                Implements:Refreshable
```

```
    public boolean isDestroyed();                                          Implements:Destroyable
    public final byte[ ] getEncoded();
    public final java.util.Date getEndTime();
    public final boolean[ ] getFlags();
    public final boolean isForwardable();
    public final boolean isForwarded();
    public final boolean isInitial();
    public final boolean isPostdated();
    public final boolean isProxiable();
    public final boolean isProxy();
    public final boolean isRenewable();
    public final java.util.Date getRenewTill();
    public final KerberosPrincipal getServer();
    public final javax.crypto.SecretKey getSessionKey();
    public final int getSessionKeyType();
    public final java.util.Date getStartTime();
// Methods Implementing Destroyable
    public void destroy() throws javax.security.auth.DestroyFailedException;
    public boolean isDestroyed();
// Methods Implementing Refreshable
    public boolean isCurrent();
    public void refresh() throws javax.security.auth.RefreshFailedException;
// Public Methods Overriding Object
    public String toString();
}
```

JAAS

ServicePermission — Java 1.4

javax.security.auth.kerberos — *serializable permission*

This java.security.Permission class protects access to the Kerberos tickets used to access a specified service. The target name of of a ServicePermission is the Kerberos principal name of the service. The action for the ServicePermission is either "initiate" for clients or "accept" for servers.


```
public final class ServicePermission extends java.security.Permission implements Serializable {
// Public Constructors
    public ServicePermission(String servicePrinicipal, String action);
// Public Methods Overriding Permission
    public boolean equals(Object obj);
    public String getActions();
    public int hashCode();
    public boolean implies(java.security.Permission p);
    public java.security.PermissionCollection newPermissionCollection();
}
```

Package javax.security.auth.login — Java 1.4

This package defines the LoginContext class which is one of the primary JAAS classes used by application programmers. To authenticate a user, an application creates a LoginContext object, specifying the application name (used to lookup the type of authentication required for that application in the Configuration) and usually specifying a javax.security.auth.callback.CallbackHandler for communication between the user and the underlying login modules. Next, the application calls the login() method of the LoginContext to perform the actual login. If this method returns without throwing a LoginException, then the user was successfully authenticated, and the getSubject() method of LoginContext returns a javax.security.auth.Subject representing the user. The code might look like this:

```
import javax.security.auth.*;
import javax.security.auth.callback.*;
import javax.security.auth.login.*;

// Get a default GUI-based CallbackHandler
CallbackHandler h = new com.sun.security.auth.callback.DialogCallbackHandler();

// Try to create a LoginContext for use with this application
LoginContext context;
try {
  context = new LoginContext("MyAppName", h);
}
catch(LoginException e) {
  System.err.println("LoginContext configuration error: " + e.getMessage());


  System.exit(-1);
}

// Now use that context to authenticate the user
try {
  context.login();
}
catch(LoginException e) {
  System.err.println("Authentication failed: " + e.getMessage());
  System.exit(-1);  // Or we could allow them to try again.
}

// If we get here, authentication was successful, so get the Subject that represents the authenticated user
Subject subject = context.getSubject();
```

In order to make this kind of authentication work correctly, a fair bit of configuration is required in various files in the jre/lib/security directory of the Java installation and possibly elsewhere. In particular, a login configuration file is required to specify which login modules are required to authenticate users for a particular application (some applications may require more than one). A description of how to do this is beyond the scope of this reference. See the Configuration class for a run-time representation of the login configuration information, however.

Classes:

public class **AppConfigurationEntry**;
public static class **AppConfigurationEntry.LoginModuleControlFlag**;
public abstract class **Configuration**;
public class **LoginContext**;

Exceptions:

public class **LoginException** extends java.security.GeneralSecurityException;
└ public class **AccountExpiredException** extends LoginException;

```
└ public class CredentialExpiredException extends LoginException;
└ public class FailedLoginException extends LoginException;
```

AccountExpiredException — Java 1.4

javax.security.auth.login — *serializable checked*

This exception signals that login failed because the user's account has expired.

Object ─ Throwable ─ Exception ─ GeneralSecurityException ─ LoginException ─ AccountExpiredException
(Throwable implements Serializable)

```
public class AccountExpiredException extends LoginException {
// Public Constructors
   public AccountExpiredException();
   public AccountExpiredException(String msg);
}
```

AppConfigurationEntry — Java 1.4

javax.security.auth.login

An instance of this class represents a login module to be used for user authentication for a particular application. It encapsulates three pieces of information: the class name of the javax.security.auth.spi.LoginModule implementation that is to be used, a "control flag" that specifies whether authentication by that module is required or optional, and a java.util.Map of arbitrary string name/value pairs of options for the login module.

```
public class AppConfigurationEntry {
// Public Constructors
   public AppConfigurationEntry(String loginModuleName,
                              AppConfigurationEntry.LoginModuleControlFlag controlFlag, java.util.Map options);
// Inner Classes
   public static class LoginModuleControlFlag;
// Public Instance Methods
   public AppConfigurationEntry.LoginModuleControlFlag getControlFlag();
   public String getLoginModuleName();
   public java.util.Map getOptions();
}
```

Returned By: Configuration.getAppConfigurationEntry()

AppConfigurationEntry.LoginModuleControlFlag — Java 1.4

javax.security.auth.login

This inner class defines a "control flag" type and four specific instances of that type. The following constants defined by this class specify whether a login module is required or optional:

REQUIRED
: Authentication by this module must be successful, or the overall login process will fail. However, even if authentication fails for this module, the LoginContext continues to attempt authentication with any other modules in the list. (This can disguise the source of the authentication failure from an attacker.)

REQUISITE
: Authentication by this module must be successful, or the overall login process will fail. If authentication fails for this module, the LoginContext does not try any further login modules.

SUFFICIENT
: Authentication by this module is not required, and the overall login process can still succeed if all REQUIRED and REQUISITE modules successfully authenticate the user. However, if authentication by this module does succeed, the LoginContext does not try any further login modules, but instead returns immediately.

OPTIONAL
: Authentication by this module is not required. Whether or not it succeeds, the LoginContext continues to with any other modules on the list.

```
public static class AppConfigurationEntry.LoginModuleControlFlag {
// No Constructor
// Public Constants
   public static final AppConfigurationEntry.LoginModuleControlFlag OPTIONAL;
   public static final AppConfigurationEntry.LoginModuleControlFlag REQUIRED;
   public static final AppConfigurationEntry.LoginModuleControlFlag REQUISITE;
   public static final AppConfigurationEntry.LoginModuleControlFlag SUFFICIENT;
// Public Methods Overriding Object
   public String toString();
}
```

Passed To: AppConfigurationEntry.AppConfigurationEntry()

Returned By: AppConfigurationEntry.getControlFlag()

Type Of: AppConfigurationEntry.LoginModuleControlFlag.{OPTIONAL, REQUIRED, REQUISITE, SUFFICIENT}

Configuration — Java 1.4

javax.security.auth.login

This abstract class is a representation of the system and user login configuration files. The static getConfiguration() method returns the global Configuration object, and the static setConfiguration() allows that global object to be replaced with some other implementation. The instance method refresh() causes a Configuration to re-read the underlying configuration files. getAppConfigurationEntry() is the key method: it returns an array of AppConfigurationEntry objects that represent the set of login modules to be used for applications with the specified name. LoginContext uses this class to determine which login modules to use to authenticate a user of the named application. Application programmers do not typically need to use this class themselves. See the documentation for your Java implementation for the syntax of the underlying login configuration files.

```
public abstract class Configuration {
// Protected Constructors
   protected Configuration();
// Public Class Methods
   public static Configuration getConfiguration();                     synchronized
   public static void setConfiguration(Configuration configuration);
// Public Instance Methods
   public abstract AppConfigurationEntry[ ] getAppConfigurationEntry(String applicationName);
   public abstract void refresh();
}
```

Passed To: Configuration.setConfiguration()

Returned By: Configuration.getConfiguration()

CredentialExpiredException — Java 1.4

javax.security.auth.login — *serializable checked*

This signals that a login failed because a credential (such as a password) has expired and is no longer valid.

Object ─ Throwable ─ Exception ─ GeneralSecurityException ─ LoginException ─ CredentialExpiredException
Serializable

```
public class CredentialExpiredException extends LoginException {
// Public Constructors
   public CredentialExpiredException();
   public CredentialExpiredException(String msg);
}
```

FailedLoginException — Java 1.4

javax.security.auth.login — *serializable checked*

This signals that login failed. Typically this is because an incorrect username, password, or other information was presented. Login modules that throw this exception may provide human-readable details through the getMessage() method.

Object ─ Throwable ─ Exception ─ GeneralSecurityException ─ LoginException ─ FailedLoginException
Serializable

```
public class FailedLoginException extends LoginException {
// Public Constructors
   public FailedLoginException();
   public FailedLoginException(String msg);
}
```

LoginContext — Java 1.4

javax.security.auth.login

This is one of the most important classes in the JAAS API for application programmers: it defines the login() method (and the corresponding logout() method) that allows an application to authenticate a user. Create a LoginContext object using one of the four public constructors. The constructor expects to be passed the name of the application, and, optionally, the javax.security.auth.Subject that is to be authenticated and a javax.security.auth.callback.CallbackHandler that is to be used for communication between the underlying login module (or modules) and the user. If no Subject is specified, then the LoginContext will instantiate a new one to represent the authenticated user. If a Subject is supplied, then the LoginContext adds new entries to its sets of principals and credentials. If no CallbackHandler is specified, then the LoginContext attempts to instantiate one using the class name specified by the auth.login.defaultCallbackHandler property in the system's security properties file.

Once a LoginContext is successfully created, you can authenticate a user simply by calling the login() method, and then calling getSubject() to obtain the Subject object that represents the authenticated user. When this Subject is no longer required, you can log them out by calling the logout() method.

```
public class LoginContext {
// Public Constructors
   public LoginContext(String name) throws LoginException;
   public LoginContext(String name, javax.security.auth.Subject subject) throws LoginException;
   public LoginContext(String name, javax.security.auth.callback.CallbackHandler callbackHandler)
       throws LoginException;
   public LoginContext(String name, javax.security.auth.Subject subject,
                       javax.security.auth.callback.CallbackHandler callbackHandler) throws LoginException;
// Public Instance Methods
   public javax.security.auth.Subject getSubject();
   public void login() throws LoginException;
   public void logout() throws LoginException;
}
```

LoginException — Java 1.4

javax.security.auth.login — *serializable checked*

This signals that something went wrong while creating a LoginContext or during the login or logout process. The subclasses of this class represent more specific exception types.

Object — Throwable — Exception — GeneralSecurityException — LoginException

Serializable

```
public class LoginException extends java.security.GeneralSecurityException {
// Public Constructors
   public LoginException();
   public LoginException(String msg);
}
```

Subclasses: AccountExpiredException, CredentialExpiredException, FailedLoginException

Thrown By: LoginContext.{login(), LoginContext(), logout()}, javax.security.auth.spi.LoginModule.{abort(), commit(), login(), logout()}

Package javax.security.auth.spi — Java 1.4

This package defines the "service provider interface" for JAAS: it defines a single LoginModule interface that must be implemented by developers of login modules.

Interface:

public interface **LoginModule**;

LoginModule — Java 1.4

javax.security.auth.spi

Developers of login modules to be used with the JAAS authentication API must implement this interface. Because this interface is not typically used by application developers, its methods are not documented here.

```
public interface LoginModule {
// Public Instance Methods
   public abstract boolean abort() throws javax.security.auth.login.LoginException;
   public abstract boolean commit() throws javax.security.auth.login.LoginException;
   public abstract void initialize(javax.security.auth.Subject subject,
                                   javax.security.auth.callback.CallbackHandler callbackHandler,
                                   java.util.Map sharedState, java.util.Map options);
```

```
    public abstract boolean login() throws javax.security.auth.login.LoginException;
    public abstract boolean logout() throws javax.security.auth.login.LoginException;
}
```

Package javax.security.auth.x500 — Java 1.4

This package defines classes for use with authentication schemes for on X.500 principals. Instances of these classes are designed to be stored in the principals and private credentials sets of Subject objects, and although application programmers may occasionally find the X500Principal class useful, they are primarily of interest to system-level programmers writing X.500-based javax.security.auth.spi.LoginModule implementations See also the java.security.cert package which contains a class representing an X.509 certificate.

Classes:

```
public final class X500Principal implements java.security.Principal, Serializable;
public final class X500PrivateCredential implements javax.security.auth.Destroyable;
```

JAAS

X500Principal — Java 1.4

javax.security.auth.x500 — *serializable*

This class implements the java.security.Principal interface for entities represented by X.500 distinguished names (such as "CN=David,O=davidflanagan.com,C=US"). The constructor methods can accept the distinguished name in string form or in binary encoded form. getName() returns the name in string form, using the format defined by one of the three constant values. The no-argument version of getName() (the one defined by the Principal interface) returns the distinguished name formatted as specified by RFC 2253. Finally, getEncoded() returns a binary-encoded form of the name.

Object — X500Principal

Principal, Serializable

```
public final class X500Principal implements java.security.Principal, Serializable {
// Public Constructors
    public X500Principal(java.io.InputStream is);
    public X500Principal(String name);
    public X500Principal(byte[ ] name);
// Public Constants
    public static final String CANONICAL;                    =[quot ]CANONICAL[quot ]
    public static final String RFC1779;                      =[quot ]RFC1779[quot ]
    public static final String RFC2253;                      =[quot ]RFC2253[quot ]
// Public Instance Methods
    public byte[ ] getEncoded();
    public String getName(String format);
// Methods Implementing Principal
    public boolean equals(Object o);
    public String getName();
    public int hashCode();
    public String toString();
}
```

Returned By: java.security.cert.X509Certificate.{getIssuerX500Principal(), getSubjectX500Principal()}, java.security.cert.X509CRL.getIssuerX500Principal()

X500PrivateCredential — Java 1.4

javax.security.auth.x500

This class associates a java.security.cert.X509Certificate with a java.security.PrivateKey for that certificate, and, optionally, the keystore alias used to retrieve the certificate and key from a java.security.KeyStore. The class defines methods to retrieve the certificate, key, and alias, and implements the methods of the javax.security.cert.Destroyable interface.

Object ─ X500PrivateCredential ··· Destroyable

```
public final class X500PrivateCredential implements javax.security.auth.Destroyable {
// Public Constructors
   public X500PrivateCredential(java.security.cert.X509Certificate cert, java.security.PrivateKey key);
   public X500PrivateCredential(java.security.cert.X509Certificate cert, java.security.PrivateKey key, String alias);
// Public Instance Methods
   public String getAlias();
   public java.security.cert.X509Certificate getCertificate();
   public java.security.PrivateKey getPrivateKey();
// Methods Implementing Destroyable
   public void destroy();
   public boolean isDestroyed();
}
```

CHAPTER 21

javax.xml.parsers, java.xml.transform, and Subpackages

JAXP

This chapter documents the javax.xml.parsers package and the javax.xml.transform package and its subpackages. These packages comprise the Java API for XML Processing, or JAXP. Before being integrated in Java 1.4, JAXP was available as a standard extension, which explains the "javax" prefix in the package names. The packages in this chapter are:

javax.xml.parsers
: This package defines parser classes that serve as a wrapper around underlying DOM and SAX XML parsers, and also defines factory classes that are used to obtain instances of those parser classes.

javax.xml.transform
: This package defines classes and interfaces for transforming the representation and content of an XML document with XSLT. It defines Source and Result interfaces to represent a source document and a result document. Sub-packages provide implementations of these classes that represent documents in different ways.

javax.xml.transform.dom
: This package implements the Source and Result interfaces that represent documents as DOM document trees.

javax.xml.transform.sax
: This package implements the Source and Result interfaces to represent documents as sequences of SAX parser events. It also defines other SAX-related transformation classes.

javax.xml.transform.stream
: This package implements the Source and Result interfaces that represent documents as streams of text.

Package javax.xml.parsers — Java 1.4

This package defines classes that represent XML parsers and factory classes for obtaining instances of those parser classes. DocumentBuilder is a DOM-based XML parser created from a DocumentBuilderFactory. SAXParser is a SAX-based XML parser created from a SAXParserFactory. Note that this package does not include parser implementations. Instead, it is an implementation-independent layer that supports "pluggable" XML parsers. Furthermore, this package does not define a DOM or SAX API for working with XML documents. The DOM API is defined in org.w3c.dom, and the SAX API is defined in org.xml.sax and its subpackages.

Classes:

public abstract class **DocumentBuilder**;
public abstract class **DocumentBuilderFactory**;
public abstract class **SAXParser**;
public abstract class **SAXParserFactory**;

Exception:

public class **ParserConfigurationException** extends Exception;

Errors:

public class **FactoryConfigurationError** extends Error;

DocumentBuilder — Java 1.4

javax.xml.parsers

This class defines a high-level API to an underlying DOM parser implementation. Obtain a DocumentBuilder from a DocumentBuilderFactory. After obtaining a DocumentBuilder, you can provide org.xml.sax.ErrorHandler and org.xml.sax.EntityResolver objects, if desired. (These classes are defined by the SAX API but are useful for DOM parsers as well.) You may also want to call isNamespaceAware() and isValidating() to ensure that the parser is configured with the features your application requires. Finally, use one of the parse() methods to read an XML document from a stream, file, URL, or org.xml.sax.InputSource object, parse that document, and convert it into a org.w3c.dom.Document tree. Note that DocumentBuilder objects are not typically thread-safe.

If you want to obtain an empty Document object (so that you can build the document tree from scratch, for example) call newDocument(). Or use getDOMImplementation() to obtain the org.w3c.dom.DOMImplementation object of the underlying DOM implementation from which you can also create an empty Document.

See the org.w3c.dom package for information on what you can do with a Document object once you have used a DocumentBuilder to create it.

```
public abstract class DocumentBuilder {
// Protected Constructors
   protected DocumentBuilder();
// Property Accessor Methods (by property name)
   public abstract org.w3c.dom.DOMImplementation getDOMImplementation();
   public abstract boolean isNamespaceAware();
   public abstract boolean isValidating();
// Public Instance Methods
   public abstract org.w3c.dom.Document newDocument();
   public abstract org.w3c.dom.Document parse(org.xml.sax.InputSource is) throws org.xml.sax.SAXException,
        java.io.IOException;
   public org.w3c.dom.Document parse(java.io.InputStream is) throws org.xml.sax.SAXException, java.io.IOException;
   public org.w3c.dom.Document parse(String uri) throws org.xml.sax.SAXException, java.io.IOException;
   public org.w3c.dom.Document parse(java.io.File f) throws org.xml.sax.SAXException, java.io.IOException;
   public org.w3c.dom.Document parse(java.io.InputStream is, String systemId) throws org.xml.sax.SAXException,
        java.io.IOException;
```

```
    public abstract void setEntityResolver(org.xml.sax.EntityResolver er);
    public abstract void setErrorHandler(org.xml.sax.ErrorHandler eh);
}
```

Returned By: DocumentBuilderFactory.newDocumentBuilder()

DocumentBuilderFactory — Java 1.4

javax.xml.parsers

A DocumentBuilderFactory is a factory class for creating DocumentBuilder objects. You can obtain a DocumentBuilderFactory by instantiating an implementation-specific subclass provided by a parser vendor, but it is much more common to simply call newInstance() to obtain an instance of the factory that has been configured as the default for the system. Once you have obtained a factory object, you can use the various set methods to configure the properties of the DocumentBuilder objects it will create. These methods allow you to specify whether the parsers created by the factory will:

- Coalesce CDATA sections with adjacent text nodes
- Expand entity references or leave them unexpanded in the document tree
- Omit XML comments from the document tree
- Omit ignorable whitespace from the document tree
- Handle XML namespaces correctly
- Validate XML documents against a DTD or other schema

In addition to the various implementation-independent set methods, you can also use setAttribute() pass an implementation-dependent named attribute to the underlying parser implementation. Once you have configured the factory object as desired, simply call newDocumentBuilder() to create a DocumentBuilder object with the all of the attributes you have specified. Note that DocumentBuilderFactory objects are not typically thread-safe.

The javax.xml.parsers package allows parser implementations to be "plugged in." This plugability is provided by the newInstance() method, which follows the following steps to determine which DocumentBuilderFactory implementation to use:

- If the javax.xml.parsers.DocumentBuilderFactory system property is defined, then the class specified by that property is used.
- Otherwise, if the *jre/lib/jaxp.properties* file exists in the Java distribution and contains a definition for the javax.xml.parsers.DocumentBuilderFactory property, then the class specified by that property is used.
- Otherwise, if any of the JAR files on the classpath includes a file named *META-INF/services/javax.xml.parsers.DocumentBuilderFactory*, then the class named in that file is used.
- Otherwise, a default implementation provided by the Java implementation is used.

```
public abstract class DocumentBuilderFactory {
// Protected Constructors
    protected DocumentBuilderFactory();
// Public Class Methods
    public static DocumentBuilderFactory newInstance() throws FactoryConfigurationError;
// Property Accessor Methods (by property name)
    public boolean isCoalescing();
```

JAXP

```
   public void setCoalescing(boolean coalescing);
   public boolean isExpandEntityReferences();
   public void setExpandEntityReferences(boolean expandEntityRef);
   public boolean isIgnoringComments();
   public void setIgnoringComments(boolean ignoreComments);
   public boolean isIgnoringElementContentWhitespace();
   public void setIgnoringElementContentWhitespace(boolean whitespace);
   public boolean isNamespaceAware();
   public void setNamespaceAware(boolean awareness);
   public boolean isValidating();
   public void setValidating(boolean validating);
// Public Instance Methods
   public abstract Object getAttribute(String name) throws IllegalArgumentException;
   public abstract DocumentBuilder newDocumentBuilder() throws ParserConfigurationException;
   public abstract void setAttribute(String name, Object value) throws IllegalArgumentException;
}
```

Returned By: DocumentBuilderFactory.newInstance()

FactoryConfigurationError — Java 1.4

javax.xml.parsers — *serializable error*

This signals a nonrecoverable problem instantiating a parser factory. This usually means that a pluggable parser implementation has been incorrectly plugged in and the newInstance() method cannot locate the specified factory implementation class.

Object — Throwable — Error — FactoryConfigurationError
Serializable

```
public class FactoryConfigurationError extends Error {
// Public Constructors
   public FactoryConfigurationError();
   public FactoryConfigurationError(Exception e);
   public FactoryConfigurationError(String msg);
   public FactoryConfigurationError(Exception e, String msg);
// Public Instance Methods
   public Exception getException();                                default:null
// Public Methods Overriding Throwable
   public String getMessage();                                     default:null
}
```

Thrown By: DocumentBuilderFactory.newInstance(), SAXParserFactory.newInstance()

ParserConfigurationException — Java 1.4

javax.xml.parsers — *serializable checked*

This exception signals a parser configuration problem that prevents a parser factory object from creating a parser object.

Object — Throwable — Exception — ParserConfigurationException
Serializable

```
public class ParserConfigurationException extends Exception {
// Public Constructors
   public ParserConfigurationException();
```

```
    public ParserConfigurationException(String msg);
}
```

Thrown By: DocumentBuilderFactory.newDocumentBuilder(), SAXParserFactory.{getFeature(), newSAXParser(), setFeature()}

SAXParser **Java 1.4**

javax.xml.parsers

The SAXParser class is a wrapper around an org.xml.sax.XMLReader class and is used to parse XML documents using the SAX version 2 API. Obtain a SAXParser from a SAXParserFactory. Call setProperty() if desired to set a property on the underlying parser. (See *http://www.saxproject.org* for a description of standard SAX properties and their values.) Finally, call one of the parse() methods to parse an XML document from a stream, file, URL, or org.xml.sax.InputSource. The SAX API is an event-driven one. A SAX parser does not build a document tree to describe an XML document like a DOM parser does. Instead, it describes the XML document to your application by invoking methods on an object the application provides. This is the purpose of the org.xml.sax.helpers.DefaultHandler object that is passed to the parse() method: you subclass this class to implement the methods you care about, and the parser will invoke those methods at appropriate times. For example, when the parser encounters an XML tag in a document, it parses the tag, and calls the startElement() method to tell you about it. And when it finds a run of plain text, it passes that text to the characters() method.

Instead of using one of the parse() methods of this class, you can also call getXMLReader() to obtain the underlying XMLReader object and work with it directly to parse the desired document. SAXParser objects are not typically thread-safe.

Note that the getParser() method as well as the parse() methods that take an org.xml.sax.HandlerBase object are based on the SAX version 1 API and should be avoided.

```
public abstract class SAXParser {
// Protected Constructors
    protected SAXParser();
// Property Accessor Methods (by property name)
    public abstract boolean isNamespaceAware();
    public abstract org.xml.sax.Parser getParser() throws org.xml.sax.SAXException;
    public abstract boolean isValidating();
    public abstract org.xml.sax.XMLReader getXMLReader() throws org.xml.sax.SAXException;
// Public Instance Methods
    public abstract Object getProperty(String name) throws org.xml.sax.SAXNotRecognizedException,
        org.xml.sax.SAXNotSupportedException;
    public void parse(java.io.File f, org.xml.sax.helpers.DefaultHandler dh) throws org.xml.sax.SAXException,
        java.io.IOException;
    public void parse(org.xml.sax.InputSource is, org.xml.sax.HandlerBase hb) throws org.xml.sax.SAXException,
        java.io.IOException;
    public void parse(org.xml.sax.InputSource is, org.xml.sax.helpers.DefaultHandler dh)
        throws org.xml.sax.SAXException, java.io.IOException;
    public void parse(java.io.InputStream is, org.xml.sax.helpers.DefaultHandler dh) throws org.xml.sax.SAXException,
        java.io.IOException;
    public void parse(java.io.InputStream is, org.xml.sax.HandlerBase hb) throws org.xml.sax.SAXException,
        java.io.IOException;
    public void parse(String uri, org.xml.sax.HandlerBase hb) throws org.xml.sax.SAXException, java.io.IOException;
    public void parse(String uri, org.xml.sax.helpers.DefaultHandler dh) throws org.xml.sax.SAXException,
        java.io.IOException;
```

```
    public void parse(java.io.File f, org.xml.sax.HandlerBase hb) throws org.xml.sax.SAXException, java.io.IOException;
    public void parse(java.io.InputStream is, org.xml.sax.HandlerBase hb, String systemId)
        throws org.xml.sax.SAXException, java.io.IOException;
    public void parse(java.io.InputStream is, org.xml.sax.helpers.DefaultHandler dh, String systemId)
        throws org.xml.sax.SAXException, java.io.IOException;
    public abstract void setProperty(String name, Object value) throws org.xml.sax.SAXNotRecognizedException,
        org.xml.sax.SAXNotSupportedException;
}
```

Returned By: SAXParserFactory.newSAXParser()

SAXParserFactory — Java 1.4

javax.xml.parsers

This class is a factory for SAXParser objects. Obtain a SAXParserFactory by calling the newInstance() method which instantiates the default SAXParserFactory subclass provided with your Java implementation, or instantiates some other SAXParserFactory that has been "plugged in."

Once you have a SAXParserFactory object, you can use setValidating() and setNamespaceAware() to specify whether the parsers it creates will be validating parsers or not and whether they will know how to handle XML namespaces. You may also call setFeature() to set a feature of the underlying parser implementation. See *http://www.saxproject.org* for the names of standard parser features that can be enabled and disabled with this method.

Once you have created and configured your factory object, simply call newSAXParser() to create a SAXParser object. Note that SAXParserFactory implementations are not typically thread-safe.

The javax.xml.parsers package allows parser implementations to be "plugged in." This plugability is provided by the newInstance() method, which follows the following steps to determine which SAXParserFactory subclass to use:

- If the javax.xml.parsers.SAXParserFactory system property is defined, then the class specified by that property is used.
- Otherwise, if the *jre/lib/jaxp.properties* file exists in the Java distribution and contains a definition for the javax.xml.parsers.SAXParserFactory property, then the class specified by that property is used.
- Otherwise, if any of the JAR files on the classpath includes a file named *META-INF/services/javax.xml.parsers.SAXParserFactory*, then the class named in that file is used.
- Otherwise, a default implementation provided by the Java platform is used.

```
public abstract class SAXParserFactory {
// Protected Constructors
    protected SAXParserFactory();
// Public Class Methods
    public static SAXParserFactory newInstance() throws FactoryConfigurationError;
// Public Instance Methods
    public abstract boolean getFeature(String name) throws ParserConfigurationException,
        org.xml.sax.SAXNotRecognizedException, org.xml.sax.SAXNotSupportedException;
    public boolean isNamespaceAware();
    public boolean isValidating();
    public abstract SAXParser newSAXParser() throws ParserConfigurationException, org.xml.sax.SAXException;
```

```
    public abstract void setFeature(String name, boolean value) throws ParserConfigurationException,
        org.xml.sax.SAXNotRecognizedException, org.xml.sax.SAXNotSupportedException;
    public void setNamespaceAware(boolean awareness);
    public void setValidating(boolean validating);
}
```

Returned By: SAXParserFactory.newInstance()

Package javax.xml.transform — Java 1.4

This package defines a high-level, implementation-independent API for using an XSLT engine or other document transformation system for transforming XML document content, and also for transforming XML documents from one form (such as a stream of text in a file) to anther form (such as a tree of DOM nodes). The Source interface is a very generic description of a document source. Three concrete implementations that represent documents in text form, as DOM trees, and as sequences of SAX parser events are defined in the three sub-packages of this package. The Result interface is a similarly high-level description of what form the source document should be transformed into. The three sub-packages define three Result implementations that represent XML documents as streams or files, as DOM trees, and as sequences of SAX parser events.

The TransformerFactory class represents the document transformation engine. The implementation provides a default factory that represents an XSLT engine. A TransformerFactory can be used to produce Templates objects that represent compiled XSL stylesheets (or other implementation-dependent forms of transformation instructions). Documents are actually transformed from Source to Result with a Transformer object, which is obtained from a Templates object, or directly from a TransformerFactory.

Interfaces:

```
public interface ErrorListener;
public interface Result;
public interface Source;
public interface SourceLocator;
public interface Templates;
public interface URIResolver;
```

Classes:

```
public class OutputKeys;
public abstract class Transformer;
public abstract class TransformerFactory;
```

Exceptions:

```
public class TransformerException extends Exception;
  └ public class TransformerConfigurationException extends TransformerException;
```

Errors:

```
public class TransformerFactoryConfigurationError extends Error;
```

ErrorListener — Java 1.4

javax.xml.transform

This interface defines methods that Transformer and TransformerFactory use for reporting warnings, errors, and fatal errors to an application. To use an ErrorListener, an application must implement this interface and pass an implementing object to the setErrorListener() method of Transformer or TransformerFactory. The argument to each method of this interface is a TransformerException object, and the implementation of these methods can throw that exception if it chooses, or it can simply log the warning or error in some way and return. A Transformer or TransformerFactory is not required to continue processing after reporting a non-recoverable error with an invocation of the fatalError() method.

If you are familiar with the SAX API for parsing XML documents, you'll recognize that this interface is very similar to org.xml.sax.ErrorHandler.

```
public interface ErrorListener {
// Public Instance Methods
   public abstract void error(TransformerException exception) throws TransformerException;
   public abstract void fatalError(TransformerException exception) throws TransformerException;
   public abstract void warning(TransformerException exception) throws TransformcrExccption;
}
```

Passed To: Transformer.setErrorListener(), TransformerFactory.setErrorListener()

Returned By: Transformer.getErrorListener(), TransformerFactory.getErrorListener()

OutputKeys — Java 1.4

javax.xml.transform

This class defines string constants that hold the names of the attributes of an <xsl:output> tag in an XSLT stylesheet. These are also legal key values for the Properties object returned by Templates.getOutputProperties() and passed to Transformer.setOutputProperties().

```
public class OutputKeys {
// No Constructor
// Public Constants
   public static final String CDATA_SECTION_ELEMENTS;          =[quot ]cdata-section-elements[quot ]
   public static final String DOCTYPE_PUBLIC;                  =[quot ]doctype-public[quot ]
   public static final String DOCTYPE_SYSTEM;                  =[quot ]doctype-system[quot ]
   public static final String ENCODING;                        =[quot ]encoding[quot ]
   public static final String INDENT;                          =[quot ]indent[quot ]
   public static final String MEDIA_TYPE;                      =[quot ]media-type[quot ]
   public static final String METHOD;                          =[quot ]method[quot ]
   public static final String OMIT_XML_DECLARATION;            =[quot ]omit-xml-declaration[quot ]
   public static final String STANDALONE;                      =[quot ]standalone[quot ]
   public static final String VERSION;                         =[quot ]version[quot ]
}
```

Result — Java 1.4

javax.xml.transform

This interface represents, in a very general way, the result of an XML transformation. setSystemId() specifies the system identifier of the result as a URL. This is useful when the result is to be written as a file, but it can also be useful for error reporting and for resolution of relative URLs even when the Result object does not represent a file. All other methods related to the result are the responsibility of the concrete implementation of this interface. See the DOMResult, SAXResult and StreamResult implementations in the three subpackages of this package.

```
public interface Result {
// Public Constants
   public static final String                         = [quot ] javax.xml.transform.disable-output-escaping [quot ]
       PI_DISABLE_OUTPUT_ESCAPING;
   public static final String                         = [quot ] javax.xml.transform.enable-output-escaping [quot ]
       PI_ENABLE_OUTPUT_ESCAPING;
// Public Instance Methods
   public abstract String getSystemId();
   public abstract void setSystemId(String systemId);
}
```

Implementations: javax.xml.transform.dom.DOMResult, javax.xml.transform.sax.SAXResult, javax.xml.transform.stream.StreamResult

Passed To: Transformer.transform(), javax.xml.transform.sax.TransformerHandler.setResult()

Source — Java 1.4

javax.xml.transform

This interface represents, in a very general way, the source of an XML document. setSystemId() specifies the system identifier of the document in the form of a URL. This is useful for resolving relative URLs and for error reporting even when the document is not read directly from a URL. All other methods related to the document source are the responsibility of the concrete implementation of this interface. See the DOMSource, SAXSource and StreamSource implementations in the three sub-packages of this package.

JAXP

```
public interface Source {
// Public Instance Methods
   public abstract String getSystemId();
   public abstract void setSystemId(String systemId);
}
```

Implementations: javax.xml.transform.dom.DOMSource, javax.xml.transform.sax.SAXSource, javax.xml.transform.stream.StreamSource

Passed To: Transformer.transform(), TransformerFactory.{getAssociatedStylesheet(), newTemplates(), newTransformer()}, javax.xml.transform.sax.SAXSource.sourceToInputSource(), javax.xml.transform.sax.SAXTransformerFactory.{newTransformerHandler(), newXMLFilter()}

Returned By: TransformerFactory.getAssociatedStylesheet(), URIResolver.resolve()

SourceLocator — Java 1.4

javax.xml.transform

This interface defines methods that return the system and public identifiers of an XML document, and return a line number and column number within that document. SourceLocator objects are used with TransformerException and TransformerConfigurationException objects to specify the location in an XML file at which the exception occurred. Note, however that system and public identifiers are not always available for a document, and so getSystemId() and getPublicId() may return null. Also, a Transformer is not required to track line and column numbers precisely, or at all, so getLineNumber() and getColumnNumber() may return –1 to indicate that line and column number information is not available. If they return a value other than –1, it should be considered an approximation to the actual value. Note that lines and columns within a document are numbered starting with 1, not with 0.

If you are familiar with the SAX API for parsing XML, you'll recognize this interface as a renamed version of org.xml.sax.Locator.

```
public interface SourceLocator {
// Public Instance Methods
   public abstract int getColumnNumber();
   public abstract int getLineNumber();
   public abstract String getPublicId();
   public abstract String getSystemId();
}
```

Implementations: javax.xml.transform.dom.DOMLocator

Passed To: TransformerConfigurationException.TransformerConfigurationException(), TransformerException.{setLocator(), TransformerException()}

Returned By: TransformerException.getLocator()

Templates **Java 1.4**

javax.xml.transform

This interface represents a set of transformation instructions for transforming a Source document into a Result document. The javax.xml.transform package is theoretically independent of type of transformation, but in practice, an object of this type always represents the compiled form of an XSLT stylesheet. Obtain a Templates object from a TransformerFactory object, or with a javax.xml.transform.sax.TemplatesHandler. Once you have a Templates object, you can use the newTransformer() method to create a Transformer object for applying the templates to a Source to produce a Result document.

getOutputProperties() returns a java.util.Properties object that defines name/value pairs specifying details about how a textual version of the Result document should be produced. These properties are specified in an XSLT stylesheet with the <xsl:output> element. The constants defined by the OutputKeys are legal output property names. The returned Properties object contains explicitly properties directly, and contains default values in a parent Properties object. This means that if you query a property value with getProperty(), you'll get an explicitly specified value of a default value. On the other hand, if you query a property with the get() method (inherited by Properties from its superclass) you'll get a property value if it was explictly specified in the stylesheet, or null if it was not specified. The returned Properties object is a clone of the internal value, so you can modify it (before passing it to the setOutputProperties() method of a Transformer object, for example) without affecting the Templates object.

Templates implementations are required to be thread-safe. A Templates object can be used to create any number of Transformer objects.

```
public interface Templates {
// Public Instance Methods
   public abstract java.util.Properties getOutputProperties();
   public abstract Transformer newTransformer() throws TransformerConfigurationException;
}
```

Passed To: javax.xml.transform.sax.SAXTransformerFactory.{newTransformerHandler(), newXMLFilter()}

Returned By: TransformerFactory.newTemplates(), javax.xml.transform.sax.TemplatesHandler.getTemplates()

Transformer **Java 1.4**

javax.xml.transform

Objects of this type are used to transform a Source document into a Result document. Obtain a Transformer object from a TransformerFactory object, from a Templates object created by a TransformerFactory, or from a TransformerHandler object created by a SAXTransformer-Factory (these last two types are from the javax.xml.transform.sax package).

Once you have a Transformer object, you may need to configure it before using it to transform documents. setErrorListener() and setURIResolver() allow you to specify ErrorListener and URLResolver object that the Transformer can use. setOutputProperty() and setOutputProperties() allow you to specify name/value pairs that affect the text formatting of the Result document (if that document is written out in text format). OutputKeys defines constants that represent the set of standard output property names. The output properties you specify with these methods override any output properties specified (with an <xsl:output> tag) in the Templates object. Use setParameter() to supply values for any top-level parameters defined (with <xsl:param> tags) in the stylesheet. Note that if the name of any such parameter is a qualified name, then it appears in the stylesheet with a namespace prefix. You can't use the prefix with the setParameter() method, however, and you must instead specify the parameter name using the URI of the namespace within curly braces followed by the local name. If no namespace is involved, then you can just use the simple name of the parameter with no curly braces or URIs.

Once you have created and configured a Transformer object, use the transform() method to perform a document transformation. This method transforms the specified Source document and creates the transformed document specified by the Result object.

Transformer implementations are not typically thread-safe. You can reuse a Transformer object and call transform() any number of times (just not concurrently). The output properties and parameters you specify are not changed by calling the transform() method and can be reused.

```
public abstract class Transformer {
// Protected Constructors
   protected Transformer();
// Property Accessor Methods (by property name)
   public abstract ErrorListener getErrorListener();
   public abstract void setErrorListener(ErrorListener listener) throws IllegalArgumentException;
   public abstract java.util.Properties getOutputProperties();
   public abstract void setOutputProperties(java.util.Properties oformat) throws IllegalArgumentException;
   public abstract URIResolver getURIResolver();
   public abstract void setURIResolver(URIResolver resolver);
// Public Instance Methods
   public abstract void clearParameters();
   public abstract String getOutputProperty(String name) throws IllegalArgumentException;
   public abstract Object getParameter(String name);
   public abstract void setOutputProperty(String name, String value) throws IllegalArgumentException;
   public abstract void setParameter(String name, Object value);
   public abstract void transform(Source xmlSource, Result outputTarget) throws TransformerException;
}
```

Returned By: Templates.newTransformer(), TransformerFactory.newTransformer(), javax.xml.transform.sax.TransformerHandler.getTransformer()

TransformerConfigurationException — Java 1.4

javax.xml.transform — *serializable checked*

This exception signals a problem creating a Transformer object. This may occur, for example, if there is a syntax error in the XSL stylesheet that contains the transformation instructions. Use the inherited getLocator() method to obtain a SourceLocator that describes the document location at which the exception occurred.

```
Object ─ Throwable ─ Exception ─ TransformerException ─ TransformerConfigurationException
            ⋮
        Serializable
```

```
public class TransformerConfigurationException extends TransformerException {
// Public Constructors
   public TransformerConfigurationException();
   public TransformerConfigurationException(Throwable e);
   public TransformerConfigurationException(String msg);
   public TransformerConfigurationException(String message, SourceLocator locator);
   public TransformerConfigurationException(String msg, Throwable e);
   public TransformerConfigurationException(String message, SourceLocator locator, Throwable e);
}
```

Thrown By: Templates.newTransformer(), TransformerFactory.{getAssociatedStylesheet(), newTemplates(), newTransformer()}, javax.xml.transform.sax.SAXTransformerFactory.{newTemplatesHandler(), newTransformerHandler(), newXMLFilter()}

TransformerException — Java 1.4

javax.xml.transform — ***serializable checked***

This exception signals a problem while reading or transforming a document. Call getLocator() to obtain a SourceLocator object that describes the document location where the exception occurred.

```
Object ─ Throwable ─ Exception ─ TransformerException
            ⋮
        Serializable
```

```
public class TransformerException extends Exception {
// Public Constructors
   public TransformerException(String message);
   public TransformerException(Throwable e);
   public TransformerException(String message, Throwable e);
   public TransformerException(String message, SourceLocator locator);
   public TransformerException(String message, SourceLocator locator, Throwable e);
// Public Instance Methods
   public Throwable getException();
   public String getLocationAsString();
   public SourceLocator getLocator();
   public String getMessageAndLocation();
   public void setLocator(SourceLocator location);
// Public Methods Overriding Throwable
   public Throwable getCause();
   public Throwable initCause(Throwable cause);                    synchronized
   public void printStackTrace();
   public void printStackTrace(java.io.PrintStream s);
   public void printStackTrace(java.io.PrintWriter s);
}
```

Subclasses: TransformerConfigurationException

Passed To: ErrorListener.{error(), fatalError(), warning()}

Thrown By: ErrorListener.{error(), fatalError(), warning()}, Transformer.transform(), URIResolver.resolve()

TransformerFactory Java 1.4

javax.xml.transform

An instance of this abstract class represents a document "transformation engine" such as an XSLT processor. A TransformerFactory is used to create Transformer objects that perform document transformations, and can also be used to process transformation instructions (such as XSLT stylesheets) into compiled Templates objects.

Obtain a TransformerFactory instance by calling the static newInstance() method. newInstance() returns an instance of the default implementation for your Java installation, or, if the system property javax.xml.transform.TransformerFactory is set, then it returns an instance of the implementation class named by that property. The default TransformerFactory implementation provided with the Java distribution transforms XML documents using XSL stylesheets.

You can configure a TransformerFactory instance by calling setErrorListener() and setURIResolver() to specify an ErrorListener object and a URIResolver object to be used by the factory when reading and parsing XSL stylesheets. The setAttribute() and getAttribute() methods can be used to set and query implementation-dependent attributes of the transformation engine. The default engine supplied by Sun does not define any attributes. The getFeature() method is used to test whether the factory supports a given feature. For uniqueness, feature names are expressed as URIs, and each of the Source and Result implementations defined in the three subpackages of this package define a FEATURE constant that specifies a URL that you can use to test whether a TransformerFactory supports that particular Source or Result type.

Once you have obtained and configured your TransformerFactory object, you can use it in several ways. If you call the newTransformer() method that takes no arguments, you'll obtain a Transformer object that transforms the format or representation of an XML document without transforming its content. For example, you could use a Transformer created in this way to transform a DOM tree (represented by a javax.xml.transform.dom.DOMSource object) to a stream of XML text stored in a file named by a javax.xml.transform.stream.StreamResult.

Another way to use a TransformerFactory is to call the newTemplates() method, passing in a Source object that represents an XSL stylesheet. This produces a Templates object, which you can use to obtain a Transformer object that applies the stylesheet to transform document content. Alternatively, if you do not plan to create more than one Transformer object from the Templates object, you can combine the two steps and simply pass the Source object representing the stylesheet to the one-argument version of newTransformer().

XML documents may include references to XSL stylesheets in the form of an xml-stylesheet processing instruction. The getAssociatedStylesheet() method reads the XML document represented by a Source object and returns a new Source object that represents the stylesheet (or the concatenation of all the stylesheets) contained in that document that match the media, title, and charset constraints defined by the other three parameters (which may be null). If you want to process an XML document using the stylesheet that it defines itself, use this method to obtain a Source object that you can pass to newTransformer() to create the Transformer object that you can use to transform the document.

Typically, TransformerFactory implementations are not thread-safe.

```
public abstract class TransformerFactory {
// Protected Constructors
```

```
  protected TransformerFactory();
// Public Class Methods
  public static TransformerFactory newInstance() throws TransformerFactoryConfigurationError;
// Public Instance Methods
  public abstract Source getAssociatedStylesheet(Source source, String media, String title, String charset)
      throws TransformerConfigurationException;
  public abstract Object getAttribute(String name) throws IllegalArgumentException;
  public abstract ErrorListener getErrorListener();
  public abstract boolean getFeature(String name);
  public abstract URIResolver getURIResolver();
  public abstract Templates newTemplates(Source source) throws TransformerConfigurationException;
  public abstract Transformer newTransformer() throws TransformerConfigurationException;
  public abstract Transformer newTransformer(Source source) throws TransformerConfigurationException;
  public abstract void setAttribute(String name, Object value) throws IllegalArgumentException;
  public abstract void setErrorListener(ErrorListener listener) throws IllegalArgumentException;
  public abstract void setURIResolver(URIResolver resolver);
}
```

Subclasses: javax.xml.transform.sax.SAXTransformerFactory

Returned By: TransformerFactory.newInstance()

TransformerFactoryConfigurationError — Java 1.4

javax.xml.transform — *serializable error*

This error class signals a fatal problem while creating a TransformerFactory. It usually signals a configuration problem, such as the system property javax.xml.transform.TransformerFactory has a value that is not a valid classname, or that the class path does not contain the specified factory implementation class.

Object — Throwable — Error — TransformerFactoryConfigurationError
Throwable ··· Serializable

```
public class TransformerFactoryConfigurationError extends Error {
// Public Constructors
  public TransformerFactoryConfigurationError();
  public TransformerFactoryConfigurationError(String msg);
  public TransformerFactoryConfigurationError(Exception e);
  public TransformerFactoryConfigurationError(Exception e, String msg);
// Public Instance Methods
  public Exception getException();                                    default:null
// Public Methods Overriding Throwable
  public String getMessage();                                         default:null
}
```

Thrown By: TransformerFactory.newInstance()

URIResolver — Java 1.4

javax.xml.transform

This interface allows an application to tell a Transformer how to resolve the URIs that appear in an XSLT stylesheet. If you pass a URIResolver to the setURIResolver() method of a Transformer or TransformerFactory, and then the Transformer or TransformerFactory encounters a URI, it first passes that URI, along with the base URI to the resolve() method of the URIResolver. If resolve() returns a Source object, then the Transformer will use that Source. If a Transformer or TransformerFactory has no URIResolver registered, or if the resolve() method returns null, then the transformer or factory will attempt to resolve the URI itself.

```
public interface URIResolver {
// Public Instance Methods
   public abstract Source resolve(String href, String base) throws TransformerException;
}
```

Passed To: Transformer.setURIResolver(), TransformerFactory.setURIResolver()

Returned By: Transformer.getURIResolver(), TransformerFactory.getURIResolver()

Package javax.xml.transform.dom — Java 1.4

This package contains Source and Result implementations that work with DOM document trees and subtrees.

Interfaces:

public interface **DOMLocator** extends javax.xml.transform.SourceLocator;

Classes:

public class **DOMResult** implements javax.xml.transform.Result;
public class **DOMSource** implements javax.xml.transform.Source;

DOMLocator — Java 1.4

javax.xml.transform.dom

This class extends SourceLocator to define a method for retrieving a DOM Node object, which is typically used to indicate the source of an error in the transformation process. See SourceLocator and TransformerException.

SourceLocator ·· DOMLocator

```
public interface DOMLocator extends javax.xml.transform.SourceLocator {
// Public Instance Methods
   public abstract org.w3c.dom.Node getOriginatingNode();
}
```

DOMResult — Java 1.4

javax.xml.transform.dom

This class is a Result implementation that writes XML content by generating a DOM tree to represent that content. If you pass an org.w3c.dom.Node to the constructor or to setNode(), the DOMResult will create the result tree as a child of the specified node (which should typically be a Document or Element node). If you do not specify a node, the DOMResult will create a new Document node when it creates the result tree. You can retrieve this Document with getNode().

Object — DOMResult ·· Result

```
public class DOMResult implements javax.xml.transform.Result {
// Public Constructors
   public DOMResult();
   public DOMResult(org.w3c.dom.Node node);
   public DOMResult(org.w3c.dom.Node node, String systemID);
```

```
// Public Constants
   public static final String FEATURE;          = [quot ] http://javax.xml.transform.dom.DOMResult/feature [quot ]
// Public Instance Methods
   public org.w3c.dom.Node getNode();                                                              default:null
   public void setNode(org.w3c.dom.Node node);
// Methods Implementing Result
   public String getSystemId();                                                                    default:null
   public void setSystemId(String systemId);
}
```

DOMSource — Java 1.4

javax.xml.transform.dom

This class is a Source implementation that reads an XML document from a DOM document tree or subtree. Pass the org.w3c.dom.Node object that represents the root of the tree or subtree to the constructor or to setNode(). When possible, it is also useful to provide a system id (a filename or URL) for use in error messages and for resolving relative URLs contained in the document.

Object — DOMSource ··· Source

```
public class DOMSource implements javax.xml.transform.Source {
// Public Constructors
   public DOMSource();
   public DOMSource(org.w3c.dom.Node n);
   public DOMSource(org.w3c.dom.Node node, String systemID);
// Public Constants
   public static final String FEATURE;          = [quot ] http://javax.xml.transform.dom.DOMSource/feature [quot ]
// Public Instance Methods
   public org.w3c.dom.Node getNode();                                                              default:null
   public void setNode(org.w3c.dom.Node node);
// Methods Implementing Source
   public String getSystemId();                                                                    default:null
   public void setSystemId(String baseID);
}
```

Package javax.xml.transform.sax — Java 1.4

This package defines Source and Result implementations that work with SAX events. In addition, it includes an extension to the TransformerFactory class that has additional methods for returning TemplatesHandler and TransformerHandler objects. These objects implement SAX handler interfaces and are able to work with a SAX parser object to turn a series of SAX parse events into a Templates object or into a Result document. SAXSource and SAXResult adapt the org.xml.sax framework for use in the javax.xml.transform framework. By contrast, SAXTransformerFactory, TemplatesHandler, and TransformerHandler adapt the javax.xml.transform framework for use within the org.xml.sax parsing framework.

Interfaces:

```
public interface TemplatesHandler extends org.xml.sax.ContentHandler;
public interface TransformerHandler
      extends org.xml.sax.ContentHandler, org.xml.sax.DTDHandler, org.xml.sax.ext.LexicalHandler;
```

Classes:

public class **SAXResult** implements javax.xml.transform.Result;
public class **SAXSource** implements javax.xml.transform.Source;
public abstract class **SAXTransformerFactory** extends javax.xml.transform.TransformerFactory;

SAXResult **Java 1.4**

javax.xml.transform.sax

This class is a Result implementation that describes the content of a transformed document by triggering the methods of the specified ContentHandler. That is, a SAXResult acts like a org.xml.sax.XMLReader object, invoking the methods of the specified org.xml.sax.ContentHandler object as it parses the transformed document. You may also provide a org.xml.sax.ext.LexicalHandler object whose methods will be invoked by the SAXResult by calling setLexicalHandler(), or by supplying a ContentHandler object that also implements the LexicalHandler interface.

Object — SAXResult ··· Result

```
public class SAXResult implements javax.xml.transform.Result {
// Public Constructors
   public SAXResult();
   public SAXResult(org.xml.sax.ContentHandler handler);
// Public Constants
   public static final String FEATURE;          = [quot ] http://javax.xml.transform.sax.SAXResult/feature [quot ]
// Public Instance Methods
   public org.xml.sax.ContentHandler getHandler();                                default:null
   public org.xml.sax.ext.LexicalHandler getLexicalHandler();                     default:null
   public void setHandler(org.xml.sax.ContentHandler handler);
   public void setLexicalHandler(org.xml.sax.ext.LexicalHandler handler);
// Methods Implementing Result
   public String getSystemId();                                                   default:null
   public void setSystemId(String systemId);
}
```

SAXSource **Java 1.4**

javax.xml.transform.sax

This class is a Source implementation that describes a document represented as a series of SAX event method calls. A SAXSource requires an org.xml.sax.InputSource object that describes the stream to parse, and may optionally specify the org.xml.sax.XMLReader or org.xml.sax.XMLFilter that generates the SAX events. (If no XMLReader or XMLFilter is specified, then the Transformer object will create a default XMLReader.) Note that since an InputSource is required, a SAXSource does not behave significantly differently than a StreamSource unless an XMLFilter is used.

SAXSource also has one static method, sourceToInputSource(), which returns a SAX InputSource method derived from the specified Source object, or null if the specified Source cannot be converted to an InputSource.

Object — SAXSource ··· Source

```
public class SAXSource implements javax.xml.transform.Source {
// Public Constructors
   public SAXSource();
   public SAXSource(org.xml.sax.InputSource inputSource);
```

```
   public SAXSource(org.xml.sax.XMLReader reader, org.xml.sax.InputSource inputSource);
// Public Constants
   public static final String FEATURE;          = [quot ] http://javax.xml.transform.sax.SAXSource/feature [quot ]
// Public Class Methods
   public static org.xml.sax.InputSource sourceToInputSource(javax.xml.transform.Source source);
// Public Instance Methods
   public org.xml.sax.InputSource getInputSource();                                   default:null
   public org.xml.sax.XMLReader getXMLReader();                                       default:null
   public void setInputSource(org.xml.sax.InputSource inputSource);
   public void setXMLReader(org.xml.sax.XMLReader reader);
// Methods Implementing Source
   public String getSystemId();                                                       default:null
   public void setSystemId(String systemId);
}
```

SAXTransformerFactory — Java 1.4

javax.xml.transform.sax

This class extends TransformerFactory to define additional factory methods that are useful when working with documents that are represented as sequences of SAX events. Pass the FEATURE constant to the getFeature() method of your TransformerFactory object to determine whether the newTemplatesHandler() and newTransformerHandler() methods are supported and whether it is safe to cast your TransformerFactory object to a SAXTransformerFactory. Use the FEATURE_XMLFILTER constant with getFeature() to determine if the newXMLFilter() methods are also supported.

newTemplatesHandler() returns a TemplatesHandler object that you can use as an org.xml.sax.ContentHandler object to receive SAX events generated by a SAX parser and transform those events into a Templates object.

The newTransformerHandler() methods are similar: they return a TransformerHandler object that can receive SAX events and representing a source document and transform them into a Result document. The no-argument version of newTransformerHandler() creates a TransformerHandler that simply modifies the form of the document without applying a stylesheet to its content. The other two versions of newTransformerHandler() use a stylesheet specified either as a Source or Templates object.

The newXMLFilter() methods, if supported, return an org.xml.sax.XMLFilter object that can acts as both a sink and a source of SAX events and filters those events by applying the transformation instructions specified by the Templates or Source objects.

Object — TransformerFactory — SAXTransformerFactory

```
public abstract class SAXTransformerFactory extends javax.xml.transform.TransformerFactory {
// Protected Constructors
   protected SAXTransformerFactory();
// Public Constants
   public static final String        = [quot ] http://javax.xml.transform.sax.SAXTransformerFactory/feature [quot ]
      FEATURE;
   public static final String   = [quot ] http://javax.xml.transform.sax.SAXTransformerFactory/feature/xmlfilter [quot ]
      FEATURE_XMLFILTER;
// Public Instance Methods
   public abstract TemplatesHandler newTemplatesHandler() throws
      javax.xml.transform.TransformerConfigurationException;
```

```
    public abstract TransformerHandler newTransformerHandler() throws
        javax.xml.transform.TransformerConfigurationException;
    public abstract TransformerHandler newTransformerHandler(javax.xml.transform.Source src)
        throws javax.xml.transform.TransformerConfigurationException;
    public abstract TransformerHandler newTransformerHandler(javax.xml.transform.Templates templates)
        throws javax.xml.transform.TransformerConfigurationException;
    public abstract org.xml.sax.XMLFilter newXMLFilter(javax.xml.transform.Source src)
        throws javax.xml.transform.TransformerConfigurationException;
    public abstract org.xml.sax.XMLFilter newXMLFilter(javax.xml.transform.Templates templates)
        throws javax.xml.transform.TransformerConfigurationException;
}
```

TemplatesHandler — Java 1.4

javax.xml.transform.sax

This interface extends org.xml.sax.ContentHandler and adds a getTemplates() method. An object that implements this interface can be used to receive method calls from some source of SAX events and process those events (as an XSL stylesheet) into a Templates object. Obtain a TemplatesHandler from a SAXTransformerFactory. Register it with the setContentHandler() method of an org.xml.sax.XMLReader and invoke the parse() method of the reader. When parse() returns, call the getTemplates() method to obtain the Templates object.

ContentHandler → TemplatesHandler

```
public interface TemplatesHandler extends org.xml.sax.ContentHandler {
// Public Instance Methods
    public abstract String getSystemId();
    public abstract javax.xml.transform.Templates getTemplates();
    public abstract void setSystemId(String systemID);
}
```

Returned By: SAXTransformerFactory.newTemplatesHandler()

TransformerHandler — Java 1.4

javax.xml.transform.sax

This interface extends org.xml.sax.ContentHandler and related interfaces so that it can consume SAX events generated by a org.xml.sax.SAXReader or org.xml.sax.XMLFilter. Create a TransformerHandler by calling one of the newTransformerHandler() methods of a SAXTransformerFactory.

Next, call the setResult() method to specify a Result object that describes the result document you'd like the transformation to produce. You may also call getTransformer() to get the Transformer object associated with this TransformerHandler if you need to set output properties or parameter values for the transformation.

Now, register the TransformerHandler with the XMLReader or XMLFilter object by calling setContentHandler(), setDTDHandler(), and setProperty(). Use the property name "http://www.xml.org/sax/properties/lexical-handler" in the call to setProperties() to register the TransformerHandler as a org.xml.sax.ext.LexicalHandler for the parser or filter.

Finally, invoke one of the parse() methods on your XMLReader or XMLFilter object. This will cause the reader or filter to start parsing the source document and translating it into method calls on the TransformerHandler. The TransformerHandler will transform those calls as specified in the Templates or Source object (if any) that was passed to the original call to newTransformerHandler() and generate a result document as directed by the Result object that was passed to setResult().

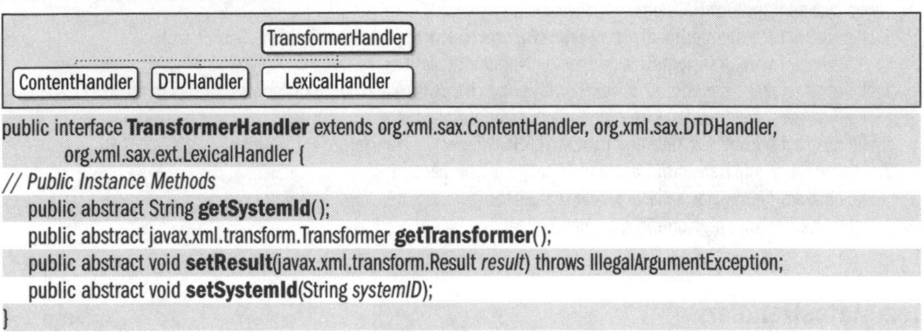


```
public interface TransformerHandler extends org.xml.sax.ContentHandler, org.xml.sax.DTDHandler,
        org.xml.sax.ext.LexicalHandler {
// Public Instance Methods
   public abstract String getSystemId();
   public abstract javax.xml.transform.Transformer getTransformer();
   public abstract void setResult(javax.xml.transform.Result result) throws IllegalArgumentException;
   public abstract void setSystemId(String systemID);
}
```

Returned By: SAXTransformerFactory.newTransformerHandler()

Package javax.xml.transform.stream — Java 1.4

This package contains Source and Result implementations that work with files and streams.

Classes:

```
public class StreamResult implements javax.xml.transform.Result;
public class StreamSource implements javax.xml.transform.Source;
```

StreamResult — Java 1.4

javax.xml.transform.stream

This class is a Result implementation that writes a textual representation of a transformed document to stream or file. Because XML documents define their own encoding, it is usually preferable to construct a StreamResult using a File or OutputStream instead of a character-based Writer which may use a different encoding than that specified within the document.

Object ─ StreamResult ··· Result

```
public class StreamResult implements javax.xml.transform.Result {
// Public Constructors
   public StreamResult();
   public StreamResult(java.io.File f);
   public StreamResult(String systemId);
   public StreamResult(java.io.Writer writer);
   public StreamResult(java.io.OutputStream outputStream);
// Public Constants
   public static final String FEATURE;        = [quot ] http://javax.xml.transform.stream.StreamResult/feature [quot ]
// Property Accessor Methods (by property name)
   public java.io.OutputStream getOutputStream();                                  default:null
   public void setOutputStream(java.io.OutputStream outputStream);
   public String getSystemId();                                     Implements:Result default:null
   public void setSystemId(java.io.File f);
   public void setSystemId(String systemId);                                    Implements:Result
   public java.io.Writer getWriter();                                               default:null
   public void setWriter(java.io.Writer writer);
// Methods Implementing Result
```

```
    public String getSystemId();                                                    default:null
    public void setSystemId(String systemId);
}
```

StreamSource **Java 1.4**

javax.xml.transform.stream

This class is a Source implementation that reads the textual format of an XML document from a file, byte stream, or character stream. Because XML documents declare their own encoding, it is preferable to create a StreamSource object from an InputStream instead of from a Reader, so that the XML processor can correctly handle the declared encoding. When creating a StreamSource from a byte stream or character stream, you should provide the system ID (i.e., the filename or URL) by using one of the two-argument constructors or by scaling setSystemId(). The system ID is required if the XML file to be processed includes relative URLs to be resolved.

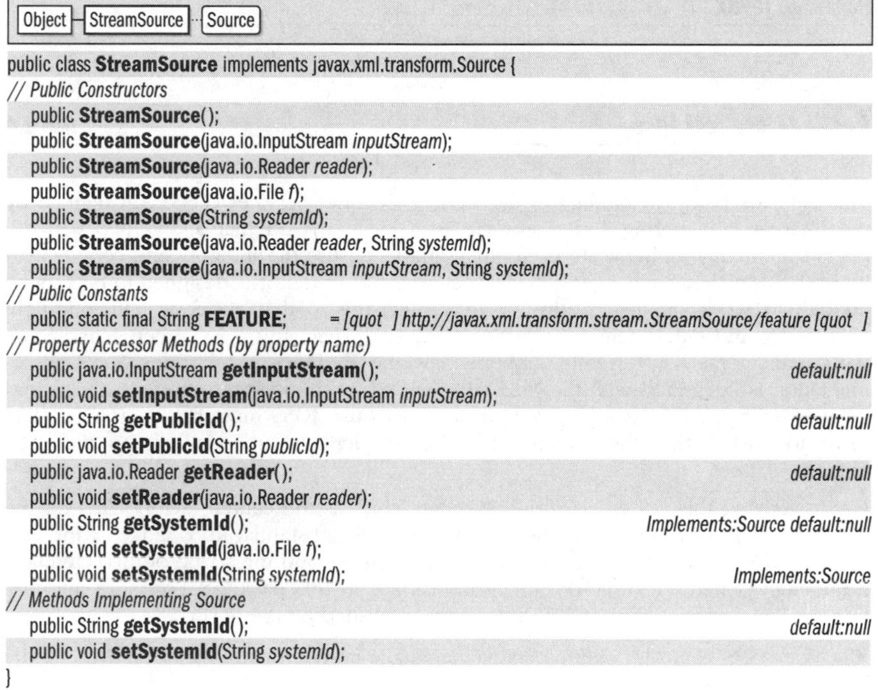


```
public class StreamSource implements javax.xml.transform.Source {
// Public Constructors
    public StreamSource();
    public StreamSource(java.io.InputStream inputStream);
    public StreamSource(java.io.Reader reader);
    public StreamSource(java.io.File f);
    public StreamSource(String systemId);
    public StreamSource(java.io.Reader reader, String systemId);
    public StreamSource(java.io.InputStream inputStream, String systemId);
// Public Constants
    public static final String FEATURE;     = [quot ] http://javax.xml.transform.stream.StreamSource/feature [quot ]
// Property Accessor Methods (by property name)
    public java.io.InputStream getInputStream();                                    default:null
    public void setInputStream(java.io.InputStream inputStream);
    public String getPublicId();                                                    default:null
    public void setPublicId(String publicId);
    public java.io.Reader getReader();                                              default:null
    public void setReader(java.io.Reader reader);
    public String getSystemId();                                 Implements:Source default:null
    public void setSystemId(java.io.File f);
    public void setSystemId(String systemId);                                  Implements:Source
// Methods Implementing Source
    public String getSystemId();                                                    default:null
    public void setSystemId(String systemId);
}
```

CHAPTER 22

org.ietf.jgss

Package org.ietf.jgss **Java 1.4**

This package is a Java binding of the Generic Security Services (GSS) API defined by the Internet Engineering Task Force (IETF). GSS is an API that allows two network peers to mutually authenticate each other, and to ensure the integrity and confidentiality of the data they exchange. GSS is a "generic" API in that it is designed to be general enough to work on top of any "security mechanism" that supports authentication, encryption, and data integrity protection. One such mechanism is Kerberos, and Sun's JGSS implementation currently supports only the Kerberos mechanism. Sun's implementation is integrated with the JAAS API defined by the javax.security.auth package and its sub-packages. Clients and servers that want to use JGSS must first perform a JAAS login to ensure that the required Kerberos credentials are available to the JGSS implementation.

Begin studying this package with GSSManager, which is the central factory class for the API. Understanding and using this package requires substantial knowledge of the GSS API and of Kerberos. Because these topics are well beyond the scope of this reference, no attempt is made to fully document the classes in this package. For more information, please read the relevant RFC documents published by the IETF:

- The GSS API is defined in a language-independent way by RFC 2743: *http://www.ietf.org/rfc/rfc2743.txt.*
- The Java binding of the GSS API is defined by RFC 2853: *http://www.ietf.org/rfc/rfc2853.txt.*
- The Kerberos Network Authentication Service is defined by RFC 1510: *http://www.ietf.org/rfc/rfc1510.txt.*
- A Kerberos security mechanism for GSS is defined by RFC 1964: *http://www.ietf.org/rfc/rfc1964.txt.*

In addition to these primary sources, Sun includes JGSS documentation and tutorials in its documentation bundle for Java 1.4. You can find them at: *http://java.sun.com/j2se/1.4/docs/guide/security/jgss/tutorials/index.html.*

Interfaces:

public interface **GSSContext**;
public interface **GSSCredential** extends Cloneable;
public interface **GSSName**;

Classes:

public class **ChannelBinding**;
public abstract class **GSSManager**;
public class **MessageProp**;
public class **Oid**;

Exception:

public class **GSSException** extends Exception;

ChannelBinding — Java 1.4

org.ietf.jgss

A ChannelBinding object is used to provide additional constraints, such as the Internet addresses of the client and server, upon the establishment of a security context.

```
public class ChannelBinding {
// Public Constructors
   public ChannelBinding(byte[ ] appData);
   public ChannelBinding(java.net.InetAddress initAddr, java.net.InetAddress acceptAddr, byte[ ] appData);
// Public Instance Methods
   public java.net.InetAddress getAcceptorAddress();
   public byte[ ] getApplicationData();
   public java.net.InetAddress getInitiatorAddress();
// Public Methods Overriding Object
   public boolean equals(Object obj);
   public int hashCode();
}
```

Passed To: GSSContext.setChannelBinding()

GSSContext — Java 1.4

org.ietf.jgss

This interface represents the "security context" within which authentication, encryption, and data integrity protection take place. A GSSContext object is obtained from a GSSManager factory. Before a GSSContext can be used to exchange data with a network peer, the security context must first be "established" (this typically involves mutual authentication) in a "context establishment loop" in which the client repeatedly calls initSecContext() and the server repeatedly calls acceptSecContext(), until the isEstablished() method returns true. Once a context has been established, you can use wrap() to apply security services (such as encryption) to an array of bytes or to a stream and can use unwrap() to reverse this process. You can also use getMIC() and verifyMIC() to generate and verify a "message integrity code" to protect the integrity of data that is transmitted in the clear.

```
public interface GSSContext {
// Public Constants
   public static final int DEFAULT_LIFETIME;                                =0
   public static final int INDEFINITE_LIFETIME;                    =2147483647
```

```
// Property Accessor Methods (by property name)
   public abstract boolean getAnonymityState();
   public abstract boolean getConfState();
   public abstract boolean getCredDelegState();
   public abstract GSSCredential getDelegCred() throws GSSException;
   public abstract boolean isEstablished();
   public abstract boolean isInitiator() throws GSSException;
   public abstract boolean getIntegState();
   public abstract int getLifetime();
   public abstract Oid getMech() throws GSSException;
   public abstract boolean getMutualAuthState();
   public abstract boolean isProtReady();
   public abstract boolean getReplayDetState();
   public abstract boolean getSequenceDetState();
   public abstract GSSName getSrcName() throws GSSException;
   public abstract GSSName getTargName() throws GSSException;
   public abstract boolean isTransferable() throws GSSException;
// Public Instance Methods
   public abstract void acceptSecContext(java.io.InputStream inStream, java.io.OutputStream outStream)
        throws GSSException;
   public abstract byte[ ] acceptSecContext(byte[ ] inToken, int offset, int len) throws GSSException;
   public abstract void dispose() throws GSSException;
   public abstract byte[ ] export() throws GSSException;
   public abstract void getMIC(java.io.InputStream inStream, java.io.OutputStream outStream,
                               MessageProp msgProp) throws GSSException;
   public abstract byte[ ] getMIC(byte[ ] inMsg, int offset, int len, MessageProp msgProp) throws GSSException;
   public abstract int getWrapSizeLimit(int qop, boolean confReq, int maxTokenSize) throws GSSException;
   public abstract int initSecContext(java.io.InputStream inStream, java.io.OutputStream outStream)
        throws GSSException;
   public abstract byte[ ] initSecContext(byte[ ] inputBuf, int offset, int len) throws GSSException;
   public abstract void requestAnonymity(boolean state) throws GSSException;
   public abstract void requestConf(boolean state) throws GSSException;
   public abstract void requestCredDeleg(boolean state) throws GSSException;
   public abstract void requestInteg(boolean state) throws GSSException;
   public abstract void requestLifetime(int lifetime) throws GSSException;
   public abstract void requestMutualAuth(boolean state) throws GSSException;
   public abstract void requestReplayDet(boolean state) throws GSSException;
   public abstract void requestSequenceDet(boolean state) throws GSSException;
   public abstract void setChannelBinding(ChannelBinding cb) throws GSSException;
   public abstract void unwrap(java.io.InputStream inStream, java.io.OutputStream outStream,
                               MessageProp msgProp) throws GSSException;
   public abstract byte[ ] unwrap(byte[ ] inBuf, int offset, int len, MessageProp msgProp) throws GSSException;
   public abstract void verifyMIC(java.io.InputStream tokStream, java.io.InputStream msgStream,
                                  MessageProp msgProp) throws GSSException;
   public abstract void verifyMIC(byte[ ] inToken, int tokOffset, int tokLen, byte[ ] inMsg, int msgOffset, int msgLen,
                                  MessageProp msgProp) throws GSSException;
   public abstract void wrap(java.io.InputStream inStream, java.io.OutputStream outStream, MessageProp msgProp)
        throws GSSException;
   public abstract byte[ ] wrap(byte[ ] inBuf, int offset, int len, MessageProp msgProp) throws GSSException;
}
```

Returned By: GSSManager.createContext()

GSSCredential — Java 1.4

org.ietf.jgss — *cloneable*

This interface defines a high-level API to a generic security credential, such as a Kerberos ticket or a Kerberos key.

Cloneable ··· GSSCredential

```
public interface GSSCredential extends Cloneable {
// Public Constants
   public static final int ACCEPT_ONLY;                                    =2
   public static final int DEFAULT_LIFETIME;                               =0
   public static final int INDEFINITE_LIFETIME;                            =2147483647
   public static final int INITIATE_AND_ACCEPT;                            =0
   public static final int INITIATE_ONLY;                                  =1
// Public Instance Methods
   public abstract void add(GSSName name, int initLifetime, int acceptLifetime, Oid mech, int usage)
       throws GSSException;
   public abstract void dispose() throws GSSException;
   public abstract boolean equals(Object another);
   public abstract Oid[ ] getMechs() throws GSSException;
   public abstract GSSName getName() throws GSSException;
   public abstract GSSName getName(Oid mech) throws GSSException;
   public abstract int getRemainingAcceptLifetime(Oid mech) throws GSSException;
   public abstract int getRemainingInitLifetime(Oid mech) throws GSSException;
   public abstract int getRemainingLifetime() throws GSSException;
   public abstract int getUsage() throws GSSException;
   public abstract int getUsage(Oid mech) throws GSSException;
   public abstract int hashCode();
}
```

Passed To: GSSManager.createContext()

Returned By: GSSContext.getDelegCred(), GSSManager.createCredential()

GSSException — Java 1.4

org.ietf.jgss — *serializable checked*

This exception class is used to signal all exceptions in the org.ietf.jgss package. getMajor() returns a GSS error code, which should be one of the integer constants defined by this class. getMajorString() returns an error message that corresponds to that error code. getMinor() and getMinorString() return an error code and error string that are specific to the underlying security mechanism.

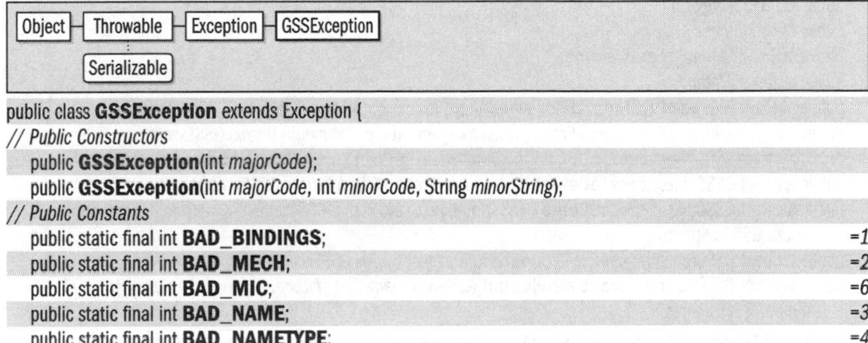


```
public class GSSException extends Exception {
// Public Constructors
   public GSSException(int majorCode);
   public GSSException(int majorCode, int minorCode, String minorString);
// Public Constants
   public static final int BAD_BINDINGS;                                   =1
   public static final int BAD_MECH;                                       =2
   public static final int BAD_MIC;                                        =6
   public static final int BAD_NAME;                                       =3
   public static final int BAD_NAMETYPE;                                   =4
```

```
    public static final int BAD_QOP;                                              =14
    public static final int BAD_STATUS;                                           =5
    public static final int CONTEXT_EXPIRED;                                      =7
    public static final int CREDENTIALS_EXPIRED;                                  =8
    public static final int DEFECTIVE_CREDENTIAL;                                 =9
    public static final int DEFECTIVE_TOKEN;                                      =10
    public static final int DUPLICATE_ELEMENT;                                    =17
    public static final int DUPLICATE_TOKEN;                                      =19
    public static final int FAILURE;                                              =11
    public static final int GAP_TOKEN;                                            =22
    public static final int NAME_NOT_MN;                                          =18
    public static final int NO_CONTEXT;                                           =12
    public static final int NO_CRED;                                              =13
    public static final int OLD_TOKEN;                                            =20
    public static final int UNAUTHORIZED;                                         =15
    public static final int UNAVAILABLE;                                          =16
    public static final int UNSEQ_TOKEN;                                          =21
// Public Instance Methods
    public int getMajor();
    public String getMajorString();
    public int getMinor();
    public String getMinorString();
    public void setMinor(int minorCode, String message);
// Public Methods Overriding Throwable
    public String getMessage();
    public String toString();
}
```

Thrown By: Too many methods to list.

GSSManager — Java 1.4

org.ietf.jgss

This is the central factory class of the org.ietf.jgss package. Obtain the default GSSManager with the static getInstance() method or by instantiating some vendor-supplied subclass. Call getMechs() to query the security mechanisms supported by the manager. (The default GSSManager supplied by Sun supports only the Kerberos mechanism.) Call createContext() to create a GSSContext. Call createCredential() to create a GSSCredential. Call createName() to create a GSSName.

```
public abstract class GSSManager {
// Public Constructors
    public GSSManager();
// Public Class Methods
    public static GSSManager getInstance();
// Public Instance Methods
    public abstract void addProviderAtEnd(java.security.Provider p, Oid mech) throws GSSException;
    public abstract void addProviderAtFront(java.security.Provider p, Oid mech) throws GSSException;
    public abstract GSSContext createContext(GSSCredential myCred) throws GSSException;
    public abstract GSSContext createContext(byte[ ] interProcessToken) throws GSSException;
    public abstract GSSContext createContext(GSSName peer, Oid mech, GSSCredential myCred, int lifetime)
        throws GSSException;
    public abstract GSSCredential createCredential(int usage) throws GSSException;
    public abstract GSSCredential createCredential(GSSName name, int lifetime, Oid mech, int usage)
        throws GSSException;
    public abstract GSSCredential createCredential(GSSName name, int lifetime, Oid[ ] mechs, int usage)
        throws GSSException;
```

```
    public abstract GSSName createName(String nameStr, Oid nameType) throws GSSException;
    public abstract GSSName createName(byte[ ] name, Oid nameType) throws GSSException;
    public abstract GSSName createName(String nameStr, Oid nameType, Oid mech) throws GSSException;
    public abstract GSSName createName(byte[ ] name, Oid nameType, Oid mech) throws GSSException;
    public abstract Oid[ ] getMechs();
    public abstract Oid[ ] getMechsForName(Oid nameType);
    public abstract Oid[ ] getNamesForMech(Oid mech) throws GSSException;
}
```

Returned By: GSSManager.getInstance()

GSSName **Java 1.4**

org.ietf.jgss

A GSSName represents an entity, such as a user or a network server, that participates in a GSS session. The constants defined by this class represent the allowed set of "name types."

```
public interface GSSName {
// Public Constants
    public static final Oid NT_ANONYMOUS;
    public static final Oid NT_EXPORT_NAME;
    public static final Oid NT_HOSTBASED_SERVICE;
    public static final Oid NT_MACHINE_UID_NAME;
    public static final Oid NT_STRING_UID_NAME;
    public static final Oid NT_USER_NAME;
// Public Instance Methods
    public abstract GSSName canonicalize(Oid mech) throws GSSException;
    public abstract boolean equals(Object another);
    public abstract boolean equals(GSSName another) throws GSSException;
    public abstract byte[ ] export() throws GSSException;
    public abstract Oid getStringNameType() throws GSSException;
    public abstract int hashCode();
    public abstract boolean isAnonymous();
    public abstract boolean isMN();
    public abstract String toString();
}
```

Passed To: GSSCredential.add(), GSSManager.{createContext(), createCredential()}, GSSName.equals()

Returned By: GSSContext.{getSrcName(), getTargName()}, GSSCredential.getName(), GSSManager.createName(), GSSName.canonicalize()

MessageProp **Java 1.4**

org.ietf.jgss

This utility class is used with the wrap(), unwrap(), getMIC() and verifyMIC() methods of GSSContext to pass and return properties related to the message or message integrity code.

```
public class MessageProp {
// Public Constructors
    public MessageProp(boolean privState);
    public MessageProp(int qop, boolean privState);
// Property Accessor Methods (by property name)
    public boolean isDuplicateToken();
    public boolean isGapToken();
```

```
    public int getMinorStatus();
    public String getMinorString();
    public boolean isOldToken();
    public boolean getPrivacy();
    public void setPrivacy(boolean privState);
    public int getQOP();
    public void setQOP(int qop);
    public boolean isUnseqToken();
// Public Instance Methods
    public void setSupplementaryStates(boolean duplicate, boolean old, boolean unseq, boolean gap,
                                       int minorStatus, String minorString);
}
```

Passed To: GSSContext.{getMIC(), unwrap(), verifyMIC(), wrap()}

Oid — Java 1.4

org.ietf.jgss

An Oid is a universal "object identifier" based on a hierarchical numbering system. The Oid class is used in this package to uniquely identify security mechanisms and name types. The Oid for the Kerberos security mechanism is 1.2.840.113554.1.2.2.

```
public class Oid {
// Public Constructors
    public Oid(String strOid) throws GSSException;
    public Oid(java.io.InputStream derOid) throws GSSException;
    public Oid(byte[ ] data) throws GSSException;
// Public Instance Methods
    public boolean containedIn(Oid[ ] oids);
    public byte[ ] getDER() throws GSSException;
// Public Methods Overriding Object
    public boolean equals(Object other);
    public int hashCode();
    public String toString();
}
```

Passed To: Too many methods to list.

Returned By: GSSContext.getMech(), GSSCredential.getMechs(), GSSManager.{getMechs(), getMechsForName(), getNamesForMech()}, GSSName.getStringNameType()

Type Of: GSSName.{NT_ANONYMOUS, NT_EXPORT_NAME, NT_HOSTBASED_SERVICE, NT_MACHINE_UID_NAME, NT_STRING_UID_NAME, NT_USER_NAME}

CHAPTER 23

org.w3c.dom

Package org.w3c.dom — Java 1.4

This package defines the Java binding to the core and XML modules of the DOM Level 2 API defined by the World Wide Web Consortium (W3C). DOM stands for Document Object Model, and the DOM API defines a way to represent an XML document as a tree of nodes. It includes methods that allow document trees to be traversed, examined, modified, and built from scratch. Node is the central interface of the package. All nodes in a document tree implement this interface, and it defines the basic methods for traversing and modifying the tree of nodes. Most of the other interfaces in the package are extensions of Node that represent specific types of XML content. The most important and commonly used of these sub-interfaces are Document, Element and Text. A Document object serves as the root of the document tree and defines methods for searching the tree for elements with a specified tag name or ID attribute. The Element interface represents an XML element or tag and has methods for manipulating the element's attributes. The Text interface represents a run of plain text within an Element, and has methods for querying or altering that text. NodeList and DOMImplementation do not extend Node but are also important interfaces.

Interfaces:

public interface **Attr** extends Node;
public interface **CDATASection** extends Text;
public interface **CharacterData** extends Node;
public interface **Comment** extends CharacterData;
public interface **Document** extends Node;
public interface **DocumentFragment** extends Node;
public interface **DocumentType** extends Node;
public interface **DOMImplementation**;
public interface **Element** extends Node;
public interface **Entity** extends Node;
public interface **EntityReference** extends Node;
public interface **NamedNodeMap**;

public interface **Node**;
public interface **NodeList**;
public interface **Notation** extends Node;
public interface **ProcessingInstruction** extends Node;
public interface **Text** extends CharacterData;

Exception:

public class **DOMException** extends RuntimeException;

Attr **Java 1.4**

org.w3c.dom

An Attr object represents an attribute of an Element node. Attr objects are associated with Element nodes, but are not directly part of the document tree: the getParentNode() method of an Attr object always returns null. Use getOwnerElement() to determine which Element an Attr is part of. You can obtain an Attr object by calling the getAttributeNode() method of Element, or you can obtain a NamedNodeMap of all Attr objects for an element with the getAttributes() method of Node.

getName() returns the name of the attribute. getValue() returns the attribute value as a string. getSpecified() returns true if the attribute was explicitly specified in the source document through a call to setValue(), and returns false if the attribute represents a default obtained from a DTD or other schema.

XML allows attributes to contain text and entity references. The getValue() method returns the attribute value as a single string. If you want to know the precise composition of the attribute however, you can examine the children of the Attr node: they may consist of Text and/or EntityReference nodes.

In most cases the easiest way to work with attributes is with the getAttribute() and setAttribute() methods of the Element interface. These methods avoid the use of Attr nodes altogether.

Node → Attr

```
public interface Attr extends Node {
// Public Instance Methods
   public abstract String getName();
   public abstract org.w3c.dom.Element getOwnerElement();
   public abstract boolean getSpecified();
   public abstract String getValue();
   public abstract void setValue(String value) throws DOMException;
}
```

Passed To: javax.imageio.metadata.IIOMetadataNode.{removeAttributeNode(), setAttributeNode(), setAttributeNodeNS()}, org.w3c.dom.Element.{removeAttributeNode(), setAttributeNode(), setAttributeNodeNS()}

Returned By: javax.imageio.metadata.IIOMetadataNode.{getAttributeNode(), getAttributeNodeNS(), removeAttributeNode(), setAttributeNode(), setAttributeNodeNS()}, org.w3c.dom.Document.{createAttribute(), createAttributeNS()}, org.w3c.dom.Element.{getAttributeNode(), getAttributeNodeNS(), removeAttributeNode(), setAttributeNode(), setAttributeNodeNS()}

CDATASection Java 1.4

org.w3c.dom

This interface represents a CDATA section in an XML document. CDATASection is a subinterface of Text and does not define any methods of its own. The content of the CDATA section is available through the getNodeValue() method inherited from Node, or through the getData() method inherited from CharacterData. Although CDATASection nodes can often be treated in the same way as Text nodes, note that the Node.normalize() method does not merge adjacent CDATA sections.

Node ··· CharacterData ··· Text ··· CDATASection

```
public interface CDATASection extends Text {
}
```

Returned By: org.w3c.dom.Document.createCDATASection()

CharacterData Java 1.4

org.w3c.dom

This interface is a generic one that is extended by Text, CDATASection (which extends Text) and Comment. Any node in a document tree that implements CharacterData also implements one of these more specific types. This interface exists simply to group the string manipulation methods that these text-related node types all share.

The CharacterData interface defines a mutable string. getData() returns the "character data" as a String object, and setData() allows it to be set from a String object. getLength() returns the number of characters of character data, and substringData() returns just the specified portion of the data as a string. The appendData(), deleteData(), insertData(), and replaceData() methods mutate the data by appending a string to the end, deleting region, inserting a string at the specified location, and replacing a region with a specified string.

Node ··· CharacterData

```
public interface CharacterData extends Node {
// Public Instance Methods
   public abstract void appendData(String arg) throws DOMException;
   public abstract void deleteData(int offset, int count) throws DOMException;
   public abstract String getData() throws DOMException;
   public abstract int getLength();
   public abstract void insertData(int offset, String arg) throws DOMException;
   public abstract void replaceData(int offset, int count, String arg) throws DOMException;
   public abstract void setData(String data) throws DOMException;
   public abstract String substringData(int offset, int count) throws DOMException;
}
```

Implementations: Comment, Text

Comment Java 1.4

org.w3c.dom

A Comment node represents a comment in an XML document. The content of the comment (i.e., the text between <!-- and -->) is available with the getData() method inherited from CharacterData, or through the getNodeValue() method inherited from Node. This content may be manipulated using the various methods inherited from CharacterData.

Node ··· CharacterData ··· Comment

```
public interface Comment extends CharacterData {
}
```

Returned By: org.w3c.dom.Document.createComment()

Document **Java 1.4**

org.w3c.dom

This interface represents a DOM document, and an object that implements this interface serves as the root of a DOM document tree. Most of the methods defined by the Document interface are "factory methods" that are used to create various types of nodes that can be inserted into this document. Note that there are two versions of the methods for creating attributes and elements. The methods with "NS" in their name are namespace-aware and require the attribute or element name to be specified as a combination of a namespace URI and a local name. You'll notice that throughout the DOM API, methods with "NS" in their names are namespace-aware. Other important methods include the following.

getElementsByTagName() and its namespace-aware variant getElementsByTagNameNS() search the document tree for Element nodes that have the specified tag name and return a NodeList containing those matching nodes. The Element interface defines methods by the same names that search only within the sub-tree defined by an Element.

getElementById() is a related method that searches the document tree for a single element with the specified unique value for an ID attribute. This is useful when you use an ID attribute to uniquely identify certain tags within an XML document. Note that this method does not search for attributes that are named "id" or "ID". It searches for attributes whose XML type (as declared in the document's DTD) is ID. Such attributes are often named "id", but this is not required.

An XML document must have a single root element. getDocumentElement() returns this Element object. Note, however that this does not mean that a Document node has only one child. It must have exactly one child that is an Element, but it can also have other children such as Comment and ProcessingInstruction nodes. The getDoctype() method returns the DocumentType object (or null if there isn't one) that represents the document's DTD. getImplementation() returns the the DOMImplementation object that represents the DOM implementation that created this document tree.

Node ··· Document

```
public interface Document extends Node {
// Public Instance Methods
   public abstract Attr createAttribute(String name) throws DOMException;
   public abstract Attr createAttributeNS(String namespaceURI, String qualifiedName) throws DOMException;
   public abstract CDATASection createCDATASection(String data) throws DOMException;
   public abstract Comment createComment(String data);
   public abstract DocumentFragment createDocumentFragment();
   public abstract org.w3c.dom.Element createElement(String tagName) throws DOMException;
   public abstract org.w3c.dom.Element createElementNS(String namespaceURI, String qualifiedName)
       throws DOMException;
   public abstract EntityReference createEntityReference(String name) throws DOMException;
   public abstract ProcessingInstruction createProcessingInstruction(String target, String data)
       throws DOMException;
```

```
    public abstract Text createTextNode(String data);
    public abstract DocumentType getDoctype();
    public abstract org.w3c.dom.Element getDocumentElement();
    public abstract org.w3c.dom.Element getElementById(String elementId);
    public abstract NodeList getElementsByTagName(String tagname);
    public abstract NodeList getElementsByTagNameNS(String namespaceURI, String localName);
    public abstract DOMImplementation getImplementation();
    public abstract Node importNode(Node importedNode, boolean deep) throws DOMException;
}
```

Implementations: org.w3c.dom.html.HTMLDocument

Returned By: javax.imageio.metadata.IIOMetadataNode.getOwnerDocument(), javax.xml.parsers.DocumentBuilder.{newDocument(), parse()}, DOMImplementation.createDocument(), Node.getOwnerDocument(), org.w3c.dom.html.HTMLFrameElement.getContentDocument(), org.w3c.dom.html.HTMLIFrameElement.getContentDocument(), org.w3c.dom.html.HTMLObjectElement.getContentDocument()

DocumentFragment — Java 1.4

org.w3c.dom

The DocumentFragment interface represents a portion—or fragment—of a document. More specifically, its represents one or more adjacent document nodes, and all of the descendants of each. DocumentFragment nodes are never part of a document tree, and getParentNode() always returns null. Although a DocumentFragment does not have a parent, it can have children, and you can use the inherited Node methods to add child nodes (or delete or replace them) to a DocumentFragment.

DocumentFragment nodes exhibit a special behavior that makes them quite useful: when a request is made to insert a DocumentFragment into a document tree, it is not the DocumentFragment node itself that is inserted, but each of the children of the DocumentFragment instead. This makes DocumentFragment useful as a temporary placeholder for a sequence of nodes that you wish to insert, all at once, into a document.

You can create a new, empty, DocumentFragment to work with by calling the createDocumentFragment() method of the desired Document.

Node — DocumentFragment

```
public interface DocumentFragment extends Node {
}
```

Returned By: org.w3c.dom.Document.createDocumentFragment()

DocumentType — Java 1.4

org.w3c.dom

This interface represents the Document Type Declaration (DTD) of a document. Because the DTD is not part of the document itself, a DocumentType object is not part of DOM document tree, even though it extends the Node interface. If a Document has a DTD, then you may obtain the DocumentType object that represents it by calling the getDoctype() method of the Document object.

getName(), getPublicId(), getSystemId(), and getInternalSubset() all return strings (or null) that contain the name, public identifier, system identifier, and internal subset of the document type. getEntities() returns a read-only NamedNodeMap that represents the a name-to-value mapping for all internal and external general entities declared by the DTD. You can use this NamedNodeMap to lookup an Entity object by name. Similarly, getNotations()

DOM

returns a read-only NamedNodeMap that allows you to look up a Notation object declared in the DTD by name.

DocumentType does not provide access to the bulk of a DTD, which usually consists of element and attribute declarations. Future versions of the DOM API may provide more details.

Node ··· DocumentType

```
public interface DocumentType extends Node {
// Property Accessor Methods (by property name)
    public abstract NamedNodeMap getEntities();
    public abstract String getInternalSubset();
    public abstract String getName();
    public abstract NamedNodeMap getNotations();
    public abstract String getPublicId();
    public abstract String getSystemId();
}
```

Passed To: DOMImplementation.createDocument()

Returned By: org.w3c.dom.Document.getDoctype(), DOMImplementation.createDocumentType()

DOMException — Java 1.4

org.w3c.dom — *serializable unchecked*

An instance of this class is thrown whenever an exception is raised by the DOM API. Unlike many Java APIs, the DOM API does not define specialized subclasses to define different categories of exceptions. Instead, a more specific exception type is specified by the public field code. The value of this field will be one of the constants defined by this class, which have the following meanings:

INDEX_SIZE_ERR
: Indicates an out-of-bounds error for an array or string index.

DOMSTRING_SIZE_ERR
: Indicates that a requested text is too big to fit into a String object. Exceptions of this type are intended for DOM implementations for other languages and should not occur in Java.

HIERARCHY_REQUEST_ERR
: Indicates that an attempt was made to illegally place a node somewhere in the document tree hierarchy.

WRONG_DOCUMENT_ERR
: Indicates that an attempt was made to use a node with a document that is different than the document that created the node.

INVALID_CHARACTER_ERR
: Indicates that an illegal character is used (for example, in an element name).

NO_DATA_ALLOWED_ERR
: Not currently used.

NO_MODIFICATION_ALLOWED_ERR
: Indicates that an attempt was made to modify a node that is read-only and does not allow modifications. Entity, EntityReference, and Notation nodes, and all of their descendants, are read-only.

NOT_FOUND_ERR
: Indicates that a node was not found where it was expected to be.

NOT_SUPPORTED_ERR
: Indicates that a method or property is not supported in the current DOM implementation.

INUSE_ATTRIBUTE_ERR
: Indicates that an attempt was made to associate an Attr with an Element when that Attr node was already associated with a different Element node.

INVALID_STATE_ERR
: Indicates that an attempt was made to use an object that is not yet, or is no longer, in a state that allows such use.

SYNTAX_ERR
: Indicates that a specified string contains a syntax error. Exceptions of this type are not raised by the core module of the DOM API described here.

INVALID_MODIFICATION_ERR
: Exceptions of this type are not raised by the core module of the DOM API described here.

NAMESPACE_ERR
: Indicates an error involving element or attribute namespaces.

INVALID_ACCESS_ERR
: Indicates that an attempt was made to access an object in a way that is not supported by the implementation.

Object — Throwable — Exception — RuntimeException — DOMException
Serializable

```
public class DOMException extends RuntimeException {
// Public Constructors
   public DOMException(short code, String message);
// Public Constants
   public static final short DOMSTRING_SIZE_ERR;                          =2
   public static final short HIERARCHY_REQUEST_ERR;                       =3
   public static final short INDEX_SIZE_ERR;                              =1
   public static final short INUSE_ATTRIBUTE_ERR;                         =10
   public static final short INVALID_ACCESS_ERR;                          =15
   public static final short INVALID_CHARACTER_ERR;                       =5
   public static final short INVALID_MODIFICATION_ERR;                    =13
   public static final short INVALID_STATE_ERR;                           =11
   public static final short NAMESPACE_ERR;                               =14
   public static final short NO_DATA_ALLOWED_ERR;                         =6
   public static final short NO_MODIFICATION_ALLOWED_ERR;                 =7
   public static final short NOT_FOUND_ERR;                               =8
   public static final short NOT_SUPPORTED_ERR;                           =9
   public static final short SYNTAX_ERR;                                  =12
   public static final short WRONG_DOCUMENT_ERR;                          =4
// Public Instance Fields
   public short code;
}
```

DOM

Thrown By: Too many methods to list.

DOMImplementation — Java 1.4

org.w3c.dom

This interface defines methods that are global to an implementation of the DOM rather than specific to a particular Document object. Obtain a reference to the DOMImplementation object that represents your implementation by calling the getImplementation() method of any Document object. createDocument() returns a new, empty Document object which you can populate with nodes that you create using the create methods defined by the Document interface.

hasFeature() allows you to test whether your DOM implementation supports a specified version of a named feature, or module, of the DOM standard. This method should return true when you pass the feature name "core" and the version "1.0", or when you pass the feature names "core" or "xml" and the version "2.0". The DOM standard includes a number of optional modules, but the Java platform has not adopted the subpackages of this package that define the API for those optional modules, and therefore the DOM implementation bundled with a Java implementation is not likely to support those modules.

The javax.xml.parsers.DocumentBuilder class provides another way to obtain the DOMImplementation object by calling its getDOMImplementation() object. It also defines a shortcut newDocument() method for creating empty Document objects to populate.

```
public interface DOMImplementation {
// Public Instance Methods
   public abstract org.w3c.dom.Document createDocument(String namespaceURI, String qualifiedName,
                                                        DocumentType doctype) throws DOMException;
   public abstract DocumentType createDocumentType(String qualifiedName, String publicId, String systemId)
       throws DOMException;
   public abstract boolean hasFeature(String feature, String version);
}
```

Implementations: org.w3c.dom.css.DOMImplementationCSS, org.w3c.dom.html.HTMLDOMImplementation

Returned By: javax.xml.parsers.DocumentBuilder.getDOMImplementation(), org.w3c.dom.Document.getImplementation()

Element — Java 1.4

org.w3c.dom

This interface represents an element (or tag) in an XML document. getTagName() returns the tagname of the element, including the namespace prefix if there is one. When working with namespaces, you will probably prefer to use the namespace-aware methods defined by the Node interface. Use getNamespaceURI() to get the namespace URI of the element, and use getLocalName() to the local name of the element within that namespace. You can also use getPrefix() to query the namespace prefix, or setPrefix() to change the namespace prefix (this does not change the namespace URI).

Element defines a getElementsByTagName() method and a corresponding namespace-aware getElementsByTagNameNS() method, which behave just like the methods of the same names on the Document object, except that they search for named elements only within the subtree rooted at this Element.

The remaining methods of the Element interface are for querying and setting attribute values, testing the existence of an attribute, and removing an attribute from the Element. There are a confusing number of methods to perform these four basic attribute operations. If an attribute-related method has "NS" in its name, then it is namespace-aware. If it has "Node" in its name, then it works with Attr objects rather than with the simpler string representation of the attribute value. Attributes in XML documents may contain entity references. If your document includes entity references in attribute values, then you may need to use the Attr interface because the expansion of such an entity reference can result in a sub-tree of nodes beneath the Attr object. Whenever possible, however, it is much easier to work with the methods that treat attribute values as plain strings. Note also that in addition to the attribute methods defined by the Element interface you can also obtain a NamedNodeMap of Attr objects with the getAttributes() method of the Node interface.

Finally, note that getAttribute() and related methods and hasAttribute() and related methods return the value of or test for the existence of both explicitly specified attributes, and also attributes for which a default value is specified in the document DTD. If you need to determine whether an attribute was explicitly specified in the document, obtain its Attr object, and use its getSpecified() method.

Node ··· Element

```
public interface Element extends Node {
// Public Instance Methods
   public abstract String getAttribute(String name);
   public abstract Attr getAttributeNode(String name);
   public abstract Attr getAttributeNodeNS(String namespaceURI, String localName);
   public abstract String getAttributeNS(String namespaceURI, String localName);
   public abstract NodeList getElementsByTagName(String name);
   public abstract NodeList getElementsByTagNameNS(String namespaceURI, String localName);
   public abstract String getTagName();
   public abstract boolean hasAttribute(String name);
   public abstract boolean hasAttributeNS(String namespaceURI, String localName);
   public abstract void removeAttribute(String name) throws DOMException;
   public abstract Attr removeAttributeNode(Attr oldAttr) throws DOMException;
   public abstract void removeAttributeNS(String namespaceURI, String localName) throws DOMException;
   public abstract void setAttribute(String name, String value) throws DOMException;
   public abstract Attr setAttributeNode(Attr newAttr) throws DOMException;
   public abstract Attr setAttributeNodeNS(Attr newAttr) throws DOMException;
   public abstract void setAttributeNS(String namespaceURI, String qualifiedName, String value)
       throws DOMException;
}
```

Implementations: javax.imageio.metadata.IIOMetadataNode, org.w3c.dom.html.HTMLElement

Passed To: org.w3c.dom.css.DocumentCSS.getOverrideStyle(), org.w3c.dom.css.ViewCSS.getComputedStyle()

Returned By: Attr.getOwnerElement(), org.w3c.dom.Document.{createElement(), createElementNS(), getDocumentElement(), getElementById()}

Entity **Java 1.4**

org.w3c.dom

This interface represents an entity defined in an XML DTD. The name of the entity is specified by the getNodeName() method inherited from the Node interface. The entity content is represented by the child nodes of the Entity node. The methods defined by this interface return the public identifier and system identifier for external entities, and the notation name for unparsed entities. Note that Entity nodes and their children are not part of the document tree (and the getParentNode() method of an Entity always returns null). Instead, a document may contain one or more references to an entity. See the EntityReference interface.

Entities are defined in the DTD (document type definition) of a document, either as part of an external DTD file, or as part of an "internal subset" that defines local entities that are specific to the current document. The DocumentType interface has a getEntities() method that returns a NamedNodeMap mapping entity names to Entity nodes. This is the only way to obtain an Entity object; because they are part of the DTD, Entity nodes never appear within the document tree itself.

Entity nodes and all descendants of an Entity node are read-only and cannot be edited or modified in any way.

Node → Entity

```
public interface Entity extends Node {
// Public Instance Methods
   public abstract String getNotationName();
   public abstract String getPublicId();
   public abstract String getSystemId();
}
```

EntityReference — Java 1.4

org.w3c.dom

This interface represents a reference from an XML document to an entity defined in the document's DTD. Character entities and predefined entities such as < are always expanded in XML documents and do not create EntityReference nodes. Note also that some XML parsers expand all entity references. Documents created by such parsers do not contain EntityReference nodes.

This interface defines no methods of its own. The getNodeName() method of the Node interface provides the name of the referenced entity. The getEntities() method of the DocumentType interface provides a way to look up the Entity object associated with that name. Note however, that the DocumentType may not contain an Entity with the specified name (because, for example, nonvalidating XML parsers are not required to parse the external subset of the DTD.) In this case, the EntityReference is a reference to a named entity whose content is not known, and it has no children. On the other hand, if the DocumentType does contain an Entity node with the specified name, then the child nodes of the EntityReference are a copy of the child nodes of the Entity, and represent the expansion of the entity. (The children of an EntityReference may not be an exact copy of the children of an Entity if the entity's expansion includes namespace prefixes that are not bound to namespace URIs.)

Like Entity nodes, EntityReference nodes and their descendants are read-only and cannot be edited or modified.

Node → EntityReference

```
public interface EntityReference extends Node {
}
```

Returned By: org.w3c.dom.Document.createEntityReference()

NamedNodeMap — Java 1.4

org.w3c.dom

The NamedNodeMap interface defines a collection of nodes that may be looked up by name or by namespace URI and local name. It is unrelated to the java.util.Map interface.

Use getNamedItem() to look for and return a node whose getNodeName() method returns the specified value. Use getNamedItemNS() to look for and return a node whose getNamespaceURI() and getLocalName() methods return the specified values. A NamedNodeMap is a mapping from names to nodes, and does not order the nodes in any particular way. Nevertheless, it does impose an arbitrary ordering on the nodes and allow them to be looked up by index. Use getLength() to find out how many nodes are contained in the NamedNodeMap, and use item() to obtain the Node object at a specified index.

If a NamedNodeMap is not read-only, you can use removeNamedItem() and removeNamedItemNS() to remove a named node from the map, and you can use setNamedItem() and setNamedItemNS() to add a node to the map, mapping to it from its name or its namespace URI and local name.

NamedNodeMap objects are live, which means that they immediately reflect any changes to the document tree. For example, if you obtain a NamedNodeMap that represents the attributes of an element, and then add a new attribute to that element, the new attribute is automatically available through the NamedNodeMap: you do not need to obtain a new NamedNodeMap to get the modified set of attributes.

NamedNodeMap is returned only by relatively obscure methods of the DOM API. The most notable use is as the return value of the getAttributes() method of Node. It is usually easier to work with attributes through the methods of the Element interface, however. Two methods of DocumentType also return read-only NamedNodeMap objects.

```
public interface NamedNodeMap {
// Public Instance Methods
   public abstract int getLength();
   public abstract Node getNamedItem(String name);
   public abstract Node getNamedItemNS(String namespaceURI, String localName);
   public abstract Node item(int index);
   public abstract Node removeNamedItem(String name) throws DOMException;
   public abstract Node removeNamedItemNS(String namespaceURI, String localName) throws DOMException;
   public abstract Node setNamedItem(Node arg) throws DOMException;
   public abstract Node setNamedItemNS(Node arg) throws DOMException;
}
```

Returned By: javax.imageio.metadata.IIOMetadataNode.getAttributes(), DocumentType.{getEntities(), getNotations()}, Node.getAttributes()

Node **Java 1.4**

org.w3c.dom

All objects in a DOM document tree (including the Document object itself) implement the Node interface, which provides basic methods for traversing and manipulating the tree.

getParentNode() and getChildNodes() allow you to traverse up and down the document tree. You can enumerate the children of a given node by looping through the elements of the NodeList returned by getChildNodes(), or by using getFirstChild() and getNextSibling() (or getLastChild() and getPreviousSibling() to loop backwards). It is sometimes useful to call hasChildNodes() to determine whether a node has children or not. getOwnerDocument() returns the Document node of which the node is a descendant or with which it is associated. It provides a quick way to jump to the root of the document tree.

Several methods allow you to add children to a tree or alter the list of children. appendChild() adds a new child node at the end of this nodes list of children. insertChild() inserts a node into this nodes list of children, placing it immediately before a specified child node. removeChild() removes the specified node from this node's list of children. replaceChild() replaces one child node of this node with another node. For all of these methods, if the node to be appended or inserted is already part of the document tree, it is first removed from its current parent. Use cloneNode() to produce a copy of this node. Pass true if you want all descendants of this node to be cloned as well.

Every object in a document tree implements the Node interface, but also implements a more specialized subinterface, such as Element or Text. The getNodeType() method provides an easy way to determine which subinterface a node implements: the return value is one of the _NODE constants defined by this class. You might use the return value of getNodeType() in a switch statement, for example, to determine how to process a node of unknown type.

getNodeName() and getNodeValue() provide additional information about a node, but the interpretation of the strings they return depends on the node type as shown in the table below. Note that subinterfaces typically define specialized methods (such as the getTagName() method of Element and the getData() method of Text) for obtaining this same information. Note also that unless a node is read-only, you can use setNodeValue() to alter the value associated with the node.

Node type	*Node name*	*Node value*
ELEMENT_NODE	The element's tag name	null
ATTRIBUTE_NODE	The attribute name	The attribute value
TEXT_NODE	"#text"	The text of the node
CDATA_SECTION_NODE	"#cdata-section"	The text of the node
ENTITY_REFERENCE_NODE	The name of the referenced entity	null
ENTITY_NODE	The entity name	null
PROCESSING_INSTRUCTION_NODE	The target of the PI	The remainder of the PI
COMMENT_NODE	"#comment"	The text of the comment
DOCUMENT_NODE	"#document"	null
DOCUMENT_TYPE_NODE	The document type name	null
DOCUMENT_FRAGMENT_NODE	"#document-fragment"	null
NOTATION_NODE	The notation name	null

In documents that use namespaces, the getNodeName() method of a Element or Attr node returns the qualified node name, which may include a namespace prefix. In documents that use namespaces, you may prefer to use the namespace-aware methods getNamespaceURI(), getLocalName() and getPrefix().

Element nodes may have a list of attributes, and the Element interface defines a number of methods for working with these attributes. In addition, however, Node defines the hasAttributes() method to determine if a node has any attributes. If it does, they can be retrieved with getAttributes().

Text content in an XML document is represented by Text nodes, which have methods for manipulating that textual content. The Node interface defines a normalize() method which has the specialized purpose of normalizing all descendants of a node by deleting empty Text nodes and coalescing adjacent Text nodes into a single combined node. Document trees usually start off in this normalized form, but modifications to the tree may result in nonnormalized documents.

Most of the other interfaces in this package extend Node. Document, Element and Text are the most commonly used.

```
public interface Node {
// Public Constants
    public static final short ATTRIBUTE_NODE;                                    =2
    public static final short CDATA_SECTION_NODE;                                =4
    public static final short COMMENT_NODE;                                      =8
    public static final short DOCUMENT_FRAGMENT_NODE;                            =11
    public static final short DOCUMENT_NODE;                                     =9
    public static final short DOCUMENT_TYPE_NODE;                                =10
    public static final short ELEMENT_NODE;                                      =1
    public static final short ENTITY_NODE;                                       =6
    public static final short ENTITY_REFERENCE_NODE;                             =5
    public static final short NOTATION_NODE;                                     =12
    public static final short PROCESSING_INSTRUCTION_NODE;                       =7
    public static final short TEXT_NODE;                                         =3
// Property Accessor Methods (by property name)
    public abstract NamedNodeMap getAttributes();
    public abstract NodeList getChildNodes();
    public abstract Node getFirstChild();
    public abstract Node getLastChild();
    public abstract String getLocalName();
    public abstract String getNamespaceURI();
    public abstract Node getNextSibling();
    public abstract String getNodeName();
    public abstract short getNodeType();
    public abstract String getNodeValue() throws DOMException;
    public abstract void setNodeValue(String nodeValue) throws DOMException;
    public abstract org.w3c.dom.Document getOwnerDocument();
    public abstract Node getParentNode();
    public abstract String getPrefix();
    public abstract void setPrefix(String prefix) throws DOMException;
    public abstract Node getPreviousSibling();
// Public Instance Methods
    public abstract Node appendChild(Node newChild) throws DOMException;
    public abstract Node cloneNode(boolean deep);
    public abstract boolean hasAttributes();
    public abstract boolean hasChildNodes();
    public abstract Node insertBefore(Node newChild, Node refChild) throws DOMException;
    public abstract boolean isSupported(String feature, String version);
    public abstract void normalize();
    public abstract Node removeChild(Node oldChild) throws DOMException;
    public abstract Node replaceChild(Node newChild, Node oldChild) throws DOMException;
}
```

Implementations: Attr, CharacterData, org.w3c.dom.Document, DocumentFragment, DocumentType, org.w3c.dom.Element, org.w3c.dom.Entity, EntityReference, Notation, ProcessingInstruction

Passed To: Too many methods to list.

Returned By: Too many methods to list.

Type Of: javax.imageio.metadata.IIOInvalidTreeException.offendingNode

NodeList — Java 1.4

org.w3c.dom

This interface represents a read-only ordered collection of nodes that can be iterated through. getLength() returns the number of nodes in the list, and item() returns the Node

DOM

at a specified index in the list (the index of the first node is 0). The elements of a NodeList are always valid Node objects: a NodeList never contains null elements.

Note that NodeList objects are live—they are not static but immediately reflect changes to the document tree. For example, if you have a NodeList that represents the children of a specific node, and you then delete one of those children, the child will be removed from your NodeList. Be careful when looping through the elements of a NodeList if the body of your loop makes changes to the document tree (such as deleting nodes) that may affect the contents of the NodeList!

```
public interface NodeList {
// Public Instance Methods
   public abstract int getLength();
   public abstract Node item(int index);
}
```

Implementations: javax.imageio.metadata.IIOMetadataNode

Returned By: javax.imageio.metadata.IIOMetadataNode.{getChildNodes(), getElementsByTagName(), getElementsByTagNameNS()}, org.w3c.dom.Document.{getElementsByTagName(), getElementsByTagNameNS()}, org.w3c.dom.Element.{getElementsByTagName(), getElementsByTagNameNS()}, Node.getChildNodes(), org.w3c.dom.html.HTMLDocument.getElementsByName()

Notation — Java 1.4

org.w3c.dom

This interface represents a notation declared in the DTD of an XML document. In XML notations are used to specify the format of an unparsed entity or to formally declare a processing instruction target.

The getNodeName() method of the Node interface returns the name of the notation. getSystemId() and getPublicId() return the system identifier and the public identifier specified in the notation declaration. The getNotations() method of the DocumentType interface returns a NamedNodeMap of Notation objects declared in the DTD and provides a way to look up Notation objects by notation name.

Because notations appear in the DTD and not the document itself, Notation nodes are never part of the document tree, and the getParentNode() method always returns null. Similarly, since XML notation declarations never have any content, a Notation node never has children and getChildNodes() always returns null. Notation objects are read-only and cannot be modified in any way.

Node — Notation

```
public interface Notation extends Node {
// Public Instance Methods
   public abstract String getPublicId();
   public abstract String getSystemId();
}
```

ProcessingInstruction — Java 1.4

org.w3c.dom

This interface represents an XML processing instruction (or PI) which specifies an arbitrary string of data to a named target processor. The getTarget() and getData() methods return the target and data portions of a PI, and these values can also be obtained using the getNodeName() and getNodeValue() methods of the Node interface. You can alter the data portion of a PI with setData() or with the setNodeValue() method of Node. ProcessingInstruction nodes never have children.

Node ··· ProcessingInstruction

```
public interface ProcessingInstruction extends Node {
// Public Instance Methods
   public abstract String getData();
   public abstract String getTarget();
   public abstract void setData(String data) throws DOMException;
}
```

Returned By: org.w3c.dom.Document.createProcessingInstruction()

Text **Java 1.4**

org.w3c.dom

A Text node represents a run of plain text that does not contain any XML markup. Plain text appears within XML elements and attributes, and Text nodes typically appear as children of Element and Attr nodes. Text nodes inherit from CharacterData, and the textual content of a Text node is available through the getData() method inherited from CharacterData or through the getNodeValue() method inherited from Node.

Text nodes may be manipulated using any of the methods inherited from CharacterData. The Text interface defines one method of its own: splitText() splits a Text node at the specified character position. The method changes the original node so that it contains only the text up to the specified position. Then it creates a new Text node that contains the text from the specified position on and inserts that new node into the document tree immediately after the original one. The Node.normalize() method reverses this process by deleting empty Text nodes and merging adjacent Text nodes into a single node.

Text nodes never have children.

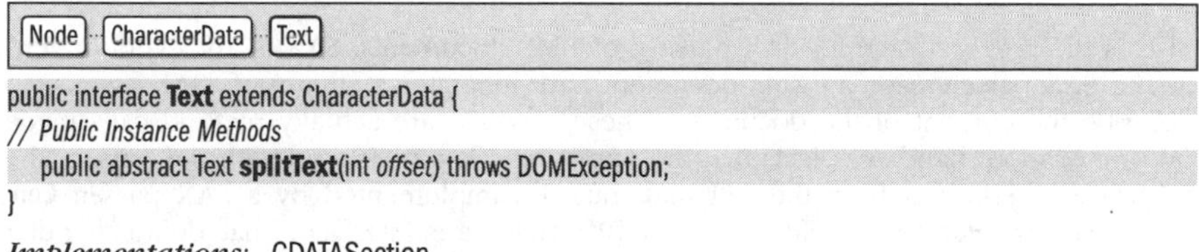


```
public interface Text extends CharacterData {
// Public Instance Methods
   public abstract Text splitText(int offset) throws DOMException;
}
```

Implementations: CDATASection

Returned By: org.w3c.dom.Document.createTextNode(), Text.splitText()

DOM

CHAPTER 24

org.xml.sax, org.xml.sax.ext, and org.xml.sax.helpers

This chapter documents the org.xml.sax package and its subpackages. org.xml.sax defines the Simplified API for XML, or SAX, a de facto standard for parsing XML documents. The org.xml.sax.ext package defines optional extensions to the SAX API, and the org.xml.sax.helpers package defines helper classes that are often useful with SAX. These packages have been incorporated into Java 1.4 but are not defined by Sun, which is why they have an "org.xml" prefix rather than a "java" prefix.

Package org.xml.sax — Java 1.4

This is the core package for SAX parsing of XML documents. SAX is an "event-driven" API: a SAX parser reads an XML document and generates a stream of "SAX events" to describe the content of the document. These "events" are actually method calls made on one or more handler objects that the application has registered with the parser. The XMLReader interface defines the API that must be implemented by a SAX parser. ContentHandler, ErrorHandler, EntityResolver, and DTDHandler are interfaces that define handler objects. An application registers objects that implement one or more of these interfaces with the XMLReader.

This package defines both the SAX1 and SAX2 interfaces. The AttributeList, DocumentHandler and Parser interfaces, as well as the HandlerBase class are part of the SAX1 API and are now deprecated in favor of Attributes, ContentHandler, XMLReader and org.xml.sax.helpers.DefaultHandler.

Interfaces:

public interface **AttributeList**;
public interface **Attributes**;
public interface **ContentHandler**;
public interface **DocumentHandler**;
public interface **DTDHandler**;
public interface **EntityResolver**;
public interface **ErrorHandler**;

public interface **Locator**;
public interface **Parser**;
public interface **XMLFilter** extends XMLReader;
public interface **XMLReader**;

Classes:

public class **HandlerBase** implements DocumentHandler, DTDHandler, EntityResolver, ErrorHandler;
public class **InputSource**;

Exceptions:

public class **SAXException** extends Exception;
  └ public class **SAXNotRecognizedException** extends SAXException;
  └ public class **SAXNotSupportedException** extends SAXException;
  └ public class **SAXParseException** extends SAXException;

AttributeList — Java 1.4; Deprecated in Java 1.4

org.xml.sax

This interface is part of the SAX1 API and has been deprecated in favor of the SAX2 Attributes interface, which supports XML namespaces.

```
public interface AttributeList {
// Public Instance Methods
   public abstract int getLength();
   public abstract String getName(int i);
   public abstract String getType(String name);
   public abstract String getType(int i);
   public abstract String getValue(String name);
   public abstract String getValue(int i);
}
```

Implementations: org.xml.sax.helpers.AttributeListImpl

Passed To: DocumentHandler.startElement(), HandlerBase.startElement(), org.xml.sax.helpers.AttributeListImpl.{AttributeListImpl(), setAttributeList()}, org.xml.sax.helpers.ParserAdapter.startElement()

Attributes — Java 1.4

org.xml.sax

This interface represents a list of attributes of an XML element and includes information about the attribute names, types, and values. If the SAX parser has read a DTD or schema for the document, this list of attributes will include attributes that are not explicitly specified in the document but which have a default value specified in the DTD or schema.

The most commonly used method is getValue(), which returns the value of a named attribute (there is also a version of this method that returns the value of a numbered attribute; it is discussed later). If the SAX parser is not processing namespaces, you can use the one-argument version of getValue(). Otherwise, use the two argument version to specify the URI that uniquely identifies the namespace, and the "local name" of the desired attribute within that namespace. The getType() methods are similar, except that they return the type of the named attribute, rather than its value. Note that getType() can only return useful information if the parser has read a DTD or schema for the document and knows the type of each attribute.

SAX

In XML documents the attributes of a tag can appear in any order. Attributes objects make no attempt to preserve the document source order of the tags. Nevertheless, it does impose an ordering on the attributes so that you can loop through them. getLength() returns the number of elements in the list. There are versions of getValue() and getType() that return the value and type of the attribute at a specified position in the list. You can also query the name of the attribute at a specified position, although the way you do this depends on whether the parser handles namespaces or not. If it does not process namespaces, use getQName() to get the name at a specified position. Otherwise, use getURI() and getLocalName() to obtain the URI and local name pair for the numbered attribute. Note that getQName() may return the empty string when namespace processing is on, and getLocalName() may return the empty string if namespace processing is off.

```
public interface Attributes {
// Public Instance Methods
   public abstract int getIndex(String qName);
   public abstract int getIndex(String uri, String localPart);
   public abstract int getLength();
   public abstract String getLocalName(int index);
   public abstract String getQName(int index);
   public abstract String getType(String qName);
   public abstract String getType(int index);
   public abstract String getType(String uri, String localName);
   public abstract String getURI(int index);
   public abstract String getValue(String qName);
   public abstract String getValue(int index);
   public abstract String getValue(String uri, String localName);
}
```

Implementations: org.xml.sax.helpers.AttributesImpl

Passed To: org.xml.sax.ContentHandler.startElement(), org.xml.sax.helpers.AttributesImpl.{AttributesImpl(), setAttributes()}, org.xml.sax.helpers.DefaultHandler.startElement(), org.xml.sax.helpers.XMLFilterImpl.startElement(), org.xml.sax.helpers.XMLReaderAdapter.startElement()

ContentHandler — Java 1.4

org.xml.sax

This interface is the key one for XML parsing with the SAX API. An XMLReader tells your application about the content of the XML document it is parsing by invoking the various methods of the ContentHandler interface. In order to parse documents with SAX, you must implement this interface to define methods that take whatever actions are necessary when they are invoked by the parser. Because this interface is so critical to the SAX API, the methods are explained individually:

setDocumentLocator()
: The parser usually calls this method (but is not required to do so) before calling any others to pass a Locator object to the ContentHandler. Locator defines methods that return the current line and column number of the document being parsed, and if the parser supplies a Locator object, it guarantees that its methods will return valid values during any other ContentHandler invocations that follow. A ContentHandler can call the methods of this object when printing error messages, for example.

startDocument(), endDocument()
: The parser calls these methods once, at the beginning and end of parsing. startDocument() is the first method called except for the optional setDocumentLocator() call, and endDocument() is always the last method call on a ContentHandler.

startElement(), endElement()
: The parser calls these methods for each start tag and end tag it encounters. Both are passed three arguments describing the name of the tag: if the parser is doing namespace processing, then the first two arguments of both methods return the URI that uniquely identifies the namespace, and the local name of the tag within that namespace. If the parser is not doing namespace parsing, then the third argument provides the full name of the tag. In addition to these tag name arguments, startElement() is also passed an Attributes object that describes the attributes of the tag.

characters()
: This method is invoked to tell the application that the parser has found a string of text in the XML document. The text is contained within the specified character array, at the specified start position, and continuing for the specified number of characters.

ignorableWhitespace()
: This method is like characters(), but parsers may use it to tell the application about "ignorable whitespace" in XML element content.

processingInstruction()
: The parser calls this method to tell the application that it has encountered an XML Processing Instruction (or PI) with the specified target and data strings.

skippedEntity()
: If the XML parser does encounters an entity in the document, but does not expand and parse its content, then it tells the application about it by passing the name of the entity to this method.

startPrefixMapping(), endPrefixMapping()
: These methods to tell the application about a namespace mapping from the specified prefix to the specified namespace URI.

DTDHandler is another interface like ContentHandler. An application can implement this interface to receive notification of DTD-related events from the parser. Similarly, the org.xml.sax.ext package defines two "extension" interfaces that can be used (if the parser supports these extensions) to obtain even more information about the document (such as comments and CDATA sections) and about the DTD (including the full set of element, attribute and entity declarations). The org.xml.sax.helpers.DefaultHandler class is a useful one. It implements ContentHandler and three other interfaces that are commonly used with the XMLReader class and provides empty implementations of all their methods. Applications can subclass DefaultHandler only need to override the methods they care about. This is usually more convenient that implementing the interfaces directly.

```
public interface ContentHandler {
// Public Instance Methods
   public abstract void characters(char[ ] ch, int start, int length) throws SAXException;
   public abstract void endDocument( ) throws SAXException;
   public abstract void endElement(String namespaceURI, String localName, String qName) throws SAXException;
   public abstract void endPrefixMapping(String prefix) throws SAXException;
   public abstract void ignorableWhitespace(char[ ] ch, int start, int length) throws SAXException;
   public abstract void processingInstruction(String target, String data) throws SAXException;
   public abstract void setDocumentLocator(Locator locator);
   public abstract void skippedEntity(String name) throws SAXException;
   public abstract void startDocument( ) throws SAXException;
   public abstract void startElement(String namespaceURI, String localName, String qName,
                                     org.xml.sax.Attributes atts) throws SAXException;
```

SAX

```
    public abstract void startPrefixMapping(String prefix, String uri) throws SAXException;
}
```

Implementations: javax.xml.transform.sax.TemplatesHandler, javax.xml.transform.sax.TransformerHandler, org.xml.sax.helpers.DefaultHandler, org.xml.sax.helpers.XMLFilterImpl, org.xml.sax.helpers.XMLReaderAdapter

Passed To: javax.xml.transform.sax.SAXResult.{SAXResult(), setHandler()}, XMLReader.setContentHandler(), org.xml.sax.helpers.ParserAdapter.setContentHandler(), org.xml.sax.helpers.XMLFilterImpl.setContentHandler()

Returned By: javax.xml.transform.sax.SAXResult.getHandler(), XMLReader.getContentHandler(), org.xml.sax.helpers.ParserAdapter.getContentHandler(), org.xml.sax.helpers.XMLFilterImpl.getContentHandler()

DocumentHandler — Java 1.4; Deprecated in Java 1.4

org.xml.sax

This interface is part of the SAX1 API and has been deprecated in favor of the SAX2 ContentHandler interface, which supports XML namespaces.

```
public interface DocumentHandler {
// Public Instance Methods
    public abstract void characters(char[ ] ch, int start, int length) throws SAXException;
    public abstract void endDocument( ) throws SAXException;
    public abstract void endElement(String name) throws SAXException;
    public abstract void ignorableWhitespace(char[ ] ch, int start, int length) throws SAXException;
    public abstract void processingInstruction(String target, String data) throws SAXException;
    public abstract void setDocumentLocator(Locator locator);
    public abstract void startDocument( ) throws SAXException;
    public abstract void startElement(String name, org.xml.sax.AttributeList atts) throws SAXException;
}
```

Implementations: HandlerBase, org.xml.sax.helpers.ParserAdapter

Passed To: org.xml.sax.Parser.setDocumentHandler(), org.xml.sax.helpers.XMLReaderAdapter.setDocumentHandler()

DTDHandler — Java 1.4

org.xml.sax

This interface defines methods that an application can implement in order to receive notification from a XMLReader about notation and unparsed entity declarations in the DTD of an XML document. Notations and unparsed entities are two of the most obscure features of XML, and they (and this interface) are not frequently used. To use a DTDHandler, define a class that implements the interface, (or simply subclass the helper class org.xml.sax.helpers.DefaultHandler) and pass an instance of that class to the setDTDHandler() method of an XMLReader. Then, if the parser encounters any notation or unparsed entity declarations in the DTD of the document, it will invoke the notationDecl() or unparsedEntityDecl() method that you have supplied. Unparsed entities can appear later in a document as the value of an attribute, so if your application cares about them, it should somehow make a note of the entity name and system ID for later use.

```
public interface DTDHandler {
// Public Instance Methods
    public abstract void notationDecl(String name, String publicId, String systemId) throws SAXException;
```

```
    public abstract void unparsedEntityDecl(String name, String publicId, String systemId, String notationName)
        throws SAXException;
}
```

Implementations: javax.xml.transform.sax.TransformerHandler, HandlerBase, org.xml.sax.helpers.DefaultHandler, org.xml.sax.helpers.XMLFilterImpl

Passed To: org.xml.sax.Parser.setDTDHandler(), XMLReader.setDTDHandler(), org.xml.sax.helpers.ParserAdapter.setDTDHandler(), org.xml.sax.helpers.XMLFilterImpl.setDTDHandler(), org.xml.sax.helpers.XMLReaderAdapter.setDTDHandler()

Returned By: XMLReader.getDTDHandler(), org.xml.sax.helpers.ParserAdapter.getDTDHandler(), org.xml.sax.helpers.XMLFilterImpl.getDTDHandler()

EntityResolver — Java 1.4

org.xml.sax

An application can implement this interface to help the parser resolve external entities, if required. If you pass an EntityResolver instance to the setEntityResolver() method of an XMLReader, then the parser will call the resolveEntity() method whenever it needs to read an external entity. This method should use the public identifier or system identifier to return an InputSource that the parser can use to read the content of the external entity. If the external entity includes a valid system identifier, then the parser can read it directly without the need for an EntityResolver, but this interface is still useful for mapping network URLs to locally cached copies, or for mapping public identifiers to local files, for example. The helper class org.xml.sax.helpers.DefaultHandler includes a stub implementation of this interface, so if you subclass DefaultHandler you can override its resolveEntity() method.

```
public interface EntityResolver {
// Public Instance Methods
    public abstract InputSource resolveEntity(String publicId, String systemId) throws SAXException,
        java.io.IOException;
}
```

Implementations: HandlerBase, org.xml.sax.helpers.DefaultHandler, org.xml.sax.helpers.XMLFilterImpl

Passed To: javax.xml.parsers.DocumentBuilder.setEntityResolver(), org.xml.sax.Parser.setEntityResolver(), XMLReader.setEntityResolver(), org.xml.sax.helpers.ParserAdapter.setEntityResolver(), org.xml.sax.helpers.XMLFilterImpl.setEntityResolver(), org.xml.sax.helpers.XMLReaderAdapter.setEntityResolver()

Returned By: XMLReader.getEntityResolver(), org.xml.sax.helpers.ParserAdapter.getEntityResolver(), org.xml.sax.helpers.XMLFilterImpl.getEntityResolver()

SAX

ErrorHandler — Java 1.4

org.xml.sax

Before parsing an XML document, an application should provide an implementation of this interface to the XMLReader by calling the setErrorHandler() method of the XMLReader. If the reader needs to issue a warning or report an error or fatal error, it will call the appropriate method of the ErrorHandler object you supplied. The error() method is used to report recoverable errors, such as document validity problems. The parser continues parsing after calling error(). The fatalError() method is used to report nonrecoverable errors, such as well-formedness problems. The parser may not continue parsing after calling fatalError(). An ErrorHandler object may respond to warnings, errors, and fatal errors however it likes, and may throw exceptions from these methods.

Instead of implementing this interface directly, you may also subclass the helper class org.xml.sax.helpers.DefaultHandler and override the error reporting methods it provides. The warning() and error() methods of a DefaultHandler do nothing, and the fatalError() method throws the SAXParseException object that was passed to it.

```
public interface ErrorHandler {
// Public Instance Methods
   public abstract void error(SAXParseException exception) throws SAXException;
   public abstract void fatalError(SAXParseException exception) throws SAXException;
   public abstract void warning(SAXParseException exception) throws SAXException;
}
```

Implementations: HandlerBase, org.xml.sax.helpers.DefaultHandler, org.xml.sax.helpers.XMLFilterImpl

Passed To: javax.xml.parsers.DocumentBuilder.setErrorHandler(), org.xml.sax.Parser.setErrorHandler(), XMLReader.setErrorHandler(), org.xml.sax.helpers.ParserAdapter.setErrorHandler(), org.xml.sax.helpers.XMLFilterImpl.setErrorHandler(), org.xml.sax.helpers.XMLReaderAdapter.setErrorHandler()

Returned By: XMLReader.getErrorHandler(), org.xml.sax.helpers.ParserAdapter.getErrorHandler(), org.xml.sax.helpers.XMLFilterImpl.getErrorHandler()

HandlerBase — Java 1.4; Deprecated in Java 1.4

org.xml.sax

This class is part of the SAX1 API and has been deprecated in favor of the SAX2 org.xml.sax.helpers.DefaultHandler class.

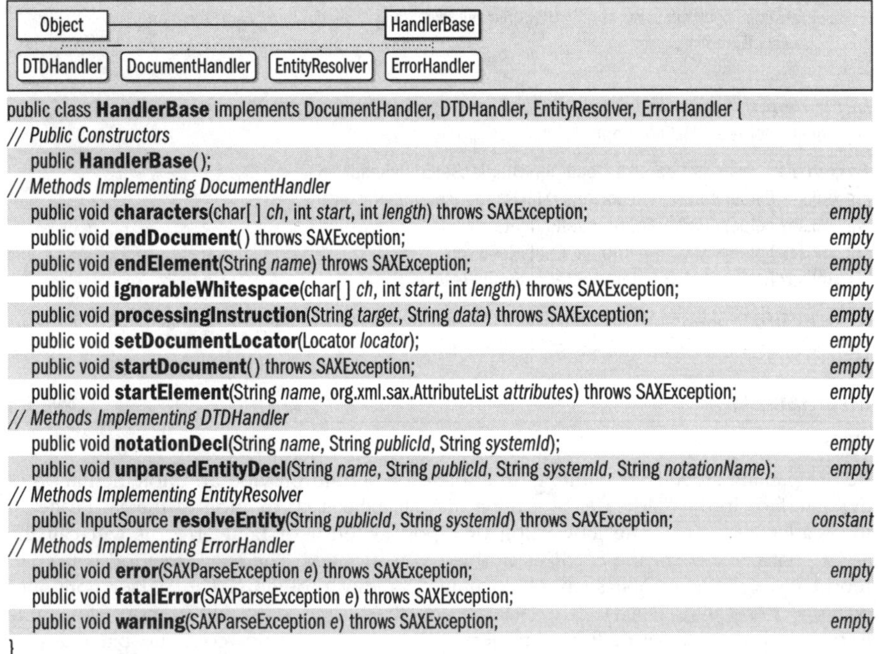


```
public class HandlerBase implements DocumentHandler, DTDHandler, EntityResolver, ErrorHandler {
// Public Constructors
   public HandlerBase();
// Methods Implementing DocumentHandler
   public void characters(char[ ] ch, int start, int length) throws SAXException;              empty
   public void endDocument() throws SAXException;                                              empty
   public void endElement(String name) throws SAXException;                                    empty
   public void ignorableWhitespace(char[ ] ch, int start, int length) throws SAXException;     empty
   public void processingInstruction(String target, String data) throws SAXException;          empty
   public void setDocumentLocator(Locator locator);                                            empty
   public void startDocument() throws SAXException;                                            empty
   public void startElement(String name, org.xml.sax.AttributeList attributes) throws SAXException;  empty
// Methods Implementing DTDHandler
   public void notationDecl(String name, String publicId, String systemId);                   empty
   public void unparsedEntityDecl(String name, String publicId, String systemId, String notationName);  empty
// Methods Implementing EntityResolver
   public InputSource resolveEntity(String publicId, String systemId) throws SAXException;    constant
// Methods Implementing ErrorHandler
   public void error(SAXParseException e) throws SAXException;                                 empty
   public void fatalError(SAXParseException e) throws SAXException;
   public void warning(SAXParseException e) throws SAXException;                               empty
}
```

Passed To: javax.xml.parsers.SAXParser.parse()

InputSource — Java 1.4

org.xml.sax

This simple class describes a source of input for an XMLReader. An InputSource object can be passed to the parse() method of XMLReader, and is also the return value of the EntityResolver.resolveEntity() method.

Create an InputSource() with one of the constructor methods, specifying the system identifier (a URL) of the file to be parsed, or specifying a byte or character stream that the parser should read the document from. In addition to calling the constructor, you may also want to call setSystemId() to specify and/or setPublicId() to provide identifiers for the document being parsed. Having a filename or URL is useful if an error arises, and your ErrorHandler object needs to print an error message, for example. If you specify the document to parse as a URL or as a byte stream, you can also call setEncoding() to specify the character encoding of the document. The parser will use this encoding value if you supply it, but XML documents are supposed to describe their own encoding in the <?xml?> declaration, so the parser ought to be able to determine the encoding of the document even if you do not call setEncoding().

This class allows you to specify more than one input source. The XMLReader will first call getCharacterStream() and use the returned Reader if there is one. If that method returns false, then it calls getByteStream() and uses the InputStream it returns. Finally, if no character or byte stream is found, then the parser will call getSystemId() and will attempt to read an XML document from the returned URL.

An XMLReader will never use any of the set() methods to modify the state of an InputSource object.

```
public class InputSource {
// Public Constructors
   public InputSource();
   public InputSource(java.io.Reader characterStream);
   public InputSource(java.io.InputStream byteStream);
   public InputSource(String systemId);
// Property Accessor Methods (by property name)
   public java.io.InputStream getByteStream();                        default:null
   public void setByteStream(java.io.InputStream byteStream);
   public java.io.Reader getCharacterStream();                        default:null
   public void setCharacterStream(java.io.Reader characterStream);
   public String getEncoding();                                       default:null
   public void setEncoding(String encoding);
   public String getPublicId();                                       default:null
   public void setPublicId(String publicId);
   public String getSystemId();                                       default:null
   public void setSystemId(String systemId);
}
```

Passed To: javax.xml.parsers.DocumentBuilder.parse(), javax.xml.parsers.SAXParser.parse(), javax.xml.transform.sax.SAXSource.{SAXSource(), setInputSource()}, org.xml.sax.Parser.parse(), XMLReader.parse(), org.xml.sax.helpers.ParserAdapter.parse(), org.xml.sax.helpers.XMLFilterImpl.parse(), org.xml.sax.helpers.XMLReaderAdapter.parse()

Returned By: javax.xml.transform.sax.SAXSource.{getInputSource(), sourceToInputSource()}, EntityResolver.resolveEntity(), HandlerBase.resolveEntity(), org.xml.sax.helpers.DefaultHandler.resolveEntity(), org.xml.sax.helpers.XMLFilterImpl.resolveEntity()

Locator **Java 1.4**

org.xml.sax

An XMLReader may pass an object that implements this interface to the application by calling the setDocumentLocator() method of the application's ContentHandler object before it invokes any other methods of that ContentHandler. The ContentHandler can use methods of this Locator object from within any of the other methods called by the parser in order to determine what document the parser is parsing and what line number and column number it is parsing at. This information is particularly useful when displaying error or warning messages, for example. getSystemId() and getPublicId() return the system and public identifiers of the document being parsed, if this information is available to the parser, and otherwise return null. getLineNumber() and getColumnNumber() return the line number and column number of the next character that the parser will read (line and column numbers are numbered starting at 1, not at 0). The parser is allowed to return an approximate value from these methods, or to return –1 if it does not track line and column numbers.

```
public interface Locator {
// Public Instance Methods
   public abstract int getColumnNumber();
   public abstract int getLineNumber();
   public abstract String getPublicId();
   public abstract String getSystemId();
}
```

Implementations: org.xml.sax.helpers.LocatorImpl

Passed To: org.xml.sax.ContentHandler.setDocumentLocator(), DocumentHandler.setDocumentLocator(), HandlerBase.setDocumentLocator(), SAXParseException.SAXParseException(), org.xml.sax.helpers.DefaultHandler.setDocumentLocator(), org.xml.sax.helpers.LocatorImpl.LocatorImpl(), org.xml.sax.helpers.ParserAdapter.setDocumentLocator(), org.xml.sax.helpers.XMLFilterImpl.setDocumentLocator(), org.xml.sax.helpers.XMLReaderAdapter.setDocumentLocator()

Parser **Java 1.4; Deprecated in Java 1.4**

org.xml.sax

This interface is part of the SAX1 API and has been deprecated in favor of the SAX2 XMLReader interface, which supports XML namespaces.

```
public interface Parser {
// Public Instance Methods
   public abstract void parse(InputSource source) throws SAXException, java.io.IOException;
   public abstract void parse(String systemId) throws SAXException, java.io.IOException;
   public abstract void setDocumentHandler(DocumentHandler handler);
   public abstract void setDTDHandler(DTDHandler handler);
   public abstract void setEntityResolver(EntityResolver resolver);
   public abstract void setErrorHandler(ErrorHandler handler);
   public abstract void setLocale(java.util.Locale locale) throws SAXException;
}
```

Implementations: org.xml.sax.helpers.XMLReaderAdapter

Passed To: org.xml.sax.helpers.ParserAdapter.ParserAdapter()

Returned By: javax.xml.parsers.SAXParser.getParser(), org.xml.sax.helpers.ParserFactory.makeParser()

SAXException — Java 1.4

org.xml.sax — *serializable checked*

This signals a problem while parsing an XML document. This class serves as the general superclass for more specific types of SAX exceptions. The parse() method of an XMLReader can throw an exception of this type. The application can also throw a SAXException from any of the handler methods (of ContentHandler and ErrorHandler, for example) invoked by the parser.

Object — Throwable — Exception — SAXException
Serializable

```
public class SAXException extends Exception {
// Public Constructors
   public SAXException(String message);
   public SAXException(Exception e);
   public SAXException(String message, Exception e);
// Public Instance Methods
   public Exception getException();
// Public Methods Overriding Throwable
   public String getMessage();
   public String toString();
}
```

Subclasses: SAXNotRecognizedException, SAXNotSupportedException, SAXParseException

Thrown By: Too many methods to list.

SAXNotRecognizedException — Java 1.4

org.xml.sax — *serializable checked*

This signals that the parser does not recognize a feature or property name. See the setFeature() and setProperty() methods of XMLReader.

Object — Throwable — Exception — SAXException — SAXNotRecognizedException
Serializable

```
public class SAXNotRecognizedException extends SAXException {
// Public Constructors
   public SAXNotRecognizedException(String message);
}
```

Thrown By: Too many methods to list.

SAXNotSupportedException — Java 1.4

org.xml.sax — *serializable checked*

This signals that the parser recognizes, but does not support, a named feature or property. The property or feature may be entirely unsupported, or it may be read-only, in which case this exception will be thrown by the setFeature() or setProperty() method, but not by the corresponding getFeature() or getProperty() method of XMLReader.

Object — Throwable — Exception — SAXException — SAXNotSupportedException
Serializable

SAX

```
public class SAXNotSupportedException extends SAXException {
// Public Constructors
   public SAXNotSupportedException(String message);
}
```

Thrown By: Too many methods to list.

SAXParseException Java 1.4

org.xml.sax *serializable checked*

An exception of this type signals an XML parsing error or warning. SAXParseException includes methods to return the system and public identifiers of the document in which the error or warning occurred, as well as methods to return the approximate line number and column number at which it occurred. A parser is not required to obtain or track all of this information, and the methods may return null or –1 if the information is not available. (See Locator for more information.)

Exceptions of this type are usually thrown by the application from the methods of the ErrorHandler interface. The parser never throws a SAXParseException itself, but does pass an appropriately initialized instance of this class to each of the ErrorHandler methods. It is up to the application's ErrorHandler object to decide whether to actually throw the exception, however.

Object — Throwable — Exception — SAXException — SAXParseException
Throwable ⋮ Serializable

```
public class SAXParseException extends SAXException {
// Public Constructors
   public SAXParseException(String message, Locator locator);
   public SAXParseException(String message, Locator locator, Exception e);
   public SAXParseException(String message, String publicId, String systemId, int lineNumber, int columnNumber);
   public SAXParseException(String message, String publicId, String systemId, int lineNumber, int columnNumber,
                            Exception e);
// Public Instance Methods
   public int getColumnNumber();
   public int getLineNumber();
   public String getPublicId();
   public String getSystemId();
}
```

Passed To: ErrorHandler.{error(), fatalError(), warning()}, HandlerBase.{error(), fatalError(), warning()}, org.xml.sax.helpers.DefaultHandler.{error(), fatalError(), warning()}, org.xml.sax.helpers.XMLFilterImpl.{error(), fatalError(), warning()}

XMLFilter Java 1.4

org.xml.sax

An XMLFilter extends XMLReader and behaves like an XMLReader except that instead of parsing a document itself, it filters the SAX events provided by a "parent" XMLReader object. Use the setParent() method to link an XMLFilter object to the XMLReader that it is to serve as a filter for.

An XMLFilter serves as both a source of SAX events, and also as a recipient of those events, so an implementation must implement ContentHandler and related interfaces so that it can obtain events from the parent object, filter them, and then pass the filtered events on to the ContentHandler object that was registered on the filter. See the helper class org.xml.sax.helpers.XMLFilterImpl for a bare-bones implementation of an XMLFilter that implements the XMLReader interface and the ContentHandler and related handler interfaces. XMLFilterImpl does no filtering—it simply passes passes all of its method invocations through. You can subclass it and override only the methods that need filtering.

XMLReader ··· XMLFilter

```
public interface XMLFilter extends XMLReader {
// Public Instance Methods
   public abstract XMLReader getParent();
   public abstract void setParent(XMLReader parent);
}
```

Implementations: org.xml.sax.helpers.XMLFilterImpl

Returned By: javax.xml.transform.sax.SAXTransformerFactory.newXMLFilter()

XMLReader — Java 1.4

org.xml.sax

This interface defines the methods that must be implemented by a SAX2 XML parser. Since it is an interface, XMLReader cannot define a constructor for creating an XMLReader. To obtain an XMLReader, object, you can instantiate some implementation-specific class that implements this interface. Alternatively, you can keep your code independent of any specific parser implementation by using the SAXParserFactory and SAXParser classes of the javax.xml.parsers package. See those classes for more details. Note that the XMLReader interface has no relationship to the java.io.Reader class or any other character stream classes.

Once you have obtained an XMLReader instance, you must register handler objects on it, so that it can invoke methods on those handlers to notify your application of the results of its parsing. All applications should register a ContentHandler and an ErrorHandler with setContentHandler() and setErrorHandler(). Some applications may also want to register an EntityResolver and/or a DTDHandler. Applications can also register DeclHandler and LexicalHandler objects from the org.xml.sax.ext package, if the parser implementation supports these extension handler interfaces. DeclHandler and LexicalHandler objects are registered with setProperty(), as explained below.

In addition to registering handler objects for an XMLReader, you may also want to configure the behavior of the parser using setFeature() and setProperty(). Features and properties are both name/value pairs. For uniqueness, the names of features and properties are expressed as URLs (the URLs usually do not have any web content associated with them: they are merely unique identifiers). Features have boolean values, and properties have arbitrary object values. Features and properties are an extension mechanism, allowing an application to specify implementation-specific details about how the parser should behave. But there are also several "standard" features and properties that are supported by many (or all) SAX parsers. They are listed below. If a parser does not recognize the name of a feature or property, the setFeature() and setProperty() methods (as well as the corresponding getFeature() and getProperty() query methods) throw a SAXNotRecognizedException. If the parser recognizes the name of a feature or property, but does not support the feature or property, the methods instead throw a SAXNotSupportedException. This exception is also thrown by the set methods when the parser allows the feature or property to be queried but not set.

The standard features are the following. Their names are all URLs that begin with the prefix "http://www.xml.org/sax/features/". For brevity, this prefix has been omitted

SAX

below. Note that only two of these features must be supported by all parsers. The others may or may not be supported in any given implementation:

namespaces
: If true (the default), the parser supports namespaces and provides the namespace URI and localname for element and attribute names. Support for this feature is required in all parser implementations.

namespace-prefixes
: If true, the parser provides the qualified name (or "qName") that for element and attribute names. A qName consists of a namespace prefix, a colon, and the local name. The default value of this feature is false, and support for the feature is required in all parser implementations.

validation
: If true, the parser will validate XML documents, and will read all external entities.

external-general-entities
: If true, the parser handles external general entities. This is always true if the validation feature is true.

external-parameter-entities
: If true, the parser handles external parameter entities. This is always true if the validation feature is true.

lexical-handler/parameter-entities
: If true, the parser will report the beginning and end of parameter entities to the LexicalHandler extension interface.

string-interning
: If true, the parser will use the String.intern() method for all strings (element, attribute, entity and notation names, and namespace prefixes and URIs) it returns. If the application does the same, it can use == equality testing for these strings rather than using the more expensive equals() method.

The standard properties are the following. Like the features, their names are all URLs that begin with the prefix "http://www.xml.org/sax/properties/" (omitted in the following list). Note that support for all of these properties is optional.

declaration-handler
: An org.xml.sax.ext.DeclHandler object to which the parser will report the contents of the DTD.

lexical-handler
: An org.xml.sax.ext.LexicalHandler object on which the parser will make method calls to describe the lexical structure (such as comments and CDATA sections) of the XML document.

xml-string
: This is a read-only property that can be queried only from within a handler method invoked by the parser. The value of this property is a String that contains the document content that triggered the current handler invocation.

dom-node
: An XMLReader that "parses" a DOM tree rather than the textual form of an XML document uses the value of this property as the org.w3c.dom.Node object at which it should begin parsing.

Finally, after you have obtained an XMLReader object, have queried and configured its features and properties, and have set a ContentHandler, ErrorHandler, and any other required handler objects, you are ready to parse an XML document. Do this by calling one of the parse() methods, specifying the document to parse either as a system identifier (a URL) or as an InputSource object (which also allows the use of streams).

```
public interface XMLReader {
// Public Instance Methods
   public abstract org.xml.sax.ContentHandler getContentHandler();
   public abstract DTDHandler getDTDHandler();
   public abstract EntityResolver getEntityResolver();
   public abstract ErrorHandler getErrorHandler();
   public abstract boolean getFeature(String name) throws SAXNotRecognizedException, SAXNotSupportedException;
   public abstract Object getProperty(String name) throws SAXNotRecognizedException, SAXNotSupportedException;
   public abstract void parse(String systemId) throws java.io.IOException, SAXException;
   public abstract void parse(InputSource input) throws java.io.IOException, SAXException;
   public abstract void setContentHandler(org.xml.sax.ContentHandler handler);
   public abstract void setDTDHandler(DTDHandler handler);
   public abstract void setEntityResolver(EntityResolver resolver);
   public abstract void setErrorHandler(ErrorHandler handler);
   public abstract void setFeature(String name, boolean value) throws SAXNotRecognizedException,
      SAXNotSupportedException;
   public abstract void setProperty(String name, Object value) throws SAXNotRecognizedException,
      SAXNotSupportedException;
}
```

Implementations: XMLFilter, org.xml.sax.helpers.ParserAdapter

Passed To: javax.xml.transform.sax.SAXSource.{SAXSource(), setXMLReader()}, XMLFilter.setParent(), org.xml.sax.helpers.XMLFilterImpl.{setParent(), XMLFilterImpl()}, org.xml.sax.helpers.XMLReaderAdapter.XMLReaderAdapter()

Returned By: javax.xml.parsers.SAXParser.getXMLReader(), javax.xml.transform.sax.SAXSource.getXMLReader(), XMLFilter.getParent(), org.xml.sax.helpers.XMLFilterImpl.getParent(), org.xml.sax.helpers.XMLReaderFactory.createXMLReader()

Package org.xml.sax.ext — Java 1.4

This package defines extensions to the basic SAX2 API. Neither SAX parsers nor SAX applications are required to support these extensions, but when they do, the interfaces defined here provide a standard way for the parser to provide additional information about an XML document to the application. DeclHandler defines methods for reporting the content of a DTD, and LexicalHandler defines methods for reporting the lexical structure of an XML document.

At the time of this writing, a "SAX2 Extensions 1.1" release is in preparation. The current beta version adds three new interfaces to this package: Attributes2, EntityResolver2, and Locator2. Because these new extensions are not yet released, they are not documented here. See *http://www.saxproject.org* for details.

Interfaces:

```
public interface DeclHandler;
public interface LexicalHandler;
```

DeclHandler — Java 1.4

org.xml.sax.ext

This extension interface defines methods that a SAX parser can call to notify an application about element, attribute, and entity declarations in a DTD. If your application requires this information about a DTD, then pass an object that implements this interface to the setProperty() method of an XMLReader, using the property name "http://www.xml.org/sax/properties/declaration-handler". Because this is an extension handler, SAX parsers are not required to support it, and may throw a SAXNotRecognizedException or a SAXNotSupportedException when you attempt to register a DeclHandler.

```
public interface DeclHandler {
// Public Instance Methods
   public abstract void attributeDecl(String eName, String aName, String type, String valueDefault, String value)
       throws org.xml.sax.SAXException;
   public abstract void elementDecl(String name, String model) throws org.xml.sax.SAXException;
   public abstract void externalEntityDecl(String name, String publicId, String systemId)
       throws org.xml.sax.SAXException;
   public abstract void internalEntityDecl(String name, String value) throws org.xml.sax.SAXException;
}
```

LexicalHandler — Java 1.4

org.xml.sax.ext

This extension interface defines methods that a SAX parser can call to notify an application about the lexical structure of an XML document. If your application requires this kind of information (for example if it wants to create a new document that has a similar structure to the one it reads), then pass an object that implements this interface to the setProperty() method of an XMLReader, using the property name "http://www.xml.org/sax/properties/lexical-handler". Because this is an extension handler, SAX parsers are not required to support it, and may throw a SAXNotRecognizedException or a SAXNotSupportedException when you attempt to register a DeclHandler.

If a LexicalHandler is successfully registered on an XMLReader, then the parser will call startDTD() and endDTD() to report the beginning and end of the document's DTD. It will call startCDATA() and endCDATA() to report the start and end of a CDATA section. The content of the CDATA section will be reported through the characters() method of the ContentHandler interface. When the parser expands an entity, it first calls startEntity() to specify the name of the entity it is about to expand, and then calls endEntity() when the entity expansion is complete. Finally, whenever the parser encounters an XML comment, it calls the comment() method.

```
public interface LexicalHandler {
// Public Instance Methods
   public abstract void comment(char[ ] ch, int start, int length) throws org.xml.sax.SAXException;
   public abstract void endCDATA( ) throws org.xml.sax.SAXException;
   public abstract void endDTD( ) throws org.xml.sax.SAXException;
   public abstract void endEntity(String name) throws org.xml.sax.SAXException;
   public abstract void startCDATA( ) throws org.xml.sax.SAXException;
   public abstract void startDTD(String name, String publicId, String systemId) throws org.xml.sax.SAXException;
   public abstract void startEntity(String name) throws org.xml.sax.SAXException;
}
```

Implementations: javax.xml.transform.sax.TransformerHandler

Passed To: javax.xml.transform.sax.SAXResult.setLexicalHandler()

Returned By: javax.xml.transform.sax.SAXResult.getLexicalHandler()

Package org.xml.sax.helpers Java 1.4

This package contains utility classes that are useful for programmers working with SAX parsers. DefaultHandler is the most commonly used: it is a default implementation of the four standard handler interfaces, suitable for easy subclassing by an application. XML-ReaderFactory provides a layer implementation-independence, allowing an application to use an XMLReader implementation specified in a system property. XMLFilterImpl is a no-op implementation of the XMLFilter interface that also implements the various handler interfaces necessary to connect the filter to its "parent" XMLReader. It does no filtering of its own, but is easy to subclass to add filtering. If you need to work with legacy APIs that expect or return SAX1 Parser objects, you can use ParserAdapter to make a Parser object behave like a SAX2 XMLReader object, or use an XMLReaderAdapter to make an XMLReader behave like a Parser.

Classes:

```
public class AttributeListImpl implements org.xml.sax.AttributeList;
public class AttributesImpl implements org.xml.sax.Attributes;
public class DefaultHandler implements org.xml.sax.ContentHandler, org.xml.sax.DTDHandler,
        org.xml.sax.EntityResolver, org.xml.sax.ErrorHandler;
public class LocatorImpl implements org.xml.sax.Locator;
public class NamespaceSupport;
public class ParserAdapter implements org.xml.sax.DocumentHandler, org.xml.sax.XMLReader;
public class ParserFactory;
public class XMLFilterImpl implements org.xml.sax.ContentHandler, org.xml.sax.DTDHandler,
        org.xml.sax.EntityResolver, org.xml.sax.ErrorHandler, org.xml.sax.XMLFilter;
public class XMLReaderAdapter implements org.xml.sax.ContentHandler, org.xml.sax.Parser;
public final class XMLReaderFactory;
```

AttributeListImpl Java 1.4; Deprecated in Java 1.4

org.xml.sax.helpers

This deprecated class is an implementation of the deprecated SAX1 org.xml.sax.AttributeList interface. They have been deprecated in favor of the AttributesImpl implementation of the SAX2 org.xml.sax.Attributes interface.

Object — AttributeListImpl ··· AttributeList

```
public class AttributeListImpl implements org.xml.sax.AttributeList {
// Public Constructors
    public AttributeListImpl();
    public AttributeListImpl(org.xml.sax.AttributeList atts);
// Public Instance Methods
    public void addAttribute(String name, String type, String value);
    public void clear();
    public void removeAttribute(String name);
    public void setAttributeList(org.xml.sax.AttributeList atts);
// Methods Implementing AttributeList
    public int getLength();                                                    default:0
    public String getName(int i);
    public String getType(int i);
    public String getType(String name);
    public String getValue(String name);
```

```
    public String getValue(int i);
}
```

AttributesImpl — Java 1.4

org.xml.sax.helpers

This utility class is a general-purpose implementation of the Attributes interface. In addition to implementing all the methods of Attributes, it also defines various set methods for setting attribute names, values, and types, an addAttribute() method for adding a new attribute to the end of the list, a removeAttribute() method for removing an attribute from the list, and a clear() method for removing all attributes. Also, there is an AttributesImpl() constructor that initializes the new AttributesImpl object with a copy of a specified Attributes object. This class is useful for XMLFilter implementations that want to filter the attributes of an element, or for ContentHandler implementations that need to make and save a copy of an Attributes object for later use.

Object — AttributesImpl ··· Attributes

```
public class AttributesImpl implements org.xml.sax.Attributes {
// Public Constructors
    public AttributesImpl();
    public AttributesImpl(org.xml.sax.Attributes atts);
// Public Instance Methods
    public void addAttribute(String uri, String localName, String qName, String type, String value);
    public void clear();
    public void removeAttribute(int index);
    public void setAttribute(int index, String uri, String localName, String qName, String type, String value);
    public void setAttributes(org.xml.sax.Attributes atts);
    public void setLocalName(int index, String localName);
    public void setQName(int index, String qName);
    public void setType(int index, String type);
    public void setURI(int index, String uri);
    public void setValue(int index, String value);
// Methods Implementing Attributes
    public int getIndex(String qName);
    public int getIndex(String uri, String localName);
    public int getLength();                                                    default:0
    public String getLocalName(int index);
    public String getQName(int index);
    public String getType(String qName);
    public String getType(int index);
    public String getType(String uri, String localName);
    public String getURI(int index);
    public String getValue(int index);
    public String getValue(String qName);
    public String getValue(String uri, String localName);
}
```

DefaultHandler — Java 1.4

org.xml.sax.helpers

This helper class implements the four commonly-used SAX handler interfaces from the org.xml.sax package and defines stub implementations for all of their methods. It is usually easier to subclass DefaultHandler and override the desired methods than it is to implement all of the interfaces (and all of their methods) from scratch. DefaultHandler implements ContentHandler, ErrorHandler, EntityResolver and DTDHandler, so you can pass an instance of this class, (or of a subclass you define) to the setContentHandler(), setErrorHandler(), setEntityResolver(), and setDTDHandler() methods of an XMLReader. You can also pass an instance of a DefaultHandler subclass directly to one of the parse() methods of a javax.xml.parsers.SAXParser. The SAXParser will take care of calling the four relevant methods of its internal XMLReader.

All but two of the methods of DefaultHandler have empty bodies and do nothing. The exceptions are resolveEntity() which simply returns null to tell the parser to resolve the entity itself, and fatalError() which throws the SAXParseException object that is passed to it.

Object — DefaultHandler
ContentHandler | DTDHandler | EntityResolver | ErrorHandler

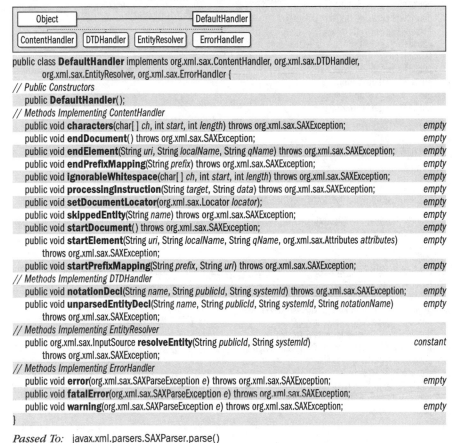

```
public class DefaultHandler implements org.xml.sax.ContentHandler, org.xml.sax.DTDHandler,
        org.xml.sax.EntityResolver, org.xml.sax.ErrorHandler {
// Public Constructors
    public DefaultHandler();
// Methods Implementing ContentHandler
    public void characters(char[ ] ch, int start, int length) throws org.xml.sax.SAXException;            empty
    public void endDocument() throws org.xml.sax.SAXException;                                            empty
    public void endElement(String uri, String localName, String qName) throws org.xml.sax.SAXException;   empty
    public void endPrefixMapping(String prefix) throws org.xml.sax.SAXException;                         empty
    public void ignorableWhitespace(char[ ] ch, int start, int length) throws org.xml.sax.SAXException;   empty
    public void processingInstruction(String target, String data) throws org.xml.sax.SAXException;       empty
    public void setDocumentLocator(org.xml.sax.Locator locator);                                          empty
    public void skippedEntity(String name) throws org.xml.sax.SAXException;                              empty
    public void startDocument() throws org.xml.sax.SAXException;                                          empty
    public void startElement(String uri, String localName, String qName, org.xml.sax.Attributes attributes)  empty
        throws org.xml.sax.SAXException;
    public void startPrefixMapping(String prefix, String uri) throws org.xml.sax.SAXException;           empty
// Methods Implementing DTDHandler
    public void notationDecl(String name, String publicId, String systemId) throws org.xml.sax.SAXException;  empty
    public void unparsedEntityDecl(String name, String publicId, String systemId, String notationName)       empty
        throws org.xml.sax.SAXException;
// Methods Implementing EntityResolver
    public org.xml.sax.InputSource resolveEntity(String publicId, String systemId)                     constant
        throws org.xml.sax.SAXException;
// Methods Implementing ErrorHandler
    public void error(org.xml.sax.SAXParseException e) throws org.xml.sax.SAXException;                  empty
    public void fatalError(org.xml.sax.SAXParseException e) throws org.xml.sax.SAXException;
    public void warning(org.xml.sax.SAXParseException e) throws org.xml.sax.SAXException;                empty
}
```

Passed To: javax.xml.parsers.SAXParser.parse()

SAX

LocatorImpl — Java 1.4

org.xml.sax.helpers

This helper class is a very simple implementation of the Locator interface. It defines a copy constructor that create a new LocatorImpl object that copies the state of a specified Locator object. This constructor is useful because it allows applications to copy the state of a Locator and save it for later use.

```
public class LocatorImpl implements org.xml.sax.Locator {
// Public Constructors
   public LocatorImpl();
   public LocatorImpl(org.xml.sax.Locator locator);
// Property Accessor Methods (by property name)
   public int getColumnNumber();                          Implements:Locator default:0
   public void setColumnNumber(int columnNumber);
   public int getLineNumber();                            Implements:Locator default:0
   public void setLineNumber(int lineNumber);
   public String getPublicId();                           Implements:Locator default:null
   public void setPublicId(String publicId);
   public String getSystemId();                           Implements:Locator default:null
   public void setSystemId(String systemId);
// Methods Implementing Locator
   public int getColumnNumber();                                          default:0
   public int getLineNumber();                                            default:0
   public String getPublicId();                                           default:null
   public String getSystemId();                                           default:null
}
```

NamespaceSupport — Java 1.4

org.xml.sax.helpers

This utility class exists to help SAX parser implementors handle XML namespaces. It is not commonly used by SAX applications.

```
public class NamespaceSupport {
// Public Constructors
   public NamespaceSupport();
// Public Constants
   public static final String XMLNS;        = [quot ] http://www.w3.org/XML/1998/namespace [quot ]
// Public Instance Methods
   public boolean declarePrefix(String prefix, String uri);
   public java.util.Enumeration getDeclaredPrefixes();
   public String getPrefix(String uri);
   public java.util.Enumeration getPrefixes();
   public java.util.Enumeration getPrefixes(String uri);
   public String getURI(String prefix);
   public void popContext();
   public String[ ] processName(String qName, String[ ] parts, boolean isAttribute);
   public void pushContext();
   public void reset();
}
```

ParserAdapter — Java 1.4

org.xml.sax.helpers

This adapter class behaves like a SAX2 XMLReader object, but gets its input from the SAX1 Parser object that is passed to the constructor. In order to make this work, it implements the deprecated SAX1 DocumentHandler interface so that it can receive events from the Parser. ParserAdapter provides its own layer of namespace processing to convert a namespace-unaware Parser into a namespace-aware XMLReader. This class is useful when working you are working with a legacy API that supplies a SAX1 Parser object, but want to work with that parser using the SAX2 XMLReader API: to use it, simply pass the Parser object to the ParserAdapter() constructor and use the resulting object as you would use any other XMLReader object.

There is not perfect congruence between the SAX1 and SAX2 APIs, and a Parser cannot be perfectly adapted to a XMLReader. In particular, a ParserAdapter will never call the skippedEntity() handler method because the SAX1 Parser API does not provide notification of skipped entities. Also, it does not attempt to determine whether two namespace-prefixed attributes of an element actually resolve to the same attribute.

See also XMLReaderAdapter, an adapter that works in the reverse direction to make a SAX2 parser behave like a SAX1 parser.

```
public class ParserAdapter implements org.xml.sax.DocumentHandler, org.xml.sax.XMLReader {
// Public Constructors
   public ParserAdapter() throws org.xml.sax.SAXException;
   public ParserAdapter(org.xml.sax.Parser parser);
// Methods Implementing DocumentHandler
   public void characters(char[ ] ch, int start, int length) throws org.xml.sax.SAXException;
   public void endDocument() throws org.xml.sax.SAXException;
   public void endElement(String qName) throws org.xml.sax.SAXException;
   public void ignorableWhitespace(char[ ] ch, int start, int length) throws org.xml.sax.SAXException;
   public void processingInstruction(String target, String data) throws org.xml.sax.SAXException;
   public void setDocumentLocator(org.xml.sax.Locator locator);
   public void startDocument() throws org.xml.sax.SAXException;
   public void startElement(String qName, org.xml.sax.AttributeList qAtts) throws org.xml.sax.SAXException;
// Methods Implementing XMLReader
   public org.xml.sax.ContentHandler getContentHandler();
   public org.xml.sax.DTDHandler getDTDHandler();
   public org.xml.sax.EntityResolver getEntityResolver();
   public org.xml.sax.ErrorHandler getErrorHandler();
   public boolean getFeature(String name) throws org.xml.sax.SAXNotRecognizedException,
      org.xml.sax.SAXNotSupportedException;
   public Object getProperty(String name) throws org.xml.sax.SAXNotRecognizedException,
      org.xml.sax.SAXNotSupportedException;
   public void parse(String systemId) throws java.io.IOException, org.xml.sax.SAXException;
   public void parse(org.xml.sax.InputSource input) throws java.io.IOException, org.xml.sax.SAXException;
   public void setContentHandler(org.xml.sax.ContentHandler handler);
   public void setDTDHandler(org.xml.sax.DTDHandler handler);
   public void setEntityResolver(org.xml.sax.EntityResolver resolver);
   public void setErrorHandler(org.xml.sax.ErrorHandler handler);
   public void setFeature(String name, boolean state) throws org.xml.sax.SAXNotRecognizedException,
      org.xml.sax.SAXNotSupportedException;
   public void setProperty(String name, Object value) throws org.xml.sax.SAXNotRecognizedException,
      org.xml.sax.SAXNotSupportedException;
}
```

SAX

ParserFactory — Java 1.4; Deprecated in Java 1.4

org.xml.sax.helpers

This deprecated SAX1 class is a factory for deprecated SAX1 Parser objects. New applications should use the SAX2 XMLReaderFactory as a factory for SAX2 XMLReader objects.

```
public class ParserFactory {
// No Constructor
// Public Class Methods
   public static org.xml.sax.Parser makeParser() throws ClassNotFoundException, IllegalAccessException,
      InstantiationException, NullPointerException;
}
```

```
    public static org.xml.sax.Parser makeParser(String className) throws ClassNotFoundException,
        IllegalAccessException, InstantiationException, ClassCastException;
}
```

XMLFilterImpl **Java 1.4**

org.xml.sax.helpers

This class is implements an XMLFilter that does no filtering. You can subclass it to override whatever methods are required to perform the type of filtering you desire.

XMLFilterImpl implements ContentHandler, ErrorHandler, EntityResolver and DTDHandler so that it can receive SAX events from the "parent" XMLReader object. But it also implements the XMLFilter interface, which is an extension of XMLReader, so that it acts as an XMLReader itself, and can send SAX events to the handler objects that are registered on it. Each of the handler methods of this class simply invoke the corresponding method of the corresponding handler that was registered on the filter. The XMLReader methods for getting and setting features and properties simply invoke the corresponding method of the parent XMLReader object. The parse() methods do the same thing: they pass their argument to the corresponding parse() method of the parent reader to start the parsing process.

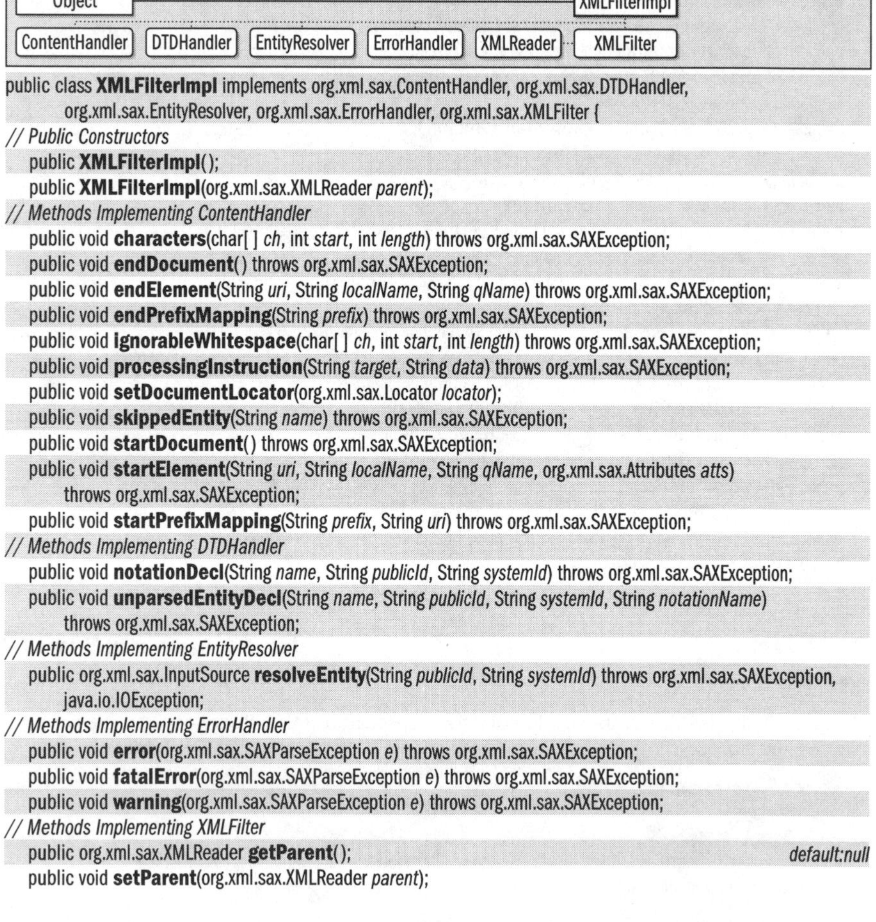


```
public class XMLFilterImpl implements org.xml.sax.ContentHandler, org.xml.sax.DTDHandler,
        org.xml.sax.EntityResolver, org.xml.sax.ErrorHandler, org.xml.sax.XMLFilter {
// Public Constructors
    public XMLFilterImpl();
    public XMLFilterImpl(org.xml.sax.XMLReader parent);
// Methods Implementing ContentHandler
    public void characters(char[ ] ch, int start, int length) throws org.xml.sax.SAXException;
    public void endDocument( ) throws org.xml.sax.SAXException;
    public void endElement(String uri, String localName, String qName) throws org.xml.sax.SAXException;
    public void endPrefixMapping(String prefix) throws org.xml.sax.SAXException;
    public void ignorableWhitespace(char[ ] ch, int start, int length) throws org.xml.sax.SAXException;
    public void processingInstruction(String target, String data) throws org.xml.sax.SAXException;
    public void setDocumentLocator(org.xml.sax.Locator locator);
    public void skippedEntity(String name) throws org.xml.sax.SAXException;
    public void startDocument( ) throws org.xml.sax.SAXException;
    public void startElement(String uri, String localName, String qName, org.xml.sax.Attributes atts)
        throws org.xml.sax.SAXException;
    public void startPrefixMapping(String prefix, String uri) throws org.xml.sax.SAXException;
// Methods Implementing DTDHandler
    public void notationDecl(String name, String publicId, String systemId) throws org.xml.sax.SAXException;
    public void unparsedEntityDecl(String name, String publicId, String systemId, String notationName)
        throws org.xml.sax.SAXException;
// Methods Implementing EntityResolver
    public org.xml.sax.InputSource resolveEntity(String publicId, String systemId) throws org.xml.sax.SAXException,
        java.io.IOException;
// Methods Implementing ErrorHandler
    public void error(org.xml.sax.SAXParseException e) throws org.xml.sax.SAXException;
    public void fatalError(org.xml.sax.SAXParseException e) throws org.xml.sax.SAXException;
    public void warning(org.xml.sax.SAXParseException e) throws org.xml.sax.SAXException;
// Methods Implementing XMLFilter
    public org.xml.sax.XMLReader getParent( );                                    default:null
    public void setParent(org.xml.sax.XMLReader parent);
```

```
// Methods Implementing XMLReader
    public org.xml.sax.ContentHandler getContentHandler();                    default:null
    public org.xml.sax.DTDHandler getDTDHandler();                            default:null
    public org.xml.sax.EntityResolver getEntityResolver();                    default:null
    public org.xml.sax.ErrorHandler getErrorHandler();                        default:null
    public boolean getFeature(String name) throws org.xml.sax.SAXNotRecognizedException,
        org.xml.sax.SAXNotSupportedException;
    public Object getProperty(String name) throws org.xml.sax.SAXNotRecognizedException,
        org.xml.sax.SAXNotSupportedException;
    public void parse(String systemId) throws org.xml.sax.SAXException, java.io.IOException;
    public void parse(org.xml.sax.InputSource input) throws org.xml.sax.SAXException, java.io.IOException;
    public void setContentHandler(org.xml.sax.ContentHandler handler);
    public void setDTDHandler(org.xml.sax.DTDHandler handler);
    public void setEntityResolver(org.xml.sax.EntityResolver resolver);
    public void setErrorHandler(org.xml.sax.ErrorHandler handler);
    public void setFeature(String name, boolean state) throws org.xml.sax.SAXNotRecognizedException,
        org.xml.sax.SAXNotSupportedException;
    public void setProperty(String name, Object value) throws org.xml.sax.SAXNotRecognizedException,
        org.xml.sax.SAXNotSupportedException;
}
```

XMLReaderAdapter **Java 1.4**

org.xml.sax.helpers

This adapter class wraps a SAX2 XMLReader object and makes it behave like a SAX1 Parser object. It is useful when working with a legacy API that requires a deprecated Parser object. Create an XMLReaderAdapter by passing an XMLReader to the XMLReaderAdapter() constructor. Then use the resulting object exactly as you would use any other SAX1 Parser object. This class implements ContentHandler so that it can receive SAX events from the XMLReader. But it also implements the Parser interface so that it can have a SAX1 DocumentHandler registered on it. The methods of ContentHandler are implemented to invoke the corresponding methods of the registered DocumentHandler.

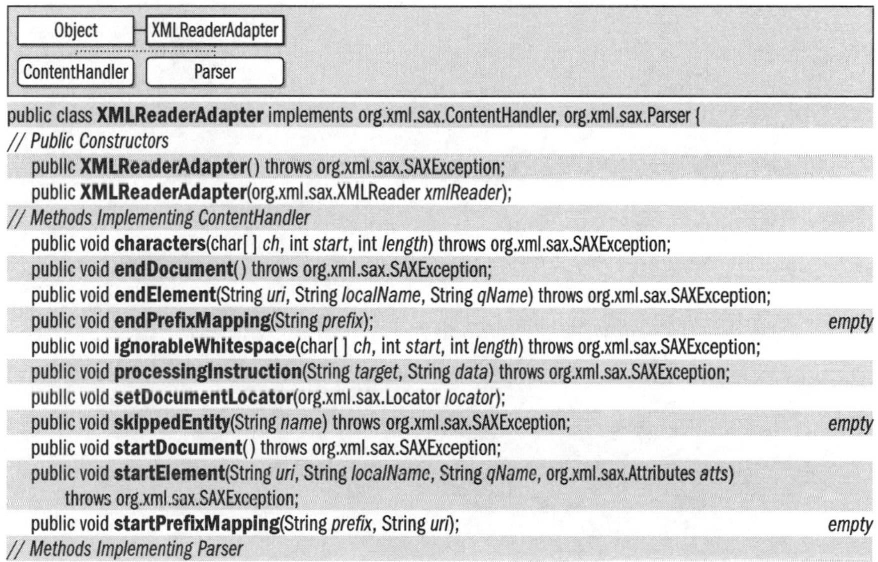


```
public class XMLReaderAdapter implements org.xml.sax.ContentHandler, org.xml.sax.Parser {
// Public Constructors
    public XMLReaderAdapter() throws org.xml.sax.SAXException;
    public XMLReaderAdapter(org.xml.sax.XMLReader xmlReader);
// Methods Implementing ContentHandler
    public void characters(char[ ] ch, int start, int length) throws org.xml.sax.SAXException;
    public void endDocument() throws org.xml.sax.SAXException;
    public void endElement(String uri, String localName, String qName) throws org.xml.sax.SAXException;
    public void endPrefixMapping(String prefix);                                     empty
    public void ignorableWhitespace(char[ ] ch, int start, int length) throws org.xml.sax.SAXException;
    public void processingInstruction(String target, String data) throws org.xml.sax.SAXException;
    public void setDocumentLocator(org.xml.sax.Locator locator);
    public void skippedEntity(String name) throws org.xml.sax.SAXException;           empty
    public void startDocument() throws org.xml.sax.SAXException;
    public void startElement(String uri, String localName, String qName, org.xml.sax.Attributes atts)
        throws org.xml.sax.SAXException;
    public void startPrefixMapping(String prefix, String uri);                        empty
// Methods Implementing Parser
```

```
    public void parse(String systemId) throws java.io.IOException, org.xml.sax.SAXException;
    public void parse(org.xml.sax.InputSource input) throws java.io.IOException, org.xml.sax.SAXException;
    public void setDocumentHandler(org.xml.sax.DocumentHandler handler);
    public void setDTDHandler(org.xml.sax.DTDHandler handler);
    public void setEntityResolver(org.xml.sax.EntityResolver resolver);
    public void setErrorHandler(org.xml.sax.ErrorHandler handler);
    public void setLocale(java.util.Locale locale) throws org.xml.sax.SAXException;
}
```

XMLReaderFactory — Java 1.4

org.xml.sax.helpers

This factory class defines two static factory methods for creating XMLReader objects. One method takes the name of a class as its argument. It dynamically loads and instantiates the class, then casts it to an XMLReader object. The second factory method takes no arguments; it reads the system property named "org.xml.sax.driver" and uses the value of that property as the name of the class XMLReader implementation class to load and instantiate. An application that instantiates its SAX parser using the no-argument method of XMLReaderFactory gains a layer of independence from the underlying parser implementation. The end user or system administrator of the system on which the application is deployed can change the parser implementation simply by setting a system property. Note that the javax.xml.parsers package provides a similar, but somewhat more useful SAXParserFactory.

```
public final class XMLReaderFactory {
// No Constructor
// Public Class Methods
    public static org.xml.sax.XMLReader createXMLReader() throws org.xml.sax.SAXException;
    public static org.xml.sax.XMLReader createXMLReader(String className) throws org.xml.sax.SAXException;
}
```

CHAPTER 25

Class, Method, and Field Index

The following index allows you to look up a class or interface and find what package it is defined in. It also allows you to look up a method or field and find what class it is defined in. Use it when you want to look up a class but don't know its package, or when you want to look up a method but don't know its class.

A

B

C

D

Class Index

E

Class Index

F

G

Class Index

Class Index

H

I

Class Index

Class Index

J

K

Class Index

L

M

N

O

P

Class Index

S

Class Index

Class Index

U

V

W

X

Y

Z

Index

Symbols

A

B

C

D

E

F

G

H

I

J

K

L

M

N

O

P

Q

R

S

T

U

V

W

X

Z

About the Author

David Flanagan is a computer programmer who spends most of his time writing about Java and JavaScript. His other books with O'Reilly include *Java Examples in a Nutshell, Java Foundation Classes in a Nutshell*, and *JavaScript: The Definitive Guide.* David has a degree in computer science and engineering from the Massachusetts Institute of Technology. He lives with his wife and son in the U.S. Pacific Northwest between the cities of Seattle, Washington and Vancouver, British Columbia.

Colophon

Our look is the result of reader comments, our own experimentation, and feedback from distribution channels. Distinctive covers complement our distinctive approach to technical topics, breathing personality and life into potentially dry subjects.

The animal on the cover of *Java in a Nutshell, Fourth Edition* is a Javan tiger. It is the smallest of the eight subspecies of tiger and has the longest cheek whiskers, which form a short mane across the neck. The encroachment of the growing human population, along with increases in poaching, have led to the near-extinction of the Javan tiger. The Indonesian government has become involved in trying to preserve the tiger. It is to be hoped that the remaining subspecies of tiger will be helped by increasing awareness and stricter protections.

Tigers are the largest of all cats, weighing up to 660 pounds and with a body length of up to 9 feet. They are solitary animals and, unlike lions, hunt alone. Tigers prefer large prey, such as wild pigs, cattle, or deer. Tigers rarely attack humans, although attacks on humans have increased as the increasing human population more frequently comes into contact with tigers. Tiger attacks usually occur when the tiger feels that it or its young are being threatened. In such cases, the tiger almost never eats its human victim. There are some tigers, however, who have developed a taste for human flesh. This is a particularly bad problem in an area of India and Bangladesh called the Sunderbans.

Matt Hutchinson was the production editor and copyeditor for *Java in a Nutshell, Fourth Edition.* Rachel Wheeler and Emily Quill provided quality control. Ellen Troutman-Zaig and Brenda Miller wrote the index. Lenny Muellner provided XML support.

Edie Freedman designed the cover of this book, using a 19th-century engraving from the Dover Pictorial Archive. David Futato designed the interior layout based on a series design by Nancy Priest. The print version of this book was created by translating the DocBook XML markup of its source files into a set of gtroff macros using a filter developed at O'Reilly & Associates by Norman Walsh. Steve Talbott designed and wrote the underlying macro set on the basis of the GNU *troff–gs* macros; Lenny Muellner adapted them to XML and implemented the book design. The GNU groff text formatter Version 1.11.1 was used to generate PostScript output. The text and heading fonts are ITC Garamond Light and Garamond Book; the code font is Constant Willison. The hierarchy diagrams that appear in the quick-reference section of this book were produced in encapsulated PostScript format by a Java program written by David Flanagan. This colophon was written by Clairemarie Fisher O'Leary.